INDIAN MONASTIC BUDDHISM

VOLUME 59

INDIAN MONASTIC BUDDHISM

Collected Papers on Textual, Inscriptional and Archaeological Evidence

GREGORY SCHOPEN

Two parts bound together

Part One - i - 298
Part Two - i - 423

MOTILAL BANARSIDASS PUBLISHERS
PRIVATE LIMITED • DELHI

First Indian Edition: Delhi, 2010
First Published by the University of Hawai'i Press in 2 Vols.
(Vol. 1) Bones, Stones, and Buddhist Monks: Collected Papers on the Archaeology, Epigraphy and Texts of Manastic Buddhism in India *(1997) and*
(Vol. 2) Buddhist Monks and Business Matters: Still More Papers on Monastic Buddhism in India *(2004)*
Reprinted in single volume with permission

ISBN: 978-81-208-3411-8

MOTILAL BANARSIDASS
41 U.A. Bungalow Road, Jawahar Nagar, Delhi 110 007
8 Mahalaxmi Chamber, 22 Bhulabhai Desai Road, Mumbai 400 026
203 Royapettah High Road, Mylapore, Chennai 600 004
236, 9th Main III Block, Jayanagar, Bangalore 560 011
Sanas Plaza, 1302 Baji Rao Road, Pune 411 002
8 Camac Street, Kolkata 700 017
Ashok Rajpath, Patna 800 004
Chowk, Varanasi 221 001

Dust Cover : A Buddhist Monastery (Number 51) at Sanchi. The background uses a page of the Mūlasarvāstivāda vinaya found at Gilgit. Courtesy of Alexander von Rospatt

PRINTED IN INDIA

By Jainendra Prakash Jain at Shri Jainendra Press,
A-45 Naraina, Phase-I, New Delhi 110 028
and published by Narendra Prakash Jain for
Motilal Banarsidass Publishers Private Limited,
Bungalow Road, Delhi 110 007

FOREWORD
to this single volume edition

UNTIL THE LATE TWENTIETH century, scholars of Indian Buddhism focused almost exclusively on Buddhist scriptural and commentarial sources—sources that depict Buddhism in an idealized and prescriptive fashion. Accordingly, Buddhist monks and nuns were imagined as celibate renunciants engaged in sophisticated philosophical debate and austere meditative practices leading to enlightenment. Little attention was paid to the kinds of textual and archaeological materials that go beyond mere prescription and shed light on the lived realities of Buddhist monastic culture. What was life in monasteries actually like? How did monks (and nuns!) sustain themselves and administer their establishments? What kind of ritual and devotional practices did they engage in, and what were their relations with the laity? Gregory Schopen, in a series of seminal essays that have appeared since the 1980s, addresses precisely such questions. His many papers demonstrate that monastics, far from being reclusive practitioners living in poverty and engaging in meditation and other forms of ascetic ritual, were active members of society and participated in its economy. Monastics owned property, borrowed and lent money, inherited family estates, hired laborers, employed servants and even owned slaves. Monastics also oversaw a variety of devotional activities commonly regarded as outside their domains: they commissioned images, stupas, and worship halls (*caitya*), while sponsoring their upkeep. Schopen's papers also highlight the funerary practices of monastics, further testifying to the shared community of customs governing both monastic and lay life.

Schopen's most important source has been the voluminous *Mūlasarvāstivādavinaya*, which was redacted in Northwestern India in the first centuries C.E. Surviving partly in the Sanskrit original and completely in Tibetan translation, this *vinaya* sheds invaluable light on the realities of monastic life at the time of its compilation. In masterly fashion, Schopen has identified numerous critical passages and subjected them to close reading. In addition, he has reexamined archaeological and epigraphical evidence, such as donor inscriptions, that bear witness to the activities of monastics and lay Buddhists and contribute to our understanding of early Indian Buddhist culture. Schopen also makes extensive use of such non-Buddhist sources as the *arthaśāstra* and *dharmśāastra*, decisively demonstrating the degree to which Buddhist monastic culture was indebted to Brahmanical lore. This wide array of hitherto neglected materials allows Schopen to present Indian Buddhist monasticism in a new light, and the resulting papers represent something of a paradigm shift in the field; Buddhism is no longer approached as a doctrinal and soteriological teaching alone, but also as a complex social institution that shaped Indian culture and civilization writ large, and was shaped by it in turn.

The present volume unites twenty-three papers published between 1984 and 2001. These papers appeared in a variety of American and European academic journals and edited volumes, many of which are difficult to access outside the West. Taken together they lay a foundation for the study of early monastic Indian Buddhism as well as the rise of Mahāyāna. Besides being of broad interest to social and institutional historians, these studies help us better understand the social context out of which developed the intricacies of Buddhist doctrine and exegesis; as such they are equally relevant for scholars whose interest lies in Indian Buddhist doctrinal development. In short, Schopen's work is required reading not only for students of Indian Buddhism, but also for anyone with a serious interest in Indian religions and its underlying socioeconomic realities.

ERNST STEINKELLNER ALEXANDER VON ROSPATT

Part I
Bones, Stones and Buddhist Monks

Dedicated to the taxpayers
and working women and men of
Canada and Australia who paid
for this foreigner's education

CONTENTS

PREFACE

THE COLLEGIATE INSTITUTE for the Study of Buddhist Traditions of the University of Michigan is very pleased to be able to present this collection of papers by Professor Gregory Schopen as the second volume in its series. Through his meticulous studies of a wide range of neglected or forgotten sources, many of which are carved in stone, Professor Schopen has effected a major shift in the direction of Buddhist Studies, a shift away from the sometimes excessive focus upon the rarefied categories of the scholastic productions by monastic elites, and a shift toward a recognition of the importance of the materiality of "popular" practice. These practices not only occupied the concerns of a much larger segment of the Buddhist communities of India, both monastic and lay, but served as the inevitable context for the formulation and elaboration of scholastic doctrine.

Professor Schopen's work, published over the last fifteen years in a wide range of scholarly journals, has been focused broadly on two issues in the history of Indian Buddhism: monastic life and the rise of the various movements that we refer to as the Mahāyāna. Monastic Buddhism in India is the subject of the current volume. Professor Schopen's highly influential papers on the rise of the Mahāyāna, which have called into question both the coherence of the category as well as its date, are currently being edited for publication as the next volume in our series.

The present volume provides an essential foundation for a social history of Indian Buddhist monasticism. Challenging the popular stereotype that represented the accumulation of merit as the domain of the layperson while monks concerned themselves with more sophisticated realms of doctrine and meditation, Professor Schopen problematizes many assumptions about the lay-monastic distinction by demonstrating that monks and nuns, both the scholastic elites and the less learned, participated actively in a wide range of ritual practices and institutions that have heretofore been judged "popular," from the accumulation and transfer of merit; to the care of deceased relatives (a practice once assumed to have been part of "the Chinese transformation of Buddhism"); to serving as sponsors and donors, rather than always as the recipients, of gifts; to (possibly) the coining of counterfeit currency. A particular emphasis of the current volume is the role played by monks in the disposition of their own dead, combining a close examination of the various rules for monastic funerals contained in the *vinaya* with an analysis of the available epigraphical and archaeological evidence. In addition, Professor Schopen provides fascinating perspectives on the role of the deceased Buddha in the particulars of Indian Buddhist monastic life, both as a relic whose presence bestows sanctity on its environs and as a permanent resident and property holder in the monastic economy. Taken together, the studies contained in this volume represent the basis for a new historiography of Buddhism, not only for their critique of many of the *idées reçues* of Buddhist Studies but for the compelling connections they draw between apparently disparate details.

All of these papers have been published previously and have been revised slightly here to provide a greater consistency of style. Despite the fact that they have appeared elsewhere, it was the opinion of the faculty of the Institute for the Study of Buddhist Traditions that their importance warranted their being gathered from far and wide into a single volume because of the edification and intellectual stimulation they provide as we continue to call into question past assumptions and to ask increasingly difficult questions about the elusive category we call Buddhism.

DONALD S. LOPEZ, JR.
Institute for the Study of
Buddhist Traditions

ACKNOWLEDGMENTS

THE PERSON TO BLAME for this volume is Donald Lopez. He was, I think, abetted early on by Robert Sharf. When the former first proposed reprinting a collection of some of my articles, I thought that doing so would probably not unduly retard the progress of the human race and I saw at least one distinct advantage: it would give me the opportunity to acknowledge in a more enduring way the help and benefit I have received from a large number of people over a long period of time.

To start at the beginning, I have always liked the opening words of *The Life and Opinions of Tristram Shandy*: "I wish either my father or mother, or indeed both of them, as they were in duty both equally bound to it, had minded what they were about when they begot me . . ." It, and the rest of Sterne's first two chapters, make it wonderfully apparent how much depends on the fact that most parents don't. By not, I suspect, minding overmuch about what they were doing, my parents inadvertently assured that I would be part of a remarkable family. My mother is deeply devout and hopelessly irreverent; my father—who never finished grade school—had a wonderful collection of strange books (including, of course, *Tristram Shandy*) and begot a family of six. Of the four that made it three have Ph.D.s—the laggard is my youngest sister Barbara who is arguably the funniest and certainly the smartest. My brother Bernard has published three novels; my sister Ann skies marathons at over fifty. Though none of them has the quiet wisdom of my father, and though we all share his capacity for error, they have all encouraged me on my way. All have been, and continue to be, important teachers.

In terms of my formal education I owe a great deal to Professor Jan Yün-hua, now retired from McMaster University in Canada. Although I was working in a different field, he supported and encouraged me with humor and good sense in my early and very precarious years of graduate school. He embodies the very best of the Confucian Gentleman Scholar. I owe a great deal to Professor J. W. de Jong now retired from the Australian National University. A man of enormous knowledge, he tried to teach me not to be sloppy in source or sense. But perhaps more than for anything else I owe him deeply for having allowed and encouraged me to go my own way, although, again, he might now be inclined to reconsider the wisdom of it. Here too I must thank my Sensei in Tibetan: Professor Shoryu Katsura, now of Hiroshima University, then at the University of Toronto, taught me the rudiments of Classical Tibetan with a clarity and precision I will never forget, although, unfortunately, I frequently forget the actual Tibetan, through no fault of his.

I owe a great deal to two of my Ph.D. examiners, even though that particular ritual function was only the beginning. Professor David Ruegg not only read my dissertation and survived, but has for many years encouraged me at a distance in many ways. The other of my examiners continues to be one, not by his position so much as by his integrity, good sense and learning. Not only was Luis Gómez one of my examiners, he was also my first Sanskrit teacher at the University of Washington. He is, I think, fond of pointing out that I dropped the class. He also gave me the second job I had after I had finished my Ph.D.—the first was as a nightwatchman in a sawmill in Wyoming—and he has continued to be both a model, a teacher, and most importantly, a friend.

In terms of friends I have been lucky beyond any conceivable expectations. I owe a very great deal to a prematurely follicularly disadvantaged theologian with a terrible jumpshot: John Thiel of Fairfield University was the first to read several of the papers republished in this volume, and every one he read was improved through his reading. Especially the piece entitled "Archaeology and Protestant Presuppositions in the Study of Indian Buddhism" owes a great deal to his editorial skills and his eye for errant rhetoric. He continues to be an important teacher and a friend, and I am very grateful.

An equally old and important friend is Hal Roth. Many of the things in these papers were first forged in long conversations with him on the phone (usually at my expense—but then also to my profit), and his sense of humor and taste in clothes has been a constant source of amazement. He too remains a teacher and a friend.

Not long after making the acquaintance of these gentlemen I met my first real exotic: a Pacific islander who spoke a quaint dialect of what, he assured me, was English. In spite, though, of the language barrier, in spite of the intervening miles and misadventures—not to mention years—Paul Harrison has too remained a very important friend and teacher. His occasional good sense still astounds me.

There are still others. I am grateful to Phyllis Granoff who over the years has published my work and given me the consolation of good conversation and shared with me her observations and her always nimble wit. I am grateful to Charles Hallisey for his encouragement and for sharing some of his boundless capacity to be interested in almost everything; to Jonathan Silk for his enthusiasm and unwillingness to accept easy answers; to Jan Nattier for her early and continued encouragement, and her ability to fruitfully frame questions on just about everything; and to Richard Salomon for his skepticism about religious studies and his scholarly standards.

Further afield, I owe a great deal to several scholars in Europe who have helped me in many ways even though I had no claim on their time and generosity. Gérard Fussman has let me profit enormously from his work and taught me much by not being easily convinced. Oskar von Hinüber has done the same, has provided one model of solid scholarship, and has supported me by numerous letters at crucial points in my academic career. K. R. Norman has both provided yet another model of scholarly excellence and taught me much by his generous correspondence. Akira Yuyama not only made it possible for me to study for a year in Tokyo, but he also taught me how to wear a tie, how to keep things in perspective, and the value of precision. To all of these I am extremely grateful.

With colleagues in the more strictly institutional sense I have also been extremely lucky. Patrick Olivelle gave me my first permanent academic job more than ten years ago at Indiana. He was then—as he is now in Austin—not only a very fine Sanskritist but nothing short of the best chairman and the best colleague someone working on Classical India could have: I trust his judgment and his wisdom, and I gain from his learning almost daily—he does not come in on Mondays. He has supported me always, even on those occasions (and I fear they were not rare) when I tried his patience. Also at Texas Richard Lariviere has been a fine colleague, a needed teacher, and an almost inexhaustible source of tall tales. More recently Janice Leoshko has done what she could to educate my lack of visual acuity, though she has yet to get me to use a slide projector. All have been good friends.

Closest to home are three women. Lynn, in the early days, who put up with being a vagabond and sharing her life with boxes full of old books, has remained a very good friend—Lynn's parents also were crucial: one of the papers included here was dedicated to the memory of her father, a man I came to greatly admire. Alice, who has put up with even more boxes and still more moves, has kept me alive to the things of greater importance. She may yet get me up on her beloved high mountains where—I suspect—a good deal of her spirit comes from. I look forward to her attempts. And Morgan—without a doubt the finest accident to have occurred in my life because, yes, her father, too, did not mind what he was about, although he trusts that she will!

Finally, to come full circle, this volume owes most to those who put it together. The collection of papers it contains were written over many years and many moods. Few, if any, had benefited from the hands of a good copyeditor. It was therefore a final happy accident that the decision was made to reset the papers and that the project was taken on by Mimi Mayer and Reiko Ohnuma. The former went carefully through the papers and suggested many minor stylistic changes which have made, I think, a major improvement in their readability. The latter made even further refinements, brought some order to the chaos of my references, and put up with my long delays with good humor. I thank them both, and so should the reader. Given the enormity of their task, however, it should not be surprising that neither succeeded in imposing anything like an ordered consistency on what was inherently inconsistent material. In fact enough "variety" remains to excite even the moderately obsessive or anally retentive: hyphenation of Sanskrit compounds is erratic; the use of diacritics in place-names—especially in the titles of books and articles—is equally so, and there is even some variation in the spelling of such names; common terms involving *anusvāra* or nasals are spelled in every conceivable way (e.g., *saṅgha, saṃgha,* etc.); although Tibetan is usually transliterated using the so-called Wylie system, the discerning reader will occasionally find the older system that used diacritics; and so on. One can only hope that at least Emerson might approve.

Although the style of the papers, and their readability, have been improved, the content—alas—has not. I have silently corrected typos and misprints that I noticed in the original publications, but resetting the papers has probably created just as many new ones. And although I have inserted a few more recent references in square brackets into the notes, or added them at the end of the notes, I have made no attempt to revise any of the papers and no substantive changes have been made. Such changes—the important revisions and corrections—are, I think, rightly left to others. I have had my chance.

ABBREVIATIONS

AI	*Ancient India*
ABORI	*Annals of the Bhandarkar Oriental Research Institute*
ArA	*Artibus Asiae*
ARASI	*Annual Report of the Archaeological Survey of India*
ArO	*Ars Orientalis*
BEFEO	*Bulletin de l'école française d'extrême-orient*
BEI	*Bulletin d'études indiennes*
BHSD	F. Edgerton, *Buddhist Hybrid Sanskrit Dictionary* (New Haven: 1953)
BHSG	F. Edgerton, *Buddhist Hybrid Sanskrit Grammar* (New Haven: 1953)
BSOAS	Bulletin of the School of Oriental and African Studies
Derge	The Sde-dge Mtshal-par Bka'-'gyur, A Facsimile Edition of the 18th Century Redaction of Si-Tu Chos-kyi-'byuṅ-gnas. Prepared under the Direction of H. H. the 16th Rgyal-dbaṅ Karma-pa, Vols. 1–103 (Delhi: 1976ff). Cited by volume, folio number in the facsimile (not by original pagination), and line.
EI	*Epigraphia Indica*
EW	*East and West*
EZ	*Epigraphia Zeylanica*
Gilgit Buddhist Manuscripts	R. Vira and L. Chandra, eds., *Giglit Buddhist Manuscripts (Facsimile Edition)*, Sata-Piṭaka Series, Vol. 10, Part 6 (New Delhi: 1974). Cited

	by part number, folio number assigned in the facsimile, and line.
Gilgit Manuscripts	N. Dutt, ed., *Gilgit Manuscripts*, Vol. III, Part 1 (Srinagar: 1947); Vol. III, Part 2 (Srinagar: 1942); Vol. III, Part 3 (Srinagar: 1943); Vol. III, Part 4 (Calcutta: 1950). Cited by volume, part, page, and line.
Histoire du bouddhisme indien	Ét. Lamotte, *Histoire du bouddhisme indien, des origines à l'ére Śaka* (Louvain: 1958).
HJAS	*Harvard Journal of Asiatic Studies*
IA	*Indian Antiquary*
IIJ	*Indo-Iranian Journal*
IHQ	*The Indian Historical Quarterly*
IBK	*Indogaku bukkyōgaku kenkyū*
JA	*Journal asiatique*
JAIH	*Journal of Ancient Indian History*
JAOS	*Journal of the American Oriental Society*
JASBom	*Journal of the Asiatic Society of Bombay*
JBomBRAS	*Journal of the Bombay Branch of the Royal Asiatic Society*
JBORS	*The Journal of the Bihar and Orissa Research Society*
JESI	*Journal of the Epigraphical Society of India*
JIABS	*The Journal of the International Association of Buddhist Studies*
JIH	*The Journal of Indian History*
JIP	*Journal of Indian Philosophy*
JPTS	*Journal of the Pali Text Society*
JRAS	*Journal of the Royal Asiatic Society of Great Britain and Ireland*
MASI	*Memoirs of the Archaeological Survey of India*
MCB	*Mélanges chinois et bouddhiques*
Peking	D. T. Suzuki, ed., *The Tibetan Tripitaka, Peking Edition, Reprinted under the Supervision of the Otani University, Kyoto*, Vols. 1–169 (Tokyo and Kyoto: 1955–1961). Cited by volume, page, folio, and line.

RHR	*Revue de l'histoire des religions*
Saṅghabhedavastu	R. Gnoli, ed., *The Gilgit Manuscript of the Saṅghabhedavastu. Being the 17th and Last Section of the Vinaya of the Mūlasarvāstivādin*, Parts I–II, Serie Orientale Roma, XLIX, 1–2 (Roma: 1977–78). Cited by volume, page, and line.
Śayanāsanavastu and Adhikaraṇavastu	R. Gnoli, ed., *The Gilgit Manuscript of the Śayanāsanavastu and the Adhikaraṇavastu. Being the 15th and 16th Sections of the Vinaya of the Mūlasarvāstivādin*, Serie Orientale Roma, L (Roma: 1978). Cited by page and line.
StII	*Studien zur Indologie und Iranistik*
Tog	*The Tog Palace Manuscript of the Tibetan Kanjur*, Vols. 1–109 (Leh: 1975–1980). Cited by volume, folio number assigned in the reprint (not by original pagination), and line.
TP	*T'oung Pao*
UCR	*University of Ceylon Review*
WZKS	*Wiener Zeitschrift für die Kunde Südasiens*
ZDMG	*Zeitschrift der Deutschen Morgenländischen Gesellschaft*

CHAPTER I

Archaeology and Protestant Presuppositions in the Study of Indian Buddhism

THE WAY IN WHICH the history of Indian Buddhism has been studied by modern scholars is decidedly peculiar. What is perhaps even more peculiar, though, is that it has rarely been seen to be so. This peculiarity is most readily apparent in what appears at first sight to be a curious and unargued preference for a certain kind of source material. This curious preference, although it may not be by any means uniquely characteristic of the study of Indian Buddhism, is particularly evident there; so too is the fact that it has no obvious scholarly justification. We might first look at a small sample of statements expressing this preference and at its consequences. Then we must at least ask what can possibly lie behind it.

When Europeans first began to study Indian Buddhism systematically there were already two bodies of data available to them, and the same is true today. There was, and is, a large body of archaeological and epigraphical material, material that can be reasonably well located in time and space,[1] and material that is largely unedited and much of which was never intended to be "read."[2] This material records or reflects at least a part of what Buddhists—both lay people and monks—actually practiced and believed.[3] There was, and is, an equally large body of literary material that in most cases cannot actually be dated[4] and that survives only in very recent manuscript traditions.[5] It has been heavily edited,[6] it is considered canonical or sacred, and it was intended—at the very least—to inculcate an ideal.[7] This material records what a small, atypical part of the Buddhist community wanted that community to believe or practice. Both bodies of material, it is important to note, became available to Western scholars more or less simultaneously.[8] The choice of sources for the scholar interested in knowing what Indian Buddhism had been would seem obvious.

Originally published in *History of Religions* 31 (1991): 1–23. Reprinted with stylistic changes with permission of The University of Chicago Press.

But the choice made was, apparently, not based on an assessment of the two kinds of sources as historical witnesses, but on some other kind of an assumption. This assumption, it appears, more than anything else has determined the status and use of archaeological and epigraphical sources in the study of Indian Buddhism, and this assumption, apparently, accounts for the fact that an overriding textual orientation was in place very early in Buddhist studies.

In discussing Burnouf, who died in 1852 and whom he calls "the brilliant founder of the study of Buddhism," de Jong, himself the most recent historian of Buddhist studies, says: "Burnouf stressed the fact that Indian Buddhism had to be studied on the basis of the Sanskrit *texts* from Nepal and the Pāli *texts* from Ceylon. . . . Burnouf was well aware of the fundamental importance of the study of *texts* for the history of Buddhism. His idea with regard to India at the time of the Buddha, the doctrine of the Buddha and its later development, the relation of Buddhism to caste, etc., which he develops in the *Introduction*, are all based on a careful study of the *texts*" (emphasis added).[9]

De Jong himself has made a number of statements that clearly indicate that the position he ascribes to Burnouf in the first half of the nineteenth century is very much his own position in the second half of the twentieth: "Each of these vehicles [the three main "divisions" of Buddhism] has produced a rich literature. Undoubtedly, this literature is the most important source of knowledge of Buddhism. Buddhist art, inscriptions, and coins have supplied us with useful data, but generally they cannot be fully understood without the support given by the texts. Consequently, the study of Buddhism needs first of all to be concentrated on the texts. . . ."[10]

De Jong's statement is of interest both because it is recent and representative and because it makes explicit some of the assertions and assumptions that lie behind it. Notice first that de Jong gives a variant version of the all-too-common, simplistic view of archaeology as "the handmaiden of history."[11] But he goes even further: not only must archaeology be the handmaiden of literary sources, it and the evidence it brings forth can only be "fully understood" with "the support given by the texts"; not only must archaeology support and amplify the literary sources, it must also be supported and amplified by them; otherwise, it has no real use. It cannot be an independent witness. It cannot, therefore, tell a different story.

But notice too that this position, which gives overriding primacy to textual sources, does not even consider the possibility that the texts we are to study to arrive at a knowledge of "Buddhism" may not even have been known to the vast majority of practicing Buddhists—both monks and laity. It is axiomatically assumed that the texts not only were known but were also important, not only were read but were also fully implemented in actual practice. But no evidence in support of these assumptions, or even arguments for them, is ever presented.[12]

Notice too that no mention is made of the fact that the vast majority of the textual sources involved are "scriptural," that is to say, formal literary expressions of normative doctrine.[13] Notice, finally, that no thought is given to the fact that even the most artless formal narrative text has a purpose, and that in "scriptural" texts, especially in India, that purpose is almost never "historical" in our sense of the term.[14] In fact, what this position wants to take as adequate reflections of historical reality appear to be nothing more or less than carefully contrived ideal paradigms. This is particularly clear, for example, in regard to what these canonical texts say about the monk. But in spite of this, scholars of Indian Buddhism have taken canonical monastic rules and formal literary descriptions of the monastic ideal preserved in very late manuscripts and treated them as if they were accurate reflections of the religious life and career of actual practicing Buddhist monks in early India. Such a procedure has, of course, placed archaeology and epigraphy in a very awkward position. If, then, archaeology and epigraphy are to be in the service of a "history" based on written sources of this kind, then they are going to have to "support and amplify" something that very probably did not exist: they are going to have to sit quietly in the corner spinning cloth for the emperor's new clothes.

That this is largely what has happened and continues to happen is again not difficult to document. We might, as a simple example, cite a series of passages from a variety of scholars that address in one way or another the question of whether individual monks owned personal property—a question of considerable importance, since it bears on the character of Buddhist monasticism and because Buddhism has been presented as "the world-renouncing religion *par excellence.*"[15]

Bühler, in discussing the second or first century B.C.E. donative inscriptions from Sāñcī, said: "Proceeding to the inscriptions which mention donations made by monks and nuns, the first point, which must strike every reader, is their great number, . . . *As the Buddhist ascetics could not possess any property,* they must have obtained by begging the money required for making the rails and pillars. This was no doubt permissible, as the purpose was a pious one" (emphasis added).[16] Discussing the Bhārhut donative inscriptions, which may slightly predate those from Sāñcī, Lüders said much the same thing: "It is perhaps striking to find monks and nuns making donations, *as they were forbidden to own any personal property* besides some ordinary requisites. Probably we have to suppose that they collected the money required for some pious purpose by begging it from their relatives and acquaintances" (emphasis added).[17]

Arguing that a "small jar" from Haḍḍa that had a Kharoṣṭhī inscription on it containing the name of a monk was not a gift made to that monk but rather "a funerary jar" intended to hold his ashes, Fussman said, in part: "Surtout il paraît surprenant que le don soit fait à un moine en particulier. *C'est contraire aux prescriptions du vinaya;* . . . On peut donc penser que la jarre était destinée à l'inhumation du moines"—to which he adds in a note: "*En ce cas il n'y aurait pas violation des règles du vinaya*" (emphasis added).[18] Marshall, commenting on one of the numerous hoards of coins found at the monastic site surrounding the Dharmarājikā at Taxila, said: "Probably the hollow block of kañjūr was merely a secret hiding place where one of the monks hid his store of coins . . . the possession of money by a monk *was contrary, of course, to the rule of the Church,* but the many small hoards that have been found in monasteries of the early medieval period leave little room for doubt that by that time the rules had become more or less a dead letter."[19] Finally, Spink, in an overview of Ajaṇṭā, said: "A number of inscriptions at Ajaṇṭā also prove that some of the caves, and numerous separate images, were donated by the monks themselves. This is an interesting commentary on the changing of Buddhism in India, for it suggests that monks, far from having renounced all worldly goods, were sometimes men of considerable wealth. It is doubtful that Buddhabhadra, the chief donor of the elaborate cave 26—a man who proclaims himself the friend of kings—spent very much time humbly wandering from village to village with his begging bowl *as his predecessors in the early days of Buddhism certainly did*" (emphasis added).[20]

The point here is not whether individual monks or nuns did or did not possess private property; the evidence we have, from all periods, indicates that they did. The point is that every time epigraphers, archaeologists, or art historians encountered evidence that even suggested the possibility that monks or nuns owned personal property, they first signaled their surprise ("It is perhaps striking, . . ." "Above all it appears surprising . . .") and then immediately invoked either explicitly or implicitly the rules in the canonical monastic codes against it to assert, in one way or another, that they were not really seeing what they saw. Either that, or they neutralized what they were seeing by attributing it to a "late change" or implied "decline" within the tradition. They all axiomatically assumed that the textual ideal either was or had been actually in operation, that if it said so in a text it must have been so in reality.

There appears to be, however, no actual evidence that the textual ideal was ever fully or even partially implemented in actual practice; at least none is ever cited. And even though the mere existence of rules against it might suggest that monks did own personal property,[21] and even though it is clear that in the textual ideal itself the infraction of those rules was a "minor offence,"[22] and even though it is almost certain that in a strictly legal sense "the monk might retain the ownership of the property that he had abandoned,"[23] still all material evidence that monks did have personal property must be explained away: Bühler's "they must have obtained by begging," Lüders' "Probably we have to suppose." This is an archaeology truly in the service of written sources, no matter how idealized the latter may be, an archaeology that will find itself forced to retire in the face of frequently indelicate situations. One example must suffice.

We know that Longhurst's Monastery 1 at Nāgārjunikoṇḍa was the gift of a lay-sister (*upāsikā*) named Bodhiśrī, and that it was the property of "the Theravādin teachers of Ceylon." These same "teachers" are further described in the epigraphy of Nāgārjunikoṇḍa as "skilled in the exegesis of both the letter and meaning of the ninefold instruction of the teacher and the preservers of the tradition of the holy lineage."[24] It is of some significance that it was in this monastery, belonging to this group, that Longhurst discovered in one of the cells "a large number of small lead coins of the usual South Indian type of about the second century A.D." But he also found, together with these coins, "a lump of lead ore and an earthenware die for the manufacture of coins of this size and pattern." Longhurst says simply that this indicates "that the monks made their own coins."[25] No mention is made of the fact that the authority for minting coins in early India was vested in the state, or in guilds of traders or "moneyers" by the power of the state.[26] This would suggest either that the monk or monks who lived in Monastery 1 at Nāgārjunikoṇḍa were involved in trading and commercial enterprises and were empowered by the state to do so, or that they were involved in counterfeiting. It is difficult to say which possibility is the more likely, but either alternative is interesting for what it might say about the character of actual, historical Buddhist monasticism. Evidence for such activities is, moreover, by no means limited to Nāgārjunikoṇḍa.[27]

The question of ownership by Buddhist monks of private wealth is, of course, not the only question that has been handled in this curious way. Another important example we might look at concerns the so-called doctrine of *karma.*

There are hundreds of short, simple donative inscriptions on the railings surrounding the *stūpas* at Sāñcī and Bhārhut that have been assigned to the second or first century B.C.E. Almost every one of them says something like *vajigutasa dānaṃ,* "the gift of Vajiguta," or *ghosāye dānaṃ,* "the gift of Ghosā," or one or another of hundreds of names, frequently with a title added indicating the donor's religious or secular status. That is all. The intention of the donor, the reason behind the gift, is—with only one exception—simply never stated. Confronted with this situation, Lamotte, in a book entitled *Histoire du bouddhisme indien,* a book that is *the* standard authority in the field, was able to say: "At this time the mentality remains strictly orthodox, that is to say it conforms to the spirit of the Buddha. By their charity, the generous donors [at Bhārhut and Sāñcī] never hope to reach the level of *Nirvāṇa,* but simply intend to benefit from the five advantages of the gift signaled by the *Aṅguttara* (III p. 38–41)."[28] Putting aside the fact that it is difficult to know how Lamotte knew exactly what "the spirit of the Buddha" was, still it is interesting to notice what happens here. The inscriptions themselves—again with one exception—say nothing about intention, nothing about what the donors' "hope" or what they "intended." There is, moreover, no evidence that the *Aṅguttara* was ever known at either Bhārhut or Sāñcī. Nevertheless, Lamotte not only imputes to actual individuals very specific intentions where none are actually expressed, he also assigns these intentions to a very specific text that he cannot, in fact, actually place at either site. This is at best a curious kind of history, a kind of history that—to put it most simply—seems to assume if it says so in a canonical text, it must have been so in reality. It does not seem to matter, again, that there is no actual evidence that this formal doctrine was ever a part of actual Buddhist practice.[29]

If this assumption is able to override the absence of evidence, it is also important to notice that it is also able to override the presence of contrary evidence. After ascribing to the donors at Bhārhut and Sāñcī the very specific intention of "benefiting from the five advantages" described in the canonical *Aṅguttara*, Lamotte goes on to say: "There can be no question [at Bhārhut and Sāñcī] of transferring the merit [of their gift] to someone else, nor moreover of formulating intentions which the mechanism of the retribution of acts would render inoperative."[30] Notice again that there can be no question either of transferring the merit or even of formulating a particular intention because, by implication, the mechanism of the retribution of acts would render both inoperative: that is to say, real donors—actual people—could only intend or want what was in conformity with a textual doctrine. There are, of course, a number of problems here, not the least of which is that it has never been established that a strict doctrine of retribution of acts was ever actually recognized outside of texts; it has never been established that it had any impact on actual behavior. In fact, what we know from contemporary anthropological studies of both Buddhist and Hindu communities where this doctrine is officially recognized suggests otherwise. It suggests that, where the doctrine is known at all, it is generally invoked in very limited and specific contexts, and people's behavior and their motivations are largely governed by other ideas or forms of a doctrine of *karma* that differ, sometimes very markedly, from the classical, textual doctrine.[31] Moreover, epigraphical data suggest that this has always been the case. Oddly enough, this is clear even at Bhārhut and Sāñcī, the sites Lamotte is specifically referring to.

As we have seen, the vast majority of donors at both sites do not record their intentions. There is only one exception. But in this single case in which the donor actually states his own intention, that intention is exactly what Lamotte says is impossible: it is exactly what the textual doctrine of the retribution of acts would render inoperative. However, Sagharakhita, the donor in question, does not seem to know that. He makes his gift *mātāpituna aṭhāyā*, "for the benefit of his mother and father."[32] This, in fact, is one of the earliest expressions of and the *only* actually attestable form of the actual—as opposed to the ideal—Buddhist doctrine of *karma* and giving current at Bhārhut and Sāñcī. But because it does not conform to and confirm the existence of the textual doctrine, it is said, "It cannot possibly be." Textuality overrides actuality. And actuality—as expressed by epigraphical and archaeological material—is denied independent validity as a witness. It may not be altogether surprising to note that the more we come to know about what real donors actually did, the clearer it becomes how defective our textual sources can be as historical witnesses.

Since Lamotte wrote the remarks quoted above, a number of important early inscriptions have come to light. In 1968 a number of donative inscriptions on what was a railing surrounding a *stūpa* were discovered at Pauni in Maharashtra. In both style and paleography they are very similar to the inscriptions found at Bhārhut and Sāñcī, and like them, have been assigned to the second or first century B.C.E. At Pauni, again as at Bhārhut and Sāñcī, the majority of donors do not express their intentions, but there is at least one exception. This exception indicates that the donor, one Visamitā, gave her gift "for the happiness of all beings" (. . . *(yā)ya visamitāya dana sukhāya hotu savasātāna*).[33] The other early inscriptions of interest to us come from Sri Lanka and are almost certainly even earlier than those from Bhārhut, Sāñcī, and Pauni. One of these inscriptions, according to Paranavitana, is among "the earliest in Ceylon that can be definitely attributed to a particular ruler" and dates to the period between 210 and 200 B.C.E. It reads: *gamaṇi-uti-maharajhaha(jhita abi-ti)śaya leṇe daśa-diśaśa sagaye dine mata-pitaśa aṭaya:* "The cave of the princess (Abi) Tissā, daughter of the great king Gāmaṇī-Uttiya, is given to the Saṅgha of the ten directions, for the benefit of (her) mother and father."[34] Additionally, we now have four virtually identical inscriptions that record gifts of caves and that may even predate Abi Tissā's inscription. All four end by saying that the gift was given *aparimita-lokadatuya śatana śita-śukaye,* ("for the welfare and happiness of beings in the boundless universe").[35]

Known epigraphical evidence, therefore, proves that the earliest actually attestable Buddhist doctrine of *karma* and giving—and this is now attested from the third century B.C.E. and at very widely separated geographic sites—always involves exactly what Lamotte, on the basis of textual sources, said "could not possibly be the case." The intentions of actual donors at Bhārhut, Pauni, and very early Sri Lanka, whenever they are actually expressed, indicate that they all wished in one sense or another "to transfer the merit to another": to their parents, or to all beings, or to "all beings in the boundless universe." These same inscriptions give no indication that any other doctrine, textual or otherwise, was ever known at these sites.

A final example we might cite concerns the disposal of the dead. Here, the assigning of primary status to literary sources has not so much determined how the archaeological record should be read. It has, rather, determined that it should not be read at all.

We know from the scholarly secondary literature on literary sources the precise views of several obscure monk-scholars on exactly how many angels can dance on the head of an abhidharmic pin, and yet that same literature tells us nothing about how the Indian Buddhist community disposed of its dead. Even de La Vallée Poussin, in writing the entry entitled "Death and Disposal of the Dead (Buddhist)" for Hastings' *Encyclopaedia of Religion and Ethics,* was able to say almost nothing about disposal of the dead and filled the entry instead with scholastic definitions and descriptions of the process of death itself.[36] Again, the reasons for this are not difficult to determine. T. W. Rhys Davids says: "Nothing is known of any religious ceremony having been performed by the early Buddhists in India, whether the person deceased was a layman, or even a member of the Order. *The Vinaya Pitaka, which enters at so great length into all the details of the daily life of recluses, has no rules regarding the mode of treating the body of a deceased bhikkhu*" (emphasis added).[37] Rhys Davids, writing in 1900, makes it clear at least why nothing is known about the ritual disposal of the monastic dead: because the canonical literature known to him says nothing about it, the inference being, of course, that it therefore did not occur. But evidence that it did occur, that early Buddhist monastic communities were, in fact, preoccupied not only with disposing of their dead but with ritually and elaborately housing them as well, had been published nearly fifty years before Rhys Davids and sixty before de La Vallée Poussin. But this was only material, physical evidence of what actually occurred—archaeological evidence—not canonical evidence.

As early as 1854, Cunningham published the results of his cursory excavations of the Central Indian monastic sites around Sāñcī. Here already was clear evidence that indicated the existence of an extensive "cemetery" associated with the Buddhist monastic site at Bhojpur before the common era; here too at Sāñcī itself and at Sonārī and Andher was clear evidence for the elaborate housing and worshiping of the remains of the monastic dead.[38] The epigraphical material we have makes it clear that the construction and embellishing of the monumental reliquaries that contained these remains resulted from activity undertaken and paid for by a disproportionately large number of monks and nuns.[39] Only eight years later, in 1862, West published the first description of what he correctly identified as an extensive monastic cemetery that formed a part of the Buddhist monastic complex at Kānheri on the western coast of India.[40] In 1883 Burgess published a description of what is clearly another monastic cemetery in the midst of the monastic cave complex at Bhājā.[41] All of this evidence was available to both Rhys Davids and de La Vallée Poussin, but for them, it seems, Indian Buddhism and Indian Buddhist practice were contained in canonical texts. What

Indian Buddhists actually did was of no consequence. And since this was true, Buddhist archaeology and epigraphy also were of no consequence.

It would appear, then, that the ascription of primacy to textual sources in Buddhist studies not only effectively neutralizes the independence of archaeological and epigraphical sources as witnesses, it also effectively excludes what practicing Buddhists did and believed from the history of their own religion. We can see something more of this in, for example, another statement of de Jong's:

> Missionaries came into contact with Theravāda Buddhism in Ceylon, Burma, Siam, and Indochina and with different forms of Mahāyāna Buddhism in China and Japan. Their knowledge was based upon what they observed, and on discussions with Buddhist priests, but very rarely on the study of Buddhist literature itself. For these reasons it must have been very difficult to gain a clear notion of the main Buddhist ideas. A religion like Buddhism which is based upon principles which are very different from the guiding principles of Christianity cannot be understood without a thorough study of its scriptures.[42]

Without wanting in any sense to defend "missionaries," still there are a number of statements here that one would like to unpack, although we can deal with only a few of the most important. Notice only that it is again clear that, for this position, Buddhism is based on texts, that it can be really—do we dare to say "correctly"?—understood only by a study of its scriptures. The implicit judgment, of course, is that real Buddhism is textual Buddhism. Notice that "Buddhist ideas"—at least "correct" "Buddhist ideas"—apparently do not reside in what Buddhists actually did or in what their "priests" said in conversation. Notice that knowledge based on observation of actual behavior is not adequate. But if actual religious behavior cannot tell us about religious "ideas" then this, again of necessity, has radical implications for the uses of archaeology and epigraphy: since archaeology and epigraphy tell us what people actually did, they cannot tell us about "real" or "correct" religion. "Real" or "correct" religion, we are given to understand, and it is assumed, resides in scriptural texts, in formal doctrine.

It is precisely this curious assumption concerning the location of real religion that lies behind the equally curious history of the study of Indian Buddhism. But the fact that it is so firmly fixed in Buddhist studies, and was operational from the very beginning, and the fact that this is a discipline largely formed—if not fully founded—within the Western intellectual tradition, might well suggest that this assumption too is rooted there, and that it might occur elsewhere as well. And indeed it does. It is not only found in fact in a variety of similar disciplines, it is much more nakedly expressed in other fields. I cite here only three examples.

Charles Thomas, one of the foremost figures in the archaeology of Early Britain, starts his book entitled *The Early Christian Archaeology of North Britain* with some important observations. He says:

> It would now be possible to build, slowly, a reliable framework for the Christian events of those centuries [the fifth to the sixth], using no more than archaeological, artistic and architectural data . . . So much that we can today detect through the exercise of archaeological methods—the primacy of the Christian cemetery, the direct Mediterranean contacts, the introduction of full monasticism, and the interplay of art styles in different media—is nowhere explicitly described in what literature has survived. Conversely, much that *is* contained in literary guise alone is not, as yet, reflected in visible or tangible evidence from this period.[43]

These observations—all of which point toward the importance of archaeological remains as independent sources for the history of a religion—are, however, followed by an otherwise curious *apologia:*

> The Christian reader may find many features of insular Christianity explained below in terms of pagan or prehistoric monuments. . . . This requires, perhaps, a short clarification. The central message of the New Testament, that redemption and the means of grace were provided for us, the priesthood of all believers, through God's assumption of manhood and his crucifixion in the person of Jesus Christ, remains untouched. It is a message conveyed by the Gospels, by patristic writing, and additionally through the means of symbols; these apart, it does not and cannot require any material reflection. On the other hand, the outward and visible form assumed by humanly constructed burials or burial-grounds, by the commemoration of dead humans by living humans, by the retention of skeletal fragments and like trivia as relics, and by the building of structures specially designed for the ceremonies of worship, are man's accretions in response to this message. As such, they are independent of the Word, and for the most part devoid of direct biblical authority. They are no more than the handiworks of what Professor Mircea Eliade has called "religious man." They are, moreover, the Christian versions of certain ideas . . . which prove, upon examination, to occur widely and commonly in the outward manifestations of most known religions both past and present.[44]

Thomas' statements, taken from a work of historical archaeology published in 1971 by Oxford University Press, provide us with a startling example of how the assumption as to where religion is located neutralizes the significance of material remains and, *ipso facto,* the role of human behavior in the history of a religion. Thomas makes it very clear that because "they are independent of the Word, and for the most part devoid of direct biblical authority," the material remains that characterize the early *Christian* archaeology of North Britain—"the primacy of the *Christian* cemetery" (emphasis added), etc.—cannot be, paradoxically, in any way essentially and historically *Christian*. In fact, he hastens to assign them to some bloodless, ahistorical abstraction called "religious man" who seems to have behaved much the same everywhere and at all times.

Virtually the same position—though made even more explicit—is maintained by Snyder in an even more recent work on "the archaeological evidence of church life before Constantine." Snyder makes a number of moves that are similar to those of Thomas, although they are more neutral in their expression. He too seems anxious to make sure that "the central message of the New Testament . . . remains untouched," but he goes about it in a somewhat different way: "In this study," he says, "there is a resolve to use only archaeological data as derived from the early Christians themselves. For a study of the New Testament, there is no such possibility. It is a basic assumption of this study that there never will be such data available for the study of the New Testament period."[45] This, of course, rather effectively neutralizes the significance of any material remains that might turn up from early first century Capernaum, for example, simply because they could not be Christian.[46]

If this suggests to the disinterested reader that what early Christian people did or how they lived has nothing to do with the history of early Christianity, Snyder is quick to confirm this when he finally encounters material remains that are clearly "derived from the early Christians themselves" and therefore indicative of what they actually did: they are, in the end, also not allowed any significance for the history of Christianity.

Snyder first asserts that "the interpretive edge today rests with the Bonn School, which proposes to study early Christian remains contextually as a *Volkreligion.*" He then goes on to say:

> If archaeological data belong to the realm of popular religious practice, the interpreter, or historian, must state clearly how the evidence of archaeology does relate to the literary material, or, to state it another way, how the popular religion relates to ecclesiastical tradition. The issue raised belongs not to the disciplines of patristics, history, or theology, but to the sociology of religion.[47]

The position here is as straightforwardly contradictory as was that of Thomas. The historian must clearly relate the archaeological evidence to the literary material, but that relationship—"The issue raised"—does not belong to the discipline of history. Early Christian remains and archaeological data belong, according to Snyder, "to the realm of popular religious practice." They must represent then, at the very least, what early Christian people actually did. But again according to Snyder, the relationship of what early Christian people actually did, or actually believed, to "the literary material" falls outside the purview of the historian of Christianity. Christianity, like Buddhism, apparently only exists in texts.

It is here also worth noting incidentally that, as Thomas' reference to Eliade suggests, the same assumption concerning religion and where it is located occurs in widely different kinds of work. The fact that a scholar like Eliade, whose concerns differ widely from those of Thomas and Snyder, also implicitly accepts this is only confirmation of how pervasive and perverse it has been.

Eliade, in speaking about "the customs and beliefs of European peasants," says:

> It is true that most of these rural European populations have been Christianized for over a thousand years. But they succeeded in incorporating into their Christianity a considerable part of their pre-Christian religious heritage, which was of immemorial antiquity. It would be wrong to suppose that for this reason European peasants are not Christians. But we must recognize that their religion is not confined to the historical forms of Christianity. . . . We may speak of a primordial, ahistorical Christianity; becoming Christian, the European cultivators incorporated into their new faith the cosmic religion that they had preserved from prehistoric times.[48]

Although there is much here that would require clarification, for our purposes it is sufficient to notice that like Thomas and Snyder—but toward a very different end—Eliade separates what Christians actually did or do, their "customs and beliefs," from "the historical forms of Christianity." What European Christian peasants do or believe is excluded from the history of their own religion and is assigned to something called "ahistorical Christianity." Once again the implications are clear: the historical forms of Christianity—whatever they are, and these are assumed to be self-evident—have little to do with actual Christians.

It is a curious fact that Thomas, Snyder, and Eliade—although each deals with a different period, a different location, and different kinds of evidence—all end by doing the same thing: they all want to exclude in one way or another actual Christian behavior and belief from the history of Christianity. Thomas wants to assign it to generalized "religious man"; Snyder assigns it to "popular religious practice," the domain of the sociologist of religion; and Eliade attributes it to "immemorial antiquity" or "ahistorical Christianity." None of them will admit it into the history of Christianity, and this can only be because they all share a common conception of where "essential," "real," or true Christianity is located. For them it appears to reside in texts. It would appear, then, that Buddhist scholars, archaeologists of early Britain, and historians of religion are all working from the same assumption as to where religion is located. But at least in its origin, this may not be an assumption at all.

Although most Buddhist scholars, archaeologists, or historians would probably resist the suggestion, this assumption in regard to the sources for the understanding of religions looks, on closer inspection, very much like it might itself be a religious or theological position. Embedded, for example, in apparently neutral archaeological and historical method might very well be a decidedly nonneutral and narrowly limited Protestant assumption as to where religion is actually located.[49]

The methodological position frequently taken by modern Buddhist scholars, archaeologists, and historians of religion looks, in fact, uncannily like the position taken by a variety of early Protestant reformers who were attempting to define and establish the locus of "true religion." The unknown author of the tract "On the Old and the New God" proposes, according to Eire, "that Christians should not seek religion in outward things, but rather in scripture."[50] Karlstadt, again according to Eire, "began to strike out against the prevailing religious externalism of his day, hoping he would be able to reassert the primacy of the Word." His position "is clearly revealed in this dictum: Only the Spirit vivifies, and the Spirit works through the Word, not through material objects. 'The Word of God is spiritual, and it alone is useful to believers.' "[51] In his *Commentary on True and False Religion,* Zwingli declared that "we ought to be taught by the word of God externally, and by the spirit internally, those things that have to do with piety, and not by sculpture wrought by the artist's hands."[52] Calvin too saw material things—"images and like things"—not as integral and vital parts of "religion," but as "innumerable mockeries . . . which pervert religion" and must be excluded from it. They are not "spiritually ordained by the Word."[53]

There are other and probably better passages that could be cited, but the point at least, I think, is clear: there is a remarkable similarity between the value assigned literary sources in modern historical and archaeological studies and the argument of Protestant reformers concerning the location of true religion. This suggests, at least, the distinct possibility that historical and archaeological method—if not the history of religions as a whole—represents the direct historical continuation of Reformation theological values; it further suggests that if Karlstadt's hope was to "reassert the primacy of the Word," he may have succeeded in doing just that in some very unlikely and unforeseen ways.

There are other considerations that point in the same direction. It is not just the assigning of primacy to literary materials in the study of religion in both modern archaeological and historical studies that shows several signs of possibly being rooted in sixteenth-century Protestant tracts. The concomitant disinclination of archaeologists and historians to consider material remains as independent, critical sources for the history of a religion also looks very much like a more recent manifestation of the sixteenth-century Protestant distrust and devaluation of actual religious and historical human behavior. Sixteenth-century material objects—reliquaries, shrines, and images—were for Protestant reformers apparently irrefutable evidence of what Christian people were actually doing.

They refer to them constantly in their polemics: Calvin, in fact, drew up "an inventory of relics" to show, from his point of view, just how bad things were.[54] This inventory, ironically, is an extremely valuable historical document because it allows us to see what was actually occurring during his lifetime in specific geographical locations. But what is a boon for us was a bane for Calvin. In fact, the problem for the reformers was, in part at least, precisely what was actually occurring and what had been historically practiced. Given the nature of the case they were trying to advance, they did not—more pointedly, could not—allow actual religious practice to have any meaningful place in defining the nature of true religion. To have done so would have been to concede to their perceived opponents the validity of a substantial portion of the argument from "tradition." Proponents of this new and historically peculiar conception of religion, therefore, were of necessity forced to systematically devalue and denigrate what religious people actually did and to deny that it had any place in true religion.[55] This devaluation, not surprisingly but in fact almost obsessively, focused on material objects. The religious power and importance of these objects are, however, only underlined by the fact that they frequently had to be forcefully removed and destroyed and always had to be fulsomely denounced with an otherwise curious ardor. We, it seems, may have inherited both tendencies: the unwillingness to allow actual practice a meaningful place in the definition of religion and the devaluation of any sources that express it.

Merely stating the striking similarity between the arguments of sixteenth-century Protestant reformers and the assumptions of modern Buddhist scholars, archaeologists, and historians of religion, does not, of course, prove anything. It does, however, suggest some possibilities. It is possible that the curious history of the study of Indian Buddhism is neither curious nor unique. It begins to appear as only one instance in which a particular assumption concerning the location of religion has dictated and determined the value assigned to various sources.[56] It is possible that what originated as a sixteenth-century Protestant polemical conception of where "true" religion is located has been so thoroughly absorbed into the Western intellectual tradition that its polemical and theological origins have been forgotten and now it is taken too often entirely as a given.[57] It is possible then, that it is this conception that has determined the history of the study of Indian Buddhism and that—as a consequence—our picture of Indian Buddhism may reflect more of our own religious history and values than the history and values of Indian Buddhism. It is possible, finally, that the old and ongoing debate between archaeology and textual studies is not—as is frequently assumed—a debate about sources. It may rather be a debate about where religion as an object of investigation is to be located. It is possible, perhaps, that the Reformation is not over after all.

Notes

1. There is, of course, no single, systematic survey of Buddhist archaeological remains in India. The best attempt so far is D. Mitra, *Buddhist Monuments* (Calcutta: 1971). It, however, was not only not intended to be exhaustive but is now also some twenty years out of date. For inscriptional remains we have, for the period up to 1910, H. Lüders, *A List of Brahmi Inscriptions from the Earliest Times to about* A.D. *400 with the Exception of Those of Aśoka,* Appendix to *EI* 10 (Calcutta: 1912). It is, though, by now badly outdated and, as its title indicates, does not list material beyond "about A.D. 400." Both more comprehensive and much more recent is Shizutani Masao, *Indo bukkyō himei mokuroku* (Catalog of Indian Buddhist Inscriptions) (Kyoto: 1979), but it too is already dated and contains serious omissions—cf. Shizutani's listings of the Kharoṣṭhī inscriptions, e.g., with those in G. Fussman, "Gāndhārī écrite, gāndhārī parlée," *Dialectes dans les littératures indo-aryennes,* ed. C. Caillat (Paris: 1989) 444–451. Shizutani is especially unreliable now for important sites like Mathurā (only one of the finds from Govindnagar is included) and like Amarāvatī (none of the early inscriptions brought to light in the "clearance-operation" in 1958–1959, e.g., are included; see A. Ghosh, "The Early Phase of the Stupa at Amaravati, Southeast India," *Ancient Ceylon* 3 [1979] 97–103).

2. On the curious fact, e.g., that a considerable number of Buddhist inscriptions were never intended to be seen, let alone read, see H. Lüders, "The Manikiala Inscription," *JRAS* (1909) 660; S. Konow, *Kharoshṭhī Inscriptions with the Exception of Those of Aśoka,* Corpus Inscriptionum Indicarum, Vol. II, Pt. 1 (Calcutta: 1929) 31; A. V. Naik, "Inscriptions of the Deccan: An Epigraphical Survey (*circa* 300 B.C.–1300 A.D.)," *Bulletin of the Deccan College Research Institute* 11 (1948) 3–4; etc.

3. This point in regard to archaeological evidence in general has been made a number of times. See, for example, R. Grenet, *Les pratiques funeraires dans l'asie centrale sedentaire de la conquete grecque à l'islamisation* (Paris: 1984) 7, who, in referring to Zoroastrianism, contrasts "canonical or clerical texts—always untiringly scrutinized although the narrowness of the milieux which produced them is ever more clearly evident," with archaeological materials "which allow us the most direct access to the religion as it was lived and practised by all social classes." Much the same has also been said of epigraphical sources. For example, L. H. Kant, in speaking of Jewish inscriptions from the Greco-Roman world, says "inscriptions, in contrast to most other written records, reflect a broad spectrum of society—from nearly illiterate poor, who wrote many of the Roman catacomb inscriptions, to the apparently wealthy patrons of funerary poetry and from tradesmen such as shoemakers and perfume sellers to educated persons such as rabbis and disciples of sages. It is also striking that, unlike many written texts, the inscriptions express for us religious views that have not been filtered by a subsequent normative literary tradition" ("Jewish Inscriptions in Greek and Latin," *Aufstieg und Niedergang der römischen Welt: Geschichte und Kultur Roms in Spiegel der Neueren Forschung,* Teil 2, *Principat,* Band 20, Halbband 2, ed. W. Haase [Berlin: 1987] 674). Likewise, in regard to "les inscriptions latines chrétiennes," Sanders has said: "De la sorte, les inscriptions nous renseignent aussi de manière privilégiée sur la masse, sur la majorité oubliée par la littérature à hauts talons, le majorité silencieuse, l'homme de la rue, sa vie privée, son imbrication dans son monde à lui, telle qu'elle fut définie par les coordonnées du temps, de l'espace, des conditions sociales, du climat religieux et émotionnel . . ." (G. Sanders, "Les chrétiens face à l'épigraphie funéraire latine," *Assimilation et résistance à la culture gréco-romaine dans le monde ancien: Travaux du VIe congrès international d' études classiques,*

ed. D. M. Pippidi [Paris: 1976] 285). For the points of view represented in Indian Buddhist inscriptions and the role of the "lettré," whether "moine ou sculpteur," see the important remarks in G. Fussman's review of *Epigraphical Hybrid Sanskrit,* by Th. Damsteegt, *JA* (1980) 423–424. It should be noted, finally, that inscriptions are, of course, written sources, but they are most easily and clearly distinguishable from literary sources by the simple fact that they were not meant to be circulated.

4. For some representative recent views, see K. R. Norman, "The Value of the Pali Tradition," *Jagajjyoti Buddha Jayanti Annual* (Calcutta: 1984) 1–9. He points out that it is now known that "the Pali canon is a translation from some earlier tradition" (4), that, in fact, "all traditions which we possess have been translated at least once" (5). See also L. O. Gómez, "Buddhism in India," *Encyclopedia of Religion,* ed. M. Eliade (London: 1987) 352ff ("Textual sources are late, dating at the very least five hundred years after the death of the Buddha"); G. Schopen, "Two Problems in the History of Indian Buddhism" Ch. II below, 23–25.

5. This, ironically, is especially true for the so-called early canonical literature. For Pāli, see O. von Hinüber, "Pāli Manuscripts of Canonical Texts from North Thailand—a Preliminary Report," *Journal of the Siam Society* 71 (1983) 75–88 ("most of the surviving [Pāli] manuscript material is hardly older than the late 18th century" [78]); and the material cited in G. Schopen, "The *Stūpa* Cult and the Extant Pāli *Vinaya,*" Ch. V below, n. 23. For Central Asian Sanskrit material, see L. Sander, *Paläographisches zu den Sanskrithandschriften der Berliner Turfansammlung,* Verzeichnis der orientalischen Handschriften in Deutschland, Supplementband 8 (Wiesbaden: 1968) 51 ("Unter den in die Tausende gehenden, von den vier preussischen Expeditionen [1902–1914] im Norden Ostturkistans gefundenen fragmentarischen Sanskrithandschriften gibt es, soweit mir bekannt ist, nur sieben mit den charakteristischen Merkmalen der Kuṣāṇa-Brāhmī," and so on).

6. I. B. Horner, *Women under Primitive Buddhism* (London: 1930) xx: "Still another inherent difficulty in dealing with the Pāli texts arises from the various editions, glosses, and revisions which they have undergone at the hands of the monks"; etc.

7. A. K. Warder, e.g., starts his discussion of the Pāli Canon as a "historical record" by saying "the Buddhists . . . were ready to turn everything to account in developing and popularizing their ideas and in presenting a comprehensive 'world view,' " and ends it by saying: "The bias of the repeaters [of the canon] sometimes intrudes itself, often very clumsily"; see "The Pali Canon and Its Commentaries as an Historical Record," *Historians of India, Pakistan and Ceylon,* ed. C. H. Philips (London: 1961) 46–47.

8. For the history of the study of the archaeological and epigraphical material, see D. K. Chakrabarti, *A History of Indian Archeology: From the Beginning to 1947* (New Delhi: 1988); there is also some interesting material for the earliest period in P. Mitter, *Much Maligned Monsters: History of European Reactions to Indian Art* (Oxford: 1977); and some useful data in A. Imam, *Sir Alexander Cunningham and the Beginnings of Indian Archaeology* (Dacca: 1966). For the study of literary sources, the most recent and reliable work is J. W. de Jong, *A Brief History of Buddhist Studies in Europe and America,* 2nd rev. ed. (Delhi: 1987); see also H. de Lubac, *La recontre du bouddhisme et de l'occident* (Paris: 1952); R. Schwab, *The Oriental Renaissance: Europe's Rediscovery of India and the East, 1680–1880,* trans. G. Patterson-Black and V. Reinking (New York: 1984); W. Halbfass, *India and Europe: An Essay in Understanding* (Albany, N.Y.: 1988).

9. J. W. de Jong, "The Study of Buddhism: Problems and Perspectives," *Studies in Indo-Asian Art and Culture,* Vol. IV, ed. P. Ratnam (New Delhi: 1975) 21, and *A Brief History of Buddhist Studies in Europe and America,* 20.

10. De Jong, "The Study of Buddhism," 14.

11. Archaeologists themselves have contributed heavily to the currency of this view; see G. Daniel, *A Short History of Archaeology* (London: 1981) 13; J. A. Alexander, "The Archaeological Recognition of Religion: The Examples of Islam in Africa and 'Urnfields' in Europe," *Space, Hierarchy and Society,* ed. B. C. Burnham and J. Kingsbury, British Archaeological Reports, No. 559 (Oxford: 1979) 215; cf. D. P. Dymond, *Archaeology and History: A Plea for Reconciliation* (London: 1974).

12. Epigraphical evidence, at least, does not support the idea that Buddhist literature was widely known in actual Buddhist communities, but in fact points in the opposite direction; see, most recently, G. Schopen, "A Verse from the Bhadracarīpraṇidhāna in a 10th Century Inscription Found at Nālandā," *JIABS* 12.1 (1989) 149–157, and the sources cited in the notes there.

13. In speaking about "early Christian archaeology," G. F. Snyder refers to "three mistaken assumptions" about "sacred" literature: "It is assumed the literature represents rather accurately the historical situation when actually it may have a tendentious purpose. . . . It is assumed the literature speaks *cum solo voce* when actually other voices have been ignored, repressed, or assimilated. . . . It is assumed the literature represents a reflective or literary level of popular religion whereas actually literature and practice often stand in tension with each other" (*Ante Pacem: Archaeological Evidence of Church Life before Constantine* [Macon, Ga.: 1985] 8). Snyder's formulation is, of course, suggestive of what has been assumed in Buddhist studies as well; but cf. below pp. 11–12.

14. It is worth noting that even those South Asian Buddhist literary sources that have been taken to most closely approximate "historical" documents in our sense of the term were intended, by their authors or transmitters, to fulfill a very different function. The chapter colophons of the *Mahāvaṃsa,* e.g., uniformly say: Here ends such and such a chapter "in the *Mahāvaṃsa,* compiled for the faith and exhilaration of good men" (*sujanappasādasaṃvegatthāya*). See W. Geiger, *Mahāvaṃsa* (London: 1908) 11, 15, 20, etc.; see also the opening exhortatory verses in H. Oldenberg, *The Dīpavaṃsa: An Ancient Buddhist Historical Record* (London and Edinburgh: 1879) 13.

15. So R. C. Zaehner in his foreword to P. Olivelle's *The Origin and Early Development of Buddhist Monasticism* (Colombo: 1974).

16. G. Bühler, "Votive Inscriptions from the Sānchi Stūpas," *EI* 2 (1894) 93; cf. J. Marshall, A. Foucher, and N. G. Majumdar, *The Monuments of Sāñchī,* Vol. I (Delhi: 1940) 34 and n. 2.

17. H. Lüders, *Bharhut Inscriptions,* Corpus Inscriptionum Indicarum, Vol. II, Pt. 2, rev. by E. Waldschmidt and M. A. Mehendale (Ootacamund: 1963) 2. Like Bühler before him, and in similar terms, Lüders points out that a comparison of Buddhist with Jain inscriptions makes it very difficult to avoid the fact that, in Buddhist inscriptions, the monks themselves appear as donors—they are not acting as organizers or agents of others: "The wording of the Bhārh[ut] inscriptions refers to the Buddhist clergyman in such a way, as if he himself had made the donation" (2).

18. G. Fussman, "Une inscription Kharoṣṭhī à Haḍḍa," *BEFEO* 56 (1969) 8–9.

19. J. Marshall, *Taxila: An Illustrated Account of Archaeological Excavations Carried out at Taxila under the Orders of the Government of India between the Years 1913 and 1934,* Vol. I (Cambridge: 1951) 240. Such hoards are, in fact, found in Buddhist monasteries that are very much earlier than "the early medieval period"; see R. B. D. R. Sahni, *Archaeological Remains and Excavations at Bairat* (Jaipur: 1937) 21–22; D. B. Diskalkar, "Excavations at Kasrawad," *IHQ* 25 (1949) 12ff; etc.

20. W. Spink, "Ajanta: A Brief History," *Aspects of Indian Art: Papers Presented in a Symposium at the Los Angeles County Museum of Art, October 1970*, ed. P. Pal (Leiden: 1972) 51. For yet other examples, see D. D. Kosambi, "Dhenukākaṭa," *JASBom* 30.2 (1955) 52–53; R. A. L. H. Gunawardana, *Robe and Plough: Monasticism and Economic Interest in Sri Lanka* (Tucson: 1979) 81–86; N. A. Falk, "The Case of the Vanishing Nun: The Fruits of Ambivalence in Ancient Indian Buddhism," *Unspoken Worlds: Women's Religious Lives in Non-Western Cultures*, ed. N. A. Falk and R. M. Gross (San Francisco: 1980) 223, n. 2; H. P. Ray, *Monastery and Guild: Commerce under the Sātavāhanas* (Delhi: 1986) 104.

21. Compare W. Wassilieff, "Le bouddhisme dans son plein développement d'après les vinayas," *RHR* 34 (1896) 321: "pour le vie en communauté, même dans les autres religions, les règles établies ne peuvent sortir du cadre connu."

22. See, for the sake of convenience, C. S. Prebish, *Buddhist Monastic Discipline: The Sanskrit Prātimokṣa Sūtras of the Mahāsāṃghikas and Mūlasarvāstivādins* (University Park, Pa.: 1975) 13–14, 70–71; I. B. Horner, "The Pattern of the Nissaggiyas," *IHQ* 16 (1940) 268–291; M. Wijayaratna, *Le moine bouddhiste selon les textes du Theravāda* (Paris: 1983) 93–104.

23. R. Lingat, "Vinaya et droit laïque: Études sur les conflits de la loi religieuse et de la loi laïque dans l'indochine hinayaniste," *BEFEO* 37 (1937) 415–477, esp. 431ff; cf. H. Oldenberg, *Buddha: His Life, His Doctrine, His Order*, trans. W. Hoey (London: 1882) 355 and n.

24. J. Ph. Vogel, "Prakrit Inscriptions from a Buddhist Site at Nagarjunikonda," *EI* 20 (1929–1930) 22–23.

25. A. H. Longhurst, *The Buddhist Antiquities of Nagarjunakonda, Madras Presidency*, MASI, No. 54 (Delhi: 1938) 10; cf. I. K. Sarma, "A Coin Mould-Piece from Nāgārjunakoṇḍa: New Light on the Silver Coinage of the Sātavāhanas," *Journal of the Economic and Social History of the Orient* 16 (1973) 89–106, which deals with an even earlier mold from the site.

26. K. D. Bajpai, "Authority of Minting Coins in Ancient India," *Journal of the Numismatic Society of India* 25 (1963) 17–21; D. C. Sircar, "Note on Chinchani Plate of Krishna III," *EI* 37 (1968) 277–278; etc.

27. Evidence for the manufacture of coins at Buddhist monastic sites is both early and widespread. For such evidence at Kasrawad, see Diskalkar, *IHQ* 25, 15; for Nālandā, B. Kumar, *Archaeology of Pataliputra and Nalanda* (Delhi: 1987) 212; S. S. P. Sarasvati, *Coinage in Ancient India: A Numismatic, Archaeochemical and Metallurgical Study of Ancient Indian Coins*, Vol. I (Delhi: 1986) 202ff; and so on.

28. *Histoire du bouddhisme indien*, 456. I have elsewhere discussed this same passage from a somewhat different point of view; see my "Two Problems in the History of Indian Buddhism," Ch. II below, 41–42.

29. There has been very little discussion of the assumptions and method that lie behind this important book. The only serious attempt to get at some of the problems involved is, as far as I know, M. Pye, "Comparative Hermeneutics in Religion," *The Cardinal Meaning: Essays in Comparative Hermeneutics, Buddhism and Christianity*, ed. M. Pye and R. Morgan (The Hague: 1973) 1–58, esp. 31ff. At least some of the problems, moreover, appear to be directly related to Lamotte's declared intentions, which, on the surface, appear to be mutually contradictory. He first says, "Notre premier souci a été de replacer le bouddhisme dans le cadre historique qui lui manquait, de le retirer du monde des idées où il se confinait volontairement pour le ramener sur terre," but then says: "En laissant au merveilleux la place qu'il a toujours occupée dans les sources, on

pense donner un reflet plus fidèle de la mentalité des disciples du Buddha. C'est cette mentalité qui constitue l'objet propre de notre enquête et non une fuyante et insaisissable certitude historique" (Lamotte, vi, x). Note that H. Durt has already pointed out that "certes, l'*Histoire du bouddhisme indien* n'est pas une 'histoire des mentalités' au sense contemporain du terme" in "Étienne Lamotte, 1903–1983," *BEFEO* 74 (1985) 14.

30. *Histoire du bouddhisme indien,* 456.

31. Even the most steadfastly conservative have had to admit this in regard to contemporary Buddhism. See, for example, R. F. Gombrich, *Precept and Practice: Traditional Buddhism in the Rural Highlands of Ceylon* (Oxford: 1971) 243: "The canonical theory of *karma* survives intact—cognitively; affectively its rigour is sometimes avoided. Similarly, though the doctrine of *anatta* can be salvaged by the claim that the personality continuing through a series of births has as much reality as the personality within one life, *prārthanā* for happy rebirths and the transfer of merit to dead relatives show that the *anatta* doctrine has no more affective immediacy with regard to the next life than with regard to this, and that belief in personal survival after death is a fundamental feature of Sinhalese Buddhism in practice." Interestingly, something very like this had been pointed out more than a hundred years ago; see P. E. de Foucaux, *Le Lalitavistara: Devéloppement des jeux, contenant l'histoire du Bouddha Çakya-muni, depuis sa naissance jusqu' à sa prèdication,* Vol. I (Paris: 1884) xvi, n. 2, and xvii, nn. 1 and 2. For the Hindu context, see, among many possibilities, U. Sharma, "Theodicy and the Doctrine of Karma," *Man* 8 (1973) 347–364.

32. Lüders, *Bharhut Inscriptions,* 55 (A 108).

33. V. B. Kolte, "Brahmi Inscriptions from Pauni," *EI* 38 (1969) 174 (D); S. B. Deo and J. P. Joshi, *Pauni Excavation (1969–1970)* (Nagpur: 1972) 38, no. 2.

34. S. Paranavitana, *Inscriptions of Ceylon,* Vol. I, *Containing Cave Inscriptions from 3rd Century B.C. to 1st Century A.C. and Other Inscriptions in the Early Brahmi Script* (Ceylon: 1970) no. 34; see also lii–liii.

35. Paranavitana, *Inscriptions of Ceylon,* Vol. I, nos. 338–341; see also lii–liii.

36. L. de La Vallée Poussin, "Death and Disposal of the Dead (Buddhist)," *Encyclopaedia of Religion and Ethics,* ed. J. Hastings, Vol. IV (Edinburgh: 1911) 446–449.

37. T. W. Rhys Davids, *Buddhist Suttas,* Sacred Books of the East, Vol. XI (Oxford: 1900) xliv–xlv.

38. A. Cunningham, *The Bhilsa Topes: Or, Buddhist Monuments of Central India* (London: 1854) 211–220, Bhojpur—at which *Stūpa* 8c, e.g., contained numerous large bones; 184–189, Sāñcī, *Stūpa* no. 2; 203–205, Sonārī, *Stūpa* no. 2; 223–226, Andher, *Stūpas* nos. 2 and 3.

39. This is beyond doubt, for example, in regard to Sāñcī *Stūpa* no. 2; see Schopen, "The *Stūpa* Cult and the Extant Pāli *Vinaya,*" Ch. V below, 92 and n. 32. M. Bénisti has recently argued that this *stūpa* is older even than Bhārhut in "Observations concernant le stūpa no. 2 de Sāñcī," *BEI* 4 (1986) 165–170.

40. W. West, "Description of Some of the Kanheri Topes," *JBomBRAS* 6 (1862) 116–120; S. Gokhale, "The Memorial Stūpa Gallery at Kanheri," *Indian Epigraphy: Its Bearing on the History of Art,* ed. F. M. Asher and G. S. Gai (New Delhi: 1985) 55–59; etc.

41. J. Burgess, *Report on the Buddhist Cave Temples and Their Inscriptions,* Archaeological Survey of Western India, Vol. IV (London: 1883) 7; see Mitra, *Buddhist Monuments,* 153.

42. De Jong, *A Brief History of Buddhist Studies in Europe and America,* 11.

43. C. Thomas, *The Early Christian Archaeology of North Britain* (London: 1971) 1.

44. Ibid., 3–4.

45. Snyder, *Ante Pacem*, 10.

46. This same assumption also makes it impossible for archaeological investigation to critically comment on the nature of the New Testament as a historical document; cf. the remarks in E. M. Meyers and J. F. Strange, *Archaeology, Rabbis and Early Christianity* (Nashville: 1981) 58–59, on the absence of a first-century synagogue at Capernaum in spite of the fact that Mark 1:21 places one there. For other problems concerning Capernaum in the New Testament, see J. Blenkinsopp, "The Literary Evidence," in V. Tzaferis, *Excavations at Capernaum, Vol. I, 1978–1982* (Winona Lake, Ind.: 1989) 201ff.

47. Snyder, 7, 9.

48. M. Eliade, *The Sacred and the Profane: The Nature of Religion* (San Diego: 1959) 164.

49. "Protestant" is used here in the broadest and most general sense, and the assumption involved is probably only meaningfully so-called in regard to its origins. It has, it seems, been so generalized and fully assimilated into Western intellectual and cultural values that, in its present form, it is probably most simply characterized as "Western." Elements of this assumption were, of course, much older. There was, to begin with, the "Second Commandment" and its long and convoluted history; see J. Gutmann, "The 'Second Commandment' and the Image in Judaism," *Hebrew Union College Annual* 32 (1961) 161–174, and "Deuteronomy: Religious Reformation or Iconoclastic Revolution?" in *The Image and the Word: Confrontations in Judaism, Christianity and Islam*, ed. J. Gutmann (Missoula, Mont.: 1977) 5–25. There was Vigilantius, of whom Saint Jerome, at least, was not fond and the later Iconoclastic controversies; see W. H. Fremantle, *The Principal Works of St. Jerome*, Select Library of Nicene and Post-Nicene Fathers of the Christian Church, Ser. 2, Vol. 4 (Grand Rapids, Mich.: 1983) 417–423, and, among an immense bibliography, D. J. Sahas, *Icon and Logos: Sources in Eighth-Century Iconoclasm* (Toronto: 1986) along with the select bibliography given there. There was Guibert of Nogent's *De Pignoribus sanctorum*; see K. Guth, *Guibert von Nogent und die hochmittelalterliche Kritik an der Reliquienverehrung* (Ottobeuren: 1970), but see also J. F. Benton's discussion of Guibert's character in *Self and Society in Medieval France: The Memoirs of Abbot Guibert of Nogent* (New York: 1970) 1–33; and even Erasmus in *Ten Colloquies*, trans. C. R. Thompson (Indianapolis: 1979) 56–91. But none of these in and of themselves had lasting cultural influence, and almost all are more significant in retrospect—that is to say, in the way in which they were perceived and used during and after the Reformation.

50. C. M. N. Eire, *War against the Idols: The Reformation of Worship from Erasmus to Calvin* (Cambridge: 1986) 76.

51. Ibid., 55, 59.

52. Ulrich Zwingli, *Commentary on True and False Religion*, ed. S. M. Jackson and C. N. Heller (Durham, N.C.: 1981) 331–332.

53. "The Lausanne Articles," No. 7, *Calvin: Theological Treatises*, ed. J. K. S. Reid, Library of Christian Classics, Vol. 22 (Philadelphia: 1954) 36.

54. "An Admonition, Showing the Advantages which Christendom might Derive from an Inventory of Relics," *Tracts Relating to the Reformation by John Calvin*, trans. H. Beveridge (Edinburgh: 1844) 289–341.

55. This can be illustrated by a number of passages from the *Institutes of the Christian Religion by John Calvin*, ed. J. Allen, Vol. II, 4th ed. (Philadelphia: 1843). In reference to the intercession of saints, 3.20.21: "Therefore, since the Scripture calls us away from all others to Christ alone . . . it would be a proof of great stupidity, not to say insanity, to be so desirous of procuring an admission by the saints, as to be seduced from him, without whom they have no access themselves. But that this has been practised in some

ages, and is now practised wherever Popery prevails, who can deny?"; 4.9.14: "Of purgatory, the intercession of saints, auricular confession, and similar fooleries, the Scriptures contain not a single syllable. But, because all these things have been sanctioned by the authority of councils, or, to speak more correctly, have been admitted into the general belief and practice, therefore every one of them is to be taken for an interpretation of Scripture"—a position Calvin, of course, denies; 4.10.1: "Whatever edicts have been issued by men respecting the worship of God, independently of His word, it has been customary to call ***human traditions.*** Against such laws we contend."

56. This, of course, is not to deny that other factors were involved. P. C. Almond, for example, has recently discussed the textualization of Buddhism as an instrument of colonialist ideology: a "Victorian Buddhism . . . constructed from textual sources increasingly located in and therefore regulated by the West" (*The British Discovery of Buddhism* [Cambridge: 1988] 24ff). A striking example of the effects of this textualization may be seen in S. Hardy, *A Manual of Buddhism in Its Modern Development,* 2d ed. (London: 1880) 412: "The difficulties attendant upon this peculiar dogma [the textual conception of *anatta*] may be seen in the fact that it is almost universally repudiated. Even the sramana priests, at one time, denied it; but when the passages teaching it were pointed out to them in their own sacred books, they were obliged to acknowledge that it is a tenet of their religion." See also L. Rocher, "Max Müller and the Veda," *Mélanges Armand Abel,* ed. A. Destrée, Vol. III (Leiden: 1978) 221–235. That the textualization of Hinduism by Indian "reformers"—in imitation of the Protestant missionary model of religion—had the same consequences for the evaluation of Indian religious practice as the Protestant location of religion had had on the evaluation of European practice, at least at the intellectual level, is painfully clear from a number of sources. Rāmmohan Roy said, e.g., "My constant reflections on the inconvenient, or rather injurious rites introduced by the peculiar practice of Hindoo idolatry which more than any other pagan worship, destroys the texture of society, together with compassion for my countrymen, have compelled me to use every possible effort to awaken them from their dream of error; and *by making them acquainted with their Scriptures,* enable them to contemplate with true devotion the unity and omnipresence of nature's God"; quoted in G. Richards, *A Source-Book of Modern Hinduism* (London: 1985) 5 (my emphasis); see also 6–9, 24, 30–33, 45, 48–50, etc. It is undoubtedly and notoriously difficult to separate the religious and the political in colonialist ideology, but since both were also at work in founding the Archaeological Survey of India (Imam [n. 8 above] 40–41), the ideological concern could not itself have been a sufficient cause for the dominance of the textual orientation.

57. This, again, is not to say that there were not powerful competing conceptions, but only to say that they did not culturally win. Early on, the "Catholic" conception held its own and produced, as a consequence, some important scholarly works: "Catholic scholars tended to anchor their investigation of Christian religious observance in ancient tradition. It was the study of this tradition that inspired the monumental and often reprinted *Annales Ecclesiastici* and the work on the Roman martyrs by Cesare Baronio, as well as Bosio's *Roma sotterranea,* the first major archaeological account of the Roman catacombs. On the other hand, when Protestants discussed the practice of Christian piety, they most often appealed to reason and to theological and philosophical principles. . . . In the words of John Calvin, a Christian should have 'no use [for] place apart from the doctrine of godliness' which could be taught anywhere at all"; see S. MacCormack, "Loca Sancta: The Organization of Sacred Topography in Late Antiquity," *The Blessings of Pilgrimage,* ed. R. Ousterhout (Urbana, Ill., and Chicago: 1990) 8–9. But recent scholar-

ship, which has tended to see "the Counter-Reformation and the Protestant Reformation as analogous social and religious processes" (so Badone in her introduction to *Religious Orthodoxy and Popular Faith in European Society*, ed. E. Badone [Princeton, N.J.: 1990] 12), has also pointed clearly to the strong textualizing responses in the former; so J. Delumeau, in *La Catholicisme entre Luther et Voltaire* (Paris: 1971): "De l'extraordinaire intérêt qu'on marqua pour les choses de la religion, au moins dans le public qui savait lire, témoignent les statistiques concernant l'édition . . . l'histoire religieuse et celle des mentalités ne peuvent négliger ce fait quantitatif: jamais autant les livres de spiritualité—souvent de petits formats et en langue vulgaire—, jamais autant d'éloges de la vierge n'avaient été mis en circulation" (84); "Surtout, l'époque de l'humanisme vit l'essor de la théologie *positive* . . . qui est l'étude de l'Ecriture, aidée par les interprétations des Pères et des conciles" (85); "En 1654, Godeau, évêque de Vence, donna dans ses mandements des listes de livres à lire à ses prêtres. En 1658 l'archevêque de Sens, Godrin, demanda à ses curés de se procurer 47 ouvrages qu'ils devaient, le cas échéant, présenter lors des visites pastorales et, parmi eux, une Bible, le catéchisme romain" (271); cf. also B. Baroni, *La contre-réforme devant la Bible: La question biblique* (Lausanne: 1943). Delumeau's remarks raise, as well, the question of the sheer influence of the development of printing on the location of religion in texts, and it undoubtedly played a role. But any argument contending that printing in itself is a sufficient explanation must take into account the fact that printing served a very different function in the Far East—especially in the earlier periods. There, sacred texts were printed not so they could be read, but so they could empower sacred objects. The earliest extant examples of printing in Japan, e.g., contain "versions of Sanskrit charms [*dhāraṇīs*] transliterated into Chinese characters," and, even if they had been seen, they would have had little or no literal meaning for a literate Japanese. But they, in fact, were never intended to be seen. They were meant to be inserted into miniature *stūpas;* see J. Needham, *Science and Civilization in China,* Vol. V, *Chemistry and Chemical Technology,* Pt. 1, *Paper and Printing,* by Tsien Tsuen-hsuin (Cambridge: 1985) 336–337; see also 321–322.

* * *

[For some further observations on the early inscriptions from Sāñcī see now: G. Schopen, "What's in a Name: The Religious Function of the Early Donative Inscriptions," *Unseen Presence: The Buddha and Sanchi*, ed. V. Dehejia (Bombay: 1996) 58–73. For monks and private property, see Schopen, "Monastic Law Meets the Real World: A Monk's Continuing Right to Inherit Family Property in Classical India," *History of Religions* 35 (1995) 101–123. For Buddhist disposal of the dead, see chs. VII, IX, and X below.]

CHAPTER II

Two Problems in the History of Indian Buddhism

The Layman/Monk Distinction and the Doctrines of the Transference of Merit

I.

IN AN AREA like Indian Buddhist doctrinal history, where there is constant discussion but little proof, it might sometimes be useful if we try to draw up lists of what we actually know. Such lists might be even more useful if we distinguish clearly, in so far as this is possible, what we know from what we have conjectured or reconstructed or hypothesized. This is what I have tried to do here in regard to two particular problems: the problem of the Layman/Monk Distinction in Indian Buddhism, and the problem of the Doctrine, or Doctrines, of the Transference of Merit in Indian Buddhism. If, however, we begin with the purpose of limiting ourselves to what we can actually know in regard to these problems, then the conventional evaluation and use of literary sources in discussions of Buddhist doctrinal history becomes, in fact, our first problem, and it is here that we must begin.

II.

We know, and have known for some time, that the Pāli canon as we have it—and it is generally conceded to be our oldest source—cannot be taken back further than the last quarter of the first century B.C.E., the date of the Alu-vihāra redaction, the earliest redaction that we can have some knowledge of,[1] and that—for a critical history—it can serve, at the very most, only as a source for the Buddhism of this period. But we also know that even this is problematic

---

Originally published in *Studien zur Indologie und Iranistik* 10 (1985):9–47. Reprinted with stylistic changes with permission of *Studien zur Indologie und Iranistik*.

since, as Malalasekera has pointed out: ". . . how far the *Tipiṭaka* and its commentary reduced to writing at Alu-vihāra resembled them as they have come down to us now, no one can say."[2] In fact, it is not until the time of the commentaries of Buddhaghosa, Dhammapāla, and others—that is to say, the fifth to sixth centuries C.E.—that we can know anything definite about the actual contents of this canon.

We also know that there is no evidence to indicate that a canon existed prior to the Alu-vihāra redaction. Although Aśoka in his Bhābrā Edict specifically enjoined both monks and laymen to recite certain texts, which he named,[3] he nowhere in his records gives any indication that he knew of a canon, or the classification of texts into *nikāyas.*[4] We do know, however, that the epithet *pañcanekāyika* occurs in the Bhārhut and Sāñcī inscriptions, but we also know that Lamotte has shown that it is unlikely that this refers to the five collections of the *Suttapiṭaka.*[5] And even if it could be shown to refer to the *nikāyas* as codified collections, this would still not push the data for the collection of at least some texts into *nikāyas* much beyond the first century B.C.E., the approximate date of the inscriptions from Bhārhut and Sāñcī. The earliest known reference to the *Tripiṭaka* is still later. It is found in an inscription published in 1974 by Fussman that is dated by him to year 5 of Kaniṣka.[6] And finally, we also know that it is not until Nāgārjunikoṇḍa and Amarāvatī—and then only in the South—that we find specific reference to the *Dīgha-, Majjhima-,* and, probably, to the *Saṃyutta-nikāyas* in inscriptions.[7]

The occurrence of the titles *sutaṃtika, sutātika,* etc., "one who knows the *sutta*" (once at Bhārhut, three times at Sāñcī), or *vinayadhara,* "one who knows the *vinaya*" (once at Sāñcī), or *peṭakin,* "one who knows the *Piṭaka*" (once at Bhārhut);[8] proves that just prior to, or contemporaneous with, the date of the Alu-vihāra redaction at least some Buddhist literature had been classified as *sutta* and *vinaya,* and that some idea of a *Piṭaka* had already emerged. But we have no idea what these classifications included.

What we definitely know of the Pāli texts that preceded the Alu-vihāra redaction, or perhaps better, the *Aṭṭhakathā* redaction—the redaction known to Buddhaghosa, et al.—is limited. We do know that at least two collections of texts, the *Aṭṭhakavagga* and the *Pārāyaṇavagga,* preceded the first redaction of the canon that we have; both collections are quoted or referred to by name in other texts of that canon; both collections have already received commentaries by the time of the earliest known redaction, and they are the only texts that have; finally, the commentaries on both collections are themselves already considered canonical in that early redaction.[9] We also know that at least seven texts (*dhammapaliyāya*) were known to Aśoka since he refers to them by name in his Bhābrā Edict, but unfortunately only three of these have been identified with anything approaching unanimity (*Muni-Gāthā* = *Suttanipāta* vss. 207–221; *Moneya-Sūte*

= *Nālaka-sutta, Suttanipāta* vss. 699–723; *Upatisa-pasine* = *Sāriputta-sutta, Suttanipāta* vss. 955–975) and even these are not certain.[10] If, however, we can take the *Aṭṭhakavagga*, the *Pārāyaṇavagga* and perhaps the three Aśokan texts as we now have them as representing something like their original form, then we know, in addition, that those texts that are demonstrably old are all short texts in verse, and that none of them in form and—it now appears—in content are anything like the finished *suttas* of the *nikāya/āgamas*, especially the first and second *nikāyas*.[11] This is of importance for the study of doctrinal history, since the majority of proof texts cited usually come from these two *nikāyas*.

We also know that Lüders has argued that the reliefs and their accompanying labels on the railings of Bhārhut presuppose actual texts,[12] but this, again, has been called into question by Lamotte.[13] An interesting point, however, is that if Lüders were to be correct, then the texts that we would once again have early evidence for are, again, unlike the finished *suttas* of the *nikāyas:* if the Bhārhut railings give evidence of actual texts, those texts are in content almost entirely *jātaka* or *avadāna* texts.[14] And it is interesting to note that the donors who commissioned illustrations from these "texts" were—as we shall see in a considerable number of cases—monks or nuns.

We know too that the earliest source we have in an Indian language other than Pāli—and this, according to Norman, is a translation[15]—appears to be the Gāndhārī *Dharmapada*, the manuscript of which may date to the second century C.E.[16] Of our Sanskrit sources, almost all from Central Asia, probably none is earlier than the fifth century,[17] and the Gilgit Manuscripts, which appear to contain fragments of an *Ekottarāgama*,[18] are still later. Our Chinese sources do not really begin until the second half of the second century, and it is, in fact, probably not until we arrive at the translations of the *Madhyamāgama* and the *Ekottarāgama* by Dharmanandin in the last quarter of the fourth century that we have the first datable sources which allow us to know—however imperfectly—the actual doctrinal content of at least some of the major divisions of the *nikāya/āgama* literature.[19] It is from this period, then, from the end of the fourth century, that some of the doctrinal content of Hīnayāna canonical literature can finally be definitely dated and actually verified. Not before.

III.

I am, of course, aware of the fact that it has been maintained that "higher criticism" is able to take us back to a point considerably before our earliest known redaction. Unfortunately, I am also aware of the fact that there are certain fundamental problems involving the cardinal tenet of this "higher criticism" and that tenet's application, which have not been critically examined. The cardinal tenet of this criticism states, in effect, if all known sectarian versions of a text or passage agree, that text or passage must be very old; that is, it must come from a presectarian stage of the tradition. This principle, in one form or another, underlies virtually all of the important historical and chronological statements formulated by Bareau, Frauwallner, et al.[20] But in applying this principle, almost no account has been given to two important sets of facts.

First, we do not actually know when the sectarian period began. We do know, as Bareau says, that "Les ouvrages qui nous ont transmis les tableaux et listes de sectes ne sont pas très anciens. Aucun ne remonte avec certitude au delà de 300 ap. J.-C., c'est-à-dire quelque 500 ans après les événements qu'ils rapportent."[21] There is, as Bareau clearly shows, a good deal of agreement between these late sources, and they have much in common. One of the most striking common elements, however, is that they all give different dates for the appearance of the schisms. Of those sources that Bareau classifies as "Les traditions de la première époque," the *Dīpavaṃsa* says that "tous les schismes se seraient produits dans la courant du IIe s. après la Nirvāṇa"; the Sammatīya tradition says that the first took place in 137 E.N. (= "ère du Nirvāṇa"), the second in 200 E.N., and the third in 400 E.N.; "La tradition cachemirienne" has schisms taking place in 100 E.N. and in the IIe, IIIe, and IVe centuries E.N., but according to the *Mañjuśrīparipṛcchāsūtra* "tous les schismes auraient eu lieu dans la Ier s. de l'ère du Nirvāṇa."[22] We also know, again as Bareau says, that on the basis of epigraphical sources "l'existence de la quasi-totalité des sectes est un fait certain," but that "nous n'avons plus d'autres renseignements avant le IIe s. de notre ère. A cette époque, les inscriptions nous apprennent la présence des Sarvāstivādin: près de Peshawer, dans l'Ouest du Cachemire, à Mathurā et à Çrāvastī; des Mahāsāṅghika: à Mathurā, à Karle, etc." We know, in other words, that it is not until the second century C.E. that we begin to find references to actual "schools" in inscriptions.[23] They simply do not occur in the earlier periods of known Buddhist inscriptions. Not at Bhārhut and Sāñcī—although both sites testify to the existence of the beginnings of the division of labor (*sutaṃtika, vinayadhara,* etc.) that some have argued was an important precondition to the eventual emergence of the sects.[24] And not in the known Aśokan inscriptions. In spite of the fact that there appears to have been some kinds of internal problems within the *Saṃgha,* Aśoka always speaks of it as "the *Saṃgha*" or "the *Bhikṣu-Saṃgha.*"[25] We know, therefore, that there is no actual evidence for the emergence of the schools prior to the second century C.E. The precise value of the literary tradition—especially the *vinayas*—in regard to this question leads us to the second group of problems involved in the application of this particular method of criticism.

In applying the principle that says, in effect, if all known versions of a text or passage agree, that text or passage must be very old, almost no account has been given to the fact that all the material to which it is applied is very late:

the Pāli sources, as we have already seen, cannot be taken back beyond 29 to 17 B.C.E. (the Alu-vihāra redaction), and we cannot know anything definite about their actual contents until the fifth or sixth centuries (the *Aṭṭhakathā* redaction); probably none of the Chinese sources go back beyond the second century C.E. and most are considerably later; the Sanskrit sources for the early literature—and here we are talking about manuscripts—are, with few exceptions, even later (from the fifth century on); and the Tibetan sources later still (not before the seventh century). The textual critic is therefore comparing texts from uniformly late stages of the literary tradition. Once this is taken fully into account, any agreement between the sources is open to a very different, if not the very opposite interpretation. The cardinal tenet may then have to be framed in the following form: If all known versions of a text or passage agree, that text or passage is probably late; that is, it probably represents the results of the conflation and gradual leveling and harmonization of earlier existing traditions.

This idea, of course, is not new. Wassilieff, for example, in an old paper which raised a number of points that have never been answered, says:

> Ordinairement pour établir l'ancienneté de la composition des Vinayas on insiste sur ce trait que, dans toutes les rédactions ou dans toutes les écoles ils sont à peu près identiques. . . . Mais à notre avis ce trait même prouve que les Vinayas parvenus à nous ont été rédigés à une époque tardive, quand la question de la vie ascétique ne constituait plus un sujet de discussion, et que toutes les écoles étaient déjà fort tranquillement établies dans des monastères, et avaient pris en conséquence une teinte monotone, parce que pour la vie en communauté, même dans les autres religions, les règles établies ne peuvent sortir du cadre connu.[26]

More recently Lamotte has said in his remarks on Frauwallner's *The Earliest Vinaya and the Beginnings of Buddhist Literature* that

> Si dans le canevas de ces derniers [i.e., the various *vinayas*]—et nous songeons surtout aux Vinaya Pāli, Mahīśāsaka et Dharmagupta—on constate de remarquables similitudes, le fait s'explique par un développement parallèle. Les communautés bouddhiques ne vivaient pas en vase clos; elles suivaient avec intérêt les travaux exécutés par leurs voisins. Il n'y a donc rien d'étonnant à ce qu'elles aient travaillé selon les mêmes méthodes et en suivant pratiquement le même plan.[27]

And Bareau himself notes that "les exemples de bonne entente entre moines de sectes différentes abondent." He then says, as an example, that "Dans l'Uḍḍiyāṇa, les Mahāsāṅghika, les Sarvāstivādin, les Mahīśāsaka, les Dharmaguptaka, et les Kāśyapīya vécurent durant des siècles en parfait accord et meme en véritable symbiose . . ."[28] But perhaps even more important than these general considerations is the fact that something like what I have suggested can, I think, actually be shown to be the case in those instances where we are fortunate enough to have an unrevised version of a text or passage still preserved.

The fact, for example, that the Pāli version as well as the Mahāsāṅghika, Mahīśāsaka, and Dharmaguptaka versions of the account of the remains of the Buddha Kāśyapa studied by Bareau all agree in placing a *stūpa* of Kāśyapa at Toyikā cannot result from the fact that this is an old, presectarian tradition. On the contrary, the fact that they all agree in this seems to result from the very opposite; it seems to result from the fact that they all represent later, revised, and conflated versions of an earlier tradition that knew nothing of a *stūpa*. Here, unfortunately, I can give only a very condensed summary of this important case, but it is clear that we have in this instance a fine example of how the accepted principle of this "higher criticism" is supposed to work, and—as we shall see—when we can actually check it, it is also clear that it does not seem to work very well at all.

To begin with what Bareau has collected, we have three versions of what is clearly the same text: a Mahāsāṅghika, a Mahīśāsaka, and a Dharmaguptaka version. These three versions, according to Bareau, "sont étroitement apparentées et proviennent manifestement d'un même récit antérieur."[29] We also have a Pāli version of this text, which appears to be the latest of all the versions and is also obviously related to the other three.[30] These four versions have a number of elements in common, and although each has been padded out with one or more of a variety of subplots and literary clichés taken from the common stock of Buddhist story literature,[31] the basic elements of the text are, in each version, still clearly visible and can be separated out: the Buddha is traveling in Kosala; he reaches a spot near a village called Tou-i, Tou-tseu, Todeyya (all = Skt. Toyikā); he has an encounter with a man working in a nearby field as a result of which it becomes known that the *stūpa* of the Buddha Kāśyapa lies buried under this spot; the Buddha then makes the *stūpa* appear momentarily and, after it disappears, he and/or the monks construct a *stūpa* on that spot from mud ("boue", "boule de boue"; in the Pāli account a *stūpa* of stone appears; the Mahīśāsaka account adds "ce fut le premier *stūpa* élevé alors sur le territoire du Jambudvīpa"); this then is followed—in one case preceded—by instructions on how a *stūpa* should be built and/or by verses praising the merit of building or worshipping *stūpas*. Since all four versions agree on these basic elements of the text, and since each version belongs to a separate school, we can conclude—according to the accepted principle—that the essential elements of this account must go back to a very old or presectarian stage of the tradition. As a matter of fact, on the basis of the agreement between the three Chinese versions set alongside his interpretation of the Nigālī Sāgar Edict of Aśoka, Bareau concludes that "cette légende paraît antérieure à Aśoka."[32] Here, however, unlike in the overwhelming majority of such cases, we can actually check both the conclusion and procedure, since yet another version of this text—a version of an unusual kind—is in this case also available.

What is clearly a fifth version of this account of the remains of the Buddha Kāśyapa is now found once in the *Mūlasarvāstivāda-vinaya* from Gilgit[33] and twice in the *Divyāvadāna.*[34] And, although this version clearly belongs to the same group and has the same basic narrative structure (the Buddha going to Toyikā, his encounter with the man working in the field, his "miraculous" raising of the relics for the monks to see, etc.) it differs from the other four in at least two important ways. First, it has none of the various subplots found in the other versions—a fairly sure sign of priority[35]—and, second, it knows absolutely nothing about a *stūpa* at Toyikā or its construction. Here, it is not a *stūpa* that the Buddha makes appear, but only "the undivided mass of relics of the Saṃyaksaṃbuddha Kāśyapa (*kāśyapasya samyaksaṃbuddhasyāvikopitaḥ śarīrasaṃghāta ucchrāpitaḥ*)." The text, in fact, knows only these relics, *which are buried in the ground,* and is concerned solely with the sacralization of that otherwise unmarked piece of ground by acts of worship and the establishment of a festival (*maha*). The merit it praises arises, first of all, from activities undertaken in regard to this *pṛthivīpradeśa* and, secondly, in regard to *buddhacaityas* (always plural), a term which here quite clearly has nothing to do with *stūpas.* This version, in short, reflects a tradition—apparently later revised—that only knew a form of the relic cult in which the *stūpa* did not yet have a part.[36]

The existence of this version is somewhat puzzling, but I think it is impossible to see it as anything else but an old account that, for some reason, was never revised. The simple narrative structure, the absence of the well-known subplots and literary clichés, the absence, especially, of any reference to a *stūpa*—all make it impossible, I think, to put it any place but at the beginning of the known history of this particular text. We have, then, what appears to be the earliest known account that knows nothing of a *stūpa* at Toyikā—and this is an important *stūpa*—set ovei against the versions of the Mahāsāṅghika, Mahīśāsaka, Dharmaguptaka, and the Theravāda, all of which must be later and all of which agree that there was a *stūpa* of Kāśyapa at Toyikā. It would appear, then, that the original version, represented now by the Mūlasarvāstivāda account, was revised at some point in time, and that once this revision was made in one school's account, it was accepted and incorporated into the accounts of all schools other than—and here probably only by an oversight—the Mūlasarvāstivāda. In any case, here it appears in one of the very few cases where we actually have the means to check the conclusions that would be generated by our "higher criticism," that the Mahāsāṅghika, Mahīśāsaka, Dharmaguptaka, and Theravāda accounts agree not because they represent the old presectarian version, but because they almost certainly represent later, conflated, and fundamentally altered versions of an earlier tradition.[37]

IV.

But if we know that we cannot know anything definite about the actual doctrinal content of the *nikāya/āgama* literature much before the fourth century C.E., we also know that a very considerable number of Buddhist inscriptions predate by several centuries the old Chinese translations of the *Madhyamāgama* and the *Ekottarāgama*, and that if we want to look at the oldest verifiable sources for the question of the layman/monk distinction in Indian Buddhism—and this is one of the questions we are concerned with here—we must look first at these inscriptions.

This inscriptional material has at least two distinct advantages. First, much of it predates what we can definitely know from literary sources. Second, and perhaps of greater importance, this material tells us not what some literate, educated Indian Buddhist wrote, but what a fairly large number of practicing Buddhists actually did. In Buddhist studies, scholars intent on generating historical statements have consistently used textual sources as if they were somehow descriptions of actual behavior, and little explicit consideration has been given to the almost certain noncongruency between an ideal and the actual. This is particularly well illustrated in a long series of statements concerning the Monk. Implicit in almost everything that has been said about him is the assumption that the scheme of the religious life for the monk preserved in our literary sources is not a normative and carefully contrived ideal paradigm, but an adequate historical reflection of the actual career of the typical Buddhist monk of the early centuries. I think we need cite here only a single example—enormously influential—which is particularly germane to our topic. In the sole paragraph devoted to the *stūpa*/relic cult in his classic *Buddha, sein Leben, seine Lehre, seine Gemeinde,* Oldenberg stated flatly in reference to the *stūpa* cult that "the order of monks as such has nothing to do with this pompous show of veneration; the old rules of the order have not a word to say about it."[38] Our donative inscriptions, however, would seem to indicate otherwise.

V.

The earliest donative inscriptions that we have come from the railings of Bhārhut and Sāñcī and date from about 120 to 80 B.C.E.[39] Here already, we know for certain that a considerable proportion of the donors—those donors actively involved with establishing and embellishing sacred objects and sacred sites, those donors actively involved with the *stūpa* cult and donative, merit-making activity—were monks or nuns. At Bhārhut, for example, almost 40 percent of the donors were either monks (twenty-four) or nuns (fourteen).[40] We also know that a considerable proportion of these individuals were not simply monks, but doctrinal specialists: six are called *bhānakas,* "reciters"; one is called *sutaṃtika,* "one who knows the *sutta*"; one is called a *peṭakin,* "one who knows the *Piṭaka*"; and one is referred to as a *pacanekāyika,* "one who [according to Lamotte] was versed in the canonical doctrine taken as a whole."[41]

A very similar picture emerges from an analysis of the Kharoṣṭhī inscriptions edited by Konow. Here, if we restrict ourselves to donations that are connected with the *stūpa* cult or the cult of images, we find that again more than 40 percent of the donors are monks (sixteen) and the rest laymen of different categories (nineteen).[42] Here too, although titles are much less common in the Kharoṣṭhī inscriptions, at least one of the monk-donors is called a *venaea,* a *vainayika,* "one who knows the *vinaya,*" and another is called a *trepiḍaka,* "one who knows the *Tripiṭaka.*"[43]

We also know from other donative inscriptions that the proportion of monastic donors increases. For example—and it is a representative example—in the Mathurā inscriptions collected by Lüders, which are certainly Buddhist and in which the name of the donor is given or preserved, well over 50 percent of those donors are monks or nuns.[44] Among these we find a monk who is called both a *bhāṇaka* and a *caturvidya* (which Lüders takes to mean one "who knows the fourfold scriptures"); another who is called a *dharmakathika,* "a preacher of the *Dharma*"; and two monks who are called *prāhaṇīkas* or, according to Lüders, "practisers of meditation"; we also find a nun-donor who is said to be the niece of another nun who is a *trepiṭaka* and the pupil of a monk who is given the same title.[45]

In the inscriptions from the "Buddhist cave temples" collected by Burgess, if again we restrict ourselves to donations connected with cult forms (images, *caityagṛhas,* relics, etc.) and exclude gifts of residences (cells, caves, cisterns) and endowments for the material support of the residences and the monks living there, we find that slightly more than 65 percent of the donors were monks or nuns (twenty-eight) and fewer than 35 percent were laymen.[46]

Finally, if we go further and look at those inscriptions that, as I have recently attempted to show, are probably Mahāyāna, the figures are even more striking. In those inscriptions that appear to be Mahāyāna—and here we are talking about nearly eighty individual inscriptions—the donors in more than 70 percent of the cases are monks or nuns, mostly the former, and only 20 percent are laymen.[47]

None of this accords very well, if at all, with received views on the matter, with the views that maintain that there was a sharp distinction between the kinds of religious activities undertaken by monks and the kinds of religious activity undertaken by laymen, and with the view that cult and religious giving were essentially and overwhelmingly lay concerns in the Indian Buddhist context.[48] In fact, if we stick to what we can actually know, it would appear that something very like the opposite was the case: we know for certain from inscriptions that from ca. 150 B.C.E.—that is to say, from our earliest knowable donative inscriptions and well before we can have any definite knowledge of the textual tradition—monks and nuns formed a substantial proportion of those involved in donative, merit-making activities connected with the *stūpa* cult and, somewhat later, the cult of images, and that this proportion increased continually as time passed. We also know that, in a considerable number of cases, these individuals were not just ordinary monks, but doctrinal specialists (*trepiṭakas, vainayikas,* etc.) and the acknowledged transmitters of Buddhist teaching (*bhānakas*). Finally, it is also worth noting that the Mahāyāna figures are particularly significant. We know on the basis of these figures that, from its first appearance in inscriptions, the Mahāyāna was a monk-dominated movement, and that it continued to be so until the thirteenth century, the date of our last known Mahāyāna inscription. But this is not all that we can know from these donative inscriptions.

VI.

The donations recorded at Bhārhut and Sāñcī concern gifts of posts, railings, sculpted medallions, and the like—that is to say, gifts intended to embellish and mark the *stūpa* as an object of worship. The Kharoṣṭhī inscriptions too, at least in their earlier phases, are often connected with the *stūpa*/relic cults, although we also find a number of inscriptions connected with images. But the donations recorded in the Mathurā inscriptions as well as the inscriptions from the "cave temples," while still including gifts connected with *stūpas* and the so-called establishment of relics, are increasingly more concerned with the setting up of images, and the Mahāyāna inscriptions are almost exclusively so. So, while the purely epigraphic evidence of the monastic control and dominance of the *stūpa* cult—at least in our samples—is perhaps not quite so clear, there is absolutely no doubt that the cult of images was overwhelmingly a monastic concern. In the eighteen Kharoṣṭhī inscriptions edited by Konow that record the setting up of an image and in which the name of the donor is given or preserved, almost two-thirds or thirteen of eighteen of the donors are monks.[49] The figures for Lüders' Mathurā inscriptions are almost exactly the same: in the twenty-eight inscriptions that have or preserve a name and that record the gift of an image, eighteen of twenty-eight of the donors are monks and nuns—again almost two-thirds.[50] In the seventeen "cave temple" inscriptions collected by Burgess that are connected with an image, the donor in every case but one is a monk.[51] In the inscriptions I have identified as Mahāyāna, virtually all of which are concerned with the making or setting up of images, more than 70 percent of the donors are monks or nuns (mostly, again, the former).[52]

But we know even more than this. We know that not only was the image cult overwhelmingly a monastic concern, it was also, on the basis of the available information, a monastically initiated cult. We know that the earliest Buddha images accompanied by a dated donative inscription—and these are some of the earliest datable examples of both Mathurā and Gandhāra art—were all set up by monks or nuns. We can cite, for example, the images set up by the ubiquitous *Bhikṣu* Bala or his pupils at Kosam, Sārnāth, Sēt-Mahet, and Mathurā,[53] or the image set up by Buddhānanda in the fifth year of Kaniṣka.[54] Note too that, once again, we know for certain that in many cases these monastic donors were not just average monks. Both Bala and Buddhānanda are specifically said to be *trepiṭakas*, that is to say, "those who know the *Tripiṭaka*"; a little later at Jauliāñ we find an image that was the gift "of the friar versed in the Vinaya" (*v(e)nae(i)asa bhikshusa*).[55] All of these monks were doctrinal specialists, and they were all actively engaged in and concerned with popular cult practice.

VII.

The earliest donative inscriptions that we know clearly establish the active and sizable participation of monks in the *stūpa* cult from at least 150 B.C.E. This again, we know, is fully confirmed by archaeology and the history of monastic architecture. We know, again from the very beginning of our actual evidence (e.g., the early cave complexes at Kondivte, Nadsur, Pitalkhorā, Ajaṇṭā, and so forth) that, as Nagao has inadvertently shown, "the caitya was already part of the monastic complex," and that "the stūpa was not merely approved and accepted by the monastic community but actually adopted by it, integrated into cenobitic life as one of its most important elements."[56] I think, however, it is only fair to say that Nagao probably did not intend to show that from the very beginning of our actual evidence, the *caitya* was already part of the monastic complex, etc. Like a number of other authors, he posits several earlier phases for the development of monastic architecture. Unfortunately, that there is evidence for these phases is less than clear. For example, for the first of these phases, Nagao takes several passages from the *vinaya* as evidence for the fifth or fourth century B.C.E. after he himself has already said that the *vinaya* "took its present textual form only about the beginning of the Christian era," and that "these texts [the *vinayas*], though they refer to many incidents contemporaneous with the Buddha himself, reflect the thinking of a much later time, the time of their own redaction." He bases the next of his phases on an overstatement of the archaeological facts. He refers to what might or might not be the Jīvakāmravaṇa—or Jīvakārāma (Pāli: Jīvakāmbavana), the *ārāma* supposedly given to the Buddha by the famous physician Jīvaka—and draws a number of conclusions from what he sees there. But again, we do not know anything definite about the nature or purpose of the building in question; we do not even know whether it was a monastery, let alone whether it was *the* Jīvakāmravaṇa, and we still do not have anything like a full report on what the excavation brought to light. There are, as a matter of fact, a number of other "Elliptical Structures" similar to the so-called Jīvakāmravaṇa, and, according to Sarkar who has made a study of them, at least two of these buildings, "are identified as *stūpas*"![57] Nagao's discussion of actual, verifiable monastic architecture begins then only with his remarks on the "cave temples" and, importantly, the place of the *stūpa* at those sites.

The history of Buddhist monastic architecture, however, does not simply confirm the active participation of monks in the *stūpa*/relic cult. It would also seem to indicate something more than this; it would seem to indicate that the cult was, from the very beginning of our evidence, both monastically controlled and monastically dominated. That this was the case seems to follow from the fact that the *stūpas* that we know are almost always found in close association with monastic complexes and very frequently fully incorporated into such complexes. The significance of this relationship is reinforced when we note that only very rarely do we find *stūpas* or *caityagṛhas* disassociated from monastic establishments. The only instance, in fact, that I am able to cite is Sirkap.[58]

We can also add to this two pieces of epigraphical evidence not yet specifically mentioned. First, everywhere, but especially noticeable in the Kharoṣṭhī inscriptions, even when relics or *stūpas* are given by laymen, they are almost always given "in the acceptance of" or "for the acceptance of" (*parigrahe, pratigrahe*) one or another monastic community or school.[59] Either that or they are specifically said to be given in conjunction with a *saṃghārāma* or *vihāra* or to a particular *vihāra*.[60] Second, we might note an interesting Kharoṣṭhī inscription that is yet to be fully understood. This particular inscription seems to record that, on the date that "the pole of the *stūpa* was erected" (*yaṭhiṃ aropayata*), "a laywoman" (*upasika*) gave in addition to—assuming Konow's interpretation of *ṭhapa(i)chaṃ* is right—the "setting up of the pole" (*yaṭhipratiṭhana*), the "surrounding structure" as well. It is clear that the erection of the *yaṣṭi* was a significant event; the inscription is dated on the day that this took place, and it probably indicated the completion of the *stūpa* and signaled its inauguration as an object of worship. The significant point here is that although both the setting up of the *yaṣṭi* and the "surrounding structure" were the gifts of a laywoman, it was expressly stated that it was a monk, a "preacher of the *Dharma*" (*dharmakathika*), who performed the ceremony that appears to have officially marked the *stūpa* as an object of worship.[61]

VIII.

We also know a few more specific things about doctrinal history on the basis of our donative inscriptions. We read, for example, in an inscription dated in the year 51 of Huveṣka from Mathurā:

(I) . . . (a)sya (p)u(rva)yā (bhi)kṣu(ṇā) (b)uddh(a)varmaṇā (bhagava)taḥ (śāk)y(am)u . . . pratimā pratiṣṭāpita sarva(b)uddhapūjārt(th)a(m) anana d(e)yadharmaparityāgen(a) upadhy(ā)yasya saghadāsasya (n)irvā(n)ā(va)ptaye = (s)t(u) mātāp(it) . . . buddh(a)varmas(y)a sarvad(u)khopaśamāya sarvasatvahitasukh(ā)r(th)a . . .

Lüders, *Mathurā Inscriptions* §29

. . . on this date an image of the Blessed One Śākyamuni was set up by the Monk Buddhavarman for the worship of all Buddhas. Through this religious gift may his Preceptor Saṅghadāsa attain *nirvāṇa,* (may it also be) for the cessation of all suffering of his parents . . . (and) for the welfare and happiness of all beings.

In another inscription on an image pedestal, again from Mathurā, we find:

(II) bhikhusa budhav(ā)lasa dān(a) māt(ā)pit(r)in(a) pujāye savasav(ā)n(a) ca

Lüders, *Mathurā Inscriptions* §90

(This is) the gift of the Monk Buddhapāla (which is made) as an act of *pūjā* for his parents and all beings.

Even more interesting are two inscriptions, one on a pillar base from the Jamālpur Mound, the other a Kharoṣṭhī inscription on an image "said to have come from near Peshawar":[62]

(III) +[63] (d)ā(na)ṃ bh(ik)ṣus(y)a b . . . + . . . m(i)trasya v(o)jya + (vaśi)kasya — (mātap)i + (tṛ)ṇa (abhyat)itaka + laga(tā)nāṃ pujāy(e) + bhavatu sa(dh)yivi + harīsya dharma(d)ev(a)s(y)a + ar(o)g(a)dākṣiṇ(a)y(e) (bha)vat(u)

Lüders, *Mathurā Inscriptions* §44

(This is) the gift of the Monk . . . mitra, the Vojyavaśika (?).[64] May it be an act of *pūjā* for his deceased parents. May it (also) be for the granting of health to his companion Dharmadeva.

(IV) sa(ṃ) 4 1 phagunasa masasa di paṃcami budhanadasa trepiḍakasa danamukhe madapidarana adhvadidana puyaya bhavatu

Fussman, *BEFEO* 61 (1974) 54

Year 5, on the fifth day of the month Phalguna. This is the gift of Buddhānanda who knows the *Tripiṭaka.* May it be an act of *pūjā* for his deceased parents.

Finally, we might cite yet another inscription on a pillar base found at the Jamālpur Mound:

(V) *ayaṃ ku(ṃ)bhako dānaṃ bhikṣunaṃ śurīyasya buddharakṣitasya ca prāhaṇīk(ā)-n(aṃ) an(e)n(a) deryadharmmaparītyāgen(a) sarvveṣ(a)ṃ pr(ā)haṇīkānaṃ arogyadakṣiṇ(ā)ye bhavat(āṃ)*

Lüders, *Mathurā Inscriptions* §46

This pillar base is the gift of the Monks Śurīya and Buddharakṣita who are practisers of meditation.[65] May this offering of a religious gift be for granting health to all practisers of meditation.

What we want to note are the basic ideas expressed in these records. It is, for example, clear that it was held that someone could be expected to obtain *nirvāṇa* as the result of an act of *pūjā* undertaken on his behalf by another. It was held that acts of *pūjā* could be undertaken for one's parents, whether living or dead. It was also held that acts of *pūjā* could be undertaken for the sake of conferring health on others. These are the expressed ideas and intentions of the individual donors. And we know beyond the shadow of a doubt that these ideas and goals were held and, more importantly, acted upon by members of the monastic community, that these were, in fact, monastic ideas and goals. We can add to this that, here again, the members of the monastic community in question were not, at least in two cases, just average monks. In one case they refer to themselves and the intended beneficiaries of their act as "practisers of meditation"; in another the donor is said to be one "who knows the *Tripiṭaka.*"

IX.

Fussman, in his remarks on the Kharoṣṭhī inscription cited above (no. IV), introduces our second problem. He explicitly recognizes that this inscription is a concrete expression of "la doctrine . . . du transfert des mérites." In fact, the same is true for all of the inscriptions just cited. All of these are individual applications of a single basic idea, the idea that the results of a religious act undertaken by one individual may be assigned or "transferred" to others, and even to all others—an act is undertaken "for the welfare and happiness of all beings" (*sarvasatvahitasukhārthaṃ*), or "as an act of *pūjā* for one's parents" (*mātāpitrina pujāye*), or "for the granting of health" (*arogyadakṣiṇāye*) to one or another individual. But in recognizing this fact, Fussman makes a number of statements that are more difficult to accept. He says:

> Je crois plutôt qu'il [the gift made in honor of the donor's deceased parents in IV cited above] implique l'existence de la doctrine mahāyāniste du transfert des mérites . . . Si notre interprétation est correcte, ce relief a été offert par un sectateur du Mahāyāna . . . Nous avons, donc, pour la première fois, une preuve de l'existence de courants mahāyānistes dans l'Inde du Nord-Ouest, à la fin du premier siècle de n.e.[66]

Fussman is almost certainly right in seeing here a doctrine of the transference of merit, but I think—and I think it can be shown—that the doctrine of the transference of merit which occurs in these inscriptions is not a Mahāyāna doctrine, and that none of the inscriptions I have cited, including his Kharoṣṭhī inscription, are Mahāyāna inscriptions.

We know that the formula "May it be an act of *pūjā* for his deceased parents" (*madapidarana adhvadidana puyaya bhavatu*) found in Fussman's inscription is also found elsewhere. He himself refers to the similar formula found in the inscription from the Jamālpur Mound that I have cited above (III), and Damsteegt refers to at least fifteen examples (including Fussman's and the Jamālpur inscription) of what he calls the "shorter" and "extended" forms of this expression.[67] From a survey of these we know that, in at least five instances, this formula appears in conjunction with a specifically named school and that in every instance that school is a Hīnayāna school: in a Mathurā inscription edited by Sircar that records a gift to the Mahāsāṅghikas, we find the expression *mātāpitraṇa abhatitana(ṃ)*. . . .[68] In an inscription from Kānheri dating from the Sātavāhana period in which we find the phrase *(mā)tapitūnaṃ abhatītā(naṃ) . . . pūjāya*, the donation is made in conjunction with the Bhādrāyaṇīyas.[69] Three instances of what Damsteegt calls the "shorter" form—*mātāpit(r)ina pujāya*, etc.,—also occur in association with the name of a school: at Nāgārjunikoṇḍa we find *mātāpituno pūjā* . . . in conjunction with the Aparamahāvinaseliyas (Aparaśailas);[70] at Kārli *mātapituna pūjā(ya)* in association with the Mahāsāṅghikas;[71] and the shorter form also occurs in a Kharoṣṭhī inscription from Wardak, again in association with the Mahāsāṅghikas.[72] It is, I think, clear from this that whenever expressions like *madapidarana adhvadidana puyaya, mātapituna pūjāya*, occur in any inscription that also contains the name of a school, that school is always a Hīnayāna school (the Bhādrāyaṇīyas once, the Aparaśailas once, and the Mahāsāṅghikas three times). The other side of this is that the expression *madapidarana adhvadidana puyaya* or any of its variants is never found in association with the name Mahāyāna, or with the titles *Śākyabhikṣu/-bhikṣuṇī* or *Paramopāsaka/-opāsikā* (which, as I have tried to show, were used at first by the group we now call the Mahāyāna), and here again we are talking about nearly eighty inscriptions from several periods and from almost all parts of India.[73] Exactly the same pattern recurs if we look at any of the other formulae found in the five inscriptions I have cited above.

In the second inscription of this group, the Monk Buddhapāla makes his donation "as an act of *pūjā* for his parents and all beings" (*māt(ā)pit(r)in(a) pujāye savasav(ā)n(a) ca*). In the first, the Monk Buddhavarman sets up an image and specifies that this act—that is to say, the resulting merit—is to be for, in part, "the welfare and happiness of all beings" (*sarvasatvahitasukh(ā)r(th)a*). This latter formula, which again clearly "implique l'existence de la doctrine . . . du transfert des mérites," is found very frequently in Buddhist inscriptions of almost all periods, and in a number of instances it is also found in conjunction with a specifically named school, but never in conjunction with the name *mahāyāna* or the titles *śākyabhikṣu* and the like. At Mathurā it occurs in conjunction with the Sarvāstivādins once and twice with the Mahāsāṅghikas;[74] at Kārli it again occurs in association with the Mahāsāṅghikas,[75] and in yet another Kharoṣṭhī inscription edited by Fussman it occurs in association with the Dharmaguptakas;[76] it occurs in two inscriptions from Kānheri in connection with the Bhādrāyaṇīyas;[77] and in one inscription from Nāgārjunikoṇḍa published by Vogel it occurs in conjunction with the Mahīśāsaka,[78] while in another from the same place it is associated with the Vibhajyavādins;[79] finally, it appears again associated with the Sarvāstivādins in a Kharoṣṭhī inscription published by Konow[80] and in an inscription from Kāman published by Bühler.[81] We know, therefore, that whenever the expression *sarvasatvahitasukhārtha,* or some variant thereof, occurs in any inscription that also contains the name of a school, that school is always a Hīnayāna school, and that the expression is never found in inscriptions associated with the groups we now call the Mahāyāna.[82]

I think that, in light of this material, Fussman's remarks on the possible Mahāyāna character of his inscription must be put aside. But in the process of testing his hypothesis, we have discovered at least one very important fact: we know now, beyond any doubt, that virtually all of the Hīnayāna schools mentioned in inscriptions accepted gifts that were given with an implicit doctrine of the transference of merit explicitly attached to them, that they accepted gifts that were expressly stated to have been made, for example, "as an act of *pūjā* for one's dead parents." This, coupled with the fact that, in at least some cases, the donors were monks presumably belonging to the same schools, would seem to indicate that we can legitimately conclude that all of these schools, the Mahāsāṅghikas, Sarvāstivādins, Bhādrāyaṇīyas, and so on, had and held a doctrine of the transference of merit. But at the same time, we also know that the groups we now call the Mahāyāna did not have and did not hold this same doctrine of the transference of merit. We know this from the fact that the formulae that express this doctrine are completely absent from what appear to be Mahāyāna inscriptions. We also know it from the formulae actually found in inscriptions that appear to belong to the Mahāyāna group.

X.

As we have seen above, the doctrine of the transference of merit, which in inscriptions is explicitly associated with the named Hīnayāna schools, is expressed in a number of formulae. An act may be undertaken "for the welfare and happiness of all beings," or "as an act of *pūjā* for . . . (deceased) parents," or more specifically "for the granting of health" to one individual or another.[83] We might also note that the act might also be undertaken, as in the first inscription from Mathurā cited above, for the attainment of *nirvāṇa* by someone other than the donor, or, as in the Taxila Silver Scroll Inscription, for a generalized, nonspecific attainment of *nirvāṇa.*[84] But this is not a frequently expressed intention of religious donations in Hīnayāna inscriptions.[85] The actual transference in the doctrine of the transference of merit associated with the Sarvāstivādins, Mahāsāṅghikas, and so on, is, therefore, not consistently oriented toward one specific goal. In most cases, it seems to simply involve the assignment of merit by one individual (the donor) to another (the expressed beneficiary) for no specific purpose other than, presumably, increasing the recipient's store of merit. When a more specific purpose is also stated, it is, on occasion, the attainment of *nirvāṇa,* but more frequently, it is something less than the religious goal sanctioned by the literary tradition: granting health or conferring long life on some specified individual, for example.[86] In what appear to be Mahāyāna inscriptions, by contrast, apart from a very small number of questionable exceptions,[87] the act or gift recorded is always undertaken, first of all, for "all beings"—even if, as we shall see, certain individuals within the category of "all beings" are, in many cases, particularly singled out. And, again in virtually every case, the transference of merit to "all beings" in the Mahāyāna inscriptions is explicitly stated to be for a single, specific purpose, the simplest form of this being *yad atra puṇyaṃ tad bhavatu sarvasatvānām anuttarajñānāvāptaye:* "what here is the merit, may that be for the obtaining of supreme knowledge by all beings." That is to say, the merit of the act in Mahāyāna inscriptions is always said to be intended specifically for the attainment of *anuttarajñāna.*[88] This is apparent from the very beginning of our Mahāyāna inscriptions and is found even in what might be called, from a purely epigraphical point of view, an early proto-Mahāyāna inscription from Mathurā.

This proto-Mahāyāna inscription, published first by Nakamura and more recently by Mukherjee,[89] is of importance for a number of reasons, not the least of which is the fact that it contains the earliest, indeed the only, reference to the Buddha Amitābha in Indian inscriptions and is, therefore, one of the few hard facts we have concerning this Buddha and his cult in India proper.[90] The inscription records the fact that in the year 26 of Huveṣka an "image of the Blessed One, the Buddha Amitābha, was set up for the worship of the Buddha" (*bhagavato buddha amitābhasya pratimā pratiṣṭhapita buddha pūjāye*) by an individual named Nāgarakṣita or Sāmrakṣita.[91] He is not given a title, although his son is called a *sārthavāha*, "caravan merchant" or "itinerant trader," and his grandfather is called a *śreṣṭhin*, "banker" or the "head of a guild." The record then concludes with the words *imena kuśalamulena sarva(satana)anuttarajñānaṃ prātp(i)m* (rd:*prāptim) (bha) (va) (tu):* "through this root of merit may there be the attainment of supreme knowledge by all beings."

Although this inscription does not yet have all of the features that characterize those inscriptions that can, I think, be shown to be Mahāyāna, it is clearly related to them: its donor, unlike the donors of the majority of our typical Mahāyāna inscriptions,[92] does not refer to himself as a *paramopāsaka* or a *śākyopāsaka* (he appears to be, by the way, almost certainly a layman); where the typical Mahāyāna inscriptions always use the phrase *yad atra puṇyaṃ tad . . .* , the present inscription uses the phrase *imena kuśalamulena* (a phrase that, according to Damsteegt, also occurs in three Kharoṣṭhī inscriptions and one from Bodh-Gayā, but one which does not occur elsewhere, even at Mathurā);[93] finally, the present inscription, instead of the final construction standard in our Mahāyāna inscriptions—*tad bhavatu . . . anuttarajñānāvāptaye*—has *anuttarajñānaṃ prāptiṃ bhavatu.* In spite of these differences, I think it is obvious that the present inscription represents a stage in the development toward the classical form of Mahāyāna inscriptions. When we bear in mind that it is earlier by at least two centuries than the earliest of our typical Mahāyāna inscriptions, I think that we can legitimately see it as an early prototype of the latter. It is significant, therefore, that this early prototype already contains the two features which distinguish the doctrine of the transference of merit associated with the group now known as the Mahāyāna from that associated with the Hīnayāna schools: it explicitly declares that the merit from the act undertaken is to be assigned to "all beings," and that merit so assigned is intended specifically for "the attainment of supreme knowledge" by those beings.[94]

We can compare one other formula found in inscriptions associated with the Hīnayāna schools with its counterparts in Mahāyāna inscriptions. In the former inscriptions, as we have seen, donors frequently present their gift "as an act of *pūjā* for their parents" or "as an act of *pūjā* for their deceased parents." This, again, is always expressed simply as a "transference" of merit from donor to parent; the merit is never said to be for any specified end. The corresponding formula found in the Mahāyāna inscriptions—and it is very frequently found—is once again quite different. The simplest forms of the expression are *yad atra puṇyaṃ tad bhavatu mātāpitṛpūrvaṅgamaṃ kṛtvā sarvasatvānāṃ anuttarajñānāvāptaye,* "What here is the merit, may that, having placed my parents in the forefront, be for the obtaining of supreme knowledge by all beings"; or *yad atra puṇyaṃ tad bhavatu mātāpitroḥ sarvasatvānāñ cānuttarajñānāvāptaye,* "What here is the merit, may that be for the obtaining of supreme knowledge by my parents and all beings." Here again, using the same basic formula as before, the donor declares that he wishes that the merit from his act should go for the obtainment of *anuttarajñāna* by the category "all beings," but here he adds a kind of subclause to the formula specifically singling out certain individuals within that category. Either that, or he simply joins the specific individuals he wants to mention and the larger category with an "and." But in any case, whenever parents or other specific individuals are mentioned in Mahāyāna inscriptions as the intended beneficiaries of a donor's act, they are never mentioned by themselves as they are in Hīnayāna inscriptions, but always in conjunction with the category of "all beings," either together with that category (*mātāpitroḥ sarvasatvānāñ ca*) or, more commonly, as a subgroup within it (*mātāpitṛpūrvaṅgamaṃ kṛtvā sarvasatvānāṃ*). And note again that, in inscriptions associated with the Mahāyāna, whether the donor directs his merit only to the general category "all beings" or whether in addition he specifically singles out his parents or other individuals within that larger group, the merit from his act is *always* explicitly stated to be for the obtainment of "supreme knowledge."[95] Finally, we might note that in none of our Mahāyāna inscriptions is merit ever transferred to deceased parents or for such things as conferring health or granting long life. These seem to have been—at least epigraphically—exclusively Hīnayāna ideas.

XI.

There is very little doubt about which of the two basic forms of the doctrine of the transference of merit found in inscriptions is—epigraphically—the oldest. If we put aside the proto-Mahāyāna inscription from Mathurā, none of our Mahāyāna inscriptions are earlier than the fourth century C.E.[96] This means that a very considerable number of the inscriptions associated with the Hīnayāna predate them by at least one or more centuries. As a matter of fact, we know that at least some form of the doctrine of the transference of merit associated in later inscriptions with the various schools of the Hīnayāna is as old as Bhārhut. We know because, in the single instance where the intention of a donor is actually stated, it is said, as Lamotte has pointed out, that the act was undertaken *mātāpituna aṭhāyā*, "pour le bénéfice de sa mère et de son père." It should be noted, however, that Lamotte draws from this somewhat different conclusions.

Lamotte says:

> A cette époque [of Bhārhut and Sāñcī], la mentalité demeure strictement orthodoxe, c'est-à-dire conforme à l'esprit du Buddha. Par leurs aumônes, les généreux donateurs n'espèrent nullement accéder de plain-pied au Nirvāṇa, mais entendent simplement bénéficier des cinq avantages du don signalés par l'*Aṅguttara* (III. p. 38–41) . . . Bien plus, ils savent que ces oeuvres méritoires sont leur bien propre . . . et qu'ayant été seuls à les accomplir, ils devront seuls en recueillir le fruit. Il ne peut être question de transférer ce mérite à des tiers, ni même de formuler des intentions que le mécanisme de la rétribution des actes rendrait inopérantes.[97]

This, however, is conjecture and the imputation of very specific views where almost none are expressed. In actual fact, we simply do not know what the intentions of the vast majority of donors at Bhārhut and Sāñcī were. What we do know is that in the lone case in which a donor himself expresses his intentions, they are just exactly what Lamotte says is out of the question: "Parmi les nombreux donateurs de Bhārhut et de Sāñcī de l'époque Śuṅga, Sagharakhita fut le seul à avoir accompli son oeuvre pie 'pour le bénéfice de sa mère et de son père.' " The rest of the donors—and, as Lamotte says, "ils sont des centaines"—simply do not express their intentions.[98] Lamotte's views have also been implicitly queried from yet another point of view. Agasse, after quoting the above passage from *Histoire,* says:

> Pourtant si 'innovation' il y a eu, ce n'est pas sans que les textes y aient invité et Sagharakhita, pour isolé qu'il soit, aurait pu lui aussi après tout, prétendre à quelque 'orthodoxie'. Car cette pratique [the transference of merit] . . . appartient bel et bien au corps de doctrine originel et les textes canoniques en portent témoignage en plusieurs endroits.[99]

Now, however, several important inscriptions have come to light that were not available to Lamotte. Although none of these were found at Bhārhut or Sāñcī, one appears to be contemporaneous with the inscriptions from these sites, and several others may be considerably earlier. The first of these comes from Pauni and palaeographically seems to belong to the "late Maurya/early Śuṅga" period. It is found on a coping stone and appears to be missing a few *akṣaras* at the beginning: . . . *ya visamitāya dana(ṃ) sukhāya hotu savasatānaṃ,* "the gift of Visamitā . . . may it be for the happiness of all beings."[100] The other inscriptions, interestingly enough, all come from Ceylon. The first of these inscriptions is one of "the earliest inscriptions in Ceylon that can be definitely attributed to a particular ruler" and dates, according to Paranavitana, "to the period between 210 and 200 B.C.": *gamaṇi-uti-maharajhaha(jhita abi-ti)śaya leṇe daśa-diśaśa sagaye dine mata-pitaśa aṭaya,* "The cave of princess (Abi) Tissā, daughter of the great king Gāmaṇī-Uttiya, is given to the Saṅgha of the ten directions, for the benefit of (her) mother and father."[101] In addition to this, we find four virtually identical inscriptions recording the gifts of caves to the *Saṅgha* by "Princess (Abi) Anurādhī, daughter of King Nāga and wife of King Uttiya, and King Uttiya," all of which end by saying that the act was done *aparimita-lokadatuya śatana śita-śukaye,* "for the welfare and happiness of beings in the boundless universe." Although less certain, it is possible that these four inscriptions are even slightly earlier than the record of the Princess Tissā.[102]

All of this renders Lamotte's interpretation less and less likely: the occurrence of the formula *mātāpituna aṭhāyā* at Bhārhut, of *sukhāya hotu savasatānaṃ* at Pauni, of *mata-pitaśa aṭaya* and *aparimita-lokadatuya śatana śita-śukaye* in third century B.C.E. Ceylon, clearly proves that the doctrine of the transference of merit associated with the Hīnayāna schools in later inscriptions was both very old and very widespread.

XII.

In concluding, we can note that all of this is of some interest in regard to the problem of the transference of merit in the Pāli canon and in modern Theravāda Buddhism in Southeast Asia. Bechert, among others, has written extensively on the subject and, although his exact position is not always immediately clear, he seems to want to say that the doctrine of the transference of merit is a "Mahāyāna idea." He says, for example:

> The fact that the possibility of transferring merit—a concept originating from the very beginnings of Mahāyāna Buddhism—has been acknowledged by all Buddhists—by the adherents of the 'Great Vehicle' as well as the Theravādins—confirms clearly to what extent this theory has to be considered as a logical consequence of the doctrines of early Buddhism. Thus we must not be astonished if we find traces of the Bodhisattva ideal in many texts of the Sarvāstivādins, e.g., the Avadānaśataka. These traces are not to be explained as outside influences; i.e., influences from Mahāyāna doctrines. On the contrary, these ideas followed quite naturally from the dynamics of early Buddhist thought—and Mahāyāna was based on these (the earlier German version of this passage says simply "Vielmehr ergaben sich diese Gedanken zwanglos aus der Entwicklung der buddhistischen Lehre").[103]

The position here is, as I have said, not altogether clear, although in a later paper Bechert appears to be a little more straightforward.[104]

If then, in the end, Bechert wants the doctrine of the transference of merit to be a "Mahāyāna idea" in the Theravāda Buddhism of Ceylon, there appear to be only two problems. The first is that this ignores the early and massive presence of *the* doctrine in Hīnayāna inscriptions. The second is that he does not give us the means by which we could know where what he presents as the "Mahāyāna idea" of the transference of merit actually comes from. His references are always in the form "in den Mahāyāna-Texten," but those texts are never cited nor are we ever given specific references. Moreover, the implication here is that there is a single, unified, and unchanging conception of the "idea" in Mahāyāna texts. But on the basis of a limited acquaintance with Mahāyāna *Sūtra* literature, this does not, to me, seem very likely, and in any case is yet to be demonstrated. What we need is a thorough study of the idea (or ideas) of the transference of merit in Mahāyāna literature. Then we will have something to compare and contrast with the material presented most recently by Agasse. For the moment, we can only observe that we know that the Pāli material that Agasse has analyzed is quite clearly much closer to the doctrine of the transference of merit which is associated epigraphically with the Hīnayāna schools than it is to the doctrine found in Mahāyāna inscriptions. But again, Bechert, by formulating an interesting hypothesis, has opened up new ground for what promises to be some very interesting exploration.

Notes

The research and writing of this paper were made possible by a grant from the Translations Program of the National Endowment for the Humanities, to which I will always be grateful. I should like to thank Professors L. O. Gómez and H. Durt for having read this paper and for allowing me to benefit from their observations. Also I must especially thank my friend Dr. John Thiel for having made a heroic attempt—not always successful—to make it more readable.

1. See, most recently, O. von Hinüber, "On the Tradition of Pāli Texts in India, Ceylon and Burma," *Buddhism in Ceylon and Studies on Religious Syncretism*, Abhandlungen der Akademie der Wissenschaften in Göttingen, Phil.-Hist. Klasse. Dritte Folge. Nr. 108, ed. H. Bechert (Göttingen: 1978) 48–49.

2. G. P. Malalasekera, *The Pāli Literature of Ceylon* (Colombo: 1928) 44.

3. J. Bloch, *Les inscriptions d'Aśoka* (Paris: 1950) 154.

4. Cf. E. Senart, *Les inscriptions de Piyadasi*, T. II (Paris: 1886) 103; *Histoire du bouddhisme indien*, 258–259.

5. *Histoire du bouddhisme indien*, 157; cf. 164–165; cf. H. Lüders, *Bharhut Inscriptions*, Corpus Inscriptionum Indicarum, Vol. II, Pt. 2 (Ootacamund: 1963) 71; B. M. Barua and K. G. Sinha, *Barhut Inscriptions* (Calcutta: 1926) 28–30. Note too that the epithet *pacanikāyika* also occurs once in the Brāhmī inscriptions from Pauni that appear to date from approximately the same period as the Bhārhut and Sāñcī inscriptions; see V. B. Kolte, "Brahmi Inscriptions from Pauni," *EI* 38 (1969) 171–172, 173 (A); S. B. Deo and J. P. Joshi, *Pauni Excavation (1969–1970)* (Nagpur: 1972) 39, no. 8.

6. G. Fussman, "Documents épigraphiques kouchans," *BEFEO* 61 (1974) 54–61. [This is incorrect. The earliest reference actually occurs in an inscription of the year 2 of Kaniṣka; cf. G. Schopen, "On Monks, Nuns, and 'Vulgar' Practices: The Introduction of the Image Cult into Indian Buddhism," Ch. XI below, and the sources cited there in n. 18.]

7. J. Ph. Vogel, "Prakrit Inscriptions from a Buddhist Site at Nāgārjunikoṇḍa," *EI* 20 (1929) C1; J. Burgess, *The Buddhist Stūpas of Amarāvatī and Jaggayyapeta*, Archaeological Survey of Southern India, Vol. I (London: 1887) 35; C. Sivaramamurti, *Amarāvatī Sculptures in the Madras Government Museum*, Bulletin of the Madras Government Museum, N. S., Vol. IV (Madras: 1956) 34.2; cf. N. Dutt, "Notes on the Nāgārjunikoṇḍa-Inscriptions," *IHQ* 7 (1931) 633–653; D. L. Barua, "On Some Terms in the Nāgārjunikoṇḍa Inscriptions," *Indian Culture* 1 (1934) 107–111. It should also be noted here that the title *majhimabaṇaka* occurs three times, the title *ekautirika-baṇaka (=Ekottarika°-)* once, and the title *śayutaka-baṇaka (=Saṃyuttaka)* once in the Brāhmī inscriptions of Ceylon; see S. Paranavitana, *Inscriptions of Ceylon*, Vol. I, *Containing Cave Inscriptions from 3rd Century B.C. to 1st Century A.C. and Other Inscriptions in the Early Brāhmī Script* (Ceylon: 1970) nos. 330, 708, 852; 407; 666. Unfortunately, none of these titles occur in inscriptions that also contain the name of a king, so it is impossible to date them with any precision. They could date anywhere from the third or second century B.C.E. to the first century C.E., or even much later; cf. P. E. E. Fernando, "Palaeographical Development of the Brahmi Script in Ceylon from the 3rd Century B.C. to the 7th Century A.D.," *UCR* 7 (1949) 282–301. It is interesting to note that the title *pacanikāyika* does not seem to occur anywhere in the Ceylonese Brāhmī inscriptions. Finally, it is worth noting that

Lévi at least has seen in the epithet *saṃyuktāgaminaḥ* found in "L'inscription de Mahānāman à Bodh-gaya" a clear reference to the *Saṃyuktāgama*, but this epithet, indeed the whole of this inscription, is associated with monks from Ceylon; see S. Lévi, "L'inscription de Mahānāman à Bodh-gaya, Essai d'Exêgèse appliquée à l'épigraphie bouddhique," *Indian Studies in Honor of Charles Rockwell Lanman* (Cambridge, Mass.: 1929) 46.

8. Cf. *Histoire du bouddhisme indien*, 164–165. Note that the title *sutata-pāḷi-bāṇaka* occurs once, and the title *vinayadhara* twice in the Ceylonese Brāhmī inscriptions (Paranavitana, *Inscriptions of Ceylon*, Vol. I, nos. 1202; 1178, 1207), but all three occurrences are found in inscriptions that Paranavitana classifies as "Later."

9. For details see, at least, S. Lévi, "Sur la recitation primitive des textes bouddhiques," *JA* (1915) 401–447; B. M. Barua, "Aṭṭhakavagga and Pārāyaṇavagga as Two Independent Buddhist Anthologies," *Proceedings and Transactions of the Fourth Oriental Conference* (Allahabad: 1928) 211–219; "Some Points Concerning the Mahāniddesa," *Fifth Indian Oriental Conference, Proceedings*, Vol. I (Lahore: 1930) 603–615; N. A. Jayawickrama, "The Sutta Nipāta: Its Title and Form," *UCR* 6 (1948) 78–86; "The Vaggas of the Sutta Nipāta," *UCR* 6 (1948) 229–256; "Sutta Nipāta: Some Suttas from the Aṭṭhaka Vagga," *UCR* 8 (1950) 244–255; "The Sutta Nipāta: Pucchās of the Pārāyaṇa Vagga," *UCR* 9 (1951) 61–68; "A Critical Analysis of the Pāli Sutta Nipāta Illustrating its Gradual Growth: General Observations," *UCR* 9 (1951) 113–124.

10. N. A. Jayawickrama, "The Vaggas of the Sutta Nipāta," *UCR* 6 (1948) 229–232; *Histoire du bouddhisme indien*, 256–259.

11. See the two interesting articles published by L. O. Gómez ("Proto-Mādhyamika in the Pāli Canon," *Philosophy East and West* 26 [1976] 137–165) and H. Nakamura ("A Process of the Origination of Buddhist Meditations in Connection with the Life of Buddha," *Studies in Pali and Buddhism* [*Kashyap Volume*], ed. A. K. Narain [Delhi: 1979] 269–277). The doctrinal discontinuity noted especially by Nakamura, but also by Gómez, between the *Aṭṭhaka-* and the *Pārāyaṇa-vaggas* and the Pāli canon as a whole is also suggested from yet another angle by the lack of parallels to the former in the latter; cf. R. Otto Franke, "Die Suttanipāta-Gāthās mit ihren Parallelen," *ZDMG* 63 (1909) 1–64, 255–286, 551–586; 64 (1910) 760–807; 66 (1910) 204–260, 706–708 (= *Kleine Schriften* [Wiesbaden: 1978] 474–777).

12. H. Lüders, *Bhārhut und die buddhistischen Literatur*, Abhandlungen für die Kunde des Morgenlandes, XXVI.3 (Leipzig: 1941) 136–176.

13. *Histoire du bouddhisme indien*, 444–445.

14. It could be argued that there is at least one exception to this. It could be argued that the relief labeled *ajātasata bhagavato vaṃdate* in which "three stages of the visit of the king to Buddha are shown, as described in the *Sāmaññaphala-sutta*" presupposes the existence of this particular text; see E. J. Thomas, *The Life of Buddha as Legend and History*, 3rd ed. (London: 1949) x. In fact, however, it seems to presuppose only the text's narrative frame since it appears very likely that, as Thomas says, the doctrinal content of the *Sāmaññaphala-sutta* has been "inserted in a legend of king Ajātasattu, who is said to have come to Buddha after having inquired of the leaders of six rival schools" (ibid., 179). The inscription and the relief presuppose only this "legend." Note that the essential doctrinal components of this text occur verbatim again and again throughout the *Sīlakkhandha-vagga* of the *Dīgha* (*Suttas* 1–13) and almost certainly had an independent existence (178). Note too that essentially the same narrative frame—although with different characters—was also used by the author of the *Milindapañha*.

15. K. R. Norman, "The Gāndhārī Version of the Dharmapada," *Buddhist Studies in Honour of I. B. Horner.* ed. L. Cousins et al. (Dordrecht/Boston: 1974) 171–179.

16. J. Brough, *The Gāndhārī Dharmapada*, London Oriental Series, Vol. VII (Oxford: 1962) 55–56.

17. J. W. de Jong, "The Study of Buddhism. Problems and Perspectives," in J. W. de Jong, *Buddhist Studies*, ed. G. Schopen (Berkeley: 1979) 19. [This is in reference to canonical texts only; see also p. 16 n. 5 above.]

18. O. von Hinüber, "Die Erforschung der Gilgit-Handschriften (Funde buddhistischer Sanskrit-Handschriften I)," *Nachrichten der Ak. d. W. in Göttingen*, I. Phil.-hist. Kl., Jahrgang 1979, Nr. 12 (Göttingen: 1979) 341, no. 4a.

19. E. Zürcher, *The Buddhist Conquest of China. The Spread and Adaptation of Buddhism in Early Medieval China*, Vol. I (Leiden: 1959), notes, however, that "the versions [of the *Madhyamāgama* and *Ekottarāgama*] which now figure in the canon seem to be a later redaction of Dharmanandin's translation, executed by Saṅghadeva at the very end of the fourth century" (204). This statement must be supplemented by the more detailed remarks in Ét. Lamotte, "Un sūtra composite de l'Ekottarāgama," *BSOAS* 30 (1967) 104ff; see also E. Waldschmidt, "Central Asian Sūtra Fragments and their Relation to the Chinese Āgamas," *Die Sprache der ältesten buddhistischen Überlieferung*, Abhandlungen der Akademie der Wissenschaften in Göttingen, Phil.-Hist. Klasse. Dritte Folge. Nr. 117, ed. H. Bechert (Göttingen: 1980) 169ff. There were, of course, isolated pieces of the *nikāya/āgama* literature translated prior to this time; cf. *L'inde classique*, T. II (Paris: 1953) 2070, 2082–2083.

20. For Bareau, see especially *Recherches sur la biographie du Buddha dans les Sūtrapiṭaka et les Vinayapiṭaka anciens: de la quête de l'éveil à la conversion de Śāriputra et de Maudgalyāyana* (Paris: 1963); *Recherches sur la biographie du Buddha dans les Sūtrapiṭaka et les Vinayapiṭaka anciens: les derniers mois, le parinirvāṇa et les funérailles*, T. I (Paris: 1971); T. II (Paris: 1971); see also n. 36 below. For Frauwallner, *The Earliest Vinaya and the Beginnings of Buddhist Literature*, Serie Orientale Roma, VIII (Rome: 1956); "The Historical Data We Possess on the Person and the Doctrine of the Buddha," *EW* 7 (1957) 309–312. For a few typical examples of the invocation of this principle, see Ét. Lamotte, "Lotus et buddha supramondain," *BEFEO* 69 (1981) 32–33; Brough, *The Gāndhārī Dharmapada*, xviii; K. R. Norman, "Four Etymologies from the Sabhiya-Sutta," *Buddhist Studies in Honour of Walpola Rahula*, ed. S. Balasooriya et al. (London: 1980) 179 (§ 8.1). But note too that the acceptance of this principle is not limited to textual scholars but has been taken up by a wide variety of modern scholars dealing with Buddhism; see, for example, J. Ph. Vogel, "The Past Buddhas and Kāśyapa in Indian Art and Epigraphy," *Asiatica, Festschrift Friedrich Weller* (Leipzig: 1954) 808; F. E. Reynolds, "The Many Lives of Buddha: A Study of Sacred Biography and Theravāda Tradition," *The Biographical Process, Studies in the History and Psychology of Religion*, ed. F. E. Reynolds and D. Capps (The Hague: 1976) 41; etc.

21. A. Bareau, *Les sectes bouddhiques du petit véhicule* (Paris: 1955) 16.

22. Bareau, *Les sectes bouddhiques*, 16–19.

23. Bareau, *Les sectes bouddhiques*, 27, 36. The second century date is Bareau's. It may be possible to push it somewhat further back, but this depends on the date of the famous Mathurā Lion Capital Inscription, which is highly controversial. See, for example, R. Salomon, "The Kṣatrapas and Mahākṣatrapas of India," *WZKS* 17 (1973) 11; A. K. Narain, *The Indo-Greeks* (Oxford: 1957) 142ff.

24. N. Dutt, *Early Monastic Buddhism*, Vol. II (Calcutta: 1945) 14.

25. For some of the hypotheses that Aśoka's "Schismenedikt" has generated, see L. Alsdorf, "Aśoka's Schismen-Edikt und das dritte Konzil," *IIJ* 3 (1959) 161–174 (= *Kleine Schriften* [Wiesbaden: 1974] 414–427); H. Bechert, "Aśoka's 'Schismenedikt' und der Begriff Sanghabheda," *WZKS* 5 (1961) 18–52; H. Bechert, "The Importance of Aśoka's So-called Schism Edict," *Indological and Buddhist Studies. Volume in Honour of Professor J. W. de Jong on his Sixtieth Birthday*, ed. L. A. Hercus et al. (Canberra: 1982) 61–68.

26. W. Wassilieff, "Le bouddhisme dans son plein développement d'après les vinayas," *RHR* 34 (1896) 318–325. It is interesting to note that, in 1896, S. Lévi, who translated Wassilieff's paper into French, added a short preface to it in which he found it necessary to say that Wassilieff's "opinions . . . puissent choquer les idées courantes," and to add: "Il va sans dire que le traducteur n'entend pas se solidariser avec l'auteur: comme indianiste, il se voit même obligé d'exprimer les réserves les plus formelles sur les conclusions hardies de M. Wassilieff." But about ten years later in an article of his own Lévi, after quoting with approval the conclusions of Wassilieff's article, says "A mon tour, je me pose la même question"; then follows nearly a page of questions of almost exactly the same purport as Wassilieff's—none of which, again, have been answered. See S. Lévi, "Les éléments de formation du Divyāvadāna," *TP* 8 (1907) 116–117 and n. 1.

27. *Histoire du bouddhisme indien*, 197.

28. Bareau, *Les sectes bouddhiques*, 48. See also L. Renou and J. Filliozat, *L'inde classique. Manuel des Études indiennes*, T. II (Paris-Hanoi: 1953) 517 (§ 2245); H. Bechert, "Notes on the Formation of Buddhist Sects and the Origins of Mahāyāna," *German Scholars on India*, Vol. I (Varanasi: 1973) 10, 11.

29. A. Bareau, "La construction et le culte des stūpa d'après les Vinayapiṭaka," *BEFEO* 50 (1960) 257–261, esp. 260.

30. H. C. Norman, *The Dhammapadaṭṭhakathā*, Vol. III (London: 1906–1915) 250–255; cf. E. W. Burlingame, *Buddhist Legends*, Pt. 3, Harvard Oriental Series, Vol. 30 (Cambridge, Mass.: 1921) 68–69.

31. For example, "the smile of the Buddha," found also at *Aṅguttara*, iii, 214; *Majjhima*, ii, 45, 74 (cf. *Saṃyutta*, ii, 254; *Vinaya*, iii, 105—all references to the Pāli texts are to the Pali Text Society editions); *Mahāvastu* (Senart ed.), i, 317; *Divyāvadāna* (Cowell and Neil ed.), 67ff, 138ff, 265ff, etc. Or the stories of King Kṛkin and Kāśyapa found also at *Mūlasarvāstivāda-vinaya, Gilgit Manuscripts*, iii 1, 191, 195, 200; iii 2, 77–78; iii 4, 190–193 = *Divyāvadāna* (Cowell and Neil ed.), 22–24; *Avadānaśataka* (Speyer ed.), II, 76, 124–125; *Avadānakalpalatā* (Vaidya ed.), i, 95 (vss. 147–148), 145 (vss. 132–133), 279 (vss. 16–17); *Ratnamālāvadāna* (Takahata ed.), 132; etc.

32. Bareau, "La construction et le culte des stūpa," 261.

33. *Gilgit Manuscripts*, iii 1, 73.16–79.2; *Peking*, 41, 179-3-6 to 180-4-2. In light of what follows, it is of some significance to note that the *Mūlasarvāstivāda-vinaya* appears to be a fairly late compilation; cf. *Histoire du bouddhisme indien*, 187, 196; Ét. Lamotte, "La légende du Buddha," *RHR* 134 (1948) 61–62. See, however, the more recent observations in *Saṅghabhedavastu*, i, xxff. Note that neither the Chinese versions nor the Pāli version of this account are noted in J. L. Panglung, *Die Erzählstoffe des Mūlasarvāstivāda-vinaya analysiert auf Grund der tibetischen Übersetzung*, Studia Philologica Buddhica, Monograph Series III (Tokyo: 1981) 34; nor has he noted that the verses of the text are also found elsewhere; see H. Lüders, "Weitere Beiträge zur Geschichte und Geographie von Ostturkestan," *Philologica Indica* (Göttingen: 1940) 612; E. Waldschmidt, "Der Buddha preist die Verehrungswürdigkeit seiner Reliquien," *Von Ceylon bis Turfan* (Göttingen: 1967) 424–427.

34. E. B. Cowell and R. A. Neil, *The Divyāvadāna* (Cambridge: 1886) 76.10–80.9, 465.10–469.18.

35. Particularly significant in this regard is the absence of any reference to the King Kṛkin since Buddhist Sanskrit literary tradition consistently associates the Buddha Kāśyapa, and especially his funeral and the deposition of his bodily remains, with this king; cf. M. Hofinger, *Le congrès du lac Anavatapta I: Légendes des anciens (Sthavirāvadāna)* (Louvain: 1956) 225, n. 1. Not only is this association consistent, but—as a glance at the references in n. 31 will reveal—it is also widespread. The fact that our Sanskrit text knows nothing of this association is, therefore, as I have said, particularly significant.

36. Note that the existence of a text which knew only a "pre-*stūpa*" form of the relic cult creates some problems for Bareau's recent attempts to reconstruct the origin of the *stūpa* and its cult. This is particularly so since the text in question appears to represent perhaps the oldest tradition we have that is connected with one of the Previous Buddhas, and since we know from the Nigālī Sāgar Edict that the cult of the Previous Buddhas was, at the very least, pre-Aśokan. Cf. A. Bareau, "Sur l'origine des piliers dits Aśoka, des stūpa et des arbres sacrés du bouddhisme primitif," *Indologica Taurinensia* 2 (1974) 9–36; "Le parinirvāṇa du Buddha et la naissance de la religion bouddhique," *BEFEO* 61 (1974) 275–299; "Les récits canoniques des funérailles du Buddha et leurs anomalies: nouvel essai d'interprétation," *BEFEO* 62 (1975) 151–189.

37. Note that there appears to be at least one other instance in Buddhist literature where a "text" appears to have undergone a process of revision similar to that which we have found here. The "text" in question is the *Vyāghrī-jātaka,* and although the various versions of this "text" have yet to be systematically studied from this point of view, it is clear that at one stage, represented by the *Jātakamālā* version (Ch. I), the "text" knew nothing of a *stūpa,* and that at another stage, represented by the *Suvarṇabhāsottama* (Ch. XVIII), reference to a *stūpa* had been fully incorporated into the tale and has become an integral part of it. In fact, the manuscript tradition of the *Suvarṇabhāsottama* by itself seems to preserve two distinct stages of the revision.

In a more general vein, we must also note that there have, of course, been other more purely philological attempts to get beyond the earliest known redaction of the canon; cf. S. Lévi, "Observations sur une langue précanonique du bouddhisme," *JA* (1912) 495–514; H. Lüders, *Beobachtungen über die Sprache des buddhistischen Urkanons,* Abh. d. Deutschen Akad. d. Wiss. zu Berlin, Kl. f. Sprachen, Lit. u. Kunst. Jg. 1952 Nr. 10, Hg. v. E. Waldschmidt (Berlin: 1954); but see also the more recent work of O. von Hinüber, "Pāli Kaṭhati: ein Beitrag zur Überlieferungsgeschichte des Theravāda-Kanons," *IIJ* 21 (1979) 21–26, and the paper cited in n. 1 above. Unfortunately, the results of these important studies—when not controverted—have so far been rather limited from a larger historical point of view.

38. H. Oldenberg, *Buddha, sein Leben, seine Lehre, seine Gemeinde* (Stuttgart: 1923; first pub. 1881) 424; trans. *Buddha: His Life, His Doctrine, His Order* (London: 1882) 377.

39. R. P. Chanda, *Dates of the Votive Inscriptions on the Stupas at Sanchi,* MASI, No. 1 (1919); A. H. Dani, *Indian Palaeography* (Oxford: 1963) 62–65; V. Dehejia, *Early Buddhist Rock Temples, A Chronological Study* (London: 1972) 35–36, 186–188. I follow Dehejia here.

40. *Histoire du bouddhisme indien,* 455. Lüders, *Bharhut Inscriptions,* 1–2, counts twenty-five monk donors, sixteen nuns, and ninety-four lay. The figures for Sāñcī are virtually the same: out of a total of four hundred thirty seven (nineteen are either

fragmentary or nondonative), there are one hundred sixty three monastic donors. See G. Bühler, "Votive Inscriptions from the Sānchi Stūpas," *EI* 2 (1899) 87–116; Bühler, "Further Inscriptions from Sānchi," *EI* 2 (1899) 366–408.

41. M. Shizutani, *Indo bukkyō himei mokuroku* [*Catalogue of Indian Buddhist Inscriptions*] (Kyoto: 1979) §§ 206, 210, 217, 223, 231, 254; 226; 277; 288; *Histoire du bouddhisme indien*, 157.

42. S. Konow, *Kharoshṭhī Inscriptions with the Exception of Those of Aśoka*, Corpus Inscriptionum Indicarum, Vol. II, Pt. 1 (Calcutta: 1929). Monks: XXXV.1, XXXVI.1, 2, 4, 5, 6, 7, 8, XL, XLII, XLIII, XLIV, LII, LVIII, LXXXVIII, plus the inscription edited by Fussman, *BEFEO* 61 (1974) 54–58. Note that the donors in XL, XLII, XLIII, and XLIV are taken as monks on the basis of the terms *sadaviyarisa, sadayarisa*, etc.; cf. H. Lüders, *A List of Brāhmī Inscriptions from the Earliest Times to about* A.D. *400 with the Exception of Those of Aśoka*, Appendix to *EI* 10, 1909/10 (Calcutta: 1912) 223; Brough, *The Gāndhārī Dharmapada*, 177 and xx–xxi; Konow (107) equates the terms with *sārdhaṃchara* or *sārdhaṁvihārin*. Note that all these donors appear to have monastic names and that, in at least one case (XLIII), Konow has reconstructed the reading as *sa[dharmarata-śamanasa sadayarisa*] although this is admittedly somewhat odd. Laymen: I, II, XIII, XV, XVII, XXI, XXVII, XXXI, XXXII, XXXV.4, XLVI, XLVII, XLIX, LXXIV, LXXVI, LXXVII, LXXX, LXXXII, LXXXVI.

43. Konow, *Kharoshṭhī Inscriptions*, XXXVI.7; Fussman, *BEFEO* 61 (1974).

44. H. Lüders, *Mathurā Inscriptions*, Abh. d. Akad. d. Wiss. in Göttingen, Philo-Hist. Klasse, Dritte Folge, Nr. 47, ed. K. L. Janert (Göttingen: 1961) §§ 4(?), 8, 24, 29, 31, 32, 33a, 33b, 35a, 35b, 36, 37, 38, 39a, 39b, 40a, 40b, 41, 44, 45, 46, 52, 53, 54, 55, 56, 58, 59, 67, 80 (?), 90, 103, 121, 126, 152, 154, 157, 179, 185, 186.

45. Lüders, *Mathurā Inscriptions*, §§ 33a, 33b, 35b; 46 [on *prāhaṇīka* cf. *BHSD*, 389 s.v. *prahāṇa*: 390 s.v. *prahāṇika* ("characterized by religious strenuosity"); 394 s.v. *prāhāṇika* ("engaging in [ascetic] exertion"); Th. Damsteegt, *Epigraphical Hybrid Sanskrit. Its Rise, Spread, Characteristics and Relationship to Buddhist Hybrid Sanskrit* (Leiden: 1978) 247; Lüders, *Mathurā Inscriptions*, 83, n. 2]; 24.

46. J. Burgess, *Report on the Buddhist Cave Temples and Their Inscriptions*, Archaeological Survey of Western India, Vol. IV (London: 1883; repr. Varanasi: 1975) IV.7, 8, 9, 10, 20 (?); VI.2; VII.3, 8, 9, 12, 13, 14, 16, 17; VIII.17; XI.6, 7, 9; XII.1, 3, 5, 7, 8, 10, 11, 12, 13, 14, 15, for monastic donors.

47. G. Schopen, "Mahāyāna in Indian Inscriptions," *IIJ* 21 (1979) 1–19, esp. 9. It should be noted that there is a certain amount of overlap among the "Mathurā Inscriptions," the "Cave Temple Inscriptions," and those grouped under the heading "Mahāyāna." A number of inscriptions from the first two groups are also included in the third.

48. See Oldenberg's statement quoted above. That this position is still very much current is clear, for example, from H. Bechert, "Contradictions in Sinhalese Buddhism," *Religion and the Legitimation of Power in Sri Lanka*, ed. B. L. Smith (Chambersburg, PA: 1978) 192–193. We can, however, also cite two recent exceptions to these views: R. F. Gombrich, *Precept and Practice. Traditional Buddhism in the Rural Highlands of Ceylon* (Oxford: 1971) 319, and D. Seyfort Ruegg, "A Recent Work on the Religions of Tibet and Mongolia," *TP* 61 (1976) 313–314.

49. Konow, *Kharoshṭhī Inscriptions*, monastic: XXXVI.1, 2, 4, 5, 6, 7, 8, XL, XLII, XLIII, XLIV, LVIII, LXXXVIII; an inscription reported by Fussman, *BEFEO* 61 (1974), would be one more. Konow's lay inscriptions are: XXI, XXXV.4, XLVI, XLVII, XLIX.

50. Lüders, *Mathurā Inscriptions*. monastic: §§ 4, 8, 24, 29, 41, 67, 80, 90, 103, 121, 126, 152, 154, 155, 157, 179, 185, 186; lay: §§ 1, 74, 76, 81, 135, 136, 150, 167, 172, 180. Note that §§ 8, 67, 152, 179, 185, 186 also fall into the inscriptions grouped under the heading "Mahāyāna."

51. Burgess, *Report on the Buddhist Cave Temples*. IV.7, 8, 9, 10; XI.7, 9; XII.1, 3, 5, 7, 8, 11, 12, 13, 14, 15, all monastic; XII.2 is the one exception. Here, the overlap with the Mahāyāna group is much greater. Only five of the seventeen inscriptions considered here are non-Mahāyāna: XII.2, 3, 7, 11, 13.

52. Schopen, "Mahāyāna in Indian Inscriptions," 9.

53. Lüders, *A List of Brāhmī Inscriptions*. §§ 918, 919, 925, 926, 927; K. G. Goswami, *EI* 24 (1938) 210ff; Lüders, *Mathurā Inscriptions*. § 24; Damsteegt, *Epigraphical Hybrid Sanskrit*, 152, 178–180; A. K. Coomaraswamy, *History of Indian and Indonesian Art* (London: 1927) 58–59; O. Takata, "On the Dated Buddha Images in the Kushan Art of Mathurā," *Bijutsu Kenkyu* 184 (1956) 223–240.

54. J. C. Harle, "A Hitherto Unknown Dated Sculpture from Gandhāra: A Preliminary Report," *South Asian Archaeology 1973*, ed. J. E. van Lohuizen-De Leeuw and J. M. M. Ubaghs (Leiden: 1974) 128–135. The inscription on this image is the same one published by Fussman in *BEFEO* 61; see n. 6; cf. K. W. Dobbins, "Gandhāra Buddha Images with Inscribed Dates," *EW* 18 (1968) 281–288.

55. Konow, *Kharoshṭhī Inscriptions*, XXXVI.7.

56. G. Nagao, "The Architectural Tradition in Buddhist Monasticism," *Studies in History of Buddhism*, ed. A. K. Narain (Delhi: 1980) 194, 195; cf. G. Nagao, *The Ancient Buddhist Community in India and its Cultural Activities* (Kyoto: 1971); D. Mitra, *Buddhist Monuments* (Calcutta: 1971) 20–52; Dehejia, *Early Buddhist Rock Temples*. 71–113.

57. H. Sarkar, *Studies in Early Buddhist Architecture of India* (Delhi: 1966) 15–24, esp. 22.

58. Sarkar, *Studies*, 53, 55; note, however, that there has been some doubt expressed as to whether these are Buddhist *stūpas*; cf. Mitra, *Buddhist Monuments*. 124.

59. Konow, *Kharoshṭhī Inscriptions*. XV, LXXII, LXXX, LXXXVI.

60. Konow, *Kharoshṭhī Inscriptions*. XIII, XXVII, LXXVI, etc.

61. See Konow, *Kharoshṭhī Inscriptions*. 140, where he discusses the interpretations of Hoernle and Majumdar as well as his own. There can, however, be little doubt that *yaṭhi* here refers to the "pole" (*yaṣṭi*) of the *stūpa*. There are textual parallels for both *yaṭhipratiṭhana* and *yaṭhiṃ aropayata*. We find *yūpa-yaṣṭir abhyantare pratipāditā*. for example, in the much-studied *stūpa* passage at *Divyāvadāna* (Cowell and Neil ed.), 244.7; see most recently G. Roth, "Bemerkungen zum Stūpa des Kṣemaṃkara," *StII* 5/6 (1980) 181–190, esp. 184–186; cf. F. B. J. Kuiper, "Yūpayaṣṭi- (Divy. 244.11)," *IIJ* 3 (1959) 204–205. And *yaṣṭim āropayed* occurs repeatedly in a short text, three copies of which I have identified among the Gilgit Manuscripts, entitled the *Adbhutadharmaparyāya*. See O. von Hinüber, "Die Erforschung der Gilgit-Handschriften. Nachtrag," *ZDMG* 130.2 (1980) *25*–*26* nos. 11, 13d, and 18; here in the repeated description of a miniature *stūpa*, we read *yo vā . . . mṛtpiṇḍād āmalakapramāṇaṃ stūpaṃ pratiṣṭhāpayet sūcīmātrāṃ yaṣṭim āropayed*. etc. [See G. Schopen, "The Ritual Obligations and Donor Roles of Monks in the Pāli *Vinaya*," Ch. IV, below; and Y. Bentor, "The Redactions of the *Adbhutadharmaparyāya* from Gilgit," *JIABS* 11.2 (1988) 21–52.]

62. Harle, "A Hitherto Unknown Dated Sculpture from Gandhāra," 128.

63. The crosses mark an interesting feature of this inscription. Lüders says, "The

text contains eight *maṅgala* symbols which are engraved generally after the seventh *akṣara* irrespective of the meaning of the words" (*Mathurā Inscriptions*, 80).

64. According to Lüders, "Vojyavaśika (?) probably refers to the native place of the donor" (*Mathurā Inscriptions*, 80).

65. This is Lüders' translation of *prāhaṇīka:* see n. 45 above.

66. Fussman, "Documents épigraphiques kouchans," *BEFEO* 61 (1974) 56.

67. Damsteegt, *Epigraphical Hybrid Sanskrit*, 164–165 and notes.

68. D. C. Sircar, *EI* 30 (1953–1954) 184; Damsteegt, *Epigraphical Hybrid Sanskrit*, 164, n. 50; Shizutani, *Indo bukkyō himei mokuroku*, § 639. Here, I follow Damsteegt.

69. J. Burgess, *Report on the Elura Cave Temples and the Brahmanical and Jaina Caves of Western India*. Archaeological Survey of Western India, Vol. V (London: 1883) II. Kānheri Inscriptions, no. 7; Damsteegt, *Epigraphical Hybrid Sanskrit*, 186.

70. D. C. Sircar, *EI* 35 (1963–1964) 7ff, no. 2 (A, B); Shizutani, *Indo bukkyō himei mokuroku*, 715.

71. Burgess, *Report on the Buddhist Cave Temples*, IX.21.

72. Konow, *Kharoshṭhī Inscriptions*, LXXXVI; Damsteegt, *Epigraphical Hybrid Sanskrit*, 160, 165, n. 51.

73. Schopen, "Mahāyāna in Indian Inscriptions," 17, n. 24.

74. Lüders, *Mathurā Inscriptions*, §§ 2; 125, 157.

75. Burgess, *Report on the Buddhist Cave Temples*. IX.21.

76. Fussman, "Documents épigraphiques Kouchans," *BEFEO* 61 (1974) IV. "Vase inscrit de Qunduz," 58–61.

77. Burgess, *Report on the Elura Cave Temples*. II.4, 27; Shizutani, *Indo bukkyō himei mokuroku*, §§ 464, 482.

78. J. Ph. Vogel, *EI* 20 (1929–1930) H; Shizutani, *Indo bukkyō himei mokuroku*. § 708.

79. D. C. Sircar, *EI* 33 (1959–1960) 250; Shizutani, *Indo bukkyō himei mokuroku*. § 712.

80. Konow, *Kharoshṭhī Inscriptions*. LXXII; Shizutani, *Indo bukkyō himei mokuroku*. § 1775.

81. G. Bühler, *EI* 2 (1892) 212, no. 42; Shizutani, *Indo bukkyō himei mokuroku*. § 460.

82. There is one possible, though I think doubtful, exception to this. Lüders gives his Mathurā Inscription § 135 as: *(Ś)ā(ky)opāsakasya Suṣasya Hāruṣasya—dānaṃ Budhaprat(i)mā Ūttarasya H(ā)ruṣa(sya) vihāre sahā mātāpitihi—sarvasatvānaṃ hitasukhartha(ṃ)*. Note that what Lüders reconstructed as *(Ś)ā(ky)opāsakasya*. Cunningham and Vogel read as *upāsakasya*. Note too that if Lüders' reconstruction were to be accepted, this would be the only instance in the forty-five inscriptions associated with *Śākyabhikṣu/-bhikṣuṇīs, Śākyopāsikas*. etc., where the formula *sarvasatvānaṃ hitasukharthaṃ* occurs. And it is not only the occurrence of this formula which is odd here. The whole structure of Mathurā § 135 differs from what we find everywhere else associated with *Śākyabhikṣus*. etc. *Dānaṃ* never occurs with the latter, but always *deyadharmo 'yaṃ*. and neither the term *budhapratimā*. nor the phrase *sahā mātāpitihi* is ever found in their inscriptions. All of this, I think, puts Lüders' reconstruction in doubt.

83. The direct evidence for the affiliation of the formula *arogyadakṣiṇāye* is not so abundant as for some other formulae. It occurs three times in the Mathurā inscriptions (§§ 44, 46, 180) and, according to Damsteegt, in seven Kharoṣṭhī inscriptions (*Epigraphical Hybrid Sanskrit*, 162). Unfortunately, the name of a school appears to occur in only one of these inscriptions, the Wardak Vase Inscription (Konow, *Kharoshṭhī Inscriptions*.

LXXXVI) where *sarvasatvaṇa arogadakshiṇae* is found in association with the Mahāsāṅghikas. We also find the phrase *atmaṇasya arogada(kṣ)i(ṇa . . .)* in an inscription from Haḍḍa published more recently by Fussman in association with the Sarvāstivādins (*BEFEO* 66 [1969] 5–9). We can say only that, in the two instances in which the formula occurs in association with a specifically named school, that school is a Hīnayāna school, and that the formula never occurs in inscriptions associated with the Mahāyāna or *Śākyabhikṣus,* etc.

84. Konow, *Kharoshṭhī Inscriptions,* XXVII; S. S. Ram, "Taxila Silver Scroll Inscription, Year 136," *Indological Studies* 2 (1974) 45–52.

85. In addition to Mathurā Inscription § 29 cited above, it is also found, for example, at Konow, *Kharoshṭhī Inscriptions,* XXVII and LXXXII; in an inscription from Kalawān edited by Konow, *JRAS* (1932) 949ff (cf. Shizutani, *Indo bukkyō himei mokuroku,* § 1745); and in several inscriptions from Nāgārjunikoṇḍa in Vogel, *EI* 20 (1929–1930) C3, B4, B5, C2, C5; Sircar, *EI* 35 (1963–1964) 11–13, no. 4; cf. N. Dutt, *Buddhist Sects in India* (Calcutta: 1970) 124–125.

Since we have traced the affiliation of all the other formulae that occur in the five inscriptions I have quoted above, we might note that the formula *sarvabuddhapūjārtham* is also consistently associated with the Hīnayāna schools. It occurs three times in the Mathurā Inscriptions in association with the name of a school: once with the Sammitīyas (§ 80) and twice with the Mahāsāṅghikas (§§ 86, 157); it occurs in the Mathurā Lion Capital Inscription in association with the Sarvāstivādins in Konow, *Kharoshṭhī Inscriptions,* XV; and again it occurs in association with the Mahāsāṅghikas in a Mathurā inscription published by Sircar in *EI* 30 (1953–1954) 181; Shizutani, *Indo bukkyō himei mokuroku,* § 639.

86. Health and longevity are mentioned, for example, in two inscriptions from Nāgārjunikoṇḍa associated with the Aparamahāvinaseliyas (Vogel, *EI* 20 [1929–1930] E; and Sircar, *EI* 35 [1963–1964] 7ff, no. 2 [A, B]; Shizutani, *Indo bukkyō himei mokuroku,* §§ 684, 715), and in an inscription from Tor Ḍherai in conjunction with the Sarvāstivādins (Konow, *Kharoshṭhī Inscriptions,* XCII).

87. There are four possible exceptions: MadP i, Aj iii 4, Bih ii, and Sa i B(b)59; the key to any abbreviations used here (e.g. MadP i) and in what follows will be found in Schopen, "Mahāyāna in Indian Inscriptions," *IIJ* 21 (1979) 2–4. Of these, MadP i is very carelessly done and is full of omissions as can be seen in the text it gives for the *Pratītyasamutpādagāthā,* and it is therefore safe to assume that our formula—which makes up the second half of the inscription and which reads only *yad atra puṇyaṃ tat bhavatu mātāpitarebhyaḥ*—has suffered the same mutilation. Aj iii 4 reads: *deyadharmo 'yam śākyabhi(kṣor) bhadanta-dha(rma) devasya /// mātāpitro(:) -dasya ya(d atra) pu(ṇyaṃ tad bha)vatu cā(nutta)rājñanāvāptaye.* But again this has obviously been badly written and is corrupt. Note that the *yad atra* clause and the *mātāpitṛ* clause have been inverted. But note especially the *ca* preceding *anuttara-.* This is a good indication that *sarvasatvānām* has probably been inadvertently omitted. Bih ii, which reads *deyadharmo 'yaṃ pravaramahāyāna-yāyinyā(ḥ) paramopāsikā-śau(śrī)-santoṣa-vadhu-maharokāyā yad atra puṇyaṃ tad bhavatv iti,* is—in spite of the *iti,* or perhaps because of it (*iti* = etc.)—obviously incomplete. There is neither person nor thing for which the merit is supposed to be. The last case, Sa i B(b)59, is in the main well written and correct: *deyadharmo 'yaṃ śākyabhikṣo(r) buddhapri(ri)yasya yad atra puṇyaṃ tad bhavatu anuttarajñānāvātma(pta)ye.* But in light of the fact that in every other occurrence of our formula *sarvasatvānām* is either present or its absence can be accounted for, it is probably safe to assume that it has simply been accidentally omitted here.

These remarks concerning the presence of both *sarvasatva-* and *anuttarajñāna-* in virtually all instances of the formula do not agree with some statements made in my earlier paper. The latter, however, must be corrected. Cf. the following note.

88. There are again some apparent exceptions in which *anuttarajñānāvāptaye* appears to be omitted: MadP i, Bih ii, Ma i 185, MadP ii B, Aj iii 3, and Aj iii 5. But the first two of these are, as we have already seen, faulty or incomplete (cf. n. 87), and Ma i 185 also, according to Lüders, is probably incomplete (*Mathurā Inscriptions*, 211, n. 4). MadP ii B is one of four inscriptions on a set of seven images from Phophnar Kalan, two of which are very short, and two of which contain a formula. One of these formulae—*yad atra puṇyam tad bhavatu aparimita-lokadhātustha-sarvv-ānuśaya-{ba}ndhan-āvabaddha-satva-lokasy-ānāvaraṇa-jñān-āvāptaye*—is very unusual and, as Gai has pointed out, "is not met with anywhere else in epigraphs" (G. S. Gai, Post-script to M. Venkataramayya and C. B. Trivedi, "Four Buddhist Inscriptions from Phophnar Kalan," *EI* 37 [1967] 150). We have, therefore, some grounds for suspecting that the other formula—which reads only *yad atra puṇya(ṃ} tad {bhavatu sa}rvva-(sa}tvānām*, omitting *anuttarajñānāvāptaye*—is also unusual, since it too is found nowhere else in complete and otherwise unproblematic inscriptions. Finally, Aj iii 3 and 5 are perhaps somewhat more complicated. Aj iii 5 has *yad atra (puṇyam) tad bhavatu mā(tāpitroḥ) sarvvasatvā(nān) ca*, but Dhavalikar says, "The inscription consists of three lines while there are traces of some letters in the fourth line" (M. K. Dhavalikar, "New Inscriptions from Ajaṇṭa," *ArO* 7 [1968] 151). Aj iii 3 has virtually the same reading, but here Dhavalikar says that the second sentence of the inscription states "that the merit accruing to the pious act of Mitradharma was meant for the attainment of the supreme knowledge by all sentient beings including his parents and others" (150). On the basis of this remark it would seem that Dhavalikar has probably omitted one line in his transcription.

After having looked at the same material from a different point of view it is clear, as I said in the previous note, that a number of statements in my earlier paper "Mahāyāna in Indian Inscriptions" must be corrected. Without going into details here, let me simply say that lines 8–17 on p. 5 of that paper should be deleted, as well as the related statement at lines 32–33. And it should be noted that the simplest, certainly attestable form of the formula appears now to be *yad atra puṇyaṃ tad bhavatu sarvasatvānām anuttarajñānāvāptaye*, found for example at Ma i 186, Bo i 72, and Na ii.

89. Cf. Shizutani, *Indo bukkyō himei mokuroku*, § 1823; B. N. Mukherjee, "A Mathura Inscription of the Year 26 and of the Period of Huvishka," *JAIH* 11 (1977–1978) 82–84. The same inscription was also published in R. C. Sharma, "New Buddhist Sculptures from Mathura," *Lalit Kalā* 19 (1979) 25–26; R. C. Sharma, *Buddhist Art of Mathurā* (Delhi: 1984) 232, n. 169. Neither of these editions appear to be altogether satisfactory and the publication of both a good facsimile and a critical edition is very much needed. [See now G. Schopen, "The Inscription on the Kuṣān Image of Amitābha and the Character of the Early Mahāyāna in India," *JIABS* 10.2 (1987) 99–134.]

90. For what appears to be "the earliest datable literary reference" to Amitābha, see P. Maxwell Harrison, "Buddhānusmṛti in the Pratyutpannabuddhasammukhāvasthita-samādhi-sūtra," *JIP* 6 (1978) 42–44, and for a recent view on at least certain aspects of the "cult" of Amitābha in India, see G. Schopen, "Sukhāvatī as a Generalized Religious Goal in Sanskrit Mahāyāna Sūtra Literature," *IIJ* 19 (1977) 177–210, esp. 204–205, and the additions and corrections to this in G. Schopen, "The Five Leaves of the Buddhabalādhā-naprātihāryavikurvāṇanirdeśa-sūtra Found at Gilgit," *JIP* 5 (1978) 335, n. 2. See also J.

C. Huntington, "A Gandhāran Image of Amitāyus' Sukhāvatī," *Annali dell' Instituto Orientale di Napoli* 40 (1980) 651–672; Huntington, "Mathurā Evidence for the Early Teachings of Mahāyāna," to be published in a volume of papers read at an International Seminar on Mathurā at Mathurā in January 1980 [since published in D. M. Srinivasan, ed., *Mathurā. The Cultural Heritage* (New Delhi: 1988) 85–92] (I should like to thank Prof. Huntington for sending me copies of his papers, but I also must add that I think that there are a number of things in both papers that require further discussion); J. Brough, "Amitābha and Avalokiteśvara in an Inscribed Gandhāran Sculpture," *Indologica Taurinensia* 10 (1982) 65–70. (This, too, I think requires further discussion.)

91. Nakamura reads *nāgarakṣita* (cf. Shizutani, *Indo bukkyō himei mokuroku*, § 1823), Mukherjee, *sāmrakṣita* (cf. *JAIH* 83.3).

92. There are, however, at least six inscriptions where the Mahāyāna donative formula is also used by a donor who does not use a title, but gives only his name. Cf. Schopen, "Mahāyāna in Indian Inscriptions," 9, and the parenthetical statement at the bottom of 11.

93. Damsteegt, *Epigraphical Hybrid Sanskrit*, 185. A phrase very like it, however, occurs frequently in Sanskrit literary sources; e.g., *Ajitasenavyākaraṇanirdeśa*. *Gilgit Manuscripts*, i, 129.10: *anena kuśalamūlena sarvasatvā anuttarāṃ samyaksaṃbodhim abhisaṃbudhyante;* S. Bagchi, *Mūlasarvāstivādavinayavastu*, Vol. I (Darbhanga: 1967) 210.18: *yan mayā bhagavataḥ kāśyapasya samyaksaṃbuddhasya {sat}kārāḥ kṛtāḥ / anena mama kuśalamūlena bahavaḥ putrā bhaveyur iti:* Bagchi, *Mūlasarvāstivādavinayavastu*, Vol. II (Darbhanga: 1970) 170.20; P. L. Vaidya, *Avadānaśataka* (Darbhanga: 1958) 2.15, 5.11, 12, 16, etc.

94. Although they cannot be discussed here, it should be pointed out that Shizutani has collected six inscriptions from the Gupta period which he thinks belong to the Mahāyāna (M. Shizutani, "Mahāyāna Inscriptions in the Gupta Period," *IBK* 10.1 [1962] 47–50). However, apart from the first two of these, which I also have classified as Mahāyāna, there appears to be no direct evidence for their affiliation. They do, though, certainly merit fuller discussion. I might also add that after writing the paper "Mahāyāna in Indian Inscriptions," an inscription published by Bühler ("The New Inscription of Toramana Shaha," *EI* 1 [1890] 238–241) came to my attention in which, if we could accept Bühler's reconstruction, the formula *yad atra puṇyaṃ*. etc. would seem to appear in conjunction with the Mahīśāsakas. But there are some serious doubts about the text and Bühler's reconstruction, which in the end make his interpretation, I think, unacceptable. (This, too, must be discussed at a future time.)

95. Although it is usually the donor's parents who are thus singled out, references to his *upādhyāyācārya*. his "teacher and preceptor," are not rare, and it can occur that they are mentioned even where his parents are not. We can find, then, either *ācāryopādhyāye mātāpitṛpūrvaṅgamaṃ kṛtvā* as at Bih iii 69, Bo i 76, Ma i 67, etc., or simply *upādhyāyācāryapūrvaṃgamaṃ kṛtvā* as at Bih iii 51. The transference of merit to *upādhyāyācāryas* found in these inscriptions is interesting. Something like it occurs less frequently in non-Mahāyāna inscriptions; cf. *Mathurā Inscriptions*. § 29 cited above, and *upajayasa* + name + *puyae* in Konow, *Kharoshṭhī Inscriptions*. LXXXVIII. And yet, according to Woodward, one of the earliest references in Pāli to the doctrine of the transference of merit is in the *Upasampadakammavaca* where the candidate for ordination transfers his merit to the ordaining monk; see F. L. Woodward, "The Buddhist Doctrine of Reversible Merit," *The Buddhist Review* 6 (1914) 38–50, esp. 38–39; see also, however, R. Gombrich, "Merit Transference in Sinhalese Buddhism. A Case Study of the Interaction between Doctrine and Practice," *History of Religions* 11 (1971) 205. For a more detailed discussion of the

place of parents in Indian Buddhist inscriptions, see G. Schopen, "Filial Piety and the Monk in the Practice of Indian Buddhism," Ch. III below (which was written after this paper).

96. See the very approximate chronological summary in Schopen, "Mahāyāna in Indian Inscriptions," 13–14.

97. *Histoire du bouddhisme indien,* 456.

98. For some views on the development of the formulae by which donors express their intentions and some of the concepts found in them, see E. Senart, "Notes d'épigraphie indienne," *JA* (1890) 119–123, and Damsteegt, *Epigraphical Hybrid Sanskrit.* Ch. III.

99. J.-M. Agasse, "Le transfert de mérite dans le bouddhisme pāli classique," *JA* (1978) 311–332, esp. 312–313. On Agasse and on the transfer of merit, see the short but important paper by J. Filliozat, "Sur le domaine sémantique de *puṇya,*" *Indianisme et Bouddhisme. Mélanges offerts à Mgr. Étienne Lamotte* (Louvain-La-Neuve: 1980) 101–116.

100. Deo and Joshi, *Pauni Excavation,* 38, no. 2; Kolte, *EI* 38 (1969) 174 (D).

101. Paranavitana, *Inscriptions of Ceylon,* Vol. I, no. 34; see also lii–liii; cf. W. S. Karunaratne, "The Date of the Brāhmī Inscriptions of Ceylon," *Paranavitana Felicitation Volume* (Colombo: 1965) 243–250.

102. Paranavitana, *Inscriptions of Ceylon,* Vol. I, nos. 338–341; see also lii–liii.

103. H. Bechert, "Notes on the Formation of Buddhist Sects and the Origins of Mahāyāna," *German Scholars on India,* Vol. I (Varanasi: 1973) 17–18; "Zur Frühgeschichte des Mahāyāna-Buddhismus," *ZDMG* 113 (1964) 535.

104. H. Bechert, "Buddha-feld und Verdienstübertragung: Mahāyāna-ideen im Theravāda-Buddhismus Ceylons," Académie Royale de Belgique, *Bulletin de la Classe des Lettres et des Sciences Morales et Politiques,* 5e série, T. 62 (1976) 27–51, esp. 48–49. Bechert cites and discusses most of the previous discussions of the problem of the transference of merit in a Theravāda context on 37ff; but see in addition D. S. Ruegg's review of N. A. Jayawickrama, *The Sheaf of Garlands of the Epochs of the Conqueror, JAOS* 92 (1972) 180–181, and his "Pāli Gotta/Gotra and the Term Gotrabhū in Pāli and Buddhist Sanskrit," *Buddhist Studies in Honour of I. B. Horner,* ed. L. Cousins et al. (Dordrecht: 1974) 207 and n. 37. It is also worth pointing out that two old papers by H. S. Gehman have been consistently overlooked in discussion of the transfer of merit: "Ādisati, anvādisati, anudisati, and uddisati in the Petavatthu," *JAOS* 43 (1923) 410–421; "A Pālism in Buddhist Sanskrit," *JAOS* 44 (1924) 73–75.

* * *

[For some critical remarks on some aspects of this paper, see H. Bechert, "Buddha-Field and Transfer of Merit in a Theravāda Source," *IIJ* 35 (1992) 95–108, esp. 104–106; see also G. Fussman, "Documents épigraphiques kouchans (V). Buddha et bodhisattva dans l'art de mathura: deux bodhisattvas inscrits de l'an 4 et l'an 8," *BEFEO* 57 (1988) 5–25, esp. 10–11; L. Schmithausen, "An Attempt to Estimate the Distance in Time between Aśoka and the Buddha in Terms of Doctrinal History," *The Dating of the Historical Buddha / Die Datierung des historischen Buddha,* ed. H. Bechert (Göttingen: 1992) Pt. 2, 111 and n. 9; 113 and nn. 15, 17, 18; 130, n. 142; 143, n. 231.]

CHAPTER III

Filial Piety and the Monk in the Practice of Indian Buddhism

A Question of "Sinicization" Viewed from the Other Side

In memory of my father-in-law, V. L. Thorpe

IN HIS CATALOG of Indian Buddhist epigraphical material, the final version of which was published in Kyoto in 1979, Shizutani Masao lists more than two thousand separate inscriptions.[1] These inscriptions come, of course, from all periods and virtually every part of India and have been thoroughly mined by historians, but not, unfortunately, by Buddhist scholars. Buddhist scholars, in fact, have shown very little interest in this material, especially those scholars writing on the development of Buddhist doctrine—this in spite of the fact that this material contains considerable information about such important matters as the conception of the Buddha or Buddhas, the conception or conceptions of merit and religious acts, and the nature of the actual, as opposed to the ideal goals of religious activity among practicing Indian Buddhists. In fact, this epigraphical material has, as I have said elsewhere, at least two distinct advantages. First, much of it predates by several centuries our earliest actually datable literary sources. Second, it tells us what a fairly large number of Indian Buddhists actually did, as opposed to what—according to our literary sources—they might or should have done.[2] But in addition to these two advantages, there is a third: this material, in a considerable number of cases, tells us what individuals themselves—whether laymen or monks—hoped to accomplish by those religious acts which they chose to record.

Originally published in *T'oung Pao, Revue internationale de sinologie* 70 (1984):110–126. Reprinted with stylistic changes with permission of E. J. Brill.

The failure of Buddhist scholars to take this epigraphical material into account has generated a number of distortions both within the realm of Indian studies and beyond. One particular example will concern us here.

Ch'en, in his deservedly well known book on Buddhism in China, says in reference to the Lung-men inscriptions that date from the very end of the fifth to the beginning of the sixth century that:

> . . . the frequent references to filial piety in the inscriptions testify to the change that had taken place in Buddhism after its introduction into China. Buddhism started as a religion renouncing all family and social ties, yet in the inscriptions one meets again and again with prayers for the well-being of deceased ancestors, uttered even by monks and nuns. These expressions of piety indicate that although the monks and nuns had joined the monastic order, their ties to family and ancestors still remained strong and enduring. *This is a specific example of how Buddhism had adapted itself to contemporary social conditions in China* (emphasis added).[3]

It should be noted here that I have not cited Ch'en's remarks because they are in any way unique. Quite the contrary. I cite them because they are a particularly clear formulation of a very widely held notion concerning the transformation of Indian Buddhism in China,[4] and because they so clearly reflect the conception of the Indian Buddhist monk presented by even our best modern authorities. The implications of Ch'en's remarks are clear: there is not supposed to be in Indian Buddhism anything like the kind of "filial piety" he finds expressed in the Lung-men inscriptions, and even if there were, Indian Buddhist monks most certainly would not be involved in it. This second point, of course, accords very well with the accepted view of the Indian Buddhist monk. The Indian monk is rather consistently presented as a radical ascetic who had severed all ties with his family and who was not involved in cult activity and, especially, not in religious giving. According to the accepted view, these practices were the province of the laity.[5] Questions remain, however, whether Ch'en's interpretation of his material is acceptable, whether there is not comparable material in India, and whether the current conception of the practicing Indian Buddhist monk accurately reflects what we can actually know about him. We want to know, then, two things: first, do our sources for Indian Buddhism give any indication of a concern similar to that expressed at Lung-men for the "well-being of deceased ancestors," or for departed or living parents; and second, if such a concern is, in fact, attested, is there any indication that this was an active concern of Indian monks and nuns. If we look at Indian epigraphical material, the answer to both of our questions is, I think, quite clear.

Most of our very earliest Buddhist donative inscriptions do not indicate the intentions of the donor. They say, for example, only *ghosāye dānaṃ*, "the gift of Ghosā" (Bhārhut),[6] or *vajigutasa dānaṃ*, "the gift of Vajiguta" (Sāñcī).[7] There are, however, exceptions, two of which are of particular interest. The first of these exceptions comes from Ceylon. I cite it here as Indian evidence because it is in effect an Indian inscription: it is written in early Brāhmī script and dates from a period during which an indigenous Ceylonese Buddhism could not have been developed. It is, in fact, one of "the earliest inscriptions in Ceylon that can be definitely attributed to a particular ruler" and dates, according to Paranavitana, "to the period between 210 and 200 B.C."[8] The inscription concerns the gift of a cave and reads: *gamaṇi-uti-maharajhaha{jhita abi-ti}śaya leṇe daśa-diśaśa sagaye dine mata-pitaśa aṭaya*, "The cave of princess (Abi) Tissā, daughter of the great king Gāmaṇī-Uttiya, is given to the Saṅgha of the ten directions, for the benefit of (her) mother and father."[9] The second exception comes from Bhārhut and is probably to be dated about a hundred years later than the Ceylonese inscription. Here on a *suci* we read: *sagharakhitasa mātāpituna aṭhāyā dānam:* "The gift of Sagharakhita, for the benefit of (his) mother and father."[10]

Here already in very early Buddhist Ceylon and at Bhārhut, we have inscriptions in which the donors themselves say that they performed acts of religious giving for the "benefit" or profit of their parents. In either case, we do not know if the parents were deceased when the gifts were made, although we do know that these inscriptions are six- and seven-hundred years older than those found at Lung-men. We also know that wording very like that which we find in our Ceylonese and Bhārhut inscriptions is also frequently found in the Kharoṣṭhī inscriptions.

Our Kharoṣṭhī inscriptions come predominantly from Northwest India. The earliest of them may date from around the middle of the first century B.C.E., but most appear to fall in the first few centuries of the Common Era. Of the Kharoṣṭhī inscriptions edited by Konow—and this is our single, most important collection—twenty-nine contain statements in which the individual donors express the intentions for which they undertook the religious act recorded in the inscription.[11] Of these twenty-nine, fourteen, or almost exactly one-half, indicate that the religious act was in whole or in part undertaken on behalf of the donors' parents.[12] Similar statements are also found in at least five additional Kharoṣṭhī inscriptions published after Konow's collection.[13] The donors' intentions may be expressed in as simple a form as . . . *matapitu puyae*, "(this is done) as an act of *pūjā* for my parents" (XXXVII. 6),[14] or they might add in addition to reference to their parents any number of other elements. They might say . . . *kue karite matapitae puyae sarvasatvaṇa hidasuhae*, ". . . this well was made as an act of *pūjā* for my parents (and) for the advantage and happiness of all beings" (XXIII), or . . . *par{i}vara {sha}dhadana . . . mira boyaṇasa erjhuṇa kapasa puyae madu pidu puya{e}*, "(this) chapel is the religious gift of . . . (name) . . . as an act of *pūjā* for Mira, the Saviour [a royal title] (and) Prince Kapa, as an act of *pūjā* for my mother and father" (XX). We can note here, however, that although these and other additional elements occur in the donors' expressions of their intentions, reference to benefiting their parents is the single most frequent element. We can also note at least one more additional fact: in one of our Kharoṣṭhī inscriptions, it is specifically said that the gift recorded was made for the donor's *deceased* parents (. . . *danamukhe madapidarana adhvadidana puyaya bhavatu*).[15]

It is clear then that "benefiting" parents, both living and dead, was, in the Kharoṣṭhī inscriptions, the most frequently mentioned purpose for religious giving. It was, it seems, a major preoccupation of those who engaged in such activities. But this means that this preoccupation occurs already in inscriptions that predate those found at Lung-men by several centuries. Again in regard to China, we might also note that, already more than twenty years ago, Brough published a Kharoṣṭhī inscription—which he would date "with some reservations . . . towards the end of the second century A.D.,"—that was found at or around Lo-yang. This might suggest that we are dealing here with a case of direct contact between two widely separated bodies of Buddhist inscriptions.[16]

This same preoccupation also appears elsewhere in Indian inscriptions which predate Lung-men. In the Mathurā inscriptions published by Lüders, there are thirty-nine Buddhist inscriptions in which the donors' intentions are expressed. Of these thirty-nine at least one-fourth or nine indicate that the donation was made in whole or in part for the sake of the donors' parents;[17] and in at least two other inscriptions not included in Lüders' collection, the donors' parents are, again, the intended beneficiaries of the religious act.[18] Here again the intentions of the donors can be expressed in a number of ways. The donor may say that the gift was made "as an act of *pūjā* for his mother and father and all living beings" (*māt{ā}pit{r}in{a} pujāye savasav{ā}n{a} ca* § 90);[19] or he may conclude his inscription by declaring that "what here is the merit [of my act] may that be for my parents" (*yad attra puṇyaṃ mātāpi{t}tra sya* § 78). And here again, although in the majority of cases we do not know if the donors' parents were living or dead, in at least one of our Mathurā inscriptions the donor explicitly says that he intends his act "as an act of *pūjā* for his *deceased* parents" (*{mātāp}i{tṛ}ṇa {abhyat}itakalaga{tā}nāṃ pujāye bhavatu* § 44). And another fragmentary Mathurā inscription also appears to make explicit reference to deceased parents (*mātāpitraṇa abhatitana{ṃ}* . . .).[20]

Like the Kharoṣṭhī inscriptions, the inscriptions from Mathurā also predate those found at Lung-men by several centuries. Although Lüders classifies a few as belonging to the Śuṅga period, the majority belong to the Kṣatrapa, the Kuṣāṇa, and—to a lesser extent—the Gupta periods.[21] But we also find a considerable number of inscriptions that fall into these same periods elsewhere in India in which an act of religious giving is expressly stated to have been undertaken for the benefit of the donors' parents. This is the case, for example, at Bodh-Gayā, where a donor ends the record of his gift by saying "by this root of merit may it be as an act of *pūjā* for my mother and father" (*imenā kuśala-mūlena mātāpitṛṇā(ṃ) pūjāye bhavatu* . . .),[22] or again at Bodh-Gayā, but in a record more nearly contemporaneous with Lung-men: "Whatever merit may have been acquired by me by all this, may this be for the benefit of my parents at first . . ." (*tad etat sarvvaṃ yan mayā puṇyopacitasambhāraṃ tan mātāpitroḥ p(ūrvaṃgamaṃ kṛtvā* . . .).[23] This is also the case at Nāgārjunikoṇḍa, where the donors frequently state that they made their gifts so that, first, they could "transfer" their act of giving to their mothers or to their families by birth and marriage. In several instances it is specifically said that the "transfer" is to be made to past, present, and future members on both sides of the donors' families. We find, for example,

> . . . this stone pillar was set up in order to transfer [it, i.e., the act and the fruit of the act] to her mother and for procuring the attainment of *nirvāṇa* for herself . . .
>
> *. . . apano mātaraṃ hammasiriṇikaṃ parinamatuna atane ca nivāṇasaṃpatisaṃpādake imaṃ selathaṃbhaṃ patithapitaṃ . . .*
>
> C2; cf. C4[24]

or, more elaborately,

> . . . this pillar was set up in order to transfer (it) to past, future, and present members of both of her families for the attainment of benefits and ease in both worlds, and for the procuring of the attainment of *nirvāṇa* for herself, and for the attainment of benefits and ease by all the world . . .
>
> *. . . apano ubhayakulasa atichhitam-anāgata-vaṭamānakānaṃ parināmetunaṃ ubhayalokahitasukhāvahathanāya atano ca nivāṇasaṃpatisaṃpādake savalokahitasukhāvahathanāya ca imaṃ khaṃbhaṃ patithapitaṃ ti . . .*
>
> C3; cf. B2, B4, E

We also have a comparatively large number of inscriptions from Sārnāth and Ajaṇṭā that either predate or are nearly contemporaneous with the Lung-men inscriptions. And here again the donors frequently state that their intention in making their religious gift was, in whole or in part, to benefit their parents. Among the inscriptions from Sārnāth that have been taken as belonging either to the Gupta period or, more specifically, to the fourth, fifth, or sixth centuries, I have noticed at least ten inscriptions in which the donors' parents are specifically listed among the intended beneficiaries.[25] We find donors saying:

> What here is the merit acquired by me after having had this image made, may that be for the obtainment of cessation for my parents and *gurus* and the world.
>
> *yad atra puṇyaṃ pratimāṃ kārayitvā mayā bhṛtam/mātāpittror gurūṇāṃ ca lokasya ca śamāptaye.*[26]

or, perhaps more typically,

> What here is (my) merit, may that be for the obtaining of supreme knowledge by my mother and father and all living beings.
>
> *yad atra puṇyaṃ tad bha{va}tu mātāpi{troḥ} sarvva{sattvā}nāñ ca anuttarajñānāvāptaye.*[27]

This second formula is, in fact, also very common at Ajaṇṭā.

The inscriptions from Ajaṇṭā, the last group of inscriptions we shall look at here, are of particular interest. If Spink is right—and the chances of this seem to be very good—most, if not all, activity ceased at Ajaṇṭā in the last quarter of the fifth century.[28] This would mean that the inscriptions at Ajaṇṭā are close in time to those at Lung-men and yet clearly predate them. Moreover, Ajaṇṭā and Lung-men are not only close in time, they are also sites of essentially the same kind. Both are complexes of excavated cave shrines; both received royal patronage, and yet a large number of individual, nonroyal donative inscriptions have been found at both sites.

I have been able to find twenty-one inscriptions from Ajaṇṭā that have a donative formula. Of these more than 90 percent, or nineteen inscriptions, declare that the intended beneficiaries of the gifts recorded are, in whole or in part, the donors' parents.[29] In eleven, or slightly more than half of these, the donors' intentions are expressed by means of variants of a single basic formula. In its simplest form at Ajaṇṭā it occurs as

> What here is his merit, may that be for the obtaining of supreme knowledge by his mother and father and all living beings.
>
> *yad atra {pu}ṇyaṃ tad bhavatu mātāpitro{ḥ} sarvva{sa}tvānāñ cānuttarajñānāvāp{t}aye.*[30]

This, of course, is almost exactly the same version of the formula as in our second example found at Sārnāth, and this or some other variant of the basic formula occurs, as I have said, in eleven of the nineteen inscriptions from Ajaṇṭā in which the donors name their parents as beneficiaries. But other donors at Ajaṇṭā express their intentions without having recourse to this particular formula. We find, for example, the donor saying simply: "This is the religious gift of . . . Śīlabhadra (made) in the name of his father and mother" (*deyaddharmmo yam . . . śīlabhadrasya mātāpitaram udi{śya}*).[31] The expression used here, *mātāpitaram uddiśya,* "in the name of his mother and father," is of particular interest and occurs in at least four other inscriptions from Ajaṇṭā.[32] In fact, the use of the term *uddiśya* seems to imply—as Senart appears to have suggested some time ago, and as its occurence in a variety of literary sources also would suggest—that the individuals concerned are deceased.[33] This would seem to be more clearly the case in The *Praśasti* of Buddhabhadra in Cave XXVI. Here Buddhabhadra says his gift was made "in the name of Bhavvirāja and also his [Buddhabhadra's] mother and father" (*taṃ bhavvirājam uddiśya mātāpitaram eva ca*), and then a little later he says "what merit is here, may that be for them [i.e., Bhavvirāja and his parents] and for the world for the attainment of the fruit of great awakening and the accumulation of all pure qualities" (*yad atra puṇyaṃ tat teṣā{ṃ} jagatāṃ ca bhavatv idaṃ sarvvāmalaguṇavyāta-*[read *vrāta-*] *mahābodhiphalāptaye*). But Buddhabhadra has already specifically indicated right before the *uddiśya* passage that Bhavvirāja, at least, was dead (. . . *pitaryy uparate*).[34]

We are now in a position to answer our first question. Indian epigraphical sources prove beyond any doubt that the basic elements of the inscriptions from Lung-men, which Ch'en interpreted as indications of "filial piety," occur already in Indian Buddhist inscriptions that predate those from Lung-men by as much as seven centuries. They prove that concern for the "well-being" of both deceased and living parents was a major preoccupation of Buddhist donors in India; that one of the most frequently stated reasons for undertaking acts of religious giving was to benefit the donors' parents, both living and dead; and that this concern was both very old and very widespread in India.[35] But if we have answered our first question, we still must discover whether there are any indications that this concern for the well-being of their parents was an active concern of Indian Buddhist monks. This, perhaps, is an even more interesting question and, once again, I think our answer can be unequivocal.

Our two earliest donative inscriptions that refer to benefiting the donors' parents both record the gifts of laymen. We know, however, that the Bhārhut inscription is only one of a large number from that site recording similar gifts, and that in thirty-six cases, or almost 40 percent of these inscriptions, the donors were monks or nuns. In several instances the individual monks involved are specifically said to be *bhānakas* or "reciters"; one is called a *sutaṃtika,* "one who knows the sutta", another a *peṭakin,* "one who knows the Piṭaka," and yet another is referred to as a *pacanekāyika,* "one who is versed in the canonical doctrine as a whole."[36]

We also know that perhaps as many as one-fourth of the Kharoṣṭhī inscriptions that refer to benefiting the donors' parents record the gifts of monks.[37] One of these inscriptions, interestingly enough, is also the single Kharoṣṭhī inscription in which there is specific reference to deceased parents. The whole inscription reads:

> Year 5, on the fifth day of the month Phalguna. This is the gift of Buddhānanda who is one who knows the *Tripiṭaka.* May it be an act of *pūjā* for his deceased parents.
>
> *sa{ṃ} 4 1 phagunasa masasa di paṃcami budhanadasa trepiḍakasa danamukhe madapidarana adhvadidana puyaya bhavatu.*[38]

Here, then, not only is a gift given by an individual for the benefit of his deceased parents, but this individual, to judge by his title, is not a simple, uneducated, village monk. He appears to have been, like many of the monk-donors at Bhārhut, a religious specialist. He is "one who knows the *Tripiṭaka,*" one who has mastered the Buddhist literature of his time.

Our Mathurā inscriptions present us with a similar—and perhaps even more definite—set of facts. There are eight inscriptions from Mathurā that record gifts made for the benefit of the donors' parents in which the donors' names or titles have been preserved. In six cases, or in 75 percent of these inscriptions, the donors were monks.[39] In the one instance where reference is specifically made to deceased parents, the donor is again a monk:

> (This is) the gift of the monk . . . mitra, the Vojyavaśika (?). May it be an act of *pūjā* for his deceased parents. May it (also) be for the granting of health to his companion Dharmadeva.
>
> *(d)ā(na)ṃ bh(ik)ṣus(y)a b . . . + . . . m(i)trasya v(o)jya + (vaśi)kasya — (mātap)i + (tṛ)ṇa (abhyat)itaka + laga(tā)nāṃ pujāy(e) + bhavatu sa(dh)yivi + harīsya dharma(d)ev(a)s(y)a + ar(o)g(a)dākṣiṇ(ā)y(e) (bha)vat(u).*[40]

At least one other of the monk-donors at Mathurā who intended their gifts for the benefit of their parents is given a title that appears to indicate that he was a learned monk, a religious specialist: he is referred to as a *dha(r)mma(kathi)ka,* "a preacher of the Dharma."[41]

In one of the two inscriptions I have cited above from Bodh-Gayā the donor is, again, a monk. Here, the donor who declares that his act was intended to benefit his parents describes himself as either "a monk who preserves the Vinaya" (*vinayadhara*) or the "companion" or "co-resident" of such a monk (*sadhevihārī*), and as a "preacher of the *Dharma*" (*dharmakathika*).[42]

If the evidence in all of these inscriptions is clear, it is equally if not more clear in those Indian inscriptions from the Gupta period—especially those from the fourth and fifth centuries—or in those inscriptions that are in date near to, though somewhat earlier than, the inscriptions found at Lung-men. At Sārnāth, for example, in the ten inscriptions that record gifts made for the benefit of the donors' parents, four-fifths or eight of the donors were monks.[43] In the nineteen inscriptions from Ajaṇṭā that express a similar intention, thirteen of the donors were certainly monks, two more were probably monks, and in one case it is impossible to say. In only three of the nineteen inscriptions were the donors certainly laymen.[44]

We have looked so far at the Kharoṣṭhī inscriptions, at inscriptions from Mathurā, Bodh-Gayā, Sārnāth, and Ajaṇṭā, and we have found a recurring pattern. Before, however, we can summarize our findings, we must deal briefly with an apparent exception: in none of the fairly numerous inscriptions from Nāgārjunikoṇḍa in which the merit of the act is transferred to the donors' parents or family is the donor a monk. At first sight, this could be significant. But seen in a larger context it is probably only another indication of the atypical character of all the Nāgārjunikoṇḍa inscriptions connected with the Ikṣvaku dynasty. There is, first of all, the atypical character of the vocabulary of these inscriptions. Several set expressions and terms are found in these inscriptions that are not found anywhere else in Indian inscriptions. This is the case with *ubhayakula,* with the expression *dhātuvaraparigahita* used to describe a *stūpa,* with the verb *parināmetuna* that is always used to express the intended "transfer." This is also the case with the formula *ubhayalokahitasukha* and the formula *atano ca nivāṇasaṃpatisaṃpādake.* All of these elements are found again and again in inscriptions of this period at Nāgārjunikoṇḍa but nowhere else at any period in India.[45] An equally atypical characteristic of the Ikṣvaku inscriptions from Nāgārjunikoṇḍa is the fact that monastic donors are extremely rare.[46] This is in marked contrast with what—as I have said elsewhere—we find everywhere else in India. From Bhārhut and Sāñcī and thereafter, monks and nuns everywhere constituted a considerable portion of the active donors at religious sites: almost 40 percent of the donors at both Bhārhut and Sāñcī were monks or nuns; well over 50 percent of the donors in the Mathurā inscriptions were also monks or nuns; 40 percent of the donors in the Kharoṣṭhī inscriptions, 65 percent of the donors in the inscriptions of the Western Cave Shrines, and 70 percent of the donors in those inscriptions that I have argued belong to the Mahāyāna were members of the monastic community.[47] Even at Amarāvatī, also in the South, twenty-four of the sixty-five individual donors were either monks or nuns.[48] Clearly then, Ikṣvaku Nāgārjunikoṇḍa is atypical and should be treated as such. It represents an isolated, very narrowly localized aberration both in terms of geography and in terms of time; all three of the Sanskrit inscriptions from this area published by Ramachandran date from the fifth century and record the gifts of monks.[49]

Having established the purely local and markedly atypical character of the material from Ikṣvaku Nāgārjunikoṇḍa, we can now summarize our findings. Indian epigraphical material establishes that not only was one of the most frequently stated reasons for undertaking acts of religious giving in Buddhist India to benefit the donors' parents—both living and dead—and that this was a major preoccupation of Buddhist donors in India, it also clearly establishes that this concern for the well-being of deceased and living parents was an active concern and major preoccupation of Indian Buddhist monks in particular. In the Kharoṣṭhī inscriptions, as many as one-fourth of the donors who indicated that their act was undertaken to benefit their parents were monks; at both Mathurā and Ajaṇṭā 75 percent of such donors were monks. At Sārnāth the percentage is even higher: there, in eight out of the ten inscriptions in which the donors indicated that their acts were undertaken to benefit their parents, those donors were monks. In fact, if we take the total number of inscriptions in our sample, it would appear that not only was the concern for their parents—both living and dead—a major preoccupation among our monk-donors, *but it was perhaps a special concern of this group:* in more than 60 percent of all of the Indian inscriptions in our sample in which acts were undertaken to benefit the donors' parents, the donors were monks, and the percentage of monk-donors is considerably higher, as we have seen, at Mathurā, Ajaṇṭā, and Sārnāth. It is also worth noting again that at least three of the monk-donors who made religious gifts for the benefit of their parents, or their deceased parents, were not average, uneducated village monks: one is called a *trepiḍaka;* one is called a *dharmakathika;* and a third was either a *vinayadhara,* or the "co-resident" of a *vinayadhara,* as well as a *dharmakathika.* These monks appear to have been the teachers and transmitters of "official" Buddhist literature.[50]

In light of what we have found in Indian epigraphical material, and in light of the fact that all of the material we have looked at predates—in some cases by five or more centuries—the inscriptions from Lung-men, it hardly seems necessary to emphasize the fact that Ch'en's interpretation of his Lung-men data is unacceptable. Clearly, "the frequent references to filial piety in the inscriptions" from Lung-men do not testify to any "change that had taken place in Buddhism after its introduction into China"; nor is the fact that monks make up a considerable number of the donors at Lung-men who are concerned with deceased or living parents "a specific example of how Buddhism had adapted itself to contemporary social conditions in China." But the merit of Professor Ch'en's interpretation of the Lung-men data is that it forces us to focus on an aspect of the practice of Indian Buddhism that has been almost completely ignored by Buddhist scholars: in answering the questions raised by Professor Ch'en's remarks, we have come to see that "filial piety" was an old, an integral, and a pervasive part of the practice of Indian Buddhism from the earliest periods of which we have any definite knowledge, and that in actual practice the idea of benefiting one's parents, whether living or dead, by making religious gifts on their behalf was a major, if not a specific preoccupation of Indian Buddhist monks. Once again, the actual monk of the first to the fifth centuries C.E. in India turns out to be—when we can catch a glimpse of him—something quite different from the picture of the monk that has been abstracted from our textual sources.[51] This is, in fact, the second point of merit in Ch'en's interpretation: it makes clear the very real dangers that arise when making historical statements on the basis of textual sources alone, when treating literary elaborations of doctrine as if they were records of actual description. We have just seen that it is clear from Buddhist inscriptions beginning from the time of Bhārhut that the donation of religious gifts was as much a part of the monk's religious life as it was of the layman's. And although this is contrary to what virtually all our modern authorities want us to believe, and although it receives no very definite support in early textual sources, it is nevertheless a demonstrable fact.

But there are also at least two curious qualities found in the inscriptions that reveal this fact, both of which bear on how we are to understand this type of religious giving in an Indian Buddhist context. First, although our inscriptions constantly refer to the objects made or presented as "gifts" (*dāna, deyadharma*), there is at least one essential component of the classic Indian definition of the "gift" which is missing: although there is always a giver and an object given, there is, in the vast majority of epigraphical cases, no recipient. Moreover, in the great majority of the inscriptions we have looked at here, the thing given is of no economic value: it is not land, housing, clothing, or food. On the contrary, the gifts recorded are almost all relics or *stūpas* or images or paintings. We have then a giver and items of no economic value given to no specific recipient. Clearly, there seems to be little here which even approaches the classic definition of a "gift" as a "transaction": there is no exchange; no conception of incurred debt; no notion of reciprocity. In itself this might seem somewhat odd, but the situation appears even stranger when we add to this the fact that the inscriptions that record these gifts were in a considerable number of cases—as Lüders and Konow pointed out long ago—never meant to be read by anyone.[52] These factors combine to leave only more questions. For example, if our inscriptions were never meant to be read, why did the individual donors take such care in recording not only their names, titles, and their places of residence, but also the exact date on which the donations were made?

The answer to at least some of these puzzles may be found, I think, in a fuller understanding of what our donors were giving and in the conceptions of merit which they held. It is true that, on one level, the laymen and monks who made these gifts were giving objects, but because these objects were of a specific kind, they were actually giving more than mere objects: they were giving objects of worship, objects that, in fact, made worship possible. They were, then, really giving to any of their fellow beings who ritually approached those objects both the means and the opportunity to make merit; they were providing for all both the opportunity and the means to further their religious lives. But this would also seem to suggest that the initial gift of the actual object only marked the first moment in the donor's act of giving. Each time the object was approached, he or the persons to whom he transferred his act of giving was to be credited with having provided an additional opportunity for someone else to make merit. Each opportunity was a separate act of giving. The donor's act of giving and its consequent merit, then, were continually repeated over time in every act of worship directed toward the object he had provided.[53] It was the donor's initial act that in a very concrete sense made each consecutive act of worship possible.

It was because the donor's act was continually repeated over time, because it took place again and again long after the donor himself had disappeared, that it was necessary to clearly record the donor's name, the moment of the initial act, and—most importantly—the donor's intentions. And it was no small matter to transfer such an act to the donor's parents. By doing so, the donor denied to himself but provided for his parents a source of merit which would continue and be maintained long after the donor himself was dead. This, it would seem, is true filial piety.

Notes

1. Shizutani Masao, *Indo bukkyō himei mokuroku* (Kyoto: 1979).

2. G. Schopen, "Two Problems in the History of Indian Buddhism," Ch. II above.

3. K. K. S. Ch'en, *Buddhism in China. A Historical Survey* (Princeton: 1964) 179; cf. K. K. S. Ch'en, "Filial Piety in Chinese Buddhism," *HJAS* 28 (1968) 81–97, and *The Chinese Transformation of Buddhism* (Princeton: 1973) 14ff. These last two works deal with filial piety in Chinese Buddhism on the basis of literary sources, and it is from the second of these (p. 5) that I have borrowed the term "sinicization" that occurs in my title. It is perhaps worth pointing out that in the appendix on *yü-lan-p'en* in the same volume (61–64) Ch'en has overlooked at least two important papers: J. Przyluski, "Les rites d'avalambana," *MCB* 1 (1931–1932) 221–225, and J. Jaworski, "L'avalambana sutra de la terre pure," *Monumenta Serica* 1 (1935–1936) 82–107. For the inscriptions from Lung-men, see E. Chavannes, *Mission archéologique dans la Chine septentrionale.* T. I, deuxième partie (Paris: 1915) 320–561, and Mizuno Seiichi and Nagahiro Toshio, *Ryūmon sekkutsu no kenkyū* (Tokyo: 1941).

4. Cf. P. Demiéville, "Le bouddhisme chinois," *Encyclopédie de la Pléiade. Histoire des Religions,* T. I (Paris: 1970) 1273 (repr. in *Choix d'études bouddhiques* [Leiden: 1973] 389); A. F. Wright, *Buddhism in Chinese History* (New York: 1969) 59; etc.

5. *Histoire du bouddhisme indien.* 59, 68, 81, 698f; cf. more recently, J. Holt, "Assisting the Dead by Venerating the Living, Merit Transfer in the Early Buddhist Tradition," *Numen* 28 (1981) 1–28. Unfortunately, even apart from the fact that he ignores the epigraphical material, Holt's analysis is rather badly distorted since he unaccountably chose to ignore the fact that the *Petavatthu*—the text on which his paper is supposed to be based—contains a number of stories in which it is not a layman who gives a gift to release his deceased kinsmen, but a monk. The most striking instance of the monk-donor occurs in the story of Sāriputta's mother in N. A. Jayawickrama, *Vimānavatthu and Petavatthu,* Vol. II (London: 1977) 2.14, but there are several others.

6. B. Barua and K. G. Sinha, *Barhut Inscriptions* (Calcutta: 1926) 31, no. 56.

7. G. Bühler, "Further Inscriptions from Sānchi," *EI* 2 (1892) 370, no. 25.

8. S. Paranavitana, *Inscriptions of Ceylon.* Vol. I, *Containing Cave Inscriptions from 3rd Century B.C. to 1st Century A.C. and Other Inscriptions in the Early Brāhmī Script* (Ceylon: 1970) lii–liii.

9. Paranavitana, *Inscriptions of Ceylon,* Vol. I, no. 34.

10. Barua and Sinha, *Barhut Inscriptions.* 22, no. 28; for several different views of the significance of this inscription, see *Histoire du bouddhisme indien.* 456; Schopen, "Two

Problems in the History of Indian Buddhism," now Ch. II above; J-M. Agasse, "Le transfert de mérite dans le bouddhisme pāli classique," *JA* (1978) 312–313. On Agasse, and the question of the transfer of merit generally, see the important paper by J. Filliozat, "Sur le domaine sémantique de puṇya," *Indianisme et buddhisme, Mélanges offerts à Mgr Étienne Lamotte* (Louvain-La-Neuve: 1980) 101–116.

11. S. Konow, *Kharoshṭhī Inscriptions with the Exception of Those of Aśoka,* Corpus Inscriptionum Indicarum, Vol. II, Pt. 1 (Calcutta: 1929) I, II, XIII, XV, XX, XXIII, XXIV, XXVI, XXVII, XXXI, XXXV.2, XXXVII.6, XLVI, LV.c, LVII, LVIII, LX, LXIII, LXXII, LXXIV, LXXV, LXXVI, LXXX, LXXXI, LXXXII, LXXXV, LXXXVI, LXXXVII, XCII.

12. Konow, *Kharoshṭhī Inscriptions,* II, XIII, XX, XXIII, XXVII, XXXI, XXXV.2, XXXVII.6, LV.c, LXXV, LXXVI, LXXXV, LXXXVI, XCII.

13. These five Kharoṣṭhī inscriptions are: 1. S. Konow, "Charsadda Kharoṣṭhī Inscription of the Year 303," *Acta Orientalia* 20 (1947) 107–119; 2. G. Fussman, "Documents épigraphiques kouchans," *BEFEO* 61 (1974) 54–58 (the same inscription read and translated by J. Brough was published in J. C. Harle, "A Hitherto Unknown Dated Sculpture from Gandhara: A Preliminary Report," in J. E. van Lohuizen-De Leeuw and J. M. M. Ubaghs, *South Asian Archaeology 1973* [Leiden: 1974] 128–136); 3. G. Fussman, "Documents épigraphiques kouchans (II)," *BEFEO* 67 (1980) 55; 4. G. Fussman, "Nouvelles inscriptions śaka: ère d'Eucratide, ère d'Azès, ère Vikrama, ère de Kaniṣka," *BEFEO* 67 (1980) 6; 5. H. W. Bailey, "Two Kharoṣṭhī Casket Inscriptions from Avaca," *JRAS* (1978) 3. This same inscription has also been published in B. N. Mukherjee, "An Interesting Kharoṣṭhī Inscription," *JAIH* 11 (1977–1978) 93–114; G. Fussman, *BEFEO* 67 (1980) 3–4; R. Salomon, "The 'Avaca' Inscription and the Origin of the Vikrama Era," *JAOS* 102 (1982) 59–68. [See now also R. Salomon and G. Schopen, "The Indravarman (Avaca) Casket Inscription Reconsidered: Further Evidence for Canonical Passages in Buddhist Inscriptions," *JIABS* 7.1 (1984) 107–23.]

14. All parenthetical roman numerals refer to the inscription numbers in Konow, *Kharoshṭhī Inscriptions.*

15. Fussman, *BEFEO* 61 (1974) 54; Brough in Harle's *South Asian Archaeology 1973*. 129 and n. 1.

16. J. Brough, "A Kharoṣṭhī Inscription from China," *BSOAS* 24 (1961) 517–530.

17. H. Lüders, *Mathurā Inscriptions.* ed. K. L. Janert, Abhandlungen der Akademie der Wissenschaften in Göttingen, Philologisch-Historische Klasse, Dritte Folge, Nr. 47 (Göttingen: 1961) 1, 2, 3, 8, 24, 29*, 31, 35, 41, 44*, 46, 50, 60, 61, 62, 67*, 73, 76, 78*, 80, 81, 86, 87, 89, 90*, 125*, 126, 128, 135, 136, 153, 154, 157, 179*, 180*, 184*, 185, 186, 187. Here and in the notes that follow, those inscriptions in which the donations were made for the sake of the donors' parents are marked with an asterisk.

18. D. C. Sircar, "Mathura Image Inscription of Vasudeva," *EI* 30 (1953–1954) 181–184 (cf. n. 20 below); Sircar, "Brahmi Inscriptions from Mathura," *EI* 34 (1961–1962) 9–13, no. 1.

19. All numbers marked with § refer to the inscription numbers in Lüders, *Mathurā Inscriptions.*

20. Sircar, *EI* 30 (1953–1954) 184, reads *mātāpitreṇa abha(s)i(ta)naṁ:* the reading cited above, however, is that proposed by Th. Damsteegt, *Epigraphical Hybrid Sanskrit. Its Rise. Spread. Characteristics and Relationship to Buddhist Hybrid Sanskrit* (Leiden: 1978) 164 and n. 50; cf. 119.

21. Lüders, *Mathurā Inscriptions,* 22–23.

22. B. M. Barua, "A Bodh-Gayā Image Inscription," *IHQ* 9 (1933) 419.

23. B. M. Barua, "Old Buddhist Shrines at Bodh-Gayā," *IHQ* 6 (1930) 27–28. The translation here is Barua's; the end of the line is missing and he has supplied a *bhavatu,* although it is possible that more than just a *bhavatu* has been lost.

24. All the letter and number references refer to J. Ph. Vogel, "Prakrit Inscriptions from a Buddhist Site at Nagarjunikonda," *EI* 20 (1929–1930) 1–37.

25. D. R. Sahni, *Catalogue of the Museum of Archaeology at Sarnath* (Calcutta: 1914) 53(B[b]60)*, 85(B[b]292), 85(B[b]293)*, 239(D[f] l)*; H. Hargreaves, "Excavations at Sārnāth," *ARASI 1914–1915* (Calcutta: 1920) XIV*, XV*, XVI*, XVII*, XVIII*, XIX.

26. Hargreaves, *ARASI 1914–1915,* XVI, XVII.

27. Sahni, *Catalogue of the Museum of Archaeology at Sarnath,* 85(B[b]292).

28. W. Spink, "Ajanta: A Brief History," *Aspects of Indian Art* (Leiden: 1972) 49–58, esp. 56–59; Spink, "The Splendours of Indra's Crown: A Study of Mahāyāna Developments at Ajaṇṭā," *Journal of the Royal Society for the Encouragement of Arts, Manufactures, and Commerce* (1974) 743–767; cf. J. G. Williams, *The Art of Gupta India, Empire and Province* (Princeton: 1982) 181ff.

29. J. Allan, "A Note on the Inscriptions of Cave II," Appendix to G. Yazdani, *Ajanta,* Part II: Text (Oxford: 1933) Cave II.11 (fragmentary, note . . . *pitṛm:*) N. P. Chakravarti, "A Note on the Painted Inscriptions in Caves VI–XVII," Appendix to G. Yazdani, *Ajanta,* Part III: Text (Oxford: 1946) Cave VI; Cave IX.1*, IX.6*; Cave X.2, X.10*, X.11*, X.12, X.17, X.21*; Cave XVI.1*, XVI.2*, XVI.3*; N. P. Chakravarti and B. Ch. Chhabra, "Notes on the Painted and Incised Inscriptions of Caves XX–XXVI," Appendix to G. Yazdani, *Ajanta,* Part IV: Text (Oxford: 1955) Cave XX(Inc.) n. 3*; Cave XXII(P) n. 4*; Cave XXVI.1*, XXVI.2*; D. C. Sircar, "Inscription in Cave IV at Ajanta," *EI* 33 (1960) 262; M. K. Dhavalikar, "New Inscriptions from Ajaṇṭā," *ArO* 7 (1968) nos.3, 4*, 5*. The two inscriptions that do not make reference to the donors' parents are Cave VI, and X.2.

30. Yazdani, *Ajanta,* Part III, Cave XVI .3. On this formula, see G. Schopen, "Mahāyāna in Indian Inscriptions," *IIJ* 21 (1979) 1–19, and corrections to this in the second half of Schopen, "Two Problems in the History of Indian Buddhism," Ch. II above.

31. Yazdani, *Ajanta,* Part III, Cave X.21.

32. Yazdani, *Ajanta,* Part III, Cave X.10, 11, 12; Yazdani, *Ajanta,* Part IV, Cave XXVI.1.

33. E. Senart, "The Inscriptions in the Caves at Nasik," *EI* 8 (1905) 64; L. de La Vallée Poussin, "Staupikam," *HJAS* 2 (1935) 283; H. Kern and B. Nanjio, *Saddharmapuṇḍarīka* (St. Petersburg: 1908–1912) 50.9, 241.6, 340.6; C. Bendall, *Śikṣāsamuccaya* (St. Petersburg: 1897–1902) 309.6.

34. Yazdani, *Ajanta,* Part IV, Cave XXVI.1.

35. It should be noted here that there are a considerable number of other Indian inscriptions in which we find reference to parents, but the interpretation of these inscriptions is uncertain. They almost always contain a formula, the key element of which is *sahā.* Lüders, *Mathurā Inscriptions,* § 126 is a typical example: . . . *bh(i)khuṇiye budhadevāye bodhisatvo pratithāpito sahā mātāpitīhi sarvasat(v)ahitasukh(a)ye.* Lüders translates: ". . . the Bodhisattva was set up by the nun Budhadevā (Buddhadevā), . . . together with her parents for the welfare and happiness of all sentient beings." But there are at least three possible interpretations here. First, the inscription may record a donation that was actually made jointly by the nun and her parents. Secondly, it may be that the nun-donor simply

used the *sahā* formula as a way of sharing the merit of her act with her parents by associating them with that act. That is to say, she shares or transfers the act rather than the merit, although the end result is the same. Thirdly, it is possible that the syntax of the formula has not been properly understood and that we should translate: ". . . the Bodhisattva was set up by the nun Budhadevā for the welfare and happiness of all sentient beings together with her parents" (cf. *yad atra puṇyaṃ tad bhavatu mātāpitṛpūrvaṅgamaṃ kṛtvā sarvasatvānāñ anuttarajñānāvāptaye* or *yad atra puṇyaṃ tad bhavatu mātāpitroḥ sarvasatvānāñ cānuttarajñānāvāptaye;* Schopen, "Two Problems in the History of Indian Buddhism," Ch. II, above). There are a number of cases where the first interpretation is almost certainly impossible. This is the case, for example, at Sahni, *Catalogue of the Museum of Archaeology at Sarnath,* 35 (B[a]1), where, if we adopted the first interpretation, we would have a single image that was the actual gift of a monk named Bala, his parents, his preceptors, teachers, fellow monks, pupils, a nun, the Satrap Vanaṣpara, and the fourfold Buddhist community (i.e., all monks, nuns, laymen, and laywomen). This appears rather unlikely, and we must adopt either the second or third interpretation. But adopting either of these last two interpretations would mean that all such inscriptions would then have to be added to our list of inscriptions that record an act undertaken—in whole or in part—for the benefit of the donor's parents. This, of course, would only further and more fully confirm the observations we have already made. [See G. Schopen, "On Monks, Nuns and 'Vulgar' Practices," Ch. XI, below; and Fussman, *BEFEO* 57 (1988) 10, n. 27.]

36. Cf. Schopen, "Two Problems in the History of Indian Buddhism," Ch. II above, and the sources cited there in nn. 40 and 41.

37. Konow, *Kharoshṭhī Inscriptions,* XXIII (cf. 64), LV.c, XCII; Fussman, *BEFEO* 61 (1974) III.

38. Fussman, *BEFEO* 61 (1974) III.

39. Lüders, *Mathurā Inscriptions,* §§ 29, 44, 67, 90, 179; Sircar, *EI* 34 (1961–1962) no. 1.

40. Lüders, *Mathurā Inscriptions,* § 44.

41. Sircar, *EI* 34 (1961–1962) no. 1.

42. Barua, *IHQ* 9 (1933) 419.

43. I.e., those inscription numbers marked with an asterisk in n. 25 above.

44. In those inscriptions marked with an asterisk in n. 29 above, the donors are definitely monks.

45. For occurrences of these terms and formulae, see the glossary in Vogel, *EI* 20 (1929–1930) 26–35.

46. Cf. Vogel, *EI* 20 (1929–1930) C1 (p. 17).

47. Schopen, "Two Problems in the History of Indian Buddhism," now Ch. II above.

48. G. Sivaramamurti, *Amarāvati Sculptures in the Madras Government Museum,* Bulletin of the Madras Government Museum, N.S., Vol. IV (Madras: 1956) 271–304. There are one hundred and twenty six inscriptions collected here, but six are nondonative, in eleven the donor has no title, and forty are too fragmentary to be intelligible. In four a *nigama* is given as a collective donor.

49. T. N. Ramachandran, *Nāgārjunakoṇḍa 1938,* MASI, No.71 (Calcutta: 1953) 28–29.

50. The fairly massive participation of monks in cult activity and religious giving that our inscriptions document raises a number of interesting points. In this regard it is well to note—as Bühler noted many years ago—that the role of the monk in Jaina inscriptions differs very markedly from the role of the monk in Buddhist inscriptions.

Bühler says, in specific reference to Sāñcī: "Proceeding to the inscriptions which mention donations made by monks and nuns, the first point, which must strike every reader, is their great number . . . But it is interesting to note the different proceedings of the Jaina ascetics, who, according to the Mathurā and other inscriptions, as a rule, were content to exhort the laymen to make donations and to take care that this fact was mentioned in the votive inscriptions" (G. Bühler, "Votive Inscriptions from the Sānchi Stūpas," *EI* 2 [1892] 93). For examples of the kind of thing Bühler is referring to in Jaina inscriptions, see Lüders, *Mathurā Inscriptions,* §§ 13, 14, 93, 140, where the key term is *nirvartana-* (on which, see Damsteegt, *Epigraphical Hybrid Sanskrit.* 75, 171, 173, 252). Other Jaina inscriptions express the same thing with a different vocabulary; cf. D. C. Sircar, "Indological Notes 7, Vidiśa Jain Image Inscriptions of the Time of Rāmagupta," *JAIH* 3 (1969–1970) 150–151. It is also worth quoting a wise old art historian here. Walter Spink says: "A number of inscriptions at Ajanta also prove that some of the caves, and numerous separate images, were donated by the monks themselves. This is an interesting commentary on the changing of Buddhism in India, for it suggests that monks, far from having renounced all worldly goods, were sometimes men of considerable wealth. It is doubtful that Buddhabhadra, the chief donor of the elaborate Cave 26—a man who proclaims himself the friend of kings—spent very much time humbly wandering from village to village with his begging bowl as his predecessors in the early days of Buddhism certainly did" (Spink, "Ajanta: A Brief History," *Aspects of Indian Art,* 51). The question, of course, is whether the facts from Ajaṇṭā that Spink refers to reflect any change at all. In fact, we simply do not know what Buddhabhadra's "predecessors in the early days of Buddhism" *actually* did. We do know, however, that from the very beginning of our actual epigraphical evidence (Bhārhut, Sāñcī, etc.), a large number of monks were doing exactly what the data indicate they were doing at Ajaṇṭā; cf. Schopen, "Two Problems in the History of Indian Buddhism," Ch. II above. What we do not know is what else they were doing.

51. Cf. Schopen, "Two Problems in the History of Indian Buddhism," Ch. II above.

52. H. Lüders, "The Manikiala Inscription," *JRAS* (1909) 660 (repr. H. Lüders, *Kleine Schriften,* hrsg. O. von Hinüber [Wiesbaden: 1973] 335); Konow, *Kharoshṭhī Inscriptions,* 31.

53. Cf. the eighth verse of the *praśasti* of the monk Buddhabhadra from Cave XXVI at Ajaṇṭā: *yāvat kīrttir lloke tāvat svarggeṣu modati ca dehī / candrārkkakālakalpā kāryyā kīrttir mahīdhreṣu//:* "And as long as the shrine (he built) remains in the world, so long does that man enjoy the heavens. So a shrine equal in duration to the sun and moon should be built on the mountains." Text cited from Yazdani, *Ajanta,* Part IV, 115.

CHAPTER IV

The Ritual Obligations and Donor Roles of Monks in the Pāli *Vinaya*

MORE THAN ONCE recently it has again been suggested that Buddhist monks had little or no role in life-cycle ceremonies in early India.[1] I do not know on what evidence these suggestions are based, but it does not seem that it could be the Pāli texts. In fact, Buddhist *vinaya* texts in Pāli, Sanskrit, and what Roth calls "Prākrit-cum-Sanskrit" seem to suggest quite otherwise. They seem to suggest and assume that monks regularly had a role in such ceremonies and that their ritual presence and performance at such ceremonies was of some importance. Most passages, indeed, employ language that suggests "obligation" (*karaṇīya*). The same texts suggest and assume that Buddhist monks were active donors to their own monastic community.

Ironically, the one life-cycle ceremony in which a significant place for monks has been explicitly conceded—the funeral—is also the one which is not explicitly included in the list of such ceremonies that appears in the Pāli *Vinaya* passage that seems most concerned with such matters. But although the funeral is not explicitly mentioned there, the passage may allude at least to death rituals as Edgerton sometime ago seemed to surmise: it speaks of "illness" (*gilāna*), and the illness in question seems to be, to judge by context, terminal.[2]

The passage occurs in the *Vassupanāyika-khandhaka,* the section dealing with the "beginning of the rains." In the Pali Text Society edition, the only one available to me, this passage is rather badly chopped up in an apparent attempt by editor or scribe to abbreviate repetitions. It deals in general with the occasions or situations when a monk could legitimately break the rain-retreat during which he was otherwise strictly forbidden to travel. One of these reasons—but only one—has been widely cited: a monk may be away for up to seven days if he goes to learn from a lay-brother (*upāsaka*) a "recognized *sūtra*" (*abhiññātaṃ . . . suttantaṃ*) that might otherwise be in danger of being lost. There are, however, a number of other equally legitimate reasons.[3]

Originally published in *Journal of the Pali Text Society* XVI (1992):87–107. Reprinted with stylistic changes with permission of the Pali Text Society.

The enumeration of these reasons begins in Horner's translation as follows:

> This is a case, monks, where a dwelling-place for an Order comes to have been built by a layfollower (*idha pana bhikkhave upāsakena saṃghaṃ uddissa vihāro kārāpito hoti*). If he should send a messenger to monks, saying: "Let the revered sirs come, I want to give a gift and to hear *dhamma* and to see the monks" (*āgacchantu bhaddantā, icchāmi dānañ ca dātuṃ dhammañ ca sotuṃ bhikkhū ca passitun ti*), you should go, monks, if you are sent for (*pahita*) and if the business (*karaṇīya*) can be done in seven days, but not if you are not sent for.
>
> (I, 139.27; IV, 186.16)

This is followed by a long list of the kinds of buildings, including "bathrooms" and other constructions ("a lotus pond"), which a lay-brother has built for "an Order," or "for several monks" or "for one monk," and so on, in regard to which the same instructions are given. Since in these cases the order or the monks are the recipients of the constructions, it is perhaps not remarkable that their presence on these occasions was considered important enough to justify breaking the rain-retreat. The same considerations, however, will not account for their presence on other occasions.

The passage continues:

> This is a case, monks, where a dwelling comes to have been built by a layfollower for himself (*idha pana bhikkhave upāsakena attano atthāya nivesanaṃ kārāpitaṃ hoti*) . . . a sleeping room (*sayanighara*) . . . a stable (*uddosita*) . . . a hall in the bathroom . . . a lotus pond . . . a shed . . . a park . . .
>
> (I, 140.27; IV, 187.22)

This list—an abbreviation of an already abbreviated text—is much longer and contains almost every conceivable kind of domestic construction. Here, there is no question of these constructions being presented to the monks; they are explicitly said to have been made for the lay-brother himself. The monks in these cases cannot be there as recipients, and their presence must have been sought, and allowed, for other reasons. Since the text expresses the lay-brother's request using the formula "I want to give a gift and to hear *dhamma* and to see the monks," it would seem reasonable to assume that not just here, but even in the prior cases where the monks were the intended recipients, the reason for the monks' presence was essentially ritualistic. It would appear that the text allows as legitimate and even requires the presence of the monks at some sort of ceremony marking the completion (the verbal form is *kārāpita*) of construction of all sorts of domestic structures owned by laymen at which monks would receive gifts and recite religious texts. It is, in fact, hard to interpret the text otherwise. But two further points should be noted: it appears to have been assumed by the redactors of the text that monks would regularly receive such requests, and that their compliance with such requests was important enough to justify their temporary absence from the rain-retreat.

If what we see here looks very much like sanctioned and assumed monastic participation in the domestic house-dedication rituals that are frequently found in traditional cultures, then what follows in the passage can only verify this impression. To the list of house-dedications the text then adds at least three other occasions of traditional domestic rituals:

> This is the case, monks, where a dwelling comes to have been built by a layfollower for himself . . . a sleeping room . . . a park . . . , or there comes to be his son's marriage (*puttassa vā vāreyyaṃ hoti*), or there comes to be his daughter's marriage (*dhītuyā vā vāreyyaṃ hoti*), or he becomes ill (*gilāno vā hoti*) . . .
>
> (I, 140.35; IV, 188.3)

In each of these cases—as in those that precede them—monks, if requested through the formulaic request, are required to go. Since the reason or occasion that immediately follows concerns preserving "a recognized *sūtra*" that is in danger of being lost, and since no distinction is made between it and the marriages of sons or daughters, for example, it would seem that the redactors of the *Theravāda-vinaya* considered the latter occasions to have the same importance as the former; in other words, the presence of monks at weddings was as important as the preservation of *sūtras*. It is, moreover, difficult to avoid the impression that this passage presupposes something like a client relationship between monks and lay-brothers. That there was some sense of obligation in this relationship seems virtually certain: the text does not say the monk *may* go, but that—if sent for and if it can be accomplished in seven days—he "*must* go" (*gantabba*).

The clarity of the text here renders elaborate discussion, I think, unnecessary. It is all but self-evident that the redactors of the Pāli *Vinaya* assumed and insisted upon monastic presence at and participation in a whole series of purely domestic or life-cycle rituals. Our passage is not simply of interest for its clear articulation of a set of ritual obligations bearing on Buddhist monks, however, because it also assumes that requests for the ritual presence of monks will not be made by laymen only. It goes on to enumerate in very nearly the same language another series of individuals who have dwelling places and monasteries built for the order and themselves, and who also request the ritual presence of the monks on such occasions:

> This is a case, monks, where a dwelling place . . . a site for a monastery for an Order . . . for several monks . . . for him-(her-)self is built by a monk . . . a nun . . . a probationer . . . a novice (*idha pana bhikkhave bhikkhunā saṃghaṃ uddissa, bhikkhuniyā saṃghaṃ uddissa . . . attano atthāya vihāro kārā-*

> *pito hoti*). If he (she) should send a messenger to monks, saying: "Let the revered sirs (masters) come. I want to give a gift and to hear *dhamma* and to see the monks," you should go, monks, if you are sent for and if the business can be done in seven days . . .
>
> (I, 141.31; IV, 189.11)

Here too, I think, the text has an elegant clarity. The redactors of our passage could only have assumed and taken very much for granted that—exactly like laymen—monks, nuns, "probationers" (*sikkhamāna*), and novices (*sāmaṇera*) all had monasteries and monastic buildings regularly constructed both for the order and for themselves, and—again like laymen—all had on such occasions need for the ritual presence of fellow monks. The text does not rule on, but assumes, that monks and nuns can and do act as major donors. We need not again belabor the fact that this kind of assumption by the redactors of the *Theravāda-vinaya* fits awkwardly, if at all, in the picture of monastic Buddhism found in our handbooks but very nicely with the actions of monks and nuns recorded in Indian inscriptions.[4] Nor is the role of monks in domestic rituals a commonplace in modern presentations of monastic Buddhism. The apparent discordancy—since we prefer so often the pictures in our *own* books—might suggest some suspicion in regard to the present passage, or perhaps that it is just another aberration peculiar to the Pāli *Vinaya.*[5] That such suspicions are unfounded seems to follow from two further quite different texts.

The *Mūlasarvāstivāda-vinaya* found at Gilgit has a section—the *Varṣāvastu*—that corresponds in the main to the Pāli *Vassupanāyika-khandhaka.* There is, as well, in the Gilgit *Varṣāvastu* a long passage that corresponds to the Pāli passage cited above and enumerates the occasions on which the monks may legitimately be away during the rain-retreat. Both the enumeration and language here are similar to what occurs in the Pāli *Vinaya,* but by no means are they the same. The *Varṣāvastu* passage starts with a list of obligations (*karaṇīya*) owed to *upāsakas* or lay-brothers. Unfortunately, the description of the very first of the occasions on which a monk must go when sent for by a layman involves a textual—and perhaps lexical—problem that I cannot solve. It is, however, virtually certain that it had something to do with the marriage of the lay-brother.[6] I therefore cite what is, in fact, the last occasion enumerated to give an example of the formulaic character of the language used in the *Varṣāvastu:*

> There is moreover a further obligation to a lay-brother (*upāsakasya karaṇīyam*). It may occur that a lay-brother has a sickness, suffering, a serious illness. He will send a messenger to the monks (saying) "Will the Venerable Ones give a recitation" (*āryā vācaṃ dāsyanti*). A monk should go, having been authorized for seven days, through this obligation to a lay-brother (*gantavyaṃ bhikṣuṇā saptāham adhiṣṭhāya upāsakasya karaṇīyena*).[7]

The *Mūlasarvāstivāda-vinaya,* like the *Vinaya* of the Theravāda, then assumes and requires the presence of monks at certain lay, domestic life-cycle ceremonies. It does not list all of the same occasions, however, referring explicitly only to marriage and serious, if not terminal, illness. The *Mūlasarvāstivāda-vinaya* does not seem to refer to house-dedication rituals; it certainly does not contain the long list of different kinds of structures found in the Pāli. But it does contain some of the same occasions found in the Pāli that are more specifically Buddhist. It refers, for example, to a lay-brother having a *vihāra* constructed, although here too it uses a different language: "It may occur that a lay-brother wishes to have erected a monastery for the community of monks from the four directions" (*yathāpi tad upāsakaś cāturdiśe bhikṣusaṃghe vihāraṃ pratiṣṭhāpayitukāmo bhavati*). It also lists a number of more specifically Buddhist occasions not found in the Pāli *Vinaya:* a lay-brother "desiring to donate bedding and seats to that monastery" (. . . *asminn eva vihāre śayanāsanam anupradātukāmo bhavati*), "wanting to designate a permanent alms-giving" in it (. . . *asminn eva vihāre dhruvabhikṣāṃ prajñapayitukāmo bhavati*), and, interestingly, "wanting to have erected a *stūpa* for the body of the Tathāgata in that monastery" (. . . *tasminn eva vihāre tathāgatasya śarīra-stūpaṃ pratiṣṭhāpayitukāmo bhavati*).[8] In all of these cases—as in the case of marriage and illness—if the monks are sent for, and if they can return within seven days, they are, of course, required to go. One such occasion, however, may be particularly important because we may be able to connect it with a record that can be much more securely placed in time and place.

The Gilgit text gives one of the more specifically Buddhist occasions in the following form:

> There is moreover a further obligation to a lay-brother. It may occur that a lay-brother wants to donate the raising of a staff on that *stūpa,* the raising of an umbrella, the raising of a flag, the raising of a banner . . . he sends a messenger to the monks . . . a monk should go . . .
>
> *aparam apy upāsakasya karaṇīyam. yathāpi tad upāsakas tasminn eva stūpe yaṣṭy-āropaṇaṃ chatrāropaṇaṃ dhvajāropaṇaṃ patākāropaṇam . . . anupradātukāmo bhavati . . . sa bhikṣūṇāṃ dūtam anupreṣayati . . . gantavyaṃ bhikṣuṇā* . . .[9]

Admitting that the exact sense of *yaṣṭi*—although much discussed[10]—is uncertain, it is still difficult not to see in this passage a regulation that corresponds almost exactly to the record of an actual event that appears to have occurred at a *stūpa* near Bahāwalpur in the first century of the Common Era. This event was recorded in a Kharoṣṭhī inscription, the language of which one might call "a Sanskritized Prākrit." Although there have been some differences of opinion in regard to its interpretation, Konow's—as usual—appears to be basically correct:

> The eleventh year—year 11—of the Great King, the King Surpassing Kings, the Son of Devas, Kaniṣka, in the month of Daisios, on the eighteenth

> day—day 18—when the monk (*bhikṣu*) Nāgadatta, a narrator of *Dharma* (*dha{rma}kathi*), the student (*śiṣya*) of the teacher (*acarya*) Damatrāta, the student's student of the teacher Bhava, raised the staff (*yaṭhiṃ aropayata*) here in Damana, the mistress of the monastery (*viharasvamiṇi*), the lay-sister (*upasika*) Balānandī and the matron, her mother Balajayā, also gave, in addition to the setting up of the *yaṣṭi* (*imaṃ yaṭhipratiṭhanaṃ*), the enclosure (*parivara*). May this be for the benefit and ease of all living beings.[11]

Here we seem to have the record of almost precisely the kind of occasion envisioned in the text. A lay-sister donates "the setting up of the *yaṣṭi*" at a *stūpa*, but the presence of a monk—if not his actual direction of the event—is carefully recorded, using in at least one case exactly the same wording as the *Vinaya* passage. The importance of the epigraphical record lies, of course, in the fact that it allows us to say that what was promulgated, in at least this *Vinaya*, appears to actually have been occurring by the first century.[12]

Apart from these points, and apart from noting that the Mūlasarvāstivāda passage also lists as one occasion the recitation of texts by a lay-brother, we need only note that this *Vinaya* not only confirms the kind of participation of monks in the domestic rituals that was taken for granted in the Pāli *Vinaya*, it also assumes—again as in the Pāli—that monks will regularly act as donors. The first of a monk's obligations to fellow monks occurs in the following form:

> What is the obligation to a monk (*bhikṣoḥ karaṇīyam*). It may occur that a monk wants to present a park to the community of monks from the four directions (*yathāpi tad bhikṣuś cāturdiśe bhikṣusaṃghe ārāmaṃ niryātayitukāmo bhavati*). By him there an abundance of material things and worldly things are brought together (*tena tatra prabhūto vastulābha āmiṣalābhaś ca samupānīto bhavati*). He sends a messenger to the monks (saying) "Come! The Reverends will enjoy." A monk should go, having been authorized for seven days, through this obligation to a monk.[13]

In referring to bringing together "material things and worldly things," the text uses exactly the same formulaic wording it had used several times previously in regard to lay-brothers. Moreover, immediately after this passage the text also lists in abbreviated form virtually all the occasions it had enumerated in detail in regard to obligations to lay-brothers: *yathāpi tad bhikṣur asminn evārāme vihāraṃ śayanāsanaṃ dhruvabhikṣāṃ tathāgatasya śārīrastūpam, . . .*[14] As in the section dealing with lay-brothers, so here the section ends with reference to a monk's obligation to attend to a sick or dying fellow monk by giving a recitation: *yathāpi tad bhikṣur ābādhiko duḥkhito vāḍhaglāno bhavati. sa bhikṣūṇāṃ dūtam anupreṣayati. āgacchantv āyuṣmanto vācāṃ bhā{ṣi}ṣyanti, . . .*[15]

We have then two apparently distinct *vinaya* traditions—the Theravāda and Mūlasarvāstivāda—that both assume and enjoin monastic participation in at least some domestic, lay life-cycle rituals and take as a given the fact that monks—exactly like laymen—make both major and minor religious donations, and that when they do, other monks are obliged to be present. There is, moreover, at least a third *vinaya* tradition in which we find something very similar.

The *Abhisamācārikā*, the "Prākrit-cum-Sanskrit" text of which was discovered in Tibet by Sankrityayana, belongs to the Mahāsāṅghika-Lokottaravāda monastic tradition. In its formal structure it does not contain divisions corresponding to the Pāli *Vassupanāyika-khandhaka* nor to the Gilgit *Varṣāvastu* and, as a consequence, we do not find in it a passage that formally corresponds to those we have discussed. We do find, however, the expression of the same sorts of assumptions and ideas. Its first chapter,[16] for example, which deals in large part with the duties of a senior monk (*saṃgha-sthavira*), says that one of the duties of such a monk is to determine, when an invitation to a meal has been received by the monks, what the occasion for the meal is (*jānitavyaṃ. kim ālambanaṃ bhaktaṃ*). He is to determine whether, significantly, the invitation is "connected with a birth, connected with a death, connected with a marriage, connected with a housewarming" (*jātakaṃ mṛtakam vā vevāhikam vā gṛha-praveśakam vā*).[17] These are the occasions, apparently, on which it was assumed monks would receive and accept invitations from the laity, and they, as in the Pāli and Gilgit *Vinayas*, are all connected with domestic life-cycle rituals. The text goes on to say that, in addition to the occasion, the senior monk must also determine the source of the invitation; he must determine whether it comes from "a visitor, a villager, a householder, or a renunciant" (*āgantukasya gamikasya gṛhasthasya pravrajitasya*). It is clear from the instructions given by the senior monk to the person sent to determine these matters that when the invitation is made by a householder, he is generally assumed to be a lay-brother or *upāsaka*: *tena gacchiya pṛcchitavyam, koci imaṃ hi itthannāmo nāma upāsako*. It is equally clear from similar instructions that the inviter could be a monk or nun: *ko nimantreti, bhikṣu bhikṣuṇī upāsakopāsikā āgantuko gamiko vāṇijako sārthavāho*.[18]

After indicating how all of this should be determined, the text goes on to specify how on each occasion the transfer of merit apparently expected from the monks should be performed, citing—curiously—both an inappropriate and an appropriate verse to be recited that in every case is tailored to the specific occasion. Typical are the instructions concerning an invitation "connected with a death":

> Now, then, when it is an occasion connected with a death, it is not permissible to direct the reward thus (*nāyaṃ kṣamati evaṃ dakṣiṇā ādiśituṃ*):
>
> "Today for you is a very good day, very efficacious. At present has arrived an auspicious moment.
> Today for you in the well-ordained, through the well-ordained, the reward in the most excellent vessel shines."

Not in this way is the reward to be directed, but rather the reward should be directed (*atha khalu dakṣiṇā ādiśitavyā*):

"All living beings will die. Indeed life ends in death. As was their action so they will go, going towards the result of good or bad.
There is hell for those of bad action; good being done, they go to heaven.
Having developed the noble path they without further consequences enter *nirvāṇa.*"

In this way the reward is to be directed.[19]

The monks on each occasion are required to recite an appropriate verse and "to direct the reward" that results from this. Although not frequently, the expression used here to refer to the "transfer of merit"—*dakṣiṇā ādiś*—does occur in the Pāli canon, and there, as here, is also associated with the recitation of verses. It is far more frequent and firmly anchored in the *Mūlasarvāstivāda-vinaya* and related sources, where again it is frequently connected with the recitation of verses or *Dharma.* And it is referred to as well in other Mahāsāṅghika sources.[20] The appropriate verse here, as in most other cases, occurs elsewhere in canonical literature.[21] But for our present purposes the most important point to be noted is, of course, that the *Abhisamācārikā,* though representing yet another distinct *vinaya* tradition, assumes, and makes rules to govern, the participation of monks in domestic life-cycle rituals, and assumes as well that monks and nuns act as donors. Though minor details may vary, it has in common a set of basic assumptions and ideas with both the Theravāda and Mūlasarvāstivāda monastic traditions and codes. All share the assumption and acceptance of a monk's obligation to be present at, and to have an active role in, a variety of domestic, life-cycle rituals connected with birth, marriage, house construction, sickness, and death. All promulgate rules governing such obligations.[22] All recognize as perfectly regular that monks and nuns will act as donors. The texts, I think, are unambiguous on these points, although there is, as well, an important qualification in all of them.

The qualification or restriction that appears to apply to the obligations monks owe to others is highlighted in, for example, another discussion in the Pāli *Vinaya.* The case involves a monk whose mother falls ill and sends for him during the rain-retreat. The monk is made to recall the Buddha's ruling on the matter, but it apparently does not cover this particular case because the monk says: *ayañ ca me mātā gilānā sā ca anupāsikā. kathaṃ nu kho mayā paṭipajjitabban ti,* "This is my mother who is fallen ill, *but she is not a lay-sister.* How now should I proceed?" The Buddha responds by adding the monk's mother and father to the previously established list of individuals—all otherwise formally connected with the Buddhist community—to whom a monk had a clear obligation in such circumstances: a monk, a nun, a probationer, a novice, a woman novice, and lay-brothers and -sisters.[23]

This case confirms and makes explicit what all of our texts, whether Theravāda, Mūlasarvāstivāda, or Mahāsāṅghika, seem to imply: the obligation of monks to attend and participate in lay life-cycle ceremonies is not owed to the *total* lay population, but only to individuals who are formally designated as lay-brothers (*upāsakas*) or lay-sisters (*upāsikās*). To which the Pāli tradition, at least, adds a monk's mother and father, even if the parents are not formally connected with the Buddhist community. This restriction is significant for understanding the social dynamics of the Buddhist community as it was understood by *vinaya* masters. It is also significant because epigraphical material seems strongly to suggest that only a small number of those people who made gifts at Buddhist sites identified themselves as *upāsakas* or *upāsikās*.[24] The ritual clientele of Buddhist monks may necessarily have been limited in early India. The problem that remains, then, is determining what "early" can mean here.

This situation is not new. It recurs repeatedly in the study of early Buddhist canonical sources, especially when textual sources transmitted by more than one Buddhist monastic order are consulted. In this instance, we have texts redacted and transmitted by the Theravāda, Mūlasarvāstivāda, and Mahāsāṅghika that, although they differ in regard to detail, share or have in common a set of rules and a common assumption in regard to monastic participation in domestic ritual. To account for such shared or common elements, two basic theories have been used: one says that common elements in discrete textual and monastic sources must go back to a period which predates the development of schisms; the other says that such common elements result from contamination, mutual borrowing, and a process of leveling, and, therefore, are late.[25] The first theory depends on the assumption that Buddhist monastic groups can be meaningfully treated as so-called sects—this has been repeatedly questioned.[26] It depends on the assumption that, once developed, these sects existed in isolation, hermetically sealed, with no significant contact or interchange—this is contrary to all our evidence.[27] It depends on the assumption that we actually know when the splits or schisms occurred—but we do not. The textual sources, all very late, give a variety of discordant dates, and epigraphical sources suggest that discrete monastic orders appeared centuries later than our textual sources say.[28] Finally, this theory assumes that "orthodoxy" or uniformity among related religious groups is established first and then, only over time, do significant differences develop—this is contrary to almost everything church historians and sociologists have discovered: if uniformity is ever achieved, it is achieved over more or less long periods of time through a complex process of mutual influence, borrowing, and sometimes violent leveling that works on originally discrete and competing groups and voices.[29] The second theory seems to avoid these problems.

A similar, in fact related, set of questions concerns the date of the various *Vinayas.* But it too seems that the old observations and arguments of Wassilieff and Lévi remain unrefuted and best account for what seem to be the facts. The former said some years ago that it appears that "les Vinayas parvenus à nous ont été rédigés à une époque tardive," and the evidence seems to be mounting in his favor.[30]

Fortunately, however, the dates of the *vinayas* need not here be decided. It is probably true that, in terms of absolute chronology, *all* of the *vinayas* are late. But from the point of view of relative chronology, they also represent the earliest codification of monastic rules that we have. For our specific purposes, this means that monastic presence and participation in a range of domestic life-cycle rituals is assumed, judged important, and prescribed in the earliest *vinaya* literature that we have, and that our earliest *vinaya* sources assume that monks and nuns will regularly act as donors and rule on the obligations of fellow monks when they do.

We still, of course, do not know if monks actually participated in domestic rituals. We only know that the monk redactors of several *vinayas* assumed they did and said they should. That monks and nuns acted as donors, however, is certain. Not only do those same monk redactors assume they did, and formulate rules for governing the behavior of other monks when they would, but Indian inscriptions put this beyond any doubt. Once again, the isolated, socially disengaged "early" Buddhist monk of modern scholars and Mahāyāna polemics is difficult to find.[31]

Notes

1. H. Bechert and R. Gombrich, eds., *The World of Buddhism: Buddhist Monks and Nuns in Society and Culture* (London: 1984) 14; R. Gombrich, *Theravāda Buddhism. A Social History from Ancient Benares to Modern Colombo* (London: 1988) 124. That these sorts of remarks represent the received wisdom probably does not require documentation. Similar—if not stronger—suggestions have also been frequently made in regard even to monks' participation in more specifically "Buddhist" ritual and cult practice, but see G. Schopen, "Monks and the Relic Cult in the *Mahāparinibbāna-sutta:* An Old Misunderstanding in Regard to Monastic Buddhism," Ch. VI below.

2. F. Edgerton, "The Hour of Death. Its Importance for Man's Future Fate in Hindu and Western Religions," *Annals of the Bhandarkar Institute* 8.3 (1926–1927) 234; for the participation of monks in monastic funerals in both the Pāli and, especially, the Mūlasarvāstivāda *Vinayas,* see G. Schopen, "On Avoiding Ghosts and Social Censure: Monastic Funerals in the *Mūlasarvāstivāda-vinaya,*" Ch. X below.

3. All the Pāli citations below come from H. Oldenberg, *The Vinaya Piṭakaṃ,* Vol. I (London: 1879) 139–142; the translations are from I. B. Horner, *The Book of The Discipline,* Vol. IV (London: 1951) 185–189.

4. See G. Schopen, "Filial Piety and the Monk in the Practice of Indian Buddhism," Ch. III above; Schopen, "Two Problems in the History of Indian Buddhism," Ch. II above; Schopen, "On Monks, Nuns, and 'Vulgar' Practices," Ch. XI below.

5. The presence in the Pāli canonical *Vinaya* of rules governing the obligatory presence of monks at weddings, for example, is particularly intriguing in light of what has recently been said about the modern "change" and "transformation" of Buddhism in Sri Lanka; see R. Gombrich and G. Obeyesekere, *Buddhism Transformed. Religious Change in Sri Lanka* (Princeton: 1988) 265–273; H. L. Seneviratne, *Rituals of the Kandyan State* (Cambridge: 1978) 129.

6. *Gilgit Manuscripts,* iii 4, 138.9, prints the text as follows: *kim upāsakasya karaṇīyena / yathāpi tad upāsakasya gṛha-kalatraṃ pratyupasthitaṃ bhavati ātmano veṣṭanaṃ . . . sa bhikṣūṇāṃ dūtam anupreṣayati. . . .* On at least two occasions immediately prior to this passage, a householder is described in similar terms: *tatra . . . gṛhapatiḥ prativasati / tasya gṛha-kalatraṃ pratyupasthitam / ātmano veṣṭanaṃ. . .* (136.15, 137.13; see also 140.22). Unfortunately, in all of these cases, the manuscript seems to read not *gṛha-kalatram,* but *gṛha-kanutram* (*Gilgit Buddhist Manuscripts,* vi, 733.8, 734.3, 734.7, 736.1), and I do not know what *-kanutram* means. I suspect that Dutt also did not and—as he so often did—silently "corrected" the text on the basis of the Tibetan: *dge bsnyen gyi bya ba gang zhe na / 'di ltar yang dge bsnyen gyis khyim du rang gi 'ching ba bag ma blangs te /* (*Tog.* I, fol. 692.2; cf. fols. 689.2, 690.6, 696.1). Although, again, I do not fully understand the phrase *khyim du rang gi 'ching ba,* the Tibetan text has certainly understood its text to be referring to the lay-brother's marriage.

7. *Gilgit Manuscripts,* iii 4, 140.17.

8. *Gilgit Manuscripts,* iii 4, 138.14–139.11.

9. *Gilgit Manuscripts,* iii 4, 139.11–139.17.

10. For *yaṣṭi,* see F. Weller, "Divyāvadāna 244.7f," *Mitteilungen des Instituts für Orientforschung* 1 (1953) 268–276; L. Alsdorf, "Der Stūpa des Kṣemaṃkara," *Studia Indologica (Festschrift für Willibald Kirfel)* (Bonn: 1955) 9–16; M. Bénisti, "Étude sur le stūpa dans l'Inde ancienne," *BEFEO* 50 (1960) 37–116, esp. 76f; F. B. J. Kuiper, "Yūpayaṣṭi- (Divy. 244,11)," *IIJ* 3 (1959) 204–205; G. Roth, "Bemerkungen zum Stūpa des Kṣemaṃkara," *StII* 5/6 (1980) 181–192; etc.

11. For Konow's edition and translation, see S. Konow, *Kharoshṭhī Inscriptions with the Exception of Those of Aśoka,* Corpus Inscriptionum Indicarum, Vol. II, Pt. 1 (Calcutta: 1929) 139–141 (no. LXXIV), pl. XXVI—my translation is heavily indebted to his. For some earlier interpretations of the record, see A. F. R. Hoernle, "Readings from the Arian Pāli," *IA* 10 (1881) 324–331; B. Indraji, "A Baktro-Pāli Inscription of Sui Bāhāra," *IA* 11 (1882) 128–129; N. G. Majumdar, "The Suë Vihar Copper-plate of the Reign of Kaniṣka," *Sir Asutosh Mookerji Silver Jubilee Volumes,* III, 1 (Calcutta: 1922) 459–474.

12. If our *Mūlasarvāstivāda-vinaya* passage strongly argues for Konow's interpretation of the Kharoṣṭhī inscription, it is less helpful for understanding the references to *yaṣṭis* or *laṣṭis* in a series of records from Western India. See B. Indraji, "The Western Kshatrapas," *JRAS* (1890) 652; R. D. Banerji, "The Andhau Inscriptions of the Time of Rudradaman," *EI* 16 (1921–1922) 19–25 (two of these *might* be Buddhist); S. Gokhale, "Andhau Inscription of Caṣṭana, Śaka 11," *JAIH* 2 (1969) 104–111; D. C. Sircar, "Andhau Fragmentary Inscription of Caṣṭana, Year 11," *JIH* 48 (1970) 253–257; S. Sankaranarayanan, "A New Early Kushana Brahmi Inscription," *Śrīnidhiḥ. Perspectives in Indian Archaeology, Art and Culture. Shri K. R. Srinivasan Festschrift,* ed. K. V. Raman et al. (Madras: 1983) 277–284; etc. Although the references that I know are late, it is

worth noting that—like our *Mūlasarvāstivāda* passage—Hindu inscriptions also refer to a ritual *dhvajāroha* or *dhvajārohaṇa.* See R. Sharma, "Udayapur Inscription of Paramara Udayaditya, Vikrama 1137," *EI* 38 (1970) 281ff; S. L. Katare, "Kalanjara Inscription of V. S. 1147," *EI* 31 (1955–1956) 163ff; etc.

13. *Gilgit Manuscripts.* iii 4, 141.1f.

14. *Gilgit Manuscripts.* iii 4, 141.6f. It will have been noticed that where the *Mūlasarvāstivāda-vinaya* makes full reference to *stūpas* the *Theravāda-vinaya* has none. On this pattern, see G. Schopen, "The *Stūpa* Cult and the Extant Pāli *Vinaya.*" Ch. V below, and the responses to it in O. von Hinüber, "*Khandhakavatta.* Loss of Text in the Pali Vinaya," *JPTS* 15 (1990) 127–138; C. Hallisey, "Apropos the Pāli Vinaya as a Historical Document. A Reply to Gregory Schopen," ibid, 197–208; R. Gombrich, "Making Mountains Without Molehills: The Case of the Missing *Stūpa.*" ibid, 141–143. What has come out of this discussion—apart from some light entertainment provided by Professor Gombrich—seems to be: an increased awareness of the complexity and extent of Pāli *Vinaya* literature, and a promising suggestion that there is something like an "ideal" *Vinaya* (the canonical *Vinaya*) and an "actually used" *Vinaya* (the various summaries and "different monastic handbooks"), with the consequent confirmation of the suggestion "that the canonical *Vinaya* text is not as useful as once thought as a ready source for extracting usable historical data" (Hallisey, 207). It seems too that the suggestion of "the loss of text" is weaker even than I thought, but some problems remain. Though the *Katikāvata* passage might be neutralized by invoking the *du* or *ca.* this will not affect the *Visuddhimagga* passages. They, as Hallisey says, "are more difficult to explain." There is, moreover, what appears to be a much more likely case of "loss of text"—here again concerning "relics"—in the Sri Lankan manuscripts of the *Saṃyutta:* see G. Schopen, "An Old Inscription from Amarāvatī and the Cult of the Local Monastic Dead in Indian Buddhist Monasteries," Ch. IX below, 191–192 and 203, n. 111. Finally, it seems absolutely certain—given Professor Gombrich's agreement—that it can no longer be said that the Pāli *Vinaya* does not contain any references to *stūpas.* He seems to have been so convinced by my suggestion that the references to *cetiyas* in the *Sutta-Vibhaṅga* are to be understood as referring to *stūpas* that he wants to use them against me (140). But the presence of such rules in one part of the Pāli *Vinaya,* but not in another, does not seem to puzzle.

15. *Gilgit Manuscripts.* iii 4, 142.5. Elsewhere in the *Mūlasarvāstivāda-vinaya*—in its *Cīvaravastu*—there are even more specific rules governing the performance of a "worship of the Teacher (= Buddha)" (*śāstuś ca pūjā*) for a sick and dying monk and how that *pūjā* should be financed; see *Gilgit Manuscripts.* iii 2, 124.11–125.9.

16. The whole text was first edited in B. Jinananda, *Abhisamācārikā {Bhikṣuprakīrṇaka}* (Patna: 1969). The first chapter has been again edited and translated—though the latter, at least, is far from satisfactory—in S. Singh and K. Minowa, "A Critical Edition and Translation of Abhisamācārikā Nāma Bhikṣu-Prakīrṇakaḥ," *Buddhist Studies. The Journal of the Department of Buddhist Studies. University of Delhi* 12 (1988) 81–146; see also M. Prasad, *A Comparative Study of Abhisamācārikā* (Patna: 1984).

17. Singh and Minowa, 91.26; Jinananda, 17.8.

18. Singh and Minowa, 91.27, 89.32, 95.27; Jinananda, 17.9, 14.9, 25.1.

19. Singh and Minowa, 92.15f; Jinananda, 18.13f.

20. For references in both primary and secondary sources and some discussion concerning the expression *dakṣiṇā ādiś-*, see Schopen, "On Avoiding Ghosts and Social Censure," Ch. X below, esp. n. 43. It has yet, however, to be fully studied. [See also

G. Schopen, "Doing Business for the Lord: Lending on Interest and Written Loan Contracts in the *Mūlasarvāstivāda-vinaya*," *JAOS* 114 (1994) 527–554; esp. 545f.]

21. This verse or variants of it occur at *Mahāvastu*, ii, 66; *Saṃyutta*, i, 97; etc.

22. The various *vinayas* obviously do not list all the same ritual occasions. The *Abhisamācārikā* list is the most inclusive, and the Pāli *Vinaya* puts considerable emphasis on "house dedication" rituals. The *Mūlasarvāstivāda-vinaya* is noticeably the most restrictive in terms of the kind of domestic rituals at which monks are obliged to be present. The explanation for these differences is not yet determined. It may be related to the cultural and geographical milieu in which the various codes were redacted rather than to chronology. We may see in the restrictive character of the *Mūlasarvāstivāda-vinaya*, for example, another indication that it was redacted by, and for, a Buddhist monastic community in close contact with brahmanical or significantly brahmanized groups in which domestic ritual was already in the hands of other religious specialists. The needs or requirements of a monastic group in "tribal" or partially brahmanized areas could differ markedly. Cf. Schopen, "On Avoiding Ghosts and Social Censure," Ch. X below.

23. Pāli *Vinaya*, i, 147.20ff.

24. A thorough study of *upāsakas* and *upāsikās* in Indian Buddhist inscriptions has yet to be done. But at Sāñcī *Stūpa* no. 1, for example, only eighteen of the more than three hundred twenty-five lay donors call themselves *upāsakas* or *upāsikās*: at Bhārhut none do; at Nāsik only four of twenty-three; at Kārli only two of twenty-two; and I very much suspect a similar pattern will hold throughout until at least the fifth or sixth century.

25. Cf. L. O. Gómez, "Buddhism in India," *Buddhism and Asian History*, ed. J. M. Kitagawa and M. D. Cummings (New York: 1989) 64, and L. Schmithausen, Preface, *Earliest Buddhism and Madhyamaka*, Panels of the VIIth World Sanskrit Conference, Vol. II (Leiden: 1990) 1–2.

26. See H. Bechert, "Zur Geschichte der buddhistischen Sekten in Indien und Ceylon," *La nouvelle clio* 7–9 (1955–1957) 311–360; Bechert, "On the Identification of Buddhist Schools in Early Sri Lanka," *Indology and Law: Studies in Honor of Professor J. Duncan M. Derrett*, ed. G. D. Sontheimer and P. K. Aithal (Wiesbaden: 1982) 60–76.

27. *Histoire du bouddhisme indien*, 197.

28. See Schopen, "Two Problems in the History of Indian Buddhism," Ch. II above, 26.

29. See, for example, the now classic W. Bauer, *Orthodoxy and Heresy in Earliest Christianity* (Philadelphia: 1971). Something similar has occasionally been argued in the development of Indian Buddhism—but only occasionally. J. Przyluski, for example, in discussing the *pratītyasamutpāda* formula said many years ago: "En somme, nous ne pouvons admettre qu'il y eût à l'origine du Bouddhisme une série de douze 'conditions' dont les autres listes ne seraient que des déformations récentes. Plus haut nous remontons dans le passé, plus grande est la diversité que nous constatons. C'est probablement à une époque assez tardive qu'on s'efforça de concilier les thèses divergentes et que finit par prévaloir la série: *avidyā . . . jarāmaraṇa*" (J. Przyluski, "La roue de la vie à Ajaṇṭā," *JA* [1920] 327–328).

30. W. Wassilieff [V. Vasilyev], "Le bouddhisme dans son plein développement d'après les vinayas," *RHR* 34 (1896) 318–325, esp. 321ff; S. Lévi, "Les éléments de formation du Divyāvadāna," *TP* 8 (1907) 116–117 and n. 1; Lévi, "Les saintes écritures du bouddhisme," *Mémorial Sylvain Lévi* (Paris: 1937) 82–84: "De plus, la vie du couvent, qui allait en se développant sans cesse, proposait ainsi sans cesse des problèmes pratiques

qu'il fallait résoudre au nom du fondateur de l'ordre. Les couvents les plus riches, les mieux fréquentés, se créaient ainsi des collections qui se perpétuaient en s'accroissant. Les religieux errants, qui circulaient toujours nombreux de couvent en couvent, maintenaient dans ce vaste ensemble une communication constante qui tendait à niveler les divergences trop accusées. Réduits par élagage à leurs éléments communs, les Vinaya de toutes les écoles se ramènent sans effort à une sorte d'archétype unique, qui n'est pas le Vinaya primitif, mais la moyenne des Vinaya."

31. The influence of the characterizations of "early" monks found in Mahāyāna *sūtra* literature on modern scholarly characterizations is a subject not yet studied, but one which may well be of particular significance. There are cases, for example, where what appears to be Mahāyāna polemical caricature has been used to account for historical development. Dayal has said that ". . . it seems that the Buddhist monks . . . in the second century B.C. . . . emphasized a few duties to the exclusion of others. They became too self-centered and contemplative, and did not evince the old zeal for missionary activity among the people. They seem to have cared only for their own liberation from sin and sorrow. They were indifferent to the duty of teaching and helping all human beings. . . . The *bodhisattva* ideal can be understood only against this background of a saintly and serene, but inactive and indolent monastic order" (H. Dayal, *The Bodhisattva Doctrine in Buddhist Sanskrit Literature* [London: 1932] 2–3). This explanation of a historical occurrence has, in a variety of forms, often been repeated (see *Histoire du bouddhisme indien*, 73, 78, 699), but no evidence for it is ever cited, and it appears to be little more than a paraphrase of the polemical position taken in Mahāyāna *sūtras*. There is, moreover, little, if any, indication in Indian inscriptions that monks—either before or after the beginning of the Common Era—were "self-centered," "cared only for their own liberation," and "were indifferent to . . . helping all human beings." In fact, the indications are quite otherwise. They suggest a monk very active in giving, concerned with benefiting parents, teachers, friends, and "all beings," and very much engaged in the social world; see the references in n. 1 above. We see this monk in Indian inscriptions that date to almost exactly the period during which we think Mahāyāna *sūtras* were first composed. Obviously, much remains to be learned here.

* * *

[For a short response to this paper see R. Gombrich, "The Monk in the Pāli Vinaya: Priest or Wedding Guest?" *JPTS* 21 (1995) 193–197. For more on the title translated here as "mistress of the monastery," see now G. Schopen, "The Lay Ownership of Monasteries and the Role of the Monk in Mūlasarvāstivādin Monasticism," *JIABS* 19.1 (1996) 81–126.]

CHAPTER V

The *Stūpa* Cult and the Extant Pāli *Vinaya*

ONE OF THE MORE curious things about the Pāli *Vinaya* as we have it is that it contains no rules governing the behavior of monks in regard to *stūpas.* In this respect it is, among the various *vinayas* that have come down to us, unique: "tous les *Vinayapiṭaka . . . à la seule exception du vinaya pāli,* contiennent," according to Bareau, "d'intéressantes données concernant la construction et le culte des *stūpa*" (emphasis added).[1] Bareau seems to see the absence of such "données" in the Pāli *Vinaya* as a function of the chronology of the compilation of the various *vinayas* and seems to suggest that the absence of such material results from the relatively earlier date of the closing of its compilation.[2] Roth explains the absence of such rules in the Pāli *Vinaya* in a somewhat different way: "The Pāli tradition apparently did not include such a section, as the compilers of the ancient Pāli canon were governed by a tradition according to which the construction and worship of a *stūpa* was the concern of laymen and not of monks. Therefore, there was felt to be no need for a particular *stūpa*-section to be included in the *Khandhaka*-section of the Pāli *Vinaya.*"[3] There is, however, a passage in a twelfth century Sinhalese *Katikāvata,* or monastic code, a passage in the *Visuddhimagga,* and several passages in the *Sutta-vibhaṅga,* that might suggest quite a different possible explanation.

The *Mahā-Parākramabāhu Katikāvata,* which has come down to us in a twelfth century inscription from Galvihāra,[4] was promulgated as a part of one of the many attempts to "purify" or "reform" the Sri Lankan *Saṅgha,* and its authors claim that it "was formulated also without deviating from the tradition of the lineage of preceptors [*ädurol* = *ācārya-kula*] and after the consultation of Dhamma and Vinaya."[5] One of the sections intended to regulate the daily life of the monks says, in part, in Ratnapala's translation:

Originally published in *Journal of the Pali Text Society* XIII (1989):83–100. Reprinted with stylistic changes with permission of the Pali Text Society.

> They should rise at dawn and pass the time walking up and down (for the sake of bodily exercise). Thereafter they should wear the cīvara covering themselves properly with it and after they have finished cleaning the teeth and have attended to *the duties specified in the Khandhaka such as the duties pertaining to Stūpas,* the great bodhi-tree, the temple terrace, the teachers, the Theras, the sick and the lodging places (*dahagab māmbo aṅgaṇa-vatu-du äduru-vat tera-vat gilan-vat senasun-vat ä kandu-vatu-du sapayā*), should if need arise enter the refectory . . . (emphasis added).[6]

It would appear from his translation that Ratnapala understood the *Katikāvata* to be saying that all the "duties" enumerated here were "specified" in the *Khandhaka,* and that he assumes that *Khandhaka* here refers to the portion of the *Vinaya* so named. But this would suggest, *if* Ratnapala's interpretation of the text is correct, that the authorities who drafted this *Katikāvata* in the twelfth century knew—and presupposed that their intended audience knew—a *Khandhaka* which contained rules concerning "duties pertaining to Stūpas." The *Khandhaka-vatta,* or duties specified in the *Khandhaka,*" were, again according to Ratnapala, specifically identified by Mahāsvāmi Śāriputra, a leading figure and *vinaya* authority contemporary with the promulgation of the *Katikāvata,* with "the major and minor duties enumerated in the *Vatta-khandhaka,* i.e., *Vinaya* ii 207–230."[7] Śāriputra, then, also understood *Khandhaka-vatta* to refer to the text of the *Vinaya,* and his specificity, in fact, should make it easy to locate these rules. But when we look at *Vinaya* ii 207–230, it becomes clear that, although there are now rules there regarding "the teachers, the Theras, the sick and the lodging places," *Vinaya* ii 207–230, *as we have it,* does not contain a word about *stūpas.* This might suggest either that Śāriputra was wrong in his identification of the *Khandhaka-vatta* with these specific pages, or that the compilers of the *Katikāvata* knew—and expected contemporaries to have—a *Vinaya* different from the one we have, a *Vinaya* which had a fuller text of *Vinaya* ii 207–230 than the one that has come down to us. Oddly enough, even if Śāriputra was wrong in his specific identification, we are still left in much the same position: even if the *Katikāvata* is not specifically referring to *Vinaya* ii 207–230, it must at least be referring to the *Vinaya.*[8] And it is not in just *Vinaya* ii 207–230 that there are no references to "duties pertaining to Stūpas"; there are no references to such duties anywhere in the Pāli *Vinaya* that we know. It is, however, not just the authors of our *Katikāvata* who appear possibly to have known a Pāli *Vinaya* different from the one we have.

Buddhaghosa refers on several occasions in his *Visuddhimagga* to the *Khandhaka* and there is, I think, no doubt about what he understood by the term. In one place he says: *ubhato-vibhaṅgapariyāpannaṃ vā ādibrahmacariyakaṃ, khandhakavattapariyāpannaṃ ābhisamācārikaṃ,* which Pe Maung Tin translates as "Or, that which is included in both the Vibhangas is the 'major precept'; that which is included in the Khandhaka duties is the 'minor precept'."[9] At another place he refers to the "proper duties" promulgated by the Blessed One in the *Khandhaka* (*yan taṃ bhagavatā . . . khandhake sammāvattaṃ paññattaṃ*) and then quotes a passage similar to that found in our *Katikāvata* that is found now in *Vinaya* ii 231.[10] It seems fairly obvious, then, that when Buddhaghosa uses the terms *Khandhaka* or *Khandhaka-vatta,* he is always referring to the text of the canonical *Vinaya* which he knew. This is of some importance because in yet another passage in his *Visuddhimagga,* he refers his readers to the *Khandhaka* for rules regarding many of the same things that the *Mahā-Parākramabāhu-Katikāvata* refers to. The passage in question reads:

> *āgantukaṃ pana bhikkhuṃ disvā āgantukapaṭisanthāro kātabbo va. avasesāni pi cetiyaṅgaṇavatta-bodhiyaṅgaṇavatta-uposathāgāravatta-bhojanasālājantāghara-ācariyupajjhāya-āgantuka-gamikavattādīni sabbāni khandhakavattāni pūretabbān' eva*

which Pe Maung Tin translates as:

> On seeing a guest-monk, he should give him the greetings due to a guest. All the remaining *Khandhaka* duties should be performed, such as the duties of the shrine-yard, the yard of the Bo-tree, the sacred-service hall, the dining-hall, the fire-room, the duties towards the teacher, the preceptor, guests.[11]

It is clear from his translation that Pe Maung Tin understood *Khandhaka* in the *Visuddhimagga* to be a proper name or the title of a work. T. W. Rhys Davids and Stede before him understood the term in the *Visuddhimagga* in the same way. Citing the same passages we have cited above from the *Visuddhimagga,* Rhys Davids and Stede defined *khandhaka-vatta* as "duties or observances specified in the v. khandha or chapter of the Vinaya which deals with these duties."[12] But if these scholars are correct, then it is hard to avoid concluding from the passage just cited that, like the authors of the *Katikāvata* who knew a *Khandhaka* containing rules "pertaining to *Stūpas,*" Buddhaghosa knew a *Khandhaka* that contained rules concerning "the shrine-yard" or *cetiyaṅgaṇa.* Since he was—like the authors of the *Katikāvata*—giving practical instructions to his readers, it is again difficult to avoid the assumption that he assumed that they would know or be able to consult a similar *Khandhaka.* But, although the Mahāsāṅghika *Vinaya* preserved in Chinese, for example, has rules concerning what Bareau translates as "l'enceinte du *stūpa,*"[13] and although the Sanskrit version of the *Mūlasarvāstivāda-vinaya* has rules regarding the *stūpāṅgaṇa,*[14] the Pāli *Vinaya as we have it* does not have a single reference to the *cetiyāṅgaṇa* or *stūpāṅgaṇa.*[15]

Unless Ratnapala, Pe Maung Tin, Rhys Davids, and Stede are all wrong in their interpretations of the compound *khandhakavatta,* unless, in short, we do not understand what the term actually refers to, these two passages—one from the fifth century *Visuddhimagga,* the other from a twelfth century Sinhalese

Katikāvata—seem to suggest that there is a distinct probability that the Pāli *Vinaya,* like virtually all the other *vinayas* known to us, had once contained specific "duties pertaining to *Stūpas*" and "duties of the shrine-yard." It is, moreover, not just sources external to the Pāli *Vinaya* like the *Visuddhimagga* and *Mahā-Parākramabāhu Katikāvata* that seem to suggest that this *Vinaya* may have originally contained such rules. There are indications within the Pāli *Vinaya* itself that would seem to point to much the same conclusion.

Although, as we have already noted, the Pāli *Vinaya* as we have it, and more particularly the *Khandhaka,* have no rules specifically governing behavior in regard to *stūpas, stūpas*—or at least *cetiyas*—are taken for granted as an integral part of the monastic life in at least four passages in the *Sutta-vibhaṅga.* We might look briefly at these.

In discussing the passage from the *Visuddhimagga* above, I have assumed that Buddhaghosa's *cetiyaṅgaṇa* was the Pāli equivalent of the Mūlasarvāstivādin *stūpāṅgaṇa* and of the "l'enceinte du *stūpa*" found in the Chinese *vinayas.* Given the narrative uses and descriptions of the *cetiyaṅgaṇa* in Buddhaghosa, it would be hard to argue otherwise. But if this equivalence of *cetiya* and *stūpa* holds here, it may hold elsewhere as well. Two of the four passages from the *Sutta-vibhaṅga* that concern us, for example, deal with property rights in, and the tripartite economic structure of, Buddhist monastic establishments. The first of these, *Vinaya* iii 266, reads:

> *saṃghassa pariṇataṃ aññasaṃghassa vā cetiyassa vā pariṇāmeti, āpatti dukkaṭassa. cetiyassa pariṇataṃ aññacetiyassa vā saṃghassa vā puggalassa vā pariṇāmeti, āpatti dukkaṭassa. puggalassa pariṇataṃ aññapuggalassa vā saṃghassa vā cetiyassa vā pariṇāmeti, āpatti dukkaṭassa.*

And Horner translates the passage as:

> If he appropriates what was apportioned to the Order for another (part of the) Order or for a shrine, there is an offence of wrong-doing. If he appropriates what was apportioned to a shrine for another shrine or for an Order or for an individual, there is an offence of wrong-doing. If he appropriates what was apportioned to an individual for another individual or for an Order or for a shrine, there is an offence of wrong-doing.[16]

This passage, and the virtually identical passage at *Vinaya* iv 156, can, I think, only represent the Pāli versions of similar discussions of property rights found in Sanskrit in the *Mūlasarvāstivāda-vinaya* and in several *vinayas* now preserved in Chinese. In the *Mūlasarvāstivāda-vinaya,* for example, we find:

> *bhagavān āha / sarvasaṃghaṃ sannipātyāsau lakṣitavyaḥ / kiṃ sambhinnakārī na vā iti / yadi sambhinnakārī / sāṃghikaṃ staupikaṃ karoti / staupikaṃ vā sāṃghikam / evam adhārmikam /*

> The Blessed One said: 'Having assembled the whole community, this is to be considered: is this a (case for) making a full division [or: mixed distribution], or is it not? If there is a full division (and) it takes what belongs to the *Saṅgha* as what belongs to the *stūpa*, or what belongs to the *stūpa* as what belongs to the *Saṅgha*—such (a procedure) is not in conformity with the *Dharma* (*de lta bu chos dang mi mthun pa yin pas*).[17]

In regard to the Chinese *vinayas*, Bareau notes, for example, that "les Sarvāstivādin parlent aussi des biens inépuisables du *stūpa*, qui sont inaliénables. Les biens qui sont donnés en offrande au *stūpa* ne peuvent être utilisés à d'autres fins. On ne doit pas les mélanger avec les biens de la Communauté des quatre directions, ni avec les biens consistant en nourriture, ni avec les biens à partager."[18]

It would seem fairly certain that the *Sutta-vibhaṅga* passage, the *Mūlasarvāstivāda-vinaya* passage, and the Sarvāstivādin material summarized by Bareau are all dealing with the same basic concern: the distribution of property to, and the ownership rights of, the different corporate or juristic entities within a monastic establishment. The fact that, in exactly similar contexts, the Sarvāstivādin and Mūlasarvāstivādin *Vinayas* speak of *stūpas* or that which "belongs to the *stūpas*" (*staupika*) and the Pāli *Sutta-vibhaṅga* speaks of *cetiyas* would seem again to suggest that the two terms are equivalent, that *cetiya* in these contexts is the Pāli equivalent for *stūpa*. It is interesting to note that the Pāli preference for *cetiya* may, in fact, represent a relatively late South Indian influence on the vocabulary of the Pāli *Vinaya*. At Nāgārjunikoṇḍa, for example, what elsewhere would be called a *stūpa* is, in the inscriptions, consistently referred to as a *cetīya*.[19]

But if *cetiya* in these contexts and in the compound *cetiyaṅgaṇa* is the Pāli equivalent of *stūpa*, then it is equally possible that it is being used in the same way in the two remaining passages we must mention from the *Sutta-vibhaṅga*. *Saṅghādisesa* V prohibits monks from acting as "go-betweens" (*sañcaritta*) but notes that "there is no offence if it is for the Order, or for a shrine, or if he is ill; if he is going on business, if he is mad, if he is a beginner" (*anāpatti saṃghassa vā cetiyassa vā gilānassa vā karaṇīyena gacchati, ummattakassa, ādikammikassā ti*).[20] Similarly, in the *Bhikkhunīvibhaṅga, Pācittiya* XLIV, which prohibits nuns from doing household work, cooking, etc., it is said that "there is no offence if it [cooking, etc.] is a drink of conjey, if it is for the Order; if it is for worship at a shrine . . ." (*anāpatti yāgupāne saṃghabhatte cetiya-pūjāya . . .*).[21] If Pāli *cetiya* in these two passages does not refer to what in other *Vinayas* would be called *stūpas*, it is hard to know what it could refer to. The *cetiya* in these passages is an "object" for whose worship nuns can properly prepare food and for whose sake monks can engage in activities otherwise forbidden to them. It is unlikely, therefore, that the term here could be referring to local or non-Buddhist "shrines"—the only other "objects" generally referred to by the term in Pāli canonical literature.[22] These considerations, and the fact that the use of Pāli *cetiya* for *stūpa* is virtually assured, as we have seen, elsewhere in the *Sutta-vibhaṅga* would certainly support the possibility that it is so used here as well.

If we keep in mind, then, the equivalence of *cetiya* and *stūpa* that seems virtually certain in two cases in the Pāli *Sutta-vibhaṅga,* and likely in two more, it would appear that the Pāli *Sutta-vibhaṅga* (although it has no rules specifically governing behavior in regard to *stūpas* or *cetiyas)* takes such behavior and the existence of *stūpas* or *cetiyas* very much for granted when it deals with other matters. The rules governing the division of property, acting as a "go-between," cooking foods, etc., take the *stūpa* or *cetiya* and activity undertaken in regard to it as established and fully integrated elements of the monastic life. This, of course, makes the complete absence of rules specifically concerned with *stūpas* or *cetiyas* in the *Khandhaka* even more striking and would seem to provide yet another argument for concluding that the Pāli *Khandhaka* must originally have contained such rules. But if—as the *Mahā-Parākramabāhu Katikāvata,* the *Visuddhimagga,* and the *Sutta-vibhaṅga* seem to suggest—the Pāli *Vinaya* had originally contained such rules, then the fact that they are no longer found in the *Vinaya* known to us could, apparently, only be explained by assuming that either they had inadvertently dropped out of the manuscripts or, perhaps, that they were intentionally written out.

The comparatively recent date of the vast majority of the surviving manuscripts for texts in the Pāli canon,[23] coupled with the long and troubled history of their transmission—especially after the twelfth century—could easily account for the loss of material from these texts on a fairly large scale and makes an uninterrupted transmission of our Pāli texts extremely unlikely. In fact, the historical situation would suggest that the transmission was probably interrupted not once but on several different occasions.[24] It is, therefore, possible to think that the loss of "the duties pertaining to Stūpas" could have occurred in just this way. There is at least one consideration, however, that renders this possibility less forceful and may, in fact, suggest quite a different process.

In the *vinayas* surveyed by Bareau—those of the Mahīśāsaka, Dharmaguptaka, Mahāsāṅghika, Sarvāstivādin, and Mūlasarvāstivādin—the rules regarding *stūpas,* although concentrated in the various *Kṣudrakavastus,* are scattered throughout this *vastu* and, in some of the collections, in other *vastus* or divisions of the *vinaya* as well.[25] They do not occur as a single block. Assuming that much the same held for the Pāli *Vinaya,* and that although concentrated in a single *vastu,* rules regarding *stūpas* would have been scattered throughout it and elsewhere in the *Skandhaka,* it would be easy enough to see how some of these scattered rules could have been lost through accidents of transmission. But that all such rules would have been lost in this way seems very unlikely. In light of this, the total absence of rules regarding *stūpas* in the Pāli *Vinaya* would seem to make sense only if they had been systematically removed.

But acknowledging the possibility—if not the likelihood—of such a systematic removal having actually occurred is one thing; knowing why it might have occurred is something else again. One might be tempted to try to explain any removal from the Pāli *Vinaya* of rules regarding *stūpas* by referring to the purported prohibition of monastic participation in the *stūpa*/relic cult that is supposed to occur in the *Mahāparinibbāna-sutta*. This, however, will raise many more questions than answers and, in fact, leads us to much the same conclusion that consideration of the *Katikāvata*, the *Visuddhimagga*, and the *Sutta-vibhaṅga* suggests. First of all—as I hope to show in some detail elsewhere—the injunction addressed to Ānanda concerning *sarīra-pūjā* has nothing to do with an ongoing cult of relics or *stūpas.*[26] Not only can this be shown from the *Mahāparinibbāna-sutta* and related texts, but it is equally clear from other sources that any discomfiture with monastic participation in *stūpa* or relic cult activity is distinctly modern. In the *Udāna* version of the story of "Bāhiya of the Bark Garment," for example, there is a clear directive to monks to build *stūpas:*

> . . . having seen (the body of Bāhiya, the Blessed One) addressed the monks: 'You, monks, must take up the body of Bāhiya of the Bark Garment! Having put it on a bier, having carried it out, you must cremate it, and you must build a *stūpa* for it! For monks, a fellow-monk has died.'
>
> *. . . disvāna bhikkhū āmantesi: gaṇhatha bhikkhave Bāhiyassa dārucīriyassa sarīrakaṃ mañcakaṃ āropetvā nīharitvā jhāpetha thūpañ c'assa karotha, sabrahmacārī vo bhikkhave kālaṅkato ti.*[27]

The *Apadāna* version of the same story has the Buddha saying to the monks: . . . *thūpaṃ karotha pūjetha,* "You must build a *stūpa!* You must worship it!"[28]

That these texts give expression to very early practice concerning the disposal of the monastic dead is confirmed by some of the earliest archaeological and epigraphical evidence that we have. There are, for example, the group of *stūpas* of the local monastic dead at the monastery complex at Bhājā, "probably one of the oldest Buddhist religious centres in the Deccan";[29] or the old *stūpa* of the "forest-dweller" Gobhūti built by his monk pupil at Bedsā;[30] or *Stūpa* no. 2 at Sāñcī, which held the mortuary remains of the local monastic dead, and which Bénisti has recently argued is older even than Bhārhut:[31] this *stūpa* appears to have been established and largely funded by monks and nuns.[32] The same early kind of evidence proves the early and massive monastic participation in the cult of the relics and *stūpas* of the historical Buddha at Bhārhut, Sāñcī, and Pauni.[33] Clear evidence for the active participation of monks and nuns in the *stūpa*/relic cult is found as well at other sites. At Pangoraria in Madhya Pradesh at a very old monastic site, the *yaṣṭi,* or shaft, and umbrella of the main *stūpa,* both of which were very finely worked, were the gift of a *bhikṣuṇī* and her disciples according to the inscription on the shaft that dates to the second century B.C.E.[34]

The inscriptions on the Bhaṭṭiprolu relic caskets, which have been dated variously from the third to the first centuries B.C.E., show that monks (*samana*) took an active and prominent part in the enshrinement of the relics of the Buddha (*budhasarira*) there, both as donors and members of the *gothi* or "committee" that undertook the project.[35] Of the many early inscriptions from Amarāvatī recording gifts of monks connected with the *stūpa* cult, we might note the one "in Maurya characters" that records the gift of a *dhamakathika* or "preacher of the Dharma."[36] An inscription dating from the second or first century B.C.E. from Guṇṭupalle indicates that the "steps leading to the circular brick chaitya-griha" were the gift "of the pupil of the Thera, the Venerable Namda."[37] An early first century C.E. inscription from Kārli says: "a pillar containing a relic (*sasariro thabho*), the gift of the Venerable Satimita, a reciter (*bhāṇaka*) belonging to the Dharmottariya School, from Soparaka."[38] A Kharoṣṭhī inscription from 32 B.C.E. records the gift of relics made by a monk that were given to "the Mahīśāsaka teachers."[39] If it is true, therefore, as T. W. Rhys Davids asserted long ago, that the Pāli *Vinaya* "enters at so great length into *all* the details of the daily life of the recluses" (emphasis added),[40] then, oddly enough, this archaeological and epigraphical evidence would seem to argue for the fact that either the Pāli *Vinaya* must have originally contained rules referring to such activity, or that the Pāli *Vinaya* was unknown or had no influence at these early Indian sites—and they are among the earliest sites that we can know.

Sri Lankan literary data also suggests monastic concern with and involvement in the *stūpa*/relic cult from the very beginning and, in so doing, would strongly suggest that premodern Sri Lankan tradition could not have understood the injunction in the *Mahāparinibbāna-sutta*—or any other passage in the canon—as prohibiting monastic participation in the cult. Mahinda, the monk *par excellence* and nominal founder of Sri Lankan monasticism, is presented by the tradition itself as intending to leave the island because "it is a long time since we have seen the Perfect Buddha, the Teacher . . . There is nothing here for us to worship." The reigning king is puzzled and responds, "But, sir, did you not tell me that the Perfect Buddha has entered *nirvāṇa?*"; to which the Monk Mahinda responds in turn: "When the relics are seen [or: "are present"], the Buddha is seen [or: "is present"]". The king promises to build a *stūpa;* the Monk Mahinda appoints another monk to fly to India to procure relics; he succeeds; and Mahinda stays.[41] The moral of this tale, written by a monk about a monk, seems obvious: the continuance of Buddhist monasticism in Sri Lanka depended on procuring a relic and building a *stūpa* so that the monks would have an object of worship. The relic and *stūpa* cults were, therefore, seen by the author of the *Mahāvaṃsa* as a primary concern of the monastic community and a necessary prerequisite for its continuance. That such a pivotal part of the institution would have been left out of the rules that governed the early community seems very unlikely.

It would seem, then, that there is much to suggest the likelihood of the interpretation of the *Katikāvata* and *Visuddhimagga* passages, and of the data in the *Sutta-vibhaṅga*, presented here. But even if this interpretation turns out not to be entirely correct, in considering it we have come upon further considerations that seem to indicate, at least, that the absence of rules regarding *stūpas* in the Pāli *Vinaya* is much more problematic for the historian than has heretofore been recognized. If the interpretation presented here is correct, the Pāli *Vinaya*, like all the *vinayas*, had such rules, and they were removed at a comparatively recent date. If this interpretation is not correct, and if the Pāli *Vinaya* did not contain such rules, then it either could not have been the *Vinaya* which governed early Buddhist monastic communities in India, or it presents a very incomplete picture of early and actual monastic behavior and has, therefore, little historical value as a witness for what we know actually occurred on a large scale at all of the earliest monastic sites in India that we have some knowledge of. The whole question clearly deserves further consideration.

Notes

1. A. Bareau, "La construction et le culte des stūpa d'après les Vinayapiṭaka," *BEFEO* 50 (1960) 229.

2. Bareau, *BEFEO* 50 (1960) 230, 267–268, 273–274.

3. G. Roth, "Symbolism of the Buddhist Stūpa according to the Tibetan Version of the Caitya-vibhāga-vinayodbhāva-sūtra, the Sanskrit Treatise Stūpa-lakṣaṇa-kārikā-vivecana, and a Corresponding Passage in Kuladatta's Kriyāsaṃgraha," *The Stūpa. Its Religious. Historical and Architectural Significance,* ed. A. L. Dallapiccola and S. Z. Lallemant (Wiesbaden: 1980) 186. K. R. Norman, *Pāli Literature. Including the Canonical Literature in Prakrit and Sanskrit of all the Hīnayāna Schools of Buddhism.* A History of Indian Literature, ed. J. Gonda, Vol. VII, Fasc. 2 (Wiesbaden: 1983) 23, cites Roth's explanation as probable.

4. This inscription was first published in E. Müller, *Ancient Inscriptions in Ceylon,* 2 Vols. (London: 1883) Text: 87–90, 120–124, pl. 137. It was reedited in D. M. de Zilva Wickremasinghe, "Polonnaruva, Gal-Vihara: Rock-Inscription of Parakrama Bahu I," *Epigraphia Zeylanica* 2 (1928) 256–283, and most recently in N. Ratnapala, *The Katikāvatas. Laws of the Buddhist Order of Ceylon from the 12th Century to the 18th Century,* Münchener Studien zur Sprachwissenschaft, Beiheft N (München: 1971) 37–44, 127–135.

5. Ratnapala, *The Katikāvatas,* 38, 129, 304.

6. Ratnapala, *The Katikāvatas,* 40, § 12 (text); 131–132 (translation). Exactly the same reading of the text was given earlier by de Zilva Wickremasinghe, and his translation of it differs only very slightly: ". . . and have attended to the duties specified in the Khandhaka, such as those rules of conduct in respect of the Dāgābas, etc." (*Epigraphia Zeylanica* 2 [1928] 271, 275). The version of this passage repeated in the *Dam̆badeṇi Katikāvata,* which "belongs to the reign of king Parākramabāhu II (1236–1270 A.D.)," differs slightly: *dahagab mahabō an̆gana-vatu-du äduru-vat tera-vat gilan-vat senasun-vat ä vatu-du sapayā* (61, § 96). It is hard to know for certain whether the omission here of

kandu- is anything but scribal. It is not noted by Ratnapala nor reflected in his translation, 158, § 96.

7. Ratnapala, *The Katikāvatas,* 193, 197; cf. 290. References to the Pāli *Vinaya* are here and throughout to the Pali Text Society edition by H. Oldenberg.

8. Cf. T. W. Rhys Davids and W. Stede, *The Pali Text Society's Pali-English Dictionary* (London: 1921–1925) 234; Pe Maung Tin, *The Path of Purity,* Pali Text Society Translation Series, Nos. 11, 17, 21 (London: 1923–1931; repr. 1971) 14, n. 4; 117, n. 3; etc.; these are discussed more fully below.

9. H. C. Warren and D. Kosambi, *Visuddhimagga of Buddhaghosācariya,* Harvard Oriental Series, Vol. 41 (Cambridge: 1950) I.27, 10; Pe Maung Tin, *The Path of Purity,* 14. In addition to the instances in the *Visuddhimagga,* Buddhaghosa frequently refers to the *Khandhakavatta* in the *Samantapāsādikā;* see H. Kopp, *Samantapāsādikā. Buddhaghosa's Commentary on the Vinaya Piṭaka,* Vol. VIII, Indexes to Vols. I–VII, Pali Text Society Text Series, No. 167 (London: n.d.) 1511. Although these references add some detail, they do not seem to suggest a referent for the term other than the text of the *Vinaya.* It should, however, be noted that the "conclusions" drawn in what follows about the *Khandhaka* known to Buddhaghosa raise some serious questions about the relationship of the *Samantapāsādikā* to the text of the *Vinaya* it was commenting on, and the nature and extent of that text. Such problems will only be resolved by a careful and thorough study of this massive commentary in comparison with the *Vinaya* as we have it. Such a study remains to be done.

10. Warren and Kosambi, *Visuddhimagga,* III. 71, 82; Pe Maung Tin, *The Path of Purity,* 117. For other similar *Vinaya* passages, see *Vinaya,* ii, 223; i, 46ff.

11. Warren and Kosambi, *Visuddhimagga,* VI.60, 153; Pe Maung Tin, *The Path of Purity,* 215.

12. Rhys Davids and Stede, *The Pali Text Society's Pali-English Dictionary,* 234.

13. Bareau, *BEFEO* 50 (1960) 251, 253.

14. *Śayanāsanavastu and Adhikaraṇavastu,* 38.29, 39.2.

15. Questions concerning "duties in regard to the yard of the Bo-tree" in the Pāli and other *Vinayas* will also have to be investigated, but given our ignorance in regard to the place of "Bo-trees" in Indian monastic communities, and given the great importance assigned to their presence in Sri Lanka, this will require a separate study. It is, however, perhaps worth noting here that the only clear reference I know in Indian inscriptional sources to a shrine connected with a Bo-tree explicitly connects that shrine with a Sri Lankan monastic community. The Second Apsidal Temple Inscription F from Nāgārjunikoṇḍa records the benefactions of the Upāsikā Bodhisiri. One of these is said to have been the construction of "a shrine for the Bodhi-tree at the Sīhaḷa-vihāra" (*sīhaḷa-vihāre bodhi-rukha-pāsādo*); see J. Ph. Vogel, "Prakrit Inscriptions from a Buddhist Site at Nagarjunikonda," *EI* 20 (1929–1930) 22–23.

16. I. B. Horner, *The Book of the Discipline,* Vol. II (London: 1940) 162.

17. *Gilgit Manuscripts,* iii 2, 145.15–146.1; *Peking,* 41, 284-2-2ff. I am not altogether sure I have completely understood this passage. The text is extremely terse, and the technical meaning of *sambhinnakārī* is not well established. I have followed my understanding of the Tibetan translation, and the problems do not, in any case, affect my point here: discussions of property rights similar to those in the Pāli *Sutta-vibhaṅga* occurring in the *Mūlasarvāstivāda-vinaya* refer frequently to *staupika* or indicate that what is *buddhasantaka* is to be used for the *stūpa;* cf. *Gilgit Manuscripts,* iii 2, 143.11; *Peking,* 44, 95-3-4ff; etc.

18. Bareau, *BEFEO* 50 (1960) 257; cf. J. Gernet, *Les aspects économiques du bouddhisme dans la société chinoise du Ve au Xe siècle* (Paris: 1956) 61ff, 159ff. For the persistence in Mahāyāna *sūtra* literature of both the vocabulary and conception of ownership found in the various *Vinayas*, see G. Schopen, "Burial *Ad Sanctos* and the Physical Presence of the Buddha in Early Indian Buddhism", Ch. VII below, 128–131.

19. Cf. G. Schopen, "On the Buddha and His Bones" Ch. VIII below, 159–160. Apart from the odd rule, "qui interdisent de faire un *stūpa* avec la nourriture puis de le démolir et de le manger," that the Pāli *Vinaya* shares with that of the Mūlasarvāstivāda according to Bareau in *BEFEO* 50 (1960) 271 (if that is what *thūpikata* actually means), the only actual occurrence of the term *stūpa* in the Pāli *Vinaya* occurs in the bizarre story concerning "the group of six nuns" found at *Vinaya*, iv, 308–309. Here it is said that "the Venerable Kappitaka, the Venerable Upāli's preceptor" destroyed the *stūpa* that "the group of six" had built for one of their deceased members. This story of an uncharacteristically violent and almost sacrilegious act may be particular to the Pāli *Vinaya*. The same rule appears to be explained by a very different story in the *Mahāsāṃghika-Bhikṣuṇī-Vinaya*, for example, in A. Hirakawa, *Monastic Discipline for the Buddhist Nuns. An English Translation of the Chinese Text of the Mahāsāṃghika-Bhikṣuṇī-Vinaya*, Tibetan Sanskrit Works Series, No. XXI (Patna: 1982) 284–286. [For reference to a Mūlasarvāstivādin story about a monk destroying a *stūpa* built by a group of nuns, see G. Schopen, "Ritual Rights and Bones of Contention: More on Monastic Funerals and Relics in the *Mūlasarvāstivāda-vinaya*," *JIP* 22 (1994) 71 and n. 85.] It may also be related to what appears to be an explicitly local Sri Lankan resistance to *stūpas* for the local monastic dead. At least, the argument against the erection of *stūpas* for "virtuous puthujjana monks" found in the Sri Lankan commentaries is a purely local one: *puthujjanabhikkhūnaṃ hi thūpe anuññāya-māne tambapaṇṇadīpe gāmapaṭṭanānaṃ okāso ca na bhaveyya tathā aññesu ṭhānesu*, "for were a *stūpa* to be allowed for *puthujjana* monks there would be no room for any villages or cities in Tambapaṇṇadīpa (Ceylon), likewise in other places"; see P. Masefield, *Divine Revelation in Pali Buddhism* (London: 1986) 23. To what degree this resistance was purely literary remains to be seen, although Longhurst already long ago noted that "the *stūpas* erected over the remains of ordinary members of the Buddhist community were very humble little structures. The ashes of the dead were placed in an earthenware pot and covered with a lid, and the humble little *stūpa* erected over it. Plenty of Buddhist *stūpas* of this class may still be seen in the Madras Presidency and also in Ceylon"; see A. H. Longhurst, *The Story of the Stūpa* (Colombo: 1936) 14.

20. I. B. Horner, *The Book of the Discipline*, Vol. I (London: 1938) 243; *Vinaya*, iii, 143.

21. I. B. Horner, *The Book of the Discipline*, Vol. III (London: 1942) 329; *Vinaya*, iv, 301.

22. Cf. B. C. Law, "Cetiya in the Buddhist Literature," *Studia Indo-Iranica. Ehrengabe für Wilhelm Geiger*, hrsg. v. W. Wüst (Leipzig: 1931) 42–48. That *cetiya* is *always* used in Pāli literature to refer to a *stūpa* is, of course, not being asserted here.

23. See, at least, O. von Hinüber, "On the Tradition of Pāli Texts in India, Ceylon and Burma," *Buddhism in Ceylon and Studies on Religious Syncretism in Buddhist Countries*, Abhandlungen der Akademie der Wissenschaften in Göttingen, Phil.-Hist. Klasse. Dritte Folge. Nr. 108, ed. H. Bechert (Göttingen: 1978) 48–57; O. von Hinüber, "Notes on the Pāli Tradition in Burma," *Nachrichten der Akademie der Wissenschaften in Göttingen*, I. Phil.-Hist. Klasse Jg. 1983, Nr. 3, 67–79; O. von Hinüber, "Pāli Manuscripts of Canonical Texts from North Thailand—A Preliminary Report," *Journal of the Siam Society* 71 (1983)

75–88; O. von Hinüber, "Two Jātaka Manuscripts from the National Library in Bangkok," *JPTS* 10 (1985) 1–22; O. von Hinüber, "The Pāli Manuscripts Kept at the Siam Society, Bangkok. A Short Catalogue," *Journal of the Siam Society* 75 (1987) 9–74; O. von Hinüber, "The Oldest Dated Manuscript of the Milindapañha," *JPTS* 11 (1987) 111–119; P. E. E. Fernando, "A Note on Three Old Sinhalese Palm-Leaf Manuscripts," *The Sri Lanka Journal of the Humanities* 8 (1982, actually 1985) 146–157.

24. As one of the many possible sources for the troubled history—both internal and external—of the Sri Lankan Saṅgha from the twelfth century on, see Ratnapala, *The Katikāvatas,* 219–232; for Burma, see E. M. Mendelson, *Sangha and State in Burma. A Study of Monastic Sectarianism and Leadership* (Ithaca and London: 1975) 31–118; for Thailand, Y. Ishii, *Sangha. State and Society. Thai Buddhism in History* (Honolulu: 1986) 59–66; etc.

25. Bareau, *BEFEO* 50 (1960) 229–230.

26. The supposed injunction occurs, of course, at *Dīgha,* ii, 141.18 (= *Mahāparinibbānasutta,* V.10). Although the details will have to be given elsewhere, it can, I think, be convincingly shown both that *sarīra-pūjā* does not refer to "worship of the relics" but to what we might call "preparation of the body" prior to cremation, and that even as late as the *Milindapañha* the injunction at *Dīgha,* ii, 141 was not understood to apply to all monks. Moreover, if this injunction, by itself, were to account for the absence of rules regarding *stūpas* in the Pāli *Vinaya,* we would expect to find that other schools who had a similar text of the *Mahāparinirvāṇa-sūtra* would also have no such rules in their *Vinayas.* But this is not the case. [See G. Schopen, " Monks and the Relic Cult in the *Mahāparinibbāna-sutta,*" Ch. VI below.]

27. P. Steinthal, *Udāna* (London: 1885) 8, 21 (I.10).

28. Bhikkhu J. Kashyap, *The Apadāna (II)—Buddhavaṃsa-Cariyāpiṭaka (Khuddakanikāya,* Vol. VII), Nālandā-Devanāgarī-Pāli-Series (Bihar: 1959) 125.16 (54.6.216).

29. See S. Nagaraju, *Buddhist Architecture of Western India (c. 250 B.C.–c. A.D. 300)* (Delhi: 1981) 113–130, 329–330. On the inscriptions associated with these *stūpas,* see also D. D. Kosambi, "Dhenukākaṭa," *JASBom* 30.2 (1955) 70–71.

30. Nagaraju, *Buddhist Architecture of Western India,* 107–108, 329.

31. M. Bénisti, "Observations concernant le stūpa n° 2 de Sāñcī," *BEI* 4 (1986) 165–170.

32. For the donative inscription connected with the mortuary deposit, see J. Marshall, A. Foucher, and N. G. Majumdar, *The Monuments of Sāñchī,* Vol. I (Delhi: 1940) 294, although its interpretation there is perhaps not entirely free of problems. Of the ninety-three donative inscriptions from *Stūpa* no. 2 at Sāñcī published by Majumdar, nearly 60 percent, or fifty-two, record the gifts of monastics: monks, nos. 631, 638, 640, 644, 646, 647, 648, 655, 656, 657, 669, 675, 677, 688, 691, 693, 694, 695, 702, 709, 716, 719, Büh xvii, xviii, xix, xx, 803, 820; nuns, nos. 662, 663, 664, 668, 672, 674, 678, 700, 703, 706, 708, 713, 714, Büh xxi, 759, 812; female disciples, nos. 637, 645, 673, 704; male disciples, nos. 632, 633, 634, 671.

33. For monastic donors at Bhārhut and Sāñcī, see G. Schopen, "Two Problems in the History of Indian Buddhism," Ch. II above, 30–31 and notes, although the Sāñcī count there is based on the old publications. For Pauni, see S. B. Deo and J. P. Joshi, *Pauni Excavation (1969–1970)* (Nagpur: 1972) 37–43.

34. H. Sarkar, "A Post-Asokan Inscription from Pangoraria in the Vindhyan Range," *Sri Dinesacandrika. Studies in Indology. Shri D. C. Sircar Festschrift,* ed. B. N. Mukherjee et al. (Delhi: 1983) 403–405.

35. G. Bühler, "The Bhattiprolu Inscriptions," *EI* 2 (1894) 323–329; H. Lüders, "Epigraphische Beiträge. I Die Inschriften von Bhaṭṭiproḷu," *Philologica Indica* (Göttingen: 1940) 213–229; D. C. Sircar, *Select Inscriptions Bearing on Indian History and Civilization,* Vol. I, 2nd ed. (Calcutta: 1965) 224–228.

36. J. Burgess, *The Buddhist Stūpas of Amaravati and Jaggayyapeta in the Krishna District, Madras Presidency, Surveyed in 1882,* Archaeological Survey of Southern India, Vol. I (London: 1887) 94, pl. LVI no. 3.

37. I. K. Sarma, "Epigraphical Discoveries at Guntupalli," *JESI* 5 (1975) 51.

38. E. Senart, "The Inscriptions in the Caves at Karle," *EI* 7 (1902–1903) 55, no. 9.

39. G. Fussman, "Nouvelles inscriptions—śaka (iv)," *BEFEO* 74 (1985) 47–51.

40. T. W. Rhys Davids, *Buddhist Suttas,* Sacred Books of the East, Vol. XI (Oxford: 1900) xlv.

41. W. Geiger, *The Mahāvaṃsa* (London: 1908) XVII.2–XVII3. On the conception of a relic articulated here, see E. W. Adikaram, *Early History of Buddhism in Ceylon* (Colombo: 1946) 136ff; Schopen, "Burial *Ad Sanctos* and the Physical Presence of the Buddha in Early Indian Buddhism," now Ch. VII below; Schopen, "On the Buddha and His Bones," Ch. VIII below.

* * *

[At least three responses to this paper were quickly published; for references, see above, Ch. IV, n. 14. For both the rule and the stories about destroying *stūpas* referred to in n. 19, see now also G. Schopen, "The Suppression of Nuns and the Ritual Murder of Their Special Dead in Two Buddhist Monastic Texts," *JIP* 24 (1996) 563–592.]

CHAPTER VI

Monks and the Relic Cult in the *Mahāparinibbāna-sutta*

An Old Misunderstanding in Regard to Monastic Buddhism

It is almost always instructive to look at the actual evidence for what are taken to be established facts in the history of Indian Buddhism. If nothing else, such an exercise makes it painfully obvious that most of those established facts totter precariously on very fragile foundations. One example only will concern us here.

It is—and has been—consistently asserted that there was in early Buddhism a fundamental difference between the religious activities of monks and the religious activities of lay persons, especially in regard to worship and participation in cult. Moreover, this fundamental difference is said to distinguish not only the religious lives of monks from the religious lives of lay persons in early Buddhism, it is also said to distinguish the Mahāyāna monk from his non-Mahāyāna coreligionists. All of this is, of course, asserted as fact, and far-reaching implications are made to follow from it. But this so-called fact—as I have pointed out several times now—stands in jarring contrast to everything we know from Indian epigraphy and archaeology.[1] It is, indeed, the accumulating weight of this epigraphical and archaeological material that, in the first instance, forces us to reexamine the evidence on which the fact of this asserted difference is founded. That evidence—not surprisingly given the history of Buddhist Studies—turns out to be exclusively literary. But it is not just exclusively literary evidence on which this fact rests: it rests entirely, it seems, on a less-than-careful

---

Originally published in Koichi Shinohara and Gregory Schopen, eds., *From Benares to Beijing: Essays on Buddhism and Chinese Religion* (Oakville, Ontario: Mosaic Press, 1991), pp. 187–201. Reprinted with stylistic changes with permission of the editors.

reading of a single passage of a single text. The passage in question is, of course, *Mahāparinibbāna-sutta* V.10:

> *kathaṃ mayaṃ bhante tathāgatassa sarīre paṭipajjāmāti avyāvaṭā tumhe ānanda hotha tathāgatassa sarīra-pujāya, iṅgha tumhe ānanda sadatthe ghaṭatha, sadattham anuyuñjatha, sadatthe appamattā ātāpino pahitattā viharatha. sant' ānanda khattiya-paṇḍitā pi brāhmaṇa-paṇḍitā pi gahapati-paṇḍitā pi tathāgate abhippasannā te tathāgatassa sarīra-pūjaṃ karissantīti.*[2]

This, in T. W. Rhys Davids' still-standard English translation of the passage, appears as:

> 'What are we to do, lord, with the remains of the Tathāgata?'
> 'Hinder not yourselves, Ānanda, by honouring the remains of the Tathāgata. Be zealous, I beseech you, Ānanda, in your own behalf! Devote yourselves to your own good! Be earnest, be zealous, be intent on your own good! There are wise men, Ānanda, among the nobles, among the brahmins, among the heads of houses, who are firm believers in the Tathāgata; and they will do due honour to the remains of the Tathāgata.'[3]

This single, short passage, probably one of the most frequently quoted passages of Buddhist canonical literature, has been taken to establish, for example, that "śarīrapūjā, the worship of relics, is the concern of the laity and not the bhikṣusaṃgha,"[4] that "advanced monks were not to occupy themselves with such worship of stūpas," and that "the worship of stūpas should be left to the laity alone."[5] But, even if we bracket the distinct possibility raised by Bareau that this passage—and a number of related passages—are to be considered as interpolations in the *Mahāparinibbāna-sutta,*[6] the passage *as we have it* simply will not support the conclusions modern scholars have drawn from it.[7] First of all, nowhere in the passage is there a reference to monks. The injunction, if it is an injunction, is addressed to Ānanda, not to all monks. It is true that plural pronominal and verbal forms are used in the Pāli version of this passage. But if the plural forms are used there as inclusive of the category "monk," then they should be used in that same way at, for example, *Mahāparinibbāna* V.7, where the same thing occurs. That, however, as the context makes absolutely clear, is out of the question since the plural *mayaṃ,* "we," is actually used there in such a way as to *exclude* "monks in different districts." Likewise in VI.1, where a first person plural form of the pronoun is used, Rhys Davids himself recognized that it could not be intended to include all monks: he translates *siyā kho pan' ānanda tumhākam evam assa* as " 'It may be, Ānanda, that *in some of you* the thought may arise' " (emphasis added). Moreover, when in the *Mahāparinibbāna-sutta* we actually find explicit reference to rules governing the *Saṅgha* as a whole—as we do in the passage dealing with the abolition of the "lesser and minor precepts" at VI.3—it is explicitly stated to be a matter for the entire *Saṅgha.* But these considerations, although consistently overlooked, may not necessarily be, in the end, the most important ones. The fact would remain that, even if it could somehow be argued that the injunction was intended for the entire *Saṅgha,* it would still be difficult to establish that that injunction had anything to do with the *stūpa*/relic cults.

There has been more than the usual degree of inconsistency in translating the text of the injunction and virtually no attempt to determine the precise meaning of the term *sarīra-pūjā* as it is used there. Even the great de La Vallée Poussin gives at least four different translations of the injunction, two of them in the same book:

> "Ne vous occupez pas du culte de mes reliques."[8]
> "Ne vous occupez pas des funérailles."
> "Ne vous occupez pas du culte des reliques."[9]
> "Ne vous préoccupez pas d'honorer mon corps."[10]

This kind of inconsistency, which can slip so easily into confusion, is still with us. Recently, for example, Hirakawa said:

> During the early period of Buddhism offerings to the Buddha's relics (*śarīra-pūjā*) were made by laymen. According to the Mahāparinibbāna Suttanta, the Buddha was asked by Ānanda what type of ceremony should be held for the Buddha's remains. The Buddha replied, 'you should strive for the true goal [*sadattha*] of emancipation [*vimokṣa*].' The Buddha thus prohibited monks from having any connection with his funeral ceremonies and instead called upon wise and pious lay believers to conduct the ceremonies.[11]

Here in four sentences, *śarīra-pūjā* is glossed in three different ways: as offerings to relics, as ceremony for remains, and as "funeral ceremonies."

The problem, of course, with de La Vallée Poussin's and with Hirakawa's treatments is, as it is with virtually all treatments of the passage, that they make no attempt to establish the precise meaning of *śarīra-pūjā* and, as a consequence, may be inadvertently conflating what are typologically two quite distinct phenomena: funeral ceremonies and cult activity directed toward relics or reliquaries are fundamentally different forms of religious behavior. In this instance the texts—*as we have them*—seem clearer than their interpreters.

In arguing for his interpretation of the curious statement at the end of the Ahraurā version of Aśoka's First Minor Rock Edict, Norman says "that in Sanskrit *śarīra* means 'body,' not 'relics,' which is its meaning in the plural."[12] That the same holds for the Pāli *sarīra* in the *Mahāparinibbāna-sutta* is, uncharacteristically, beyond doubt. Before a certain point in the narrative, the term is never used in the plural, always in the singular, and can only mean "body": in V.2, for example, the trees burst into bloom out of season and scatter their flowers on the *body* of the dying, but not yet dead, Buddha (*te tathāgatassa sarīraṃ okiranti*); in V.11 the *body* of a *cakkavattin* is said to be wrapped in a new cloth (*cakkavattissa sarīraṃ ahatena vatthena veṭhenti*); in VI.13 the Mallas are said to have approached the *body* "with dancing and hymns, and music, and with garlands and perfumes" (*yena bhagavato sarīraṃ ten' upasaṃkamiṃsu, upasaṃkamitvā bhagavato sarīraṃ naccehi gītehi . . . pūjentā*); in VI.18 the *body* is said to have been wrapped (*bhagavato sarīraṃ veṭhetvā*), "placed on the pyre" (*bhagavato sarīraṃ citakaṃ āropesuṃ*), etc. Wherever, therefore, the term *sarīra* occurs in the singular in the *Mahāparinibbāna,* it unambiguously means *body,* and it occurs in the singular throughout the entire description of the actual funeral. It is, in fact, only after the funeral proper, only after the cremation, that we find *sarīra* in the plural, and it is only here that the text could be speaking about "relics." We can actually watch—in VI.23—the transition in both grammatical number and meaning as it takes place in a single paragraph. The only question that remains, then, is which of the two possible meanings of *sarīra* is in play in the injunction delivered to Ānanda.

Since the text of the injunction uses *sarīra* in compound—*avyāvaṭā tumhe ānanda hotha tathāgatassa sarīra-pujāya*—we have no formal indication of the implied grammatical number and, therefore, of the intended meaning of *sarīra.* But even in the absence of a formal indicator, the contextual indication is virtually certain. The injunction is not an unsolicited declaration; it is a response or answer to a very specific question, and the question itself does have the formal indication of grammatical number that we need. The question is put in the following form: *kathaṃ mayaṃ bhante tathāgatassa sarīre paṭipajjāmāti. Sarīre* here is almost certainly a locative singular used in the sense of "in regard to" exactly as in the immediately preceding *mātugāme,* which is constructed with the same verb: *kathaṃ mayaṃ bhante mātugāme paṭipajjāmāti* (V.9). Rhys Davids translates the latter as "How are we to conduct ourselves, lord, with regard to womankind?" If the construction of the question leading to our injunction is analogous, and if *sarīre* there is in the locative singular, it would accordingly have to be translated: "How are we to conduct ourselves in regard to the body of the Tathāgata?" To argue that *sarīre* is not a locative singular, moreover, would be difficult. The only other thing it could be, as far as I know, is an accusative plural, but there is much evidence against this. A neuter accusative plural in *-e,* though found on occasion elsewhere, would be distinctly out of place in the language of the *Mahāparinibbāna-sutta;*[13] when *sarīra* occurs elsewhere in the *Mahāparinibbāna-sutta* in the accusative plural—and it does so at least five times—it always occurs with the normal neuter plural ending, *-āni;* in the one other instance where *sarīre* occurs in the final sections of the *Mahāparinibbāna-sutta,* it forms a part of a locative absolute so there can be no doubt about its interpretation: *daḍḍhe kho pana bhagavato sarīre.* VI.23.

All of this is only to say that it seems virtually certain that Ānanda, in his question, was not asking about his or anyone else's participation in the relic cult. He was asking about how the *body* of the Buddha should be treated *immediately* after his death, about that which we would call "the funeral arrangements."[14] But if the question is about funeral arrangements, it is at best disingenuous to suggest that the answer and the injunction is about something else. In fact, the text of the injunction itself also seems to indicate that *sarīra-pūjā,* the activity Ānanda was not to be preoccupied with, was intended to refer to only funeral activities.

The text says in V.11 that "the body of the Tathāgata" is to be treated in the same way as "the body of a wheel-turning king" is treated. It is this that the "wise men . . . among the nobles, among the brahmins, among the heads of houses" are to do, and it is this that Ānanda is not to be overly concerned with. But the treatment accorded to the body of a dead king that is detailed in the Pāli text makes no reference either to relics or to an ongoing cult. The *sarīra-pūjā* of a dead king's body described in the text involves the following steps: the body is wrapped elaborately in cloth; the body is then placed in an "oil vessel of iron"; a funeral pyre is built; the body is cremated; and a *stūpa* is built. That is all. "This is the way they treat the body of a wheel-turning king, Ānanda," the text says, and then goes on:

> *yathā kho ānanda rañño cakkavattissa sarīre paṭipajjanti evaṃ tathāgatassa sarīre paṭipajjitabbaṃ. cātummahāpathe tathāgatassa thūpo kātabbo. tattha ye mālaṃ vā gandhaṃ vā vaṇṇakaṃ vā āropessanti abhivādessanti vā cittaṃ vā pasādessanti tesaṃ taṃ bhavissati dīgharattaṃ hitāya sukhāya.*
>
> As indeed, Ānanda, they proceed in regard to the body of a wheel-turning king, so in regard to the body of the Tathāgata the procedure is to be followed. At the main crossroads a *stūpa* of the Tathāgata is to be made. Who will take a garland or perfume or paint there, or will salute, or will cause their mind to be tranquil, that will be for their benefit and ease for a long time.

It may be of some importance to note the shift in verbal forms that takes place in this passage, since that shift would seem to indicate that the final sentence was not intended as a part of the instructions concerning the treatment of the Buddha's body and that, therefore, the activities it describes were not thought to form a part of *sarīra-pūjā.* When the text refers to what is to be done in regard to the body of the Buddha, it uses future passive participles to indicate what must be done by the wise laymen who will perform the *sarīra-pūjā:* the procedure followed in regard to a deceased king *is to be followed* in regard to the Buddha; a *stūpa of the Tathāgata is to be made.* These are clear injunctions in both grammar and sense. But the injunctions end here. The final sentence, which contains the only references in the passage to what might be called cult practices, constitutes not an injunction, but a statement about the future. The text shifts from future passive participles with an imperative sense to simple futures, from "it is to be done" to "those who will do." Notice too that the final sentence also introduces a new grammatical subject: context suggests that the injunctions are addressed to the wise laymen who will perform the *sarīra-pūjā,* but the subject of the final sentence is the indefinite *ye* which Rhys Davids renders by "whosoever." All of this, again, would appear to indicate that all of those activities that we associate with an ongoing relic cult did not—for the author of our text—form a part of *sarīra-pūjā,* and that *sarīra-pūjā* was used to refer only to funeral activities that began with the wrapping of the body and ended with cremation and constructing a *stūpa* and had—like the injunction as a whole—nothing to do with relics.

That this was indeed the original meaning of *sarīra-pūjā* is, in fact, further demonstrated by a number of passages in Hīnayāna literature where we have clear references to monastic funerals. In an interesting passage from the *Mūlasarvāstivāda-vinaya* we find, for example:

> Again on that occasion another monk, being sick, died in his cell. Having brought him to the burning ground, having performed *the worship of the body,* that monk was burnt. Then the monks returned to the monastery (. . . *sa bhikṣur ādahanaṃ nītvā śarīra-pūjāṃ kṛtvā dagdhas, tato vihāram āgatā*).[15]

To that passage from the *Mūlasarvāstivāda-vinaya* we might add another from the same source:

> Again on that occasion another monk died. The monks, having carried out his body, having simply thrown it into the burning grounds (. . . *tan 'bhinirhṛtya evam eva śmaśāne chorayitvā*), returned to the monastery. The distributor of robes entered the dead monk's cell saying 'I distribute the bowl and robe.' He—the dead monk—having been reborn among nonhuman beings appeared there wielding a club. He said: 'Until you perform *the worship of the body* for me (*yāvan mama śarīra-pūjāṃ kurutha*), do you now distribute (my) bowl and robe?'
>
> The monks asked the Blessed One concerning this matter.
>
> The Blessed One said: 'By the monks *the worship of the body* for the deceased is first to be performed (*bhikṣubhis tasya pūrvaṃ śarīra-pūjā karttavyeti*). After that the bowl and robe are to be distributed.'[16]

Both of these passages enumerate a sequence of activities involved in the disposal of the body of a monk who has died in his cell. In both it is clear that *śarīra-pūjā*—whatever it involved—took place after the body had been removed and taken to the cremation ground, but before it was cremated, before there could have been anything like what we call "relics." It is again fairly certain that *śarīra-pūjā* involved the ritual handling or treatment of the body prior to cremation since the second passage contrasts it with—and insists that it replace—"having simply thrown the body into the burning grounds." That it is the body and not relics that is the object of this treatment is both clear here and made even more explicit elsewhere.

The forty-eighth *avadāna* of the *Avadānaśataka* looks very much like a literary elaboration of the much simpler narratives concerning the disposal of the monastic dead found in the *Mūlasarvāstivāda-vinaya,* two examples of which have already been cited. It leaves us in no doubt as to the object toward which *śarīra-pūjā* is directed. It says a certain monk:

> . . . *kālagataḥ svake layane preteṣūpapannaḥ / tato 'sya sabrahmacāribhir muṇḍikāṃ gaṇḍīṃ parāhatya śarīrābhinirhāraḥ kṛtaḥ / tato 'sya śarīre śarīrapūjāṃ kṛtvā vihāram āgatāḥ /*
>
> . . . died and was reborn in his own cell as a hungry ghost (*shi nas rang gi gnas khang du yi dags su skyes so*). Then his fellow monks, having struck the *muṇḍikā* gong ("la cloche funèbre"), performed the removal of the body. Then, having performed the worship of the body on his body, they returned to the monastery.[17]

Virtually every element of this passage from the *Avadānaśataka* also occurs in the *Mūlasarvāstivāda-vinaya.* The "*muṇḍikā* gong," or "cloche funèbre,"[18] for example, is referred to in the latter more intelligibly as the *mṛta-gaṇḍī* or "gong for the dead."[19] It is, however, not just the elements of the funeral procedure that are essentially the same in the two works; the sequence in which they are said to occur is also basically the same. It is, therefore, significant that where the *Mūlasarvāstivāda-vinaya* has *śarīra-pūjāṃ kṛtvā,* "having performed the worship of the body," the *Avadānaśataka* has corresponding to it the even more explicit *śarīre śarīra-pūjāṃ kṛtvā,* "having performed the worship of the body on his body." This construction leaves no doubt about the object of the *pūjā* involved.[20] Nor is this in doubt in another instance where the construction is used. In the Sanskrit version of the *Mahāparinirvāṇa-sūtra* (48.8) when Mahākāśyapa meets an Ājīvika coming from Kuśinagarī, he asks him if he knows his teacher. The Ājīvika answers:

> *jāne / śramaṇo gautamaḥ / parinirvṛtas te āyuṣmañ chāstā / adya (gate saptāhe va)rtate śarīre śarīra-pūjā.*
>
> I know him. He is the *Śramaṇa* Gautama. But sir, your teacher is dead. For seven days now the worship of the body on his body is performed.[21]

But since the Buddha had not yet been cremated, it is here not just the construction, but the context too that makes it certain that *śarīra-pūjā* was understood to be an activity directed toward the body of the deceased that took place after the individual's death, but before or as a part of his cremation. It could not, therefore, have anything to do with relics for the simple reason that there were no relics.

All of this is richly confirmed by a variety of other passages as well. In the account of the funeral of Mahāprajāpatī and her companions found in the *Vinaya-kṣudraka-vastu* of the *Mūlasarvāstivāda-vinaya*, for example, in which prominent monks come from afar to undertake the full performance of the worship of her body (*de'i lus la mchod pa lhag par bya ba la brtson par byas*), the text says: "Then, having performed the great worship and having removed the bodies, they set the biers down at an appropriate and isolated spot" (*de nas mchod pa chen po byas te khyer nas sa phyogs bar skabs dben par khyogs rnams bzhag go*). Only after the great worship was performed and the bodies were removed did the cremation take place (*de nas . . . bsregs so*).[22] In the terse account of the end of Aśoka found in the *Divyāvadāna*, the text says that the ministers thought of enthroning the new king only "after having carried out (Aśoka's body) on dark blue and yellow biers, after having performed the worship of the body, and after having cremated him" (*yāvad amātyair nīlapītābhiḥ śivikābhir nirharitvā śarīra-pūjāṃ kṛtvā dhmāpayitvā rājānaṃ pratiṣṭhāpayiṣyāma iti*).[23] Here again, "worship of the body" precedes cremation; it takes place before there could be any relics.

Still other passages make it clear that *śarīra-pūjā* also took place prior to the erection of a *stūpa*. The *Saṅghabhedavastu* of the *Mūlasarvāstivāda-vinaya*, describing the events that followed the death of a former Buddha, says:

> A great crowd of people, after having performed the worship of the body in regard to his body, established a great *stūpa* on an isolated spot.
>
> *tasya mahājanakāyena śarīre śarīra-pūjāṃ kṛtvā viviktāvakāśe pṛthivīpradeśe mahān stūpaḥ pratiṣṭhāpitaḥ.*[24]

Similarly, in the description of events that followed the death of a series of former Buddhas found in the *Avadānaśataka*—a description that is repeated at least eleven times—the text says:

> The king . . . , after having performed the worship of the body in regard to the body of the Blessed One, established a *stūpa* a *yojana* in circumference, etc.
>
> *tato rājñā . . . bhagavataḥ śarīre śarīra-pūjāṃ kṛtvā samantayojanastūpaś caturatnamayaḥ pratiṣṭhāpitaḥ krośam uccatvena.*[25]

Significantly, in several instances, this statement is completed with the phrase "and a festival of the *stūpa* was instituted" (*stūpamahaś ca prajñaptaḥ*). In all of these cases then, *śarīra-pūjā* could not possibly have been thought to be connected with activity in regard to *stūpas* since it was only after *śarīra-pūjā* had been completed that a *stūpa* was established. Moreover, in those cases in which it was said that "a festival of the *stūpa* was instituted"—and, therefore, something like an ongoing cult is referred to—this too took place after *śarīra-pūjā* had been performed. *Śarīra-pūjā* did not form a part of any ongoing activity.

We might consider here one final and perhaps particularly interesting passage from the Sanskrit text of the *Mahāparinirvāṇa-sūtra* (49.15). In this version, when Mahākāśyapa approaches the funeral pyre of the Buddha, he takes the lid off the oil vessel, removes the cloths wrapped around the body, and "pays reverence to the uncovered body of the Blessed One" (*bhagavataḥ śarīram avigopitaṃ vandate*). Then the following thought occurs to him: *yan nv ahaṃ svayam eva bhagavataḥ śarīra-pūjāyām autsukyam āpadyeya,* "What if I myself, indeed, were to be zealous in regard to the worship of the body of the Blessed One." Having thought this, he brings other cloths, wraps the body with them, puts it back into the vessel, closes the lid, makes a(nother) pyre, and stands to one side. That is all. It is apparently just this sequence of activities that the text intends by the term *śarīra-pūjā.* Although it looks to us like "worship," what Mahākāśyapa does in regard to the body when he has initially uncovered it is not even included; that activity is expressed by a completely different word: *vandate.*

It is also important to note that, in the Sanskrit text, Mahākāśyapa does precisely what Ānanda is earlier told not to be concerned with, and the two passages use virtually the same words. Ānanda's question is expressed as *kathaṃ vayaṃ . . . bhagavataḥ śarīra-pūjāyām autsukyam āpadyemahi* (36.2) and the injunction as *alpotsukas tvam ānanda bhava śarīra-pūjāyāḥ* . . . (36.3), while Kāśyapa's intention appears as *yan nv ahaṃ svayam eva bhagavataḥ śarīra-pūjāyām autsukyam āpadyeya* (49.19). Since we know what Kāśyapa did when he involved himself in *śarīra-pūjā,* we also know quite precisely what Ānanda was not to be concerned with and, again, it has nothing to do with the relic cult.[26] But since the Sanskrit text goes to the trouble to point out that Kāśyapa was a monk of the highest standing, one of only four *Mahāsthaviras* alive at the time (49.16), and since it is precisely this *Mahāsthavira* who is said to have engaged in *śarīra-pūjā,* we also know that it is extremely unlikely that the authors of the text understood the earlier injunction addressed to Āṇanda to apply to all monks or to forbid monastic involvement in such activity. In fact, if there were any restrictions on participation in *śarīra-pūjā,* they appear from the Sanskrit text to have been of a very different order. Since, again, the Sanskrit text takes the trouble to point out that Kāśyapa was not only one of only four *Mahāsthaviras,* but was also—in Buddhist monastic terms—rich and famous,[27] and since he involved himself actively in behaviors Ānanda was counseled not to be concerned with, the text may be suggesting almost the opposite of what we would expect: it may be suggesting that participation in that part of monastic funerals known as *śarīra-pūjā* was—in, at least, important funerals—the prerogative of advanced monks of high status.[28] Since Ānanda, at this stage, appears to have been neither, this may only confirm from an unexpected angle that the injunction addressed to him was fundamentally *ad hominem.*

All of the evidence we have, then, would seem to argue for the fact that *śarīra-pūjā* did not originally mean "the worship of relics" and did not have anything to do with a relic cult. It would seem to strongly suggest—if not establish—that, originally, it referred to that part of the funeral ceremony that took place primarily between the time of death and the cremation and construction of a *stūpa,* and involved primarily what we would call "preparation of the body." The construction of a *stūpa*—if it is included at all—signaled the end of *śarīra-pūjā,* not its beginnings.

But if the available evidence suggests that *śarīra-pūjā* was not connected with an ongoing relic cult, that same evidence suggests the injunction concerning it as it was delivered to Ānanda was not intended to apply to all monks. The restricted range of the injunction is confirmed from an unexpected source.

The injunction delivered to Ānanda created problems, apparently, for the later Theravāda tradition. It reappears as one "lemma" of an interesting dilemma in the Fourth Book of the *Milindapañha.* This dilemma is particularly important for our discussion since it allows us to see at least something of how the injunction was understood in Sri Lanka in about the fifth century C.E.[29] In presenting the dilemma Milinda points out that the Buddha said both "Do not you, Ānanda, be occupied with honouring the Tathāgata's bodily remains," and—in the *Vimānavatthu* 82, vs. 8—"Venerate that relic of him who is to be venerated (*pūjetha naṃ pūjaniyassa dhātuṃ*); by doing so, you will go from here to heaven."[30] It is clear from the conjunction of these two passages that by the time this Book was added to the *Milinda* a change in the meaning of *sarīra-pūjā* had occurred; it is clear by the way in which the dilemma is framed that *sarīra-pūjā* was now considered equivalent to "venerating a relic," and could now mean that. But it is also clear from Nāgasena's response that even then, and even when taken to refer to relic worship, the injunction addressed to Ānanda had not yet been understood to apply to all monks. If the injunction had already been understood to apply to all monks, or if this interpretation had been widely or fully accepted, Milinda's dilemma could not have arisen and Nāgasena's response would have made no sense.

The response of Nāgasena comes in the following form:

bhāsitam p'etaṃ mahārāja bhagavatā: abyāvaṭā tumhe ānanda hotha tathāgatassa sarīrapūjāyāti. puna ca bhaṇitaṃ:
pūjetha naṃ pūjaniyassa dhātuṃ
evaṃkarā saggam ito gamissathāti
tañ ca pana na sabbesaṃ. jinaputtānaṃ yeva ārabbha bhaṇitaṃ: abyāvaṭā tumhe ānanda hotha tathāgatassa sarīrapūjāyāti. akammaṃ h'etaṃ mahārāja jinaputtā-

> *naṃ yad idaṃ pūjā; sammasanaṃ sankhārānaṃ, yoniso manasikāro, saṭipaṭṭhānānupassanā, ārammaṇa-sāraggāho, kilesayuddhaṃ sadatthamanuyuñjanā, etaṃ jinaputtānaṃ karaṇīyaṃ; avasesānaṃ devamanussānaṃ pūjā karaṇīyā.*

Taking into account the new meaning attributed to *sarīra-pūjā,* this can be translated as:

> Great King, this was indeed spoken by the Blessed One: 'You, Ānanda, should not be concerned with worshipping the relics of the Tathāgata!' And again it was said (by him):
>
> 'Worship the relic of one who is to be worshipped!
> Acting thus, you will go from here to heaven.'
>
> But that (which was said) was not (intended) for everyone. Only in reference to the sons of the Conqueror was it said: 'You, Ānanda, should not be concerned with worshipping the relics of the Tathāgata!' For this, Great King, is not an action for the sons of the Conqueror, namely, worship. Thoroughly understanding the conditioned; concentrating the mind; realizing the establishment of mindfulness; taking hold of the most excellent foundations; destroying the impurities; pursuing the highest goal—this is what is to be done by sons of the Conqueror. By the remainder of gods and men worship is to be performed.

The primary purpose of this passage and of the elaborate series of metaphors that follow it is readily apparent. Its primary, if not its sole purpose was to establish the meaning of the injunction delivered to Ānanda by establishing to whom that injunction was to apply. The mere fact that this was a dilemma can, again, only mean that, at the time that this passage was written, it had not yet been established for whom the injunction was meant; it had not been determined that—as modern scholarship would have it—the injunction was meant for all monks. In fact—and this is the significance of the passage—even this late book of the *Milinda* does not understand the passage in this way.

According to the *Milinda,* the injunction did not apply to monks but to what it calls *jinaputtas,* "sons of the Conqueror." But, first of all, this could not have been the intention of the original injunction since the *Dīgha* as a whole is completely ignorant of such a group. "The compound [*jinaputta*] appears to occur," according to Horner, "three times in Buddv. [= *Buddhavamṣa*], but nowhere else in the Pāli Canon."[31] Moreover, what little we know about this term comes from a single passage in the *Madhuratthavilāsinī,* a commentary on the *Buddhavaṃsa,* which in Horner's words "is late."[32] It says simply *jinaputtā ti dīpankarassa satthuno sāvakā,* "the sons of the Conqueror means the disciples of the Teacher Dīpaṅkara."[33] The equation *jinaputta* = *sāvaka* is, of course, not terribly helpful. It has recently been pointed out that it is not always easy to determine who was understood to be included in the category *sāvaka,* that it certainly included monks—but by no means, perhaps, all monks—and certainly, at times, included some laymen.[34] The group designated *sāvaka* is not, therefore, certainly coterminous with the group designated *bhikkhu* and, given its vagueness, the group designated *jinaputta* seems even less so. It would, as a consequence, be difficult to argue even that the author of this Book of the *Milinda* was moving *toward* the modern interpretation, which wants to see in the injunction a prohibition of monastic involvement in the relic cult. But even if this argument were to be made, it would have to be conceded that even that author is yet a long way from articulating it with any precision. That interpretation, even as late as the Fourth Book of the *Milinda,* simply has not been made. Had it been, the dilemma would not have arisen; had it been, the author of Book Four, instead of using a term like *jinaputta,* could have simply used the word *bhikkhu.* The fact that he did not is important; the fact that he used a metaphoric epithet rather than an ecclesiastical title may also be important.

Bhikkhu and *jinaputta* are fundamentally different kinds of designations. *Bhikkhu* is a title conferred on an individual as a result of having undergone a set of formal ecclesiastical procedures for induction into a particular group. It designates his formal membership in that group. That membership is not subject to interpretation or opinion; it is subject to recognized procedure. Anyone who undergoes the procedure is a monk. The same, of course, is not true of an epithet like *jinaputta,* if for no other reason than it obviously cannot be taken literally. An individual so designated cannot literally be "a son of the Conqueror." Moreover, there are no formally recognized procedures that make one such a "son" and no formally recognized criteria for determining membership in this group. It, in effect, does not designate membership in a particular group, but conformity to an ideal notion of what the religiosity of a follower of the Buddha—whether that follower be a layman or a monk—ought to be. This, of course, is decidedly a matter of interpretation and not a matter of ecclesiastical procedure. It may well be, then, that the author of the Fourth Book of the *Milinda* saw in the injunction addressed to Ānanda support for *his* view that *pūjā* was not an activity of what he thought was a *true* monk, but even he could not see in the injunction support for the view that it prohibited all monks from such activity. The contrast for him, in fact, continues to be not that between social groups (laymen and monks), but that between different styles of religiosity (meditative and devotional), and a particular religious style had not yet been identified exclusively with any particular group.

It would seem, then, that if the arguments and observations presented here turn out to be even approximately correct, we will be required to admit that a good deal of what has been said about early monastic Buddhism is based on a misunderstanding. If *sarīra-pūjā* in the *Mahāparinibbāna-sutta* has nothing to do with relics or an ongoing cult of relics, then the only textual basis for asserting that monks were not allowed to be involved with either activity disappears. If the injunction concerning *sarīra-pūjā*—however the latter be precisely understood—was not addressed to all monks, then, once again, we are left without any warrant for one of our favorite claims, and we must rethink what we thought we knew about the acultic character of early monastic Buddhism. Once again, it seems, we have encountered material—this time literary—that appears to suggest that our view of the Indian Buddhist monk is in need of more than a little revision.[35]

Notes

1. See especially G. Schopen, "Two Problems in the History of Indian Buddhism," Ch. II above, 30ff; Schopen, "The *Stūpa* Cult and the Extant Pāli *Vinaya*," Ch. V above, 92ff.
2. T. W. Rhys Davids and J. E. Carpenter, *The Dīgha Nikāya*, Vol. II (London: 1903) 141. All references to the Pāli text are to this edition.
3. T. W. and C. A. F. Rhys Davids, *Dialogues of the Buddha*, Part II (London: 1910) 154.
4. A. Hirakawa, "The Rise of Mahāyāna Buddhism and Its Relationship to the Worship of Stupas," *Memoirs of the Toyo Bunko* 22 (1963) 102.
5. N. Dutt, "Popular Buddhism," *IHQ* 21 (1945) 250–251.
6. A. Bareau, "La composition et les étapes de la formation progressive du mahāparinirvāṇa-sūtra ancien," *BEFEO* 66 (1979) 45–103.
7. As a small sample—and it is only that—of these "conclusions," see H. Oldenberg, *Buddha. Sein Leben, seine Lehre, seine Gemeinde* (Berlin: 1897) 428; N. Dutt, "Place of Laity in Early Buddhism," *IHQ* 21 (1945) 164; Ét. Lamotte, "Le bouddhisme des läics," *Studies in Indology and Buddhology. Presented in Honour of Professor Susumi Yamaguchi on the Occasion of his Sixtieth Birthday* (Kyoto: 1955) 80; *Histoire du bouddhisme indien*, 81; D. L. Snellgrove, "Śākyamuni's Final Nirvāṇa," *BSOAS* 36 (1973) 410; A. Bareau, "Le parinirvāṇa du buddha et la naissance de la religion bouddhique," *BEFEO* 61 (1974) 283–284; G. Nagao, "The Architectural Tradition in Buddhist Monasticism," *Studies in History of Buddhism*, ed. A. K. Narain (Delhi: 1980) 193–194; M. Wijayaratna, *Le moine bouddhiste. Selon les textes du theravāda* (Paris: 1983) 183; R. Gombrich, *Theravāda Buddhism. A Social History from Ancient Benares to Modern Colombo* (London and New York: 1988) 119–124. See also the works cited in nn. 4 and 5 above and nn. 8–11 below; etc.
8. L. de La Vallée-Poussin, *Nirvāṇa* (Paris: 1924) 7.
9. L. de La Vallée-Poussin, *Le dogme et la philosophie du bouddhisme* (Paris: 1930) 64, 191.
10. L. de La Vallée-Poussin, *L'inde aux temps des mauryas et des barbares, grecs, scythes, parthes et yue-tchi* (Paris: 1930) 141.
11. A. Hirakawa, "Stupa Worship," *The Encyclopedia of Religion*, ed. M. Eliade, Vol. 14 (New York: 1987) 93.
12. K. R. Norman, "Notes on the Ahraurā Version of Aśoka's First Minor Rock Edict," *IIJ* 26 (1983) 278.
13. W. Geiger, *Pāli Literature and Language*, trans. by B. Ghosh (Calcutta: 1943) § 78.7; see also *Mahāparinibbāna* V.11 quoted below.

14. This seems clear, as well, in *Mahāparinibbāna* V.17, where Ānanda tries to dissuade the Buddha from passing away in Kusinārā.

15. *Gilgit Buddhist Manuscripts*, vi, fol. 852.8; *Gilgit Manuscripts*, iii 2, 127.13; *Peking*, 41, 281-1-1: *de'i tshe dge slong nad pa zhig gnas khang du shi nas de dge slong rnams kyis dur khrod du khyer te ro la mchod pa byas bsregs nas de nas gtsug lag khang du lhags pa dang* /.

16. *Gilgit Buddhist Manuscripts*, vi, fol. 852.6ff; *Gilgit Manuscripts*, iii 2, 127.4ff; *Peking*, 41, 280-5-6ff: *de'i tshe dge slong zhig shi nas dge slong rnams kyis de phyung ste / dur khrod du de bzhin du bor nas . . . re shig kho bo'i ro la mchod pa yang ma byas par . . . dge slong rnams kyis sngar de'i ro la mchod pa byas la. . . .* This and the preceding passage are two of a series of interesting passages dealing with monastic funerals that occur in the *Mūlasarvāstivāda-vinaya;* I am now working on a detailed study of this material. [See G. Schopen, "On Avoiding Ghosts and Social Censure," Ch. X below; and Schopen, "Ritual Rites and Bones of Contention: More on Monastic Funerals and Relics in the *Mūlasarvāstivāda-vinaya*." *JIP* 22 (1994) 31–80.]

17. J. S. Speyer, ed., *Avadānaçataka. A Century of Edifying Tales belonging to the Hīnayāna*, Vol. I (St. Petersburg: 1906–1909; repr. The Hague: 1958) 271.15ff; *Peking*, 40, 184-1-8ff. On the sectarian affiliation of the *Avadānaśataka*, see, most recently, J.-U. Hartmann, "Zur Frage der Schulzugehörigkeit des Avadānaśataka," *Zur Schulzugehörigkeit von Werken der Hīnayāna-Literatur*, hrsg. H. Bechert, Erster Teil (Göttingen: 1985) 219–224.

18. So L. Feer, *Avadāna-Çataka. Cent légendes bouddhiques*, Annales du musée guimet, T. XVIII (Paris: 1891) 185.

19. *Gilgit Manuscripts*, iii 2, 120.6ff.

20. For similar cognate constructions, see *Saṅghabhedavastu*, i, 59.18: *atithīnām atithipūjā kartavyā* (the reading here, however, is not absolutely certain; see 59, note b); *Gilgit Manuscripts*, iii 4, 177.9: *jñātīnāṃ vā jñātipūjā na kriyate*, etc.

21. For the Sanskrit text of the *Mahāparinirvāṇa-sūtra*, I refer throughout to the edition in E. Waldschmidt, *Das Mahāparinirvāṇasūtra. Text in Sanskrit und Tibetische, verglichen mit dem Pāli nebst einer Übersetzung der chinesischen Entsprechung im Vinaya der Mūlasarvāstivādins*, T. I–III (Berlin: 1950–1951). All references are to the paragraph numbers imposed on the text by Waldschmidt.

22. For the Tibetan text of the *Vinaya-kṣudraka-vastu*, I have used the *Derge* edition. The account of the death of Mahāprajāpatī is found at *Derge*, 10, 224.6ff.

23. E. B. Cowell and R. A. Neil, eds., *The Divyāvadāna. A Collection of Early Buddhist Legends* (Cambridge: 1886) 433.13–433.16; S. Mukhopadhyaya, ed., *The Aśokāvadāna. Sanskrit Text compared with Chinese Versions* (New Delhi: 1963) 132.7. The text is cited from the latter; for variants, see 132, n. 6.

24. *Saṅghabhedavastu*, i, 161.14.

25. Speyer, *Avadānaśataka*, i, 349.6, 352.16, 357.3, 361.14, 365.13, 369.18, 373.10, 377.12, 383.2, 387.5; ii, 5.17.

26. It is worth noting here that in the Sanskrit text of the injunction, singular pronominal and verbal forms are used, and it is clearly addressed to Ānanda alone.

27. . . . *āyuṣmān mahākāśyapo jñāto ma(hā)puṇyo lābhī cīvarapiṇḍapātaśayan(āsana)-gl(ā)napratyayabhaiṣajyapariṣkārāṇāṃ*, 49.17.

28. On Mahākāśyapa's place in the text as a whole, see Bareau, "La composition et les étapes de la formation progressive du mahāparinirvāṇasūtra ancien," 70ff; Bareau refers to the incidents involving Kāśyapa as "la série des récits inventés par les auteurs de *Vinayapiṭaka* pour glorifier Mahākāśyapa."

29. In dating the section in the *Milinda* in which our passage occurs, I follow P. Demiéville, "Les versions chinoises du milindapañha," *BEFEO* 24 (1924) 34–35; *Histoire du bouddhisme indien,* 465; I. B. Horner, *Milinda's Questions,* Vol. I (London: 1963) xxx–xxxi; cf. the discussion in K. R. Norman, *Pāli Literature. Including the Canonical Literature in Prakrit and Sanskrit of All the Hīnayāna Schools of Buddhism,* A History of Indian Literature, ed. J. Gonda, Vol. VII, Fasc. 2 (Wiesbaden: 1983) 110–113.

30. The text cited here and throughout is from V. Trenckner, ed., *The Milindapañho. Being Dialogues between King Milinda and the Buddhist Sage Nāgasena* (London: 1880) 177ff; the translation here is from Horner, *Milinda's Questions,* i, 249ff.

31. Horner, *Milinda's Questions,* i, 250, n. 1.

32. I. B. Horner, ed., *Madhuratthavilāsinī. The Commentary on Buddhavaṃsa of Bhadantācariya Buddhadatta Mahāthera* (London: 1946) vi.

33. Horner, *Madhuratthavilāsinī,* 99; I. B. Horner, *The Clarifier of the Sweet Meaning (Madhuratthavilāsinī). Commentary on the Chronicle of Buddhas (Buddhavaṃsa) by Buddhadatta Thera* (London: 1978) 142.

34. P. Masefield, *Divine Revelation in Pali Buddhism* (London: 1986) 1–36. Masefield's conclusions are not infrequently overstated and problematic, but he clearly shows that the Pāli texts will not support a simple equation of *sāvaka* and *bhikkhu.*

35. Cf. G. Schopen, "Filial Piety and the Monk in the Practice of Indian Buddhism," Ch. III above; Schopen, "On Monks, Nuns, and 'Vulgar' Practices," Ch. XI below.

CHAPTER VII

Burial *Ad Sanctos* and the Physical Presence of the Buddha in Early Indian Buddhism

A Study in the Archaeology of Religions

IT IS HARDLY REVOLUTIONARY to suggest that, had the academic study of religions started quite literally on the ground, it would have been confronted with very different problems. It would have had to ask very different questions, and it would have produced very different solutions. It would, in short, have become not the History of Religions—which was and is essentially text-bound—but the Archaeology of Religions. It would have used texts, of course, but only those that could be shown to have been actually known or read at a given place at a given time, or to have governed or shaped the kind of religious behavior that had left traces on the ground. In fact, texts would have been judged significant only if they could be shown to be related to what religious people actually did. This Archaeology of Religions would have been primarily occupied with three broad subjects of study then: religious constructions and architectures, inscriptions, and art historical remains. In a more general sense, though, it would have been preoccupied *not* with what small, literate, almost exclusively male and certainly atypical professionalized subgroups wrote, but rather, with what religious people of all segments of a given community actually did and how they lived.

All of this—since it did not happen—is, of course, totally academic. But—and this is the beauty of it—since the History of Religions is also totally academic, it still might. In fact, what I will present here is meant as a small push in that direction. In what follows, I want to look at Indian Buddhism on the ground. It is, however, very clear to me that, since this is something of a

---

Originally published in *Religion* 17 (1987): 193–225. Reprinted with stylistic changes with permission of Academic Press Limited.

first attempt,[1] the results that it will produce will necessarily be somewhat tentative. My data can and should be supplemented. My methods may have to be refined. My conclusions and interpretations may have to be modified and perhaps, in part, rejected. But it should be an interesting discussion, and once the discussion is engaged, I very much suspect it will become an unavoidable part of Buddhist Studies and, I hope, of the academic study of religions in general.

Starting on the Ground

If, then, our study of Indian Buddhism is to start on the ground, the first and most noticeable things we encounter are Buddhist sacred sites. Like so many sacred sites elsewhere, these sites immediately appear to be connected, at least in part, with the way in which the early Buddhist tradition disposed of and behaved toward its "very special dead."[2]

From two inscriptions of Aśoka we know that, already in the third century B.C.E., the Buddhism that he knew had developed two geographically fixed sacred sites. In fact, both of these sites are probably pre-Aśokan. One of them most certainly is. Although these two sites appear to us to be different in kind, Aśoka himself behaves in regard to both in exactly the same way. In both inscriptions when he initially describes what he did, he uses exactly the same wording: "King Priyadarśī . . . came in person (and) worshipped (here)" (*devānapiyena . . . attana āgācca mahīyite,* Rummindei; and *devānaṃpiyena . . . attana āgacca mahīyite,* Nigliva).[3] The places in question are Lumbini, the birthplace of the Buddha Śākyamuni, and the *stūpa* or monumental reliquary of the past Buddha Konākamana.[4] In regard to the latter, it should be noted that some years before "coming in person," Aśoka had the reliquary doubled in size (*thube dutiyaṃ vaḍḍhite).* In regard to the former, he also effected some construction at the site, and he describes it in an important way. He says:

> King Priyadarśī . . . came in person (and) worshipped, saying 'Here the Buddha was born, Śākyamuni,' he had a stone wall made and erected a stone pillar. Saying 'Here the Blessed One was born,' the village of Lummini was freed from tax and put at one-eighth.

> *devānapiyena . . . attana āgācca mahīyate hida buddhe jāte sakyamunī ti silāvigaḍabhī cā kālāpita silātthabhe ca ussapāpite hida bhagavaṃ jāte ti luṃminigāme ubbalike kaṭe aṭṭhabhāgiye ca.*

The statement "here the Blessed One was born," however, is almost certainly not Aśoka's, but an old ritual formula that was to be spoken by any individual upon arriving at the sacred site. It is almost certainly an actual quotation or direct paraphrase as is indicated, at least in part, by the particle *ti* (Skt. *iti*), although this has not always been understood.[5] This quotation, or direct paraphrase, makes it highly likely that Aśoka knew some version of a short text now preserved in somewhat different forms in the various versions of the *Mahāparinirvāṇa-sūtra.* The earliest actually datable Indian version—which is also closest to the wording found in Aśoka—has the Buddha say:[6]

> After I have passed away, monks, those making the pilgrimage to the shrines, honoring the shrines, will come [to these places], they will speak in this way: 'Here the Blessed One was born,' 'here the Blessed One attained the highest most excellent awakening,' etc.
>
> *āgamiṣyanti bhikṣavo mamātyayāc caityaparicārakāś caityavandakās* (Tib. *mchod rten bskor ba daṅ mchod rten la phyag 'tshal ba;* cf. Pāli, though not here, *cetiyacārika) ta evaṃ vakṣyanti / iha bhagavāñ jātaḥ /,* etc., 41.7–41.8.

The similarity in context and wording between the *Mahāparinirvāṇa* text and the Aśokan inscription is too close to be coincidental.

If Aśoka knew a version of the text that was similar to the one that has come down to us—and the fact that Aśoka quotes or paraphrases what he does indicates that some version of it was very old and predated him—then we are able to recover a number of other points. First, there is the question as to whether or not Aśoka's action was unique and purely individual in its motivation; a predated text would suggest otherwise. It would suggest that he was only doing what was prescribed for "a devout son of good family." The extant Sanskrit version of the old text says:

> Monks, there are these four places which are to be/must be visited by a devout son or daughter of good family during their life.
>
> *catvāra ime bhikṣavaḥ pṛthivīpradeśāḥ śrāddhasya kulaputrasya kuladuhitur vā yāvajjīvam anusmaraṇīyā* (but read with the ms. *abhigamanīyā*[7]) *bhavanti,* 41.5.

The Pāli text is, interestingly, even stronger. It says:

> Ānanda, there are these four places that a devout son of good family must do *darśan* of, and powerfully experience.
>
> *cattār' imāni ānanda saddhassa kulaputtassa dassanīyāni saṃvejanīyāni ṭhānāni.*

In both cases, there are future passive participles that blend into and frequently replace the imperative in both languages. Both versions make it clear that there must be direct contact with these places, and the verbs in the Pāli version are particularly striking.[8] It is worth noting that, despite the fact that it has dropped out of the English translations in particular, the final sections of the Pāli version of the *Mahāparinibbāna-sutta* are clearly marked with the notion and importance of *darśan,* and *darśan* is about direct, intimate contact with a living presence.[9] In fact, the idea that Bodh-Gayā was a place at which one did *darśan* must have persisted for a very long time. We find reference to it again in an inscription written in Devanāgarī that may be as late as the fifteenth century.[10]

It is also worth noting, in light of a common misconception, to whom these injunctions were directed. A *kulaputra,* "a son of good family," was no more the actual son of a family of a certain socioeconomic class than an *ārya* was a member of a specific racial group. "Son of good family" was simply an honorific title, a title applied as frequently to monks as to laymen. Note that in the Sanskrit version the injunction is delivered to monks and in the Pāli version to a specific monk. A few lines later in the same passage, the Sanskrit version replaces "devout son of good family" with two other titles: "one who makes the pilgrimage to the shrines," and an "honorer of shrines"—and we know from early inscriptions from Amarāvatī that the second of these, at least, was a monastic title.[11] The Pāli version makes an even more specific substitution. For its "devout son of good family," it substitutes later in the same passage "devout monks, nuns, laymen, and laywomen" (*saddhā bhikkhubhikkhuniyo upāsaka-upāsikāyo).*[12] In fact, all of the early epigraphical material confirms a predominately monastic preoccupation with Bodh-Gayā. The greater part of the surviving first century B.C.E. railing appears to have been the gift of a single nun; all of the Kushan and Gupta inscriptions in which the status of the donor is clear record the donations of monks—monks from as far away as Sri Lanka.[13]

Again, if we can assume that Aśoka knew a version of the old text that was similar to the oldest actually datable version we have, then we can make at least two other important statements about the early Buddhist conception of sacred sites. After having the Buddha say "After I have passed away, monks, those making the pilgrimage to the shrines . . . will come, they will speak in this way, . . . " that version has him then say:

> Those who during that time die here with a believing mind *in my presence,*
> all those who have *karma* still to work out, go to heaven.
>
> *atrāntarā ye kecit prasannacittā mamāntike kālaṃ kariṣyanti te sarve svargopagā ye kecit sopadhiśeṣāḥ,* 41.9 and 14.

First, it seems fairly clear that the monk redactor of the text thought that the Buddha was, after his *parinirvāṇa,* in some sense actually present at the places where he is known to have formerly been. The text is hard to read in any other way. Second, it is equally clear that the monk redactor of the text accepted as fact that a devout death that occurred within the range of this presence assured for the individuals involved—and these were both monks and laymen—rebirth in heaven. The Pāli version of the text, while it differs somewhat in articulation, confirms the essentials:

Indeed, Ānanda, whosoever being engaged in visiting the shrines with a devout mind dies, they all after the breakup of their body, after death, will be reborn in heaven.

ye hi keci ānanda cetiyacārikaṃ āhiṇḍantā pasannacittā kālaṃ karissanti sabbe te kāyassa bhedā param maraṇā sugatiṃ saggaṃ lokaṃ uppajjissantīti.

One cannot help but suspect that both of these ideas are somehow connected with a curious but consistent pattern clearly observable in the archaeological record of Buddhist sacred sites.[14]

An Archaeological Pattern

Everywhere in the Indian Buddhist archaeological record, the exact spot at which the former presence of the Buddha was marked had a clear and pronounced tendency to draw to it other deposits. Bodh-Gayā, although a much disturbed site, is a fine example. Crowded in a jumbled mass around the central point of the site, the exact point of former contact, are hundreds and thousands of small *stūpas* of various sizes, and what we see today is only the lowest strata. Above this strata, according to Cunningham, were at least:

> four tiers of similar monuments . . . carved stones of an early date were frequently found in the bases of the later monuments, and as the soil got silted up, the general level of the courtyard was gradually raised, and the later stūpas were built over the tops of the earlier ones in successive tiers of different ages . . . so great was the number of these successive monuments, and so rapid was the accumulation of stones and earth that the general level of the courtyard was raised about 20 feet above the floor of the Great Temple.[15]

However, it is not just at spots at which the former presence of the Buddha was marked that we find this pattern; exactly the same configuration occurred around *stūpas* containing relics. Here, the presence of the relic has had exactly the same effect that the presence of the point of former contact with the Buddha's physical body had. It has drawn to it a jumble of minor *stūpas* which crowd around it in an ever increasing state of disarray. The Dharmarājikā *Stūpa* in Taxila is a good, early example. Although, as Marshall himself admits, there is no surviving evidence to actually prove that the main *stūpa* is Mauryan, it is unlikely that it is much later; a second century B.C.E. date is not unlikely.[16] Within a century this main *stūpa* was surrounded by a tight circle of smaller *stūpas* crowding around it, some of which can be dated by coin finds more specifically to the first century B.C.E. A similar situation is found at Jauliāñ, a later but particularly well-preserved site that had not been overwhelmed by successive layers of building. Here, there is a central *stūpa* on a well-planned oblong plinth, but crowded around it are at least twenty-one smaller *stūpas* of varying size that, by their irregular placement, were clearly not a part of the original plan, and that were clearly added at different times wherever space allowed. When space ran out, these *stūpas* spilled down to a lower level where five more are found.[17] Likewise at Mīrpūr-Khas in Sind—a site both badly preserved and badly reported—around the main *stūpa* at the upper level was "a regular forest of smaller stūpas" that, much like at Bodh-Gayā, had been built directly on top of still earlier levels of still earlier minor *stūpas.* Cousens thinks that the main *stūpa* at least cannot be later than 400 C.E. and may be earlier.[18]

This clustering apparently occurred even at sites where it is no longer visible. The main *stūpa* at Sāñcī, for example, today rises somewhat awesomely straight out of the flat, clear ground that surrounds it. This, however, was not always the case. Marshall says "Time was when the Great Stūpa was surrounded, like all the more famous shrines of Buddhism, by a multitude of *stūpas* of varying sizes crowded together on the face of the plateau. The majority of these appear to have been swept away during the operations of 1881–1883, when the ground around the Great Stūpa was cleared for a distance of some 60 feet from the outer rail."[19] Only a very few of these smaller *stūpas* survived the destruction.

The Mortuary Associations of the Pattern

These smaller *stūpas* have, by habit, been taken to be votive *stūpas* and a number of imaginative scenarios created to explain their presence. But in a significant number of cases this simply cannot be so. These cannot be "votive" in any meaningful sense of the term because these smaller *stūpas* contain things, and the things they contain are of particular interest. All of the earliest smaller *stūpas* crowding around the Dharmarājikā described by Marshall contained "relic" deposits; that is, anonymous bones and ashes.[20] That these bones and ashes did not belong to Śākyamuni may be inferred from the fact attested almost everywhere, that, when his relics were deposited, they were accompanied with an inscriptional label of some sort indicating that they were his.[21] Moreover, his relic was already present in the main *stūpa.* Likewise at Jauliāñ, where only the bases of most of the smaller *stūpas* survive, still, at least three of these contained anonymous burial deposits or chambers that once contained such deposits.[22] At Mīrpūr-Khas "all the smaller stūpas of the upper level, which had been opened, had funerary associations, as they contained urns with pieces of bone. Below the floor of these stūpas were found some earlier minor stūpas, which included two of clay, one with bones."[23] Even at Sāñcī, at least one of the very few surviving "votive" *stūpas* contained such an anonymous burial deposit.[24]

The situation at Bodh-Gayā is a little more complex, but equally interesting. Cunningham says in regard to the "votive" *stūpas* found in such large numbers at Bodh-Gayā that "the pinnacles of the tall mediaeval stūpas were always more or less broken, and even the solid hemispheres of the earlier structural stūpas were mostly displaced."[25] That is to say that almost all of these *stūpas* had no "pinnacle" or elaborate finial. Cunningham attributes this "loss" to the construction of new structures on top of the old, but there is now evidence to suggest that his explanation may not be correct.

Excavations of the site at Ratnagiri in Orissa have revealed very similar "votive" *stūpas* in numbers equaling, if not surpassing, those found at Bodh-Gayā.[26] Here, it is even more clear than at Bodh-Gayā that a considerable number of these *stūpas* were portable; that is they were brought from somewhere else and deposited near the main *stūpa.* But here—to judge by the photographs—most of these *stūpas* appear never to have had pinnacles. Most appear to have a socket on top into which plugs of various shapes were inserted.[27] Indeed, a very considerable number of these so-called votive *stūpas* from both sites seem to correspond in form, at least, to what I-tsing in his *Record of The Buddhist Religion as Practised in India and the Malay Archipelago* called a "*kula.*" However, these *kulas* had a very specific use. I-tsing says: "They [Buddhist monks in India] sometimes build a thing like a stūpa for the dead, to contain his *śarīra* (or relics). It is called a '*kula,*' which is like a small stūpa, but without the cupola on it."[28] That at least some of the monolithic "votive" *stūpas* at Ratnagiri corresponded, not only in form but also in function, to I-tsing's *kula* is beyond doubt. Mitra, in referring to the smaller monolithic *stūpas* at Ratnagiri, says: "They are mostly votive in nature, with or without some inscribed texts in their cores, but in a few cases their funerary character was obvious, for they contained charred bone relics either within sockets plugged by stone lids or in urns."[29] It may not be these cases only that are funerary. If, as appears likely, the sockets on the top of these *stūpas* that previously have been taken to be meant for the insertion of some kind of finial were actually intended for and held ash or bone, then the funerary character of a very large number of these *stūpas* is established.[30] But there is still something more of interest in what Mitra says.

The Mortuary Associations of Inscribed *Dhāraṇīs*

Mitra refers here, and elsewhere, to the presence of "inscribed texts" in the cores of some of these *stūpas,* and the same thing has been noticed at Bodh-Gayā, Nālandā, Paharpur, and at other sites. A significant number of these texts are *dhāraṇīs,* at least in later *stūpas.* Although largely ignored, it has recently been shown that these are not *ad hoc* compositions but specific *dhāraṇīs* taken from a specific group of texts. And these texts tell us quite explicitly why these *dhāraṇīs* were placed in *stūpas.*[31] Although this group of texts is only now beginning to be studied, even a preliminary survey makes it clear that all of them are preoccupied with the problem of death and with either the procurement of a means to avoid rebirth in the hells or other unfortunate destinies, or with the release of those already born there. The latter, in fact, is one of the primary reasons for placing *dhāraṇīs* in *stūpas.* I cite here a typical example from the Tibetan translation of the *Raśmivimalaviśuddhaprabhādhāraṇī:*

> Moreover, if someone were to write this *dhāraṇī* in the name of another (who is deceased) and were to deposit it in a *stūpa* and earnestly worship it, then the deceased, being freed (by that) from his unfortunate destiny, would be reborn in heaven. Indeed, being reborn in the region of the Tuṣita gods, through the empowering of the Buddha he would (never again) fall into an unfortunate destiny.
>
> *yaṅ gaṅ la la źig gis gsaṅ sṅags yi ger bris pa gźan gyi miṅ nas smos te / mchod rten gyi naṅ du bcug la nan tan du mchod pa byas na śi ba gaṅ yin pa de naṅ soṅ gi gnas nas thar te mtho ris su skye bar 'gyur ro / yaṅ na dga 'ldan gyi lha'i ris su skye bar 'gyur te / saṅs rgyas kyi byin gyis brlabs kyis ṅan soṅ du ltuṅ bar mi 'gyur ro /*[32]

But these *dhāraṇīs* are also connected with Buddhist mortuary practices in a variety of other ways as well. Again, a typical example can be seen in the *Sarvakarmāvaraṇaviśodhanidhāraṇī:*

> If one, reciting (this *dhāraṇī*) over earth or sesame or white mustard or water, were to scatter it over the corpse, or if, having washed (the body), one afterwards were to either cremate it or deposit and preserve it in a *stūpa,* writing this *dhāraṇī* and attaching it to the top (or head), then the deceased—although already reborn in an unfortunate destiny—being freed, would without a doubt after seven days be reborn in a blessed heaven, or else he would be reborn through the power of his own vow.
>
> *sa 'am til lam yuṅs kar ram chu gaṅ yaṅ ruṅ ba la bzlas brjod byas te śi ba'i lus la gtor ram/khrus byas nas de'i 'og tu bsreg pa 'am/yaṅ na mchod rten gyi naṅ du bcug ste bźag la/rig sṅags kyaṅ bris te mgo bo la btags na de naṅ soṅ du skyes pa yaṅ źag bdun gyis gnod mi za bar thar te bde 'gro mtho ris kyi 'jig rten du skye bar 'gyur ba am/yaṅ na raṅ gi smon lam gyi dbaṅ gis skye bar 'gyur ro/*[33]

Finally, it is perhaps worth noting that similar, although more complicated, funerary rituals involving the same kinds of uses of written *dhāraṇīs* are to be found in the *Sarvadurgatipariśodhanatantra* published in 1983 by Skorupski—a text which, though a fully developed *tantra,* is clearly related both narratively and doctrinally to our group.[34]

That the *dhāraṇīs* found at Ratnagiri and elsewhere had funerary associations is suggested not only by the texts that they were taken from, but also by the fact that they are almost always found in exactly the same archaeological contexts as are the anonymous deposits of bone and ash. This again is particularly clear at Ratnagiri. In addition to the small *kula*-like monolithic *stūpas*, there are also a considerable number of small structural *stūpas* crowded around the main *stūpa* at Ratnagiri, and an even larger number of them still contained undisturbed their original deposits of anonymous bones. Mitra specifically mentions that in *Stūpas* 3, 4, 23, 24, 25, and 115—all structural—bone deposits were found; however, she then adds that "there is every reason to believe that there were many more *śārīrika stūpas* (i.e., those containing bone or ash). For, stray bones with or without reliquaries were found in the *Stūpa* area. Apparently, they must have got dislodged from structural *stūpas*, many of which are reduced to the lowest part of the base or platform."[35] All eight of the *dhāraṇīs* found at Ratnagiri—exactly like the anonymous bone deposits—were found in the cores of structural *stūpas*.[36]

The Archaeological Pattern Recapitulated

The archaeological record of Buddhist sacred sites exhibits, then, from the very beginning of our actual evidence, at least one curious but consistent pattern. This pattern, significantly, is most distinctly and directly visible at our very earliest undisturbed sites. The Dharmarājikā at Taxila, which dates to the second century B.C.E., is a fine example. But there are also clear indications that the same pattern held at other very early sites like Sāñcī and Bhārhut until these sites, by different agents, were irrevocably altered or virtually destroyed. It continues to hold through the fourth and fifth centuries C.E.—for example, at Jauliāñ and Mīrpūr-Khas—and is found at Ratnagiri still in its full disorderly effervescence in the tenth and twelfth centuries. What we find is a large central structure that marks one of two things: either the presence of a spot that was formerly in direct contact with the physical body of the Buddha, or—more commonly—the presence of an actual physical piece of that body. Around this structure, closely packed, in increasing disorder, are a large number—increasingly so—of other smaller structures that frequently contain anonymous bones or bone ash or other items connected with mortuary deposits. That these smaller structures were added at different times is apparent from the fact that they are not part of any discernible original or ordered plan. In fact, they frequently appear to violate any preexisting orderly plan of the sites. The only concern that appears to have governed their placement was an apparent desire to have them as close as possible to the main structure. All of this would suggest, in turn, that these mortuary deposits were purposely brought here, again at different times, from somewhere else. In fact, a considerable number of the smallest of these structures were obviously portable.[37] This, in outline, is what we see. What we want to know, of course, is what it means.

Some Archaeological Parallels

It is worth noting, however briefly, some remarkably similar archaeological configurations found elsewhere. In at least some of these other instances, we know a considerable amount about the ideational systems that produced these parallel configurations, and they are, therefore, at least suggestive of what the configuration in Buddhist India might have meant.

Ariès condensed into a few sentences a large body of archaeological literature that is of interest to us. He says:

> Over the saint's tomb a basilica would be built . . . Christians sought to be buried close to this structure. Diggings in the Roman cities of Africa or Spain reveal an extraordinary spectacle concealed by subsequent urban growth: piles of stone sarcophagi in disorder, one on top of the other, several layers high, especially around the walls of the apse, close to the shrine of the saint.[38]

This, again according to Ariès, "is what one finds in Tipasa, Hippo, and Carthage. The spectacle is just as striking in Ampurias, in Catalonia . . . [and] . . . the same situation is found in our Gallo–Roman cities, but it is no longer visible to the naked eye and has to be reconstructed beneath the successive deposit of history."[39]

Notice that, apart from the technical vocabulary ("basilica," "sarcophagi," etc.), Ariès' description of the archaeological record in the Roman cities of Africa, Spain, and France could almost serve equally well as a description of what was seen at Bodh-Gayā, Taxila, and other South Asian sites. Another site of interest to us differs from these two groups in only one significant way: the successive waves of mortuary deposits, rather than being heaped one on top of the other, have spread out in horizontal layers to cover an immense area, to produce in effect what has been called "the greatest cemetery of Japan." This is the cemetery on Mount Kōyasan. Here, a dense jumble of graves and markers covering many acres crowds around the tomb of Kōbō Daishi, the eighth or ninth century monk who, among a multitude of other accomplishments, founded Shingon Buddhism. Casal notes that "the number of graves . . . is indeed very large . . . But not all the graves contain a body or its ashes; it suffices to bury a bone, or even some hair or a tooth. The important thing is that one's symbol be interred near the great teacher. . . ."[40]

It is interesting to note that the ideas that produced the configuration of crowding or clustering of mortuary deposits around a central structure in both the Roman cities of Africa and Spain and on Mount Kōyasan appear to be reducible—in both cases—to two basic sets. The first set is perhaps the easier to describe because there is an established vocabulary that can be applied to it. The ideas grouped here are essentially eschatological: in the Christian case, they concern the Doctrine of the Resurrection of the Dead; in the case of Kōyasan, they concern the coming of Maitreya, the Future Buddha. The Christian case can be illustrated by some remarks of Geary: "Early Christians took literally Christ's promise of the resurrection and thus expected that on the last day the martyrs' physical bodies would be taken up again by their owners . . . Christians believed that physical proximity to these bodies was beneficial, and that those buried near a saint's tomb would be raised up with the saint on the day of judgment."[41] Similar ideas were also certainly associated with the tomb of Kōbō Daishi, although one might dispute the exact wording of those scholars who have described them. Lloyd, for example, says: "The Shingon are firm believers in Maitreya . . . It is their conviction that the body of Kōbō Daishi, which never decays, is awaiting the advent of Maitreya in his tomb at Kōya San, and Shingonists often send the bones of their dead, after cremation, to Kōya San, so as to be near to Kōbō at the resurrection, which will take place when Maitreya makes his appearance."[42]

The eschatological set, although clearly present in both cases, is only one of two sets and probably is not the most important. The second set—again present in both cases—is based on the notion that the tomb or shrine contains an actual living presence. It was thought, to quote Hakeda, that "Kukai had not died but had merely entered into eternal Samādhi and was still quite alive on Mt. Kōya as a savior to all suffering people."[43] Here, there is no preoccupation with some distantly future eschatological event. Burial in close physical proximity to the living presence, in fact, effects an immediate result: it assures that the individual whose bones or ashes are placed there will gain rebirth in paradise, in the Pure Land of Amitābha, in Sukhāvatī.[44] Christian notions that fall into this second set are much more richly documented. "It was commonly believed," says Wilson, ". . . that, far from inhabiting any distant heaven, the saint remained present in his shrine. Delehaye wrote that, for those who followed his cult, St. Menas 'resided, invisible, in his basilica' in the Mariut, near Alexandria."[45] Here too, eschatological notions are largely absent, and a different set of functions comes into play. Ariès first quotes St. Paulinus, who had had the body of his son buried beside the Saints at Aecola. Paulinus writes: "We have sent him [his dead son] to the town of Complutum so that he may lie with the martyrs in the union of the grave, and so that from the blood of the saints he may draw that virtue that refines our souls like fire." Ariès himself then adds the following observation: "We see here that the saints not only grant protection from the creatures of Tartarus, they also communicate to the deceased who is associated with them a little of their virtue, and post-mortem, redeem his sins."[46]

The Buddhist Conception of Relics as "Living Entities"

We know, then, that the above ideas produced the essentially similar archaeological configurations that are to be seen at Carthage and Kōyasan, and we might well expect that similar thinking produced the same configuration at Bodh–Gayā and Taxila. In India, however, the first set seems not to have been operational. There is no evidence of any kind of a connection between the presence of the relic—whether it be a contact relic, like a spot of earth, or an actual bone—and any eschatological event.[47] In fact, if there is any eschatological thinking in India, it takes a decidedly different form. This would seem to suggest that if the configuration found at Bodh–Gayā and Taxila was produced by ideas similar to those that produced Carthage and Kōyasan, then the ideas involved would probably belong not to the first set, but to the second. But if this were the case, we might expect to find at least some indications that the relic in early Buddhist India was thought of as an actual living presence. And we have some evidence for this.

The first piece of evidence that might be brought forward is the old text we started with, which is now preserved in the various versions of the *Mahāparinirvāṇa-sūtra.* Notice that the redactor of the Sanskrit version seems clearly to have thought that the Buddha, although dead, was somehow actually present at the places where he was formerly known to have been. Notice too that he explicitly indicates that a death in physical proximity to that actual presence produces specific and positive results, that it, like burial near a Saint or close to Kōbō Daishi, resulted in "heaven." In other words, death at Bodh–Gayā and burial *ad sanctos* at Carthage and Kōyasan have exactly the same result, although the heaven in each case is somewhat differently appointed. In fact, the key concept in this old text—only very slightly extended—is probably able to account by itself for what is seen in the archaeological record of several Buddhist sacred sites in India. The extension would only be from *death* to *deposition of the already dead* in close physical proximity to that actual presence.[48]

However, strictly speaking, the old text is referring only to geographically fixed points of former contact with the physical body of the Buddha: Bodh–Gayā, Sārnāth, and so on. The text says he is present at these places, and yet the archaeological pattern appears to indicate burial *ad sanctos* not just at these sites, but also at sites where there is only a bodily relic. This archaeological evidence, if we are correct in our interpretation of it, would suggest that, at these sites too, the Buddha was thought to be actually present and alive. There is, again, some evidence that would indicate this to be the case.

One of the earliest Indian inscriptions after Aśoka is written on the broken lid of a relic casket that came from Shinkot. It records, very laconically, the deposition of a relic of the Buddha Śākyamuni in the reign of the Indo-Greek king, Menander, who ruled in the second century B.C.E. All are agreed—Majumdar, Konow, Sircar, Narain, and Lamotte[49]—that it said on the rim:

> . . . [on] the 14th day of the month Kārttika, the relic of the Blessed One Śākyamuni which is endowed with life was established.
> *kārttikasya {māsasya} divase 14 prāṇasametaṃ {śarīraṃ} {bhagavataḥ śākyamuneḥ} pratiṣṭhāpitam.*[50]

Similar wording to this also occurs on the inner face of the lid:

> [This is] a relic of the Blessed One Śākyamuni which is endowed with life.
>
> *prāṇasametaṃ śarīraṃ bhagavataḥ śākyamuneḥ.*

What this seems to mean is, of course, what Konow and Lamotte have already said: "The relics were looked upon as living entities"; "la relique corporelle . . . c'est un être vivant 'doué de souffle.' " However, neither of these authors noted—perhaps because it did not seem germane to their particular point—that this is the earliest actually datable reference to the relics of the historical Buddha, and that, in fact, the conception of the relic as "un être vivant" is the earliest actually attestable conception that we have.

Other early sources indicate that the physical relics of Śākyamuni were endowed with more than just "life" or "breath." They were "informed," "parfumée," "saturated," "pervaded," "imbued" with just those characteristics that defined the living Buddha. Statements to this effect are found in a wide variety of sources. The Inscription of Senavarma is a good example. This inscription, which dates to the early first century C.E., is "la plus longue des inscriptions Kharoṣṭhī jusqu' ici connues," and has proven to be difficult.[51] The portion which concerns us, however, is clear. Senavarma says in part:

> I establish these relics which are infused with morality, infused with concentration, wisdom, emancipation, and knowledge and vision.
>
> *ima dhadu śila(pari)bhavita samasiprañavimutiñaṇadra(śa)paribhavita . . . pratiṭhavemi.*

The list of faculties and qualities given here looks very much as though it may have been intended for, or is perhaps a haplography of what the Pāli tradition calls the five *sampadās* or "attainments" and, of course, normally only a living person can be "infused" with such "attainments." Yet another Kharoṣṭhī inscription, which can be dated more exactly to 25 to 26 C.E., has a similar characterization of the relics of Śākyamuni. Here, the relics are said to be *śilaparibhavida sama(s)iparibhavemtu ·prañaparibhavida* or "infused with morality, infused with concentration, infused with wisdom."[52] That is to say, the relics themselves were thought to retain—to be "infused with," impregnated with—the qualities that animated and defined the living Buddha.

Something of the same vocabulary found in these two inscriptions is also found in Aśvaghoṣa's *Buddhacarita.* In fact, both of these inscriptions and Aśvaghoṣa may have been closely contemporaneous. Johnston dates the latter to "between 50 B.C. and 100 A.D. with a preference for the first half of the first century A.D."[53] It is not, however, just his date that makes Aśvaghoṣa important for us. Both of our inscriptions record the gifts of laymen, although they, or the redactors of their inscriptions, had some apparent familiarity with accepted Buddhist doctrines.[54] Aśvaghoṣa, on the other hand, was most decidedly a monk, an extremely literate and very widely learned monk, and his conception of relics is important because of that: they are the conceptions of a monk exceptionally well-versed in Buddhist doctrine.[55] In the passage that concerns us, Aśvaghoṣa says, for example, that the relics of Śākyamuni, like "the sphere (*dhātu*) of the chief of the gods (*Brahmā*) in heaven at the end of the aeon," cannot be destroyed by the final cosmic conflagration, that these relics "cannot be carried even by Viṣṇu's Garuda," that "though cool, they burn our minds" (*bsil ba yin kyaṅ bdag cag rnams kyi yid rnams sregs).* But Aśvaghoṣa also uses less overwrought expressions, like those found in our inscriptions. The relics, he says, are "full of virtue" (*dge legs gaṅ ba*), and "informed (*paribhāvita?*) with universal benevolence (*maitrī*)" (*byams pas yoṅs su rnam par bsgoms pa).*[56]

There are also other witnesses, at least one of which is hostile. The *Aṣṭasāhasrikāprajñāpāramitā* is one of the earliest Mahāyāna texts translated into Chinese, and some version of it was very probably contemporaneous with both our inscriptions and Aśvaghoṣa.[57] Like the *Suvarṇaprabhāsottama,* the *Buddhabalādhāna,* the *Saddharmapuṇḍarīka,* and a number of other, later texts, it is in part preoccupied with sometimes sustained arguments intended to devalue—if not altogether deny the value—of relics.[58] In fact, it devotes large parts of at least three chapters to such arguments. As a part of these arguments, the *Aṣṭasāhasrikā* on two occasions concedes that there are good reasons for worshipping relics, and, in so doing, uses much the same vocabulary as is found in our two inscriptions and in Aśvaghoṣa's *Buddhacarita.* It is stated quite explicitly that:

> the relics of the Tathāgata are worshipped because they are saturated with the Perfection of Wisdom.
>
> *api tu khalu punar bhagavaṃs tāni tathāgataśarīrāṇi prajñāpāramitāparibhāvitatvāt pūjāṃ labhyante.*[59]

The final instance that we might cite here where relics are said to be "saturated" or "infused" or "pervaded" with specific qualities comes from the Fourth Book of the *Milindapañha*, a book which Demiéville has shown was almost certainly added to the *Milinda* in Ceylon at a date not much earlier than the fifth century C.E.[60] It is, therefore, noteworthy that despite the fact that it is separated from the Senavarma Inscription by 500 years, the *Milindapañha*—as Fussman has already pointed out—contains an almost exact verbal parallel to that inscription. Here too, the relic is described as "infused with morality, concentration, wisdom, emancipation, and the knowledge and vision of emancipation" (*sīlasamādhipaññāvimuttivimuttiñāṇadassanaparibhāvitaṃ dhāturatanañ*).

Each of these passages comes from a distinctly different kind of source, and yet they all use exactly the same participle, *paribhāvita*, in characterizing the relics of the Buddha. The same participle is, of course, used elsewhere, and its characteristic usages are worth noting. One of the most common usages of the term in canonical Pāli, oddly enough, has to do with chicken's eggs. In a frequently found simile, eggs are described as "sat on" (*adhisayita*), "heated" (*parisedita*), and "pervaded or infused" (*paribhāvita*) by a hen. It is this that makes the eggs "live." In fact, the point of the simile is that, if this is not done properly, the chicks do not live.[61] Apart from this, the term is more usually applied to living persons. A particularly interesting usage occurs twice in the *Sarvatathāgatādhiṣṭhānasattvāvalokanabuddhakṣetrasandarśanavyūha-sūtra* from Gilgit. Here, the negative *aparibhāvitakāya*, "having an unpervaded or uninvigorated body" is twice paired with *alpāyuṣka*, "having little life."[62] In the *Mahāvastu* [Senart ed., Vol. i, 153.12], *bodhisattvas*, like relics in Aśvaghoṣa, are said to be "completely saturated with virtue" (*kuśalaparibhāvita*); likewise in *Milindapañha* 361.23, those who fulfill the ascetic practices, like the relics in our two inscriptions, are said to be "saturated with the lovely and excellent unparalleled sweet perfume of morality" (*sīlavarapavara-asamasucigandha-paribhāvito hoti*). Again like relics in Aśvaghoṣa, a *bodhisattva* is said in the *Saddharmapuṇḍarīka* [Kern-Nanjio ed., 3.1] to "have his body and mind saturated with benevolence" (*maitrīparibhāvitakāyacitta*). From these and other passages, it seems evident that *paribhāvita* implies "filled or infused with life," "invigorated," "strengthened or made strong," "impregnated," "animated," and that, according to our passages, is what relics are.

The *Stūpa* as a "Legal Person"

A set of three imprecatory inscriptions on the gateways of *Stūpa* no. 1 at Sāñcī also deserves our attention. The substance of these three inscriptions—which are very much alike and which are as early as at least the first century B.C.E.—is fully expressed in the following passage from the inscription on the West Gateway:

> He who dismantles, or causes to be dismantled; the stone work from this Kākaṇāva [i.e., the old name for the *Stūpa* at Sāñcī], or causes it to be transferred to another house of the teacher, he shall go to the [same terrible] state as those who commit the five sins that have immediate retribution.
>
> *pac-ānatariya-kārakāna gati{ṃ} gacheya yo ito kākaṇāvāto selakame upā{ḍeya} upāḍ{ā}peya vā anaṃ vā ācariyakulaṃ saṃkāmeyā. . . .*[63]

There are two points that should be noted here. First, the *Stūpa* or reliquary at Sāñcī appears to be implicitly classified as an *ācariya-kula,* a "house of the teacher" [i.e., the Buddha]. Bühler long ago suggested that this is a comparable expression, a parallel expression, to the common Indian term for a temple, *devakula,* "a house of the *deva.*" But if this is the case, we know that *devakula* was taken quite literally, that is, it was the place where the *deva* lived, where he was actually and powerfully present, and it is rather unlikely that an *ācariya-kula* would have been conceived of any differently.[64]

The second point to be noted here is that these inscriptions indicate that a set of important ideas known only from later literary sources was already operational at Sāñcī in the first century B.C.E. In a very useful study of the material found in the various monastic codes (*vinayas*) dealing with "la construction et le culte des *stūpas*" Bareau noted that "comme toute personne, le *stūpa* a le droit de possession . . . et ce droit doit être protégé." He goes on to say, for example:

> Les Sarvāstivādin parlent aussi des biens inépuisables du *stūpa,* qui sont inaliénables. Les biens qui sont donnés en offrande au *stūpa* ne peuvent être utilisés à d'autres fins. On ne doit pas les mélanger avec les biens de la Communauté des quatre directions, ni avec les biens consistant en nourriture, ni avec les biens à partager.[65]

From these same texts, it is clear that the property belonging to the *stūpa* or reliquary included real property such as land in the form of gardens with productive fruit and flowering trees and ponds.

What Bareau did not note was that "le droit de possession" of the *stūpa* was referred to and elaborated in sources other than the *Vinayas.* These other sources are important for two reasons: first, they are still later than the *Vinayas* and, therefore, indicate the long continuity of these ideas; second, at least some of these sources must be considered, again, as hostile witnesses since they are Mahāyāna *Sūtras,* the majority of which perhaps are at best ambivalent in regard to the value of relics and *stūpas,* if they are not explicitly engaged in actually devaluing them.[66] The number of these references in Mahāyāna literature is also impressive. Edgerton, under the term *staupika,* cites two passages from the *Śikṣāsamuccaya,* two from the *Bodhisattvabhūmi,* and one each from the *Rāṣṭrapāla* and *Gaṇḍavyūha.*[67] However, there are at least four more in the *Śikṣā* and two also now available in the *Upālipariprcchā.*[68]

The strength of the ideas concerning the *stūpa's* rights of ownership is clear from a long passage from the *Ratnarāśi-sūtra* quoted in the *Śikṣā* (56.9). The substance of this passage is this: although funds of the local order—if there is a surplus and unanimous agreement—can be used to make up a deficit in the ecumenical order (normally such funds must be kept strictly separated), funds belonging to the *stūpa,* even if there is an excess, must never be handed over to either the local or ecumenical order (*yadi punaḥ kāśyapa kiyad bahur api staupiko lābho bhavet / sa vaiyāvṛtyakareṇa na saṃghe na cāturdiśasaṃghe upanāmayitavyaḥ*). The text, in fact, goes so far as to say that "a robe (or piece of cloth) given to the *stūpa must* be allowed to go to ruin on the *stūpa* through the wind and sun and rain," that such a robe cannot be exchanged for a sum of money, and that nothing that belongs to a *stūpa* can have a commercial price set on it (*yac ca stūpe cīvaraṃ niryātitaṃ bhavati tat tatraiva tathāgatacaitye vātātapavṛṣṭibhiḥ parikṣayaṃ gacchatu / na punaḥ staupikaṃ cīvaraṃ hiraṇyamūlyena parivartayitavyaṃ / na hi staupikasya kaścid argho*).[69] The reason given for this is of some interest: "Whatever belongs to a *stūpa,* even if it is only a single fringe that is given . . . that itself is a sacred object for the world together with its gods" (*yā staupikā antaśa ekadaśāpi . . . niryātitā bhavati / sā sadevakasya lokasya caityaṃ*). That is to say, an object given to a *stūpa* becomes itself a sacred object (*caitya*). However, we know that there is only one way for objects to become sacred in a Buddhist context: they must be owned or used by a sacred *person.* In fact, the Chinese version of the above passage translates *staupika* or "belonging to the *stūpa*" by characters which mean "belonging to the Buddha."[70]

We should also notice that some of these Mahāyāna texts—exactly like the gateway inscriptions at Sāñcī—explicitly associate or equate taking property belonging to the *stūpa* with "the five acts with immediate retribution"; for example, this is true of the *Ākāśagarbha-sūtra* and the *Upālipariprcchā.*[71] This, if nothing else, indicates the extremely serious nature of such an act, as these five acts are the most serious offenses known to the Indian Buddhist tradition. However, the association of theft or destruction of property belonging to a *stūpa* with this set of five offenses is probably more than just a way of indicating its terrible seriousness. "The five acts with immediate retribution" are: taking the life of one's mother; taking the life of one's father; taking the life of an *arhat;* causing a division within the *Saṅgha;* and wounding or causing physical harm to a Buddha. Four of the five, then, have to do with seriously harming living persons of rank. That harm done to a *stūpa* or reliquary is explicitly equated with acts of this kind would suggest, again, that the *stūpa* was cognitively classified as a "living person of rank." If this were not the case, it would be difficult to understand the extreme seriousness with which such harm was viewed.

In noting that the *stūpa* or reliquary "comme toute personne" had the right to, and did in fact, possess personal real property, and in noting that the ideas surrounding this right were both old and markedly tenacious, it is of some interest to point out that we find ourselves again in front of a phenomenon noted elsewhere. In discussing the "Thefts of Relics in the Central Middle Ages," Geary repeatedly insists that "in a very basic sense, men in the Central Middle Ages perceived relics as being alive . . . relics were actually the saints themselves, continuing to live among men." One body of evidence he uses to establish this view parallels exactly at least a part of what we have just seen in regard to the Buddhist *stūpa.* He says, "Relics even had legal rights; they received gifts and offerings made specifically to them and owned churches and monasteries, which were technically the property of the saints who lay in their crypts."[72]

The Functional Equivalence of the Relic and the Living Buddha

If Buddhist reliquaries and the relics they contained were legal persons, that is to say, if they had and exercised the rights of living persons, and if harm done to them was explicitly equated with harm done to living persons of rank, then the reverse of the second equation in particular should also hold: honor or worship done to them should be explicitly equated with honor or worship done to living persons. And so it is. An instance of exactly this equation is found, for example, in a text now preserved in the Gilgit *Mūlasarvāstivādin-vinaya.* which has the appearance of being very old. This text, in fact, seems to reflect a period prior to the development of the monumental *stūpa* when relics were simply buried in the ground at specific places.[73]

The text says the Buddha in company with Ānanda went to a place called Toyikā. When he arrived there, there was a *brahmin* plowing his field. This gentleman saw the Buddha and said to himself, "If I approach the Blessed One Gautama and pay honor to him, my work will suffer; but if I do not approach him and pay honor to him, my merit will suffer. What can I do to avoid both a loss of work and a loss of merit?" He decided—being a clever *brahmin*—to remain where he was, but to pay honor to Gautama from a distance, which he did still—as the text pointedly notes—holding his goad. Gautama, of course, was not terribly impressed with this expedient—the text calls it an *upāya*—and he said, in part, to Ānanda:

> 'Mistaken, Ānanda, is this brahmin. Had he approached this spot then when he did honor here, he would himself have known "on this spot the undisturbed mass of relics of the Perfect Buddha Kāśyapa is present." Had he approached I would have been honored by him, indeed honor would have been done by him to two Perfect Buddhas. Why is that? Because, Ānanda, at this spot the undisturbed mass of relics of the Perfect Buddha Kāśyapa is present.'

> *kṣūṇa ānanda eṣa brāhmaṇaḥ / {anenopakramyāsmin pradeśe abhivādane kṛte} sati pratyātmaṃ jñānadarśanaṃ pravartate / etasmin pradeśe kāsyapasya samyaksaṃbuddhasyāvikopito 'sthisaṃghātas tiṣṭhatīti / aham anenopakramya vandito bhaveyam / evam anena dvābhyāṃ samyaksaṃbuddhābhyāṃ vandanā kṛtā bhavet / tatkasya hetoḥ / asminn ānanda pradeśe kāśyapasya samyaksaṃbuddhasyāvikopito 'sthisaṃghātas tiṣṭhati /*[74]

The implications here are that there is no distinction between a living Buddha and a collection of relics—both make the sacred person equally present as an object of worship, and the presence of either makes available the same opportunity to make merit. In case his reader missed the point, the redactor of the text adds a set of verses that make it explicit in slightly different terms:

> He who would worship a living (Buddha), and he who would worship one who has entered final *nirvāṇa,* having made their minds equally devout—between them there is no distinction of merit.
>
> *tiṣṭhantaṃ pūjayed yaś ca yaś cāpi parinirvṛtam / samaṃ cittaṃ prasādyeha nāsti puṇyaviśeṣatā /* 78.8.

That such ideas were both common and durable would seem to be suggested by the fact that this same verse, or close variants of it, occurs in what Waldschmidt calls a "sondertext" of the Sanskrit *Mahāparinirvāṇa-sūtra,* in the *Caityapradakṣiṇa-gāthā* manuscripts of which have been found at Gilgit, in the "Schenkungsformular" manuscript from Turkistan published by Lüders, and in the Khotanese text of the *Pradakṣiṇa-sūtra.*[75] Yet another version of this verse has come down to us in the work of the learned Monk Aśvaghoṣa:

> The learned should know the qualities of the Buddha, and that if one worships with similar devotion the Seer when he is present, or if one worships his relic after he has entered final Nirvāṇa, the result is the same.
>
> *draṅ sroṅ bźugs ba la ni mchod pa sbyaṅ nas sam / yoṅs su mya ṅan 'das pa'i gduṅ la phyag byas nas / yid kyi daṅ ba mñam na 'bras bu mñan pa ste / saṇs rgyas yon tan rnams ni mkhas rnams śes par mdzod /*[76]

Notice that all of these texts emphasize that the individual is to "make his mind equally devout" in regard to the actual presence and the relic (*samaṃ cittaṃ prasādya; same cittaprasāde hi; sems dge ba ni mtshuṅs 'gyur na; yid kyi daṅ ba mñam na;* etc.). That is to say, one is to adopt the same frame of mind toward the relic as is adopted in regard to the living presence. For the believer they are to be taken as the same. They have the same function. They make possible the same result.

It is interesting too to note that one of the clearest expressions of these ideas is to be found in the *Mahāvaṃsa,* the fifth century Pāli chronicle of

Buddhism in Sri Lanka written by the Monk Mahānama. The passage concerned is supposed to be the record of a conversation which took place in the third century B.C.E. between the Monk Mahinda, who is credited with the conversion of Sri Lanka, and the reigning Sri Lankan king, Devānaṃpiyatissa. Mahinda, who according to the *Dīpavaṃsa* is on the verge of leaving Sri Lanka, complains to the king: "For a long time O King, we have not seen the Perfect Buddha, the Teacher. We have lived without a Master. There is nothing here for us to worship"; to which the king replies: "But, sir, did you not tell me that the Perfect Buddha has entered *nirvāṇa?*" The Monk Mahinda answers—and his answer perfectly condenses much of our discussion—"when the relics are seen [or: are present], the Buddha is seen [or: is present]" (*ciradiṭṭho hi saṃbuddho satthā no manujādhipa / anāthavāsaṃ vasimha natthi no pūjiyaṃ idha // bhāsittha nanu bhante me: saṃbuddho nibbuto iti / āha dhātusu diṭṭhesu diṭṭho hoti jino iti*). The king, of course, promises to build a *stūpa,* and Mahinda appoints another monk to fly to India to procure relics.[77]

The Public Value Placed on Relics

Before our findings up to this point are summarized, it is worth looking briefly at one final piece of evidence, not because it provides further indications that the relic was thought of as a living presence—that, I think, is already sufficiently clear—but because it is an early piece of evidence for what we might call, in the absence of a better term, the communal or public value placed on relics. The evidence in question is an old tradition concerning what has come to be called the War of the Relics. Already in the oldest surviving Buddhist art—at Sāñcī, Bhārhut, Amarāvatī, and in Gandhāra—we have illustrations of this episode,[78] although the narrative details are now known only from later texts. After the cremation of the Buddha, the Mallas of Kusinārā "surrounded the bones of the Exalted One in their council hall with a lattice work of spears, and with a rampart of bows." Seven other groups representing distinct and apparently competing political entities also came, however, armed for war to claim a share of the relics. They were initially refused. Interestingly enough, imminent conflict was avoided only by the intervention of a brahmin who pointed out the incongruency of waging war over the remains of one who was a teacher of forbearance (*khantivāda*).[79]

We might note that this old tradition, however the details might fall, forcefully articulates in the strongest possible contemporary political idiom the extreme value placed on these remains. Bareau has noted:

> Qu'elle [this tradition] raconte un fait historique ou qu'elle soit pure légende, peu importe ici, l'essentiel pour notre propos est que . . . les fidèles, dont les hagiographes reflètent l'esprit, ont cru à la réalité de cet épisode,

> ont regardé comme parfaitement vraisemblable que la dévotion de leurs prédécesseurs ait poussé ces derniers à se disputer les restes corporels du bienheureux, les armes à la main. Cela prouve qu'au temps où la première version de ce récit fut composée, les fidèles trouvaient normal et même édifiant un tel excès de zèle . . .[80]

And, but for one small detail, Bareau's remarks are very much to the point: unless he wants to assert that it was written by a layman—and I doubt that he would—"la première version de ce récit," or any other for that matter, can tell us nothing directly about some hypothetical and generalized "fidèles." What it can and does prove, however, is what "les hagiographes" who composed it—almost certainly monks—"trouvaient normal et même édifiant." This, of course, is a very different matter.

Conclusions

Several different kinds of data have been presented here. There are the archaeological data that show a seemingly characteristic, repeatedly encountered configuration of material remains at Buddhist sacred sites. This configuration consists of a central structure marking either a spot known to have been formerly in direct contact with the physical body of the Buddha, or housing an actual part of that physical body. Around this central structure are crowded in increasing disarray large numbers of smaller structures, a considerable number of which contain anonymous mortuary deposits—bone and ash—or other objects known to be associated with mortuary practices. These mortuary deposits have been purposely brought and placed here at different times. They do not form a part of an original or ordered plan.

In addition, an old literary tradition exists that indicates that the Buddha was thought to be actually present at certain spots with which he was known to have had direct physical contact. There is also a whole series of epigraphical and literary documents that prove that the physical relic of the Buddha was thought to be possessed of "life" or "breath," and to be impregnated with the characteristics that defined and animated the living Buddha, that show that the relic or the reliquary that contained it had and exercised the right to own personal property—that it was legally a person—and that it was cognitively classified with living persons of rank. Some of these literary documents, at least one of which is very old, also establish that the presence of the relic was thought to be the same thing as the presence of the actual Buddha, that the two were religiously the same, and that the same behavior was required in regard to both.

This, in turn, means that the central structures at both types of Buddhist sacred sites contained or located the actual living presence of the Buddha, and it was this presence that drew to it the secondary mortuary deposits and a host of subsidiary structures.

Another part of the same old literary tradition proves that it was thought that a death in the presence of the Buddha resulted in rebirth in heaven. In addition, there are the parallels in conception and mortuary practice in the Roman cities of Spain and Africa and on Mount Kōyasan.

We have, it would seem, reason to believe that Indian Buddhists also practiced and believed in some form of what in the Latin West was called *depositio ad sanctos,* and that—regardless of what some canonical texts might occasionally suggest and what some scholastic texts definitely state—the Buddha was and continued to be an actual living presence in the midst of the Buddhist community.

Notes

I would like to thank my colleagues Gérard Fussman and Patrick Olivelle for their helpful comments on different drafts of this paper.

1. There have been other attempts to draw archaeological and art historical sources into the mainstream of Buddhist Studies, most notably those of P. Mus. See the bibliography in G. Moréchand, "Paul Mus (1902–1969)," *BEFEO* 57 (1970) 25–42, but note that Mus' *Barabuḍur. Esquisse d'une histoire du bouddhisme fondée sur la critique archéologique des textes* (Hanoi: 1935), deux tomes, has since been reprinted by Arno Press (New York: 1978), both volumes in one. There are, however, some very real problems with Mus' work. He ignored Indian epigraphy—which is surprising in light of the work he did in Indo-China—and he was very little concerned with chronology. He also used textual material very indiscriminately, citing texts of widely different periods and widely different provenances without ever asking if this material could ever have been known to any actual Buddhist in the premodern period. In religious studies, generally, the last published work of S. G. F. Brandon was also clearly moving in the direction of what I would call the Archaeology of Religions; see Brandon's *Man and God in Art and Ritual. A Study of Iconography, Architecture and Ritual Action as Primary Evidence of Religious Belief and Practice* (New York: 1975).

2. The category "the very special dead" is, of course, borrowed from Peter Brown, *The Cult of the Saints. Its Rise and Function in Latin Christianity* (Chicago: 1981) 69ff. Although he applied it to Christian saints as a whole, I will here be almost exclusively concerned not with Buddhist "saints" as a group, but with the historical Buddha Śākyamuni. This is not to say that there was not a "cult of the saints" or other "very special dead" in Indian Buddhism. There is both epigraphical and archaeological evidence that indicates otherwise, but a discussion of this material must await another time. [See G. Schopen, "An Old Inscription from Amarāvatī," Ch. IX below.]

3. J. Bloch, *Les inscriptions d'Asoka* (Paris: 1950). The Prakrit cited here and below all comes from Bloch's edition. The two inscriptions in question are from Rummindei (Paderia), 157, and Nigālī Sāgar (Nigliva), 158. Unlike the bulk of the Aśokan material, these two inscriptions are not edicts. They, at least together with the Barabar Inscription,

constitute the earliest surviving Indian donative inscriptions. Whether or not the Aśokan material establishes that Bodh–Gayā was an established sacred site at the time of Aśoka depends very much on how one interprets the word *saṃbodhi* in the 8th Rock Edict. Since A. L. Basham reopened the question, it has yet to be resolved; see "Saṃbodhi in Aśoka's 8th Rock Edict," *JIABS* 2 (1979) 81–83. Therefore, this is not taken into account here, although my own position is much closer to the one most recently expressed by R. Lingat, "Encore *ayāya saṃbodhim* à propos de l'inscription gréco-araméenne d'Aśoka," *JA* (1967) 195–198.

4. On the Past Buddhas, see J. Ph. Vogel, "The Past Buddhas and Kāśyapa in Indian Art and Epigraphy," *Asiatica Festschrift Friedrich Weller* (Leipzig: 1954) 808–816; R. Gombrich, "The Significance of Former Buddhas in the Theravādin Tradition," *Buddhist Studies in Honour of Walpola Rahula*, ed. S. Balasooriya et al. (London: 1980) 62–72; A. Vergati, "Le culte et l'iconographie du buddha dīpankara dans la vallée de Kathmandou," *Arts asiatiques* 37 (1982) 22–27.

5. See, for example, Bloch, *Les inscriptions d'Asoka*, 49, 157, nn. 2 and 4. Note that Aśoka here uses the absolutive form of *ā√gam* to describe his coming to Lummini, and, according to Bloch's index, this root is used only here and in the related Nigālī Sāgar inscription. Both the Sanskrit and Pāli versions of our passage also use forms of *ā√gam*. Note too that while neither of the two instances of the *hida* statement in Aśoka corresponds with the Pāli, the second, *hida bhagavaṃ jāte*, corresponds exactly with the Sanskrit *iha bhagavāñ jātaḥ*.

6. I here refer to, and cite throughout, the Sanskrit version of the *Mahāparinirvāṇa-Sūtra* edited by E. Waldschmidt (*Das Mahāparinirvāṇasūtra*, Teil I, II, III, Abh. DAW Berlin, Kl. f. Spr., Lit. u. Kunst, Jg. 1949, No. 1; Jg. 1950, No. 2 und Jg. 1950, No. 3 [Berlin: 1950, 1951, 1951]; I cite the text according to Waldschmidt's paragraph numbers). Since the Sanskrit text is based primarily on the Turfan materials, this means that we have actual manuscripts for it that are centuries earlier than anything we have for the Pāli text, and, in this sense at least, its readings are the earliest actually attestable readings that we have for the text in an Indian language. On the Turfan manuscript material, see L. Sander, *Paläographisches zu den Sanskrithandschriften der Berliner Turfan-sammlung*, Verzeichnis der Orientalischen Handschriften in Deutschland, Supplementband 8 (Wiesbaden: 1968). For Pāli manuscripts, see H. Smith, *Saddanīti, La grammaire palie d'aggavaṃsa* (Lund: 1928) v; O. von Hinüber, "On the Tradition of Pāli Texts in India, Ceylon and Burma," *Buddhism in Ceylon and Studies on Religious Syncretism in Buddhist Countries*, Abh. d. Akad. d. Wiss. in Göttingen, Phil.-Hist. Kl. Dritte Folge. Nr. 108, ed. H. Bechert (Göttingen: 1978) 48: "The big gap between the first redaction of our Pāli canon and the basis of the texts as we have them today, becomes evident at once, if we bear in mind that there is no manuscript older than about 400 years, with the only exception, as far as I know, of a tenth century Vinaya-fragment in Pāli found in Nepal." [See O. von Hinüber, *The Oldest Pāli Manuscript. Four Folios of the Vinaya Piṭaka from the National Archives, Kathmandu*, Akademie der Wissenschaften und der Literatur, Mainz, Abhandlungen der Geistes- und Sozialwissenschaftlichen Klasse, Jahrgang 1991, Nr. 6 (Stuttgart: 1991).] More recently, von Hinüber has said "that most of the surviving manuscript material [for the Pāli canon] is hardly older than the late 18th century." He also refers to "an extremely old manuscript dated as early as A.D. 1412," and adds "if this date is correct, this would be the oldest dated Pāli manuscript known so far" in "Pāli Manuscripts of Canonical Texts From North Thailand—A Preliminary Report," *Journal of the Siam Society* 71 (1983) 78. Note too that, in terms of Pāli literature, a

slightly shorter version of the *Mahāparinibbāna* passage on pilgrimage also occurs at *Aṅguttara,* ii, 120. In light of these passages, it is difficult to understand what A. Bharati meant when he said, "Although pilgrimage figures importantly in the religions of India, it never had any canonical status in non-tantric traditions" (*The Tantric Tradition* [London: 1965] 85).

7. Waldschmidt's *anusmaraṇīyā* appears to be reconstructed on the basis of Tibetan *rjes su dran par 'gyur bar bya.* In fact, in neither of the two manuscript fragments for 41.5 has the actual reading been preserved. But in the restatement of 41.5 that occurs in 41.10, the one manuscript in which the actual reading has been preserved has quite clearly *abhigamanīyā;* see Teil I, 43, 113.2. Note that this passage of the *Mahāparinirvāṇa-Sūtra* has been reedited by F. Edgerton in *Buddhist Hybrid Sanskrit Reader* (New Haven: 1953) 34–35; cf. n. 14 below.

8. For the range of meanings of *saṃvejanīya,* "to be powerfully experienced," see A. K. Coomaraswamy, "*Saṃvega:* Aesthetic Shock," *HJAS* 7 (1943) 174–179, repr. in *Coomaraswamy* 1. *Selected Papers. Traditional Art and Symbolism,* ed. R. Lipsey (Princeton: 1977) 179–185. He translates *saṃvejanīya* from our passages of the *Mahāparinibbāna-sutta* as "should be deeply moved." For an interesting use of *vega/pravega* in early Mahāyāna *sūtra* literature, see *Vajracchedikā Prajñāpāramitā* (Conze ed.) 14A: *atha khalv āyuṣmān subhūtir dharmavegenāśrūṇi* [the Gilgit text has *-pravegenā-*] *prāmuñcat,* etc.

9. J. Gonda has clearly demonstrated the antiquity of many of the ideas that most secondary literature associates only with the much later "classical" *bhakti* conception of *darśan* in *Eye and Gaze in the Veda,* Verhandelingen der Koninklijke Nederlandse Akademie van Wetenschappen, Afd. LetterKunds. Nieuwe Reeks-Deel 75 (Amsterdam: 1970). On *darśan* generally, see the fine little book by D. L. Eck, *Darśan. Seeing the Divine Image in India* (Chambersburg: 1981). In light of the pervasiveness and age of these Indian ideas about "seeing" and what it entails, it would appear that many of our translations, at the very least, miss the nuance and may, in fact, miss the whole point. The exhortation that Ānanda was directed by the Buddha to deliver to the Mallas is a good example. Ānanda was told to go and tell the Mallas that the Buddha would enter *parinibbāna* during the last watch of that night, and he was supposed to say to them: *abhikkhamatha . . . abhikkhamatha . . . mā pacchā vippaṭisārino ahuvattha: amhākañ ca no gāmakkhette tathāgatassa parinibbānaṃ ahosi, na mayaṃ labhimhā pacchime kāle tathāgataṃ dassanāyâti,* which Rhys Davids translates as: "Be favourable . . . be favourable. Give no occasion to reproach yourselves hereafter, saying: 'In our own village did the death of our Tathāgata take place, and we took not the opportunity of visiting the Tathāgata in his last hours' "; see T. W. and C. A. F. Rhys Davids, *Dialogues of the Buddha,* Pt. II (London: 1910) 162. The Rhys Davids' translation is, of course, not really wrong, but unless the reader has the etymology of the English word clearly in mind, to translate *dassana* by "visit," from Latin, *visere* "to go to see," *videre, visum* "to see," is at best terribly flat. In a culture where "casting one's eyes upon a person and touching him were related activities" (Gonda, 19), where there was strong "belief in the beneficial results of visual contact" (46), and where there were large numbers of old "ritual texts prescribing a conscious and directed look by which the spectator was . . . believed to benefit, or ritual acts performed to derive some advantage from looking on a mighty being . . . to participate in its nature or essence, to be purified or raised to a higher level of existence by being *vis-à-vis* with such a man" (55)—in such a culture, to go to "see" a man, especially an exceptionally holy man, clearly involves much more than a "visit." In fact, the Upavāṇa Incident in the *Mahāparinibbāna-sutta* makes it absolutely clear that, for this text, the important

aspect of *dassana* was direct visual contact and that such contact was very highly valued. In this remarkable incident, the Buddha is lying on his deathbed and the Monk Upavāṇa is standing in front of him fanning him. But then the Buddha "spoke harshly" to Upavāṇa (*apasādesi*—a very strong verb and an action very uncharacteristic of the textual Buddha), saying "Get away, Monk! Don't stand in front of me!" (*apehi bhikkhu mā me purato aṭṭhāsīti*). Ānanda is puzzled (shocked, cf. Skt. 35.4) and asks about the Buddha's behavior. The latter calmly explains that the *devas* from all the ten directions have come together to gaze upon/behold/see him (*devatā sannipatitā tathāgataṃ dassanāya*), but they are "grumbling" (*ujjhāyanti*), saying "we have come from great distances to gaze upon/etc. the Tathāgata . . . but this eminent Monk standing in front of the Blessed One is preventing it and we do not get to gaze on the Tathāgata in his final moments" (*na mayaṃ labhāma pacchime kāle tathāgataṃ dassanāyâti*). Clearly, here again the *devas* did not come simply "to visit," and, in fact, here Rhys Davids was almost forced to translate *dassana* as "behold." It is also worth noting that there is Buddhist evidence for other aspects of the conception of *darśan* usually associated with mediaeval *bhakti* which is, relatively speaking, much earlier. Both Coomaraswamy (*Mediaeval Sinhalese Art,* 2nd ed. [New York: 1956] 70–75) and Gombrich ("The Consecration of a Buddhist Image," *The Journal of Asian Studies* 26 [1966] 23–36) have pointed out that Buddhaghosa, already in the fifth century C.E., refers to the ritual empowerment of an image by painting in its eyes, and there is a clear allusion to the same idea in the *Ratnaguṇasaṃcayagāthā* (Yuyama ed.) VII.2 that is almost certainly several centuries earlier than Buddhaghosa.

10. A. Cunningham, *Mahābodhi or the Great Buddhist Temple under the Bodhi Tree at Buddha-Gaya* (London: 1892) 82–83; B. M. Barua, "Old Buddhist Shrines at Bodh-Gayā," *IHQ* 6 (1930) 30–31. There may, in fact, have been several more inscriptions of roughly the same period that refer to *darśan,* but it is not possible to be sure from Cunningham's presentation. He says that in Slabs F and G, "The pilgrim offers his adoration to Mahābodhi, for the benefit of his father and mother," but he does not give the actual reading of the inscriptions. Since, however, he translates . . . *jina dasakena sri man mahābodhi bhandāraka darsana kritam yadatra punyam tad bhavati mātapittri purvaga* . . . as " . . . Jina Dasaka . . . adoration was made at the Temple of Sri-man Mahābodhi, for the benefit of his father and mother, etc." (83), it is possible that F and G also had this same reading; see Barua for a much better reading of Slabs F and G.

11. In H. Lüders, *A List of Brahmi Inscriptions from the Earliest Times to about* A.D. *400 with the Exception of Those of Aśoka,* Appendix to *EI* 10 (Calcutta: 1912) no. 1223, a gift made by "The Elder *(thera),* the Chaitya worshipper *(Chetiyavaṃdaka) bhayaṃta (bhadunta)* Budhi"; no. 1263, a gift made by "Papin (Pāpin), brother of *bhayaṃta (bhadanta)* Budhi (Buddhi), the Chaitya worshipper *(Chetiavadaka).*" As both of these inscriptions come from Amarāvatī and are roughly contemporaneous, there is a good chance that the monk named Budhi referred to in both is the same person. But if this is true, there is an equally good chance that the Monk Budhi who is called a *cetiyavandaka* in these two inscriptions is the same Monk Budhi who is called a *mahāvinayadhara,* "a great preserver/knower of the Vinaya," in two other contemporaneous Amarāvatī inscriptions found in Lüders, no. 1270, and in H. Sarkar, "Some Early Inscriptions in the Amarāvatī Museum," *JAIH* 4 (1970–1971) 9, no. 63, and a *dhamakathika,* "a preacher of Dharma," in a third inscription in Lüders, no. 1267. This would seem to indicate that some, at least, of the "honorers of shrines" were the acknowledged transmitters of Buddhist doctrine and monastic rules and monks of considerable standing.

12. In the Pāli canon, in the *Araṇavibhaṅgasutta* (*Majjhima*, iii, 237), the Monk Subhūti is called a *kulaputta;* in the *Dhātuvibhaṅga-sutta* (*Majjhima*, iii, 238–247), the Monk Pukkasāti is repeatedly referred to as a *kulaputta;* in a recurring "arhat formula," *kulaputtas* are the ones said to properly go forth from the house to the houseless state (*Aṅguttara*, i, 282; *Dīgha*, ii, 153; etc.); etc. In very early Mahāyāna *sūtra* literature, it is clear that not only did the title *kulaputra* apply both to monks and laymen, but it was also a title that could be applied to followers of both what we usually call the Mahāyāna and the Hīnayāna. In the *Pratyutpannabuddhasaṃmukhāvasthitasamādhisūtra, byaṅ chub sems dpa' khyim pa 'am/ rab tu byuṅ ba,* "both householder and renunciant bodhisattvas," are equated with *rigs kyi bu 'am rigs kyi bu mo,* "sons and daughters of good family"; see P. M. Harrison, *The Tibetan Text of the Pratyutpannabuddhasaṃmukhāvasthitasamādhisūtra* (Tokyo: 1978) 7B; see also 8G, where *kulaputras* who seek arhatship are referred to; 9E, which refers to *kulaputras* who are "adherents of the *Śrāvakayāna*"; etc. Likewise, in the equally early *Akṣobhyatathāgatasyavyūha,* we find *byaṅ chub sems dpa'i theg pa pa daṅ ñan thos kyi theg pa pa'i rigs kyi bu 'am/rigs kyi bu mo gaṅ dag khyim gyi gnas nas ṅes par byuṅ źiṅ rab tu byuṅ bar gyur pa dag . . . Peking,* 22, 132-5-4; cf. 137-1-2, 154-4-6, 156-1-7, 2-3, 3-1, etc. On this important but until recently little studied text, see now J. Dantinne, *La splendeur de l'inébranlable (Akṣobhyavyūha),* T. I (Louvain-la-neuve: 1983). For a much later occurrence, see *Suvikrāntavikrāmiparipṛcchā* (Hikata ed.) 64.14.

13. See Barua's "Old Buddhist Shrines at Bodh-Gayā," 6ff, esp. 20, and his "A Bodh-Gayā Image Inscription," *IHQ* 9 (1933) 416–419. A Kushan inscription records the gift of a monk who is called a *dharmakathika,* "preacher of *Dharma,*" and who is associated with a *vinayadhara,* a "preserver/transmitter of the Vinaya"; see J. F. Fleet, *Inscriptions of the Early Gupta Kings and Their Successors,* Corpus Inscriptionum Indicarum, Vol. III (Calcutta: 1888) nos. 71, 72, 76.

14. A. Wayman translates the Sanskrit *atrāntarā ye kecit prasannacittā mamāntike kālaṃ kariṣyanti,* etc., as "among these places, whoever with pure thought will die in my presence, all those belong to heaven *(svarga),* whoever are with remainder" in "Buddhism," *Historia Religionum. Handbook for the History of Religions,* Vol. II, ed. C. J. Bleeker and G. Widengren (Leiden: 1971) 401, taking *kālaṃ kariṣyanti* as that which takes place *mamāntike* and not *prasannacittā.* This is worth noting because the Tibetan translation appears to do just the opposite: *kha cig ṅa la sems dad pas dus byas pa* (v. 1. *te*) *de thams cad mtho ris su 'gro'o / kha cig ni phuṅ po lhag ma daṅ bcas par ro,* "Some with devout thoughts in regard to me die, they all go to heaven. Some are possessed with a substratum (i.e., still have *karma* to work out)." But the Tibetan is either translating a Sanskrit text that differs from the one we have, or it is only a very loose rendering. It has nothing corresponding to *atrāntarā,* and it suggests a text that read: *ye kecin mamāntike prasannacittāḥ kālaṃ kariṣyanti.* The genitive + *antike* can of course mean "in regard to," but Edgerton's examples in *BHSD,* 40, make it clear that the genitive + *antike* is always followed by and never preceded by the action concerned: *daridrapuruṣas tasya gṛhapater antike pitṛsaṃjñāṃ utpādayet,* SP 107.4; *devānām . . . antike cittāni pradūṣayitvā,* Mv i 30.9; etc. This is the construction regardless of the sense in which *antike* is used, and this makes it difficult to see in *mamāntike kālaṃ kariṣyanti* anything but "those who will die in my presence." To say "those who will die in regard to/in reference to me" makes no sense. It is possible, however, that the Tibetan translation did not result from the fact that it was based on a different original, nor from a misunderstanding. It may represent an intentional alteration of the text. Notice that the Tibetan corresponding to 41.9, as well as—if not more so than—that corresponding to 41.14 (*kha cig ni ṅa la sems dad pas dus byas pa* [v. 1. *te*]

de thams cad mtho ris su 'gro'o / kha cig ni phuṅ po lhag ma daṅ bcas par ro / ji ltar mṅon du 'gro bar bya ba de ltar rjes su dran par bya'o) looks very much like an attempt to retain the benefit of rebirth in heaven while no longer requiring an actual pilgrimage. The Tibetan appears to want to make a *mental* pilgrimage equal to the *actual* pilgrimage, or at least to make the former an option. Notice that its *ji ltar mṅon du 'gro bar bya ba de ltar rjes su dran par bya'o* is clearly an addition. There is nothing corresponding to it in either Sanskrit or Pāli and, while we do not actually have manuscript readings for the Sanskrit of 41.5, where the Pāli has *dassanīyāni saṃvejanīyāni,* i.e., a reference to direct visual contact, the Tibetan has *rjes su dran par 'gyur bar bya'o* = *anusmaraṇīya,* meaning "mental recalling" or "visualization." When we do have an actual manuscript reading for the Sanskrit, as in 41.10, it is *abhigamanīya.* The substitution or option that the Tibetan translation appears to be introducing is also clearly visible in the Chinese version of the text translated by Waldschmidt: "Wenn man an diesen vier Plätzen entweder persönlich seine Verehrung bezeigt oder (ihnen) aus der Ferne seine Achtung übermittelt, sehnsuchtsvoll und aufrichtig reinen Glauben entstehen lässt und beständig die Gedanken daran heftet, wird man nach Lebensende Geburt im Himmel erlangen." Here too, one can *either* go in person to the four places *or* call them to mind from afar; cf. A. Bareau, *Recherches sur la biographie du Buddha dans les sūtrapiṭaka et les vinayapiṭaka anciens: II Les derniers mois, le parinirvāṇa et les funérailles,* T. II (Paris: 1971) 29–32. Bareau, however, takes Waldschmidt's reconstructed *anusmaraṇīya* at 41.5 without comment, and this affects some of what he says. All of this would seem to suggest that, as long as the text remained in India, the original readings like *dassanīya, saṃvejanīya,* and probably *abhigamanīya*—all of which required actual pilgrimage—were not a problem, but that when the texts moved outside of India—where actual pilgrimage would have been extremely difficult—new readings, like *anusmaraṇīya,* and new options, like visualization "aus der Ferne," had to be introduced into the text. It is in this light, I think, that the Tibetan translation and some of the Chinese translations of our passage are to be viewed. There were, of course, other ways of dealing with the problem of actual pilgrimage. See, for example, the interesting paper by A. B. Griswold, "The Holy Land Transported: Replicas of the Mahābodhi Shrine in Siam and Elsewhere," *Paranavitana Felicitation Volume,* ed. N. A. Jayawickrama (Colombo: 1965) 173–222.

15. Cunningham, *Mahābodhi,* 46–49; for a recent study of the surviving "minor" *stūpas* at Bodh-Gayā, see M. Bénesti, *Contribution à l'étude du stūpa bouddhique indien: les stūpa mineurs de Bodh-gayā et de Ratnagiri,* T. I and II (Paris: 1981).

16. J. Marshall, *Taxila: An Illustrated Account of Archaeological Excavations Carried Out at Taxila under the Orders of the Government of India between the Years 1913 and 1934,* Vol. I (Cambridge: 1951) 235; see Vol. III, pl. 45, for a clear ground plan of the whole Dharmarājikā complex.

17. Marshall, *Taxila,* Vol. I, 368–387; see Vol. III, pl. 101, for the ground plan of Jauliāñ. A slightly fuller acccount of the excavations at Jauliāñ had been published earlier in J. Marshall, *Excavations at Taxila: The Stūpas and Monasteries at Jauliāñ,* MASI, No. 7 (Calcutta: 1921).

18. H. Cousens, *The Antiquities of Sind,* Archaeological Survey of India, Vol. XLVI, Imperial Series (Calcutta: 1929) 82–97; D. R. Bhandarkar, "Excavations near Mirpur Khās," *Progress Report of the Archaeological Survey of India, Western Circle, for the Year Ending 31st March, 1917,* 47–48; D. Mitra, *Buddhist Monuments* (Calcutta: 1971) 132–133.

19. J. Marshall, *A Guide to Sanchi* (Calcutta: 1918) 87–88.

20. Marshall, *Taxila*, Vol. I, 240ff. Marshall does not specifically describe all the earliest smaller *stūpas*, but of those that he does all contain bone or ash (i.e., R5, S8, S9, B6, B3). Other contemporary *stūpas* that contain bone or ash are J2, N7, and Q1. *Stūpas* of varying date scattered around the complex that are specially said to contain "relic" deposits are G4, G5, T12, K3, P6, S10, N11, N10, N9, P10, P12, U1.

21. See, for example, "The Piprāhwā Buddhist Vase Inscription" in Lüders, *List*, no. 931, with bibliography; G. Bühler, "The Bhattiprolu Inscriptions," *EI* 2 (1894) 323–329; J. Ph. Vogel, "Prakrit Inscriptions from a Buddhist Site at Nagarjunikonda," *EI* 20 (1929–1930) 1–36 (where the *stūpa* itself appears to be repeatedly described as containing the relics of the Buddha, although Vogel, I think, has misunderstood this and the construction is somewhat odd; see Āyaka Pillar Inscriptions C3, B2, B4, B5, C2, C4, C5. The key instance for the correct interpretation of the construction appears to be the First Apsidal Temple Inscription E: *saṃma-saṃbudhasa dhātuparigahitasa mahāchetiya-pādamūle*); R. Salomon and G. Schopen, "The Indravarman (Avaca) Casket Inscription Reconsidered: Further Evidence for Canonical Passages in Buddhist Inscriptions," *JIABS* 7 (1984) 107–123; P. R. Srinivasan, "Devni-Mori Relic Casket Inscription of Rudrasena, Kathika Year 127," *EI* 37 (1967) 67–69; etc.

22. Marshall, *Taxila*, Vol. I, 373, A11; 373, D5; 374, A16. There was also at least one reliquary found in the debris between *Stūpas* A7 and A8.

23. Mitra, *Buddhist Monuments*, 133; Cousens, *The Antiquities of Sind*, 97

24. Marshall, *A Guide to Sanchi*, 88.

25. Cunningham, *Mahābodhi*, 48–49.

26. A. Ghosh, ed., *Indian Archaeology 1957–58—A Review* (New Delhi: 1958) 39–41, pls. XLIX–LIII; D. Mitra, "Ratnagiri. Unearthing of a New Buddhist Site in Orissa," *Indo-Asian Culture* 9 (1960) 160–175; D. Mitra, *Ratnagiri (1958–61)*, Vol. I, MASI, no. 80 (New Delhi: 1981). For the configuration and numbers of the smaller *stūpas* around the main *stūpa* at Ratnagiri, see the siteplan of the *stūpa* area, Mitra, *Ratnagiri*, 26, fig. 3; this can be compared with that for Bodh-Gayā published by Cunningham, *Mahābodhi*, pl. XVIII. For a study of the smaller *stūpas* at Ratnagiri, see M. Bénisti, *Contribution à l'étude du stūpa bouddhique indien*, T. 1, 93ff, figs. 119ff, and Mitra, *Ratnagiri*, 44–138, pls. LX–LXXXI.

27. See Mitra, *Ratnagiri*, pls. IX, XX–XXI, XXXIV, XLII, LVI–LVIII, etc.

28. I-tsing, *A Record of the Buddhist Religion as Practised in India and the Malay Archipelago (A.D. 671–695)*, trans. J. Takakusu (London: 1896; repr. 1966) 82. An additional, but I do not think an alternative, explanation for the absence of a finial on *some* Buddhist votive *stūpas* is suggested by U. Wiesner in "Nepalese Votive Stūpas of the Licchavi Period: The Empty Niche," *The Stūpa—Its Religious, Historical and Architectural Significance*, Bieträge zur Südasien-Forschung Südasien-Institut Universität Heidelberg 55, ed. A. L. Dallapiccola et al. (Wiesbaden: 1980) 170–172. What Wiesner says about an intentional sectarian "revision" of the form of the *stūpa*, however, *could* only apply to those found on the surface. The vast majority of the *stūpas* we are concerned with only came to light during excavation, having been covered over by newer levels of building.

29. Mitra, *Indo–Asian Culture* 9 (1960) 166.

30. Notice that Mitra, in the final excavation report published (*Ratnagiri*, 31–32), comes close to suggesting something similar. She says first that "a limited number of these monolithic *stūpas* were doubtless used for enshrining the bone-relics of the departed: for this purpose they were provided with sockets, usually at the base, to hold charred bones." However, she then adds that "most of the sockets of these *śārīrika stūpas* were

found empty, and only a few (*stūpas* 112 and 188 for instance), which were found plugged by stone blocks, retained the relics." This raises the real possibility that many more might have contained relics, a possibility that she clearly states in discussing the structural *stūpas,* as we will see below. Notice too that she incidently notes (44n) that "the relics were noticed mostly during the conservation of the *stūpas,*" i.e., the possibilities of the presence of bone deposits were not in any way systematically studied.

31. G. Schopen, "The Text on the 'Dhāraṇī Stones from Abhayagiriya': A Minor Contribution to the Study of Mahāyāna Literature in Ceylon," *JIABS* 5 (1982) 100–108; G. Schopen, "The Bodhigarbhālaṅkāralakṣa and Vimaloṣṇīṣa Dhāraṇīs in Indian Inscriptions: Two Sources for the Practice of Buddhism in Medieval India," *WZKS* 29 (1985) 119–149. In the second of these papers, I was able to show that the "*dhāraṇī*-text" on the Cuttack Stone Inscription published by A. Ghosh (*EI* 26 [1941] 171–174) was an incomplete Sanskrit version of a text called the *Bodhigarbhālaṅkāralakṣadhāraṇī.* Although Mitra refers to Ghosh (*Ratnagiri,* 31), she apparently did not recognize that the two *dhāraṇīs* found on eight plaques at Ratnagiri that she transliterated (43, 99) were the same *dhāraṇī* that he had transliterated. The same *dhāraṇī* is also found on at least two plaques from Nālandā and on a "cachet" from Qunduz.

32. *'Phags pa 'od zer dri ma med pa rnam par dag pa'i 'od ces bya ba'i gzuṅs, Peking,* 7, 190-1-4. It is interesting to note that the two earliest known examples of printing—one from Korea and one from Japan—both contain the *Raśmivimala,* and in both countries were found inside *stūpas;* see L. Carrington Goodrich, "Printing: Preliminary Report on a New Discovery," *Technology and Culture* 9 (1967) 376–378; T. F. Carter, *The Invention of Printing in China and Its Spread Westward,* 2nd ed. rev. L. Carrington Goodrich (New York: 1955) 46–53; B. Hickman, "A Note on the Hyakumantō Dhāraṇī," *Monumenta Nipponica* 30 (1975) 87–93.

33. *'Phags pa las kyi sgrib pa thams cad rnam par sbyoṅ ba źes bya ba'i gzuṅs, Peking,* 11, 252-1-6. It is very likely that the *dhāraṇī* from this text was one of the *dhāraṇīs* deposited by the Monk Bu Ston in the *stūpa* he built for his deceased mother; see D. S. Ruegg, *The Life of Bu Ston Rin Po Che, With the Tibetan Text of the Bu Ston rNam Thar,* Serie Orientale Roma, XXXIV (Rome: 1966) fol. 29a, 5 and 136.

34. T. Skorupski, *The Sarvadurgatipariśodhana Tantra* (Delhi: 1983). Notice that, although the *dramatis personae* and the setting differ in each case, the *Raśmivimalaviśuddhaprabha,* the *Samantamukhapraveśaraśmivimaloṣṇīṣaprabhāsasarvatathāgatahṛdayasamayavilokita* (*Peking,* 7, no. 206), and the *Sarvadurgatipariśodhanī-uṣṇīṣavijaya* (*Peking,* 7, no. 198) *dhāraṇīs* and the *Sarvadurgatipariśodhana Tantra* (Skorupski, 4, 122.29ff) are all introduced by essentially the same thematic kind of narrative. The introductions to the *dhāraṇīs* are summarized in *Mkhas Grub Rje's Fundamentals of the Buddhist Tantras. Rgyud sde spyiḥi rnam par gźag pa rgyas par brjod,* trans. F. D. Lessing and A. Wayman (The Hague: 1968) 104–107, 115–117. On *dhāraṇīs* in funerary rites in the *Sarvadurgati Tantra,* see Skorupski, 81, 242.22ff.

35. Mitra, *Ratnagiri,* 28. For a brief description of three of the "dislocated reliquaries," see 28–29.

36. Mitra, *Ratnagiri,* 43, 98–99. It should be noted that a more complete and systematic survey of Buddhist sites than the one I have been able to present here promises—despite the deficiencies of much of the published archaeological literature—to produce much fuller evidence for the funerary functions of the minor *stūpas* found at almost all Buddhist sites. For now I can only mention the following points. It is possible that "les stūpa à avancée" or "les stūpa à cella" which occur at both Bodh-Gayā

(Cunningham, *Mahābodhi,* 48, pl. XXIII.k; Bénisti, *Contribution à l'étude du stūpa,* T. i, 20–22; T. ii, figs. 23–26, 28, 29, 31, 33) and Ratnagiri (Mitra, *Ratnagiri,* pls. XXIa. 102, XXIb. 107, XLVIIA.228) and which have been taken—on very weak evidence—to have been meant for images, may, in fact, have been intended and used for funerary deposits. It has been reported, at least at Mainamati, that "the hoard of miniature baked and unbaked clay stūpas" found there "contained bone relics or small sealings or sometimes both" ("Mainamati Excavations," *Pakistan Archaeology* 5 [1968] 173). These miniature *stūpas* have a very wide distribution indeed; see M. Taddei, "Inscribed Clay Tablets and Miniature Stūpas from Gaznī," *EW* 20 (1970) 85–86. Finally, G. Fussman has already published two Kharoṣṭhī inscriptions that he thinks are funerary in "Une inscription kharoṣṭhī à Haḍḍa," *BEFEO* 56 (1969) 5–9, and "Documents épigraphiques kouchans," *BEFEO* 61 (1974) 58–61. There are, according to a personal communication from Prof. Fussman, also a number of similar inscriptions from Haḍḍa that have yet to be published. A. H. Dani has also published a number of Kharoṣṭhī inscriptions that appear to be funerary in "Shaikhan Dheri Excavation (1963 and 1964 Seasons)," *Ancient Pakistan* 2 (1965–1966) 109–113. All of these things deserve to be studied much more fully.

37. Mitra, however, has indicated that, at Ratnagiri at least, there is some evidence to indicate that the "portable monolithic *stūpas*" were made locally (*Ratnagiri,* 32).

38. P. Ariès, *Western Attitudes Towards Death: From the Middle Ages to the Present* (Baltimore: 1974) 16–17.

39. P. Ariès, *The Hour of Our Death* (New York: 1981) 34.

40. U. A. Casal, "The Saintly Kōbō Daishi in Popular Lore (A.D. 774–835)," *Journal of Far Eastern Folklore. Folklore Studies* 18 (1959) 143.

41. P. Geary, *Furta Sacra. Thefts of Relics in the Central Middle Ages* (Princeton: 1978) 33–34; see also S. Wilson's Introduction to *Saints and Their Cults. Studies in Religious Sociology, Folklore and History,* ed. S. Wilson (Cambridge: 1983) 10.

42. A. Lloyd, "Death and Disposal of the Dead (Japanese)," *Encyclopaedia of Religion and Ethics,* Vol. 4, ed. J. Hastings (Edinburgh: 1911) 491; see also Casal, "The Saintly Kōbō Daishi," 139, 143.

43. Y. S. Hakeda, *Kukai: Major Works* (New York: 1972) 60.

44. O. Statler, *Japanese Pilgrimage* (New York: 1983) 94–96, 128, 175, etc., taking as his "basic source" S. Gorai, *Koya Hijiri* (Tokyo: 1965).

45. Wilson, *Saints and Their Cults,* 11; see also P. Brown, *The Cult of the Saints. Its Rise and Function in Latin Christianity* (Chicago: 1981) 3–4.

46. Ariès, *The Hour of Our Death,* 33.

47. There is, of course, the old story of Kāśyapa awaiting the coming of Maitreya entombed in the "Kukkuṭapada" or "Gurupada" mountain that has some obvious similarities with some of the ideas connected with Kōbō Daishi; see T. Watters, *On Yuan Chwang's Travels in India,* Vol. II (London: 1905) 143ff, and literature cited therein, but this has nothing to do with relics as such. Outside of India, G. Obeyesekere refers to a "Sinhalese myth which states that in the flood that heralds the destruction of this age all the Buddha *dhātu* found in various parts of the world will assemble together through *ridhi* and the Buddha himself will be refashioned out of these substances. He will then utter a last sermon" ("The Buddhist Pantheon in Ceylon and Its Extensions," *Anthropological Studies in Theravada Buddhism* [New Haven: 1966] 9). M. E. Spiro cites several instances of a similar "myth" in Burma: "Just prior to his [Maitreya's] arrival, the relics of the present Buddha, Gautama, will be recombined to form his physical body. By worshiping him, the *weikza* will automatically achieve nirvana" (*Burmese Supernaturalism. A Study in the*

Explanation and Reduction of Suffering [Englewood Cliffs: 1967] 231, 165–66, 191). The Indian antecedents of the Sri Lankan and Burmese materials are very vague. Both are undoubtedly related to the *Anāgatavaṃsa;* see J. Minayeff, "Anāgatavaṃsa," *JPTS* (1886) 36; cf. H. C. Warren, *Buddhism in Translation* (Cambridge: 1896) 484–485, but this text is itself sometimes presented as a *sutta* (e.g., Minayeff's Ms. B from Rangoon) while at other times it is considered an authored work attributed to a Coḷiyan monk named Kassapa who probably lived between 1160 and 1230 C.E.; see J. Minayeff, "The Gandha-Vaṃsa," *JPTS* (1886) 60–61, 66, 70; A. P Buddhadatta and A. K. Warder, *Mohavicchedanī Abhidhammamātikatthavaṇṇanā* (London: 1961) x–xi, xvi–xviii. The *Anāgatavaṃsa* itself clearly owes much to Buddhaghosa's *Manorathapūraṇī* (*Histoire du bouddhisme indien,* 216). To complicate matters even further, two versions of an *Anāgatavaṃsa* exist in the Tibetan Kanjur (*Peking,* nos. 751 and 1010), both of which were co-translated by a Sri Lankan Monk, Ānandaśrī, in the thirteenth century; see G. Schopen, "Hīnayāna Texts in a 14th Century Persian Chronicle: Notes on Some of Rashid al'Din's Sources," *Central Asiatic Journal* 26 (1982) 231, n. 9, and sources cited therein; and S. Lévi, "Maitreya le consolateur," *Études d'orientalisme publiées par le musée guimet à la mémoire de Raymonde Linossier,* T. II (Paris: 1932) 379–380; Lévi's discussion of the Tibetan translations, 377, needs, in part, to be corrected. Sorting all this out requires and deserves a good deal of future work, but it would appear at this stage that the ideas expressed in the *Anāgatavaṃsa,* etc., are too late to have had any real formative role in producing the archaeological configuration that concerns us.

48. See D. L. Eck, *Banaras: City of Light* (New York: 1982) 215: "Those who die in Kāshī, assured of liberation, will be cremated on the banks of the river of Heaven at this most sacred of *tīrthas.* If one cannot die in Kāshī, then cremation by the Ganges anywhere along her banks is desirable. If even this is impossible, then relatives might later bring the ashes of the deceased to the Ganges at Kāshī, or even send them to Kāshī parcel post."

49. N. G. Majumdar, "The Bajaur Casket of the Reign of Menander," *EI* 24 (1937) 1–8; S. Konow, "New Traces of the Greeks in India," *New Indian Antiquary* 2 (1939/40) 639–648; Konow, "Note on the Bajaur Inscription of Menandros," *EI* 27 (1947–1948) 52–58; D. C. Sircar, "A Note on the Bajaur Casket of the Reign of Menander," *EI* 26 (1942) 318–321; Sircar, *Select Inscriptions Bearing on Indian History and Civilization,* Vol. I, 2nd ed. (Calcutta: 1965) 102–106; A. K. Narian, *The Indo-Greeks* (Oxford: 1957) pl. VI; Ét. Lamotte, "De quelques influences grecques et scythes sur le bouddhisme," *Académie des inscriptions et belles-lettres. Comptes rendus des séances de l'année 1956,* 485–504, esp. 494; *Histoire du bouddhisme indien,* 464, 474ff. Essentially a reworking of the first paper, much of what Lamotte says in both places in regard to "influences grecques et scythes" is highly conjectural, and some of it can now be shown to be wrong. On the historical setting of the Bajaur Inscription, see most recently R. Salomon, "The 'Avaca' Inscription and the Origin of the Vikrama Era," *JAOS* 102 (1982) 62–65. [See G. Fussman, "L'indo-grec Ménandre ou Paul Demiéville revisité," *JA* (1993) 61–138.]

50. I cite here, and below, Sircar's Sanskritized text from *Select Inscriptions,* 105. It should be noted that this inscription is very fragmentary, and not all of the inscriptions on the lid go back to the time of Menander.

51. First edited by H. W. Bailey, "A Kharoṣṭhī Inscription of Senavarma, King of Oḍi," *JRAS* (1980) 21–29; edited anew, with much better results, by G. Fussman, "Documents épigraphiques kouchans (III). L'inscription kharoṣṭhī de Senavarma, roi d'Oḍi: Une nouvelle lecture," *BEFEO* 71 (1982) 1–46; yet another edition, by R.

Salomon, is forthcoming. I quote below Salomon's edition (Bailey line 7; Fussman 7a–7d). [See R. Salomon, "The Inscription of Senavarma, King of Oḍi," *IIJ* 29 (1986) 261–293.]

52. G. Fussman, "Nouvelles inscriptions śaka (II)," *BEFEO* 73 (1984) 38 ('5. reliquaire [en l'honneur de?] Kopśakasa'); Fussman translates: "ces reliques . . . parfumées de moralité, parfumées de concentration, parfumées de discernement."

53. E. H. Johnston, *The Buddhacarita or Acts of the Buddha,* Pt. II (Calcutta: 1935–1936; repr. Delhi: 1972) xvii; cf. F. Wilhelm, "Kanika and Kaniṣka—Aśvaghoṣa and Mātṛceta," *Papers on the Date of Kaniṣka,* ed. A. L. Basham (Leiden: 1968) 337–345; B. Bhattacharya, *Aśvaghoṣa: A Critical Study* (Santiniketan: 1976) 20.

54. On the important question of the role of "le rédacteur" in Buddhist inscriptions, see Fussman, *BEFEO* 56 (1969) 7, and his review of Th. Damsteegt, *Epigraphical Hybrid Sanskrit, JA* (1980) 424.

55. See Johnston, *Buddhacarita,* Pt. II, xxiv–lxxix.

56. Cantos XV–XXVIII of the *Buddhacarita* are known to us only in the Tibetan and Chinese translation. Johnston has published an English translation of the Tibetan text in "The Buddha's Mission and Last Journey; Buddhacarita, XV–XXVIII," *Acta Orientalia* 15 (1937) 26–111, 231–292. For the passage that concerns us, XXVII, 77–79, I follow Johnston, 276. The Sanskrit equivalents in parentheses are his; the Tibetan in parentheses is cited from *Peking,* 129, no. 5656, 169-4-8 to 169-5-3, the only version that was available to me.

57. See L. R. Lancaster, "The Oldest Mahāyāna Sūtra: Its Significance for the Study of Buddhist Development," *The Eastern Buddhist* 8 (1975) 30–41.

58. See G. Schopen, "The Phrase 'sa pṛthivīpradeśaś caityabhūto bhavet' in the Vajracchedikā: Notes on the Cult of the Book in Mahāyāna," *IIJ* 17 (1975) 147–181, esp. 163–167, for the *Saddharmapuṇḍarīka;* also J. Nobel, *Suvarṇabhāsottamasūtra. Das Goldglanz Sūtra. Ein Sanskrittext des Mahāyāna Buddhismus* (Leipzig: 1937) 6–19; G. Schopen, "The Five Leaves of the Buddhabalādhānaprātihāryavikurvāṇanirdeśa-sūtra Found at Gilgit," *JIP* 5 (1978) 329ff, and *Peking,* 34, 191-4-6ff. The translation offered in *JIP* 5 is a rather awful piece of English. This is, in part at least, because I tried to translate the Sanskrit and Tibetan at the same time—an exercise I would now never repeat—and because I tried to be unnaturally literal. But I also occasionally did not understand the text. One instance of this occurs on 332, where the passage beginning "As-so-ever he sees . . ." up to "does not (exist in the Tathāgata)" should be translated from the Tibetan: "As he sees those beings who will not honor the Teacher, who do not have faith in the Tathāgata, who are the lowest dregs (*kaśaṭṭaka*) and who can (only) be trained through (his manifesting) a final *nirvāṇa* and through relics, as he sees those, just so he manifests a final *nirvāṇa,* but a Tathāgata does not come and does not go." I am now working on a revised edition of the Sanskrit fragments and an edition of the complete Tibetan translation of the *Buddhabalā.* [Unfortunately, I am still working on it.]

59. U. Wogihara, *Abhisamayālaṃkārālokā Prajñāpāramitāvyākhyā,* fasc. 3 (Tokyo: 1934) 272.16, 273.5.

60. The passage in question is *Milindapañho* (Trenckner ed.) 98; see P. Demiéville, "Les versions chinoises du Milindapañha," *BEFEO* 24 (1924) 29, 34–35.

61. *Majjhima,* i, 104, 357; *Saṃyutta,* iii, 153; *Aṅguttara,* iv, 125, 176; *Vinaya,* iii, 3.

62. *Gilgit Manuscripts,* i, 50.19, 51.6.

63. The text is cited from Majumdar's edition published in J. Marshall, A. Foucher,

and N. G. Majumdar, *The Monuments of Sāñchī,* Vol. I (Delhi: 1940) 342, no. 404; see also nos. 389 and 396.

64. There is disagreement about the meaning of *ācariya-kula* here. I have followed G. Bühler, "Further Votive Inscriptions from the Stūpas at Sāñchi (II)," *EI* 2 (1894) 396 and n. 1; Lüders, *A List of Brahmi Inscriptions,* nos. 340 and 350; and Sircar, *Indian Epigraphical Glossary* (Delhi: 1966) 4. In *Monuments of Sāñchī,* Vol. I, 298, however, Majumdar connects the term found in the Sāñcī inscriptions with the *ācariyavāda* found in the much later *Mahāvaṃsa* in a very different context (see W. Geiger, *The Mahāvaṃsa* [London: 1908] 5.4 and 5.11, and *ācariya-kulavādakathā niṭṭhitā* which occurs as a kind of sectional colophon on 29). Majumdar then makes a number of very tenuous assertions concerning the demography of early Buddhist sects on the basis of his "connection." In "Buddhist Schools as Known from Early Indian Inscriptions," *Bharati. Bulletin of the College of Indology* 2 (1957/58) 28–29, A. M. Shastri questions some of the assertions but not Majumdar's basic "connection." The whole question needs further study in light, especially, of other epigraphical imprecations and the now much richer inscriptional materials in which named "schools" appear. [See also G. Schopen, "Doing Business for the Lord: Lending on Interest and Written Loan Contracts in the *Mūlasarvāstivāda-vinaya,*" *JAOS* 114 (1994) 527–554, esp. 550–551.]

65. A. Bareau, "La construction et le culte des stūpa d'après les Vinayapiṭaka," *BEFEO* 50 (1960) 253, 257; cf. J. Gernet, *Les aspects économiques du bouddhisme dans la société chinoise du Ve au Xe siècle* (Paris: 1956) 61ff, 159ff. For literature other than the *Vinayas,* see the remarks of M. Hofinger, "Le vol dans la morale bouddhique," *Indianisme et bouddhisme. Mélanges offerts à Mgr. Étienne Lamotte* (Louvain-La-Neuve: 1980) 185, which indicate the existence of a broader range of opinions.

66. In "La construction et le culte des stūpa," Bareau did, however, point out that these interdictions were maintained regardless of whether a given sect maintained "que le don au Buddha ou le culte rendu à un *stūpa* ne produisent pas de grands fruits." In fact, of the schools that he named as holders of such a view—Mahīśāsaka, Vetullaka, Caitika, Pūrvaśaila, and Aparaśaila—at least the last three are Mahāsāṅghika, and it is just the Mahāsāṅghika who most explicitly and with the greatest detail "interdisent de prendre ou d'utiliser les biens du stūpa" (253).

67. *BHSD,* 608–609; *Śikṣā,* 56.5, 170.3; *Bbh,* 163.11, 166.20; *RP,* 29.8; *Gv,* 228.21.

68. *Śikṣāsamuccaya* (Bendall ed.) 59.13, 63.15, 169.3, 269.4; P. Python, *Vinaya-Viniścaya-Upāli-Paripṛcchā. Enquête d'Upāli pour une exégèse de la discipline* (Paris: 1973) paragraphs 22 (*Śikṣā,* 169.3) and 25 (*Śikṣā,* 170.3).

69. Bendall's text here is mispunctuated; as a consequence the translation by Bendall and Rouse (*Śikshā-Samuccaya. A Compendium of Buddhist Doctrine* [London: 1922; repr. 1971] 57) is also off the mark; cf. *Ratnarāśi-Sūtra, Peking,* 24, 212-4-7ff.

70. Bendall and Rouse, *Śikshā-Samuccaya,* 57, n. 2; cf. Gernet, *Les aspects économiques du bouddhisme,* 67 and n. 5.

71. *Śikṣāsamuccaya* (Bendall ed.) 54.13ff (*Ākāśagarbhasūtra*); *Vinaya-Viniścaya-Upāli-Paripṛcchā* (Python ed.) paragraph 22.

72. Geary, *Furta Sacra,* 152–53.

73. I have discussed this interesting text in more detail in G. Schopen, "Two Problems in the History of Indian Buddhism," Ch. II above, 28–29.

74. *Gilgit Manuscripts,* iii 1, 73.9 (*Bhaiṣajyavastu* of the *Vinaya* of the Mūlasarvāstivādin; the same text also occurs twice in the *Divyāvadāna* [Cowell and Neil ed.]), 76.10–80.9, 465.10–469.18.

75. E. Waldschmidt, "Der Buddha preist die Verehrungswürdigkeit seiner Reliquien. Sondertext I des Mahāparinirvāṇasūtra," *Von Ceylon bis Turfan* (Göttingen: 1967) 426; *Caityapradakṣiṇagāthā, Peking,* 39, 86-2-8; cf. O. von Hinüber, "Die Erforschung der Gilgit-Handschriften, Neue Ergebnisse," *ZDMG* 131 (1981) nos. 13b, 13d, 60; H. Lüders, "Weitere Beiträge zur Geschichte und Geographie von Ostturkestan," *Philologica Indica* (Göttingen: 1940) 613; H. W. Bailey, "The Pradakṣiṇa-Sūtra of Chang Tsiang-Kuin," *Buddhist Studies in Honour of I. B. Horner,* ed. L. Cousins et al. (Dordrecht: 1974) 16.

76. *Buddhacarita,* XXVIII.69; Tibetan text, *Peking,* 129, 171-5-4; cf. Johnston, *Acta Orientalia* 15 (1937) 285.

77. *Mahāvaṃsa* (Geiger ed.) XVII.2–.3; cf. W. Geiger, *The Mahāvaṃsa or the Great Chronicle of Ceylon* (London: 1912) XVII.2–.3; H. Oldenberg, *The Dīpavaṃsa. An Ancient Buddhist Historical Record* (London: 1879; repr. New Delhi: 1982) XV 1–5. It should be noted that Pāli *diṭṭha,* though literally meaning "seen," blends into—like *dṛṣṭa* in Buddhist Hybrid Sanskrit—"visible," "present," "here," cf. the idiom *diṭṭhe dhamme, dṛṣṭe dharme,* in contrast to *samparāya*. The Sri Lankan Chronicles are rich in references to relics, and a careful study of them would undoubtedly produce interesting results. On the other hand, references to relics in the anthropological literature on Sri Lanka and Southeast Asia generally are few and rather disappointing. A notable exception, however, are the remarks of G. Obeyesekere, "The Buddhist Pantheon in Ceylon and Its Extensions" (see n. 47 above), 5–9.

78. Marshall et al., *The Monuments of Sāñchī,* Vol. I, 214, pl. 61.2; A. K. Coomaraswamy, *La Sculpture de Bharhut* (Paris: 1956) fig. 15, planche V; C. Sivaramamurti, *Amaravati Sculptures in the Madras Government Museum* (Madras: 1977) pls. xiv.2, xliii.1; A. Foucher, *Les bas-reliefs gréco-bouddhiques du gandhāra* (Paris: 1905) figs. 31, 288, 289, 291–295, 297–300; H. Ingholt, *Gandhāran Art In Pakistan* (New York: 1957) figs. 149–154, 158; etc.

79. For the literary sources and an analysis of them, see A. Bareau, *Recherches sur la biographie du buddha dans les sūtrapiṭaka et les vinayapiṭaka anciens: II. Les derniers mois, le parinirvāṇa et les funérailles,* T. II (Paris: 1971) 265ff.

80. A. Bareau, "Le parinirvāṇa du buddha et la naissance de la religion bouddhique," *BEFEO* 61 (1974) 287.

* * *

[See now also G. Schopen, "*Stūpa* and Tīrtha: Tibetan Mortuary Practices and an Unrecognized Form of Burial Ad Sanctos at Buddhist Sites in India," *The Buddhist Forum, Volume III, 1991–93, Papers in Honour and Appreciation of Professor David Seyfort Ruegg's Contribution to Indological, Buddhist and Tibetan Studies,* ed. T. Skorupski and U. Pagel (London: 1994) 273–293.]

CHAPTER VIII

On the Buddha and His Bones

The Conception of a Relic in the Inscriptions of Nāgārjunikoṇḍa

NĀGĀRJUNIKOṆḌA, WHICH LIES NOW at the bottom of a man-made lake, was a rich source not only of Buddhist and Hindu archaeological and art historical remains, but also of inscriptions. It has proved to be, as a consequence, an equally rich source of conundrums and a well-watered ground for speculation. There has been a persistent series of attempts, for example, to see elements of the Mahāyāna in the early phases of Nāgārjunikoṇḍa, in spite of the fact that there is no actual epigraphical or art-historical evidence for this movement anywhere in the Andhra area prior to the fifth or sixth centuries C.E., and in spite of the fact that what epigraphical and art-historical evidence we actually have richly documents the presence there of non-Mahāyāna groups.[1]

The inscriptions from Nāgārjunikoṇḍa are difficult. They are difficult because of "the want of precision of which they show ample evidence." Vogel has noted that, "considering that these inscriptions were meant to be perpetual records of pious donations made by ladies of royal blood, the careless manner in which they have been recorded is astonishing." [2] They are also difficult because they are, in many ways, atypical. They contain a number of phrases and formulae not found elsewhere in Indian Buddhist inscriptions so that we do not have, in many cases, parallels to assist us.[3] This difficulty is offset in part by the fact that these inscriptions tend to be highly repetitive; there are frequently numerous "copies" of the same basic inscription. I would like here to look at one of these atypical phrases that has important implications for Buddhist doctrinal history and to exploit the advantage that the existence of multiple copies presents us with.

Most of the pillar inscriptions connected with the *Mahācetiya*[4] are structured

---

Originally published in *Journal of the American Oriental Society* 108 (1988):527–537. Reprinted with stylistic changes with permission of American Oriental Society.

in exactly the same way. They begin with (1) the word *sidhaṃ,* "success!"; this is followed usually by (2) an invocation to the Buddha, which consists of the word *namo,* "adoration to," followed by a string of epithets of the Buddha in the genitive. Then come (3) the name of the place at which the gift recorded was made, put in the locative; (4) the name of the donor, her pedigrees and relationships; (5) the purpose or intent behind her gift; (6) the nature of the gift, etc. We will be concerned here only with the second and third elements: the invocation consisting of the *namo* plus the string of epithets in the genitive, and the name of the place at which the gift was made in the locative.

The first thing to notice is that the number of epithets in the string of genitives following *namo* varies. The fullest form of the formula containing the invocation and the name of the location at which the gift was made is, in the Prakrit original:

> *namo bhagavato deva-rāja-sakatasa supabudha-bodhino savaṃñuno sava-sat-ānukaṃpakasa jita-rāga-dosa-moha-vipamutasa mahāgaṇi-vasabha-gaṃdha-hathisa saṃma-saṃbudhasa dhātuvara-parigahitasa mahācetiye* . . .(C3)

Sircar translates this into Sanskrit as:

> *namaḥ bhagavate devarājasatkṛtāya suprabuddhabodhaye sarvajñāya sarvasattvānukampakāya jitarāgadoṣamoha-* (= *āsaktighṛṇājñāna-*)*-vipramuktāya mahāgaṇi-vṛṣabhagandhahastine* (= *bahusaṅkhyakaśiṣya-mahācāryeṣu pradhānaḥ*) *samyaksaṃbuddhāya dhātuvara-parigṛhītāya* (= *nirvāṇaprāptāya*) {*asmin*} *mahācaitye* . . .[5]

and Vogel puts it into English as:

> Adoration to the Lord, the Supreme Buddha, honoured by the Lord of the gods, omniscient, compassionate towards all sentient beings, freed from lust, hatred and delusion which have been conquered by him, the bull, and musk-elephant among great spiritual leaders, the perfectly Enlightened One, who is absorbed by the best of the elements (i.e., by Nirvāṇa). At the Mahāchetiya . . .[6]

At least four "copies" of this same inscription omit everything after *deva-rāja-sakatasa* up to *saṃma-saṃbudhasa,* reading as a consequence:

> *namo bhagavato deva-rāja-sakatasa saṃma-saṃbudhasa dhātuvara-parigahitasa mahācetiye* . . .[7]

Vogel's interpretation of what he takes to be the last of the string of epithets—*dhātuvara-parigahita,* "absorbed by the best of the elements (i.e., by Nirvāṇa)" —was suggested to him by de La Vallée Poussin, who added: "If the inscriptions belonged to the Mahāsanghikas, a conjectural explanation of *dhātu-*

vara as *Dharmadhātu* would not be excluded. The *Dharmadhātu* was sometimes a kind of Buddhist Brahman for the followers of the Mahāyāna."[8] Sircar also has taken the term in much the same way, glossing it with *nirvāṇaprāpta,* and Dutt, who translates the compound by "possessed of the excellent *dhātu,*" wants to see in it evidence that raises "the presumption that the Andhaka conception of *Nirvāṇa* was different from that of the Theravādins or their subsect the Mahīśāsakas,"[9] which de La Vallée Poussin, at least, does not query.[10] A. M. Shastri, finally, sees in the expression evidence indicating that "the Andhakas . . . upheld the docetic theory and believed that the Buddha was supramundane," and, following de La Vallée Poussin, that it "most probably alludes to the Kāya doctrine of the Mahāyānists for whom the Buddha was not a historical personality."[11]

This line of interpretation, which connects the expression with the development of Mahāyāna scholastic definitions and conceptions of the Buddha, did not go unquestioned. In editorial notes added to Vogel's initial publication of the inscriptions in *Epigraphia Indica,* Sastri said, "to me it does not appear to be impossible that the Mahāchetiya has been specified in these inscriptions as 'protected by the corporeal remains of the Buddha' and that the genitive case is used here to discriminate this *stūpa* from others not similarly consecrated."[12] Longhurst too was inclined toward this interpretation.[13] Even Dutt, three years before his "notes" on Vogel's treatment of the inscriptions, seems to have gone in this direction: he refers to one of the inscriptions and says it records "the gift of a pillar . . . to the *caitya,* enshrining a *dhātu* of Sammāsambuddha."[14]

There are basically two problems here. The interpretation of Vogel et al. takes *dhātuvara-parigahita* as one of the series of epithets governed by the initial *namo.* Sastri et al. want it rather to be a kind of "partitive" genitive constructed with the following *mahācetiye.* This is the first problem. The second, quite simply, is the meaning of *dhātuvaraparigahita,* the discussion so far having turned almost entirely on the significance of the final member of the compound.

The first problem arises in large part from the fact that the inscriptions are not punctuated. To quote again only the short form, we find:

> *namo bhagavato deva-rāja-sakatasa saṃma-saṃbudhasa dhātuvara-parigahitasa mahācetiye . . .*

Vogel et al. understand a *daṇḍa* or full stop after *dhātuvaraparigahitasa.* Sastri's interpretation, however, implies a full stop after *saṃma-saṃbudhasa.* But at least two other inscriptions from Nāgārjunikoṇḍa indicate that neither of these constructions of the text is correct. Āyaka-pillar Inscription B2 opens not with the invocation to the Buddha but with several lines praising the donor's father. The reference to the site at which the gift was made does not occur until almost the very end of the inscription and reads:

bhagavato saṃma-sa{ṃ}budhasa dhātuvaraparigahītasa mahācetiye imaṃ khaṃbhaṃ patidhapaṃta {rd. *patiṭhāpitaṃ*} *ti* . . .

Here, where the *namo* construction does not interfere, it is clear that the genitives are constructed with *mahācetiye* and that *dhātuvaraparigahīta* is an adjective modifying *saṃma-saṃbudhasa.* This is fully confirmed by the First Apsidal Temple Inscription E. This inscription also opens, like Āyaka-pillar Inscription B2, with the praise of a relative of the donor. Here, the gift recorded is said to have been made at:

saṃma-saṃbudhasa dhātu-{vara}[15]*-parigahitasa mahācetiya-pādamūle* . . .

Once again, without the *namo* plus genitive construction, there is no doubt as to how the text is to be constructed. In light of these two unambiguous cases, it seems fairly sure that *dhātuvaraparigahitasa* everywhere must be an adjective modifying *saṃma-saṃbudhasa,* and that *saṃma-saṃbudhasa dhātuvaraparigahitasa* everywhere must be taken, not as a part of the string of epithets in the genitive governed by *namo,* but as a separate adjectival phrase modifying *mahācetiye.* This is only more fully confirmed if we notice that, although almost all of our Nāgārjunikoṇḍa inscriptions open with or contain a *namo* invocation consisting of strings of *different* epithets of the Buddha, the collocation *saṃma-saṃbudhasa dhātuvara-parigahitasa* occurs *only* in inscriptions that make reference to the *mahācetiya* and *always* immediately precedes the noun *mahācetiya* in the locative. Just this observation allows some improvement in our understanding of the text that, in the short form of the formula, might now be read:

namo bhagavato deva-rājasakatasa {//} *saṃma-saṃbudhasa dhātuvaraparigahitasa mahācetiya* . . .

Homage to the Blessed One, he who is honored by the King of the Gods! At the Great Shrine of the Perfectly Enlightened One who is *dhātuvaraparigahita* . . .

While this is an improvement, it still leaves us, obviously, with the problem of the meaning of *dhātuvaraparigahita.* Although most previous discussions have concerned the meaning of the final member of the compound and, only correlatively, the first, the meaning of the middle term may also be of significance.

Dhātu- in our inscriptions has been taken by most interpreters—as we have seen—in the sense of "sphere," "state," "condition," and assimilated to *nirvāṇa-dhātu* or even *dharmadhātu.* This interpretation is, however, put forth without any justification—de La Vallée Poussin refers to his suggestion as "a conjectural explanation" —and it appears in fact to be unjustifiable. While not uncommon in this sense in abhidharmic, scholastic, and learned literature, or even in the technical vocabulary of the *sūtras,*[16] *dhātu* by itself is never certainly found with this meaning anywhere in Buddhist donative inscriptions dating prior to the medieval period, and even after this period one would be hard pressed to find a single unambiguous instance in donative inscriptions of this use.

Where it occurs in contemporaneous or—by Indian standards—nearly contemporaneous Buddhist donative inscriptions, *dhātu* always and unambiguously appears to mean "relic."[17] This is the case whether the term occurs in association with an explicit reference to the person of the Buddha—as it does in several Kharoṣṭhī inscriptions—or without such an association, as in a pillar inscription from Amarāvatī. We find, for example, *śastakhadhatu,* "the collar-bone relic of the Lord," in the Mathurā Elephant Inscription;[18] or *bhagavato śakamuni{sa} dhatuve pratiṭhavita,* "des reliques du Bienheureux Śākyamuni ont été déposées" in both the Bhagamoya and Kopśakasa Reliquary Inscriptions;[19] or, again, in both the Taxila Silver Scroll Inscription and the Taxila Gold Plate Inscription, we find reference to the deposition of *bhagavato dhatu,* "relics of the Blessed One."[20] The Amarāvatī pillar inscription already referred to records the gift of "a chaitya pillar with a relic," *cetiyakhabho sadhāduko dānaṃ,* without specifying to whom the relic "belongs."[21]

But if the term *dhātu* always appears to be used in the sense of "relic" in Buddhist inscriptions connected with shrines—*stūpas, caityas,* pillars, etc.—the same is true of its usage in literary texts wherever it occurs in narrative passages dealing with shrines. *Dhātu,* in the sense of "sphere," "condition," and so on, never appears to be found in such contexts unless it is specifically compounded with *nirvāṇa,* and *dhātu* alone is never used to stand for *nirvāṇa-dhātu.*[22] There would be little point in surveying all such passages, but it is worth noting an exact parallel to the first two members of our compound, *dhātuvara,* which occurs in an "historical" literary text that—again, by Indian standards—is quite close in time to our inscriptions, and quite near in geographical location. This parallel seems to render the equations *dhātuvara = dharmadhātu,* or *dhātuvara = nirvāṇa-dhātu,* altogether untenable.

We know from two inscriptions that there was during the period under discussion—the late third to the early fourth centuries C.E.—a community of Sri Lankan monks at Nāgārjunikoṇḍa.[23] It is, therefore, of some interest that the term *dhātuvara* occurs at least three times in the *Dīpavaṃsa,* which was "composed" sometime in the fourth century,[24] in a particularly important context. When Sumana was given instructions to go to Pāṭaliputta to get what would become one of the most important relics in Sri Lanka, an "object" which would make it possible for the monks living there "to see the Buddha," he was told to ask Aśoka: *dehi dhātuvaraṃ tassa,* "grant him the most excellent of relics." When Sumana arrives he says to Asóka: "Your friend, Great King, has faith in the teaching of the Buddha. Grant him the most excellent of relics. He is going to make a *stūpa* for the Teacher" (*sahāyo te mahārāja pasanno buddhasāsane / dehi dhātuvaraṃ tassa thūpaṃ kāhati satthuno*). Sumana then goes and makes a similar request to Kosiya (Indra) in almost exactly the same words: *devānampiyo rājā so pasanno buddhasāsane / dehi dhātuvaraṃ tassa karissati thūpam uttamaṃ.*[25]

Although seemingly a small point, it is worth noting the language used in the request Sumana was told to, and did, make to Aśoka: *dhātuvara* and "the Teacher" do not appear to have been thought of here as different things. The *stūpa* that was to be built to house the *dhātuvara* is specifically said to be "for the Teacher," not—be it noted—for a part of the Teacher or for something belonging to the Teacher. And if the language here only suggests that the relic was not thought of as merely a part of the physical remains of the Buddha, but was thought to be the Buddha himself, it—like so much else in the *Dīpavaṃsa*—is explicitly stated in the *Mahāvaṃsa*. In the *Mahāvaṃsa* account of the same events narrated in our passages from the *Dīpavaṃsa*, Mahinda complains to Devānaṃpiya, saying: "For a long time, O King, we have not seen the Perfect Buddha, the Teacher" (*ciradiṭṭho hi saṃbuddho satthā no manujādhipa*); to which the King replies: "But did you not tell me, Revered Sir, that the Perfect Buddha is extinguished/dead?" (*bhāsittha nanu bhante me: saṃbuddho nibbuto iti*); to which Mahinda replies in turn: "When the relics are seen (or 'are present'), the Buddha is seen (or 'is present')" (*dhātusu diṭṭhesu diṭṭho hoti jino iti*).[26]

It is also worth noting that *dhātuvara* continues to be used in the *vaṃsa* literature. It occurs twice, for example, in the *Thūpavaṃsa,* which probably dates to the thirteenth century; once in the rather florid opening verse, and once to refer to the same relic that the *Dīpavaṃsa* also referred to as *dhātuvara.*[27] It occurs again in the *Chakesadhātuvaṃsa,* which, though of unknown author or date, is clearly later and yet gives clear expression to the same conception of a relic as is found at the very beginning of the *vaṃsa* literature in the *Dīpa-* and *Mahāvaṃsa.* In one passage, for example, we find the enshrinement of a relic described in the following terms:

> . . . having taken the relic of the Buddha from his head [where he had placed it out of respect], having bathed it with water from Sakka's jar, saying: 'May the Reverend Blessed One live/dwell at this place for five thousand years for the benefit of all living things,' he enshrined it.
>
> . . . *dasabalassa dhātuṃ sīsato oropayitvā sakkabhiṅkārodakena nhāpetvā bhante bhagavā imasmiṃ ṭhāne sakalajanahitatthaṃ pañcavassasahassapamāṇaṃ tiṭṭhā 'ti vatvā ṭhapesi.*[28]

We might notice again the language used in this passage from the *Chakesadhātuvaṃsa.* Notice, for example, that in speaking to the relic, the same titles are used as are used in addressing the Buddha himself: *bhante bhagavā;* rephrased, the request to dwell or live for a long time at the place in question, although spoken to the relic, is addressed to the Buddha. Again, the relic and the Buddha do not appear to have been thought of as separate things.

Of course, the *Chakesadhātuvaṃsa* is a late text, but its conception of a relic is not. The same conception is already found, as we have seen, in the *Mahā-* and *Dīpavaṃsa,* the latter especially being only slightly later than our inscriptions from Nāgārjunikoṇḍa. Something like it is also found, as I have already pointed out elsewhere, in inscriptions and textual sources which are somewhat earlier than our Nāgārjunikoṇḍa epigraphs.[29] In the Kopśakasa Reliquary Inscription, for instance, which has been dated to 26 C.E. and which records the deposition of "reliques du Bienheureux Śākyamuni," these relics (*dhaduve*) are said to be *śila-paribhavida sama(s)i-paribhaveṃtu prañā-paribhavida,* "saturated/invigorated/enlivened by morality, concentration, and wisdom." The Inscription of Senavarma, King of Oḍi, that also dates to the early first century C.E., also contains a very similar characterization of the relics of Śākyamuni. Here the relics (*dhadu*) are characterized as *śila(pari)bhavita samasiprañavimutiñaṇadra(śa)paribhavita,* "saturated/invigorated/enlivened by morality, saturated/invigorated/enlivened by concentration, wisdom, emancipation, knowledge, and vision."[30]

At the very least, this must mean that the relics are characterized by—full of—exactly the same spiritual forces and faculties that characterize, and, in fact, constitute and animate the living Buddha. To speak of an inanimate object in these terms, to speak of an inanimate object as "saturated or invigorated by morality or concentration" would at least require some explanation. But as a matter of fact, with one apparent exception, Buddhist sources do not speak of inanimate objects in such terms. When *paribhāvita,* the participle in these inscriptions, is used in literary sources, it is always used—again, with one apparent exception—in reference to two related categories of "things": (1) "living persons"—like ascetics or *bodhisattvas*—or that which distinguishes those persons from inanimate objects: their mental faculties, minds, or consciousness (*citta, manas, vijñāna,* etc.); and (2) "objects" that contain life or are capable of being enlivened, like a body or an egg that is being incubated.[31] It is, for example, as a result of being "sat on" (*adhisayita*), "heated" (*parisedita*), and "saturated/invigorated" by a hen that a chicken's egg "lives."[32] Conversely, in at least one text, *aparibhāvitakāya,* "having an uninvigorated body," is twice paired with *alpāyuṣka,* "having a short life."[33] The necessary connection suggested here between being *paribhāvita* by something and continuing to live is made even more explicit elsewhere. There is, in fact, at least one remarkable passage that has come down to us in both Pāli and Sanskrit that indicates that what is "invigorated with morality and wisdom"—as relics are said to be—is what continues to live after the breakup of the body. The Pāli version of this passage, which is now found in the *Saṃyutta-nikāya,* provides us the fullest indication of its setting: a devout layman from Kapilavatthu expresses to the Buddha the anxieties he has about what will happen to him after death (*imamhi cāhaṃ samaye kālaṃ kareyyaṃ kā mayhaṃ gati ko abhisamparāyo iti*). The Buddha reassures him (*mā bhāyi . . . mā bhāyi . . .*) and tells him that, after the destruction of the body:

> the mind that is for a long time saturated/invigorated/enlivened by faith, saturated/invigorated by morality, learning, renunciation, and wisdom, goes upward, goes to distinction.
>
> *cittaṃ dīgharattaṃ saddhāparibhāvitam sīla-suta-cāga(paññā)-paribhāvitaṃ, tam uddhagāmi hoti visesagāmi.*[34]

When *paribhāvita* is used in Buddhist literary sources, it appears, then, always to express something like "impregnated with active force," "invigorated or enlivened by," and is used—with one exception—in reference to living persons and to that which animates living persons, or to objects that contain life. The exception is, of course, relics, whether the term used is *dhātu* or *śarīra*. Literary sources too, like inscriptions, characterize relics as "saturated or invigorated with virtue and wisdom." We might look at just two examples that are somewhat earlier than the Nāgārjunikoṇḍa inscriptions, but probably nearly contemporaneous with the Senavarma and Kopśakasa Reliquary Inscriptions.

A particularly interesting example comes from the *Aṣṭasāhasrikāprajñāpāramitā*, which some have associated—though not necessarily convincingly—with South India and the area around Nāgārjunikoṇḍa.[35] Here we find it said that:

> *itaḥ prajñāpāramitāto nirjātāni tāni tathāgataśarīrāṇi pūjāṃ labhante yad uta prajñāpāramitāparibhāvitatvāt.*
>
> These relics of the Tathāgata, being born from the Perfection of Wisdom, receive worship—that is to say from the fact that they are invigorated by the Perfection of Wisdom.[36]

Here, *paribhāvita* is glossed by *nirjāta*, "to be born, given life." Elsewhere in the text it is, for example, the "all knowledge" of the Buddha that is said to be "born from the Perfection of Wisdom" (*prajñāpāramitānirjātā hi . . . tathāgatānām arhatāṃ samyaksaṃbuddhānāṃ sarvajñatā*).[37] What gives life to and animates the "all knowledge" of the Buddha, gives life to and animates the relic.

The second passage we might cite comes from a very different type of literature and is particularly significant because of that. Aśvaghoṣa in his *Buddhacarita* characterizes the relics (*khams, dhātu*) of Śākyamuni as "full of virtue" (*dge legs gaṅ ba*). He then intentionally plays on several senses of the word *dhātu:*

> The jars hold the great relics . . . like the jewelled ore (*dhātu*) of a great mountain, and the relics (*dhātu*) are unharmed by fire, just as the sphere (*dhātu*) of the chief of the gods (Brahmā) in heaven (is unharmed by the fire at the end of the aeon).

"These bones," he says, are "informed (*paribhāvita?*) with universal benevolence (*maitrī*)" (*byams pas yoṅs su rnam par bsgoms pa*):[38]

Notice that when *dhātu* is used here in the sense of "sphere," that sense is secondary and forced and occurs in a context of contrived and learned wordplay. This sort of learned artfulness is absent from our Nāgārjunikoṇḍa inscriptions. The primary meaning of *dhātu* in Aśvaghoṣa is, as everywhere in passages dealing with the physical remains of Śākyamuni, "relic." Notice too that Aśvaghoṣa, who can be dated fairly firmly to the first century C.E., characterizes relics as full of what can only be human qualities—"virtue" and "universal benevolence"—and, in doing so, appears to use at least once the same participle, or something very near to it, as was used by both contemporary or nearly contemporary canonical *sūtra* texts and Indian inscriptions.

Aśvaghoṣa was, of course, no ordinary monk. His work exhibits immense learning and broad culture. The range of sources he was able to draw upon is, as Johnston has shown, daunting.[39] For just that reason, the conception of relics articulated in the *Buddhacarita* is particularly important: it represents a conception current not among "the masses" or village monks, but a conception current among the most learned, cultured, and educated of monastic circles. The fact that there is a marked consistency in both conception and vocabulary with regard to relics in such diverse sources as Buddhist epigraphical records, canonical or paracanonical texts, historical or *vaṃsa* literature, and learned poetical works of "high" literature, makes it possible justifiably to assert that this conception of the relic—the conception that takes the relic as a living presence animated and characterized by the same qualities that animated and characterized the living Buddha—is the one conception that had general currency in the Buddhist world in the period that both preceded and followed the Nāgārjunikoṇḍa inscriptions. This same material also clearly establishes the wide currency of the term *dhātu* in the sense of "relic" for the same period. It is, therefore, virtually certain that it is this sense of the word *dhātu* and this conception of a relic that is to be expected in the Nāgārjunikoṇḍa inscriptions as well. To assert otherwise would require clear evidence, and this is not forthcoming.

The occurrence of the expression *dhātuvara* in the *vaṃsa* literature, where the sense of the second element is fairly obvious, supports the derivation of *vara,* the second member of the Nāgārjunikoṇḍa compound, from $\sqrt{2}$ *vṛ,* and suggests the likelihood that the interpreters of the Nāgārjunikoṇḍa inscriptions were correct in assigning to it there the sense of "the most excellent," "the best," etc. But in light of the fact that *dhātuvara* occurs in the inscriptions in close association with the term *mahācetiya,* the latter denoting a *stūpa* or monumental reliquary, one other *possible* derivation suggests itself. It is *possible*—but only that—to derive *-vara-* from $\sqrt{1}$ *vṛ* and see in it the meaning "enclosing," "surrounding," and, therefore, "room" or "chamber." *Dhātuvara-* would then be almost perfectly parallel to *dhātugarbha,* "relic chamber," which is, of course, well attested. This interpretation of *-vara-*, moreover, may receive some support from at least one other Buddhist inscription, the Sui Vihār Copper-Plate Inscription of the Year 11, which was recovered from the chamber of a ruined *stūpa. Although it is itself not without difficulties,* it appears to record in addition to the "foundation of the staff" [of the *stūpa*] (*yaṭhipratiṭhanaṃ ṭhapa(i)chaṃ*), the gift of the *pari-vara* or *anu-pari-vara* as well. As one possible meaning of the latter, Konow suggests that *anu-pari-vara* must have the same meaning as he assigned to *pari-vara*—"cover," "surrounding wall or hedge," "enclosure"—and must "refer to the chamber raised around the relics, after the *yaṭhi* had been put up."[40] That *vara* might have this sense in the Nāgārjunikoṇḍa inscriptions is possible and only that. To establish that it did would require much fuller and less uncertain evidence.

Parigahita, the final element of the Nāgārjunikoṇḍa compound, has been taken in one of two ways: either "absorbed (by)" or "protected (by)." But the participle occurs in several other compounds in the Nāgārjunikoṇḍa inscriptions. It occurs several times in an adjectival compound used to describe a male member of the ruling family. He is called *virūpakhapatimahāsena-parigahita,* which Vogel translates as "absorbed by Mahāsena the Lord of Virūpakhas" in one place, but as "favoured (absorbed?) by Mahāsena, etc." in another.[41] Although it proved awkward, since Vogel had translated *parigahita* in our compound by "absorbed," he appears to have felt it should have the same force in this compound. Others, like Sastri and Sircar, have taken the term here to mean "protected by."[42]

Parigahita also occurs in Vogel's C1 and C2:

> *ācariyānaṃ aparamahāvinas(e)liyāna(ṃ) suparigahitaṃ imaṃ mahācetiyana-vakaṃma(ṃ).*
>
> This new construction, the Great Shrine, was fully received (or 'taken possession of') by the Teachers of the Aparamahāvinaseliya sect.[43]

Yet another usage is attested in the First Apsidal Temple Inscription E, and in two other places where the gifts recorded are said to be *savaniyuta(ṃ) cātusala-parigahitaṃ sela-maṃṭava(ṃ);* Vogel translates as "a stone shrine [Skt. *maṇḍapa*] surrounded by a cloister and provided with everything."[44]

Having established with a fair degree of probability what *dhātuvara* means in our inscriptions allows us to eliminate some of the meanings ascribed to *parigahita.* Although the meaning "protected" fits well in several contexts, since our compound, *dhātuvaraparigahita,* describes the Buddha, and not the *Mahācetiya,* it seems unlikely there: the Buddha almost certainly would not be, nor need to be "protected" by "the most excellent relic." It also seems unlikely that he would be described as "taken possession of" by the relic. Vogel's "absorbed in," though not impossible, is a meaning that is both rather far from the primary meaning of *parigahita* and not easily attested. This would seem to leave only "surrounded by" or "enclosed in" —a sense that is quite close to the literal meaning of *parigahita* and, therefore, involves the least amount of conjecture.

Our discussion, then, generates at least one clear alternative to the previous interpretations of the formula found in the Nāgārjunikoṇḍa inscriptions, and one other interpretation that is at least possible. The short form of the formula might, in light of our discussion, be better translated as:

> Homage to the Blessed One, he who is honored by the king of the gods! At the Great Shrine of the Perfectly Enlightened One *who is enclosed within the most excellent relic . . .*

or possibly—but again only that—we might be able to translate *saṃma-saṃbud-hasa dhātuvaraparigahitasa mahāchetiye* . . . as:

> At the Great Shrine of the Perfectly Enlightened One who is enclosed in the relic chamber . . .

If we adopt the first and most likely of these interpretations, the wording of our Nāgārjunikoṇḍa inscriptions would seem to indicate that their redactor *did not* think of the *dhātu* or "relic" as a piece or a part of the Buddha. He seems, in fact, to have thought of it as something that contained or enclosed the Buddha himself, something in which the Buddha was wholly present. But if the Buddha was present in the relic, the relic could not represent—as has sometimes been argued—a token or reminder of the past and "dead" Buddha: for the Buddha to be present, he would have to have been thought of as alive. And such a living "relic" could, of course, be characterized as "saturated or invigorated with morality, knowledge, and wisdom."

Even if we adopt the second interpretation, the resultant meaning is much the same. In this case, the inscriptions do not refer to the relic of the Buddha in the shrine but to the Buddha himself being enclosed within its "relic" chamber. The wording again would indicate that it is not a part or a piece of the departed Buddha that is there in the chamber but the Buddha himself who is wholly present there. In both interpretations the conception of a "relic" seems to be very much the same. Both interpretations are only variant forms of the conception of a "relic" already articulated in the Senavarma and Kopśakasa Reliquary Inscriptions, in Aśvaghoṣa and the *Aṣṭasāhasrikā,* and both suggest that the redactor of the Nāgārjunikoṇḍa inscriptions—almost certainly a monk—thought of the Buddha as a living presence dwelling in his shrine.

Although we do not necessarily know anything about the redactor of our inscriptions, we do know something about the individual who "completed" the construction of the shrine and the erection of the pillars on which the inscriptions are inscribed. He is described in two of the inscriptions where we find, in Vogel's translation:

> . . . this pious foundation of the Mahāchetiya has been completed by the Reverend Ānanda, who knows the *Dīgha-* and the *Majjhima-nikāyas* by heart, (who is) a disciple of the masters of the Ayira-haṃgha (Skt. *Ārya-saṅgha*) who are resident in Paṃṇagāma and who are preachers and preceptors of the *Dīgha*, the *Majjhima{-nikāya}* and of the five *Mātukas*. This pious work, the Mahāchetiya, was completed and the pillars were erected.[45]

The Reverend Ānanda—although not specifically designated as such here—appears to have been the *navakammika*, the monk appointed as the superintendent of construction of religious buildings.[46] The construction of the *cetiya* and the erection of the pillars was overseen by him. As a consequence, even if he was not himself the redactor of the inscriptions incised on the pillars, he would still have been responsible for their content, and they would have to have been approved by him. This would mean that the views expressed in the inscriptions—notably, the conception of a relic—must represent the view and conceptions that were either dictated by or redacted under the auspices of a very learned monk, a monk "who knew by heart both the *Dīgha-* and *Majjhima-nikāyas*." They do not, again, represent the views of an uneducated village monk. They do not represent a popular conception of a relic, but an official, monastic conception.

We also know that the Mahācetiya at Nāgārjunikoṇḍa was "accepted or taken possession of by," or "belonged to," the Aparamahāvinaseliya teachers (*ācariyānaṃ aparamahāvinas{e}liyāna{ṃ} suparigahitaṃ imaṃ mahācetiyanavakaṃma{ṃ}*, C1, C2). But what little we think we know about the doctrinal position of the Aparamahāvinaseliya group—and this is on the generous assumption that it is the same as the Aparaśaila—*appears* not to set altogether well with this fact. Both Vasumitra and Vinītadeva maintain that one of the tenets of this school was: *mchod rten la mchod pa ni 'bras bu mchog tu gyur pa ma yin no,* "l'acte de vénérer (*pūjākara*) un reliquaire (*stūpa*) ne procure pas un grand fruit."[47] Rosen has taken the *appearance* at face value and offered the following explanation:

> Amongst their [the Aparamahāvinaseliyas'] doctrines, according to Vasumitra, we find it stated that the worship of a *stūpa* or the worship of a *caitya* does not produce much fruit. Nevertheless, the fact that one of the largest *stūpas* in India was built for the benefit of this sect, indicates that they were willing to alter their practices to fit more modern times.[48]

Rosen, in referring to both *stūpas* and *caityas,* has been misled in part by Bareau's paraphrase of Vasumitra.[49] The Tibetan text has only *mchod rten,* and, while it is true that we cannot be sure whether this translated *stūpa* or *caitya,* both Bareau and Masuda translate their texts by *stūpa.*[50] It is also true that one of the most notable characteristics of the Aparamahāvinaseliya inscriptions at Nāgārjunikoṇḍa is the complete avoidance of the term *stūpa.* Although it is used everywhere else in Buddhist inscriptions in India, the term never occurs at Nāgārjunikoṇḍa. There Buddhist "shrines" are always called *cetiyas.* This usage shows every sign of being intentional and very likely reflects a regional influence in the vocabulary applied to Buddhist sacred sites. In addition to these considerations, our inscriptions make it clear that the Mahācetiya at Nāgārjunikoṇḍa was not conceived of as "un reliquaire," but as a structure housing the living presence of the Buddha: any worship of "it" would actually be of *him.*

But these considerations aside, Rosen's argument is still—in at least one aspect—a little startling. It is not known who among the several Vasumitras who appear in the history of Buddhist scholasticism was the author of the work on "les sectes bouddhiques" assigned to that name. What appears to be known is that the first translation of the work into Chinese took place at "la fin du ive siècle ou début du ve siècle de notre ère." There is also general agreement that its author, whoever he was, was a Sarvāstivādin.[51] We have, then, an assertion by an unknown Sarvāstivādin author, of unknown geographic provenance, in a work of about the fourth century purporting to express the views of a group to which he did not belong. Over against this we have an historical record either written by, or redacted under the auspices of, a learned Aparamahāvinaseliya monk from Nāgārjunikoṇḍa in the third century that was intended to record what a community of Aparamahāvinaseliya monks there actually did. By any criteria, the historical value of the two sources for the history of the Aparamahāvinaseliya cannot be the same. It is, therefore, curious that Rosen takes as somehow more representative of the Aparamahāvinaseliya position not what Aparamahāvinaseliya monks in the third century actually did, but what a Sarvāstivādin author of the fourth century said. This perfunctory preference for formal literary sources—which is quite common in historical works on Indian Buddhism—can only result in histories of Buddhism that have little relationship to what practicing Buddhists actually did. At the very least, it rather effectively impedes an adequate appraisal or appreciation of other kinds of sources. But it is, in fact, precisely because our inscriptional formula from Nāgārjunikoṇḍa is one of these "other kinds of sources" that it is important.

If, for example, the phrase *saṃma-saṃbudhasa dhātuvaraparigahitasa mahācetiye* means what I have suggested it does, then it would appear to be another piece of nontextual evidence that indicates that we have not yet understood at all well the Buddhist conception of "relics" or the nature of Buddhist sacred sites. Elsewhere I have recently presented evidence indicating that the earliest actually attestable Buddhist conception of relics was that "la relique corporelle . . . c'est un être vivant 'doué de souffle' "; "that relics were thought to retain—to be infused with, impregnated with—the qualities that animated and defined the living Buddha"; that the *stūpa* or reliquary was cognitively classified as a "living person of rank" and that it was—like the Hindu image—a "juristic personality" and owned property; that, finally, the Indian Buddhist community practiced a form of what in the West was called "burial *ad sanctos*" and that this can only be accounted for by the belief that the *stūpa* contained a living presence.[52] The formula found in the Nāgārjunikoṇḍa inscriptions appears to be yet one more piece of this ever-more-clearly emerging complex of actual beliefs—as opposed to the formal literary doctrines—of practicing Indian Buddhists, both monastic and lay.

Notes

1. N. Dutt, "Discovery of a Bone-Relic at an Ancient Centre of Mahāyāna," *IHQ* 5 (1929) 794–796; Dutt, "Notes on the Nāgārjunikoṇḍa Inscriptions," *IHQ* 7 (1931) 633–653; H. Sarkar, *Studies in Early Buddhist Architecture of India* (Delhi: 1966) 74–96; E. S. Rosen, "Buddhist Architecture and Lay Patronage at Nāgārjunikoṇḍa," in A. L. Dallapiccola and S. Z. Lallemant, eds., *The Stūpa: Its Religious, Historical and Architectural Significance* (Wiesbaden: 1980) 112–126; A. and H. Wayman, *The Lion's Roar of Queen Śrīmālā* (New York: 1974) 1–4; A. Wayman, "The Mahāsāṃghika and the Tathāgatagarbha," *JIABS* 1 (1978) 42–43; etc. On the Mahāyāna in Andhra art, see D. Barrett, "The Later School of Amarāvatī and Its Influence," *Art and Letters* 28.2 (1954) 41–53; D. Barrett, *Sculptures from Amaravati in the British Museum* (London: 1954) 59; Ét. Lamotte, "Mañjuśrī," *TP* 68 (1960) 4; on the Mahāyāna in epigraphical sources, see G. Schopen, "Mahāyāna in Indian Inscriptions," *IIJ* 21 (1979) 1–19; Schopen, "The Inscription on the Kuṣān Image of Amitābha and the Character of the Early Mahāyāna in India," *JIABS* 10.2 (1987) 99–137. Since writing the first of these, I have come across a single instance of the Mahāyāna formula in an inscription from the Andhra area; it dates to the fifth century; see T. N. Ramachandran, *Nāgārjunikoṇḍa 1938*, MAŚI, No. 71 (Calcutta: 1953) 29 (III).

2. J. Ph. Vogel, "Prakrit Inscriptions from a Buddhist Site at Nāgārjunikoṇḍa," *EI* 20 (1929) 11–12.

3. Cf. G. Schopen, "Filial Piety and the Monk in the Practice of Indian Buddhism," Ch. III above, 63–64.

4. Vogel, *EI* 20 (1929) A2–A4, B1–B5, C1–C5, D2–D4, and X. Citations in the text are made following Vogel's letter/number system.

5. D. C. Sircar, *Select Inscriptions Bearing on Indian History and Civilization*, 2nd ed. (Calcutta: 1965) 230. I have silently corrected two misprints in the passage cited.

6. Vogel, *EI* 20 (1929) 17.

7. Vogel, *EI* 20 (1929) 16, n. 2; B3, C1, D2, and D4.

8. Vogel, *EI* 20 (1929) 29, n. 1.

9. Dutt, "Notes on the Nāgārjunikoṇḍa Inscriptions," 649–650, and N. Dutt, *Buddhist Sects in India* (Calcutta: 1970) 124–125.

10. L. de La Vallée Poussin, "Notes et bibliographie bouddhiques," *MCB* 1 (1931–1932) 383.

11. A. M. Shastri, *An Outline of Early Buddhism (A Historical Survey of Buddhology, Buddhist Schools and Sanghas Mainly Based on the Study of Pre-Gupta Inscriptions)* (Varanasi:

1965) 29–30; cf. A. M. Shastri, "The Legendary Personality of the Buddha as Depicted in Pre-Gupta Indian Inscriptions," *The Orissa Historical Research Journal* 8 (1960) 172–173.

12. Vogel, *EI* 20 (1929) 29, n. 1.

13. A. H. Longhurst, *The Buddhist Antiquities of Nāgārjunikoṇḍa, Madras Presidency*, MASI, No. 54 (Delhi: 1938) 18.

14. Dutt, "Discovery of a Bone-Relic at an Ancient Centre of Mahāyāna," 794.

15. The "scribe" has omitted *-vara-* here, but this is almost certainly only another instance of the "carelessness" in these records noted by Vogel; cf. also *EI* 20 (1929) 21, n. 2.

16. See the long entry on *dhātu* in *BHSD*, 282–284.

17. Cf. the very problematic passage in the Senavarma Reliquary Inscription, *ime śarireṇa tadagada-prava-diśaṇivaṇa-dhatu-gade ta pratiṭhavemi* (7c–7d), where, if *dhatu* were to be constructed with the preceding *ṇivaṇa-*, we might have an instance where the sense of "sphere," etc. was in play. But this passage, in spite of the efforts of Bailey, Fussman, and Salomon remains, as the last of these scholars says, "highly obscure"; H. W. Bailey, "A Kharoṣṭhī Inscription of Senavarma, King of Oḍi," *JRAS* (1980) 21–29; G. Fussman, "Documents épigraphiques kouchans (III). L'inscription kharoṣṭhī de senavarma, roi d'oḍi: une nouvelle lecture," *BEFEO* 71 (1982) 1–45; R. Salomon, "The Inscription of Senavarma, King of Oḍi," *IIJ* 29 (1986) 261–293.

18. S. Konow, *Kharoshṭhī Inscriptions with the Exception of Those of Aśoka*, Corpus Inscriptionum Indicarum, Vol. II, Pt. 1 (Calcutta: 1929) 49–50, XVI.

19. G. Fussman, "Nouvelles inscriptions śaka (II)," *BEFEO* 73 (1984) 33–38, 38–46; R. Salomon, "The Bhagamoya Relic Bowl Inscription," *IIJ* 27 (1984) 107–120.

20. Konow, *Kharoshṭhī Inscriptions*, 70–77, XXVII; 83–86, XXXI.

21. C. Sivaramamurti, *Amaravati Sculptures in the Madras Government Museum*, Bulletin of the Madras Government Museum, N.S. Vol. IV (Madras: 1977) 283, no. 47.

22. But see Aśvaghoṣa's use of *dhātu* cited below.

23. Vogel, *EI* 20 (1929) 22; D. C. Sircar and A. N. Lahiri, "Footprint Slab Inscription from Nagarjunikoṇḍa," *EI* 33 (1960) 247–250.

24. K. R. Norman, *Pāli Literature. Including the Canonical Literature in Prakrit and Sanskrit of All the Hīnayāna Schools of Buddhism*, A History of Indian Literature, ed. J. Gonda, Vol. VII, Fasc. 2 (Wiesbaden: 1983) 115ff.

25. H. Oldenberg, *The Dīpavaṃsa: An Ancient Buddhist Historical Record* (London and Edinburgh: 1879) 79.14, 79.21, 80.8.

26. W. Geiger, *The Mahāvaṃsa* (London: 1908) XVII.2–XVII.3; on the relationship of the *Mahāvaṃsa* to the *Dīpavaṃsa*, see Norman, *Pāli Literature*, 115.

27. N. A. Jayawickrama, *The Chronicle of the Thūpa and the Thūpavaṃsa*, Sacred Books of the Buddhists, Vol. XXVII (London: 1971) 147.1, 201.1; on the date of the *Thūpavaṃsa*, see Norman, *Pāli Literature*, 142–143.

28. I. P. Minayeff, "The Cha-kesa-dhātu-vaṃsa," *JPTS* (1885) 10.11, 8.15; cf. B. C. Law, "An Account of the Six Hair Relics of the Buddha (Chakesadhātuvaṃsa)," *JIH* 30 (1952) 193–204; on the date of the *Chakesadhātuvaṃsa*, see Norman, *Pāli Literature*, 143.

29. G. Schopen, "Burial *Ad Sanctos* and the Physical Presence of the Buddha in Early Indian Buddhism," Ch. VII above, 125–128.

30. Fussman, *BEFEO* 73 (1984) 38ff; Fussman, *BEFEO* 71 (1982) 4, 7a–7b; Salomon, *IIJ* 29 (1986) 265. There are several additional references to "relics" in the Senavarma Inscription that seem to point in the same direction. I hesitate to cite them, however, since in spite of the fine efforts of both Fussman and Salomon they remain obscure. Note

only that in 12b the "relic" deposited by Senavarma seems clearly to be characterized as "immortal" or "deathless" (*amudae dhatue*), and cf. n. 17 above.

31. Schopen, "Burial *Ad Sanctos* and the Physical Presence of the Buddha in Early Indian Buddhism," Ch. VII above, 128.

32. *Majjhima*, i, 104, 357; *Saṃyutta*, iii, 153; *Aṅguttara*, iv, 125, 176; *Vinaya*, iii, 3. All references to canonical Pāli sources are to the editions published by the Pāli Text Society.

33. *Gilgit Manuscripts*, i, 50.19, 51.6.

34. *Saṃyutta*, v, 369–370; the Sanskrit version of this passage is cited in L. de La Vallée Poussin, *L'Abhidharmakośa de Vasubandhu*, T. II (Paris: 1923–1931; repr. 1971) 95, n. 1. For Hindu and Jain instances of the use of the participle *-bhāvita* in similar contexts, see Edgerton, "The Hour of Death," *ABORI* 8.3 (1927) 225, 227.

35. See, for example, E. Conze, *The Prajñāpāramitā Literature*, 2nd ed. (Tokyo: 1978) 1ff.

36. P. L. Vaidya, *Aṣṭasāhasrikā Prajñāpāramitā*, Buddhist Sanskrit Texts, No. 4 (Darbhanga: 1960) 49.6.

37. Vaidya, *Aṣṭasāhasrikā*, 36.1.

38. *Buddhacarita*, XXVII.77–XXVII.79; I cite here the translation and Sanskrit equivalents given in E. H. Johnston, "The Buddha's Mission and Last Journey; Buddhacarita, XV–XXVIII," *Acta Orientalia* 15 (1937) 276; the Tibetan is cited from *Peking*, 129, no. 5656, 169-4-8 to 169-5-3.

39. For a discussion of both Aśvaghoṣa's date and his learning, see E. H. Johnston, *The Buddhacarita or Acts of the Buddha*, Pt. II (Calcutta: 1935–1936; repr. 1972) xvii, xxiv–lxxix; B. Bhattacharya, *Aśvaghoṣa: A Critical Study* (Santiniketan: 1976) 20; etc.

40. S. Konow, *Kharoshṭhī Inscriptions*, 141; see also—for other meanings of *parivara*—38, 60, 170. For earlier interpretations of the inscription, see the sources cited in Konow, 141, nn. 2–6; more recently, D. R. Patik, "The Origin of Memorial Stones," in S. Settar and G. D. Sontheimer, eds., *Memorial Stones. A Study of Their Origin, Significance and Variety* (Dharwad: 1982) 52–53; G. Schopen, "Two Problems in the History of Indian Buddhism," Ch. II above, 34. [See also G. Schopen, "Ritual Obligations and Donor Roles of Monks in the Pāli *Vinaya*," Ch. IV above.] There are at least two other sources that might also suggest that *dhātu-vara* was intended to refer to a structure holding relics. Sircar sees in vs. 16 of the Mandasor stone inscription of the time of Prabhākara the expression *dhātuvara*, and the term here—if this is the correct reading—is clearly used interchangeably with the term *stūpa*. Sircar says in a note: "*Dhātu-vara* really means the relics of the Buddha; but here it means a *stūpa* built on the Buddha's relics. Such *stūpas* were usually called *dhātu-garbha*" (Sircar, *Select Inscriptions*, 409 and n. 3). Unfortunately Garde, the first to read the inscription, read not *dhātu-vara*, but *dhātu-dhara* (M. B. Garde, "Mandasor Inscription of Malava Samvat 524," *EI* 27 [1947–1948] 15), although Agrawala, to whom we owe the most recent edition, reads—as did Sircar—*dhātuvara* in P. K. Agrawala, *Imperial Gupta Epigraphs* (Varanasi: 1983) 81. In fact, the reading in the published facsimiles is problematic. A comparison of the third *akṣara* of the compound with the *akṣara -va-* elsewhere in the inscription (line 1, eighth *akṣara*; line 5, fifteenth *akṣara*; etc.) would argue against reading the *akṣara* in our compound as *-va-*, but a comparison of it with the *-dhā-* of the immediately preceding *dhātu-* does not unambiguously support Garde either. On balance, all we can say is that the *akṣara* is uncertain, although it looks to me more like *-dha-* than *-va-*. (Incidentally, this verse in the Mandasor inscription, like the verse from the *Buddhacarita* cited above, seems to

contain a pun or wordplay involving the word *dhātu*). The second source that may use the compound *dhātu-vara* to refer to a structure holding relics is literary. In G. Sastri's edition of the *Rājavyākaraṇa-parivarta* of the *Mañjuśrīmūlakalpa*, the term *dhātu-vara* occurs repeatedly in contexts that make it certain that it is being used interchangeably with the term *stūpa*, and the Tibetan version supports this: it consistently translates *dhātu-vara* by *mchod rten*. But almost as consistently, Sāṅkṛtyāyana "corrects" every occurrence of *dhātu-vara* into *dhātu-dhara*. Since it is not clear if Sāṅkṛtyāyana's "corrections" are based on anything but the Tibetan, and since the manuscript tradition of the *Mañjuśrīmūlakalpa* is notoriously problematic, it is difficult to cite this material with confidence; see K. P. Jayaswal, *An Imperial History of India* (Lahore: 1934) vss. 427, 431, 531, 588, 589, etc.; cf. vss. 416, 574, etc.

41. Vogel, *EI* 20 (1929) 17, 21.

42. Vogel, *EI* 20 (1929) 29, n. 1; 30, n. 2 (notes marked "Ed."); Sircar, *Select Inscriptions*, 230, n. 3.

43. Elsewhere in the inscriptions from Nāgārjunikoṇḍa, *parigahe* (E; J. Ph. Vogel, "Additional Prakrit Inscriptions from Nāgārjunikoṇḍa," *EI* 21 [1931] M2, M3) is found in the same context—once (H) *suparigahe*. *Parigahe* is more in conformity with Buddhist epigraphical usage elsewhere.

44. *Cātusāla-parigahita* also occurs in Vogel, *EI* 21 (1931) M4, and in H. Sarkar, "A Note on Some Fragmentary Inscriptions from Nāgārjunikoṇḍa," *EI* 38 (1969) 176.

45. Vogel, *EI* 20 (1929) 17 (C1), 19 (C2).

46. Cf. M. Njammasch, "Der *navakammika* und seine Stellung in der Hierarchie der buddhistischen Klöster," *Altorientalische Forschungen* 1 (1974) 279–293.

47. E. Teramoto and T. Hiramatsu, *Vasumitra's (dByig-Gi bÇes-gÑen) Samaya-Bhedo-paracana-Cakra (gShuṅ-Lugs-kyi Bye-Brag bKod-Paḥi ḥKhor Lo)*, etc. (Kyoto: 1935) 9 (V), 42; A. Bareau, "Trois traités sur les sectes bouddhiques attribués à Vasumitra, Bhavya et Vinītadeva," *JA* (1954) 248 (VIII.2), etc.

48. Rosen, "Buddhist Architecture and Lay Patronage at Nāgārjunikoṇḍa," 114.

49. A. Bareau, *Les sectes bouddhiques du petit véhicule* (Paris: 1955) 105.

50. Bareau, "Trois traités sur les sectes bouddhiques," 248; J. Masuda, "Origin and Doctrines of Early Indian Buddhist Schools," *Asia Major* 2 (1925) 38.

51. Bareau, *JA* (1954) 231.

52. Schopen, "Burial *Ad Sanctos* and the Physical Presence of the Buddha in Early Indian Buddhism," Ch. VII above.

* * *

[There is what appears to be a response to this paper in A. Wayman and E. Rosen, "The Rise of Mahāyāna Buddhism and Inscriptional Evidence at Nāgārjunakoṇḍa," *The Indian Journal of Buddhist Studies* 2.1 (1990) 49–65, but I cannot claim to have understood it.]

CHAPTER IX

An Old Inscription from Amarāvatī and the Cult of the Local Monastic Dead in Indian Buddhist Monasteries

ALTHOUGH THEY HAVE yet to be carefully studied, scattered throughout extant Buddhist literature are references to permanently housing the mortuary remains of deceased monks. In both the Pāli *Udāna* and *Apadāna,* for example, there is a clear injunction addressed to monks—and monks alone—directing them not only to perform the funeral rites for a "fellow-monk" (*sabrahmacārin*), but to build a mortuary *stūpa* for him as well and to worship it.[1] In the Pāli *Vinaya* there is an account that describes, in part, a group of nuns performing the funeral rites and building a *stūpa* for a deceased member of their group.[2] In the account of the deposition of the remains of Śāriputra preserved in the Tibetan version of the *Mūlasarvāstivāda-vinaya,* there is a passage in which the placement of the monastic dead within the monastery complex is directly addressed. Here, the Buddha first gives instructions concerning the form of mortuary *stūpa* appropriate to different categories of individuals, starting with a *buddha* and ending with "stream-winners" (*rgyun du zhugs pa*) and "ordinary good men" (*so so'i skye bo dge ba*). He then says:

> As Śāriputra and Maudgalyāyana sat (in relation to the Buddha) when the Tathāgata was sitting, just so should their mortuary *stūpas* be placed as well. Moreover, the *stūpas* of various elders (*sthavira*) should be aligned in accordance with their seniority. *Stūpas* of ordinary good men should be placed outside the monastery (*dge 'dun gyi kun dga' ra ba, saṃghārāma*).[3]

The *Mahāsāṃghika-vinaya*—according to de La Vallée Poussin—also contains such passages: "D'après le Mahāsāṃghikavinaya," he says, "des moines hommes du commun (*pṛthagjana*) ont aussi droit au *stūpa,* à savoir le Vinayadharadharmācārya, le Vaiyāpṛtyabhikṣu, le Vertueux-bhikṣu. Comme ils ne sont pas des Āryas,

---

Originally published in *Journal of the International Association of Buddhist Studies* 14.2 (1991) 281–329. Reprinted with stylistic changes with permission of the editor.

il n'y a pas de *lou-pan* ["dew-dish"] et [le stūpa] est dans un lieu caché. Péché à faire autrement."[4]

There is also—although, again, not yet systematically studied—an important body of independent evidence for the monastic preoccupation with permanently housing their dead from well preserved cave sites like Bhājā, Bedsā, and Kānheri. But with a few exceptions, little certain evidence has been noted for such activity at structural monastic sites. Evidence of this sort would, in fact, be difficult to detect at such structural sites for several reasons. The first and most general reason is, of course, that structural sites in India are far less well-preserved than the Western Cave Complexes. Those same cave complexes suggest, in addition, that the structures associated with the local monastic dead at structural sites would very likely have been small, and very well might have been situated some distance away from the main *stūpa* or center of the site. Neither of these factors would have favored the detection of such structures. Moreover, very few structural monastic sites in India have been extensively investigated or excavated horizontally; generally, attention and effort have been focused on the main *stūpa* of such sites. Anything not in the immediate vicinity would only accidentally have been noted.[5] The fact that such small structures would have required—and, therefore, would have left—no substantial foundations, that their superstructures would not only have been exposed to the elements, but also would have been easy prey for those who used such sites for building materials suggests that even horizontal surveys may have noted little. In such circumstances, stray epigraphical evidence for the housing of the local monastic dead is the most likely certain evidence to survive at structural sites; even then, such incidents of survival may not be numerous, and each possible piece should be carefully studied. The present essay concerns one such possible piece from Amarāvatī.

Amarāvatī must have been a striking monastic site. The main *stūpa* stood on a plain between the old city of Dharaṇikoṭa and the neighboring hills "where," said Burgess, "so many dolmans or rude-stone burying places are still to be seen."[6] "Upwards of 10,000 to 12,000 [carved] figures" were—according to Fergusson's calculations—associated with the *stūpa.* He calls it, perhaps without undue inflation, "a wonderful pictorial Bible of Buddhism as it was understood at the time of the erection of the monument."[7] But through the work of *zamindars,* zealous treasure seekers, and untrained if well-intentioned British civil servants, most of the complex—one of the longest lasting in India—has disappeared.[8] As a consequence, we know next to nothing about the monastic quarters there and very little about any secondary structures at the site. We do know that there were a number of mortuary *stūpas* clustered around the main *stūpa.* Burgess, in 1882, referred to two of these, in one of which he found "a small *chatti* [a type of pot] . . . and a quantity of calcined bones." A similar "*chatti*" had earlier been recovered from another.[9] Rea also excavated several secondary *stūpas,* one of which still had its lower portion encased in sculptural slabs,[10] as well as another that overlay a group of seventeen "megalithic" urn burials.[11] In fact, the site plan published by Rea in 1909 shows almost twenty small *stūpas* and at least one "earthenware tomb." We do not, unfortunately, know anything more about these *stūpas* except for the fact that their placement and contents conform to a pattern found at a considerable number of other Buddhist sites in India and seem to reflect the practice that I—on analogy with the Christian West—have called "burial *ad sanctos*."[12] The inscription we will be primarily concerned with here may have been associated with one such *stūpa*.

The stone on which our inscription is inscribed was not found in its original position. It had already been displaced and could even have been moved a considerable distance, given its size and shape. Burgess describes it as "a circular slab 2 feet 1 inch in diameter . . . with a mortise hole in the centre surrounded by a lotus, and this again by a sunk area carved with rays. The outer border is raised . . ." and it is on this raised border that our record—"a well-cut inscription"—occurs.[13] This "circular slab"—a good photograph of which was also published by Burgess[14]—is clearly the "umbrella" (*chata, chattra*) referred to in the inscription. That this "umbrella" was intended for a shrine (*cediya*) or *stūpa* is clear as well from the inscription, and the comparatively small size of the *chattra* is sufficient to indicate that the *stūpa* was a small one. We do not, however, know exactly where this small *stūpa* stood.

With a few minor exceptions, the readings of this "well-cut" record were not difficult to establish, and, after something of a false start in the first transcription published in Burgess' *Notes*, the basic text was quickly established. In the "Additional Notes" added to that same volume, in fact, Hultzsch had already come very close to his final version, which appeared a year later.[15] The text is printed there as:

> *uvāsikāya cadaya budhiṇo mātuya saputikāya sadutukāya aïrānaṃ*
> *utayipabhāhīnaṃ cediyasa chata deyadhamaṃ*

and this is the basic text accepted by Lüders,[16] Franke,[17] and Sivaramamurti.[18] Sivaramamurti does, however, read *-pabhāhinaṃ* rather than *-pabhāhīnaṃ*, and notes that the "nasal"—he means *anusvāra*—"is not quite clear in *aïrānaṃ* and *utayipabhāhinaṃ*," although this is more true of the latter than the former.

Hultzsch first translated the text as:

> An umbrella (*chhattra*), a meritorious gift to the Chaitya (?) of the venerable Utayipabhāhins by the female worshipper Chadā (Chandrā), the mother of Budhi, together with her sons, together with her daughters

He added as well the following note: "*Utayipabhāhin* seems to be the name of a school like *Dharmottarīya* . . . Perhaps *utara* (= *uttara*) is to be read for *utayi*, and *pabhāhin* = *prabhāsin*."[19] But a year later he published a slightly different rendering:

> Ein Sonnenschirm (*chattra*), die verdienstliche Gabe der Laiin *Cadā* (*Candrā*), der Mutter des Budhi (*Buddhi*), mit ihren Söhnen, mit ihren Töchtern, an die (Schule der) ehrwürdigen *Utayipabhāhis* (?) (und) an das *Caitya*[20]

The English translation of the record that appears in Burgess' later report looks like a somewhat garbled version of Hultzsch's second translation, and here too, *Utayipabhāhin* appears to have been taken as the name of a Buddhist school. Burgess adds to it the following note: "May this not be synonymous with Uttaraparvatas, or Uttaraśelas."[21] Although he proposed no emendation or equivalent, Lüders lists *Utayipabhāhi* in his index of personal names as the name of a Buddhist "school," and translates the portion of the record that most concerns us as: "Gift of a parasol (*chhata*) to the Chaitya (*chediya*) of the venerable (*aïra*) Utayipabhāhis, . . ."[22] In fact, Sivaramamurti alone *seems* to have considered other possible interpretations of the text, but his translation—as printed—is also garbled and without explanation or comment: "Meritorious gift of umbrella for the caitya (cediya) of the worthy airānam Utayipabhāhi, etc." What "*airānaṃ*," still carrying its case ending, is doing in the translation is, of course, far from clear, especially since it already seems to have been translated by "worthy." Moreover, Sivaramamurti lists *Utayipabhāhi* in his glossary as "probably Uttaraseliyas."[23]

The inclination to see in *utayipabhāhin* the name of a school has had, in fact, a wide currency. Lamotte says:

> Les donations religieuses signalées par les inscriptions proviennent, non seulement de particuliers, mais encore de clans (*kula*), de groupes (*gaṇa*) et d'associations (*sahaya*). Parmi ces dernières, quelques-unes peuvent avoir été des sectes bouddhiques, non mentionées en littérature,

and as one example of such a group he cites the "aïra (*ārya*) Utayipabhāhi" of our inscription.[24] In a later paper, Furtseva has said: "The epigraphic data gives evidence of the existence of the schools unknown to any tradition. These are such schools as, for example, Utayibhāhī in Amaravati, . . ." again citing our inscription.[25]

Although this interpretation of our record has received wide currency, and although Furtseva, for example, seems to take it as an established fact that the inscription refers to a Buddhist school, the evidence for this was never firm: Hultzsch had said *utayipabhāhin* only "*seems* to be the name of a school," Burgess, "may this not be . . . ," Sivaramamurti, "probably," and so on. In fact, there are a number of reasons to reject seeing in the inscription a reference to a shrine or *caitya* that "belonged" to a specific Buddhist school, and much evidence that suggests a much more supportable interpretation.

Although the evidence is sadly fragmentary, it appears, as has already been indicated, that the main *stūpa* at Amarāvatī was—as Marshall says of Sāñcī—"surrounded, like all the more famous shrines of Buddhism, by a multitude of *stūpas* of varying sizes crowded together."[26] The *stūpa* or *caitya* to which our umbrella was donated appears to have been just one of such a multitude and, to judge by the size of the *chattra,* a comparatively small one at that. That one of such a multitude of secondary *stūpas* close to—or in the vicinity of—the main shrine would have been claimed as the special property of a specific school seems very unlikely. That monastic orders accepted as gifts and, therefore, "owned," specific forms of property—relics, fields, buildings, images, and so on—is virtually certain. It is equally certain that specific schools "owned" the main *stūpa* at certain sites. But there is no other case, in so far as I know, where one of the small secondary *stūpas* was so "owned." Whether near the main shrine or situated elsewhere in the complex, secondary *stūpas* at Buddhist sites are almost always uninscribed and anonymous. There are, however, a small number of significant exceptions, and it is this group of exceptions that may point toward a better understanding of the record on our small umbrella from Amarāvatī.

The first exception may come from Amarāvatī itself. If we can accept Sivaramamurti's reading of his no. 103 as even approximately correct, then the one other secondary *stūpa* that had an associated inscription at Amarāvatī was "the small cetiya of the mendicant monk Nāgasena." Sivaramamurti gives the text of his no. 103 in the following form:

> *sidham (namo) bhagavato gāmmamahivathasa peṇḍavatikasa nāgasenasa khuda-cetiya . . . haghavāṇikiniya patiṭhapitam savasatamata a . . .*[27]

If we put aside *gāmmamahivathasa,* which is clearly wrong (although it just as clearly indicated the place of residence of Nāgasena), and if we follow—however reluctantly—Sivaramamurti's interpretation of . . . *haghavāṇikiniya* as "by the merchant's wife, Haghā," this could be translated as:

> Success. (Homage) to the Blessed One. The small *cetiya* of the mendicant monk Nāgasena who lived in . . . established by the merchant's wife Haghā for the . . . of all . . .

We do not know where the sculptured slab on which this record was inscribed was discovered. Already by the time of Burgess (1887), it had been removed to Bejwāḍā, "possibly," says Burgess, by Colonel Mackenzie.[28] On the basis of the expression *khudacetiya,* "small *cetiya*" in the record itself, Sivaramamurti assumes that the slab formed a part of one of what he calls the "smaller votive *stūpas.*" That the inscribed slab did, in fact, belong to a secondary *stūpa* appears likely. The problem remains, however, that Sivaramamurti's reading of the record cannot actually be verified with the published material at hand. Although Burgess and

Stern and Bénisti both provide illustrations of the slab on which the record occurs, in neither case is the photograph sufficiently clear to allow the inscription to be read with any confidence.[29] Sivaramamurti also reproduces the record reduced to such a degree that no certain reading is possible,[30] and in cases where his readings can be checked, they are by no means always as careful as one might wish. Given this situation, the most that one could say is that it appears—although it is not certain—that, in the one other case at Amarāvatī in which a secondary *stūpa* had an associated inscription, that inscription does not refer to the *stūpa* as "belonging" to a specific school, but seems to describe it as "belonging" to an individual monk, a monk who appears to have been of purely local stature and who is otherwise unknown.

But this itself raises some further questions that it would be well to deal with here. The exact sense of the genitive construction used here in *nāgasenasa khudacetiya,* and in other records connected with *stūpas* "of" local monks, is not at first sight immediately clear. This, in part at least, is related to the fact that in inscriptional Prakrits, much as in the Prakrits generally, the dative case—although it has not entirely disappeared—is very much attenuated, and dative functions have been taken over by an already elastic conception of the genitive. Given these linguistic realities, *nāgasenasa khudacetiya,* for example, can be understood, at least on one level, in two ways: "the small *cetiya of* Nāgasena," or "the small *cetiya for* Nāgasena." It could be argued that the intended meaning here is more like "the small *cetiya* built *for the merit* of Nāgasena by Haghā," but the one certain case I know of that does record something like this is not only late but articulated in a very different way. The case in point occurs in a tenth century inscription from Nālandā where the disciple of a monk is said to have raised "a *caitya* of the Blessed One, the Sugata" (*bhagavataḥ sugatasya caityaḥ*) with the expressed hope or intention that his teacher, through the merit of the disciple's act, might "obtain the unsurpassed station of a *buddha*" (*puṇyenānena labdhāsau bauddham padam anuttaram*).[31] In fact, from the earliest Buddhist inscriptions that record acts undertaken for another, the statement of purpose almost always involves an explicit expression of that fact: the construction is usually something like *aṭhāyā* (*arthāya,* "for the sake of"), either in compound with the name of the person or persons involved, or with the latter in the genitive (*mātāpituna aṭhāyā*), or a construction like *sukhāya hotu savasatānaṃ* ("for the happiness of all beings") is used.[32] The transaction involved is very rarely, if at all, expressed by the simple genitive or dative. In the rare and still uncertain cases in which the simple genitive or dative might be used, it appears that the name of the person for whose benefit a gift is given is put not in the genitive, but in the dative. On what Rao calls "an āyaka pillar" found near the second *stūpa* at Sannati, for example, we find: *ahimarikāya nāganikāya arikā-bhātuno giridatanakasa.* This would appear to indicate that the "pillar" in question was the gift of Giridatanaka, brother of Arikā, "for or in honor of"—expressed by the simple dative—Nāganikā of Ahimara, the latter being a place name.[33] Considerations of this sort would seem to rule out *nāgasenasa khudacetiya* in our Amarāvatī inscription as being intended to convey "the small *cetiya* for the benefit or merit of Nāgasena"; so too does the fact that, although now fragmentary, there seems to have been a separate dedicative statement at the end of the record (compare the better-preserved record from Mathurā cited below).

If, then, *nāgasenasa khudacetiya* does not mean "the small *cetiya* for the benefit or merit of Nāgasena," it—and similarly constructed records elsewhere—must mean "the small *cetiya* of or for Nāgasena" in some other sense. Since *stūpas* or *cetiyas*—whether they were memorials or mortuary containers—were never, as far as we know, erected *for* anyone who was not physiologically dead,[34] this would mean, if our inscription in fact refers to "the small *cetiya* of or for Nāgasena," that Nāgasena must have been not just a local monk, but a *deceased* local monk. But in that case it is important to note that, although Nāgasena was "dead," the *cetiya* was not said to be "of" or "for" his relics or remains, but "of" or "for" him—period. Exactly the same thing is, of course, said elsewhere at Amarāvatī and at other Andhra sites in regard to the *cetiya* of the Buddha. On more than one occasion at Amarāvatī we meet with something like *bhagavato mahāc(e)tiyasa,* "for the Great Shrine of the Blessed One," or *bhagavato mahacetiya-padamale* [rd: *-mūle*], "at the foot of the Great Shrine of the Blessed One."[35] Similar phrasing is also found, for example, at Jaggayyapeṭa: *bhagavato budhasa mahācetiye,* "at the Great Shrine of the Blessed One, the Buddha."[36] In all of these cases, the genitive phrasing was almost certainly intended to express both the fact that the *cetiya* "belonged" to the Blessed One—that is to say, he "owned" it—and the fact that it contained, or was thought to contain, the Buddha himself.[37] It is again important to notice that where we might want to say the *cetiya* was "of" or contained the relics of the Buddha, these inscriptions themselves never use a term for "relics": they say the *cetiya* was "of" or "for" the Buddha himself. He—not his remains—was, apparently, thought to reside inside. But if this is true in regard to the *cetiyas* "of" the Buddha, it would be hard to argue that exactly the same genitive phrasing applied to the *cetiya* "of Nāgasena"—or to the *stūpa* "of" any other local monk—could have meant something different. This secondary *stūpa*—actually called a "small shrine" if we can accept Sivaramamurti's reading—must either have contained, or had been thought to contain, what we would call the "relics" of a local mendicant monk named Nāgasena, but what the composer of the inscription called Nāgasena himself.[38]

It would seem, then, that in the one other possible case at Amarāvatī where we have an inscription associated with a secondary *stūpa,* there is no support for the interpretation of the record on the small umbrella from the same site proposed by Hultzsch, Burgess, Lüders, and others. The former inscription makes no reference to a "school," but rather points towards a very different possibility and set of ideas. It suggests the possibility at least that *utayipabhāhin* in the umbrella inscription may not be the name of a "school" but the name of a deceased local monk. This possibility receives further support when we look elsewhere since, although there are no other instances where a secondary *stūpa* is said to be "owned" by a specific "school," there are a small but significant number of cases where secondary *stūpas* are explicitly said to be "of" or "for" the local monastic dead. At least one of these other cases comes from another sadly dismembered structural site.

It is ironic that, although we have a large number of inscriptions and a far larger number of sculptural and architectural pieces from Mathurā, we know very little really about the structures they were associated with, about what the Buddhist complexes at the site looked like, or how these complexes were laid out. We have only a large number of fragments and disassociated pieces.[39] On one such piece occurs an inscription which van Lohuizen-de Leeuw has read in the following fashion:

> *sa 90 2 he 1 di 5 asya pū(r)vvaye*
> *vi(or kha)ṇḍavihare vasthavyā bhikṣusa grāha-*
> *dāsikasa sthuva prāṣṭhāpāyati sa-*
> *rva sav(v)anaṃ hitasukhaye*

She translates the record as:

> In the year 92, the first (month of) winter, on the 5th day, on this occasion as specified, the inhabitants of the Viṇḍa Monastery erected a stūpa for the monk Grāhadāsika. May it be for the welfare and happiness of all beings.[40]

More than a dozen years later, this same inscription was edited again by Sircar, who seems to have been under the impression that the record was discovered in 1958. Although his reading differs on several minor points from van Lohuizen-de Leeuw's, it is significantly different in only one regard: where van Lohuizen-de Leeuw reads *vasthavyā* plural ("inhabitants"), Sircar reads *vastavya-* and takes it in compound with the following *bhikṣusa.* But this makes for an odd compound and, more importantly, results in a text in which there is no possible subject for the main verb, which Sircar reads as *pra(ti*)ṣṭhāpayati.*[41] The absence of such a subject renders Sircar's construction of the text highly problematic, and suggests that, for the moment, van Lohuizen-de Leeuw's is to be preferred. From the paleographic point-of-view, however, Sircar's *vastavya*—with short final *-a*—appears likely, and this would give a singular subject for the singular verb. The result would be a slight alteration of van Lohuizen-de Leeuw's translation: ". . . an inhabitant of the Viṇḍa Monastery erected a *stūpa* for the Monk Grāhadāsika."

Here, of course, there is no possibility of taking the text to mean "for the benefit or merit of the Monk Grāhadāsika." The text ends with an explicit statement indicating for whom the act was undertaken, and it was not Grāhadāsika, but "all beings." Sircar says: "the object of the inscription is to record the erection of a *stūpa* of the Buddhist monk Grāmadesika"; this is his reading of the name. But he adds: "In the present context, the word *stūpa* mean[s] a memorial structure enshrining the relics of the monk in question."[42] Such an interpretation seems very likely, although here too it is important to note that where Sircar speaks of "relics," the composer of our record—although he certainly could have—does not. For the composer, the *stūpa* does not seem to have been a structure for enshrining relics, but a structure for enshrining, in some sense, the monk himself.

We do not, again, know where the *stūpa* of Grāhadāsika stood. Van Lohuizen-de Leeuw assumes that it "was erected in the monastery," but that is not terribly helpful. The slab on which the inscription is inscribed appears to have been a small one—the writing covers a space that is only nine-and-one-half inches long and four inches high. More than anything else, it seems to resemble the small engraved slabs—to be discussed more fully below—associated with the brick *stūpas* of the local monastic dead at Kānheri, where the writing covers a space of almost the same dimensions. It would appear, then, that the *stūpa* at Mathurā was a small one situated somewhere within the confines of one of the monastic complexes. But in spite of the uncertainties concerning the exact location of the *stūpa* it mentions, this Mathurā record—like Sivaramamurti's Amarāvatī no. 103—does not lend any support to the view that sees in the inscription on the small *chattra* from Amarāvatī a reference to a *stūpa* "belonging" to a specific monastic school. On the contrary, both this Mathurā inscription and Amarāvatī no. 103 would seem to indicate that when secondary *stūpas* or *cetiyas* in this period are inscribed, those *stūpas* or *cetiyas* are *stūpas* or *cetiyas* "of" deceased local monks. That this is so, not just for this period but also for periods long before and after, will become evident below. But these two cases are already sufficient to establish the suspicion that the record on the Amarāvatī umbrella is, again, also referring to such a *stūpa.* Neither Amarāvatī no. 103 nor the Mathurā inscription, however, account for a peculiarity of the Amarāvatī umbrella record, which has undoubtedly exerted considerable influence on previous interpretations.

The Amarāvatī umbrella record does not at first sight appear to be referring to a *cetiya* of a *single* monk. The reading—which is virtually certain apart from the final *anusvāras*—is *aïrāna(ṃ) utayipabhāhīna(ṃ) cediyasa. Aïra,* a Prakrit form of *ārya,* is certainly in the plural, and the following *utayipabhāhin*—though the form is not so well recognized—was almost certainly also intended for a plural. But this use of the plural, rather than suggesting that the *cetiya* "belonged" to a group of monks, may in fact confirm the possibility that the reference is to a single, *deceased* individual.

There are more than a dozen inscriptions that can be cited to demonstrate that the name and titles of a monk for whom a *stūpa* was built were commonly put in the genitive plural. Two are particularly informative: one from Bedsā, which Nagaraju assigns to the first century B.C.E., and one from Kānheri, which he dates to the early second century C.E.[43] In both instances, we are dealing with small secondary *stūpas* whose precise location relative to the main shrine is known. In both instances, these small secondary *stūpas* are inscribed and can therefore be certainly identified as *stūpas* "of" local monks. And in both instances, the individual local monk in question is referred to in the plural.

Less than twenty-five feet to the left of the entrance to the main *caityagṛha* at Bedsā there is "a tiny apsidal excavation" containing a small *stūpa.* On the back wall of this "excavation" there is a short "much weatherworn" inscription in two lines. Some syllables at the beginning of both lines appear to have been lost, but what remains can be fairly certainly read, and the general sense of the record is clear in spite of the missing syllables. Burgess published the following reading in 1883:

> . . . *ya gobhūtinaṃ āraṇakāna peḍapātikānaṃ mārakuḍavāsinā thupo*
> . . . *(aṃte)vāsinā bhatāsāḷa(ḷha)mitena kārita (//)*[44]

In spite of the fact that Gobhūti's name and all his epithets are in the genitive plural, this can only mean:

> The *stūpa* of . . . Gobhūti, a forest-dweller, a mendicant monk who lived on Māra's Peak—caused to be made by his pupil, the devoted Asāḷamita.

At Kānheri as well we have to do with a small excavation containing a *stūpa*. The steps leading up to the chamber containing this *stūpa* are no more than twelve feet to the left of the steps that lead to the main "hall of worship" at the site. On the *harmika* of the small *stūpa* the following record occurs:

> *sidhaṃ heranikasa dhamanakasa bhayā-a*
> *sivapālitanikāya deyadhaṃma*
> *therāna bhayata-dhaṃmapālānaṃ*
> *thuba (//)*[45]

Likewise here we have the name of a monk and his title in the genitive plural, and this can only refer to a single individual:

> Success. The religious gift of Sivapālitanikā, the wife of the treasurer Dhamanaka—the *stūpa* of the Elder, the Reverend Dhaṃmapāla.

Bearing in mind again that *stūpas* were, in so far as we know, erected only for individuals who were dead, these two cases from Bedsā and Kānheri present us with two clear cases where a deceased local monk is referred to in the plural. These cases can only represent a specific application of the *pluralis majestaticus* or plural of respect, and it is important to note that in this regard they are not, apparently, exceptions, but represent something of a rule. Plurals of respect are certainly the rule in the numerous *stūpa* labels found in association with the two monastic "cemeteries" that have been identified at Western Cave sites.

At Bhājā, "probably one of the oldest Buddhist religious centres in the Deccan," a group of fourteen small *stūpas* are clustered together in what Mitra alone has explicitly noted "may be regarded as the cemetery."[46] Nagaraju suggests that these *stūpas* "belong to different dates ranging from late third century B.C. to about the end of the second century A.D."[47] Although Burgess seems to have been of the opinion that a larger number of these *stūpas* had originally been inscribed, in his day only five such inscriptions still remained, in part or in whole. One of the two inscriptions that appeared to be complete reads:

> *therānāṃ bhayaṃta-aṃpikiṇakānaṃ thūpo {//}*
>
> The *stūpa* of the Elder, the Reverend Aṃpikiṇaka.

The other complete record is of exactly the same form, and enough survives of the other three of the five inscriptions to show that, in every case, the name of the monk for whom the *stūpa* was built and his titles were always in the genitive plural.[48] The use of the *pluralis majestaticus* in referring to deceased local monks appears from the Bhājā cemetery labels, then, to have been both an early and a continuous practice over time. But the evidence from the Bhājā cemetery not only confirms this linguistic usage noted previously at Bedsā and Kānheri, it confirms as well the assumed character and contents—in at least one sense—of *stūpas* built "for" deceased local monks. Fergusson and Burgess note that on the capitals of at least four of these *stūpas* there were "holes on the upper surface as if for placing relics . . . and in two cases there is a depression round the edge of the hole as if for a closely fitting cover."[49] The fact that Deshpande discovered at Pitalkhorā exactly the same sort of "holes" still plugged with "a closely fitting cover" and—as a consequence—still containing their relic deposits, makes it highly likely that the "holes" in the *stūpas* at Bhājā—and perhaps all such "holes" in rock-cut *stūpas* in the Western Caves—originally held relics: such *stūpas* were, as a consequence, by no means simply "commemorative" but contained the mortuary deposits of the monks mentioned in their accompanying inscriptions.[50]

The Bhājā cemetery, however, is not the only monastic cemetery in the Western Caves that provides evidence for the use of the *pluralis majestaticus* in referring to deceased monks. The character of the large monastic cemetery at Kānheri was almost immediately surmised. In 1862, West had already said in regard to these groups of *stūpas:* "It seems likely that these topes have contained the ashes of the priesthood and that this gallery has been the general necropolis of the caves."[51] In 1883, Burgess had described this "gallery"—which at that time was assigned the number 38—in the following terms: "No. 38 is the long terrace under the overhanging rock on the brow of the hill, where are the bases of numerous brick stūpas, being the monuments over the ashes of numerous Bauddha sthaviras or priests who died there . . . a vast number fill this gallery"—more than a hundred according to the most recent count—"which is about 200 yards in length; many of them, however, are covered over with the débris of decayed bricks and rock and all seem to have been rifled long ago of any relics or caskets they contained."[52] Although West had already published in 1861 an eye-copy of at least one inscription connected with "the Kaṇheri Bauddha Cemetery"—his no. 58—it was never read;[53] it was not until 1974 or 1975 that further and fuller epigraphical data came in the form of a considerable number of small inscribed slabs, which had originally been inset into the brick *stūpas,* but which—after these *stūpas* had decayed—had either fallen or been thrown into the ravine on the edge of which the gallery sits. The exact number of inscribed insets recovered is not clear—Gokhale says in one place that there were nearly fifteen but in another nearly twenty; Gorakshkar put the number at about forty, but Rao at twenty-nine.[54] Gokhale has edited eight of these inscriptions, but not always well, and the published photographs are not always easy to read.

In spite of these problems, some important points are sufficiently clear. Like the inscriptions associated with the *stūpas* of the local monastic dead at Bhājā, none of the inscriptions so far available from the Kānheri cemetery are donative. They are all labels, and—like the Bhājā inscriptions although more elaborate—they are all consistently patterned. Both considerations are enough to indicate that these labels—like all labels at Buddhist sites—are not the result of individual donative activity but the results of endeavors by the monastic community or its "administration" at their respective sites. Again, as in the Bhājā labels, in all the Kānheri labels that are available—including that published long ago by West—the name and titles of each individual monk for whom a *stūpa* was erected are in the genitive plural. I cite here just two examples that can be checked against the photos:[55]

> *therāṇaṃ ayya-vijayaseṇāṇaṃ tevijāṇaṃ arahantāṇaṃ thūbhaṃ*
>
> The *Stūpa* of the Elder, the Venerable Vijayasena, One Possessed of the Three Knowledges, an Arhat
>
> *therāṇaṃ bhadata-dāmāṇaṃ anāgāmiṇam thū(bhaṃ)*
>
> The *Stūpa* of the Elder, the Reverend Dāma, a Nonreturner

These labels—obviously written by someone familiar with the technical textual terminology of Buddhist conceptions of "sainthood"—establish that at Kānheri, as at Bedsā and Bhājā, deceased local monks were individually referred to in the plural. The use of the *pluralis majestaticus* was, in fact, the rule in referring to such individuals. But if the Bhājā labels establish this usage long before our Amarāvatī umbrella inscription, those from Kānheri establish its continued currency for a long time after. Gokhale had first suggested a date of "between 550 A.D. and 700 A.D." for the Kānheri labels; later they are said to be "written in the late fifth- or early sixth-century boxheaded variety of Brāhmī."[56] In any case, they date from a period long after our Amarāvatī record.

The material presented so far from Amarāvatī itself and from Mathurā, Bedsā, Bhājā, and Kānheri must bear heavily on any interpretation of the Amarāvatī umbrella inscription. This material establishes at least two consistent patterns: first, it would appear that all secondary *stūpas* from Buddhist sites that have associated inscriptions and that date from well before the Common Era to at least the sixth century C.E. are—in every case—*stūpas* raised for deceased local monks; second, with some exceptions that prove the rule, the names and titles of deceased individual monks that occur in *stūpa* inscriptions or labels from this period are put in the genitive plural. The Amarāvatī umbrella record comes from the same period, was associated with a small secondary *stūpa*, and has a name in the genitive plural preceded by a title commonly given to monks. Since, therefore, it conforms in every other respect to records connected with the shrines of deceased local monks, and since *Utayipabhāhin* is nowhere certainly attested as the name of a "school," nor is there any other instance where a secondary *stūpa* is said to belong to such a "school," it is very difficult—if not impossible—to avoid the conclusion that *Utayipabhāhin* in the Amarāvatī umbrella inscription is the name of a local monk. Such a conclusion, it seems, must be accepted until there is clear and incontrovertible evidence to the contrary.[57]

There is, however, one further point in regard to this name that is worth noting, a point that involves us again with yet other *stūpas* of the local monastic dead. Sivaramamurti said that "the term *Utayipabhāhi* is puzzling," and there has, in fact, been some uncertainty in regard even to the stem form of what appears in the inscription as *utayipabhāhīnaṃ* or *utayipabhāhinaṃ*. Originally, Hultzsch seems to have preferred *utayipabhāhin,* but later he and almost everyone else seems to have preferred *utayipabhāhi.*[58] Given the morphological variation in inscriptional Prakrits, a genitive plural form that ends in *-īnaṃ* or *-inaṃ* could have been made from either an *i*-stem or a stem in *-in.* In the present case there is, therefore, no certain formal means of determining the stem, but this—in the end—may not pose a serious problem. It is perhaps more important to note that Hultzsch had proposed *-prabhāsin* as the Sanskrit equivalent of *-pabhāhin*[59] and this—the only equivalent that has been suggested—seems likely: the change of *s* to *h* is well attested in the South.[60] In fact, whether the stem form is taken to have been *-pabhāhin*—which seems preferable—or *-pabhāhi,* it seems fairly certain that, in either case, we would have a derivative from *pra√bhās,* "to shine, be brilliant," etc. It may, therefore, be of interest to note that other derivations from *pra√bhās* occur as the final element of a name or title in—interestingly enough—two other inscriptions connected with the local monastic dead.

Almost one hundred forty years ago, Cunningham published an account of his explorations and "excavations" of the Sāñcī ruins and the Buddhist monuments of central India. Much work has, of course, been done since on Sāñcī—its art, architecture, and inscriptions—but the other related sites in this complex, Sonārī, Satdhāra, Bhojpur, and Andher, have been almost completely ignored. In fact, it is hard to find a reference to them after Cunningham. Also ignored is the fact that this cluster of related sites, among the earliest structural sites that we know, produced some of the clearest and most concrete evidence for the monastic cult of the local monastic dead. Cunningham discovered that the remains of ten individual monks—representing at least three generations—had been deposited in *Stūpa* no. 2 at Sāñcī. The remains of some of these same monks also had been deposited in Sonārī *Stūpa* no. 2, which contained the relics of five individuals, and in *Stūpas* nos. 2 and 3 at Andher.[61] In all of these cases, the deposits had been carefully labeled, and the inscription on one of the Andher deposits reads: *sapurisasa gotiputasa kākanāvapabhāsanasa koḍiñagotasa,* which Majumdar renders as: "(Relics) of the saint Gotiputa, the Kākanāva-pabhāsana, of the Koḍiña-gota."[62] Majumdar notes as well that "the expression *kākanāva-pabhāsana* is used as an epithet of Gotiputa and means 'the Light of Kākanāva,' " Kākanāva being, of course, the old name for Sāñcī.[63] A variant of the epithet also occurs at Sāñcī itself in the one donative record connected with the deposits in *Stūpa* no. 2. Majumdar reads and translates the latter as *kākanava-pabhāsa-siha(n)ā dana,* "the gift of the pupils of the Light of Kākanava," and says here that *kākanava-pabhāsa* "may be taken as standing for Gotiputa himself."[64] If Majumdar is correct in his interpretation of these inscriptions—and the chances are good that he is[65]—they may provide a possible parallel for the "name" that occurs in the Amarāvatī umbrella inscription. *Kākanava-pabhāsana* or *-pabhāsa* is, at Sāñcī and Andher, used both as an epithet of a local monastic "luminary" named Gotiputa and—by itself—as an alternative designation or name of that same individual. This may suggest that *utayipabhāhin* too could have been both an epithet and an alternative name for a prominent deceased local monk from a place named Utayi, which was situated somewhere in the region of Amarāvatī, that *-Pabhāsa* or *-Pabhāsin* might have been an ecclesiastical title of some currency, and that *Utayipabhāsin* might be translated "the Light or Luminary of Utayi"—all of this, at least, would seem a reasonable possibility.

As a result of our discussion so far, we are, then, in a position to do two things: we can offer a new and defensible translation of the old inscription on the small umbrella found long ago at Amarāvatī, and we can make some preliminary and perhaps promising observations on the cult of the local monastic dead in Indian Buddhist monasteries.

The Amarāvatī record can now be translated—keeping close to the syntax of the original—as follows:

> Of the lay-sister Cadā, the mother of Budhi, together with her sons, together with her daughters, to the shrine of the Venerable Luminary from Utayi, the umbrella is a religious gift.

Interpreted and translated in this way, the Amarāvatī inscription takes its place as one among a limited series of significant inscriptions or labels associated with *stūpas* of the local monastic dead. It is significant in regard to Amarāvatī itself because it would provide a much more certain piece of evidence than Sivaramamurti's inscription no. 103 for the presence of such *stūpas* at the site. The presence of such *stūpas* at Amarāvatī is, in turn, significant because it allows us to add it to the list of structural sites for which we have firm epigraphical evidence to prove the presence of *stūpas* of the local monastic dead: epigraphical evidence for the presence of this type of *stūpa* at structural sites has come from Sāñcī, Sonārī, Andher, Mathurā, and now from Amarāvatī. But the Amarāvatī inscription has broader significance as well. It provides us with an especially clear case in which the *stūpa* of a deceased local monk is presented with "gifts" exactly like the *stūpas* of the Buddha himself were, a clear instance in which such a *stūpa* receives the same kind of accoutrement—an umbrella—as did the *stūpas* of the Buddha. This is welcome corroboration of what we learn from the donative inscriptions associated with *Stūpa* no. 2 at Sāñcī, which indicate that coping stones, crossbars, rail-pillars, and pavement slabs, etc., were donated to this *stūpa* of the local monastic dead, just as they were to the *stūpa* of the Buddha at the site. In neither form nor content do the inscriptions associated with *Stūpa* no. 2 differ from those associated with *Stūpa* no. 1. The two sets are virtually indistinguishable, and, in fact, may have had some of the same donors.[66] But in arriving at our interpretation and translation of the Amarāvatī umbrella inscription, we have had to look at virtually all the parallel records that are known, and even our limited discussion of this group of inscriptions allows for some interesting provisional generalizations.

The first and perhaps most obvious generalization might be stated as a simple fact: the remains of the local monastic dead were permanently housed at a significant number of monastic complexes, the majority of which are very early: we have epigraphical evidence from Sāñcī, Sonārī, Andher, Mathurā, Amarāvatī, Bedsā, Bhājā, and Kānheri. These remains, moreover, were permanently housed in the same type of architectural structure as were the remains of the Buddha. I have elsewhere collected epigraphical, archaeological, and literary evidence that suggests that the mortuary remains or relics of the Buddha were thought to be possessed of "life" or "breath," that—as Lamotte says—"la relique corporelle . . . c'est un être vivant,"[67] that they were thought "to be impregnated with the characteristics that defined and animated the living Buddha," that "relics" are addressed as persons and treated as persons.[68] Bareau had, in fact, already noted that the "culte bouddhique des reliques . . . s'inspire en effet d'abord des marques de vénération que l'on adresse aux personnes vivantes."[69] But the fact alone that the remains of the local monastic dead were both treated and housed in the same way as the remains of the Buddha makes it again very difficult to argue that they were thought to be, in any essential way, different. Bareau has also said that "dès avant notre ère, donc, le *stūpa* est plus que le symbole du Buddha, c'est le Buddha lui-même."[70] To argue that the *stūpa* of Utayipabhāhin or the *stūpa* of Gobhūti were thought of any differently would require clear evidence. What evidence is available does not now favor such an argument.

The parallelism between the remains of the Buddha and the remains of the local monastic dead is not limited to the kinds of structures used to house them. There is, as well, a strict parallelism in the way in which these similar structures are referred to. As we have already seen, although we might describe a *stūpa* as a structure "for" relics or a container "of" relics, our inscriptions do not. They refer to *stūpas* or *cetiyas* "for" *persons* or "of" *persons.* This—again as we have seen—is clearly the case for *stūpas* "of" or "for" the Buddha or Blessed One (*bhagavato mahāc(e)tiya-, bhagavato budhasa mahācetiye,* etc.). But it is also the case for *stūpas* "of" or "for" deceased local monks (*aïrānaṃ utayipabhāhīnaṃ cediya-, bhikṣusa grāhadāsikasa sthuva, gobhūtinaṃ āraṇakāna . . . thupo,* etc.). Exactly the same construction and phrasing are used without distinction and regardless of the person "for" whom the *stūpa* was intended. But if this genitive phrasing suggests that, in the case of the Buddha, the *stūpa* "of" the Buddha was thought to contain him, or to be owned or possessed by him, or to be—in some sense—the Buddha himself, then the *stūpas* "of" Utayipabhāhin or Grāhadāsika or Gobhūti, since they are referred to in exactly the same way, could hardly have been thought of differently. In other words, parallel linguistic usage points in the same direction as parallel architectural form.

There may be yet another parallel as well. If we stick to actually datable *stūpas* of the historical Buddha—and put aside the not infrequent assertions of an "Aśokan" date for what are usually hypothetical "earlier" or "original" forms of extant structures—then it will be possible to see that there may be few or no clear chronological gaps between the earliest actually datable *stūpas* of the historical Buddha and the earliest examples of *stūpas* for the local monastic dead that we know. We might take Bhārhut as an example. Scholarly consensus, at least, would place it at or very near the beginning of the known sequence of *stūpas* for the historical Buddha. But Bénisti has recently argued that at least the rail that surrounded the Bhārhut *stūpa* was not the earliest such rail. She has said:

> . . . la décoration qu'offre la *vedikā* qui entoure le *Stūpa* n° 2 de Sāñcī . . . remonte, dans sa quasi totalité, à la première moitié du IIe siècle avant notre ère; elle est donc, de peu, antérieure à celle du *stūpa* de Bhārhut . . . et, très sensiblement, antérieure à celle des *toraṇa* du grand *Stūpa* n° 1 de Sāñcī.[71]

Since "le *Stūpa* n° 2 de Sāñcī" is a *stūpa* of the local monastic dead, this would seem to mean either that this *stūpa* for the local monastic dead predates both the Bhārhut and Sāñcī *stūpas* of the historical Buddha "de peu" and "très sensiblement," or—at least—that it was the first of these to receive the kind of rail we associate with *stūpas* of the Buddha and, therefore, may have been considered, in some sense, more important. However this might ultimately be decided, it would appear—again, at the very least—that, at these early sites, there is no clear or considerable chronological gap between *stūpas* of the local monastic dead and *stūpas* for the historical Buddha; rather, in regard to these structural sites, there appears to be a broad contemporarity between the two types of *stūpas*. This same contemporarity appears to hold for the Western Caves as well. The main *caityagṛha* at Bhājā—Bhājā no. 12—has, for example, been called "the earliest of rock-cut chetiyagharas of [the] Western Deccan" and assigned by Nagaraju to the third century B.C.E.[72] But some of the labeled *stūpas* of the local monastic dead at Bhājā have been assigned to the same period. There is, again, no clear chronological gap. Even at somewhat later sites, *stūpas* for the Buddha and *stūpas* for the local monastic dead seem to appear simultaneously. The inscription in Cave 7—the main *caityagṛha* at Bedsā—is assigned by Nagaraju to his "series III" (60 B.C.E.), but that associated with Gobhūti's *Stūpa* he places in his "series IVa" (60 B.C.E. to 100 C.E.), and he says that it "probably" falls toward the end of the first century B.C.E.[73] Given the fact that paleography alone is rarely capable of making such fine distinctions, it is clear that the two inscriptions—and, therefore, the two *stūpas*—belong to the same broad period. Although the question requires and deserves much fuller study, it appears now that there is possibly little, if any, chronological gap between *stūpas* for the historical Buddha and *stūpas* for the local monastic dead, little clear evidence for the kind of gap that could suggest that practices connected with the former's remains were, over time, extended or generalized to the remains of the latter. Archaeologically and epigraphically, the two types of *stūpas* appear now as roughly contemporary with, in some cases, some indication that *stūpas* of the local monastic dead may actually have predated those of the Buddha. It is interesting to note, moreover, that if we look at the internal chronology or narrative time taken for granted in our Buddhist literary sources, it would appear that their redactors also considered *stūpas* for the local monastic dead to predate those of the Buddha. Both of the *stūpas* mentioned in the *Udāna* and *Apadāna*, and that referred to in the Pāli *Vinaya*, for example, long preceded—according to the narrative time assumed by our texts—those erected for the Buddha.[74] It might, in fact, some day be possible to argue that the relic cult and *stūpas* of the historical Buddha represent only a special and particularly well-known instance of what was a common and widespread monastic practice. It may, indeed, have been much more widespread than our certain evidence now indicates.

It is certain that there were *stūpas* of the local monastic dead at Sāñcī, Sonārī, Andher, Mathurā, Amarāvatī, Bhājā, Bedsā, and Kānheri. This is certain because, at all of these sites, we have either donative inscriptions or inscribed labels that prove it. These inscribed and, therefore, certain instances are, of course, important in themselves. But they also have an importance that goes beyond their respective individual sites. Given the poor state of preservation of most Buddhist sites in India and the virtually complete absence of contemporary documentation concerning them, we often must, and can, argue—as in archaeology in general—from those cases that are certain to those that are less so. In this situation, the individual labeled *stūpas* in their own small separate shrines placed near the main shrine at Bedsā and Kānheri, the clearly labeled *stūpas* in the ordered monastic cemeteries at Bhājā and Kānheri, and the multiple labeled deposits in *Stūpa* no. 2 at Sāñcī—all have considerable indexical or typological importance. They establish the important fact that *all* secondary *stūpas* at monastic sites situated in small separate shrines near the main *stūpa* or in ordered groups away from the hub of the complex or that contain multiple deposits are—in *every* case in which they are *labeled* and it can therefore be determined—mortuary *stūpas* of the local monastic dead. In light of this, it would seem that unless, and until there is evidence to the contrary forthcoming, we are obliged to assume that those *stūpas* found at monastic sites that are similar, but not actually labeled, are also *stūpas* of the local monastic dead. On this basis, we may be able to identify a considerable number of additional *stūpas* of this category.

We may note, for example, using Nagaraju's numbers, that Cave 1 at Bedsā, and Caves 2c, 2d, and 2e at Kānheri are all—like the shrines of Gobhūti at Bedsā and Dhaṃmapāla at Kānheri—excavations grouped around the main *caitya*-hall at their respective sites; they are all small chambers; they all contain a single *stūpa*.[75] If these are not mortuary *stūpas* for the local monastic dead like those of Gobhūti and Dhaṃmapāla, they have no readily explicable function. We may note as well that, at both cave and structural sites, there are groups of unlabeled small *stūpas* that look remarkably like the labeled monastic cemeteries at Bhājā and Kānheri.

Among the Western Caves, Sudhagarh provides an early example. Here, in "a large low-roofed cell," Kail found a group of eight *stūpas* ranging in height from three-and-one-half to four-and-one-half feet. Without citing his evidence or good illustration, Kail said these "are not devotional *stūpas* but are funerary mounds, the relics . . . of a Buddhist saint being enshrined in a hollow receptacle in the square abacus."[76] Nadsur also provides a good example. In Cave 3—which measures thirty-four by twenty feet—there are twelve *stūpas* differing somewhat in size, form, and type of construction, making it virtually certain that they were neither cut nor constructed at the same time. In fact, four of these *stūpas* were structural, and, in the most complete of these, Cousens found "a handful of old rice husks, and about as much grey ash."[77] We might cite Pitalkhorā as a final example from the caves. At Pitalkhorā, on the side of the ravine opposite the main *caityagṛha* and the living quarters, Deshpande describes a cluster of four excavations, all of which contain at least one small *stūpa* and one of which contains three, again dating to different periods. None of this cluster of small *stūpas* are well preserved, but in at least one, Deshpande noted "two holes," one with "a ledge . . . to receive a cover," that—in analogy with similar still-plugged holes containing relics in the *stūpa* of his Cave 3—could only have been used to hold mortuary deposits.[78]

There are no inscriptions associated with these *stūpas* at Sudhagarh or Nadsur or Pitalkhorā, but at all of these sites, we seem to see a number of common characteristics. In so far as we can tell from the reports, there is evidence at all three sites that these were mortuary *stūpas.* At all three sites, these *stūpas* had been placed together in orderly groups over more or less long periods of time. In so far as we can tell—and this is particularly clear at Pitalkhorā—these groups were situated well away from the public areas of their complexes. All three cases—in analogy with similar but inscribed and, therefore, certain cases at Bhājā and Kānheri—can only have been, it seems, cemetery shrines for the local monastic dead. This same kind of argument could be made for several structural sites as well.

This argument could be made for Bhojpur, for example, where at least fifty small *stūpas* whose mortuary character is strikingly evident—large deposits of bones being found in several—are placed together away from the hub of the complex in a way that parallels the placement of the local monastic dead in the cemeteries of the Western Caves and, significantly, at the structural site at Sāñcī.[79] It could be made for the orderly rows of mortuary *stūpas* at Guṇṭupalle in Andhra, which Longhurst long ago suggested could represent "the ruined tombs of monks who died" at the site.[80] It could be made for the area "to the east and north-east of monastery 19" at Śrāvastī, which "seems to have been specifically utilized for the erection of *stūpas.*"[81] It could, as well, be made in regard to the still-curious orderly arrangement of secondary *stūpas* at Lauṛiyā Nandangaṛh, whose mortuary character is again clear and whose Buddhist affiliation now seems sure.[82] All of these sites—and a number of others—have all or several of the characteristics that define inscribed and, therefore, certain monastic cemetery shrines, and this would suggest that they too belong to this category.

It is, however, not just individual labeled shrines or labeled monastic cemeteries that have uninscribed parallels. The certain cases of the deposition of the mortuary remains of a number of local monks together in a single *stūpa* at Sāñcī, Sonārī, and Andher argue well for Longhurst's interpretation of the deposits he discovered in at least two *stūpas* at Nāgārjunikoṇḍa. Longhurst found in the spaces created by the "spokes" and crosswalls of the foundations of his *Stūpa* no. 4 "twelve water-pots covered with inverted food bowls . . . together with six large begging-bowls . . . placed on the floor of the chamber near the other vessels. The pots were in small groups of three or four and filled with a mixture of bone ash and fine red earth." By itself, in a separate space, he also found a distinctively shaped "globular" pot inside of which was a silver "casket" that contained in turn "a tiny gold reliquary." Longhurst suggests that this *stūpa* "was built to contain the remains of twelve monks and the ashes of some important divine" from the monastery in front of which it stands. In his *Stūpa* no. 5, Longhurst again discovered six "water-pots and bowls" of the same form and content, and again suggested that this *stūpa* too "was erected to contain the remains of monks or priests" belonging to its associated monastery.[83]

None of the deposits in the two *stūpas* at Nāgārjunikoṇḍa were labeled, and Longhurst does not cite the Sāñcī, Sonārī, and Andher deposits that are. The latter sites, however, establish a sure precedent for the deposition of the mortuary remains of a number of local monks together in a single *stūpa,* and they indicate again that, until we have equally sure evidence or examples to the contrary, we must assume—even in the absence of inscriptions—these *stūpas* at Nāgārjunikoṇḍa also contained, as Longhurst suggested, the remains of the local monastic dead. The same may apply as well to other instances. At Śrāvastī, for example, Marshall discovered in the northeast corner of a very early *stūpa* three "earthen jars . . . filled," he says, "with a mixture of sand and clay."[84]

To round out the range of the possible, we might cite several examples in which there are neither associated inscriptions nor parallels with such inscriptions, but that nevertheless have been interpreted as possible *stūpas* for the local monastic dead. For instance, in referring to the still badly reported Ghoṣitārāma monastery at Kauśāmbī, Ghosh has said:

> the portion presently excavated contained the foundations of a large number of small *stūpas* and pavements with numerous roughly circular postholes. It appears that ordinary monks were memorialized by the erection of small pillars, their relics being buried in earthen pots in the floors adjoining the small *stūpas.*[85]

In *vihāras* at Taxila, Kālawān, and Mohṛā Morādu, Marshall found small *stūpas* built in what originally could only have been the living quarters of individual monks. He suggested that these *stūpas* were funeral monuments intended "as memorials to signalise the sanctity of the cell where some specifically holy *bhikshu* had lived and died," that these *stūpas* "probably" contained the ashes of these monks, or "doubtless contained the bodily relics" of a former resident.[86]

It would appear, then, that the list of certain, probable, and possible monastic sites for which there is evidence for the permanent housing or enshrinement of the local monastic dead is already a long one: Sāñcī, Sonārī, Andher, Mathurā, Bedsā, Kānheri, Bhājā, Amarāvatī, Sudhagarh, Nadsur, Pitalkhorā, Bhojpur, Guṇṭupalle, Śrāvastī, Lauṛiyā Nandangaṛh, Nāgārjunikoṇḍa, Kauśāmbī, Taxila, Kālawān, and Mohṛā Morādu. This list—which is nothing more than preliminary and provisional—is startling if for no other reason than it reflects only what a superficial survey has turned up in reports of explorations and excavations that were almost completely unconcerned with, and uninformed about, the treatment of the local monastic dead. A good deal could be said about early archaeological methods in India and the character of the published reports, much of which would not be kind. One matter, however, is clear: Buddhist historical archaeology in India was from the beginning—and to a large degree remains—text bound.[87] Unfortunately, the texts that were, and to some degree continue to be, the best known are coming more and more to be seen as the least representative and—at least as they were interpreted—less-than-sure guides to actual practice.[88] This meant, of course, that investigators of Buddhist monastic sites often did not know what to look for or did not recognize what they were seeing. Since, for example, it was taken on good scholarly authority that "the *Vinaya*" contained no rules governing the disposal of the monastic dead,[89] it is hardly surprising that no attempt was made to survey sites for evidence of such practices. What is, however, surprising is that especially the early investigators sometimes actually noted such evidence, and in some cases accurately identified it for what it was. It is still more surprising that, in spite of the lack of anything even approaching a systematic attempt to locate evidence for the treatment of the monastic dead, our list of sites for which there is such evidence—however casually or incidentally reported—is as long as it is. Had there been any attempt to locate such evidence, it is reasonable to assume our list would have been far longer.

But this list is impressive not just by its length. It contains a considerable number of early sites and several of the earliest sites that we have certain knowledge of (Sāñcī, Sonārī, Andher, Bhājā, Bhojpur, Pitalkhorā); it includes some of the main Buddhist sites referred to in *nikāya/āgama* literature (Śrāvastī, Kauśāmbī); it includes sites from the South (Amarāvatī, Guṇṭupalle, Nāgārjunikoṇḍa), from the West (Bedsā, Kānheri, Sudhagarh, Nadsur, etc.), from the Northwest (Taxila, Kālawān, Mohṛā Morādu), from Central India (Sāñcī, Sonārī, etc.), and from the Buddhist heartland. In short, this list testifies to a preoccupation with permanently housing or enshrining the local monastic dead that was very early and very widespread geographically.

Again, if nothing else, this preoccupation with local monks forces us toward a long-overdue recognition of the limited character of the so-called great tradition, and an acknowledgment of the potential significance of the purely local in actual Buddhist communities. In an interesting sociological study of the monasteries and modern monks of Bhubaneswar, Miller and Wertz found that when people were asked to name a "holy man," by far the greatest number of them (38.2 percent) named contemporary ascetics *in the local community.* Only 11.3 percent named historical religious figures such as the Buddha, Guru Nanak, or Śaṅkara.[90] These figures must, at least, remind us of the distinct possibility that, whereas *we* tend to locate the "holy" almost exclusively in major historically known Indian religious men, actual Indian communities—including monastic communities—may never have done so. In fact, the mere existence of the architecturally marked presence of the local monastic dead in so many Buddhist monastic complexes already suggests that those who lived in such complexes located the holy at least as often in purely local figures as they did in pan-Buddhist figures such as the Buddha or Śāriputra and Maudgalyāyana. We are, moreover, already able to say a little more about who or what these local figures were, and about the individuals or groups who were preoccupied with preserving their permanent presence.

Information regarding the individual local monks whose remains were preserved at Buddhist monastic sites is, of course, limited to what is contained in the inscriptions and labels associated with their *stūpas* or the deposits of their relics. In some cases, there are indications of a monk's place of origin or residence, but, in all cases, the individual monk involved is given an ecclesiastical title or a title indicative of his religious practice and status or both. It is, however, almost immediately obvious that these titles—whether ecclesiastical or religious—are not, until very late, elaborate. There is little indication that these individuals were "great saints," at least in terms of what we might have expected from textual descriptions of religious achievements.[91] Nor is there much indication that they were high ecclesiastics or "pontiffs." Grāhadāsika in the Mathurā record is simply called a *bhikṣu,* a monk. Dhaṃmapāla at Kānheri, and all the monks in the Bhājā cemetery, are referred to only as "Elders" (*thera*) and given the title "Reverend" (*bhadanta*). The monks whose remains were deposited in *Stūpa* no. 2 at Sāñcī may be referred to collectively as *vināyakas,* which should mean "guide, leader, trainer, or discipliner," but it may be an alternative expression for *vinayadhara,* "preserver of the *vinaya,*" or "*vinaya* master." However, only one of the monks is individually so-called; two are called *ara,* but the significance of this term is unclear. Most scholars have taken it to be equivalent to *arhat,* although that is not likely.[92] The term *arhat* occurs in the Prakrit inscriptions of Central India not infrequently as *arahata, araha, ariha, arāha,* but never as *ara. Ara* could, in fact, just as easily be from *ārya,* although the common form of *ārya* in these same inscriptions is *aya.*[93] One of these monks is also called an *ācārya* and one is called an *ātevāsin,* "pupil." Most significantly, however, *all* of these monks are individually referred to as *sapurisa,* and, in eight out of the ten individual labels, that is all that they are called. At Sonārī, too, *sapurisa* is the only religious title that occurs in the four labels; and at Andher, although one individual is again called a "pupil" and another a *pabhāsana* or "luminary," both are called *sapurisa,* and the two other individuals named there are called only that. The one quality, then, that all of these monks had in common—in addition to the fact that their remains had been enshrined in a set of Central Indian *stūpas*—was classification as a *sapurisa.* Unfortunately, what such a classification meant is not very clear. *Sapurisa* in Pāli seems to mean little more than "a good, worthy man" and is cited as "equal to *ariya*";[94] in Sanskrit sources too, it is said to mean literally a "worthy or true man." Edgerton says that "they are evidently a lay category" and that "the term *satpuruṣa* may include monks."[95] Although the monk in our Amarāvatī umbrella inscription may have a title (*-pabhāhin*) that may be related to one of the titles that occurs at Andher (*-pabhāsana*), and although he is also referred to as an *ārya,* the title *sapurisa* occurs neither in this inscription nor in any of the other inscriptions or labels associated with the local monastic dead. It seems to reflect a purely local classification and—at the very least—one which has no demonstrable connection with canonical or textual definitions of religious achievement or "sainthood." In fact, only two of the early inscriptions connected with the local monastic dead contain references to a distinct type of religious practitioner recognized by the textual tradition. In Amarāvatī no. 103, Nāgasena is called a *peṇḍavatika,* a "mendicant monk," and in the *stūpa* inscription from Bedsā, Gobhūti is called both a *peḍapātika* and an *āraṇaka,* a "forest-dweller," as well. Both *piṇḍapātika* and *āraṇyaka* are, of course, known in the literature, primarily as two of the twelve or thirteen *dhutaṅgas* or *dhutaguṇas.* But the status and value placed on these "ascetic practices"—especially in Pāli sources—are less than clear. *The Pali Text Society Dictionary,* for example, refers to a passage that occurs twice in the *Parivāra* "deprecating such practices," and says that each of the *dhutaṅgas* is "an ascetic practice not enjoined in the Vinaya." It notes as well that "the Milinda devotes a whole book (chap. VI) to the glorification of these 13 *dhutaṅgas,*" but says "there is no evidence that they were ever widely adopted." That there was a certain amount of ambivalence toward these practices in at least some of the literary sources seems fairly sure, and it appears that nowhere were they considered obligatory or an integral part of the career of the *arhat.* It is therefore curious that they, and they alone, find mention in Buddhist epigraphs that refer to significant individuals in actual communities.[96] What is perhaps even more significant, however, is what is absent in these epigraphs. Nowhere in these early inscriptions that refer to local monks whose remains were treated like those of the Buddha is there any reference to the classical textual definitions of Buddhist "sainthood," no certain references to *arhats* or any of the levels of spiritual attainment associated with or preliminary to this ideal. There are, in fact, no indications—apart from references to *piṇḍapātikas* or *āraṇyakas*—that canonical or textual definitions of religious achievement or "sainthood" ever penetrated actual early monastic communities in India, no indications in these records that they were known at all.

The absence of such indications in early records connected with the local monastic dead is in itself striking. But it is even more so in light of the fact that such indications are frequently found—in spite of what might have been expected—in the latest series of such inscriptions, long after, one might have thought, the *arhat* ideal had lost its predominant place. It is not until the sixth or seventh century, and even then only at Kānheri, that we find in records associated with the local monastic dead certain references to *arhats*—seven of the eight Kānheri labels published by Gokhale in 1985 refer to monks who are called *arhats*—and to characteristics associated with textual definitions of "sainthood": *tevija, ṣaḍabhijñāna, anāgāmin,* etc. This situation is, again, not what might have been expected, and deserves fuller study. But it would appear, at the very least, that we have here yet another case indicating that we need not—and probably should not—assume that the presence of an idea in a canonical Buddhist text necessarily means that that same idea was current in actual Buddhist communities. The two need not—and probably often did not—have any necessary connection, chronological or otherwise. Our inscriptions, for example, suggest that the significance of the individual local monks whose remains were carefully and permanently preserved at early monastic sites was not linked to their having achieved the religious ideals articulated in what are taken to be early texts; such a linkage occurs, in fact, only later, long after we think those early texts were composed. Although it would lead too far afield to discuss it here, it is also at least worth noting that nowhere in these inscriptions—even very late and at Kānheri—is there the slightest hint or trace of the religious ideals we associate with the Mahāyāna. When we do finally encounter textual definitions of the ideal, they are definitions articulated in traditions firmly rooted in the *nikāyas* and *āgamas,* and show no influence of the Mahāyāna *Sūtras,* even though a very large number of the latter seem to have been composed long before.[97]

If, then, epigraphical data tell us something about the local monks for whom *stūpas* were raised and whose remains were preserved in early India, if these tell us that such monks were not thought—until very late—to have been *arhats,* but are instead said to be *theras* or *bhadantas* or, sometimes, *piṇḍapātikas,* these same materials also tell us something, finally, about the people who made considerable efforts to ensure the permanent presence of those *theras* and *bhadantas* in their midst, who established, honored, and adored the structures that housed them. Our best information concerning these matters comes, perhaps, from *Stūpa* no. 2 at Sāñcī.

Among the labels found on the deposits in *Stūpa* no. 2 at Sāñcī there is, as we have seen, one donative inscription. Majumdar reads the latter as: *kākanava-pabhāsa-siha{n}ā dana,* and translates it: "the gift of the pupils of the Light of Kākanāva"—"the Light of Kākanāva" being the monk and *sapurisa* Gotiputa mentioned also in an Andher label. If Majumdar's reading and interpretation are correct, then so too must be his conclusion:

> It may, therefore, be concluded that the casket on which this inscription occurs was the gift of the disciples of Gotiputa, the *Kākanava-pabhāsa.* It is highly probable that the other three caskets, which do not bear any donative inscription but were deposited along with this one in the stone box, were likewise contributed by the same persons.[98]

Although Majumdar's derivation of what he reads as *siha* from Sanskrit *śaikṣa* is not entirely free of problems,[99] his interpretation of the record appears to be the most satisfying to date, and it suggests that the deposition of the monastic remains in *Stūpa* no. 2 at Sāñcī was the result of monastic endeavors. But even if this suggestion cannot be taken as entirely certain, even if some doubt might remain concerning the donors of the deposit itself, there can be no doubt that the structure that housed this deposit was disproportionately paid for by monks and nuns. There are ninety-three donative records connected with *Stūpa* no. 2 at Sāñcī in which the status of the donor is clear, and which record the gifts of coping stones, crossbars, rail-pillars, pavement slabs, and berm and stairway balustrades. Forty-four of these inscriptions record the gifts of monks (twenty-eight) and nuns (sixteen), and eight more the gifts of pupils (*antevāsin*) of monks and nuns.[100] This means that well over half of the donors who contributed to the construction and adornment of this *stūpa* of the local monastic dead were monks and nuns, some of whom were *sutaṃtika,* "versed in the *Suttantas,*" and *bhāṇakas,* "reciters (of the *Dharma*)." Unless one would want to argue that monks and nuns made up more than half of the population in the area around Sāñcī, it would appear that monks and nuns not only made up an absolute majority of the donors concerned with *Stūpa* no. 2, but that their numbers were disproportionately large in light of the fact that they almost certainly constituted only a small percentage of the local population; Sāñcī, after all, was very near "the famous and populous city of Vidiśa" and, perhaps, a "nodal point" on an important commercial route between Andhra and the north.[101] It should, therefore, have had a large lay·catchment area.

It is unfortunate that we do not have comparably rich data for other *stūpas* of the local monastic dead. But what data we do have point very much in the same direction. We know, for example, that the *stūpa* of Gobhūti at Bedsā was "caused to be made" by the monk-pupil of Gobhūti. It is also virtually certain that the *stūpa* of Grāhadāsika at Mathurā was erected either by a monk or by a group of monks who resided in the Viṇḍa Monastery. The labeled *stūpas* in the monastic cemeteries at both Bhājā and Kānheri could have been erected and maintained only—almost certainly—by the monks of their respective establishments. Had they had individual "donors," it is reasonable to assume that those donors would have been named—as they are at Bedsā, Mathurā, and elsewhere—in their associated inscriptions. But no donors are mentioned. Moreover, the labels at Kānheri especially could only have been written by persons familiar with the textual, technical definitions of "sainthood," and this too would suggest monks. Even in the case of the uninscribed *stūpas,* it is difficult to avoid the conclusion that the monks themselves were responsible for the deposit of the remains of what appear to be local monastic dead. At Nāgārjunikoṇḍa, for example, neither *Stūpa* nos. 4 nor 5 were the main *stūpas* at the site. Both appear to have been the private *stūpas* of the monasteries with which they are closely and physically associated. Again, it is unlikely that anyone but the monks could have established and maintained the orderly groups of *stūpas* at, for example, Sudhagarh and Nadsur. Moreover, and much more broadly, there is evidence to indicate that, from the very beginning, construction activities at monastic sites were—not surprisingly—under the supervision and control of specifically designated monks, and that, as a consequence, what we see at such sites is the reflection of monastic choices and monastic values. Already at Bhārhut and Sonārī, at Amarāvatī, Nāgārjunikoṇḍa, Kānheri, and so on, we find evidence for the presence of *navakammikas,* monks "appointed by the Chapter as a superintendent of the building operations."[102] Njammasch has, in fact, gone some ways toward showing that "Der *navakammika* war offenbar eine wichtige Persönlichkeit in der Struktur der indischen buddhistischen Klöster."[103] The earliest *navakammika* that we have reference to is Isipālita at Bhārhut, and he appears to have been by no means an average monk: in addition to being a "Superintendent of Works," he is also called a *bhadanta,* an *ārya,* and a "Reciter (of *Dharma*)" (*bhāṇaka*);[104] at Amarāvatī, the *Navakammika* Budharakhita is called both a *thera* and a *bhadanta*—that is to say, he belonged to the same class as did so many of the monks for whom *stūpas* were built;[105] at Nāgārjunikoṇḍa, the three *navakammikas* mentioned in the Second Apsidal Temple Inscription F are all called *theras,* the monk responsible for the construction of the *cetiya* and *vihāra* referred to in Detached Pillar Inscription H is called "the Master, the Great Preacher of the Law, the *Thera* Dhaṃma[gho]sa" (*acariyena mahādhaṃmakāthik(e)na dhaṃma(gho)sa-therena anuthitaṃ*), and the *Mahācetiya* was said to have been brought to completion by "the

Reverend Ānanda, who knows the *Dīgha-* and the *Majjhima-nikāyas* by heart" (*dīgha-majhima-nikāya-dharena bhajaṃtānadena nithapitaṃ*).[106] Monks—and oftentimes learned monks—supervised and controlled building activities at monastic sites; they determined, it would appear, what was and what was not built and where it was to be placed. Their choices and their values are, again, what we see expressed at Buddhist monastic sites. These monastic choices and monastic values have almost certainly determined the presence—whether they are inscribed or not—of the *stūpas* of the local monastic dead at so many sites in India.

Although the evidence that we have primarily points directly and indirectly to monastic initiative for the deposition of the remains of the local monastic dead and the establishment of permanent structures to house them, and although this same evidence suggests that monks would have been predominantly preoccupied with and active in any cult of the local monastic dead, there is, as well, some evidence to indicate that the laity were not entirely excluded. The Amarāvatī umbrella inscription, for example, records the gift of an *upāsikā* or "lay-sister" to the *stūpa* of a local monk, although the *stūpa* itself seems, obviously, already to have been in existence.[107] At Kānheri, however, "the *stūpa* of the Elder, the Reverend Dhaṃmapāla" is explicitly said to be "the religious gift of Sivapālitanikā, the wife of the treasurer Dhamanaka."[108] In addition to these records, there are the donative inscriptions from *Stūpa* no. 2 at Sāñcī that also reveal lay participation in activity connected with the local monastic dead. But that participation at Sāñcī, as everywhere else, seems to have been overshadowed by that of the monks. The place and participation of the laity in activity connected with the local monastic dead seems everywhere to have been restricted, and this, in turn, may be reflected in the literature.

Conflict—potential or actual—is a consistent theme in literary accounts of the deposition of the Buddhist dead. The War of the Relics, never actually launched, is an established element of the accounts of the death of the Buddha.[109] Ānanda's death and the deposition of his remains also takes place in a context marked by the threat of war between competing claimants for his remains.[110] But the conflict over the remains of Śāriputra may be of particular interest. Although the only canonical Pāli account of the death of Śāriputra has either suffered—or been intentionally altered—in transmission, still it is clear from the *Saṃyutta-nikāya* account that the collection and preservation of Śāriputra's remains was thought to have been an exclusively monastic affair.[111] The account of these same events in the *Mūlasarvāstivāda-vinaya,* however, presents a much more complicated situation.[112] Although, here too, the initial collection of Śāriputra's remains was undertaken by a monk, and they were taken possession of by the Elder Ānanda, another monk, in this account, the monastic claim to exclusive possession and access is challenged by the wealthy layman Anāthapiṇḍada. He approaches Ānanda and asks for the remains, but Ānanda flatly refuses. This conflict between the monastic and lay claims then has to be mediated by the Buddha himself, who initially seems to favor Anāthapiṇḍada, and instructs Ānanda to hand over the remains. But that the redactors of this version did not see this either as a happy solution or as signaling the end of monastic control seems apparent from what follows: Anāthapiṇḍada takes the remains and enshrines them in his own house, but this only restricts access to these relics in another way. People come to Anāthapiṇḍada's house, but find the door locked. They complain to the Buddha, who, as a result, indicates that *stūpas* for deceased monks—although they might be erected by laymen—have to be erected within the confines of the monastery.

Although this quick summary does not do justice to the text, a text which deserves to be translated in full, it at least suggests that its author assumed or asserted the priority of an exclusive monastic claim to the remains of the monastic dead; it suggests that that claim at some point had been challenged, and that the monastic response to the challenge had been, at best, ambivalent: it allowed lay participation and involvement, but it restricted it to the confines of the monastery and indicated that lay participation was to be governed by monastic rules.

The account of the deposition of the remains of Śāriputra in the *Mūlasarvāstivāda-vinaya* is—in so far as we can now tell—only a story; as such, it can only tell us what its compiler or redactor thought or wanted his intended audience to think. The same applies, as well, to the accounts in the Pāli *Udāna* and *Apadāna* in which the Buddha is presented as directing monks, and monks alone, to perform the funeral and build a *stūpa* for a deceased fellow monk, or to the account in the Pāli *Vinaya* concerning a group of nuns doing the same for one of their deceased members.[113] As of now there is, of course, no way to relate any of these geographically unlocalizable and largely undatable documents directly to any of our sites. The most that we can say is it appears that all of the compilers or redactors of these stories assumed or asserted that concern for the local monastic dead was originally and primarily a concern of monks and nuns, that the laity, if they were involved at all, were thought, or directed to be, only secondarily, even tangentially, involved. This assumption or assertion, moreover, would appear to have been widespread.

These and other passages from the canonical literature deserve to be much more carefully studied for what they can tell us about attitudes and ideas concerning the local monastic dead that various authors or redactors attributed to the Buddha. It is, however, very likely that they will not tell us very much, and this, perhaps, gives rise to the broadest generalization that we can make. The epigraphical and archaeological material we have looked at—although it too requires much fuller study—already tells us some important things about the limitations of our literary sources. We know from the epigraphical and archaeological sources, not only that the remains of the *local* monastic dead were housed in permanent structures that paralleled structures used to house the remains of the Buddha, but we know too that the relationship between the *local* dead and the structures that housed their remains was expressed exactly as was the relationship between the "dead" Buddha and his *stūpa*—that, in both cases, the structure was said to be "of" or "for" the person, not "of" or "for" his remains. We know that there was little, if any, chronological gap between *stūpas* for the Buddha and *stūpas* for the *local* monastic dead; that a considerable amount of effort and expenditure went toward ensuring the continuing presence of deceased purely *local* monks in their respective communities; that the remains of *local* monks were deposited in separate shrines near the main *stūpa* of some sites, or that the remains of several *local* monks were deposited together in a single *stūpa*, or—most commonly—in ordered groups of individual *stūpas* placed away from the central hub of the complex. We know that there were *local*, perhaps regional, definitions of "sainthood," and that the status of *bhadanta* or *thera* appears to have had more than merely ecclesiastical significance in *actual* communities; that the preoccupation with the *local* monastic dead was primarily and predominantly a monastic concern and activity. Finally—and perhaps most importantly—we know that these conceptions and practices concerning the *local* monastic dead were certainly current at Sāñcī, Sonārī, Andher, Mathurā, Amarāvatī, Bhājā, Bedsā, and Kānheri, and probably at a dozen or more widely separated *actual* sites, and that such activity was not only widespread, but in most cases very early. We know all of this from epigraphical and archaeological material.

But almost none of this could have been clearly perceived, precisely understood, or even known from our canonical sources for the simple reason that all of it took place at a *local* level in actual monastic communities, and our canonical sources know nothing of—or say nothing about—the vast majority of the actual local sites at which we know early monastic Buddhism was practiced. There is, moreover, for the vast majority of such sites, no evidence that the canonical sources we know were known or used by the communities that lived there. These sources have, in this sense, no *direct* documentary value at all. If the study of Indian Buddhism is ever to be anything other than a study of what appears to be an idealizing and intentionally archaizing literature, if it is ever to deal directly with how this religion was actually practiced in actual local monasteries, these facts will have to be fully confronted, however uncomfortable that might be.

Notes

1. P. Steinthal, *Udāna* (London: 1885) 8.21; Bhikkhu J. Kashyap, *The Apadāna (II)—Buddhavaṃsa-Cariyā-Piṭaka* (*Khuddakanikāya*, Vol. VII), Nālandā-Devanāgarī-Pāli-Series (Bihar: 1959) 125.16 (54.6.216).

2. H. Oldenberg, *The Vinaya Piṭakaṃ,* Vol. IV (London: 1882) 308–309; cf. G. Schopen, "The *Stūpa* Cult and the Extant Pāli *Vinaya,*" Ch. V above, n. 19.

3. For the Tibetan text, see *Peking,* 44, 95-2-1. Certain aspects of this text—largely shorn of their context—have been discussed several times: W. W. Rockhill, *The Life of the Buddha and the Early History of His Order Derived from Tibetan Works in the Bkah-hgyur and Bstan-hgyur* (London: 1884) 111; L. de La Vallée Poussin, "Staupikam," *HJAS* 2 (1935) 276ff; A. Bareau, "La construction et le culte des stūpa d'après les Vinayapiṭaka," *BEFEO* 50 (1960) 236, 240, 247, 264; G. Roth, "Symbolism of the Buddhist Stūpa According to the Tibetan Version of the Caitya-vibhāga-vinayodbhāva-sūtra, the Sanskrit Treatise Stūpa-lakṣaṇa-kārikā-vivecana, and a Corresponding Passage in Kuladatta's Kriyāsaṃgraha," *The Stūpa. Its Religious, Historical and Architectural Significance,* ed. A. L. Dallapiccola and S. Z. Lallemant (Wiesbaden: 1980) 183ff.

4. de La Vallée Poussin, "Staupikam," 288.

5. For a survey of the kind and character of the "excavation" work done on Buddhist sites up until the '50s—and comparatively little major work has been done on such sites since then—see D. K. Chakrabarti, *A History of Indian Archaeology from the Beginning to 1947* (New Delhi: 1988).

6. J. Burgess, "Is Bezawāḍa on the Site of Dhanakaṭaka?" *IA* 11 (1882) 97–98. There is a good drawing of the plan and elevation of one of these "dolmens or rude-stone burying places" at Amarāvatī in J. Fergusson, "Description of the Amarāvatī Tope in Guntur," *JRAS* (1868) 143, fig. 6. Amarāvatī is not the only Buddhist site in Andhra built on or near proto-historical burials. There is evidence of such burials at Nāgārjunikoṇḍa; see R. Subrahmanyam et al., *Nagarjunakonda (1954–60),* Vol. I, MASI, No. 75 (New Delhi: 1975) 165ff. For Yeleswaram, see M. A. W. Khan, *A Monograph on Yelleshwaram Excavations* (Hyderabad: 1963) 4ff; for Jaggayyapeṭa, see R. Sewell, *Quelques points d'archéologie de l'inde méridionale* (Paris: 1897) 5–6; for Goli, see K. P. Rao, *Deccan Megaliths* (Delhi: 1988) 23; etc. The association of Buddhist sites with proto-historical burials is also by no means limited to Andhra—see, for convenience's sake, D. Faccenna, *A Guide to the Excavations in Swat (Pakistan) 1956–62* (Roma: 1964) 62, 65—and deserves to be much more fully studied as a general pattern. [See G. Schopen, "Immigrant Monks and the Proto-Historical Dead: The Buddhist Occupation of Early Burial Sites in India," *Festschrift Dieter Schlingloff,* ed. F. Wilhelm (Reinbek: 1996) 215–238.]

7. Fergusson, "Description of the Amarāvatī Tope in Guntur," 138, 140.

8. For the modern history of the site and a summary account of the work done on it, see N. S. Ramaswami, *Amaravati. The Art and History of the Stūpa and the Temple* (Hyderabad: 1975) 14–23. There is epigraphical evidence of Buddhist devotional and donative activity at the site in the eleventh century (E. Hultzsch, "A Pallava Inscription from Amaravati," *Madras Journal of Literature and Science for 1886–87* [Madras: 1887] 59–62), in the twelfth and thirteenth centuries (E. Hultzsch, "Two Pillar Inscriptions at Amaravati," *EI* 6 [1900–1901] 146–160), and in the fourteenth century (S. Paranavitana, "Gaḍalādeṇiya Rock-Inscription of Dharmmakīrtti Sthavira," *EZ* 4 [1935] 90–110). Some of the earliest work on the site had already revealed stray sculptures, relief work, and plaques that belonged to a "late" period, and in 1954 D. Barrett had made an attempt to describe "the Later School of Amaravati," which he situated between the seventh and tenth centuries in "The Later School of Amaravati and its Influence," *Arts and Letters* 28.2 (1954) 41–53. More recently, a certain amount of attention has been focused on what is rather loosely called "tantric" material from Amarāvatī and other Andhra sites; see K. Krishna Murthy, *Iconography of Buddhist Deity Heruka* (Delhi: 1988)

and K. Krishna Murthy, *Sculptures of Vajrayāna Buddhism* (Delhi: 1989). Although the latter work is often careless and badly done, still it makes clear that we have much to learn about the later phases of Buddhism in Andhra and suggests that it persisted far longer than we are wont to think. There is, moreover, evidence for this persistence not just at Amarāvatī but at Sālihuṇḍam (R. Subrahmanyam, *Salihundam. A Buddhist Site in Andhra Pradesh* [Hyderabad: 1964] 91ff), Guṇṭupalle (I. K. Sarma, *Studies in Early Buddhist Monuments and Brāhmī Inscriptions of Āndhra Deśa* [Nagpur: 1988] 59–91), Gummaḍidurru (M. H. Kuraishi, "Trail Excavations at Alluru, Gummadidurru and Nagarjunakonda," *ARASI 1926–27* [Calcutta: 1930] 150–161), and at a number of other sites.

9. J. Burgess, *Notes on the Amaravati Stupa* (Madras: 1882) 4, 9.

10. A. Rea, "Excavations at Amarāvatī," *ARASI 1905–06* (Calcutta: 1909) 118–119 and pl. L. Rea's pl. XLVII.6 reproduces "evidently a late example" of the kind of sculpture referred to in n. 8.

11. A. Rea, "Excavations at Amarāvatī," *ARASI 1908–09* (Calcutta: 1912) 90–91 and figs. 1 and 2. Rea called these burials "neolithic pyriform tombs," but Rao (*Deccan Megaliths*, 46) has pointed out that ". . . taking into account the recent evidence, we can safely assign them to the megalithic period." Note the "late" sculptures illustrated in Rea's pls. XXVIIId and XXXId.

12. G. Schopen, "Burial *Ad Sanctos* and the Physical Presence of the Buddha in Early Indian Buddhism," Ch. VII above.

13. Burgess, *Notes on the Amaravati Stupa*, 49.

14. J. Burgess, *The Buddhist Stupas of Amaravati and Jaggayyapeta in the Krishna District, Madras Presidency, Surveyed in 1882* (London: 1887) pl. xlv.6.

15. Burgess, *Notes on the Amaravati Stupa*, 49 (no. 88b), 55 (88b). Hultzsch's final version appeared in E. Hultzsch, "Amarāvatī-Inschriften," *ZDMG* 37 (1883) 555–556, no. 24.

16. H. Lüders, *A List of Brahmi Inscriptions from the Earliest Times to about* A.D. *400 with the Exception of those of Aśoka*, Appendix to *EI* 10 (Calcutta: 1912) no. 1276.

17. R. O. Franke, "Epigraphische Notizen," *ZDMG* 50 (1896) 600.

18. C. Sivaramamurti, *Amaravati Sculptures in the Madras Government Museum*, Bulletin of the Madras Government Museum, N.S. Vol. IV (Madras: 1942) 295, no. 92.

19. Burgess, *Notes on the Amaravati Stupa*, 55 and n. 2.

20. Hultzsch, "Amarāvatī-Inschriften," 555–556, no. 24.

21. Burgess, *The Buddhist Stupas of Amaravati and Jaggayyapeta*, 87.

22. Lüders, *A List of Brahmi Inscriptions*, no. 1276.

23. Sivaramamurti, *Amaravati Sculptures in the Madras Government Museum*, 295, no. 92; 342.

24. *Histoire du bouddhisme indien*, 583–584.

25. O. R. Furtseva, "On the Problem of the Territorial Distribution of the Buddhist Schools in Kushana Age (According to the Epigraphic Data)," *Summaries of Papers Presented by Soviet Scholars to the VIth World Sanskrit Conference, October 13–20, 1984, Philadelphia, Pennsylvania, U.S.A.* (Moscow: 1984) 55; see also A. M. Shastri, "Buddhist Schools as Known from Early Indian Inscriptions," *Bhāratī, Bulletin of the College of Indology* 2 (1957/1958) 48; etc.

26. J. Marshall, *A Guide to Sanchi* (Calcutta: 1918) 87.

27. Sivaramamurti, *Amaravati Sculptures in the Madras Government Museum*, 298.

28. Burgess, *The Buddhist Stupas of Amaravati and Jaggayyapeta*, 72.

29. Burgess, *The Buddhist Stupas of Amaravati and Jaggayyapeta*, pl. xxxi.6; Ph. Stern and M. Bénisti, *Évolution du style indien d'Amarāvatī* (Paris: 1961) pl. lxvi.

30. Sivaramamurti, *Amaravati Sculptures in the Madras Government Museum*, pl. lxv.8.

31. G. Schopen, "A Verse from the Bhadracarīpraṇidhāna in a 10th Century Inscription found at Nālandā," *JIABS* 12.1 (1989) 149–157.

32. See for references G. Schopen, "Two Problems in the History of Indian Buddhism," Ch. II above, nn. 97–102.

33. M. S. Nagaraja Rao, "Brāhmī Inscriptions and their Bearing on the Great Stūpa at Sannati," *Indian Epigraphy. Its Bearing on the History of Art*, ed. F. M. Asher and G. S. Gai (New Delhi: 1985) 41–45, esp. 42, no. 8. There are a number of problems concerning the inscriptions from this recently discovered site in Karnataka, and their nature is not fully understood. For example, although Rao takes the record cited above as a donative inscription and says it occurs on "an āyaka pillar," it is very likely—to judge by the illustration in his pl. 62—that it is a memorial pillar, not an *āyaka* pillar, and the record might simply be a label.

34. Literary sources do, of course, refer to *keśanakha-stūpas*, "*stūpas* for the hair and nail clippings," and these are—as Feer has said—presented as a kind of "monument élevé à un Buddha de son vivant" (*Avadāna-Çataka. Cent légendes bouddhiques* [Paris: 1891] 482). References to this type of *stūpa* occur widely: in the *Avadānaśataka* (J. S. Speyer, *Avadānaçataka. A Century of Edifying Tales belonging to the Hīnayāna* [St. Petersburg: 1906–1909] i, 123.1, 307.1ff; ii, 71.3; etc.); in the *Divyāvadāna* (P. L. Vaidya, *Divyāvadāna* [Darbhanga: 1959] 122.1–122.25: *dharmatā khalu buddhānāṃ bhagavatāṃ jīvatāṃ dhriyamāṇānāṃ yāpayatāṃ keśanakhastūpā bhavanti* . . . —this is a particularly important passage, and a part of it is quoted as well by Śāntideva in C. Bendall, *Çikshāsamuccaya. A Compendium of Buddhistic Teaching* [St. Petersburg: 1897–1902] 148.13, where he attributes it to the Sarvāstivādins: *ārya-sarvāstivādānāṃ ca paṭhyate*); and scattered throughout the *vastus* of the *Mūlasarvāstivāda-vinaya*: the *Cīvaravastu* (*Gilgit Manuscripts*, iii 2, 143.12), the *Pārivāsikavastu* (*Gilgit Manuscripts*, iii 3, 98.4), the *Śayanāsanavastu* (*Śayanāsanavastu and Adhikaraṇavastu*, 28.1, 5), the *Kṣudrakavastu* (*Derge*, 10, 9.6, 7), etc. There are also a number of references to a *keśanakha-stūpa* in some of the versions of the meeting of the Buddha with Trapuṣa and Bhallika; for some of these—and for further references to *keśanakha-stūpas* in general—see A. Bareau, *Recherches sur la biographie du buddha dans les sūtrapiṭaka et les vinayapiṭaka anciens: de la quête de l'éveil a la conversion de śāriputra et de maudgalyāyana* (Paris: 1963) 106–123; A. Bareau, "La construction et le culte des stūpa d'après les Vinayapiṭaka," *BEFEO* 50 (1960) 261–263; de La Vallée Poussin, "Staupikam," 285–87; etc. But in spite of the fact that there are numerous references in literary sources to such *stūpas*, and in spite of the fact that the Chinese pilgrims refer to them (Li Yung-hsi, *A Record of Buddhist Countries by Fa-hsien* [Peking: 1957] 32; S. Beal, *Buddhist Records of the Western World*, Vol. II [London: 1884] 80, 173; etc.), there is as yet no archaeological or epigraphical evidence to confirm their actual existence. Moreover, the texts themselves indicate that though such *stūpas* were thought to have been built while the *buddhas* in question were still alive, such *stūpas* were built only for *buddhas*, certainly not for local monks like Nāgasena. Finally, it might be noted that the possibility of *cetiyas* being made during the lifetime of the Buddha is also explicitly raised in the Pāli *Kāliṅgabodhijātaka: Sakkā pana bhante tumhesu dharantesu yeva cetiyaṃ kātun* (V. Fausbøll, *The Jātaka together with its Commentary*, Vol. IV [London: 1887] 228.17), and—although the text is not entirely clear—what we normally think of as *stūpas*, *sāririka-cetiyas*, are clearly and obviously ruled out. Things like the *bodhi*-tree, which the Buddha had "used," are alone

clearly allowed; cf. de La Vallée Poussin, "Staupikam," 284–285. The classification of *cetiyas* into *sārīrika*, *pāribhogika*, and *uddesika* found in the *Kāliṅgabodhijātaka* and other Pāli sources, although frequently cited, shows several signs of being very late; cf. E. W. Adikaram, *Early History of Buddhism in Ceylon* (Colombo: 1946) 135, but note that he has overlooked the *Jātaka* passage.

35. Sivaramamurti, *Amaravati Sculptures in the Madras Government Museum*, nos. 102, 118; cf. no. 51.

36. G. Bühler, "Inscriptions from the Stupa of Jaggayyapeṭā," *IA* 11 (1882) 258 (II.6), 259 (.6); also in Burgess, *The Buddhist Stupas of Amaravati and Jaggayyapeta*, 110, no. 2, 1.5; no. 3, 1.4.

37. For both ideas, see Schopen, "Burial *Ad Sanctos* and the Physical Presence of the Buddha in Early Indian Buddhism," Ch. VII above, esp. 128–131; Schopen, "The Buddha as an Owner of Property and Permanent Resident in Medieval Indian Monasteries," Ch. XII below, 272–274.

38. It is worth noting here that it is in Andhra alone that structures connected with the local monastic dead are called *cetiyas*. Elsewhere, even in the Deccan, they are referred to as *stūpas*. A similar—but not exactly the same—pattern seems to hold as well in regard to structures connected with the "dead" Buddha: in Andhra they are consistently called *cetiyas*, usually *mahā-cetiyas*, while elsewhere in inscriptions—apart from the Western Caves—such structures are usually called *stūpas*. In the Western monastic cave complexes there is evidence to suggest that the structures connected with the "dead" Buddha were called *cetiyas* (e.g. *caityagṛha*), while the word *stūpa* was used "primarily to denote" what Sarkar calls "small-sized memorial *stūpas* raised in honour of some elder *thera*" (H. Sarkar, *Studies in Early Buddhist Architecture of India* [Delhi: 1966] 4). Obviously these regional differences must be more fully studied and precisely plotted, but it is worth noting that some canonical Pāli literature—like Andhran epigraphy—shows a clear preference for the term *cetiya*, and that this shared preference may evidence mutual contact and influence; cf. Schopen, "The *Stūpa* Cult and the Extant Pāli *Vinaya*," Ch. V above, 89–91.

39. Although it is neither well written nor well documented, C. Margabandhu, "Archaeological Evidence of Buddhism at Mathurā—A Chronological Study," *Svasti Śrī. Dr. B. Ch. Chhabra Felicitation Volume*, ed. K. V. Ramesh et al. (Delhi: 1984) 267–280, provides an overview of work on the site. For attempts to reconstruct even the basic outlines of the development of the site, see M. C. Joshi and A. K. Sinha, "Chronology of Mathurā—an Assessment," *Puratattva* 10 (1978–1979) 39–44; R. C. Gaur, "Mathura-Govardhana Region: An Archaeological Assessment in Historical Perspective," *Indological Studies. Prof. D. C. Sircar Commemoration Volume*, ed. S. K. Maity and U. Thakur (New Delhi: 1987) 103–113; S. C. Ray, "Stratigraphic Evidence of Coins from Excavations at Mathura," *Sraddhāñjali. Studies in Ancient Indian History (D. C. Sircar Commemoration Volume)*, ed. K. K. Das Gupta et al. (Delhi: 1988) 375–384; M. C. Joshi, "Mathurā as an Ancient Settlement," *Mathurā. The Cultural Heritage*, ed. D. M. Srinivasan (New Delhi: 1988) 165–170; etc. There are two papers that—for different reasons—are particularly important for the site, neither of which is directly connected with Buddhist material: K. W. Folkert, "Jain Religious Life at Ancient Mathurā: The Heritage of Late Victorian Interpretation," *Mathurā. The Cultural Heritage*, 103–112, which discusses some of the distortions in interpretation that have arisen, at least in part, from the piecemeal discovery and publication of the material from Mathurā; and H. Härtel, "Some Results of the Excavations at Sonkh. A Preliminary Report," *German Scholars on India. Contributions to Indian Studies*, Vol. II (New Delhi: 1976) 69–99, which establishes a clear, datable

stratigraphical sequence, and—by contrast—makes clear what could have been gained by systematic excavation of specific complexes at Mathurā.

40. J. E. van Lohuizen-de Leeuw, *The "Scythian" Period. An Approach to the History, Art, Epigraphy and Palaeography of North India from the 1st Century B.C. to the 3rd Century A.D.* (Leiden: 1949) 181–183; van Lohuizen-de Leeuw refers to a still earlier treatment of the record in V. S. Agrawala, "New Sculptures from Mathurā," *Journal of the United Provinces Historical Society* 11.2 (1938) 66–76, but I have been unable to consult this paper.

41. D. C. Sircar, "Brahmi Inscriptions from Mathurā," *EI* 34 (1961–1962) 9–13, esp. 10–11 and pl.

42. Sircar, "Brahmi Inscriptions from Mathurā," 11.

43. S. Nagaraju, *Buddhist Architecture of Western India (c. 250 B.C.—c. A.D. 300)* (Delhi: 1981) 113 (a reading of the Bedsā record is given on 329 as well); chart iii places the Kānheri inscription early in the period between A.D. 100 and A.D. 180 (see also 333, no. 6 under Kānheri). V. Dehejia, *Early Buddhist Rock Temples. A Chronology* (London: 1972) 177, assigns the record from Bedsā to "c. 50–30 B.C."; for Kānheri, see 183–184.

44. J. Burgess, *Report on the Buddhist Cave Temples and Their Inscriptions*, Archaeological Survey of Western India, Vol. IV (London: 1883) 89 (VI.2) and pl. xlvii; see also D. D. Kosambi, "Dhenukākaṭa," *JASBom* 30.2 (1955) 50–71, esp. 70. For the spatial location of this *stūpa* within the Bedsā complex, the most useful site plan is that published in A. A. West, "Copies of Inscriptions from the Caves near Beḍsa, with a Plan," *JBomBRAS* 8 (1864–1866) 222–224 and 2 pl.—this contains as well an eye-copy of the inscription.

45. J. Burgess, *Report on the Elura Cave Temples and the Brahmanical and Jaina Caves in Western India*, Archaeological Survey of Western India, Vol. V (London: 1883) 78, no. 10, and pl. li. For the position of this small "shrine" within the complex, see Nagaraju, *Buddhist Architecture of Western India*, 197–198 and fig. 39; J. Fergusson and J. Burgess, *The Cave Temples of India* (London: 1880) pl. liii.

46. D. Mitra, *Buddhist Monuments* (Calcutta: 1971) 153.

47. Nagaraju, *Buddhist Architecture of Western India*, 129. Dehejia, in *Early Buddhist Rock Temples*, 47–48, 154, assigns the inscriptions to c. 70–50 B.C.

48. For these records from Bhājā, see Burgess, *Report on the Buddhist Cave Temples and Their Inscriptions*, 82–83 (I.2–I.5); Kosambi, "Dhenukākaṭa," 70–71; Nagaraju, *Buddhist Architecture of Western India*, 330; etc.

49. Fergusson and Burgess, *The Cave Temples of India*, 228.

50. M. N. Deshpande, "The Rock-cut Caves of Pitalkhorā in the Deccan," *AI* 15 (1959) 66–93, esp. 72–73. On "relic" deposits in monolithic or rock-cut *stūpas*, see also Fergusson and Burgess, *The Cave Temples of India*, 186, n. 1; H. Cousens, *The Antiquities of Sind. With Historical Outline* (Calcutta: 1929) 105, referring to Kārli; etc.

51. W. West, "Description of Some of the Kānheri Topes," *JBomBRAS* 6 (1862) 116–120, esp. 120.

52. Burgess, *Report on the Buddhist Cave Temples and Their Inscriptions*, 67. On the same page there is a good woodcut illustrating what a part of the cemetery looked like in his day.

53. E. W. West, "Copies of Inscriptions from the Buddhist Cave-Temples of Kānheri, etc. in the Island of Salsette, with a Plan of the Kānheri Caves," *JBomBRAS* 5 (1861) 1–14, esp. 12, no. 58.

54. S. Gokhale, "New Inscriptions from Kānheri," *JESI* 5 (1975) 110–112, esp. 110; S. Gokhale, "The Memorial Stūpa Gallery at Kānheri," *Indian Epigraphy. Its Bearing on the History of Art*, ed. F. M. Asher and G. S. Gai (New Delhi: 1985) 55–59, esp. 55,

and pls. 94–101; S. Gorakshkar, "A Sculptured Frieze from Kānheri," *Lalit Kalā* 18 (1977) 35–38, esp. 35, and pls. xvi–xviii; M. S. Nagaraja Rao, ed., *Indian Archaeology 1983–84—A Review* (New Delhi: 1986) 154; cf. M. S. Nagaraja Rao, ed., *Indian Archaeology 1982–83—A Review* (New Delhi: 1985) 122.

55. Gokhale, "The Memorial Stūpa Gallery at Kānheri," 56, no. 1, pl. 95; 57, no. 4, pl. 98.

56. Gokhale, "New Inscriptions from Kānheri," 110; Gokhale, "The Memorial Stūpa Gallery at Kānheri," 56.

57. Before leaving the question of the use of plurals of respect in Buddhist inscriptions—a question that also requires further study—it is important to note that the use of such plurals, although characteristic of records referring to the local monastic dead, is not restricted to records of this kind. See, for example: E. Senart, "The Inscriptions in the Caves at Nasik," *EI* 8 (1905–1906) 76; Burgess, *Report on the Buddhist Cave Temples and Their Inscriptions*, 85, no. 7; 87, no. 22; 95, no. 17 (etc.); D. C. Sircar, *Epigraphic Discoveries in East Pakistan* (Calcutta: 1975) 11 (there is here, however, the additional problem that the inscription Sircar is referring to may not be Buddhist—cf. S. Siddhanta, "The Jagadishpur Copper Plate Grant of the Gupta Year 128 (A.D. 44–48)," *Journal of the Varendra Research Museum* 1.1 [1972] 23–37); Schopen, "The Buddha as an Owner of Property and Permanent Resident in Medieval Indian Monasteries," Ch. XII below, 264, referring to the Valabhī grants; etc.

58. Burgess, *Notes on the Amaravati Stupa*, 55, no. 88b and n. 2; Hultzsch, "Amarāvatī-Inschriften," 555–556; Burgess, *The Buddhist Stupas of Amaravati and Jaggayyapeta*, 87; Lüders, *A List of Brahmi Inscriptions*, no. 1276; Sivaramamurti, *Amaravati Sculptures in the Madras Government Museum*, 295, no. 92.

59. Burgess, *Notes on the Amaravati Stupa*, 55, n. 2.

60. M. A. Mehendale, *Historical Grammar of Inscriptional Prakrits* (Poona: 1948) 122 (§232, c ii); O. von Hinüber, *Das Ältere Mittelindisch im Überblick* (Wien: 1986) 111 (§221).

61. A. Cunningham, *The Bhilsa Topes; or Buddhist Monuments of Central India* (London: 1854) esp. 184–189, 203–205, 223–236. The local character of the monks whose remains were deposited in the *stūpas* at Sāñcī and related sites has been obscured by an early and persistent tendency to identify some of these monks with some of the monks involved in the so-called Third Council, which is known only from Sri Lankan sources. This sort of identification started with Cunningham himself (184–189) and has been reasserted—with variation and differing degrees of certitude—over the years: see J. F. Fleet, "Notes on Three Buddhist Inscriptions," *JRAS* (1905) 681–691; W. Geiger, *The Mahāvaṃsa or the Great Chronicle of Ceylon* (London: 1912) xix–xx; E. Frauwallner, *The Earliest Vinaya and the Beginnings of Buddhist Literature*, Serie Orientale Roma, VIII (Roma: 1956) 14–15; *Histoire du bouddhisme indien*, 333–334; etc. Such identifications have not, however, gone entirely unquestioned, and recently Yamazaki has presented an argument that has put the question of the "council" and the identification of the monks named on the Sāñcī area deposits in an entirely new light: see G. Yamazaki, "The Spread of Buddhism in the Mauryan Age—with Special Reference to the Mahinda Legend," *Acta Asiatica* 43 (1982) 1–16. It is important to note that even if we were to accept that *some* of the monks whose remains were deposited in *stūpas* at Sāñcī, Sonārī, and Andher were connected with a "Third Council," the majority were not. At least seven of the ten monks—like the named monks at Bedsā, Bhājā, Kānheri, Mathurā, and Amarāvatī—are completely unknown in the so-called Great Tradition and could only have been local monastic "saints."

62. J. Marshall, A. Foucher, and N. G. Majumdar, *The Monuments of Sāñchī,* Vol. I (Delhi: 1940) 294.

63. For more recent remarks on Kākanāva/Sāñcī, see P. H. L. Eggermont, "Sanchi-Kākanāda and the Hellenistic and Buddhist Sources," *Deyadharma. Studies in Memory of Dr. D. C . Sircar,* ed. G. Bhattacharya (Delhi: 1986) 11–27.

64. Marshall et al., *The Monuments of Sāñchī,* Vol. I, 294.

65. Majumdar's interpretation of *siha,* which he says "can be equated with Arddha-Māgadhī *seha,* corresponding to Sanskrit *śaiksha,*" remains, however, problematic; see below n. 99.

66. For the inscriptions from Sāñcī *Stūpa* no. 2, see Marshall et al., *The Monuments of Sāñchī,* Vol. I, 363–375, nos. 631–719, nos. xvi–xxi, and nos. 803, 812, 819–821.

67. *Historie du bouddhisme indien,* 474.

68. Schopen, "Burial *Ad Sanctos* and the Physical Presence of the Buddha in Early Indian Buddhism," Ch. VII above, 125–133; Schopen, "On the Buddha and His Bones," Ch. VIII above, esp. 152–156ff.

69. Bareau, "La construction et le culte des stūpa d'après les Vinayapiṭaka," 268.

70. Bareau, "La construction et le culte des stūpa d'après les Vinayapiṭaka," 269.

71. M. Bénisti, "Observations concernant le Stūpa n° 2 de Sāñcī," *BEI* 4 (1986) 165–170, esp. 165.

72. Nagaraju, *Buddhist Architecture of Western India,* 119, 129.

73. Nagaraju, *Buddhist Architecture of Western India,* 112–113.

74. For references, see nn. 1 and 2 above.

75. Nagaraju, *Buddhist Architecture of Western India,* 107, 191.

76. Very little work has been done on the Buddhist caves at Sudhagarh, the primary source of information on them being O. C. Kail, "The Buddhist Caves at Sudhagarh," *JASBom,* N.S. 41/42 (1966/1967) 184–189, figs. 1–7. Kail assigns the caves to a period ranging from 200 B.C.E. to 150 B.C.E. (188).

77. H. Cousens, *An Account of the Caves at Nadsur and Karsambla* (Bombay: 1891) esp. 3–4 and pl. II. See also J. E. Abbott, "Recently Discovered Buddhist Caves at Nadsur and Nenavali in the Bhor State, Bombay Presidency," *IA* 20 (1891) 121–123. Cousens says: ". . . I think we cannot be far wrong in ascribing to these caves as early a date as Bhājā or Kondāne, i.e., about B.C. 200" (10); Dehejia, *Early Buddhist Rock Temples,* assigns the sculpture at Nadsur to "the period of Sanchi II" (118), but the inscriptions to "around 70 B.C." (153).

78. Deshpande, "The Rock-cut Caves of Pitalkhorā in the Deccan," esp. 78–79. See also W. Willetts, "Excavation at Pitalkhorā in the Aurangabad District of Maharashtra," *Oriental Art,* N.S. 7.2 (1961) 59–65, and Mitra, *Buddhist Monuments,* 174. The latter says: "Curiously enough, all the four caves of this group are associated with *stūpas* . . . evidently made in memory of some distinguished resident-monks as at Bhājā."

79. A. Cunningham, *The Bhilsa Topes; or Buddhist Monuments of Central India,* 211–220.

80. A. H. Longhurst, "The Buddhist Monuments at Guntupalle, Kistna District," *Annual Report of the Archaeological Department, Southern Circle, Madras, for the Year 1916–17* (Madras: 1917) 30–36 and pls. xvii–xxvii, esp. 31 and 35; see also R. Sewell, "Buddhist Remains at Guṇṭupalle," *JRAS* (1887) 508–511; A. Bareau, "Le site bouddhique du Guntupalle," *Arts Asiatiques* 23 (1971) 69–78 and figs. 1–32. Bareau noted that "de tels alignements de petits *stūpa* se retrouvent sur d'autres sites bouddhiques," and evidence for the mortuary character of these *stūpas* is accumulating; see A. Ghosh, ed., *Indian*

Archaeology 1961–62—A Review (New Delhi: 1964) 97, and B. B. Lal, ed., *Indian Archaeology 1968–69—A Review* (New Delhi: 1971) 64. For other results of recent work on the site, see I. K. Sarma, "Epigraphical Discoveries at Guntupalli," *JESI* 5 (1975) 48–61 and pls. i–ix (pl. i gives a good photograph of the rows of *stūpas* on the middle terrace), and Sarma, *Studies in Early Buddhist Monuments and Brāhmī Inscriptions of Āndhradeśa,* 57–91.

81. See, for convenience's sake, M. Venkataramayya, *Śrāvastī* (New Delhi: 1981) 15.

82. T. Bloch suggested that "the funeral mounds in Lauriya go back to the pre-Mauryan epoch" and hinted at a "Vedic" connection in "Excavations at Lauriya," *ARASI 1906–07* (Calcutta: 1909) 119–126. Bloch's views are still occasionally referred to (e.g., P. V. Kane, *History of Dharmaśāstra,* Vol. IV [Poona: 1953] 234, 254), in spite of the fact that Majumdar's later work on the site (N. G. Majumdar, "Explorations at Lauriya-Nandangarh," *ARASI 1935–36* [Delhi: 1938] 55–66 and pls. xix–xxi; N. G. Majumdar, "Excavations at Lauriya Nandangarh," *ARASI 1936–37* [Delhi: 1940] 47–50 and pls. xxi–xxiv) "proved that many of the mounds at Lauriya are Buddhist in character, enclosing *stūpas*" (so G. N. Das, "Coins from Indian Megaliths," *Bulletin of the Deccan College Research Institute* 8 [1947] 208; cf. Mitra, *Buddhist Monuments,* 83–85). A good survey of work on the site may be had in J. E. van Lohuizen-de Leeuw, "South-East Asian Architecture and the Stūpa of Nandangarḥ," *ArA* 19 (1956) 279–290, esp. 281ff.

83. For both *stūpas* and Longhurst's comments, see A. H. Longhurst, *The Buddhist Antiquities of Nāgārjunakoṇḍa, Madras Presidency,* MASI, No. 54 (Delhi: 1938) 20–21. There may as well be a third *stūpa* of this type at Nāgārjunikoṇḍa—see A. Ghosh, ed., *Indian Archaeology 1955–56—A Review* (New Delhi: 1956) 25, under "Site XXV."

84. J. H. Marshall, "Excavations at Saheṭh-Maheṭh," *ARASI 1910–11* (Calcutta: 1914) 4.

85. A. Ghosh, ed., *Indian Archaeology 1955–56—A Review* (New Delhi: 1956) 9; see also G. R. Sharma, "Excavations at Kauśāmbī, 1949–55," *Annual Bibliography of Indian Archaeology* 16 (Leyden: 1958) xlii–xliii.

86. J. Marshall, *Taxila. An Illustrated Account of Archaeological Excavations carried out at Taxila under the Orders of the Government of India between the Years 1913 and 1934,* Vol. I (Cambridge: 1951) 246, 335, 361; J. Marshall, *Mohenjo-Daro and the Indus Civilization. Being an Official Account of Archaeological Excavations at Mohenjo-Daro carried out by the Government of India between the Years 1922 and 1927,* Vol. I (London: 1931) 120–121. See also R. D. Banerji, *Mohenjodaro. A Forgotten Report* (Varanasi: 1984) 59ff. The burial deposits in what has been taken to be a Buddhist monastery at Mohenjo-daro may also be connected with the local monastic dead, but the interpretation of these data remains controversial.

87. Cf. G. Schopen, "Archaeology and Protestant Presuppositions in the Study of Indian Buddhism," Ch. I above.

88. Schopen, "The *Stūpa* Cult and the Extant Pāli *Vinaya,*" Ch. V above, 92–93; Schopen, "Monks and the Relic Cult in the *Mahāparinibbāna-sutta,*" Ch. VI above.

89. See H. Oldenberg, *Buddha. Sein Leben, seine Lehre, seine Gemeinde* (Berlin: 1881) 384, n. 3; H. Oldenberg, *Buddha: His Life, His Doctrine, His Order,* trans. W. Hoey (London: 1882) 376 and note (which contains a significant addition); T. W. Rhys Davids, *Buddhist Suttas,* Sacred Books of the East, Vol. XI (Oxford: 1900) xliv–xlv; and G. Schopen, "On Avoiding Ghosts and Social Censure," Ch. X below.

90. D. M. Miller and D. C. Wertz, *Hindu Monastic Life. The Monks and Monasteries of Bhubaneswar* (Montreal: 1976) 100, table 8.

91. See most recently—although limited to Pāli sources—G. D. Bond, "The Ara-

hant: Sainthood in Theravāda Buddhism," *Sainthood. Its Manifestations in World Religions,* ed. R. Kieckhefer and G. D. Bond (Berkeley: 1988) 140–171.

92. Marshall et al., *The Monuments of Sāñchī,* Vol. I, 290, n. 5.

93. Mehendale, *Historical Grammar of Inscriptional Prakrits,* 169 (§294), 166 (§290 b, i).

94. T. W. Rhys Davids and W. Stede, *The Pali Text Society's Pali-English Dictionary* (London: 1921–1925) 680.

95. *BHSD,* 554.

96. These references to "ascetic" monks—one specifically called a "forest-dweller"—may suggest that what has been noted recently in regard to such monks in modern Thailand and Sri Lanka may have a long history; see S. J. Tambiah, *The Buddhist Saints of the Forest and the Cult of Amulets* (Cambridge: 1984); S. J. Tambiah, "The Buddhist Arahant: Classical Paradigm and Modern Thai Manifestations," *Saints and Virtues,* ed. J. S. Hawley (Berkeley: 1987) 111–126; M. Carrithers, *The Forest Monks of Sri Lanka. An Anthropological and Historical Study* (Delhi: 1983); etc.

97. There are also epigraphical references to the Mahāyāna, or related to what we call "the Mahāyāna," that almost certainly predate the Kānheri labels—at least two at Kānheri itself; see G. Schopen, "Mahāyāna in Indian Inscriptions," *IIJ* 21 (1979) 1–19; Schopen, "Two Problems in the History of Indian Buddhism," Ch. II above, 38–41; Schopen, "The Inscription on the Kuṣān Image of Amitābha and the Character of the Early Mahāyāna in India," *JIABS* 10.2 (1987) 99–134; Schopen, "The Buddha as an Owner of Property and Permanent Resident in Medieval Indian Monasteries," Ch. XII below, n. 49.

98. Marshall et al., *The Monuments of Sāñchī,* Vol. I, 294.

99. Elsewhere at Sāñcī itself we find *sijhā-* for *śaikṣā-*, and *sejha-* for *śaikṣa-*, which suggests a development different from that suggested by Majumdar; see Mehendale, *Historical Grammar of Inscriptional Prakrits,* 151 (§267.b, §286.a iv); also von Hinüber, *Das Ältere Mittelindisch im Überblick,* 114–116 (§§232–236).

100. See Schopen, "The *Stūpa* Cult and the Extant Pāli *Vinaya,*" Ch. V above, n. 32, for a detailed tabulation.

101. Marshall, *A Guide to Sanchi,* 2; H. P. Ray, "Bhārhut and Sanchi—Nodal Points in a Commercial Interchange," *Archaeology and History. Essays in Memory of Shri A. Ghosh,* ed. B. M. Pande and B. D. Chattopadhyaya, Vol. II (Delhi: 1987) 621–629. It should be noted that Ray's figures and remarks concerning the donors at both Sāñcī and Bhārhut are unreliable; they are entirely based on Lüders' *List* and do not take into account the much fuller and more complete collections of inscriptions from both sites published after 1912.

102. This is the definition of *navakammikas* given by J. Ph. Vogel, "Prakrit Inscriptions from a Buddhist Site at Nagarjunikonda," *EI* 20 (1929–1930) 30.

103. M. Njammasch, "Der *navakammika* und seine Stellung in der Hierarchie der buddhistischen Klöster," *Altorientalische Forschungen* 1 (1974) 279–293, esp. 293; but see also P. V. B. Karunatillake, "The Administrative Organization of the Nālandā Mahāvihāra from Sigillary Evidence," *The Sri Lanka Journal of the Humanities* 6 (1980) 57–69, esp. 61–63; G. Fussman, "Numismatic and Epigraphic Evidence for the Chronology of Early Gandharan Art," *Investigating Indian Art,* ed. W. Lobo and M. Yaldiz (Berlin: 1987) 67–88, esp. 80–81 and the sources cited there.

104. H. Lüders, *Bharhut Inscriptions,* Corpus Inscriptionum Indicarum, Vol. II, Pt. 2, ed. E. Waldschmidt and M. A. Mehendale (Ootacamund: 1963) 38 (A59).

105. Sivaramamurti, *Amaravati Sculptures in the Madras Government Museum,* 290, no. 69.

106. Vogel, "Prakrit Inscriptions from a Buddhist Site at Nagarjunikonda," 22, 24 (for an important correction to Vogel's reading of the "Detached Pillar Inscription H," see K. A. Nilakanta Sastri and K. Gopalachari, "Epigraphic Notes," *EI* 24 [1937–1938] 279, VI), 17.

107. See above 167–168; 179.

108. See above 174.

109. See, for convenience's sake, A. Bareau, *Recherches sur la biographie du buddha dans les sūtrapiṭaka et les vinayapiṭaka anciens: II. Les derniers mois, le parinirvāṇa et les funérailles,* T. II (Paris: 1971) 265–288.

110. *Peking,* 44, 243-3-5ff; cf. J. Przyluski, "Le partage des reliques du buddha," *MCB* 4 (1935–1936) 341–367, esp. 347ff.

111. The account of Śāriputra's death occurs at L. Feer, *Saṃyutta-nikāya,* Pt. V (London: 1898) 161–163, and is translated in F. L. Woodward, *The Book of the Kindred Sayings,* Pt. V (London: 1930) 140–143. The text as it appears in Pāli has a close parallel in the Tibetan *Kṣudrakavastu* (*Peking,* 44, 93-1-7ff) as well. The textual situation for the Pāli version is complicated. In the text as printed by Feer, when Cunda announces Śāriputra's death he says: *āyasmā bhante sāriputto parinibbuto idam assa pattacīvaran ti,* "Sir, the Venerable Sāriputta has passed away—here are his robe and bowl." This reading represents the Sri Lanka manuscripts, but Feer notes that one of his Burmese manuscripts has . . . *idam assa pattacīvaraṃ idaṃ dhātuparibhāvanan ti,* and Woodward's note suggests this reading is characteristic of the Burmese manuscripts. What *dhātuparibhāvana* means is not immediately obvious, but it almost certainly contains a reference to relics. In fact, the text of the *Saṃyutta* on which Buddhaghosa wrote his commentary—the *Sāratthappakāsinī*—also appears to have had a reference to relics. Buddhaghosa, citing the text, says: ***idam assa pattacīvaran ti*** *ayam assa hi paribhoga-patto.* ***idam dhātu-parissāvaṇan*** *ti evaṃ ekekam ācikkhi* (F. L. Woodward, *Sāratthа-Pakāsinī,* Vol. III [London: 1937] 221.28): " 'This is his robe and bowl' [means] this is indeed the bowl [actually] used by him. 'This is the [or 'a' or 'his'] water strainer [full] of relics'—he described them thus one by one." Where the Burmese manuscripts have the difficult *dhātu-paribhāvana,* the text cited by Buddhaghosa had, then, the more immediately intelligible *dhātu-parissāvaṇa,* "water strainer [full] of relics." The latter, in fact, may well represent a "correction" introduced by a scribe who also had had difficulty with the meaning of *-paribhāvana.* The Tibetan version, though it has nothing corresponding to either *-paribhāvana* or *-parissāvaṇa,* also clearly refers to relics. When Śāriputra's death is announced it is done so in the following words: *btsun pa śā ri'i bu ni yongs su mya ngan las 'das te / de'i ring bsrel dang / lhung bzed dang / chos gos kyang 'di lags so /:* "The Venerable Śāriputra has passed away. These are his relics and his bowl and robe." All of this will require further study to sort out, but it seems virtually certain that the Pāli text as we have it is defective. It appears that in the only canonical Pāli account of the death of Śāriputra reference to the preservation of his relics has either dropped out, or been written out, of the Sri Lankan manuscripts of the *Saṃyutta.*

112. What follows here is based on the Tibetan translation—see above n. 3. [See now G. Schopen, "Ritual Rights and Bones of Contention: More on Monastic Funerals and Relics in the *Mūlasarvāstivāda-vinaya,*" *JIP* 22 (1994) 31–80, esp. 45ff.]

113. For references, see above nn. 1 and 2.

CHAPTER X

On Avoiding Ghosts and Social Censure

Monastic Funerals in the *Mūlasarvāstivāda-vinaya*

FUNERAL RITES and burial practices in Indian Buddhist monasteries have received very little scholarly attention. This is perhaps because such rites and practices, like those in so many other religious traditions, call clearly into question the degree to which purportedly official and purportedly central doctrines were known to the members of actual Buddhist monastic communities, or, if known, the degree to which they had actual impact on behavior. This may be particularly annoying to modern scholars of Buddhism because they seem to like official literary doctrine and seem to want to think—in spite of the apparent absence of good evidence—that it somehow had importance beyond a narrow circle of scholastic specialists. It is, however, perhaps more certainly true that certain statements made by early and good scholars did little to direct attention toward such rites and practices. Oldenberg, as early as 1881, said ". . . the Vinaya texts are nearly altogether silent as to the last honours of deceased monks. To arrange for their cremation was perhaps committed to the laity."[1] T. W. Rhys Davids went even further only eighteen years later. "Nothing is known," he said, "of any religious ceremony having been performed by the early Buddhists in India, whether the person deceased was a layman, or even a member of the order. The Vinaya Piṭaka, which enters at so great length into all details of the daily life of the recluses, has no rules regarding the mode of treating the body of a deceased Bhikkhu."[2]

That such statements would not have encouraged further research would hardly be surprising. If, too, they were entirely correct, there would be little need for it. But they are not. There are at least two things wrong with statements

---

Originally published in *Journal of Indian Philosophy* 20 (1992):1–39. Reprinted with stylistic changes with permission of Kluwer Academic Publishers.

of this kind. First of all, both Oldenberg and Rhys Davids—like so many scholars still—axiomatically assumed that evidence for Buddhist practices can only be found in texts, that texts and texts alone reflect what actually occurred. It does not seem to matter that there was and is clear epigraphical and archaeological evidence that proves that Buddhist monastic communities at Sāñcī, Sonārī, Andher, and Bhojpur, at Bhājā, Bedsā, and Kānheri, at Amarāvatī and Mathurā were concerned—even preoccupied—with ritually depositing and elaborately housing the remains of at least some of the local monastic dead. It does not seem to matter that a good deal of this evidence was available long before either Oldenberg or Rhys Davids were writing, or that a good deal of it dates to the earliest period of Buddhist monasticism of which we have certain knowledge.[3] But even if we put aside—as we must here—this epigraphical and archaeological evidence,[4] the fact remains that both Oldenberg's and Rhys Davids' statements are still distortive. Both refer to "*the Vinaya,*" which meant for them, as it still means for many, only the Pāli *Vinaya.* We now know, however, that the Pāli *Vinaya,* in fact the Pāli canon as a whole, is—in Norman's words—"a translation from some earlier tradition, and cannot be regarded as a primary source," that in some cases the Pāli *Vinaya* is "markedly inferior" to the other *Vinayas,* and in some cases appears decidedly later.[5] Moreover, Csoma's analysis of the Tibetan *'dul ba,* published almost fifty years before Oldenberg, contained enough in summary form to make it clear that if the Pāli *Vinaya* as we have it had "no rules regarding the mode of treating the body of a deceased *Bhikkhu,*" the *Mūlasarvāstivāda-vinaya* did.[6] Rockhill's extracts from the same *Vinaya,* which were published only two years after Oldenberg and six years before Rhys Davids, should have put this beyond all doubt.[7]

This Mūlasarvāstivāda material was, and has remained, largely ignored while Oldenberg's, and especially Rhys Davids', assertions—although demonstrably distorted, if not entirely wrong—have come to be taken as established fact. Kane, for example, in his influential *History of Dharmaśāstra,* simply paraphrases Rhys Davids' remarks concerning the Buddhist treatment of their dead.[8] This clearly will not do, and the Mūlasarvāstivāda material—available in part in Sanskrit in the Gilgit Manuscripts,[9] in part in a partial and far-from-perfect Chinese translation,[10] and in its entirety in the Tibetan Kanjur—needs to be brought into the discussion. There have already been limited and partial attempts to do this, notably by de La Vallée Poussin.[11] What follows, I hope, is a more concerted attempt to be added to those that have gone before though it remains very much in the category of the tentative: it is based on a far-from-full familiarity with two *Vinayas;* it does not take into account the important monastic codes preserved in Chinese (but I hope might stimulate others to do so); it does not solve—but, in fact, exiles to the forest of footnotes or ignores—numerous lexical, terminological, and textual problems encountered in these legalistic codes; it merely suggests and does not necessarily establish some possible lines of interpretation that might or might not prove fruitful. It does, I think, make more fully available some interesting data.

There are literally dozens of references to the death of a local monk in both the Pāli *Vinaya* and the *Vinaya* of the Mūlasarvāstivādins, but the bulk of these in both *Vinayas* occur in what at first sight might seem an unlikely place. In both *Vinayas,* the death of a local monk is treated most fully in their respective "section on robes or robe-material" (*Cīvara-vastu, Cīvarakkhandhaka*). The explanation for this, however, seems to be that the death of a local monk raised for the *vinaya* masters one of the same problems that death in almost every community, whether secular or religious, raises: the problem of property and inheritance. Since the "robe" was one of the primary pieces of personal property that belonged to a monk, and since inheritance might be an important means by which other monks might acquire robes, it is only natural that the disposition of a deceased monk's property would be discussed together with the other means of legitimately acquiring robes and the rules governing such acquisition. In the Pāli *Cīvarakkhandhaka,* inheritance of a monk's property is neither heavily legislated nor encumbered. The formal rules are kept to a minimum. Typical is the first promulgation in this regard: two monks tend to a sick monk who dies. They take the deceased monk's robe and bowl and report his death to the Buddha. The latter says:

> Monks, the Order is the owner of the bowl and robes of a monk who passed away. But truly those who tend the sick are of great service. I allow you, monks, to give through the Order the three robes and the bowl to those who tended the sick.[12]

The formal procedure is then explained. This relatively simple legislation becomes more complicated when the property of a dead monk is more extensive, when, for example, it involves both what the texts call "biens légers" (*lahu-bhaṇḍa, lahu-parikkhāra*) and "biens lourds" (*garu-bhaṇḍa, garu-parikkhāra*).[13] But on the whole, the Pāli *Vinaya* legislates far fewer situations than does the *Mūlasarvāstivāda-vinaya* and limits itself to the enunciation of a few general principles. The *Mūlasarvāstivāda-vinaya,* on the other hand, devotes nearly thirty-five pages to the disposition of a dead monk's property, taking pains to make detailed rulings on a large range of specific situations.[14]

There has been a clear tendency to explain differences of this sort in the *vinayas* as reflections of differences of chronology, to see an increase in number and specificity of rules as an indication of later composition. But this explanation—although a favorite of Western scholars—is only one explanation, and a very narrow one at that. It completely overlooks a number of other equally possible explanations. For example, what has been taken as a reflection of a chronological difference may, in fact, reflect "sectarian" differences in legal rigorism that need not involve any chronological component at all. Looked at in this light, the Pāli rules governing the disposition of a deceased monk's property may simply have been loose, if not lax. They would have allowed a fair amount of ambiguity and leeway for individual judgment. The compilers of the *Mūlasarvāstivāda-vinaya* appear to have intended to prevent both situations and to frame a far stricter and more comprehensive code, a code in which little was left to an individual's or local community's discretion. The *Mūlasarvāstivāda-vinaya* may, then, represent a far stricter rule rather than a later one.

The *Mūlasarvāstivāda-vinaya* also appears to be straightforward about the kind and range of problems that could have arisen in the distribution of a dead monk's property. It contains, for example, the following detailed case about a monk named Upananda, who had amassed a considerable estate.[15] After establishing its right to the estate, which was initially impounded by the King, the community at Śrāvastī proceeded to distribute it among its resident monks. But then the monks from Sāketā heard about Upananda's death and came to claim a share (*asmākam api bhadantopanandaḥ sabrahmacārī. asmākam api tatsantako lābhaḥ prāpadyata iti*). As a result, the text says: *bhikṣubhiḥ pātayitvā taiḥ sārdhaṃ punar api bhājitaḥ*, "after having brought (the estate) together again, the monks (of Śrāvastī) once more divided it together with those (monks from Sāketā)." But this was not the end. Monks from Vaiśālī, Vārāṇasī, Rājagṛha, and Campā came, and the whole procedure had to be repeated again and again. The situation reached the point that, according to the text: *bhikṣavaḥ pātayanto bhājayantaś ca riñcanty uddeśaṃ pāṭhaṃ svādhyāyaṃ yogaṃ manasikāram*, "the monks (because they were always) bringing together and dividing (estates), abandon (their) instruction, recitation, study, yoga, and mental concentration."[16] The Buddha is informed of the situation and as a consequence he declares:

> *pañca karaṇāni lābhavibhāge. katame pañca. gaṇḍī tridaṇḍakaṃ caityaṃ śīlākā jñaptiḥ pañcakam. yo mṛtagaṇḍyām ākoṭyamānāyām āgacchati, tasya lābho deyaḥ. evaṃ tridaṇḍake bhāṣyamāṇe caityavandanāyāṃ kriyamāṇāyāṃ śīlākā{yām ā}caryamāṇāyām. tasmāt tarhi bhikṣavaḥ sarvaṃ mṛtapariṣkāraṃ jñaptiṃ kṛtvā bhājayitavyam. akopyaṃ bhaviṣyati.*[17]

> There are five occasions for the distribution of (a deceased monk's) possessions. Which five? The gong; the *Tridaṇḍaka;* the *caitya;* the ticket; the formal motion is the fifth. Who, when the gong for the dead is being beaten, comes—to him something is to be given. It is the same for when the *Tridaṇḍaka* is being recited, when the worship of the *caitya* is being performed, when tickets are being distributed, [when a formal motion is being made].[18] Therefore, then, monks, having made a formal motion concerning all of the personal belongings of the deceased, they are to be distributed. It will be a fixed procedure [which is then described].[19]

A passage such as this is an explicit recognition that Buddhist monastic communities had a wide range of potentially conflicting concerns and preoccupations, all of which were accepted as legitimate. Notice that concern with the distribution of a deceased monk's property is not here—nor in the Pāli *Cīvarakkhandhaka*—in itself ever criticized. It is presented as perfectly legitimate. A problem arises or a situation requiring legislation appears only when that concern distracts monks or communities from other legitimate concerns. In the present case, there is no hint that one set of concerns was considered more important than the other; the problem was to accommodate both. Since there is no legislation in the Pāli *Vinaya* for the particular situation addressed in this Mūlasarvāstivādin passage, and yet we know that the kinds of activities involved were known to, and recognized as legitimate concerns of a monastic community by, the compilers of the Pāli *Vinaya,* we might be able to see in this Mūlasarvāstivādin passage another good example of the consistent tendency on the part of its compilers to insist on a far stricter and more comprehensive code than was framed in the Pāli *Vinaya.* Again, chronological considerations need not enter in. It is, finally, also important to note that this passage presents us with the first direct indication of the intimate connection in the *Cīvara-vastu* of the *Mūlasarvāstivāda-vinaya* between the distribution of a deceased monk's property and what it presents as the proper performance of his funeral: the first of the *occasions* for the distribution mentioned in this passage, and very probably the second and third as well, are—as we shall see—particular moments in a Mūlasarvāstivādin monastic funeral. We know—again as we shall see—from a variety of Mūlasarvāstivādin sources that the sounding of "the gong or bell for the dead" (called variously the *mṛta-, anta-* or *muṇḍikā gaṇḍī* in Sanskrit,[20] and *shi ba'i gaṇḍī* or *gaṇḍī mjug* (v.l. *'jug*) *med pa* in Tibetan[21]) was used "pour l'annonce d'une mort" and appears to have signaled the beginning of the formal funeral proceedings.[22] We also know that the recitation of the "Tridaṇḍaka,"[23] or giving a recitation of *Dharma* (*dharmaśravaṇaṃ dattaṃ*),[24] or of the *Dharma* connected with the impermanent" (*mi rtag pa dang ldan pa'i chos dag bshad nas*),[25] took place at the end of or during the cremation, and that "worshipping the *Stūpa* or *caitya*" (*mchod rten la phyag 'tshal bar bya'o*) appears to have formally terminated the proceedings as a whole.[26]

The moments chosen for the distribution of a dead monk's property do not appear to have been arbitrary but appear initially to have been closely linked to significant moments in his funeral. The order in which they occur also does not appear to be arbitrary; it seems to reflect a sequence of moments that are increasingly removed from the moment of death and would appear to involve a decreasing degree of participation in the funeral activities. He "who, when the gong for the dead is being beaten, comes" is present and participates from the very commencement of the funeral. But he who comes "when the worship of the *caitya* is performed" need only be present at the end, and he who comes only "when a formal motion is being made" need not have been present at all. That the first moment is first in more than just a numerical sense and involves both a priority in time and a priority of rights to inherit is virtually certain. If the distribution takes place at the first moment, there will be no others, and only those present at that moment could partake in the distribution. Priority of rights, therefore, seems directly linked to degree of participation in the funeral. Even if, it is important to note, one might argue that the recitation of the *Tridaṇḍaka* and "the worship of the *caitya*" referred to here need not necessarily refer to moments in the funeral (both activities, as we shall see below, occur in other contexts as well), still the principle holds: preference and priority are still given to those individuals "who, when the gong for the dead is being beaten, come"; there can be no doubt about whether this refers to participation in the funeral. It is also worth noting that the commencement of the funeral with the sounding of the gong significantly underlines its communal character; this means of summons is used only for activities that concern the entire community: it is used "pour la convocation des moines, . . . l'appel au travail, . . . pour le repas," and "pour annoncer un danger."[27] It is perhaps unnecessary to point out that by making physical presence at key moments of the funeral the determining factor in defining who had first rights to participate as a recipient in the distribution of the estate, the compilers of the *Mūlasarvāstivāda-vinaya* assured or reinforced the communal character of the proceedings.

The linkage between the distribution of a deceased monk's property and the performance of his funeral is, in fact, a central theme of one of the two promulgations of rules governing monastic funerals found in the *Mūlasarvāstivāda-vinaya* that we will look at here. This promulgation is the least known and consists of three interlocked texts that mark out individually what appear to have been considered the important elements of a monastic funeral. They are now found together, one after the other in the *Cīvara-vastu.* The edition of these texts published by Dutt is not always satisfactory; although I cite his edition here, I have inserted in brackets at least the more important "corrections" that a study of the manuscript itself has indicated are required. Occasionally, I have also inserted the corresponding Tibetan in parentheses:

> I. *śrāvastyāṃ nidānam. tena khalu samayenânyatamo bhikṣur glāno layane kālagataḥ. amanuṣyakeṣūpapannaḥ. cīvarabhājako bhikṣus taṃ layanaṃ praveṣṭum ārabdhaḥ. pātracīvaraṃ bhājayāmîti. sa tīvreṇa paryavasthānena laguḍam ādāyôtthitaḥ kathayati: yāvan māṃ abhinirharatha* [but ms: *mamābhinirharatha*] *tāvat pātracīvaraṃ bhājayatheti (re zhig kho bo dur khrod du yang ma phyung bar lhung bzed dang gos 'ged par byed dam). sa saṃtrasto niṣpalāyitaḥ.*
>
> *etat prakaraṇaṃ bhikṣavo bhagavata ārocayanti.*

bhagavān āha: pūrvaṃ tāvan mṛto bhikṣur abhinirhartavyaḥ; paścāt tasya pātracīvaraṃ bhājayitavyam iti.[28]

Although the sense of this text is generally clear, it is still not always easy to arrive at an altogether smooth or satisfying translation. This is in large part due to the language of the greater part of the *Mūlasarvāstivāda-vinaya,* to what Lévi calls "ses étrangetés," and to its "almost colloquial style."[29] There is, for example, a heavy reliance on pronouns, and sometimes the same pronominal form is used in close proximity with two entirely different referents. This, together with an even more general tendency toward elliptical expression, sometimes requires that a good deal of padding be added to any translation. The Tibetan translators have sometimes been forced in this direction. Moreover, each of the texts in this series employs a *yāvat . . . tāvat* construction, the exact sense of which is neither easy to determine nor easy to render into English, and there is some disquieting variation. The Tibetan translations—although sufficiently clear—seem to presuppose a slightly different text as well. Either that, or they have settled for a far looser translation than usual. With these provisos, the first text may be translated:

> I. The setting was in Śrāvastī. On this occasion a certain monk, being sick, died in his cell. He was reborn among the nonhuman beings. The monk who was the distributor-of-robes started to enter the cell (of the dead monk) saying "I distribute the bowl and robes." (But) he (the deceased monk) appeared there with intense anger wielding a club and said: "When you perform for me the removal of the body, (only) then do you effect a distribution of (my) bowl and robe" (Tibetan: "How could one who had not even carried me out to the cremation ground effect a distribution of (my) robe and bowl?").[30] He (the distributor-of-robes) was terrified and forced to flee.
>
> The monks ask the Blessed One concerning this matter.
>
> The Blessed One said: "Now first the removal of a dead monk is to be performed. Then his robe and bowl are to be distributed."

Here we have legislated what appears to be the minimum funereal procedure that must be effected before any distribution of a dead monk's property can take place. This procedure is here expressed by forms of the verb *abhi-nir-*$\sqrt{}$*hṛ*. This verb, or close variants of it with or without the initial *abhi-,* is in fact something of a technical expression for the initial act of funereal procedures described in a variety of Buddhist sources.[31] It also occurs in Jain texts dealing with funerals.[32] But even when this exact expression is not used, we find a whole series of parallel expressions—*ādahanaṃ nītvā, śmaśānaṃ nītvā, tam ādāya dahanaṃ gatāḥ, ro bskyal nas,* etc.[33]—that indicate that the removal of the body, undoubtedly ritualized, was a first and minimal procedure involved in carrying out a monastic funeral or a funeral of any kind. It would appear, however, that the compilers of the

Mūlasarvāstivāda-vinaya did not consider this minimum procedure to be necessarily sufficient. After the passage cited above, the second in the series immediately follows:

> II. *śrāvastyāṃ nidānam. tena khalu samayenânyatamo bhikṣuḥ kālagataḥ. bhikṣavas tam abhinirhṛtya evam eva śmaśāne chorayitvā vihāram āgataḥ. cīvarabhājakas tasya layanaṃ praviṣṭaḥ pātracīvaraṃ bhājayāmîti. so 'manuṣyakeṣûpapannaḥ; laguḍam ādāyotthitaḥ sa kathayati: yāvan mama śarīrapūjāṃ kurutha tāvat pātracīvaraṃ bhājayatheti (re zhig kho bo'i ro la mchod pa yang ma byas par chos gos dang lhung bzed 'ged par byed dam zhes).*
>
> *etat prakaraṇaṃ bhikṣavo bhagavata ārocayanti.*
>
> *bhagavān āha: bhikṣubhis tasya pūrvaṃ śarīrapūjā kartavyeti. tataḥ paścāt pātracīvaraṃ bhājayitavyam. eṣa ādīnavo {na} bhaviṣyatîti (nyes dmigs 'dir mi 'gyur ro,* supporting Dutt's *{na}*).[34]

> II. The setting was in Śrāvastī. On that occasion a certain monk died. The monks, having performed the removal of that one('s body), having simply thrown it into the burning ground, returned to the *vihāra.* The distributor-of-robes entered his (the dead monk's) cell saying "I distribute the bowl and robe." He (the dead monk) was reborn among the nonhuman beings. Wielding a club he appeared (in his cell) and said: "When you perform the worship of the body for me, (only) then do you distribute (my) bowl and robe?" (Tibetan: "How could one who had not even performed the worshipping of my body effect a distribution of (my) robe and bowl?").
>
> The monks asked the Blessed One concerning this matter.
>
> The Blessed One said: "By the monks the worship of the body for him (the deceased monk) is first to be performed. After that (his) bowl and robe are to be distributed. This will (otherwise) be a danger" (Tibetan: "There would not be in this case a calamity/fault").

This second text, while indicating that the first procedure was still required, indicates as well that it might not prove sufficient and provides separate legislation for what appears to have been considered a second necessary component of a Mūlasarvāstivādin monastic funeral. This procedure is called here—and in a considerable number of other places—*śarīra-pūjā.* And this is a term that, although widely cited, has not been carefully studied and perhaps, has been misunderstood. It has commonly been taken to refer to the worship of relics, but I have recently tried to demonstrate "that *śarīra-pūjā*—whatever it involved—took place after the body had been removed and taken to the cremation ground, but before it was cremated, before there could have been anything like what we call 'relics,'. . ." and that it is "fairly certain that *śarīra-pūjā* involved the ritual handling or treatment of the body prior to cremation . . ."[35] Not surprisingly, this second text played a part in that attempted demonstration: it, perhaps better than any other passage, points toward what *śarīra-pūjā* involved by clearly stating what its opposite was. *Śarīra-pūjā* is presented in our passage as the opposite of, and correct alternative for "having simply thrown the body into the burning ground," or unceremoniously dumping it. That this alternative involved what we understand by the term "worship" seems unlikely, and, from this point of view at least, "worship of the body" is undoubtedly not a very good translation of *śarīra-pūjā*. I have retained it only to maintain some consistency with the way in which the term *pūjā* is generally rendered.[36] The Pāli sources here offer little aid. In fact the term *śarīra-pūjā,* although found throughout Mūlasarvāstivāda literature, is curiously uncommon in Pāli canonical literature outside of the *Mahāparinibbāna-sutta* where it is not impossible that it—like several other lexical items there—may represent a borrowing from continental Sanskrit sources.[37] Although uncommon as well, a Pāli parallel expression may be had in the term *sarīra-kicca,* but it, too, lacks a precise definition, being defined only as "the duties of the body, i.e., funeral rites."[38]

We have, then, in these two texts the legislation of two distinct funereal procedures that appear to have been considered necessary to keep angry ghosts at bay and to allow the distribution of a dead monk's property to go forward unobstructed. These same two procedures, however, are by no means exclusive to a dead monk's funeral; they are also components of, for example, the funerals of the Kings Aśoka (. . . *śibikābhir nirharitvā śarīrapūjāṃ kṛtvā*) and Prasenajit (. . . *dur khrod du skyol cig . . . 'di'i khog pa la mchod pa lhag par bya ba*),[39] and, therefore, do not specifically define a monastic funeral. Something more would appear to be required, and this is precisely what we find in the third and final text of this series:

> III. *śrāvastyāṃ nidānam. tena khalu samayenânyatamo bhikṣur glāno layane kālagataḥ. sa bhikṣur ādahanaṃ nītvā śarīrapūjāṃ kṛtvā dagdhaḥ. tato vihāram āgataḥ* [but ms: *āgatā*]. *cīvarabhājakas tasya layanaṃ praviṣṭaḥ. sa laguḍam ādāyotthitaḥ, tat tāvan* [but ms. clearly *na tāvan,* in this instance agreeing with Tibetan] *māṃ uddiśya dharmaśravaṇam anuprayacchatha tāvac cīvarakāṇi bhājayatheti (re zhig bdag gi ched du chos bsgrags pa ma byas par chos gos rnams 'ged par byed dam).*
>
> *etat prakaraṇaṃ bhikṣavo bhagavata ārocayanti.*
>
> *bhagavān āha: tam uddiśya dharmaśravaṇaṃ dattvā dakṣiṇāṃ uddiśya paścāc cīvarakāṇi bhājayitavyānîti (de'i ched du chos bsgrags pa dang / de'i ched du yon bsngo ba byas nas chos gos rnams bgo bar bya'o).*[40]
>
> III. The setting was in Śrāvastī. On that occasion a certain monk, being sick, died in his cell. After having brought him to the burning ground, (and) having performed (for him) the worship of the body, that (deceased) monk was cremated. After that they (the monks who had performed these procedures) returned to the *vihāra.* The distributor-of-robes entered that

(dead monk's) cell. He (the dead monk) appeared wielding a club, saying "You do not yet give a recitation of *Dharma* for my sake, (but only) then are you to effect a distribution of my monastic robes" (Tibetan: "How could one who had not performed a recitation of *Dharma* for me effect a distribution of (my) robes?").

The monks ask the Blessed One concerning this matter.

The Blessed One said: "Having given a recitation of *Dharma* in his (the deceased's) name, having directed the reward (to him), after that his monastic robes are to be distributed."

In this third and final text of the series, the monks, although they have performed the removal of the body as well as "the worship of the body," are still confronted by the belligerent ghost. He still has not relinquished ownership rights to his property. For that to happen one further—and, by implication, final—procedure appears to be required. This procedure is the most distinctively Buddhist of those so far met and appears to be particularly—perhaps exclusively—associated with monastic funerals. Although, as we have seen, both the "removal" and "the worship of the body" occur in the descriptions of the funerals of the Kings Prasenajit and Aśoka, there is no reference in either account to a recitation of *Dharma* having been made for their sake or a transfer of the resulting merit to their account. This stands in clear contrast with what we often find in the accounts of funerals performed for monks or nuns. In the latter accounts, there is occasional reference either to a recitation of *Dharma* or to the transfer of merit or both.[41] The recitation and the transfer of merit are the last and apparently sufficient elements of a monastic funeral separately legislated here. They appear to achieve the definitive separation of the deceased monk from his property and to allow the distribution of that property to go forward unencumbered. It is important to note that the monks who participate in the funeral generate the merit by giving a recitation of *Dharma,* and it is the monks who assign the merit to the deceased. This appears to be a straightforward case of religious merit being transferred or assigned to one who did not produce it.[42] This straightforward transfer of merit is, in fact, characteristic of many parts of the *Mūlasarvāstivāda-vinaya,* and this *Vinaya* contains as well numerous indications of its compilers' concerns with making such transfers to several categories of the dead.[43] There is, however, more here.

It is, of course, not simply the merit itself that allows the distribution of a dead monk's property to go forward. It is perhaps more the proper and complete performance of his funeral by the monks in attendance. The distribution, therefore, would appear to turn on two points: one, before the property is unencumbered, before any distribution can take place, a set of ritual procedures must be performed or a set of ritual obligations owed to the deceased must be met; two, those who participate in these rituals or in meeting these obligations are—as the account of Upananda's estate makes clear—precisely the same individuals who have a first and prior claim on the estate: "Who, when the gong for the dead is being beaten, comes—to him something is to be given. . . ." It is, moreover, almost certainly not accidental that the monks who perform or participate in the dead monk's funeral are the monks who have the first rights and opportunities to receive or inherit the deceased's property. In fact, such an arrangement would appear to suggest that—at least—these Buddhist monastic regulations governing the distribution of a dead monk's property were framed to conform to, or be in harmony with, classical Hindu laws or Dharmaśāstric conventions governing inheritance. In his *History of Dharmaśāstra* Kane says, for example, that "there was a close connection between taking the estate of a man and performing the rites after death up to the 10th day," and "that it was obligatory on everyone who took the estate of another . . . to arrange for the rites after death and *śrāddha.*"[44] The *Baudhāyana-Pitṛmedha-sūtra* says that "proper cremation-rites" should be performed not only for one's mother, father, preceptor, etc., but also for any "person who leaves inheritance for one, whether he belongs to one's gotra or not."[45] This congruency between Buddhist monastic rule and Hindu law is not only interesting,[46] it is also in striking contrast with the apparent lack of congruency between the same *Vinaya* rule and formal Buddhist doctrine.

There can be little question that the promulgation of this set of rules is based on a belief in an individual "personality" that survives after death. That "personality," moreover, was thought to retain an active interest in, and ownership rights to, his former possessions. The claims of that "person" had to be compensated before any distribution of those possessions could take place. This belief—it is important to keep in mind—was assumed and articulated by monks in a code of behavior meant to govern monks. It is not part of some ill-defined lay or popular Buddhism; it is an element of official monastic Buddhism, and, precisely for that reason, its seemingly total lack of congruency with the supposedly fundamental Buddhist doctrine of the absence of a permanent self is even more striking. In speaking of the "traditional Buddhism" of the rural highlands of modern Sri Lanka, Gombrich has said that:

> though the doctrine of *anatta* can be salvaged by the claim that the personality continuing through a series of births has as much reality as the personality within one life, *prārthanā* for happy rebirths and the transfer of merit to dead relatives show that the *anatta* doctrine has no more affective immediacy with regard to the next life than with regard to this, and that belief in personal survival after death is a fundamental feature of Sinhalese Buddhism in practice.[47]

The set of rules governing monastic funerals and inheritance that we have been looking at suggests the very real possibility that there is nothing new in the modern Sri Lankan case. It suggests, as well, the distinct possibility that purportedly "fundamental" Buddhist doctrine may not only have had little influence on lay Buddhist behavior, it may as well have had equally little influence on even highly educated, literate monks.[48] The implications of this possibility are, of course, far reaching, and there are some equally interesting implications for our understanding of monastic Buddhism in a second promulgation of rules concerning monastic funerals found in the *Mūlasarvāstivāda-vinaya.*

Unlike the set of rules for monastic funerals that occur in the *Cīvara-vastu,* the second promulgation, perhaps because it is preserved as well in Chinese, has been referred to several times in the scholarly literature. In fact, apart from short or incidental references, we also have several paraphrases or summaries of the text: the earliest, perhaps, by Rockhill, based on the Tibetan;[49] the fullest, based on the Chinese, by de La Vallée Poussin;[50] and the most recent, again based on the Chinese, by Seidel.[51] None of these paraphrases or summaries are, however, entirely satisfactory from at least one point of view. This text, which is preserved in Tibetan in the *Vinaya-kṣudraka-vastu,* does not link the proper performance of a monastic funeral with the distribution of a deceased monk's property as do the texts preserved in the *Cīvara-vastu.* The text in the *Kṣudraka-vastu* is, rather, preoccupied with yet another problem that the death of a local monk would have raised for a Buddhist community. Unlike the *Cīvara-vastu* texts, which appear to respond to the kind of problems that such a death would occasion within the group—to what might be called "internal problems"—the text in the *Kṣudraka-vastu* appears to have been intended to respond to the kind of problems that such a death could occasion between that group and the larger world that surrounded it and on which it was almost entirely dependent. These external problems are most fully articulated not so much in the rules themselves but in the frame story that accounts for their promulgation, and it is this frame story that has suffered the most in the paraphrases. As a consequence, there are good reasons for citing here the Tibetan text as a whole. The text I cite is based on the three Kanjurs available to me: the Derge, Peking, and Tog Palace:[52]

sangs rgyas bcom ldan 'das mnyan yod na rgyal bu rgyal byed kyi tshal mgon med zas sbyin gyi kun dga' ra ba na[a] *bzhugs so /*

mnyan yod na khyim bdag cig[b] *gnas pa des rigs mnyam pa las chung ma blangs te / de de dang lhan cig ces bya ba nas / bu pho zhig btsas te de*[c] *btsas*[d] *pa'i btsas ston zhag bdun gsum nyi shu gcig tu rgya cher byas nas rigs dang mthun*[e] *pa'i ming btags te bsrings bskyed*[f] *nas chen por gyur to zhes bya ba'i bar snga ma bzhin no /*

ji tsam dus gzhan zhig na legs par gsungs pa'i chos 'dul ba la rab tu byung ba dang / de'i khams ma[g] *mnyam nas na bar gyur te / de rtsa ba dang / sdong bu dang / me tog dang / 'bras bu'i sman dag gis rim gro byas na ma phan te dus las 'das so /*

de dge slong dag gis lhung bzed dang bcas / chos gos dang bcas par[h] *lam dang nye ba zhig tu bor ro /*

ji tsam na lam de nas bram ze dang khyim bdag 'gro ba de[i] *dag gis de mthong ste / de ni*[j] *kha cig gis smras pa / shes*[k] *ldan dag śākya'i bu*[l] *zhig dus las 'das so / gzhan dag gis smras pa / tshur sheg*[m] *blta bar bya'o /* [n]*de dag gis mthong nas ngo shes te de dag gis smras pa / shes ldan dag 'di ni khyim bdag che ge mo'i bu yin te / dge sbyong śākya'i bu pa mgon med pa rnams kyi nang du rab tu byung bas gnas skabs 'di 'dra bar gyur to / 'di dag gi nang du rab tu byung bar ma gyur na de*[o] *nye du dag gis 'di rim gro byas par 'gyur ba zhig /*

skabs de bcom ldan 'das la dge slong dag gis gsol ba dang / bcom ldan 'das kyis bka' stsal pa / dge slong dag de lta bas na gnang gis dge slong shi ba'i rim gro bya'o / bcom ldan 'das kyis dge slong shi ba'i rim gro bya'o zhes gsungs[p] *pa dang / dge slong dag ji ltar rim gro bya ba mi shes nas / bcom ldan 'das kyis bka' stsal pa / bsreg*[q] *bar bya'o /*

bcom ldan 'das kyis bsreg par bya'o zhes gsungs pa dang / bcom ldan 'das la tshe dang ldan pa nye ba 'khor gyis zhus pa / btsun pa bcom ldan 'das kyis lus 'di la srin bu'i rigs brgyad khri yod do zhes gang gsungs pa de dag ji lta bu lags / bcom ldan 'das kyis bka' stsal pa / nye ba[r] *'khor de skyes*[s] *ma thag tu de dag kyang skye la / shi ba'i tshe de dag kyang 'chi mod kyi 'on kyang rma'i sgo rnams su brtags te bsreg par bya'o /*

bcom ldan 'das kyis bsreg par bya'o zhes gsungs[t] *ba dang / shing ma 'byor nas skabs de bcom ldan 'das la dge slong dag gis gsol ba dang / bcom ldan 'das kyis bka' stsal pa / chu klung dag tu dor bar bya'o / chu klung med nas bcom ldan 'das kyis bka' stsal pa / sa brkos te gzhug par bya'o / dbyar kha sa yang 'thas la shing yang srog chags can du gyur nas / bcom ldan 'das kyis bka' stsal pa / thibs po'i phyogs su mgo byang phyogs su bstan te sngas su rtsva'i*[u] *bam po bzhag la glo g-yas pas bsnyal te rtsva*[v] *'am lo ma'i tshogs kyis*[w] *g-yogs la yon bsngo zhing rgyun*[x] *chags gsum gyi chos mnyan pa byin nas 'dong bar bya'o /*

dge slong dag de bzhin du dong ba dang / bram ze dang khyim bdag dag śākya'i bu'i dge sbyong rnams ni ro bskyal nas khrus mi byed par de bzhin 'dong ste gtsang sbra med do / zhes 'phya bar byed nas / skabs de bcom ldan 'das la dge slong dag gis gsol ba dang / bcom ldan 'das kyis bka' stsal pa / de bzhin du 'dong bar mi bya'i 'on kyang khrus bya'o / de dag thams cad bkru bar brtsams pa dang / bcom ldan 'das kyis bka' stsal pa / thams cad krus mi bya'i gang dag reg pa de dag gis gos dang bcas te bkru bar bya'o / gzhan dag gis ni rkang lag nyi tshe bkru bar bya'o /

de dag mchod rten la phyag mi 'tshal nas / bcom ldan 'das kyis bka' stsal pa / mchod rten[y] *la phyag 'tshal bar bya'o*

NOTES

a. P omits *na.* b. P *gcig.* c. P omits *btsas te de.* d. P *bcas.* e. P *'thun.* f. P *bskyad.* g. T *mi.* h. P *bad.* i. P *da.* j. T *na.* k. P *shas.* l. T adds *pa* after *bu.*

m. T *shog.* n. T has an additional *de* before *de dag gis.* o. T omits *de.* p. P *gsangs.* q. P *bsregs.* r. P, T *bar*; the name is commonly spelled *nye bar 'khor.* s. T *skyed.* t. P *gsung.* u. P *rtsa'i.* v. P *rca.* w. P *kyas.* x. P, T *rgyud.* y. P, T both add *dag* after *rten.*

The Buddha, the Blessed One, dwelt in Śrāvastī, in Prince Jeta's Grove, in the park of Anāthapiṇḍada.

In Śrāvastī there was a certain householder. He took a wife from a family of equal standing and, having laid with her, a son was born. Having performed in detail for three times seven, or twenty-one, days the birth ceremonies for the newborn son, he was given a name corresponding to his *gotra* (*trīṇi saptakāny ekaviṃśatidivasāni vistareṇa jātasya jātimahaṃ kṛtvā; gotrānurūpaṃ nāmadheyaṃ vyavasthāpitaṃ*).[53] His upbringing, to his maturity, was as before.[54]

When, at another time, he (the householder's son)[55] had entered (the Order of this) well-spoken *Dharma* and *Vinaya,* his bodily humors having become unbalanced, he fell ill. Although he was attended with medicines made from roots and stalks and flowers and fruits, it was of no use and he died (*sa . . . mūlagaṇḍapatrapuṣpaphalabhaiṣajyair upasthīyamāno na svasthībhavati . . . sa ca kālagataḥ*).[56]

The monks left him (i.e., his body), together with his robe and bowl, near a road.

Later, brahmins and householders who were out walking saw him from the road. One said, referring to him: "Good Sirs, a Buddhist monk (*śākyaputra*) has died." Others said: "Come here! Look at this!" When they looked, they recognized the dead monk and said: "Good Sirs, this is the son of such and such a householder. This is the sort of thing that happens when someone joins the Order of those lordless Buddhist *śramaṇas.* Had he not joined their Order, his kinsmen would have performed the funeral ceremonies for him."[57]

The monks reported this matter to the Blessed One, and the Blessed One said: "Now then, monks, with my authorization, funeral ceremonies for a (deceased) monk are to be performed" ("Bhikṣus, il faut rendre les derniers devoirs au cadavre").[58] Although it was said by the Blessed One "funeral ceremonies for a deceased monk are to be performed," because the monks did not know how they should be performed, the Blessed One said: "(A deceased monk) is to be cremated."

Although the Blessed One said: "(A deceased monk) should be cremated," the Venerable Upāli asked the Blessed One: "Is that which was said by the Reverend Blessed One—that there are 80,000 kinds of worms in the human body—not so?" The Blessed One said: "Upāli, as soon as a man is born, those worms are also born, so, at the moment of death, they too surely die. Still, (only) after examining the opening of any wound, is the body to be cremated" ("Quand le corps présente des ulcères, on doit voir s'il n'y a pas d'animaux, et alors le brûler." "Si le cadavre a des plaies, on ne peut le brûler qu'après avoir vérifié s'il n'y a pas de vers").[59]

Although the Blessed One said (a deceased monk) is to be cremated, when wood was not at hand, the monks asked the Blessed One concerning this matter, and the Blessed One said: "The body is to be thrown into a river." When there is no river, the Blessed One said: "Having dug a grave, it is to be buried." When it is summer and both the earth is hard and the wood is full of living things ("En été, la terre est humide et fourmille d'animaux"; "[et] en été, [quand] la terre est humide et fourmille de vers et d'insects?"),[60] the Blessed One said: "In an isolated spot, with its head pointing north, having put down a bundle of grass as a bolster, having laid the corpse on its right side, having covered it with bunches of grass or leaves, having directed the reward (to the deceased),[61] and having given a recitation of the *Dharma* of the *Tridaṇḍaka,* the monks are to disperse."[62]

The monks dispersed accordingly. But then brahmins and householders derided them saying: "Buddhist *śramaṇas,* after carrying away a corpse, do not bathe and yet disperse like that. They are polluted." The monks asked the Blessed One concerning this matter, and the Blessed One said: "Monks should not disperse in that manner, but should bathe." They all started to bathe, but the Blessed One said: "Everyone need not bathe. Those who came in contact (with the corpse) must wash themselves together with their robes. Others need only wash their hands and feet."

When the monks did not worship the *stūpa,* the Blessed One said: "The *stūpa* (v.l. *stūpas*) is to be worshipped" ("Rentrés au couvent, ils ne vénéraient pas le *caitya.* Le Bouddha dit: 'Il faut vénérer le *caitya*' ").[63]

Anyone who has read even a little *Vinaya* will immediately recognize this promulgation of rules as yet another instance—although perhaps a particularly striking one—of the preoccupation of the compilers of these codes with avoiding social censure. This preoccupation—which not infrequently appears obsessive—has been described in a number of ways. Horner has said, for example, in referring to the Pāli *Vinaya:*

> For the believing laity, though naturally not to the forefront in the *Vinaya,* are in a remarkable way never absent, never far distant . . . thus the *Vinaya* does not merely lay down sets of rules whose province was confined to an internal conventual life. For this was led in such a way as to allow and even to encourage a certain degree of intercommunication with the lay supporters and followers, no less than with those laypeople who were not adherents of the faith. What was important, was that the monks should neither abuse their dependence on the former, nor alienate the latter, but should so regulate their lives as to give no cause for complaint. With these aims in view, conduct that was not thought seemly for them to indulge in had to be carefully defined, and it became drafted in rule and precept.[64]

Elsewhere, Horner again says: "It must be remembered that it was considered highly important to propitiate these [lay followers], to court their admiration, to keep their allegiance, to do nothing to annoy them."[65] But she also raises another point that may be germane to our *Kṣudraka-vastu* passage and—when seen in a certain light—only underscores the curious absence of such a passage in the Pāli *Vinaya.* She says: "We cannot tell with any degree of accuracy the historical order in which the rules [in the *Vinaya*] were formulated," but she notes that "it is, however, more likely that the majority of the rules grew up gradually, as need arose, and are the outcome of historical developments that went on within the Order."[66]

Horner's observations concerning the monastic sensitivity to lay values are important for a full understanding of our passage because there can hardly be a doubt that this passage—and the rules promulgated there—concern two related topics on which any even partially brahmanized social groups would have been acutely sensitive: death and pollution. Malamoud has not only said that "le rituel funéraire est le *saṃskāra* par excellence," but has noted as well that "les injonctions, les instructions techniques et les justifications théologiques qui traitent de la manière dont les vivants doivent se comporter à l'égard des morts forment une part considérable de la littérature normative de l'Inde brâhmanique (hymnes védiques, Brāhmaṇa, Kalpasūtra, Dharmasūtra et Dharmaśāstra). Le rituel funéraire . . . frappe par sa richesse, sa complexité, sa cohérence." "Le service des morts," he says, "l'institution des morts pèsent d'un poids très lourd dans la vie des Indiens qui se rattachent en quelque manière au brâhmanisme."[67] Much the same, of course, has been said of "purity" and "pollution." "Normative literature," says Dumont, "the literature of the *dharma* or religious law, has purification *(śuddhi)* as one of its main themes, the impurity resulting from birth and death being specially designated *āśauca* . . . Family impurity is the most important: it is that of birth *(sūtaka)* and above all death."[68]

As the sources cited especially by Malamoud would indicate, the brahmanical preoccupation with the proper ritual treatment of the dead was not only broad but very old. It would presumably have informed and presumably have framed the attitudes of any brahmanical or brahmanized community that Buddhist monastic groups came into contact with, and such contact must have been early and frequent, at least in the middle Gangetic plains: the area including Śrāvastī, Kauśāmbī, Rājagṛha, Vaiśālī, etc. Any disregard of such set attitudes in the surrounding population, especially of those touching on the treatment of the dead and pollution, would have opened the Buddhist monastic community to immediate criticism and opprobrium. Such criticism would have been especially strong if the case involved a deceased individual who had originally been a member of the local group, an individual whose history and birth were widely known. The compiler of our *Kṣudraka-vastu* passage seems, in fact, to have encountered or envisioned just such a situation. He seems to have taken some pains to clearly indicate that the deceased monk had been born from a perfectly regular, normatively sanctioned marriage; that the full complement of normative birth rituals had been performed for him; that he had been named according to his *gotra*. The proper performance of ritual that accompanied his birth, however, only provides a stronger contrast for the initial total disregard of normative procedures in regard to his death on the part of the Buddhist monastic community. The response such disregard is said to have provoked seems entirely believable—even the language seems particularly appropriate here: "Come here! Look at this! . . . This is the sort of thing that happens when someone joins the order of those lordless Buddhist *śramaṇas*." Such behavior would most certainly have alienated "those laypeople who were not adherents of the faith," and almost certainly would not have been long-tolerated by either that group or—importantly—the Buddhist community that had to interact with and depend on it. In fact, unless the extent and depth of brahmanical attitudes among actual communities have been badly overestimated—and this is not impossible—it is almost inconceivable that such blatant disregard of established custom and local feeling would not have been immediately checked and regulated "in rule and precept." But this would, in turn, suggest that such rules, regardless of where they now occur, would probably have been in place very early on, and would suggest that a *Vinaya* which—like the Pāli *Vinaya*—did not contain such rules would have been poorly equipped to deal with monastic communities in close contact with brahmanical societies. The first of these suggestions has historical implications: it may be that this set of rules—like much else in the *Mūlasarvāstivāda-vinaya*—is very old indeed.[69] The second may underscore the importance of geography for understanding the various monastic codes: a monastic code framed in a predominantly brahmanical area would almost certainly—regardless of chronological considerations—contain rules and sets of rules that may differ from or not be included in codes redacted in, or meant for, communities in, say, predominantly "tribal" areas. Local or regional standards may have determined a good deal.

But if this second promulgation of rules concerning the local monastic dead in the *Mūlasarvāstivāda-vinaya* was, unlike the first, intended to respond to a particularly sensitive concern of the larger social group with which Buddhist monastic communities had to interact, and from which they drew recruits and economic support, still the funereal procedures that it prescribed were essentially similar to those of the first promulgation. Formal removal of the body—*abhinirhāra*—though not explicitly mentioned in the rules, is taken for granted throughout: the body is not to be casually dumped by the road side; there is clear reference to the monks having carried away the corpse *(śākya'i bu'i dge sbyong rnams ni ro bskyal nas)* in the remarks of the brahmins and householders concerning monks not having washed. Although the term *śarīra-pūjā / ro la mchod pa* is not explicitly used, *rim gro bya ba*—which generally translates some form of *sat*$\sqrt{}$*kṛ*—is, contextually, clearly its equivalent here: whereas in *Cīvara-vastu* II *śarīra-pūjā* is the prescribed alternative to simply dumping the body in the burning ground, *satkāra* here is the prescribed alternative to throwing it unceremoniously alongside the road.[70] The *Kṣudraka-vastu* passage differs, to be sure, in stipulating certain contingencies when alternative means of disposal could be used, but, in doing so, it only emphasizes the fact that the first choice in normal circumstances was cremation. The two related elements in the *Cīvara-vastu* monastic funeral that appear to be both most peculiarly Buddhist and, perhaps, restricted to funerals for monks—the recitation of *Dharma* and the transfer of merit—are also both explicitly mentioned and taken for granted. Although only actually mentioned after the last of the series of alternative means of disposal, it seems fairly certain it was to be understood that both the recitation and the transfer of merit were to follow whichever alternative was undertaken.[71]

We have seen, then, in this quick look at these passages from the *Mūlasarvāsti-vāda-vinaya* two sets of similar and mutually supplementary rules meant to govern a monastic funeral. Contrary to the old and established conventional wisdom, they establish that Buddhist *Vinaya* texts are by no means "nearly altogether silent as to the last honours of deceased monks," and they point to yet another concern in regard to which the Pāli *Vinaya,* as we have it, appears to be markedly deficient and possibly unrepresentative. Together with various narrative accounts scattered throughout Mūlasarvāstivādin literature, they also allow us to reconstruct the complete outline of a Mūlasarvāstivādin monastic funeral, from the tolling of the bell to the postfuneral bath, and they indicate that the laity were allowed no place in these procedures, that the funeral of a local monk was an exclusively monastic affair where participation was limited to monks and monks alone.[72] Even more than this, they allow us entrée into the mentality and concerns of the *Vinaya* masters who framed this code. They allow us to see learned monks and *Vinaya* authorities framing rules that were intended to avoid ghosts[73] and were preoccupied with the problems of inheritance and estates; monks concerned with carefully regulating behavior to avoid social censure; and monks—perhaps most importantly—who appear to have been influenced and motivated as much by Indian mores, beliefs, and legal conventions as by specifically Buddhist doctrines. They allow us to see, in short, a Buddhist monk who is far more human, and far more Indian, than the monk we usually meet in the works of Western scholarship.[74]

Textual Sources Cited and Abbreviations

The following notes contain several abbreviated titles of textual sources that differ from the listing at xv–xvii. These include:

ACF = *Annuaire du collège de france*

Aṅguttara = R. Morris and E. Hardy, eds., *The Aṅguttara-Nikāya,* Vols. i–v (London: 1885–1900). Cited by volume number and page.

Avadānaśataka = J. S. Speyer, ed., *Avadānaçataka. A Century of Edifying Tales belonging to the Hīnayāna,* Bibliotheca Buddhica, III, Vols. i and ii (St.-Pétersbourg: 1906–1909). Cited by volume, page, and line.

Divyāvadāna = P. L. Vaidya, ed., *Divyāvadāna,* Buddhist Sanskrit Texts, 20 (Darbhanga: 1959). Cited by page and line.

JOIB = *Journal of the Oriental Institute, Baroda*

Mahāparinirvāṇa-sūtra = E. Waldschmidt, ed., *Das Mahāparinirvāṇasūtra. Text in Sanskrit und Tibetisch, verglichen mit dem Pāli nebst einer Übersetzung der chinesischen Entsprechung im Vinaya der Mūlasarvāstivādins,* Teil I, Abhandlungen der Deutschen Akademie der Wissenschaften zu Berlin, Philosophisch-Historische Klasse, Jahrgang 1949, Nr. 1 (Berlin: 1950); Teil II, Abhandlungen . . . zu Berlin, Klasse für Sprachen, Literatur und Kunst, Jahrgang 1950, Nr. 2 (Berlin: 1951); Teil III, Abhandlungen . . . und Kunst, Jahrgang 1950, Nr. 3 (Berlin: 1951). Cited according to the "Vorgänge" and section numbers imposed on his restored text by Waldschmidt.

Pāli *Vinaya* = H. Oldenberg, *The Vinaya Piṭakaṃ. One of the Principal Buddhist Holy Scriptures in the Pāli Language,* Vols. i–v (London: 1879–1885). Cited by volume, page, and line.

Pravrajyāvastu = C. Vogel and K. Wille, eds., *Some Hitherto Unidentified Fragments of the Pravrajyāvastu Portion of the Vinayavastu Manuscript found near Gilgit,* Nachrichten der Akademie der Wissenschaften in Göttingen I. Philologisch-Historische Klasse, Jahrgang 1984, Nr. 7 (Göttingen: 1984). Cited by page or folio number and line.

Rab tu 'byuṅ ba'i gźi = H. Eimer, ed., *Rab tu 'byuṅ ba'i gźi. Die tibetische Übersetzung des Pravrajyāvastu im Vinaya der Mūlasarvāstivādins,* Teil i–ii, Asiatische Forschungen, Bd. 82 (Wiesbaden: 1983). Cited by volume, page, and line.

Udāna = P. Steinthal, *Udāna* (London: 1885). Cited by page and line.

Notes

1. H. Oldenberg, *Buddha. Sein Leben, seine Lehre, seine Gemeinde* (Berlin: 1881) 384 n; H. Oldenberg, *Buddha. His Life, His Doctrine, His Order,* trans. W. Hoey (London: 1882) 376 n.

2. T. W. Rhys Davids, *Buddhist Suttas,* Sacred Books of the East, XI (Oxford: 1900) xliv–xlv. In light of the references by both Oldenberg and Rhys Davids to the *Vinaya,* it is worth noting that there is good evidence for suggesting that the *Mahāparinibbāna-sutta*—which contains, of course, elaborate rules for funerals—was originally a part of the Pāli *Vinaya;* see L. Finot, "Textes historiques dans le canon pāli," *JA* (1932) 158; Finot, "Mahāparinibbāna-sutta and Cullavagga," *IHQ* 8 (1932) 241–246; E. Obermiller, "The Account of the Buddha's Nirvāṇa and the First Councils according to the Vinayakṣudraka," *IHQ* 8 (1932) 781–784; E. Frauwallner, *The Earliest Vinaya and the Beginnings of Buddhist Literature,* Serie Orientale Roma, VIII (Roma: 1956) 42ff. There are also indications that when read as a piece of *vinaya* a number of puzzling elements in the *Mahāparinibbāna-sutta* begin to make much better sense; see below nn. 46 and 72.

3. For a discussion of the differential treatment of archaeological/epigraphical and

textual sources, see G. Schopen, "Archaeology and Protestant Presuppositions in the Study of Indian Buddhism," Ch. I above. One might suspect, moreover, that the inclination to locate Buddhism in canonical texts has had an inhibiting influence even on anthropological investigations. C. F. Keyes, for example, says, quoting Rhys Davids: "Because both men [i.e. two modern Thai "Saints"] were considered to be Buddhist saints, their deaths were interpreted in terms of Buddhist ideas about death and its aftermath. *There is really only one source for these ideas,* particularly since nothing is said in the Vinaya, the discipline incumbent upon monks, about the disposal of the corpses of members of the Sangha (Rhys Davids: xlv); and that is in the account of the death of the Buddha himself as given in the *Mahāparinibbāna sutta*" (C. F. Keyes, "Death of Two Buddhist Saints in Thailand," *Charisma and Sacred Biography,* ed. M. A. Williams, JAAR Thematic Studies, XLVIII/3 and 4 [n.d.] 154; my emphasis). This seeming restriction of "Buddhist ideas" to canonical texts appears especially odd coming from an anthropologist. In fact, Keyes himself has done perhaps more than anyone else writing on Southeast Asia to show that "Buddhist ideas about death" can come from a variety of sources: C. F. Keyes, "Tug-of-war for Merit: Cremation of a Senior Monk," *Journal of the Siam Society* 63.1–63.2 (1975) 44–62; P. K. Anusaranaśāsanakiarti and C. F. Keyes, "Funerary Rites and the Buddhist Meaning of Death: An Interpretative Text for Northern Thailand," *Journal of the Siam Society* 68.1 (1980) 1–28; cf. S. J. Tambiah, "The Ideology of Merit and the Social Correlates of Buddhism in a Thai Village," *Dialectic in Practical Religion,* ed. E. R. Leach (Cambridge: 1968) 41–121, esp. 88–99; etc. To my knowledge there has been no work done on monastic funerals and little on the disposal of the dead in general in Sri Lanka, for example, in spite of the fact that we have a reasonably detailed description of a monastic funeral which took place there in the fifth century from Fa-hsien, *A Record of the Buddhist Countries,* trans. Li Yung-hsi (Peking: 1957) 83–84. (For some incidental references to monastic funerals in Tibet and Tibetan speaking areas, see T. Wylie, "Mortuary Customs at Sa-Skya, Tibet," *HJAS* 25 [1964–1965] 229–242; M. Brauen, "Death Customs in Ladakh," *Kailash* 9 [1982] 319–332; C. Ramble, "Status and Death: Mortuary Rites and Attitudes to the Body in a Tibetan Village," *Kailash* 9 [1982] 333–356; T. Skorupski, "The Cremation Ceremony according to the Byang-gter Tradition," *Kailash* 9 [1982] 361–376; etc.) It is, finally, worth noting that although an immense amount of work has been done on Medieval Christian monasticism, relatively little has been done on monastic funerals; see, however, for some interesting comparative and contrastive material, L. Gougaud, "Anciennes coutumes claustrales. La mort du moine," *Revue mabillon* (1929) 283–302; J. Leclercq, "Documents sur la mort des moines," *Revue mabillon* (1955) 165–179; (1956) 65–81; J.-L. Lemaitre, "L'inscription dans les necrologes clunisiens, XIe–XIIe siecles," *La mort au moyen âge. Colloque de l'association des historiens médiévistes français réunis à Strasbourg en juin 1975 au palais universitaire* (Strasbourg: 1977) 153–167; J.-L. Lemaitre, "La mort et la commémoration des défunts dans les prieurés," *Prieurs et prieurés dans l'occident médiéval,* ed. J.-L. Lemaitre (Genève: 1987) 181–190; L. Gougaud, *Dévotions et pratiques ascétiques du moyen age* (Paris: 1925) 129–142 ("Mourir sous le froc"); etc.

4. For a preliminary survey and discussion of this evidence, see G. Schopen, "An Old Inscription from Amarāvatī," Ch. IX above.

5. K. R. Norman, "The Value of the Pāli Tradition," *'Jagajjyoti' Buddha Jayanti Annual* (Calcutta: 1984) 1–9, esp. 4, 7; cf. K. R. Norman, "Pāli Philology and the Study of Buddhism," *The Buddhist Heritage,* Buddhica Britannica, Series Continua I (Tring,

U.K.: 1989) 29–53; also see the much earlier S. Lévi, "Observations sur une langue précanonique du bouddhisme," *JA* (1912) 495–514, esp. 511.

6. A. Csoma de Körös, "Analysis of the Dulva," *Asiatic Researches* 20 (1836) 41–93, esp. 71, 89; cf. A. Csoma de Körös, *Analyse du Kandjour,* traduite et augmentée par L. Feer, Annales du musée guimet, 2 (Lyon: 1881) 175, 192, 194.

7. W. W. Rockhill, *The Life of the Buddha and the Early History of His Order derived from Tibetan Works in the Bkah-hgyur and Bstan-hgyur* (London: 1884) 112, 116, 150, etc.

8. P. V. Kane, *History of Dharmaśāstra,* Vol. IV (Poona: 1953) 234–235. The idea that "the Vinaya" treats "all details of the daily life of the recluses" rather than simply the staggering number of areas in which there were problems remains with us: "As the *saṅgha* evolved, regulations developed governing the cenobitical life. These ordinances, preserved in the Vinaya Piṭaka of the Pāli Canon, detail every aspect of the lives of monks and runs [read: nuns] in the *saṅgha*"; K. G. Zysk, *Asceticism and Healing in Ancient India. Medicine in the Buddhist Monastery* (Oxford: 1991) 39. If such characterizations of the scope of "the Vinaya" are accepted, then we are stuck with an interesting irony: ". . . les *Vinayapiṭaka* . . . ne soufflent mot des nombreuses pratiques spirituelles, méditations, recueillements, etc., qui constituaient l'essence même de la 'religion' bouddhique" (A. Bareau, "La construction et le culte des stūpa d'après les Vinayapiṭaka," *BEFEO* 50 [1960] 249). To say that the *Vinayas* "ne soufflent mot" about such matters is too strong, but the point remains: if we had to judge by the *Vinayas,* we would have to conclude that "pratiques spirituelles" had little, if any, place in the daily life of monks and nuns.

9. See most recently A. Yuyama, *Systematische Übersicht über die buddhistische Sanskrit-Literatur.* Erster Teil. *Vinaya-Texte,* Hrsg. H. Bechert (Wiesbaden: 1979) 12–33; K. Wille, *Die Handschriftliche Überlieferung des Vinayavastu der Mūlasarvāstivādin,* Verzeichnis der Orientalischen Handschriften in Deutschland. Supplementband 30 (Stuttgart: 1990).

10. *Histoire du bouddhisme indien,* 187, for example, refers to the Chinese translation as "médiocre et incomplète"; E. Frauwallner, *The Earliest Vinaya and the Beginnings of Buddhist Literature,* 195, says it "is not only incomplete but also full of gaps." "The Chinese translation," he says, "is also much less exact than the Tibetan one." Lévi, *JA* (1912) 509, had even earlier said: "Du Vinaya des Mūla-Sarvāstivādins, nous avons deux traductions: une en chinois, par Yi-tsing, du type des 'belles infidèles'; une autre en tibétain, scrupuleusement littérale." J. W. de Jong, "Les *sūtrapiṭaka* des sarvāstivādin et des mūlasarvāstivādin," *Mélanges d'indianisme à la mémoire de Louis Renou* (Paris: 1968) 401, has, "en comparant les versions chinoise et tibétaine du *Vinaya* des Mūlasarvāstivādin," argued that some of these characterizations are unjustified, that some of the omissions in I-tsing's translation can be accounted for since "les manuscrits de Gilgit prouvent qu'il [I-tsing] a dû traduire une recension plus brève"; but see also E. Huber, "Études bouddhiques I.—Les fresques inscrites de Turfan," *BEFEO* 14 (1914) 13–14.

11. See below and n. 50.

12. Pāli *Vinaya,* i, 302ff; I. B. Horner, *The Book of the Discipline,* Vol. IV (London: 1951) 434ff; for some discussion on the problems of inheritance and the Pāli *Vinaya,* see U. Gaung, *A Digest of the Burmese Buddhist Law concerning Inheritance and Marriage,* Vol. I (Rangoon: 1908) 447–468; R. Lingat, "Vinaya et droit laique. Etudes sur les conflits de la loi religieuse et de la loi laïque dans l'indochine hinayaniste," *BEFEO* 37 (1937) 415–477, esp. 443ff.

13. See J. Gernet, *Les aspects économiques du bouddhisme dans la société chinoise du ve au xe siècle* (Paris: 1956) 61ff. Although dealing primarily with China, Gernet's study is

still probably the best thing we have on the economic structures of Indian Buddhist monasteries as they are described in texts of Indian origin.

14. *Gilgit Manuscripts*, iii 2, 113–148.

15. *Gilgit Manuscripts*, iii 2, 117ff.

16. For *yogaṃ manasikāram*, the Tibetan translation has only *yid la byed pa* (*Derge*, 3, 204; *Tog*, 3, 267; *Peking*, 41, 279-5). Compare the list of activities ignored in the Mūlasarvāstivāda passage with the similar but divergent list found at Pāli *Vinaya*, i, 190 (*riñcanti uddesaṃ paripucchaṃ adhisīlaṃ adhicittaṃ adhipaññaṃ*—said of monks preoccupied with making and ornamenting shoes), and iii, 235 (said of nuns preoccupied with washing, dyeing, and combing sheep's wool).

17. *Gilgit Buddhist Manuscripts*, vi, fol. 848.7–848.9; *Gilgit Manuscripts*, iii 2, 120.3–120.4—Tibetan: *Derge*, 3, 204; *Tog*, 3, 267; *Peking*, 41, 279-5.

18. Tibetan *gsol ba byed pa na*, and context, both suggest that something like *jñaptyāṃ kriyamāṇāyāṃ* has dropped out of the Gilgit manuscript; cf. the following note.

19. The *Cīvaravastu*, the *vastu* in which this passage occurs in the Sanskrit text, may not have been translated by I-tsing into Chinese; see Frauwallner, *The Earliest Vinaya and the Beginnings of Buddhist Literature*, 195. Durt, however, refers to a very similar list of "five occasions" that occurs in the *Vinaya-saṃgraha* (*Taishō* 1458): "1° battement de gong . . . 2° récitation du Sankei Mujōkyō . . . le sūtra tripartite . . . 3° salutation profonde . . . 4° distribution de Bâtonnets . . . 5° proclamation d'une motion . . ." in H. Durt, "Chū," *Hôbôgirin*, cinquième fascicule (Paris/Tokyo: 1979) 437; and I-tsing certainly knew the *Cīvaravastu*. At least one entire chapter of his *Record* is, in fact, a translation of a long passage from this *vastu*, as N. Dutt pointed out long ago (*Gilgit Manuscripts*, iii 2, x–xi). The chapter in question is number xxxvi; see *A Record of the Buddhist Religion as Practiced in India and the Malay Archipelago by I-tsing*, trans. J. Takakusu (London: 1896) 189–193. The failure to recognize that this chapter of the *Record* was a translation of part of the *Mūlasarvāstivāda-vinaya* has misled a number of scholars who have presented it as a reflection of actual monastic practice in India at the time of I-tsing's visit: cf. Lingat, *BEFEO* 37 (1937) 464; Gernet, *Les aspects économiques du bouddhisme dans la société chinoise du ve au xe siècle*, 71–73; A. Bareau, "Indian and Ancient Chinese Buddhism: Institutions Analogous to the Jisa," *Comparative Studies in Society and History* 3 (1961) 447; A. Bareau, "Etude du bouddhisme. Aspects du bouddhisme indien décrits par I-tsing," *ACF* 1989–1990, 631–640. The fact that the *Cīvaravastu* is not now found in the *Taishō* may only indicate that it was one of I-tsing's works that was lost after his death; cf. A. Hirakawa, *Monastic Discipline for the Buddhist Nuns* (Patna: 1982) 12. For a detailed description of the procedure involved in distributing "tickets" mentioned in our passage, see the article by Durt mentioned above.

20. *Gilgit Manuscripts*, iii 2, 120.6; *Gilgit Manuscripts*, iii 4, 79.13; *Avadānaśataka*, i, 272.1; cf. L. Feer, *Avadāna-çataka. Cent légendes bouddhiques* (Paris: 1891) 185, who translates *muṇḍikā gaṇḍī* as "la cloche funèbre."

21. *Peking*, 41, 279-5; *Gilgit Manuscripts*, iii 4, 79, n. 3; *Peking*, 40, 184-3.

22. This is especially clear in the monastic funeral described in *Avadānaśataka*, i, 271ff: *tato 'sya sabrahmacāribhir muṇḍikāṃ gaṇḍīṃ parāhatya śarīrābhinirhāraḥ kṛtaḥ / tato 'sya śarīre śarīrapūjāṃ kṛtvā vihāram āgatāḥ /*. It is almost equally clear that this *avadāna* is a narrative elaboration of the much simpler accounts in the *Cīvaravastu* of the *Mūlasarvāstivāda-vinaya* in which the first set of rules governing monastic funerals is presented; see below. On the "sectarian" affiliation of the *Avadānaśataka*, see J.-U. Hartmann, "Zur

Frage der Schulzugehörigkeit des Avadānaśataka," *Zur Schulzugehörigkeit von Werken der Hīnayāna-Literatur,* Hrsg. H. Bechert, Erster Teil (Göttingen: 1985) 219–224.

23. See below n. 62.

24. *Gilgit Manuscripts,* iii 2, 144.14, in the account of the death of a monk who had left his bowl and robe in the keeping of others: *viṣūcitaḥ kālagataḥ | sa bhikṣubhiḥ śmaśānaṃ nītvā dagdhaḥ | dharmaśravaṇaṃ dattam | anupūrveṇa vihāraḥ praviṣṭaḥ |.*

25. *Derge,* 10, 226.2, in an account of the funeral of Mahāprajāpatī in which the Buddha himself is given a prominent part.

26. See below n. 63.

27. M. Helffer, "Le gandi: un simandre tibétain d'origine indienne," *Yearbook for Traditional Music* 15 (1983) 112–125; I. Vandor, "The Gandi: A Musical Instrument of Buddhist India Recently Identified in a Tibetan Monastery," *The World of Music* 17 (1975) 24–27; cf. S. Lévi and Éd. Chavannes, "Quelques titres énigmatiques dans la hiérarchie ecclésiastique du bouddhisme indien," *JA* (1915) 213–215. References to the use of the *gaṇḍī* are frequent in the *Mūlasarvāstivāda-vinaya*—see, as a sample, *Gilgit Manuscripts,* iii 2, 145, 156, 158; iii 3, 9; iii 4, 35, 36, 37, 81, 92; *Saṅghabhedavastu,* ii, 83; *Śayanāsanavastu and Adhikaraṇavastu,* 41, 55, 85, 106; etc. It is interesting to note that striking "la tablette du cloître . . . cette sorte de gong funèbre," also signaled the beginning of monastic funerals in Medieval Western monasteries (Gougaud, *Revue mabillon* [1929] 281, 290), and its function there marks the communal nature of the event; see Lemaitre, *Prieurs et prieurés dans l'occident médiéval,* 185: ". . . on sonne la claquoir (*tabula*) pour réunir les frères . . ."

28. *Gilgit Buddhist Manuscripts,* vi, fol. 852.3–852.5; *Gilgit Manuscripts,* iii 2, 126.17–127.3—Tibetan: *Derge,* 3, 210.2–210.4; *Tog,* 3, 275.5–276.1; *Peking,* 41, 280-5-4 to 280-5-6.

29. S. Lévi, "Les éléments du formation du Divyāvadāna," *TP* 8 (1907) 105–122, esp. 122: "De ce point de vue, la langue du Mūla Sarvāstivāda Vinaya prend, par ses étrangetés même, une importance exceptionnelle; elle montre le sanscrit de Pāṇini entraîné par la circulation de la vie réelle, en voie d'altération normale, sur les confins des pracrits . . ."; *Saṅghabhedavastu,* i, xx, n. 2.

30. Both here and in II and III below, the Tibetan translators appear to have construed the dead monk's speech as a rhetorical question. The Tibetan, in fact, looks like it might be translating an interrogative *mā* construction (cf. *BHSG,* §§ 42.12–42.16); in III, the final text in this series cited below, the manuscript itself has a negative in the parallel construction, but it is *na* not *mā.*

31. *Gilgit Manuscripts,* iii 2, 127.5 (*bhikṣavas tam abhinirhṛtya,* of the dead body of an ordinary monk); *Pravrajyāvastu,* fol. 12r.2 (*bahir api nirhṛtya,* of the dead body of the teacher Saṃjayin); *Divyāvadāna,* 281.30 (*śibikābhir nirharitvā,* of the dead body of Aśoka); *Avadānaśataka,* i, 272.1 (*sabrahmacāribhir . . . śarīrābhinirhāraḥ kṛtaḥ,* of the body of a dead monk); *Udāna,* 8.21 (*sarīrakaṃ mañcakaṃ āropetvā nīharitvā,* of the dead body of an ascetic); Pāli *Vinaya,* iv, 308 (*bhikkuniyo taṃ bhikkhuniṃ nīharitvā,* of the dead body of a nun); etc. There are, of course, other technical meanings for *abhinirhāra;* cf. M. H. F. Jayasuriya, "A Note on Pali *abhinīhāra* and Cognate Forms in the Light of Buddhist Hybrid Sanskrit," *Añjali. Papers on Indology and Buddhism,* O. H. de A. Wijesekera Volume (Peradeniya: 1970) 50–54.

32. J. Jain, *Life in Ancient India as Depicted in the Jain Canon and Commentaries. 6th Century* B.C. *to 17th Century* A.D., 2nd ed. (New Delhi: 1984) 281–284, esp. 283 where *nīharaṇa* is cited as the term for "the ceremony of taking out the dead."

33. *ādahanaṃ nītvā: Gilgit Manuscripts,* iii 2, 127.13 (*dur khrod du khyer te,* of the body of a monk); iii 2, 125.14 (*sreg tu khyer nas,* of the body of a monk); *śmaśānaṃ nītvā: Gilgit Manuscripts.* iii 2, 144.14 (*dur khrod du bsregs nas,* of the body of a monk); *tam ādāya dahanaṃ gatāḥ: Gilgit Manuscripts,* iii 2, 118.15 (*de khyor te sreg tu dong ngo,* of the body of a monk). Cf. *Saṅghabhedavastu,* i, 70, 163; *Derge,* 10, 224ff, 444, 472; *Divyāvadāna,* 428; etc. It will, perhaps, be clear from even the small sample cited here that the Tibetan translations of the terms and phrases involved are neither consistent nor exact; cf. n. 38 below.

34. *Gilgit Buddhist Manuscripts,* vi, fol. 852.5–852.8; *Gilgit Manuscripts,* iii 2, 127.4–127.11—Tibetan: *Derge,* 3, 210.4–210.6; *Tog,* 3, 276.1–276.5; *Peking,* 41, 280-5-6 to 281-1-1.

35. G. Schopen, "Monks and the Relic Cult in the *Mahāparinibbāna-sutta,*" Ch. VI above.

36. On the meaning of the term *pūjā* and the kinds and range of activities it can refer to, see J. Charpentier, "The Meaning and Etymology of Pūjā," *IA* 56 (1927) 93–99, 130–136; L. de La Vallée Poussin, "Totémisme et Végétalisme," *Bulletins de la classe des lettres et des sciences morales et politiques, Académie Royale de belgique,* 5ᵉ série, T. XV (1929) 37–52; P. Thieme, "Indische Wörter und Sitten," *ZDMG* 93 (1939) 105–139, esp. 105–123; A. L. Basham, "The Evolution of the Concept of the Bodhisattva," *The Bodhisattva Doctrine in Buddhism,* ed. L. S. Kawamura (Waterloo: 1981) 19–59, esp. 35–36; G. E. Ferro-Luzzi, "*Abhiṣeka,* the Indian Rite that Defies Definition," *Anthropos* 76 (1981) 707–742; A. Ostor, *Puja in Society* (Lucknow: 1982); D. D. Malvania, "The Word Pūjā and Its Meaning," *Indologica Taurinensia* 14 (1987–1988) 269–273; etc.

37. See below n. 43.

38. T. W. Rhys Davids and W. Stede, *The Pali Text Society's Pali-English Dictionary* (London: 1921–1925) 698 s.v. *sarīra.* It is worth noting here that the handling of the term *śarīra-pūjā* by the Tibetan translators is far from satisfactory and a long way from their usual consistency. In this passage and in III cited below, *śarīra-pūjā* is translated by *ro la mchod pa, ro la mchod pa byas la,* and *ro la mchod pa byas; ro* means first "dead body, corpse, carcass," then "body," then "residue, remains, sediment." *Avadānaśataka,* ii, 272.2, however, which reads *śarīrābhinirhārah kṛtaḥ / tato 'sya śarīre śarīra-pūjāṃ kṛtvā,* is translated *rus bu phyir phyung ngo / de nas de'i rus bu la rus bu'i mchod pa byas nas.* Here, then, where the first occurrence of *śarīra,* and almost certainly the second and third, can only mean "body," the Tibetan translates it in all three instances by *rus ba* which can only mean "small bone" or "bones in general." Again, especially in the first instance, *śarīra* cannot possibly mean "bone" since the context makes it certain that it refers to a newly dead "body" which has not even been removed from the monk's cell, let alone cremated. Likewise, in the *Mahāparinirvāṇa-sūtra,* there are several occurrences of the term *śarīra-pūjā* in passages narrating events that preceded the cremation; that is to say, prior to the time that there could have been any "bones" or "relics." At 36.2, where Ānanda asks what should be done with the body of the Buddha after his death, *śarīra-pūjāyām autsukyam āpadyemahi* is translated by *sku gdung la . . . mchod pa ji snyed cig brtson par bgyi lags* (similarly at 46.4); at 48.8, where the wandering Ājīvika tells Mahākāśyapa that the Buddha is dead and that his body was honored for seven days, *śarīre śarīrapūjā* is translated by *sku gdung la mchod pa bgyis pa;* but at 49.19, where Kāśyapa formulates his intention to personally repeat the *śarīra-pūjā* of the Buddha's body that had already been performed by the Mallas, he says: *yan nv ahaṃ svayam eva bhagavataḥ śarīrapūjāyām autsukyam āpadyeya,* and this is translated into Tibetan by *ma la bdag nyid kyis bcom ldan*

'das la mchod pa'i las bya'o snyam du spro ba bskyed nas. In other words, in the same text, *śarīra* is sometimes translated by *sku gdung,* which is the respect form of *rus* and means first of all—if not exclusively—"bone," in contexts where there could not yet have been any "bone"; or it is sometimes not translated at all: 49.19, where the Sanskrit text has "worship of the body of the Blessed One," the Tibetan has simply "worship of the Blessed One" himself. There are, moreover, numerous instances where we do not have the Sanskrit original, but where it was almost certainly *śarīra-pūjā.* Here too there is considerable variation: at *Derge,* 10, 480, for example, immediately after Śāriputra's death, a fellow monk is said to have *śā ri'i bu'i ring bsrel la lus kyis mchod pa byas te.* Context makes it virtually certain that this can only refer to funeral procedures, and it is very likely that the original read *śarīre śarīrapūjā,* but in spite of this the Tibetan literally means something like "performing the worship with the body on the *relics* of Śāriputra." Later in the same account—Derge, 10, 488—where again the original almost certainly had *śarīre śarīrapūjā,* and where the reference is undoubtedly to post-cremation remains, the Tibetan has *ring bsrel la ring bsrel gyi mchod pa bgyi'o.* In the account of the death of Mahāprajāpatī (*Derge,* 10, 224ff), we find *lus la mchod pa;* in the account of the death of Prasenajit (*Derge,* 10, 174), we find both *khog pa la mchod pa* and *lus la mchod pa;* in the account of the death of the Monk Gavāṃpati, *rus pa la rus pa'i mchod pa* (*Derge,* 10, 606)—in all these cases the original was almost certainly *śarīrapūjā* or *śarīre śarīrapūjā.* It is not impossible that a systematic survey of the Tibetan handling of the term might reveal meaningful patterns in what now appears to be confusion, but such a survey has yet to be done. It is also worth noting that, although rare, there are traces of the use of the term *śarīra-pūjā* to refer to honor directed toward post-cremational remains and not to a funereal procedure. This appears to be the case several times in the account concerning the remains of Śāriputra at *Derge,* 10, 488ff; likewise, at *Divyāvadāna,* 252.10, when Aśoka expresses his desire to honor the *stūpas* of the Buddha's famous disciples, the Sanskrit text has him say *teṣāṃ śarīrapūjāṃ kariṣyāmi;* J. Przyluski, *La légende de l'empereur Açoka (Açoka-avadāna) dans les textes indiens et chinois,* Annales du musée guimet, 32 (Paris: 1923) 257, however, translates the parallel passage in the *A-yü-wang-chuan* (*Taishō* 2042) as " 'Je veux maintenant honorer les *stūpa* des grands disciples . . . ' "; see also Schopen, "Monks and the Relic Cult in the *Mahāparinibbāna-sutta,*" Ch. VI above, 108ff. Note, finally, that the Sanskrit sources themselves do not always use the term *śarīra-pūjā;* cf. n. 70.

39. *Divyāvadāna,* 281.30 (note that for Vaidya's *śibikābhir nirharitvā śarīrapūjāṃ kṛtvā rājānaṃ pratiṣṭhāpayiṣyāma,* the text given in S. Mukhopadhyaya, *The Aśokāvadāna. Sanskrit Text compared with Chinese Versions* [New Delhi: 1963] 132.7, provides an important variant: *śivikābhir nirharitvā śarīrapūjāṃ kṛtvā dhmāpayitvā rājānaṃ pratiṣṭhāpayiṣyāma*—this reading makes it very clear that *śarīrapūjā* preceded cremation); *Derge,* 10, 174. The fact that known kings—including and especially Aśoka—did not receive the funeral of a *Cakravartin* only emphasizes the purely ideal, if not entirely artificial, character of both the idea and the description of such a funeral in the texts, as well as the fourfold classification of those "worthy of a *stūpa*"; cf. A. Bareau, *Recherches sur la biographie du buddha dans les sūtrapiṭaka et les vinayapiṭaka anciens: II. Les derniers mois, le parinirvāṇa et les funérailles,* T. II (Paris: 1971) 50ff; G. de Marco, *I "Kuṣāṇa" nella vita del Buddha. Per una Analisi del Rapporto tra Potere Politico e Religione nell' Antico Gandhāra,* Supplemento n. 34 agli *Annali* (Napoli: 1983) 47–54; etc.

40. *Gilgit Buddhist Manuscripts,* vi, fol. 852.8–852.10; *Gilgit Manuscripts,* iii 2, 127.12–127.18—Tibetan: *Derge,* 3, 210.7–211.2; *Tog,* 3, 276.5–277.1; *Peking,* 41, 281-1-1 to 281-1-3.

41. *Gilgit Manuscripts,* iii 2, 144.14; *Derge,* 10, 472.2ff; *Derge,* 10, 224.6ff; *Avadānaśataka,* i, 272ff; etc.—reference to both or either is not, however, invariably found in references to monastic funerals. Sometimes such references contain only phrases like *tam ādahane saṃskārya* or *tam ādahanaṃ nītvā saṃskārya* (*Gilgit Manuscripts,* iii 2, 118.16, 125.4), where a recitation of *Dharma* and transfer of merit are probably simply understood. For the importance of performing a "*pūjā* of the teacher (i.e. the Buddha)" (*śāstuś ca pūjā*) for a dying but not yet dead monk, see *Gilgit Manuscripts,* iii 2, 124.11ff. It is again worth noting the similar procedures stipulated in "les coutumiers monastiques" composed in the Medieval West: ". . . on annonce la nouvelle au chapitre et l'on fait aussitôt un office pour le défunt, avec sonnerie de cloches"; "les frères résidant dans cette dépendance (prieuré, prévôté, etc. . . .) font pour le mort ce qui se fait dans le monastère, c'est-à-dire l'office des morts pendant sept jours, avec glas le premier jour, distribution d'une pitance (*justicia*) pendant trente jours avec chant du psaume *Verba mea* (Ps. 141) et de cinq autres psaumes pour le défunt." See Lemaitre, *Prieurs et prieurés dans l'occident médiéval,* 185; Gougaud, *Revue mabillon* (1929) 281ff.

42. For what is probably still the best discussion of the subtleties sometimes involved in what is called the "transfer of merit," see J. Filliozat, "Sur le domaine sémantique de *puṇya,*" *Indianisme et bouddhisme. Mélanges offerts à Mgr. Étienne Lamotte* (Louvain-la-neuve: 1980) 102–116.

43. See—noting the language used to express such "transfers"—*Gilgit Manuscripts,* iii 1, 220.12 (*nāmnā dakṣiṇām ādiśeyam,* to *pretas* who were the deceased relatives of a group of laymen); *Gilgit Manuscripts,* iii 4, 181.5, 18; 182.12 (*nāmnā dakṣiṇām ādeśaya,* to deceased relatives); *Derge,* 10, 472.2ff (*yon bsngo zhing,* to a deceased monk); *Śayanāsanavastu and Adhikaraṇavastu,* 37.7 (*nāmnā dakṣiṇā ādeṣṭavyā* 37.11; *nāmnā dakṣiṇām uddiśasi,* both to deceased donors who had given *vihāras* to the Order); *Gilgit Manuscripts,* iii 4, 161.1 (*nāmnā dakṣiṇām ādekṣyati,* to deceased parents by a son); *Rab tu 'byuṅ ba'i gźi,* ii, 41.9 (*miṅ gis yon bsṅo ba byed par gyur cig,* to deceased parents by a son); for literature related to this *Vinaya,* see *Avadānaśataka,* i, 272.13 (*nāmnā dakṣiṇā ādiṣṭā,* to a deceased monk by the Buddha); *Divyāvadāna,* 1.23, 286.24; *Avadānaśataka,* i, 15.1, 197.3, 277.2; etc., all to deceased parents by a son. There are, as well, instances which use the same vocabulary but where the transfer is directed to living beings: *Saṅghabhedavastu,* i, 199.25 (*dakṣiṇā ādiṣṭā,* by the Buddha to his father); *Gilgit Manuscripts,* iii 4, 80 (*dakṣiṇādeṣṭavyeti,* connected with the *Poṣadha,* cf. the last verse of the *Mūlasarvāstivāda Prātimokṣa Sūtra: prātimokṣasamuddeśād yat puṇyaṃ samupārjitaṃ / aśeṣas tena lokoyaṃ maunīndraṃ padam āpnuyāt //* in A. C. Banerjee, *Two Buddhist Vinaya Texts in Sanskrit* [Calcutta: 1977] 56); *Mahāparinirvāṇa-sūtra,* 6.10, 6.13 (*nāmnā dakṣiṇām ādiśava; dakṣiṇām ādiśet,* to local devas). In his work on the Pāli *Petavatthu,* H. S. Gehman noted and carefully studied parallel expressions in "Ādisati, Anvādisati, Anudisati and Uddisati in the Petavatthu," *JAOS* 43 (1923) 410–421. In a short note written long before the Sanskrit text of the *Mūlasarvāstivāda-vinaya* was available, he also argued that expressions like *nāmnā dakṣiṇādeśana* in the *Avadānaśataka* were "Pālisms" in "A Pālism in Buddhist Sanskrit," *JAOS* 44 (1924) 73–75. But, in fact, it now appears that such expressions are much more firmly anchored in Sanskrit—especially Mūlasarvāstivāda—sources and are of limited and late occurrence in Pāli sources; they occur frequently only in texts like the *Petavatthu,* very rarely elsewhere: at *Aṅguttara,* iii, 43 (*petānaṃ dakkhiṇaṃ anuppadassati*), and once in the Pāli *Mahāparinibbāna-sutta* (I.31: *tāsaṃ dakkhiṇam ādise*—the same expression in the same verse also appears in the parallel accounts to the *Mahāparinibbāna* passage that are now found at *Udāna,* 85ff, and Pāli *Vinaya,* i, 228ff). This pattern of occurrence of

the expression *dakkhiṇaṃ ādis-* in Pāli sources, noting especially its occurrence in the *Mahāparinibbāna-sutta*, parallels that of the term *śarīra-pūjā*. Both are firmly rooted and frequent in Mūlasarvāstivāda sources (see above n. 38), both are rare in anything but "late" Pāli sources, but both occur prominently in the Pāli *Mahāparinibbāna-sutta;* cf. J. P. McDermott, *Development in the Early Buddhist Concept of Kamma/Karma* (New Delhi: 1984) 41ff, although his views are not themselves free of problems. It is possible that we may have in both expressions indications of the influence of continental sources on canonical Pāli. It is also worth noting that at least the expression *dakṣiṇādeśana* is not limited to Mūlasarvāstivāda sources. In the *Sphuṭārthā Śrīghanācāra-saṃgraha-ṭīkā* of Jayarakṣita, for example, the term occurs and is provided with a "definition": *dakṣiṇādeśanañ ca dānagāthāpāṭhaḥ*, in Sanghasena, ed., *Sphuṭārthā Śrīghanācārasaṅgrahaṭīkā,* Tibetan Sanskrit Works Series, XI (Patna: 1968) 36.10: " 'Assignment of gift' is the reading of gift-verses" (J. D. M. Derrett, *A Textbook for Novices. Jayarakṣita's "Perspicuous Commentary on the Compendium of Conduct by Śrīghana,"* Pubblicazioni di Indologica Taurinensia, XV [Torino: 1983] 44). This work, it appears, is affiliated with the Mahāsāṅghika; cf. M. Shimoda, "The *Sphuṭārthā Śrīghanācārasaṅgrahaṭīkā* and the Chinese *Mahāsāṅghika Vinaya,*" *IBK* 39.1 (1990) 495–942. Finally, for some interesting suggestions concerning the background of the expression, see B. Oguibenine, "La dakṣiṇā dans le Ṛgveda et le transfert de mérite dans le bouddhisme," *Indological and Buddhist Studies. Volume in Honour of Professor J. W. de Jong on his Sixtieth Birthday.* ed. L. A. Hercus et al. (Canberra: 1982) 393–414.

44. Kane, *History of Dharmaśāstra,* Vol. IV, 257.

45. *Śrautakośa. Encyclopedia of Vedic Sacrificial Literature,* Vol. I, English Section; Part II (Poona: 1962) 1037.

46. This same congruency may also allow us a better understanding of some otherwise puzzling elements in the *Mahāparinirvāṇa-sūtra.* The Sanskrit version, for example, goes to some trouble to indicate that, although the funereal *śarīra-pūjā* had already been performed for the Buddha when Mahākāśyapa finally reached Kuśinagara, he nevertheless is made to repeat the entire procedure himself (49.18–49.20). This at first sight seems both odd and unnecessary. But it makes perfect sense if—as is not unlikely—the compiler of the text "knew" that Kāśyapa was the chief heir of the Buddha (cf. *Gilgit Manuscripts,* iii 1, 259–260), and if he "knew" that, for a monk to inherit, he must perform or participate in the funeral of the deceased. Seen from this point of view, Kāśyapa could not be what he was supposed to be unless he had performed the *śarīra-pūjā* or had participated in the funeral. Kāśyapa's role in the Pāli version of the text—although slightly less odd—can also be explained in this way.

47. R. F. Gombrich, *Precept and Practice. Traditional Buddhism in the Rural Highlands of Ceylon* (Oxford: 1971) 243.

48. Something similar has somewhat hesitantly been noted by Knipe in regard to Hindu funereal practice: "The doctrines of transmigration and liberation transformed the whole of ancient Indian speculation and practice, but the rites accorded the ancestors bear a stamp of rigorous antiquity. They appear to endure beside the newer sentiments of *saṃsāra* and *mokṣa.*" "The ritual world view of early vedic religion could abide through several strenuous periods via the directives of the *sūtras* and *śāstras* for individual funeral and ancestral rites, with remarkably little tampering from innovative doctrines, theologies, and cosmographies that gradually eroded the official, institutional structures of vedic religion. Although the concern shifted from the early vedic desire for a state of perpetual non-death or immortality to the dilemmas of *saṃsāra* and the ideal of *mokṣa,* the intention

of the *śrāddhas* survived, and the understanding of the passage of the deceased as a cosmogonic progression, with an individual's salvation dependent on the correct ritual activity of his descendants, permitted these archaic ceremonies for the dead to continue to the present day"; D. M. Knipe, "*Sapiṇḍīkaraṇa:* the Hindu Rite of Entry into Heaven," *Religious Encounters with Death. Insights from the History and Anthropology of Religions,* ed. F. E. Reynolds and E. H. Waugh (University Park and London: 1977) 111–124, esp. 112, 121–122.

49. Rockhill, *The Life of the Buddha and the Early History of His Order,* 112.

50. L. de La Vallée Poussin, "Staupikam," *HJAS* 2 (1935) 286-287.

51. A. Seidel, "Dabi," *Hôbôgirin,* sixième fascicule (Paris/Tokyo: 1983) 577f.

52. *Derge,* 10, 472.2-474.1; *Tog,* 9, 704.7–707.5; *Peking,* 44, 91-4-3 to 92-1-1. The footnote letters inserted into the text refer to the separate critical apparatus that follows it and in which variants—most of little consequence—are recorded.

53. This entire paragraph is made up of stereotypical phrases used to describe an orthodox union and birth; cf. *Gilgit Manuscripts,* iii 2, 1–2, 52; iii 4, 6, 15, 23, 24, 28, 29, 53; *Śayanāsanavastu and Adhikaraṇavastu,* 13; *Saṅghabhedavastu,* i, 27; *Rab tu 'byuṅ ba'i gźi,* ii, 7, 21, 23, 42; *Pravrajyāvastu,* 312; *Divyāvadāna,* 2; *Avadānaśataka,* i, 206, 261, 295; etc.

54. For the whole of what has been abbreviated here, see Feer, *Avadāna-çataka,* 3; *Pravrajyāvastu,* 16.

55. As with the Sanskrit texts from the *Cīvaravastu* treated above, so here in the Tibetan text the style is sometimes elliptical, and there is a considerable reliance on pronouns whose referents sometimes need to be drawn out.

56. The Sanskrit is cited from *Gilgit Manuscripts,* iii 2, 140.14.

57. For the Sanskrit underlying much of this paragraph, cf. *Gilgit Manuscripts,* iii 1, 285.17ff: (said of a monk bitten by a snake) *sa tathā vihvalo brāhmaṇagṛhapatibhir dṛṣṭaḥ / te kathayanti / bhavantaḥ katarasyâyaṃ gṛhapateḥ putra iti / aparaiḥ samākhyātam / amukasya iti / te kathayanti / anāthānāṃ śramaṇaśākyaputrīyāṇāṃ madhye pravrajitaḥ / yadi na pravrajito 'bhaviṣyat jñātibhir asya cikitsā kāritā abhaviṣyad iti /;* see also *Gilgit Manuscripts,* iii 1, ix.10, although the passage there involves considerable reconstruction. Note that our text has no word for "funeral," which I supply both here and below. A literal translation would be more like "would surely have performed the honors/ceremonies," "honors/ceremonies for a (deceased) monk are to be performed," etc. For Sanskrit phrases which might lie behind *rim gro byas par 'gyur ba,* etc., see below n. 70.

58. So de La Vallée Poussin, *HJAS* 2 (1935) 286, translates the Chinese. In a note he suggests the Chinese was translating *śarīra-pūjā,* but the Tibetan would not support this; cf. n. 38 above.

59. So de La Vallée Poussin, *HJAS* 2 (1935) 286; Seidel, *Hôbôgirin,* sixième fasc., 578.

60. So de La Vallée Poussin, *HJAS* 2 (1935) 286; Seidel, *Hôbôgirin,* sixième fasc., 578; cf. J. Przyluski, "Le partage des reliques du buddha," *MCB* 4 (1935–1936) 341–367, esp. 345–346.

61. It is virtually certain that Tibetan *yon bsngo zhing* here is translating some form of *dakṣiṇām ādiś-;* cf. *Mahāparinirvāṇa-sūtra,* 6.10: *nāmnā dakṣiṇām ādiśasva = yon sngo ba mdzad du gsol;* 6.13: *dakṣiṇām ādiśet = yon bsngo byas; Gilgit Manuscripts,* iii 2, 127.18: *dakṣiṇām uddiśya = yon bsngo ba byas nas;* etc.

62. Determining the precise referent of the term or title *Tridaṇḍaka* is not as easy as one might expect. Modern scholars, on the basis of good Chinese evidence (I-tsing, colophons from Tun-Huang), have with differing degrees of certainty seen in *Tridaṇḍaka*

a reference to a specific text. *Taishō* 801, the text in question, has in fact been assigned in various Chinese sources two titles: *(Fo shuo) wu ch'ang ching*, "Sūtra (Spoken by the Buddha) on Impermanency," a title which has been taken as a translation of a Sanskrit title something like *Anityatā-sūtra*, and *San ch'i ching*, "Sūtra des Trois Ouvertures" or "les trois 'informations.' " Sometimes the second title is given as an alternative, sometimes the two titles are simply combined into one: *Fo shuo wu ch'ang san ch'i ching;* de La Vallée Poussin renders the Chinese corresponding to our *Kṣudraka* passage by "récite les trois 'informations', *K'i* [et] le Sūtra sur l'impermanence," *HJAS* 2 (1935) 287. *Taishō* 801, or the *Anityatā-sūtra*, would appear to be well suited for a funeral text; see the Sanskrit version edited in I. Yamada, "Anityatāsūtra," *IBK* 20.2 (1972) 1001–1996. It appears, moreover, from at least Takakusu's translation, that I-tsing says in his description of a monastic funeral in his *Record* that "while the corpse is burning . . . the 'Sūtra on Impermanence' (*Anitya-sūtra*) is recited" (Takakusu, *A Record of the Buddhist Religion as Practiced in India and the Malay Archipelago*, 81–82). Bareau, however, in summarizing the passage says only: "Un moine récite un bref sermon (*sūtra*) sur l'impermanence (*anityatā*) . . . ," *ACF* 1989–90, 636. In the account of the funeral of Mahāprajāpatī in the *Kṣudraka*, finally, the Buddha himself is said to have "expounded teachings connected with impermanence" (*mi rtag pa dang ldan pa'i chos dag bshad nas: Derge*, 10, 226.2). All of this would seem to argue for identifying the *Tridaṇḍaka* with the *Anityatā-sūtra*. But there are still other indications that would seem to suggest that the *Tridaṇḍaka* was not, in fact, a specific text but a kind of ritual formulary into which any given text could be inserted. Although I-tsing does not appear to refer to the *Tridaṇḍaka* in his description of a monastic funeral, he does refer to it elsewhere in his *Record* and his description of it is of considerable interest. Lévi has translated the passage as follows: "Dans les pays occidentaux, l'adoration des caitya et le service ordinaire se font à la fin de l'après-midi ou au crépuscule . . . Quand tout le monde est définitivement assis, un maître des sūtra monte sur le siège aux lions (*siṃhāsana*) et déclame *un peu de sūtra* . . . Quant aux textes sacrés qu'on récite, c'est surtout les Trois Ouvertures qu'on récite. C'est un recueil dû au vénérable *Ma ming* (Aśvaghoṣa). La première partie compte dix vers; l'objet du texte est d'exalter les Trois Joyaux. Ensuite vient un texte sacré proprement dit, prononcé par le Buddha en personne. Après l'hymne et le récitation, il y a encore plus de dix vers, qui ont trait à la déflexion des mérites (*pariṇāmanā*) et à la production du voeu (*praṇidhāna*). Comme il y a trois parties qui s'ouvrent successivement, on appelle ce texte sacré les Trois Ouvertures"; see S. Lévi, "Sur la récitation primitive des textes bouddhiques," *JA* (1915) 401–447, esp. 433–434; cf. Takakusu, *A Record of the Buddhist Religion as Practiced in India and the Malay Archipelago*, 152–153, and R. Fujishima, "Deux chapitres extraits des mémoires d'I-tsing sur son voyage dans l'inde," *JA* (1888) 411–439, esp. 416–418. This passage is important in at least two ways. First, the *Tridaṇḍaka* described here is not a specific text, but a set form of recitation consisting of three parts: (1) praise of the three precious things followed by (2) the recitation of "un texte sacré proprement dit" with the sequence concluded by, (3) a formal transfer of merit. The "texte sacré" is unspecified and can apparently be any text suitable to the occasion of the recitation. The second important thing that I-tsing's description indicates would point in the same direction. We have seen so far in the *Mūlasarvāstivāda-vinaya* that the recitation of the *Tridaṇḍaka* is one of the specified moments for the distribution of a deceased monk's estate, and that it is recited as a part of a monastic funeral. I-tsing's description, however, makes it clear that these were not the only ritual contexts in which the *Tridaṇḍaka* was used. His description would seem to indicate that it was also used during the daily "adoration des caitya et le service ordinaire," and to these ritual moments we can add others. The *Poṣadhavastu* of the *Mūlasarvāstivāda-vinaya*, for example, associates the recitation of the *Tridaṇḍaka* with the fortnightly communal recitation of the *Prātimokṣa*, which is often presented as the most important congregational ritual in Buddhist monasticism (see *Gilgit Manuscripts*, iii 4, 80.5, where details concerning the appropriate length of its recitation are given). This association is repeated in the *Bod rgya tshig mdzod chen mo*, which characterizes the *Tridaṇḍaka* as a procedure or method of practice connected with the Upoṣadha: *gso sbyong gi sbyor chog cig ste;* its description of the *Tridaṇḍaka* as a recitative formulary corresponds almost exactly to I-tsing's: . . . *phyag 'tshal ba'i rgyud / mdo 'don pa'i rgyud / bsngo ba'i rgyuḍ de rgyud gsum dang ldan pa'i sgo nas tshul khrims rnam dag gi mdo la sogs pa'i chos bshad cing nyan par byed pa'o /* in Kraṅ dbyi sun, ed., *Bod rgya tshig mdzod chen mo*, Vol. I (Beijing: 1985) 577. Elsewhere in the *Mūlasarvāstivāda-vinaya*, moreover, the recitation of the *Tridaṇḍaka* is prescribed in the ritual required before cutting down a tree; see the text cited in K. Tokiya, "The Anityatā-sūtra Quoted in the Tibetan Version of a Mūlasarvāstivāda Text," *IBK* 34.1 (1985) 164; etc. It is, therefore, not just the structure of the *Tridaṇḍaka* as it is described by I-tsing, but also its use in a variety of different ritual contexts that suggests that it might well have been not a specific text but a specific set type of recitation or an established formulary into which any given *sūtra* text could be inserted. The Chinese identification of the *Tridaṇḍaka* with the *Anityatā-sūtra* may have resulted from the fact that I-tsing sent home the version of the formulary used for monastic funerals into which the *Anityatā* had been inserted and this came to be considered the only version. All of this will, of course, require further research to settle; so too will the attribution of the formulary to Aśvaghoṣa. For material bearing on both questions, see—in addition to the sources already cited—P. Demiéville, "Bombai," *Hôbôgirin*, Premier fasc. (Tokyo: 1929) 93ff; R. Sāṅkṛtyāyana, "Search for Sanskrit Mss. in Tibet," *JBORS* 24.4 (1938) 157–160; E. H. Johnston, "The *Tridaṇḍamālā* of Aśvaghoṣa," *JBORS* 25 (1939) 11–14; Lin Li-Kouang, *L'aide-mémoire de la vraie loi* (Paris: 1949) 303–305; L. Giles, *Descriptive Catalogue of the Chinese Manuscripts from Tunhuang in the British Museum* (London: 1957) 114–115; Durt, *Hôbôgirin*, cinquième fasc., 437; P. Demiéville, "Notes on Buddhist Hymnology in the Far East," *Buddhist Studies in Honour of Walpola Rahula*, ed. S. Balasooriya et al. (London: 1980) 50, n. 31; Seidel, *Hôbôgirin*, sixième fasc., 577–578; etc.

63. de La Vallée Poussin, *HJAS* 2 (1935) 287. Here again we have a case where what should be a straightforward referent turns out not to be so. The problems start with an old one. Tibetan translations almost never distinguish between *stūpa* and *caitya*, both terms almost always being rendered by *mchod rten;* there are apparent exceptions, but they are extremely rare—see the *Mchod rten gcig btab na bye ba btab par 'gyur pa'i gzungs* (*Peking*, 6, 151-2-2 to 151-3-2; 11, 168-4-8 to 164-5-8) where the transliteration *tsai tya* appears several times. The original that was translated in our passage by *mchod rten la phyag mi 'tshal nas* and *mchod rten la phyag 'tshal bar bya'o* cannot, therefore, be determined. There is also the fact that the Tibetan versions are not in agreement as to whether the text is referring to one or to several *mchod rtens:* the *Derge* has in the second occurrence *mchod rten la*, but both *Tog* and *Peking* have *mchod rten dag la* (de La Vallée Poussin translates the Chinese as singular). Both considerations may bear on an even more important point: we do not know to whom the *mchod rten* or *mchod rtens* belonged; we do not know whether the reference is to a *stūpa* or *stūpas* of the Buddha, or to the *stūpa* or *stūpas* of the local monastic dead—it is now clear that the latter were found in considerable numbers at a considerable number of mostly very early monastic sites in

India; cf. Schopen, "An Old Inscription from Amarāvatī," Ch. IX above; for some regional variation in regard to whether such structures were called *stūpas* or *caityas,* see 197 and n. 38. Taking this category into account it is, of course, not impossible that our text might be referring to a *stūpa* built for the deceased monk whose funeral has just been performed. It appears, however, that at least Mūlasarvāstivāda texts do not seem to link funereal activity *per se* with the erection of *stūpas* for the local monastic dead. In none of the numerous references to monastic funerals in Mūlasarvāstivāda literature that I know is there any reference to erecting a *stūpa.* In fact, the erection of *stūpas* for the local monastic dead is legislated separately in the *Mūlasarvāstivāda-vinaya*, not in an account of a funeral, but in an account concerning the post-funereal "relics" of Śāriputra (*Derge,* 10, 488ff). This would suggest, I think, that in this *Vinaya* funeral ceremonies and cult activity directed toward relics or reliquaries of the local monastic dead were conceived of as fundamentally different forms of religious behavior. (It is—in so far as I know—only in a few Pāli narrative passages that funeral ceremonies for local monks or nuns are directly linked with the erection of *stūpas* for them; cf. *Udāna,* 8.21; Pāli *Vinaya,* iv, 308.) [See now G. Schopen, "Ritual Rights and Bones of Contention: More on Monastic Funerals and Relics in the *Mūlasarvāstivāda-vinaya,*" *JIP* 22 (1994) 31–80.] In light of these considerations, it might be well to assume—until it can be shown otherwise—that *mchod rten (dag) la phyag 'tshal bar bya'o* in our passage refers to worshipping the *stūpa* or *stūpas* of the Buddha, and that such an act was the final moment of a monastic funeral. What "external" evidence we have also would seem to indicate that funeral activity and activity connected with *stūpas* were thought of as distinct. I-tsing in his *Record* refers to something "like a *stūpa*" for the local monastic dead, but he seems to indicate that such was not always erected and that when it was it was made an indeterminate time after the funeral: the monks, he says, "on returning [from the cremation] to their apartments, . . . cleanse the floor with powdered cow-dung. All other things remain as usual. There is no custom as to putting on a mourning-dress. They sometimes build a thing like a *stūpa* for the dead, to contain his *śarīra* (or relics). It is called a '*kula,*' which is like a small *stūpa,* but without the cupola on it"; see Takakusu, *A Record of the Buddhist Religion as Practiced in India and the Malay Archipelago,* 82; cf. Bareau, *ACF* 1989–1990, 636: "Après la crémation, on recueille les restes corporels (*śarīra*) et on élève sur eux un petit tumulus appelé *kula.* Celui-ci ressemble à un *stūpa,* mais on ne dresse pas de parasols (*chattra*) à roues (*cakra*) à son sommet . . ." For an attempt to identify what I-tsing calls a *kula* with what is found at a number of monastic sites in India, see G. Schopen, "Burial *Ad Sanctos* and the Physical Presence of the Buddha in Early Indian Buddhism," Ch. VII above, esp. 120. Note too that Rockhill's summary of our text is particularly unsatisfactory at this point: "Previously to being interred the body must be washed. A cairn or tchaitya (*mchod rten*) must be raised over the remains" (*The Life of the Buddha and the Early History of His Order,* 112). There is no justification in the text itself for his interpretation of either injunction: it is the monks who participated in the funeral who must wash, and the *mchod rten* is to be worshipped, not "raised."

64. I. B. Horner, *The Book of the Discipline,* Vol. I (Oxford: 1938) xvi–xvii.

65. Horner, *The Book of the Discipline.* Vol. I, xxix.

66. Horner, *The Book of the Discipline,* Vol. I, xv.

67. Ch. Malamoud, "Les morts sans visage. Remarques sur l'idéologie funéraire dans le brâhmanisme," *La mort, les morts dans les sociétés anciennes,* ed. G. Gnoli et J.-P. Vernant (Cambridge and Paris: 1982) 441–453, esp. 441, 445, 449.

68. L. Dumont, *Homo Hierarchicus. The Caste System and Its Implications,* completely revised English ed. (Chicago: 1980) 49–50.

69. Jain has recently argued that the "elaborate rules for disposing of the dead bodies of Jain monks" found in Jain literature are also early: "The material contained in the *Bhag{avatī} Ārā{dhanā}* belongs to the time of early Jainism when the division of Śvetāmbara and Digambara did not exist in the Jain *Saṅgha*" (J. Jain, "Disposal of the Dead in the Bhagavatī Ārādhanā," *JOIB* 38 [1988] 123–31. Though a late text, see the interesting description of "The Funeral of a Renouncer" in J. P. Olivelle, ed., *Saṃnyāsapaddhati of Rudradeva,* The Adyar Library Series, 114 [Madras: 1986] 63ff). It should be noted that the scholarly literature in regard to the date of the *Mūlasarvāstivāda-vinaya* is marked by ambivalence and seeming contradictions. Lamotte, for example, notably on the basis of the fact that this *Vinaya* contains a "prediction" relative to Kaniṣka and was not translated into Chinese until the eighth century, asserts that "on ne peut attribuer à cet ouvrage une date antérieure aux IVe–Ve siècles de notre ère" in *Histoire du bouddhisme indien,* 727. But Huber, already in 1914, had drawn very different conclusions from the presence of this prediction relative to Kaniṣka. He had said: "Ce petit fait vient s'ajouter à un certain nombre d'autres déjà connus qui tendent à montrer que le Vinaya des Mūla-Sarvāstivādins a subi un remaniement aux environs de l'ère chrétienne," and then added: "Sans discuter la date exacte du roi Kaniṣka, on peut dire que la mention de son nom nous reporte vers le même temps." See E. Huber, "Études bouddhiques III.—Le roi kaniṣka dans le vinaya des mūlasarvāstivādins," *BEFEO* 14 (1914) 19; Gnoli, *Saṅghabhedavastu,* i, xix, has more recently made much the same observation. Moreover, and again long before Lamotte, Lévi had already counseled against attributing too much significance to the date of the Chinese translation: "La date tardive de la traduction chinoise . . . ne doit pas non plus nous entraîner trop vite à tenir l'ouvrage pour récent" in *TP* 8 (1907) 115f. To this might be added the fact that dating the compilation of a work does not necessarily date its specific contents: "dans l'état fragmentaire de nos connaissances sur le bouddhisme indien, la date récente du document qui nous fait connaître une légende, ne permet nullement de conclure à la formation récente de la légende elle-même" (Huber, *BEFEO* 14 [1914] 17). This is made strikingly evident in regard to the *Mūlaṣarvāstivāda-vinaya* in another series of observations and investigations. Although he repeatedly characterizes the *Mūlasarvāstivāda-vinaya* as "tardif" or "le plus récent de tous les recueils disciplinaires," Bareau says as well that the form of the *stūpa* it describes appears to be the "most ancient" in A. Bareau, "La construction et le culte des stūpa d'après les Vinayapiṭaka," *BEFEO* 50 (1960) 233. Elsewhere, while still pointing to its "late" character, he says: ". . . d'après des études comparatives approfondies mais très partielles, le *Vinayapiṭaka* des Mūlasarvāstivādin paraît nettement plus archaïque que celui des Sarvāstivādin et même que le plupart des autres *Vinayapiṭaka*" (A. Bareau, *Les sectes bouddhiques du petit véhicule* [Paris: 1955] 154). More specifically, Lévi, in a detailed study of certain linguistic forms in the *Vinaya,* says for example: "L'interdiction de 'boire à la sangsue', promulgée d'abord dans un dialecte qui pratiquait l'adoucissement de la sourde intervocalique, est arrivée telle quelle aux rédacteurs du canon pali qui n'ont plus reconnu sous son altération le terme original; ainsi des autres écoles, à l'exception des Mūla-Sarvāstivādins, qui montrent encore sur d'autres points du canon une incontestable supériorité," *JA* (1912) 510; M. Hofinger, in his study of the Second Council, argues that the oldest extant accounts of these events are preserved in the *Mūlasarvāstivāda-* and *Mahāsāṅghika-vinayas* (M. Hofinger, *Étude sur le concile de vaiçālī* [Louvain: 1946] 235–241, 256); I myself have suggested that the account of the remains of the former

Buddha Kāśyapa found in the *Mūlasarvāstivāda-vinaya* appears from every angle to be earlier than the standardized, revised, and probably conflated accounts found in our other *Vinayas* in "Two Problems in the History of Indian Buddhism," Ch. II above, 28–29. If these divergent opinions and observations suggest a state of some uncertainty concerning the date of the *Mūlasarvāstivāda-vinaya,* then their presentation has succeeded in representing the actual state of our knowledge. We simply know very little that is definitive about it; the illusion, of course, is that we know anything more about the dates of our other *Vinayas,* including that preserved in Pāli. It does, however, seem that there is mounting evidence that the *Mūlasarvāstivāda-vinaya*—whatever its date or the degree of its "remaniement"—contains a good deal of very early material. The rules concerning monastic funerals may, in fact, be just another case in point.

70. For the Sanskrit translated by *rim gro bya ba,* see L. Chandra, *Tibetan-Sanskrit Dictionary* (New Delhi: 1961) 2268–2269, and note that Sanskrit *satkāra,* when not actually a "w.r. for *saṃskāra,*" can itself in one form or another mean "doing (the last) honour (to the dead), cremation of a corpse, funeral obsequies," "to pay the last honours to (acc.), cremate," etc.; M. Monier-Williams, *A Sanskrit-English Dictionary* (Oxford: 1899) 1134. As stated earlier, Sanskrit accounts of monastic funerals do not always use the expression *śarīra-pūjā:* at *Gilgit Manuscripts,* iii 2, 118.15, for example, we find *bhikṣavas tam ādāya dahanaṃ gatāḥ . . . bhikṣavas tam ādahane saṃskārya vihāram āgatāḥ;* at iii 2, 125.14: *bhikṣavas tam ādahanaṃ nītvā saṃskārya vihāram āgatāḥ.*

71. Although it contains some details not yet found in the texts, I-tsing's description of a monastic funeral also contains, in one form or another, the same basic elements; see Takakusu, *A Record of the Buddhist Religion as Practiced in India and the Malay Archipelago,* 81–82, and Bareau, *ACF* (1989–1990) 636.

72. It would appear from Jain's remarks in *Life in Ancient India as Depicted in the Jain Canon and Commentaries,* 281–284, and *JOIB* 38 (1988) 123–131, that the funeral of a dead Jain monk was by preference and, when at all possible, an exclusively monastic affair. But Jain sources explicitly legislate for contingencies: "The question of carrying the dead [monk] for disposal was rather complicated . . . If there were only one single monk and it was not possible for him to carry the dead, ascetics belonging to non-Jain religion or laymen should be called, or help should be taken from the members of the Mallagaṇa, the Hastipālagaṇa or the Kumbhakāragaṇa, or in the absence of these a village-headman, *cāṇḍalas,* people from degraded castes, sweepers, barbers and others should be approached." It is not impossible that the Buddhist *Vinayas* also contained such legislation and it simply has not been recognized as such. The well-known passage that we associate with the *Mahāparinirvāṇa-sūtra,* which has been taken wrongly to establish that "śarīrapūjā, the worship of relics, is the concern of the laity and not the bhikṣusaṃgha" (Schopen, "Monks and the Relic Cult in the *Mahāparinibbāna-sutta,*" now Ch. VI above, 100–101), may be, in fact, just such legislation. In the passage in question (Sanskrit 36.2–36.3; Pāli V.10), Ānanda asks how the funereal *śarīra-pūjā* for the Buddha could be performed, and the Buddha responds in the Sanskrit version: *alpotsukas tvam ānanda bhava śarīrapūjāyāḥ. prasannā brāhmaṇagṛhapataya etad āpādayiṣyanti.* All of the other known versions are essentially similar: Pāli, " 'ne soyez pas occupés (*avyāvaṭā tumhe hotha*) du culte [à rendre au] corps du Tathāgata' "; Chinese D, " 'ne vous souciez pas de cette affaire' "; Chinese A and C, " 'restez tranquilles' "; etc. All versions, as well, indicate essentially the same reason why Ānanda need not be concerned: " 'les pieux brahmanes et maîtres de maison (*gṛhapati*) s'en chargeront' "; all quotations are from Bareau, *Recherches sur la biographie du buddha dans les sūtrapiṭaka et les vinayapiṭaka anciens: II. Les derniers*

mois, le parinirvāṇa et les funérailles, T. II, 36–37. Previous interpretations of this passage—and they have been many—have, it seems, never asked why Ānanda should have been so concerned in the first place. Moreover, they have failed to take into account, among other things, that the *Mahāparinirvāṇa-sūtra* was almost certainly a piece of *vinaya;* that the Buddha's declaration came at almost the very end of the various *Vinayas* and certainly at the very end of the narrative time or internal chronology assumed by the canonical texts; and that—finally—Ānanda found himself, in so far as we can tell, alone. This would mean in terms of the *Mūlasarvāstivāda-vinaya,* for example, that by the time the reader or redactor of this *Vinaya* had reached this passage, he would have seen or inserted both sets of rules governing monastic funerals that we have looked at here and a host of narrative descriptions of monastic funerals, in all of which it was monks and monks alone who did and were explicitly directed to perform the funeral of a fellow-monk. But again, in so far as we can tell, Ānanda found himself alone or virtually so. He could not, therefore, fulfill the *vinaya* rule. This situation can explain well Ānanda's concern, the Buddha's assurance, and the sense of the passage: the Buddha was allowing an exception to the rule. This interpretation, although differing markedly from others, is perhaps worth pursuing. It is also perhaps worth noting that it—or some residual sense that Ānanda had indeed broken the rule—may also explain one of the charges brought against Ānanda by Mahākāśyapa at "the council of Rājagṛha." Among other things and in all versions, Ānanda is criticized, in fact charged with a fault (*duṣkṛta*), for having allowed apparently unauthorized individuals—nuns, laymen, and especially laywomen—to participate in what could only have been the funereal *śarīra-pūjā;* most of the versions emphasize that the women saw the Buddha's penis, and that could only have happened during the preparation of the body before it was wrapped. See, for the various accounts, J. Przyluski, *Le concile de rājagṛha. Introduction a l'histoire des canons et des sectes bouddhiques* (Paris: 1926–1928) 15, 50–51, 64, 153, 157, etc.

73. The role of ghosts, demons, etc., in the promulgation of *vinaya* rules would make an interesting topic of study. In both the Pāli *Vinaya* (i, 149ff) and the *Mūlasarvāstivāda-vinaya* (*Gilgit Manuscripts,* iii 4, 149ff), for example, problems with or the presence of *piśāca* or *amanuṣyas* are cited as legitimate causes for cutting short the rain-retreat, an act which otherwise was forbidden. Again in the Pāli *Vinaya* the case of a monk who had "a non-human affliction" (*amanussikābādha*) or was "possessed" prompted the Buddha to allow monks to eat raw flesh and drink blood (Pāli *Vinaya,* i, 202; I. B. Horner, *The Book of the Discipline,* Vol. IV [London: 1951] 274, n. 6); etc. It would appear, moreover, from Jain's remarks that many of the rules governing Jain monastic funerals were also connected with the fear of "ghosts": "If these rites are not followed, it is possible that some deity might enter the dead body, rise, play and create disturbances to the saṅgha" (*JOIB* 38 [1988] 127).

74. Unfortunately, the material studied here makes little specific reference to nuns, and in this it is probably typical of textual sources on the whole and unrepresentative of what actually occurred; see G. Schopen, "Monks, Nuns, and 'Vulgar' Practices," Ch. XI below, esp. 248ff. It is true, however, that none of the inscribed—and therefore certain—*stūpas* of the local monastic dead found at Indian monastic sites were erected for a nun; see Schopen, "An Old Inscription from Amarāvatī," now Ch. IX above. The subject requires, and will undoubtedly reward, future research.

CHAPTER XI

On Monks, Nuns, and "Vulgar" Practices

The Introduction of the Image Cult into Indian Buddhism

THERE IS A CURIOUS consistency in the way in which major doctrinal changes and innovations in the history of Indian Buddhism have been explained. Some variant of a single explanatory model has been used to account for such diverse phenomena as the initial split within the Buddhist community that produced the Mahāsāṅghika and the beginnings of Buddhist sectarianism, the appearance and growth of relic worship and the *stūpa* cult, and the appearance of the Mahāyāna, "celestial *bodhisattvas,*" the cult of images, and Buddhist tantric practices. The same model has been used, as well, to account for the disappearance of Buddhism from India.

It is equally curious that we owe the most recent and perhaps most clearly articulated statement of this model to a classicist working in "late antiquity." Brown, in talking about the rise of the cult of the saints in Latin Christianity, speaks of "a particular model of the nature and origin of the religious sentiment," which he calls the " 'two-tiered' model." In this model:

> The views of the potentially enlightened few are thought of as being subject to continuous upward pressure from habitual ways of thinking current among "the vulgar" . . .
>
> When applied to the nature of religious change in late antiquity, the "two-tiered" model encourages the historian to assume that a change in the piety of late-antique men, of the kind associated with the rise of the cult of saints, must have been the result of the capitulation by the enlightened elites of the Christian church to modes of thought previously current only

---

Originally published in *Artibus Asiae* 49:1–2 (1988–1989):153–168. Reprinted with stylistic changes with permission of *Artibus Asiae*.

> among the "vulgar." The result has been a tendency to explain much of the cultural and religious history of late antiquity in terms of drastic "landslips" in the relation between the elites and the masses. Dramatic moments of "democratization of culture" or of capitulation to popular needs are held to have brought about a series of "mutations" of late-antique and early medieval Christianity.[1]

That this view or "model" has become an almost unnoticed part of our scholarly method could be easily documented on every side. That it is deeply embedded in even the best standard works on Indian Buddhism is clear from any number of statements in Lamotte. The latter, under the heading "influence du milieu laïc," says, for example:

> Le bouddhisme n'est pas qu'une philosophie mystique à l'usage des candidats au Nirvāṇa. Ce fut aussi une religion qui sortit du cadre étroit des couvents pour se répandre à travers toutes les couches de la population. Il n'est pas douteux que, sur certains points de la doctrine et du culte, les religieux n'aient dû composer avec les aspirations des laïcs . . . les succès croissants de la propagande eurent pour effet de transformer le bouddhisme, de message philosophico-mystique qu'il était primitivement, en une véritable religion comportant un Dieu (plus exactement un buddha divinisé), un panthéon, des saints, une mythologie et un culte. Cette religion ne tarda pas à s'infiltrer dans les monastères et à influencer, peu ou prou, les savants docteurs.[2]

Later in the same work and at the end of his short discussion of the cult of images, Lamotte says:

> Dans l'ensemble, en face des exigences multipliées du sentiment populaire, la réaction cléricale n'a manqué ni de souplesse ni d'adresse . . . Dans la vie courante, les autorités spirituelles évitaient de prendre position, tolér-aient sans permettre, concédaient sans accorder . . .[3]

In fact, this attitude and the " 'two-tiered' model" has particularly affected our understanding of such things as the introduction of the cult of images into Indian Buddhism almost from the very beginning of the discussion. Sixty years ago Coomaraswamy said:

> . . . it may well be asked how it came to pass that Hinduism, Buddhism, and Jainism alike became "idolatrous" religions. The answer to this question was admirably expressed by Jacobi over forty years ago: 'I believe that this worship had nothing to do with original Buddhism or Jainism, that it did not originate with the monks, but with the lay community, when the people in general felt the want of a higher cult than that of their rude deities and demons, when the religious development of India found in Bhakti the supreme means of salvation. Therefore instead of seeing in the Buddhists the originals and in the Jainas the imitators, with regard to the

> erection of temples and worship of statues, we assume that both sects were . . . brought to adopt this practice by the perpetual and irresistible influence of the religious development of the people in India.[4]

That this model is still very much current can be seen in even the most recent discussions of the early image cult.[5]

The position here is an odd one. It starts with the assumption—another old one—that Indian Buddhism was a religion dominated by a religious elite. But then it almost immediately asserts that these "enlightened elites"—"les savants docteurs," "les autorités spirituelles," "the monks"—were apparently able only to react: change and innovation were apparently out of their hands and were the result of the pressure of popular, lay feeling; it was the laity, it seems, who stimulated change and innovation. But apart from the fact that this would have been an almost complete reversal of the role that "autorités spirituelles" have always had in Indian culture, every indication that we have in regard to the cult of images, for example, suggests something like the very opposite.

Precisely because it was a later innovation in Indian Buddhism, the development of the cult of images can be much more easily followed than many other, earlier developments. This is especially true of its introduction and its earlier phases at individual sites. By means of one of the most important and most unaccountably little-used sources for the history of Indian Buddhism, we are able to actually document the role of the Indian Buddhist monastic in this process. In fact, even a preliminary analysis of the large collection of donative inscriptions that have come down to us clearly indicates the preponderant place that the monks and nuns had in the entire enterprise. We might start late and with Sārnāth.

There are twenty-two image inscriptions from Sārnāth in which the donor is clear that date to the Kuṣān and Gupta periods. In fifteen of these, including the *very earliest,* the donor of the image is a monastic.[6] In only three is the donor specifically said to be a layman, and one of these is uncertain.[7] In four others, only the name of the donor is given without any indication of his status. Even if we assume that this last group were laymen, still there are more than twice as many monk donors as lay donors. The numbers for monastic donors are almost certainly far out of proportion with the actual number of monks in the general population. They are also in striking contrast with what we find at Sārnāth at the end of what Sahni calls "the Mediaeval Period": 1100–1200 C.E. Here we find six lay donors, and possibly two more, but not a single monk.[8] Monastics initiated and disproportionately supported the cult of images at Sārnāth in the early periods.

In the Western Cave Temples we can even more clearly watch the introduction of the cult of images. The caves at Ajaṇṭā were excavated in two main phases. In the early phase, which goes back to the first century B.C.E., there are no images. In the second phase, which started in the fifth century C.E., images were an integral part of the new excavations and were introduced into many of the older caves as well. Here, there is no doubt about who was responsible for their introduction. We have thirty-six donative inscriptions connected with images from Ajaṇṭā in which the status of the donor can be determined. In only three of these inscriptions are the donors laymen, and one of these cases is doubtful. The other thirty-three donors were all monks. Ninety-four percent of these images were given by monks.[9]

Although less overwhelming, the evidence from other cave sites in Western India always points in the same direction. Eighteen of our donative inscriptions from Kānheri record the gifts of laymen: caves, cisterns, seats, and so on. Seven show monks and nuns making the same kind of gifts. But although laymen never donated images, two additional inscriptions indicate that monks did. The two inscriptions from Kānheri connected with images both indicate they were given by monks.[10] Moreover, if Leese is right about "the earliest extant figures of the Buddha at Kaṇheri," it is worth noting that the figures she identifies resulted either entirely or in large part from the patronage of a group of five monks.[11] The pattern is very much the same at Kuda. Here eighteen inscriptions record the gifts of laymen: caves, cisterns, a bathing tank, and so on. In only one case did a layman give an image. There are six additional inscriptions from Kuda that record the gifts of monks: in two of these, monastic individuals donated caves; in one, the object given is unclear; the remaining three inscriptions all record the gifts of images by monks.[12] At both Kuda and Kānheri the images found are intrusive—they were not part of the original plan. They were introduced onto the site, and in five out of six cases they were introduced by monks. Many of the images at Ajaṇṭā were also intrusive, and virtually all of them were introduced by monks.

The monastic role in the cult of images is also apparent in the Kharoṣṭhī inscriptions—some quite early—from the Northwest. There are eighteen Kharoṣṭhī inscriptions in the old collection edited by Konow that record the gifts of images and in which the donor's name is preserved. Of these eighteen, more than two-thirds (or thirteen) record the gifts of monks.[13] When we add to these the image inscriptions that have been published recently, the figures change somewhat but not markedly. I know of nine newly discovered Kharoṣṭhī inscriptions connected with images, but in three of these the status of the donor is unclear or problematic.[14] In five others, the donors are lay persons, and in one—the *earliest* dated piece of Gandhāran sculpture—the donor is a monk.[15] It is worth noting that even if in all three of the new inscriptions in which the donor's status is unclear the donor is assumed to be a lay person, this would still mean that almost 60 percent of the inscribed images from Gandhāra now known were given by monks, and this figure, again, is certainly way out of proportion in terms of the percentage of monks in the total population. It is also worth noting that both of the earliest actually dated Gandhāran images were the gifts of monks.

Because images are much more frequently inscribed and much more frequently and precisely dated at Mathurā, Mathurān images are probably our most important single source of information on the cult of images, especially in its early phase. Here too, the monastic element disproportionately predominates. Of the twenty-six inscriptions published in Lüders' collection that record the gift of an image and preserve the donors' names, seventeen—or almost two-thirds—record the gifts of monks or nuns.[16] When we add the ten more recently published inscriptions in which the donors are clear[17] and the six inscriptions on early images found elsewhere (Kauśāmbī, Sārnāth, or Śrāvastī) but known to have come from Mathurā,[18] we arrive at a total of forty-two. Of these forty-two images, seventeen were donated by lay persons, but twenty-five by monks or nuns: here again, almost two-thirds. But because many of the Mathurān images are more precisely dated, we can make an even more precise chronological analysis of them.

Since the four image inscriptions assigned by Lüders to the Kṣatrapa period (*MI* nos. 1, 72, 80, 86) are not actually dated, our analysis will be limited to dated Kuṣān inscriptions on images of Mathurān origin in which the status of the donor is clear. (See Table 1. I include the two Kharoṣṭhī inscriptions dated in an early Kuṣān year, marked with an asterisk.)[19]

The first feature that strikes the eye is the proportionately high number of monastic donors: two-thirds of the donors of images in dated Kuṣān inscriptions were monks or nuns. But for the hazards of time, this number would have been higher. Only two of the Kuṣān image inscriptions recording the gift of lay persons lacked a year date and were therefore excluded from the analysis. But four of the inscriptions recording monastic gifts lacked such a date and had to be excluded. The second striking feature of our table is the clustering of monastic donors *at the very beginning of the period.*

Apart from one exception, every image set up in the first dozen years of the period was set up by a monk or a nun. The exception—number v in our table—is itself very doubtful. Lüders says "owing to the deplorable state of the inscription, the reading of the date is not absolutely reliable." Sahni reads it as year 30, and Lüders in a note says "it may have been 4 or 40."[20] There is a distinct possibility that it belongs much further down in our table. However this may be, we need go no further in our analysis to conclude that, on the basis of the actual evidence, the cult of images in the Kuṣān period—the earliest period we can actually reach—was almost entirely, and very probably exclusively, a monastically initiated and supported cult.

But these inscriptions can tell us even more about the individuals involved

Table 1. Status of Donors in Kuṣān Period: Inscriptions from Mathurā

	Kuṣān Year	*Type of Donor*	*Location*	*Source*
i	2	monastic	Kauśāmbī	*EI* 24, 210ff
ii	3	monastic	Sārnāth	*EI* 8, 173ff
iii	3[a]	monastic	Śrāvastī	*EI* 8, 181
iv	4	monastic	Mathurā	*EI* 34, 9ff
v	4 or 40?	lay	Mathurā	*MI* No. 172
vi	5*	monastic	Peshawar(?)	*BEFEO* 61, 54
vii	6	monastic	Kauśāmbī	*Central Asia in the Kushan Period.* Vol. II, 15
viii	8	monastic	Mathurā	*MI* No. 154
ix	14	lay	Mathurā	*MI* No. 81
x	16	monastic	Mathurā	*MI* No. 157
xi	17	lay	Mathurā	*MI* No. 150
xii	23	lay	Mathurā	*MI* No. 136
xiii	26	lay	Mathurā	*JIABS* 10.2, 101
xiv	31	monastic	Mathurā	*MI* No. 103
xv	32	monastic	Ahicchatra	*JASB* 21, 67
xvi	33	monastic	Mathurā	*MI* No. 24
xvii	39	monastic	Mathurā	*MI* No. 126
xviii	45	lay	Mathurā	*MI* No. 180
xix	46	lay	Mathurā	*JAIH* 13, 277ff
xx	51	monastic	Mathurā	*MI* No. 29
xxi	89*	monastic	Mamāne Ḍheri	*KI* LXXXVIII

[a]The year has not actually been preserved in this inscription, but since the same donor set up images in the years 2 and 6, the year 3 is a reasonable approximation; cf. the following discussion.

in this monastic innovation. If we set aside the doubtful lay inscription of the year 4 or 40, then we can see that the donors of five of the first Buddhist cult images known in India (i, ii, iii, vi, vii) had at least one more quality in common in addition to the fact that they were all monastics: these donors are all called *trepiṭakas*, those "who know the Three *Piṭakas*," those who knew the whole of Buddhist sacred literature as it existed at the time. This would suggest that they were not average monks, but high ecclesiastics of wide religious knowledge.

It would also mean—as we shall see in greater detail in a moment—that the earliest dated cult images set up at a minimum of three major Buddhist sites in the Ganges Basin—at Sārnāth, Śrāvastī, and Kauśāmbī—and in Gandhāra (i, ii, iii, vi, vii), were set up by learned monastics, by individuals who "knew the Three *Piṭakas.*" It is also interesting to note that one of the two inscribed images introduced at Kānheri was the gift of a pupil of yet another *trepiṭaka,*[21] and that the donor of the other image dated in the year 4 at Mathurā (iv) was a companion monk to another monk who is called a "preacher of Dharma," a *dha{r}mma-{kathi}ka.* The connection between the beginnings of the image cult and learned monastics is everywhere, so to speak, carved in stone.

Yet other things about the donors of these early images emerge from their accompanying inscriptions. The latter indicate that at least five of these images were set up by a group of monastics who knew one another—perhaps intimately. They also allow us a rare insight into the life and multifarious relationships of one learned monk at the beginning of the Kuṣān period.

The learned monk, the *Bhikṣu* Bala "who knew the Three *Piṭakas,*" himself "caused to be set up" (*pratiṣṭhāpito*) an image in the third year of Kaniṣka at Sārnāth. This is a huge image, ten-feet high and three-feet wide. Both the stone it is made of and its style indicate that it came from Mathurā, which—as the crow flies—is 300 miles away. He "caused it to be set up" at Sārnāth "at the place where the Lord [i.e., the Buddha] used to walk" (*bhagavato caṃkame*); that is to say, on the "promenade, terrace, place for walking" at Sārnāth that local tradition apparently maintained the Buddha had actually used. He also provided this huge image with a large stone umbrella.[22] Some time before or after—the exact year is unsure—this same learned monk "caused to be set up" another image at Śrāvastī. This image is also huge—eleven-feet, eight-inches high—and it too was made in Mathurā, which—again, as the crow flies—is more than 200 miles away. At Śrāvastī also Bala caused this monumental image to be set up "at the place where the Lord used to walk." Here as well he provided the image with a stone umbrella.[23]

As Vogel has already said, all the evidence points to the fact that these were the first images set up at Śrāvastī and Sārnāth, two of the most important Buddhist sacred sites in India. It is, therefore, of considerable significance that the person responsible was at both places the same learned monk, and all of the evidence indicates that he alone was responsible, in spite of the fact that the cost of having the images made and having them transported must have been very great. There is no question about this in regard to the Śrāvastī image: although he attached two separate inscriptions to his gift—one on the base of the image and one on the umbrella shaft—Bala himself is the only donor mentioned. The inscription on the base reads:

> *{mahārājasya devaputrasya kaniṣkasya saṃ . . . di} 10 9 etaye purvaye bhikṣusya puṣya{vu}-*
> *{ddhis}ya saddhy{e}vihārisya bhikṣusya balasya trepiṭakasya dānaṃ b{o}dhisatvo chātraṃ dāṇḍaś ca śāvastiye bhagavato caṃkame*
> *kosaṃbakuṭiye acaryyāṇāṃ sarvastivādinaṃ parigahe*
>
> (*EI* 8 [1905–1906] 181)
>
> [In the year [3] of the Great King, the Devaputra Kaniṣka, in the . . . the month of . . ., on the] 19th [day], on this date the gift of the Monk Bala, who knows the Three *Piṭakas* and is a companion of the Monk Puṣyavuddhi, [i.e.,] a *Bodhisattva,* an umbrella, and its shaft [were set up] in Śrāvastī, on the Blessed One's Promenade, in the Kosaṃbakuṭi, for the possession of the Sarvāstivādin Teachers.

Here, although Bala identifies himself in part by reference to a fellow monk—Puṣyavuddhi—that fellow monk is not associated with his gift. The gift is said to be Bala's alone. Note that what was almost certainly the first cult image set up at Śrāvastī—one of the most important of Buddhist sites—was not only given *by* a learned monk, it was also given *to* a group of learned monks, "the Sarvāstivādin Teachers."

The inscription on the umbrella shaft belonging to the Śrāvastī image, although very fragmentary at the beginning, almost certainly is worded exactly the same as the inscription on the base. No more. In this, the inscriptions on the Sārnāth image differ.

There are three separate inscriptions associated with the Sārnāth image: one on the umbrella shaft, which is the longest, one on the front of the image pedestal, and one on the back of the image between the feet. The last of these reads:

> *mahārajasya kaṇiṣ{kasya} saṃ 3 he 3 di 2{2}*
> *etaye purvaye bhikṣusya balasya trepiṭa{kasaya}*
> *bodhisatvo chatrayaṣṭi ca {pratiṣṭhāpito}*
>
> (*EI* 8 [1905–1906] 179)
>
> The year 3 of the Great King Kaniṣka, the 3rd month of winter, the 22nd day. On this date, by the Monk Bala who knows the Three *Piṭakas*, a *Bodhisattva*, an umbrella, and its shaft were caused to be set up.

Here, Bala is the only donor mentioned. He alone is said to be responsible for setting up "the *Bodhisattva,* an umbrella, and its shaft." But the inscription on the front of the pedestal says that the *Bodhisattva* at least—the umbrella and shaft are not mentioned—was "caused to be set up" by Bala *mahākṣatrapena kharapallānena sahā kṣatrapena vanaṣparena,* which on the face of it means: "together with the Great Satrap Kharapallāna and the Satrap Vanaṣpara." The inscription on the shaft is even fuller. It records that the *Bodhisattva,* umbrella, and shaft were set up by the Monk Bala, who is here identified as "the companion of the Monk Puṣyavuddhi"—thus identifying the Bala of the Śrāvastī image with the Bala named here at Sārnāth. But it goes on to say that this was done "together with his mother and father, together with his preceptors and teachers, his companions and pupils, together with Buddhamitrā who knows the Three *Piṭakas,* together with the Satrap Vanaṣpara and Kharapallāna, and together with the Four Assemblies, for the welfare and happiness of all beings."

The situation appears somewhat contradictory here. The inscription on the back of the image says that Bala alone set up the image, umbrella, and shaft. The other two inscriptions say that the same act was done—following the usual interpretation of *saha*—"together with" a number of named individuals. The seeming contradiction turns on the interpretation of *saha:* if it is taken literally, the inscriptions recording the same event are saying different things; if it does not literally mean "together with," they are not. There are internal indications that seem to indicate that *saha* was not intended to be understood in its literal sense.

The last group mentioned in the shaft inscription according to the way Vogel has printed it, is "the Four Assemblies"; that is, "all monks, nuns, laymen, and laywomen." The universalistic character of this group is even clearer if we read *sahā ca sarvāhi pariṣāhi,* "and together with all assemblies," instead of *sahā ca(tu)hi pariṣāhi,* "together with the Four Assemblies." Vogel admits he hesitated between the two readings.[24] In fact, both are possible. But the important point here is that, in either case, it is very difficult to believe that the inscription intended to say that the image at Sārnāth was "caused to be set up" by Bala "together with"—*literally*—"all monks, nuns, laymen, and laywomen." In fact, several individuals and subgroups who would fall into the larger categories such as "monks" have already been specifically mentioned. It seems much more likely that the *saha* construction is used here—and perhaps everywhere in Buddhist donative inscriptions—as a means by which the donor can share the merit of his act by explicitly associating others with it. He shares or "transfers" the *act* rather than, as is frequent elsewhere, the *merit* resulting from it. The end result in either case is the same.[25]

Whether Bala's gift was literally made "together with" the groups or individuals named, or whether—as appears to be more likely the case—he chose to associate these groups or individuals with his meritorious act, it would seem obvious that he had a special relationship with them, especially with those he specifically names. The Satraps Vanaṣpara and Kharapallāna were clearly important local political figures, and it appears likely that the Monk Bala, like the Monk Buddhabhadra later at Ajaṇṭā, was "the friend of kings." Like Buddhabhadra again, he must also have been a man "of considerable wealth."[26] But the one other specifically named individual he associates with his act has no counterpart in Buddhabhadra's inscription. Bala specifically names, in addition to the Satraps, only Buddhamitrā: a woman—she is called here neither a nun nor a pupil—who "knows the Three *Piṭakas.*" This is of particular importance, both for what it reveals about Bala's preoccupations and for the fact that it establishes that he knew and apparently had a special relationship with a woman named Buddhamitrā who—like himself and apparently on the same footing—"knew the Three *Piṭakas*" or the whole of Buddhist canonical literature as it existed at the time. This, in turn, is important because it suggests that he probably knew the woman who, on at least two occasions—the year 2 and the year 6 of Kaniṣka—"caused to be set up" the first cult images at Kauśāmbī, yet another major Buddhist sacred site.

The earliest dated cult image set up at Kauśāmbī was, like Bala's images at Sārnāth and Śrāvastī, a very large standing image very probably made at Mathurā, which was more than 200 miles away. It, again like both Bala's images, was set up "on the promenade of the Blessed One, the Buddha" (*bhagavato buddhasa ca{ṃ}kame*). These facts alone would suggest that the installation of these three images—the first of their kind at these important sites—was the result of a patterned and coordinated effort: all three originated from the same place, and all three were set up on a "promenade" associated with the Buddha. This suggestion is further strengthened by the fact that the Kauśāmbī image was set up by a woman named Buddhamitrā who, according to the inscription, "knew the Three *Piṭakas.*" This Buddhamitrā, called here "a nun" (*bhikhuṇī*), can hardly be anyone else than the Buddhamitrā "who knows the Three *Piṭakas*" that Bala mentions in his inscription from Sārnāth. This same Buddhamitrā set up at least three separate images "on the promenade of the Blessed One" at Kauśāmbī: the first in the year 2, another in the year 6, and a third in an unknown year.[27]

The nature of the relationship between Bala and Buddhamitrā is curiously unstated. Buddhamitrā is the only specifically named individual—apart from the Satraps—whom Bala associates with his gift. But he does not say that she was a nun, nor does he indicate that she was his pupil. Buddhamitrā, although specifically mentioned by Bala, does not mention him at all in any of her three inscriptions. She indicates that she was a nun but gives no indication of whom her teacher was. This is of some significance, since it was a common practice already for monks or nuns to identify themselves by reference to the monastic who was their teacher. The association of Bala and Buddhamitrā with one another, as well as their association with Mathurā, is, however, both confirmed and given specificity by the donative inscription of yet another nun who seems to have carried on their joint project. This inscription records the fact that, in the year 33, a nun named Dhanavatī "caused to be set up" at Mathurā an image. Dhanavatī describes herself both as a nun and as "the sister's daughter of the nun Buddhamitrā, who knows the *Tripiṭaka,* the female pupil of the monk Bala, who knows the *Tripiṭaka*" (*bhīkṣusya balasya {t}repiṭakasya antevā{si}n{ī}y{e} {bhi}kṣuṇīye tre{pi-*

ṭi)(kā)ye buddha(mi)trāy(e) bhāgineyīye, MI no. 24). Thirty years after Buddhamitrā set up her first image at Kauśāmbī, her maternal niece set up an image at Mathurā. The niece identified herself exclusively in terms of her relationship to Buddhamitrā, and identified Buddhamitrā in turn as a "pupil" of Bala. That neither of the latter made reference to Buddhamitrā's "pupilhood" is curious, but it is clear that their names were still linked by the generation that followed them.

If the connection between learned monastics and the beginnings of the image cult is everywhere apparent, it is even more specifically so in the Bala-Buddhamitrā inscriptions. We seem to see here something like an intentional, organized, even coordinated distribution of early images from a central point. The earliest cult images at three of the most important Buddhist sites in the Ganges Basin—Kauśāmbī, Śrāvastī, and Sārnāth—almost certainly came from Mathurā, where scholarly opinion is more and more inclined to locate the production of the first Buddha images.[28] The production, transportation, and installation of all these images—again, the first at these sites—was effected by at least two monastics who knew one another in one or more capacities. And both of these individuals were, in their contemporary idiom, very learned. All of the evidence suggests that these learned monastics were, in Basham's words, "propagandists for a new cult,"[29] and that this propaganda was effected in a systematic fashion. This can only mean that the only "autorités spirituelles" whom we have actual knowledge of, far from "taking no position," were the sponsors and initiators of one of the most radical and far-reaching innovations in Indian Buddhist cult practice. That some of these "autorités spirituelles" were women brings us to the last aspect of the question that we can deal with here.

If, because of an almost exclusive reliance on textual sources, our picture of the actual Indian Buddhist monk is more than a little skewed, the picture of the Indian Buddhist nun—for the same reason—has been almost obliterated. Oldenberg, for example, says:

> In number they [Buddhist nuns] were apparently far behind monks, and therefore it is to be doubted also, whether at any time there was inherent in the spiritual sisterhood a degree of influence which could be felt, bearing on the Buddhist community as a whole. The thoughts and forms of life of Buddhism had been thought out and moulded solely by men and for men.[30]

That this is off-the-mark on several counts can be surmised on the basis of what we have seen already of the nun Buddhamitrā: her activities at Kauśāmbī would almost certainly have had profound "influence" there "on the Buddhist community as a whole." It was she who introduced at Kauśāmbī the cult image. In fact, nuns, and laywomen as well, seem to have been very actively involved in the development of the "new cult." This will be easily apparent if we rewrite our table containing the data for the image cult connected with Mathurā in such a way as to show gender differences. (See Table 2.)

If we set aside the two Kharoṣṭhī inscriptions, we can note that, of the nineteen individuals associated with Mathurā who "caused images to be set up" in the Kuṣān period, six were monks, two were laymen, six were nuns, and five were laywomen. Nuns here, rather than being "far behind monks," had parity with them both in terms of numbers and in terms of learned titles. This parity was not new. It occurred before in the earlier inscriptions recording donations connected with the *stūpa*/relic cult at Sāñcī: there were at Sāñcī one hundred twenty-nine monk donors, and one hundred twenty-five nuns. At least four inscriptions from Sāñcī record the gift of a nun named Avisinā who is called one "who is versed in the *Sūtras*,"[31] and at least three nun donors at Sāñcī had "pupils" (*antevāsin*).[32] The figures for other early sites show a similar pattern: at Pauni there were three monk donors and five nuns;[33] at Bhārhut, sixteen nuns and twenty-five monks;[34] at Amarāvatī, twelve monk donors and twelve nun donors.[35] The one striking exception from the early period comes from our Kharoṣṭhī inscriptions: in Konow's collection there are sixteen monk donors but not a single nun. There are, as well, no nuns in the more recently published Kharoṣṭhī inscriptions. The reasons for this are not yet clear. It may well have to do with the fact that the geographic area from which our Kharoṣṭhī inscriptions came is precisely that area which has always been most open to foreign influence and occupation, and this influence and occupation may have determined a differ-

Table 2. Gender Differences of Donors in Kuṣān Period Inscriptions from Mathurā

	Kuṣān Year	*Donor*		*Kuṣān Year*	*Donor*
i	2	nun	xii	23	laywoman
ii	3	monk	xiii	26	layman
iii	(3)	monk	xiv	31	nun
iv	4	monk	xv	32	monk
v	4 or 40?	laywoman	xvi	33	nun
vi	5*	monk	xvii	39	nun
vii	6	nun	xviii	45	laywoman
viii	8	nun	xix	46	layman
ix	14	laywoman	xx	51	monk
x	16	monk	xxi	89*	monk
xi	17	laywoman			

ent attitude toward the participation of women in monastic lives.[36] But however this might eventually be explained, it is clear already that, in addition to geographical factors affecting the degree of participation of nuns in recorded Buddhist activities, there is a marked chronological component as well.

From the very earliest period up to and through the Kuṣān period, nuns were everywhere—apart from the Kharoṣṭhī area and Nāgārjunikoṇḍa—present as active donors in numbers similar to those of monks. When we move from the Kuṣān to the Gupta period (the fourth to fifth centuries C.E.), this pattern changes radically. Among the donors of images associated with Mathurā in the Kuṣān age, for example, there were, as we have seen, six monks and six nuns. But in the Gupta inscriptions from Mathurā, while there are six monk donors, there is only a single nun.[37] This marked drop in the number of nun donors at Mathurā occurred in conjunction with at least one other change that can be detected there: a new kind of monk appeared at Mathurā in the fourth to fifth centuries. Five of the six Gupta monk donors appear to have belonged to the same group. They all refer to themselves as *śākyabhikṣus*—a title unknown in previous periods.[38] That the presence of these monks is related to the decline or disappearance of nun donors is suggested as well at other sites, perhaps most dramatically at Ajaṇṭā and Sārnāth. At Ajaṇṭā there were thirty-three monastic donors of images, all of the fifth century, and every one of them was a monk. There was not a single nun. Of these thirty-three monks, at least twenty-five specifically referred to themselves as *śākyabhikṣus*.[39] The same pattern is found in the Gupta inscriptions from Sārnāth: there were thirteen monk donors of images but only a single nun. Here too eleven of the thirteen monk donors referred to themselves as *śākyabhikṣus*.[40]

Although the full details have yet to be worked out, it appears that the appearance or presence of monks calling themselves *śākyabhikṣus* everywhere in the fourth to fifth centuries C.E. occurred in conjunction with the marked decline or disappearance of the participation of nuns in recorded Buddhist religious activity. The fact that these *śākyabhikṣus* were almost certainly Mahāyāna monks may seem curious, but it appears that the emergence of the Mahāyāna in the fourth to fifth centuries coincided with a marked decline in the role of women of all kinds in the practice of Indian Buddhism.[41] What is important for us to note here, however, is that until that time—contrary to Oldenberg—nuns, indeed women as a whole, appear to have been very numerous, very active, and, as a consequence, very influential in the actual Buddhist communities of early India. The female monastics who, like their male counterparts, were so active in religious giving and the cults of relics and images were, again like their male counterparts, oftentimes of high ecclesiastical standing: they were "masters of the Three *Piṭakas*," "versed in the *Sūtras*," and many of them had groups of disciples.

Before we formulate any general conclusions regarding the material we have seen so far, at least one point should be clearly emphasized. In dealing with the earliest phase of the image cult—primarily but not exclusively at Mathurā—I have intentionally restricted myself to inscribed, dated images in which the status of the donor is clear. The reasons for this are very simple: there are no images that can be proved to be earlier, and there are no earlier data on the donors of images. Whether these are *absolutely* the earliest images cannot, in fact, be known. But even if there were earlier images, they could not have been many, and, almost all would agree, they could not have been much earlier. It is, therefore, extremely unlikely that their inclusion would alter the pattern of patronage we have uncovered. In a rough sort of way this can actually be demonstrated. Although none of them are actually dated, Lüders assigns four image inscriptions to the Kṣatrapa period. In two of these, the status of the donor is unclear (nos. 72, 86); in one, the donor is a laywoman (no. 1); in the other, the donor is a monk (no. 80). (A fifth inscription, no. 155, cannot definitely be connected with an image.)

These same considerations apply with even greater force to true cult images. While there may have been earlier representations of the Buddha in human form in narrative or even decorative contexts, what evidence we have argues against any long-standing *Buddhist* tradition of monumental cult images in a medium other than stone.[42] Unquestionably, early monumental Buddhist cult images in stone—like those of Bala and Buddhamitrā at Sārnāth, Śrāvastī, and Kauśāmbī—presuppose not a previously established, Buddhist cult-image tradition, but an image tradition of a different kind:

> All these early images [in stone] from Mathurā and the surrounding area are closely related with the local *yakṣa* figures and with images of Kuṣāna emperors. They belong to the same world, where the concepts of overlordship, of fame and of fortune (*bhāga*) predominate . . . It has been pointed out that the standing Buddha image is really a replica of the earlier standing *yakṣa* or royal image, but lacking the regalia and insignia of royalty.[43]

Surely if there had been a prior tradition of any standing of Buddhist cult images in wood or clay, the stone images that we have would not still be borrowing so heavily from non-Buddhist models. The fact that our earliest extant monumental cult images in stone represent a tradition still groping for its own types and iconography, still working with non-Buddhist models, virtually precludes any long-standing development of *Buddhist* cult images in clay or wood. The monumental cult images we have in stone from Sārnāth, Śrāvastī, and elsewhere are probably the earliest that there were.

Although this is but a preliminary study of Buddhist donative inscriptions associated with images, still a number of points are already clear. We have seen that the first cult images at several major Buddhist sacred sites—Sārnāth, Śrāvastī, Kauśāmbī, Mathurā—in the early Kuṣān period were set up by learned nuns and monks. We have seen that the earliest dated images in the Northwest were the gifts of learned monks, that it was monks who introduced images of the Buddha into the monastic cave complexes at Kānheri, Kuda, and—massively—at Ajaṇṭā in the fourth to fifth centuries C.E., and that it was monks who donated new images in the fifth-century revitalization at Sārnāth. Although images were introduced at different times at different sites, they were almost always introduced by the same group everywhere: either monks or nuns. It would appear that the image and its attendant cult were major preoccupations of nuns and monks; that they everywhere introduced the cult and everywhere disproportionately supported it.[44] These were not the monks and nuns our textual sources have presented to us; but those monks and nuns, it is coming to be clear, were not in any case the real Indian monastics.

A picture of the actual Indian Buddhist monk and nun is gradually emerging; he and she differ markedly from the ideal monk and nun who have been presented on the basis of textual material alone. The actual monk, for example, unlike the textual monk, appears to have been deeply involved in religious giving and cult practice of every kind from the very beginning. He is preoccupied not with *Nirvāṇa* but, above all else, with what appears to have been a strongly felt obligation to his parents, whether living or dead. He is concerned as well, for example, with the health of his companions and teachers. He appears, in short, as very human and very vulnerable.[45] We do not yet understand him well by any means, but the work of Brown, with which we started the present essay, may not only provide us with an alternative model for change and innovation, it may also give us a clue concerning where we might begin to look in trying to understand this actual monk.

Speaking again about the cult of the saints in Latin Christianity, Brown says "it is not surprising, perhaps, that the cult of the patron saint spread most quickly in ascetic circles." In fact, although he has been criticized for using the term, he refers to "the remarkable generation of Christian leaders" from these circles as the *impresarios* of the cult: "for the *impresarios* of the new cult are precisely those who had taken on themselves the crushing weight of holiness demanded by the ascetic way of life."[46] As Brown himself notes, this suggests that change and innovation "come from a very different direction from that posited by the 'two-tiered' model" and that "the evidence of the pressure from 'mass conversions' "—compare Lamotte's "les succès croissants de la propagande" cited above—"has been exaggerated. Nor is there any evidence that the *locus* of superstitious practice lay among the 'vulgar'. Indeed, it is the other way round . . ."[47] Our donative inscriptions would suggest an Indian situation in the first centuries of the Common Era that was remarkably parallel in essentials: changes in cult practice came from, and were supported by, learned "ascetic circles." But the possible parallel may go further and may provide a partial explanation for the Indian case.

Brown again says: "For the *impresarios* of the cult of saints were studiously anxious men. Sulpicius and Paulinus shared the strong link . . . of having very recently and at no small cost of suffering and scandal, abandoned their previous social identities," and it was they who sought "the face of a fellow human being where an earlier generation had wished to see the shimmering presence of a bodiless power . . ."[48] Again there appear to be clear parallels in the Indian situation. The renunciation of the household life—especially for high-class brahmins—would have entailed the wrenching loss of their "social identity." To judge by the textual sources, it was a move fraught with difficulty and generated strong familial reactions.[49] To judge by the inscriptional sources, it created a disproportionately strong sense of anxiety in regard to their "abandoned" parents on the part of individual monks and nuns. These concerns, again, would have pressed particularly hard on monks from brahmin families, and it is precisely this group that apparently made up the majority of the Buddhist elite.[50] Although much else remains to be understood, it appears that it was this same group that introduced and promoted the cult of images, that sought "the face of a fellow human being where an earlier generation had wished to see the shimmering presence of a bodiless power."

Notes

1. P. Brown, *The Cult of the Saints. Its Rise and Function in Latin Christianity* (Chicago: 1981) 16–18.

2. *Histoire du bouddhisme indien,* 686–687.

3. *Histoire du bouddhisme indien,* 705.

4. A. K. Coomaraswamy, "The Origin of the Buddha Image," *The Art Bulletin* 9 (1927) 297; the quotation from Jacobi is from his *Gaina Sutras,* Sacred Books of the East, XXII (Oxford: 1884) xxi.

5. E.g., J. C. Huntington, "The Origin of the Buddha Image: Early Image Traditions and the Concept of Buddhadarśanapunyā," in A. K. Narain, *Studies in Buddhist Art of South Asia* (New Delhi: 1985) 27, 28, 35, etc.; S. L. Huntington, with contributions from J. C. Huntington, *The Art of Ancient India. Buddhist, Hindu, Jain* (New York and Tokyo: 1985) 124.

6. D. R. Sahni, *Catalogue of the Museum of Archaeology at Sārnāth* (Calcutta: 1914) B(a)1, B(b)59*, B(b)60*, B(b)172*, B(b)175*, B(b)179*, B(b)293*, B(b)294*, B(b)295*, B(b)300*; H. Hargreaves, "Excavations at Sārnāth," *ARASI* 1914–15 (Calcutta: 1920) nos. XIV, XV, XVI*, XVII*, XVIII (123–127). Hargreaves' nos. XV, XVI, XVII have been reedited in J. M. Rosenfield, "On the Dated Carvings of Sārnāth," *ArA* 26 (1962) 11ff. Asterisks indicate *śākyabhikṣus*, cf. nn. 40 and 41.

7. Sahni, *Catalogue*, B(b)299[?], B(d)1; Hargreaves, *ARASI 1914–15,* no. XIX.

8. Certain: Sahni, *Catalogue,* B(d)13, B(d)20, B(e)1, B(e)10, B(f)15; possible: B(d)42; certain in Hargreaves, *ARASI 1914–15,* no. XXV; possible: nos. XXI, XXII—same donor in both.

9. Lay: G. Yazdani, *Ajanta,* Part II: Text (Oxford: 1933) no. 11 (64); *Ajanta,* Part III: Text (Oxford: 1946) no. IX.2 (89); M. K. Dhavalikar, "New Inscriptions from Ajaṇṭā," *ArO* 7 (1968) no. 3. Monastic: Yazdani, *Ajanta,* II: no. 9*; Yazdani, *Ajanta,* III: VI*, IX. 1*, .3*, .4*, .5*, .6*, .7*, .11*, .12; X.2, .3*, .7*, .8*, .9, .10*, .11*, .12*, .13*, .15*, .16*, .18, .19, .21; XVI.1*, .2*, .3*; *Ajanta,* Part IV: Text (Oxford: 1955) XXII*, XXVI.2*, .4*; Dhavalikar, "Inscriptions," nos. 4*, 5; D. C. Sircar, "Inscription in Cave IV at Ajanta," *EI* 33 (1960) 262 (uncertain).

10. J. Burgess, *Report on the Elura Cave Temples and the Brahmanical and Jaina Caves in Western India* (London: 1883) nos. 6, 7 (77).

11. M. Leese, "The Early Buddhist Icons in Kaṇheri's Cave 3," *ArA* 41 (1979) 83–93.

12. J. Burgess, *Report on the Buddhist Cave Temples and Their Inscriptions,* Archaeological Survey of Western India, Vol. IV (London: 1883). Lay: no. 7; monastic: nos. 8, 9, 10.

13. S. Konow, *Kharoshṭhī Inscriptions with the Exception of Those of Aśoka,* Corpus Inscriptionum Indicarum, Vol. II, Pt. 1 (Calcutta: 1929) nos. XXXVI.1, .2, .4, .5, .6, .7, .8; XL, XLII, XLIII, XLIV, LVIII, LXXXVIII. It should be noted that all but two of these inscriptions (nos. LVIII, LXXXVIII) come from only two sites. Nos. XL, XLII, XLIII, and XLIV are from Loriyān Tangai. The *stūpa* there has been assigned to "perhaps the second century A.D.," and the characters of the inscriptions are said to be "evidently late" (Konow, 106). Nos. XXXVI.1, .2, .4, .5, .6, .7, .8, all come from Jauliāñ, and the situation there is complicated. The images with which the inscriptions are associated, and the inscriptions themselves, have been assigned by Marshall to the second half of the fifth century C.E., but they are a part of the redecoration of much older *stūpas.* Konow, however, is inclined to think, on the basis of the oddly mixed paleography of the inscriptions, that "some of the inscriptions are copies of older ones, executed when the old images and decorations were restored or repaired" (92–93).

14. S. Konow, "Kharoṣṭhī Inscription on a Begram Bas-relief," *EI* 22 (1933–1934) 11–14; J. Brough, "Amitābha and Avalokiteśvara in an Inscribed Gandhāran Sculpture," *Indologica Taurinensia* 10 (1982) 65–70; A. K. Narain, "A Note on Two Inscribed Sculptures in the Elvehjem Art Center of the University of Wisconsin, Madison," *Indian Epigraphy. Its Bearing on the History of Art,* ed. F. M. Asher and G. S. Gai (New Delhi: 1985) 73–74.

15. Lay: G. Fussman, "Documents épigraphiques kouchans (II)," *BEFEO* 67 (1980) 54–55, 56–58; H. W. Bailey, "Two Kharoṣṭhī Inscriptions," *JRAS* (1982) 149; G. Fussman, "Deux dédicaces kharoṣṭhī," *BEFEO* 74 (1985) 34; G. Fussman, "Un buddha inscrit des débuts de notre ère," *BEFEO* 74 (1985) 43–45. Monk: Fussman, *BEFEO* 61 (1974) 54–58. This last inscription is dated in the year 5 "d'une ère qui ne peut être que l'ère de Kaniṣka" (Fussman). The assignment of the year has not been universally accepted (e.g., S. J. Czuma, *Kushan Sculpture: Images from Early India* [Cleveland and Bloomington: 1985] 198–199; K. Khandalavala, "The Five Dated Gandhāra School Sculptures and Their Stylistic Implications," *Indian Epigraphy. Its Bearing on the History of Art,* 68–69), although the arguments against it are not convincing.

16. H. Lüders, *Mathurā Inscriptions,* ed. K. L. Janert, Abhandlungen der Akademie der Wissenschaften in Göttingen, Philo.-Hist. Kl., Dritte Folge, Nr. 47 (Göttingen: 1961) nos. 4, 8, 24, 29, 41, 67, 80, 90, 103, 121, 126, 152, 154, 157, 179, 185, 186.

17. R. C. Sharma, *Buddhist Art of Mathurā* (Delhi: 1984) lay: 181, n. 41; 191, n. 63; 226, n. 153; 226, n. 154; 228, n. 159; monk: 223, n. 148; lay: P. R. Srinivasan, "Two Brahmi

Inscriptions from Mathura," *EI* 39 (1971) 10–12; B. N. Mukherjee, "A Mathura Inscription of the Year 26 and of the Period of Huviṣka," *JAIH* 11 (1977–1978) 82–84 (= R. C. Sharma, "New Buddhist Sculptures from Mathura," *Lalit Kalā* 19 [1979] 25–26; Sharma, *Buddhist Art of Mathurā*, 232, n. 169; G. Schopen, "The Inscription on the Kuṣān Image of Amitābha and the Character of the Early Mahāyāna in India," *JIABS* 10.2 [1987] 99–134); B. D. Chattopadhyaya, "On a Bi-scriptual Epigraph of the Kuṣaṇa Period from Mathura," *JAIH* 13 [1980–1982] 277–284 (cf. B. N. Mukherjee, "A Note on a Bi-scriptual Epigraph of the Kuṣaṇa Period from Mathurā," *JAIH* 13 [1980–1982] 285–286); monk: D. C. Sircar, "Brahmi Inscriptions from Mathurā," *EI* 34 (1961–1962) 9–13.

18. Ahicchatrā: D. Mitra, "Three Kushan Sculptures from Ahichchhatrā," *Journal of the Asiatic Society*, Letters, 21 (1955) 67; Sārnāth: J. Ph. Vogel, "Epigraphical Discoveries at Sarnath," *EI* 8 (1905–1906) 173–179; Śrāvastī: T. Bloch, "Two Inscriptions on Buddhist Images," *EI* 8 (1905–1906) 180–181, and his "Inscription on the Umbrella Staff of the Buddhist Image from Sahet Mahet," *EI* 9 (1907–1908) 290–291; Kauśāmbī: K. G. Goswami, "Kosam Inscription of the Reign of Kanishka, the Year 2," *EI* 24 (1938) 210–212 (cf. A. Ghosh, "Kosam Inscription of Kanishka," *IHQ* 10 [1934] 575–576; Ghosh reads the date "the 22nd (?) year of Mahārāja Kaniṣka"); G. Sharma and J. Negi, "The Saka-Kushans in the Central Ganga Valley (Mainly a Review of the New Data from Kausambi)," *Central Asia in the Kushan* Period, Vol. II, ed. B. G. Gafuron et al. (Moscow: 1975) 15ff. In all of these inscriptions, the donors are monastics.

19. Several images fairly certainly of Mathurān origin and having low-numbered year dates have been excluded because of the uncertainty concerning the date or the identity of the king referred to in them. This is the case, for example, with the two inscriptions—assigned to the Kuṣān period—on images found at Sāñcī but thought to have come from Mathurā; cf. J. Marshall, A. Foucher, and N. G. Majumdar, *The Monuments of Sāñchī*, Vol. I (Delhi: 1940) 385–387, nos. 828 and 830; J. M. Rosenfield, *The Dynastic Arts of the Kushans* (Berkeley: 1967) 112; A. L. Basham, *Papers on the Date of Kaniṣka, Submitted to the Conference on the Date of Kaniṣka, London, 20–22 April, 1960* (Leiden: 1968) 108ff, 267ff, 283, 290–291. This is also the case with the image from Bodh-Gayā dated in the year 64; cf. B. M. Barua, "A Bodh-Gayā Image Inscription," *IHQ* 9 (1933) 417–419, etc.

20. Lüders, *Mathurā Inscriptions*, 200 and n. 6.

21. Burgess, *Report on the Elura Cave Temples*, no. 6 (77).

22. Vogel, *EI* 8 (1905–1906) 173ff.

23. Cf. note to Table 1 and Bloch, *EI* 8 (1905–1906) 180–81, *EI* 9 (1907–1908) 290–291.

24. Vogel, *EI* 8 (1905–1906) 176, s.v. L9.

25. Cf. G. Schopen, "Two Problems in the History of Indian Buddhism," Ch. II above, 36ff.

26. W. Spink, "Ajanta: A Brief History," *Aspects of Indian Art. Papers Presented in a Symposium at the Los Angeles County Museum of Art, October 1970*, ed. P. Pal (Leiden: 1972) 51; Yazdani, *Ajanta*, IV, 114–118.

27. See the sources cited for Kauśāmbī in n. 18 above.

28. On the wide distribution of Mathurān images, see J. E. van Lohuizen-de Leeuw, "Gandhāra and Mathurā: Their Cultural Relationship," *Aspects of Indian Art*, 39 and notes; J. E. van Lohuizen-de Leeuw, "New Evidence with Regard to the Origin of the Buddha Image," *South Asian Archaeology 1979*, ed. H. Härtel (Berlin: 1981) 393–394.

29. A. L. Basham, "The Evolution of the Concept of the Bodhisattva," *The Bodhisattva in Buddhism*, ed. L. S. Kawamura (Waterloo: 1981) 30.

30. H. Oldenberg, *Buddha: His Life, His Doctrine, His Order,* trans. W. Hoey (London: 1882) 381; or *Buddha, sein Leben, seine Lehre, seine Gemeinde* (Berlin: 1881) 389–390.

31. Marshall et al., *Sāñchī,* Vol. I, nos. 304, 305, 540, 680.

32. Marshall et al., *Sāñchī,* Vol. I, nos. 118, 645, 804.

33. S. B. Deo and J. P. Joshi, *Pauni Excavation (1969–70)* (Nagpur: 1972). Monks: nos. 5, 7, 8; nuns: nos. 9, 12, 13, 14, 21.

34. H. Lüders, *Bharhut Inscriptions,* Corpus Inscriptionum Indicarum, Vol. II, Pt. 2, ed. E. Waldschmidt and M. A. Mahendale (Ootacamund: 1963) 2 and nn. 1 and 2.

35. C. Sivaramamurti, *Amaravati Sculptures in the Madras Government Museum* (Madras: 1977). Monks: nos. 5, 10, 11, 19, 30, 33, 34, 38, 63, 99, 112, 113; nuns: 31, 62, 68, 69, 70, 74, 80, 83, 93, 96, 99, 100. A number of these inscriptions record joint donations.

36. The inscriptions from Ikṣvaku Nāgārjunikoṇḍa would be another exception, but they are atypical in several other ways as well; cf. G. Schopen, "Filial Piety and the Monk in the Practice of Indian Buddhism," Ch. III above, 63–64.

37. Monks: Lüders, *Mathurā Inscriptions,* nos. 67, 152, 179, 185, 186; Sharma, *Buddhist Art of Mathurā,* 223, n. 148; nuns: Lüders, *Mathurā Inscriptions,* no. 8.

38. The exception is Sharma, *Buddhist Art of Mathurā,* 223, n. 148. On the *śākyabhikṣus* and the emergence of the Mahāyāna in the fourth to fifth centuries C.E., see M. Shizutani, "On the Śākyabhikṣu as Found in Indian Buddhistic Inscriptions," *IBK* 2 (1952) 104–105 (in Japanese); and his "Mahāyāna Inscriptions in the Gupta Period," *IBK* 19 (1962) 355–358; H. Sarkar, *Studies in Early Buddhist Architecture of India* (Delhi: 1966) 106–107; G. Schopen, "Mahāyāna in Indian Inscriptions," *IIJ* 21 (1979) 1–19; Schopen, "The Inscription on the Kuṣān Image of Amitābha and the Character of the Early Mahāyāna in India," *JIABS* 10.2 (1987) 99–137.

39. All those marked with an asterisk in n. 9 above.

40. All those marked with an asterisk in n. 6 above; the single nun is in Hargreaves, *ARASI 1914–15,* no. XIV.

41. The possible connection between the emergence of the Mahāyāna and the decline and disappearance of the nun has not been made before, but it—like the fourth to fifth century emergence of the Mahāyāna itself—requires much fuller study. I am now working on a larger project involving both. In general, the nun in Buddhist epigraphy has received little attention; see B. C. Law, "Bhikshunis in Indian Inscriptions," *EI* 25 (1940) 31–34; A. S. Altekar, "Society in the Deccan during 200 B.C.–A.D. 500," *JIH* 30 (1952) 63ff; A. M. Shastri, *An Outline of Early Buddhism (A Historical Survey of Buddhology, Buddhist Schools and Sanghas Mainly Based on the Study of Pre-Gupta Inscriptions)* (Varanasi: 1965) 141–144; S. Nagaraju, *Buddhist Architecture of Western India (c. 240 B.C.–c. A.D. 300)* (Delhi: 1981) 32.

42. Cf. Huntington in *Studies in Buddhist Art of South Asia,* 23–58, where conjecture, especially but not exclusively in regard to texts, is very much in evidence.

43. D. L. Snellgrove, *The Image of the Buddha* (Paris and Tokyo: 1978) 53–54.

44. It is equally clear that the sectarian affiliation of these monks and nuns has little, if any, bearing on their association with the image cult. While the monks promoting the cult in the fourth to fifth centuries at Ajaṇṭā, Sārnāth, and Mathurā were predominately Mahāyāna monks, those involved in the same cult at Śrāvastī, Kauśāmbī, Mathurā, etc., in the Kuṣān period almost certainly were not. The widespread assumption that connects the image cult with the Mahāyāna is simply not well founded; cf. Schopen, "Mahāyāna in Indian Inscriptions," 16, n. 7; D. Snellgrove, *Indo-Tibetan Buddhism. Indian Buddhists and Their Tibetan Successors,* Vol. I (Boston: 1987) 49.

45. Cf. Schopen, "Filial Piety and the Monk in the Practice of Indian Buddhism," now Ch. III above, and "Two Problems in the History of Indian Buddhism," now Ch. II above, 30ff. In the first of these earlier pieces especially I have not always distinguished clearly between monk and nun donors and have used the term "monk" when I should have used the term "monastic." The degree of concern for their parents on the part of nuns as a separate category is therefore not clearly discernible there.

46. Brown, *The Cult of the Saints,* 30, 57, 67; for the criticism, see J. Fontaine, "Le culte des saints et ses implications sociologiques. Réflexions sur un récent essai de Peter Brown," *Analecta Bollandiana* 100 (1982) 17–41, esp. 23ff.

47. Brown, *The Cult of the Saints,* 32.

48. Brown, *The Cult of the Saints,* 63–64, 51.

49. A. Bareau, "Les réactions des families dont un membre devient moine selon le canon bouddhique pali," *Malalasekera Commemoration Volume,* ed. O. H. de A. Wijesekera (Colombo: 1976) 15–22.

50. B. C. Gokhale, "The Early Buddhist Elite," *JIH* 43 (1965) 391–402.

CHAPTER XII

The Buddha as an Owner of Property and Permanent Resident in Medieval Indian Monasteries

PROBABLY ALL WOULD AGREE that understanding the way in which the person of the Buddha was understood is central to any attempt to characterize the Indian groups that came to coalesce around that person. In fact, understanding how that person was understood or perceived has, it appears, oftentimes determined how a great many other matters were understood. The old Anglo-German school of Pāli scholarship, for example, saw the Buddha as a kind of sweetly reasonable Victorian Gentleman. Such a view dominated not only the scholarly world, but as Almond has recently shown,[1] the popular press of the day. It is, therefore, hardly surprising that the "religion" attributed to him was understood as an orderly system of sweetly reasonable, rational Victorian ethics, a system that—significantly—was seen to carry an implicit "native" criticism of the actual, observable religions of nineteenth century India, and to point up their "decline."[2]

This view, like virtually every other one that followed it, was built up almost exclusively from a particular, if not peculiar, selected reading of literary sources. The later views, the views of the so-called Franco-Belgian school, in this regard at least differed not at all. They treated later sources, to be sure, but still literary sources only. They took seriously the works of the later Vasubandhu, of Asaṅga and Haribhadra—works of the early medieval and medieval periods. They determined, for example, that "the extreme Mahāyāna reduced the Buddha to two elements: . . . indescribable reality and the suprarational intuition of this reality"; that the Buddha was understood to have not one, but two, three, or—eventually—four bodies, each thought of in ever-increasing abstract terms; that, finally, the real Buddha was thought to be "the Dharmakāya which has no flesh or blood or bones."[3] In light of this understanding of the Buddha, the Buddhism of this period was understood as a collection of loosely connected, increasingly convo-

---

Originally published in *Journal of Indian Philosophy* 18 (1990):181–217. Reprinted with stylistic changes with permission of Kluwer Academic Publishers.

luted systems of abstract theory. This understanding still confronts the neophyte when he or she approaches the standard textbooks dealing with Mahāyāna Buddhism.

It is at least curious that this particular Buddhology, based as it is almost exclusively on a narrowly limited corpus of highly specialized literature, has persisted in virtually all of the work done by modern scholars on the medieval period. It is curious because, already sixty years ago, de La Vallée Poussin—a man whose knowledge of Buddhist scholastic literature has probably not yet been equaled—unequivocally declared it to be incomplete and merely partial. At the end of his long discussion "sur les corps du Bouddha," itself largely taken up with the beginnings of the increasingly abstract conceptions of the early medieval period, de La Vallée Poussin said: "La description des théories abstraites n'est qu'une partie, non négligeable, de l'histoire de la bouddhologie."[4] Buddhist Studies has been slow to realize the implications of this, and many other, observations scattered throughout the still-astounding body of work left by this Belgian scholar.

Because of this slowness, the "abstract theories" have by default been left to stand as the sole representatives of medieval Buddhist conceptions of the Buddha, and this, in turn, has left an almost permanent distortion of the doctrinal record, a distortion that would require the availability of other sources to remove. But such sources—at least some of them—have been available for a very long time, and de La Vallée Poussin, at the head of the same discussion already referred to, had already pointed us in a promising direction: "la vénération des corps," he said, "occupe une place notable dans l'épigraphie."[5] De La Vallée Poussin was referring here primarily to the various "hymns" (*stava*) found, not commonly it now appears, in Buddhist inscriptions. But he was, at least, still pointing to an important source, a source which we too might do well to consider, although with a broader and less self-consciously literary selection.[6]

There are considerable numbers of Buddhist donative records and land grants that have survived from the medieval period.[7] We might look at a sample of these—and it is *only* a sample—paying particular attention to their language, to what they say about both the Buddha's location and about where he was thought to be and to what they say about his role in the transactions being recorded.

Earlier inscriptions already contain some hints of what is to come, but they are somewhat ambiguous or can, at least, be understood in more than one way. An inscribed first century slab from Kauśāmbī that has the Buddha's footprints carved on it says, for example: "(this) slab was caused to be made . . . in the residence of the Buddha, in the Ghoṣitārāma" (. . . *budhāvāse ghoṣitārāme . . . śilā kā(ritā)*).[8] Given the traditions that assert that the Buddha had actually lived on occasion at Kauśāmbī, the "residence of the Buddha" referred to here may not refer to a *current* residence, but to a structure or room where the Buddha was thought to have *formerly* resided.[9]

Similarly, the inscription on a faceted stone pillar from Mithouri that "may be assigned to the 2nd Century A.D." may also be interpreted in more than one way. It says the donor "caused an umbrella to be set up for the Blessed One, the Pitāmaha, the Fully and Completely Awakened One, in the Saptaparṇṇa Monastery" (. . . *saptaparṇṇa-vihāre bhagavat-pitāmahasya samyaksaṃbuddhasya . . . cha{traṃ pra}tiṣṭhāpayati).*[10] Although, in the end, the differences in possible meaning may be small, the inscription can be understood to be saying either that the umbrella was set up for the Buddha who was himself in the monastery, or it may be saying that the umbrella itself was set up in the monastery *for* the Buddha without specifying where the latter actually was. But even this second interpretation would suggest, at least, that things intended "for," or at least "belonging to," the Buddha were "set up" in this monastery.

If, however, the language of these and a small number of other early inscriptions remains ambiguous and not altogether explicit, the same cannot be said of a large number of inscriptions and land grants that belong to the medieval period. Starting from the fourth to fifth centuries, the language of inscriptions becomes ever increasingly unambiguous and straightforward in regard to the Buddha's location, his proprietorship, and his permanent residency in local monasteries. The fifth century inscriptional record of the foundation of Cave XVI at Ajaṇṭā, for example, explicitly refers to this cave as the "excellent dwelling to be occupied by the Best of Ascetics"; that is, the Buddha (*udāraṃ . . . veśma yatī{ndra-sevyam}*),[11] but this cave is not a "shrine" or *caityagṛha.* It is a *vihāra* containing seventeen residential cells, only one of which—the central cell in the back wall—seems to have been intended for the Buddha.[12] Moreover, in spite of the fact that this cave—Cave XVI—was intended to provide residential quarters for monks, while the closely contemporaneous Cave XXVI was a *caitya-gṛha,* both are referred to by the same term: *veśman,* "dwelling."[13]

If the Ajaṇṭā text locates the Buddha in monastic living quarters, a fifth or sixth century inscription from Cave VI at Kuda provides us with an early instance of his being the recipient of real property. It says:

> This is the gift of the Śākyabhikṣu Saṃghadeva. And having here attached the Cheṃdina field it is given to the Buddha as capital for lamps. Whoever would disrupt [this endowment] would incur the five great sins.
>
> *deyadharmmoyaṃ śākyabhikṣoḥ saṃghadevasya atra ca cheṃdinakhetra{ṃ} badhvā dīpamūlya-buddhasya dattaṃ {//} yo lopaye{t} pa{ṃ}ca-mahāpātakaba{saṃ}yukto bhave{t}.*[14]

While the full technical sense of *badhvā* is not entirely clear, I have translated it as "having attached," intending by that some of the legal sense of the English phrase. It is, however, clear from the imprecation that we are dealing with an ongoing endowment. It is equally clear that the field was given directly to the Buddha, and that the profit realized from it was to be applied to his service.

Equally interesting—although from a somewhat different angle—are two fifth- or sixth-century copperplate land grants, one from Bāgh in Madhya Pradesh, the other from Gunaighar in Bengal. The first of these records the gift of a village that was "to be used" to provide perfumes, incense, and flowers, and the like "*for* the Blessed One, the Buddha," *and* to provide the requisites for the monks, both of whom—the language of the record makes clear—were thought to reside "in the monastery called Kalāyana . . . caused to be constructed by Dattaṭaka" (*dattaṭaka-kārita-kalāyana-vihāre. . . bhagavato buddhāya gandhadhūpa-mālyabalisatropayojyaḥ . . . āryya-bhikṣu-saṅghasya cāturddiśābhyāgatakasya cīvara-piṇḍapāta-glāna-pratyaya-śeyyāsana-bhaiṣajya-hetor . . .*)[15] This "monastery" is almost certainly Cave II, the cave in which the plate was found. It, like Cave XVI at Ajaṇṭā, was a residential *vihāra* having twenty-one cells, the central cell in the back wall being reserved for the Buddha.[16]

Although, geographically speaking, it was written a long way from Bāgh, the Gunaighar grant is quite similar. It records the gift of five clearly delimited parcels of land:

> for the perpetual employment, three times a day, of perfumes, flowers, lamps, incense, etc., for the Blessed One, the Buddha, (who is) in the monastery in the Aśrama of Avalokiteśvara, which is the property of the community of irreversible Mahāyāna monks received through just this Teacher [Śāntideva], and for the provision of robes, bowls, beds, seats, medicines, etc., for the community of monks (in the monastery).
>
> *-āryyāvalokiteśvarāśrama-vihāre anenaivācāryyeṇa pratipādita-* [read: *-te*] *māhāyānika-vaivarttika-* [read: *-āvaivarttika-*] *-bhikṣu-saṃghanām* [read: *ānām*] *parigrahe bhagavato buddhasya satataṃ triṣkālaṃ gandha-puṣpa-dīpa-dhūpādi-pra{varttanāya} {ta}sya bhikṣusaṃghasya ca cīvara-piṇḍapāta-śayanāsana-glāna-pratyayabhaiṣajyādi-paribhogāya.*[17]

As in the land grant from Bāgh, the grammatical structure of the Gunaighar grant would seem to indicate that the locative phrase situates *both* the Blessed One, the Buddha, *and* the community of monks in the same establishment, and the donors' intention seems to have been to provide for both. These two land grants have—as their very name implies—something else in common. Like most of the remaining inscriptions that will be cited here, these are not religious texts or panegyrics. Both the Bāgh and Gunaighar grants are legal documents authorizing and recording the transfer of property. Their language, therefore, in regard to this transfer, is not likely to have been casual but must have been chosen to articulate specifically perceived and legally acknowledged realities.

Much the same sort of evidence as is found at Bāgh and Gunaighar occurs also in the rich collection of Buddhist land grants from Valabhī in Gujarat, even when—and that not infrequently—the vocabulary used is somewhat different. We find, for example, in a grant of Dharasena II dated to 575 C.E. that two villages were given, in part:

> for the sake of furthering the activity—through flowers, incense, perfumes, lamps, oils, etc.—of/for the Blessed Ones, the Buddhas, in the monastery of the worthy Śrī Bappa which the Ācārya-Bhadanta-Sthiramati had caused to be built.
>
> *ācāryya-bhadanta-sthiramati-kārita-śrī-bappa-pādīya-vihāre bhagavatāṃ buddhānāṃ puṣpa-dhūpa-gandha-dīpa-tailādi-kriyotsarppaṇārthaṃ.*[18]

Elsewhere in the Valabhī grants the same expression is applied to monks in a given monastery, the only difference being that their activity is "furthered" through robes, bowls, and the other monastic requisites: *-vihāre nānādigabhyāgatāṣṭādaśa-nikāyābhyantarāryya-bhikṣu-saṅghāya grāsācchādana-śayanāsana-glāna-bhaiṣajyādi-kriyotsarppaṇārthaṃ.*[19]

When taken together, statements of this sort would seem to suggest that the Valabhī grants were intended to provide for the needs of two groups, both of which appear to have been thought of as residing in the local monasteries: Buddhas and monks. Although their specific needs might differ, it appears to have been thought that both groups must be provided for, and both were conceptually considered residents of a single kind of establishment. This, of course, must strike us as odd because we think of the members of the two groups as conceptually and completely different, and we are not in the habit of thinking that the Buddha—let alone several Buddhas—actually lived in any seventh century monastery in Valabhī or anywhere else for that matter. But the wording of these grants, and all of the records we have seen and will see further on, suggests that their drafters thought otherwise. Modern scholars have seen in these and similar passages references to what we call "images." But although this may be correct from at least our own culturally limited frame of reference, and although the concrete referent in these passages may, in fact, have been an object of stone that we would call an "image," the drafters of these grants and all the inscriptions we will deal with here never use a word that could—however unsuitably—be translated as "image." They talk about "*persons*," not objects; and these "*persons*"—like the monks who are also to be provided for—always live in monasteries.[20]

But if medieval records consistently locate these "*persons*" in monasteries, some of them specify even more precisely that location. Yet another Valabhī grant of Dhruvasena I appears to provide us one such instance:

> *{ā}cāryya-bhadanta-buddhadāsa-kārita-vihāra-kuṭyāṃ pratiṣṭāpita-bhagavatāṃ ssamya{ksaṃbu}-{ddhānāṃ buddh}-ānām gandha-dhūpa-puṣpa-dīpa-tailopayogi . . . catur-ddiś-ābhyāgatobhaya-vihāra-prativāsi-bhikṣu-saṅghasya {pi}ṇḍapāta-śayanāsana-glāna-pratyaya-bhaiṣajya-pariṣkāropayogārtthaṃ ca pra{tip}āditaḥ {//*}.*[21]
>
> Given for the acquisition of perfumes, incense, flowers, lamps, oils, etc., for the Blessed Ones, the Fully and Completely Awakened Buddhas established in the chamber in the monastery built by the Ācarya-Bhadanta-Buddhadāsa . . . and for the acquisition of the requisites—bowls, beds, seats, and medicines—for the community of monks dwelling in the monastery from the four directions.[22]

There are at least two points worth noting here. First, the Buddhas are specifically said to be "established" not just in the monastery, but "in the chamber (*kuṭī*) in the monastery." The specificity intended here, however, seems oddly incomplete: although the text as it now stands seems to want to indicate a precise location, it uses a generic term without further qualification, and which "chamber" was intended does not now appear to be indicated. This oddity, taken together with both epigraphical and textual parallels, would seem to suggest that we have here a scribal error and that the intended reading was almost certainly *gandha-kutyāṃ*. In the only other occurrences of the term *kuṭī* in the Valabhī grants, for example, the term always occurs in compound with a preceding *gandha-*: a grant of Śīlāditya III reads *gandha-kuṭī* [read: *-kutyāṃ?*] *ca bhagavatāṃ buddhānāṃ pūjā-snapana-gandha-dhūpa-puṣpādi-paricaryyārthaṃ*, "for serving the Blessed Ones, the Buddhas, and (or, in) the Perfume Chamber with worship, baths, perfumes, incense, flowers, etc.";[23] in a recently published plate of Dharasena IV, the grant is said to be in part *gandhakutyāś ca khaṇḍa-sphuṭita-pratisaṃskaraṇāya*, "for repairing the cracks and breaks in the Perfume Chamber. . . ."[24] Not only do these passages support the emendation suggested above for the grant of Dhruvasena I but they indicate that the *gandhakuṭī* was an established and important element of the monasteries at Valabhī. Moreover, we have—as we shall see—a significant amount of evidence that indicates that this was the case as well in a considerable number of medieval Buddhist monasteries elsewhere in India,[25] and we know that "the Perfume Chamber' " was supposed to be the central cell in a Buddhist monastery reserved as the residence of the Buddha himself.

The second point to be noted is that our passage says that the Buddhas were "established" (*pratiṣṭ{h}āpita-*) in the monastery, but the monks were "dwelling" (*prativāsi-*) in it. This verbal difference may be thought to be significant, and perhaps it is. However, it is important to remember that the first meaning of *prati* $\sqrt{}$*sthā* is "to stand, stay, abide, dwell," and that the causative—which we have here—has marked tones of "permanence," "fixity," and "continued existence over time." *Prati* $\sqrt{}$*3. vas*, on the other hand, need imply none of this and is not infrequently used in the sense of "to lodge, receive as a guest." The Buddhas, then, may have been considered the only permanent residents of a monastery.

It is also worth noting, as shown in these passages, the Valabhī grants frequently refer to Buddhas in the plural. This may be because there actually were several, or we may have here—as Sircar, for example, has suggested we have elsewhere—"the plural number signifying *gaurava* (venerableness)," the *pluralis majestaticus.*[26] Although the use of the plural predominates, the fact that the use of the singular in virtually the same context and construction is not rare may well argue for the plurals being plurals of respect. In any case, references to a plurality of Buddhas are not infrequently found in Indian inscriptions from very early on.[27]

The language of the Valabhī grants provides us, then, with important information on monastic conceptions of the Buddha in medieval Gujarat, but this, of course, is not the only area for which we have records from this period. A roughly contemporaneous record from Nālandā, for example, provides us with a particularly striking instance of the language of personal presence in a form that we have not yet seen. The record in question, the Stone Inscription of Yasovarmmadeva, has been variously dated to the sixth or eighth century.[28] It is written in an elaborate *kāvya* style and as a consequence is not always easy to interpret. It would appear that its primary purpose was to record a series of benefactions made by the son of a royal minister. Among these is a "permanent endowment" specifically said to be "for the Blessed One, the Buddha" (*akṣaya-nīvikā bhagavate vuddhāya*); the same donor provided the monks with food and gave to "the sons of the *Śākya*" a *layana,* a "residence" or "house." The most interesting statement, however, occurs as a part of the concluding imprecation and constitutes a clear warning:

> Whoever would create an obstacle to this gift which is to last as long as the created world (he should know that) the Conqueror in person, the Blessed One, dwells always here within on the Diamond Throne.
>
> *yo dānasyāsya kaścit kṛtajagadavadher antarāyaṃ vidadhyāt sākṣād vajrāsanastho jina iha bhagavān antarasthaḥ sadāste* /[29]

The language is very strong here, and the sense of personal presence (*sākṣād, iha*) and permanent abiding (*sadāste*) is pronounced. Although the style of our record sometimes makes it difficult to understand, this much is certain. It is equally certain that the permanent endowment was given directly to the Buddha himself, and reasonably certain that the place wherein the Blessed One is said to "always" dwell was the *layana* or "residence" that had been given to the monks.[30]

Yet other forms of expression involving both the sense of legal recognition and personal presence are found in other grants. In the Toramāṇa Inscription from the Salt Range in the Punjab, for example, which Sircar dates to the sixth century, the statement that seems to have been intended as a description of the primary act being recorded reads:

> This religious gift, the establishment of a monastery for the Community of Monks from the Four Directions which is headed by the Buddha.
>
> *buddha-pramukha* [read: *-khe*] *cāturdiśe bhikṣusaṃghe deyadharmo (')ya(ṃ) vihāra-pratiṣṭhāpana.*[31]

Fortunately, we have a fairly good idea of how such an expression would have been understood from both literary sources and contemporary or near-contemporary epigraphical records.

Strikingly similar expressions occur throughout both Pāli and Sanskrit canonical literature in passages that, of course, narrate events that are supposed to have occurred while the Buddha was very much alive and a living presence. Some of these passages are so commonplace as to be clichés. In a typical passage describing the feeding of the Buddha and his disciples, for example, that group is described as *buddhapramukhaṃ bhikṣusaṃghaṃ* or *buddhapamukhaṃ bhikkhusaṃghaṃ,* "the community of monks headed by the Buddha."[32] T.W. Rhys Davids translates one such passage in the *Mahāparinibbāna-sutta* by: "And the Exalted One robed himself early, took his bowl with him, and repaired, with the brethren [*saddhiṃ bhikkhusaṃghena*], to the dwelling-place of Sunīdha and Vassakāra . . . and with their own hands they set the sweet rice and the cakes before the brethren with the Buddha at their head [*buddhapamukhaṃ bhikkhusaṃghaṃ*].[33] Equally interesting is another passage from the same text. Ambapāli's gift of the "mango grove" is there expressed in the following form: *imāhaṃ bhante ārāmaṃ buddhapamukhassa bhikkhusaṃghassa dammīti. paṭiggahesi bhagavā ārāmaṃ;* "Reverend," Ambapāli says, "I give this grove to the community of monks with the Buddha at their head. The Blessed One accepted the grove."[34] That the monastic recipients of gifts of food and real property should be described in this way in texts narrating events set during the lifetime of the Buddha is not surprising. Such a description says nothing more than that the actual community that received these gifts was headed by the still-living Buddha, and that it was he—explicitly at least in the case of Ambapāli's grove—who accepted or took possession of them. But if that is what *buddhapamukhassa bhikkhusaṃghassa* means in other Buddhist texts, it is hard to see how *buddha-pramukhe cāturdiśe bhikṣusaṃghe* could mean anything essentially different in the Toramāṇa Inscription, an inscription that shows clear signs of having been authored by someone familiar with even the most technical textual definitions of the Buddha.[35] It is hard to argue that the conception changed if the expression remained constant, regardless of how much time intervened.

Much the same point is reached if we look at epigraphical usage. At the end of an inscription from Nāgārjunikoṇḍa that makes provision for the maintenance, etc., of a *devakula* or temple, the body charged with the ultimate responsibility for seeing that the work was done is called the *seṭhi-pamakha* [= Skt. *śreṣṭhi-pramukha*] *-nigamo,* "the council of citizens headed by the banker."[36] Similarly, in a sixth-century land grant from Andhra Pradesh, the order transferring the land is addressed to the *rāṣṭrakūṭa-grāma-vṛddha-pramukha-viṣaya-(ni)vāsinaḥ,* "to the inhabitants of the district headed by the elders of the village and district officer"[37]

The Nāgārjunikoṇḍa inscription and the Andhra land grant are, of course, describing corporate or legal entities with a particular structure. But the fact that a Buddhist monastic community could be described in the same way in a document like the Toramāṇa Inscription dealing in part with the transfer of property would seem to suggest that it, too, was considered to be organizationally similar. This, in turn, would mean that if "the council of citizens" were legally or corporately recognized as headed "by the banker," the sixth-century Buddhist monastic community in the Salt Range must have been thought of as legally or corporately headed "by the Buddha." Moreover, in the same way the council and particularly its head, were charged with the responsibility for making sure the provisions of the gift were fulfilled, the monastery whose erection was recorded in the inscription of Toramāṇa must have been intended for *both* the monastic community and, particularly, its corporate head. Finally—and perhaps most significantly—these epigraphical parallels appear to indicate that the designation *-pramukha* was never applied "symbolically," but always referred to actual individuals holding certain responsible positions.

This corporate or legal language continued to be used for a very long time, and when it was not used, it was not infrequently replaced with an even more interesting turn of phrase. It was used, for example, in a twelfth century inscription from Śrāvastī recording the grant of six villages together with "all water and dry land, mines of iron and salt, repositories (i.e., ponds) of fish, etc.," within their boundaries. These six villages are said to be granted to:

> *śrīmaj-jetavana-mahāvihāra-vāstavya-buddha-bhaṭṭāraka-pramukha-parama-ārya-(ś)ākyabhikṣu-saṃghāya* . . .[38]
>
> The Community of Excellent Venerable Śākya-Monks which is headed by the Lord Buddha who resides in the Great Monastery in the Illustrious Jetavana.

or:

> The Community of Excellent Venerable Śākya-Monks headed by the Lord Buddha which resides in the Great Monastery in the Illustrious Jetavana.

However this long compound is nuanced, it seems fairly certain that ownership of the villages in question was being transferred to the monastic community as a corporate group, that, in terms of the transfer, the Buddha was considered to be the legal head of the group, and that both the Buddha and the monastic community were thought to reside in the same monastery. This last point, at least, again draws support from the living arrangements reflected in the ground plan of the monastery in question. Monastery 19 is described as having "an open courtyard in the centre surrounded by rows of [residential] cells on all sides . . . The central chamber in the row facing the entrance forms the shrine and is situated directly opposite the main entrance-gate, so that the statue that it enshrined was the first object coming to the view of the visitor . . ."[39]

This same sense of personal presence and of ownership by the Buddha however, is by no means restricted to passages in which he is designated as *-pramukha* of the community. We have already seen one instance—the Yasovarmmadeva Inscription—in which this vocabulary does not occur. An early ninth-century copperplate grant of Devapāla from Nālandā is yet another. In this grant we find the gift of five villages being made, in part, to provide the resident Buddha with an income:

> *suva(rṇṇa)dvīpādhipama(hā)rājaśrībālaputradevena dūtakamukhena vayam vijñāpitāḥ yathā mayā śrīnālandāyām vihāraḥ kāritas tatra bhagavato buddhabhaṭṭārakasya prajñāpāramitādisakaladharmmanetrīsthānasyāyārthe . . . pratipādit(ā)ḥ*[40]

> We, being requested to by the Mahārāja, the Illustrious Bālaputradeva, the king of Suvarṇṇadvīpa, through an ambassador, (declare): 'As I have had constructed a monastery in Illustrious Nālandā [the previously mentioned villages] . . . are granted for the sake of providing an income to the Blessed One (residing) there, the Worshipful Buddha, the Storehouse of All Methods of Dharma, the Perfection of Wisdom, etc.'

As in the Yasovarmmadeva Inscription, the sense of presence is clear: the Buddha in question is "*there*" (*tatra*) in the monastery. As in the Yasovarmmadeva Inscription where a permanent endowment is given directly to the resident Buddha, here too the Buddha himself is provided with an "income" (*āya*) in his own right and not as the head of the *Saṅgha.* The implication here is that some of these villages are transferred directly to the Buddha himself, that he himself owns them. This again is very clear in yet other copperplate grants.

In the so-called Larger Leiden Plates, for example, the wording is straightforward. These plates—which date to the eleventh century—record the gift of a village *atiramaṇīyañ cūḷāmaṇivarmma-vihāram adhivasate buddhāya,* "to the Buddha residing in the surpassingly beautiful Cūḷāmaṇivarma Monastery" in Nāgapaṭṭinam.[41] Here again, there is no reference to the Buddha as the head of the monastic community, and the village is given to him directly as an individual; he and he alone became the "owner" by the terms of the grant. Here too, the explicit wording of the grant leaves no room to doubt that the Buddha himself was thought to actually reside in the specifically named monastery. It is, moreover, worth noting that there was official, *external* recognition of the Buddha's legal ownership of land, even in non-Buddhist records that record gifts similar to those recorded in both the Nālandā Grant of Devapāla and the Larger Leiden Plates. A Chandella copperplate grant of the twelfth century, for example, records the donation of a village to a number of brāhmaṇas. But it explicitly excludes from the grant five *halas* of land within the village that already belonged to the Buddha: *deva-śrī-bauddha-satka-pañcahalāni bahiḥkṛtya.*[42]

The last examples we might look at refer—like some of the Valabhī grants—to the *Gandhakuṭī*, "the Perfume Chamber." Sircar, for example, has noted that originally the term *Gandhakuṭī* referred to "the room occupied by the Buddha at Śrāvastī, but later indicated the Buddha's private chamber in any Buddhist establishment,"[43] and Edgerton has noted literary uses that seem "to imply that any monastery might be provided with one."[44] The epigraphical sources confirm both.

The earliest inscriptional reference to the *Gandhakuṭī* occurs in a label from Bhārhut, and it is clear that here the term is applied to the original chamber at Śrāvastī.[45] But the epigraphical sources also indicate that from the fourth or fifth century on, the *Gandhakuṭī* was an established part of Buddhist monastic establishments everywhere. There is a third- or fourth- century reference to a *Gandhakuṭī* in the inscriptions from Ghaṇṭaśala;[46] a late-fourth-century reference in an inscription from Hyderabad to the *Gandhakuṭī* in the monastery named after Govindarāja, the founder of the Viṣṇukuṇḍi dynasty;[47] references in inscriptions from Ajaṇṭā,[48] Kānheri,[49] and Kauśāmbī[50]—all probably dating from around the fifth century; several references in inscriptions from Sārnāth dating from the fourth or fifth century to the eleventh,[51] and from Bodh-Gayā[52] covering much the same period; references from Valabhī (sixth or seventh century),[53] for Kurkihar (ninth to eleventh centuries),[54] and from Nālandā.[55] Both the geographical and the chronological range of these references establish that a large number of Buddhist monasteries had, in the medieval period, a private chamber reserved for the Buddha. In addition, some of these references make it very clear that these private chambers were formally recognized as distinct organizational components of their monasteries and had specifically titled monks or groups of monks attached to them.

The monk donor in the Hyderabad inscription, for example, is called a *gaṃdhakuṭī-vārika,* and we have a reasonably good idea of what this might have meant from a series of similarly constructed monastic titles, all of which have *-vārika* as the final element. Literary sources know, for instance, *bhājana-vārika,* "(monks) in charge of receptacles," *pānīya-vārika,* "(monks) in charge of beverages," *upadhi-vārika,* "(monks) in charge of physical properties," or a "beadle, or provost of a monastery," etc.[56] Titles ending in *-vārika,* would appear, then, to have been used to designate the monk or monks who were officially in charge of important administrative and material areas or aspects of a functioning monastery. To judge by his title, a *gandhakuṭī-vārika* must have been a similar official, a monk or the monk "in charge of the Perfume Chamber." The fact that such an office was formally instituted and acknowledged would argue for the importance this chamber had in the life of the community, and would seem to indicate that it was already a fully integrated institutional element of medieval Buddhist monasteries. The same conclusions would seem to follow from the fact that references to "monks in charge of the Perfume Chamber" are found not only in Andhra Pradesh, but also at such widely separated sites as Kānheri and Nālandā: in a fourth or fifth-century donative record from the former site, the monk donor is called a *mahā-gandhakuṭī-vārika,* "one who is in charge of the Great Perfume Chamber";[57] from the latter come a number of interesting sealings, two of which refer to two distinct groups of *gandhakuṭī-vārikas.* The first of these reads:

> *śrī-nālandāy(āṃ) śrī-bālāditya-gandhakuḍī-vārika-bhikṣū(ṇām)*[58]
>
> Of/for/belonging to the monks in charge of the Perfume Chamber of Śrī-Bālāditya at Śrī-Nālandā.

and the second:

> *śrī-nā-dharmapāladeva-gandha-kuṭī-vārika-bhikṣūṇā(ṃ)*[59]
>
> Of/for/belonging to the monks in charge of the Perfume Chamber of Dharmapāladeva at Śrī-Nālandā.

These sealings are, however, important not just because they help to establish the wide geographic spread of the *Gandhakuṭī* as a formally recognized component of Buddhist monastic establishments; they also indicate that in at least some cases it was not a single monk who was charged with the oversight of the Perfume Chamber but a group of monks. They confirm, as well, the fact that different individual monasteries at a single site each had its own *Gandhakuṭī* and suggest that, like the monasteries themselves, these *Gandhakuṭīs* could be individually named after their chief sponsors or donors. Finally, the mere existence of these sealings would suggest that within the monastery, the *Gandhakuṭī* functioned as a distinct and individual entity that either owned its own movable property or had its own official correspondence with other monasteries or concerns. In fact, the two primary uses of such sealings appear to have been either to mark ownership of the property to which they were attached, or to "vouch for the genuineness" of the letters or documents that were sent or circulated under their seal.[60]

But if the sealings from Nālandā indicate that the *Gandhakuṭī* as a corporate entity either owned its own property or had its own official correspondence, yet another type of sealing indicates that this was true as well for the individual who resided in it. Several specimens of such sealings have been found at Sārnāth—Marshall and Konow refer to "a number" of them in their report for the year 1907,[61] and Hargreaves recorded two more.[62] These sealings have all been dated to the sixth or seventh century, and the text on all of them is essentially the same:

> *śrī-saddharmmacakkre mūla-gandhakuṭyāṃ bhagavataḥ*

Although the meaning of this seems to be straightforward, the treatment of the text has been somewhat disingenuous. Vogel, for example, has translated it as:

> at the Saddharmacakra in the principal Gandhakuṭī of the Lord.[63]

But Vogel's translation—suggesting as it does that it is the *Gandhakuṭī* that is "of the Lord"—violates what little syntax the sealing provides and differs markedly from his translation of other similarly constructed texts on other sealings. A seal-die from Kasia, for example, which has a legend with virtually the same grammatical construction, reads *śrī-viṣṇudvīpavihāre bhikṣusaṅghasya.* Here, Vogel takes the final inflected form for what it most obviously is—an independent genitive—and translates the legend as "of the community of friars at the Convent of Holy Viṣṇudvīpa."[64] Bearing in mind that "an independent genitive is used . . . on seals and personal belongings to name the owner of the object,"[65] the sense of the Kasia legend is clear: the document or property to which the sealing was attached was "of," "from," or "belonged to" the monks in the Viṣṇudvīpa Monastery. In light of this Kasia legend, and others like it, the sense of the Sārnāth sealing must almost certainly be the same and must almost certainly be translated:

> of/belonging to the Blessed One in the original Perfume Chamber in the Śrī-Saddharmacakra (Monastery).

Understood in this way, these Sārnāth sealings—which date from the sixth or seventh century—would seem to indicate that it was not just the monks attached to the *Gandhakuṭī* who owned their own property or carried on their own distinct official business. The same apparently was true of "the Blessed One in the original Perfume Chamber." The language of the legend and what we know of the function of such sealings would seem to allow little room for other conclusions. Moreover, by using the designation "original," these sealings would seem to suggest that—as Marshall and Konow noted long ago—"there were also other *gandhakuṭīs* in Sārnāth,"[66] that at Sārnāth, as at Nālandā and probably at Kānheri,[67] there were several. But if nothing else, these sealings provide us with yet another kind of evidence indicating that the Buddha was thought to have been a current resident and an abiding presence in medieval Buddhist monasteries. The language of the sealings makes it clear that the Blessed One himself was thought to be *in* the Perfume Chamber. It was this location and it alone that was noted on these sealings, sealings whose mere existence would seem to indicate that the Blessed One resident in the Perfume Chamber had certain active functions that required an official documentation. In fact, these sealings of the Blessed One are like—perhaps more than anything else—those that contemporary living kings attached to their land grants and other official records.[68]

The apparent emphasis on the Blessed One's presence in the *Gandhakuṭī* is not, however, found at Sārnāth only on these sealings. It is expressed, as well, in at least one donative record from the site. The record occurs on an old rail-pillar that appears to have been recut and reused as a lampstand in the Gupta period. Although now fragmentary, its restoration is fairly sure. It reads:

> *deyadharmmo yam paramopā- / -sika-sulakṣmaṇāya mūla- / {gandhakuṭyāṃ bha}-gavato buddhasya / pradīpaḥ*[69]
>
> This is the religious gift of the excellent laywoman Sulakṣmaṇā: a lamp for the Blessed One, the Buddha, in the original Perfume Chamber.

When the laywoman Sulakṣmaṇā gave a lamp to the Buddha, apparently she did not think of him as gone or unlocatable but as present in and available at the Perfume Chamber, the cell or room reserved for him in the monastery. In this she perhaps differed from the authors of medieval Buddhist *śāstras;* or, at least, from the views they formally stated. But as we have seen, she differed very little from a large number of other donors, or from those fully literate and probably monkish scribes who throughout the medieval period likewise appear to have had no doubts about where the Buddha was.

Sulakṣmaṇā's record—in fact medieval epigraphic material as a whole—appears then to provide us with conceptions of the Buddha that otherwise have not been noted, conceptions that are embedded in and underlie a whole series of legal or quasi-legal documents connected in the main with the transfer of property, and conceptions that differ markedly from those that are articulated in formal Buddhist literary and doctrinal sources of much the same period. These epigraphical conceptions are, moreover, not limited to a specific region but are pan-Indian. They are expressed from the fifth century on in "documents" from Andhra Pradesh, Bihar, and Bengal, from Uttar Pradesh and Maharastra, and from Gujarat and the Punjab. These are conceptions that—without the usual exaggeration implied in the phrase—can be said to occur everywhere.

This epigraphical material is, however, sometimes fragmentary, sometimes elusive, and not infrequently difficult to interpret. Fortunately, we are not without some means to test our interpretation. If the interpretation of the epigraphical material presented above is correct—if the Buddha was actually thought to reside in monasteries—then we should find, for example, clear evidence in monastic architecture of accommodations being provided for him. Moreover, if the Buddha was considered to be an actual individual within the monastic community that owned or had a claim to certain property, we should expect to find at least some rulings or regulations within the monastic codes or *Vinayas* to confirm this. Happily, we find both, and in fact a bit more, but none of this can be treated in detail here. We can simply note, for example, that the *Mūlasarvāstivāda-vinaya*—the one *Vinaya* for which we have some evidence of use in medieval Indian monastic communities[70]—contains numerous passages that explicitly treat the Buddha as a juristic personality and describe the appropriate procedures for dealing with *buddhasantaka*, "that which belongs to the Buddha."

Typical of such passages is that in the *Adhikaraṇa-vastu* where pearls are given "one part for the Buddha, one part for the *Dharma,* and one part for the *Saṅgha*" (*ekaṃ buddhāya ekaṃ dharmāya ekaṃ saṃghāya*), and where the Buddha is made to specify how each part is to be used:

> *ato yo buddhasya bhāgas tena gandhakuṭyām pralepaṃ dadata; yo dharmasya sa dharmadharāṇām pudgalānāṃ; yaḥ saṃghasya taṃ samagraḥ saṃgho bhajayatu,*[71]
>
> what of this is the Buddha's share, with that you should plaster the Perfume Chamber; what belongs to the *Dharma,* that is for the persons preserving the *Dharma;* what belongs to the *Saṅgha,* the entire *Saṅgha* should share that!

Likewise, in a *Cīvara-vastu* passage dealing with the distribution of the estate of a wealthy layman who had intended to become a monk but who had died before he could do so, we find:

> *suvarṇaṃ ca hiraṇyaṃ cānyacca kṛtākṛtaṃ trayo bhāgāḥ kartavyāḥ; eko buddhasya, dvitīyo dharmasya, tṛtīyaḥ saṃghasya. yo buddhasya tena gandhakuṭyāṃ keśanakha-stūpeṣu ca khaṇḍachuṭṭaṃ pratisaṃskartavyam; yo dharmasya tena buddhavacanaṃ lekhayitavyaṃ siṃhāsane vā upayoktavyam; yaḥ saṃghasya sa bhikṣubhir bhājayitavyaḥ*[72]
>
> The coined and uncoined gold and other worked and unworked metal is to be divided into three shares—one for the Buddha, a second for the *Dharma,* a third for the *Saṅgha.* With that which belongs to the Buddha, the dilapidation and damage in the Perfume Chamber and on the hair and nail *stūpas* is to be repaired; with that which belongs to the *Dharma,* the word of the Buddha is to be copied, or it is to be used on the Lion Throne; that which belongs to the *Saṅgha* should be shared by the monks.

Elsewhere in the *Cīvara-vastu* a similar threefold division is to be effected, and it is said *buddhasantakena buddhapūjā vā gandhakuṭyāṃ stūpe vā navakarma kartavyam,*[73] "with that belonging to the Buddha, worship of the Buddha is to be performed, or new work in the Perfume Chamber or on the *stūpa* is to be undertaken." Yet another passage from the *Cīvara-vastu* refers to two distinct categories of real wealth that belong to the Buddha and indicates that both could be drawn on to finance *pūjās* of the Buddha undertaken for sick or dying monks. The monastic community could use—among other things—"that belonging to the perpetual endowment for the Buddha" (*buddhākṣayanīvisantakaṃ*), or they could "sell" (*vikrīya*) an "umbrella or flag or banner or jewel on the *tathāgata-caitya* or in the Perfume Chamber" (*tathāgata-caitye vā gandhakuṭyāṃ vā chatraṃ vā dhvajaṃ vā patākā vā ābharaṇakaṃ vā*); in either case, the funds obtained were then to be used to attend to the sick or dying monk and to perform a *pūjā* of the Teacher on his behalf (*upasthānaṃ kartavyaṃ śāstuś ca pūjā*). Should the latter recover, he is to be told "that belonging to the Buddha was used for you" (*yad buddhasantakaṃ tavopayuktam iti*), and he should make every effort to repay it (*tena yatnam āsthāya dātavyam*).[74] There is, finally, at least one passage in the *Vinaya-kṣudraka-vastu* where the otherwise fairly consistent, anachronizing language of these passages appears to break down, and the "share" apparently belonging to the Buddha appears to be specifically assigned to an "image." Here, in the account of events surrounding the housing of Śāriputra's relics, the text says the monks received precious jewels and pearls but did not know how they should be distributed. In response to the situation, the Buddha is made to say:

> *bud dud gang yin pa de dag ni shing 'dsam bu'i grib ma na bzhugs pa'i sku gzugs la dbul bar bya'o / gzhan yang chung shas shig ni shâ ri'i bu'i mchod rten de'i bcos legs bya bar bzhag la lhag ma ni dge 'dun tshogs pas bgo bar bya'o / de de bzhin gshegs pa'i mchod rten gyi ma yin gyi / shâ ri'i bu'i mchod rten gyi yin te / de lta bas na 'gyod par mi bya'o /*[75]
>
> Which are for the Buddha, those are to be given to the image which is sitting in the shadow of the *jambu* tree. A small part is to be put aside to repair the *stūpa* of Śāriputra. The remainder is to be divided by the community of monks—this does not belong to the *stūpa* of the *Tathāgata,* it belongs to the *stūpa* of Śāriputra: therefore, there is no fault [in the latter usage].

The translation of the first clause given here is tentative. I do not know what *bud dud* means, although this reading appears in all of the Kanjurs available to me: the Peking, Derge, and Tog Palace.[76] Context and similar passages suggest that it might be the equivalent of *buddhasya, buddhasantaka,* or *bauddha,* and I have translated it accordingly. It may, however, be the name of a specific gem or precious jewel. But in either case, the passage indicates that a "share" of valuable property was explicitly assigned to an "image." An instance of just such an image may be had in the headless figure discovered at Sāñcī that bears on its base a Kuṣān inscription indicating, it seems, that it is "a stone (image depicting) the 'Jambu-shade' (episode) of the Bhagavat (Śākyamuni)" (*bhagava-{sya} . . . sya jambuchāyā-śīlā*).[77]

These passages and others like them scattered throughout the *Mūlasarvāsti-vāda-vinaya* deserve and require a thorough study; they need to be studied in light of the similar passages and conceptions signaled by Gernet in *Vinayas* extant now only in Chinese;[78] they need to be studied further in connection with medieval Indian land grants and inscriptions that make explicit provision for copying texts.[79] For the moment, though, we need only note that the *Vinaya* that may well have governed the majority of medieval monastic communities in eastern India, and perhaps as well those residing at Ajaṇṭā and similar sites, contains exactly what we would expect if our interpretation of the epigraphical material is correct. It contains explicit rules that acknowledge, at the very least, the juristic personality and presence of the Buddha within the midst of the monastic community that it envisions. It contains explicit rules concerning the property and real wealth owned by this "person." And it contains specific directions concerning the central accommodations provided for him. This Buddha, at least, was a force and a factor in almost every aspect of everyday medieval monastic life.

What is almost unavoidably indicated by the epigraphical material and monastic codes is, however, only confirmed more fully by what we know about the development of Buddhist monastic architecture. Dehejia says "the early rock-cut caves of western India . . . are all Buddhist monasteries. Each site consists of one or more *caityas*—chapels for congregational worship—and several *vihāras* which were residential halls for the monks."[80] What needs to be emphasized however, is that although each early site necessarily had both "chapels" and residential quarters, they were kept spatially and architecturally distinct and each separated one from the other. The Buddha resided, as it were,[81] in his own separate quarters, in the *stūpa* housed in a separate excavation that was used for public and "congregational worship." Exactly the same pattern occurs at the much less numerous and much less well-preserved early structural sites. For example, even though the earliest monastic residential quarters at the Dharmarājikā at Taxila face the "Great *Stūpa*," they are separated from it.[82] This pattern becomes even clearer in the Taxila area with somewhat later *vihāras*. They are typically quadrangular structures having an open court surrounded by rows of residential cells, usually on all four sides. The main entrance to these monasteries almost always faces directly—and, if possible, is symmetrically aligned with—the main *stūpa*, which is outside of and separated from the monastic residential quadrangle.[83] There are, of course, some variations and some movement toward a different arrangement—attempts toward tentatively drawing the two types of "residence" into a tighter intimacy. Sometimes the *stūpa* is placed in the middle of the residential court, and although remaining distinct, it is surrounded by the living quarters of the monks.[84] But these attempts remain tentative and pale in comparison with a major rearrangement that began to appear everywhere in the fifth century—at exactly the time that we start to get clear epigraphical references to the Buddha as an actual resident of Indian monasteries.

Vogel was perhaps the first to sense the significance of this rearrangement, first at Kasia,[85] then at Bāgh, where he alludes at least to its possible connection with the *Gandhakuṭī.*[86] It has, however, been most fully studied at the Western Cave sites in several works by Dhavalikar. Dhavalikar notes that in the early Western Caves "the standard *vihāra* plan from the beginning consisted of a squarish hall with cells in side and back walls," and that the *caityagṛha,* "the shrine proper for the congregation" was separate from the *vihāra,* which "was for the residence of monks." Then, through a reconstructed sequence the details of which may or may not be entirely acceptable, he clearly shows that the later *vihāras,* too, "were squarish pillared halls, with cells in side and back walls," but they now also had "a shrine in the centre of the back wall containing a Buddha image. The vihāra," he now says, "also thus served the purpose of a shrine."[87] He also notes "that by the middle of the fifth century the typical . . . plan of the shrine-cum-vihara was completely standardized."[88] We have already noted this "plan" at the *vihāra* Cave XVI at Ajaṇṭā, *vihāra* Cave II at Bāgh, Monastery 19 at Śrāvastī, and Monastery I at Nālandā—all sites from which we have contemporary inscriptional records that speak of the Buddha as residing *in* these specific monasteries. Two additional very clear structural examples of this "shrine-cum-*vihāra*" plan are provided by Sirpur Monastery[89] and Monastery 1 at Ratnagiri.[90]

This plan—both pervasive and standardized after the fifth century—is not difficult to describe. It was achieved by only a slight modification of the typical layout for early Buddhist monasteries: structural examples were formerly quadrangular structures surrounding an open court with rows of residential cells on all four sides, or, occasionally, on only three. But in this new plan, what would have previously been only another monastic residential cell in the middle of the back wall facing the main entrance has been architecturally set apart as a very special room. The old plan had been altered to accommodate a new and equally special resident: the Buddha has moved into private monastic quarters. This new addition is, however, in at least one important sense, only a return to a much earlier tradition, and, in a sense, the Buddha has only reoccupied his old quarters.

In the *Śayanāsana-vastu* a householder in Vārāṇasī named Kalyāṇabhadra asks permission of the Buddha to build a *vihāra* for "the disciples of the Blessed One" (*bhagavataḥ śrāvakāṇāṃ vihāraṃ kārayeyam iti*). The Buddha grants permission, but Kalyāṇabhadra is presented as not knowing how such a structure should be made. At this point the Buddha is made to give specific instructions:

> *bhagavān āha: yadi trilayanaṃ kārayasi madhye gandhakuṭiḥ kārayitavyā dvayoḥ pārśvayor dve layane; evaṃ triśāle nava layanāni; catuḥśāle madhye dvārakoṣṭhakābhimukhaṃ gandhakuṭiḥ dvārakoṣṭhakapārśvayor dve layane.*[91]
>
> The Blessed One said: if you have three cells made, the Perfume Chamber is to be made in the middle, the two (other) cells on each side; likewise, if there are nine cells in three wings; in a quadrangular (*vihāra*) the Perfume Chamber (is to be placed) in the middle (of the back wall) facing the main entrance, two cells on each side of the entrance.

That these instructions constitute a virtually exact description of what Dhavalikar called "the shrine-cum-vihara" plan—a plan found almost everywhere after the fifth century—is probably obvious. We need only note that this correspondence between *vinaya* rule and actual groundplan allows us to label more precisely the special cell in the middle of the back wall of post-fifth-century Buddhist monasteries: although called by Dhavalikar and others simply a "shrine," it could hardly have been intended as anything other than the *Gandhakuṭī.* This means, of course, that the monastic architects at Ajaṇṭā, Bāgh, Nālandā, and numerous other post-fifth-century sites provided—exactly like Kalyāṇabhadra in early Benares and Anāthapiṇḍika at Śrāvastī—special accommodations in their monasteries that were reserved for the Buddha himself. It was apparently in such monastic quarters that, from the fifth to the fourteenth centuries, the Buddha was thought to live.[92]

There may, however, be one final bit of archaeological evidence that further confirms what epigraphical, architectural, and *vinaya* sources all suggest. If the "images" housed in medieval monastic *Gandhakuṭīs* were cognitively classified with the living Buddha, if such stone Buddhas were actually thought to *live* in these establishments, they also—at least occasionally, and in spite of their unusually hardy constitutions—must have *died* there. The remains of such "dead" Buddhas—if, again, our interpretation is correct—should have been treated not as mere objects; they should have been treated as the mortuary remains of any other "dead" Buddha had been treated.

And that, it seems, is exactly what occurred. When Marshall opened a ninth- or tenth-century *stūpa* at Śrāvastī, he did not find human remains. Instead, he found the remains of an old and broken image, an image that was probably made in the Kuṣān period at Mathurā.[93] This was not an isolated find. In *Stūpa* no. 9 at the same site yet another similar broken image had been deposited. This *stūpa* was "also of the Medieval Period," although the image was much older.[94] Marshall noted at least three additional instances of such "burials" in the medieval *stūpas* at Sāñcī[95] and still other instances at Sārnāth.[96] More recently, yet another instance was discovered at the latter site.[97] Marshall, more than forty years ago, had already drawn a first, obvious conclusion: ". . . the burial of older cult statues, whole or fragmentary, in Buddhist *stūpas* is a practice which appears to have been common during the medieval age."[98] It would seem then, again in "the medieval age," that the remains of dead images were ritually treated and permanently housed exactly like the mortuary remains of dead Buddhas; that, in fact, the equivalence of image and actual person that we have noted held not just during the life of the image but in its death as well.[99]

If nothing else, the convergence here of these distinct, and very different kinds of sources is remarkable. Epigraphical, architectural, *vinaya,* and archaeological sources all come together toward the same point: all document in different ways a conception of the Buddha that was very widely and very deeply held. This conception is important for the history of Indian religion because it is—in many respects—strikingly similar to the conception of divinity which predominates in medieval Hindu Temple Religion and raises, therefore, the question of the relationship, chronological and otherwise, between the two.[100] But it is also important—and perhaps most interesting—because it tells us a great deal that we otherwise could not know about "the abstract theories" concerning the "person" of the Buddha. It confirms and gives specificity to the wisdom of de La Vallée Poussin's observation: "the abstract theories" were, indeed, "one part," but "only one part of the history of Buddhology" or the conception of the Buddha. That part, to be sure, was not "insignificant," but it was, apparently, not unduly significant either. Bearing in mind that our inscriptions, for example, did not express the views of the masses, but were obviously written by literate individuals familiar with Buddhist doctrines of the day, it would appear that "the abstract theories"—which, significantly, were being developed at virtually the same time—had little, if any, direct *detectable* influence on a large segment of even the already limited number of literate members of the Buddhist society of their day, most of whom were probably monks.

This is particularly striking if we bear in mind that two of the sites that have produced some of the fullest epigraphical documentation for the conception of the Buddha as a permanent monastic resident were, during the period from which this documentation comes, the two most important centers of Buddhist scholasticism in Northern India. I-tsing, for example, says that in his day (the seventh century), "After having studied this commentary [the *Kāśikāvṛtti*], students begin to learn composition in prose and verse, and devote themselves to logic (*hetuvidyā*) and metaphysic (*abhidharmakosha*) . . . Thus instructed by their teachers and instructing others they pass two or three years, generally in the Nālandā monastery in Central India, or in the country of Valabhī (Walā) in Western India." These two places, he says, "are like Chin-ma, Shih-ch'ü, Lung-men and Ch'ue-li"—the foremost seats of learning in China.[101] May says:

Quant à l'idéalisme proprement dit, il connaît, parallèlement à l'école des

> logiciens, une brillante floraison: il se scinde en deux écoles principales . . . L'une, est l'école de Valabhī . . . L'autre école, celle de Nālandā, eut une destinée brillante et devint le plus important centre d'études bouddhiques dans les derniers siècles du bouddhisme indien.[102]

The synchronism between, for example, both the epigraphical and architectural sources and the development of the abstract theories points us, as well, toward another curious observation: language expressing the personal presence and permanent abiding of the Buddha began to appear explicitly in inscriptions at almost exactly the same time—the fourth or fifth century—as monastery ground plans began to show that specific and elaborate accommodations were beginning to be provided for the Buddha in Indian monasteries. But both of these phenomena began to appear, then, at or during the period when some of the most abstract theories concerning the person of the Buddha were beginning to take definitive shape. This, of course, would suggest that all three developments were not unrelated, but specifying the nature of the relationship is not easy. Several possibilities present themselves. It is conceivable that the security, if you will, of dwelling in daily domestic intimacy with the Buddha provided a certain freedom of thought on the theoretical level—that increased etherealization and abstraction were possible precisely because the domestic presence of the Buddha was firmly established. It is conceivable, as well, that the abstract theories constituted a kind of minority report and were, in fact, a reaction to the apparently pervasive sense of the Buddha's personal presence, that they were in intent, at least, an attempt at reformation. It is also conceivable, finally, that the reaction went in the opposite direction: the increasing emphasis on the abiding presence of the Buddha, and the architectural efforts to assure daily domestic contact with him, were fueled by the anxieties engendered by the increasingly abstract and ethereal character of current theoretical discussions. All of these are possibilities but all have one thing in common: they all indicate that any attempt to assess the actual historical significance of Buddhist *śāstric* notions must take into account a far broader range of sources than has heretofore been considered. They remind us—if such a reminder be required—that Indian Buddhism is very much more than the sum of its *śāstras.*

Notes

1. P. C. Almond, *The British Discovery of Buddhism* (Cambridge: 1988) esp. 77–79. The first half of Ét. Lamotte, "La légende du Buddha," *RHR* 134 (1948) 37–71, contains a still-useful sketch of the changing scholarly perceptions of the historical Buddha.

2. Almond, *The British Discovery of Buddhism,* 70–77. Curiously, it was also explicitly argued that the promotion of archaeological work could provide a useful critique of

nineteenth-century "Brahmanism" by showing that "Brahmanism, instead of being an unchanged and unchangeable religion which has subsisted for ages, was of comparatively modern origin, and had been constantly receiving additions and alterations. . . ." see A. Imam, *Sir Alexander Cunningham and the Beginnings of Indian Archaeology* (Dacca: 1966) 39–41.

3. L. de La Vallée Poussin, *Vijñaptimātratāsiddhi. Le siddhi de Hiuan-tsang,* T. II (Paris: 1929) 762–813, esp. 774, 776, 788–791.

4. de La Vallée Poussin, *Vijñaptimātratāsiddhi,* T. II, 811.

5. de La Vallée Poussin, *Vijñaptimātratāsiddhi,* T. II, 763.

6. de La Vallée Poussin does refer to the "invocation" of at least one inscription, but his example is non-Indian, and he does not pursue the possibilities further. In fact, similar "invocations" or *maṅgalas* are frequently found at the head of several varieties of the more elaborate types of Buddhist inscriptions, and they constitute a rich potential source for future study. A cursory study of some of the epithets applied to the Buddha in pre-Gupta inscriptions has been published by A. M. Shastri, "The Legendary Personality of the Buddha as Depicted in Pre-Gupta Indian Inscriptions," *The Orissa Historical Research Journal* 8 (1960) 168–176, reprinted with few alterations as 22–35 of A. M. Shastri, *An Outline of Early Buddhism (A Historical Survey of Buddhology, Buddhist Schools and Sanghas Mainly Based on the Study of Pre-Gupta Inscriptions)* (Varanasi: 1965).

7. "Medieval" is used here in a very broad and very loose sense to cover the period from the fifth to about the fourteenth century C.E.—cf. A. L. Basham, *The Wonder That was India,* 3rd rev. ed. (New York: 1967) xxi–xxii. This periodization reflects the fact that what is usually called—using an unsatisfactory dynastic terminology—the "late Gupta" represents not an end, but the beginnings of a number of new developments in the form and content of Indian Buddhist inscriptions. For a recent attempt to catalog the Buddhist inscriptions of this period, although already now somewhat outdated, see Shizutani Masao, *Indo bukkyō himei mokuroku* (Kyoto: 1979) 159–232.

8. A. Ghosh, "Buddhist Inscription from Kausambi," *EI* 34 (1961–1962) 14–16. The inscription is fragmentary and its interpretation consequently not sure.

9. Cf. E. J. Thomas, *The Life of Buddha as Legend and History,* 3rd ed. (London: 1949) 115, n. 2: "It is doubtful if Buddha ever went so far west as Kosambī. There were later important monasteries there, and this is sufficient to explain the existence of legends attached to it."

10. P. R. Srinivasan, "Two Brahmi Inscriptions," *EI* 39 (1971 but 1985) 123–128.

11. V. V. Mirashi, *Inscriptions of the Vākāṭakas,* Corpus Inscriptionum Indicarum, Vol. V (Ootacamund: 1963) 103–211, esp. 109, line 18. The reading is in part a reconstruction but is fairly sure; cf. *(ya)ti* as a title of the Buddha in line 1 of this same inscription, and note that he is also referred to elsewhere at Ajaṇṭā as *munīndra-* (Cave XVII inscription [Mirashi] 127, line 28).

12. For the plan of Cave XVI, see J. Fergusson and J. Burgess, *The Cave Temples of India* (London: 1880) pl. xxxiii, 1; see also the discussion and plans in W. Spink, "Ajaṇṭā's Chronology: The Crucial Cave," *ArO* 10 (1975) 143–169, and W. Spink, "The Splendours of Indra's Crown: A Study of Mahāyāna Developments at Ajaṇṭa," *Journal of the Royal Society of Arts* 122, no. 5219 (1974) 743–767, esp. 758–760 and figs. 13a–13d.

13. For the Cave XXVI inscription, see G. Yazdani, *Ajanta,* Part IV: Text (London: 1955) 114–118, vs. 14. What in vs. 14 is called a *veśma* is called a *śaila-gṛhaṃ . . . śāstuḥ,* "a stone residence . . . for the Teacher," in vs. 6, and a *sugatā(layaṃ),* "a house for the Sugata," in vs. 13.

14. J. Burgess, *Report on the Buddhist Cave Temples and Their Inscriptions*, Archaeological Survey of Western India, Vol. IV (London: 1883) 86, no. 10.

15. V. V. Mirashi, *Inscriptions of the Kalachuri-Chedi Era*, Corpus Inscriptionum Indicarum, Vol. IV, Pt. 1 (Ootacamund: 1955) 19–21, esp. 20, line 5ff. I have omitted here, and in a number of the grants quoted below, the portion explicitly providing for the maintenance and upkeep of the monastery. Such a provision is a common, even a standard, element in land grants to Buddhist monasteries. The failure to take this into account in specific regard to the Bāgh grant has, unfortunately, affected Spink's attempt to date the caves. Spink argues in part that the presence of such a provision in the Bāgh grant indicates that Subandhu actually made "repairs" to the caves and that they were, therefore, excavated earlier than had been previously thought. But the provision, of course, need not imply any of this; see W. M. Spink, "Bagh: A Study," *Archives of Asian Art* 30 (1976/1977) 53–84, esp. 54, 56, 58, 83. It might also be noted that Mirashi's translation of the grant is not free of problems. The key phrase "for the Blessed One, the Buddha," has, for example, been entirely omitted.

16. For the plan of Cave II at Bāgh, see J. Marshall et al., *The Bagh Caves in the Gwalior State* (London: 1927) pl. I.

17. D. C. Bhattacharyya, "A Newly Discovered Copper-plate from Tippera [the Gunaighar Grant of Vainyagupta: The Year 188 Current (Gupta Era)]," *IHQ* 6 (1930) 45–60; D. C. Sircar, *Select Inscriptions Bearing on Indian History and Civilization*, Vol. I, 2nd rev. ed. (Calcutta: 1965) 340–345; P. K. Agrawala, *Imperial Gupta Epigraphs* (Varanasi: 1983) 113–116. The preservation of the plate is not entirely satisfactory, nor is anything certain known about the monastery referred to, the plate being an accidental find; see, however, F. M. Asher, *The Art of Eastern India, 300–800* (Delhi: 1980) 16, 32, 63. The identity of the *Ācārya* Śāntideva mentioned in this record also remains unclear.

18. G. Bühler, "Further Valabhī Grants," *IA* 6 (1877) 9–12, esp. 12, line 3. The Sthiramati of this record has been persistently identified with the Yogācāra author of the same name; see S. Lévi, "Les donations religieuses des roi de Valabhī," *Bibliothèque de l'école des hautes-études, sciences religieuses, études de critique et d'histoire*, 2° série, 7° vol. (1896) 75–100, reprinted in *Mémorial Sylvain Lévi* (Paris: 1957) 218–234, esp. 231; Y. Kajiyama, "Bhāvaviveka, Sthiramati and Dharmapāla," *WZKS* 12–13 (1968–1969) 193–203; etc.

19. G. Bühler, "Grants from Valabhī," *IA* 5 (1876) 204–221, esp. 207, line 7.

20. This, of course, is not to say that words for "images" do not occur in Buddhist records and inscriptions of this period. They do occur, but not commonly; see, for example, the seventh to eighth century inscription from Nālandā in D. C. Sircar, "Nalanda Inscription of King Prathamasiva," *EI* 39 (1971 but 1985) 117–122, esp. 122, line 10 (*bhagavato buddhasya bimbaṃ*), line 12 (*pratikṛtir . . . śās(tu)r*). The occurrence of such terms in a small number of medieval inscriptions may or may not point to the not unlikely possibility that different groups had different conceptions of these "objects," but terms like *bimba, pratikṛti, pratimā*, etc. must be much more fully studied and much more carefully nuanced before this will become clear; to translate them all automatically and indiscriminately as "image" is, to say the least, not helpful. For some remarks on the patterned occurrence and nonoccurrence of the term *pratimā* in the pre-Gupta inscriptions from Mathurā, see G. Roth, "The Physical Presence of the Buddha and its Representation in Buddhist Literature," in M. Yaldiz and W. Lobo, eds., *Investigating Indian Art. Proceedings of a Symposium on the Development of Early Buddhist and Hindu Iconography Held at the Museum of Indian Art, Berlin, in May 1986* (Berlin: 1987) 306, n. 8, and the sources

cited there. For the Khotanese terms *pratäbimbaa* (Skt. *pratibimba*) and *pe'ma, pema, paima* (Skt. *pratimā*) and some interesting material illustrating Khotanese conceptions of Buddhist "images," see H. W. Bailey, "The Image in Gaustana," in N. A. Jayawickrama, ed., *Paranavitana Felicitation Volume* (Colombo: 1965) 33–36: "The Buddhas were conceived to be in these images. Thus we have the Khotanese verse *ramanī tcaṣū paima bīsai jista bai'ysa,* 'the deva Buddha resident in the delightful splendid image' "; etc. These Khotanese conceptions are particularly interesting because they are articulated in sources that are broadly contemporaneous with a considerable number of the Indian inscriptions cited here. See also n. 39 below. Although further afield, see H. Delahaye, "Les antécédents magiques des statues chinoises," *Revue d'esthétique* 5 (1983) 45–53, and the very interesting paper by B. Frank, "Vacuité et corps actualisé: la problème de la presence des 'personnages vénérés' dans leurs images selon la tradition du bouddhisme japonais," *JIABS* 11.2 (1988) 53–86.

21. Th. Bloch, "An Unpublished Valabhī Copper-plate Inscription of King Dhruvasena I," *JRAS* (1895) 379–384, esp. 383, line 18.

22. Note that Lévi, "Les donations religieuses des roi de Valabhī," 232, identifies the *Ācārya* Buddhadasa with the scholastic of the same name who "était l'élève d'Asaṅga."

23. D. B. Diskalkar, "Some Unpublished Copper-plates of the Rulers of Valabhī," *JBomBRAS* 1 (1925) 13–64, esp. 63, line 53. This text is faulty, and it is not impossible that the intended reading was *-kutyāṃ,* not *-kuṭī.* In any case *-kuṭī* is, as it stands, almost certainly a scribal error. In form it could only be either a stem form without grammatical marker or a nominative singular. Context and syntax, however, make the second alternative virtually impossible.

24. P. R. Srinivasan, "Two Fragmentary Charters of Maitraka Dharasena IV," *EI* 35 (1970 but 1976) 219–224, esp. 223, line 8.

25. See below 268ff.

26. D. C. Sircar, *Epigraphic Discoveries in East Pakistan* (Calcutta: 1973) 11; 62, line 9; D. C. Sircar, "Jagadishpur Plate of the Gupta Year 128," *EI* 38 (1970 but 1979) 247–252, esp. 249. In the passage he is dealing with here, Sircar sees a reference to a Buddhist establishment, but it might very well be Jain; cf. S. Siddhanta, "The Jagadishpur Copper Plate Grant of the Gupta Year 128 (A.D. 447–448)," *Journal of the Varendra Research Museum* 1 (1972) 23–37. If the record is in fact referring to Jain *Arhats,* its language would provide an early and striking Jain parallel to what we find in Buddhist records from Valabhī and elsewhere. An equally early and more certainly Jain parallel may be seen in K. N. Dikshit, "Paharpur Copper-Plate Grant of the [Gupta] Year 159," *EI* 20 (1929–1930) 59–64: *kāśika-pañca-stūpa-nikāyika-nigrantha-śramaṇācāryya-guhanandi-śiṣya-praśiṣyādhiṣṭhita-vihāre bhagavatām arhatāṃ gandha-dhūpa-sumano-dīpādy-arthan . . .,* etc. Asher (*The Art of Eastern India,* 15) has expressed some doubt about the Jain character of this record, but the epithet *pañca-stūpa-nikāyika-* makes it virtually certain that it is Jain; see A. K. Chatterjee, *A Comprehensive History of Jainism (up to 1000 A.D.)* (Calcutta: 1978) 105–106. The mere fact that it is not always easy to distinguish Buddhist and Jain inscriptions of this sort is, however, in itself significant.

27. See G. Schopen, "The Inscription on the Kuṣān Image of Amitābha and the Character of the Early Mahāyāna in India," *JIABS* 10.2 (1987) 99–134, esp. 105–106, 121–122.

28. H. Sastri, "Nalanda Stone Inscription of the Reign of Yasovarmmadeva," *EI* 20 (1929–1930) 37–46; H. Sastri, *Nalanda and its Epigraphic Material,* MASI, No. 66 (Delhi: 1942) 78–82; D. C. Sircar, *Select Inscriptions Bearing on Indian History and Civilization,*

Vol. II (Delhi: 1983) 229–232; S. M. Mishra, "The Nālandā Stone Inscription of the Reign of Yaśovarmadeva—A Fresh Appraisal," *Studies in Indian Epigraphy* 3 (1977) 108–115.

29. Sastri, *EI* 20 (1929–1930) 44, line 9.

30. The last assertion at least may, perhaps, draw some support from the fact that the inscription of Yasovarmmadeva "was found buried in the debris of the southern verandah of the old *vihāra*—now called Monastery I" at Nālandā. Sastri says of this *vihāra* and the others in the eastern row: "The [monastic] quadrangles had a projecting porch on one side which gave the entrance to the monastery . . . Directly opposite to the entrance was the shrine wherein the principal image of Tathāgata was enthroned as we see in Monastery No. 1 where the chapel still preserves the remains of a colossal figure of the Buddha . . ." (*Nalanda and Its Epigraphic Material,* 22). What this means, of course, is that Monastery I—in fact, all the *vihāras* in the eastern row—had exactly the same basic layout as Cave XVI at Ajaṇṭā and Cave II at Bāgh: although all were primarily intended as monastic residences and consisted of individual residential cells, each had the central cell in the back wall specially reserved for the Buddha. For the layout at Nālandā, see pl. 23 in B. Kumar, *Archaeology of Pataliputra and Nalanda* (Delhi: 1987) esp. 181–182. On the uncertainties concerning the second half of the verse quoted above, see Sastri, *EI* 20 (1929–1930) 39 and n. 1; 46, n. 3; etc.

31. G: Bühler, "The New Inscription of Toramana Shaha," *EI* 1 (1892) 238–241, esp. 240, line 6; Sircar, *Select Inscriptions,* Vol. I, 422–424. Bühler's notes to his edition reflect the curious character of the language of this record: "a mistake," "a monstrous form," "utterly wrong," "the utter loss of all feeling for the rules of the language"; cf. É. Senart, "L'inscription du vase de Wardak," *JA* (1914) 581.

32. T. W. Rhys Davids and J. E. Carpenter, eds., *The Dīgha Nikāya,* Vol. II (London: 1903) 88, 97, etc.; E. Waldschmidt, ed., *Das Mahāparinirvāṇasūtra,* T. II (Berlin: 1951) 152 (6.9), 188 (12.4), 256 (26.15), etc.; cf. G. von Simson, *Zur Diktion einiger Lehrtexte des buddhistischen Sanskritkanons* (München: 1965) 16.7, 16.9, 16.11, etc.; J. S. Speyer, ed., *Avadānaçataka,* Vol. I (St. Petersbourg: 1906) 9.8, 58.5, 64.9, etc.

33. T. W. and C. A. F. Rhys Davids, *Dialogues of the Buddha,* Pt. II (London: 1910) 93.

34. Rhys Davids and Carpenter, *Dīgha,* ii, 98.

35. Among the various epithets applied to the Buddha in the Toramāṇa Inscription we find, for example, *daśabalabalinacatuvaiśāradyacatasrapratisaṃ(vidā)aṣṭādaśāveṇīkādbhutadharmasamanvāgatasya sarvasatvavatsalamahākāruṇikasya* (Bühler, *EI* 1 [1892] 240, lines 5ff). These qualities or characteristics are not only textual, but were involved in "the controversy about the nature of the *āveṇikabuddhadharmas* . . . reflected in a number of important Sanskrit Buddhist scholastic texts"; see Y. Bentor, "The Redactions of the *Adbhutadharmaparyāya* from Gilgit," *JIABS* 11.2 (1988) 21–52, esp. 25–26 and notes.

36. D. C. Sircar, "More Inscriptions from Nagarjunikonda," *EI* 35 (1963) 1–36, esp. 7, line 7; cf. D. C. Sircar, "Note on Nagarjunikonda Inscription of 333 A.D.," *EI* 38 (1969 but 1971) 183–185.

37. S. S. Ramachandra, "Hyderabad Museum Plates of Prithivi-Sri-Mularaja," *EI* 38 (1969 but 1971) 192–195, esp. 194, line 15. For some earlier instances of the use of the term *-pramukha,* see H. Lüders, *Mathurā Inscriptions* (Göttingen: 1961) §§47–51 (all of which are associated with what Lüders translates as "the commissioners of the Community": *saṅghaprakṛtān(ā)ṃ bh(ad)raghoṣa-pramukhā(nāṃ),* "the commissioners of the Community headed by Bhadraghoṣa," etc.), and §27.

38. D. R. Sahni, "Saheth-Maheth Plate of Govinda-Chandra [Vikrama-]Samvat 1186," *EI* 11 (1911–1912) 20–26, esp. 24, line 20.

39. M. Venkataramayya, *Śrāvastī* (New Delhi: 1956) 13–15. Khotanese material again provides some interesting parallels. First of all, according to Bailey, "In Khotanese texts the Sanskrit *pramukha* 'chief' is used in various dialectal forms as the title of the head of a Buddhist monastery (*vihāra*)"; see H. W. Bailey, "Iranica," *BSOAS* 11 (1943–1946) 2. Elsewhere, Bailey cites as examples *tcarmaja prramāha maledaprañā,* "Maledaprañā principal [*pramukha*] of Tcarma," and—notably—*drūttīrai prraumāha' ttathāgatta śrībhadra,* "the Tathāgata Śrībhadra principal [*pramukha*] of Dro-tir"; see H. W. Bailey, "Hvatanica IV," *BSOAS* 10 (1940–1942) 921. Bailey's second example would seem to explicitly designate a Buddha as the head of a monastery. Notice too the invocation to P. 2026 treated in the same paper (894–895) where Buddhas dwelling in two local communities are referred to: "Homage, reverence to the Buddha dwelling in Brrūya; homage, reverence to the Buddha in Khāṃhyape." For even more generalized uses of *pramukha* as a monastic title in Khotanese and in Tibetan sources dealing with Khotan, see H. W. Bailey, *Indo-Scythian Studies. Being Khotanese Texts,* Vol. IV (Cambridge: 1961) 24 (7), 82ff; H. W. Bailey, *The Culture of the Sakas in Ancient Iranian Khotan* (Delmar: 1982) 66, both dealing with a letter in which several monks are referred to by name with titles: *Dvipiṭaka Ācārya Pramukha* Yaśaḥ-prajña, *Tripiṭaka Ācārya Pramukha* Puṇya-mitra, etc.); R. E. Emmerick, *Tibetan Texts Concerning Khotan* (London: 1967) 60.3, 137 (*par-mog* = *pramukha*).

40. H. Shastri, "The Nalanda Copper-plate of Devapala-deva," *EI* 17 (1923–1924) 310–327, esp. 322, line 38; Sastri, *Nalanda and Its Epigraphic Material,* 92–102, esp: 98, line 38.

41. K. V. Subrahmanya Aiyer, "The Larger Leiden Plates (of Rajaraja I)," *EI* 22 (1933–1934) 213–266, esp. 242, lines 83–84.

42. R. B. Hiralal, "Four Chandella Copper-plate Inscriptions," *EI* 20 (1929–1930) 125–136, esp. 130, line 14; see also R. K. Dikshit, "Land-grants of the Chandella Kings," *Journal of the Uttara Pradesh Historical Society* 23 (1950) 228–251, esp. 239.

43. D. C. Sircar, *Some Epigraphical Records of the Medieval Period From Eastern India* (New Delhi: 1979) 32.

44. *BHSD,* 209.

45. H. Lüders, *Bharhut Inscriptions,* Corpus Inscriptionum Indicarum, Vol. II, Pt. 2, rev. E. Waldschmidt and M. A. Mehendale (Ootacamund: 1963) 107–108 (B 34).

46. J. Ph. Vogel, "Prakrit Inscriptions from Ghantasala," *EI* 27 (1947–1948) 1–4, esp. 3, A and B. The same inscriptions were published some twenty years later as recent discoveries and without reference to Vogel in M. S. Sarma, "Some Prākṛit Inscriptions from Ghaṇṭaśāla," *Epigraphia Āndhrica* 2 (1979) 1–3. None of these inscriptions contain a date. Two of them are virtually identical and record the construction of a "stone *maṇḍapa* with a *gandhakuṭī,* a railing (*vedikā*) and a *toraṇa.*"

47. P. V. P. Sastry, "Hyderabad Prakrit Inscription of Govindaraja Vihara," *JESI* 11 (1984) 95–100. This inscription is poorly edited here and must be studied again. For now, the readings marked "[ed.]" in the notes are to be preferred. The donor in this record, a monk, is called among other things *goviṃdarāja-vihārasa gaṃdhakuṭi-vārika,* the sense of which has been misunderstood; see below n. 56.

48. Mirashi, *Inscriptions of the Vākāṭakas,* 120–129 (no. 27), esp. 127, line 27. This is the "Inscription in Ajaṇṭā Cave XVII." It records the "construction" of, among other things, a *Gandhakuṭī* but because it is badly preserved and fragmentary there is some uncertainty about which of the extant excavations at Ajaṇṭā it refers to.

49. J. Burgess, *Report on the Elura Cave Temples and the Brahmanical and Jaina Caves in Western India* (London: 1883) 77 (no. 6). The inscription records the gift of a *śākyabhikṣu*

(*śākya-* has been inadvertently omitted from the reading published here but is easily read in the facsimile, pl. LI); this monk is also called *mahāgandhakuṭī-vārika;* cf. below, 269ff.

50. G. R. Sharma, "Excavations at Kauśāmbī, 1949–1955," *Annual Bibliography of Indian Archaeology,* Vol. XVI (Leyden: 1958) xliv: "Inscription on a lotus-shaped lamp (pl. Vc and d). The inscription records the donation of the lotus-shaped lamp by Bhikṣu Pradipta for the use in the Gandhakuṭī of the monastery." Although the bibliography of B. Ch. Chhabra's work published in *Svasti Śrī Dr. B. Ch. Chhabra Felicitation Volume,* ed. K. V. Ramesh et al. (Delhi: 1984) lists the "Ghoshitarama Terracotta Lamp Inscription" and says it was "published twice in English and once in Sanskrit," it gives no further details and I have yet to locate it. In the photograph published by Sharma the whole inscription is not clearly readable.

51. E. Hultzsch, "The Sarnath Inscription of Mahipala," *IA* 14 (1885) 139–140; and see below nn. 61, 62, and 69.

52. B. Indraji, "An Inscription at Gayā Dated in the Year 1813 of Buddha's Nirvana, with Two Others of the Same Period," *IA* 10 (1881) 341–347, esp. 342, line 13; Th. Bloch, "Notes on Bodh Gayā," *ARASI 1908–09* (Calcutta: 1912) 139–158, esp. 153, line 1; R. D. Banerji, *The Palas of Bengal,* Memoirs of the Asiatic Society of Bengal, Vol. V, No. 3 (Calcutta: 1915) 35, line 3; D. C. Sircar, "Three East Indian Inscriptions of the Early Medieval Period," *JAIH* 6 (1972–1973) 39–59.

53. See above nn. 21, 23, and 24.

54. A. Banerji-Sastri, "Ninety-three Inscriptions on the Kurkihar Bronzes," *JBORS* 26 (1940) 236–251, esp. nos. 31 and 32.

55. See below nn. 58 and 59.

56. *BHSD,* 477 s.v. *vārika.* Edgerton cites as the usual Tibetan equivalent *zhal (l)ta pa,* "guard, superintend(ent)." Curiously, this Buddhist material has not been taken into account in an exchange between Sircar and S. P. Tewari concerning the meaning of *vārika* in inscriptions. See S. P. Tewari, "A Note on Varika of the Inscriptions," *JESI* 9 (1982) 34–36 (also in Tewari, *Contributions of Sanskrit Inscriptions to Lexicography* [Delhi: 1987] 208–211); D. C. Sircar, "The Designation 'Varika'," *Vajapeya: Essays on Evolution of Indian Art and Culture. Prof. K. D. Bajpai Felicitation Volume,* Vol. I, ed. A. M. Sastri et al. (Delhi: 1987) 111–112. The Buddhist usage clearly favors Sircar.

57. See n. 49 above.

58. Sastri, *Nalanda and Its Epigraphic Material,* 38 and n. 4 (S.I. 675).

59. Sastri, *Nalanda and Its Epigraphic Material,* 43 (S.I. 730), but accepting the emendation proposed in P. V. B. Karunatillaka, "The Administrative Organization of the Nālandā Mahāvihāra from Sigillary Evidence," *The Sri Lanka Journal of the Humanities* 6.1 and 2 (1980) 62. See also the more general discussion on 61–64 of the term *vārika.* There is a third sealing published in Sastri (40, S.I. A, 357) that refers to a *Gandhakuṭī,* but it does not contain the term *vārika: śrīdevapāla-gandhakuḍyāṃ.*

60. See Sastri, *Nalanda and Its Epigraphic Material,* 27, for example. It is a pity that in one of the very few studies connected with the *Gandhakuṭī* the title *gandhakuṭīvārika* and a considerable number of other things have been so carelessly treated. J. S. Strong, "Gandhakuṭī: The Perfumed Chamber of the Buddha," *History of Religions* 16 (1977) 390–406, referring to the Kānheri inscription (n. 18 above), cites the title as "*gandhakuṭī-bhārika.*" This, of course, is wrong and had he actually checked the work he cites as his primary source—Lüders' list in *EI* 10 (1909–1910) no. 989—he would have seen that it was so. "*Gandhakuṭī-bhārika*" is an invention of S. Dutt (*Buddhist Monks and Monasteries in India* [London: 1962] 149), which is nowhere attested, and certainly not at Kānheri.

The form found at Kānheri is, as given by Lüders, "*mahāgandhakuṭīvārika?*," the question mark reflecting the uncertainty expressed in Burgess (n. 49 above) concerning the possibility of reading-*cārika* instead of *-vārika*, an uncertainty that was removed by the publication of the Nālandā seals. In both Lüders and Burgess the title is translated as "the guardian of the great gandhakuṭī," but because, apparently, Strong wants the title to "confirm" a story in the *Avadānaśataka* about a monk sweeping the *Gandhakuṭī*, Strong himself invents a quotation that he attributes to Dutt: He says that the title means "according to Sukumar Dutt, a 'monk in charge of keeping the sanctuary clean'." What Dutt actually says is " . . . *Gandhakuṭī-bhārika* who was in charge of the sanctuary (Lüders, no. 989 at Kanheri) and probably had to keep it clean and make arrangements for the daily worship." The Nālandā material, long available, should have indicated to Dutt and Strong how unlikely it was that the term referred to a janitor. Strong says of the *Gandhakuṭī* that it was "never itself a canonical tradition, figuring only sporadically in a few popular texts." But unless he wants to argue that the *Mūlasarvāstivāda-vinaya* is not "canonical," this is contradicted in one of his own notes. In his n. 19 he says: ". . . there are two references to the *gandhakuṭī* in the Vinaya of the Mūlasarvāstivādins"; he then cites, probably only by coincidence, the only two passages that occur in Bagchi's index, and adds: "the first of these is just a passing reference: the second specifies the location of the *gandhakuṭī* as being in the middle of the monastery. Together they add little to the Pāli materials we have reviewed . . ." There are several problems here. First, there are many more references to the *Gandhakuṭī* in the *Mūlasarvāstivāda-vinaya* than the two in Bagchi's index. This is clear from the fact that the passage he refers to as "just a passing reference" is only one of a series of passages indicating that certain kinds of material possessions and moveable wealth that "belonged" to the Buddha had to be lodged in or used on the *Gandhakuṭī* and that—since such wealth frequently consisted of items like jewels and pearls—the *Gandhakuṭī* was not only a central unit in the monastic economy but also one of the wealthiest. See *Gilgit Manuscripts*, iii 2, 142.10, 143.12, 146.3; *Gilgit Manuscripts*, iii 4, 210.4; *Śayanāsanavastu and Adhikaraṇavastu*, 68.22; and below. More could be added here, but it is probably clear that few of the facts and perhaps even less of the interpretation in Strong's paper can be taken with confidence.

61. J. H. Marshall and S. Konow, "Sārnāth," *ARASI 1906–07* (Calcutta: 1909) 97. See also J. H. Marshall and S. Konow, "Excavations at Sārnāth 1908," *ARASI 1907–08* (Calcutta: 1911) 66.

62. H. Hargreaves, "Excavation at Sārnāth," *ARASI 1914–15* (Calcutta: 1920) 127.

63. J. Ph. Vogel, "Seals of Buddhist Monasteries in Ancient India," *Journal of the Ceylon Branch of the Royal Asiatic Society*, N.S. 1 (1950) 27–32, esp. 27.

64. Vogel, "Seals of Buddhist Monasteries in Ancient India," 30.

65. G. Fussman, "Numismatic and Epigraphic Evidence for the Chronology of Early Gandharan Art," *Investigating Indian Art*, ed. M. Yaldiz and W. Lobo (Berlin: 1987) 80.

66. Marshall and Konow, *ARASI 1906–07*, 99.

67. The presence of more than one *Gandhakuṭī* at Kānheri is at least suggested by the designation *mahā-gandhakuṭī-vārika* (above n. 48), "the superintendent of the *Great Gandhakuṭī*," the specificity added by the *mahā-* being otherwise unnecessary.

68. See, for example, H. Shastri, "The Nalanda Copper-plate of Devapaladeva," *EI* 17 (1923–1924) 310–327, esp. 310, where the seal reads simply *śrī-devapāladevasya*, "of the Illustrious Devapāladeva," and D. C. Sircar, "Lucknow Museum Copper-plate

Inscription of Surapala I, Regnal Year 3," *EI* 40 (1973 but 1986) 4–16, esp. 5, which reads *śrīśūrapāladevasya,* "[this] belongs to the Illustrious Śūrapāladeva."

69. The text cited here is that found in D. R. Sahni, *Catalogue of the Museum of Archaeology at Sārnāth* (Calcutta: 1914) 211. A second similar inscription on yet another recut pillar was also found at the site. It reads: *deyadharmmo yaṃ paramopa- / -{sa}ka-kīrtteḥ {mūla-ga}ndhaku- / {tyāṃ pra}dī{p . . . ddhaḥ}* (also Sahni, 211). What remains of both inscriptions, taken together with the sealings already discussed, allows for a fairly certain restoration.

70. The most direct evidence comes, of course, from Gilgit. To judge by the manuscript material recovered from this site, the monastic community at Gilgit was governed by this *Vinaya,* although the rest of the literature it had available was primarily—although not exclusively—Mahāyāna. See O. von Hinüber, "Die Erforschung der Gilgit-Handschriften (Funde buddhistischer Sanskrit-Handschriften, I)," *Nachrichten der Akademie der Wissenschaften in Göttingen I. Philo-Hist. Klasse,* Jahrgang 1979, Nr. 12 (Göttingen: 1979) 329–359; O. von Hinüber, "Die Bedeutung des Handschriftenfundes bei Gilgit," *ZDMG,* Supplement V, XXI. Deutscher Orientalistentag vom 4 bis. 29 März 1980 in Berlin (Wiesbaden: 1982) 47–66; etc. That virtually the same situation is mirrored in the Tibetan Kanjur—primarily Mahāyāna *sūtra* literature, but only the *Mūlasarvāstivāda-vinaya*—would seem to argue for the pervasiveness of this *Vinaya* in the primarily Mahāyāna Indian communities from which Tibet got its Buddhism, and may, in fact, suggest that this was the standard *Vinaya* in Eastern India at the time. I-tsing, *A Record of the Buddhist Religion as Practised in India and the Malay Archipelago,* points in the same direction. More specifically, his remarks suggest the importance of this *Vinaya* at Tāmralipti and Nālandā (the latter, incidentally, has produced the only epigraphic reference I know to the Mūlasarvāstivāda; see S. L. Huntington, *The "Pāla-Sena" Schools of Sculpture* [Leiden: 1984] 225–226, no. 34). There are, moreover, indications of a connection between this *Vinaya* and Ajaṇṭā: J. Przyluski, "La roue de la vie à Ajaṇṭā," *JA* (1920) 313–331; M. Lalou, "Trois récits du dulva reconnus dans les peintures d'Ajaṇṭā," *JA* (1925) 333–337; M. Lalou, "Notes sur la décoration des monastères bouddhiques," *Revues des arts asiatique* 5.3 (1930) 183–185; D. Schlingloff, *Studies in the Ajanta Paintings. Identifications and Interpretations* (Delhi: 1987) 14, 34, 70–71, 77–78, 153, etc.

71. *Śayanāsanavastu and Adhikaraṇavastu,* 68.9ff.

72. *Gilgit Manuscripts,* iii 2, 143.10. This passage—like a number of other passages from the *Mūlasarvāstivāda-vinaya*—has been incorporated by I-tsing in his *Record;* see J. Takakusu, *A Record of the Buddhist Religion as Practised in India and the Malay Archipelago* (London: 1896) 192.

73. *Gilgit Manuscripts,* iii 2, 146.3.

74. *Gilgit Manuscripts,* iii 2, 124.1ff. There are a number of textual problems in the passage as a whole—Dutt, for example, makes several emendations—and the Tibetan translation (*Peking,* 41, 280-3-6ff) differs here, as it frequently does, just enough so that it does not provide a sure guide. However, the general sense of the passage is not in doubt.

75. *Peking,* 44, 95-3-5ff.

76. Given the not infrequent difficulty in distinguishing *d/ng,* especially but not exclusively, in the Peking edition, it is not impossible to read *bud dung,* etc. *Dung* can mean "a kind of shell or conch." [See G. Schopen, "Ritual Rights and Bones of Contention: More on Monastic Funerals and Relics in the *Mūlasarvāstivāda-vinaya,*" *JIP* 22 (1994) 59–60 for a much better discussion of the term.]

77. J. Marshall, A. Foucher, and N. G. Majumdar, *The Monuments of Sāñchī,* Vol. I

(Delhi: 1940) 385–386; Vol. III, pl. 124b. The inscription is fragmentary and has given rise to somewhat different interpretations. Two interesting studies of this "episode"—the so-called "First Meditation"—have recently been published: H. Durt, "La 'visite aux laboureurs' et la 'méditation sous l'arbre *jambu*' dans les biographies sanskrites et chinoises du buddha," *Indological and Buddhist Studies. Volume in Honour of Professor J. W. de Jong on His Sixtieth Birthday,* ed. L. A. Hercus et al. (Canberra: 1982) 95–120, and D. Schlingloff, "Die Meditation unter dem Jambu-Baum," *WZKS* 31 (1987) 111–130 (118, n. 32: "Die Inschrift [on the Sāñcī figure] vermeldet die Errichtung einer Statue des Erhabenen, der sich auf einem Steinsitz (?) unter dem Schatten des Rosenapfelbaumes befindet"). The passage cited above is not the only one in the *Mūlasarvāstivāda-vinaya* to refer to this image; see *Gilgit Manuscripts,* iii 2, 142.1: *yaṣṭa(yo yā) āyatās tā jambūcchāyikāḥ pratimāyā dhvajavaṃśāḥ kārayitavyāḥ,* and Takakusu, *A Record of the Buddhist Religion,* 190.

78. J. Gernet, *Les aspects économiques du bouddhisme dans la société chinoise du ve au xe siècle* (Paris: 1956) esp. 61–70, 149–162. Gernet, given his primary focus, justifiably paid little attention to the *Mūlasarvāstivāda-vinaya:* "Le Vinaya des Mūlasarvāstivādin, traduit au début du viiie siècle par Yi-tsing, et venu trop tard n'a pu avoir sur la constitution des institutions monacales autant d'influence que les précédents"; 62, n. 1. See also A. Bareau, "La construction et le culte des stūpa d'après les Vinayapiṭaka," *BEFEO* 50 (1960) 229–274, esp. 230, 242–243, 244, 256–257; A. Bareau, "Indian and Ancient Chinese Buddhism: Institutions Analogous to the Jisa," *Comparative Studies in Society and History* 3.4 (1961) 443–451. For traces of similar ideas in the Pāli *Vinaya,* see G. Schopen, "The *Stūpa* Cult and the Extant Pāli *Vinaya,* "Ch. V above, esp. 89–90; and, for the strong continuance of such ideas in Mahāyāna *sūtra* literature, G. Schopen, "Burial *Ad Sanctos* and the Physical Presence of the Buddha in Early Indian Buddhism," Ch. VII above, esp. 128–131. See, finally, for some brief remarks on some of these ideas in the *Abhidharmakośa* and *Mahāvibhāṣā,* M. Hofinger, "Le vol dans la morale bouddhique," *Indianisme et bouddhisme. Mélanges offerts à Mgr. Étienne Lamotte* (Louvain-La-Neuve: 1980) 177–189, esp. 185.

79. See, for example, from Valabhī, G. Bühler, "Additional Valabhī Grants, Nos. IX–XIV," *IA* 7 (1878) 66–72, esp. 67, line 5: . . . *tasya gandhapuṣpadhūpadīpatailādikriyotsarppaṇārthaṃ saddharmmasya pustakopakra . . . ānādeśasamatvāgatāṣṭādaśanikāy(ābhyantarā) ryyabhikṣu(saṃgha)sya cīvirapiṇḍapā(ta) . . . -vihārasya ca khaṇḍasphuṭitaviśīrṇṇapratisaṃskāraṇārtham . . .;* from Nālandā, Shastri, *EI* 17 (1923–1924) 322, line 38: . . . *bhagavato buddhabhaṭṭārakasya. . . āyārthe. . . cāturddiśāryabhikṣu-saṅghasya balicarusatracīvarapiṇḍapātaśayanāsanaglānapratyaya-bhaiṣajyādyarthaṃ dharmaratnasya lekhanādyarthaṃ vihārasya ca khaṇḍasphuṭitasamādhānārthaṃ;* from Kailan, D. C. Sircar, "The Kailan Copper-plate Inscription of King Śrīdhāraṇa Rāta of Samataṭa," *IHQ* 23 (1947) 221–241, esp. 239, line 22: . . . *bhagavatas tathāgataratnasya gandhadhūpadīpa-mālyānulepanārthan tadupadiṣṭamārggasya dharmmasya lekhanavācanārtham āryasaṅghasya ca cīvarapiṇḍapātādivividhopacārārtha. . . .* All of these make clear provision for copying texts as well.

80. V. Dehejia, *Early Buddhist Rock Temples. A Chronology* (London: 1972) 71.

81. On the Buddha as a living presence in his *stūpa* and relics, see Bareau, "Le construction et le culte des stūpa d'après les Vinayapiṭaka," 269: "D'autre part, la participation du *stūpa* au caractère sacré des reliques et de la personne du Buddha ou du saint tend à personnaliser le monument . . . le *stūpa* est plus que le symbole du Buddha, c'est le Buddha lui-même"; Schopen, "Burial *Ad Sanctos* and the Physical Presence of the Buddha in Early Indian Buddhism," Ch. VII above; and Schopen, "On the Buddha and His Bones," Ch. VIII above.

82. J. Marshall, *Taxila. An Illustrated Account of Archaeological Excavations carried out at Taxila under the Orders of the Government of India between the Years 1913 and 1934,* Vol. I (Cambridge: 1951) 275.

83. Marshall, *Taxila,* Vol. I, 315, 316, 317, 318, etc.

84. Marshall, *Taxila,* Vol. I, 365.

85. J. Ph. Vogel, "Excavations at Kasiā," *ARASI 1906–07* (Calcutta: 1909) 44–67, esp. 48–49.

86. Marshall et al., *The Bagh Caves in the Gwalior State,* 27–28.

87. M. K. Dhavalikar, *Late Hinayana Caves of Western India* (Poona: 1984) 79, 3. Dhavalikar uses here and elsewhere "Hīnayāna" to refer to "early" caves and "Mahāyāna" to refer to the "later" caves. I have avoided these sectarian usages in the belief that their accuracy has yet to be fully demonstrated.

88. M. K. Dhavalikar, "Evolution of the Buddhist Rock-cut Shrines of Western India," *JASBom* 45/46 (1970/1971) 50–61, esp. 53; see also M. K. Dhavalikar, "The Beginnings of Mahayana Architecture at Ajanta," *Madhu. Recent Researches in Indian Archeology and Art History. Shri M. N. Deshpande Festschrift,* ed. M. S. Nagaraja Rao (Delhi: 1981) 131–38.

89. A. Ghosh, ed., *Indian Archaeology 1954–55—A Review* (New Delhi: 1955) 24–26, esp. fig. 6.

90. D. Mitra, *Ratnagiri (1958–61),* MASI, No. 80 (New Delhi: 1981) Vol. I, 152ff, esp. fig. 8. It should, perhaps, be noted that the central cell in the back wall of Cave II at Bāgh houses a *stūpa,* not an image. This, however, may only represent a formal, and not a conceptual difference in the articulation of the sense of the Buddha's presence; see n. 81 above. The question needs further study.

91. *Śayanāsanavastu and Adhikaraṇavastu,* 10.20ff.

92. That constructional activity at Buddhist monastic sites was under the supervision of specifically designated monks is clear from both literary and inscriptional sources; see M. Njammasch, "Der *navakammika* und seine Stellung in der Hierarchie der buddhistischen Klöster," *Altorientalische Forschungen* 1 (1974) 279–293. For the construction of the *Gandhakuṭī* at Śrāvastī in Pāli sources, see V. Fausbøll, *The Jataka,* Vol. I (London: 1877) 92.21 (*so majjhe dasabalassa gandhakuṭiṃ kāresi*).

93. J. H. Marshall, "Excavations at Saheth-Maheth," *ARASI 1910–11* (Calcutta: 1914) 11–12 and pl. VIa; see also D. R. Sahni, "A Buddhist Image Inscription from Śrāvastī," *ARASI 1908–09* (Calcutta: 1912) 133–138.

94. Marshall, "Excavations at Saheth-Maheth," 12 and pl. VIb.

95. Marshall et al., *The Monuments of Sāñchī,* Vol. I, 47–49.

96. Marshall and Konow, "Excavations at Sārnāth, 1908," 68, etc.

97. A. Ghosh, ed., *Indian Archaeology 1962–63—A Review* (New Delhi: 1965) 97, 107; cf. M. C. Joshi, "Studies in Early Indian Art in Uttar Pradesh and Neighbouring Areas: Summary and Suggestions," *Archaeology and History. Essays in Memory of Shri A. Ghosh,* ed. B. M. Pande and B. D. Chattopadhyaya, Vol. II (Delhi: 1987) 495–506, esp. 501 and pl. 134.

98. Marshall et al., *The Monuments of Sāñchī,* 47.

99. The above remarks should not be taken to imply that all "images" found in *stūpas* are to be interpreted in this way. There are some instances where other ideas—although not unrelated—appear to be intended. See, for example, the carefully arranged set of images found in the core of the main *stūpa* at Devnimori in R. N. Mehta and S. N. Chowdhary,

Excavation at Devnimori (A Report of the Excavation conducted from 1960 to 1963) (Baroda: 1966) 49ff.

100. See as a sampling for the aspects which have most concerned us here: A. B. Keith, "The Personality of an Idol," *Journal of Comparative Legislation and International Law*, 3rd series, 7 (1925) 255–257; J. N. Banerjea, *The Development of Hindu Iconography* (Calcutta: 1956) esp. 36–107; G.-D. Sontheimer, "Religious Endowments in India: The Juristic Personality of Hindu Deities," *Zeitschrift für vergleichende Rechtswissenschaft* 67 (1965) 44–100; J. D. M. Derrett, "The Reform of Hindu Religious Endowments," *South Asian Politics and Religion*, ed. D. E. Smith (Princeton: 1966) 311–336; H. von Stietencron, "Orthodox Attitudes Towards Temple Service and Image Worship in Ancient India," *Central Asiatic Journal* 21 (1971) 126–138; D. L. Eck, *Darśan. Seeing the Divine Image in India*, 2nd rev. ed. (Chambersburg: 1985).

101. J. Takakusu, trans., *A Record of the Buddhist Religion as Practised in India and the Malay Archipelago*, 176–177.

102. J. May, "La philosophie bouddhique idéaliste," *Asiatische Studien / Études asiatiques* 25 (1971) 256–323, esp. 298.

Index of Archaeological Sites and Inscriptions

Index of Texts

Index of Words, Phrases, and Formulae

Index of Subjects

Part II
Buddhist Monks and Business Matters

Dedicated to the taxpayers
and working men and women of
Indiana, Texas, and California,
whose labor paid for
my scholarly leisure

CONTENTS

ACKNOWLEDGMENTS

THE PERSON TO BLAME for this volume is Patricia Crosby. She was abetted by Luis Gómez, but it was largely as a result of her . . . uh . . . persistence that vague and evasive promises on my part were somehow transformed into a project, then a schedule, then a manuscript. Her motives remain inscrutable, but given her roots, it might be assumed that she still has a soft spot for old cowboys. I am, in any case, grateful to her, and to Professor Gómez, who, indeed, remains for me a Professor.

I am also, again, grateful to the members of my family, all of whom—although a little worse for wear—are still going. Their perspective on things remains important and is nicely exemplified by an encounter that my niece—also a Schopen—had at an American university that shall remain nameless. When the professor of an anthropology course she was taking asked her if she was related to the Schopen who was a "buddhologist," she promptly and emphatically denied it—she did not know what the word meant, but it did not sound like anybody she knew.

I remain grateful to old friends: John Thiel and Hal Roth—a theologian and a Sinologist—an odd cluster, perhaps, but deep, and old, and true. Our conversations are still about books and ideas even if there are increasingly frequent references to aches and pains, receding hair, or bulging waistlines. I continue to be grateful to my old boss and friend Patrick Olivelle, and I continue to be amazed by his scholarship, his high spirits, and his apparently boundless energy. I am also grateful to another—if unlikely—boss: one Carl Bielefeldt. He had to watch my misguided attempt to make myself over into a member of the faculty of that bastion of free enterprise and liberal politics that is Stanford University. It could not have been a pretty sight, and yet he never seemed to lose his sense of humor. I am grateful to him for this, and for the time spent at Stanford—at least one of the papers in this volume was written there. I am equally grateful to Bernard Faure, at Stanford still, for his friendship and conversation. Our occasional trips to Berkeley in quest of books, and even our trip to the Palo Alto dump, are among my favorite memories of those otherwise benighted days.

My new boss too had to watch, but, as befits the only monk I know who looks really good in a three-piece suit, Robert Buswell never lost his composure. Also at UCLA, William Bodiford (an amazing source of the most disparate kinds of information) and John Duncan (a fellow country boy) were welcoming from the start. Robert Brown—who, if I remember correctly, started the whole convoluted process that led to Los Angeles—has become a very good reason for going to campus, has put up with a lot of teasing, and generously allowed me access to his personal library (most of which is made up of books checked out of the university library for the next two hundred years). More recently, a young man I have known for many years has joined us, and his enthusiasm for scholarship has, as always, been infectious: Jonathan Silk has never been at a loss for words about my work or anyone else's, has lent me books, provided me references (even when I did not want them), and, even more important for world peace, is learning how to be polite. It is nice to have him near at hand. To all these gentlemen I am very grateful.

I am equally grateful to all the students (or at least most of them)—both undergraduate and graduate—whom I have had the good fortune to meet in the classroom. They have kept me young and curious, some in particular: long ago in Bloomington, Yael Bentor and Daniel Boucher—the first soft-spoken, the second decidedly not; Jason Neelis, who had the good sense to go to study with Richard Salomon; at UCLA, Nicholas Morrissey (who scanned all the papers in this volume) and Shayne Clarke, who has done yeoman's work on this cantankerous task. I have learned a great deal from them all and look forward to learning more.

I continue to be in debt to several others who are farther afield. To Richard Salomon in Seattle and Jan Nattier in Bloomington, who, in different ways, have kept me on my toes. To Phyllis Granoff and Koichi Shinohara in the frozen North, to Gérard Fussman in France, Oskar von Hinüber in Germany, and K. R. Norman in England—my debt to them all is old and continuous. In Japan, I continue to be grateful to Shoryu Katsura, and I have a special debt to Nobuchiyo Odani, who invited me to Otani University, made my time there productive and fun, translated my lectures into Japanese, and saw to their publication in a handsome little volume. I am also grateful to a whole string of young scholars who have sent me offprints and their books and thereby taught me much—in Japan, Shizuka Sasaki, Satoshi Hiraoka, Nobuyuki Yamagiwa, Masahiro Shimoda, and Seishi Karashima, in particular; in Germany, Petra Kieffer-Pülz and Ute Hüsken, especially; in England, Andrew Skilton and Kate Crosby.

My debt to all of those so far mentioned is substantial and deeply felt. It is exceeded only by the debt I owe to two young women: Morgan—young in years—

who gives me hope; and Fleming—young in spirit—who gives me meaning. Neither could I do without.

Some details—all but one of the papers in this volume have been previously published. There is in this volume, as in its predecessor, a certain amount of repetition, and some passages of the *Mūlasarvāstivāda-vinaya* in particular are translated more than once. In such cases I have made no attempt to make my renderings exactly alike, and I do not offer any apologies for this. I have left these variant translations because they so nicely show that all translations are only approximate—the same phrase can be legitimately rendered in more than one way. In this volume too there is some variation in the spelling of place-names that has not always been removed, and copious other minor inconsistencies in hyphenation, capitalization, and other matters of national security. These remain in spite of the *fact* that once again—as with the first volume—these papers have fallen into the hands of an excellent copy editor. Working in Austin, where many of these papers were first written, Rosemary Wetherold has *in fact* removed *at least* a *very* large number of stylistic infelicities (she will most fully appreciate the italicization). Those that remain are my fault, as is the substance, which has been changed not at all. I am grateful to her, and to the University of Hawai'i Press for taking yet another chance.

ABBREVIATIONS

Adhikaraṇavastu (Gnoli)	R. Gnoli, *The Gilgit Manuscript of the Śayanāsanavastu and the Adhikaraṇavastu. Being the 15th and 16th Sections of the Vinaya of the Mūlasarvāstivādin* (Serie Orientale Roma 50) (Rome: 1978)
ArA	*Artibus Asiae*
ARASI	*Annual Report of the Archaeological Survey of India*
ArO	*Ars Orientalis*
Avadānaśataka (Speyer)	J. S. Speyer, *Avadānaçataka. A Century of Edifying Tales Belonging to the Hīnayāna* (Bibliotheca Buddhica 3.1–2) (St. Petersburg: 1902–1909)
Bauddhavidyāsudhākaraḥ	*Bauddhavidyāsudhākaraḥ. Studies in Honour of Heinz Bechert on the Occasion of His 65th Birthday* (Indica et Tibetica 30), ed. P. Kieffer-Pülz and J.-U. Hartmann (Swisttal-Odendorf: 1997)
BD	I. B. Horner, *The Book of the Discipline* (Oxford and London 1938–1966) 6 Vols.
BEFEO	*Bulletin de l'école française d'extrême-orient*
BEI	*Bulletin d'études indiennes*
BHSD	F. Edgerton, *Buddhist Hybrid Sanskrit Grammar and Dictionary.* Vol. II: Dictionary (New Haven, Conn.: 1953)
BSBM	G. Schopen, *Bones, Stones, and Buddhist Monks. Collected Papers on the Archaeology, Epigraphy,*

	and Texts of Monastic Buddhism in India (Honolulu: 1997)
Bod rgya tshig mdzod chen mo	*Bod rgya tshig mdzod chen mo*, ed. Zhang Yisun et al. (Beijing: 1985) 3 Vols.
BSOAS	*Bulletin of the School of Oriental and African Studies*
CAJ	*Central Asiatic Journal*
CII	*Corpus Inscriptionum Indicarum*
Derge	*The Tibetan Tripitaka. Taipei Edition*, ed. A.W. Barber (Taipei: 1991)
Divyāvadāna (Cowell and Neil)	E. B. Cowell and R. A. Neil, *The Divyāvadāna. A Collection of Early Buddhist Legends* (Cambridge, U.K.: 1886)
DPPN	G. P. Malalasekera, *Dictionary of Pāli Proper Names* (London: 1937) 2 Vols.
'Dul ba pha'i gleng bum chen mo	L. Chandra, *The Collected Works of Bu-ston*, Part 23 (Ḥa) (Śata-Piṭaka Series 63) (New Delhi: 1971)
EB	*Eastern Buddhist*
EI	*Epigraphia Indica*
EW	*East and West*
FFMB	G. Schopen, *Figments and Fragments of a Mahāyāna Buddhism in India. More Collected Papers* (Honolulu: forthcoming)
GBMs	R. Vira and L. Chandra, *Gilgit Buddhist Manuscripts* (Facsimile Edition) (Śata-Piṭaka Series 10.6) (New Delhi: 1974), Part 6
GMs	N. Dutt, *Gilgit Manuscripts*, Vol. III, Pt. 1 (Srinagar: 1947); Vol. III, Pt. 2 (Srinagar: 1942); Vol. III, Pt. 3 (Srinagar: 1943); Vol. III, Pt. 4 (Calcutta: 1950)
HJAS	*Harvard Journal of Asiatic Studies*
HR	*History of Religions*
IA	*Indian Antiquary*
IAR	*Indian Archaeology: A Review*
IBK	*Indogaku bukkyōgaku kenkyū*
IHQ	*Indian Historical Quarterly*

IIJ	*Indo-Iranian Journal*
JA	*Journal asiatique*
JAOS	*Journal of the American Oriental Society*
JASBom	*Journal of the Asiatic Society of Bombay*
Jäschke	H. A. Jäschke, *A Tibetan-English Dictionary* (London: 1881)
JBomBRAS	*Journal of the Bombay Branch of the Royal Asiatic Society*
JIABS	*Journal of the International Association of Buddhist Studies*
JIH	*Journal of Indian History*
JIP	*Journal of Indian Philosophy*
JPTS	*Journal of the Pali Text Society*
JRAS	*Journal of the Royal Asiatic Society of Great Britain and Ireland*
Kaṭhinavastu (Chang)	Kun Chang, *A Comparative Study of the Kaṭhinavastu* (Indo-Iranian Monographs 1) (The Hague: 1957)
Konow, *Kharoshṭhī Inscriptions*	S. Konow, *Kharoshṭhī Inscriptions with the Exception of Those of Aśoka* (Corpus Inscriptionum Indicarui Vol. II, Pt. 1) (Calcutta: 1929)
Lamotte, *Histoire du bouddhisme indien*	Ét. Lamotte, *Histoire du bouddhisme indien. Des origines à l'ère śaka* (Bibliothèque du muséon 43) (Louvain: 1958)
Lüders, *Bharhut Inscriptions*	H. Lüders, *Bharhut Inscriptions* (Corpus Inscriptionum Indicarum Vol. II, Pt. 2), rev. E. Waldschmidt and M. A. Mehendale (Ootacamund: 1963)
Lüders, *Mathurā Inscriptions*	H. Lüders, *Mathurā Inscriptions* (Abhandlungen der Akademie der Wissenschaften in Göttingen. Philologisch-Historische Klasse. Dritte Folge, Nr. 47), ed. K. L. Janert (Göttingen: 1961)
Mahāparinirvāṇasūtra (Waldschmidt)	E. Waldschmidt, *Das Mahāparinirvāṇasūtra. Text in Sanskrit und Tibetisch, verglichen mit dem Pāli neb. einer Übersetzung der chinesischen Entsprechung im Vinaya der Mūlasarvāstivādins* (Abhandlungen der Deutschen Akademie der Wissenschaften zu

	Berlin. Philologisch-Historische Klasse. Jahrgang 1949, Nr. 1; Klasse für Sprachen, Literatur und Kunst. Jahrgang 1950, Nr. 2–3) (Berlin: 1950–1951) Teil I–III
MASI	*Memoirs of the Archaeological Survey of India*
Pāli *Vinaya*	H. Oldenberg, *The Vinaya Piṭakaṃ: One of the Principal Buddhist Holy Scriptures in the Pāli Language* (London: 1879–1883) 5 Vols
Panglung, *Die Erzählstoffe des Mūlasarvāstivāda-Vinaya*	J. L. Panglung, *Die Erzählstoffe des Mūlasarvāstivāda-Vinaya. Analysiert auf Grund der tibetischen Übersetzung* (Studia Philologica Buddhica Monograph Series 3) (Tokyo: 1981)
Poṣadhavastu (Hu-von Hinüber)	H. Hu-von Hinüber, *Das Poṣadhavastu. Vorschriften für die buddhistische Beichtfeier im Vinaya der Mūlasarvāstivādins* (Studien zur Indologie und Iranistik. Monographie 13) (Reinbeck, Germany: 1994)
Pravrajyāvastu (Eimer)	H. Eimer, *Rab tu 'byuṅ ba'i gẑi. Die tibetische Übersetzung des Pravrajyāvastu im Vinaya der Mūlasarvāstivādins* (Asiatische Forschungen 82) (Wiesbaden: 1983) 2 Teil
Pravrajyāvastu (Näther/Vogel/Wille)	V. Näther, C. Vogel, and K. Wille, "The Final Leaves of the *Pravrajyāvastu* Portion of the Vinayavastu Manuscript Found near Gilgit. Part I Saṃgharakṣitāvadāna," in *Sanskrit-Texte aus dem buddhistischen Kanon: Neuentdeckungen und Neueditionen III* (Sanskrit-Wörterbuch der buddhistischen Texte aus den Turfan-Funden. Beiheft 6) Bearbeitet von G. Bongard-Levin et al. (Göttingen: 1996) 241–296
Pravrajyāvastu (Vogel and Wille)	C. Vogel and K. Wille, *Some Hitherto Unidentified Fragments of the Pravrajyāvastu Portion of the Vinayavastu Manuscript Found near Gilgit.* Nachrichten der Akademie der Wissenschaften in Göttingen I. Philologisch-Historische Klasse. Jahrgang 1984, Nr. 7 (Göttingen: 1984) 299–337
RAA	*Revue des arts asiatiques*
RHR	*Revue de l'histoire des religions*
SAA	*South Asian Archaeology*

Saṅghabhedavastu (Gnoli)	R. Gnoli, *The Gilgit Manuscript of the Saṅghabhedavastu. Being the 17th and Last Section of the Vinaya of the Mūlasarvāstivādin* (Serie Orientale Roma 49.1–2) (Rome: 1977–1978)
Śayanāsanavastu (Gnoli)	see *Adhikaraṇavastu* above
Schopen, *Daijō bukkyō kōki jidai*	G. Schopen, *Daijō bukkyō kōki jidai: Indo no sōin seikatsu*, trans N. Odani (Tokyo: 2000)
StII	*Studien zur Indologie und Iranistik*
Tog	*The Tog Palace Manuscript of the Tibetan Kanjur* (Leh: 1975–1980)
TP	*T'oung Pao*
TSD	L. Chandra, *Tibetan-Sanskrit Dictionary* (New Delhi: 1959–1961; repr. Kyoto: 1971)
UCR	*University of Ceylon Review*
Vinayasūtra (Bapat and Gokhale)	P. V. Bapat and V. V. Gokhale, *Vinayasūtra and Auto-Commentary on the Same by Guṇaprabha* (Tibetan Sanskrit Works Series 22) (Patna: 1982)
Vinayasūtra (Sankrityayana)	R. Sankrityayana, *Vinayasūtra of Bhadanta Guṇaprabha* (Singhi Jain Śāstra Śikṣāpītha. Singhi Jain Series 74) (Bombay: 1981)
WZKS	*Wiener Zeitschrift für die Kunde Südasiens*
ZDMG	*Zeitschrift der Deutschen Morgenländischen Gesellschaft*

CHAPTER I

The Good Monk and His Money in a Buddhist Monasticism of "the Mahāyāna Period"

It is probably fair to say that, because of the way they have been studied, neither Indian Buddhist monasticism nor the Buddhist monastery in India has been allowed to have anything like a real history. Whether implicitly or explicitly, conscious or not, most modern scholars have either unquestioningly assumed, or worked hard to show, that extant monastic or *vinaya* sources, for example, must be early, some even asserting—or again assuming—that they must go back to the Buddha himself. But the necessary consequences of this assumption have rarely been examined: if the extant *vinaya* sources are early, if they go back anywhere near the time of the Buddha, then Buddhist monasticism could not have any real institutional history—it could only have sprung all but fully formed from the head of the Buddha. Moreover, since these extant *vinaya* sources already know and are meant to govern fully developed, well-organized, walled monasteries that had infirmaries, refectories, bathrooms, steam rooms, locks, and keys, the Buddhist monastery too could have had no real development and, consequently, no actual history. It would have been architecturally finished from its very start.

Such pictures—one is tempted to say fantasies—fit, of course, not at all well with what is known about monasticisms elsewhere. More importantly, and in specific regard to the Indian Buddhist monastery for which we have some independent, nonliterary sources as well, it does not fit at all with what is found in the archaeological record of Buddhist monastic sites in India. The earliest Buddhist "monasteries" that are known in India—and none of these are pre-Aśokan—are not "monasteries" at all. They are either [86]* only barely improved, unorganized, natural caverns or caves, or poorly constructed and ill-organized shelters built of

Originally published in *The Eastern Buddhist* n.s. 32.1 (2000) 85–105. Reprinted with stylistic changes with permission of The Eastern Buddhist Society.

*To allow for easy cross-reference, the page numbers of the original publications have been inserted into the text in square brackets.

rubble or other cheap materials.[1] Communities living in these environments could not have produced our elaborate *vinayas*, nor would they have had any use for them. Since such communities had no steam rooms (*jentāka*), for example, how could they possibly have generated elaborate rules governing their construction and use?

Clearly there is something curiously wrong here, and the early history of Buddhist monasticism and Buddhist monasteries in India must be fundamentally rethought and reexamined. But there are other equally interesting projects that also must be undertaken. Once it is allowed that, yes, both Buddhist monasticism and Buddhist monasteries had histories, that both developed and changed over time, then "early" Buddhist monasticisms—and we should probably begin to use the plural seriously here—and the "early" Buddhist monastery, become only one, and certainly not the only important, object of investigation. We need no longer be implicitly or explicitly concerned primarily with the question of what Buddhist monasticisms originally were. We might be equally—and probably more fruitfully—concerned with what at given places at given points in time they had become. We might begin to meaningfully talk about "early" and "early medieval" and "medieval" and "late" Buddhist monasticisms and to study each of these in their own right and not, for example, as mere exemplifications of the decline and degeneration of some "early" and largely assumed single "ideal." Each of these monasticisms will need to be understood and evaluated on its own terms, and this, of course, will not be easy.

If, for example, we want to know what Buddhist monasticism had become in North India in the period between the mature Kuṣān and the fifth through sixth centuries—the period that for lack of a better term might be called "the early medieval," and the period that is generally taken to be that of "the Mahāyāna"—then the *Mūlasarvāstivāda-vinaya* becomes a primary source. There is an almost general agreement that this *Vinaya* is "late" and was redacted and used during this period. There is the same sort of agreement that during this period this *vinaya* had clear connections with North India, [87] with Gandhāra, Mathurā, and perhaps Kashmir.[2] This is the good part. The bad part follows almost immediately: the *Mūlasarvāstivāda-vinaya* is enormous. Sylvain Lévi has described it as "a vast compilation," as "nearly epic," as an "immense pot-pourri of the Buddhist discipline," as "monstrous" and "in itself an already complete canon." Huber, too, refers to it as "this enormous compilation," and Lalou as "this enormous *vinaya*"—here too there is general agreement and it is not difficult to see why.[3] The Tibetan version of the *Mūlasarvāstivāda-vinaya* in, for example, the Derge edition is almost four thousand folios long and takes up thirteen volumes, and even it may not be complete. It seems to lack two texts often quoted by Guṇaprabha entitled the *Mātṛkā* and the *Nidāna*, although both may now be represented in the Tibetan traditions by what is there called the *Uttaragrantha(s)*.[4] Large portions of its *Vinayavastu* have also been preserved in Sanskrit in the manuscripts from Gilgit,[5] and significant portions of its *Vibhaṅga* are also available—usually in truncated or crudely condensed form—in the *Divyāvadāna*.[6] There is as well a Chinese translation, although it is incom[88]plete, "full of gaps," and "much less exact than the Tibetan one." Lamotte, in fact, characterizes it as "mediocre."[7]

The bulk of the *Mūlasarvāstivāda-vinaya* is, however, only a part of the bad news. Not only is this *Vinaya* huge, but it has also been little studied, and only a tiny portion of it has been critically edited in any language. This means—at the very least—that anything said about it at this stage can be only tentative and provisional.

These are all serious problems, but an equally serious obstacle to any understanding of this "monster" is the fact that much of what it seems to contain does not correspond to what we thought we knew about the character and defining characteristics of monastic Buddhism. It has, for example, been commonly assumed or asserted that becoming a Buddhist monk involved—or even required—renouncing all personal property. But the *Mūlasarvāstivāda-vinaya* seems to assume, or even require, something quite different. According, for example, to the Mūlasarvāstivādin ordination formulary that has come down to us in a Sanskrit manuscript from Tibet, the candidate for ordination must be asked: "Do you have any debt (*deya*, *bu lon*), either large or small, to anyone?" If he says yes, then he must be asked: "Will you be able to repay this *after* you have entered the order (*śakṣyasi pravrajyāyaṃ dātum*)?" If he says no, the text says he must be sent away and he cannot be admitted into the order. Only if he says that he will be able to pay can the ordination proceed.[8] Here, in other words, the expectation—indeed the rule—is that a successful candidate for Mūlasarvāstivādin ordination would not renounce private wealth but would retain it and be responsible for and able to pay any debt that was contracted prior to ordination.

These sorts of expectations are moreover found elsewhere in this *Vinaya* in a startling variety of contexts. The *Vinayavibhaṅga*, for example, repeat[89]edly assumes that monks will be subject to tolls and road taxes and gives rules that require monks to pay them (Derge Ca 72b.6ff). This must mean that the redactors of this *Vinaya* also assumed two other things: that monks while traveling would be transporting taxable goods, and that monks would have the means to pay the taxes. That it was assumed that these were their own personal goods, and that the payments were to be made from their own resources, is made virtually certain by the fact that the *Vibhaṅga* has a separate set of rules dealing with the payment of tolls on goods that are for ritual purposes and are corporately owned, that is, that belong to the Buddha or the Dharma or the Saṅgha—in such cases it is explicitly stated that the tolls must be paid from corporate funds (Derge Ca 76b.4–78a.4). In the *Kṣudrakavastu* there is a rule explicitly stating that when a monk borrows (*brnyas pa*) a mat from another monk, and that mat is damaged by him, the borrowing monk must compensate the owner: "He must either give him the price of its full value or what will satisfy him" (*ri ba'i rin sbyin par bya ba 'am / de'i sems mgu bar bya'o*—Derge Tha 49a.1). In the same *Vastu*, monks are explicitly told that when their property is stolen, they must not take the thieves to court but must buy back from them what they stole, even if they have to give the full price (*rgyal po'i pho brang du sbron par mi bya'i 'on kyang sngar chos bshad nas bslang bar bya'o / gal te mi ster na rin phyed kyis blang bar bya'o / gal te de ltar yang mi ster na rin tshang bar byin la blang bar bya ste*—Derge Tha 233b.2). And the *Kṣudrakavastu* also explicitly declares that monks must carry seals (*rgya bcang bar bya'o*). Such seals were meant to mark property, and the text, again, explicitly says there are two sorts of seals—seals of the community and seals of individuals (*rgya ni gnyis te / dge 'dun gyi dang gang zag gi'o*—Derge Tha 7b.6–8a.7; cf. *Vinayavibhaṅga*, Derge Ca 79b). The distinction here is particularly interesting as one of numerous instances where this *Vinaya* formally acknowledges the existence of individual private property (*paudgalika*) and distinguishes it from corporate or communal property (*sāṃghika*). Yet another example occurs in the *Cīvaravastu*. Here the problem is that terminally ill monks were dying on bedding belonging to the community (*glānāḥ asaṃviditā eva sāṃghike śayanāsane kālaṃ kurvanti*). As a consequence, the Buddha himself is made to order the attending monk to watch closely for the signs of imminent death and, when they occurred, to move the dying monk on some pretext onto his personal bedding (*śarīrāvasthāṃ jñātvā paudgalike śayanāsane vyājenāvatārya śāyitavya iti*—GMs iii 2, 123.16). And this same distinction also comes into play elsewhere in the *Cīvaravastu* in regard to dying monks. [90] In one passage, for example, it is clearly assumed that monks normally owned or were expected to pay for any medicines they required or for any rituals that were performed on their behalf. This seems at least to follow from the fact that only in the case of very poor monks (*alpajñāta*) could these be paid for out of corporate funds (*sāṃghika*), and even then those corporate funds were to be repaid if at all possible (GMs iii 2, 124.11–125.9; cf. 128.1–131.15). The acknowledgement of *paudgalika*, of a monk's private property, occurs even in the Mūlasarvāstivādin *Prātimokṣa*.[9]

The mere existence of the distinction between *sāṃghika* and *paudgalika*, and the formal acknowledgment of the latter in Mūlasarvāstivādin monastic law, should in themselves put to rest any doubts about whether Mūlasarvāstivādin monks were expected to have personal property. But to well and truly bury them we probably need only glance again at the last part of the *Cīvaravastu*. There are there more than thirty-five pages detailing what can only be called Mūlasarvāstivādin monastic inheritance law. There are rules detailing what should happen to the property of a monk from one "residence" (*āvāsa*) who dies in another (GMs iii 2, 113.14–117.4); rules dealing with the disposition of the estate of a monk some of whose property was held in trust (*prativastu*) by other monks or even laymen (143.15–145.13); rules laying down the formal procedures (*karman*) required when the community takes formal possession (*adhitiṣṭhati*) of a deceased monk's estate in order to distribute it (117.8–121.5 and 145.2–.9); rules establishing the proper times for distributing a dead monk's estate and for determining who can participate in that distribution (120.3–.20); and so on. Rules dealing with monastic estates are, moreover, not found only in the *Cīvaravastu*. There are, for example, rules in the *Kṣudrakavastu* stipulating that property that a monk "designates" (*bsngo ba*) for another monk while he is alive reverts to his estate upon his death (Derge Tha 254a.1–.6) and, conversely, that property that was "designated by one monk for another does not belong to the latter's estate when he dies, but continues to belong to the former" (Derge Tha 254a.6–b.2). There is as well a large number of rules governing monastic estates and inheritance law in the *Uttaragrantha(s)*, rules—for example—governing what must happen [91] when a monk borrows money from a layman (*dge slong gzhan zhig gis khyim bdag cig las kār shā pa ṇa zhig bskyes pa* . . .) but dies without repaying the loan (Derge Pa 132b.7–133a.3; see also Derge Pa 85a.3–86a.2, 86a.2–.6, 86a.6–b.4, 86b.4–.7, 86b.7–87a.4, etc.).[10] The size, finally, of some of the monastic estates that are mentioned is also impressive, and it seems clear that the redactors of this *Vinaya* assumed that some monastic estates would be very large indeed. One such estate is described as worth or consisting of "a great deal of gold, three hundred thousand of gold" (*prabhūtaṃ suvarṇaṃ tisraḥ suvarṇalakṣāḥ*—GMs iii 2, 118.11), and this elicits no comment in the text and appears to pass as completely acceptable. In fact, the *Cīvaravastu* even has a set of rules specifically framed to deal with large estates left by monks who were "rich and famous" (*jñātamahāpuṇya*—GMs iii 2, 123.10–15), and here again there is not the slightest indication that such estates were considered irregular or undesirable.

At least two things, it seems, are then already reasonably clear from the material quickly summarized to this point. A great deal of the *Mūlasarvāstivāda-vinaya* takes for granted that the monks it was meant to govern had and were expected—even required—to have personal property and private wealth. If Buddhist monks were ever required to renounce private property—and there are good reasons for doubting this—they certainly were not by the time the *Mūlasarvāstivāda-vinaya* was redacted. Some Mūlasarvāstivādin monks, those who were "well known and of great merit," were even expected to be quite wealthy. Rather than suggest that such wealth should be renounced or avoided, this *Vinaya* redacted detailed rules to transmit that wealth to other monks and to shelter it from the state. The estates of men who died *aputra*, "sonless"—and monks at least normally did—otherwise went to the king, and this issue of law is twice directly addressed in the *Cīvaravastu* (GMs iii 2, 118.11ff, 140.14ff).

In fact, a preoccupation with specifically legal issues is the second seemingly characteristic feature of Mūlasarvāstivādin monasticism to emerge. The redactors of this *Vinaya* appear to have been just as much jurists [92] as they were monks. They appear to apply to the questions of ownership and inheritance, for example, the same sort of care and precision that their colleagues working on the *Abhidharma* applied to the classification and definition of *dharmas*. Indeed, how much the "style" of thinking that dominates the *Abhidharma* owes to these monastic jurists is an open and emerging question.[11] It may be that many of the techniques and styles of exposition were first employed in constructing the *vinayas*. The two bodies of material at the very least have many methods in common, and Vasubandhu, for example, deals not infrequently with what are issues of monastic law. One of the best examples, perhaps, is his treatment of the rights and status of a monk who violated one of the *pārājika* rules but who had no intention of concealing it (Shastri, ii 646)—the same topic is treated as well in the *Kṣudrakavastu* (Derge Tha 102a.5–104b.2). But even putting these considerations aside, what we have seen so far would seem to suggest that in regard to legal questions the *Mūlasarvāstivāda-vinaya* has a degree of sophistication that is certainly notable, and it appears that the redactors of this *Vinaya* were certainly concerned with legal precision. But this same legal sophistication and concern is also found elsewhere in the *Mūlasarvāstivāda-vinaya*.

The redactors of the *Mūlasarvāstivāda-vinaya* either adapted or invented a significant number of sophisticated financial instruments and economic devices—they knew and made rules governing the use of both oral and written wills, written loan contracts, permanent endowments, monetary deposits, interest-bearing loans, negotiable securities, and even what might be called a form of health insurance. The *Cīvaravastu*, for example, disallows the use of nuncupative, or oral, wills by monks to dispose of their property in favor of other monks (GMs iii 2, 124.1–10). But this rule is also amended and clarified in both the *Kṣudrakavastu* and the *Uttaragrantha(s)*, where it is explicitly established that Buddhist monastic law does not apply to laymen and that, therefore, a nuncupative will made by a layman in favor of monks is both allowable and valid (Derge Tha 252b.3–254a.1 and Pa 130a.4–131a.3).[12] The oral disposition of property prior to death was, of course, a subject of discussion in *dharmaśāstric* law as well. More striking [93] still is the sanctioned use of a written will (*patrābhilekhya*, *patrābhilikhita*) by a layman of sorts to leave all of a considerable fortune to the Community (GMs iii 2, 140.14ff). This is most certainly the earliest reference to a written will in all of Indian literature and—apart from a possible second reference in the *Divyāvadāna*'s account of the death of Aśoka—virtually unique.[13] Not quite so unusual are the detailed rules in both the *Vibhaṅga* and the *Uttaragrantha(s)* requiring monks to accept permanent endowments of cash (*akṣayanīvī*) and to lend that cash out on interest (Derge Ca 154b.3–155b.2 and Pa 265a.6–b.2)—both the rate of interest and the instructions to be followed in writing up the loan contract here are very close to what is found in *dharmaśāstric* sources, especially in *Yājñavalkya.*[14] And although in the *Vibhaṅga*, but not in the *Uttaragrantha(s)*, it is the monks themselves who are to lend out the money, draw up the contract, and service the loan, the *Kṣudrakavastu* contains a passage describing an arrangement, sanctioned by the Buddha, whereby a monetary deposit for the benefit of the monks is made by a layperson with a merchant, who in turn uses it as venture capital, the profit from which—how much is not specified—is to be distributed to the monks (Derge Tha 258a.3–259a.3). There is good inscriptional evidence for just such arrangements, especially from the Western Caves.[15] There are also references in our *Vinaya* to both monks and nuns making use of what might be called negotiable securities or promissory notes (*patralekhya, chags rgya*). Our *Vinaya* even distinguishes between two sorts of such notes and gives separate rules for dealing with each. The *Cīvaravastu* rules that when promissory notes come to the Community as a part of an estate, whatever is realized from those that can be quickly liquidated (*yacchīghraṃ śakyate sādhayituṃ*) must be distributed among the monks, [94] whereas those that cannot be so liquidated must be deposited in the strong room as property in common for the Community of the Four Directions (GMs iii 2, 143.7–.9). In the *Bhikṣuṇī-vibhaṅga* the nun Sthūlanandā all but forces a layman to give her a promissory note (*chags rgya*), which he is holding, as a "gift" for reciting the Dharma for him. Neither the practice nor the note is presented as problematic. The problem arises only when Sthūlanandā tries to collect on it. She goes to the debtor and demands quick payment. The debtor, apparently a little surprised, asks, "Do you, Noble One, own this (i.e., the note—*'phags ma khyod mnga' 'am*)?" Her answer—from the point of view of monks, nuns, and private property—is both interesting and unequivocal: She says, "I am the owner (*bdag dbang ngo*)." And this too is not problematic. The only problem is that the nun then threatens to take the man to court to collect on the debt—this, and this alone, is an offense against monastic rule, and even it is allowed, or at least involves no offense, if the nun is "one who earns with some difficulty" (*tshegs chung ngus khugs pa*—Derge Ta 123a.5–124a.2).

The final example of a financial instrument that we might note here is not formally contractual and requires a short excursus. Although the whole topic has received little attention, it appears that Buddhist monasteries in India, and Buddhist monastic communities of the sort envisioned in the *Mūlasarvāstivāda-vinaya*, were ideally suited to provide care to the old and infirm and to the sick and dying. There was, moreover, a distinct social need for such services, or at least the redactors of our *Vinaya* seem to have thought so. They seem to have thought that because of taboos concerning purity and pollution, brahmanical groups at least were not willing to provide services of this sort, even for their own. This much it seems can be deduced, for example, from texts like one that is found in the *Śayanāsanavastu* (Gnoli) 13.24–.33. Here it is said that a young brahmin was staying in a hostel for young brahmins (*māṇavakaśālā*),[16] but he fell ill with vomiting and diarrhea. Rather than attend to him, however, the other brahmins, "from fear of pollution" (*aśucibhayād*), threw him out and abandoned him. It is only the Buddhist monks Śāriputra and Maudgalyāyana who, when they chanced upon him, "cleaned him with a bamboo brush, rubbed him with [95] white earth and bathed him." Because they also "taught" the Dharma for him—and here this almost certainly can refer only to a kind of deathbed recitation—he died in a good state of mind and was reborn in heaven. The function of Buddhist monks here is hard to miss—they, not one's fellow brahmins, care for the sick and dying.

This story, however, concerns a chance encounter. Buddhist monasteries, on the other hand, at least those envisioned by the *Mūlasarvāstivāda-vinaya*, were—unlike brahmanical hostels—ideologically, organizationally, and even architecturally suited to provide such services. Such monasteries not only would have had "infirmaries" but also would have had the manpower and organization to provide nurses and care to those who would otherwise not have them. The *Mūlasarvāstivāda-vinaya*, moreover, put a great deal of emphasis on just such services. We have already seen a rule that was designed to provide funding for such services for poor monks who could not themselves afford it, and this is not the only rule of this kind. Elsewhere (GMs iii 2, 128.1–131.15), when the Buddha himself finds another poor monk sick and "lying in his own urine and excrement," he does exactly what Śāriputra and Maudgalyāyana had done for the young brahmin—with his own hands he cleans and bathes the sick monk. He then gives orders to the monks:

> "Monks, apart from you, their fellow-monks, those who are sick have no mother, nor father, nor other relative. As a consequence, fellow-monks must attend to one another (*tasmāt sabrahmacāribhiḥ parasparam upasthānaṃ karaṇīyam*)! A preceptor (*upādhyāya*) must do so for his co-residential pupil (*sārdhaṃvihārin*); a co-residential pupil for his preceptor; a teacher (*ācārya*) for his disciple (*antevāsin*); a disciple for his teacher . . . etc., etc. One who is bereft of an assembly and little known (*alpajñāta*), to him the community must give an attendant monk after determining the state of his illness—one or two or many, even to the extent that the entire community must attend to him!"

This is a remarkable passage. If, for example, the roles of preceptor (*upādhyāya*) and teacher (*ācārya*) were ever conceived of primarily in terms of teaching functions, they certainly are not here. Here both roles are defined exclusively in terms of caregiving functions, and they are also so defined elsewhere in the *Mūlasarvāstivāda-vinaya*. Entering into the relationship of "preceptor/co-residential pupil" or "teacher/disciple" is known as "entering [96] into dependence" (*gnas bcas pa*), and this is the one essential and indispensable relationship that every Mūlasarvāstivādin monk must enter into. The *Kṣudrakavastu*, for example, says that a monk can be without a recitation teacher (*klog pa'i slob dpon*), but not without a monk on whom he is dependent (Derge Tha 214a.6); in the same *Vastu*, monks are forbidden to travel without a monk in regard to whom they have entered into dependence; and numerous monasteries were said to have passed ordinances denying traveling monks who lacked such a supporting monk the right to accommodations for even one night (Derge Tha 71b.7–72b.4). And it is repeatedly said: "The Blessed One has ordered entering into dependence for the sake of assisting one another, and for the purpose of attending to the sickness of those who are ill" (*bcom ldan 'das kyis kyang . . . gcig gis gcig bstang zhing na ba'i nad g-yog bya ba'i phyir gnas bca' bar gnangs ba*—Derge Tha 213a.1)—not, be it noted, for the purposes of instruction.

These rules make, of course, for a very attractive arrangement, which if implemented would have provided for Mūlasarvāstivādin monks unparalleled security for long-term care. Given that this arrangement would have been embedded in a "permanent" enduring institution, there would have been nothing like it in early medieval India—these monks would have been very well looked after in their final days, and this, in turn, may have been a powerful motivating factor in an individual's decision to enter the order. It is at least notable that in the overwhelming majority of cases in our *Vinaya* in which a motive is given for individuals' becoming monks, that motive is connected with the fact that the individual concerned is either old or poor or without living relatives or sonless, and usually it is a combination of all four. Examples of this may be found throughout the *Mūlasarvāstivāda-vinaya*, in the *Vibhaṅga* (Derge Ca 90b.6, 61a.4), in the *Pravrajyāvastu* (Eimer ii 193), in the *Kṣudraka* (Derge Tha 100a.4, 114b.6; Da 138b.5), and so on.

There are, of course, parallels for some of the arrangements and facilities at least envisioned by the redactors of the *Mūlasarvāstivāda-vinaya*. David Knowles, for example, has said in regard to medieval England that "in the fully developed monastery of the twelfth century facilities for care of the sick were probably greater than in any other place in the kingdom."[17] But in the English case—indeed in much of medieval European monasticism—we know that such "facilities" came to be an important part of monastic [97] economies and important sources of revenue, by being made available, on a limited basis, not to the poor but to the rich laity. By a series of arrangements—none of which were precisely defined—"confraternity," "corrodies," entry "*ad succurrendum*," the old, the sick, and the almost certainly terminally ill were allowed the benefits of a monk and of the monastic facilities while they were alive, with the expectation, and sometimes formal promise, that when they died, some, all, or a good share of their estates would go to the monastery.[18] Although the bald "exchange" or "purchase" nature of these arrangements was often muted in the documents that recorded them, the effect was not, and both the basic arrangement and the verbal vagueness seem to have a parallel in the *Mūlasarvāstivāda-vinaya*.

The parallel occurs again in the *Cīvaravastu* in a passage already referred to—it is the text that makes explicit reference to the use of a written will. It concerns a wealthy layman who, in spite of repeated attempts and repeated invocations of various gods, remains childless. As a consequence, the text says, he repudiates all the gods and comes to have faith in the Blessed One (*sarvadevatāḥ pratyākhyāya bhagavaty abhiprasannaḥ*—GMs iii 2, 139.20), though the transition here is rather abrupt. He approaches a monk and asks for admission into the order. The initial motivating factor is that the man is "sonless"; the implications are that he is also old; and—as we shall see—he is about to become seriously ill. The monk shaves the man's head and begins to give him the rules of training (*śikṣāpada*), but the rich man becomes ill, which creates an obstacle to his admission into the order (*pravrajyāntarāyakareṇa ca mahatā jvareṇābhibhūtaḥ*). Here it is hard to miss the hand of the monastic lawyer: whoever wrote this little narrative must have been fully aware that there were rules against admitting the sick into the order and deftly avoided that difficulty by having the man's illness become manifest only after the initial and most visible aspects of his admission—the shaving of his head—had occurred. The result, of course, was a thoroughly ambiguous situation from the point of view of monastic law, which involved the status of the "shaven-headed householder"—visibly a monk—who had not been fully admitted into the order. What obligations did the monastic community have in regard to such individuals? The monks, as was their usual practice in such ambiguous [98] situations, ask the Buddha—that is to say, our text would have been seen as providing a definitive solution. The Buddha rules that monastic care must be provided for the sick man (*upasthānam asya karaṇīyam*); he rules in other words that, in this regard at least, such an individual must be treated as a member of the community—Guṇaprabha, incidentally, makes this interpretation explicit.[19] But the Buddha then specifically adds that such an individual must not be given the rules of training until he recovers (*na tāvac chikṣāpadāni deyāni yāvat svasthaḥ saṃvṛttaḥ*—140.5), and the Buddha specifically rules that the monks themselves must attend to him. The Buddha's rulings in effect create a new category: a sick layman who has undergone the most visible act of admission to the order but who cannot, because of his illness, be fully admitted. The text goes on to indicate that the monks are obligated to attend to such individuals even if they are taken back to their own homes. This seems to clearly indicate that the redactor was fully conscious of the fact that he was inventing a new category. He says: "In regard to him [the sick householder] the designation 'shaven-headed householder' arose" (*tasya muṇḍo gṛhapatir iti saṃjñā saṃvṛttā*—140.13).

The obligations of the monks to "shaven-headed householders" were then made matters of explicit monastic rules, but what of the obligations of the "shaven-headed householders" to the monks: what did they owe the monks? As in the case of medieval European monasticism, the language used in regard to this question is careful and ambiguous, avoiding any direct reference to sale or purchase. We move from a language of rule and obligation to a situation of unexpressed—but probably nonetheless definite—expectation. We are simply told that when the "shaven-headed householder" knew he was on the point of death, he drew up a will leaving all of his enormous estate to the monastic community, and we are explicitly told that the state itself (i.e., the king) confirmed the monastic community's rightful ownership of such an estate. The arrangement here was, then, not a formally contractual one; it was rather a matter of unstated but understood practice. A wealthy layman without heirs could undergo the initial and most visible aspects of the ritual of admission into the Mūlasarvāstivādin order. As a result, the monks [99] would be obliged to care for him, especially in his final days, even if he remained at home. He in turn was *expected*, though not contractually obligated, to leave his entire estate to the Community, and the state formally acknowledged the legitimacy of such an arrangement.

It is also worth noting that the redactors of the *Mūlasarvāstivāda-vinaya* seem to have anticipated that such an arrangement would or could have resulted in considerable amounts of cash or precious materials going directly to individual monks. This, again, would seem to follow from the provisions they put in place for dealing with specific forms of property or wealth that might form a part of such an estate. They stipulated, for example, that any *maṇi* gems, lapis lazuli, or conch shells included in the estate must be divided into two lots, one for the Dharma and one for the Community, and that, further, the Community's share must then be divided among the monks (GMs iii 2, 143.1). They stipulated that if the estate included any books or manuscripts containing non-Buddhist *śāstras* (*bahiḥśāstrapustaka*), those books must be sold (*vikrīya*) and the profit, again, divided among the monks (143.7). They stipulated too that any gold, money, or other precious metals, either worked or unworked (*suvarṇaṃ ca hiraṇyaṃ cānyac ca kṛtākṛtaṃ*), must be divided into three shares, and the share for the Community must again be divided among the monks themselves.[20] These provisions are completely in line, moreover, with a host of rules and practices throughout the *Mūlasarvāstivāda-vinaya*. In the passage already mentioned from the *Kṣudrakavastu* that deals with monetary deposits made by donors with merchants, the Buddha himself explicitly orders the monks to accept money (*kārṣāpaṇas*) from the merchants (Derge Tha 258a.3–259a.3).[21] In yet another passage from the *Kṣudrakavastu*, the Buddha himself also orders monks not to divide certain kinds of expensive cloth that is given to them, but he insists that the monks must first sell the cloth for money and then divide the money among themselves (*de lta bas na dge 'dun la gos kyi rnyed pa de lta bu grub pa gang yin pa de kār shā pa ṇa dag tu bsgyur la / kār shā pa ṇa dag bgo bar bya'o*—Derge Tha 263a.6). In the *Cīvaravastu*, again monks are told that they must divide the profits among themselves after they have sold (*vikrīya*) property that makes up part of the [100] estate of a deceased monk (GMs iii 2, 121.2; see also 119.14). In the *Kṣudraka*, the *Vibhaṅga*, and the *Uttaragrantha(s)*, finally, monks volunteer to act as "assistants for merit" (both the terms *puṇya-sahāya* and *dharma-sahāya* are used) on construction projects paid for by laymen and meant for the monks. In this role the monk receives the money (*kārṣāpaṇas*)—usually a substantial amount—from the laymen; hires, oversees, and pays the laborers; buys the necessary tools; and is told, for example, to use the construction funds for his food, that is to say, to buy it (*mkhar len byed pas mkhar len gyi nor kho na las bsod snyoms yongs su spyad par bya'o*—Derge Tha 193b.7; see also Derge Ca 146a.2–148a.6 and Pa 123a.7–124a.6; cf. GMs iii 4, 139.9).

There are, of course, rules in the Mūlasarvāstivādin *Prātimokṣa* that have been understood at least by modern scholars to forbid monks from engaging in almost all of these activities—handling "money," buying and selling, and so forth. And here we have a particularly interesting problem. It is almost certainly not safe to assume that the *Vinayadharas*, the monastic lawyers who compiled, shaped, and probably wrote the *Vinayavastus* and the *Vinayavibhaṅga*, were unfamiliar with their own *Prātimokṣa*, especially given that the *Vibhaṅga* is at least structurally based on it. But if the *Vinayadharas* knew their *Prātimokṣa*, then there would seem to be at least two possible explanations for what we have seen here. It is possible that the *Vinayadharas* chose to ignore the *Prātimokṣa*—and could so choose—indicating that it was much less binding and authoritative than has been assumed. At the very least we may have to look much, much more carefully at the differences and divergencies between the *prātimokṣas* and the other expository parts of the *vinaya*. Those differences may be much broader and more significant than even Schlingloff has said.[22] Certainly the differences between the Mūlasarvāstivādin *Bhikṣuṇī-prātimokṣa* and *Bhikṣuṇī-vibhaṅga*, for example, are so great that Bu-ston at least thought that the *Vibhaṅga* was not Mūlasarvāstivādin at all.[23] We may also have much to learn about the force and construction of monastic rules from medievalists working on Western monastic codes. Louis Lekai, for example, in discussing early Cistercian [101] monastic legislation has said: "The founders of Cîteaux assumed a peculiarly ambivalent attitude toward the Rule of Saint Benedict. They declared their utter devotion to it, but in fact they used that venerable document with remarkable liberality. They invoked and applied it when it suited their purpose, ignored or even contradicted it when they thought that they had better ideas."[24] Even more helpful perhaps is what he says about the form of early Cistercian legislation:

> A further proof of both the tentative nature of new regulations and the broad-minded, always compromising disposition of the chapter fathers is the wording of virtually countless statutes before as well as after 1180. The beginning of such a paragraph is always a firm command or rigid prohibition, but the end lists the exceptions, often enfeebling the text to such an extent that it can hardly qualify for more than a fatherly advice.[25]

The last sentence in particular here could do good service as a description of the *Prātimokṣa* rules as they occur in the *Vibhaṅga*: they almost all begin with a "firm command or rigid prohibition" but end with a list of "exceptions" (*anāpatti*) which—in the Buddhist case as well—can render them little more than "fatherly advice." An example of this sort of thing has already been cited above, where the rule stated unequivocally that it is an offense if a nun goes to court to collect on a promissory note, but the exception, which immediately follows, says there is, however, no offense if the nun is "one who earns with some difficulty." In the Buddhist case it has been assumed or argued that these "exception" clauses represent a later chronological stratum,[26] but this need not necessarily be the case. In the case of the Cistercian texts, it is known that such exemption clauses were a part of the original legislation—they were there from the beginning—and their presence has been taken at least by Lekai as evidence for "a tolerant and flexible attitude" and, he says, should be taken not as "a sign of decay" but as "evidence of health and vitality."[27] In fact, we do not know for sure if in the early days the [102] *Prātimokṣas* were ever—apart from liturgical contexts—used without their *Vibhaṅgas*. It is at least hard to imagine that their rulings were ever actually applied without interpretation or discussion. But even if the *anāpattis*—the exemptions, exclusions, extenuations—turn out to be later additions, that will make them not less but even more important for tracking the development and gradual maturation of Buddhist monastic rules.

A second possible explanation for what we have seen—although this is rarely the explanation of our first choice—is that Mūlasarvāstivādin *Vinayadharas* may have known their texts far better than we do and applied to them a far more sophisticated exegesis than we can. The *Prātimokṣa* rule that has been taken to forbid the "handling" of "money" by monks may be a case in point. We do not actually know what activity is forbidden. The verb in the Sanskrit text of the Mūlasarvāstivādin *Prātimokṣa* is *udgṛhṇīyād*, but this has a wide range of possible meanings, none of which are very close to "accept" or "have" (this would be rather *pari* or *prati* √*grah*), and it has been translated in an equally wide range of ways.[28]

Worse still, we do not actually know what was intended or understood by *jātarūparajata*, the object of the action that was forbidden, which is conventionally translated as "gold and silver." What, however, is clear to even us—and we must therefore assume was far clearer to Mūlasarvāstivādin monastic lawyers—is that the rule does not refer to *suvarṇa* or *hiraṇya* or *kārṣāpaṇas* ("gold," "silver," "money"), and it is these things that monks own, accept, handle, and inherit in the *Vibhaṅga*, the *Vinayavastus*, and the *Uttaragrantha(s)*. This can hardly be an accident and must point again to the fact that *Vinaya* texts, like *Abhidharma* texts, represent a sophisticated system of thought that works from a particular and precise definition of terms. It, again, can hardly be an accident that what is called the "old commentary" that is embedded in the *Vibhaṅga* is—as Norman says of the Pāli *Vinaya*—"really an analysis of words (*pada-bhājanīya*)."[29] And conversely—even perversely—a part of [103] this sophistication may be an element of intentional ambiguity. Here too an observation by Lekai in regard to Cistercian texts may not be inappropriate: "In other cases the careful reader of the records may come under the impression that the wording of important statutes was made deliberately so vague or complicated that it left open a number of possible interpretations."[30] Unless I am much mistaken, this too will have numerous parallels in Buddhist *vinayas*. The Mūlasarvāstivādin rule that has been understood to mean that monks are forbidden to engage in "buying and selling" may be another case in point.[31] It does not refer to unqualified "buying and selling"; nor does it refer—which it could easily have—to "all" (*sarva*) "buying and selling." It refers to *nānā-prakāraṃ kraya-vikrayaṃ*, which, of course, could mean "buying and selling of various sorts" or "buying and selling of many sorts." Neither interpretation precludes "all," but neither requires it either. Mūlasarvāstivādin exegesis, moreover, clearly did not take it to have absolute application. The *Vibhaṅga*, for example, says that there is no fault in engaging in both unqualified buying and selling if a monk is not seeking to gain (*dge slong gis rnyed pa mi 'dod pas nyo bar byed cing rnyed pa mi 'dod pas 'tshong bar byed na gnyis ka la ltung ba med do*; Derge Cha 156b.3).

But what can be learned specifically about the *Mūlasarvāstivāda-vinaya* from our larger discussion? We now know that the Buddhist monks who wrote or redacted it in early medieval North India did not share our assumptions about Buddhist monks and the renunciation of private wealth or property, and we—under the enormous influence of St. Benedict—think that this is an important element of any monastic ideal.[32] Those same monks also apparently did not have the same attitude that we do in regard to monks' involvement with money. They either knew monks who did, or wanted monks to do, all sorts of things that do not fit our assumptions: Pay debts and tolls and transport taxable goods; own their own furniture and have the means to pay for any damage they might do to that of other monks; carry personal seals; pay for their own medicine and healing rituals; leave estates, sometimes huge; borrow money from laymen; inherit property [104] from both other monks and laymen; accept and service permanent endowments; make loans and charge interest; accept and use negotiable securities; provide care for sick and dying laymen, with the understanding that, when the layman died, his estate would go to the monastery; and receive precious and semiprecious materials, sell books, receive gold in various forms, accept money (*kārṣāpaṇas*), sell the property of deceased monks, hire and oversee laborers, and buy food. And this, of course, is only a provisional list of the sorts of things that Mūlasarvāstivādin monks were—in most cases—not only expected but also *required* to do by their own monastic rule. If they did not, then—at least in terms of monastic discipline—they would not be "good" monks. Exactly how many such "good" monks there were we obviously do not know, although it is at least certain that Indian monks accepted permanent endowments and monetary deposits made with merchants; it is also certain that some Indian monks had personal seals.[33] But whether all the things described in our *Vinaya* actually happened matters far less than the fact that Buddhist monks who were, presumably, the acknowledged authorities on monastic discipline spent a great deal of time thinking about them in North India in the early medieval period. These were—again presumably—monks who were in a position to influence actual communities, literate monks who were concerned with things other than asceticism, meditation, and doctrinal study, monks who, again in their own terms, were the "good" monks. That they had a different perspective from ours is confirmed by at least one further observation: Unlike modern scholars, these "good" monks did not have much good to say about monks who did engage in asceticism, meditation, and doctrinal learning. If they mention them at all—and they do so infrequently—it is almost always with a tone of marked ambivalence, if not actual ridicule. Ascetic monks, meditating monks, and learned monks appear in our *Vinaya* by and large only as slightly ridiculous characters in unedifying, sardonic, and funny stories or as nasty customers that "good" monks do not want to spend much time around.[34] [105]

The monks that the redactors of the *Mūlasarvāstivāda-vinaya* envisioned, and the monks that modern scholarship has imagined, are then radically different, and this difference is extremely important for the historian of Buddhism in India. The monastic ideal found in the *Mūlasarvāstivāda-vinaya*, for example, is almost certainly one of the most prominent monastic ideals that the authors of the Mahāyāna *sūtras* encountered, and much of what these Mahāyāna authors said is probably fully intelligible only as a reaction against this ideal. If we are ever to understand more about the Mahāyāna, we obviously are going to have to know, then, much, much more about what they were reacting to. This is our future task.

Notes

1. For some brief remarks on the "early" archaeological and inscriptional evidence for *vihāras*, see G. Schopen, "Doing Business for the Lord: Lending on Interest and Written Loan Contracts in the *Mūlasarvāstivāda-vinaya*," *JAOS* 114 (1994) 527–554, esp. 547–552 [= Ch. III below].

2. See the discussion and sources cited in G. Schopen, "The Bones of a Buddha and the Business of a Monk: Conservative Monastic Values in an Early Mahāyāna Polemical Tract," *JIP* 27 (1999) 279–324, esp. 292ff [= *FFMB* Ch. III]. That in fact *all* "les Vinayas parvenus à nous ont été rédigés à une époque tardive" was suggested already long ago by Wassilieff (W. Wassilieff, "Le bouddhisme dans son plein développement d'après les vinayas," *RHR* 34 [1896] 318–325), and this suggestion came as well to be seconded by S. Lévi ("Les éléments de formation du divyāvadāna," *TP* 8 [1907] 116–117).

3. S. Lévi, "Les saintes écritures du bouddhisme. Comment s'est constitué le canon sacré," in *Mémorial Sylvain Lévi* (Paris: 1937) 78, 80, 84; Ed. Huber, "Études bouddhiques. III—Le roi kaniṣka dans le vinaya des mūlasarvāstivādins," *BEFEO* 14 (1914) 18; M. Lalou, "Notes sur la décoration des monastères bouddhiques," *RAA* 5.3 (1930) 183. According to a notice published by L. de la Vallée Poussin in 1929, Lalou "travaille à l'*Analyse et Bibliographie du Vinaya des Mūlasarvāstivādins*, vaste compilation pleine de documents indispensables" (*Académie royale de belgique. Bulletin de la classe des lettres et des sciences morales et politiques* 5 série—T. 15 [1929] 366).

4. G. Schopen, "Marking Time in Buddhist Monasteries. On Calendars, Clocks, and Some Liturgical Practices," in *Sūryacandrāya. Essays in Honour of Akira Yuyama on the Occasion of His 65th Birthday* (Indica et Tibetica 35), ed. P. Harrison and G. Schopen (Swisttal-Odendorf: 1998) 157–179, esp. 171–172 and nn. 51–54 [= Ch. IX below].

5. K. Wille, *Die handschriftliche Überlieferung des Vinayavastu der Mūlasarvāstivādin* (Verzeichnis der orientalischen Handschriften in Deutschland, Suppl. Bd. 30) (Stuttgart: 1990).

6. See most recently S. Hiraoka, "The Relation between the *Divyāvadāna* and the *Mūlasarvāstivādavinaya*," *JIP* 26 (1998) 419–434 and the sources cited.

7. E. Frauwallner, *The Earliest Vinaya and the Beginnings of Buddhist Literature* (Serie Orientale Roma 8) (Rome: 1956) 194–195; Lamotte, *Histoire du bouddhisme indien* 187.

8. B. Jinananda, *Upasampadājñaptiḥ* (Tibetan Sanskrit Works Series VI) (Patna: 1961) 15.5; *Pravrajyāvastu* (Eimer) ii 142.13. The Tibetan version of this entire *vastu* is in part translated and in part closely—if not always correctly—paraphrased in A. C. Banerjee, *Sarvāstivāda Literature* (Calcutta: 1957) 100–186; see esp. 120.

9. A. C. Banerjee, *Two Buddhist Vinaya Texts in Sanskrit* (Calcutta: 1977) 32.17: *yaḥ punar bhikṣuḥ pūrvaṃ samanujño bhūtvā tataḥ paścād evaṃ vaded* [*yathā*] *saṃstutikayāyuṣmantaḥ sāṃghikaṃ lābhaṃ pariṇatam ātmanaḥ paudgalikaṃ pariṇāmayantīti pāyantikā* /.

10. Almost all the provisions of Mūlasarvāstivādin monastic inheritance law have been collected together and digested by Guṇaprabha at *Vinayasūtra* (Sankrityayana) 85.3–86.5 (= *'dul ba'i mdo*, Derge, bstan 'gyur, 'dul ba Wu 68a.2–69a.5—for the commentaries, see *Svavyākhyāna* Zu 126b.1–132b.7; *Ṭīkā* Yu 178a.6–185a.3; *Vyākhyāna* Ru 197b.7–200b.3;

Vṛtti Lu 250b.5–254a.4); also Bu-ston in his *'Dul ba pha'i gleng 'bum chen mo* (Collected Works, L. Chandra ed. Part 23) 'A 290a.2–295a.3, and now G. Schopen "Dead Monks and Bad Debts: Some Provisions of a Buddhist Monastic Inheritance Law," *IIJ* 44 (2001) 99–148 [= Ch. V below].

11. Cf. O. von Hinüber, "Vinaya und Abhidhamma," *StII* 19 (1994) 109–122.

12. The *Kṣudraka* text is discussed in some detail in G. Schopen, "Monastic Law Meets the Real World: A Monk's Continuing Right to Inherit Family Property in Classical India," *HR* 35 (1995) 101–123 [= Ch. VI below]—when this was written, I was not aware of the text in the *Uttaragrantha(s)*.

13. The *Cīvaravastu* text is translated—without notes—in G. Schopen, "Deaths, Funerals, and the Division of Property in a Monastic Code," in *Buddhism in Practice*, ed. D. S. Lopez Jr. (Princeton, N.J.: 1995) 498–500 [= Ch. IV below]. For the possible reference to a written will in the *Divyāvadāna*, see Schopen, "If You Can't Remember, How to Make It Up: Some Monastic Rules for Redacting Canonical Texts," in *Bauddhavidyāsudhākaraḥ*, 580 n. 27 [= Ch. XIV below].

14. On the *Vibhaṅga* text, see Schopen, "Doing Business for the Lord," 527ff—here again, when this was written, I did not know of the *Uttaragrantha(s)* text.

15. See, for example, E. Senart, "The Inscriptions in the Caves at Nasik," *EI* 8 (1905–1906) nos. 12 and 15, but see also no. 17, where an endowment of 100 *kārṣāpaṇas* is given *saṃghasa hathe*.

16. Gnoli prints *mānavakaḥ śālāṃ*, but the facsimile clearly has *māṇavakaśālāṃ* (GBMs vi 948.2), and the Tibetan (Derge Ga 195a.3) *bram ze'i khye'u zhig gi khyim du*.

17. D. Knowles, *The Monastic Order in England. A History of Its Development from the Times of St. Dunstan to the Fourth Lateran Council 943–1216* (Cambridge, England: 1949) 477.

18. Knowles, *The Monastic Order in England*, 475ff; J. H. Lynch, *Simoniacal Entry into Religious Life from 1000 to 1260. A Social, Economic and Legal Study* (Columbus, Ohio: 1976) 26–36.

19. For the passage in question, we have a Sanskrit text for both the *Sūtra* and Guṇaprabha's auto-commentary, *pravrajitavat atra prārabdha-talliṅgaḥ* / . . . *yaḥ pravrajyārthaṃ muṇḍanādinā veṣamātreṇa yojitaḥ nādyāpi pravrājitaḥ sa pravrajitavat draṣṭavyaḥ* / *Vinayasūtra* (Bapat and Gokhale) 46.19. A few lines later Guṇaprabha actually uses the term *muṇḍagṛhapati*, and Bu-ston (*'Dul ba pha'i gleng 'bum chen mo* 'A 55b.5) gives our *Cīvara* text as Guṇaprabha's source.

20. In all three cases the wording is similar and explicit: *yaḥ saṃghasya sa bhikṣubhir vikrīya bhājayitavyaḥ* in the first and third cases; *bhikṣubhir vikrīya bhājayitavyāḥ* in the second.

21. In this case it is also made explicit that the money then belongs absolutely to the monks: *kār shā pa ṇa dag blangs nas ci 'dod par yongs su spyad par bya ste* /.

22. D. Schlingloff, "Zur Interpretation des *Prātimokṣasūtra*," *ZDMG* 113 (1964) 536–551.

23. C. Vogel, "Bu-ston on the Schism of the Buddhist Church and on the Doctrinal Tendencies of Buddhist Scriptures," in *Zur Schulzugehörigkeit von Werken der Hīnayāna-Literatur*, Erster Teil, Hrsg. H. Bechert (Göttingen: 1985) 110; and *Bu-ston, 'Dul ba dge slong ma'i gleng 'bum* (Ma'i) 'A 58b.5.

24. L. J. Lekai, "Ideals and Reality in Early Cistercian Life and Legislation," in *Cistercian Ideals and Reality* (Cistercian Studies Series 60), ed. J. R. Sommerfeldt (Kalamazoo, Mich.: 1978) 4–29, esp. 5.

25. Ibid., 17.

26. Schlingloff, "Zur Interpretation des *Prātimokṣasūtra*," 538 n. 22: "Diese 'Kasuistik' ist wohl der jüngste Teil des Vibhaṅga"; O. von Hinüber, *A Handbook of Pāli Literature* (Indian Philology and South Asian Studies 2) (Berlin: 1996) 14.

27. Lekai, "Ideals and Reality," 24.

28. The same verb occurs in a closely related rule, *Pāyantikā* 59: *yaḥ punar bhikṣu ratnaṃ vā [ratna] saṃmatam vā svahastam udgṛhṇīyād udgrāhayed vā* (L. Chandra, "Unpublished Gilgit Fragment of the Prātimokṣa-sūtra," *WZKS* 4 [1960] 8.6), and here can, it seems, mean only—and is almost always taken to mean—something like "pick up." See also the discussion in the *Bhaiṣajyavastu* dealing with *jāta-rūpa-rajata* where *prati√grah* and *ud √grah* are explicitly and clearly distinguished: *tasmāt śrāmaṇerakeṇodgrahītavyam / no tu pratigrahaḥ svīkartavyaḥ /* (GMs iii 1, 248.6–.16).

29. K. R. Norman, *Pāli Literature* (A History of Indian Literature Vol. VII, fasc. 2) (Wiesbaden: 1983) 19.

30. Lekai, "Ideals and Reality," 22.

31. For the Gilgit text of the rule, see Banerjee, *Two Buddhist Vinaya Texts in Sanskrit*, 29.20.

32. On Benedict's enormous influence on the study of monasticism and the conception of a monk, see S. Elm, *"Virgins of God." The Making of Asceticism in Late Antiquity* (Oxford: 1994) vii–viii, 1ff.

33. See, for example—and this seems to be the earliest example so far—R. Salomon, "Five Kharoṣṭhī Inscriptions," *Bulletin of the Asia Institute* (Studies in Honor of Vladimir A. Livshits) n.s., 10 (1996) 233–246, esp. 244–245. Salomon says: "These archaic features suggest an early date for this seal, possibly as early as the second century B.C."

34. As a sampling of such texts, see GMs iii 1, 79.3–84.2; Derge Ja 154b.2–156b.7; Tha 222b.2–224b.1; GMs iii 4, 71.6ff; GMs iii 1, 56.2ff; Derge Da 35b.2–36a.2; Tha 39a.6–39b.5; GMs iii 1, 56.20–57.18; Derge Ja 79b.7–80b.3; Tha 180b.1–181a.4, 71b.7–72b.4; GMs iii 2, 173.5–178.1; GMs iii 1, 55.8–56.19; and so on.

CHAPTER II

Art, Beauty, and the Business of Running a Buddhist Monastery in Early Northwest India

IT IS VERY DIFFICULT still to get an overview of Early North India—dates, dynasties, denominations, and deities there are still the subjects of sometimes unedifying debate. We work, of course, with what we have, and what we have are broken walls and tangled trenches, stray inscriptions and reused pots, coins, images out of context, and conclusions hanging by a thread. So much energy and erudition goes into sorting all these things out that important questions go unasked. We are usually so preoccupied with what is there that we often do not ask—do not even wonder—why it is. When, for example, so much of the raw data for North Indian numismatics comes from Buddhist monastic sites and ritual deposits, are we not obliged to ask why this is so—how is it that groups of ascetic, celibate men who were supposed to have renounced all wealth and social ties, left such largesse in the archaeological record; how is it that they, and sometimes they alone, lived in North India in permanent, architecturally sophisticated quarters, that they, and they alone, lived in intimate association with what we call art? Something is clearly wrong with this picture, and there is a good chance that we have not yet understood the people in North India who handled the coins we study or the pots we classify. As an example—and it is only that—of an important group of such people, it is perhaps worthwhile to try again to understand what exactly a Buddhist monk was in Early North India. We can do this now a little better because we now know a little better an important Buddhist monastic code that appears to have been redacted there. That the Buddhist monk in Early North India, and in this monastic code, did not look like the caricature found in modern scholarly sources will come as no surprise to those who know well what he left behind in his living quarters. The monk that we will see in this code is a construction fore-

---

Originally presented at the symposium "On the Cusp of an Era: Art in the Pre-Kushan World," held at the Nelson-Atkins Museum of Art, Kansas City, Missouri, November 8–11, 2000, and published here for the first time.

man, an art promoter, a banker, an entrepreneur, sometimes a shyster, and sometimes a saint—he should at least prove to be of some interest.

The monastic code in question—the *Mūlasarvāstivāda-vinaya*—has been known in one form or another for a long time now,[1] and although it was recognized early on that this code was compiled or redacted in Northwest India, the discussion of its date has been badly misdirected by a very red herring and the inattention of those who were supposed to be following the trail. In 1958 the great Belgian scholar Étienne Lamotte declared that this *Vinaya*, or Code, was late, that "one cannot attribute to this work a date earlier than the 4th–5th Centuries of the Christian Era."[2] This pronouncement—even at its inception based on very shaky grounds—still proved almost fatal, for Lamotte himself was forced by his own further work to change his position—and he did so several times—but few scholars seem to have noticed. By 1966, Lamotte was in fact referring to the *Mūlasarvāstivāda-vinaya* as a source of information for the first or second century of our era.[3] Ironically, other scholars then, and for a long time after, continued to quote only the Lamotte of 1958.[4]

The changes in Lamotte's views—which he never explicitly acknowledged—brought them eventually into conformity with the views of others who had specifically addressed the issue and been ignored, and today, it seems, the views of the Italian Raniero Gnoli hold the field. He said in 1977: "However, one point seems certain to me: the date of the compilation of the *Vinaya* of the MSV is to be taken back to the times of Kaniṣka."[5] And, but for a few quibbles, this would seem fine. Gnoli, as others before him, relies in part for his dating on the fact that one section of this Code—in a passage preserved in the Sanskrit manuscript from Gilgit—refers both to Kaniṣka by name and to the *stūpa* of Kaniṣka at a place it calls Kharjūrikā.[6] This passage in turn forms a part of what Sylvain Lévi long ago called "un véritable *māhātmya* du Nord-Ouest de l'Inde."[7] Both the presence of Kaniṣka's name, and the *māhātmya* as a whole, have been taken as interpolations "which tend to show that the *Vinaya* of the Mūlasarvāstivādins had undergone a rehandling around the beginning of the Christian Era."[8] But if the *māhātmya* containing the reference to Kaniṣka is an interpolation made at somewhere near his time, or if this *Vinaya* underwent a rehandling or redaction—"un remaniement"—around the beginning of the Christian era, it seems fairly obvious that it must have existed in some form or in some part even before that time. And there are other indications of this as well.

It is of course neither possible nor desirable to enter here into all the specifics, and it must suffice to simply note that the more we learn about the contents of this Code, the clearer it becomes that it explicitly deals, often in great detail, with specific religious and monastic practices, ideas, and motives that we know from epigraphical and archaeological sources were also current in North India both before and after the rise of the Kuṣāns, that it uses the same titles for learned monks and certain kinds of laymen, and describes—often again in great detail—some of the same elements of material culture that we find there. A Kharoṣṭhī inscription from Bahāwalpur and dated in the early years of Kaniṣka, for example, illustrates in a single instance several of these shared elements. It records that a monk named Nāgadatta, who is called a *dha*[*rma*]*kathi*, "a Narrator of the Dharma"—a title or office repeatedly referred to in the *Mūlasarvāstivāda-vinaya*[9]—"raised the staff" (*yaṭhiṃ aropayata*), that is, inaugurated a *stūpa*, for "the Owner of the Monastery" (*viharasvamiṇi*) Balānandī. Not only is the title *vihārasvāmin* repeatedly found in the *Mūlasarvāstivāda-vinaya*, where it designates the key lay figure in Mūlasarvāstivādin monasticism,[10] but this Code also contains an explicit reference—using virtually the same expression—to a monk's obligation to be in attendance at "the raising of the staff" (*yaṣṭyāropaṇa*).[11] There is, moreover, a whole series of pre-Kuṣān Kharoṣṭhī inscriptions—all securely dated to the very beginning of the Common Era—which record that individuals deposited relics at "a previously unestablished place" (*apratiṭhavita-prubami paḍhavi-pradeśami*), and in one case this action is specifically said to result in "the merit of Brahmā" (*brammapuñ*[*o*] *prasavati*).[12] This idea of establishing relics at previously "unconsecrated" places, an idea that appears to have motivated the actual behavior of a number of highly placed individuals in pre-Kuṣān North India, is again explicitly stated in our *Vinaya* in *exactly* the same language (*apratiṣṭhitapūrve pṛthivīpradeśe*) and is explicitly stated there to result in "the merit of Brahmā" (*brāhmam puṇyam prasavati*), raising the possibility at least that our *Vinaya* is actually being quoted in this record.[13] There are as well early Kuṣān records that refer to learned monks as *trepiḍakas*, "those who know the Three Baskets,"[14] and this title too repeatedly occurs in the *Mūlasarvāstivāda-vinaya*.[15] There is a series of records that describe religious acts undertaken by monks and "co-residential pupils" (*sārdhaṃvihārin*) for the purpose of each other's health (*arogadakshinae*),[16] and this is a characteristically Mūlasarvāstivādin idea prominently enshrined, for example, in its ordination formulary, where it is said that a newly ordained monk must be told: "You must, from this day forward and for as long as he lives, nurse your Preceptor. Your Preceptor too must attend to your illnesses until you are dead or cured."[17] In fact, the Preceptor/disciple relationship is defined almost exclusively in this Code in terms of mutual caregiving.[18] There are, finally, the Tōr Ḍherai inscribed pot fragments that refer not only to another *vihārasvāmin* but also to a *prapa*, a "hall for providing water" in a monastery,[19] and our *Vinaya* again has *very* detailed rules governing both the construction and the use of what appears to have been just such a "hall."[20]

Material of this sort—and as we will continue to see, there is a great deal of it in this enormous *Vinaya*—would appear to place this Code on the cusp of an era: many of the sorts of things it refers to are attested in the archaeological and epigraphical records of North India both before the Kuṣāns and in the early Kuṣān period itself. It seems to span what may in any case be something of an artificial divide. But at least one more shared linkage between our monastic Code and the Northwest is worth citing because, if for no other reason, it concerns one of our most important sources of knowledge for pre-Kuṣān and Kuṣān North India.

Nobody really knows where the idea of using what we call "donative inscriptions" came from in South Asia or why the Buddhists started to use them—and they were certainly the first to use them on any scale. But Emile Senart, one of the early and great masters of Indian epigraphy, recognized a long time ago that at least one of their characteristic features originated in the Northwest. He said in 1890: "It is in the Northwest that developed votive formulae first appear,"[21] and little has appeared since that would affect this observation. Given that such developments occurred in the Northwest, and that the Northwest is so comparatively rich in early inscriptions, it is again probably not coincidental that our monastic Code has a good deal to say about what we would call inscriptions, and it is—to my knowledge—the only such Code that does.[22]

Some of what our Code says about inscriptions is a little startling—even outrageous—and a glance at it not only will therefore serve the purpose of telling us something about monastic conceptions of inscriptions but also might introduce the uninitiated to the style, verve, and sometimes droll humor of this Code, as well as to the monastic world out of which it comes. The first text we might look at involves putting restrictions on the monastic use of inscriptions and tells the story of how the bowl of the famous monk Aniruddha ended up in a whorehouse.

Aniruddha, according to the text,[23] had a young disciple who looked after his bowl. But because the young disciple washed both his own and Aniruddha's bowl together, they often got confused, so the disciple wrote on Aniruddha's bowl: "The bowl of the Preceptor Aniruddha" (*des tshe dang ldan pa ma 'gags pa'i lhung bzed la slob dpon ma 'gags pa'i lhung bzed ces yi ge bris so*). Once, however, both went to a fine meal at the house of a layman. After the meal, Aniruddha left, but the disciple stayed behind to wash their bowls. While he was doing so, the layman asked to borrow a bowl so he could send some of the fine food to his favorite prostitute, and the disciple gave him Aniruddha's bowl. The layman filled it with food and sent it to his favorite whore. When she poured out the food, she saw the writing on the bottom of the bowl (*lhung bzed kyi zhabs la yi ge 'dug pa mthong nas*). When she read it—the text points out that for a woman she was clever—she thought to herself, "It is not right for me to desecrate in this way the bowl of that Noble One who is worshiped by gods and men," and she rubbed it with perfume, filled it with sweet-smelling flowers, and placed it on a painted stand (*khri'u tshon gyis bris pa*). It was, of course, bad enough that a famous monk's bowl ended up in a private shrine in a whorehouse, but more was yet to come.

When another of her customers arrived "bringing five hundred *kārṣāpaṇas*, perfume and garlands" and wanted to get right down to it, she put him off: "Wait a minute—do worship to the bowl!" He replied, "Where did this bowl come from? Whose is it, anyhow?" She told him as much as she knew, and he misunderstood even that, accusing her, in effect, of servicing renouncers (*pravrajita*). She, of course, denied what he implied, but the damage was done.

This little tale, written by a monk for other monks and bordering on burlesque, is used to justify the rule that "monks must not write what is not meant to be written!" (*de lta bas na dge slong dag mi bri ba ma bri shig*), which includes "what pertains to separate individuals" (*gang zag so so*; *paudgalika*)—that is to say, a monk should not inscribe his private property. This rule, of course, makes writing some of the sorts of inscriptions that we actually find—notably on the shards from the Buddhist levels at Mohenjo-daro—an offense, but it was clearly a minor offense, and such inscriptions are in any case surprisingly rare.[24]

A second text from our *Vinaya* that deals with inscribing objects also deals with a potentially embarrassing situation for the monastic order.[25] In this text it is said that a householder had or owned two *vihāras* (or monasteries), a forest *vihāra* and a village *vihāra* (*khyim bdag gcig la gtsug lag khang dgon pa dang / grong mtha' pa gnyis yod nas*).[26] The village *vihāra* was well and abundantly furnished, but the forest *vihāra* was not. On the occasion of a festival (*dus ston*), the forest monks wanted to borrow furnishings, bedding, and seats from the village monastery, but the village monks refused. The Buddha intervened and ordered that they must be lent. But the text does not end here, although a clear ruling had been established, because, it seems, the real issue had not yet been engaged.

The text goes on to say that at the end of the festival the forest monks thought to themselves: "This (forest) *vihāra* too belongs to that (same) householder" (*de dag gtsug lag khang 'di yang khyim bdag de'i yin no*), and they therefore did not return the goods. The Buddha again intervened and declared, however surprisingly, "They must be brought back by force!" (*mthus dgug par bya'o, balād . . . grahaṇam*). There is absolutely no doubt that this is what the text says; the same exact expression is also used elsewhere in this Code in regard to the recovery of goods.[27]

But the text even here is not yet finished, although a second clear and forceful ruling had also been established. The real issue comes—as it usually does in these texts—at the end, when the monks could not tell which goods belonged to what monastery:

> The Blessed One said: "Write on them 'these furnishings belong to the forest monastery of the householder so-and-so,' 'this belongs to the village monastery,' and as these furnishings are clearly identified, so they are to be used!" (*bcom ldan 'das kyis bka' stsal pa / gnas mal 'di ni khyim bdag che ge mo zhig gi dgon pa'i gtsug lag*

> *khang gi yin no / 'di ni grong mtha'i gtsug lag khang gi yin no zhes yi ge bri zhing gnas mal ji ltar nges par byas pa bzhin du longs spyad par bya'o*).

Although the two texts so far cited occur in two completely different sections of our Code—one in the *Uttaragrantha* and the other in the *Vibhaṅga*—the second text is clearly a pendant to the first: the latter indicates that by monastic rule a monk's private property should not be inscribed; the former that property belonging to a monastery should be. A third and here final text, however, goes beyond both.[28] It rules that the name of the donor must be inscribed on the object given and, in fact, puts in the mouth of the Buddha himself a donative formula that is virtually identical to some of what we find in actual North Indian donative inscriptions.

The text says that after King Ajātaśatru, who had been misled by the evil monk Devadatta, had killed his father, he wept whenever he saw his father's furnishings (*mal gos*). His advisers suggested that he should therefore give them to the Community of Monks, which he did. The monks, however, arranged them in the entrance hall (*sgo khang*, *dvārakoṣṭhaka*) of the monastery and thus defeated the purpose, for whenever the king visited the monastery, he saw them and once again wept. The Buddha then said that the furnishings must not be arranged in the entrance hall, so the monks first put them in an upper room (*yang thog*, *aṭṭāla*), but that did not work either, and so they put them in a residential cell (*gnas khang*, *layana*), and this turned out to be even worse. When "unbelievers" no longer saw the furnishings, they began to criticize the Community, saying "since these monks have surely sold or made away with the king's furnishings, merit from giving to them disappears!" (*ma dad pa dag gis rgyal po'i mal gos ni dge slong dag gis nges par btsongs te zos pas na / de ste phul ba'i bsod nams mi snang ngo zhes dpyas pa /*).[29] This of course would not do, and the Buddha then ordered that the furnishings be periodically displayed, but this served only to confuse the Community's critics because sometimes they saw the goods and sometimes they didn't. This whole comedy of errors—and countless texts in this *Vinaya* are structured as such—finally results in the definitive ruling. The Buddha, in the end, said simply to the monks: "You must write on the ends: 'This thing is a religious gift of King Bimbisāra' and display it!" (*yon du phul ba'i dngos po 'di ni rgyal po gzugs can snying po'i yin no zhes mtha' ma la yi ger bris te zhog shig /*).

Fortunately we have a Sanskrit text too for what the Buddha ordered should be written. In his *Vinayasūtra*—a digest of our Code—Guṇaprabha gives it as *deyadharmo 'yam amukasya*,[30] and if we bracket the ever expanding "pious wishes," this is almost exactly what we find, for example, on some of the inscribed pots recently published by Richard Salomon in his remarkable book on the British Library Scrolls: *[a]yaṃ pānaya ghaḍe deyaṃdharme va[sa]vadatae susomabharyae* . . .

("This waterpot is the pious gift of Vasavadata, wife of Susoma . . .") or *aya pa[ni]ya ghaḍae hastadatae teyavarmabharyae deyadharma* . . . ("This waterpot is the pious gift of Hastadata . . . wife of Teyavarman . . .").[31] This is also very much like what we find—as Gérard Fussman has shown—on the Shah-ji-ki Dheri casket inscription: *ayaṃ gaṃdha-karaṃḍe deyadharme . . . mahasenasa saṃgharakṣidasa* . . . or on the Tōr Ḍherai shards, which share as well, as we have seen, a number of other features with our *Vinaya*: *shahi-yola-mirasya viharasvamisya deyadharmo yaṃ prapa*. . . .[32]

We have here, it seems, a remarkable congruence between text and epigraph, and yet another indication that what was stated as a rule in the *Mūlasarvāstivāda-vinaya* was actually being practiced before, on, and after the cusp of our era in Northwest India. And a few further things might be noted here. First, it is immediately obvious that the "donative formula" found in the text is, by comparison with what occurs already in the earliest inscriptions, rather undeveloped, and this might suggest that the text is therefore even earlier. Second, it is clear, but probably not so obvious, that the text, though undeveloped, already carries the seed of what will grow into full-blown formulae for the "transfer of merit." In the text it is explicitly indicated that the gift is actually given by Ajātaśatru, but the Buddha himself says that it should be inscribed as the gift of Bimbisāra, his dead father. Indeed, given the ambiguity and overlap between the genitive and dative cases not only in Sanskrit and Prakrit but in Tibetan as well, the text could just as well be translated as "You must write on the ends: 'This thing is a religious gift *for* King Bimbisāra.'" Finally, it is perhaps significant that the text I have treated here is not the only such text in our Code. Another similar one immediately follows it. The idea, it seems, was worth repeating.[33]

What we have seen so far of the *Mūlasarvāstivāda-vinaya* would seem, then, to provide good grounds for asserting both a broad contemporaneity and a close if not intimate connection between much of what it contains and the religious world of pre-Kuṣān and Kuṣān North India that is reflected in the epigraphical and archaeological records. This, of course, might not have been entirely unexpected. We know from even old inscriptions that the Sarvāstivādins were widely spread across Northwest India in these periods,[34] and our Code, or *Vinaya*, is by its title either "*the Original Vinaya of the Sarvāstivādins*" or "*the Vinaya of the Original Sarvāstivādins*," depending on how the compound is read. In fact, the apparent contemporaneity between it and early Northwest practice may actually give substance to the claim embedded in its title.[35] But our Code in any case also provides us with a glimpse into the Buddhist monastic world out of which it comes, and it already indicates how far removed this world is from that presented in popular works and textbooks and even in otherwise good scholarly work. The Buddhist monk we see even in the few passages so far cited from this Code has little in common with the Buddhist monk who lives in the Western imagination—the ascetic monk who wanders alone "like a rhinoceros" in the forest, sits at the root of a tree in deep meditation, and has cut all ties with the world. If this monk ever existed, by the time of our Code he would certainly have been an exception, and by no means a popular one.

Forty years ago André Bareau said not just about our Code but about all Buddhist monastic Codes: "It is true that the Vinayapiṭakas . . . do not breathe a word about the numerous spiritual practices, meditations, contemplations, etc., which constituted the very essence of the Buddhist 'religion.'"[36] And although this is something of an exaggeration, still it should have given all pause for thought. Our Code, for example, does refer to ascetic, meditating monks, but when it does so in any detail, such monks almost always appear as the butt of jokes, objects of ridicule, and—not uncommonly—sexual deviants.[37] They are presented as irresponsible and of the type that give the order a bad name.[38] There are texts in our Code where, for example, ascetic, cemetery monks manage only to terrify children;[39] where ascetic monks who wear robes made from cemetery cloth are not even allowed into the monastery, let alone allowed to sit on a mat that belongs to the Community;[40] tales whose only point seems to be to indicate that meditation makes you stupid;[41] texts about monks who meditate in the forest and cannot control their male member and so end up smashing it between two rocks, whereupon the Buddha tells them, while they are howling in pain, that they, unfortunately, have smashed the wrong thing—they should have smashed desire;[42] and a tale about another monk who meditated in the forest and, to avoid being seduced by a goddess, had to tie his legs shut. The goddess being put off by this then flung him through the air, and he landed—legs still tied—on top of the king, who was sleeping on the roof of his palace. The king, of course, was not amused and made it known to the Buddha that it would not do to have his monks being flung around the countryside in the middle of the night. The Buddha then actually made a rule forbidding monks to meditate in the forest![43] Texts and tales of this sort are numerous in our Code.

The monks with whom our Code is concerned are of a very different sort, as even our brief survey indicates. In the passages so far cited, we find monks who have servants and who do not even have to wash their own dishes; monks who eat fine meals in the homes of prominent laymen; monks who are concerned not about meditation but with property, with marking and maintaining control or possession of property, and who have and acknowledge personal property. Moreover, the monks with whom our Code is concerned live—whether in the forest or in the village—in monasteries that are owned by laymen, and it is becoming ever clearer on the basis of this Code that that meant that the monks were in at least some important ways in the employ of their donors. There are rules in this Code that require, for example, that monks—regardless of their own wishes—must spend a part of each day in any *vihāra* that has been "donated," to ensure that none stands empty, that all are used, and thus to continue to earn merit for their owner, even if a single monk has to move from one to another in the course of the same day.[44] There are rules that require the monks to recite verses every day for the merit of not only the owner of the monastery but also each and every donor or benefactor, and each of their individual names must every day be announced—this in a monastery of any size could easily have taken up a significant part of the day.[45] There was, however, an even more serious problem in this "employment," a systemic problem of far-reaching consequences that involved our monks—and early on it seems—in money transactions, sophisticated financial enterprises, the promotion of "art," and extensive fund-raising projects. It created situations that, for example, the administrators of the Nelson-Atkins Museum of Art, or any institution, might find uncomfortably familiar.

The problem most simply put was this: whereas, as we have seen, the obligations of the monks who lived in their monasteries were reasonably clear and enforceable, the obligations of the owner or donors were much less so. Aspects of the problem are repeatedly addressed in our Code, particularly the problems of the maintenance and upkeep of the "physical plant" and the subsistence of its residents. The problem of monasteries falling into disrepair is explicitly raised—for example, in the *Śayanāsanavastu*, "the Section on Bedding and Seats" in our Code, but the solution proposed there must have been something less than satisfying. There the Buddha says:

> The donor should be encouraged to make repairs (*dānapatir utsāhayitavyaḥ*). If just that succeeds, it is good. If it does not succeed then they are to be repaired with Community assets (*sāṃghika*). If that is not possible, insofar as it is possible, to that extent restoration is to be done. The rest must be tolerated (*anye vyupekṣitavyāḥ*).[46]

Passages of this sort suggest that the redactors of our Code understood that "donors" were not, strictly speaking, obliged to maintain their monasteries and could only be encouraged to do so. But these passages also suggest that there was an awareness, if not an expectation, that the donors might not. Other passages in this same *Vastu*, however, suggest as well that in regard to the related problem of subsistence the monks might vote, as it were, with their feet.

In one such passage,[47] for example, a householder goes to a monastery and hears the Elder of the Community reciting verses and "assigning the reward or merit" (*dakṣiṇām ādiśat*) to its deceased (*abhyatītakālagata*) donors.[48] He says to the monk: "Noble One, if I have a *vihāra* built, would you assign the merit to my name also?" (*ārya yady ahaṃ vihāraṃ kārayāmi mamāpi nāmnā dakṣiṇām uddiśasi*). The monk says yes, and the householder has a *vihāra* built, "but he gave nothing to it and it remained unoccupied" (*tatrānena na kiṃcid dattam sa śūnya evāvasthitaḥ*). The householder sees this and goes to complain to the monk: "Noble One," he says, "my *vihāra* (*madīyo vihāraḥ*) remains empty. No monk resides there." The monk says, "Sir, it should be made productive (*utsvedya*)." The householder initially misunderstands this euphemism and replies, "But, Noble One, it was built on sterile saline soil. How is it to be made productive?" To which the monk says: "Householder, I did not mean that, but rather that there was no donation (*lābha*) there." The householder says: "Noble One, who now resides in my *vihāra* (*madīye vihāre*), to him I will present cloth."

Monks could, then, in effect try to force the owner of a *vihāra* to provide for their maintenance by withdrawing or refusing to provide their services, but this of course could be a two-edged sword, and if they tried it, they might find themselves not only out of business but also without a home. Moreover, yet another structural weakness arose from the fact that donors—like the rest of us—died, and the redactors of our Code were clearly aware of what this could mean. More than one text in our Code begins with just such a situation. In a passage in the *Vinayavibhaṅga* that we will return to, we find, for example:[49]

> A devout and good householder with meritorious inclinations lived in a rural hamlet. He had a *vihāra* for the Community built in the forest that had lofty gateways and was ornamented with open galleries on the roof, latticed windows, and railings. It captivated both the heart and the eye, was like a stairway to the heavens, and had exquisite couches, benches, and furnishings.[50] The householder provided robes, alms, and all the needs of the sixty monks who lived there.
>
> But later that householder died. Because he had a son, the monks went to him and said: "Seeing, Sir, that your father had provided robes, alms, and all the needs of sixty monks, are you able as well to provide us, the sixty monks, with robes, alms, and all our needs?"
>
> The son said: "Noble Ones, although there are some who might look after a hundred, a thousand, or even a hundred thousand, because there are others, myself included, who have difficulty making ends meet, I am not able to do it."
>
> The monks then left that *vihāra*.

In the event of the death of a donor, then, the lack of clarity in regard to his obligations while alive that has already been noticed became even more pronounced in regard to the donor's heirs. The text here suggests that the redactors of our Code considered that the initial response of the monks to such an event should be to approach the heir or heirs to get a confirmation that any arrangement that the donor had entered into would continue. But it also suggests that there was a clear awareness that the heirs might—and had the right to—simply terminate any such arrangement. In fact, the death of an owner or donor created an awkward situation. The obligations of the monks to a dead donor had been put unequivocally into the Buddha's mouth: "The Blessed One said: 'Merit must be transferred to donors who have passed away and are dead!'" (*uktaṃ bhagavatā abhyatītakālagatānāṃ dānapatīnām nāmnā dakṣiṇā ādeṣṭavyā iti*).[51] The Buddha had been made to declare just as explicitly that all *vihāras* must be used. But without some provision having been made for the maintenance of both the physical monastery and any resident monks, neither would have been possible after the donors' death, even though donors might have acted on the expectation that it would. The redactors of our Code, moreover, would have us believe that this concern was explicitly articulated by donors themselves, and that it was in response to their voiced concern that the monks had begun to accept considerable sums as "permanent endowments" and to lend those sums out on interest. At least this is how these practices were justified in one of the two texts in our *Vinaya* that deal with them.

The *Vibhaṅga* text in question, which has been treated in some detail elsewhere, opens by saying:[52]

> At that time the Licchavis of Vaiśālī built houses with six or seven upper chambers. As the Licchavis built their houses, so too did they build *vihāras*. . . . As a consequence, because of their great height . . . they fell apart. When that occurred, the donors thought: "If even the *vihāras* of those who are still living . . . fall thus into ruin, how will it be for the *vihāras* of those who are dead? We should give a perpetuity to the monastic Community for building purposes."

The donors did give such a perpetuity and then encouraged the suitably reluctant monks to lend the sums they were given as endowments out on interest. The monks asked the Buddha and the Buddha said: "For the sake of the Community a perpetuity for building purposes must be lent on interest." A little later in the text this directive is extended to perpetuities for the benefit of the Buddha, the Dharma, and the Community. The text then concludes with one of the more remarkable pieces of *buddhavacana* that we have, a saying of the Buddha giving detailed instructions on how to make a loan and how to write a written loan contract:

> The Blessed One said: "Taking a pledge of twice the value (of the loan), and writing out a contract that has a seal and is witnessed, the perpetuity is to be placed. In the contract the year, the month, the day, the name of the Elder of the Community, the Provost of the monastery, the borrower, the property, and the interest should be recorded. When the perpetuity is to be placed, that pledge of twice the value is also to be placed with a trustworthy lay-brother who has undertaken the five rules of training.

Such a financial instrument or legal device is, of course, at least one viable solution to the problem of institutional maintenance over time, and this sort of thing—like the legal concept of a "juristic personality"—was very likely pioneered by Buddhist monastic communities. There is in fact inscriptional evidence for the use of such instruments by Buddhist monastic communities from as early as, perhaps, the first century of the Common Era, but unfortunately not from the Northwest.[53] This fact, however, must be tempered by the further fact that records of endowments or land grants, for example, are extremely rare—if they occur at all—in the pre-Kuṣān and Kuṣān epigraphical record from the Northwest. If such transactions occurred there, and it is hard to imagine that they did not, it appears that they were simply not recorded in inscriptions.

But in addition to permanent endowments and to lending money on interest, our Code also suggests that the monastic communities it knew or envisioned could also borrow money. We know this from a remarkable provision of what can only be called Mūlasarvāstivādin monastic inheritance law. Because the text involved is a short one and until recently virtually unknown, it is quoted here in full:[54]

> The setting was in Śrāvastī.
>
> A monk who was the Service Manager (*zhal ta byed pa*, *vaiyāpṛtyakara*) borrowed money (*nor*) from a householder for the sake of the Community and then died. When the householder heard that that monk had died, he went to the *vihāra* and asked: "Where is the monk so-and-so?"
>
> The monks said: "He's dead."
>
> The householder said: "But, Noble Ones, he borrowed some money from me."
>
> "Well, go and collect it from him then!" the monks said.
>
> "But since it was not for the sake of his parents or himself, but for the sake of the Community that he took it, you should repay it!"
>
> The monks reported to the Blessed One what had occurred, and the Blessed One said: "If it is known that he took it for the sake of the Community, then the Community must repay the loan! I, monks, will here give the rules of customary behavior for a monk like the Monk in Charge of Construction (*las gsar du byed pa*, *navakarmika*): When the Monk in Charge of Construction has asked the various Seniors (*rgan pa*), then he must take out loans! If Monks in Charge of Construction do not act in accordance with the rules of customary behavior, they come to be guilty of an offense."

Here we have put into the mouth of the Buddha—the same Buddha who is said to have declared that "all things are impermanent"—specific instructions detailing how a monastic officer must, after consultation with the senior monks, take out a loan from a layman for the use of the monastic community. Obviously, if we chose—as most scholars have—to take the one type of declaration seriously, but the other not, then we are going to be in no position to fully understand the buildings that followers of that same Buddha built, nor the pots they used, nor the money that they handled. Indeed, there may be for us a further cautionary tale in that the *navakarmika*, the monk who was not only in charge of construction but who was also to take out loans, is probably the earliest monastic officer for which we have epigraphical evidence,[55] and in the fact that just such an officer is mentioned in four separate pre-Kuṣān and early Kuṣān Kharoṣṭhī inscriptions from the Northwest.[56]

To this point, then, it seems that we can at least conclude that the redactors of our Code, who probably lived in Early Northwest India, were looking for ways, and devising means, to secure access to funds and reliable sources of income that would ensure the continuation of the institution to which they belonged, and the maintenance of the physical plants that housed it. In the process they, like so many successful fund-raisers who came after them, seem to have discovered what St. Bernard in eleventh-century France still found disconcerting. Bernard did not like elaborate monastic architecture, nor art in monasteries. He particularly did not like what he thought other monks used them for. He argued, in fact, that art and fine architecture were being used to attract donations to the monasteries, and he thought that because, very probably, they were. But in his exasperation he said: "In this way wealth is derived from wealth, in this way money attracts money, because by I know not what law, wherever the more riches are seen, there the more willingly are offerings made."[57] This same principle, or quirk of human psychology, seems—as I have already said—to already have been discovered by the redactors of our Code. They at least included in their compilation a significant number of texts that suggest that. Here we can look only at a few.

Our Code refers to beautiful monasteries in beautiful settings, to paintings on monastery walls and on cloth, and to a specific image type, one example of which, from Sahri-Bahlol, must surely be one of the most beautiful images in all of Gandhāran art.[58] But in virtually every case these references refer as well—in one way or another—to the gifts and donations that such things generate. Even in a case that might at first sight seem to be an exception to this, it turns out to be true. In a text that we have already seen, for example, an elaborate monastery with "lofty gateways" and "ornamented with open galleries on the roof," a monastery that explicitly "captivated both the heart and the eye," is abandoned after the death of its donor. But not—the text goes on to say—for long. When "merchants from the North Country" see this beautiful monastery and discover that its monks have left, they promptly re-endow it on an even more lavish scale. They say to two old monks that they find there:[59]

> Noble Ones, here is alms for three months for sixty monks. Here is alms for the festival of the eighth day, and for the fourteenth day, and the fifteenth day. Here are the requisites for medicines for the sick, a general donation, the price for robes. . . . When the rainy season is over, we will return and provide for the needs of a hundred monks.

Narratively, the merchants can be responding only to the beauty and elaborate character of the monastery, not to what the monks are or do—there are in fact no permanent resident monks there, and this interpretation is, as we will see, explicitly confirmed elsewhere. The message here in a tale told by monks to other monks must have been clear: If you want to have a monastery that can survive the death of its donor, then it too must be capable of captivating the heart and the eye—not, be it noticed, the head.[60] Such monasteries, it seems, were thought not only to survive but also to have been inordinately prosperous. That at least is the substance of another text that describes in some detail the kinds of wealth that are found in a beautiful *vihāra*. There even the cells of new novices have cloth racks "hung and heaped with cloth"; the Community has a great deal of "bedding and seats," and even new novices get the seven sorts; and the monks' cells are full of copper vessels.[61] Beauty, it seems, in part at least means overabundance, and the association between the two is made not by us but by the redactors of our Code. A third text that refers to such a monastery typifies a whole series of such texts and confirms our initial observation. It is of additional interest because it contains the authorization for monks to maintain stores of rice and to get into the rice-selling business.

The text in question is so straightforward as to be startling. In it "some merchants from the Northern Road" were traveling:[62]

> . . . they saw *vihāras* that had high arched gateways, were ornamented with windows, latticed windows, and railings, *vihāras* that captivated the eye and the heart and were like stairways to heaven, and they were deeply affected (*dad par 'gyur te, prasanna*). They went to a *vihāra* and said to the monks: "Noble Ones, we would make an offering feast (*mchod ston*) for the Community!"

The point here is probably hard to miss. The merchants are explicitly presented as responding to the appearance of the monastery, and to that alone. They are moved by its beauty—their heart and eye stolen. The Sanskrit was certainly either *prasanna* or *abhiprasanna*, and it repeatedly occurs in our passages to express an emotional state or aesthetic reaction. It is a term like *saṃvega*, which occurs in some of the same contexts, in spite of how it has sometimes been translated, and in our texts this aesthetic reaction almost invariably results—as we will see—in donations.[63] But our text also goes on to indicate that attracting donors can also involve complications.

When the merchants have declared their intentions to the monks, the monks tell them to bring what is needed for the meal, but the merchants say they have only just arrived and would prefer to give the price to the monks and then the monks can provide the rice. The monks demur, but the Buddha then gives a first directive: "When someone makes an offering feast for the sake of the Community, you must sell them rice!" (*rin gyis 'bras sbyin par bya'o*). The monks do so, but when "large numbers" made such feasts and the monks sold to all of them, "the common stores were exhausted." The Buddha then gives a second set of directives, which constitute, in effect, guidelines for running an efficient granary—that is, when rice is sold for a feast in the same *vihāra*, a little something extra might be given for the price; old rice must be sold at "a good time" and the storerooms filled with new rice; and so on. Clearly, the monks who redacted our Code realized that being in one business, the business of attracting donors, required engaging in other businesses as well, like buying and selling grain.

But if these and other texts like them in our *Vinaya* link beautiful and imposing monastic architecture with the attraction of donations, still others articulate in addition a linkage between donations and the natural beauty of a monastery's setting. One example will suffice. In the Chapter on Robes, we find:[64]

> There was a householder in a rural hamlet. He had a *vihāra* made, but only one monk entered into the rainy-season retreat there. That monk, however, was energetic. Every day he smeared that *vihāra* with cow dung and swept it well. Well maintained was that *vihāra*, and sited in a lovely isolated spot adorned with all sorts of trees, filled with the soft sounds of geese and curlews, peacocks and parrots, mainas and cuckoos, adorned with various flowers and fruits.
>
> Once a wealthy trader spent the night in that *vihāra*. When he saw the beauties of that *vihāra* (*vihāraśobhaṃ*) and the beauties of its woods (*upavanaśobhaṃ*), he was deeply moved (*abhiprasanna*), and although he had not seen the monks, he dispatched in the name of the Community a very considerable donation (*prabhūto lābhaḥ*).

This little text too probably requires little commentary, in part because in both its structure and its basic vocabulary it repeats the others we have seen, and in part because it is so clear. There are of course "new" elements of interest, but the basic account is what might already be called "the same old story." A wealthy merchant comes to a *vihāra*, and when he sees its beauties, he is struck, moved, or affected—once again the term is *abhiprasanna*—and he makes a large donation. What is different here is that although, again, the *vihāra* itself is attractive, the emphasis is not so much on it as on what might be called the aesthetics of order and cleanliness and the beauty of its setting. If the early Northwest was anything like modern India, it is not difficult to see how a clean and well-maintained monastery might make a distinct impression. But the natural beauty of the site itself is most fully described, and it is this, perhaps, that our redactors want most to emphasize. The site of the monastery is here described very much in the same terms that our Code repeatedly uses to describe the natural beauties of a park or garden (*udyāna*) in spring, and thereby it assimilates the two.[65] Though oddly little studied, Indian literature—both religious and secular—is saturated with thick and sensuous descriptions of such "parks," and they clearly had strong aesthetic appeal. Western archaeologists from Cunningham to Stein have also repeatedly remarked on the sometimes stunning natural beauty of the sites of Buddhist monasteries, and our text would seem to indicate that their selection was almost certainly not accidental.[66] Apart from these considerations, we perhaps need only note here that our text makes explicit what in the previous texts was only strongly implied: This merchant was responding solely and simply to the beauties of the *vihāra* and its setting—the text explicitly says that he never even saw the monks.

Having seen what we have in the discussion of our texts so far, when we get to what we call "art," there are no surprises. As Zürcher and others have noted, our monastic Code is comparatively rich in references to "art," although the "art" it refers to is predominantly painting.[67] Here I must limit myself to some brief remarks on two such texts whose basic point will sound perfectly familiar.

One of the texts on monastic art in our Code has been known for some time now. It deals with the famous lay-brother Anāthapiṇḍada, who was seeking and gaining permission from the Buddha to have paintings in the equally famous monastery that he "donated" to the Order.[68] The language that he is made to use, and the reasons he is made to give for wanting paintings in the monastery, are particularly interesting but can, of course, be securely attributed only to the monk or monks who composed or redacted the text. They, or Anāthapiṇḍada, did not, according to the text, want art in the monastery to instruct either the laity or the monks, nor to serve as objects of devotion or as aids to meditation. They or he wanted this art for a very different reason, and the text here too seems to be remarkably straightforward. It begins:

> When the householder Anāthapiṇḍada had given the Jetavana Monastery to the Community from the Four Directions, it occurred to him then: "Since there are no paintings, this monastery is ugly (*di ri mo ma bris pas mi sdug ste*). If, therefore, the Blessed One were to authorize it, it should have paintings." So thinking, he went to the Blessed One and sat down at one side. So seated, the householder Anāthapiṇḍada said this to the Blessed One: "Reverend, the Jetavana is ugly be-

> cause I did not have paintings made. Therefore, if the Blessed One were to authorize it, I will have paintings made there."
>
> The Blessed One said: "Householder, with my authorization, paintings therefore must be made!"[69]

As if to make sure that no one missed the point, the redactors repeat it twice: There should be paintings in the monastery because without them it is ugly or not beautiful. And no other reason is here given.[70]

The text continues with the Buddha's giving specific instructions on the placement of specific paintings—the Great Miracle and the Wheel of Rebirth are to be painted on the porch; the garland of *Jātakas* on the gallery; a *yakṣa* holding a club at the door of the Buddha's shrine; the various Elders in the meeting hall; and so on.[71] This much of the tradition has been known—if not fully appreciated—for some time, but an equally important text related to the paintings in the Jetavana that occurs in the same section of our Code has gone completely unnoticed. Its purport will be almost immediately familiar:[72]

> After the householder Anāthapiṇḍada had given the Jetavana Monastery to the Community of Monks from the Four Directions, and had had it finished both inside and out with various sorts of colors, and had had paintings done, then crowds of people who lived in Śrāvastī heard how the householder Anāthapiṇḍada had finished the Jetavana both inside and out with various sorts of colors and paintings and had made it remarkably fine, and many hundreds of thousands of people came then to see the Jetavana.

The text to this point is not subtle, and it is hard to imagine that any monk who was in charge of a monastery could miss the point: People would hear about a monastery that had paintings, and they would come—in large numbers. But the rest of the text is no more subtle. It concerns a brahmin from Śrāvastī to whom, the text says, "the king and his ministers and the local people were much devoted"—paintings will apparently attract not just people but the better sort as well. The text says that this brahmin had received from the royal court "an extremely costly woolen blanket" (*chen po la 'os pa'i la ba*), and then—by now almost predictably:[73]

> Once when he was wearing that blanket, he went to the Jetavana to see its wonders (*ltad mo, kūtahala*). Just as soon as he saw it, he was greatly moved (*dad pa chen po skyes nas*), and he gave that woolen blanket to the Community of Monks from the Four Directions.

The first thing to note here is that we again have a text that makes explicit what is only strongly implied in most others: The presence of things beautiful—in this case paintings that are explicitly said to be "a wonder" or "a marvel"—attract people. It is explicitly said that the brahmin went to the monastery to see "its wonders," not, be it noted, to see the Buddha or the monks or to hear the Dharma. Apart from this, we see only what we have already seen before: An individual sees what is beautiful, is deeply moved, and makes a large donation. It is this last that the text is most interested in, and its value is explicitly stated: The blanket not only was a royal gift but also is explicitly described as "extremely costly." Its value is further emphasized by the fact that as the text continues the brahmin tries to get it back! And it is even more strongly emphasized by the further fact that its donation requires and effects a significant change in established monastic rules. Prior to this occasion, the rule established by the Buddha was that all cloth donated to the Community must be cut up and divided equally among the monks.[74] But the donation of this costly cloth led the Buddha himself to modify that rule—to, it is easy to see, the material benefit of the monks. He is made to rule: "Henceforth, monks, whatever donation of cloth of this sort falls to the Community must be sold for cash (*kārṣāpaṇa*) and the cash divided among the monks (*de lta bas na dge 'dun la gos kyi rnyed pa de lta bu grub pa gang yin pa de kar sha pa ṇa dag tu bsgyur la kar sha pa ṇa dag bgo bar bya'o*). This ruling, which *requires* the monks to engage in commercial transactions and to act as cloth merchants is, in fact, the main point of the entire account. But between the selling of cloth and the buying and selling of rice and a whole host of other such activities, it is hardly surprising, then, that large numbers of coins have been found at Buddhist monastic sites.

These texts dealing with the paintings in the Jetavana are probably the most important texts in our Code dealing with monastic art. There are of course others, but there is little point in treating them in detail—they all in one way or another tell the same story. The well-known text dealing with the Wheel of Rebirth painted on the porch of the Jetavana is, in the end, about the donation of a monastic feast that cost five hundred *kārṣāpaṇas*, although the painting was originally intended for didactic purposes or to frighten the monks;[75] the account of the painted image of the Buddha on cloth that was sent to a Sri Lankan princess is, in the end, about a magnificent donation of pearls that provided one of the occasions on which the Buddha himself defined the threefold economic and corporate structure of the monastic Community—it culminates in a ruling that mandates how the three equal parts of such a donation must be used.[76] Even the important series of texts in our Code that deal with the specifically named "Image in the Shade of the Jambu Tree" follows the same pattern. This specifically named image not only provides another remarkable linkage between our *Vinaya* and the art of the Northwest—several clearly identifiable examples of this named image have already been recognized in the Gandhāran corpus, and there is an inscribed Kuṣān example made in Mathurā but found at Sāñcī—but the texts that deal with it also provide a unique and detailed set of rules governing monastic image processions, image processions that are explicitly said to generate large donations and are clearly meant to do so. This series of texts in fact, as now must seem perfectly fitting, ends with another set of rules governing monastic auctions, which turn those abundant offerings into cash.[77]

What we see and have seen here is, then, the monastic view of the function of beauty and what we call "art" in the monastery. There may have been other views—there almost certainly were—but they are not expressed in the *Mūlasarvāstivāda-vinaya*, an important monastic Code that almost certainly was written or redacted in Early Northwest India. In the Early Northwest those other views appear to have been expressed by dissident monks who would come to form what we call "the Mahāyāna," but they—like St. Bernard and for many of the same reasons—appear at least originally to have disapproved of art and to have had little or no interest in promoting elaborate monasteries.[78] All of this, at the very least, must be sobering. Clearly we have much more to learn about the Buddhist monks who handled the coins we collect and used the pots that we classify. They were not, it seems, what we have been told they were.

Notes

1. Examples of early work published on this *Vinaya* include, first of all, A. Csoma de Körös, "Analysis of the Dulva. A Portion of the Tibetan Work Entitled the Kah-gyur," *Asiatik Researches* 20 (1836) 41–93 (later translated into French in L. Feer, *Analyse du kandjour. Recueil des livres sacrés au tibet* [Annales du musée guimet II] [Paris: 1881] 146–198). In the 1870s, A. von Schiefner published a long series of papers under the title "Indische Erzählungen" in *Bulletin de l'académie impériale des sciences de St.-Petersbourg* (listed in detail in Panglung, *Die Erzählstoffe des Mūlasarvāstivāda-Vinaya*, 254–255), which were in turn translated into English in W. R. Ralston, *Tibetan Tales Derived from Indian Sources* (London: 1882), making available a significant sampling of the narrative literature found in this *Vinaya*—indeed the work might have been more accurately entitled "Tales or Stories from the *Mūlasarvāstivāda-vinaya*," though a very few of the "tales" came from elsewhere. W. W. Rockhill also did early important work on this *Vinaya* (Rockhill, "Le traité d'émancipation ou Pratimoksa Sutra," *RHR* 9 [1884] 3–26, 167–201; Rockhill, "Tibetan Buddhist Birth-Stories: Extracts and Translations from the Kandjur," *JAOS* 18 [1897] 1–14; Rockhill, *The Life of the Buddha and the Early History of His Order Derived from Tibetan Works in the Bkah-Hgyur and Bstan-Hgyur* [London: 1907]).

2. Lamotte, *Histoire du bouddhisme indien*, 727.

3. For references and further, sometimes overlapping discussion, see G. Schopen, "The Bones of a Buddha and the Business of a Monk: Conservative Monastic Values in an Early Mahāyāna Polemical Tract," *JIP* 27 (1999) 292–293 [*FFMB* Ch. III]; and Schopen, *Daijō bukkyō kōki jidai*, 39ff.

4. For but one prominent example, see J. W. de Jong, Review of Falk, *Schrift im alten Indien*, *IIJ* 39 (1996) 69.

5. *Saṅghabhedavastu* (Gnoli) i, "General Introduction," xix.

6. *Bhaiṣajyavastu*, GMs iii 1, 1.20–2.5—for the reading of this passage in the Gilgit manuscript itself (GBMs vi 952.2) and some discussion, see Schopen, *Daijō bukkyō kōki jidai*, 42–45.

7. In the short "Introduction" he wrote to J. Przyluski, "Le nord-ouest de l'inde dans le vinaya des mūlasarvāstivādin et les textes apparentés," *JA* (1914) 493–568—Przyluski translates here the Chinese translation of this "māhātmya" done by I-ching.

8. Ed. Huber, "Études bouddhiques. III—Le roi kaniṣka dans le vinaya des mūlasarvāstivādins," *BEFEO* 14 (1914) 18: "qui tendent à montrer que le Vinaya des Mūla-Sarvāstivādins a subi un remaniement aux environs de l'ère chrétienne." This paper of Huber's, moreover, was also translated into English shortly after its original publication in G. K. Nariman, *Literary History of Sanskrit Buddhism* (Bombay: 1919) 274–275.

9. See as a small sample: *Śayanāsanavastu* (Gnoli) 3.19; *Bhaiṣajyavastu*, GMs iii 1, 55.12; *Pravrajyāvastu*, GMs iii 4, 56.12; *Vibhaṅga*, Derge Ca 247a.7, Ja 69a.2 = *Divyāvadāna* (Cowell and Neil) 493.15; etc.

10. See G. Schopen, "The Lay Ownership of Monasteries and the Role of the Monk in Mūlasarvāstivādin Monasticism," *JIABS* 19.1 (1996) 81–126 [= Ch. VIII below]; Schopen, "Marking Time in Buddhist Monasteries. On Calendars, Clocks, and Some Liturgical Practices," in *Sūryacandrāya. Essays in Honour of Akira Yuyama on the Occasion of His 65th Birthday* (Indica et Tibetica 35), ed. P. Harrison and G. Schopen (Swisttal-Odendorf: 1998) 158–179 [= Ch. IX below]. At this stage of our ignorance, it appears that although the title *Vihārasvāmin* might not be exclusive to Mūlasarvāstivādin sources, it may well be predominantly a Mūlasarvāstivādin term. Th. Damsteegt, *Epigraphical Hybrid Sanskrit* (Leiden: 1978) 165, says that the title "is apparently not found in Pali," and it certainly does not occur in the Pāli *Vinaya*, even though the term *sassāmika* occurs in conjunction with *vihāra* there (Pāli *Vinaya* iii 156). The lack of linkages between Pāli sources and the epigraphical and archaeological records of the Northwest is consistent and points to the limited utility of the former for understanding the latter.

11. The passage in question—*Varṣāvastu*, GMs iii 4, 139.11–.17—has been discussed in some detail in G. Schopen, "The Ritual Obligations and Donor Roles of Monks in the Pāli *Vinaya*," *JPTS* 16 (1992) 87–107 [= *BSBM*, Ch. IV].

12. See, for example, R. Salomon, "The Bhagamoya Relic Bowl Inscription," *IIJ* 27 (1984) 108 (1.2); G. Fussman, "Nouvelles inscriptions śaka (II)," *BEFEO* 73 (1984) 33 (1.2), 35 (1.2), 39 (11.7–.9); Fussman, "Nouvelles inscriptions śaka (III)," *BEFEO* 74 (1985) 37 (1.3); Fussman, "Documents epigraphiques kouchans (IV). Ajitasena, pere de senavarma," *BEFEO* 75 (1986) 2 (1.5); Salomon, "The Reliquary Inscription of Utara: A New Source for the History of the Kings of Apraca," *IIJ* 31 (1988) 169. For the inscription that refers explicitly to "the merit of Brahma," see R. Salomon and G. Schopen, "The Indravarman (Avaca) Casket Inscription Reconsidered: Further Evidence for Canonical Passages in Buddhist Inscriptions," *JIABS* 7.1 (1984) 108 (1.4).

13. The passage in question—*Saṅghabhedavastu* (Gnoli) ii 206.16—has been noticed

in Salomon and Schopen, "The Indravarman (Avaca) Casket Inscription Reconsidered," 121–122, but the reservations expressed there in regard to whether or not the passage was original to this *Vinaya* need to be revisited and may well have been overstated. The same or a similar passage also occurs in the *Ekottarāgama*, for example, but given the nature of that compilation, the chances that it was the original source are certainly not better.

14. For convenience, see the references in G. Schopen, "On Monks, Nuns, and 'Vulgar' Practices: The Introduction of the Image Cult into Indian Buddhism," *ArA* 49 (1988/1989) 158–159 [= *BSBM*, 243].

15. See as a small sample: *Bhaiṣajyavastu*, GMs iii 1, 55.12; *Pravrajyāvastu*, GMs iii 4, 56.12; *Pravrajyāvastu* (Eimer) ii 259.15; *Vibhaṅga*, Derge Ca 247a.7, Ja 64b.5 (= *Divyāvadāna* [Cowell and Neil] 488.3, though the Sanskrit has been abbreviated), Ja 80a.2 (= *Divyāvadāna* [Cowell and Neil] 505.2), Ja 227a.1; etc.

16. Konow, *Kharoshṭhī Inscriptions*, LVIII (124), LXXXVIII (172); Lüders, *Mathurā Inscriptions* §§ 44, 46.

17. *Pravrajyāvastu* (Eimer) ii 163.12. For a Sanskrit text of the formulary, see B. Jinananda, *Upasampadājñaptiḥ* (Patna: 1961), esp. 26.3 for the passage cited. The *Upasampadājñaptiḥ* appears to be an extract from the *Pravrajyāvastu*, but its textual history is not actually known. A translation of the entire formulary will appear in the new Penguin *Buddhist Scriptures*, being edited by D. Lopez.

18. For some texts illustrative of this strong emphasis on the obligations of preceptors and pupils in regard to mutual caregiving, especially in times of illness, see *Kṣudrakavastu*, Derge Tha 212b.3–213b.3, 213b.3–214a.7. On similiar obligations, again in times of illness, of monks for other monks with whom they need not have a formally acknowledged relationship, see *Cīvaravastu*, GMs iii 2, 124.11–125.9, 128.1–131.15 (most of these are briefly discussed at G. Schopen, "The Good Monk and His Money in a Buddhist Monasticism of the Mahāyāna Period," *EB* n.s. 32.1 [2000] 95–96 [= Ch. I above, 8–9]). *Cīvaravastu*, GMs iii 2, 124.11ff, contains a rule requiring monks to undertake acts of worship (*pūjā*) for the benefit of (*uddiśya*) a dying fellow monk—a situation that might well lie behind several of our inscriptions—and is tentatively translated in G. Schopen, "Deaths, Funerals, and the Division of Property in a Monastic Code," in *Buddhism in Practice*, ed. D. S. Lopez Jr. (Princeton, N.J.: 1995) 495–496 [= Ch. IV below, 114–115].

19. S. Konow, "Note on the Tōr-Ḍhērai Inscriptions," in A. Stein, *An Archaeological Tour in Wazīristān and Northern Balūchistān* (MASI 37) (Calcutta: 1929) 93–97; Konow, *Kharoshṭhī Inscriptions*, XCII (173–177); cf. the series of pot inscriptions published and discussed in R. Salomon, *Ancient Buddhist Scrolls from Gandhāra. The British Library Kharoṣṭhī Fragments* (Seattle: 1999) 183–247.

20. See *Kṣudrakavastu*, Derge Tha 108a.6–110a.4; see also *Śayanāsanavastu* (Gnoli) 50.18–51.9 on monastic wells and the monks' obligation to distribute water there.

21. E. Senart, "Notes d'épigraphie indienne," *JA* (1890) 122. There is now probably no need to pursue the question raised by Senart of foreign influence ("l'imitation des formules épigraphiques de l'Occident") on the development of these formulae—they are far more explicable "par le jeu naturel des idées natives" than he could ever have seen, and a considerable amount of evidence for this is found in our Code.

22. Obviously, much more needs to be known about all the *Vinayas* preserved now only in Chinese before such statements can have any dependable force. For the moment it can only be said that no such material has been noted so far in these *Vinayas* and that no material of this kind occurs in the canonical Pāli *Vinaya*.

23. The text is found at *Uttaragrantha*, Derge Pa 99a.7–100a.6.

24. For the shards from Mohenjo-daro, see E. J. H. Mackay, *Further Excavations at Mohenjo-Daro* (Delhi: 1938) Vol. I, 187; see also Salomon, *Ancient Buddhist Scrolls from Gandhāra*, 193 (pot A inscription) and 245 (the Kara Tepe example cited). There are some other possible examples, but an explicit identification of the "owner" as a monk is generally lacking; e.g., S. R. Rao, "Excavations at Kanheri (1969)," in *Studies in Indian History and Culture*, ed. S. Ritti and B. R. Gopal (Dharwar: 1971) 45; H. Falk, "Protective Inscriptions on Buddhist Monastic Implements," in *Vividharatnakaraṇḍaka. Festgabe für Adelheid Mette* (Indica et Tibetica 37), ed. C. Chojnacki et al. (Swisttal-Odendorf: 2000) 254, and the literature cited.

25. *Vibhaṅga*, Derge Ja 15a.3–15b.1—discussed in G. Schopen, "The Lay Ownership of Monasteries and the Role of the Monk in Mūlasarvāstivādin Monasticism," 101–102 [= Ch. VIII below, 230–231].

26. For another example of this state of affairs, see *Śayanāsanavastu* (Gnoli) 40.13: *anyatamena gṛhapatinā dvau vihārau kāritau eka āraṇyakānāṃ dvitīyo grāmāntikānām.*

27. See Schopen, "The Lay Ownership of Monasteries," 102 n. 44 [= Ch. VIII below, 252 n. 44] (in the original publication "cited above 14" should be corrected to "cited above 94").

28. *Uttaragrantha*, Derge Pa 154b.6–155a.6 = Tog Na 223a.5–b.7.

29. There is a significant difference between Derge and Tog in regard to the reading for the second half of this statement. Tog has *de ste phul ba'i bsod nams mi snang ngo zhes dpyas pa*, and I have adopted this here. Derge, however, reads *de sngon snang na da mi snang no zhes dpyas pa*, "since that which was formerly visible now is not." It is possible that the reading in Derge was influenced by the reading in the corresponding passage in the very similar text that immediately follows (see n. 33 below), since there both Derge and Tog have *snga na ni snang na da* [Tog *da ni*] *mi snang no zhes 'phya ba* [Tog *dpyas pa*], but any satisfying determination will have to wait for a proper edition of the text.

30. *Vinayasūtra* (Sankrityayana) 119.2 = Derge, bstan 'gyur, 'dul ba Wu 98b.3.

31. Salomon, *Ancient Buddhist Scrolls from Gandhāra*, 198, 218.

32. G. Fussman, "Numismatic and Epigraphic Evidence for the Chronology of Early Gandharan Art," in *Investigating Indian Art*, ed. M. Yaldiz and W. Lobo (Berlin: 1987) 79; Konow, "Note on the Tōr-Ḍhērai Inscriptions," 97.

33. *Uttaragrantha*, Derge Pa 155a.6–157a.2. This second text—in essentials similar to the first, although it contains as well a sermon on the inevitability of death—deals with the furnishings (*mal gos*) of King Prasenajit's grandmother (*phyi mo*) that he gave "to the Noble Community of the Jetavana" (the same narrative frame is used at Pāli *Vinaya* ii 169.29 to a different end). In this instance, however, the "inscription" that is to be written is *yul ko sha la'i rgyal po gsal rgyal gyis phul ba'i* [*mal*] *gos*, "furnishings that were given by Prasenajit, King of Kośala." It, then, does not use a pronoun (*'di, ayam*), nor an expression like

yon du phul ba'i dngos po or *sbyin par bya ba'i chos* (*deyadharma*—so *Vinayasūtra*), and so is even less developed. It also names as the donor the actual giver of the property (Prasenajit), and not its previous and now deceased owner (Presenajit's grandmother).

34. Already noted in A. Bareau, *Les sectes bouddhiques du petit véhicule* (Paris: 1955) 36, 131–132, and the sources cited; Lamotte, *Histoire du bouddhisme indien*, 578; and repeated recently in C. Willemen et al., *Sarvāstivāda Buddhist Scholasticism* (Leiden: 1998) 103–104, 115–116. Inscriptions from the Northwest that refer to the Sarvāstivādins, moreover, continue to be published—see Salomon, *Ancient Buddhist Scrolls from Gandhāra*, 200 (pot B), 205 (pot C).

35. For some examples of the attempts to sort out the relationship(s) between the Sarvāstivādins and the Mūlasarvāstivādins, see J. W. de Jong, "Les *sūtrapiṭaka* des sarvāstivādin et des mūlasarvāstivādin," in *Mélanges d'indianisme a la mémoire de Louis Renou* (Paris: 1968) 395–402; B. Mukherjee, "On the Relationship between the Sarvāstivāda Vinaya and the Mūlasarvāstivāda Vinaya," *Journal of Asian Studies* (Madras) 2.1 (1984) 139–165; Mukherjee, "Shih-sung-lu and the Reconstruction of the Original Sarvāstivāda Vinaya," *Buddhist Studies* 15 (1991) 46–52; Willemen et al., *Sarvāstivāda Buddhist Scholasticism* 36–137; F. Enomoto, "'Mūlasarvāstivādin' and 'Sarvāstivādin,'" in *Vividharatnakaraṇḍaka*, 239–250. Referring to work by Przyluski, Hofinger, and Bareau, Willemen et al. (p. 87) say: "Comparative studies of the *Vinayapiṭaka* of the Sarvāstivādins and of the Mūlasarvāstivādins reveal that what was later called the *Mūlasarvāstivādavinaya* is older than the *Sarvāstivādavinaya*, and even older than most other *Vinayapiṭakas*."

36. A. Bareau, "Le construction et le culte des stūpa d'après les vinayapiṭaka," *BEFEO* 50 (1960) 244.

37. *Kṣudrakavastu*, Derge Tha 102a.5–104b.2.

38. *Poṣadhavastu* (Hu-von Hinüber) §§ 6.1–.8.

39. *Vibhaṅga*, Derge Ja 154b.2–156b.7.

40. *Kṣudrakavastu*, Derge Tha 222b.2–224b.1.

41. *Vibhaṅga*, Derge Ja 79b.7–80b.3 = *Divyāvadāna* (Cowell and Neil) 504.25–505.29.

42. *Kṣudrakavastu*, Derge Tha 39a.6–b.5.

43. *Kṣudrakavastu*, Derge Da 35b.2–36a.2; the *Poṣadhavastu* passage cited in n. 38 above also explicitly forbids practicing meditation in the forest: *bhagavān āha / nāraṇye yogo bhāvayitavyaḥ* (§ 6.5).

44. *Śayanāsanavastu* (Gnoli) 35.1–.10. The passage is translated and discussed in Schopen, "The Lay Ownership of Monasteries," 113ff [= Ch. VIII below, 238ff]; note in particular n. 65 in which the corresponding passage in the *Vinayasūtra* is also translated.

45. *Uttaragrantha*, Derge Pa 71b.4–74a.2—translated and discussed in Schopen, "Marking Time in Buddhist Monasteries," 173ff [= Ch. IX below, 270–271].

46. *Śayanāsanavastu* (Gnoli) 35.7; Schopen, "The Lay Ownership of Monasteries," 113 [= Ch. VIII below, 238].

47. *Śayanāsanavastu* (Gnoli) 37.6–.19; translated in full in Schopen, "The Lay Ownership of Monasteries," 92–93 [= Ch. VIII below, 325–326].

48. Both Vinītadeva's *Vinayavibhaṅgapadavyākhyāna* (Derge, btsan 'gyur, 'dul ba Tshu 64b.5) and Śīlapālita's *Āgamakṣudrakavyākhyāna* (Derge, btsan 'gyur, 'dul ba Dzu 73a.5)

make it clear that the Mūlasarvāstivādin commentarial tradition understood *dakṣiṇām ā√dis* or *ud√diś* to mean the "assigning" or "transfer" of merit. The first, commenting on *Vibhaṅga*, Derge Ca 154a.5, says *yon bshad pa zhes bya ba ni sbyin pa'i 'bras bu yongs su bsngo ba'o*, "'Assigning the reward' means: transferring the fruit of the gift"; and the second, commenting on *Kṣudrakavastu*, Derge Tha 237a.5, says *yon bsngo ba ni chos kyi sbyin pa la sogs pa las yang dag par byung ba'i bsod nams kyi 'bras bu kun du* [read: *tu*] *bgo bsha' byad* [read: *byed*] *pa'o*, "'assigning the reward' means: apportioning the fruit of the merit that arises from a religious gift, etc."

49. *Vibhaṅga*, Derge Cha 184a.1.

50. On this description of, and emphasis on, a beautiful *vihāra*, see pages 31–32 and n. 60 below.

51. *Śayanāsanavastu* (Gnoli) 37.6.

52. *Vibhaṅga*, Derge Cha 154b.3. For a more detailed treatment of the passage, see Schopen, "Doing Business for the Lord: Lending on Interest and Written Loan Contracts in the *Mūlasarvāstivāda-vinaya*," *JAOS* 114 (1994) 527–554 [= Ch. III below].

53. See, for references, Schopen, "Doing Business for the Lord," 532 nn. 22–25 [= Ch III below, nn. 22–25], to which might be added B. S. L. Hanumantha Rao et al., *Buddhist Inscriptions of Andhradesa* (Secunderabad: 1998) 192 ("Patagandigudem [Kallacheruvu] Copper Plates of Siri Ehāvala Chāntamūla"—this record was apparently discovered only in 1997 and is potentially very important. It is the only copper-plate inscription of the Ikṣvākus so far known and is the only record so far of a grant of land by an Ikṣvāku king to a Buddhist monastic community. It is therefore particularly unfortunate that it is available only in a rather primitive transcription that is not accompanied with usable plates or photographs). [See now H. Falk, "The Pātagaṇḍigūḍem Copper-Plate Grant of the Ikṣvāku King Ehavala Cāntamūla," *Silk Road Art and Archeology* 6 (1999/2000) 275–283.]

54. *Uttaragrantha*, Derge Pa 196a.7. For a discussion of the text, see now G. Schopen, "Dead Monks and Bad Debts: Some Provisions of a Buddhist Monastic Inheritance Law," *IIJ* 44 (2001) 115–118 [= Ch. V below, 137–138].

55. Its only possible competitor would be the office of *bhatudesaka*, which is referred to in a single inscription from Bhārhut (H. Lüders, *Bharhut Inscriptions* [CII Vol. II, Pt. 2], ed. E. Waldschmidt and M. A. Mehendale [Ootacamund: 1963] 20, A 17).

56. Konow, *Kharoshṭhī Inscriptions*, XIII, LXXII, LXXVI, LXXXII; see also *BSBM* 159, 190–191, and notes.

57. C. Rudolph, *The "Things of Greater Moment." Bernard of Clairvaux's Apologia and the Medieval Attitude toward Art* (Philadelphia: 1990) 280–281 (for both the Latin text and the translation cited here). For another translation, see M. Casey and J. Leclercq, *Cistercians and Cluniacs. St. Bernard's Apologia to Abbot William* (Kalamazoo, Mich.: 1970) 65; see also P. Fergusson, *Architecture of Solitude. Cistercian Abbeys in Twelfth-Century England* (Princeton, N.J.: 1984) 11ff.

58. See n. 77 below.

59. *Vibhaṅga*, Derge Cha 184a.1.

60. This description of a beautiful *vihāra* is so common in our *Vinaya* that it constitutes a cliché; for some other examples, some of which will be cited immediately below,

see *Vibhaṅga*, Derge Ca 153b.3; Cha 148b.2, 156b.4; Nya 141a.6, 146b.4, 147b.3; *Pravrajyāvastu* (Eimer) ii 271.8, 273.12; etc. The last two of these are particularly interesting examples that combine the description of a beautiful *vihāra* with another formula, discussed below, that describes the natural beauty of a park in spring; and both also contain a further characterization of the *vihāra* as *lha'i gnas ltar dpal gyis 'bar ba*. Happily we also have a Sanskrit version of this simile: *Pravrajyāvastu* (Näther/Vogel/Wille) 255.33—*devabhavanam iva śriyā jvalantam*, "like the dwelling of a god, shining with splendor." This is a remarkable figure of speech to apply to a Buddhist monastery.

61. *Vibhaṅga*, Derge Ca 153b.1ff.

62. *Vibhaṅga*, Derge Cha 156b.4.

63. For the richness of the terms *prasanna* and *abhiprasanna*, see, for now, Schopen, "The Lay Ownership of Monasteries" 98–99 and n. 39 [= Ch. VIII below, 228–229]; and note, for now, that there is almost certainly a connection between the Buddhist use of these terms in the context of donations and the *dharmaśāstric* notion of "tokens of affection" (*prasāda*) as a distinct category of property that is excluded from partition (for some examples of the latter, see L. and R. Rocher, "Ownership by Birth: The Mitākṣarā Stand," *JIP* 29 (2001) 247–248).

64. *Cīvaravastu*, GMs iii 2, 107.11.

65. *Saṅghabhedavastu* (Gnoli) ii 109.10, 121.5; *Śayanāsanavastu* (Gnoli) 32.3; etc.

66. A. Cunningham, *The Bhilsa Topes or Buddhist Monuments of Central India* (London: 1854) 320–321; A. Stein, *On Alexander's Track to the Indus* (London: 1929) 17–18, 35.

67. See E. Zürcher, "Buddhist Art in Medieval China: The Ecclesiastical View," in *Function and Meaning in Buddhist Art. Proceedings of a Seminar Held at Leiden University 21–24 October 1991*, ed. K. R. van Kooij and H. Van der Veere (Groningen: 1995) 1–20, esp. 6; and before him, A. C. Soper, "Early Buddhist Attitudes towards the Art of Painting," *Art Bulletin* 32 (1950) 147–151, and P. Demiéville, "Butsuzō," *Hōbōgirin*, troisième fascicule (Paris: 1974) 210ff.

68. For the account of the founding of this famous monastery in the *Mūlasarvāstivāda-vinaya*, and on the distinct possibility that the purchase of its site by Anāthapiṇḍada was highly illegal, see G. Schopen, "Heirarchy and Housing in a Buddhist Monastic Code. A Translation of the Sanskrit Text of the *Śayanāsanavastu* of the *Mūlasarvāstivāda-vinaya*. Part One," *Buddhist Literature* 2 (2001) 98–99 n. VIII.7.

69. *Kṣudrakavastu*, Derge Tha 225a.3ff. Though much of this account found in the *Kṣudrakavastu* was summarized or partly translated already by both W. W. Rockhill (*The Life of the Buddha*, 48 n. 2) and M. Lalou ("Notes sur la décoration des monastères bouddhiques," *RAA* 5.3 [1930] 183–185), this important opening paragraph was entirely ignored.

70. Virtually this same reason—and it alone—is repeatedly given elsewhere in the *Mūlasarvāstivāda-vinaya* to justify several significant elements of both *stūpas* and images, and several elements of the ritual activity directed toward them as well. In the *Uttaragrantha*, for example, when Anāthapiṇḍada has a *stūpa* built for the hair and nails of the Blessed One, and "when, because it was not plastered, it was ugly (*mi mdzes pa*)," he then seeks and receives permission to have it plastered, repeating in full the reason: "so long as it remains unplastered, it is ugly (*mi mdzes pa*)." In the same way it is said that a *stūpa* is not beauti-

ful when there are no lamps, when the railing surrounding it has no gateway (*rta babs = toraṇa*), when flowers given to it wither, etc., and in each case this aesthetic consideration—and it alone—results in the Blessed One's ordering that this aesthetic deficiency be remedied, that *stūpas* be provided with lamps, their railings be provided with *toraṇas*, etc. (*Uttaragrantha*, Derge Pa 114a.3ff, 120b.1). A fuller summary of these passages—not always entirely dependable—can be found in P. Dorjee, *Stupa and Its Technology. A Tibeto-Buddhist Perspective* (New Delhi: 1996) 4–7. Dorjee paraphrases *mi mdzes par gyur na/nas* as "would appear unattractive," "did not look nice," "looked unattractive"). The same "argument," using the same language, is also used to justify providing "the image of the Bodhisattva" (*byang chub sems dpa'i gzugs*; i.e., of Siddhārtha) with ornaments, with carrying the image on a wagon, with providing that wagon with flags, banners, and so on—and in each case, it is said that the reason for doing so was so that the image or processional wagon would not be ugly (*mi mdzes pa*)—*Uttaragrantha*, Derge Pa 137b.4ff.

71. A digest of this part of the text is preserved in Sanskrit—see *Vinayasūtra* (Sankrityayana) 114.16–.31.

72. *Kṣudrakavastu*, Derge Tha 262b.4.

73. *Kṣudrakavastu*, Derge Tha 262b.7.

74. *Kṣudrakavastu*, Derge Tha 205b.7–207b.3.

75. *Vibhaṅga*, Derge Ja 113b.3–122a.7. A Sanskrit version of this text has come down to us as an extract now found at *Divyāvadāna* (Cowell and Neil) 298.24–311.10. For a translation of the first part of the text from its Chinese translation, see J. Przyluski, "La roue de la vie à ajaṇṭā," *JA* (1920) 313–319; and for Sanskrit fragments of a seemingly similar text, see B. Pauly, "Fragments sanskrits de haute asie (mission pelliot)," *JA* (1959) 228–240.

76. *Adhikaraṇavastu* (Gnoli) 63.16–69.2—*ato yo buddhasya bhāgas tena gandhakuṭyām pralepaṃ dadata; yo dharmasya sa dharmadharāṇām pudgalānāṃ; yaḥ saṃghasya taṃ samagraḥ saṃgho bhajayatu*; cf. Schopen, "Deaths, Funerals, and the Division of Property in a Monastic Code," 500 [= Ch. IV below, 119].

77. The fullest treatment of these texts so far may be found in Ch. IV of *FFMB*, entitled "On Sending Monks Back to Their Books: Cult and Conservatism in Early Mahāyāna Buddhism."

78. See G. Schopen, "The Bones of a Buddha and the Business of a Monk: Conservative Monastic Values in an Early Mahāyāna Polemical Tract," *JIP* 27 (1999) 279–324; and Ch. IV of *FFMB*.

CHAPTER III

Doing Business for the Lord

Lending on Interest and Written Loan Contracts in the *Mūlasarvāstivāda-vinaya*

It is probably fair to say that there has been little discussion in Western scholarship about how Indian Buddhist monasteries paid their bills. It is possible, of course, that this is in part because money and monks have had, to be sure, an unhappy history in the West—at least as that history has often been written—and the topic may therefore be considered somehow unedifying.[1] It may also be true, as Peter Levi's "Study of Monks and Monasteries" suggests, that we like our monasteries in "ruins," as "landscape decorations and garden ornaments." "That," Levi says, "is because the ruins of monasteries speak more clearly than the real inhabited places."[2]

However this be eventually settled, it appears that this reticence or romanticism has worked less forcefully in regard to the study of China. Why this was so is again uncertain, but one effect of it is not: much that a student of Indian monastic Buddhism might find surprising in the *Mūlasarvāstivāda-vinaya*, for example, will be old hat to economic and legal historians of China. A particularly good instance of this sort of thing occurs in the *Cīvaravastu* of the *Mūlasarvāstivāda-vinaya*, where we find the following passage: *tatra bhagavān bhikṣūn āmantrayate sma. bhājayata yūyaṃ bhikṣavā upanandasya bhikṣor mṛtapariṣkāram iti. bhikṣubhiḥ saṃghamadhye avatārya vikrīya bhājitam.* On one level the meaning of this passage is straightforward: "In this case the Blessed One said to the monks: 'You, monks, must [528] divide the estate of the dead monk Upananda!' The monks, having brought it and having sold it in the midst of the community, divided (the proceeds)."[3] It looks like there was a kind of "public" sale or auction of the belongings of a dead monk that was held by the monks, and that what was realized from this sale was then distributed to the monks in attendance.

Originally published in *Journal of the American Oriental Society* 114.4 (1994) 527–553. Reprinted with stylistic changes with permission of American Oriental Society.

Although there is a second reference to "selling" the goods of a deceased monk in this same passage, this procedure, seen through the eyes of an Indianist, will almost certainly appear unusual. But readers of J. Gernet's remarkable *Les aspects économiques du bouddhisme dans la société chinoise du vᵉ au xᵉ siècle* will already be familiar with it. In discussing the "division of the clothes of the deceased among the monastic community," Gernet said—almost forty years ago—that "the documents from Tun-Huang show how the clergy of the same parish (*chieh*, Skr. *sīmā*) gathered for the auction of clothing and pieces of cloth. The proceeds were subsequently divided among the monks, nuns, and novices of both sexes."[4]

Professor Gernet, who for good reason paid less attention to the *Vinaya* of the Mūlasarvāstivādins, seems to have thought that "there is no mention in the Vinaya, however, of the sale of the clothing of deceased monks" and that "the Vinaya of the Mahāsāṃghika alone makes a very discrete allusion to this method of division," although he himself then quotes short passages from both the *Vinaya* of the Sarvāstivādins and "la Mātṛkā [des Mūlasarvāstivādin]" that refer to the sale of monastic robes,[5] and Lien-sheng Yang had already some years before noted that "a [Mūlasarvāstivādin] *vinaya* text translated in the early T'ang period, however, indicates that in India sale by auction was used to dispose of such personal belongings" of deceased monks.[6] Yang's assertion seems now, in part at least, to be confirmed by the passage from the *Cīvaravastu* cited above: that passage does not actually contain a word for "auction," but clearly refers to the sale "in the midst of the community" of a dead monk's possessions, and—although it cannot establish that this was actually practiced in India—it does confirm that Mūlasarvāstivādin *vinaya* masters thought it should or hoped it would.

Such confirmation from an extant Sanskrit text is, of course, welcome, but perhaps a more important point is that without the work of sinologists the significance of the *Cīvaravastu* passage might easily be missed. Scholars working on China have in fact often been the first to introduce and make available important Indian material bearing on the institutional and economic history of Buddhism, but this material rarely, or never, makes it into Indian studies. References to Gernet's *Les aspects économiques du bouddhisme*, for example, are extremely rare in works on Indian cultural and economic history. D. D. Kosambi long ago referred to Gernet when he raised the "fundamental question" of the extent to which Buddhist monks and monasteries in India participated directly in trade. "The documentary evidence" for such participation, Kosambi said, "exists at the other end of the Buddhist world, in Chinese records and translations," of the sort presented by Gernet.[7] But few have followed this up. André Bareau, too, relied heavily on Gernet in a short piece he published on certain forms of monastic endowments in India and China.[8] Apart from these papers, I know of little else.[9]

There are of course problems in using Chinese sources in studying India. No one, I think, would accept without serious qualifications, for example, Kosambi's assertion that "not only the art but the organization and economic management of Chinese Buddhist monasteries, especially the cave-monasteries . . . were initially copied from Indian models, so that their records can be utilized for our purpose," that is to say, to study directly Indian monasteries.[10] The use of Chinese translations of Indian texts is sometimes less problematic, but there are still serious difficulties. The process of translation often conceals, for example, the Indian vocabulary, and this is [529] especially the case with realia or financial matters. The sinologists, too, who present such Indian texts are, justifiably, often unable to recognize their broader Indian significance. Here I would like to deal with just one example that might illustrate at least some of these points.

In his survey of what the Chinese translations of the various *vinayas* have to say in regard to monks participating in "commerce" or trade or business, Professor Gernet partly paraphrases and partly translates a text from the *Vinayavibhaṅga* of the *Mūlasarvāstivāda-vinaya* that—unless I am much mistaken—is of unique importance.[11] It is important first for what it can tell us about the kinds of legal and economic ideas that were developed by at least some Indian *vinaya* writers; it is important for what it can contribute to our understanding of the laws of contract and debt in early and classical India, and because it provides another good example of Buddhist *vinaya* interacting with Indian law; it is also important for what it can contribute to the discussion concerning the uses of writing and written documents and legal instruments in India.

A Sanskrit text for this passage has not yet—as far as I know—come to light. But in addition to the Chinese version presented by Gernet, the text is also available in a Tibetan translation. This Tibetan translation has at least one advantage over the Chinese text: it is often, though not always, easier to see the Sanskrit that underlies a Tibetan translation and therefore to get at the original Indian vocabulary. Because the text has not yet been fully translated, I first give a complete translation. This will be followed by an attempt to establish the technical Indian vocabulary that the Tibetan appears to be translating, and then further discussion directed toward situating this piece of *vinaya* in the larger context of similar discussions in Indian *dharmaśāstra*, with some reference to actual legal records presented in Indian inscriptions. In the end, too, there will have to be some attempt made to get at the religious and institutional needs that might lie behind our text and the legal instruments it is concerned with.

Vinayavibhaṅga

(Derge, 'dul ba Cha 154b.3–155b.2)

The Buddha, the Blessed One, was staying in Vaiśālī, in the hall of the lofty pavilion on the bank of the monkey's pool. At that time the Licchavis of Vaiśālī built houses with six or seven upper chambers (*pura*).[12] As the Licchavis of Vaiśālī built their houses, so too did they build *vihāras* with six or seven upper chambers. As a consequence, because of their great height, having been built and built, they fell apart.[13] When that occurred, the donors thought: "If even the *vihāras* of those who are still living, abiding, continuing, and alive fall thus into ruin, how will it be for the *vihāras* of those who are dead? We should give a perpetuity (*akṣaya*) to the monastic Community for building purposes."

Having thought thus, and taking a perpetuity, they went to the monks. Having arrived, they said this to them: "Noble Ones, please accept these perpetuities for building purposes!"

The monks said: "Gentlemen, since the Blessed One has promulgated a rule of training in this regard, we do not accept them."

The monks reported this matter to the Blessed One.

The Blessed One said: "For the sake of the Community a perpetuity for building purposes is to be accepted. Moreover, (155a) a *vihāra* for a community of monks should be made with three upper chambers. A retreat house (*varṣaka*) for a community of nuns should be made with two upper chambers."

The monks, having heard the Blessed One, having accepted the perpetuity, put it into the community's depository (*koṣṭhikā*), and left it there.

The donors came along and said: "Noble Ones, why is there no building being done on the *vihāra*?"

"There is no money (*kārṣāpaṇa*)."

"But did we not give you perpetuities?"

The monks said: "Did you think we would consume the perpetuities? They remain in the Community's depository."

"But of course, Noble Ones, they would not be perpetuities if they could be exhausted, but why do you think we did not keep them in our own houses?[14] Why do you not have them lent out on interest (*prayojayati*)?" [530]

The monks said: "Since the Blessed One has promulgated a rule of training in this regard, we do not have them lent on interest."

The monks reported the matter to the Blessed One.

The Blessed One said: "For the sake of the Community a perpetuity for building purposes must be lent on interest."

Devout brahmins and householders having in the same way given perpetuities for the sake of the Buddha and the Dharma and the Community, the Blessed One said: "Perpetuities for the sake of the Buddha and the Dharma and the Community are to be lent on interest. What is generated from that, with that accrued revenue (*siddha*), worship is to be performed to the Buddha and the Dharma and the Community."

The monks placed the perpetuities among those same donors. But when they came due, that caused disputes among them. "Noble Ones," they said, "how is it that disputes have arisen from our own wealth?"

The monks reported the matter to the Blessed One.

The Blessed One said: "Perpetuities should not be placed among them."

The monks placed them among wealthy persons. But when they came due, relying on those possessed of power, those wealthy persons did not repay them. When, by virtue of their high status, they did not repay them,[15] the Blessed One said: "They should not be placed among them."

The monks (155b) placed them among poor people. But they were unable to pay them back as well.

The Blessed One said: "Taking a pledge (*ādhi/bandhaka*) of twice the value (*dviguṇa*), and writing out a contract (*likhita*) that has a seal and is witnessed (*sākṣimat*), the perpetuity is to be placed. In the contract the year, the month, the day, the name of the Elder of the Community (*saṃghasthavira*), the Provost of the monastery (*upadhivārika*), the borrower, the property, and the interest (*vṛddhi*) should be recorded. When the perpetuity is to be placed, that pledge of twice the value is also to be placed with a devout lay-brother who has undertaken the five rules of training.

The vocabulary of this passage is not always transparent and requires some discussion. We might start with two architectural terms. The Tibetan text says the Licchavis built both houses and *vihāras* of six or seven *rtseg. Rtseg* almost certainly translates Sanskrit *pura* here, as it does in the *Śayanāsanavastu* several times.[16] But the exact nature of a *pura* is not clear: Edgerton defines it as an "upper chamber" (*BHSD*, 347). In Gernet, however, where the beginning of the text seems to be omitted, the rule corresponding to "a *vihāra* for a community of monks should be made with three upper chambers, [etc.]" is rendered as "the bhikṣu's residence (*vihāra*) shall be rebuilt in three stories [étages]," which would seem to suggest that I-ching understood the term to refer to additional "stories" or "floors" of a building. Unfortunately, yet another reference to a *pura* suggests that it was something that monks fell off of. The *Poṣadhavastu*, in referring to the construction of "halls for religious exertion" (*prahāṇaśālā*), says: *te tatra na yāpayanti. bhagavān āha. upariṣṭhād dvitīyaḥ pūraḥ* [but ms.: *puraṃ*] *kartavyaḥ. na ārohati. bhagavān āha. sopānaṃ kartavyam. prapatitaṃ bhavati. bhagavān āha. vedikā parikṣeptavyā*: "The monks had no room there (in the hall). The Blessed One said: 'A second upper chamber (or story) is to be built above.' They could not get up to it. The Blessed One said: 'A staircase is to be made.' They fell off it. The Blessed One said: 'It should be enclosed with a railing.'"[17] Here, of course, neither "upper chamber" nor "story" does very well. Finally, it is worth noting that the rule given in our text concerning the number of *pura* for *vihāras* of monks and nuns does not correspond to that given elsewhere in the same *Vinaya*. In a passage in the *Śayanāsanavastu* already referred to that recounts the origin of the *vihāra*, the Buddha is made to say: *bhikṣūṇāṃ pañcapurā vihārāḥ kartavyāḥ . . . bhikṣuṇīnāṃ tu tripurā vihārāḥ kartavyāḥ*: "for monks *vihāras* are to be made with five upper chambers . . . but for nuns *vihāras* are to be made with three upper chambers."[18]

Our Tibetan text says that when monks first started accepting perpetuities, they simply put them in the community's *mdzod*, and this is the second architectural term requiring comment. Chandra's *Tibetan-Sanskrit Dictionary* (1971) gives *kośa* as the most commonly attested equivalent for *mdzod*, but a reference in a context much closer to ours than any Chandra cites suggests something more specific. The passage in question is another piece of the *Mūlasarvāstivāda-vinaya* that is of interest for the history of Indian law because it refers to a written will. In stipulating what should be done with the various sorts of things that make up an [531] estate inherited by the monastic community, the text says that "books containing the word of the Buddha"—unlike "books containing the treatises of outsiders" (*bahiḥ-śāstra-pustakā*), which are to be sold—are, in Dutt's edition, *cāturdiśāya bhikṣusaṃghāya dhāraṇakoṣṭhikāyāṃ prakṣeptavyāḥ.*[19] This, as it stands, might be translated as "are to be deposited in the place for storing (sacred books) for the Community of Monks from the Four Directions." But Dutt almost certainly has only reproduced a mistake in the manuscript and thereby created a "ghost word"—*dhāraṇa-koṣṭhikāyāṃ*—which quickly found its way into Edgerton's dictionary (s.v. *koṣṭhikā*), whose definition, "a place for storing and keeping (sacred books)," I have used in the preceding translation. What is, however, almost certainly the intended form is first of all clear from the Tibetan translation of this passage: *phyogs bzhi'i dge slong gi dge 'dun gyi ched du spyir mdzod du gzhug par bya'o.*[20] The important word here is *spyi*, a well-attested equivalent for which is *sādhāraṇa*, "in common," and the Tibetan is easily rendered as: "to be placed in the depository as common property for the Community from the Four Directions." Oddly enough, further confirmation that *dhāraṇa-* is a scribal error for *sādhāraṇa-* is found almost immediately in the same *vinaya* passage.

After stipulating what should be done with the two sorts of books, the passage moves on to discuss two sorts of what the Sanskrit text calls *patra-lekhya*, which were also included in the estate. The Sanskrit term would mean something like "written document," but both the Tibetan translation and the context indicate that the term refers to some kind of written lien or contract of debt. The Tibetan renders it by *chags rgya*, a term not found in the standard dictionaries but cited in the *Bod rgya tshig mdzod chen mo* (p. 779) as "archaic" (*rnying*) and defined there as *bu lon bda' ba'i dpang rgya*, "a witnessed marker that calls in a debt," and in Roerich's *Tibetsko . . . Slovar'* (3.70) as a "promissory note." The context too points in this direction when it indicates that there are two kinds of *patra-lekhya*, one that can be realized or liquidated quickly (*patra-lekhyaṃ yacchīghraṃ śakyate sādhayituṃ*) and one that cannot. The former are to be called in immediately and what is realized is to be divided among the monks. In regard to one that cannot be realized quickly, the text says—again in Dutt's edition—*tac cāturdiśāya bhikṣusaṃghāya dhāraṇa / koṣṭhikāyāṃ prakṣeptavyaṃ*. Here Dutt emends against both the manuscript and the Tibetan only to produce a text whose sense is not immediately clear. The manuscript has, of course, *tac cāturdiśāya bhikṣusaṃghāya sādhāraṇaṃ koṣṭhikāyāṃ prakṣeptavyaḥ*, "that is to be placed in the depository as common property for the Community from the Four Directions."[21] The Tibetan corresponds exactly to the manuscript reading and is virtually the same here as in the passage dealing with books: *de ni phyogs bzhi'i dge slong gi dge 'dun gyi ched du spyir mdzod du gzhag par bya'o.*

It would appear, then, that the term *dhāraṇa-koṣṭhikā* is not yet attested—certainly not in the *Vinaya* passage that Edgerton cites for it—and is, rather, a ghost word based on an unnoticed scribal error. For our more immediate purposes, however, it can now be said that the term *mdzod*, which occurs in our text from the *Vinayavibhaṅga* as the word for the place or thing in which the perpetuities were initially deposited, is, elsewhere in the same *Vinaya*, used to translate the Sanskrit *koṣṭhikā*, and that a *koṣṭhikā* in a Buddhist monastery was a place, probably a room, in which not only books but also legal documents and money were kept. Incidentally this may give us some indirect indication of both the value and the rarity of books at the time these texts were written—they certainly did not circulate!

When we move from architectural terms to the legal vocabulary of our text, we move as well to a somewhat different set of problems and, significantly, to a different class of literature. For the architectural terms in our Tibetan text, we had at least established Sanskrit equivalents or other *vinaya* texts in Sanskrit that would allow us to establish such equivalents. For the legal vocabulary there is often neither. Several of the technical terms that occur in our text are not listed in Chandra's *Tibetan-Sanskrit Dictionary*, for example; and most of those that are—and for which there are, therefore, at least attested Sanskrit equivalents—are cited from passages in which those terms are not used with the technical meanings that they appear to have in our text. Moreover, I know of only a single Buddhist text that deals with some of the same matter as our *Vinaya* passage, and it is itself not free of problems. If, then, the vocabulary of our passage was peculiar to known Buddhist literature, the situation would be decidedly grim. But—unless I am much mistaken—this vocabulary is by no means Buddhist but is widely attested and fully discussed in Sanskrit legal literature. This [532] *dharmaśāstra* literature will, I think, allow us to reconstruct much—though not all—of the Sanskrit vocabulary that underlies our Tibetan text, and the partial Buddhist parallel will allow us to confirm—at least in part—these reconstructions. The linkage of our text with Hindu legal literature, moreover, may also tell us something important about both the nature and the history of the *Mūlasarvāstivāda-vinaya*, if not about Buddhist *vinaya* as a whole.

Given what has been said so far, it must be immediately noted that the first term we might deal with is not, as such, attested in *dharmaśāstra*. The term is that which I have translated as "perpetuity." Gernet translates the Chinese corresponding to this as "des biens inépuisables" but is not able to cite a Sanskrit equivalent. For our Tibetan text, however, the Sanskrit original is virtually certain. The Tibetan term is *mi zad pa*. This is a well-known and widely attested translation of Sanskrit *akṣaya*, "exempt from decay" or "undecaying," hence "permanent." The problem, of course, is that *akṣaya* is in both form and function an adjective and yet was almost certainly being used in the Sanskrit underlying our Tibetan as a substantive—it referred to a "thing." What that "thing" was, moreover, is unusually clear from our text itself. It was, first of all, a kind of donation that the donors expected to continue to work long after they themselves were dead; it was the gift of, apparently, a certain sum of money, but that sum was not itself—as the donor's remarks in our text make clear—ever to be spent. It was to be lent out on interest, and the interest alone was to be used for specific purposes. It was, in short, a conditioned endowment the principal of which must remain intact and was, therefore, "permanent." Sanskrit lexicography, moreover, knows a word for exactly the kind of donation our text presents, and it is a term that is too close to *akṣaya* to be unrelated. That term is *akṣaya-nīvī*, and there are a number of interesting things about it.

A number of our Sanskrit dictionaries, Monier-Williams and Apte, for example, are able to cite only a single source for the term, which they define as "a permanent endowment"—namely, Buddhist inscriptions. And although it is true that inscriptional evidence for *akṣaya-nīvī* or variants of it is—as Derrett says—"rich," far richer than he himself indicated, it is by no means exclusively Buddhist. One of the earliest occurrences of the term does indeed come from a Buddhist record from Alluru in Andhra that has been dated to the end of the first century C.E. or to the second century;[22] and there are, for example, as many as nine inscriptions from the Satavahana period from the Buddhist site at Kānheri that refer to *akṣaya-nīvīs*.[23] But yet another of the earliest inscriptional references to this sort of endowment comes from Kuṣān Mathurā, and there the endowment was intended to feed a hundred *brāhmaṇas* and the destitute.[24] In fact, references to *akṣaya-nīvīs* continue to occur through the Gupta period and beyond in both Hindu and Jain inscriptions, as well as Buddhist.[25]

That the type of donation called an *akṣaya-nīvī* in inscriptions is the same type of donation that our *Vinaya* text calls an *akṣaya* will, I think, be clear from even a single well-preserved example of such an inscription. This example is a fifth-century Buddhist record from Sāñcī written in good Sanskrit that details several separate endowments:[26]

Success. The wife of the lay-brother (*upāsaka*) Sanasiddha, the lay-sister (*upāsikā*) Harisvāminī, has, after designating her mother and father beneficiaries (*mātā-pitaram uddiśya*), given twelve *dīnāras* as a permanent endowment (*akṣaya-nīvī*) to the Noble Community of Monks from the Four Directions in the Illustrious Mahāvihāra of Kākanādaboṭa [i.e., Sāñcī]. With the interest (*vṛddhi*) that is produced from these *dīnāras*, one [533] monk who has entered into the community is to be fed every day. Moreover, three *dīnāras* were given to the House of the Precious One (*ratna-gṛha*). With the interest (*vṛddhi*) from those three *dīnāras*, three lamps are to be lighted every day for the Blessed One, the Buddha, who is in the House of the Precious One.[27] Moreover, one *dīnāra* was given to the Seat of the Four Buddhas. With the interest from that, a lamp is to be lighted every day for the Blessed One, the Buddha, who is on the Seat of the Four Buddhas.[28] Thus was this permanent endowment (*akṣaya-nīvī*) created with a document in stone to last as long as the moon and sun (*ācandrārkka-śilā-lekhya*) by the lady, the wife of Sanasiddha, the lay-sister Harisvāminī.

The year 131—the month *Aśvayuj*—day 5.

What we see here in this fifth-century record of an actual transaction is straightforward, is typical of both earlier and later inscriptional records of *akṣaya-nīvīs*, and documents what is obviously the same sort of donation that our *Vinaya* text describes. Sums of money are given to the monastic community, but the sums themselves are not to be spent. They are to remain intact and to be used as permanent sources for generating spendable income in the form of interest. Though this particular record does not explicitly say so, such sums could generate interest only if they were lent out or invested.

We gather, then, from inscriptional evidence that endowments of the kind described in our text were in actual practice called *akṣaya-nīvī*, *akṣaya-nīvī-dharmeṇa*, and so on; that—beginning at least in the first-second centuries C.E.—such endowments or donations were, in actual practice, frequently made; and that Buddhist, Hindu, and Jain communities or establishments all, in actual practice, benefited from such endowments. Such endowments were, it seems, important legal instruments used in widely separated geographical areas—from Andhra to Mathurā to Kānheri—over a long period of time. In light of its widespread use in actual practice, it is curious—Derrett says it is "odd," "puzzling," and "enlightening"—that there are no references to this legal device "in the fundamental materials of the *dharmaśāstra*."[29] Derrett draws from this situation a "lesson" that applies as well to Buddhist *vinaya*, where it has so often been assumed that "the *Vinaya Piṭaka* . . . enters at so great length into all details of the daily life of the recluses" and that if something was not mentioned in the *vinaya*, it was of no importance or did not occur. He says:

> It struck me as odd that a word which plays so important a role in the legal *practice* of ancient and mediaeval India [i.e., *nīvī*] should not appear, in its legal sense, in the fundamental materials of the *dharmaśāstra*. There is a lesson to be learnt from this . . . *viz.* that the *śāstra*, though strong on the jurisprudence of the ancient pre-Islamic legal system, did not aim to be comprehensive when it came to its incidents. This instance is worth pondering over. The more we discover about the utility of the *śāstra* in practice in ancient times the more puzzling it remains that technical terms which had great currency should be missing from the literature.

He ends by adding:

> The absence of the term from the abundant and versatile *dharmaśāstra* literature in these technical senses is most enlightening on the nature of that *śāstra*.[30]

The "absence" in the *dharmaśāstra* that Derrett refers to may now, however, have to be seen in yet another light, because even if we bracket, for the moment, the seemingly obvious identity between the inscriptional *akṣaya-nīvī* and the *akṣaya* of our *Vinaya* text, there is at least one other certain reference to an *akṣaya-nīvī* in the *Mūlasarvāstivāda-vinaya*, and this same *Vinaya* also gives other evidence of monastic property or wealth intended for loan. The reference occurs in the Sanskrit text of the *Cīvaravastu* recovered from Gilgit and forms a part of a passage dealing [534] with the monks' obligation to attend to, and to perform acts of worship for the benefit of, a sick and dying fellow monk. The text lists a series of possible ways to fund these activities—donors might be solicited, but if that does not work, then what belongs to the Community (*sāṃghika*) might be used. If that also does not work, the text says, "That which belongs to the permanent endowment for the Buddha is to be given" (*buddhākṣaya-nīvī-santakaṃ deyam*).[31]

Though welcome, there are two unfortunate things about this explicit reference to an *akṣaya-nīvī*. One is that this passage does not appear in the Tibetan translation of the *Cīvaravastu* and therefore does not give us an established Tibetan equivalent for the term. The other is that it gives us no information about this *akṣaya-nīvī*, apart from the fact that such endowments were known. But this, in itself, may allow one further observation. This passage not only suggests that *akṣaya-nīvīs* were known to the compilers of the *Mūlasarvāstivāda-vinaya*, but that they were so well known that no description or explanation of them was felt necessary. Moreover, the *Cīvaravastu* passage also seems to indicate that the compilers of this *vinaya* knew of "permanent endowments" that were set up for more than one purpose—otherwise the qualification "for the Buddha" would appear to have been unnecessary.

All of what we have seen so far would seem to show that the compilers of the *Mūlasarvāstivāda-vinaya* recognized a category of donations meant for loan; that they were familiar with endowments, the principal of which was to be lent out at interest, which they called *akṣayas*; and that they—unlike the authors of the *dharmaśāstra*—both knew and, at least on one occasion, used the term *akṣaya-nīvī*. But this last especially leaves us with the question of why, when they referred to a financial instrument that clearly corresponds to what epigraphical sources called an *akṣaya-nīvī*, they did not use this term, even though it must have been known in their circle. In other words, the question is, what is the relationship between *akṣaya* used as a substantive and the compound *akṣaya-nīvī*? The answer—or an answer—may turn on how common such endowments were and may lead us to conclude that *akṣaya* by itself is, paradoxically, a particular kind of Sanskrit compound.

Some years ago J. Gonda, to whom we owe so many close studies bearing on issues of Sanskrit syntax, published a paper on what he called "abbreviated nominal compounds." In his usual style, he gave copious examples of such compounds: *kalpa* for *kalpānta*, "the end of a *kalpa*"; *chada* for *dantacchada*, "lip"; *śākya* for *śākya-bhikṣu*, "a Buddhist monk"; *akṣa* for *akṣa-mālā*, "a rosary"; *bhadra* for *bhadrāsana*, "a particular posture of meditation"; and *kriyā* for *kriyāpāda*, "the third division of a suit at law"; and so forth. In all but one of these cases the first element of a two-part compound has come to be used by itself with the same meaning that was originally expressed by the whole compound. Gonda suggested that this is the more common pattern of such abbreviated compounds "that the omission of the former member probably is less common than that of the latter." He also noted that in such compounds "an adjective is, as a consequence of abbreviation, sometimes used as a substantive: *śveta-* for *śvetacchatra-* 'a white sun-shade.'" Finally, he suggested that such abbreviation "is also in Sanskrit less rare than those scholars who do not mention it at all seem to assume."[32]

Given what little that can be ascertained, it does not seem unreasonable to suggest that *akṣaya* in our *Vinaya* text is yet another example of such an abbreviated nominal compound: *akṣaya* is the first part of an attested two-part compound; the first element of that compound is used by itself with the same meaning that the compound itself has—both are used to refer to exactly the same sort of financial instrument; *akṣaya* is—like *śveta*—clearly an adjective, but, like *śveta* as an abbreviated compound, is just as clearly used as a substantive in our text. This explanation may be as good as we can get without further data. But even if only tentatively accepted, this explanation has at least some further implications.

Any attempt to explain the sorts of linguistic changes that produce things like abbreviation must, of course, skate very near speculation. Gonda, however, suggests the following:

> Whenever the speakers of a language need an expression which contains more information and applies to fewer objects than any simple words in their language, they are compelled to use several words or,—if the structure of their language allows it—to form a compound. If however the longer expression becomes in general, or within a definite group of speakers, more [535] frequently used than is necessary or convenient they are often abbreviated.

Gonda then cites from English the use of the word "bulb" for what was originally called the "electric light bulb."[33]

If we were to grant that something like this process worked on the compound *akṣaya-nīvī*, then this in turn would imply that among Buddhist groups the "longer expression" became "more frequently used than is necessary or convenient" and therefore could be—though it was not always—abbreviated. This would account for the continued usage of both *akṣaya-nīvī* and *akṣaya* but suggests as well that this particular form of endowment—as inscriptions prove—was particularly well known among Buddhists and, though not exclusive to them, may have been considered as largely theirs. If, moreover, the *akṣaya-nīvī* retained a Buddhist smell, this may account for the reluctance of "orthodox" *dharmaśāstra* authors to deal with it.[34]

Though much here remains uncertain, two related things do not. It is, I hope, already clear that the study of *dharmaśāstra* might profitably be expanded to include Buddhist *vinaya*, and that the study of Buddhist *vinaya* must most assuredly include the study of *dharmaśāstra*. One might even begin to suspect that much that is found in Buddhist *vinaya*—sleeping on low beds, not evading tolls, and so on—is there because similar concerns are addressed in *dharmaśāstra*. But apart from this question, which cannot be pursued here, it will hopefully become clear from what follows that *vinaya* and *dharmaśāstra* often speak the same language.

Fortunately, most of the legal vocabulary of our *Vinaya* text is far less complicated, and for some of it we have at least one Buddhist work extant in both Sanskrit and Tibetan that will provide attested equivalents and, as already noted, confirm what can be reconstructed from Hindu *dharmaśāstra*. Our text, for example, has the Buddha himself declare: "For the sake of the Community a perpetuity for building purposes must be lent on interest" (*dge 'dun gyi phyir mkhar len gyi rgyu mi zad pa rab tu sbyor bar bya'o*). The Tibetan I have translated as "lent on interest" is *rab tu sbyor ba*. The Tibetan, of course, does not normally have this meaning, but here the underlying Sanskrit cannot easily be doubted. Several equivalents are attested, and they are all forms from *pra√yuj*: *prayukta*, *prayukti*, *prayoga*.[35] Monier-Williams gives, as the technical meaning for *pra√yuj* in *dharmaśāstra* literature, "to lend (for use or interest)"; for *prayukta*, "lent (on interest)." The glossary in *Dharmakośa* I.3 has the following: *prayukta*, "invested (sum)," *prayoga*, "lending money at interest," *prayojya*, "money lent at interest; investment," and so forth. Kangle's glossary to the *Arthaśāstra* also gives *prayoga* as "giving a loan" and *prayojaka* as "a lender of money." Our *Vinaya* text is, therefore, using not Buddhist vocabulary here but a vocabulary well established and current in *dharmaśāstra* and other Sanskrit texts dealing with legal and financial matters. Both the equivalence *rab tu sbyor ba* = *pra√yuj* and the sense "lend on interest" are, moreover, confirmed by the one Buddhist partial parallel that has already been referred to: Guṇaprabha uses a form of *pra√yuj* several times in the sense of "to lend" in his *Vinayasūtra*, and this is most often rendered into Tibetan by *rab tu sbyor ba*.[36] But here too the parallel between *dharmaśāstra* and Buddhist *vinaya* goes beyond items of vocabulary.

The compiler of our *Vinaya* text represents his monks as being aware of "rules of training" that would make lending on interest inadmissible. The declaration he attributes to the Buddha also does not negate the general principle involved but rather allows for specific purposes to which the inadmissibility does not apply. First, such activity is not only allowed but also to be pursued—the Tibetan is translating a future passive participle—for building purposes for the benefit of the Community. Then admissibility is extended to any purpose that is for the benefit of the Buddha, the Dharma, and the Community. Here our Tibetan text allows us to correct an observation made by Gernet in regard to the Chinese text. The latter has a passage corresponding to the Tibetan that I translate above as: "The Blessed One said: 'Perpetuities for the sake of the Buddha and the Dharma and the Community are to be lent on interest. What is generated from that, with that accrued revenue (*siddha*), worship is to be performed to the Buddha and the Dharma and the Community.'" But Gernet excludes it from his text and puts it in a footnote that says, "here are two phrases that presumably constitute a note."[37] [536] Our Tibetan text, however, indicates that it is an integral and important part of the text: It explicitly and categorically extends the admissibility of lending on interest to purposes beyond building activities that will benefit the Community and allows it for what we might call, categorically, "religious purposes." Significantly, we find in *Manu*, for example, the same kind of dispensation and extension expressed in simpler, if rather curious, terms.

Manu X.117 is a good example of the "one must not, *but* . . ." pattern of promulgation typical of both *dharmaśāstra* and Buddhist *vinaya*. It starts by declaring absolutely that "a *brāhmaṇa* and even a *kṣatriya* should not, indeed, lend on interest" (*vṛddhiṃ naiva prayojayet*). Our *Vinaya* text, as noted above, presented Buddhist monks as knowing that their "rules of training" placed the same restrictions on them. But like the *Vinaya* text, *Manu* too—though in somewhat different terms—then lifts the restriction in regard to loans made for a certain and essentially similar purpose: "But, however, he may on his own accord place sums at low interest with a vile man *for religious purposes*" (*kāmaṃ tu khalu dharmārthaṃ dadyāt pāpīyase 'lpikām*).[38] Here we appear to have not only another instance of shared vocabulary (*prayojayet*), but also an instance of parallel provisions for parallel purposes ("religious purposes"). And there are further examples of both.

As in the case of Tibetan *rab tu sbyor ba*, where the technical meaning "lend on interest" is not easily available in Tibetan itself, so too in the case of what I have translated as "accrued revenue." The Tibetan is *grub pa*, and the standard dictionaries give little or no indication that this term can carry such a meaning. But a well-attested Sanskrit equivalent for *grub pa* in other contexts is *siddha*, and *siddha* occurs several times in, for example, the *Arthaśāstra* with exactly this meaning.[39]

Although, as we will see, the route to the technical meanings of the Tibetan terms in our passage, or even to their Sanskrit equivalents, is not always the same or so straightforward, it invariably seems to involve going to *dharmaśāstra*. When, for example, our *Vinaya* text gets to its final instructions in regard to making a loan, it says first that one should take a "pledge of twice the value" of the loan. The Tibetan is *gta' nyi ri*, and at least the first element of this expression, *gta'*, is cited in the standard dictionaries in the meaning "pawn" or "pledge," and it occurs a couple of times in this sense in the Tibetan documents "concerning Chinese Turkestan" treated long ago by Thomas. In one of the latter, we find exactly the same expression that occurs in our *Vinaya* text, *gta' nyi ri*, but Thomas in his glossary queries his own translation, "of twice the value."[40] It is, in fact, almost certainly correct. Gernet translates the corresponding Chinese as "pledges worth twice the value of the loan," and the *Bod rgya tshig mdzod chen mo* (p. 101) defines *gta' nyis ri ba* as *bu lon gyi dmigs rten rin thang ldab ri ba*. Here, then, there is little doubt about the meaning of the Tibetan. But without a Sanskrit equivalent and some reference to *dharmaśāstra*, much might be missed.

Once again, neither *gta'* nor *nyi ri* occur in Çhandra's *Dictionary*, nor are Sanskrit equivalents easily available in known Buddhist Sanskrit sources. We do know now, however, that our *Vinaya* text shares several lexical items, not with Buddhist texts but with Indian *dharmaśāstra* sources, so that we might expect that the same might hold in this case as well. And our expectations appear to be justified. If we consider our text to be an Indian text dealing with legal matters and laws of contract, then our sought-for equivalents can hardly be in doubt: Tibetan *gta'*, which means "pawn" or "pledge," is likely to be a translation of one or another of two Sanskrit terms. In his study of the "law of debt" in ancient India, H. Chatterjee says, "to convey the sense of pledge, two terms are used in the *dharmaśāstra*—one is *ādhi* and the other is *bandhaka*." He goes on to note that "it may be supposed that the use of the word *bandhaka* is of late origin" and that "it appears that the exact difference between the two words might have been lost long before the period of the digest writers."[41] Such considerations would suggest that the Sanskrit original of our *Vinaya* text probably read either *ādhi* or *bandhaka*, although we cannot be absolutely certain which of these two actually occurred. In Guṇaprabha's text, *gta'* is twice used to render *bandhaka*. Guṇaprabha, however, is also relatively "late," so [537] we cannot be certain that this was also the term that occurred in our *Vibhaṅga* passage. But as in the case of *pra√yuj*, here too it is not just a single vocabulary item that is shared or similar between our text and *dharmaśāstra*, but an entire procedure. *Bṛhaspati* X.5, for example, stipulates—like the Buddha of our *Vinaya* text—that one should make a loan *after* having taken a pledge or deposit of full value (*paripūrṇaṃ gṛhītvādhiṃ bandhakaṃ vā*). He also says—and, as we will see, he is not alone—to get it in writing. But before we move to that point, we still have to account for our Tibetan *nyi ri*. Its significance too is clarified by *dharmaśāstra*.

Chatterjee, for example, indicates that the general understanding of a pledge of "full value" was that it was "sufficient to meet the capital with interest."[42] Our text, however, stipulates that the pledge be "of twice the value." In spite of appearance to the contrary, these two positions are almost certainly the same, their identity turning on a "general rule" of *dharmaśāstra* in regard to the allowable amount of interest that can be charged on a loan. This rule not only may explain how these two positions are essentially the same but also almost certainly provides us with the Sanskrit term that was translated by *nyi ri*. In *dharmaśāstra* this rule is known as the rule of *dvaiguṇya*, or "doubling." *Arthaśāstra* 3.11.6, for example, clearly recognizes this principle when it says that even in cases where a debt is long outstanding, the debtor still pays only double the principal (*mūlya-dviguṇaṃ dadyāt*). *Manu* VIII.151 is even more explicit when it says that interest from loans of money should, when taken at one time, not exceed double the amount of the loan (*kusīda-vṛddhir dvaiguṇyaṃ nātyeti sakṛdāhṛtā*). This principle—that "at one investment the interest and capital taken together should not be more than twice the capital"—is widely attested, even if, in time, a number of ways of getting around it were developed.[43] For our purposes, however, we need only note two things. First, although our *Vinaya* text does not explicitly refer to the rule of *dvaiguṇya*, the instructions put in the mouth of the Buddha implicitly acknowledge it. To take a pledge of twice the value of the loan is to take a pledge of the value of the loan plus the value of the maximum interest allowed by *dharmaśāstra* rule: no more, no less. Second, if one were to translate Tibetan *nyi ri* into Sanskrit, one could easily go with *mūlya-dviguṇa* (*Arthaśāstra*) or simply *dvaiguṇya* (*Manu*). In Guṇaprabha, again, *nyi ri* translates *dviguṇa*—almost exactly as we would expect.

After "taking a pledge," our text refers to "writing out a contract that has a seal and is witnessed." The Tibetan here is *dpang po dang bcas pa'i dam rgya'i glegs bu bris te* and is not entirely clear to me. I-ching may also have had some trouble with his text at this point as well. In Gernet, at least, what appears to be the corresponding clause is rendered simply as "Let there be . . . contracts drawn up. In addition, a guarantee (*pao-cheng*) shall be deposited." We might begin with what is clear.

Glegs bu, the term I translate by "contract," is once again not listed in Chandra's dictionary, but a passage in the *Cīvaravastu* that we have already referred to provides us with an attested Sanskrit equivalent. Our term occurs four times in this one passage: *glegs bu la bris te* = *patrābhilekhyaṃ kṛtvā*; *glegs bu la bris nas* = *patrābhilikhitaṃ kṛtvā*; *glegs bu la ma bris ba* = *apatrābhilikhitaṃ*; and *glegs bu la bris pa* = *patrābhilikhitam*.[44] Given that *'bri ba, bris ba* is the usual Tibetan word for "to write," or *likhati*, then *glegs bu*, strictly speaking, is here translating *patra* (*pattra*), "document," and *patrābhilikhita*, as a noun, would mean "written document." Context alone would determine that in these *Cīvaravastu* passages it means "will," whereas in our passage what was likely the same form almost certainly means "contract."

This time when we look to *dharmaśāstra* for clarification, it proves to be—at least on one level—less useful. This in large part may only be because the use of writing and the place of written documents in the *dharmaśāstra* has yet to be as systematically studied as many other topics, and the vocabulary of both is, as a consequence, not yet fully fixed.[45] What can be surmised at the moment is this: the terms *abhilikhita* and *abhilekhya*—both in the sense of "a document"—occur in *dharmaśāstra*, but very rarely; *patra* in the senses of "written document," "letter," "paper," "a leaf for writing on," and so on occurs more commonly, but *dharmaśāstra* appears to overwhelmingly prefer *likhita* or *lekhya* when referring to documents. It should be noted, however, that though it might prefer a slightly different expression, *dharmaśāstra*—like Buddhist *vinaya*—uses the same terms to refer to a wide range of what we would consider [538] different kinds of documents: *likhita* and *lekhya* are used indiscriminately to designate mortgages, deeds, contracts, and bills of sale. Here too, the partial parallel in Guṇaprabha is much less useful: the Sanskrit text—which appears to be faulty at this point—has *āropya patre*, "having recorded in a document," and this is translated into Tibetan by *dpang rgyar bris nas so*, "having written in a sealed bond." It would appear that Guṇaprabha's text was not using the same vocabulary as our *Vibhaṅga* passage. But lest it be lost sight of, the most general point that needs to be noted here—though we will come back to it—is this: Although the reference to written contracts in our *Vinaya* text may—as a piece of *vinaya*—appear unusual, even odd, it looks quite normal when seen in light of *dharmaśāstra* of a certain period. Normal, too, it seems, is at least one of the two further qualifications of the "contract" found in our text.

The Tibetan expression I have rendered into English as "is witnessed" is *dpang po dang bcas pa*, and—although absent from Chandra—there can be little doubt about the Sanskrit underlying it: *dpang* or *dpang po* is a common translation for *sākṣin*, "witness," and *dang bcas pa*—like *can*—is a good translation for the Sanskrit suffix *-mat*, "having," "possessing." Although Guṇaprabha is here of little use, having—as we will see—constructed his text differently, still *sākṣimat*, "having a witness," "witnessed," or "attested," is itself widely attested in *dharmaśāstra* in connection with documents. *Yājñavalkya* says that for any contract entered into by mutual consent there should be "a witnessed document" (*lekhyaṃ . . . sākṣimat*).[46] *Nārada* I.115 says of documents (*lekhya*) that they can be both "witnessed and unwitnessed" (*asākṣimat sākṣimac ca*). But if we are on firm ground here, we are less so in regard to the second expression applied to "contracts" in our *Vinaya* text, and that is unfortunate.

What I have translated as "has a seal" is *dam rgya* in Tibetan. Jäschke says that *dam rgya* = *dam ka*, which he defines as "a seal, stamp." The *Bod rgya tshig mdzod chen mo* (p. 1244) defines *dam rgya* first as *thel rtse*, a variant of *thel se*, which also means "a seal, stamp." It then says it is "old" for *dpang rgya* (which Thomas takes to mean "witness signature"), "attestation seal," *khrims rgya*, "legal seal," and *dam tshig gi phyag rgya*, "a seal of promise." Thomas, finally, takes it as "a signed bond,"[47] and in Guṇaprabha *dpang rgya* can only be translating *patra* if—and this is far from certain—it is translating a text similar to the Sanskrit that we have. Obviously the precise meaning of the Tibetan expression in our *Vibhaṅga* passage has yet to be determined, though its general sense of "seal" is relatively certain. The problem for us, however, is that whereas all meanings adduced for *dam rgya* would make it a noun, in our *Vinaya* text it appears to be by position and function an adjective; the construction remains, for me at least, obscure. It may be, of course, that the Tibetan *dpang po dang bcas pa'i dam rgya'i glegs bu* is translating some sort of possessive compound.

The significance of all this is that there is almost certainly lurking behind the Tibetan some form of *mudrā* or *mudrita* and that we may have in our passage, therefore, a rare reference to the use of a kind of "object" that frequently is found at Buddhist monastic sites in India. Monastic seals—more commonly sealings—have been recovered from a wide variety of monastic sites—Vaiśālī, Kasia, Kauśāmbī, Nālandā, and so on—sometimes in considerable numbers.[48] Because they almost always bear the name of a monastery, they could be, and have been, used to identify the site from which they come. But there is a problem here recognized long ago by Vogel.

Cunningham early on had identified Kasia with Kusinārā, the site of the Buddha's death. When Vogel actually excavated Kasia, he recovered a number of sealings, typical of which is one bearing the legend *Mahāparinirvāṇe cāturdiśo bhikṣusaṅghaḥ*, "The Community of Monks from the Four Directions at (the site) of the *Mahāparinirvāṇa*." Vogel assessed this new evidence in the following way:

> As long as the use of these documents [i.e., the sealings] has not been ascertained it is impossible to decide whether their evidence tends to prove or to disprove Cunningham's theory. If they belong to the spot where they [539] were found—

> and the variety of their dates and uniformity of their legends seem to point to that conclusion—they would vindicate Cunningham's identification. If, on the other hand, they were attached to letters and parcels—and this seems to be the most likely use they were put to—they would place beyond doubt that the Convent of the Great Decease is to be sought elsewhere.[49]

When the problem is formulated in this way, it is not difficult to see how our *Vinaya* passage may bear on the issue. If—as seems likely—our passage is referring to the use of such sealings on written contracts for loans made from permanent endowments held by a monastic community, and if, therefore, such sealings were used for this purpose and not for "letters and parcels," then—since we know that such documents were placed in the monastery's "depository"—our passage would support the view that such sealings "belong to the spot where they were found." Moreover, if our passage is referring to the use of sealings of this sort—and again this seems likely—then those sealings in turn could have considerable evidential value for the use of the legal instruments described in our text: If they were used to "seal" loan contracts, then their presence at Buddhist sites will allow us to date the use of such contracts in actual practice at certain sites, and they will provide some indication of the frequency of their use at certain times. They could, in short, be extremely valuable.[50]

In regard to what was to be included in such written contracts of loan, Buddhist *vinaya* and Hindu *dharmaśāstra*, beginning with *Yājñavalkya*, are again in close basic agreement, although *Yājñavalkya* is already fuller than our *Vinaya* passage. *Yājñavalkya* (11: 5.86–89) says:

> For whatever business (*artha*) is freely and mutually agreed upon, a witnessed document should be made (*lekhyaṃ vā sākṣimat kāryaṃ*). The creditor (*dhanika*) should be put first. [540]
>
> With the year, the month, the fortnight, the day, place of residence, caste, and *gotra*,
>
> With the name of a fellow student, his own, and his father's it is marked (*cihnita*).
>
> When the business (*artha*) is concluded, the debtor (*ṛṇin*) should enter his name with his own hand
>
> (Adding) "what is written above concerning this matter is approved by me, the son of so-and-so."
>
> And the witnesses, in their own hand and with their father's name first,
> Should write: "In this matter I, named so-and-so, am a witness."

Then a number of other details and conditions of validity follow, but what is cited above is surely enough to establish the fundamental similarity between the contract described in our *Vinaya* passage and the contract described by *Yājñavalkya*. The differences, insofar as they exist, reflect, in part, the concern of *Yājñavalkya* with greater detail and technicality and, in part, the fact that our *Vinaya* passage is describing a contract of loan not between individuals but between an individual and an institution. As a consequence, it is not the creditor's name, for example, that should be registered but the names of two representatives of the institution—the Elder of the Community and the Provost of the monastery—that is making the loan.[51]

But one final textual problem remains. The final sentence of our passage in its Chinese version reads, as Gernet has translated it: "Even if you are dealing with a believing *upāsaka*, one who has received the five instructions, he shall likewise be obliged to furnish pledges." Gernet sees here "a very clear sense" on the part of the redactor that business is business ("les affaires sont les affaires"), and the requirement that even a devout lay-brother must give a pledge when borrowing from the community.[52] The Tibetan text reads *gang la sbyin par bya ba dge bsnyen dad pa can bslab pa'i gzhi lnga bzung ba la yang gta' nyi ri kho nas sbyin par bya'o*, and—although it is not impossible to interpret it in a similar way—there are several things that appear to make such an interpretation difficult.

First, the verb used in the Tibetan to express the action undertaken in regard to the lay-brother—*sbyin ba*—cannot mean "to receive from." It is the same verb our passage uses more than a half a dozen times to express the "giving" or "placing" of the loan, for example, *bcom ldan 'das kyis bka' stsal pa / de dag la sbyin par mi bya'o*: "The Blessed One said: (Perpetuities) should not be placed among them.'" That it could mean anything else in this one instance, after being consistently used in all the previous instances, seems unlikely.

The careful characterization in our passage of the kind of lay-brother involved must also be considered. That lay-brother is not just any lay-brother but is explicitly said to be "a devout lay-brother who has undertaken the five rules of training" (*dge bsnyen dad pa can bslab pa'i gzhi lnga bzung ba*), and elsewhere in our *Vinaya* this kind of characterization marks a particularly trustworthy individual. In a passage in the *Vinayavibhaṅga* that comes only a few folios before our text, for example, it is said that when *vihāras* were built in "border regions" (*mtha' 'khob*), monks frequently abandoned them in times of trouble. As a consequence they were also frequently looted. In response to this situation the Buddha is made to say: "The treasure and gold belonging to the Community or the *stūpa* (*dge 'dun bye* [read: *gyi*] *'am mchod rten gyi dbyig dang gser*) should be hidden. Only then should you leave." But the monks did not know who should do the hiding. Then, the text says:

> The Blessed One said: "It should be hidden by an attendant of the *vihāra* (*kun dga' ra ba pa*) or a lay-brother."

> But then those who hide it stole it themselves. Then the Blessed One said: "It should be hidden by a devout lay-brother (*dge bsnyen dad pa can*)."[53]

From this and similar passages, it would appear that "devout"—as opposed to ordinary—lay-brothers were considered worthy of trust, especially in regard to matters involving valuable property. The chances seem good that our text should be taken as supplying another instance of the same sort of thing.

Finally, "pledges"—at least according to *dharmaśāstra*—were, or came to be, fairly complex affairs. Two basic kinds were referred to: *gopya*, or "pledges for custody," and *bhogya*, or "usufructuary pledges." The first was [541] to be kept; the second was to be used, that is to say, to generate profit. Pledges could be anything from a copper pan or cloth to female slaves, or fields, gardens, cows, or camels. There were other refinements and complexities as well.[54] How much of this was known to the redactor of our *Vinaya* is, of course, impossible to say. Our passage says nothing that would indicate his awareness. It is, however, safe to assume that, even before the stage of complexity had been reached that we see in some *dharmaśāstra*, the taking of pledges would have created some awkward problems for monastic communities. And it is, again, reasonable to assume that such monastic communities would have solved such problems by one of their favorite devices—recourse to lay middlemen. This, I think, is what our text is saying.

Now that we have come this far, all that remains is the hard part. We must at least try to determine several interrelated things. We must make some attempt to determine how important the perpetuities or permanent endowments mentioned in our text were, and what—if any—further history our text or similar *vinaya* rulings on written contracts had. We must make some attempt to determine what the religious and institutional situations were that stimulated Mūlasarvāstivādin *vinaya* masters to create or borrow these legal instruments. And we must make some attempt to place our *Vinaya* text in the still uncertain history of *dharmaśāstra*. In none of these endeavors can we expect complete success.

It of course goes without saying that we have at our disposal almost no means of determining what was and what was not particularly important in the enormous *Mūlasarvāstivāda-vinaya*. But there is at least one rough indicator of what in this *Vinaya* was thought important in the early medieval period: We are able to determine what Guṇaprabha, who has been dated to a period between the fifth and seventh centuries and who may have been from Mathurā, chose to include in his *Vinayasūtra*. Guṇaprabha's *Vinayasūtra* appears to have been the most authoritative epitome or summary of the *Mūlasarvāstivāda-vinaya*, and Bu-ston, at least, cites it as a model of the type of treatise that condenses "excessively large (portions of) scripture."[55] Given that Guṇaprabha has reduced or condensed what takes up more than four thousand folios in the Derge edition to no more than a hundred, it is obvious that he had to make some austere choices. He would have been able, presumably, to include only what would have been considered—or what he considered—essential to an understanding of the whole. His choices, therefore, can be revealing and at times—at least to some—may appear surprising. Professor Schmithausen, for example, in his fascinating paper on the "sentience of plants," has several times referred to a text in the *Vinayavibhaṅga* of the Mūlasarvāstivādins that describes a monastic ritual that must be performed before cutting down a tree.[56] The ritual contains several significant elements that also form a part of the funeral ritual for dead monks, but the text looks like a minor appendix of no great importance. Guṇaprabha, however, includes an almost complete description of the ritual in his epitome.[57] It is much the same for our rules.

Although our text, where it is now found, may also look like an appendix, and although it appears to have no known parallels in other *vinayas*, the continuing importance of at least the subject that it treats for the Mūlasarvāstivādin order would appear to be indicated by [542] what we find in Guṇaprabha's *Sūtra*. But there is also something of a surprise here. As our discussion of the vocabulary of our *Vibhaṅga* passage undoubtedly indicated, Guṇaprabha does, indeed, include lending on interest and written contracts in his *Sūtra*. And they are presented—as one would expect—in very much the same terms as in our canonical text: Guṇaprabha, like all good epitomizers, appears to be neither creative nor original. The surprise, however, is that although Guṇaprabha presents in his *Sūtra* what can, in part, easily be taken as a condensation of our text, he himself in his auto-commentary—the *Svavyākhyānābhidhāna-vinaya-sūtra-vṛtti*—actually cites another source when he comments on that material, and he gives there a frame story that would seem to indicate that our material was indeed found, as well, in a second source.

There is much to be learned both about and from Guṇaprabha's *Sūtra* and *Vṛtti*, but to date, it has received little attention. In the *Vṛtti*, for example, Guṇaprabha frequently cites or quotes his authorities and therefore gives us some indication of where he got his material. Most commonly, however, his references are given under a general rubric like *tathā ca granthaḥ*, "and thus is the text,"[58] or *ity atra granthaḥ*, "it is said in this case in the text" (*Sū*. 177, 181, 183, etc.), or *grantho 'tra*, "the text here is" (*Sū*. 193). In these general references "the text" appears to refer to the canonical *Vinaya*. Sometimes he even uses the phrase *vinaye uktam*, "it is said in the *Vinaya*" (*Sū*. 82). Such references can sometimes be particularly frustrating because, though commenting on his summary of one section of the *Vinaya*, he sometimes quotes from a completely different section. At one place in the *Vṛtti* dealing with the *Pravrajyāvastu*, for example, he quotes a passage under the rubric *ity atra granthaḥ*, which does indeed come from the canonical *Vinaya* but not from the *Pravrajyāvastu*; it comes instead from the *Cīvaravastu*.[59] Sometimes, happily, he is more specific. Occasionally, he says something like *vibhaṅgād etad śayanāsana-śikṣāpadāt*, "this is from the *Vibhaṅga*, from the rules of training in regard to beds and seats" (*Sū*. 389), or *grantho 'tra bhikṣuṇīvibhaṅge* "here is the text in the *Bhikṣuṇīvibhaṅga*" (*Sū*. 591), or *poṣadhavastu atra granthaḥ*, "the text here is the *Poṣadhavastu* (*Sū*. 646). Citations of this sort—because they can considerably reduce the range—are, of course, more suited to our needs. But even some of these more specific references can be problematic. Several times, for example, Guṇaprabha cites material under a rubric referring to an or the "Introduction": *iti nidānam*, "the *Nidāna* says" (*Sū*. 327), or *atra granthaḥ nidānāt*, "here is the text from the *Nidāna*" (*Sū*. 384), or *nidāne yad uktaṃ*, "what was said in the *Nidāna*" (*Sū*. 422). In cases such as these it is not always clear whether the reference is to a part of a work or a work entitled *Nidāna*. The material Guṇaprabha cites in commenting on lending on interest and written contracts is also cited under such a rubric.

In his auto-commentary Guṇaprabha introduces the passage of most direct interest to us with the following phrase: *'dir gzhung ni ma mo las 'di lta ste*. The translation of this seems straightforward: "here the text is from the *Mātṛkā*, namely. . . ." There is, as well, at least one similar reference in the first chapter of the *Vṛtti*, the only part of the Sanskrit text of the commentary that has been published so far: *mātṛkāyām atra granthaḥ*, "the text here is found in the *Mātṛkā*" (*Sū*. 165). Although the Tibetan translation of this second reference differs slightly from that of the first—*'dir ma mo'i gzhung las*—there can be little doubt that both are referring to the same work. The problem, of course, is that we do not—at least I do not—actually know what work this is. The Tibetan tradition does not appear to preserve a canonical *vinaya* text with this title; the Chinese canon has one text—*Taishō* 1441—whose reconstructed title is *Sarvāstivādavinaya-mātṛkā*, but this reconstruction is marked as doubtful by the *Hōbōgirin* catalog; equally doubtful apparently are the titles of two other texts—*Taishō* 1452 and 1463—which are given as "[*Mūlasarvāstivāda*]*nidānamātṛkā*?" and "*Vinayamātṛkā*?"[60] Fortunately, this does not have to be sorted out here. For our purposes we need only note that Guṇaprabha cites technical material bearing on lending on interest and written contracts that is, in the main, quite close to that found in our text in the *Vinayavibhaṅga*, but he cites at least a part of it from a different, second source. Any doubt that he got this material from—or at least knew as well—a source different from our *Vinayavibhaṅga* passage is quickly dissipated by looking at what he actually said.

The *Sūtra* itself gives the first indication that Guṇaprabha is not necessarily dependent on our [543] *Vibhaṅga* passage for his material. In speaking about a certain kind of chattel (*upakaraṇa*), Guṇaprabha says:

> It should be lent on interest for the sake of the (three) Jewel(s).
>
> When there is a monastery attendant or lay-brother, he should be used.

(It should be loaned) after taking a pledge of twice the value (of the loan and) after recording in a document the witness, the year, the month, the day, the Elder of the Community, the Provost of the monastery, the borrower, the capital, and the chattel.

prayuñjīta ratnārtham /
ārāmikopāsakayoḥ sattve niyogeta /
bandhakaṃ dviguṇam ādāya sākṣi-saṃvatsara-māsa-divasa-saṃghasthaviro(?) vārika [read: *opadhivārika*]*-gṛhītṛ-dhana-lābhān āropya patre /*

kun dga' ra ba pa 'am dg[e] bsnyen dag yod na bsko bas dkon mchog gi don du bskyed par bya'o /
gta' nyi rir blang par bya'o / dpang po dang / lo dang / zla ba dang / nyi ma dang / dge 'dun gyi gnas brtan dang / dge skos dang / len pa po dang / rdzas dang bskyed rnams dpang rgyar bris nas so /[61]

It is, of course, immediately obvious that what Guṇaprabha says about taking a "pledge" and the contents of the contract are close—though not fully identical—to what our *Vibhaṅga* passage says. But what precedes this is not. The references to the monastery attendant and the lay-brother must, at least, come from what Guṇaprabha calls in his auto-commentary the *Mātṛkā*. The auto-commentary says, in fact:

Here the text is from the *Mātṛkā*, namely: "When, after having had both a *stūpa* of the Blessed One and a domed chamber (*gtsang khang byur bu*)[62] made, the merchants of Vaiśālī consigned chattels (*yo byad*) to the monks for the maintenance (*zhig ral du mi 'gyur ba*) of *stūpas* and domed chambers, the monks, being scrupulous, did not accept them.

The monks reported the matter to the Blessed One.

The Blessed One said: "I authorize that chattels for the maintenance of a *stūpa* should be accepted by a monastery's attendant (*kun dga' ra ba* = *ārāmika*) or a lay-brother (*upāsaka*). Having accepted them, they should be used to generate interest (*bskyed par bya ste*). As much profit as is produced in that case should be used for worship of the *stūpa*."

In regard to the words "a pledge of twice the value should be taken" (*gta' nyis rir blang bar bya'o*), so that there should be no loss, this—by its force—should be considered as "a means that avoids a default" (*'di spang ba mi skyed pa'i yan lag ces bya ba shugs kyis rtogs par bya*).

It might be asked how, after having accepted it, the chattel is to be lent on interest (*sbyar bar bya*). For that reason it is said: After having written with a witnessed seal the witness, the year, the month, the day, the Elder of the Community, the Provost of the monastery, the borrower, the property, and the interest (*dpang po dang lo dang zla ba dang nyi ma dang dge 'dun gyi gnas brtan dang dge skos dang len pa po dang rdzas dang skyed rnams dpang rgyar bris nas so*), et cetera.[63]

The Tibetan text of Guṇaprabha's commentary is here—as it frequently is elsewhere—difficult, and I am not sure that I have always correctly understood it. It is, moreover, not entirely clear where the boundaries of his quotation or paraphrase of the *Mātṛkā* are. Given this, the following appear to be firm. Guṇaprabha knew where in the *Vibhaṅga* the topics of lending on interest and written contracts occurred, because in his *Sūtra* he treats these topics under the nineteenth *niḥsargika-pātayantikā* offense, and this is precisely where they are treated in our *Vibhaṅga*. But he also knew another passage—this one in the *Mātṛkā*—which dealt at least with lending on interest. The *Mātṛkā* passage dealt with chattels, not perpetuities; it also had the Buddha authorize lending activities undertaken by a monastery's attendant or a lay-brother—it did not authorize monks to do so. For lending on interest, Guṇaprabha chose to follow the *Mātṛkā* text, and this is explicitly confirmed in his auto-commentary. In regard to written contracts, it would appear either that he reverted to our *Vibhaṅga* text or that the *Mātṛkā* text had itself almost the same material as our text in the *Vibhaṅga*. There are, for example, some differences in what our *Vibhaṅga* text indicates should be included in the contract, and what is indicated in Guṇaprabha. It is, however, difficult to know what—or how much—to [544] make of this. There are also in all the sources a number of textual problems that have to be worked out.

But even if our discussion leaves a number of points and problems hanging, it does allow some observations on the importance of lending on interest and written contracts of debt in Mūlasarvāstivādin *vinaya* literature. The canonical *Vinaya* of the Mūlasarvāstivādins had at least two texts or sets of rules concerning lending on interest, and both were associated with the need to maintain durable architectural forms and finance ritual. There were as well—probably—two sets of rules regarding written contracts of debt. Both lending on interest and contracts of debt continued, moreover, to be of interest to Mūlasarvāstivādin *vinaya* masters, at least up until the seventh century—though Guṇaprabha was working with severe space limitations, he chose to include a fairly detailed discussion of both in his *Vinayasūtra*. It will have been noticed that Guṇaprabha does not specifically mention *akṣayas* or *akṣaya-nīvīs*. We might surmise that lending on interest was at first particularly associated with such endowments but by his time had come to be associated with all sorts of chattels or property. This, in turn, might explain his preference for the *Mātṛkā*. We simply do not know. It is also notable that both Guṇaprabha's presentation and apparent preference for the *Mātṛkā* appear to shift the financial activities involved away from monks and—if possible—into the hands of lay monastic functionaries. The reasons for such a shift, or any historical situation it may reflect, remain, however, undetermined.

Although questions of this sort must for now remain open, Guṇaprabha's *Vinayasūtra* may still allow us in a general way to extend the history of interest in—or at least knowledge of—Mūlasarvāstivādin monastic rules governing lending on interest and written contracts of debt. These rules, as indeed the Sanskrit text of the *Vinayasūtra* that has come down to us, were, to judge by the colophon of the text, known at the Vikramaśīla Monastery in Eastern India. Although the colophon as it is printed is difficult to make sense of, one important statement seems clear. That colophon says in part:

> *Śākyabhikṣu-Dharmakīrttinā sattvārthe likhitaṃ*
> *Śrīmad-vikramaśīlāṃ* [*sic*] *āśritya phālguṇamāse*[64]

> Copied by the Śākyabhikṣu Dharmakīrti, for the benefit of living beings, when residing at Vikramaśīla, in the month of Phālguṇa.

What information we have suggests that Vikramaśīla was founded in either the eighth or the ninth century and was probably destroyed in the twelfth,[65] so our copy of the *Vinayasūtra* can be assigned to sometime during this period.

We can, in sum, track our Mūlasarvāstivādin rules starting from the *Vinayavibhaṅga* in—as we shall see—about the first century C.E. They also occurred, with at least a different frame-story, in a text called the *Mātṛkā*. They were known and repeated by Guṇaprabha, who lived perhaps at Mathurā sometime between the fifth and seventh centuries. And Guṇaprabha's summary was itself known and copied sometime after the ninth century at the Vikramaśīla Monastery. Though such a trail is not much, it is far more than we usually have, and it testifies to the continuing currency of our rules through both time and space.

The redactor of our *Vinayavibhaṅga* text appears to have thought, or to have wanted others to think, that the Buddhist monastic community began to accept endowments, to lend on interest, and to use written contracts, not on its own initiative but in response to the concerns of lay donors about what would happen, after they were dead, to the establishments they had founded and were themselves able to maintain while they were alive. Confronted with the visible deterioration of their *vihāras* in their lifetime, lay donors are made to say—in effect—"if this happens while we are still alive, it obviously will occur even more so when we are dead." It is this concern that—according to our text—gives immediate rise to the resolve on the part of lay donors to provide the monastic community with permanent or perpetual endowments, and to ensure, in effect, that their *vihāras* remain inhabitable. For the redactor of our text all else—lending on interest, written contracts of debt—follows directly from this concern and forms an integral and necessary part of the monastic communities' response to it. Our text, however, is not the only text in the *Mūlasarvāstivāda-vinaya* where such concerns are voiced. Nor are they only about maintenance—they are, as well, inextricably about merit. A glance at two related texts from the *Śayanāsanavastu* must here suffice: they are in fact sufficient to establish something of the range of ideas connected with our *Vibhaṅga* text.

The first passage we might look at forms a part of a larger discussion about various rights and obligations in regard to *vihāras*. It starts rather abruptly with what appears to be a reference to what the Buddha had [545] already said on some other occasion; and the passage is more narrative than formally promulgatory:

> It had been said by the Blessed One: "The reward should be assigned in the name of the dead donors" (*abhyatītakālagatānāṃ dānapatīnām nāmnā dakṣiṇā ādeṣṭavyā iti*).
>
> The Elder of the Community recited the verse for the sake of deceased donors.
>
> And a certain householder had come to a *vihāra*. He heard the assigning of the reward. He approached the Elder and said: "Noble One, if I have a *vihāra* built, will you assign a reward in my name also?"
>
> The Elder said: "Have one built! I will duly make the assignment."
>
> When that householder had had a *vihāra* built, he had not given anything to it. It remained thus empty. When that householder saw that, he went to the first *vihāra* and said to the Elder: "Noble One, my *vihāra* remains empty. Not a single monk lives there."
>
> The Elder of the Community said: "Sir, it should be made productive (*utsvedya*, *snum pas so*)."
>
> The householder said: "But, Noble One, it has been built on sterile saline soil (*ūṣare jaṃgale kāritaḥ*). How is it to be made productive?"
>
> "Householder, I did not mean it in that sense (*nāham etat saṃdhāya kathayāmi*), but rather that there is no acquisition (*lābha*) there."
>
> The householder said: "Noble One, whoever now lives in my *vihāra*, to him I present cloth (*paṭenācchādayāmi*)."[66]

This is an interesting fragment for a number of reasons—it uses, for example, a term to describe the "dead" donors, *abhyatītakālagata*, which also occurs in inscriptions.[67] But for our immediate purposes it is important above all for what it can contribute to our understanding of how monks understood, or expressed, the concerns of lay donors.

The text is—as is the Sanskrit *Mūlasarvāstivāda-vinaya* as a whole—clipped and elliptical. It is, as already noted, a narrative text, not a promulgatory one. What it assumes is as revealing as what it says. It starts by explicitly stating that the Buddha had ruled that "the reward should be assigned in the name of the dead donors" of a *vihāra*. This clearly is obligatory for the monastic community. The narrative then seems to suggest that the redactor of the text assumed that this obligatory activity was a "public" ritual that took place on a recurring basis—it is otherwise hard to account for the narrative facts that it was "heard" by a householder on a random visit. The redactor also indicates that this recurring public ritual was performed by the Elder of the Community (*saṃghasthavira*) and involved the recitation of verses.

We have a fairly good idea of what—narratively—"assigning the reward" was: it was a ritualized recitation of a verse or verses that formally designated the beneficiaries of the merit produced from a specific donation or gift. Such designation could be made to both the dead—as in our passage from the *Śayanāsanavastu*—or the living. In the *Bhaiṣajyavastu*, for example, at the end of a meal given by brahmins and householders, the Buddha himself "assigns the reward" to their deceased kin who had become "hungry ghosts" (*preta*).

> Then the Blessed One, with a voice having five qualities, commenced to assign the reward to the name of those hungry ghosts (*teṣāṃ nāmnā dakṣiṇām ādeṣṭuṃ pravṛttaḥ*):
>
> > "The merit from this gift, may that go to the hungry ghosts! (*ito dānād dhi yat puṇyaṃ tat pretān upagacchatu*)
> > May they quickly rise from the dreadful world of hungry ghosts!"[68]

In the *Saṅghabhedavastu*, on the other hand, we find at the end of the account of the gift of the Nyagrodha Park:

> Śuddhodana took up a golden waterpot and presented the Nyagrodha Park to the Blessed One, and the Blessed One, with a voice having five qualities, assigned the reward (*bhagavatā . . . dakṣiṇā ādiṣṭā*):
>
> > "The merit from this gift (*ito dānād dhi yat puṇyaṃ*), may that go to the Śākyas! May they always attain the station (*pada*) desired or wished!"[69]
> > [546]

Whereas, in the first case, the assignment is explicitly to deceased kin, in the second it is to all members of the lineage, and this could have included both living and dead. In any case, it is virtually certain that a reader of the *Mūlasarvāstivāda-vinaya* would have seen in the *Śayanāsanavastu* a reference to a performance very much of this sort.

It was a ritual performance for the sake of dead donors that the *Śayanāsana* passage narratively isolates as the motive behind its householder's construction of a *vihāra*—this is what he hopes to gain: a, presumably, recurring or ongoing assignment of merit in his name after his death. But the point of the text is, of course, that the construction of a *vihāra* is not in itself sufficient to achieve this. To achieve the intended goal requires in addition that the *vihāra* be in use and inhabited, and continue to be so. It requires, in short, the presence of an Elder who will continue to perform the assignment. This, in turn, requires further donation. The requirements, however, do not fall only on the donor. Whereas he must further endow the monastery, the monks are obligated to perform the assignment. The monks, as well, have a further obligation, which is only implied here but explicitly stated in another passage in the same *vastu*.

The second passage makes it clear that if donors have obligations, so too do the monks:

> The devout had had many *vihāras* built, but few monks entered into the retreat in Śrāvastī. Those *vihāras* stood empty. For the donors there was no merit resulting from use (*dānapatīnāṃ paribhogānvayaṃ puṇyaṃ na bhavati, . . . longs spyod las byung ba'i bsod nams med cing*). And ne'er-do-wells began to inhabit them.
>
> The Blessed One said: "All *vihāras* must be assigned two, three, or four to each one individually, depending on how many there are. All must be used (*sarve paribhoktavyāḥ*)."[70]

Here the rule is presented as firm: no presumably inhabitable *vihāra* is to be allowed to stand empty. All must be used. In fact, the text here, in regard to *vihāras*, refers to a specific category of merit: "merit resulting from use." Given that a *vihāra* must be *used* to generate such merit, it would seem to follow that continuous use would generate continuous merit.

There are, in both these passages from the *Śayanāsanavastu*, in the web of mutual obligations they seem to envision between monastery and donor, some striking parallels with what is known about the relationships between donor and monastery in medieval Europe. But these cannot here be pursued.[71] What we can do here is to note that the concern of the lay donors in our *Vinayavibhaṅga* passage—the concern that gives rise to the use of endowments, lending on interest, and written contracts of debt—is, when seen in the light of the *Śayanāsana* passages, almost certainly not about maintenance only. It is as much about merit. Our endowments, and the legal instruments required to make them work, begin, in fact, to appear as devices intended to ensure not just the perpetual inhabitability of the *vihāra* but also an equally perpetual, a permanent, source of ongoing merit for its donor that would continue long after he or she were dead. Maintenance and merit are in fact closely and causally linked: without maintenance, there will not be continuing use; without continuing use, there will not be for the donor the "merit resulting from use." Without provisions for the maintenance of the *vihāra* and its residents, there will be no officiating Elder, without an officiating Elder, the assignment of merit to the donor will not continue after his death. Both our *Vibhaṅga* text and the first passage from the *Śayanāsana* explicitly identify the interests or anxieties of lay donors concerning what will occur after they are dead as the religious problem that endowments and "acquisitions" are meant to solve. Endowments were obviously seen by the monks—perhaps also by lay donors—as a *permanent* solution to the problem. They are, after [547] all, called "perpetuities" or "permanent endowments." They were intended to ensure not long-term but perpetual benefits to lay donors by ensuring a permanent source of merit.

There is, of course, at least some appreciable irony in a monastic community whose official doctrine declared that "all things are *impermanent*" devising or adopting legal and economic instruments explicitly intended to ensure *permanent* benefits to lay donors. But endowments and lending on interest were not—at least as far as they are presented in the *vinaya*—intended only to meet the religious needs of the more prominent supporters of the monastic community. They were intended as well to meet certain institutional needs, institutional needs that, indeed, might be approximately dated.

It is, I think, fairly obvious that for our *Vibhaṅga* text, and for the *Śayanāsana* passages, getting *vihāras* built or funding their initial construction was not the problem. The existence of permanent, durable *vihāras* is taken very much for granted. Our texts too take it for granted that these durable *vihāras* were already both architecturally and institutionally well organized. They assume that such *vihāras* were already considerably beyond mere shelters and were already, for example, multistoried, were already provided with separate "depositories" (*koṣṭhikā*). They take for granted that Buddhist monasteries were, significantly, already sufficiently well organized to administer the kinds of endowments they are recommending. They already know a Community with a recognized administrative and ritual division of labor. They know both the office of Elder and of Provost. They presuppose an established ritual of "assigning the reward" to dead donors, performed by the Elder. They presuppose that both Elder and Provost were already legally recognized representatives who could enter into binding contracts on behalf of the Community. In short, our texts—like all of the *vinayas* as we know them—presuppose a stage of development of the *vihāra* as both an architectural form and an institution that should be at least partially visible in the archaeological record. But here we butt directly up against an increasingly awkward problem: the stage of architectural and institutional development of the Buddhist monastery reflected in the *vinayas* as we have them can be detected in the archaeological record only at a period that is far later than that to which the composition of the *vinayas* is assigned by most scholars. This is a large problem and—as already noted—an awkward one: it seems to present us with enormous collections of rules that were composed to govern conditions that did not exist. Here of course we can only offer a sketch of the conflicting data.

Étienne Lamotte—without necessarily wanting to follow out the implications of what he said—noted some years ago:

> If remarkable similarities can be discerned in the outlines of the latter [i.e., the various *vinayas*]—and we are thinking particularly of the Pāli, Mahīśā[sa]ka and Dharmagupta *Vinayas*—this fact can be explained by a parallel development. The Buddhist communities did not live in complete isolation but were interested in the work carried out by their neighbors. It is therefore not surprising that they worked with the same methods and followed practically the same plan. If nothing is more like one Buddhist *vihāra* than another Buddhist *vihāra*, it is normal that the various known *vinayas* should reveal the close link which connected them.[72]

Lamotte's last sentence would seem to suggest that the various *vinayas* are alike because they all reflect the existence of a uniform, standardized, and well-organized *vihāra*. In fact, all our *vinayas*, as we have them, appear to presuppose such a uniform and developed monastery: they speak, for example, about doors and keys[73] and elaborate divisions of labor,[74] about bathrooms[75] and slaves or permanent labor forces,[76] about the acquisition [548] of land, ownership rights, sharecropping,[77] social obligations[78] and the problems of inheritance.[79] These are the concerns of a landed institution with durable goods and well-organized durable domiciles—the kind of institution for which maintenance could have been an important concern, and which could have administered permanent monetary endowments. But there is virtually no evidence in the archaeological record for this kind of monastic institution until late, and it is beginning to appear that both the degree and the rate of growth of Indian Buddhist monasticism have been grossly exaggerated. The history of the physical monastery, at least, points very much in this direction.

We know, for example, in at least some important areas, when the standard *vihāra* started to emerge—and it is not much before the beginning of the Common Era. Sir John Marshall, among others, has noted that "even on such important sites as Sārnāth, Bodhgayā, Rājagṛha, and Kasia, which were some of the earliest to be occupied by the Buddhists, no remains of any of these structures [i.e., those mentioned in the *vinaya*] have been found which can be referred to pre-Mauryan times."[80] He was, however, so sure that such structures simply *must* have existed that he then went to some trouble to account for their absence, and his account will have a familiar ring to those who while away their time reading Indian art history: it is the old perishable-materials argument. This argument says that no trace of such structures survive because they were made of perishable materials, and although essentially the same argument has been used in regard to Buddhist cult images, in neither case does it appear to be overwhelmingly convincing. When the perishable-materials hypothesis is applied to Buddhist cult images, the evidence frequently appears to interfere with the argument,[81] and much the same thing appears to happen when it is applied to monastic architecture.

It should be noted without fudging that the evidence for early *vihāras* is limited, but this itself may be significant. This observation holds especially for structural sites, few of which have been fully excavated. But one of the best preserved examples of an early *vihāra* occurs at Taxila. It is a "range" of irregularly sized rooms strung out in a line west of the main *stūpa*. This type of *vihāra* is, according to Marshall, characterized by its "haphazard methods of planning and its lack of security and privacy for its inmates."[82] It is, significantly, unwalled and unprotected. This sorry little structure was near the prosperous and already architecturally sophisticated settlement of Sirkap and is not later than the first century C.E. Equally unimpressive, though better preserved, are the early excavations in Western India. Bhājā, "probably one of the oldest Buddhist religious centers in the Deccan," although it continued to be added to until the first century C.E., is, for example, characterized by an almost complete lack of order or standardization, which suggests that its makers had little experience in planning a community whether in wood or stone—no two [549] caves or *vihāras* are organized the same way.[83] Likewise, the monastic complex at Junnar in its early phases shows the same lack of order. Until about the beginning of the Common Era it is little more than a string of irregularly shaped and placed single cells, not really far removed from natural caves.[84] It could, of course, be argued that some of what we see at Junnar and Bhājā can be explained by lack of experience with working in live rock, but this can hardly account for the lack of planning, nor can accumulated experience in cutting rock alone account for the fact that organized, planned *vihāras* approaching the standardized *vihāra* begin to appear at both sites at almost exactly the same time that the same organized plan begins to appear at a large number of other sites. Planned and ordered space implies a planned, ordered, and settled community—the kind of community that could have composed our *vinayas* in the full and final forms in which we have them and that could have used and administered "permanent endowments."

But what needs to be noted above all else is this: the earliest extant remains of monastic residential architecture, like the earliest cult images in stone, show again a tradition still struggling, in this case toward order, still lacking a sense of functional organization and structured use of space. Such a tradition—again like that which produced the early extant cult images—does not suggest a long period of development or directed experimentation in wood or other perishable materials preceding it. Moreover, even if, against the evidence, we grant earlier *vihāras* in perishable materials, the implications of this may have been overlooked:

such vihāras by definition could not have been durable or in any significant sense permanent. They would suggest a poor and probably little organized—both socially and economically—community, a community that had little access to, or ability to exploit, any economic surplus. This seems especially so in light of the traces of substantial works in such perishable materials, which have some chance of being Mauryan—the cyclopean city-wall of Rājagṛha and the curious elliptical structures there; the "stupendous timber palisade" at Pāṭaliputra and the massive teak wood platforms there; or the hypostyle hall found at Kumhrar—but none of these are Buddhist, and all appear to have been produced by ruling powers.[85] In other words, enduring monumental architecture in perishable materials was available, but apparently out of reach of Buddhist monastic communities.[86]

Though, again, the evidence is far from full, there are other data pointing to the lack of early permanent Buddhist dwellings. The evidence, for example, in the main body of Aśoka's inscriptions for *vihāras* is thin. In the controversial eighth Rock Edict, Aśoka uses the term *vihāra* only in a decidedly curious way—if the term had then any Buddhist sense. He there contrasts his "tours for *dharma*," *dhamma-yātta*, with the activity of earlier kings, which he calls "tours for pleasure," *vihāra-yātta*, where *vihāra* is used in the sense of "diversion, enjoyment," and the like.[87] In his so-called Schism Edict, he does not again refer to *vihāras* when he talks about the expulsion of troublesome monks but does refer to *anāvāsa* and by implication to *āvāsa*. Although much discussed, the facts remain that *āvāsa* literally means only an "inhabited" or "inhabitable" place, that Aśoka himself does not use the term *vihāra*, and that *āvāsa* does not certainly refer to an architectural form.[88] Equally curious and still difficult to understand are Aśoka's directions as to what should be done with this edict. Aśoka says, in Hultzsch's translation:

> Thus this edict must be submitted [*viṃnapayitaviye*—Bloch, probably more correctly: "Il faut faire [550] connaître . . . à"] both to the Saṃgha of monks and to the Saṃgha of nuns.
>
> Thus speaks Devānāṁpriya:
>
> Let one copy of the (edict) remain with you [i.e., the administrative officials—mahamāta-?] deposited in (your) office [*saṃsalana*]; and deposit ye another copy of the very (edict) with the lay worshippers.[89]

Here again, where one might expect a reference to monasteries, there is none. There is no indication that a "copy" of this edict was deposited in the "office" of the group it most concerned—no indication that there was such an "office" where they were located. Likewise, in the even more difficult Rummindeī Pillar Inscription, Aśoka seems to imply—especially as Hultzsch understands the text—that he was the first to mark the spot of Buddha's birth: "(He) . . . caused a stone pillar to be set up, (in order to show) that the Blessed One was born here." But contrary to what we might have expected, if there had been a permanent community at the site, he then extends his largesse not to a monastery there but to the village of Luṃmini itself: "(He) made the village of Luṃmini free of taxes, and paying (only) an eighth share (of the produce)."[90]

The only possible reference in the Aśokan material to a *vihāra* is problematic. It may occur in the "cover letter" attached to the recently discovered version of Minor Rock Edict I found at Pāṅgurāriā in Madhya Pradesh. Sircar translates the lines in question: "The king named Priyadarśin [speaks] to Kumāra Śaṃva from [his] march [of pilgrimage] to the U(O?)punitha-vihāra in Māṇema-desa (. . . *māṇema-des*[*e*] [*u*]*punitha-vihāra-*[*ya*]*tāy*[*e*])."[91] As the bristle of brackets shows, the readings are uncertain; the published facsimiles are extremely difficult to read; this statement has no parallels in the fifteen or so other versions of this edict—it is, in short, profoundly problematic. But whether or not the term *vihāra* occurs in the inscription, or whether the possible *vihāra* mentioned can be identified with the site at which the record was recovered, that site itself is of interest. It represents, at least a part of it, the remains of another Mauryan monastic site, and although it has so far been only partially published, it appears to have been a poor and unimpressive complex; many of the small *stūpas*, revetments, enclosing walls, and small monastic cells appear to have been crudely made of "rubble." These contrast with the main *stūpa* and its *chatra*, which, however, are clearly later—the nun donors of the latter may be linked with Sāñcī. What has been taken to be the main monastic complex—on the walls of which the Aśokan record occurs—as well as most of the residential cells, are little more than natural caves or rock shelters with slight improvements. To judge by the primitive rock art in some of them, these were probably old, abandoned cave-dwellings.[92] This—rather than a romantic vision of Nālandā—appears to be what a Buddhist "monastery" looked like "as late as" the time of Aśoka.

Even considerably after Aśoka, however, there are no references to *vihāras*. In none of the hundreds of donative records from Bhārhut, Sāñcī, and Pauni does the term occur. The scores of monk and nun donors at these sites identify themselves never as from or residents of any *vihāra* but rather—*exactly like lay donors*—by their natal or residential villages.[93] Even more curious, the only expression even vaguely like *vihāra* that occurs at early Sāñcī is not even a Buddhist word but rather a common *upaniṣadic* term.

On several of the gateways of the rail surrounding the main *stūpa* at Sāñcī, variant versions of the following imprecation occur:

> He shall have the fate of the perpetrators of five sins (*paṃc-ānaṃtarya*), who dismantles, or causes to be [551] dismantled, the stone work from this

> Kākaṇāva [i.e., the old name for Sāñcī], or causes it to be transferred to another church.[94]

The phrase here translated by Majumdar "to another church" is *anaṃ . . . ācariya-kulaṃ*. The use of "another" clearly implies that Kākaṇāva or Sāñcī—the whole complex—was thought of as belonging to the same category. It was not called a monastery or *vihāra*, then, but a "church" or, more accurately, "a house of the teacher." But although it occurs at least five hundred years later in a sectional colophon to the *Mahāvaṃsa*, the term *ācārya-kula* has a much closer and more significant context. It is in fact an established usage in the Upaniṣads. *Chāndogya* 2.23.1 says, for example:

> There are three branches of duty. Sacrifice, study of the Vedas, alms-giving—that is the first. Austerity, indeed, is the second. A student of sacred knowledge dwelling in the house of a teacher, settling himself permanently in the house of a teacher, is the third (*brahmacāryācārya-kula-vāsī tṛtīyo 'tyantam ātmānam ācārya-kule 'vasādayan*).[95]

All of this would seem to suggest the need for a considerable review of our notions of the degree of development of pre-Kuṣān Buddhist monasticism. But that, I submit, is exactly what we might have expected to emerge when Buddhist institutional history was treated with the same methods and criteria of evidence that pertain to every other kind of history, and when all types of sources were taken into account, without privileging the literary or canonical. Happily, however, such a review is not here our responsibility. Here we had only to make a case—however sketchy—for the unlikelihood that monastic communities like those at early Taxila or Bhājā or Junnar or Pāṇgurāriā could have compiled the monastic codes that we have, or could have even conceived of permanent endowments for purposes of maintenance, let alone written contracts of debt. It seems to me unlikely that monastic communities housed in poorly made and disorganized, impermanent structures or in open, crudely cut caves or abandoned rock-shelters could have had either the need or the means to redact elaborate codes containing rules against, for example, monks "building a fire to smoke out those who take too long in the latrine,"[96] or stipulating, for another example, that "when seeds belonging to an individual are sown on ground belonging to an Order, having given back a portion, (the rest) may be made use of" by the monks.[97]

But if, then, the *early* Buddhist monastic communities that are visible in the archaeological record appear to have been utterly incapable of compiling our *vinayas*, and completely unsuited to administering elaborate endowments, the question still remains as to when they did achieve a level of material and institutional development that would have allowed both—when, in fact, did it become true that "nothing is more like one Buddhist *vihāra* than another Buddhist *vihāra*"? A reasonably clear and closely approximate answer to this question has, oddly enough, been available for some time.

Marshall, again, noted some time ago that the *vihāra* that Lamotte seems to have had in mind, the ordered "quadrangular, high-walled monastery or *vihāra* . . . seems to have made its first appearance in the *saṅghārāmas* of the northwest during the first century A.D., and thence to have found its way southward and eastward to the rest of India." Marshall also said: "Before the close of the first century the old type of *saṅghārāma*, with its haphazard methods of planning and its lack of security and privacy for its inmates had disappeared. . . . [T]he living quarters of the monks . . . are now securely enclosed in a walled-in quadrangle."[98] The standardized, ordered *vihāra*, then, began to appear almost everywhere in the archaeological record just before and just after the beginning of the Common Era. It was then, too, that Buddhist monastic communities appear to have had access to the economic resources that would have allowed them for the first time to build on a wide scale in durable materials like stone and baked brick.

Marshall explained the observable change in type and construction of the *vihāra* by saying, in part, that [552] the wide acceptance of the standard form "was probably due in large measure to the changing character of the [Buddhist] church, which was everywhere tending to substitute regular, settled monasticism for the wandering life, and to relax its rules pertaining to strict asceticism and the possession of property."[99] The precise wording here might need some readjustment, but not, probably, the basic point. What, however, Marshall did not say needs to be stated: the development of the standard *vihāra*, the emergence of this form, is clearly visible in the archaeological record beginning around the Common Era, *but* that form—and all that it implies—is the type of *vihāra* that our *vinayas*, as we have them, are intended to govern. Unless one wants to assume that rules are written to govern behavior that does not occur, or that elaborate procedures are developed to meet needs that do not exist, then one is forced to conclude that our *vinayas* could not have been compiled in the form that we know them until after the beginning of the Common Era. It is, for example, hardly likely that a monastic code like the Pāli *Vinaya*, which contains rules in regard to planting seeds in land owned by the Community, could have been compiled before the Community owned land, and the first actual evidence for this too comes from the first century C.E.[100] It is, again, hardly likely that the rules in the Pāli *Vinaya* that have the Buddha say, "Monks, I allow them [i.e., *vihāras*] to be enclosed in three kinds of walls (*pākāra*): walls of burnt brick (*iṭṭhaka-pākāra*), walls of stone (*sila-*), walls of wood (*dāhu-*),"[101] could have been redacted before such walls were known, and they were not, until the beginning of the Common Era.

Considerations of this sort, and determining the period at which durable ordered *vihāras* were first built, allow us more specifically to determine the period before which it is unlikely that our *Vibhaṅga* text on perpetuities could have been written. Though ironic, it is almost certainly true that only the emergence of durable architecture could have created the idea and need of perpetual maintenance. Buildings in flimsy or perishable materials would have had a life expectancy considerably short of perpetual and could hardly have given rise to the notion or felt need for perpetual endowments to maintain them. Such endowments presuppose a justifiable expectation that what they were intended to support would endure. Moreover, as has already been noted, such endowments also presuppose an equally permanent and ordered institutional structure that could administer them. Our text, then, was almost certainly not written until both things were in place, and the archaeological record would seem to suggest that this could not have been the case much before the beginning of the Common Era. But if it is unlikely that our *Vibhaṅga* text could have been written much before the Common Era, it is also unlikely that it was written much after the second century, when we know that such perpetual endowments were already in use. Their effective use would seem to require rules governing both them and written or legal contracts of the sort found so far in the *Vinaya* only in our text.

A date in the first or second century of the Common Era for our *Vibhaṅga* text would seem to fit well with, and perhaps confirm—or be confirmed by—what has been said about written contracts in Hindu *dharmaśāstra*. *Manu*, for example, is generally assigned a date "between 200 B.C. and A.D. 100,"[102] and although it knows of written contracts and deeds (VIII. 168, 255), they receive little attention. *Yājñavalkya*, on the other hand, which is assigned to the first or second century, "gives preference to documentary evidence" and—as we have seen—"gives very detailed rules about the drawing up of legal documents."[103] Though it would be easy here to overextend what little evidence there is, it does seem that *Yājñavalkya* has a more developed—certainly a more detailed—treatment of written contracts,[104] and it is at least possible to suggest that our *Vibhaṅga* text falls somewhere between *Manu* and *Yājñavalkya*, but how close to the latter is not clear. *Yājñavalkya* may also be the first *dharmaśāstra* to refer explicitly to Buddhist monks.[105] [553]

One sometimes has the impression in reading works on *dharmaśāstra* that it is assumed that developments occurred within a closed system of *ideas*, or between *texts*, without reference to what occurred or was occurring *in the world*. The change from *Manu* to *Yājñavalkya* in regard to written contracts, for example, is often presented as if it were only a further refinement or sophistication in legal technique or theory that had no connection with changes in the social or economic world that that technique or theory was intended to govern. But it is possible, if not altogether more reasonable, to assume that changes in a legal system are responding to changes in the social or economic systems to which they are connected. Seen from this angle—the angle I have here taken in regard to the *vinaya*—what may well lie between *Manu* and *Yājñavalkya* is not merely our *Vibhaṅga* text but, more importantly, the emergence in India of a new type of social institution with considerable economic clout: the fully institutionalized, permanently housed, landed monastery. It is perhaps too easy to forget how remarkable and—in significant ways—unprecedented such an institution was in the social history of early India. Its cumulative impact must have been felt in many areas, and it is not unlikely that fully institutionalized Buddhist monasticism in India—like its counterpart in early medieval Europe—produced or stimulated the development of a whole range of bureaucratic and legal devices.[106] A good case could be made, for example, for suggesting that the concept of the juristic personality arose first in India in regard to the Buddhist *saṅgha* and *stūpa*, not in regard to the Hindu "Idol."[107] It is also likely that such an institution would have provided a strong impulse toward the depersonalization and formalizing of the economy in the areas in which it operated, and it would have required first such things as written contracts.

It remains true, of course, that the chronological boundaries suggested above are not firm enough on either side to rule out the distinct possibilities that our *Vibhaṅga* text and *Yājñavalkya* are, rather, close contemporaries, or even that the *Vibhaṅga* text is later than, and dependent on, *Yājñavalkya* in its rules for written contracts. Against this possibility are only the noticeable—though not great—differences in the degree of their detail. But if the *Vibhaṅga* text is later, it probably cannot be much later, given that—as already noted—Buddhist monastic communities were already dealing with perpetual endowments in the first or second century. Moreover, the *Vinaya* text explicitly and directly links the use of written contracts with such endowments, and these, at least, could not have been derived from *Yājñavalkya*, because he knows nothing of them. These and other possibilities must remain unsure.[108] What is less unsure, however, is that what *Yājñavalkya* says, for example, in regard to written contracts, or, indeed, what *dharmaśāstra* says in regard to a whole host of topics, may now have to be seen in light of similar discussions in Buddhist *vinaya*, and certainly Buddhist *vinaya*—especially, it seems, the *Mūlasarvāstivāda-vinaya*—can no longer be studied in isolation from *dharmaśāstra*. Finally, it is becoming ever clearer that the *Mūlasarvāstivāda-vinaya* may have particularly close ties to brahmanical concerns, and this, in turn, may again suggest that it was redacted by a community deeply embedded in the larger Indian, brahmanical world. It may turn out to be *the* mainstream Indian *vinaya*. Time will tell.

Notes

I would like to thank my colleagues Richard Lariviere, Janice Leoshko, and Jonathan Silk for having read a draft of this paper and for allowing me to benefit from their criticism and good sense.

1. For two important positions on monks and monasticism in Western scholarship, see L. W. Barnard, "Two Eighteenth Century Views of Monasticism: Joseph Bingham and Edward Gibbon," in *Monastic Studies: The Continuity of Tradition*, ed. J. Loades (Bangor, Wales: 1990) 283–291. Gibbon's overwhelmingly negative view has been, of course, by far the most influential. However, as a first-rate example of what more recent scholarship has been able to do on the question of monks and money, see L. K. Little, *Religious Poverty and the Profit Economy in Medieval Europe* (Ithaca, N.Y.: 1978). There has been, as well, a promising start made toward determining indigenous South Asian attitudes toward monastic wealth (see S. Kemper, "Wealth and Reformation in Sinhalese Buddhist Monasticism," in *Ethics, Wealth, and Salvation: A Study in Buddhist Social Ethics*, ed. R. F. Sizemore and D. K. Swearer [Columbia, S.C.: 1990] 152–169) and toward acknowledging the significance of economic concerns in religious developments in South Asia: see H. von Stietencron, "Orthodox Attitudes towards Temple Service and Image Worship in Ancient India," *CAJ* 21 (1971) 126–138, and G. W. Spencer, "Temple Money-lending and Livestock Redistribution in Early Tanjore," *The Indian Economic and Social History Review* 5.3 (1968) 277–293, for two interesting examples.

2. P. Levi, *The Frontiers of Paradise: A Study of Monks and Monasteries* (London: 1987) 29ff. For a more scholarly study of the theme, see M. Aston, "English Ruins and English History: The Dissolution and the Sense of the Past," *Journal of the Warburg and Courtauld Institutes* 36 (1973) 231–255.

3. *Cīvaravastu*, GMs, iii 2, 119.13.

4. J. Gernet, *Les aspects économiques du bouddhisme dans la société chinoise du ve au xe siècle* (Paris: 1956) 82. [The English translation here is taken from J. Gernet, *Buddhism in Chinese Society. An Economic History from the Fifth to the Tenth Centuries*, trans. F. Verellen (New York: 1995) 85. I have, however, not always followed the latter.]

5. Gernet, *Les aspects économiques du bouddhisme*, 83, 84 [Verellen, 87].

6. L.-S. Yang, "Buddhist Monasteries and Four Money-Raising Institutions in Chinese History," *HJAS* 13 (1950) 174–191, esp. 182. The text in question is Taishō 1452, the reconstructed title of which is given in P. Demiéville, H. Durt, and A. Seidel, *Répertoire du canon bouddhique sino-japonais*, 2d ed. (Paris and Tokyo: 1978) as "[*Mūlasarvāstivāda*]*nidānamātṛkā*?"; see below, p. 66 and n. 60. Yang's paper is reprinted in L.-S. Yang, *Studies in Chinese Institutional History* (Cambridge, Mass.: 1961) 198–215.

7. D. D. Kosambi, "Dhenukākaṭa," *JASBom* 30.2 (1955) 50–71, esp. 52–53.

8. A. Bareau, "Indian and Ancient Chinese Buddhism: Institutions Analogous to the Jisa," *Comparative Studies in Society and History* 3 (1961) 443–451.

9. For some idea of sinological work on the economic and institutional aspects of Buddhism, see the equally rich book of Stanley Weinstein, *Buddhism under the T'ang* (Cambridge, U.K.: 1987), and the sources cited there.

10. Kosambi, "Dhenukākaṭa," 53.

11. Gernet, *Les aspects économiques du bouddhisme*, 156 [Verellen, 160–161].

12. Most of the Sanskrit equivalents inserted into the translation will be discussed below.

13. *yangs pa can gyi li tstsha bī rnams kyi khang pa ji lta ba de bzhin du gtsug lag khang dag kyang drug rtseg dang bdun rtseg tu byed pas de dag mtho ches pas brtsigs shing brtsigs shing rdib nas*. . . . I am not quite sure how to take the reduplicative construction *brtsigs shing brtsigs shing*. I cite the Tibetan here and in nn. 14 and 15, where I am not sure of my translation.

14. *'phags pa dag de lta na mi zad par mi 'gyur gyi 'di ltar zad par 'gyur te ci bdag cag gi sdum pa na gnas ma mchis snyam 'am.*

15. *de dag gis phyug po dag la byin nas / de dag la 'das pa na mthu dang ldan pa la rten cing mi ster ba dang / bla'i grva'i mthus mi ster nas*. . . .

16. *Śayanāsanavastu* (Gnoli) 11.2–.5 = Tog, 'dul ba Ga 260a.3.

17. *Poṣadhavastu*, GMs iii 4, 77.1.

18. *Śayanāsanavastu* (Gnoli) 11.2.

19. *Cīvaravastu*, GMs iii 2, 143.6.

20. Tog, 'dul ba Ga 149a.5.

21. GBMs vi, fol. 861.5.

22. S. Sankaranarayanan, "A Brahmi Inscription from Alluru," *Sri Venkateswara University Oriental Journal* 20.1–2 (1977) 75–89; cf. D. C. Sircar, *Successors of the Satavahanas in Lower Deccan* (Calcutta: 1939) 228–230.

23. J. Burgess, *Report on the Elura Cave Temples and the Brahmanical and Jaina Caves in Western India* (London: 1883) 74–89, nos. 5, 15, 16, 17, 18, 21, 22, 26, 28.

24. S. Konow, "Mathura Brahmi Inscription of the Year 28," *EI* 21 (1931–1932) 55–61.

25. There are considerably more inscriptional references to *akṣaya-nīvīs* than are cited or signaled in J. D. M. Derrett, "The Development of the Concept of Property in India c. A.D. 800–1800," *Zeitschrift für vergleichende Rechtswissenschaft* 64 (1962) 46 n. 117, 68–72 [= Derrett, *Essays in Classical and Modern Hindu Law* (Leiden: 1977) ii, 39 n. 117, 61–65], or Derrett, "Nīvī," *Vishveshvaranand Indological Journal* 12.1–2 (1974) 89–95. In the first of these papers especially, Derrett might leave the impression that inscriptional references to *akṣaya-nīvīs* are largely Gupta and later, but this, of course, is definitely not the case. To the secondary sources he gives, at least the following should be added: R. G. Basak, "The Words *nīvī* and *vinīta* Used in Indian Epigraphs," *IA* 48 (1919) 13–15: M. Njammasch, "Akhaya-nivi-Schenkungen an Klöster und Tempel im Dekhan unter den Sātavāhanas," *Acta Orientalia (Hungaricae)* 24.2 (1971) 203–215.

26. The translation that follows is made from the edition of the inscription in J. F. Fleet, *Inscriptions of the Early Gupta Kings and Their Successors* (*CII*. III) (Calcutta: 1888) 260–262, no. 62.

27. The term *ratnagṛha*—the referent of which is not entirely clear—also occurs in another fifth-century inscription from Sāñcī (Fleet, *Inscriptions of the Early Gupta Kings*, 29–34, no. 5) and in what may be a considerably earlier inscription from Mathurā (H. Lüders, *Bharhut Inscriptions* [*CII*. II, II], rev. E. Waldschmidt and M. A. Mehendale [Ootacamund: 1963] 12–14).

28. It is likely that the reference here is to a spot or seat that local tradition said had been used by a series of former Buddhas and by Śākyamuni as well. References to such spots are frequent in the Chinese pilgrims' accounts of early medieval India, but rare in inscriptions. Presumably there was on a spot of this sort at Sāñcī what we call an "image," but what the inscription itself calls "the Buddha." On the concept lying behind such language, see G. Schopen, "The Buddha as an Owner of Property and Permanent Resident in Medieval Indian Monasteries," *JIP* 18 (1990) 181–217 [= *BSBM* 258–289].

29. Derrett, "Nīvī," 89–90.

30. Ibid., 89–90, 95.

31. *Cīvaravastu*, GMs iii 2, 125.3.

32. J. Gonda, "Abbreviated and Inverted Nominal Compounds in Sanskrit," in *Pratidānam: Indian, Iranian and Indo-European Studies Presented to Franciscus Bernardus Jacobus Kuiper on His Sixtieth Birthday*, ed. J. C. Heesterman et al. (The Hague: 1968) 221–246.

33. Gonda, "Abbreviated and Inverted Nominal Compounds in Sanskrit," 223–224.

34. Although it seems to have no connection with endowments, it is worth noting that the term *akṣayya* does occur in *dharmaśāstra* in connection with interest, as at *Nārada* 1.94, but as Lariviere notes, even this is not common (R. W. Lariviere, *The Nāradasmṛti* [Philadelphia: 1989] ii 60).

35. Chandra, *TSD*, 1752.

36. Guṇaprabha and his *Vinayasūtra* will be treated below in some detail.

37. Gernet, *Les aspects économiques du bouddhisme*, 156 n. 2 [Verellen, 357 n. 26].

38. See, however, R. S. Sharma, "Usury in Early Mediaeval India (A.D. 400–1200)," *Comparative Studies in Society and History* 8 (1965–1966) 56ff, esp. 58, who understands the passage differently: "the *brāhmaṇa* or the *kṣatriya* should not take interest even in times of distress, but should pay interest to people of mean avocations (*pāpīyase*) out of legal necessity."

39. *Arthaśāstra* 2.6.13, 15.

40. F. W. Thomas, *Tibetan Literary Texts and Documents concerning Chinese Turkestan*, Pt. 3 (London: 1955) 136, 134, and the references cited there.

41. H. Chatterjee, *The Law of Debt in Ancient India* (Calcutta: 1971) 211ff.; see also L. Sternbach, *Juridical Studies in Ancient Indian Law* (Delhi: 1965) i 109ff.

42. Chatterjee, *The Law of Debt*, 226.

43. Ibid., 48ff.

44. *Cīvaravastu*, GMs iii 2, 140.16, 140.20, 141.1 [= Tog, 'dul ba Ga 147b.6, 7], 148a.1–.2.

45. Much of the material for such a study has, however, already been gathered and is conveniently available in Joshi, *Dharmakośa*, i 1, 348–380. The following observations are based on it.

46. For a fuller citation of the passage, see below, p. 62.

47. Thomas, *Tibetan Literary Texts and Documents*, iii 143.

48. For a sampling of such seals and sealings, see B. Ch. Chhabra, "Intwa Clay Sealing," *EI* 28 (1949–1950) 174–175; V. A. Smith, "Vaiśālī: Seals of the Gupta Period," *JRAS* (1905) 152; J. Ph. Vogel, "Seals of the Buddhist Monasteries in Ancient India," *Journal of*

the Ceylon Branch of the Royal Asiatic Society, n.s., 1 (1950) 27–32; G. R. Sharma, "Excavations at Kauśāmbī, 1949–1955," *Annual Bibliography of Indian Archaeology* 16 (Leyden: 1958) xliv–xlv; D. Schlingloff, "Stamp Seal of a Buddhist Monastery," *The Journal of the Numismatic Society of India* 31 (1969) 69–70; H. Sastri, *Nalanda and Its Epigraphical Material* (Delhi: 1942) 36ff.; and D. C. Sircar, "Inscribed Clay Seal from Raktamrittika," *EI* 37 (1967) 25–28.

49. J. Ph. Vogel, "Some Seals from Kasia," *JRAS* (1907) 366.

50. In the case of Kasia there is, of course, other material that confirms the identity of the site—see F. E. Pargiter, "The Kasia Copper-plate," *ARASI 1910–11* (Calcutta: 1914) 73–77, esp. 77 n. 10. One further point in regard to at least some of these sealings can, I think, also be quickly clarified, and such a clarification will establish an even more specific linkage between what has been found at some Buddhist sites and the *Mūlasarvāstivāda-vinaya*. Vogel found at Kasia a number of sealings that he described as showing a "skeleton seated in meditation" or a "skeleton standing. On both sides a bird perched on a skull." Sastri, in later work at the site, also found such sealings. (See J. Ph. Vogel, "Excavations at Kasia," *ARASI 1905–06* [Calcutta: 1909] 85; Vogel, "Excavations at Kasia," *ARASI 1906–07* [Calcutta: 1909] 66; H. Sastri, "Excavations at Kasia," *ARASI 1910–11* [Calcutta: 1914] 72. In the second of the reports cited, Vogel surmised that "such figures possibly are meant to represent the corporeal relics of some Buddhist saint," p. 59, n. 1.) There is, however, a passage in the *Kṣudrakavastu* of the *Mūlasarvāstivāda-vinaya* that makes this unlikely. Vogel knew this passage but, presumably, only from the truncated summary in Csoma or Feer. In the latter it appears as "Un membre de l'ordre religieux doit avoir sur son sceau ou cachet un cercle avec deux daims se faisant vis-à-vis et au-dessous le nom du fondateur du Vihāra" (L. Feer, *Analyse du kandjour* [Lyon: 1881] 191). The Tibetan text itself says, however: *bcom ldan 'das kyis bka' stsal pa / rgya ni gnyis te / dge 'dun gyi dang / gang zag gi'o / de la dge 'dun gyi ni dbus su 'khor lo bris na / glo gnyis su ri dags / 'og tu gtsug lag khang gi bdag po'i ming bri bar bya'o / gang zag gi ni rus pa'i keng rus sam / mgo 'i thod pa bri bar bya'o* (Tog, 'dul ba Ta 11b.4): "The Blessed One said: 'There are two kinds of seals: (seals) of a Community, and (seals) of individual monks. In regard to them, that of a Community is to have a wheel engraved in the middle with a deer on both sides; below it the name of the Vihārasvāmin. That of an individual monk is to have a skeleton or a skull engraved on it.'" Vogel identified a considerable number of the seals he found at Kasia with the first type mentioned in this passage, but because he had access only to an incomplete summary of the passage, he was unable to recognize seals of the second type for what they were: those seals or sealings bearing skeletons or skulls almost certainly had nothing to do with "the corporeal relics of some Buddhist saint" but were rather simply seals of individual monks. It is worth noting too that the association between things connected with the individual and skeletons and skulls is also found elsewhere in this *Vinaya*. In a well-known passage that describes what paintings are allowed in a *vihāra*, the text says, in Lalou's translation, "dans les [individual] cellules, un squelette, des os et un crâne" are to be painted (M. Lalou, "Notes sur le décoration des monastères bouddhiques," *RAA* 5.3 [1930] 183–185). Certain individual cells at some Buddhist monastic sites have been identified as "meditation caves" because they have skeletons and skulls painted on their walls (cf. L. Feugere, "A Med-

itation Cave in Kyzil," in *SAA 1985*, ed. K. Frifelt and P. Sørensen (London: 1989) 380–386). Obviously, these *Vinaya* passages render such identifications doubtful.

51. Karunatilaka has noted what he calls an "obvious gap in the information found in the law-books": "The law-books of the early medieval times and the preceding period contain various laws pertaining to money-lending and interest payments between individuals but they pay little or no attention at all to similar transactions between individuals and institutions" (P. V. B. Karunatilaka, "Hindu Temples in Bihar and Orissa: Some Aspects of the Management of Their Monetary Endowments in Early Medieval Times," *The Sri Lanka Journal of Humanities* 13.1–2 [1987] 154).

52. Gernet, *Les aspects économiques du bouddhisme*, 156 n. 3 [Verellen, 161 and n. 27].

53. *Vibhaṅga*, Derge, 'dul ba Cha 149b.1 ff.

54. Sternbach, *Juridical Studies*, i 111ff.

55. For the sources on the life and date of Guṇaprabha, and for work on his *Vinayasūtra* and its auto-commentary, see G. Schopen, "Ritual Rights and Bones of Contention: More on Monastic Funerals and Relics in the *Mūlasarvāstivāda-vinaya*," *JIP* 22 (1994) 63–64 and nn. 63–64 [= Ch. X below]. When I wrote this essay, I was unaware that an edition of the whole of the Sanskrit text of the *Sūtra* had been published. P. V. Bapat and V. V. Gokhale had said in their introduction to their edition of the first chapter of both the *Vinayasūtra* and its auto-commentary that they had seen and used an edition of the *Sūtra* by R. Sāṅkṛtyāyana. But they also said that it was only "provisionally printed . . . not formally published." I therefore assumed, wrongly, that it was never made available. Mr. Jonathan Silk—already known for his keen bibliographic nose—was kind enough not only to point out to me that it had indeed been published (as no. 74 of the Singhi Jain Śāstra Śikṣāpīṭha, Singhi Jain Series!) but also to send me a copy. I would like to thank him very much. Unfortunately, Bapat and Gokhale may have understated the case when they referred to this edition as "very unsatisfactory." It does, however, make it possible to improve on some points in my treatment of the Tibetan translation of the *Sūtra* in the present essay, but that will have to wait.

56. L. Schmithausen, *The Problem of the Sentience of Plants in Earliest Buddhism* (Tokyo: 1991) 74. The text occurs at Derge, 'dul ba Cha 279b.3–280b.7.

57. *Vinayasūtra* (Sankrityayana) 38.11ff; *'dul ba'i mdo*, Derge, bstan 'gyur, 'dul ba Wu 30a.4ff. Note in particular: *tridaṇḍakaṃ bhāṣaṇa-dakṣiṇadeśanāṃ kṛtvā*, translated—oddly enough—by *rgyun chags gsum pa gdon pa dang sbyin pa bshad pa byas nas*.

58. All the examples that follow are cited from the edition of the Sanskrit text of the first chapter of the *Sūtra* and its commentary found in P. V. Bapat and V. V. Gokhale, eds., *Vinaya-sūtra and Auto-commentary on the Same* (Patna: 1982); references are to the *Sūtra* numbers inserted into the text.

59. *Sū.* 506 is citing the text of the *Cīvaravastu* now found at GMs iii 2, 131.13–.15.

60. Demiéville, Durt, and Seidel, *Répertoire du canon bouddhique sino-japonais*, 123, 124, 125. See note * on p. 90.

61. *Vinayasūtra* (Sankrityayana) 33.12–.14; *'dul ba'i mdo*, Derge, bstan 'gyur, 'dul ba Wu 26.b5.

62. I am not at all sure what *gtsang khang byur bu* means. *gtsang khang* in *dri gtsang*

khang seems to translate *kuṭī*; and *byur bu* is usually said to mean "heaped, a heaped measure of corn or meal," or "full, brim-full."

63. Derge, bstan 'gyur, 'dul ba Zhu 165b.1–.4.

64. *Vinayasūtra* (Sankrityayana) 124.3.

65. See S. L. Huntington, *The "Pāla-Sena" Schools of Sculpture* (Leiden: 1984) 125–126, nn. 120–125, and the sources cited there.

66. *Śayanāsanavastu* (Gnoli) 37.6–.19 = Tog, 'dul ba Ga 286a.6–b.5.

67. Lüders, *Mathurā Inscriptions*, no. 44, and 81 n. 1.

68. *Bhaiṣajyavastu*, GMs iii 1, 220.20.

69. *Saṅghabhedavastu* (Gnoli) i 199.25. For additional references to *dakṣiṇām ādiś-* in the *Mūlasarvāstivāda-vinaya* and elsewhere, see G. Schopen, "On Avoiding Ghosts and Social Censure: Monastic Funerals in the *Mūlasarvāstivāda-vinaya*," *JIP* 20 (1992) 12, 30 n. 43 [= *BSBM* 229 n. 43]; Schopen, "The Ritual Obligations and Donor Roles of Monks in the Pāli *Vinaya*," *JPTS* 16 (1992) 101–102 [= *BSBM* 79–80] [see also now Ch. II above, n. 48].

70. *Śayanāsanavastu* (Gnoli) 35.1 = Tog, 'dul ba Ga 284b.4.

71. Here it will be sufficient to cite—as one of many possible examples—Lawrence's remarks given under the heading, "The Religious Motives for Endowment": "The merit that accrued to an individual [monk] through prayer and good works could be applied to other people, and not only to living people, but also to the dead. This concept played a crucial role in Medieval religious practice. To found and endow a community of monks was to ensure for the donor an unceasing fund of intercession and sacrifice which would avail him and his relatives both in life and after death" (C. H. Lawrence, *Medieval Monasticism: Forms of Religious Life in Western Europe in the Middle Ages*, 2d ed. [London and New York: 1989] 69; see also the very rich study of M. McLaughlin, *Consorting with Saints: Prayer for the Dead in Early Medieval France* [Ithaca, N.Y.: 1994]. For what appears to be a much later (sixteenth-century?) Indian legal instrument intended in part to assure the postmortem well-being of an individual, see J. D. M. Derrett, "Kuttā: A Class of Land-Tenures in South India," *BSOAS* 21 (1958) 61–81 [= *Essays in Classical and Modern Hindu Law* (Leiden: 1976) i 280–302).

72. Ét. Lamotte, *History of Indian Buddhism: From the Origins to the Śaka Era*, trans. S. Webb-Boin (Louvain-la-neuve: 1988) 179.

73. It will perhaps be sufficient, even representative, to cite here examples from the Pāli *Vinaya*, which is still commonly held to be the "oldest" of the *vinayas*, and from the *Mūlasarvāstivāda-vinaya*, which is still commonly held to be the most recent (cf. O. v. Hinüber, "The Arising of an Offence, *apattisamuṭṭhāna*: A Note on the Structure and History of the Theravāda-Vinaya," *JPTS* 16 [1992] 68 n. 13): Pāli *Vinaya* ii 148.7ff (on doors and the three kinds of keys); GMs iii 4, 80.15 (reference to hiding the key to the "hall for religious exertion").

74. See, for convenience, the Pāli material discussed in M. Njammasch, "Hierarchische Strukturen in den buddhistischen Klöstern Indiens in der ersten Hälfte des ersten Jahrtausends unserer Zeitrechnung: Untersuchungen zur Genesis des indischen Feudalismus," *Ethnographische-archäologische Zeitschrift* 11 (1970) 515–539, esp. 529ff.

75. Pāli *Vinaya* ii 119.19ff; GMs iii 4, 79.3.

76. Perhaps the most striking example here is the story of the monk Pilindavaccha, which occurs in two separate places in the Pāli *Vinaya* (i 206.34ff and iii 248.11ff). Bimbisāra gave five hundred monastery attendants (*ārāmika*) to the monk Pilindavaccha, and the text says: "A distinct village established itself. They called it 'The Village of the Monastery Attendants' and they also called it 'Pilinda Village'" (*pāṭiyekko gāmo nivisi. ārāmika-gāmako 'ti pi naṃ āhaṃsu pilindagāmako 'ti pi naṃ āhaṃsu*—the translation is from I. B. Horner, *The Book of the Discipline*, Vol. IV [London: 1951] 282). Note that Jaworski calls this story a "légende locale" and says it "n'a pas d'équivalent en chinois" (J. Jaworski, "Le section des remèdes dans le vinaya des mahīśāsaka et dans le vinaya pali," *Rocznik Orientalistyczny* 5 [1927] 100 n. 14). For the Mūlasarvāstivādin version of the story, see G. Schopen, "The Monastic Ownership of Servants or Slaves: Local and Legal Factors in the Redactional History of Two *Vinayas*," *JIABS* 17 (1994) [= Ch. VII below].

77. Pāli *Vinaya* i 250.14: "Now at that time seeds belonging to an Order were sown on ground belonging to an individual, and seeds belonging to an individual were sown on ground belonging to an Order. They told this matter to the Lord. He said: 'When, monks, seeds belonging to an Order are sown on ground belonging to an individual, having given back a portion, (the rest) may be made use of. When seeds belonging to an individual are sown on ground belonging to an Order, having given back a portion, (the rest) may be made use of"—so Horner, *The Book of the Discipline*, iv, 347.

78. See Schopen, "The Ritual Obligations and Donor Roles of Monks," 87–107 [= *BSBM* Ch. IV].

79. The inheritance of lay estates: Pāli *Vinaya* ii 169.24; GMs iii 2, 139.6–143.14; the inheritance of a dead monk's property: Pāli *Vinaya* i 304ff; GMs iii 2, 113ff (cf. Schopen, "On Avoiding Ghosts and Social Censure," 3ff [= *BSBM* 206ff]).

80. J. Marshall et al., *The Monuments of Sāñchī* (Delhi: 1940) i 63; cf. J. Marshall, *Taxila: An Illustrated Account of Archaeological Excavations* (Cambridge, England: 1951) i 274, where he says, for example, "At the Dharmarājikā at Taxila . . . there is not a vestige of any residential quarters which can be assigned to a date much earlier than the beginning of the Christian Era."

81. Cf. G. Schopen, "On Monks, Nuns, and 'Vulgar' Practices: The Introduction of the Image Cult into Indian Buddhism," *ArA* 49.1–2 (1988–1989) 165–166 [= *BSBM* 250–251].

82. Marshall, *Taxila*, i 320.

83. See S. Nagaraju, *Buddhist Architecture of Western India (c. 250 B.C.–c. A.D. 300)* (Delhi: 1981) 113–130, and the ground plans given in figs. 23–25.

84. Ibid., 133–40, and plans in fig. 27. Nagaraju says, "Here are the earliest Buddhist excavations among the inland group of caves in Western Deccan."

85. For the sake of convenience, see B. Kumar, *The Archaeology of Pataliputra and Nalanda* (Delhi: 1987) 164ff, and the sources cited there.

86. Though it would lead too far afield to pursue it here, it is—I think—safe to say that a careful study of extant, as opposed to conjectured, early *stūpas* would arrive at the same point. Those *stūpas* that have some chance of being really early, and in regard to which

we have some actual knowledge, are all small, unimpressive affairs. This is the case with the *stūpas* at Bairat (R. B. D. R. Sahni, *Archaeological Remains and Excavations at Bairat* [Jaipur: 1937] 28ff; S. Piggott, "The Earliest Buddhist Shrines," *Antiquity* 17 [1943] 1–10), at Lauṛiya-Nandangaṛh (J. E. van Lohuizen-De Leeuw, "South-east Asian Architecture and the Stūpa of Nandangaṛh," *ArA* 19 [1956] 282ff and fig. 2), at Junnar-Tuljalena (Nagaraju, *Buddhist Architecture of Western India*, 133–134), etc.

87. E. Hultzsch, *Inscriptions of Asoka* (*CII. I*) (Oxford: 1925) 14, 36, 60, etc.; J. Bloch, *Les inscriptions d'asoka* (Paris: 1950) 111.

88. For a recent discussion, see K. R. Norman, "Aśoka's 'Schism' Edict," *Bukkyōgaku seminā* 46 (1987) 1–33, esp. 9–10, 25–26, and nn. 4, 19.

89. Hultzsch, *Inscriptions of Asoka*, 163; Bloch, *Les inscriptions d'asoka*, 152–153; cf. Norman, "Aśoka's 'Schism' Edict," 101–102.

90. Hultzsch, *Inscriptions of Asoka*, 164; Bloch, *Les inscriptions d'asoka*, 157.

91. D. C. Sircar, *Aśokan Studies* (Calcutta: 1979) 94–103, esp. 101–102; Sircar, "Panguaria Inscription of Asoka," *EI* 39 (1971, but 1981) 1–8.

92. For the site, see B. K. Thapar, ed., *Indian Archaeology 1975–76: A Review* (New Delhi: 1979) 28–30, and pls. xxxix–xli; H. Sarkar, "A Post-Asokan Inscription from Pangoraria in the Vindhyan Range," in *Sri Dinesacandrika: Studies in Indology, Shri D. C. Sircar Festschrift*, ed. B. N. Mukherjee et al. (Delhi: 1983) 403–405, and pls. 73–75. (This contains a note on the site by K. D. Banerjee and an edition of the later "chatra inscription"—the latter is also treated in S. S. Iyer, "Panguraria Brahmi Inscription," *EI* 40 (1973, but 1986) 119–120 and pl.).

93. See, for example, all the inscriptions listed under "Donations by Inhabitants of Certain Places" in Lüders, *Bharhut Inscriptions*, A5–54. Note what might be traces of the same sort of situation, of "monks" living in villages, in what are considered the oldest parts of the Pāli Canon; e.g., *Suttanipāta* 971: . . . *yatacāri gāme*, which K. R. Norman translates ". . . living in a restrained way in a village" (K. R. Norman, *The Rhinoceros Horn and Other Early Buddhist Poems* [London and Boston: 1985] 157).

94. Marshall et al., *The Monuments of Sāñchī*, i, no. 404; cf. 298.

95. S. Radhakrishnan, *The Principal Upaniṣads* (London: 1953) 374; R. E. Hume, *The Thirteen Principal Upanishads*, 2d rev. ed. (Oxford: 1931) 200–201.

96. See C. Hallisey, "Apropos the Pāli *Vinaya* as a Historical Document: A Reply to Gregory Schopen," *JPTS* 15 (1991) 207.

97. See n. 77 above.

98. Marshall, *Taxila*, i 233, 320. Cf. Marshall et al., *The Monuments of Sāñchī*, i 63–64: "As a fact, it was not until the Kushān period that the self-contained monastery, which we are wont particularly to associate with the Buddhist *saṅghārāma*, made its appearance in the Northwest of India, and not until the early Gupta Age that it found its way into Hindustān and Central India"—the last part of which is in need of revision.

99. Marshall, *Taxila*, i 324.

100. See the Alluru inscription cited above in n. 22 and the well-known Mathurā Lion Capital Inscription (*Kharoshṭhī Inscriptions*, 48–49) for two of the earliest inscriptional references to donation of land to Buddhist communities.

101. Pāli *Vinaya* ii 121.2.

102. J. D. M. Derrett, *Dharmaśāstra and Juridical Literature* (A History of Indian Literature, ed. J. Gonda, Part of Vol. IV) (Wiesbaden: 1973), 31.

103. R. Lingat, *The Classical Law of India*, trans. J. D. M. Derrett (Berkeley: 1973) 99–100.

104. There is at least one significant difference. *Yājñavalkya* (II.5.96–97) gives detailed procedures for recording partial repayments and for—when the debt is repaid—nullifying the written contract or writing a "receipt" (cf. Chatterjee, *The Law of Debt in Ancient India*, 345–348). But our *Vinaya* passage knows nothing of this.

105. But see J. Filliozat, "La valeur des connaissances gréco-romaines sur l'inde," *Journal des savants*, avril–juin (1981) 113 n. 32.

106. See, for example, J. A. Raftis, "Western Monasticism and Economic Organization," *Comparative Studies in Society and History* 3 (1961) 452–469; K. J. Conant, "Observations on the Practical Talents and Technology of the Medieval Benedictines," in *Cluniac Monasticism in the Central Middle Ages*, ed. N. Hunt (London: 1971) 77–84; etc.

107. See G. Schopen, "Burial 'Ad Sanctos' and the Physical Presence of the Buddha in Early Indian Buddhism: A Study in the Archaeology of Religions," *Religion* 17 (1987) 206–209 [= *BSBM* 128–131]; Schopen, "The Buddha as an Owner of Property and Permanent Resident," [= *BSBM* 271–274].

108. A large part of the problem has, of course, to do with what Lariviere has so gracefully called the "chronological house of cards" that has been built up for *dharmaśāstra* (Lariviere, *Nārada* ii, xix ff). Dates for *Yājñavalkya* in particular have varied widely—it has been assigned to the fourth or even sixth century C.E. (Lingat, *The Classical Law of India*, 99–100). Should such later dates turn out to be correct, then *Yājñavalkya* would be considerably later than our *Vinaya* text.

*[It is now much clearer what the *Mātṛkā* is, and the passage cited by Guṇaprabha has been identified in a section of what in the Tibetan tradition is called the *Uttaragrantha*. The section is there called the *Mātṛkā*. See above pp. 8–9, 17n. 14, and below pp. 125, 162n. 19, 270, 282n. 52.]

CHAPTER IV

Deaths, Funerals, and the Division of Property in a Monastic Code

READING BUDDHIST *vinaya* texts as we have them can be an unsettling experience. These texts are huge compilations of rules and regulations meant to govern the lives of Buddhist monks. Though they were written or compiled by monks for monks, the life of a monk they envision or take for granted has little in common with the image of the Buddhist monk that is commonly found in our textbooks, or even in many of our scholarly sources. That image—which has found its way even into modern European novels—presents the Buddhist monk as a lone ascetic who has renounced all social ties and property to wander or live in the forest, preoccupied with meditation and the heroic quest for *nirvāṇa* or enlightenment. But Buddhist monastic literature is more gritty; it presents and presupposes a different kind of monk. The monk it knows is caught in a web of social and ritual obligations, is fully and elaborately housed and permanently settled, preoccupied not with *nirvāṇa* but with bowls and robes, bathrooms and door bolts, and proper behavior in public. A French scholar, André Bareau, some years ago went so far as to say that the various monastic codes, or *vinayas*, "contain hardly a whisper about the numerous spiritual practices, meditations, contemplations, etc., which constituted the very essence of the Buddhist 'religion.'" This at least must give us pause for thought.

But even when elements of the image of the ascetic, meditating monk do appear in *vinaya* literature—and they do—they often appear in unexpected form. The various *vinayas* present the ascetic ideal, for example, in the instructions they say should be given to the candidate at his or her ordination. In the Pāli *Vinaya*, the candidate is to be told that entrance into the monastic order entails exclusive reliance on only four things, technically known as "requisites" or "means of sup-

Originally published in *Buddhism in Practice*, ed. D.S. Lopez (Princeton, N.J.: 1995): 473–502. Reprinted with stylistic changes with permission of the editor.

port": begged food or scraps; rag-robes, or robes of discarded cloth; the foot of trees as a place of residence; and urine as medicine. The candidate—the text says—is to be told this, and told that he should limit himself to these means of [474] support "for as long as he lives." But then he is immediately told, in the text as we have it, that, in addition to robes made from rags, he may also have robes made of "linen, cotton, silk, wool, and so on." In a Sarvāstivādin *Vinaya* text that describes the ordination procedure for nuns, the list of "extra allowances" is even longer and includes colored cloth, woven cloth, muslin, hemp, silk, wool, fine Banaras cloth, and linen. If this looks like a double message, another passage in the Pāli *Vinaya* puts this beyond doubt. Though the candidate for ordination is told in one place to limit himself to rag-robes, the same *Vinaya* unequivocally says in another place that wearing only rag-robes is an "offense of wrongdoing," or a violation of the *vinaya*. In a late "appendix" to the Pāli *Vinaya* called the *Parivāra*, it is even suggested that most monks who actually wear rag-robes do so "from stupidity" or "from madness, from a deranged mind," and are "of evil desires, filled with covetousness."

Other and even more extreme elements of the ascetic ideal also occur in the *vinayas*, but they too are treated in a curious way. The *Mūlasarvāstivāda-vinaya*, for example, knows and contains rules to regulate the behavior of monks who live in cemeteries or wear robes made from burial cloths. This text says, however:

> A monk who dwells in a cemetery, robing himself with burial cloth, must not enter a monastery. He must not worship a *stūpa*. If he should worship, he must not approach it any nearer than a fathom. He must not use a monastic cell. He must not even sit on monastic bedding. He must not sit among the community of monks. He must not teach Dharma to brahmans and householders who have come and assembled. He must not go to the houses of brahmans and householders, and so on.

If in the former instances the ascetic ideal is severely weakened or rendered purely symbolic by permitting "extra allowances" or calling into question the motives that lie behind it, in the case of ascetic practices connected with cemeteries—though nothing is directly said to discourage them—a set of rules is promulgated that excludes any monk who engages in such practices from any meaningful place in normal monastic life. Such a monk cannot enter or use monastic property; he is denied full access to the object of monastic worship; he cannot engage in monastic activities or interact with fellow monks; interaction with the laity—and therefore access to economic support—is also either denied him or seriously restricted. But notice too that the way in which these rules are framed inadvertently articulates the conception of normal monasticism presupposed by their authors: normal monks lived in monasteries and had free access to and use of monastic property and objects of worship; they lived communally and could interact with the laity. The norm here, the ideal, is not of ascetic practice but of sedentary, socially engaged, permanently housed monasticism. This same norm is equally evident elsewhere as well.

Much has recently been written about modern Buddhist "forest monks," and the Pāli *Vinaya* also speaks of such monks. But in one of the passages in this [475] monastic code in which the lifestyle of such monks is most clearly described, there are, again, some surprises:

> At that time the Venerable Udāyin was living in the forest. The monastery of that Venerable was beautiful, something to see, and lovely. His private chamber was in the middle, surrounded on all sides by the main house, well appointed with couch and chair, cushion and pillow, well provided with drinking water and water for washing, the grounds well kept. Many people came to see the Venerable Udāyin's monastery. A brahman and his wife approached the Venerable Udāyin and said they would like to see his monastery.
>
> "Have a look," he said, and taking the key, unfastening the bolt, and opening the door, he entered . . .

Though this is in the forest, these are not the quarters that one might expect for a monk who relied on the four requisites: he had a private room, well-appointed furniture, and lock and key, and his monastery was something of a tourist attraction. And yet this, apparently, is how the compilers of the Pāli *Vinaya* saw the forest life. Their forest life was little different from their vision of monastic life in general: both, for them, were permanently housed and well appointed, well ordered, maintained, secured by lock and key, and the focal point of lay activities.

These passages from several different *vinayas*—and a large number of other passages—make it difficult to avoid the conclusion that if the ideal of the individual rag-wearing, begging, forest-dwelling monk was in fact ever the rule in the early history of Indian Buddhism, if the ideal was ever anything more than "emblematic," then it was, by the time the *vinayas* that we have were compiled, all but a dead letter. The *vinaya* texts that we know are little interested in any individual religious quest but are concerned with the organization, administration, maintenance, and smooth operation of a complex institution that owned property and had important social obligations.

The disinclination on the part of scholars to acknowledge fully the institutional preoccupations of the *vinaya*, and the complexity of the institutions these texts presuppose, has distorted the discussion of the *vinayas*' dates and disguised their historical importance. In fact, though often pressed into service to do so, our *vinaya* texts can probably tell us very little about what early monastic Buddhism "originally" was. They can, however, almost certainly tell us a great deal about what it had—by a certain period—become. And that, for further historical developments, is far more interesting.

Many, if not most, scholars seem to want to place the canonical *vinayas* in a period close to—if not even during—the lifetime of the Buddha. But this would mean that Buddhist monasticism had little or no real history or development, since by this argument monasticism appeared fully formed at the very beginning. Such an argument requires, as well, the suppression of what little we actually know about the various *vinayas* and the history of Buddhist monasticism.

In most cases, we can place the *vinayas* we have securely in time: the *Sarvāstivāda-vinaya* that we know was translated into Chinese at the beginning of [476] the fifth century (404–405 C.E.). So were the *Vinayas* of the Dharmaguptakas (408), the Mahīśāsakas (423–424), and the Mahāsāṃghikas (416). The *Mūlasarvāstivāda-vinaya* was translated into both Chinese and Tibetan still later, and the actual contents of the Pāli *Vinaya* are only knowable from Buddhaghosa's fifth-century commentaries. Although we do not know anything definite about any hypothetical earlier versions of these *vinayas*, we do know that all of the *vinayas* as we have them fall squarely into what might unimaginatively be called the Middle Period of Indian Buddhism, the period between the beginning of the Common Era and the year 500 C.E. As we have them, then, they do not—and probably cannot—tell us what monastic Buddhism "originally" was, but they do provide an almost overwhelming amount of detail about what it had become by this time. To use these *vinayas* for what we know them to be—documents from the Middle Period—gives to them and to this period the historical importance that both deserve but that neither has yet received.

That the *vinayas* as we have them do indeed belong to and reflect the Middle Period is obvious from other evidence as well. All of our *vinayas* presuppose a standard, well-organized, walled monastery with latrines, refectories, cloisters, storerooms, dispensaries, doors, and keys; it had more or less extensive landholdings and a battery of monastic servants and laborers. But we know from archaeological sources that such an ordered and well-developed monastery did not exist before the beginning of the Common Era and appeared throughout India only in the Middle Period. Sources that know such monasteries, and are intended to regulate them, could therefore only date from the same period. We know, moreover, from inscriptional records that it was only in the Middle Period that Buddhist monastic groups started to receive large donations of land and, in fact, entire villages. But the Pāli *Vinaya*, for example, already describes one such village of five hundred "monastery attendants" that was given to a single monk.

To suggest that the Middle Period saw the compilation of huge monastic codes should not be surprising. This was, after all, the period during which equally enormous doctrinal encyclopedias like the *Abhidharmakośa* were also compiled; this was the period during which the various named monastic orders—the Sarvāstivādins, Mahāsāṃghikas, Dharmaguptakas, and so on—appeared in Indian inscriptions as the recipients of what must have been an enormous amount of surplus wealth. And there are no such records either before or after this period. What might be more surprising is that the Middle Period apparently not only saw the full institutional, economic, and doctrinal development of the monastic orders, but also was the period during which the vast majority of the texts that we call "Mahāyāna *sūtras*" were being written. And these two developments are almost certainly related; it may well be that much of Māhāyana *sūtra* literature makes good sense only in light of what else was going on when it was composed. Such a possibility gives a new importance to the *vinayas* and demands a new reading of them, for it seems likely that one of the things that those groups that we call Mahāyāna were struggling with—and against—was what monastic Buddhism had become by the Middle Period. To determine what that was, the *vinayas* will be a major source. [477]

I might cite a single broad example. Unless we know what landed, institutional monastic Buddhism had become when Mahāyāna *sūtras* were being written, it is difficult to understand the attacks on "abuses" associated with sedentary monasticism found most stridently in Mahāyāna texts like the *Rāṣṭrapālaparipṛcchā*; it is also difficult to understand similar, if less shrill, criticisms in Mahāyāna texts like the *Kāśyapaparivarta*, or the constant calls in such texts to return to a life in the forest, or why long sections of the *Samādhirāja-sūtra* are given over to extolling ascetic practices, and why the necessity and value of these same practices are a topic of sharp debate in the *Aṣṭasahāsrikā-prajñāpāramitā*. Unless we have a clear picture of what the authors of these Mahāyāna texts were surrounded by and reacting to, we will have little chance of appreciating what they were producing. And an important source for that picture will be the *vinayas* that were being compiled at the same time. It is in this light, I would suggest, that the following selections should be read.

The following selections are of interest for at least two related reasons. They provide some interesting examples of the sorts of things that institutionalized monastic Buddhism was concerned with in the Middle Period: the proper performance of funeral rituals for deceased fellow monks; the inheritance of property; the performance of death rituals for fellow monks; and negotiating ritual privileges, control of sacred relics, and economic resources. There is perhaps some added interest from the fact that such monastic concerns have rarely been identified or studied. But these selections illustrate as well how far monastic Buddhism had moved away from what we consider "spiritual" concerns—how far, in other words, it had developed strictly as an institution and become preoccupied with institutional concerns. These developments, of course, made it ripe for reformation. And this was very likely what many of the Mahāyāna groups were attempting to effect.

The selections that follow all come from a single *vinaya*, the *Mūlasarvāstivāda-vinaya*, or literature related to it, so at this stage one must be careful not to over-generalize. They are—and are only meant to be—suggestive of what we still have yet to learn. The first consists of three short texts that in their original context, as here, follow one after another. They define and present as obligatory what appear to be the three main elements of a Mūlasarvāstivādin monastic funeral: removal of the body—undoubtedly ritualized; the honor of the body (*śarīra-pūjā*)—which appears to have involved bathing the body (see section III) and other preparations prior to cremation; and the recitation of some sacred or "scriptural" text, the merit from which was to be assigned to the deceased. These actions are presented here as a set of rituals that the monks must perform before any distribution of the deceased monk's property can be undertaken. They are clearly intended to effect a definitive separation of the dead monk—here presented as a club-wielding "ghost"—from his personal belongings. Keep in mind that the expression used here, "robe and bowl," was a euphemism that covered a large variety of personal property. Notice too that these passages imply a kind of exchange relationship that is also expressed elsewhere (section VII): the monks are obligated to perform the funeral and, significantly, to transfer to the deceased [478] the reward, or "merit," that results from their ritualized recitation of the Dharma; but the deceased, in exchange, is to allow the distribution of his estate to take place unencumbered and without interference. This conception of a set of mutual obligations between the dead and the living is almost certainly only a specific instance of an established Indian norm. Indian legal texts, for example, take as a given that the property or estate of a dead person goes to the person or persons who perform his funeral rites.

The rules regarding monastic funerals in section I were presented as a response to the problem of inheritance and the distribution of monastic estates, a problem that will reappear in other selections (sections VII and VIII). The second selection presents another set of rules as a response to a different problem—that of avoiding social criticism or censure. Buddhism has often been presented as if it had been a force for social change in early India—a reaction to and an attempt to reform established Indian norms. But again, if this were ever actually true, it most certainly was not by the time the *vinayas* were compiled in the Middle Period. The *vinayas* are, in fact, preoccupied—if not obsessed—with avoiding any hint of social criticism and with maintaining the status quo at almost any cost. In terms of social norms the monks who compiled the *vinayas* were profoundly conservative men. Our second selection is but one particularly striking instance of this general trend. Here the institution of monastic funerals is presented and justified almost exclusively in terms of the need to avoid any offense to the social and religious sensibilities of the world outside the monastery. This world was particularly sensitive to the question of the proper ritual treatment of the dead and the need to avoid the "pollution" associated with death and dying. Our selection seems, again, to represent a Buddhist monastic expression of these same Indian concerns. Unlike section I, it explicitly refers to the means of final disposal of the body and, in fact, presents several alternatives designed to meet various contingencies: cremation is preferred, but disposal in water or burial are acceptable in certain circumstances. The text also implies that whatever means of disposal is used, a recitation of the Dharma and the assigning of the resultant reward to the deceased are required. Finally, in regard to this selection, it should be noted that it contains the first reference that we have seen to "the three sections" (*tridaṇḍaka*) (which is also referred to in section VII). Although it is not certain what this was, it would appear to have been a standard formulary made up of three parts that was used on a variety of ritual occasions. The first part consisted of a set of verses in praise of the Buddha, the Dharma, and the Saṅgha; the middle portion was made up of a canonical text suited to the ritual occasion; and the third part contained a formal transference of merit.

In sections I and II, where the rules governing monastic funerals are presented as obligatory, there is no reference to lay participation in these affairs. But in section III such participation is presented both as an obligation and as a particular privilege sought after by a number of competing groups. The beginning of the text—which is omitted here—sets the stage for the events that our selection narrates to justify an exception to established monastic rule. It was a rule that monks [479] were not to enter towns or villages except at certain regular times. But the need to perform proper funeral rituals for a dead monk, the need to perform "the honors for his body," was apparently considered so important by the compilers of this *Vinaya* that it was able to override or abrogate this rule. The particular case that gave rise to this exception involved the death of a monk named Udāyin, who was known as the foremost of monks who were able to convert families. A married woman who had been sleeping with the leader of a gang of thieves was worried that this monk knew what she was up to and would reveal it. She arranged with her lover to lure the monk into a house. Her lover was to wait at the door and to dispatch the monk when he came out. Our selection picks up the story from here.

In this account the Buddha begins by reiterating the obligation of monks to perform the "honors for the body" of a fellow monk. As the story develops, what starts as a monastic obligation comes to be a ritual privilege that several categories of individuals seek to secure: there is a monastic claim, but it lacks ecclesiastical specificity—these monks are presented as neither specifically co-residential monks nor ecclesiastically recognized disciples of Udāyin; there is a royal claim, but it has a purely personal or biographical basis; there is, finally, a lay claim, but one in which an institutionally recognized relationship is involved. This final claim is the one that wins. It is made by Mālikā, who declares that Udāyin was her "teacher" (*ācārya*). This would make her his "disciple" (*antevāsin*), which is an institutionally recognized formal relationship that involves a set of mutual obligations. Mālikā, however, is not a nun, but—elsewhere at least—a lay-sister, and herein lies a part of the significance of the text. Elsewhere in the *Mūlasarvāstivāda-vinaya* it is made clear that monks had a series of ritual obligations in regard to lay-brothers and lay-sisters (*upāsaka / upāsikā*). What our text seems to be suggesting is that lay-brothers and lay-sisters might, in turn, have certain ritual privileges in regard to monks. But here this is being negotiated, not asserted or made a rule. Our text seems to carefully avoid making a general rule. It simply establishes a precedent—"this happened once when . . ."—that is all. Future cases, therefore, would also have to be negotiated. The ambiguity seems to be intentional, and such ambiguity or ambivalence seems to be characteristic of all those situations in which lay participation in monastic ritual is at issue, or where control of, and access to, sacred objects is involved, and it is clearly visible again in section IV.

Section III also represents one of the rare cases in which building a *stūpa*, or permanent structural reliquary, for the postcremation remains of the deceased is specifically included as a part of the funeral. Generally these two things, although obviously related, were considered and treated separately, as in section IV. But the *stūpa* referred to here is almost certainly not of the monumental type; given that it was, as it were, built in a day, it was probably a small structure built over a pot containing the ashes of the deceased. There is Indian inscriptional evidence indicating that small *stūpas* were built for the local monastic dead, and in some cases these are explicitly said to have been erected—as in our text—by a disciple of the deceased. [480]

Section IV is particularly interesting. In Mūlasarvāstivādin literature at least—and probably in the literatures of other orders—it, and not the account of the death and funeral of the Buddha in the *Mahāparinirvāṇa-sūtra*, describes the origins of what we call the "relic cult" in monastic Buddhism. Like section III, it deals with questions of access and control and shows the monks and the laity jockeying for position; the monks win, of course, for they wrote the account. Like several other of our selections, its denouement deals not so much with devotion as with "dollars."

The selection starts with what was apparently the established monastic rule: the funeral of the Monk Śāriputra was performed by a fellow monastic. The text assumes that the remains or relics of a dead monk are the property of the monastic community. However, this position becomes the initial point of friction and the point to be negotiated. For the established monastic claim cuts off a monk in death from the laity who in life may have been his supporters and followers. Such an assertion of proprietary rights by the monks has at least the potential to disaffect that lay group, and all our *vinayas* stress the need to avoid that.

After the Novice Cunda has performed the funeral of the Monk Śāriputra and handed his relics over to the Monk Ānanda, the latter goes to the Buddha to express his dismay at Śāriputra's death. The Buddha then delivers a longish homily on the meaning of Śāriputra's death, which is omitted here. The Householder Anāthapiṇḍada, who is the prototypical generous lay donor, then hears of Śāriputra's death and goes to the Monk Ānanda to present a claim on the relics. Ānanda responds with a counterclaim in exactly the same terms and refuses to give up possession of the relics. To this point, we have monastic possession of the relics, a lay claim, a monastic counterclaim, and unresolved deadlock. Here—as in so many other cases in the *vinaya* involving friction between the lay and monastic communities—the Buddha himself is brought in to mediate. The layman Anāthapiṇḍada repeats his claim to the Buddha, and the Buddha sides with him. The Buddha summons the Monk Ānanda and tells him to turn the relics over to Anāthapiṇḍada. The Buddha is also made to say, in effect, that when monks retain exclusive possession of monastic relics, this is not beneficial to the teaching, and that monks should rather occupy themselves with the "business of a monk"—recruiting, ordaining, and instructing other monks. Here we have articulated something like a distinction that is commonly said to have existed between the religious activity of monks and the religious activity of laypersons in Indian Buddhism: monks are to be properly occupied with maintaining the institution by inducting new recruits and with transmitting the teaching; activity in regard to relics is the concern of the laity. But note that it requires the authority of the Buddha to introduce this distinction, that it is presented as an innovation and that the prior or original monastic practice did not recognize this distinction. Also note that the account as we have it implies that there was some monastic resistance; at least the compilers of the account must have anticipated such resistance, because they apparently felt compelled to add what amounts to an editorial comment. After saying that Ānanda gave the relics of Śāriputra to the householder, [481] the text adds: "This was so since the Blessed One when formerly a *bodhisattva* never violated the words of his father and mother, or of his preceptor or teacher or other persons worthy of respect." This statement is syntactically isolated and does not form a part of the ongoing narrative. It appears, rather, to be an editorial intrusion intended to make explicit how the compilers wanted the text to be read: Ānanda acquiesced not as a result of his own inclinations but strictly as a matter of obedience.

There are other indications that the compilers of the account did not see the Buddha's instructions as a satisfying solution, for the account does not end here. Both the Buddha and the reluctant Monk Ānanda are presented as acceding to lay desires to have monastic relics. But—you can almost hear the editors say—look what happened. Anāthapiṇḍada takes the relics and enshrines them in his house. Although others had some access to them, the text seems to emphasize that they virtually became the object of a private household cult. The issue came to a head because lay control of monastic relics ultimately resulted in exactly what it was intended to prevent: access to such relics, when in private hands, was restricted and could be entirely shut off. Enter, again, the Buddha. He rules that laypersons can, indeed, build *stūpas* for the relics of the monastic dead, but all such *stūpas*, except those for "ordinary" monks, must be built within the monastic complex, that is, must remain under monastic control. It is a clever piece. It makes it possible to present the Buddha as reasserting the right of monastic control solely for the sake of benefiting the laity.

Access and control, however, are not the only issues here. Relics gave rise to festivals; festivals gave rise to trade; trade gave rise to gifts and donations. It is this, in the end, that our text may be about. But to appreciate this particular monastic interest in monastic relics, an established principle of *vinaya* law must be kept in mind. Virtually all the *vinayas* contain rules stipulating that any donation made to the *stūpa* of a Buddha belongs to that *stūpa*, that is, to the Buddha himself, and could not, except under special circumstances (see section VI), be transferred to, or used by, either the monastic community or an individual monk. This legal principle, which continues in effect even in Mahāyāna *sūtra* literature, deprived the monks of an important source of revenue, and our text is almost certainly responding to this situation. It acknowledges that a token part (the "first fruit" offerings) of the donations in question is to be given to the Buddha in the form of the "Image that Sits in the Shade of the Jambu Tree." This was, apparently, an image of the Buddha that represented him in his first youthful experience of meditation. There are several references to it in the *Mūlasarvāstivāda-vinaya* (see section VIII), and an inscribed second-century image of this sort has been found at Sāñcī. A small part of the donations is also to be used to maintain the *stūpa* of Śāriputra. But the rest—and in this case that is a goodly amount—is to be divided among the monks. Our text hastens to add that in this instance there is no offense, because the donations were not made to a *stūpa* of the Buddha but to a *stūpa* of a specific disciple. The qualification to the established rule that is being introduced here, and the full range of its applicability, are stated more [482] straightforwardly in Guṇaprabha's *Vinayasūtra*, a fifth- to seventh-century monastic handbook that paraphrases our passage as "that which is given to the *stūpa* of a disciple belongs indeed to his fellow monks." Such *stūpas* could, then, come to be a legitimate source of revenue for the monks, and such a possibility may explain what Faxian, a fifth-century Chinese monk, said he saw in India: "wherever monks live they build up *stūpas* in honor of the saints Śāriputra, Maudgalyāyana, and Ānanda."

We have no idea, of course, if any of the things narrated in our account actually occurred. If, as seems very likely, this account was compiled in the Middle Period, then it was written hundreds of years after the events it is supposed to be describing and has, in one sense, no historical value at all. But in another sense it is an extremely important historical document: it shows us how Mūlasarvāstivādin *vinaya* masters in the Middle Period chose to construct and to present their past to their fellow monks; it shows us how the issue of who controlled sacred relics had—at least for this period—been settled; more generally it shows us *vinaya* masters in the Middle Period seriously engaged with questions of power, access, relics, and money. These monks almost look like real people.

Sections V and VI both deal with an aspect not of death but of dying, and both link it with property. Both texts reflect the importance attributed by a variety of Indian sources—Hindu, Jain, and Buddhist—to the moment of death. The basic idea is succinctly expressed in a Jain text: "as is the mind at the moment of death, just so is one's future rebirth"; or in the *Samādhirāja-sūtra*: "when at the moment of passing away, death, or dying, the thought of something occurs, one's consciousness follows that thought." The last moment or one's dying thought was believed, in effect, to determine one's next birth. However serious the difficulties such a belief might create for official Buddhist doctrine, it is obvious from our two texts that *vinaya* masters took it as a given. The rules they present here are solely intended either to avoid negative thoughts at the moment of death (section V) or to ensure positive thoughts at such a time. The failure on the part of the monastic community to do what is required to effect either is not only a disciplinary fault but has disastrous consequences for their dying fellow monk, who is thereby condemned to rebirth in the hells.

How important such beliefs and rituals were to the monastic community is at least suggested in both texts. In section V, although the Buddha is made to rule that "excessive attachment" to some possession on the part of a monk is a fault, still the final ruling provides for the continuing existence of such a fault. In section VI the need to ensure a positive state of mind in a monk who may be on the point of death overrides not one, but two, otherwise firm *vinaya* laws. This need is apparently so important that the monks may use assets that belong to the Buddha to meet it, though this is normally strictly forbidden: to meet this need the monks are also allowed to engage in buying and selling, and this too is normally restricted.

In terms of detail, note that section V contains a reference to the actual cremation of a dead monk as being performed by a low-caste man; this would suggest [483] again that the monks had a purely ritual role and did not do the dirty work.

In section VI, as in VIII, there is a reference to "the perfumed chamber." We know from numerous references to this chamber in the *Mūlasarvāstivāda-vinaya*, and from architectural and inscriptional evidence, that it was the residential cell directly opposite the main entrance of the typically quadrangular Indian Buddhist monastery of the Middle Period. This cell was both by position and by architectural elaboration set off from the other residential cells and was reserved for the Buddha himself. The latter permanently resided in such a cell in every fully developed monastery in the form of what we call an image, and there were specific monks assigned to this chamber or monastic shrine. Section VI also contains a reference to a permanent endowment for the Buddha. We know from inscriptions that Buddhist monastic communities received such endowments throughout the Middle Period. They were called "permanent" because they consisted of sums of money that could never be spent but were to be lent out on interest by the monks to generate usable income. The *Mūlasarvāstivāda-vinaya* contains a text that gives detailed instructions governing such monastic loans and the use of written contracts of debt. Note finally that section VI ends by invoking a principle of the Indian law of property. Buddhist *vinaya* texts, in fact, frequently reveal points of contact with Indian law, as in sections VII and VIII.

Section VII presents an interesting case of interaction between *vinaya* law and secular law and involves a sizable monastic estate: "three hundred thousands of gold." The latter may appear surprising but should not be. Reference to the private wealth of monks is frequently found. In the *Suttavibhaṅga* of the Pāli *Vinaya* it is said, for example, that if a monk asks for yarn and then has it woven into robe material, that is an offense. But if the monk does it "by means of his own wealth," the same act is not an offense. There are a dozen such references to private wealth in this section of the Pāli *Vinaya* alone. There are also clear indications in both the Pāli and Mūlasarvāstivāda *Vinayas* that seem to suggest that monastic status or reputation was directly related to a monk's material possessions. Note that in section VI the monk who was "little known" had no medicine, and in section IX the Buddha himself and the selfish monk are each described as both "widely known" and the recipients of robes, bowls, medicines, and so on. Who you were was determined by what you received and had.

Evidence that individual monks must have had considerable private means is also available in Buddhist donative inscriptions. Large numbers of monks and nuns made private gifts to their communities, and some of these were impressive. Such wealth might very well have been of interest to the state, and establishing who had jurisdiction over, or rights of possession to, such wealth in the event of its owner's death was undoubtedly a matter of some negotiation between the state and the Buddhist monastic communities. What we see in the first part of section VII is, of course, only the monastic point of view.

The remainder of section VII suggests further that dealing with monastic estates could become a major and disruptive monastic preoccupation, and some means of sorting out the various claims was required. That is the main purpose of the [484] second half of the text. The Buddha is made to declare that the division and distribution of a dead monk's estate was to take place on only five occasions. The first three of these correspond to moments in a Mūlasarvāstivādin monastic funeral: (1) "when the gong for the dead is being beaten"—the sounding of the funeral gong, we know from other sources (see section IX), marked the beginning of a monastic funeral by summoning the monks; (2) the recitation of the Three Sections—referred to also in section II; and (3) "when the shrine (*caitya*) is being honored"—which seems to have marked the end of the funeral and is also referred to in section II. The order in which these occasions are listed seems to represent the order of preference and appears to favor direct participation in the funeral. If the distribution takes place on these occasions, only those present will receive a share. The other two occasions appear to take place separately: (4) at the distribution of counting sticks—such sticks are referred to in all the *vinayas* and were used for a variety of purposes; and (5) the making of a "formal motion"—such "motions" are also widely noted in *vinaya* literature and were used for any formal act or decision that required the consent of the entire community. Of these occasions, only the procedure for the formal motion is described in detail. Note the reference to "selling" a dead monk's property. Such references also occur elsewhere, and it appears that the property was first sold and the money realized was then divided among the monks. In Chinese sources it is clear that this involved an actual auction.

Section VIII also deals with the problem of estates, but of a particular kind. The estate in question belongs to what the text calls a "shaven-headed householder." Because monks shave their heads but householders do not, such individuals obviously represented a mixed or intermediate category. Our text purports to describe the origin of this category: a wealthy layman decided to enter the order and approached a monk. The monk shaved the householder's head and began to train him for ordination. But the householder fell seriously ill and—in accordance with an established *vinaya* rule against ordaining sick people—the Buddha declared that "the rules of training" were not to be given until he recovered. The Buddha also ruled, however, that monastic attendants should be given to the sick man even when he was taken back home. The man did not recover, but at the point of death made a written will and sent it to the monastery. He died, and government officials heard of it and of the size of his estate. They reported his death to the king. Because the man was sonless, and because according to Indian law the estate of a man who dies sonless goes to the king, the state should have had jurisdiction in this case and the king should have had clear rights to the property. But our monastic text has the king declare—explicitly citing the case adjudicated in section VII—that a case of this sort too falls under the authority of the Buddha, that is, under the jurisdiction of monastic law. The king, in other words, is presented as acknowledging or confirming the religious status of the category "shaven-headed householder": the estate of such an individual is not subject to secular law.

What we see here is another instance of *vinaya* law interacting with Indian law. [485] But we probably see something else as well: this *vinaya* passage establishes a precedent and procedure that would allow a sonless man to avoid the confiscation of his estate by the state upon his death. The procedure involves a relationship of exchange and obligation that is embedded in the text without always being explicitly stated. The layman undergoes at least a ritual or symbolic ordination—his head is shaved—but it is not completed. This ritual ordination itself, however, creates an obligation for the monastic community to provide monastic attendants to look after the layman when he falls ill, whether he remains at the monastery or returns home. In other words, it provides a kind of health insurance for the layman. But in exchange, as it were, for attending to the layman in his final days—in this case, apparently for an extended period—the monastic community receives, upon his death, his entire estate. Both parties clearly gain by the arrangement. Certain rulings in the text itself suggest that what is being proposed here was intended to apply even to laymen who might have had children—there is a provision dealing specifically with what should happen to a deceased person's sons and daughters. In a case of this sort, the shaven-headed householder would have been able to divert his estate from its normal heirs.

What we have in section VIII is, then, almost certainly a Buddhist version of a ritual practice commonly found in other monastic traditions as well. Several of the Hindu *Saṃnyāsa Upaniṣads* refer to undergoing the rites of renunciation at the point of death; Jain sources, too, speak of laypersons' being initiated into the monastic order at the approach of death. But the strongest parallels are probably found in medieval Christian monastic practice: here too a layman is "ordained" at the approach of death; here too the monks are obligated to attend to him in his final days; and here too they receive his estate or substantial gifts in return.

The reference in section VIII to a written will is also of interest. Although the Pāli *Vinaya*, for example, knows and approves of the use, under certain conditions, of oral testaments or wills on the part of monks, nuns, lay-brothers and lay-sisters, or "anyone else," references to written wills are extremely rare even in Indian legal texts. There is also a reference to "written liens" or loan contracts that may form part of an estate, and to both Buddhist and non-Buddhist books. These and other such references provide important evidence for determining the history and use of writing in early India, a topic that is as yet little studied or understood. Finally, in terms of details, section VIII shows that ownership rights were clearly divided in a Mūlasarvāstivādin monastery: property belonged to the Buddha or the Dharma or the Community. In each case such property could be used only for specific purposes and normally could not be transferred to another unit or purpose (see section VI). This tripartite division of property rights, or some form of it, is recognized by virtually all the *vinayas*.

There is one more point that needs to be noted in regard to section VIII. A Chinese monk named Yijing visited and studied in India in the last quarter of the seventh century. He wrote an important account of what he observed, which has survived and been translated into English under the title *A Record of the Buddhist Religion as Practiced in India and the Malay Archipelago*. Much of this *Record* may, [486] in fact, be based on Yijing's observations, but some of it is not. The whole of his chapter 36, apart from the first and last sentences, for example, is nothing more than a Chinese translation of the *vinaya* passage that we have been discussing. The failure to recognize this, and the fact that Yijing gives the passage out of context, have misled a number of modern scholars.

Section IX does not come from the *Mūlasarvāstivāda-vinaya*. It is presented here to show how some of the concerns in the other selections were treated in more literary form. Section IX is taken from a collection of stories called the *Avadānaśataka*, *The Hundred Edifying Stories*, apparently a Mūlasarvāstivādin text. Our selection appears to be in many ways only a narrative elaboration of the rules governing monastic funerals found in sections I and II. Although it is commonly asserted that *Avadāna* or Buddhist story literature was "popular" literature meant for the laity, there is little evidence for this, and a large number of such stories were—like our selection—explicitly addressed to monks, had monastic heroes and characters, and dealt with specifically monastic concerns that would have been of little interest to the laity. It is more likely that such moralizing story literature was written for and read by ordinary monks who probably, at all periods, made up the largest segment of the Buddhist monastic population.

Section IX throws some further light on at least one particular detail. Sections I, II, and III all refer to "assigning" or "directing" a reward to the deceased monk as a part of a monastic funeral, but section IX alone actually describes the procedure. Like numerous passages in the *Mūlasarvāstivāda-vinaya*, section IX makes it clear that "assigning the reward" meant making a formal declaration designating who should receive the merit resulting from a specific act. When the Buddha assigns the reward in section IX, he recites a verse that says in part, "what, indeed, is the merit from this gift, may that go to the hungry ghost," that is, the dead monk. In this case the merit is formally designated for the same "person" who made the gift. In sections I, II, and III the merit results from the acts of a group (the monks) or an individual (Mālikā) but is assigned to someone else (the deceased). This practice—usually called the "transference of merit"—used to be considered a Mahāyāna innovation but is found even in the Pāli sources, frequently in the *Mūlasarvāstivāda-vinaya*, and almost everywhere in Buddhist donative inscriptions that have no determinable connection with the Mahāyāna.

The selections presented here are in several senses a mere sampling: they are taken from a single *vinaya*, or monastic code; they all deal with a single cluster of concerns; they all represent fragments of a large and complex literature. But they also suggest at least the possibility of a new reading of the *vinaya*, not as sources connected with the origins of Indian Buddhist monasticism but as documents of its Middle Period. They show what is to be learned by reading the *vinayas* not as documents dealing with spiritual or even ethical concerns but as works concerned with institutional, ritual, legal, and economic issues. They also show how much may have been missed or misunderstood by the modern scholarly preference for the Pāli *Vinaya*. Finally, they at least suggest how complex, rich—in [487] several senses—and remarkable an institution Buddhist monasticism might have been.

Five of the following selections are from the *Cīvaravastu* and have been translated from Sanskrit—**I**: GMs iii 2, 126.17–127.18; **V**: 125.10–126.16; **VI**: 124.11–125.9; **VII**: 117.8–121.5; and **VIII**: 139.6–143.14. One is from the *Vinayavibhaṅga* and translated from Tibetan—**III**: Derge, 'dul ba Nya 65a.2–66a.4 [the volume letter was incorrectly given as Nga in the original publication]. The remaining two *vinaya* texts are from the *Kṣudrakavastu* and are translated from Tibetan—**II**: Tog, 'dul ba Ta 352b.7–354a.5; and **IV**: Tog, 'dul ba Ta 354a.5–368a.5. **IX** is translated from Sanskrit: *Avadānaśataka* (Speyer) i 271–273.

I. Rules Governing Monastic Funerals and the Problem of Inheritance

This took place in Śrāvastī. On that occasion a certain monk who was sick died in his cell. He was reborn among the nonhuman beings. The monk who was the distributor-of-robes started to enter the cell of the dead monk, saying, "I distribute the bowl and robes." But the deceased monk appeared there with intense anger, wielding a club, and said: "When you perform for me the removal of the body, only then can you proceed with the distribution of my bowl and robe." The distributor-of-robes was terrified and forced to flee.

The monks asked the Blessed One concerning this matter.

The Blessed One said: "First the removal of the dead monk is to be performed. Then his robe and bowl are to be distributed."

This took place in Śrāvastī. On that occasion a certain monk died. The monks performed the removal of his body but simply threw it into the burning ground and returned to the monastery. The distributor-of-robes entered the dead [488] monk's cell, saying, "I distribute the bowl and robe." But the dead monk had been reborn among the nonhuman beings. Wielding a club, he appeared in his cell and said: "When you perform the honor of the body for me, only then can you proceed with the distribution of my bowl and robe."

The monks asked the Blessed One concerning this matter.

The Blessed One said: "The monks must first perform the honor of the body for a deceased monk. After that his bowl and robe are to be distributed. There will otherwise be a danger."

This took place in Śrāvastī. On that occasion a certain monk who was sick died in his cell. After having brought him to the burning ground, and having performed for him the honor of the body, that deceased monk was cremated. Then the monks returned to the monastery. The distributor-of-robes entered the dead monk's cell. The dead monk appeared wielding a club, saying, "You have not yet given a recitation of the Dharma for my sake, but only then are you to proceed with the distribution of my monastic robes."

The monks asked the Blessed One concerning this matter.

The Blessed One said: "Having given a recitation of Dharma in the deceased's name, having directed the reward to him, after that his monastic robes are to be distributed."

II. Rules Governing Monastic Funerals and the Pressure of Social Criticism

The Buddha, the Blessed One, dwelt in Śrāvastī, in the Grove of Jeta, in the Park of Anāthapiṇḍada.

In Śrāvastī there was a certain householder. He took a wife from a family of equal standing, and after he had lain with her, a son was born. The birth ceremonies for the newborn son, having been performed in detail for three times seven or twenty-one days, the boy was given a name corresponding to his clan. His upbringing, to his maturity, was of a proper sort.

Later, when that householder's son had become a Buddhist monk, his bodily humors became unbalanced and he fell ill. Though he was treated with medicines made from roots and stalks and flowers and fruits, it was of no use, and he died.

The monks simply left his body, together with his robe and bowl, near a road.

Later, brahmins and householders who were out walking saw the body from the road. One said: "Hey look, a Buddhist monk has died." Others said: "Come here! Look at this!" When they looked, they recognized the dead monk and said: "This is the son of the householder what's-his-name. This is the sort of thing that happens when someone joins the Order of those lordless Buddhist [489] ascetics. Had he not joined their Order, his kinsmen would certainly have performed funeral ceremonies for him."

The monks reported this matter to the Blessed One, and the Blessed One said: "Now then, monks, with my authorization, funeral ceremonies for a deceased monk must be performed." Although the Blessed One had said that funeral ceremonies for a deceased monk should be performed, because the monks did not know how they should be performed, the Blessed One said: "A deceased monk is to be cremated."

Although the Blessed One had said that a deceased monk should be cremated, the Venerable Upāli asked the Blessed One: "Is that which was said by the Reverend Blessed One—that there are eighty thousand kinds of worms in the human body—not so?" The Blessed One said: "Upāli, as soon as a man is born, those worms are also born, so, at the moment of death, they too surely die. Still, only after examining the opening of any wound is the body to be cremated."

Although the Blessed One had said a deceased monk is to be cremated, when wood was not at hand, the monks asked the Blessed One concerning this matter, and the Blessed One said: "The body is to be thrown into rivers." When there is no river, the Blessed One said: "After a grave has been dug, the body is to be buried." When it is summer and the earth is hard and the wood is full of living things, the Blessed One said: "In an isolated spot, with its head pointing north, having put down a bundle of grass as a bolster, having laid the corpse on its right side, having covered it with bunches of grass or leaves, having directed the reward to the deceased, and having given a recitation of the Dharma of the Three Sections (*tridaṇḍaka*), the monks are to disperse."

The monks dispersed accordingly. But then brahmins and householders derided them, saying: "Buddhist ascetics, after carrying away a corpse, do not bathe and yet go about their business. They are polluted." The monks asked the Blessed One concerning this matter, and the Blessed One said: "Monks should not disperse in that manner but should bathe." They all started to bathe, but the Blessed One said: "Everyone need not bathe. Those who came in contact with the corpse must wash themselves together with their robes. Others need only wash their hands and feet."

When the monks did not worship the shrine (*caitya*), the Blessed One said: "The shrine is to be worshiped."

III. The Death and Funeral of the Monk Kālodāyin: Negotiating Ritual Privileges

The ringleader of thieves, having pulled his sword from its sheath, waited at the door.

When the Venerable Udāyin came out, the ringleader, with a mind devoid [490] of compassion and without concern for the other world, severed his head and it fell to the ground.

An old woman saw him killing the noble one: "Who is this," she said, "who has done such a rash thing?"

The ringleader said: "You must tell no one or I will make sure that you too end up in the same condition!"

She was terrified and was then unable to speak. Thinking that perhaps someone following the tracks of the Eminent One would come by later, she—given the circumstances—remained silent.

The two of them, with minds devoid of compassion and without concern for the other world, hid the body of the Venerable Udāyin in a heap of trash and left it there.

That day the monk-in-charge-of-the-fortnightly-gathering, sitting at the seniors' end of the assembly, said: "Has someone determined the inclination of the Reverend Udāyin? The Reverend Udāyin is not here."

Then the Blessed One said to the monks: "Monks, that one who is the best of those who make families pious has been killed. His robes must be brought back, and the honors for his body must be performed!"

The Blessed One set forth but was stopped by the gate of Śrāvastī. He then caused a brightness like that of gold to shoot forth. He filled all of Śrāvastī with a light like that of pure gold.

Prasenajit, the King of Kośala, thought to himself: "Why has all of Śrāvastī been filled with a light like that of pure gold?" He thought further: "Without a doubt, the Blessed One wishes to enter!"

Together with his retinue of wives, and taking the key to the city, he unlocked the gate, and the Blessed One entered.

Prasenajit, the King of Kośala, thought: "But why has the Blessed One come into Śrāvastī at an irregular time?" But since Buddhas, Blessed Ones, are not easy to approach and are difficult to resist, he was incapable of putting a question to the Buddha, the Blessed One.

The Blessed One, together with the community of disciples, having gone ahead, Prasenajit, together with his retinue of wives, went following everywhere behind the Blessed One, until they came to that heap of trash.

The Blessed One then addressed the monks: "Monks, he who was the best of those who make families pious is hidden here. Remove him!"

He was removed, and those who had depended on the Venerable Udāyin, seeing there what had truly happened in regard to the Noble One, said: "Since he was our good spiritual friend, does the Blessed One allow us to perform the honors for his body?"

The Blessed One did not allow it.

Prasenajit, the King of Kośala, said: "Since he was a friend of mine from our youth, does the Blessed One allow me to perform the honors for his body?"

The Blessed One did not allow it.

Queen Mālikā said: "Since he was my teacher, does the Blessed One allow me to perform the honors for his body?" [491]

The Blessed One allowed it.

Queen Mālikā, then, having had the dirt removed from the body of the Venerable One with white earth, had it bathed with perfumed water. Having adorned a bier with various-colored cotton cloths, she put the body onto it and arranged it.

Then the Blessed One, together with the community of disciples, went ahead, and the king, together with his retinue of wives, followed behind them.

Having put the bier down at an open, extensive area, Queen Mālikā, heaping up a pile of all the aromatic woods, cremated the body. She extinguished the pyre with milk, and having put the bones into a golden pot, she had a mortuary *stūpa* erected at a crossing of four great roads. She raised an umbrella, a banner, and a flag and did honor with perfumes, strings of garlands, incense, aromatic powders, and musical instruments. When she had venerated the *stūpa's* feet, the Blessed One, having assigned the reward, departed.

IV. Śāriputra's Death and the Disposition of His Remains: Negotiating Control and Access to Relics

After the Venerable Śāriputra had died, the Novice Cunda performed the honors for the body on the remains of the Venerable Śāriputra and, taking the remains, his bowl, and monastic robes, set off for Rājagṛha. When in due course he arrived at Rājagṛha, he put down the bowl and robe, washed his feet, and went to the Venerable Ānanda. When he had honored with his head the feet of Ānanda, he sat down to one side. Being seated to one side, the Novice Cunda said this to the Venerable Ānanda: "Reverend Ānanda, you should know that my preceptor, the Reverend Śāriputra, has entered into final *nirvāṇa*—these are his relics and his bowl and monastic robes."

The Householder Anāthapiṇḍada heard it said that the Noble Śāriputra had passed away into final *nirvāṇa* and that his relics were in the hands of the Noble Ānanda. Having heard that, he went to the Venerable Ānanda. When he had arrived there and had honored with his head the feet of the Venerable Ānanda, he sat down to one side. Having sat down to one side, the Householder Anāthapiṇḍada said this to the Venerable Ānanda: "May the Noble Ānanda hear! Since for a long time the Noble Śāriputra was to me dear, beloved, a guru, and an object of affection, and since he passed away into final *nirvāṇa* and his relics are in your possession, would you please hand them over to me! The honor due to relics should be done to his relics!"

Ānanda said: "Householder, because Śāriputra for a long time was to me dear, beloved, a guru, and an object of affection, I myself will perform the honor due to relics for his relics."

Then the Householder Anāthapiṇḍada went to the Blessed One. When he had arrived there and had honored with his head the feet of the Blessed One, he sat down to one side. Having sat down to one side, the Householder

Anā[492]thapiṇḍada said this to the Blessed One: "May the Reverend One hear! For a long time the Noble Śāriputra was to me dear, beloved, a guru, and an object of affection. His relics are in the hands of the Noble Ānanda. May the Blessed One please grant that they be given to me! I ask for the honor due to relics for his relics."

The Blessed One then, having summoned Ānanda through a messenger, said this to him: "Ānanda, give the relics of the Monk Śāriputra to the Householder Anāthapiṇḍada! Allow him to perform the honors! In this way brahmans and householders come to have faith. Moreover, Ānanda, through acting as you have, there is neither benefit nor recompense for my teaching. Therefore you should cause others to enter the Order, you should ordain them, you should give the monastic requisites, you should attend to the business of a monk, you should cause [the teaching] to be proclaimed to monks as it was proclaimed, cause it to be taken up, teach it, and through this, indeed, you profit and give recompense for my teaching."

Then the Venerable Ānanda, by the order of the Teacher, gave the relics of Śāriputra to the Householder Anāthapiṇḍada—this was so because the Blessed One, when formerly a *bodhisattva*, never violated the words of his father and mother or of his preceptor or teacher or other persons worthy of respect.

The Householder Anāthapiṇḍada took the relics of the Venerable Śāriputra and went to his own house. When he got there, he placed them at a height in the most worthy place in his house and, together with members of his household, together with his friends, relations, and older and younger brothers, undertook to honor them with lamps, incense, flowers, perfumes, garlands, and unguents.

The people of Śrāvastī heard then that the Noble Śāriputra had passed away into final *nirvāṇa* in the village of Nalada in the country of Magadha, that the Noble Ānanda, after having obtained his relics, presented them to the Householder Anāthapiṇḍada, and that the latter, together with members of his household, together with his friends, relatives and acquaintances, and elder and younger brothers, honored them with lamps, incense, flowers, perfumes, garlands, and unguents. When Prasenajit, the King of Kośala, heard this, he went to the house of the Householder Anāthpiṇḍada together with his wife Mālikā, the Lady Varṣakārā, both Ṛṣidatta and Purāṇa, and Viśākhā, the mother of Mṛgāra, as well as many of the devout, all of them carrying the requisites for doing honor. Through paying honor to the relics with the requisites of honor, several of them there obtained accumulations of good qualities. But on another occasion when some business arose in a remote village, the Householder Anāthapiṇḍada, having locked the door of his house, went away. But a great crowd of people came then to his house, and when they saw the door locked, they were derisive, abusive, and critical, saying, "In that the Householder Anāthapiṇḍada has locked the door and gone off, he has created an obstacle to our merit."

Later the Householder Anāthapiṇḍada returned, and members of his house-[493]hold said: "Householder, a great multitude of people carrying the requisites of honor came, but seeing the door locked, they were derisive, abusive, and critical, saying, 'Anāthapiṇḍada has created an obstacle to our merit.'"

Anāthapiṇḍada thought to himself, "This indeed is what I must do," and went to the Blessed One. When he had arrived there and had honored with his head the feet of the Blessed One, he sat down to one side. Seated to one side, he said this to the Blessed One: "Reverend, when a great multitude of men who were deeply devoted to the Venerable Śāriputra came to my house carrying the requisites of honor, I, on account of some business, had locked the doors and gone elsewhere. They became derisive, abusive, and critical, saying, 'In that the Householder Anāthapiṇḍada has locked the door and gone away, he has created an obstacle to our merit.' On that account, if the Blessed One would permit it, I would build a *stūpa* for the Noble Śāriputra in a suitably available place. There the great multitudes of men would be allowed to do honor as they wish."

The Blessed One said: "Therefore, Householder, with my permission, you should do it!"

Although the Blessed One had said, "with my permission, you should do it," Anāthapiṇḍada did not know how a *stūpa* should be built.

The Blessed One said: "Make four terraces in succession; then make the base for the dome; then the dome and the *harmikā* and the crowning pole; then, having made one or two or three or four umbrellas, make up to thirteen, and place a rain receptacle on the top of the pole."

Although the Blessed One had said that a *stūpa* of this sort was to be made, because Anāthapiṇḍada did not know if a *stūpa* of such a form was to be made for only the Noble Śāriputra or also for all Noble Ones, the monks asked the Blessed One concerning this matter, and the Blessed One said: "Householder, in regard to the *stūpa* of a Tathāgata, a person should complete all parts. In regard to the *stūpa* of a Solitary Buddha, the rain receptacle should not be put in place; for an Arhat, there are four umbrellas; for One Who Does Not Return, three; for One Who Returns, two; for One Who Has Entered the Stream, one. For ordinary good monks, the *stūpa* is to be made plain."

The Blessed One had said, "In regard to a *stūpa* for the Noble Ones it has this form, for ordinary men this," but Anāthapiṇḍada did not know by whom and in which place they were to be made. The Blessed One said: "As Śāriputra and Maudgalyāyana sat when the Tathāgata was seated, just so the *stūpa* of one who has passed away into final *nirvāṇa* is also to be placed. Moreover, in regard to the *stūpas* of each individual Elder, they are to be arranged according to seniority. Those for ordinary monks are to be placed outside the monastic complex."

The Householder Anāthapiṇḍada said: "If the Blessed One were to give permission, I will celebrate festivals of the *stūpa* of the Noble Śāriputra."

The Blessed One said: "Householder, with permission, you should do it!"

Prasenajit, the King of Kośala, had heard how, when the Householder Anā[494]thapiṇḍada asked of the Blessed One permission to institute a festival of the *stūpa* of the Noble Śāriputra, the Blessed One had permitted its institution. Prasenajit, having thought, "It is excellent! I too should help in that," and having had the bell sounded, proclaimed: "Sirs, city dwellers who live in Śrāvastī, and the multitudes of men who have come together from other places, hear this: 'At the time when the festival of the *stūpa* of the Venerable Śāriputra occurs, for those who have come bringing merchandise there is to be no tax, no toll, nor transportation fee. Therefore, they must be allowed to pass freely here!'"

At that time five hundred overseas traders who had made a great deal of money from their ships arrived at Śrāvastī. They heard then how the king, sounding the bell in Śrāvastī, had ordered, "Whoever, at the time when the festival of the *stūpa* of the Noble Śāriputra occurs, comes bringing merchandise, for them there is to be no tax, no toll, nor transportation fee. Therefore, they must be allowed to pass freely here!" Some thought to themselves: "This king abides in the fruit of his own merit but is still not satisfied with his merit. Since gifts given produce merit, why should we not give gifts and make merit?" Becoming devout in mind, on the occasion of that festival they gave tortoise shells and precious stones and pearls and so on.

The monks, however, did not know how to proceed in regard to these things.

The Blessed One said: "Those gifts that are the 'first fruit' offerings are to be given to the 'Image that Sits in the Shade of the Jambu Tree.' Moreover, a small part is to be put aside for the repair of the *stūpa* of Śāriputra. The remainder is to be divided by the assembly of monks—this is not for a *stūpa* of the Tathāgata, this is for a *stūpa* of Śāriputra: therefore one does not commit a fault in this case."

V. The Death of a Monk Who Was Excessively Attached to His Bowl

This took place in Śrāvastī. A certain monk was afflicted with illness, was suffering, seriously ill, overcome by pain. His bowl was lovely, and he was excessively attached to it.

He said to the attendant monk: "Bring my bowl!" The attendant did not give it to him. The sick monk, having become angry in regard to the attendant, died attached to his bowl.

He was reborn as a poisonous snake in that same bowl.

The monks, after carrying his body to the burning ground, after performing the funeral rites, returned to the monastery.

The monks assembled. The belongings of the deceased were set up on the senior's end of the assembly by the distributor-of-robes. At that moment the Blessed One addressed the Venerable Ānanda:

"Go, Ānanda! Declare to the monks: 'No one should loosen the bowl-bag of that deceased monk. The Tathāgata alone will loosen it.'" [495]

The Venerable Ānanda told the monks. After that the Tathāgata himself loosened it. The poisonous snake, having made a great hood, held its ground.

Then the Blessed One, having aroused it with the sound *ṛvraṭā*, harnessed it. "Go!" he said, "you stupid fellow. Give up this bowl! The monks must make a distribution!"

That snake was furious. He slithered off into a dense forest. There he was burnt up by the fire of anger, and that dense forest burst into flames. Because at the moment when he was consumed by the flames he was angry with the monks, he was reborn in the hells.

Then the Blessed One addressed the monks: "You, monks, must be disgusted with all existence, must be disgusted with all the causes of existence and rebirth. Here, indeed, the body of one person was burnt up on three different occasions: in the dense forest by the fire of anger; in hell by an inhabitant of hell; in the burning ground by a low-caste man. Therefore, a monk should not form excessive attachment in regard to a possession. That to which such an attachment arises is to be discarded. If one does not discard it, he comes to be guilty of an offense. But if a sick person asks for one of his own belongings, it should indeed be very quickly given to him by the attendant monk. If one does not give it, he comes to be guilty of an offense."

VI. Undertaking Acts of Worship for Sick or Dying Fellow Monks

At that time a monk was afflicted with illness, was suffering, seriously ill. He was little known; there was no medicine for him. Realizing the nature of his condition, he said to the attendant monk: "There is nothing that can be done for me. You must perform worship for my sake!"

The attendant monk promised, but the sick monk died. He was reborn in the hells.

Then the Blessed One addressed the monks: "Monks, the monk who died, what did he say to the attendant monk?"

They related the situation as it had occurred.

"Monks, that deceased monk has fallen into a bad state. If his fellow monks had performed worship to the Three Precious Things, his mind would have been pious. Therefore, a monk should never ignore a sick fellow monk. An attendant should be given to him. When he asks for it, if there is no medicine for him, a donor is to be solicited by the attendant monk. If that succeeds, it is good. But if it does not succeed, what belongs to the Community is to be given. If that succeeds, it is good. If it does not succeed, that which belongs to the Buddha's permanent endowment is to be given. But if that too does not succeed, an umbrella or banner or flag or ornament on a shrine of a Tathāgata, or in the Perfume Chamber, which is to be preserved by the Community, is to be made use of. After selling it, the attendant monk should look after him and perform worship to the Teacher. [496] To a monk who has recovered this is to be said: 'What belongs to the Buddha was used for you.' If that monk has any means, he, making every effort, should use it for repayment. If he has none, in regard to that used for him it is said: 'The belongings of the father are likewise for the son. Here there should be no remorse.'"

VII. The Death and Property of the Monk Upananda

When he died, the Monk Upananda had a large quantity of gold—three hundred thousands of gold: one hundred thousand from bowls and robes; a second hundred thousand from medicines for the sick; a third hundred thousand from worked and unworked gold. Government officials heard about it. They reported it to the king, saying: "Lord, the Noble One Upananda has died. He had a large quantity of gold—three hundred thousands of gold. We await your orders in regard to that!"

The king said: "If it is so, go! Seal his residential cell!"

The monks, having taken up Upananda's body, had gone to the cremation.

The government officials came and sealed Upananda's cell.

After having performed the funeral ceremonies for him at the cremation ground, the monks returned to the monastery. They saw the cell sealed with the seal of the king. The monks asked the Blessed One concerning this matter. On that occasion the Blessed One said this to the Venerable Ānanda: "Go, Ānanda! In my name, ask King Prasenajit concerning his health, and speak thus: 'Great King, when you had governmental business, did you then consult the Monk Upananda? Or when you took a wife or gave a daughter, did you then consult Upananda? Or at sometime during his life, did you present Upananda with the standard belongings of a monk—robes, bowls, bedding and seats, and medicine for the sick? Or when he was ill, did you attend him?' If he were to answer no, this is to be said: 'Great King, the affairs of the house of householders are one thing; those of renouncers quite another. You must have no concern! These possessions fall to the fellow monks of Upananda. You must not acquiesce to their removal!"

Saying "Yes, Reverend," Ānanda, having understood the Blessed One, approached Prasenajit, the King of Kośala. Having approached, he spoke as he had been instructed.

The King said: "Reverend Ānanda, as the Blessed One orders, just so it must be! I do not acquiesce to their removal."

The Venerable Ānanda then reported to the Blessed One the answer of the king.

Then the Blessed One addressed the monks: "Monks, you must divide the estate left by the Monk Upananda!" Having brought it into the midst of the community, having sold it, the monks divided the return. But the monks from Sāketā heard it said: "Upananda has died. He had a great quantity of [497] gold—three hundred thousands of gold—which was divided by the monks." Making great haste, the monks of Sāketā went to Śrāvastī. They said: "We too were fellow monks of the Reverend Upananda. The possessions belonging to him fall to us as well!"

Having reassembled the estate, the monks of Śrāvastī divided it again together with the monks of Sāketā. The same thing happened with monks from six great cities, since monks from Vaiśālī, Vārāṇasi, Rājagṛha, and Campā also came. The monks, having reassembled the estate on each occasion, divided it. Reassembling and dividing the estate, the monks neglected their exposition, reading, training, and mental focus.

The monks asked the Blessed One concerning this matter.

The Blessed One said: "There are five occasions for the distribution of possessions; which five? The gong, the Three Sections (*tridaṇḍaka*), the shrine, the counting sticks, and the formal motion is the fifth. He who, when the gong for the dead is being beaten, comes—to him a portion is to be given. It is the same when the Three Sections (*tridaṇḍaka*) is being recited, when the shrine is being honored, when counting sticks are being distributed, when a formal motion is being made. Therefore, in the last case, monks, after making a formal motion in regard to all the estate, it is to be divided. The formal motion should be a fixed procedure and should be done in this way: having made a provision of seats and bedding . . . and so forth, as before, up to . . . when the entire community is seated and assembled, having placed the estate of the deceased at the senior's end of the assembly, a single monk seated at the senior's end should make a formal motion: 'Reverends, the Community should hear this! In this parish the Monk Upananda has died. This estate here, both visible and invisible, is his. If the Community would allow that the proper time has come, the Community should give consent, to wit: that the Community should take formal possession of the goods of the deceased Monk Upananda, both visible and invisible, as an estate of the deceased—this is the motion.' This, monks, is the last occasion for the distribution of the estate of the deceased—that is to say, the formal motion. A monk who comes when this motion has already been made is not to be given a portion."

The Venerable Upāli asked the Buddha, the Blessed One: "Wherever, Reverend, there is no one who makes a motion through lack of agreement in the Community—is an estate to be divided there?"

The Blessed One said: "It is not to be divided—Upāli, after having performed 'the first and last,' it is to be distributed."

But the monks did not know what 'the first and last' was.

The Blessed One said: "After selling as a unit the deceased's belongings, and then giving a little to the seniormost of the Community and to the juniormost of the Community, it is to be distributed agreeably. There is in that case no cause for remorse. When a formal motion has been made, or 'the first and last,' then the possessions belonging to the estate of a deceased monk fall to all pupils of the Buddha." [498]

VIII. The Death and Distribution of the Estate of a Shaven-Headed Householder

This took place in Śrāvastī. At that time in Śrāvastī there was a householder named Śreṣṭhin who was rich, had great wealth, possessed much property, whose holdings were extensive and wide, and who possessed the wealth of Vaiśravaṇa, equaled in wealth Vaiśravaṇa. He took a wife from a similar family. Being sonless but wanting a son, he supplicated Śiva and Varuṇa and Kubera and Śakra and Brahmā, and so on, and a variety of other gods, such as the gods of parks, the gods of the forest, the gods of the crossroads, the gods of forks in the road, and the gods who seize offerings. He even supplicated the gods who are born together with individuals, share their nature, and follow constantly behind them. It is, of course, the popular belief in the world that by reason of supplication sons and daughters are born. But that is not so. If it were so everyone—like the wheel-turning king—would have a thousand sons. In fact, sons and daughters are born from the presence of three conditions. What three? Both the mother and the father are aroused and have coupled; the mother, being healthy, is fertile; and a *gandharva* is standing by. From the presence of these three conditions, sons and daughters are born.

But when there was neither son nor daughter even through his propitiation of the gods, then, having repudiated all gods, the householder became pious in regard to the Blessed One. Eventually he approached a monk: "Noble One," he said, "I wish to enter the Order of this well-spoken Dharma and Vinaya."

"Do so, good sir!" said the monk, and in due order, after shaving the householder's head, he began to give him the rules of training. But the householder was overcome with a serious fever that created an obstacle to his entering the Order.

The monks reported this matter to the Blessed One.

The Blessed One said: "He must be attended to, but the rules of training are not to be given until he is again healthy."

Although the Blessed One had said that he was to be attended to, the monks did not know by whom this was to be done.

The Blessed One said: "By the monks."

The doctors treated the man during the day, but at night his debility grew worse. They said: "Nobles, we treat him during the day, but at night his debility grows worse. If he were taken home we could treat him at night as well."

The monks reported this matter to the Blessed One.

The Blessed One said: "He should be taken home, but there too you must give him an attendant!"

His debility turned out to be of long duration. His hair grew longer and longer. It was in regard to him that the designation "shaven-headed householder, shaven-headed householder" arose.

When he did not get better although treated with medicines made from

[499] roots, stalks, leaves, flowers, and fruits, then, realizing the nature of his condition, he said, "I am dead." After that, at the time of death, he made a written will containing all the personal wealth belonging to him and sent it to the Grove of Jeta. And he died.

His government officials reported to Prasenajit, the King of Kośala: "Lord, a shaven-headed householder without a son has died, and he had a great deal of gold and silver, elephants, horses, cows, buffaloes, and equipment. Having made a written will containing all of that, it was sent to Jeta's Grove for the Noble Community."

The king said: "Even in the absence of a written will, I did not obtain the possessions of the Noble Upananda; how much less will I obtain such goods when there is a written will. But what the Blessed One will authorize, that I will accept."

The monks reported this matter to the Blessed One.

The Blessed One said: "Monks, what is there in this case?" The monks fully described the estate.

The Blessed One said: "It is to be divided according to circumstances. Therein, property consisting of land, property consisting of houses, property consisting of shops, bedding and seats, a vessel made by an ironworker, a vessel made by a coppersmith, a vessel made by a potter—excepting a waterpot and a container—a vessel made by a woodworker, a vessel made by a canesplitter, female and male slaves, servants and laborers, food and drink, and grains—these are not to be distributed but to be set aside as property in common for the Community of Monks from the Four Directions.

"Cloths, large pieces of cotton cloth, a vessel of hide, shoes, leather oil bottles, waterpots, and water jars are to be distributed among the entire Community.

"Those poles that are long are to be made into banner poles for the 'Image that Sits in the Shade of the Jambu Tree.' Those that are quite small, having been made into staffs, are to be given to the monks.

"Sons and daughters are not to be sold at will within the Community, but when they have gained piety, they are to be released.

"Of quadrupeds, the elephants, horses, camels, donkeys, and mules are for the use of the king. Buffaloes, goats, and sheep are property in common for the Community of Monks from the Four Directions and are not to be distributed.

"And what armor and so forth is suitable for the king, all that is to be handed over to the king, except for weapons. The latter, when made into knives, needles, and staffs, are to be handed out within the Community.

"Of pigments, the great pigments, yellow, vermilion, blue, and so on are to be put in the Perfumed Chamber to be used for the image. Khaṃkhaṭika, red, and dark blue are to be distributed among the Community.

"Spirituous liquor, having been mixed with roasted barley, is to be buried in the ground. Turned into vinegar, it is to be used. Except as vinegar it is not [500] to be used but is to be thrown away. Monks, by those who recognize me as Teacher spirituous liquor must neither be given nor drunk—even as little as could be held on the tip of a blade of grass.

"Medicines are to be deposited in a hall suitable for the sick. Thence they are to be used by monks who are ill.

"Of precious jewels—except for pearls—the gems, lapis lazuli, and conch shells with spirals turning to the right are to be divided into two lots: one for the Dharma; a second for the Community. With that which belongs to the Dharma, the word of the Buddha is to be copied, and it is to be used as well on the lion seat. That which belongs to the Community is to be distributed among the monks.

"Of books, books of the word of the Buddha are not to be distributed but to be deposited in the storehouse as property in common for the Community of Monks from the Four Directions. The books containing the treatises of non-Buddhists are to be sold, and the sum received is to be distributed among the monks.

"Any written lien that can be quickly realized—the share of the money from that is to be distributed among the monks. And that which is not able to be so realized is to be deposited in the storehouse as property in common for the Community of Monks from the Four Directions.

"Gold and coined gold and other, both worked and unworked, are to be divided into three lots: one for the Buddha; a second for the Dharma; a third for the Community. With that which belongs to the Buddha repairs and maintenance on the Perfumed Chamber and on the *stūpas* of the hair and nails are to be made. With that belonging to the Dharma the word of the Buddha is to be copied or it is to be used on the lion seat. That which belongs to the Community is to be distributed among the monks."

IX. Monastic Rules Expressed in Story: The Death and Funeral of a Rich Monk in the *Avadānaśataka*

The Buddha, the Blessed One, honored, revered, adored, and worshiped by kings, chief ministers, wealthy men, city dwellers, guild masters, traders, by gods, *nāgas*, *yakṣas*, *asuras*, *garuḍas*, *kiṃnaras*, and *mahoragas*, celebrated by gods and *nāgas* and *yakṣas* and *asuras* and *garuḍas* and *kiṃnaras*, and *mahoragas*, the Buddha, the Blessed One, widely known and of great merit, the recipient of the requisites, of robes, bowls, bedding, seats, and medicines for illness, he, together with the community of disciples, dwelt in Śrāvastī, in Jeta's Grove, in the Park of Anāthapiṇḍadā.

In Śrāvastī there was a guild master who was rich, had great wealth, possessed much property, possessed the wealth of Vaiśravaṇa, equaled in wealth Vaiśravaṇa. He on one occasion went to Jeta's Grove. Then he saw the Buddha, the Blessed One, fully ornamented with the thirty-two marks of the Great Man, his limbs glorious with the eighty secondary signs, ornamented with an aureole

[501] of a full fathom, an aureole that surpassed a thousand suns—like a moving mountain of gems, entirely beautiful. And after having seen him, after having worshiped at the feet of the Blessed One, he sat down in front of him to hear the Dharma. To him the Blessed One gave an exposition of the Dharma, instilling disgust with the round of rebirths. When he had heard this and had seen the faults of the round of rebirth and the qualities in *nirvāṇa*, he entered the Order of the Blessed One. When he had entered the Order, he became widely known, of great merit, approached, a recipient of the requisites, of robes, bowls, bedding, seats, and medicines for illness. He, having accepted the requisites, obtained more and more. He accumulated a hoard but did not share with his fellow monks. He, through this selfishness, which was cultivated, developed, and extended, and being obsessed with personal belongings, died and was reborn in his own cell as a hungry ghost.

Then his fellow monks, having struck the funeral gong, performed the removal of the body. Having performed the honor of the body on his body, they then returned to the monastery. When they unlatched the door of his cell and began to look for his bowl and robe, they saw that deceased monk who was now a hungry ghost, deformed in hand and foot and eye, his body totally revolting, standing there clutching his bowl and robe. Having seen him deformed like that, the monks were terrified and reported it to the Blessed One.

Then the Blessed One, for the purpose of assisting that deceased son of good family, for the purpose of instilling fear in the community of students, and for the purpose of making fully apparent the disadvantageous consequences of selfishness, went to that place, surrounded by a group of monks, at the head of the Community of monks. Then that hungry ghost saw the Buddha, the Blessed One, fully ornamented with the thirty-two marks of the Great Man, his limbs glorious with eighty secondary signs, ornamented with an aureole of a full fathom, an aureole that surpassed a thousand suns—like a moving mountain of gems, entirely beautiful—and as soon as he had seen him, piety in regard to the Blessed One arose in him. He was ashamed.

Then the Blessed One, with a voice that was deep like that of a heavy thundercloud, like that of the kettledrum, admonished the hungry ghost: "Sir, this hoarding of bowl and robe by you is conducive to your own destruction. Through it you are reborn in the hells. Indeed, your mind should be pious in regard to me! And you should turn your mind away from these belongings—lest, having died, you will next be born in the hells!"

Then the hungry ghost gave the bowl and robe to the Community and threw himself at the Blessed One's feet, declaring his fault. Then the Blessed One assigned the reward in the name of the hungry ghost: "What, indeed, is the merit from this gift—may that go to the hungry ghost! May he quickly rise from the dreadful world of hungry ghosts!"

Then that hungry ghost, having in mind become pious toward the Blessed One, died and was reborn among the hungry ghosts of great wealth. Then the hungry ghost of great wealth, wearing trembling and bright earrings, his limbs [502] glittering with ornaments of various kinds, having a diadem of many-colored gems and his limbs smeared with saffron and tamāla leaves and spṛkka, having that very night filled his skirt with divine blue lotuses and red lotuses and white lotuses and mandāra flowers, having suffused the whole of Jeta's Grove with blinding light, having covered the Blessed One with flowers, sat down in front of the Blessed One for the sake of hearing the Dharma. And the Blessed One gave him an appropriate exposition of the Dharma. Having heard it and become pious, he departed.

The monks remained engaged in the practice of wakefulness throughout the entire night. They saw the blinding light around the Blessed One, and having seen it—being unsure—they asked the Blessed One: "Blessed One, did Brahmā, the Lord of the World of Men, or Śakra, the Leader of the Gods, or the Four Guardians of the World approach in the night for having the sight (*darśana*) of the Blessed One?"

The Blessed One said: "Monks, it was not Brahmā, the Lord of the World of Men, nor Śakra, the Leader of the Gods, nor even the Four Guardians of the World who approached for having sight of me. But it was that hungry ghost who, having died, was reborn among the hungry ghosts of great wealth. In the night he came into my presence. To him I gave an exposition of the Dharma. He, becoming pious, departed. Therefore, monks, work now toward getting rid of selfishness. Practice, monks, so that these faults of the guild master who became a hungry ghost will thus not arise for you."

This the Blessed One said. Delighted, the monks and others—*devas, asuras, garuḍas, kiṃnaras, mahoragas*, and so on—rejoiced in what the Blessed One spoke.

CHAPTER V

Dead Monks and Bad Debts

Some Provisions of a Buddhist Monastic Inheritance Law

DEBT WAS A MAJOR concern it seems for those brahmins who wrote or redacted both ancient and classical Indian religious and legal texts. It was a central piece of brahmanical anthropology—Patrick Olivelle, discussing what he, following Charles Malamoud, calls "the theology of debt" in Vedic literature, says that "the very existence, the very birth of a man creates his condition of indebtedness," and Malamoud had already said: "In the same way as the notion of debt is already there, fully formed, in the oldest texts, so does fundamental debt affect man and define him from the moment he is born."[1] Both are of course, at least in part, alluding to the famous passage in the *Taittirīya Saṃhitā* (6.3.10.5), which says: "A Brahmin, at his very birth, is born with a triple debt—of studentship to the seers, of sacrifice to the gods, of offspring to the fathers."[2]

Brahmanical literature was not, however, concerned only with man's religious or anthropological debt—it was equally occupied with real financial debt, and often the two sorts of debt are tightly entangled. Typical of the legal concern with debt is the *Nāradasmṛti*, "the only original collection of legal maxims (*mūlasmṛti*) which is purely juridical in character."[3] The first and by far the longest of its chapters dealing with "titles of law" (*vyavahārapadāni*) is devoted to "nonpayment of debt" (*ṛṇādānam*). It contains 224 verses. By comparison, the second-longest chapter, the chapter dealing with "relations between men and women" (*strīpuṃsayoga*), covers what one might have thought was a far broader range of issues but consists of only 117 verses; and the thorny issue of "partition of inheritance" (*dāyābhāga*) is treated in only 49 verses. A preoccupation with legal debt and the recovery of debt is moreover by no means limited to *Nārada*, as a glance at modern works like Chatterjee's *The Law of Debt in Ancient India* will show: the topic was similarly

---

Originally published in *Indo-Iranian Journal* 44 (2001) 99–148. Reprinted with stylistic changes with permission of Kluwer Academic Publishers.

addressed by previous *śāstrakāras* and by those who followed him, and it also forms a significant part of almost all the "digests," or *nibandhas*.[4]

Given the length to which *Nārada* pursues the topic, it is probably not surprising that we find reference in his discussion—and that fairly early on (I.7)—to ascetics who die in debt. Even though we do not often think of [100] Indian ascetics as having or entering into contractual obligations, *Nārada* says:

> *tapasvī câgnihotrī ca ṛṇavān mriyate yadi* /
> *tapaś caivâgnihotraṃ ca sarvaṃ tad dhaninām dhanam* //

which Richard Lariviere translates as

> If an ascetic or an agnihotrin dies in debt, all of the merit from his austerities and sacrifices belongs to his creditors.[5]

The exact status of the *tapasvin*, or "ascetic," here is of course not clear, and the reference to debts may refer to debts incurred or contracted before the individual undertook the practices of an ascetic. But that is not stated to have been the case. A little clearer perhaps is *Viṣṇu* 6.27: "*Viṣṇu* is explicit on this point: when a debtor dies or renounces [*pravrajita*] or is away in a distant land for twenty years, his sons and grandsons should settle the debt"; and, as Olivelle notes, *Kātyāyana* makes a similar statement.[6] Care, however, is probably best taken not to exclude the possibility that "ascetics" and/or "renouncers" were not as socially dead as some of the prescriptive texts make out. Some of these same texts contain explicit rules governing the inheritance of a deceased renouncer's property even though he was not supposed to have any—Olivelle in fact says that "the civil death of the renouncer makes him incapable of owning property."[7] Some Indian *vinaya* literature would seem to require that such questions be left open or, at the least, problematizes the civil status of both Buddhist monks and Indian renouncers and the relationship, or comparability, of the two.[8] "Some" here, however, is the operable term.

There has been a marked tendency even in scholarly literature to refer to "the *Vinaya*," as if there were only one, when in fact the actual reference is only to the Pāli *Vinaya*. This is a habit that should not be encouraged for any number of good reasons, not the least of which is that there are a half a dozen other extant *vinayas*. Moreover, the relationship of the Pāli *Vinaya* to Indian practice may not be as clear and straightforward as has been unquestionably assumed,[9] and the citation of it alone is certainly distortive, as can be seen in a case that is particularly germane to our topic. Chatterjee, for example, has said with some confidence: "The entanglement and anxieties of debt as well as corporate liability belonging to communistic life in a religious order rendered it necessary to debar any candidate from admission to the *saṅgha* who was a debtor (*Vinaya*, I.76)."[10] The only evidence actually cited for this global assertion is, of course, the Pāli *Vinaya*, and the latter does indeed contain a prohibition against ordaining debtors (*na bhikkhave iṇāyiko pabbājetabbo*).[11] But—as has been pointed out elsewhere—at least the Mūlasarvāstivādin *Vinaya* [101] has a different provision: it requires that if a candidate for ordination has debts, he must make an assurance that he will be able to pay such debts *after* his ordination.[12] Neither *Vinaya*, moreover, explicitly prohibits a monk from contracting debts once he has been ordained, and as we will shortly see, the Mūlasarvāstivādin *Vinaya*—a *vinaya* with clear points of contact with early Northwest India[13]—would seem to indicate that its monks routinely did so.

The passages from the *Mūlasarvāstivāda-vinaya* that most concern us here, those which in part deal with monks who die in debt, occur in the *Uttaragrantha*, the section of this *Vinaya* that has received the least attention, and some preliminary remarks in regard to it might therefore be useful. First of all, it should be noted that as we now have it in the Tibetan translation of the *Mūlasarvāstivāda-vinaya*, there are actually two texts in this section. Both there are given the same Sanskrit title—*Vinaya-uttaragrantha*—but each has a slightly different Tibetan title: the first text has the Tibetan title *'Dul ba gzhung bla ma*; the second *'Dul ba gzhung dam pa*. *Bla ma* and *dam pa* can be close in meaning, and whereas *bla ma* is an attested equivalent of *uttara*, *dam pa* more commonly translates *uttama*.[14] The first of the two texts appears to be incomplete, and the relationship between the two has yet to be fully worked out. Neither appears to have been preserved in Sanskrit.

Although there are then serious unanswered questions about the textual history of this section of the *Mūlasarvāstivāda-vinaya*, its importance—judged by almost any standard—is much less in doubt, and it is already clear that one of the few published general characterizations of it is widely off the mark. A. C. Banerjee says: "The *Vinaya-uttara-grantha*, just like the Pāli *Parivāra*, is an appendix to the *Vinaya*. This work tells us nothing new; it is only an abridgement of the *Vinaya* texts."[15] Nothing, however, could be further from the truth: it is in no sense an abridgement of the *Vinaya*, and most of what it contains is either found nowhere else or appears to be the basis or an earlier version of what is found elsewhere in this *Vinaya*. For example, the *Śayanāsana-*, *Pārivāsika-*, and *Kṣudrakavastus* of the *Mūlasarvāstivāda-vinaya* all take for granted that the date must be formally announced every day in a Mūlasarvāstivādin monastery, and that each day verses must be recited for the monastery's "donor" or owner, but the rule requiring both is found only in the *Uttaragrantha*.[16] Or—to cite an example closer to the topic at hand here—the *Cīvaravastu* twice refers to liquidating a deceased monk's estate by sale in the midst of the assembled community, but the "origin tale" and rule requiring this procedure are, again, found only in the *Uttaragrantha*, and the detailed rules governing the "auction" by which the sale is handled are also unique [102] to it.[17] It is already clear that this sort of pattern repeatedly occurs, but the apparent priority of texts in the *Uttaragrantha* may also be detected in another pattern as well.

There are, to be sure, instances where a version of a text found in the *Uttaragrantha* occurs elsewhere in the *Mūlasarvāstivāda-vinaya*, or a topic treated in the *Uttara* is similarly treated in some other *vastu* or section, but these are almost never exact doublets and often there is at least some indication suggesting the priority of the version in the *Uttara*. Both the *Kṣudrakavastu* and the *Uttara*, for example, have a similar text dealing with a monk's continuing right to inherit family property even after he is ordained, but—as I have pointed out elsewhere—the version found in the *Kṣudraka* has a reference to the monk's "foster mother," which makes no sense there and could only have been taken over from the version of the text found in the *Uttara*, where it also occurs and makes perfectly natural narrative sense.[18] Likewise, both the *Vinayavibhaṅga* and the *Uttaragrantha* have texts dealing with permanent endowments or perpetuities whose funds are to be lent out on interest. But whereas in the *Vibhaṅga* these loans are to be made and serviced by the monks themselves, in the *Uttara* it is explicitly said that this is to be done by a monastery's factotum (*ārāmika*) or a lay-brother (*upāsaka*), suggesting perhaps a far greater fastidiousness on the part of the *Uttara* in regard to the open engagement of monks in commercial matters, at least in this case.[19]

These sorts of patterns pointing toward the priority or importance of the *Uttaragrantha* can also be detected even beyond the boundaries of the *vinaya* proper. In recent years the Mūlasarvāstivādin affiliation of the *Avadānaśataka*, for example, has become increasingly clear, and it is even beginning to appear that the *Avadānaśataka*—like the *Divyāvadāna*—is heavily dependent on this *Vinaya*. Michael Hahn, for example, has already pointed out that the *Mūlasarvāstivāda-vinaya* has versions of both the *Śaśa* and *Dharmagaveṣin Avadānas*, which are very close to those now found in the *Avadānaśataka* (nos. 37 and 38). He says: "Except for a few redactional changes which became necessary because of the different frame stories, the Tibetan texts of the MSV *Vinaya* point to a wording which is absolutely identical with that of the *Avadānaśataka*." He goes on to say—quite rightly, I think—that "in principle, borrowing in either direction is possible, although in this particular case it seems to be more likely that the redactors of the *Avadānaśataka* extracted the two legends from the MSV *Vinaya* and furnished it with the standardized frame they used throughout their work."[20] Professor Hahn's observations are particularly relevant here, of course, because they could just as easily be describing two other texts also in the *Avadānaśataka*. Both the *Maitrakanyaka* and the [103] *Śrīmatī Avadānas*—numbers 36 and 54 in the *Avadānaśataka*—also have close parallels in the *Mūlasarvāstivāda-vinaya*, and in these cases too "the Tibetan texts of the MSV *Vinaya* point to a wording which is absolutely identical with that of the

Avadānaśataka." But whereas in one of Hahn's cases the redactors of the *Avadānaśataka* appear to have borrowed from the *Bhaiṣajyavastu*, and in the other they appear to have gotten their text from the *Kṣudrakavastu*, both the *Maitrakanyaka* and the *Śrīmatī* almost certainly were taken from the *Uttaragrantha*.[21]

A final consideration concerning the importance of the *Uttaragrantha* is related to the apparent use made of it by Guṇaprabha in his remarkable *Vinayasūtra*. The sources of Guṇaprabha's individual *sūtras* can—especially with the help of Bu ston—usually be identified with a reasonable degree of certainty, and a large number of them turn out to be based on the *Uttaragrantha*. This will be clear, perhaps, even if we limit ourselves to a single example that is particularly germane to our topic. In his sixth chapter, headed *Cīvaravastu*, Guṇaprabha has a series of *sūtras* dealing with what can only be called Mūlasarvāstivādin monastic inheritance law. According to the commentaries and Bu ston's equally remarkable *'Dul ba pha'i gleng 'bum chen mo*,[22] it would appear that these *sūtras* are based on and are digesting at least twenty-five separate canonical texts or passages. The sequence and distribution of these canonical passages is interesting and indicative of Guṇaprabha's working methods. Both can be clearly seen in the following table, which lists the canonical passages in the order in which Guṇaprabha treats them:

i.	*Uttaragrantha*—Derge	Pa 85a.3–86a.2	Bu ston	290a.2–.3[23]
ii.		Pa 86a.2–.6		290a.3–.5
iii.		Pa 86a.6–b.4		290a.5–.6
iv.		Pa 86b.4–.7		290a.6–.7
v.		Pa 86b.7–.87a.4		290a.7–b.1
		(i–v continuous)		
vi.	*Cīvaravastu*—GMs iii 2,	113.14–117.4		290b.1–291a.1
vii.		117.8–122.20		291a.1–292a.2
	(vi–vii, an *uddāna* intervenes, otherwise continuous)			
viii.	*Uttaragrantha*—Derge	Pa 88a.1–.2		292a.1
ix.	*Cīvaravastu*—GMs iii 2,	143.15–145.12		292a.1–.7
x.		147.10–148.20		292a.7–b.4 [104]
xi.		146.7–147.9		292b.4–.6
xii.		126.17–127.18		292b.6–293a.3
xiii.	*Uttaragrantha*—Derge	Pa 87a.4–.6		293a.3–.4
xiv.		Pa 132b.2–.7		293a.4–.7
xv.		Pa 132b.7–133a.3		293a.7–b.2
xvi.		Pa 133a.3–b.1		293b.2–.4
xvii.		Pa 133b.1–.4		293b.4–.5
xviii.		Pa 133b.4–134a.1		293b.5–.7
		(xiv–xviii continuous)		
xix.	*Cīvaravastu*—GMs iii 2,	145.13–146.6		293b.7–294a.2
xx.		122.20–123.15		294a.2–.5

xxi.	*Uttaragrantha*—Derge	Na 261a.1–.5	294a.5–.7
xxii.	*Cīvaravastu*—GMs iii 2,	124.1–.10	294a.7–b.2
xxiii.	*Kṣudrakavastu*—Derge	Tha 252b.3–254a.1	294b.2–.6
xxiv.	*Uttaragrantha*—Derge	Pa 130a.4–131a.3	294b.6–295a.1
xxv.	*Cīvaravastu*—GMs iii 2,	139.6–143.14	295a.1–.3

Several things are fairly obvious from this table. First, bearing in mind that the *sūtras* in the *Vinayasūtra* that digest this canonical material cover only a little more than a single large page of printed Devanāgarī in Sankrityayana's edition (thirty-five lines), it is clear that Guṇaprabha has packed a great deal—material that covers nearly ten folios, or twenty pages, of printed Tibetan, plus more than twenty printed pages of Devanāgarī in Dutt's edition of the *Cīvaravastu*—into a small space. It is equally clear that Guṇaprabha does not present his material in anything like its canonical order. He starts by summarizing in sequential order material that covers two leaves of the *Uttara*, the last section of the canonical *Vinaya*; then he summarizes, again in sequential order, material that covers nine pages of the *Cīvaravastu*, which is the sixth or seventh subsection of the first section in the canonical *Vinaya*;[24] then he jumps back to a two-line text in the *Uttara*; then back again to a block of material from the *Cīvara*, which he presents completely out of order; then again back to a block of material—this time presented in sequence—from the *Uttara*; and so on.[25] But though our table provides what might well turn out to be some good indications of Guṇaprabha's general working methods, perhaps the most important thing it shows for our immediate purposes is the significant place that the *Uttaragrantha* has in Guṇaprabha's understanding and presentation [105] of the rules governing Mūlasarvāstivādin monasticism: his presentation of Mūlasarvāstivādin inheritance law, while it makes considerable use of the *Cīvaravastu*, starts with the *Uttaragrantha*, implicitly indicating what is confirmed by the canonical text itself, that the foundational ruling for all the rest is found there. Although the *Cīvaravastu* served as the basis for many of Guṇaprabha's *sūtras* and ten of the identifiable texts he used come from it, fourteen are from the *Uttaragrantha*. The latter, therefore, could hardly have been considered by him as a mere "appendix" or "abridgement" that contained nothing not found elsewhere. To judge by this example—and there are many more like it—the *Uttaragrantha* must have been considered an integral, an important, and in many instances a foundational part of the *Mūlasarvāstivāda-vinaya*.

Our table, moreover, shows at least one other important thing as well. Because almost all of the texts that we are about to discuss dealing with debt and the death of a monk are included in the list of Guṇaprabha's sources—they are numbers xiv through xvii—it is clear that, at least as Guṇaprabha saw it, they are a part of a larger "system" of Mūlasarvāstivādin monastic inheritance law and by no means isolated or anomalous rulings that had no continuing influence. Once these rulings were enshrined in Guṇaprabha's *Vinayasūtra*, moreover, they were ensured a continuing long life in it, in the bulky commentarial tradition that quickly grew up around it, and on into the Tibetan exegetical tradition.[26]

The texts in the *Uttaragrantha* that deal with private debt and the death of a monk are typical of many other sets of texts there. They are all short and similarly structured; their narrative frame is lean and repetitive; they follow one another in a sequential order; and they deal with one issue at a time. Because these texts are little known, an edition of the Tibetan text will be given first, followed by a translation. The Tibetan texts are based on the three Kanjurs that are available to me: the Tog Palace Manuscript Kanjur (= Tog); the Derge Xylograph (= Derge); and the Peking Edition (= Peking). I reproduce the "punctuation" that is found in Tog.[27]

II. (= xiv)

Tog Na 190b.3–191a.4 = Derge Pa 132b.2–.7 = Peking Phe 129a.3–b.1

sangs rgyas bcom ldan 'das mnyan du yod pa'i dze ta'i tshal mgon med zas sbyin gyi kun dga'[1] *ra ba na bzhugs so /* [106]

dge slong gzhan zhig gis[2] *khyim bdag cig las kar sha pa ṇa*[3] *zhig bskyis ba dang / de dus kyi mtha' zhig tu ci*[4] *zhig gis dus 'das nas / dge slong de ji ltar dus*[5] *'das pa khyim bdag des thos so / dge slong de ji ltar dus 'das pa khyim bdag des thos nas / gtsug lag khang du song ste / shes bzhin du dge slong dag la dris pa / 'phags pa 'di zhes bgyi ba'i dge slong de gang na mchis /*

de dag gis smras pa / bzhin bzangs dus 'das so /

'phags pa[6] *des bdag gi kar sha pa ṇa*[3] *zhig bskyis te 'tshal lo*[7] */*

bzhin bzangs de ni dur khrod du bskyal gyis der song ste dos shig /

'phags pa khyed kyis de'i lhung bzed dang chos gos bgos na bdag gis ji ltar dur khrod du song ste bda' / khyed[8] *kyis stsol*[9] *cig ces smras pa dang / de ltar gyur pa dge slong rnams kyis bcom ldan 'das la gsol nas / bcom ldan 'das kyis bka' stsal pa / dge slong dag khyim bdag des ni legs par smras te / de'i nor las bskyis pa dge slong dag gis byin cig /*

de dag gis gang nas sbyin pa mi shes nas / bcom ldan 'das kyis bka' stsal pa / de'i lhung bzed dang chos gos yod pa las byin cig /

dge slong de dag gis lhung bzed dang chos gos de dag byin pa dang / chos gos dang lhung bzed[10] *de dag ma 'dod nas / bcom ldan 'das kyis bka' stsal pa / tshongs la byin cig /*

dge slong dag gis de dag thams cad byin no /

bcom ldan 'das kyis bka' stsal pa / ji tsam blangs pa de tsam du byin la lhag ma bgos shig /

The Buddha, the Blessed One, was staying in the Park of Anāthapiṇḍada, in the Jetavana of Śrāvastī.

1. Peking: *dga'i*. 2. Tog: omits *gis*, but cf. II. 3. Derge: *kār shā pa ṇa*. 4. Tog: *ji*. 5. Peking: *du*. 6. Peking: omits *pa*. 7. Derge, Peking: *to*. 8. Derge, Peking: *khyod*. 9. Peking: *sol*. 10. Derge, Peking: *lhung bzed dang chos gos*, reversing the items.

A certain monk had borrowed some money from a householder, and when his time had come and he had died of something, that householder heard how that monk had died. When that householder had heard how that monk had died, he went to the *vihāra* and—although he knew—asked the monks: "Noble Ones, where is that monk named so-and-so?"

"He, sir, is dead," they said.

"Noble Ones, he borrowed some of my money and I want it."

"Well, sir, since he has been carried out to the cremation grounds, you will just have to go there and collect!"

"When you, Noble Ones, have already divided his bowl and robes, how am I going to go and collect in the cremation grounds? You must repay me!," he said. And when the monks reported what had occurred to the Blessed One, the Blessed One said: "That householder, monks, speaks properly, and the monks must repay the money that was borrowed from him!"

When the monks did not know from what he was to be repaid, the Blessed One said: "He must be repaid from the bowl and robes that deceased monk had!"

The monks gave him the bowl and robes, but when he did not want robes and bowls, the Blessed One said: "You must sell them and then repay him!"

The monks gave the householder all of the proceeds.

The Blessed One said: "As much as was taken, so much must be returned, and the rest must be divided!" [107]

The first thing that might be noted about this short text—the first of the series—is that although it might not always be possible to determine the exact Sanskrit vocabulary underlying its Tibetan translation, the meaning of the text on almost every important point is virtually certain. That we are dealing here with money, for example, is absolutely certain. The key term is in every case but one transliterated, not translated, and was *kārṣāpaṇa*, the designation of a coin type of variable value that is also widely used in Sanskrit to refer in general to "money, gold and silver."[28] That the monk had "borrowed" *kārṣāpaṇas* from a layman is also not in doubt. Here the Tibetan is *bskyis ba*, the past tense of *skyi ba*, and Jäschke, for example, gives under *nor*—which also occurs once in our text in place of *kārṣāpaṇa*—*nor skyi ba*, as meaning "to borrow money."[29] Likewise, the first meaning under *skyi ba* in the *Bod rgya tshig mdzod chen mo* is *dngul sogs g-yar ba*, "to borrow silver [or money], etc."[30] Lokesh Chandra's *Tibetan-Sanskrit Dictionary* gives *uddhāra* as the Sanskrit equivalent of *skyi ba*, and a form of *uddhāra* is twice translated by the closely related *skyin po* in a passage in the *Carmavastu* of the *Mūlasarvāstivāda-vinaya* that also occurs in the *Divyāvadāna*:[31] *skyin pa* means "a loan, a thing borrowed"; and both Edgerton and Cowell and Neil recognize the meaning "debt" for *uddhāra*, a meaning it also has in Pāli, though not commonly in Sanskrit. The Sanskrit equivalent for the one other important action in our text is, finally, much more straightforward. At the end of our text the monks are told, in effect, that they must liquidate the deceased monk's estate, that they must "sell" it. The Tibetan here is *tshongs*, an imperative form of *'tshong*, which is a widely and well-attested equivalent for forms from Sanskrit *vi√krī*, perhaps the most common Sanskrit term for "to sell."[32] This is, moreover, as we will see, not the only place that monks are ordered by the Buddha to do this.

But apart from matters of vocabulary, it is also worth noting here that the deceased monk's action—a monk's borrowing money from laymen—passes entirely without comment: this is not the problem, and no rule forbidding it is provided by our text or by any other that I know of.[33] The problem that our text addresses appears, ironically, not even to have been a particular concern of the general run of monks. Their cheeky response to the layman's assertion—which, as we will see, will be repeated—is nothing if not dismissive: they tell him in effect to buzz off. But although this might be well and good for individual monks, it was precisely this sort of thing that the "author" of our ruling—who we can assume speaks through the Buddha's mouth—apparently wanted to stop.

Like the authors of all Buddhist texts, whether *sūtra* or *śāstra*, our author was almost certainly not an average or typical Indian Buddhist [108] monk. Moreover, as a *vinayadhara*, or monastic lawyer, he would have had specific and specialized concerns and would have been charged, as it were, with a particular mission. Herein, of course, lay the problem. Almost everything in the *Mūlasarvāstivāda-vinaya*—and perhaps in other *vinayas* as well—suggests that its author or authors were concerned with building and maintaining an institution and therefore avoiding social criticism. This concern appears to have prompted, especially in the *Mūlasarvāstivāda-vinaya*, any number of rulings that would accommodate and bring its version of Buddhist monasticism into line with brahmanical values and concerns. A good example of this can be seen in Mūlasarvāstivādin rules governing monastic funerals.[34] Given that they deal with a related issue, it should be no surprise that the texts we are concerned with here provide another example: they too appear to have been designed to shield the institution from criticism and to bring its practice into conformity with *dharmaśāstric* law or expectation. It probably did not escape our *vinayadhara*'s notice that by doing so they would as well provide some assurance to any potential lender or creditor that a loan to a member of a Buddhist community would not go bad. This last may have been more important than we can realize, because the *Mūlasarvāstivāda-vinaya* itself contains repeated references, put in the mouth of tradesmen, that suggest that its author or authors knew that Buddhist monks had a reputation among such folk for not paying their bills. In the *Kṣudrakavastu*, for example, when a monk's bowl begins to leak and he takes it to a smith to be repaired, the latter tries to get rid of him, thinking to himself, the text says: "Although these monks commission work, they do not pay the bill" (*de dag ni khas las byed du 'jug pa yin gyi / gla rngan ni mi ster ba*). In the *Carmavastu* a cobbler says much the same sort of thing when a monk brings him his sandals to repair: "Buddhist monks want us to work, but without wages" (*śākya'i sras kyi dge slong rnams ni rngan pa med par 'chol gyis . . .*).[35] It is, of course, almost impossible to know at this distance anything certain about the relationships between Buddhist monks and Indian tradesmen. The presence of passages like these—and many others—suggests that they had them, and that such narrative criticisms occur even in Buddhist sources may suggest that such relationships were not always good. Moreover, that several of the texts in our series also deal—as we shall see—with the same relationships would seem to indicate that our *vinayadhara* thought they were in need of careful regulation.

Considerations of this kind must of course remain conjectural. What is far more certain, though, is the effect of the ruling put in place by our text, which, again, is only the first of the series. Classical "Hindu" [109] law was clear on certain aspects of the law of debt. Chatterjee, for example, says: "Gautama prescribes that those who inherit the property of a person should discharge his debt. The idea finds place in the texts of *Yājñavalkya* and *Viṣṇu*." Gautama's text is particularly elegant: *rikthabhāja ṛṇaṃ pratikuryuḥ* (xii.37).[36] Because our text explicitly indicates that, in the case it is describing, the monks had already "inherited" (*bgos na*—translating a past tense from √*bhaj*) the dead monk's estate (his "bowl and robes"), the householder's assertion ("You [monks] must repay me!") is not—in light of *Gautama* et al.—an individual claim or private opinion but the invocation of brahmanical law or expectation. When the Buddha is made to declare that "that householder . . . speaks properly," he is only saying that he speaks in conformity with *dharmaśāstra*. And when the Buddha then immediately—and, by implication, consequently—orders that the monks must repay what was borrowed, he is in fact insisting that his monks conform to brahmanical norms.

One last observation in regard to our text concerns the good business sense of this *Vinaya*'s Buddha. Although we are not told how much money the deceased monk had borrowed, the text explicitly says that when the monks liquidated his estate, they gave everything to the lay creditor, and the clear implication—especially in light of our next text—was that this was in excess of what had been borrowed. At this point the Buddha, unasked, intervenes and insists on a much more enlightened procedure that would be far more favorable to his monks: they must repay only as much as was borrowed—nothing here is said about interest even though our redactors elsewhere required monks themselves to charge interest on money that they lent, and even though *dharmaśāstric* texts have a great deal to say about it, some of which our monks appear to have known.[37]

We have, then, in our little text a good solution to a potentially serious problem. It averts social criticism of monastic practice; it brings Buddhist monastic practice into conformity with brahmanical norms; it—incidentally—might also serve to assure members of the Buddhist monastic community continuing access to credit by providing any potential lender something like a limited guaranty. But though it was a good solution, it was not a complete solution, and the problem remained that the guaranty was based on the size of the deceased monk's estate: if the estate was equal to or in excess of what had been borrowed, then the guaranty would have effect. But what if it were not? Moreover, the ruling our text provides could be interpreted to admit, in principle, corporate liability for the debt of its individual members and to expose Community assets or those of other monks to any action for recovery. How important these considerations [110] were to our *vinayadhara* may be indicated by the fact that both points of law were explicitly addressed in a separate text that immediately follows the one we have been dealing with in the *Uttaragrantha*.

III. (= xv)

Tog Na 191a.4–b.2 = Derge Pa 132b.7–133a.3 = Peking Phe 129b.1–.4

mnyan du yod pa na dge slong gzhan zhig gis khyim bdag cig las kar sha pa ṇa[1] *zhig bskyis ba dang / de dus kyi mtha' zhig tu ji zhig*[2] *gis dus*[3] *'das pa dang / dge slong de dag gis snga ma bzhin du lhung bzed dang chos gos btsongs nas de la byin no /*

khyim bdag gis smras pa / 'phags pa des[4] *bdag las*[5] *'di tsam zhig 'tshal te / bdag la ni 'di las ma stsal gyis / gzhan yang stsol cig ces smras pa dang / de ltar*[6] *gyur pa dge slong rnams kyis / bcom ldan 'das la gsol pa dang / bcom ldan 'das kyis bka' stsal pa / de la de'i lhung bzed dang chos gos ni 'di las med do*[7] *zhes sgo*[8] *zhig / de ste yid mi ches na go bar gyis shig / go bar bsgo yang mi*[9] *btub na de*[10] *la dge 'dun gyi 'am / gang zag gzhan gyi las ni ma*[11] *sbyin cig / rigs kyi gzu bo rnams kyis go bar bsgo la thong zhig /*

In Śrāvastī a certain monk borrowed some money from a householder, and when his time had come, he died of something. Then after the monks had sold his bowl and robes as before, they repaid the householder.

The householder said: "Noble Ones, that monk took this much from me, but since you have not returned it to me from this, you must return still more!" And the monks reported to the Blessed One what had occurred, and the Blessed One said: "You must inform him saying: 'In regard to his bowl and robes there is nothing beyond this.' If he does not believe that, you must make a clear account. If, even when a clear account is declared, that is not acceptable, you must not repay him from what belongs to the Community or another individual monk! Mediators of good family must declare a clear account and settle it!"

1. Derge: *kār shā pa ṇa*. 2. Derge, Peking: *ci zhig*. 3. Derge, Peking: omit *dus*. 4. Derge, Peking: *der*. 5. Tog: *la*. 6. Derge, Peking: *de lta bur*. 7. Peking: probably *mad do*, but could also be read as *mang ngo*. 8. Peking: *bsgo*. 9. Peking: *ma*. 10. Peking: *da*. 11. Peking: *na me*.

The language here is a little crabbed, and the precise sense of some of the Tibetan vocabulary is not as clear as one might want, nor are the Sanskrit equivalents always sure. Still, the general purport of the text cannot be in doubt. That, for example, this text is a pendant to the one that precedes it is certain and even formally expressed by the shorthand reference to the sale being "as before." Moreover, the new text certainly and explicitly addresses the two questions that the preceding text left open or raised: what happens when the liquidation of the estate of the [111] monk in debt realizes less than what is owed, and is the community or are other individual monks liable for any balance that remains after the sale of the deceased monk's estate? At least a part of the answer to the first question is also clear. When the lender declares that what was realized from the estate sale is insufficient, the monks must give an "accounting"—this seems to be the best rendering of *go ba* here in such a context, but it is not certain. *Go ba* more commonly means "cause to understand," "explain," or even "convince." If this does not work, then, it seems, the case is put to independent outsiders, neither monks nor ordinary householders, but "mediators of good family." Unfortunately it is not easy to determine a precise Sanskrit equivalent for *rigs kyi gzu bo*. *Rigs* almost certainly translates *kula-*, but all I can say about *gzu bo* is that *Bod rgya tshig mdzod chen mo* defines it as *rtsod gleng bar 'dum byed mkhan*, "one who is skilled in reconciling disputes." There is no indication in the text that these individuals are state officers or officers of any court. And there is also no indication of what I have translated as "settle" really means or actually involves. It seems certain from the answer to the second question that whatever these "mediators" might do, they could only rule against the monastic community if it had dissembled. They could not require—could not expect—the Community to repay more than was realized from the sale of the estate, because all other potential assets were, by the rule of the Buddha, protected. The function of the mediators would seem, then, to have been limited to providing an independent accounting of the dead monk's estate and of what was realized from its sale. Beyond this the creditor would seem to have had no recourse.

The second and more fundamental question is almost entirely free of such lexical and procedural uncertainties, and the answer is—on one level—emphatic and unequivocal: the monastic community or corporation is not in itself liable for a debt left by one of its individual members. The individual monks to whom the estate falls and among whom it is divided—and there are elaborate rules defining who these are—are responsible, though not individually liable, for discharging such debt up to the amount realized by the liquidation of the estate, but no further. This limitation is articulated by our text in a language that uses key elements of a vocabulary that are as old, it seems, as anything in the *Vinaya*. Most scholars would maintain that the *Prātimokṣa* is the "original" or oldest part of all the *Vinayas*.[38] If this is true, then a distinction between corporate property and individual property was a part of Buddhist monasticisms from the beginning, since the terms *sāṃghika* and *paudgalika*, and their attendant conceptions, appear to be found either separately or together in all known versions of the *Prātimokṣa*.[39] These are also the same terms that occur [112] in the fundamental ruling delivered by our text—*dge 'dun gyi* and *gang zag gi* are solidly attested equivalents for, and can only be translations of, *sāṃghika* and *paudgalika*. By having, then, the Buddha himself use them when he said that, in effect, under no circumstance must "what belongs to the Community" (*sāṃghika*) or what belongs to another individual monk (*paudgalika*) be used to discharge even a portion of an individual's debt, our redactor or author not only used unambiguous and familiar conceptions but also definitively denied any corporate liability for such debt. "What belongs to the Community," or *sāṃghika*, can be used only for what are Community purposes. Because *sāṃghika* cannot be used here, the affair, by definition, is not Community business. Our redactor makes the same move, by the same means, in regard to the individual assets of the deceased's fellow monks—they too cannot be used for such a purpose.

It is, of course, in all of this hard to avoid the conclusion that the single most important goal for our author was to protect Community assets and the individual assets of other monks from any potential action on the part of the creditor. That at the same time he was apparently attempting to honor the well-established *dharmaśāstric* principle that "the right to inheritance should be followed by the obligation to discharge the debt"[40] made his task both difficult and delicate. It was difficult in part because other texts in our *Vinaya* make it clear that the *vinayadharas* had no desire at all to give up the right to inheritance, although this was one obvious way that the obligation for debt could have been avoided. On the contrary, our *Vinaya* has at least one elaborate text that was also taken up by Guṇaprabha (= vii) whose main purport was to establish the rights of a deceased monk's fellow monks (*sabrahmacārin*) to his estate, and this text is explicitly cited in another of Guṇaprabha's sources (= xxv) as a precedent binding on the state. There was, moreover, also *dharmaśāstric* precedent for "spiritual brothers" (*dharmabhrātṛ*) to inherit the estate of a co-religionist—Olivelle cites passages from both *Yājñavalkya* and even *Kauṭilya* to that effect.[41] But here we butt up against something of the same problem we started with: although *dharmaśāstra* provides for a renouncer's "spiritual brothers" to inherit his goods, it says nothing—to my knowledge—about whether debts incurred after he renounced followed that property. This silence has been *assumed* to indicate that a renouncer did not—indeed could not—incur such debts. But although this could be the case, it is by no means certain; and if it is the case, this could be another of the ways in which Indian renouncers differed from Buddhist monks.[42] A more obvious and effective difference, however, is that Indian renouncers were not, insofar as it is presently known, members of a corporation that had its own assets (*sāṃghika*) that could be at risk. The presence [113] of the latter in the Buddhist case added on yet another layer of complexity that Buddhist authors had to address.

But our *vinayadhara*'s task was not just difficult; it was—as already noted—delicate as well, and at least from a brahmanical point of view it left the deceased debtor monk's fate hanging in the balance. Two points in brahmanical sources could here intersect to devastating effect. Chatterjee, for example, has observed that "according to Hindu concept a debtor may be released from the charge of indebtedness only through payment of debt"[43]—which occurs, of course, in the Buddhist case only when the deceased monk's assets are equal to or more than his debt. But the following was also clear: "In the concept of Hindu *śāstrakāras*, repayment of a debt is not merely a legal obligation. Non-payment of debt is treated as a sin, the consequences of which follow the debtor into the next world"—and already in *Nārada* those consequences involved falling into hell (*naraka*). The idea that a debtor ends up in hell even found its way into inscriptions.[44] In light of such notions the rule in our text which, in effect, makes it all but impossible for the deceased monk's debt to be discharged when the liquidation of his estate realizes less than what is owed also, in effect, condemns him to hell—notice that according to our text neither Community assets nor those of other individual monks should be used for this purpose, and there appear to have been no other means available. That our *vinayadhara* was willing to let such a condemnation stand to avoid exposing other assets to a creditor's action is eloquent testimony to how important the latter was in principle, especially given that he actually allows the use of some of these other assets in a related circumstance.

The *Mūlasarvāstivāda-vinaya* repeatedly acknowledges that there were wide discrepancies in the personal wealth of individual monks and even makes a number of provisions specifically designed to deal with them. One of these is of particular interest here. The *Cīvaravastu* contains a text—also found digested in some detail in Guṇaprabha—that presents a case in which a monk who is said to be *alpajñāta* is sick and about to die.[45] *Alpajñāta* literally means "little known" but is consistently used in our *Vinaya*—as here—to designate monks who are poor. In the present case, for example, immediately after the text describes the monk as *alpajñāta*, it says *tasya bhaiṣajyaṃ nāsti*, "He had (or owned) no medicine" (in the *Vinayavibhaṅga*, to cite another example, a monk so designated is described as "wanting even in regard to the three robes"[46]). This poor monk realizes that he is about to die and says to the attendant monk: *mama nāsti kiṃcit. māṃ uddiśya pūjāṃ kuruṣveti*, "There is nothing else for me—you must perform an act of *pūjā* in my name!" The attendant says he will but then ignores him, and the monk [114] dies and is reborn in the hells (*apāyeṣu*). The Buddha then says that if his fellow monks had performed an act of worship to the Three Jewels, the poor monk's mind would have been made devout and this would not have happened—those who die with a devout mind do not go to hell (*yadi tasya sabrahmacāribhiḥ ratnatrayapūjā kṛtābhaviṣyat cittam asyābhiprasannam abhaviṣyat*). But the point of greatest interest here is that the Buddha himself is then made to instruct the monks that both to provide medicine for a poor monk (i.e., a monk who does not own his own) and to fund what are in effect death rituals performed on his behalf to ensure that he is not reborn in hell, they should first solicit a donor (*dānapati*). But if that does not work, then they should not only use corporate assets (*sāṃghika*) but, if necessary, even what belongs to the Buddha's permanent endowment (*buddhākṣayanīvisantaka*) or what can be realized after "selling" (*vikrīya*) the accoutrements belonging to the *Tathāgatacaitya* or the Perfume Chamber (*gandhakuṭī*). How extraordinary these provisions are is, however, immediately underlined when the text adds that, should the monk recover, he must make every effort to repay what had been used on his behalf.

The contrast between this ruling in the *Cīvaravastu* and the ruling in our text from the *Uttaragrantha* is, then, both striking and instructive. The former explicitly allows—indeed, orders—that corporate funds (*sāṃghika*) be used, if a donor cannot be found, to provide medicines for a dying indigent monk and, more significantly here, to fund ritual activity that would ensure that he would not be reborn in the hells. Even assets earmarked for the Buddha himself and property belonging to him may be so used, though the ruling does not extend to the individual or personal assets of other monks. Yet in the *Uttaragrantha* the use of *sāṃghika* to pay off the debt of a deceased monk, and thereby also ensure that he would not be reborn in hell, is just as explicitly forbidden. The only difference between the two undertakings, it seems, is that one provides an act of charity and the other establishes a legal precedent, if not principle, and although our *vinayadhara* was more than willing, both here and elsewhere, to do the first, he emphatically refused—even at the cost of a fellow monk's "soul"—to do the second. For this Buddhist monk, law had precedence over charity, and property was more important than a fellow monk's fate. This was a monk, moreover, who quite literally made the rules.

What we have seen so far is, it seems, a Buddhist monastic lawyer trying to shelter Community or corporate assets from any action on the part of potential creditors to recover debts incurred by individual monks. [115] The determining element here, however, is the word "individual," because our *vinayadhara* also provided a ruling that explicitly admitted corporate liability for *corporate* debts, this time carefully sheltering individual assets—he was nothing if not good at his job. To see this additional ruling, however, we must go outside the sequential series of texts from the *Uttaragrantha* that we started with, and will return to, but we need not go outside the *Uttaragrantha*.

The new ruling that establishes corporate liability for corporate debt also occurs in the *Uttara*, but some ninety folios beyond our series; and although it too is treated by Guṇaprabha, he treats it under a separate heading. He in fact treats it much earlier, in a section devoted to commercial activities that can be legitimately engaged in by monks for the purposes and benefits of the Community, which only emphasizes further that the rulings we have so far seen are strictly limited to actions undertaken by individual monks for their individual purposes.[47] In spite of this crucial difference the narrative involved will be familiar.

VII (=)

Tog Na 283b.6–284a.5 = Derge Pa 196a.7–b.4 = Peking Phe 189b.5–190a.1

gleng gzhi ni mnyan du yod pa na ste / zhal ta byed pa'i dge slong zhig gis / dge 'dun gyi phyir[1] *khyim pa zhig las*[2] *nor zhig bskyis ba dang / de dus*[3] *'das so /*

de dus[3] *'das so zhes thos nas / des*[4] *gtsug lag khang du 'ongs nas dris pa / dge slong ming 'di zhes bgyi ba zhig ga*[5] *re zhes smras pa dang / dge slong dag gis smras pa / de dus las 'das so /*

des smras pa / 'phags pa bdag gi nor zhig[6] *des*[7] *bskyis so /*

dge slong dag gis smras pa / song la de nyid la dos[8] *shig /*

des dge 'dun gyi phyir khyer gyi / pha ma dang bdag gi phyir ma lags kyis / khyed[9] *kyis stsol cig*[10] */*

de ltar gyur pa dge slong dag gis / bcom ldan 'das la gsol pa dang / bcom ldan 'das kyis bka' stsal pa / de ste dge 'dun gyi phyir des khyer bar shes na[11] */ dge 'dun gyis skyin pa byin cig / dge slong rnams ngas las gsar du byed pa'i mtshungs*[12] *pa'i dge slong gi*[13] *chos bca' 'o*[14] */ las gsar du byed pa'i dge slong gis bskyis ba*[15] *dag / rgan zhing rgan pa dag la dris la long zhig / las gsar du byed pa rnams*[16] *kyis mtshungs par spyad pa'i chos bcas pa bzhin du ma byas na 'das pa dang bcas par 'gyur ro /*

The setting was in Śrāvastī. A monk who was the Service Manager borrowed some money from a layman for the sake of the Community and he died.

When that layman heard that he had died, after he had gone to the *vihāra* he asked, saying "Where is the monk named so-and-so?" and the monks said: "He has died."

The layman said: "He, Noble Ones, borrowed some of my money."

The monks said: "Well, go and collect it from him!"

"But since he took it for the sake of the Community, and not for the sake of his parents or himself, you must repay it!"

The monks reported to the Blessed One what had occurred, and the Blessed One said: "If it is known that he took it for the sake of the Community, the Com-

---

1. Peking: *dga dun gya phy(i)r*. 2. Derge, Peking: *la*. 3. Derge, Peking: add *las*; Tog makes the same addition once below. 4. Tog: *de*. 5. Peking: *gi*. 6. Peking: *zhag*. 7. Tog: omits *des*. 8. Peking: *dris*. 9. Peking: *khyod*. 10. Peking: *shig*. 11. Peking: *nas*. 12. Tog, Derge: *tshungs*, but cf. below. 13. Peking: *gis*. 14. Derge, Peking: *bca'o*. 15. Derge, Peking: *bskyi ba*. 16. Tog: *byed pa'i rnams*. [116]

munity must repay the loan! I, monks, will designate the rule for a monk who is like the Monk-in-Charge-of-Construction: the Monk-in-Charge-of-Construction will borrow. And he must ask all Seniors and then obtain a loan! If the Monk-in-Charge-of-Construction does not act in accordance with the designated rule of customary behavior, he comes to be guilty of an offense."

Although the narrative frame here is unremarkably familiar, the specific and defining details are completely different. In our previous cases the tale was told about and the ruling governed generic, individual monks—"a certain monk," "you monks must repay," etc.—but here we are not talking about just monks, we are dealing with monastic officers, and this little text bristles with official titles. "Service Manager" occurs once; "Seniors" actually occurs twice; "Monk-in-Charge-of-Construction" occurs three times—all of these in a short space. We have clearly moved from the individual to the institutional, from the rank and file to the official functionary.

On one level, none of these titles presents serious difficulty—the underlying Sanskrit for all is reasonably sure. *Zhal ta byed pa* is a well-attested equivalent of *vaiyāpṛtyakara* or *vaiyāvṛtyakara*, even if the exact range of functions and status of this particular monastic officer are not clear.[48] *Rgan pa*, although it can occasionally translate *sthavira*, more commonly translates *vṛddha*, "Senior," as in *vṛddhānta*, "the Seniors' end of the assembly."[49] And *las gsar du byed pa* can only be a variant—in fact a better—rendering of *navakarmika*, which is more commonly rendered by *lag gi bla* and is probably the earliest monastic office to be mentioned in inscriptions.[50] Our cast of characters then are almost all monks having official and recognized capacities, and the use of their titles only emphasizes that they are not acting as individuals.

Our redactor does not, however, rely only on the heavy use of titles to indicate that the undertaking at issue was not a private transaction: not only does he have the layman explicitly declare that it was not, but three times—again in a short space—he explicitly signals that we are dealing with an action undertaken "for the sake of the Community" (*dge 'dun gyi phyir*). [117] The "narrator" says this at the beginning; the layman says it to the monks; and the Buddha himself says it. But perhaps more interesting is the layman's phrasing when he explicitly denies that the loan undertaken by "the monk named so-and-so" was a private transaction, in part because he by implication also thereby more clearly indicates the nature of the loans in both texts II and III. The layman says that "the monk who was the Service Manager" did not take out the loan "for the sake of his parents or himself," and this, by extension, must be the definition of a private loan and must be exactly what the monks in our two previous cases had done. That a private monastic loan was one in which an individual monk borrowed money for his own sake and purposes is perhaps by now not surprising, but that a monk would borrow money for the sake of his parents might still be, even though there are good reasons why it should not come as any surprise at all: our *Vinaya* has a detailed set of rulings establishing a monk's obligation to financially support his parents and outlining how this is to be done;[51] and even the Pāli *Vinaya* has the Buddha himself authorizing such support;[52] monastic tales in the Pāli *Jātaka* also repeatedly refer to this practice and repeatedly present monks who are called *mātiposakas*, "[Mönch, der] seine Mutter unterstützt," for example, in a positive light.[53] That all of this—and much more—has been largely overlooked should probably be far more surprising than the fact that, given this obligation, individual monks might on occasion have had recourse to loans to fulfill it. That they did so seems to be taken for granted by our text.

A final indication that we are dealing with an action undertaken by a monastic officer—if that indeed be needed—is that our text ends with what it calls a "designated rule of customary behavior." That *mtshungs par spyad pa'i chos* represents another translation of *āsamudācārika dharma* cannot be in doubt. There are dozens of texts from almost every part of the *Mūlasarvāstivāda-vinaya* in which we find the same expression, or some slight variant, as occurs here in the *Uttaragrantha* when the Buddha says "I, monks, will designate the rule for a monk who . . ." In the *Poṣadhavastu* it occurs in regard to the Monk-in-Charge-of Religious-Exertion: *prāhāṇikasyāhaṃ bhikṣavo bhikṣor āsamudācārikāṃ dharmāṃ prajñapayiṣyāmi*, "Mönche, ich lege die Verhaltensregeln für einen meditierenden Mönch fest"; in the *Śayanāsanavastu* in regard both to the Monk-in-Charge-of-the-(Monastery's)-Dogs (*kukkurapoṣaka*) and the Monk-Who-Gives-the-Explanations (*uddeśadāyaka*).[54] In all such cases—and again they are numerous—such "rules" are promulgated not for all monks but always for specific and limited categories of monks or monks who find themselves with a particular, often temporary, formal ecclesiastical status. [118]

All of these considerations, then, both condition and are condensed in what is probably the single most significant difference between our first two texts (II and III), which deal with private loans taken out by individual monks for their own purposes, and our third text (VII), which deals with a corporate loan taken out by a monastic officer for the sake of the Community. In the first the Buddha rules that *bskyis pa dge slong dag gis byin cig*, "The monks must repay what was borrowed!" But in the last the wording, although only slightly changed, is still significantly different. There the Buddha says: *dge 'dun gyis skyin pa byin cig*, "The Community must repay the loan!" In the first the responsibility falls directly on the monks almost certainly because, as we have seen, they divide or inherit the deceased's estate, and debt follows property. The *saṅgha* has no part in either and is mentioned only to exclude its assets from any involvement. But in the last it is the monks who have no part and are not mentioned, nor, significantly, is there any mention of the deceased monastic officer's estate or its partition. In the last case the monk's estate does not enter in because the true borrower in this case is the *saṅgha*, and although it has assets, it has no estate because it cannot die. There are perhaps few passages in which the corporate nature of the Buddhist *saṅgha* is so clear, nor can there be any real doubt that the net effect, if not the actual intention, of these rulings was to put into place what came much later to be a fundamental principle of Western corporate law, the principle according to which the corporation was not liable for debt incurred by its members, nor were its members responsible for the debts of the corporation—all of this as the word of the Buddha.

To this point, we are building toward something like a system of the Mūlasarvāstivādin laws of debt, but it is important to keep in mind that this emerging system is to some degree of our own making. By placing the text on corporate liability for corporate debt (VII) where we have, we have had to go outside the sequential series of texts from the *Uttaragrantha* that we started with, and we have had to treat together provisions that Guṇaprabha had placed under different headings. The divergence here from both the order of the *Uttara* and from Guṇaprabha is largely a result of the fact that the latter implicitly considered private debt as a matter of inheritance, but corporate debt as a species of commercial transaction. But it also results from an inclination to keep the categories "private" and "corporate" separate, and this may have been the stronger concern, given that in returning to the sequential *Uttara* series, we will immediately see that it too moves next to issues of private debt that arise from commercial transactions. This [119] move, in turn, brings into focus a question so far begged. In neither II nor III, nor VII for that matter, is the professional status of the lender clear. In both II and III he is described only as a *khyim bdag*, the standard translation for *gṛhapati*; in VII he is described even more generically as a *khyim pa*, an almost equally standard rendering of Sanskrit *gṛhin*. In none of these cases is there any indication that the lender was a professional moneylender, so although that is by no means impossible, there are also no means to actually know.[55] That the remaining cases in the *Uttaragrantha* deal with professionals is, by contrast, not in doubt.

IV (= xvi)

Tog Na 191b.2–192a.2 = Derge Pa 133a.3–b.1 = Peking Phe 129b.4–130a.2

gleng gzhi ni mnyan du yod pa na / dge slong zhig gis gos 'tshong ba las ras shig rin ma byin par blangs pa las / dge slong de dus 'das nas / dge slong de dus 'das so zhes gos kyi bdag po des thos nas / de gtsug lag khang du 'ongs te shes bzhin du / dge slong rnams la[1]

1. Peking: omits *la*.

'phags pa dge slong ming 'di zhes bgyi ba 'di ga la mchis zhes[2] *dris pa dang / de dag gis smras pa / bzhin bzangs dus 'das so /*

'phags pa des bdag las ras shig[3] *rin sbyin par byas te khyer ro /*

bzhin bzangs de dur khrod du bskyal gyis der song la dos shig /

'phags pa de'i chos gos dang lhung bzed ni khyed rnams kyis bgos na bdag ci'i phyir dur khrod du song ste bda' / khyed rnams[4] *kyis byin cig /*

de ltar gyur pa dge slong rnams kyis bcom ldan 'das la gsol nas / bcom ldan 'das kyis bka' stsal pa / dge slong rnams gos 'tshong ba 'di smra ba ni bden gyis de ni byin cig /

dge slong rnams kyis de'i ras nyid byin[5] *pa dang / des 'phags pa rnams bdag la des rin thang 'di tsam du 'tshal to zhes smra*[6] *pa dang / bcom ldan 'das kyis de nyid tshongs la byin cig*[7] *ces bka' stsal pa dang / dge slong rnams kyis de btsong bar brtsams pa dang / snga ma'i rin thang du ma lon nas bcom ldan 'das kyis*[8] *bka' stsal pa / lhag ma ni chos gos dang lhung bzed rnams tshongs la byin cig /*

The setting was in Śrāvastī. A monk took some cotton cloth from a cloth merchant without having paid for it, and when that monk died, and when the owner of the cloth heard that that monk had died, he went to the *vihāra*, and although he already knew, he asked the monks, saying "Noble Ones, where is the monk named so-and-so?" And they said: "He, Sir, is dead."

"Noble Ones, he took away some cloth from me without paying for it."[56] [120]

"Well, Sir, since he has been carried out to the cremation grounds, you will just have to go there and collect!"

"Noble Ones, when you have already divided his robes and bowl, why should I go to the cremation grounds and collect? You must pay me!"

When the monks reported to the Blessed One what had occurred, the Blessed One said: "Since that said by this cloth merchant is true, you, monks, must repay him!"

The monks gave him his same cotton cloth, but he said: "He was to give me a price of so much," and the Blessed One said: "You must sell that same cloth and repay him!" The monks then proceeded to sell it, but when they did not get its former price, the Blessed One said: "In regard to the balance, you must sell his robes and bowl and repay him!"

Even if it had not been signaled by its number, it would have been immediately obvious from its content that with IV we have returned to the sequence of texts that we started with. We have returned to the undertakings of an individual, generic monk—he is not a monastic officer—who has acted for his own pur-

2. Peking: *shes*. 3. Peking: adds *ni*, but the spacing suggests a correction here and both the required sense and the previous *ras shig rin ma byin par* would seem to indicate that a *ma* here has dropped out in all three witnesses. 4. Peking: omits *rnams*. 5. Peking: *sbyin*. 6. Derge, Peking: *smras*. 7. Tog: omits *cig*. 8. Peking: *kyas*.

poses. The text again explicitly refers to the dead monk's estate having already been "divided" by the monks, and once again the Buddha's ruling aligns monastic practice with the principle that "debt follows property"—there is no reference to the Community, and the liability, as before in II and III, falls not on it but on the individual monks who participated in the division. What our text adds directly to the provisions already established is simply an extension of their referent: the established provisions apply now not just to borrowed money but to unpaid bills as well. This text—unlike II and III—also explicitly indicates that it is dealing with interactions between monks and professional merchants: the creditor here is not "a householder" or a "layman" but a cloth merchant. And our present text, although it does not use a word that would correspond to "credit," is quite certainly describing what we would describe as "a monk buying goods on credit." So now we have Buddhist monks both buying *and* selling, and this calls for a short excursus, because both have been taken to constitute an infraction of monastic rule.

All the *Prātimokṣas* that I know appear to have a rule against buying and selling, and when we are lucky enough to have the ruling in an Indian language, the basic wording in all of them is close:

> Sarvāstivāda: *yaḥ punar bhikṣur nānāprakāraṃ krayavikrayaṃ samāpadyeta niḥsargikā pātayantikā*
>
> Mūlasarvāstivāda: *yaḥ punar bhikṣur nānāprakāraṃ krayavikrayaṃ samāpadyeta naisargikā pāyantikā*
>
> Lokottaravāda: *yo puna bhikṣur anekavidhaṃ krayavikrayavyavahāraṃ samāpadyeya saṃyyathīdaṃ imaṃ kriṇa ito kriṇa ettakam ettake[na krī]ṇāhīti vā vadeya nissargikapācattikaṃ*
>
> Theravāda: *yo pana bhikkhu nānappakārakaṃ kayavikkayaṃ samāpajjeyya nissaggiyaṃ pācittiyaṃ*[57] [121]

These versions are cited here merely to show that what has already been said about the Mūlasarvāstivādin version likely applies to all: "It does not refer to unqualified "buying and selling"; nor does it refer—which it could easily have—to "all" (*sarva*) "buying and selling." It refers to *nānā-prakāraṃ* [in the Lokottaravāda case cited here: *anekavidhaṃ*] *kraya-vikrayaṃ*, which, of course, could mean "buying and selling of various sorts" or "buying and selling of many sorts" [the same possibilities also hold for the Lokottaravāda]. Neither interpretation precludes "all," but neither requires it either. Mūlasarvāstivādin exegesis, moreover, clearly did not take it to have absolute application."[58] It will, of course, be important to determine if the last sentence here applies as well to the other monastic orders, or to what degree it might, and in those cases where we must rely especially on Chinese translations, this may prove difficult. Already, and even on the level of the canonical rule alone, the difficulty is apparent. The Tibetan translation of the Mūlasarvāstivādin rule, for example, seems to be strictly literal: *yang dge slong gang nyo tshong rnam pa sna tshogs byed na spang ba'i ltung byed do.*[59] But Kumārajīva's translation of the Sarvāstivādin rule does not. Huber renders it into French: "Si un bhikṣu fait des achats et des ventes de toute sorte, il y a, etc,"[60] and "de toute sorte" is not an accurate translation of *nānāprakāra* or *anekavidha*, but says precisely what the Sanskrit and Pāli do not, although modern interpreters too have made the same move Kumārajīva seems to have made. Wijayaratna, for example, in referring to the Pāli rule cited above says that it "interdit *toute sorte* de trocs," even when Horner had already translated the same rule as "Whatever monk should engage in *various kinds* of bartering there is an offence. . . ." To make matters even more complicated, Rhys Davids and Oldenberg render the rule—again the same rule!—"Whatsoever Bhikkhu shall engage in *any one of the various kinds* of buying and selling," etc.[61] The fact that the same rule and the same wording can be understood in three different ways may, however, constitute not a defect but rather a considerable advantage and may indicate an admirable flexibility intentionally built into the *Prātimokṣa* by its original drafters, an intentional ambiguity that various (*nānāprakāra*), not "all" (*sarva*), authors—both ancient and modern—have tried to override. This sort of intentional ambiguity has, as has been noted elsewhere, good parallels in the history of monastic statutes in medieval Europe[62] and—more importantly, it seems—in Indian *dharmaśāstra*. In his study of the law of debt in ancient India already referred to several times, Chatterjee says things, for example, like "And sometimes (let us presume) intentionally the laws were couched in vague language (e.g. *Manu*, viii.153; *Bṛhaspati*, x.36; x.42)," or "The [122] words are sometimes technical and precise, at times vague and ambiguous. In many cases, we fear, the ambiguity was deliberate."[63]

However all of these considerations might be sorted out remains to be seen, but it seems fairly certain even at this stage that in regard to monks' "buying and selling" the *Mūlasarvāstivāda-vinaya* is much more straightforward, and much less inclined to disguise these transactions, than the *Theravāda-vinaya*. That the latter, for example, as we have it, did not understand its own ruling as a prohibition against monks engaging in—or at least initiating—both types of transactions would seem to follow from the "casuistic" already attached to it, which says: *anāpatti aggham pucchati kappiyakārakassa ācikkhati idaṃ amhākaṃ atthi amhākañ ca iminā ca iminā ca attho 'ti bhaṇati*, "There is no offense if he [the monk] asks the value, points it out to one who makes it legally allowable [i.e., a layman in the service of the monk], saying: 'This is ours, and we want this and that.'"[64] There is, in other words, no infraction of the Theravādin rule if the individual monk uses a designated individual—and thereby a legal fiction—to buy or sell what he wants. The *Mūlasarvāstivāda-vinaya*, of course, also knows of such legal fictions, but the *kappiyakāraka* and other surrogates like him are far less common in it, and even when they do appear, their use is rarely mandatory. Even a couple of examples might be enough to give some idea of the different flavor of these two *vinayas*.

The *Uttaragrantha* itself contains a particularly good example of the Mūlasarvāstivādin recommendation of, but lack of insistence on, the use of a surrogate, and this example comes immediately after the sequential series of texts we have labeled here II–V. It says:

> When the Blessed One had said "a monk must not himself buy" (*dge slong rang gis nyo bar ma byed cig*), and the monks did not know how buying should be done, the Blessed One said: "A lay-brother (*dge bsnyen pa* = *upāsaka*) who lives in the *vihāra* must be entrusted with it! If there is no lay-brother living in the *vihāra* or one who is trustworthy (*dge bsnyen dad pa*), and a monk certainly wants to buy, he must state two or three times terms that have been determined, and he must not increase them by way of a *kārṣāpaṇa*, etc. Whether monks want to buy or do not want to buy, if they increase the terms by way of a *kārṣāpaṇa*, etc., or state their terms more than two or three times, they come to be guilty of an offense."[65]

Here, then, it is good for a Mūlasarvāstivādin monk to use a surrogate to make purchases, if there is one, but the bulk of the rule appears to assume that there may well not be and that the monk himself will be doing so—most of the rule is devoted to governing his behavior when he does. It is also fairly certain from the narrative frame, which is not cited here, and from the content of the rule that the problem for the Mūlasarvāstivādin *vinayadharas* was not monks' buying and selling, but monks' haggling, and haggling must have been a common element of the early Indian economy. [123] The "casuistic" in the Mūlasarvāstivādin *Vibhaṅga* attached to the rule on buying and selling moreover explicitly says that there is no offense in a monk's buying or selling if he is not seeking a profit (*rnyed pa mi 'dod pa*),[66] and our *Uttaragrantha* text actually ends by allowing even haggling if it is for the sake of the Buddha, the Dharma, and the Saṅgha (*sangs rgyas dang / chos dang / dge 'dun gyi phyir rin thang bskyed kang nyes med do /*).

A second example concerning the Mūlasarvāstivādin attitude toward the use of surrogates—this one from the *Vibhaṅga*—is particularly interesting because it explicitly articulates the *dharmaśāstric* notion of *āpad*, "distress" or "extremity": "A situation when normal rules do not apply."[67] The text in question occurs as one of the cases treated under the rule against monks' "touching" gold and silver—another problematic rule—but also involves the rule against digging the ground. It says that in times of danger monks fled *vihāras* that were situated in "border regions" (*mtha' khob*), but when they did, thieves looted the unoccupied *vihāras*. The text then continues:

> The Blessed One said: "The treasure and gold (*dbyig dang gser*) belonging to the Community or the *stūpa* must be hidden. Then you should go!"

> Although the Blessed One had said "It must be hidden," the monks did not know by whom it should be hidden.
>
> The Blessed One said: "It should be hidden by an attendant of the monastery (*kun dga' ra ba pa* = *ārāmika*) or a lay-brother (*dge bsnyen* = *upāsaka*)."
>
> But then those who hid it, they themselves stole it.
>
> The Blessed One said: "It must be hidden by a trustworthy lay-brother (*dge bsnyen dad pa can*)![68] When there is no trustworthy lay-brother, it must be hidden by a novice! When there is no novice, it must be hidden by the monks themselves!"

Because hiding the treasure involved, according to the text, digging a hole (*dong brko bar bya ba*), the monks also did not know who should do the digging, and the Buddha gave the same instructions for that activity too. Then the text ends with the Buddha saying: "Monks, that which I allow in times of distress should not be practiced in conditions of ease," *dge slong dag ngas phongs pa'i dus dag tu gnang ba gang yin pa de bde ba'i gnas skabs dag tu spyad par mi bya ste*—and it is virtually certain that the Sanskrit translated here by *phongs pa'i dus* was *āpatkāla*.[69]

But if texts like these show Mūlasarvāstivādin *vinayadharas* allowing—like their *dharmaśāstric* colleagues—certain conditions to determine the application of specific rules, and if they show them disinclined to rely on lay surrogates and even suspicious of them,[70] still other passages seem to show them much more inclined than their Mahāvihārin brothers to call a spade a spade. We have already seen repeated and straightforward references in the *Mūlasarvāstivāda-vinaya* to monks selling things, but one [124] particular text brings out especially clearly the differences between it and the *Theravāda-vinaya*. The text in question occurs in the *Kṣudrakavastu*[71] and concerns "a woolen blanket worth a great deal"—*chen po la 'os pa'i la ba*, which is almost perfectly translated into Pāli as *mahaggho kambalo*. This woolen blanket was donated to the Community, but because of its great value the Buddha ruled that unlike other gifts of cloth, it should not be cut up and distributed. Rather, he says: "Whatever acquisition of cloth of such kind falls to the Community, that should be sold for money and the money divided! (*de lta bas na dge 'dun la gos kyi rnyed pa de lta bu grub pa gang yin pa de kar sha pa ṇa dag tu bsgyur la kar sha pa ṇa dag bgo bar bya'o* /)." While the Tibetan here might itself involve a mild euphemism in its use of *bsgyur ba*, "to transform or change into," the Sanskrit almost certainly would not since it almost certainly had a form of *vi√krī*—forms of *vi√krī* are well-attested equivalents for *bsgyur ba*;[72] and since the Tibetan transliterates *kārṣāpaṇa*, "money," there is not the slightest doubt that the text in both languages meant "to sell." But the *Theravāda-vinaya* also has a short text—completely shorn of context—ruling on what should be done with a "woolen blanket of great value"—*mahaggho kambalo*. These two texts cannot, it seems, be unrelated,[73] and yet the language of the Pāli text is on its own—or at least as it has been translated—not immediately transparent. In the Pāli text the Buddha is made to say: *anujānāmi bhikkhave phātikammatthāya parivattetun ti*, and this has produced some awkward translations. Rhys Davids and Oldenberg have represented it by "I allow you, O Bhikkhus, to barter . . . these things in order to increase the stock of legally permissible furniture," but this, of course, is more of a paraphrase than a translation, and the added gloss—"the stock of legally permissible furniture"—itself runs into trouble because, as the attached note implies, *kambala* is nowhere declared "impermissible." Horner's translation is much less padded but no more straightforward: "I allow you, monks, to barter it for (something) advantageous," and Wijayaratna understands it to mean that the monks "were allowed to exchange it for something else."[74]

Part of the problem here must be that *phātikammatthāya* is an unusual expression. According to the recent and useful *Index to the Vinaya-Piṭaka*, it occurs in the Pāli *Vinaya* only in this passage and the one that immediately follows it. The only other related form—*phātikātum*—also only occurs once in the entire *Vinaya*.[75] The Pāli Text Society dictionary gives for *phātikamma* in our passage the meanings "increase, profit, advantage" and *phātikātum* in the phrase *na paṭibalo . . . adhigataṃ vā bhogaṃ phātikātum* at *Vinaya* i 86.12 has been [125] rendered by Horner as "I am not able . . . to increase the wealth (already) acquired."[76] Since *parivatteti* is certainly used in the *Vinaya* to mean "invert," "barter," and "exchange"—the latter once where "gold and silver" is "exchanged" for some product—it would seem that the phrase *phātikammātthāya parivattetun* should mean "to exchange/barter/sell for the purpose of making a profit" or something like that. But if it does mean that—and the Mūlasarvāstivādin parallel also would suggest it should—that meaning is not immediately obvious and requires some effort to see. Perhaps the most easily available explanation for this lack of transparency is that it is intentional, that in having the Buddha say *phātikammātthāya parivattetun* the redactors of the Pāli *Vinaya* were employing a conscious euphemism. A reluctance on the part of modern scholars to see what even Pāli texts might have been saying probably has also not helped the discussion.

The larger issue in all of this is, however, rather simple. It would appear that we have a great deal yet to learn about what has been presented as, or assumed to be, a settled issue: whether or not and to what degree Buddhist *vinaya* literature—all Buddhist *vinaya* literature—allowed, permitted, or mandated the participation of monks in commercial activity. Our *Uttaragrantha* texts make a significant contribution toward understanding the Mūlasarvāstivādin position(s) on these issues, and the text most immediately at hand here (IV) would seem to indicate not only that Mūlasarvāstivādin monks were expected to engage in monetary purchases on a regular basis but also that Mūlasarvāstivādin *vinayadharas* were redacting rules that would address some of the problems between merchants and monks that could arise from these activities. The ruling in IV seems, indeed, to have no other purpose than to establish a procedure that—again without exposing community assets—would provide merchants some assurance that credit extended to a Buddhist monk would be made good by the inheritors of his estate upon that monk's death. This ruling, even more than the others we have seen, would seem to favor the creditor over the monks: what would otherwise have gone to them must be used to make up any shortfall that results from the sale of what the deceased had bought on credit. But like the other rulings, this ruling too is most directly engaged in establishing the liabilities of monks in regard to the estate of a fellow monk, not their rights. Our *vinayadhara*, however, is not yet finished.

The vast majority of the canonical texts dealing with monastic inheritance that were digested by Guṇaprabha do not in fact deal with the issue of [126] liability. They are overwhelmingly concerned with rights. There are texts dealing with the rights of nuns to the estate of a dead monk (ii—except in the absence of other monks they have none), and vice versa (iii—to the same, though reversed, effect). There are texts detailing the rights of monks to the estate of another monk who dies between monastic boundaries (*sīmā*) (viii) or to the estate of one of a group of traveling monks who dies within the monastic boundaries of another group (xi). There are texts determining the priority of the rights of monks to the estate of a dead monk that is in the possession of a layman (xiii), and a considerable number of others. The next two texts in the sequence of texts from the *Uttaragrantha* that we are here dealing with form, then, in at least some sense, a subset of this larger group: they too deal with the rights of monks. But they also belong to our sequence because they address the issue of debt. In these two cases, however, the issue is not what a monk owed at the time of death but rather what was owed to him. These last two texts are even shorter than the others and are most conveniently treated together.

V (= xvii)

Tog Na 192a.2–.7 = Derge Pa 133b.1–.4 = Peking Phe 130a.2–.6

gleng gzhi ni mnyan du yod pa na[1] */ dge slong zhig gis tha ga pa la ras 'thag pa'i phyir skud pa dang / rngan pa byin pa las / dge slong de dus 'das nas*[2] */ dge slong rnams kyis tha ga pa la*[3] *bos te / bzhin bzangs*[4] *khyod la dge slong ming 'di zhes bya bas ras 'thag pa'i phyir skud pa dang rngan pa byin pa de slar*[5] *phul cig ces smras pa dang / des 'phags pa rnams bdag gis de la ras sbyin*[6] *par byas kyis*[7] */ skud pa dang rngan pa ni ma lags so*

1. Peking: adds *ste*. 2. Derge, Peking: have *dus 'das pa dang* instead of *dus 'das nas*. 3. Derge: omits *la*. 4. Peking: *bzang*. 5. Peking: *slab*. 6. Peking: *byin*. 7. Derge, Peking: *kyi*.

zhes smras pa dang / dge slong rnams kyis de ji ltar bya ba ma shes nas / de ltar gyur pa dge slong rnams kyis / bcom ldan 'das la gsol pa dang /) bcom ldan 'das kyis dge slong rnams tha ga pa smra ba ni bdeṇ gyis ras su long zhig ces smras pa dang[8] */ dge slong rnams kyis phra mo las bkug pa dang / des*[9] *'phags pa rnams bdag gis de la sbom po sbyin par byas so zhes smras pa dang / bcom ldan 'das kyis bka' stsal pa / dge slong de ni dus 'das kyis ci*[10] *ltar byin pa de lta bu long zhig*[11] */*

VI (= xviii)

Tog Na 192a.7–b.5 = Derge Pa 133b.4–134a.1 = Peking Phe 130a.6–b.1

gleng gzhi ni mnyan du yod pa na ste / dge slong zhig gis gos 'tshong ba la kar sha pa ṇa[1] *byin te / ras shig byin cig ces smras pa dang / dge slong de dus 'das nas / dge slong rnams kyis gos 'tshong ba la bos te / bzhing bzangs*[2] *khyod la dge slong ming 'di zhes bya bas ras kyi rin zhig byin pa de 'on cig ces*[3] *smras pa dang / des 'phags pa rnams de la*[4] *ras su sbyin par bgyis so zhes smras pa dang / dge slong rnams kyis de la ji ltar bya ba mi shes so /*

de ltar gyur pa dge slong rnams kyis bcom ldan 'das la gsol nas / bcom ldan 'das kyis dge slong rnams gos 'tshong ba de smra ba ni bden gyis / ras su long zhig[5] *ces smras pa dang / dge slong rnams kyis phra mo bkug pa dang*[6] */ des 'phags pa rnams*[7] *bdag gis de la sbom po dbul bar bgyis so zhes smras pa dang / bcom ldan 'das kyis bka' stsal pa / dge slong de ni dus 'das na ji lta bu byin pa de bzhin du long zhig*[8] */*

V (= xvii)

The setting was in Śrāvastī. When after a monk had given thread and wages to a weaver for the purpose of having cloth woven, and the monk died, the monks summoned the weaver and said: "Sir, the monk named so-and-so gave you thread and wages for the purpose of having cloth woven and you must give that back!" But the weaver said: "Noble Ones, since I was to give him cloth, there is no thread or wages." And when the monks did not know what to do in regard to that, they reported to the Blessed One what had occurred, and the Blessed One said: "Monks, since what the weaver says is true, you must accept cloth!" But the monks called for fine cloth, and the weaver said: "Noble Ones, I was to give him coarse." And the Blessed One said: "Since that monk is dead, you must accept what is given!"

VI (= xviii)

The setting was Śrāvastī. A monk gave money to a cloth merchant and said: "You must give me cloth." But when that monk died, the monks summoned the cloth

8. Derge, Peking: *bcom ldan 'das kyis dge slong rnams la bka' stsal pa tha ga pa smra ba ni bden gyis* [Peking: *gyi*] *ras su long shig ces bka' stsal pa dang*. 9. Derge: *de la*. 10. Derge, Peking: *ji*. 11. Derge, Peking: *shig*. [127]

1. Derge: *kār shā pa ṇa*. 2. Peking: *bzang*. 3. Peking: *cas*. 4. Tog: omits *de la* but has it in the similar statement below. 5. Derge, Peking: *shig*. 6. Derge, Peking: *bkug nas* instead of *bkug pa dang*. 7. Peking: omits *rnams*. 8. Derge, Peking: *shig*.

merchant and said: "Sir, the monk named so-and-so gave you the price of the cloth and you must return it!" But the cloth merchant said: "Noble One, cloth was to be given to him"; and the monks did not know what to do in regard to that.

When the monks had reported to the Blessed One what had occurred, the Blessed One said: "Monks, since what the cloth merchant says is true, you must accept cloth!" But the monks called for fine cloth, and the cloth merchant said: "Noble One, I was to give him coarse." And the Blessed One said: "In that that monk is dead, what sort is given, so you must accept!" [128]

There is a good deal that is by now not new in these two little texts, the last two in our continuous sequence from the *Uttaragrantha*. The Community or corporation (*saṅgha*) is again noticeable only by its absence; it has no role in the actions undertaken, nor in the resultant ruling. The text is dealing with the estate of an individual monk who had entered into a private transaction with another private individual, and a claim lodged by a group of individual monks. It is by now hopefully clear that for our *vinayadhara* "a group of individual monks" does not constitute a or the *Saṅgha*. Which monks are included in the group is here not explicitly stated, although context and the texts seen previously allow, or even require, the assumption that "the monks" referred to are the monks who will participate in the division of the estate—in effect the dead monk's heirs—and a large number of Guṇaprabha's canonical texts are taken up with determining who and in what circumstances these monks will be (ii–viii, xi–xiii, xx, etc.). There is, moreover, no reference in our last two texts to the monks' having already divided the estate, almost certainly because, as is clear from still other texts (vii, ix), procedure required that the content of the estate should be determined and gathered before any division takes place, and the monks in our two texts are engaged in that necessary preliminary.

In these two texts we also have, as in several earlier instances, monks interacting with merchants and tradesmen. There is another cloth merchant and also a weaver—*tha ga pa / ba* is an attested equivalent of *tantuvāya*—and, in regard to the latter, specific reference to "wages" (*rngan* = *bhṛtikā*). The *Mūlasarvāstivāda-vinaya* has a wealth of material on wage labor, but it has yet to be studied. And if there were any lingering doubts about whether our monks were thought to enter directly into financial transactions with tradesmen or to directly purchase goods from merchants, V and VI should put them at rest. Here we see monks themselves hiring weavers and themselves buying cloth. What is different here—especially from the tales of smiths and cobblers referred to above—is that in these two cases the monks actually paid in advance, and therein lay the problem.

What is new here is that in these last two cases the monks concerned did not die in debt. When they died, something in both cases was owed to them, and the primary purpose of our two texts was, it seems, to determine what that was, and what the deceased's co-religionists had a right to expect, what, in short, they could or could not legitimately seek to recover. Notice that the monks' right to institute an action for recovery was not argued or ruled upon: it was simply assumed; but notice too that it is "the monks'" [129] right to institute the action, not the Community's. This, presumably, is based on the fact that because they will inherit and therefore will be obligated—within established limits—to pay the deceased's debts, they also have the rights to anything that was owed to him. Although none of this is here explicitly stated, the assumption that the right of recovery inhered in "the monks" is at least narratively asserted to have been held by both monks and merchants: neither the weaver nor the cloth merchant challenge the monks' right to make their claim. The challenge of both is only to its terms, and here we strike an element that, while not necessarily new, is certainly far more pronounced in our last two texts.

It is something of a truism in the history of law that one of the earliest—if not indeed *the* earliest—forms of contract was debt. It is, moreover, notoriously difficult in a number of contexts to clearly separate a law of debt from contract law. That, starting with IV but more certainly with V and VI, we have moved almost imperceptibly from the former to the latter should not, then, be an undue surprise. The dispute in both V and VI—if we may call it such—is not about the rights of the monks to make a claim for recovery. That, as we have seen, is conceded. The dispute and the Buddha's ruling are about the terms, about, in other words, the terms or provisions of what would have to be called the contract. Although neither text uses a term for "contract"—and this may have some chronological significance—both carefully state the intended nature of the transaction that the dead monk had entered into: V explicitly states the purpose for which the deceased had transferred his property to the weaver—"for the purpose of having cloth woven"; in VI the deceased himself declares the merchant's obligation—"You must give me cloth." The acceptance of thread and money on the part of the weaver and the merchant—which is a narrative fact—would have signaled their acceptance of the terms of the contract, and their understanding of those terms is made explicit in response to the action of the monks. They, the Buddha, and the dead monk are all presented as understanding that the contract or agreement called for cloth.

Given the careful presentation of the "facts" by our *vinayadhara*, it is impossible not to see the action of the monks as the issue, although that action can be described in more than one way. It could be said that the monks were attempting to recover something other than what was specified in the contract; it could also be said that they were in effect seeking to abrogate or annul the contract. However phrased, this is what the Buddha is asked to adjudicate, and his ruling is unmistakably that either or both are at fault. He—like the weaver and the merchant—does not question the monks' right of recovery, but he—again like the weaver and the merchant—in effect insists [130] that that right only operates within, and is constrained by, the terms of the dead monk's agreement. What had been instituted and agreed to by the monk while alive cannot be altered by either party—notice that merchant and weaver do nothing else than insist on the original terms. The Buddha's original ruling, then, does no more nor no less than insist that his monks abide by the terms of the contract that their now deceased fellow monk had entered into with both weaver and merchant. He insists, in other words, on the rule of law, in this case the accepted law of contract, and by doing so he makes this accepted law of contract a specific element of Buddhist monastic law.[77]

The second ruling of the Buddha in both V and VI seems to be directed toward the question of witness, although no such term is used. As the case is developed the dispute comes down to the narrative fact that although both parties now agree that by terms of the original contract "cloth" was to be delivered, and the monks, in compliance with the Buddha's first ruling, are seeking only to recover that, there is a disagreement as to the quality of that cloth. In the first ruling the Buddha had declared that what the merchant said was true and the monks must act accordingly. In his second ruling, however, the Buddha does not explicitly say this, and the implications seem to be that although the existence of a contract, and the broad content of it, can both be determined in the absence of one party—the now dead monk—a determination of its finer terms must depend on, and be conceded to, its surviving witness, that is to say, the merchant. Once again, it seems, the Buddha's ruling does not necessarily favor the monks but would seem rather to accommodate the authority of lay claims and to insist once more that his monks play according to lay rules. This apparent emphasis on accommodation—whether rhetorical or real—brings us to the last text from the *Uttaragrantha* that we can look at here.

What has so far been presented here will probably suggest an unexpectedly sophisticated and developed Buddhist monastic law of debt and contract. But it is good to keep in mind that what we have seen is really only a small part—a distinct subset—of a much larger corpus of Mūlasarvāstivādin *Vinaya* texts that articulate an equally sophisticated monastic law of inheritance. When we are confronted with this substantial corpus, certain questions seem unavoidable, but the chief of these would seem to be quite simply, how did all of this happen, how did what was supposed to have been little more than groups of celibate men without possessions, social ties, or fixed addresses get tangled up with property law and [131] laws of inheritance, with *dharmaśāstra* and *kārṣāpaṇas* and commercial deals? Any answer will undoubtedly be a long time coming and complicated and may end in seeing that in fact these groups were so entangled from the start. But modern historians themselves might start with a clear awareness that they are not the first to have tried to offer some kind of answer to a part of the question—our *vinaya-dharas* had already done so in our final text.

Our final text is actually the first to occur in the *Uttaragrantha*—it occurs almost 70 folios before the sequence of texts dealing with private debts of individual monks, and more than 160 folios before the text on corporate or Community debt. There are, moreover, good reasons for thinking that it was intended as, or at least taken to be, the Mūlasarvāstivādin "origin tale" for monastic inheritance law, the textual source, in other words, for how all of this came to be. Perhaps the best evidence that this was so is that our final text was the first of the canonical sources that is given by Bu ston for Guṇaprabha's *sūtras* on inheritance—it *(I)* stands at the head of, and was by implication the foundation for, all the rest. This foundational character of I is also suggested, as we will see, by its contents. It gives a series of initial solutions—none of which worked—to the problem of what to do with the property that a deceased monk left behind, and it is presented as if it were the first of the Buddha's rulings to do so. It begins with a "period" during which a very different approach was taken to the issue, a "period" before which, it seems, the Buddha had made any ruling on the matter.

I (= i)

Tog Na 121b.2–122b.5 = Derge Pa 85a.3–86a.2 = Peking Phe 82b.5–83b.2

sangs rgyas bcom ldan 'das mnyan du yod pa na dze ta'i[1] *tshal mgon med zas sbyin gyi kun dga' ra ba na bzhugs so /*

mnyan du yod pa na khyim bdag gzhan zhig 'dug pa des / rigs mnyam pa las chung ma zhig blangs nas / de de dang lhan cig[2] *tu rtse dga' zhing*[3] *yongs su spyod do / de rtse dga' zhing yongs su spyad pa las / de'i chung ma sems can dang ldan par gyur te / de zla ba brgyad dam dgu lon pa dang bu pho zhig btsas te / de zhag bdun gsum nyi shu*[4] *gcig gi bar du btsas pa'i btsas ston chen po*[5] *rgya cher byas nas / rigs dang mthun*[6] *par ming btags*[7] *so /*

de dus phyi[8] *zhig na bcom ldan 'das kyi bstan pa la rab tu byung nas / de yang dus phyi zhig na nad kyis btab ste dus 'das pa*[9] *dang / dge slong dag gis de lhung bzed dang chos gos dang bcas te dur khrod du bor ba bram ze dang khyim bdag lam der byung ste*[10]*/ dong ba de dag gis mthong nas / de dag gcig la gcig gtam du 'dzer cing 'dong ste / kye bdag cag khyim pa khyim na gnas pas thabs*[11] *rnam pa du mas nor rdzas dag bsgrubs kyang snod spyad dang gos dag ni mi 'dor na / dge sbyong shā kya'i bu 'di dag ni sgo'i them*[12] [132] *pa brgya rgal zhing dka' bzhin du lto 'gengs shing bsod snyoms bsgrub*[13] *na / ci'i phyir lhung bzed dang chos gos 'dor zhes smra ba na / dge slong dag kyang de'i mdun nas*

1. Peking: *'dze ta'i*. 2. Peking: *gcig*. 3. Derge, Peking: omit *zhing*. 4. Derge, Peking: add *rtsa*. 5. Peking: omits *chen po*, but this looks like a "correction." 6. Peking: *'thun*. 7. Peking: *gtags*. 8. Peking: *phyis*. 9. Derge, Peking: *dus las 'das pa*. 10. Derge, Peking: *pa* instead of *ste*. 11. Peking: *thams cad* instead of *thabs*. 12. Peking: *tham*. 13. Derge, Peking: *sgrub*.

tshur 'ongs pa dang / de dag gis de dag la smras pa / 'phags pa bdag cag khyim pa khyim na gnas te / thabs rnam pa du mas nor rdzas bsgrubs kyang snod spyad dang gos mi 'dor na / khyed cag sgo'i them pa brgya rgal zhing dka' bzhin du[14] *lto 'gengs*[15] *pa'i bsod snyoms bsgrubs te / lhung bzed dang chos gos 'di ga las 'ong na de ci'i phyir khyed kyis dge slong 'di'i lhung bzed dang chos gos su bcas te dur khrod du bor zhes smras pa dang / de dag gis bcom ldan 'das kyis ma gnang ngo zhes smras pa dang / de dag cang mi zer bar dong ngo /*

de ltar gyur ba dge slong dag la smras pa dang / dge slong dag gis / bcom ldan 'das la gsol to /

bcom ldan 'das kyis bka' stsal pa / lhung bzed dang chos gos su bcas te ma dor cig/

bcom ldan 'das kyis lhung bzed dang chos gos su bcas te ma dor cig ces gsungs[16] *pa dang / dge slong dag*[17] *gis gcer bur bor nas / bcom ldan 'das kyis bka' stsal pa / gcer bur ma dor bar smad g-yogs dang rdul gzan*[18] *gyis bkris*[19] *te bor cig /*

de nas dge slong dag gis gos bzang po dang bor nas / bcom ldan 'das kyis bzang po dang ma dor cig ces bka' stsal pa dang / de dag gis ngan pa dang bor ro /

bcom ldan 'das kyis ngan pa dang[20] *yang ma dor bar 'bring po dang bor cig ces bka' stsal to' /*

bcom ldan 'das kyis lhung bzed dang chos gos su bcas te ma dor cig ces bka' stsal pa dang[21] */ dge slong dag gis ji ltar bya ba mi shes nas / bcom ldan 'das kyis dge slong gang 'phongs ba de la byin cig ces bka' stsal to /*

drug sde dag rtag tu 'phongs pa ltar byed[22] *nas / bcom ldan 'das kyis drug sde dag la ma sbyin par / ji ltar rgan rims bzhin du byin cig ces bka' stsal pa dang / gsar bu dag ma thob par gyur nas / bcom ldan 'das kyis dris pa la lan 'debs pa'i dge slong gis dge 'dun la bsgo la / dge slong gi dge 'dun thams cad 'dus shing 'khod pa dang / gtsug lag khang skyong gis dge 'dun gyi nang du rin thang bskyed par byos shig ces bka' stsal to //*

The Buddha, the Blessed One, was staying in Śrāvastī, in the Jetavana, in the Park of Anāthapiṇḍada.

When a householder living in Śrāvastī had taken a wife from a suitable family, he enjoyed himself and made love with her. From that enjoyment and lovemaking, his wife became pregnant, and, eight or nine months passing, she gave birth to a male child. When, during three times seven, or twenty-one, days, the birth festival for the newborn had been performed in detail, he was given a name that was in conformity with the family.

When at a later time the son had entered the religious life in the Order of the Blessed One, and still later had been struck with illness and had died, the monks had thrown him, together with his bowl and robes, into the burning ground. When brahmins and householders coming out and going along the road saw him, they talked among themselves as they went: "Hah! When we laymen

14. Peking: omits *du*. 15. Peking: *'grengs*. 16. Peking: *bsungs*. 17. Peking: omits *dag*. 18. Peking: has either *bran* or *zan* as the second member of the compound—it is difficult to read. 19. Derge: *dkris*; Peking: *dgris*. 20. Derge, Peking: omit *dang*. 21. Peking: omits *dang*. 22. Peking: *byaṣ*.

living in a house do not throw away vessels and garments [133] even though we can acquire money and goods in all sorts of ways, how is it that these Buddhist ascetics, when they cross a hundred thresholds and still with difficulty fill their bellies and get alms, throw away bowls and robes?" While they were saying this, monks too were returning from there, and the laymen said to them: "Noble Ones, when we laymen living in a house do not throw away vessels and garments even though we can acquire money and goods in all sorts of ways, and when you, crossing a hundred thresholds still get alms that fill your bellies with difficulty, where did these bowl and robes come from, and how is it that you have thrown that body[78] into the burning ground together with this monk's bowl and robes?" But the monks said: "The Blessed One has not authorized it otherwise," and they left without saying more.

The monks told the other monks what had occurred, and those monks reported it to the Blessed One.

The Blessed One said: "He must not be thrown out together with his bowl and robes!"

When the Blessed One had said "He must not be thrown out together with his bowl and robes," and the monks threw the corpse out naked, the Blessed One said: "It must not be thrown out naked. Rather, when you have wrapped it in an undergarment and a sweat cloth, it must be thrown out!"

Then when the monks threw it out with expensive cloth, the Blessed One said: "It must not be thrown out with the expensive!" and the monks threw it out with the cheap.

The Blessed One said: "It must also not be thrown out with the cheap, but it must be thrown out with the run-of-the-mill!"

When the Blessed One said: "He must not be thrown out together with his bowl and robes," and the monks did not know what should be done with them, the Blessed One said: "They must be given to that monk who is poor!"

When the Group of Six constantly acted as if they were poor, the Blessed One said: "They must not be given to the Group of Six, but they should be given according to seniority." But when the junior monks did not get any, the Blessed One said: "The Monk-Who-Answers-Questions[79] must summon the Community, and when the whole Community of Monks is assembled and seated, the Guardian-of-the-Monastery[80] must auction[81] them in the midst of the assembly!"

The narrative logic of our final text—the first to actually occur in the *Uttaragrantha*—is not difficult to discern if we move from the end backward. A monk's estate is sold at auction in the midst of the Community by a monastic officer to ensure an otherwise unachievable equitable distribution. (Though not explicitly stated, it is virtually certain from other references to monastic sales, like that of the valuable woolen blanket already cited, that this sale would be followed by the division among the monks of the proceeds). Some form of distribution was required because the Buddha himself had ruled that the monks could not simply throw a dead monk's property away, and it did not by implication belong to the Community either. It could not be thrown away because to do so would invite and had produced lay criticism—that criticism, which is expressed in one long sentence that is not easily turned into felicitous English, comes down to this: monks who would do so are even [134] by lay standards profligate and wasteful; and monks who could afford to do so were not what they made themselves out to be. Ergo, monks kept the estates of their deceased brethren and disposed of them responsibly to accommodate lay standards and expectations! It is a nice argument and one by which the monks win both ways: they get to keep the goods *and* what the *vinayadhara* seemed to think was their good reputation. But others might see here some loss.

The actions of the monks in our text in regard to the estate of the dead monk, prior to the Buddha's ruling, appear to be fully consonant with ascetic ideals and a life of voluntary poverty—they simply left his property with his corpse in the cemetery. It is the intervention of the Buddha and the force and consequences of his ruling that move his monks away from what might have been thought was his own ideal and, in effect, involve them with the whole issue of inheritance law and sales by auction: once the estate was kept, something had to be done with it. This movement—if movement it was—is presented by the text itself as entirely the result of lay reaction to narratively prior practice: the monks themselves did not want or seek to retain the estate; lay criticism forced it on them. This quite clearly is the subtext of the tale, and because this tale was apparently understood to stand as the foundation for all the rest of Mūlasarvāstivādin inheritance law, it would appear to represent that tradition's understanding of how, in our words, all this came to be. The charge—if there was to be a charge—was laid firmly at the feet of laymen. The Buddha did not innovate but only reacted to lay pressure; the monks did not assert their own individual or institutional interests but only accommodated lay values. The question that remains here—and it is a historical one—is, of course, whether and in what sense any of this is true. Does the traditional explanation identify an actual historical mechanism that operated in the development of Buddhist monastic orders, or is it just a tale told by monks to other monks to explain why things are as they are, an explanatory trope they used to cover their tracks? Although I am not at all sanguine that this question can ever be fully or satisfactorily answered, an attempt might at least flush out some useful observations.

There are several discomforting things about our origin tale, but the first must be that the laymen in our text criticize Buddhist monks for doing what elsewhere in our *Vinaya* laymen themselves do or are said to do. The laymen in our text say not once, but twice, that they "do not throw away vessels and garments," and, given the context, this would seem to refer to their funereal practices. But—to cite only one very clear example—the *Vinayavibhaṅga* has a text that says that laymen did the very thing they criticize monks for doing. The *Vibhaṅga* text concerns a monk with [135] the unsavory name of Mahākāla. He is described as "one who obtained everything from the burning ground" (*thams cad dur khrod pa dang ldan pa yin te*)—his bowl, robe, alms, etc. The text then goes on to explain what this means:

> What is an alms bowl from the burning ground? It is like this—his relatives throw away in the burning ground the pot of one who has died and passed away (*nye du dag gis shi zhing dus la bab pa'i rdze'u dur khrod du 'dor bar byed pa*). Then the Venerable Mahākāla, squaring the pieces and having heated them, takes possession of it as an alms bowl and keeps it. Just so is an alms bowl from the burning ground.
>
> And what is a robe from the burning ground? It is like this—his relatives throw away in the burning ground the garments of one who has died and passed away (*nye du dag gis shi zhing dus la bab pa'i gos dag dur khrod du 'dor bar byed pa*). Then the Venerable Mahākāla washes and stitches them, and having altered them, he takes possession of them as a robe, etc.[82]

Apart from noting it, it is hard to know what to do with this discrepancy. Our text has laymen saying that they do not throw away vessels and garments, and the verb here is *'dor ba*. But the *Vibhaṅga* represents them as routinely doing just that, at least in their funereal practice, and the verb here too is *'dor ba*. In light of the *Vibhaṅga* passage, the practice of Buddhist monks prior to the Buddha's ruling in the *Uttaragrantha* would have to be seen as conforming almost exactly to lay practice and, therefore, hardly open to the kind of criticism it receives. Given that there are a significant number of other passages elsewhere in this *Vinaya* referring to a variety of goods deposited in burning grounds—indeed the *śmāśānika*, a distinct category of monks, would seem to presuppose this—a Mūlasarvāstivādin monk who knew his *Vinaya* might be legitimately puzzled by the explanation offered in our text for how monks came to be required to retain the estates of a deceased member of their Community. That same monk, moreover, would almost certainly have noticed something else as well.

A Mūlasarvāstivādin monk who knew his *Vinaya* would almost certainly have noticed that the text in the *Uttaragrantha* that explained the origin of Mūlasarvāstivādin inheritance law was remarkably similar to another text about another dead monk and the problems that what he left behind had created. This other text—found in the *Kṣudrakavastu*—is one of two that explain the origin of Mūlasarvāstivādin monastic funerals. The *Kṣudrakavastu* text is now easily available[83] and can therefore be only briefly summarized here. A householder in Śrāvastī took a wife from a suitable family and lay with her, and as a consequence a son was born. The birth festival was held, and the son was named. Later the son entered the Buddhist Order but got sick and died. Up to this point, of course, the text in the *Kṣudraka* tells the same story, using much the same language, as our *Uttara* text. And the similarity continues. The former then says: "The [136] monks left him (i.e., his body), together with his bowl and robes, near a road (*de dge slong dag gis lhung bzed dang bcas / chos gos dang bcas par lam dang nye ba zhig tu bor ro /*)." Then brahmins and householders came along, saw the body discarded along the road, and scoffed at Buddhist monks and their practices. The Buddha, when told of this, then gave a detailed set of rulings governing a monk's funeral, indicating that the body must be properly and ritually treated and that ideas of death pollution must be accommodated.

Both texts are obviously built up on the same narrative armature, and in both, it seems, the Buddha's ruling moves monastic practice away from what might have been thought to be something like Buddhist doctrine. Once again the monks' behavior prior to the ruling—the casual discarding of the body, the absence of ritual, and the lack of concern for social and religious norms, especially in regard to pollution—would seem to have been far more consonant with formal Buddhist notions of "person" and body. But once again they are not allowed to stand. Once again too this movement away from Buddhist ideal and toward social convention is caused or motivated by, and explained as a reaction to, social criticism. In other words, our monk might well begin to detect an explanatory pattern. If he knew both accounts he might, moreover, not just have noticed the pattern but even have concluded that the ruling governing funerals must have preceded the ruling governing inheritance, at least in narrative time, because the monks in the *Kṣudraka* were still disposing of the bowl and robes together with the body, and this, narratively, had not yet become an issue and had not yet been ruled against by the Buddha.

The criticism spoken by the brahmins and householders in the *Kṣudraka* is also particularly interesting. When they see the discarded body, their conversation goes like this:

> One said: "Hey look, a Buddhist monk has died." Others said: "Come here! Look at this!" When they looked, they recognized the dead monk and said: "This is the son of the householder so-and-so. This is the sort of thing that happens when someone joins the Order of those lordless Buddhist ascetics. Had he not joined their Order, his kinsmen would certainly have performed funeral ceremonies for him!"

And this too would have looked familiar to our Mūlasarvāstivādin monk. If he had known his *Bhaiṣajyavastu*, he would have encountered something like it at least twice—once, for example, in a story about a young monk named Svāti who was bitten by a snake and went unattended. The text says that Svāti "fainted from the poison, fell to the ground, foamed at the mouth, and his face was contorted and his eyes rolled." Then:

> *sa tathā vihvalo brāhmaṇagṛhapatibhir dṛṣṭaḥ | te kathayanti | bhavantaḥ katarasyāyaṃ gṛhapateḥ putra iti | aparaiḥ samākhyātam | amukasya iti | te kathayanti |* [137] *anāthānām śramaṇaśākyaputrīyānāṃ madhye pravrajitaḥ | yadi na pravrajito 'bhaviṣyat jñātibhir asya cikitsā kāritā abhaviṣyad iti |*

> Brahmins and householders saw him afflicted in that way. They said: "Of which householder, Sirs, is this the son?" Others reported: "Of so-and-so." They said: "He entered into the religious life in the midst of those lordless Buddhist ascetics—if he had not entered the religious life, his kinsmen would certainly have had him medically treated!"[84]

Almost exactly the same conversation among brahmins and householders is also reported to have occurred in the *Bhaiṣajyavastu*, when they saw another Buddhist monk named Saikata wandering around insane.[85] The first of these conversations motivated the Buddha to rule that, under a doctor's orders, his monks could take "foul foods" (*vikṛta-bhojana*) and to provide them with a charm against snake bite (the *Māyūrī-vidyā*); the second led him to rule that his monks could—again under the orders of a doctor—take "raw flesh." Though less obviously, perhaps, both of these new rulings also go toward weakening the already lukewarm ascetic ideal found in the *Mūlasarvāstivāda-vinaya*. There is reference in the Mūlasarvāstivādin ordination formulary to the candidate, when a monk, relying for "medicines" on "medicinal decoctions" (*pūtimukta*) only, and although this sole reliance is already weakened in the formulary itself by a long list of "extra allowances" (*atireka*), the two rulings just cited go a long ways beyond even them.

What our Mūlasarvāstivādin monk might have made of all of this is, of course, hard to determine, but one thing at least is fairly certain, and this itself is of some importance to the historian: Mūlasarvāstivādin monks were repeatedly told by their own *Vinaya* that not just the rules governing monastic inheritance, but a whole range of practices required of them that departed from ascetic ideals and the idea of voluntary poverty, were instituted in direct response to lay criticism.[86] Whether such monks believed this or not may not be as important as the fact that their *vinayadharas* felt compelled, apparently, to repeat it. That their *vinayadharas* did so in a stereotypical way, using the same conventional trope over and over again, makes it at least doubtful that this narrative "explanation" can tell us anything certain about actual historical processes. Indeed there are good reasons for suspecting that "brahmins and householders" in India might well have been entirely indifferent to what

Buddhist monks did or did not do—it is, after all, only Buddhist literature that says otherwise, and it is perhaps painfully obvious that Buddhist monks were of absolutely no concern or importance for the authors of Indian *dharmaśāstra*: they have no place in this old, large, and continuous normative literature.[87] What we see in our *Vinaya*, then, can it seems at best tell us only about one important group of monks and how they chose to represent their community and [138] its history to other monks. This may have been an influential group of monks—they wrote or compiled the texts and thereby made the rules—but if they were, this is the same group of monks who appear to have had some knowledge of *dharmaśāstra*, even if it had virtually no knowledge of them, and who appear to have been much concerned with representing their Community to their fellow monks as sensitive to and accommodating toward the norms and values of what they took to be their surrounding community. Knowing even this may prove, perhaps, to be of some value. [139]

Notes

1. P. Olivelle, *The Āśrama System. The History and Hermeneutics of a Religious Institution* (New York and Oxford: 1993) 51; C. Malamoud, *Cooking the World. Ritual and Thought in Ancient India*, trans. D. White (Delhi: 1996) 95 (for the original French version, see C. Malamoud, "La théologie de la dette dans le brahmanisme," *Puruṣārtha: Science sociales en asie du sud* 4 [1980] 39–62); see also M. Hara, "*Ānṛṇya*," in *Langue, style et structure dans le monde indien. Centenaire de Louis Renou*, éd. N. Balbir et al. (Paris: 1996) 235–261. The redactors of the *Mūlasarvāstivāda-vinaya*, the text we will be most directly concerned with here, clearly knew something of this brahmanical anthropology. For example, the father of a newborn son is repeatedly said in this *Vinaya* to declare to his wife, in a narrative cliché, *bhadre jāto 'smākam ṛṇaharo dhanaharaḥ*, which in spite of Edgerton (s.v. *ṛṇadhara*), and in light of far more occurrences than he knew and their Tibetan translations, must mean "My dear, (both) a remover of our debt (and) a taker of our wealth has been born to us" (see for occurrences of the cliché in Sanskrit, in addition to those cited from the *Divyāvadāna* by Edgerton: *Bhaiṣajyavastu*, GMs iii 1, 87.5; *Pravrajyāvastu*, GMs iii 4, 54.1; *Saṅghabhedavastu* (Gnoli) ii 32.22, 91.9; and the commentary on the cliché in the *Vinayavastuṭīkā*, Derge, bstan 'gyur, 'dul ba Tsu 284b.l—cf. E. H. Johnston, *The Buddhacarita* (Calcutta: 1935) IX.65: *naraḥ pitṝṇām anṛṇaḥ prajābhir* . . .). Edgerton's *ṛṇadhara*, by the way, is almost certainly a ghost form that should be disregarded.

2. The translation here is Olivelle's—*The Āśrama System*, 47.

3. R.W. Lariviere, *The Nāradasmṛti*, Pts. I–II (Philadelphia: 1989). The quotation is from Pt. II, ix. All references to *Nārada* are to this careful edition.

4. H. Chatterjee, *The Law of Debt in Ancient India* (Calcutta: 1971).

5. Chatterjee, *The Law of Debt*, 86, also cites this verse, but, because he was using another edition, as IV.9.

6. P. Olivelle, "Renouncer and Renunciation in the Dharmaśāstras," *Studies in Dharmaśāstra*, ed. R.W. Lariviere (Calcutta: 1984) 81–152; here 145.

7. Olivelle, "Renouncer and Renunciation in the Dharmaśāstras," 144 (for inheritance of a renouncer's property), 143 (for the quotation).

8. Even only desultory observation would seem to indicate that some Buddhist monks, although they sometimes claimed or invoked the status of "renouncer" (*pravrajita*), did not—by the testimony of their own rules—have that status. Olivelle ("Renouncer and Renunciation," 149) has said, for example, "His vow of poverty exempted the renouncer from both tolls and taxes"; but Mūlasarvāstivādin monks at least were both subject to and expected to pay such tolls—their *Vibhaṅga* has a section of more than twenty pages (Derge Ca 72b.6–84a.6) dealing with their obligations in regard especially to road taxes. Olivelle (ibid., 143) has also said, "After renunciation he [the renouncer] can no longer inherit any property"; but again the *Mūlasarvāstivāda-vinaya* has two separate texts dealing with a Mūlasarvāstivādin monk's continuing right to inherit family property *after* his ordination (see *Kṣudrakavastu*, Derge Tha 252b.3–254a.1; *Uttaragrantha*, Derge Pa 130a.4–131a.3—the first of these has been discussed in some detail in G. Schopen, "Monastic Law Meets the Real World: A Monk's Continuing Right to Inherit Family Property in Classical India," *HR* 35.2 [1995] 101–123 [= Ch. VI below]). Moreover, as will be seen below, Mūlasarvāstivādin monks are routinely presented as inheriting the estates of deceased fellow monks. A systematic study of issues of this sort would undoubtedly bear handsome fruit and might even point to inconsistencies on some of these questions in *dharmaśāstra* itself—see n. 42 below.

9. See, as an example, G. Schopen, "The Monastic Ownership of Servants or Slaves: Local and Legal Factors in the Redactional History of Two *Vinayas*," *JIABS 17.2* (1994) 145–173 [= Ch. VII below].

10. Chatterjee, *The Law of Debt*, xxv–xxvi.

11. Pāli *Vinaya* i 76.18. Even otherwise very careful scholars have said the same sort of thing—Olivelle, "Renouncer and Renunciation," 146 n. 121: "In Buddhism detailed rules were formulated regarding those disqualified from entering the *saṅgha*. Thieves, debtors and slaves were specifically barred from entry. Cf. *Mahā-vagga* 1.39–76"; Olivelle, *The Āśrama System*, 176: "Buddhist literature also indicates that 'being without debt' was a condition for becoming a monk. . . . One of the questions put to the candidate for ordination is 'Are you without debt?' A man with debts should not be allowed to become a monk (Vin I, 76). . . . One can understand the concern of the Buddhists; they did not want their monasteries to become havens for people trying to dodge debt collectors" (see also 195 n. 38); R. S. Sharma, "Usury in Early Mediaeval India (A.D. 400–1200)," *Comparative Studies in Society and History* 8 (1965–1966) 74: "The Buddhist Order did not admit a person who had not paid off his debts." There is what appears to be an occasional reference in brahmanical sources to freedom from debt as a prerequisite (?) to renouncing; see P. Olivelle, *Rules and Regulations of Brahmanical Asceticism: Yatidharmasamuccaya* of *Yādava Prakāśa* (Albany, N.Y.: 1995) 68, 235 (IV.19); *Manu* VI.94; etc.

12. See G. Schopen, "The Good Monk and His Money in a Buddhist Monasticism of 'the Mahāyāna Period,'" *The Eastern Buddhist*, n.s., 32.1 (2000) 85–105, esp. 88ff [=

Ch. I above, 3]. For the texts, see B. Jinananda, *Upasampadājñaptiḥ* (Patna: 1961) 15.5: (The candidate for ordination must be asked:) *mā te kasyaci[t] kiñcid deyam alpaṃ vā prabhūtam vā* [?] *yadi kathayati deyam, vaktavyaṃ / śakṣyasi prabrajyāyaṃ dātuṃ* [/] *yadi kathayati na, vivaktavyam ata eva gaccha* [/] *yadi kathayati śakṣyāmīti, vaktavyaṃ*, etc. (i.e., the ordination can proceed); *Pravrajyāvastu* (Eimer) ii 142.13: *khyod la la la'i bu lon mang yang rung nyung yang rung / cung zad chags pa med dam / gal te bu lon chags so zhes zer na / khyod bsnyen par rdzogs nas 'jal nus sam zhes dri bar bya'o / gal te mi nus shes zer na / 'o na song shig ces brjod par bya'o / gal te bsnyen par rdzogs nas 'jal nus shes zer na*, etc.; Kalyāṇamitra, *Vinayavastuṭīkā*, Derge, bstan 'gyur, 'dul ba Tsu 250b.1: *khyod la la la'i bu lon mang yang rung nyung yang rung cud zad chags pa med dam zhes bya ba ni bu lon ni gzhal bar bya ba yin pas de'i phyir bu lon can rab tu dbyung ba dang rdzogs par bsnyen par mi bya'o / bu lon can thams cad rab tu dbyung ba dang rdzogs par bsnyen par mi bya ba yang ma yin te / 'di ltar gal te rdzogs par bsnyen nas 'jal nus so zhes zer na de rab tu dbyung ba dab* [Peking Dzu 283b.1 has, correctly, *dang*] *rdzogs par bsnyen par bya'o /*. Notice that there is some difference in these sources in regard to when the candidate should be able to repay the loan: in the *Upasampadājñapti* it is after he has "gone forth," or entered the order (*pravrajyā*); in the *Pravrajyāvastu* it is after he has been fully ordained (*upasampanna*); in the commentary it is after both. The "*karmavākya*" from Gilgit says in A. C. Banerjee, *Two Buddhist Vinaya Texts in Sanskrit* (Calcutta: 1977) 63.4: *mā te kasyacit kiñcid deyam alpaṃ vā prabhūtaṃ vā śaknoṣi vā upasampadaṃ dātum*, but the manuscript (GBMs i 73.5) has: *mā te kasyacit ki*[*ṃ*]*cid deyam alpaṃ vā prabhūtaṃ vā śakṣyasi vā pravrajyā dātuṃ*. See also *Vinayasūtra* (Sankrityayana) 4.1; *Vinayasūtra* (Bapat and Gokhale) 20.26; *'Dul ba'i mdo*, Derge, bstan 'gyur, 'dul ba Wu 4a.4; *Svavyākhyāna*, Derge, bstan 'gyur, 'dul ba Zhu 20b.1; etc. The statement about repayment is not found in M. Schmidt, "Bhikṣuṇī-Karmavācanā. Die Handschrift Sansk. c.25(R) der Bodleian Library Oxford," in *Studien zur Indologie und Buddhismuskunde. Festgabe des Seminars für Indologie und Buddhismuskunde für Professor Dr. Heinz Bechert zum 60. Geburtstag am 26. Juni 1992*, ed. R. Grünendahl et al. (Bonn: 1993) 239–288, esp. 254.1.

13. G. Schopen, *Daijō bukkyō kōki jidai: Indo no sōin seikatsu*, trans. Odani Nobuchiyo (Tokyo: 2000) 70–146; Schopen, "Art, Beauty, and the Business of Running a Buddhist Monastery in Early Northwest India," Ch. II above.

14. Cf. H. Eimer, "Which Edition of the Kanjur Was Used by A la ša Lha btsun in Studying the Vinaya?" in H. Eimer, *Ein Jahrzehnt Studien zur Überlieferung des tibetischen Kanjur* (Vienna: 1992) 185–189, esp. 187 n. 7. Eimer says that "in the Derge and in the Urga edition . . . the *Vinayottaragrantha* and the *Vinayottamagrantha* are not distinctly separated," but they are so at least in the Taipei reprint of the Derge; see G. Schopen, "If You Can't Remember, How to Make it Up: Some Monastic Rules for Redacting Canonical Texts," in *Bauddhavidyāsudhākaraḥ* 580 n. 30 [= Ch. XIV below].

15. A. C. Banerjee, *Sarvāstivāda Literature* (Calcutta: 1957) 99.

16. G. Schopen, "Marking Time in Buddhist Monasteries: On Calendars, Clocks, and Some Liturgical Practices," in *Sūryacandrāya. Essays in Honour of Akira Yuyama on the Occasion of His 65th Birthday*, ed. P. Harrison and G. Schopen (Swisttal-Odendorf: 1998) 157–179, esp. 172ff [= Ch. IX below, 270ff].

17. *Cīvaravastu*, GMs iii 2, 119.15, 121.2. For the *Uttaragrantha* text, see the text marked "I" below (in the present chapter), and for the auction, especially n. 81.

18. See the references in n. 8 above; and Schopen, "Marking Time in Buddhist Monasteries," 172 n. 54 [below, p. 282n. 54].

19. G. Schopen, "Doing Business for the Lord: Lending on Interest and Written Loan Contracts in the *Mūlasarvāstivāda-vinaya*," *JAOS* 114 (1994) 527–554 [= Ch. III above] (for the text in the *Uttaragrantha*—which I did not know at the time I was writing this essay—see Derge Pa 265a.6–b.2). Guṇaprabha appears to have used the *Uttara* text, though he refers to his source as "The *Mātṛkā*" (pp. 543–544) [= Ch. III above, 66–68]. (For more on the monastic use of substitutes or surrogates, see below, pp. 143–145). Although the question needs much fuller study, what appears to be another example of the pattern is worth mentioning because it concerns the *gandhakuṭī*. *Śayanāsanavastu* (Gnoli) 10–12 has an important proof text that places the *gandhakuṭī* within the *vihāra*, but this placement is attested in the archaeological record only rather late (fourth–fifth centuries) and appears to be completely absent in Gandhāra. The *Uttara*, however, has a text that places *gandhakuṭīs* around the perimeters of *stūpas* (Derge Pa 119b.2: . . . *mchod rten la mtha' ma dri gtsang khang gis bskor la* . . .), and this may be precisely what we see at, for example, the Dharmarājikā at Taxila.

20. M. Hahn, "The Avadānaśataka and Its Affiliation," in *Proceedings of the XXXII International Congress for Asian and North African Studies. Hamburg 25th–30th August 1986*, ed. A. Wezler and E. Hammerschmidt (Stuttgart: 1992) 171.

21. For the texts in the *Uttaragrantha*, see Derge Pa 104b.6–108a.4 (= *Maitrakanyaka*); Derge Pa 115b.1–119a.6 (= *Śrīmatī-Avadāna*). M. Deeg ("The Saṅgha of Devadatta: Fiction and History of a Heresy in the Buddhist Tradition," *Journal of the International College for Advanced Buddhist Studies* 2 [1999] 183–218, esp. 198–199 and n. 86) says, referring to the *Śrīmatī* in the *Avadānaśataka*, "This episode . . . is not found anywhere else in Buddhist narrative literature," but the *Uttara* version requires that this be revised. J. L. Panglung, *Die Erzählstoffe des Mūlasarvāstivāda-vinaya. Analysiert auf Grund der Tibetischen Ubersetzung* (Tokyo: 1981) has not included the *Uttara* in its survey and does not always give the parallels in the *Avadānaśataka* for stories found even elsewhere in the *Mūlasarvāstivāda-vinaya*; e.g., under what it calls "Die Bekehrung einer alten Frau" (p. 30), it does not indicate that this tale has a close parallel in *Avadānaśataka* no. 78, "Kacaṅgala." This is a particularly important parallel because the *vinaya* version is preserved in Sanskrit (*Bhaiṣajyavastu*, GMs iii 1, 20.3ff) and can therefore be directly compared with the Sanskrit text of the *Avadānaśataka*. The fourth *varga* of the *Avadānaśataka*, by the way, appears to be particularly dependent on the *Mūlasarvāstivāda-vinaya*—as many as half of the tales in the former may have come from the latter (nos. 31, 36, 37, 38, and 40).

22. This work has received little attention and has yet to be described in any detail. L.W.J. van der Kuijp ("The Yoke Is on the Reader: A Recent Study of Tibetan Jurisprudence," *CAJ* 43 [1999] 266–292, esp. 280 n. 29) has recently referred to it as a source for Buddhist *Vinaya* narrative literature bearing on legal matters, but it is also more than that. I myself have described it as "a condensed version of the entire *Mūlasarvāstivāda-vinaya*" and noted that "it follows the rearrangement of the canonical material effected by

Guṇaprabha in his *Vinayasūtra*" (Schopen, "Marking Time in Buddhist Monasteries," 178 n. 67 [= Ch. IX below, 284 n. 67]). But whereas in the *Vinayasūtra* we get only the rulings, and then too in sometimes incredibly compact *sūtra* form that renders any identification of source difficult, in Bu ston we get a more or less condensed version not only of the rulings but also of the narratives that generated them. These, of course, are much easier to recognize, though doing so requires a reasonably good knowledge of the canonical *Vinaya*. The commentaries on the *Vinayasūtra*—there are four by Indian authors—also occasionally cite something of the canonical narratives Guṇaprabha is drawing on, and a combination of these sources usually allows one to identify the texts in the canonical *Vinaya* he is digesting with at least some degree of certainty.

23. The references here are to the text of the *'Dul ba pha'i gleng 'bum chen mo* published in *The Collected Works of Bu-Ston*, Pt. 23 (Ḥa), ed. L. Chandra (New Delhi: 1971), and the numbers given are the original folio numbers.

24. On the order of the *vastus* in the *Mūlasarvāstivāda-vinaya*, see H. Hu-von Hinüber, "The 17 Titles of the *Vinaya-vastu* in the *Mahāvyutpatti*. Contributions to Indo-Tibetan Lexicography II," *Bauddhavidyāsudhākaraḥ*, 339–345.

25. No one, to my knowledge, has yet studied the thematic logic of Guṇaprabha's rearrangement of the canonical material. The study of the *Vinayasūtra* and its commentarial literature in general has moved at something less than even the usual snail's pace. Only recently, for example, have we begun to get some material for establishing better Sanskrit texts; see M. Nakagawa, "On the *Adattādāna-pārājikam* in the *Vinayasūtravṛtti*—Transcription Text on the *sūtras* no. 120–123—," *Indogaku bukkyōgaku kenkyū*, 48.2 [96] (2000) 1135–1133, and his other papers cited there in n. 1 (note, however, that this list is not complete).

26. Here it is worth noting that there appears to be at least one other attempt to systematize Buddhist monastic inheritance law that is much in need of study. S. Weinstein has said: "The importance of the question of the disposition of the property of deceased monks, technically known as *wang pi-ch'iu wu* . . . , can be seen from the fact that Tao-Hsüan, the *de facto* founder of the *Lü* (or *Vinaya*) school, wrote a work solely devoted to this subject (the *Liang-ch'u ch'ing-chung i* . . . in two fascicles . . .)" (*Buddhism under the T'ang* (Cambridge, U.K.: 1987) 183 n. 25; cf. 93–94). As far as I know, however, this work has been little more than mentioned in Western sources; e.g., J. Gernet, *Les aspects économiques du bouddhisme dans la société chinoise du vᵉ au xᵉ siècle* (Paris: 1956) 66 n. 2, 70 n. 2, etc.; J. Kieschnick, *The Eminent Monk. Buddhist Ideals in Medieval Chinese Hagiography* (Honolulu: 1997) 12 n. 43.

27. Capital roman numerals in the section heads below indicate the actual order of occurrence in the *Uttaragrantha* of the main texts presented here—the first text presented, for example, occurs in the *Uttara* at Tog Na 190b.3 and therefore after the last text presented in this chapter—i.e., text I, which occurs at Tog Na 121 b.2. This seemed a good way of highlighting the fact that in presenting texts we often rearrange them and produce a "system" that is entirely of our own making. Lowercase roman numerals in parentheses reflect the order or position of the texts treated here in Guṇaprabha's "system" and refer to the table on pp. 126–127.

28. So M. Monier-Williams, *A Sanskrit-English Dictionary* (Oxford: 1899) s.v. *kārṣāpaṇa*, though he cites only "Lexicographers"; for the *Mūlasarvāstivāda-vinaya* and related literature, see, for convenience, K. Upreti, *India as Reflected in the Divyāvadāna* (New Delhi: 1995) 40, 43, 44, 72–73, 96, 105, 130.

29. H. A. Jäschke, *A Tibetan-English Dictionary* (London: 1881)—hereafter cited simply as Jäschke.

30. Zhang Yisun et al., *Bod rgya tshig mdzod chen mo*, Vols. I–III (Peking: 1985)—hereafter cited by title only.

31. *Carmavastu*, GMs iii 4, 192.17: *mā yuṣmābhiḥ kiñcid uddhārīkṛtam* / . . . *nāsmābhiḥ kiñcid uddhārīkṛtaṃ* = Tog Ka 382b.4: *khyed kyis skyin po cung zad ma byas sam* / . . . *bdag cag gis skyin po cung zad kyang ma byas te* = *Divyāvadāna* 23.14.

32. See, for example, *Prātimokṣa* (Banerjee) 29.20 = Derge Ca 10a.6; *Saṅghabhedavastu* (Gnoli) ii 104.13 = Tog Nga 246a.1 and ii 106.22 = Tog Nga 247b.5; *Cīvaravastu*, GMs iii 2, 143.7 = Tog Ga 149a.5; *Carmavastu*, GMs iii 4, 192.13 = Tog Ka 382b.2; etc.

33. One might have thought that this would be covered by the 19th *Naisargika-pāyantikā* (*yaḥ punar bhikṣur nānāprakāraṃ rupika-*[ms.: *rūpika*]*-vyavahāraṃ samāpadyeta naisargikā pāyantikā—Prātimokṣa* [Banerjee] 29.18; GBMs i 44.2), but the treatment of this rule in the *Vibhaṅga* (Derge Cha 149b.7–155b.3) shows no sign of that. On the contrary, it is precisely under this rule that the *Vibhaṅga* authorizes monks to lend money on interest (see Schopen, "Doing Business for the Lord," 527–554 [= Ch. III above]). Moreover, the wording of this ruling is open to the same range of interpretations as is the 20th *Naisargika*, which is discussed in the text, pp. 142–143.

34. See G. Schopen, "On Avoiding Ghosts and Social Censure: Monastic Funerals in the *Mūlasarvāstivāda-vinaya*," *JIP* 20 (1992) 1–39 [= *BSBM* 204–237].

35. *Kṣudrakavastu*, Tog Ta 45a.6–46a.1 = Derge Tha 31a.5–b.4; *Carmavastu*, GMs iii 4, 210.6–.14 [though the Sanskrit text is here faulty] = Tog Ka 395b.6–396a.7 = Derge Ka 277a.6–b.5. See also *Kṣudrakavastu*, Tog Ta 306a.6–307a.5 = Derge Tha 204b.1–205a.3.

36. Chatterjee, *The Law of Debt in Ancient India*, 90–91. For *Gautama*, see now P. Olivelle, *Dharmasūtras. The Law Codes of Ancient India* (Oxford: 1999) 99—his 12.40: "Those who inherit the property of someone have to pay his debts." For the text and translation of *Yājñavalkya* and *Viṣṇu*, see, for convenience, B. N. Mani, *Laws of Dharmasastras* (New Delhi: 1989) 170.

37. Schopen, "Doing Business for the Lord," 537.

38. "Das *Prātimokṣasūtra* . . . ist nach übereinstimmender Ansicht der Forschung eines der ältesten Werke, wenn nicht das älteste Werk des buddhistischen Schrifttums überhaupt"; D. Schlingloff, "Zur Interpretation des Prātimokṣasūtra," *ZDMG* 113.3 (1964) 536.

39. For the Mūlasarvāstivādins see, for example, the 9th *Pāyantikā*, *Prātimokṣa* (Banerjee) 32.17. But note too that the occurrence alone of the term *sāṃghika* must of necessity imply the acknowledgment of other kinds of "monastic" property. For example, if all *vihāras* belonged to the Community, then the expression *sāṃghike vihāre*, "in a monastery belonging to the Community," is redundant and the specification pointless. The presence of *sāṃghika* makes no sense unless there were other kinds of *vihāras* that did not belong to the

Community. Although not yet fully studied, it is already clear that the Pāli *Vinaya* knows and takes for granted *vihāras* owned by lay-brothers (*upāsaka*—Pāli *Vinaya* ii 174.4, iii 65.38, 102.5). And there is no doubt that the *Mūlasarvāstivāda-vinaya* even more fully acknowledges the private ownership of monasteries by both laymen and monks (see G. Schopen, "The Lay Ownership of Monasteries and the Role of the Monk in Mūlasarvāstivādin Monasticism," *JIABS* 19.1 [1996] 81–126 [= Ch. VIII below], to which should be added at least two texts, one from the *Vibhaṅga* [Derge Cha 203a.4–205b.1] and one from the *Uttaragrantha* [Derge Pa 82b.1–84b.2], which deal with a dispute centered on a monastery that was the personal property of the Monk Rāhula). These considerations, moreover, would appear to place a significant restriction on a not insignificant number of *Prātimokṣa* rules. The 14th–18th *Pāyantikās*, for example, would appear to apply, by virtue of the qualification *sāṃghike vihāre* in them, *only* to Community-owned *vihāras*. In any other case the action described would not constitute an offense. I hope to return to these issues in the not too distant future.

40. Chatterjee, *The Law of Debt*, 101.

41. Olivelle, "Renouncer and Renunciation," 144–145—*dharmabhrātṛ* is another *dharmaśāstric* term found in the *Mūlasarvāstivāda-vinaya*. In the *Uttaragrantha* (Derge Pa 86a.2–.6), a nun claims the estate of a dead monk that was in her possession on the basis of the assertion that "he was also our brother in religion," *bdag cag gi yang chos kyi ming po lags so zhes smras pa*, and *chos kyi ming po* can hardly be anything other than a translation of *dharmabhrātṛ*. In a pendant to this text in which monks make a claim on a nun's estate, the assertion is "she was also our sister in religion," *de yang nged kyi chos kyi sring mo yin no* (Derge Pa 86a.6–b.4), and here the text must be translating something like the lesser-known *dharmabhaginī*. Both claims are rejected on the principle that what belonged to a member of one gender goes to others of that same gender, except when there are no others of that same gender present. All these texts are taken up by Guṇaprabha (ii–v in the table above, pp. 126–127).

42. There is as well another potential difficulty here in terms of *dharmaśāstra* itself. If, as *Yājñavalkya* says, the heirs of a renouncer (*yati*) are, in part even, his *dharmabhrātṛ*, his "spiritual brothers," then because his *dharmabhrātṛs* are also presumably renouncers, this would seem to indicate that renouncers can indeed inherit, and this would collide with Olivelle's assertion that "after renunciation he [the renouncer] can no longer inherit any property" ("Renounçer and Renunciation," 143).

43. Chatterjee, *The Law of Debt*, 122.

44. Ibid., 83; see also 84–87; *Nārada* I.6.

45. *Cīvaravastu*, GMs iii 2, 124.11–125.9. Although I cite the Sanskrit text here, it is by no means free of textual and/or lexical problems, the chief of which concern what Dutt reads as *pānīyaṃ* and *pātavyam* (nn. 2 and 3) but prints as *dānīyaṃ* and *dātavyam* (see GBMs vi 851.2–.6). These problems do not obscure the general sense, which is clear in the Tibetan (Derge Ga 104b.2–105a.1 =Tog Ga 136b.6–137a.7) and even in the *Vinayasūtra* (*Vinayasūtra* [Bapat and Gokhale] 47.2ff), but they need to be sorted out.

46. *Vinayavibhaṅga*, Derge Ca 79b.3ff: *chos gos gsum la 'chel ba*.

47. *Vinayasūtra* (Sankrityayana) 33.22—*'Dul ba'i mdo*, Derge, bstan 'gyur, 'dul ba Wu 27a.2.

48. On this title and office, see the unpublished dissertation, J. A. Silk, *The Origins and Early History of the Mahāratnakūṭa Tradition of Mahāyāna Buddhism with a Study of the Ratnarāśisūtra and Related Materials*, University of Michigan, 1994, 215ff.

49. See *Vinayasūtra* (Sankrityayana) 33.22: *nāpṛṣṭvā vṛddhām* . . . = *'Dul ba'i mdo*, Derge, bstan 'gyur, 'dul ba Wu 27a.3: *rgan rabs rgan rabs dag la ma zhugs par*. . . .

50. Though limited for its textual sources to Pāli material, see M. Njammasch, "Der *navakammika* und seine Stellung in der Hierarchie der buddhistischen Klöster," *Altorientalische Forschungen* 1 (1974) 279–293; for the Mūlasarvāstivādin tradition, see at least *Vinayasūtra* (Sankrityayana) 112.16–31.

51. *Uttaragrantha*, Derge Pa 112b.1–113a.1; see also *Vinayavibhaṅga* Derge Ca 75b.5–76b.4.

52. Pāli *Vinaya* i 297.33–298.3; see also iv 286.3.

53. O. von Hinüber, *Entstehung und Aufbau der Jātaka-Sammlung. Studien zur Literatur des Theravāda-Buddhismus I* (Akademie der Wissenschaften und der Literatur, Mainz) (Stuttgart: 1998) 23–24; also L. Feer, "Études bouddhiques. Maitrakanyaka-Mittavindaka. La piété filiale," *JA* (1878) 388–392.

54. *Poṣadhavastu* (Hu-von Hinüber) 280–281; *Śayanāsanavastu* (Gnoli) 38.30, 47.18.

55. On lenders and lending institutions in early India, see, for example, L. Gopal, "Credit Laws in Ancient India," *Felicitation Volume (A Collection of Forty-two Indological Essays) Presented to Mahamahopadhyaya Dr. V. V. Mirashi*, ed. G. T. Deshpande et al. (Nagpur: 1965) 444–458; H. S. Singh, "Institutions of Money-lending," *Journal of the Ganganatha Jha Kendriya Sanskrit Vidyapeetha* 38–39 (1982–1983) 109–124; S. Gururajachar, "Banking Practices in India (Up to A.D. 1600)," *New Trends in Indian Art and Archaeology. S. R. Rao's 70th Birthday Felicitation Volume*, ed. B. U. Nayak and N. C. Ghosh (New Delhi: 1992) Vol. 2, 573–582.

56. As already noted in the apparatus to the Tibetan text (n. 3), a negative appears to have dropped out of the text. Although it occurs in neither Tog, Derge, nor Peking—nor even in Bu ston—both the context and the previous *ma byin par* in line 1 would seem to require it, and I have supplied it in translation.

57. L. Finot, "Le prātimokṣasūtra des sarvāstivādins," *JA* (1913) 498 (no. 20); *Prātimokṣa* (Banerjee) 29 (no. 20); *Prātimokṣasūtram of the Lokottaravādimahāsāṅghika School*, ed. N. Tatia (Patna: 1976) 16 (no. 19); *Pātimokkha*, ed. R. D. Vadekar (Poona: 1939) 9 (no. 20).

58. Schopen, "The Good Monk and His Money," 103 [Ch. I above, 14].

59. S. C. Vidyabhusana, "So-sor-thar-pa; or, a Code of Buddhist Monastic Laws: Being the Tibetan Version of Prātimokṣa of the Mūla-Sarvāstivāda School," *Journal of the Asiatic Society of Bengal*, n.s. 11 (1915) 99. Notice too that the "Old Commentary" embedded in its *Vibhaṅga* glosses *rnam pa sna tshogs* (*nānāprakāra*) with *rnam pa mang po* (Derge Cha 156.7), and in the previous rule the same term is glossed by *rnam pa du ma*. *Mang po* most commonly means "many," and *du ma* virtually the same; neither carries the sense "all."

60. Huber in Finot, "Le prātimokṣasūtra des sarvāstivādins," 498. Cf L. Wieger, *Bouddhisme chinois. Vinaya. Monachisme et discipline. Hinayana, véhicule inférieur* (Paris: 1910) 233: "Si un moine fait le commerce, en quelque marchandise que ce soit, il y a transgression"—Dharmaguptaka.

61. M. Wijayaratna, *Le moine bouddhiste selon les textes du theravāda* (Paris: 1983) 97; I. B. Horner, *The Book of the Discipline* (Sacred Books of the Buddhist 11) (Oxford: 1940) Pt. 2, 111; T. W. Rhys Davids and H. Oldenberg, *Vinaya Texts* (Sacred Books of the East 13) (Oxford: 1885) 27.

62. Schopen, "The Good Monk and His Money," 100ff [Ch. I above, 12–13].

63. Chatterjee, *The Law of Debt*, xvii, xx.

64. Pāli *Vinaya* iii 242.11; Horner, *The Book of the Discipline* ii 112—see also R. Gombrich, *Theravāda Buddhism. A Social History from Ancient Benares to Modern Colombo* (London and New York: 1988) 92–93, 102–103, 162–164.

65. *Uttaragrantha*, Derge Pa 134a.1–b.7 = Tog Na 192b.5–194a.4.

66. *Vinayavibhaṅga*, Derge Cha 156b.3.

67. The definition is from W. Doniger, *The Laws of Manu* (London: 1991) 316; see also R. Lingat, *The Classical Law of India*, trans. J. D. M. Derrett (Berkeley: 1973) 39–40.

68. Notice the qualification of lay-brothers both here and in the text just cited from the *Uttara*. Both indicate that a "trustworthy" lay-brother should be used, meaning, it seems, that not all lay-brothers were so. For yet another reference to the use of a "trustworthy" lay-brother, see the text treated in Schopen, "Doing Business for the Lord," 530 [Ch. III above, 49], where *dge bsnyen dad pa can* is incorrectly translated as "a devout lay-brother."

69. For the text, see *Vinayavibhaṅga*, Derge Cha 149b.1–.7. For another instance of the use of surrogates in the *Mūlasarvāstivāda-vinaya*, see p. 125 above, and notice the difference in this regard between the *Vibhaṅga* and the *Uttara* pointed out there.

70. For some indications of the same sort of thing even in the Pāli *Vinaya*, see Gombrich, *Theravāda Buddhism*, 103.

71. *Kṣudrakavastu*, Derge Tha 262b.4–263a.6 = Tog Ta 392b.2–393b.2.

72. See, for example, *Cīvaravastu*, GMs iii 2, 119.14 = Tog Ga 133b.6; GMs iii 2, 121.2 = Tog Ga 134b.6; GMs iii 2, 125.6 = Tog Ga 137a.5.

73. At first sight at least the Pāli version looks like a much condensed or "edited" version of the text found in the *Mūlasarvāstivāda-vinaya*, and there are other instances of what seems to be the same pattern, although the whole question has yet to be carefully studied.

74. Pāli *Vinaya* ii 174.18–.24; Rhys Davids and Oldenberg, *Vinaya Texts* iii 217; Horner, *The Book of the Discipline* v 245; M. Wijayaratna, *Buddhist Monastic Life. According to the Texts of the Theravāda Tradition*, trans. C. Grangier and S. Collins (Cambridge, U.K.: 1990) 81. The original (Wijayaratna, *Le moine bouddhiste*, 97) reads: ". . . furent autorisés à l'échanger contre un article plus utile."

75. Y. Ousaka, M. Yamazaki, and K. R. Norman, *Index to the Vinaya-Piṭaka* (Oxford: 1996) 472.

76. Horner, *The Book of the Discipline* iv 109.

77. For a good idea of what could fall under contract law in *dharmaśāstra*, see *Nārada* V, VI, VIII, and IX. The binding nature of the act of acceptance of a fee is startlingly clear, for example, in *Nārada* VI.20: *śulkaṃ gṛhītvā paṇyastrī necchantī dvis tad āvahet.*

78. As is characteristic of the prose of the *Mūlasarvāstivāda-vinaya*, in both Sanskrit and Tibetan, the text here and throughout can be both elliptical and heavily dependent on the use of pronouns. The text never uses a term for "body" or "corpse," but simply the

"demonstrative pronoun" *de*. I have as a consequence sometimes translated this by supplying what I take to be the referent, and sometimes simply by "it."

79. Our text makes *dris pa la lan 'debs pa'i dge slong* . . . look like a title or designation for yet another monastic office, and yet it can hardly be anything else than an attempt to render something like the common *pṛṣṭavācikayā bhikṣūn samanuyujya* (*Kaṭhinavastu* [Chang] 52.28), which is more typically rendered: *dris pa'i tshig gis dge slong rnams la yang dag par bsgo la* (Chang 80.13). The Sanskrit phrase itself, however, especially *pṛṣṭa-* or *pṛṣṭha-vācika*, remains problematic (see Edgerton 353; *Poṣadhavastu* (Hu-von Hinüber) 212–214; H. Matsumura, "The Kaṭhinavastu from the Vinayavastu of the Mūlasarvāstivādins," in *Sanskrit-Texte aus dem buddhistischen Kanon: Neuentdeckungen und Neueditionen III* [Sanskrit-Wörterbuch der buddhistischen Texte aus den Turfan-Funden. Beiheft 6] [Göttingen: 1996] 193 n. 72). Given this, it might be useful to cite the two commentarial "definitions" that I have come across. Śīlapālita, *Āgamakṣudrakavyākhyāna*; Derge, bstan 'gyur, 'dul ba Dzu 22a.6: *dris pa'i tshig gis zhes bya ba ni ga ṇḍī brdungs ba na lam gyi phyogs na gnas pa'i dge slong gis ci'i phyir gaṇḍī brdungs ba sngon du song ba can gyi 'dus pa mdzad ces dris ba gang yin pa de la / dris nas lan du brjod pa de ni dris pa'i tshig yin no /*, which—*if* I have understood it correctly—might be translated as: "'With the pronouncement of what is asked' means: when the monk stationed to the side of the path when the *gaṇḍī* is struck is asked the question 'for what reason is an assembly preceded by striking the *gaṇḍī* called?' and he gives the answer—that is the pronouncement of what is asked." Vinītadeva, *Vinayavibhaṅgapadavyākhyāna*, Derge, bstan 'gyur, 'dul ba Tshu 91b.4: *dris pa'i tshig gis zhes bya ba ni ci'i phyir gaṇḍī brdungs zhes gzhan gyis dris pa la 'di'i phyir brdungs so zhes lan gdab pa'i tshig gis so /*: "'With the pronouncement of what is asked' means: with the pronouncement of the answer "it has been struck for this reason" when someone asks 'for what reason has the *gaṇḍī* been struck?'"

80. *gtsug lag khang skyong (ba)* can hardly be anything but a translation of something like *vihārapāla*—*gtsug lag khang* is the standard translation of *vihāra*, and *skyong ba* commonly renders forms of √*pāl*. This office is referred to elsewhere in the *Uttara* as well, at Derge Pa 72a.1 (where the *vihārapāla* is one of two officers—the other is the *saṃghasthavira*—charged with keeping track of the date; see Schopen, "Marking Time in Buddhist Monasteries," 173,175 [Ch. IX below, 271, 272]), 151a.5 (which would seem to indicate that it was a rotating office: *tshe dang ldan pa kun dga' bo la gtsug lag khang skyong gi res bab bo /*), 200b.5ff, etc. Yijing says, "Those who stand guard, administer the monastery gates, and announce the business to the community meeting are called *vihārapāla*" (Silk, *The Origins and Early History of the Mahāratnakūṭa*, 235). What is probably the same title occurs in the form *gtsug lag khang dag yongs su skyong bar byed ba* in the *Kṣudraka* (see, Schopen, "The Lay Ownership of Monasteries," 110 n. 60 [Ch. VIII below, n. 60]).

81. *rin thang bskyed pa* as a unit does not yet have an attested equivalent, but *rin thang* is given as an equivalent of *argha* and *mūlya* in the *Tibetan-Sanskrit Dictionary* (2264), and *bskyed pa* is given for *vardhana* (207). The Tibetan, then, is not far from one of the definitions that Monier-Williams (*English-Sanskrit Dictionary* 32) gives—on what authority I do not know—of the English word "auction": *varddhamānamūlyena nānādravyavikrayaḥ*. The *Uttaragrantha* has detailed rules governing this kind of sale, which include one against

monks artificially inflating the bid (Derge Pa 177b.2). But a discussion of these and other references to monastic auctions must wait for another time. Note, for the moment, only that other Buddhist monastic traditions also appear to have known such sales—see G. Roth, *Bhikṣuṇī-vinaya. Manual of Discipline for Buddhist Nuns* (Patna: 1970) 182.13 = É. Nolot, *Règles de discipline des nonnes bouddhistes* (Paris: 1991) 184.18.

82. *Vinayavibhaṅga*, Derge Ja 154b.2–156b.7.

83. Schopen, "On Avoiding Ghosts and Social Censure," 14–17 [= *BSBM* 215–218].

84. *Bhaiṣajyavastu*, GMs iii 1, 285.17.

85. *Bhaiṣajyavastu*, GMs iii 1, ix—the passage here has been in large part reconstructed by Dutt.

86. Though the story line differed, the same "explanation" was also given to justify, for example, monastic control of important relics; see G. Schopen, "Ritual Rights and Bones of Contention: More on Monastic Funerals and Relics in the *Mūlasarvāstivāda-vinaya*," *JIP* 22 (1994) 31–80, esp. 52 [= Ch. X below, 302–303].

87. It has indeed been difficult to detect even a trace of Buddhists in *dharma*-literature; see Lingat, *The Classical Law of India*, 123. See also, for examples: J. Filliozat, "La valeur des connaissances gréco-romaines sur l'inde," *Journal des savants*, avril–juin (1981) 113 n. 32; R. Gombrich, "The Earliest Brahmanical Reference to Buddhism?" in *Relativism, Suffering and Beyond. Essays in Memory of Bimal K. Matilal*, ed. P. Bilimoria and J. N. Mohanty (Delhi: 1997) 32–49. But see also Olivelle, *Rules and Regulations of Brahmanical Asceticism*, 32 n. 10; O. von Hinüber, *Das Pātimokkhasutta der Theravādin. Studien zur Literatur des Theravāda-Buddhismus II* (Akademie der Wissenschaften und der Literatur, Mainz) (Stuttgart: 1999) 23 n. 50. It is, of course, commonly suggested that "Buddhists" are included by *dharmaśāstra* writers under the term *pāṣaṇḍa*, but this is only made explicit in later commentaries; see, for example, Lariviere, *The Nāradasmṛti*, Pt. II, 130.

CHAPTER VI

Monastic Law Meets the Real World

A Monk's Continuing Right to Inherit Family Property in Classical India

ACCORDING TO WILLIAM of Saint-Thierry, the greater part of "the world" in the twelfth century was owned by monks.[1] William, of course, did not mean that it was owned by individual monks. "The Rule of St. Benedict was quite clear: personal poverty is required from the monks, but this is distinct from corporate possessions." Moreover, "the denial of private property [in the Rule] does not imply in any way a materially poor lifestyle."[2] The Rule of St. Benedict, in fact, which J. P. Greene calls "the foundation upon which the entire structure of medieval monasticism in Western Europe was eventually built,"[3] has little to say about corporate or institutional wealth or property. Its aim was directed, rather, toward "this vice of personal ownership," and on this it was, indeed, "quite clear."

Chapter 33 of the Rule, under the heading "Whether monks may have personal property," says in part: "It is of the greatest importance that this vice should be totally eradicated from the monastery. No one may take it upon himself to give or receive anything without the Abbot's permission, or to possess anything as his own, anything whatever, books or writing tablets or pen or anything at all. . . . Everything should be common to all, [102] as it is written, and no one should call anything his own or treat it as such." And chapter 55 reads: "The beds should be frequently inspected by the Abbot as a precaution against private possessions. If anyone is found to have anything which was not given him by the Abbot, he is to undergo the severest punishment; and that this vice of personal ownership may be totally eliminated, everything necessary should be given by the Abbot; namely, a cowl, a tunic, stockings, shoes, a belt, a knife, a pen, a needle, a handkerchief and writing tablets, so that all excuses about necessity are removed."[4]

The clarity in Benedict's Rule in regard to "whether monks may have per-

Originally published in *History of Religions* 35.2 (1995) 101–123. Reprinted with stylistic changes with permission of University of Chicago Press.

sonal property" must at least partially be a function of the fact that Benedict was able here—as elsewhere—to avoid sticky issues and the largely legal difficulties that could, and did, arise when an individual renounced real property. He may have been able to avoid these difficulties in part, perhaps, because one of his predecessors—the author of the only other "Rule" that he refers his monks to—had already dealt with them in some detail and in part, perhaps, because he was writing for a world on which the weight of Roman secular law was pressing much less heavily.[5]

Although Basil of Caesarea, St. Basil the Great (330–379), "wrote no Rule, his conferences and replies to questions were treated as a guide and were quoted as a rule by St. Benedict and others."[6] These were translated into Latin in 397 and circulated widely.[7]

Basil, of course, lived in a world very different from Benedict's. "It is necessary," for example, "to recall that at this period the burdensome tax system inaugurated by Diocletian is still operative throughout the Roman Empire and that monks are laymen and are not, therefore, eligible to the immunities granted the clergy." So, although Basil "states that the monk upon his entrance into the monastery has renounced all right to the ownership and use of his possessions" and—as Benedict ruled—that he has no ownership rights in the property of the monastery, still [103] Basil had to deal, for example, with prior unpaid taxes. His solution, according to M. G. Murphy, was to rule that "the monk actually renounces his rights to the ownership and administration of the funds he has brought to the monastery, but not his obligations to pay the taxes which have accrued before his entrance."[8]

Given the complexity of Roman laws of inheritance in their full vigor, this was another area with which Basil—unlike Benedict—was forced to deal. On this question, Murphy, summarizing several passages from *The Ascetic Works*, says: "In regard to the property that might come to the monk by way of inheritance or donation, St. Basil teaches that his monastic profession has deprived him of all right to ownership of this," and "in the case of the inherited property, therefore, St. Basil recommends that it be entrusted to the proper ecclesiastical authority to be disposed of as the latter deems fit."[9]

Whether in Benedict or Basil, then, what characterizes relatively early Christian monastic legislation in regard to private ownership by monks, or any continuing right of inheritance, is its clarity: monks have no ownership rights, and although they might technically inherit, the property in question does not go to them but to "the proper ecclesiastical authority to be disposed of as the latter deems fit." Two points are worth noting here. First, these issues are explicitly engaged in Christian monastic literature, and positions in regard to them are clearly articulated. Second, we seem to see here—at least on these issues—a case where the important variable affecting the complexity of monastic legislation or rule is not age or time but the surrounding legal environment: Benedict's is the later rule but also the simplest. It is Basil's, the earlier "Rule," that is also the most detailed and complex. It is possible that the same variable—and not date of composition or compilation—may have affected Buddhist monastic rules as well. [104]

Far, far less is known about Buddhist monastic rules and therefore about Buddhist monastic attitudes toward private ownership by monks and continuing rights of inheritance, but one thing appears to be certain: neither the scholarly literature nor the primary source materials bearing on such topics that have been noted so far have anything like the clarity of Basil or Benedict. Typical of the scholarly literature is the old remark of H. Oldenberg's: "So the Buddhist monk also renounces all property. No express vow imposes on him the duty of poverty; both the marriage tie and the rights of property of him who renounces the world, are regarded as *ipso facto* canceled by the 'going forth from home into homelessness.'" But to this Oldenberg immediately adds a note that begins: "More accurately expressed: the monk, *who is resolved to remain true to the spiritual life*, looks upon his marriage as dissolved, his property as given away."[10]

More recently, I. B. Horner has said similar things. She first said: "It was particularly reprehensible for a Sakyan monk to steal, since at the time of his entry into the Order he *morally* renounced his claim to all personal and private possessions." Then she said: "The Buddhist *bhikkhu* has to renounce his worldly possessions before he is ordained, and after his ordination he should own no private property, but should regard his bowl and robe and other requisites as being the communal property of the Order. . . . But . . . there were no vows for a Sakyan *bhikkhu* to take. He did not make any vows, did not bind himself by vows. If he attempted right behavior, this was because his spiritual training led to the taming of the self."[11]

The ambiguity here is palpable—this would have been a lawyer's dream or a lawyer's nightmare, depending on which side he had to argue. A Buddhist monk "renounces all property" but only if he "is resolved to remain true to the spiritual life": renunciation of property could not therefore be effected by the fact of ordination itself but would depend on the individual's spiritual resolve, and no mechanism is provided to establish that. A Buddhist monk "morally renounced his claim to all personal and private possessions," but this need not entail an actual legal act nor have legal effect or force.

Neither the fault nor the ambiguity here belongs to Oldenberg or Horner. They are simply putting the best face on what can be gathered from the Pāli, or Mahāvihārin, *Vinaya*. That this Rule is deeply ambiguous, if not straightforwardly ambivalent, in regard to the question of [105] "whether monks may have personal property" has been noted a long time ago, and R. Lingat, for example, has richly demonstrated the kinds of problems this ambiguity or ambivalence created for the Southeast Asian countries that had to deal with it in their secular legal system.[12]

It is important to note that it is not just the absence of positive statements in the Mahāvihārin *Vinaya* in regard to the legal status of a monk's property rights that creates the problems. It is as much—if not more so—the presence in this same *Vinaya* of the clear presumption that monks had and used private wealth. Oldenberg himself in the note already cited said: "In one direction the spiritual law [*geistliche Recht*] permitted a noteworthy operation of the old rights of property surrendered by the monk to take effect: in certain cases [*in gewissen Fällen*] where the receiving of any new article whatever for monastic house-keeping was forbidden, e.g., a new almsbowl, he was permitted to take the object in question, if it had been made for him 'from his own means.'" The language here is interesting: it continues the fiction that "old rights of property" had been surrendered, and it seems to put a narrow limit on when these old rights could take effect: *in gewissen Fällen*. Probably as a result of an admirable desire for brevity, Oldenberg cites only two instances of such cases, to which he adds *usw.*, "and so on." But this effectively conceals the fact that such cases are not rare in the Mahāvihārin *Vinaya*. There are at least sixteen cases in the last three sections of the Mahāvihārin *Suttavibhaṅga* alone, and it is probably not inaccurate to say that what Oldenberg is referring to is an established and common casuistry or escape clause in rulings of the Mahāvihārin *Vinaya* concerning allowable possessions. A significant number of prohibitions against accepting or possessing material properties, "e.g., a new almsbowl," are abrogated or rendered inapplicable if that property comes to the monk *attano dhanena*, "through his own, or private, wealth." The fact that monks have private wealth is therefore widely attested and assumed in this *Vinaya* and is repeatedly invoked to abrogate otherwise general rulings.[13]

It is, moreover, not just in the *Suttavibhaṅga* of the Mahāvihārin *Vinaya* that one finds it taken very much for granted that monks had and used private wealth. A particularly striking instance occurs in its *Vassupanāyika Khandhaka*, or chapter on the rainy season retreat. This chapter has a long section dealing with the legitimate reasons for which a monk might break the rain retreat, although under "normal" circumstances this was strictly [106] forbidden. A monk could, for example, legitimately break the rain retreat to be present, receive gifts, and recite Dhamma at the wedding of a lay-brother's (*upāsaka*) children or at a series of house dedication rituals. He could also go when a lay-brother donated a *vihāra* or any of its appendages to the order. Or, significantly, he could go when "a monk . . . a nun . . . a probationer [or] a novice" donated a *vihāra* for the Community or for him- or herself. Here, of course, it is again taken very much as a given that—exactly like lay-brothers—monks, nuns, probationers, and novices acted as major donors to Buddhist monastic communities and had—again, like lay-brothers—the means to do so.[14]

This *vinaya* material is interesting, but it is not alone in pointing out that Buddhist monks and nuns had and used private wealth. Inscriptional records of all periods show monks and nuns as active and substantial donors almost everywhere in India. This activity was first perceived as a problem in regard to the earliest series of donative records that have survived. H. Lüders said in regard to Bhārhut, much as G. Bühler had already said in regard to Sāñcī: "It is perhaps striking to find monks and nuns making donations, as they were forbidden to own any personal property besides some ordinary requisites. Probably we have to suppose that they collected the money required for some pious purpose by begging it from their relatives or acquaintances. It is, however, never stated in Bhārhut as in Jain inscriptions from Mathurā, that the dedication was made by a layman at the request of some clergyman. The wording of the Bhārhut inscriptions refers to the Buddhist clergyman in such a way, as if he himself had made the donation."[15]

The "wording of the Bhārhut inscriptions," as well as the distinct difference in Jain records, is significant. Equally significant, however, is that at least one Buddhist Rule, on at least three different occasions when it could have given its consent, withholds approval of monks' giving to a *stūpa* what "devout brahmins and householders" had given to them, suggests that such action would create friction with donors, and in each instance explicitly mandates an alternative action. One example from this Rule, the *Mūlasarvāstivāda-vinaya*, will suffice.[16] [107]

The passage starts by saying that "devout brahmins and householders" offered the monks perfumes, but they were refused by the monks. The Buddha then says they are to be accepted, and although the monks accept them, they then throw them away.

> The Blessed One said: "They must not be thrown away!" The monks gave them to the *stūpa* of the hair and nails. The donors said: "Noble Ones, did we not see the *stūpa* of the hair and nails of the Buddha? We gave them to you, even though we could have given them to the *stūpa* of the hair and nails of the Buddha in the first place !"[17]
>
> After that when the monks accepted perfumes, they put them on the door of their cells. But devout brahmins and householders saw that and thought those cells were the Perfume Chamber. When they paid reverence to those cells, the Blessed One said: "They must not be put on the door of your cells, but inside them."[18]
>
> But when the monks put them just inside the door, this itself became a problem.
>
> The Blessed One said: "They should not be put just inside the door, but since all good-smelling scents are beneficial for one's eyes, a perfumed palm print

should be made on one's pillow. After that it should be applied to the eyes now and then."[19]

Passages such as these were almost certainly intended to discourage, if not to disallow, the practice of monks' giving as gifts those things that had been given to them. Such action is repeatedly said to elicit comment from lay donors and to create confusion—both of which are to be avoided. Moreover, although it is indirectly stated, a monk's obligation in these passages is—as is expressly stated elsewhere in this *Vinaya*—to use what he is given. Only then does it generate merit for its donor.[20] [108]

All of this is perhaps sufficient to indicate that the Buddhist monastic literature that has been studied so far lacks both the clarity of Benedict and the detail of Basil in regard to personal ownership and the rights of inheritance of a monk. This comparative observation in itself may already allow some tentative hypotheses. The lack of clarity on personal ownership may indicate that for the writers of Buddhist monastic codes, personal ownership was not—as it was for Benedict—a vice, nor was it "of the greatest importance." Had it been either, there surely would have been much greater and more careful discussion. The absence in the *vinaya* literature so far studied of any explicit engagement of the question of a monk's continuing right to inherit family property is also suggestive. It may indicate that that literature—unlike Basil's—was composed or redacted in (or for) cultural milieus in which formal legal systems were little developed and the potential for conflict between monastic and secular law was not great. This would seem to exclude any highly brahmanized area of early India as a possible place of origin for this literature.

But the Buddhist *vinaya* literature that has so far been carefully studied—especially in the West—is only a small part of what has survived and may in no sense be representative. For a series of reasons—most of which are connected to historical accident—the Pāli, or Mahāvihārin, *Vinaya* alone has been thoroughly investigated and is easily available. There are, however, significant portions of other *vinayas* extant in Chinese and in Sanskrit fragments. There is also one other virtually complete *vinaya* preserved in Tibetan, large parts of which are also available in Sanskrit. This last *vinaya*, the *Mūlasarvāstivāda-vinaya*, contains—as is already clear—important data, as well as some surprises, and as it becomes better known, it likely will change the way in which we have thought about monastic Buddhism. The case in hand may be a case in point.[21]

Unlike the Mahāvihārin *Vinaya*, the *Mūlasarvāstivāda-vinaya* does explicitly engage the issue of a monk's continuing right to inherit family [109] property and personal wealth. But before we can deal directly with the passage that does so, we must first look at a passage from the section of the *Mūlasarvāstivāda-vinaya* called the *Cīvaravastu* that concerns an issue that, at first sight, does not seem directly related. The *Cīvaravastu* passage seems to be concerned with the issue of one monk's promising his "robe and bowl"—which is often a code word for all types of personal property—to a second monk on the condition that the second monk will take care of the first in his final illness. The theme of attending to the sick and dying is, by the way, a common one in the *Mūlasarvāstivāda-vinaya*. I translate the passage from the *Cīvaravastu* here from the Sanskrit text recovered from Gilgit.[22]

> The setting was Śrāvastī. When a certain monk who was ill knew himself that he was going to die, he said to another monk: "For as long as I live, so long you should attend to me. When I am dead, my robe and bowl are for you to treat as you please (*yathāsukham*)."
>
> The second monk began to attend to the dying monk. Some time later, the latter monk died. Then the monk who was the Distributor-of-Robes said to the attendant monk: "Bring the robe and bowl of that deceased monk! I will distribute it."
>
> The attendant monk said: "He made them over specifically to me to treat as I pleased (*yathāsukham*)."
>
> The monks reported this matter to the Blessed One.
>
> The Blessed One said: "Monks, that deceased monk did not give it when still living; how now, he being dead, will he give it? This is not an act of giving when one says 'After I am dead, it will be for him' (*nāstīdaṃ dānaṃ mamātyayād asya bhaviṣyati*). Therefore, [the Community] having taken possession of it, it is to be distributed. In this case, however, a good share is to be given to the attendant monk."

Given our great chronological and intellectual distance from documents of this sort, it would be easy enough to see in this passage just another piece of *vinaya* minutia dealing with monks cutting deals with other monks. But there is good evidence, as we will see, that Mūlasarvāstivādin monastic lawyers saw, or came to see, something here far more fundamental and potentially problematic, and there can be little doubt that a brahmanical jurist would have as well. The monastic lawyers were, or came to be, much less concerned with the specific case than with the general principle that its adjudication put in place. The case turns on something approaching absolute possession—*yathāsukham*. But the principle denies that such possession, or any valid possession, can be effected by what, for lack of a better term, might be called an oral [110] testament made prior to death: "This is not [a valid] act of giving when one says 'After I am dead, it will be for him.'" Restricted in its application to the sphere of monastic law—applied, that is, only to the actions of monks—this principle could have been, presumably, implemented without serious difficulties, although it would have placed monastic law at variance with brahmanical law. But in this case, it was not so limited but was annunciated without limitation and was therefore, presumably, intended or understood to have universal application. Such unrestricted application would, however, have put monastic law on a collision course with brahmanical law. Although scholars have argued over the vocabulary and the conditions placed on it, it is generally accepted that "the *Smṛtis* recognize in regard to the head of the household the right to proceed while still living with the partition of his property among his heirs," and Lingat has suggested that this must have frequently taken place, for example, "during the course of his last illness."[23] In other words, unless its application were to receive some restriction, the general principle delivered in our passage declares invalid what was almost certainly commonly practiced in brahmanical milieus and clearly recognized as a right by the *Smṛtis*. If the *Mūlasarvāstivāda-vinaya* had been redacted in, or was intended for use in, tribal areas or communities little influenced by brahmanical law—and there must have been many of both in early India—then this principle could have been unproblematic. But in any highly brahmanized areas—and it appears likely that most early Buddhist communities arose in such areas—something or someone would clearly have to give. The evidence suggests that it was the monks and that, in giving, they gained.

What evidence we have comes from another text in the *Mūlasarvāstivāda-vinaya*, a text that presents a situation that is almost exactly what could have been foreseen when the general principle presented in our first text operated in a brahmanical milieu and that, in fact, quotes that principle as the words of the Buddha. This second text is not, as far as I know, preserved in Sanskrit, so its citation here is based on the Tibetan translation.

The case occurs in the section called the *Kṣudrakavastu*[24] and concerns a householder (*khyim bdag/gṛhapati*) from Śrāvastī who married and had three sons, the youngest of whom entered the Buddhist Order. The father fell ill; then the text says: [111]

> Although he was treated with medicines made from roots, stalks, leaves, flowers, and fruits, his illness did not abate. When the feelings that end in death appeared and the time of death could not be far off, then, having assembled his friends, relatives, brothers, and neighbors, the father said to his two oldest sons: "Sons, however little there is in my house, bring all of that and come!"
>
> Hearing his words, they brought all of that and came.
>
> The father then said to those friends, relatives, brothers, and neighbors: "Lis-

ten, sirs! I have three sons. These are the two older; the youngest has entered the Order of the Buddhist *śramaṇas*. Therefore, whatever property there is in my house, however small, all of that must be divided equally."

When he had said this—since it has been said:

All accumulations end in destruction. All elevations end in a fall.
All unions end in separation. Life, to be sure, ends in death—

he died.[25]

We have here the description of a perfectly regular procedure: a father making, while alive but close to death, an equal partition of his estate, by oral declaration, to his sons. The only unusual element is, of course, that one of the sons is a Buddhist monk. But this is unusual only because *dharmaśāstra*, as far as I know, never directly addresses such a case. There is to this point no objection raised—although equal division among all sons was by no means free of controversy in brahmanical law itself[26]—and no one, including the two elder brothers, appears to see anything problematic here. The division should have been, and—as we will see—was taken to be, an accomplished fact.

When the youngest son, who was a monk, heard that his father had died, he is said to have thought: "I should go to recite Dharma and give consolation to my foster mother and elder brothers."[27] But this intention was formed, the text explicitly says, after the funeral and after the "two eldest sons had offered *śrāddha*." The inclusion of this bit of information was likely a calculated move on the part of the redactor: he likely knew, and expected his readers to know, that aside from a [112] preemptory oral partition made while the father was still living, "the heir is he who performs the funeral rites, who offers the rice-balls called *piṇḍas* to the ancestors."[28] Given that the monk did not know about the first and had not performed the second, he could not—the redactor implies—have had any expectation of receiving an inheritance when he returned. This could only have reinforced the explicit motives already attributed to him, although his motives will again be explained. The redactor, it seems, has thought through his case.

When the monk returns to Śrāvastī, "he put away his robe and bowl in the Jetavana Monastery and, when he had recovered from the fatigue of his journey, went to his own house"—there was here no unseemly haste. Then:

The members of the household saw him and wept. Hearing the weeping the neighbors assembled. Some, letting out cries, wept. The eyes of some filled with tears. Since the youngest son was still an ordinary monk, when he heard that large group sitting there and crying, his eyes, too, were filled with tears.

A neighbor woman said to him: "Son, do not lament! Since your father had done meritorious actions, he has gone to the land of the gods. Moreover, your father, having assembled friends, kinsmen, brothers, and neighbors, has also given a third share of his property to you."

Once again, the redactor explains to his readers the monk's action: he wept when he heard the crowd wailing—something his readers presumably would not have expected an advanced monk to do—because he was a *pṛthagjana* (*de so so'i skye bo yin pas*). This is a technical term commonly applied to ordinary monks, monks who have not yet achieved any of the seven preliminary stages that lead to the state of an *arhat*.[29] Here too, it seems, the redactor is setting up his reader, preparing him, because in what immediately follows, the neighbor woman is presented as misunderstanding the monk's tears: she implies by her reassurances that she thought that the monk was crying—at least in part—because he thought he had not received any of the inheritance. But that allows even an ordinary monk to make some major points by quoting *vinaya*—it is a clever piece. In response to the neighbor woman's assurances, the text continues:

He said:[30] "That which the Blessed One has said is indeed this: 'Saying "When I have died, this must be given to him" is not an act of giving.' Knowing [113] this, I do not therefore lament on this account. But since my father has done what is difficult to do for me, tears involuntarily appear. The Blessed One has also said: 'A father and mother do what is difficult for a son—they are nourishers, supporters, fosterers, and teachers of the world's many things. A son might carry his father on one shoulder, his mother on the other, for a full hundred years; he might establish them as lords with power over all the jewels, pearls, lapis lazuli, crystal, coral, silver, gold, emeralds, sapphires, rubies, and right-turning conches in this great earth—even by this much a son would neither profit nor repay his father and mother. But if one moved his father and mother away from the absence of devotion to complete devotion, encouraged them in it, led them to train, enter, and fully enter it; if one moved them from being confused in morality to complete morality, from avarice to complete liberality, from being confused in wisdom to complete wisdom, encouraged them in it, led them to train, enter, and fully enter it, then by this much a son would both profit and repay his father and mother.' Again, the Blessed One, in saying 'Saying "When I have died, this must be given to him" is not giving,' forbids it."

The woman remained silent.

Our ordinary monk quotes here two texts from the *vinaya*, one of them twice. One appears to have been something of a trope expressing a monastic conception of filial piety and a justification for ordination. It is also quoted, for example, in the Section on Medicine in the *Mūlasarvāstivāda-vinaya* and, consequently, in the *Divyāvadāna*. In both places it is introduced with the phrase "it has formerly been said by the Blessed One" (*pūrvam uktaṃ bhagavatā*).[31] The other text, the one that is quoted twice, is almost certainly taken from the text of the *Cīvaravastu* that we started with, dealing with the dying monk's willing his robe and bowl to another monk. Notice first that both times it is quoted, it too is introduced with a phrase indicating it was the word of the Buddha, and although there are differences in word choice between the Tibetan translation of the passage in the *Cīvaravastu* (*bdag shi nas 'di'i yin no zhes bya ba'i sbyin pa 'di ni med pa yin pas*) and the Tibetan text of our present [114] passage (*nga 'das nas 'di la byin cig ces zer ba ni med pa yin no*), there is virtually no doubt that these represent variant attempts to translate the same original.

It should be noticed, too, that the redactor's ordinary monk does not cite any of the specifics of the case presented in the *Cīvaravastu* but cites only the general principle that they gave rise to, indicating—as has already been suggested—that it was the general principle alone that had continuing significance for the tradition. Moreover, the redactor's monk applies this principle to a completely and significantly different set of circumstances, allowing us to see that, regardless of what the intent behind the original ruling was, by the time the text in the *Kṣudrakavastu* was redacted, the principle was thought to have broad, if not universal, application. The monk cites it in reaction to the neighbor woman's suspicion that he was crying in part because he thought he had been cut out of the estate. To indicate that he had had no such thoughts, he is made to say that the ruling found in the *Cīvaravastu* rendered impossible any anticipation of anything coming to him by an oral partition made by his father while still alive, and he repeats the ruling a second time to indicate that the Buddha forbade his acceptance of any property that might result from such a partition.

It is reasonable to assume that the ordinary monk's reactions represented the ordinary, established interpretation of the principle that was current at the time the redactor put together his text: regardless, again, of the original intention behind it, it was then understood to have unrestricted applicability and, significantly, to apply not only to actions of or between monks but to all such actions. What may have been only a ruling of monastic law was now understood to render all oral partition during life invalid. The neighbor lady was silent because, perhaps, she was stunned. In any case her silence here is not—as it is in formal monastic deliberative procedure—a sign of assent but of consternation and lack of clarity; she, in modern English idiom, simply does not know what to say.

The silence of an interlocutor frequently expresses such consternation elsewhere in this section of the *Mūlasarvāstivāda-vinaya*. In a passage dealing with the duties of the monk who looks after the monastery's trees, for example, pilgrims who go to Mount Vaidehaka to celebrate the festival inaugurated to mark the conversion of Śakra are oppressed by the heat. They suggest to the monks that they should plant trees there. The monks say that is not allowed by the Blessed One. The pilgrims, however, ask—quite reasonably—"But, Noble Ones, in this case what is the transgression?" The monks have no response and remain silent.[32] In [115] another interesting passage detailing the formal procedures for abandoning a *vihāra* whose donor or "owner" (*vihāraṣvāmin*) has been seized by the king (a passage that, by the way, clearly indicates that donors had continuing rights of ownership in a *vihāra*), the monks are criticized by the donor for running away before they consult the donor's relatives. In the face of this criticism, the monks were "rendered speechless and remained silent" (*de dag spobs pa med par cang mi zer bar 'dug pa*).[33] In these two instances—as in all such cases—silence calls for and receives the intervention of the Buddha to resolve the confusion and provide guidelines for future behavior. Our present case is just another example of this pattern. But it is worth noting that the Buddha intervenes here to provide guidelines for the monks, to be sure, but more important, he does so to resolve the confusion of the neighbor lady, that is to say, the lay community. This at least is how the redactor chose to present it.

The Buddha intervenes by providing an even broader general principle that modifies the general principle under discussion and thereby establishes clear limitations on the range of monastic law. Here is a piece of Buddhist legislation that rivals some of St. Basil's. The text continues:

> The monks reported this matter to the Blessed One.
>
> The Blessed One said: "Monks, what I said did not refer to laymen but was said in reference to renunciants. When laymen would die thus having attachments, this is not a renunciant. Therefore, then, when this layman thought 'When I have died, this is given to him,' this indeed was an act of giving. Moreover, because he was not a renunciant, it should be accepted. When, further, it has been accepted, it should be used as property in whatever way one wishes."[34]

The Buddha's resolution of the case obviously works in several directions at the same time and does several things. It resolves the confusion in the specific case at hand. It resolves the conflict between monastic law and brahmanical law. It allows the monk in question to accept the property in question, and by its wording—which is even fuller here than in the *Cīvaravastu*—it allows that monk full and absolute possession of that property: "It should be used as property in whatever way one wishes" (*ji ltar 'dod pa bzhin du longs spyod du yongs su spyad par bya'o*). But beyond that, it does two things of considerable consequence: it imposes clear and unequivocal limits on the operation of [116] monastic law both specifically in regard to questions of inheritance and, it seems, as a general principle; it also establishes as a general ruling a monk's right to inherit and possess absolutely any family property that comes to him by means of an oral partition made by the head of his family while still living, saying, in effect, that although monastic law disallows such an oral will between monks, this has no bearing on the validity of such instruments when used by laymen to the benefit of monks.

In regard to the first of these broader concerns, it should be noted that this is not the only place in the *Mūlasarvāstivāda-vinaya* in which the question of the relationship between lay law and monastic law is explicitly engaged. It is engaged, for example, in another case that also involves inheritance, and here too we find much the same language used. The case involves the Monk Upananda, who had accumulated a considerable fortune. He dies, and the king's agents hear of it. They go to the king to ask his determination in regard to the situation: although it is never stated, the issue here is almost certainly the law, well known in this *Vinaya* and in *dharmaśāstra*, that the estate of one who is without heirs goes to the king.[35] The king orders his men to seal Upananda's cell, which they do. The text then adds a detail that almost certainly was intended to lay some groundwork for the claim that was about to be made: the cell was sealed when the monks were away performing the funeral rites for Upananda; that is to say, the monks, by their actions, had already established themselves, even in the eyes of the secular law, as the rightful heirs. When the monks return, they report the matter to the Buddha, and he tells the Monk Ānanda to go to the king and say to him: "'Great King, when you had government business, did you then consider the Monk Upananda? Or when you took a wife or gave a daughter, did you consider Upananda? Or sometime during his lifetime, did you present Upananda with the standard belongings of a monk—robes, bowls, bedding and seats, and medicine for the sick? Or when he was ill, did you attend him?' If, Ānanda, he should answer no, this should be said: 'Great King, the affairs of the house of householders are one thing; those of renunciants quite another. You must remain unconcerned! This property falls to the fellow monks of Upananda. You must not acquiesce to its removal!'" The king's response, according to the redactor, was "Reverend Ānanda, as the Blessed One orders, just so it must be!"[36] [117]

Obviously, what we have here is only the monastic view of things. How a secular authority or brahmanical jurist would have written the account we simply do not know. But what is important is that this text, like our text from the *Kṣudrakavastu*, shows us Mūlasarvāstivādin monastic jurists grappling with the relationship of lay and monastic law and trying, in this instance, to establish limits not on monastic law but on the jurisdiction of secular law. The text allows the king the chance to assert that, in his political and domestic activities, he considered Upananda as he would a layman or that he had a specific relationship with Upananda while he was still living. But if he cannot do this—and he cannot—then he must accept the principle that "the affairs of the house of householders are one thing; those of renunciants quite another" (*pṛthaṅ mahārāja gṛhiṇāṃ gṛhakāryāṇi pṛthak pravrajitānām*).[37] The king must, in other words, acknowledge that lay law does not apply to Buddhist monks in the same way—and with the same basic vocabulary—that the Buddha rules that monastic law does not apply to laymen.

But the case of Upananda, and the broad principle that the king accepts in his determination of it, had—like the ruling against the dying monk making an oral partition of his possessions to another monk—a continuing history in the *Mūlasarvāstivāda-vinaya*. It, too, is quoted in a related case that again involves inheritance and establishing the limits or jurisdiction of lay law. This case is particularly interesting because it also involves a written will and a further determination of who does and who does not fall into the categories "renunciant" and "householder."

All the details of this particularly rich account cannot be treated here, and I limit myself to only the matter directly germane to the main issue at hand. The case concerns a wealthy householder, and, like the case of Upananda but some twenty pages later, it occurs in the *Cīvaravastu* of the *Mūlasarvāstivāda-vinaya*.[38] After failing to have a child—that is, an heir—through invoking various gods, the householder decides to enter the Buddhist order. He approaches a monk, who shaves the head of the householder and begins to give him the precepts, but then—although he has undergone at least a part of the ordination ritual and certainly one of its most visible parts—he falls ill. The text notes that it was a serious illness that created an obstacle to his "going forth" (*pravrajyāntarāyakareṇa ca mahatā jvareṇābhibhūtaḥ*). The Buddha accordingly rules that the precepts cannot be given to him until he recovers but that an attendant who is a monk should be given to him. Monks attend to him even when he is taken home, and even though he was now at home, the text explicitly says that he was designated as a "shaven-headed householder" (*tasya muṇḍo gṛhapatir* [118] *iti saṃjñā saṃvṛttā*). This designation is oddly like the terms *monachi laici*, "lay monk," and *monachi barbati*, "bearded monk," which occur in medieval European monasticism.[39] Since medieval monks were clean-shaven, a bearded monk, like a "shaven-headed householder," was—if not a contradiction in terms—clearly a mixed and conceptually messy category, and the emerging problem should be obvious: the case of Upananda established that lay law did not apply to renunciants (*pravrajita*), but where did a shaven-headed householder fall?

The shaven-headed householder, of course, does not recover but, on the point of death, prepares a written document describing all his property and wealth, sends it to the Jetavana Monastery (*tatas tena maraṇakālasamaye sarvaṃ santa*[*ka*]*svāpateyaṃ patrābhilekhyaṃ kṛtvā jetavane preṣitam*), and then dies. The king's men hear of the householder's death and report to the king. They say first, alluding to what has been noted above was an established principle of law, "Lord, a shaven-headed householder who is sonless (*aputra*) has died." They then describe his considerable estate and inform the king of the written document (*patrābhilikhitaṃ*).

The redactor of this account has cleverly placed the competing concepts in the initial sentence of the report delivered to the king: the deceased is described as both a shaven-headed householder and sonless. The king must rule as to which of these two statuses will have determining influence. By the principle of lay law that was—as already noted—widely known in both the *vinaya* and *dharmaśāstra*, the estate of one who was sonless went to the king. But if the shaven-headed householder was not a layman, then this lay law did not—could not by the king's previous decision—apply to him. The king's response to the report is interesting, although once again the redactor has already laid the groundwork for the monastic claim.

The redactor has not once but twice pointed out that monks had attended to the shaven-headed householder when he was ill. This, by an established monastic law recognized in part even in the *Cīvaravastu* case concerning the oral partition by the dying monk, establishes a claim to at least a part of the estate. More important, in the case of Upananda it was clearly implied that had the king been able to reply in the affirmative to the question "When [Upananda] was ill, did you attend to him?" he would have been able to advance a claim on the estate. The redactor has then, not surprisingly, already presented the case in a way [119] prejudicial to the king. When the redactor has the king explicitly refer to the case of Upananda, it could only have been with a grin. Oddly enough, the significance of the written document is almost discounted, and this may show some continuing unease in regard to such instruments. "The king said: 'Even in the absence of a written document, I did not obtain the possessions of the Noble Upananda; how much less will I obtain such goods when there is a written document. But what the Blessed One will authorize, that I will accept.'" The written document does not establish the case; it only strengthens it. What has actually occurred, however, is that the king, by his response, has tacitly accepted the inclusion of the shaven-headed householder in the category of renunciant by assimilating his case to that of Upananda. That this was the way the Mūlasarvāstivādin tradition understood the case is clear from Guṇaprabha's *Vinayasūtra*—a fifth- to seventh-century compendium of the *Mūlasarvāstivāda-vinaya*—which refers to it. The *Vinayasūtra* says, "Who, for the purposes of entering the Order (*pravrajyārthaṃ*), has taken on the external appearance [of a renunciant], his head being shaved, etc., although not yet entered, he is to be seen [i.e., treated] as one who has entered (*pravrajitavad*)."[40] In other words, the shaven-headed householder—one who has undergone at least a part of the ritual of ordination, who has at least assumed the outward appearance of a renunciant—is to be treated as, and has the rights of, a renunciant. One of these rights, conceded already by the king in the case of Upananda, is that his estate is not subject to lay law.

Much more could—and should—be said about this case. But not here.[41] If its rulings could have been implemented, this would have expanded enormously the number of estates that the monastic community [120] might be able to make a claim on. It also must almost immediately call to mind the upaniṣadic ritual or "custom of renouncing when a person was at the point of death" that both the *Upaniṣads* and *Purāṇas* call *āturasaṃnyāsa*,[42] or the similar practice—called "entry *ad succurrendum*"—in medieval European monasticism by which dying individuals took monastic robes and the monastic community, as a consequence, generally received at least a part of their estates.[43] For now, however, it is important to note that the case of the shaven-headed householder is yet one more instance where Mūlasarvāstivādin jurists appear to be seriously struggling with the relationship and boundaries of monastic and lay law, and one more instance where the issues are focused on questions of inheritance.

As far as I know, there is nothing like this explicit discussion of the problem of the relationship of lay and monastic law in the Pāli, or Mahāvihārin, *Vinaya*, nor does this *Vinaya* show much concern with problems of inheritance. These issues, as Lingat has so richly shown, had to be slowly, if not tortuously, worked out by the secular law of those Southeast Asian Buddhist cultures who appear to have known only—and were therefore limited by—the Pāli *Vinaya*. The Pāli *Vinaya* does in fact once engage the issue of the validity of an oral disposition, but the relationship of monastic and lay law is never mentioned there, and the discussion in the Pāli *Vinaya* is exclusively concerned with internal disputes between the community of monks and the community of nuns. It has nothing to do with a monk's family property and refers only incidentally, it seems, to lay estates.[44] The question that remains, then, is how to account for this striking difference between these two *vinayas*. [121]

There has been, and remains, a strong prejudice toward chronological explanations of such differences: the Pāli *Vinaya*, the "simplest," does not treat these issues because it is early; the *Mūlasarvāstivāda-vinaya*, the most "complex," does because it is late. But even bracketing the distinct possibility that both these *vinayas* are late, this solution—although its simplicity highly recommends it to some—does not exhaust the possible explanations. And it is here that the relationship between the Rule of Benedict and the Rules of Basil might serve as an analogy, although it can be only that.

Basil, it seems, wrote his complex, detailed rules on inheritance not because he came late in the chronological development of Western monastic rules but rather, it seems, because at an early date he and his communities had to interact with, and come to terms with, an established and powerful competing system of secular law that already governed such matters. He took up, for example, the question of the monk's obligation to pay taxes on family property not because this question related to developments that had occurred within monasticism itself but because he and his communities—if they were to develop and avoid difficulties—had to adjust themselves to the tax laws of Diocletian that were already in effect and enforced in their world. It is, I think, not unreasonable to suggest that the rulings we have found in the *Mūlasarvāstivāda-vinaya* might well have come out of similar sets of circumstances.

It has already been argued elsewhere that the redactors of the *Mūlasarvāstivāda-vinaya* developed a set of rulings governing the treatment of the monastic dead in response both to brahmanical preoccupations with purity and pollution that surrounded them and, significantly, to bring the rules of monastic inheritance into line with the rulings of *dharmaśāstra* that stipulated that, for one to inherit, he must of necessity perform the funeral rites for the deceased.[45] It seems very likely that the cases and rulings we have looked at here may have resulted from the same pressures, and, to judge by the traditional foci of brahmanical law, it would seem reasonable to expect that this occurred early. [122]

The disposition of family property was already a major preoccupation in the *dharmasūtras*. "In all the *dharma-sūtras*," Lingat says, "the rules of succession have a large place in the collection of duties which makes up *ācāra*," and some of these *dharmasūtras* have been assigned dates as early as the sixth century B.C.E.[46] Given the age and extent of such rules and preoccupations in brahmanical circles, it would seem that any Buddhist monastic community in contact with such circles, or any Buddhist community that had any hope of establishing itself in highly brahmanized communities or areas, would have to clarify—and that quickly—the relationship between monastic rule and brahmanical law. Moreover, since the Buddhist community would have been, in several important senses at least, intrusive in such areas, it would have been it—not the established local tradition—that had to adjust and work out such issues.

The absence in the Pāli *Vinaya* of such explicit discussions of the relationship between lay law and monastic law and of clear rulings on, for example, the matter of inheritance by monks of lay family property need not then point to its having been early but would seem to indicate that it was not—could not have been—redacted in, or intended for use by, a monastic community in close contact with brahmanical cultures. This indication, however, may in turn actually rule out the possibility of the Pāli *Vinaya*'s being an early Indian monastic code, because other data suggest that early Buddhism developed in proximity to brahmanical cultures, and it may point—as other data also seem to[47]—toward the possibility that the Pāli *Vinaya* was redacted in, and intended for use by, Buddhist monastic communities in Sri Lanka, where there is little evidence, until late, for any system of non-Buddhist formal law and where church and state appear to have been very little separated.[48]

The *Mūlasarvāstivāda-vinaya*, on the other hand, reveals a monastic community preoccupied with the separation of church and state, a community in the thick of negotiating their boundaries. We seem to see these negotiations at several different stages in the passages we have studied here, and the process seems to have been ongoing. This would be [123] perfectly consistent not only with Buddhist monastic communities that were living in brahmanical areas but also with Buddhist monastic communities that were living in states ruled by brahmanized kings; all of the evidence would suggest that, with few exceptions, this was precisely the kind of state that most Buddhist monastic communities in India had to deal with. Considerations of this sort must for now, of course, remain conjecture and hypothesis, but one thing need not. Regardless of its early history, which remains controversial,[49] there are good indications that the *Mūlasarvāstivāda-vinaya* was an important influence in Indian Buddhism from the Gupta period on: there is seemingly strong evidence for its presence and influence at Ajaṇṭā in the fifth century; Guṇaprabha may place it at Mathurā during the period between the fifth and seventh centuries; in the seventh century it was known and used in such widely separated places as Tāmralipti in Bengal, Nālandā in Bihar, and Gilgit in Pakistan; still later at least Guṇaprabha's compendium or summary of it was known at Vikramaśīla; and the fact that it was taken as the sole canonical text of *vinaya* by the Tibetans suggests that it had great authority everywhere in Eastern India in the communities from which the Tibetans got their Indian Buddhism.[50] It is, therefore, of considerable significance for understanding the nature of Buddhist monasticism and, perhaps, the extensive donative activity of individual Buddhist monks in these areas and periods, that this *Vinaya*—as the passages we have looked at here establish—unequivocally and explicitly acknowledged and supported the continuing right of Buddhist monks to inherit family property and to have absolute possession of such property to be used "in whatever way one wishes." Buddhist monks, under such a rule, had every right to be rich. And, it seems, many were.

Notes

1. William's *Super Cantica*, cited in C. Rudolph, *The "Things of Greater Importance": Bernard of Clairvaux's Apologia and the Medieval Attitude toward Art* (Philadelphia: 1990) 315.

2. J. Burton, *Monastic and Religious Orders in Britain, 1000–1300* (Cambridge, U.K.: 1994) 11; and L. J. R. Milis, *Angelic Monks and Earthly Men: Monasticism and Its Meaning to Medieval Society* (Woodbridge, U.K.: 1992) 18.

3. J. P. Greene, *Medieval Monasteries* (Leicester: 1992) 2.

4. Of the many translations of Benedict's Rule, I cite that recently reprinted in Abbot

Parry, trans., *The Rule of Saint Benedict* (Leominster, Mass.: 1990); also easily available is the translation in O. Chadwick, *Western Asceticism* (London: 1958). Dom Cuthbert Butler has noted that in regard to private ownership "St. Benedict speaks with quite unwonted vehemence" (Dom Cuthbert Butler, *Benedictine Monasticism: Studies in Benedictine Life and Rule*, 2d ed. (London: 1924) 146.

5. On Italy in the sixth century, see the old but still readable E. S. Duckett, *The Gateway to the Middle Ages: Italy* (Ann Arbor: 1938). I ignore here the much discussed question of Benedict's dependence on the Rule of the Master; for one recent study, see M. Dunn, "Mastering Benedict: Monastic Rules and Their Authors in the Early Medieval West," *English Historical Review* 105 (1990) 567–594.

6. D. Knowles, *From Pachomius to Ignatius: A Study in the Constitutional History of the Religious Orders* (Oxford: 1966) 4.

7. See P. J. Fedwick, "The Translations of the Works of Basil before 1400,"in *Basil of Caesarea, Christian, Humanist, Ascetic: A Sixteen-Hundredth Anniversary Symposium*, ed. P. J. Fedwick, Vol. 2 (Toronto: 1981) 457–459.

8. M. G. Murphy, *St. Basil and Monasticism* (Catholic University of America, Patristic Studies, Vol. 25) (Washington, D.C.: 1930) 54–55. See also, more recently, G. Gould, "Basil of Caesarea and the Problem of the Wealth of Monasteries," in *The Church and Wealth* (Studies in Church History, Vol. 24) ed. W. J. Sheils and D. Wood (Oxford: 1987) 15–24, esp. 18–20; and G. May, "Basilius der Grosse und der römische Staat," in *Bleibendes im Wandel der Kirchengeschichte: Kirchen-historische Studien Hans von Campenhausen gewidmet*, ed. B. Moeller and G. Ruhbach (Tübingen: 1973) 47–70. For the Long and Short Rules, see W. K. L. Clarke, trans., *The Ascetic Works of Saint Basil* (London: 1925) 145–228, 229–351; on their complicated textual history, see J. Gribomont, *Histoire du texte des ascétiques de saint basile* (Bibliothèque du muséon 32) (Louvain: 1953). Gribomont argues that Basil originally addressed himself to all Christians and only later revised the Rules to be more explicitly monastic. For a good overview of his position, see J. Gribomont, "Le monachisme au sein de l'église en syrie et en cappadoce," *Studia Monastica* 7 (1965) 7–24. For a recent biographical study of Basil, see P. Rousseau, *Basil of Caesarea* (Berkeley: 1994).

9. Murphy, *St. Basil and Monasticism*, 55–56; see Gould, "Basil of Caesarea," 19–20, and other works cited in n. 8.

10. H. Oldenberg, *Buddha: His Life, His Doctrine, His Order*, trans. W. Hoey (London: 1882), 355 n; for the original German, see H. Oldenberg, *Buddha: sein Leben, seine Lehre, seine Gemeinde*, ed. H. von Glasenapp (Stuttgart: 1959) 370, 449, n. 13; my emphasis.

11. I. B. Horner, *The Book of the Discipline* (Oxford: 1938) Vol. I, xxi, xlvii; my emphasis.

12. R. Lingat, "Vinaya et droit laïque: Etudes sur les conflits de la loi religieuse et de la loi laïque dans l'indochine hinayaniste," *BEFEO* 37 (1937) 415–477.

13. Pāli *Vinaya* iii 204.7, 16; iii 213, 215, 217, 234, 248, 257, 260; iv 48, 81, 89, 104, 190, 192, 193.

14. G. Schopen, "The Ritual Obligations and Donor Roles of Monks in the Pāli *Vinaya*," *JPTS* 16 (1992) 87–107 [= *BSBM* 72–85].

15. Lüders, *Bharhut Inscriptions*, 2; cf. G. Bühler, "Votive Inscriptions from the Sāñchi

Stūpas," *EI* 2 (1894) 93; G. Schopen, "Two Problems in the History of Indian Buddhism: The Layman/Monk Distinction and the Doctrines of the Transference of Merit," *StII 10* (1985) 9–47 [= *BSBM* 23–55].

16. *Kṣudrakavastu*, Tog, 'dul ba Ta 293b.6–294b.2; see also Ta 7a.4–8a.1, 292b.6–293b.3.

17. The *stūpas* of the hair and nails (*keśa-nakha-stūpa*) are a kind of "monument élevé à un Buddha de son vivant" containing his nail clippings and hair (for references, see G. Schopen, "An Old Inscription from Amarāvatī and the Cult of the Local Monastic Dead in Indian Buddhist Monasteries," *JIABS* 14.2 (1991) 320–321, n. 34) [= *BSBM* 196–197].

18. I suspect there is a bit of intentional humor here—the Perfume Chamber was the central cell in a Buddhist monastery reserved for the Buddha himself (see G. Schopen, "The Buddha as an Owner of Property and Permanent Resident in Medieval Indian Monasteries," *JIP* 18 (1990) 181–217, esp. 193ff) [= *BSBM* 258–289].

19. The Tibetan here reads: *sgo'i drang thad du gzhag par mi bya'i / 'on kyang dri zhim po thams cad ni mig la phan pas / sngas kyi thad kar dri'i lag ris bya zhing / de nas dus dus su bsnam par bya'o /*. The reference here to the "perfumed palm print" has a close parallel at Pāli *Vinaya* ii 123. For this and other references in Pāli, see J. Ph. Vogel, "The Sign of the Spread Hand or "Five-Finger Token" (*Pañcaṅgulika*) in Pali Literature," *Verslagen en Mededeelingen der Koninklijke Akademie van Wetenschappen: Afdeeling Letterkunde*, Vol. 5, pt. 4 (Amsterdam: 1909) 218–235. *Kṣudrakavastu*, Tog, 'dul ba Ta 7b.3, also refers to the perfumed palm print.

20. See esp. *Śayanāsanavastu* (Gnoli) 35.1ff, which explicitly refers to the "merit resulting from use" (*paribhogānvayaṃ puṇyaṃ*). Pāli *Vinaya* ii 269–270 also contains a passage in which the Buddha is made to say, "Monks, you must not give to others what was given to you for your own use" (*na bhikkhave attano paribhogatthāya dinnaṃ aññesaṃ dātabbaṃ*); here, too, the donors complain, saying, in effect: "Do these monks think we do not know how to make our own gifts?" (*mayam ha na jānāma dānaṃ dātun ti*). The obligation of monks to use what has been given to them is studied in some detail in G. Schopen, "The Lay Ownership of Monasteries and the Role of the Monk in Mūlasarvāstivādin Monasticism," *JIABS* 19.1 (1996) 81–126 [= Ch. VIII below].

21. Compare G. Schopen, "On Avoiding Ghosts and Social Censure: Monastic Funerals in the *Mūlasarvāstivāda-vinaya*," *JIP* 20 (1992) 1–39 [= *BSBM* 204–237], and "Doing Business for the Lord: Lending on Interest and Written Loan Contracts in the *Mūlasarvāstivāda-vinaya*," *JAOS* 114.4 (1994) 527–554 [= Ch. III above].

22. *Cīvaravastu*, GMs iii 2, 124.1–.10 (= Tog, 'dul ba Ga 136b.2–.6).

23. Lingat, "Vinaya et droit laïque" (n. 12 above) 461–462 and the sources cited in his notes. See also T. Mukherjee and J. C. Wright, "An Early Testamentary Document in Sanskrit," *BSOAS* 42.2 (1979) 297–320, esp. 318–320.

24. *Kṣudrakavastu*, Tog, 'dul ba Ta 377a.2–379a.4 = Derge, 'dul ba Tha 252b.3–254a.1.

25. This verse, cited editorially to explain the fact of death, occurs commonly in the *Mūlasarvāstivāda-vinaya* (see, e.g., GMs iii 4.57.9, and *Pravrajyāvastu* [Vogel and Wille] i 332; *Saṅghabhedavastu* [Gnoli] ii 38). But it also occurs in the *Mahābhārata* and in some brahmanical death liturgies (see P. V. Kane, *History of Dharmaśāstra*, 2d ed., Vol. 4 [Poona: 1973], 237).

26. R. Lingat, *The Classical Law of India*, trans. J. D. M. Derrett (Berkeley: 1973) 61–62, 192–193.

27. I am unsure here of the term I have translated as "foster mother." The Tibetan has *ma yar mo*, which appears to mean the same thing as *ma gyar* and *ma tshab*. Given that there is no other reference to the woman of the house, it is not possible to determine why this particular term might have been used. The woman's status, however, almost certainly had no bearing on the case. [See now Ch. V above, nn. 8 and 18, and Ch. IX below, n. 54].

28. Lingat, *The Classical Law of India*, 58.

29. On the term *pṛthagjana*, and for further references, see G. Schopen, "Ritual Rights and Bones of Contention: More on Monastic Funerals and Relics in the *Mūlasarvāstivāda-vinaya*," *JIP* 22 (1994): 31–80, esp. 53–55 [= Ch. X below, 304–305].

30. The Tibetan text actually reads *des bsams pa*, "he thought," but context makes it clear that this is an oversight. This sort of thing, as well as the less than careful marking of the boundaries of direct speech that also occurs in our passage, are some of the characteristics of this part of the Tibetan translation of the *Mūlasarvāstivāda-vinaya*. Long ago, Rockhill had translated a part of a colophon attached to this translation that said: "This translation is not felicitous; it is full of obsolete expressions, is badly written, and in the latter part of the volume the correctors' minds appear tired and their faculties worn out; and all this is a source of much incertitude" (W. W. Rockhill, *The Life of the Buddha and the Early History of His Order; Derived from Tibetan Works of the Bkah-Hgyur and Bstan-Hgyur* [London: 1884] 148). Although these remarks are, on the whole, apt (if a little overstated), they apply only in certain regards to the text we are dealing with here, whose basic sense is not in doubt.

31. *Bhaiṣajyavastu*, Tog, 'dul ba Ka 443a.4ff (*bcom ldan 'das kyis sngon bka' stsal pa*); *Divyāvadāna* (Cowell and Neil) 51.19 ff, trans. in E. Burnouf, *Introduction a l'histoire du bouddhisme indien* (Paris: 1844) 270.

32. *Kṣudrakavastu*, Tog, 'dul ba Ta 349b.2.

33. *Kṣudrakavastu*, Tog, 'dul ba Ta 343b.1.

34. *bcom ldan 'das kyis bka' stsal pa / dge slong dag ngas ni khyim pa las dgongs te gsungs pa ma yin gyi / 'on kyang rab tu byung ba las dgongs pa yin no / khyim pa dag ni chags pa dang bcas bzhin du 'chi bar 'gyur la rab tu byung ba ni ma yin no / de lta bas na de'i phyir khyim pa 'di snyam du / nga 'das nas 'di la sbyin no snyam du sems pa ni byin pa yin gyi / rab tu byung pa ni ma yin pas blang bar bya zhing / blangs nas kyang ji ltar 'dod pa bzhin du longs spyod du yongs su spyad par bya'o /.*

35. This law is explicitly stated, e.g., in *Adhikaraṇavastu* (Gnoli) 69.20, where a childless banker says to himself: *na me putro na duhitā. mamātyayāt sarvasvāpateyam aputraka iti kṛtvā rājavidheyaṃ bhaviṣyati iti* ("I have no son or daughter. When I pass away all of my property, having been declared 'sonless,' will come to be subject to the king").

36. *Cīvaravastu* GMs iii 2, 119.1–.10 = Tog, 'dul ba Ga 133a.6–b.4. For some preliminary remarks on this and the following text, see Schopen, "Ritual Rites and Bones of Contention," 62–63 [= Ch. X below, 311–312].

37. This is rendered into Tibetan as *khyim pa rnams kyi khyim gyi bya ba dang / rab tu byung ba rnams kyi tha dad pas*.

38. *Cīvaravastu*, GMs iii 2, 139.6–143.14; = Tog, 'dul ba Ga 146b.3–149b.2.

39. Knowles, *From Pachomius to Ignatius*, 29–30; these terms were applied to what were more generally called *conversi*. See, as a sample of the discussion, C. Davis, "The *Conversus* of Cluny: Was He a Lay-Brother," in *Benedictus: Studies in Honor of St. Benedict of Nursia*, ed. E. R. Elder (Kalamazoo, Mich.: 1981) 99–107, and the sources cited in nn. 12 and 13; D. J. Osheim, *A Tuscan Monastery and Its Social World: San Michele of Guamo, 1156–1348* (Rome: 1989) 102–112.

40. *Vinayasūtra* (Bapat and Gokhale) 46.20; on the date of Guṇaprabha, see Schopen, "Ritual Rights and Bones of Contention," 63–64, and nn. 63–64 [= Ch. X below, 312–313].

41. It should, however, be noted that this case has been known to Western scholarship in a confused form for a long time. Although his observations have passed largely unnoticed, Dutt pointed out more than fifty years ago that ch. 36 of I-tsing's *A Record of the Buddhist Religion as Practised in India and the Malay Archipelago*, which was translated by Takakusu in 1896, is little more than a translation of a part of the passage in the *Cīvaravastu* dealing with the estate of the shaven-headed householder (GMs, iii 2, xi). Takakusu, too, had suggested in a note that the "chapter" had a "verbatim" parallel in a canonical *Vinaya* text. Failure to note this has misled several scholars, including Lingat (see Lingat, "Vinaya et droit laïque," 446 ff) and J. Gernet (*Buddhism in Chinese Society: An Economic History from the Fifth to the Tenth Centuries*, trans. F. Verellen [New York: 1995] 75–77). It of course did not help that I-tsing omitted the framing story and implied in his introductory remarks that the case dealt with monks. For a translation of the Sanskrit text, see Schopen, "Deaths, Funerals, and the Division of Property in a Monastic Code," in *Buddhism in Practice*, ed. D. S. Lopez (Princeton, N.J.: 1995) 498–500 [= Ch. IV above, 117–119].

42. P. Olivelle, *Saṃnyāsa Upaniṣads: Hindu Scriptures on Asceticism and Renunciation* (Oxford: 1992) 74 and n. 19; Kane, *History of Dharmaśāstra*, Vol. 4, 184–185.

43. L. Gougaud, *Dévotions et pratiques ascétiques du moyen age* (Paris: 1925) 129–142; J. H. Lynch, *Simoniacal Entry into Religious Life from 1000 to 1260: A Social, Economic and Legal Study* (Columbus, Ohio: 1976) 27–36.

44. The passage occurs at Pāli *Vinaya* ii 267–268, and it is discussed in some detail in Lingat, "Vinaya et droit laïque," 461–466. It is interesting to note that the Pāli *Vinaya* itself accepts the validity of an oral disposition made during life by monks, nuns, lay-brothers, lay-sisters, or "anyone else" (*añña*) as long, it seems, as the beneficiary is the community of monks and nuns (the question of such a disposition between individuals is not engaged, nor is that of family property), but Buddhaghosa, the commentator, does not. Lingat says that Buddhaghosa expresses an opinion "qu'il a le soin de présenter comme indépendante du canon (*pālimuttakavinicchayo*)," according to which "entre religieux, en effet, une donation exécutoire après décès (*accayadānam*) n'est pas valable; elle est valable, au contraire, entre laïques." Lingat speculates on the reason for this difference, in the course of which he asserts that with Buddhaghosa's position "un droit religieux était né, distinct du droit laïque." The position of Buddhaghosa is, of course, close to that found in our Mūlasarvāstivādin sources, and in light of these sources—which Lingat did not know—it is at least possible to suggest that Buddhaghosa was expressing an (or the) Indian position and that we have in his remarks another instance of Mūlasarvāstivādin influence on the Pāli com-

mentaries (see E. Frauwallner, *The Earliest Vinaya and the Beginnings of Buddhist Literature* [Rome: 1956] 188, and sources cited in his n. 4; H. Bechert, "Zur Geschichte der buddhistischen Sekten in Indien und Ceylon," *La nouvelle clio* 7–9 [1955–1957] 355–356). For the larger question of the relationship between lay and monastic law in the Pāli *Vinaya*, I can only point to Pāli *Vinaya* i 138, where the Buddha allows (orders) monks to comply with requests made by kings (*anujānāmi bhikkhave rājūnaṃ anuvattitun ti*). But this case does not seem to involve questions or conflicts of law. For wills in Southeast Asia, see A. Huxley, "Wills in Theravada Buddhist S.E. Asia," *Recueils de la société Jean Bodin pour l'histoire comparative des institutions*, 62.4 (1994) 53–92; for the validity of oral disposition prior to death in the *Mahīśāsaka-vinaya*, see Gernet, *Buddhism in Chinese Society* 86–87.

45. Schopen, "On Avoiding Ghosts and Social Censure," 1–39.

46. Lingat, *The Classical Law of India*, 58, 18–27.

47. See G. Schopen, "The Monastic Ownership of Servants or Slaves: Local and Legal Factors in the Redactional History of Two *Vinayas*," *JIABS* 17.2 (1994) 145–173 [= Ch. VII below].

48. See A. Huxley, "How Buddhist Is Theravāda Buddhist Law?" in *Buddhist Forum*, ed. T. Skorupski (London: 1990) 1, 41–85; "Sri Lanka has produced no lasting tradition of written secular law texts" (p. 42), and "Sri Lankan Buddhists, despite 1800 years of literate culture, did not produce a lasting textual tradition of secular laws" (p. 82); cf. Lingat ("Vinaya et droit laïque," 466): "On s'étonne que Ceylan ait accepté sans discussion apparente l'usage du testament importé par les Anglais. Mais on est si mal renseigné sur l'état ancien du droit dans ce pays qu'on ne peut former aucune conjecture sur la véritable coutume indigène."

49. For a selection of sources on the date of the *Mūlasarvāstivāda-vinaya*, see Schopen, "On Avoiding Ghosts and Social Censure," 36 n. 69. The dates suggested or asserted for it range from the beginning of the Common Era to not before the fourth or fifth century, whereas "d'après des études comparatives approfondies mais très partielles, les *Vinayapiṭaka* des Mūlasarvāstivādin paraît nettement plus archaïque que celui des Sarvāstivādin et même que le plupart des autres *Vinayapiṭaka* (A. Bareau, *Les sectes bouddhiques du petit véhicule* [Paris: 1955] 154).

50. For sources, see Schopen, "The Buddha as an Owner of Property," 213 n. 70.

CHAPTER VII

The Monastic Ownership of Servants or Slaves

Local and Legal Factors in the Redactional History of Two *Vinayas*

WE STILL, IT SEEMS, know little about how Buddhist monastic communities became fully institutionalized in India or how such Indian monastic organizations actually functioned. This, in part, is because we still know little that is certain about the *vinaya*, and because little attention has been paid to those things that allowed such communities not only to endure over time but also to prosper and made, in fact, the monastic life possible—property, buildings, money, forced labor, and corporate organization. Historians of Indian Buddhism seem slow, if not entirely reluctant, to admit or allow what their medievalist colleagues elsewhere take as a given:

> Yet monasticism is not just about forms of Christian service, the daily round of prayer and contemplation by those who lived within the cloister. . . . Religious houses were also corporations which owned land, administered estates and enjoyed rights and privileges which needed ratifying and defending.[1]

Moreover, medievalists have been fully aware that different monastic groups or Orders could—and did—deal with these various concerns differently, at least in their formal legislation, and that these differences were often directly linked to the social, political, and [146] economic contexts in which the various monastic groups operated.[2] The study of Buddhist monasticism has, to be sure, been hampered in this regard by the availability of significantly less documentation. But it is also just possible that what documentation it has—and it is still considerable—has not been fully utilized. There is a comparative wealth of inscriptional data bearing on the economic and institutional history of monastic Buddhisms that has yet to be fully used; there are as well the monastic codes of six different Buddhist Or-

---

Originally published in *Journal of the International Association of Buddhist Studies* 17.2 (1994) 145–173. Reprinted with stylistic changes with permission of the editor.

ders, although only one of these is easily available in a translation into a European language, and the rest have been comparatively ignored.

But the study of the institutional history of Buddhist monasticisms may also have been hampered as much by some of its own assumptions. It has, for example, been commonly believed—and still is by some—that elements found to be common to all or most of the extant *vinayas* must go back to a hypothetical, single, "pre-sectarian," primitive *vinaya*.[3] This belief has had at least two consequences. First, most of the energy and effort in the study of the *vinayas* has been directed toward finding or ferreting out these common elements. This procedure has resulted in, if nothing else, a kind of homogenization of potentially significant differences and has led—at least according to Sylvain Lévi—"to a kind of single archetype, which is not the primitive *Vinaya*, but the average of the *Vinayas*."[4] Second, this same belief has almost necessarily determined that any deviation from the mean or average would have to be [147] explained in chronological terms as a "late addition" or "an isolated accretion"—as if there were no other possible explanation for such differences. We are, in short, left with little sense of how the different monastic Orders might have solved different or even common problems, or what kinds of external forces might have been working on the different Orders in different geographical and cultural areas. If I. B. Horner was right—and that is likely—about the important influence of lay values on monastic rules and legislation,[5] then, unless one wants to argue for a uniform level and type of lay culture throughout early India and Sri Lanka, the different Orders in different places could not have been subjected to the same sets of influences and must have had to adapt to a wide range of local lay values. Something like this is, indeed, explicitly allowed for in the *Mahīśāsaka-vinaya* for example:

> Le Buddha dit: . . . Bien qu'une chose ait été autorisée par moi, si dans une autre région on ne la considère pas comme pure, personne ne doit s'en servir. Bien qu'une chose n'ait pas été autorisée par moi, si dans une autre région il y a des gens qui doivent nécessairement la pratiquer, tout le monde doit la mettre en pratique.[6]

And explicit instances of adaption of monastic rule to local custom can be found in all the *vinayas*, as, for example, in the case where monks in Avanti were allowed to bathe constantly because "in the southern region of Avanti people attach importance to bathing, to purification by water."[7] The recognition of the force of local values is also a characteristic of Indian *dharmaśāstra*, where it is an accepted principle that "custom prevails over dharma."[8]

These, however, are large questions and are themselves not easily treated. Nor will any one case bring a definitive solution. But if we are to begin to make an effort toward determining the various stages in the process of the institutionalization of monastic Buddhisms, and to begin [148] to understand the external forces that might have been involved in the process, then it is probably best not to begin with generalizations—they, it seems, may already have created a considerable muddle. However tiresome it may be, we must start with particulars and particularity and look closely at how, for example, the literate members of these monastic Orders saw, or wanted others to see, particular and presumably significant moments in their own institutional histories.

Potentially, of course, there are any number of such "moments" that could be studied, but I have chosen to limit the discussion here to the accounts in only two *vinayas* of the particular circumstances in which the Buddha was said to have allowed (ordered) the use, acceptance, or ownership of a particular kind of property, property whose use or ownership would seem to have entailed and presupposed significant institutional developments. In both *vinayas* the property in question is a certain category or class of domestic servant or slave, a more precise definition of which will depend on the discussion of the texts. The choice of the two *vinayas* to be taken into account is determined by my own linguistic incompetence. But—perhaps as a small proof that at least occasionally you can indeed make a silk purse out of a sow's ear—these two *vinayas* also represent the two opposite ends of the chronological continuum conventionally assumed in most discussions of the composition of the various *vinayas*: the Mahāvihārin *Vinaya* is often believed to be the earliest of the monastic codes,[9] the Mūlasarvāstivādin *vinaya* the latest.[10] If these chronological assumptions are correct—although my own opinion is that there are no very compelling reasons to think that they are—then a close study of these two accounts will allow us to see how the same tradition was presented by two widely separated monastic codes. It might allow us as well to see if the "separation" between the two has not been determined by something other than time. [149]

We might start with the account now found in the *Bhesajja-khandhaka*, or Section on Medicines, in the Mahāvihārin *Vinaya*.[11]

> On that occasion the Venerable Pilindavaccha was clearing an overhang in Rājagṛha, wanting to make a cell. The King of Magadha, Seniya Bimbisāra, approached the Venerable Pilindavaccha, saluted him, and sat down to one side. So seated, the King of Magadha, Seniya Bimbisāra, said to the Venerable Pilindavaccha: "Reverend, what is the Elder doing?"
>
> "Great King, I am clearing an overhang to make a cell."
>
> "Reverend, does the Noble One need an attendant for a monastery (*ārāmika*)?"[12]
>
> "Great King, the Blessed One has not allowed an attendant for a monastery."
>
> "Then indeed, Reverend, when you have asked the Blessed One about this, you should inform me."

The Venerable Pilindavaccha agreed, saying, "Yes, Great King."

Then the Venerable Pilindavaccha instructed King Bimbisāra with talk connected with Dhamma, inspired, incited, and delighted him. When King Bimbisāra had been instructed with talk connected with Dhamma by the Venerable Pilindavaccha, had been inspired, incited, and delighted, he stood up from his seat, saluted the Venerable Pilindavaccha, circumambulated him, and departed. [150]

The Venerable Pilindavaccha sent a messenger then to the Blessed One to say: "Reverend, the King of Magadha, Seniya Bimbisāra, wishes to give (*dātukāma*) an attendant for a monastery. How, Reverend, should it now be done?"

When the Blessed One had given a talk on Dhamma on that occasion, he addressed the monks: "I allow [order], monks, a monastery attendant."

A second time the King of Magadha, Seniya Bimbisāra, approached the Venerable Pilindavaccha, saluted him, and sat down to one side. So seated, Bimbisāra said this to the Venerable Pilindavaccha: "Reverend, has the Blessed One allowed [ordered] a monastery attendant?"

"Yes, Great King."

"Then indeed, Reverend, I will give a monastery attendant to the Noble One (*ayyassa ārāmikaṃ dammīti*)."

Then the King of Magadha, Seniya Bimbisāra, after he had promised a monastery attendant to the Venerable Pilindavaccha and had forgotten it, after a long time remembered. He addressed a minister concerned with all affairs: "Sir, has the monastery attendant which I promised to the Noble One been given (*dinna*)?"

"No, Lord, the monastery attendant has not been given to the Noble One."

"But how long ago, Sir, since it was considered?"

The minister then counted up the nights and said to Bimbisāra: "Lord, it has been five hundred nights."

"Therefore indeed, sir, you must give (*detha*) five hundred monastery attendants to the Noble One (*ayyassa*).

The minister assented to the king, saying, "Yes, Lord," and gave (*pādāsi*) five hundred monastery attendants to the Venerable Pilindavaccha. A separate village was settled. They called it a "Village of Monastery Attendants (*ārāmikagāma*)." They called it a "Village of Pilinda."[13]

Although their reasons are not always clear or entirely well founded, a number of scholars have expressed some uneasiness in regard to this text. R. A. L. H. Gunawardana, for example, seems to want to assign the account to "the later sections of the *Vinaya Piṭaka*" but does not say why or how he has identified these "later sections."[14] J. Jaworski, having noted that the account in the Mahāvihārin *Bhesajja-khandhaka* had no parallel in the "Section des Remèdes" in the *Mahīśāsaka-vinaya*, first refers to our text as a "local legend."[15] A few years later he said, [151] for essentially the same reason: "la longue histoire sur Pilindavatsa, que nous rencontrons dans *Mahāvagga*, ne peut être qu'une interpolation tardive."[16] Neither Gunawardana nor Jaworski, then, seem to want our text to be early, and it well may not be, but that does not necessarily mean that it occurs in a "later section" or is a "late interpolation." We will have to return to this point later. For the moment, we might look first at Jaworski's suggestion that the Mahāvihārin text is a "local legend."

There are at least two things about the Mahāvihārin text that might suggest that it is local: its beginning and its end. The beginning of the text is unusual. It says that Pilindavaccha . . . *pabbhāraṃ sodhāpeti leṇaṃ kattukāmo*. Rhys Davids and Oldenberg translate this: "Pilindavaccha had a mountain cave . . . cleared out, with the object of making it into a cave dwelling-place"; Horner has: "Pilindavaccha, desiring to make a cave, had a (mountain) slope cleared." Admittedly *leṇa* can mean several things, but first and foremost it seems to mean "a cave used or made into a residential cell," and that is almost certainly its sense here. Moreover, although *sodhāpeti* might mean "clear" in the sense of "removing trees, etc.," it is hard to see why making a "cave" would require clearing a slope or hillside. Then there is the term *pabbhāra*, which the Pāli Text Society dictionary defines as, first, "a decline, incline, slope," but its Sanskrit equivalent—*prāgbhāra*—is defined by Edgerton, when it is a noun, as a "rocky overhanging crag with ledge beneath."[17]

There are a number of uncertainties here, but in large part that may be because the activity described in our text is so odd, if not entirely unique: it is not commonly described elsewhere in *Indian* literature, if at all. And it is probably safe to assume that an Indian monk would have had as difficult a time as we do understanding what was being referred to—Indian monks normally did not occupy or "improve" natural caves. Sri Lankan monks, however, most certainly did. The hundreds of early Brāhmī inscriptions from Sri Lanka are almost all engraved below the artificially made "drip-ledges" of just such cleared [152] and improved natural caves or overhangs, and these "caves" are almost always referred to in these records as *leṇas*.[18] W. Rahula, for example, has already noted that "the large number of donative inscriptions of the first few centuries of Buddhism, incised on the brows of the caves found scattered throughout the island, indicates the extent to which the caves were used by monks."[19] Yet another observation of Rahula's suggests that both the authors and the readers of the Pāli Commentaries might well have had an even more precise understanding of what Pilindavaccha was doing. Rahula says:

> Preparing a cave for the residence of monks was not an easy task. Fortunately, we get in the Pāli Commentaries casual references to the process that was in vogue at least about the fifth-century A.D. First of all, the cave was filled with

> fire-wood and the wood was then burnt; this helped to remove loose splinters of rock as well as to dispel unpleasant odours. After the cave was cleaned, walls of bricks were built on the exposed sides, and doors and windows fixed. Sometimes walls were plastered and whitewashed.[20]

To judge, for example, by Carrithers' text and photographs, some Sri Lankan monks are still living in such accommodations.[21] [153]

All of this is not to say that Indian monks never cleared and improved natural rock overhangs or caves, but the known instances of anything like this are very rare in India.[22] In Sri Lanka, on the other hand, this sort of activity was extremely common, so common that it produced a characteristic form of Sri Lankan monastic "architecture." And it is precisely this characteristically Sri Lankan activity that, I would suggest, is being described in our text of the canonical *vinaya*.

If the beginning of the Mahāvihārin account of Pilindavaccha appears to reflect not Indian but Sri Lankan practice, so too might the end. The account closes by explaining, or accounting for the origin of, two terms or names that, however, are introduced rather abruptly only in the conclusion: "Village of Monastery Attendants," *ārāmikagāma*, and "Village of Pilinda," *pilindagāma*. The second of these two is specific and has no other history as far as I know. But the first is a generic name for a category of donation that is, indeed, referred to elsewhere, but not in India. Geiger, for example, has noted in regard to early medieval Sri Lanka: "The general expression for monastery helpers was *ārāmika* (46.14; 100.218). A hundred helpers and three villages were granted by Aggabodhi IV's Queen Jeṭṭhā to a nunnery built by her (46.28)."[23] Gunawardana too has noted that in Sri Lanka *ārāmikas* "were, at times, granted in large numbers" and that "Aggabodhi I granted a hundred *ārāmikas* to the Kandavihāra, and Jeṭṭhā, the queen of Aggabodhi IV, granted a hundred *ārāmikas* to the Jeṭṭhārāma. Kassapa IV granted *ārāmikagāmas* to the hermitages he built."[24] Evidence of this sort—drawn largely from the *Cūlavaṃsa*—makes it clear that the account of Pilindavaccha now found in the canonical *vinaya* was describing practices that were curiously close to those said by the *Cūlavaṃsa* to have been current, if not common, in medieval Sri Lanka. This, of course, is not to say that *ārāmikas* were not known in Indian *vinaya* texts. There are a number of references to them in the [154] *Mūlasarvāstivāda-vinaya*, for example. But I do not know of a single reference to the gift of *ārāmikas* in any of the numerous Indian royal donations of land and villages to Buddhist monastic communities recorded in Indian inscriptions, nor does the term *ārāmikagāma* seem to occur anywhere there or in continental literary sources. In this sense, then, if in no other, what is described in the Mahāvihārin account of Pilindavaccha is characteristically Sri Lankan. There are also other indications that would suggest that groups of *ārāmikas* were a particular concern of the compilers of the Mahāvihārin *Vinaya*, and well known to them.

At the end of "the Section on Beds and Seats" in the Mahāvihārin *Vinaya*, for example, there is a well-known passage that describes the Buddha "allowing" or instituting a whole series of administrative positions. He "allowed" that an individual monk should be designated as the "issuer-of-meals" (*bhattuddesaka*), the "assigner-of-lodgings" (*senāsanapaññāpaka*), the "keeper-of-the-storeroom" (*bhaṇḍāgārika*), the "accepter-of-robes" (*cīvarapaṭiggāhaka*), etc. In regard to the second-to-the-last administrative office mentioned, the text says: "At that time the Order did not have a superintendent-of-monastery-attendants (*ārāmikapesaka*). The monastery attendants, being unsupervised, did not do their work." When the Buddha was told of this he allowed or instituted the office of "superintendent-of-monastery-attendants."[25] The corresponding passage at the end of the corresponding section of the *Mūlasarvāstivādin-vinaya* has a similar list of monastic officials, but one of the several ways in which that list differs from the Mahāvihārin list is that the former makes no reference to an *ārāmikapesaka* or anything like it. Such an office was unknown at least in this piece of Mūlasarvāstivādin legislation.[26] This is particularly interesting because this [155] office is also referred to in the Mahāvihārin *Parivāra* and *Aṅguttaranikāya*.[27]

Beyond considerations of this sort, the way itself in which the Mahāvihārin account of Pilinda is presented seems to presuppose that it was compiled after it was already commonly known what an *ārāmika* was. Notice that the text is not about how *ārāmikas* got their name or what they were. It is about how a village came to be called a "village of *ārāmikas*," or how the name for a certain category of village—*ārāmikagāma*—came to be. The text itself never says what an *ārāmika* was and proceeds as if this were already known. Notice too that the text as it stands not only abruptly introduces the term but also seems to require that *ārāmika* be taken in its technical and specifically Buddhist sense of a—for the moment—"forced laborer attached to or owned by an individual monk or monastic community," but, again, that sense has not yet been articulated. Notice finally that unless the legal status of such a "laborer" had already been established, our text would have been a lawyer's nightmare—unless, of course, it was redacted and intended for use in an environment with little legal tradition or where formal laws of ownership and property were little developed. There are otherwise far too many things left undetermined: for what purposes is an *ārāmika* allowed; in whom or what does ownership of the *ārāmika* inhere; does the donor retain some rights in regard to the *ārāmika*, and if the king is the donor, does the *ārāmika* continue to have obligations in regard to the state; what, if any, are the obligations of the donee; what are the obligations of the *ārāmika*; etc. None of this is engaged and there must be at least some question as to whether this would have been acceptable—or even possible—in an Indian world that knew anything about the *Dharmasūtras* or *Dharmaśāstras*. The issues here might be better focused if we look at our next text.

When Jaworski suggested that the account of Pilindavaccha in the Mahāvihārin *Vinaya* was a "late interpolation," and when Gunawardana wanted to assign it to "the later sections" of that collection, both were referring only to the account in the *Bhesajja-khandaka*. Neither seems to have noted that the same account also occurs in the *Suttavibhaṅga* of the same *Vinaya*,[28] and neither indicated that a clear parallel to the [156] Mahāvihārin account also occurs in the *Vibhaṅga* of at least one other *vinaya*, the Mūlasarvāstivādin *Vinayavibhaṅga* preserved in Tibetan. This Mūlasarvāstivādin parallel complicates, of course, both their observations in a number of ways, but before taking up a discussion of these, I first give a translation of the Tibetan text. The Tibetan account translated here, it should be noted, does not fall under the heading of the 23rd "Forfeiture" (*nissaggiya*) as in the Mahāvihārin *Vinaya* but forms a part of the Mūlasarvāstivādin discussion of the second of the offenses requiring expulsion from the order.[29]

> The Buddha, the Blessed One, was staying in Rājagṛha, in the Bamboo Grove and haunt of the Kalandakas. Now, it was the usual practice of King Bimbisāra (101b) to go every day to venerate the feet of the Blessed One and each of the Elder monks. On one such occasion King Bimbisāra venerated the feet of the Blessed One and sat down in his presence to hear Dharma. The Blessed One instructed with a talk connected with Dharma the King of Magadha, Śreṇya Bimbisāra, as he was seated to one side; he inspired, incited, and delighted him. When the Blessed One had instructed him in various ways with talk connected with Dharma, had inspired, incited, and delighted him, he fell silent. Then King Śreṇya Bimbisāra, when he had venerated the feet of the Blessed One, stood up from his seat and departed.
>
> He went to the *vihāra* (*gtsug lag khang*) of the Venerable Pilindaka. At that time the Venerable Pilindaka himself was doing repair and maintenance work on that *vihāra*.[30] The Venerable Pilindaka saw Śreṇya Bimbisāra, the King of Magadha, from a distance, and when he saw him, he washed his hands and feet and sat down on the seat he had prepared.
>
> Śreṇya Bimbisāra, the King of Magadha, then honored with his head the feet of the Venerable Pilindaka and sat down to one side. So seated, King Śreṇya Bimbisāra said this to the Venerable Pilindaka: "Noble One, what is this? Do you yourself do the repair and maintenance work?"
>
> "Great King, a renunciant (*rab tu byung ba, pravrajita*) is one who does his own work. Since we are renunciants (102a), what other would do the work?"
>
> "Noble One, if that is so, I will give the Noble One a servant (*zhabs 'bring ba, parivāra*)."
>
> The Great King up to four times had this polite exchange. A fifth time too

he himself said, "I will give the Noble One a servant." But finally a co-residential pupil (*sārdhamvihārika*) of the Venerable Pilindaka who spoke truthfully, consistently, and with courage said: "Great King, ever since the Great King offered servants to the Preceptor, the Preceptor, when the *vihāra* is in need of repairs, lets it fall to pieces." [157]

The King said: "Noble One, what is this? Did we not repeatedly promise servants?"

"Great King, not only on one occasion, but on five."

Because the King was forgetful, it was his usual practice when making even small promises to someone to have all that written down in a document by a man who sat behind him.[31] The King said to the man: "Hear, home minister! Is it not true that I repeatedly promised this?"

"That is true, Lord, five times."

"Therefore, since I would do what I had agreed, I will give the Noble One five hundred servants." He ordered his officers: "Present the Noble One with five hundred servants!"

The Venerable Pilindaka said: "Great King, I have renounced personal servants (*g-yog, parivāra, dāsa*). What do servants have to do with a renunciant?"

"Noble One, you must accept them for the benefit of the Community! (*dge 'dun gyi don du bzhes shig, saṃghāya gṛhāṇa*)."

"Great King, if that is the case I will ask the Blessed One."

"Noble One, ask, since that would not involve an offense!"

The Venerable Pilindaka reported the matter in detail to the Blessed One.

The Blessed One said: "Servants (*g-yog*) are to be accepted for the benefit of the Community (*dge 'dun gyi don du*)."

The Venerable Pilindaka accepted those servants (102b).

When those servants were repeatedly made to do work in the King's house, they said to the Venerable Pilindaka: "Noble One, we were given as servants (*zhabs 'bring ba*) to the Noble Ones (*'phags pa dag gi, āryānāṃ*). Given that we are delighted with that, why are we repeatedly made to do work in the King's house?"

"Good men, do not make trouble! I must speak to the King."

On another occasion Śreṇya Bimbisāra, the King of Magadha, again approached the Venerable Pilindaka, honored his feet, and sat down in front of him.

The Venerable Pilindaka said: "Great King, do you not regret having given servants (*g-yog*) for the benefit of the Community?"

"Noble One, I do not have the slightest regret."

"But why then are those servants still made to do work in the King's house?"

The King, while still seated on that very seat, ordered his ministers: "Sirs, the servants of the Noble Ones henceforth must not be made to do work in the King's house!"

When the ministers ordered others, saying: "You must do work in the King's house!" some among them said: "We belong to the Noble Ones (*bdag cag 'phags pa dag gi yin no*)."

The ministers said to the King: "Lord, we are unable to order anyone. When we say to someone "You must do work in the King's house!" they say 'We belong to the Noble Ones.'"

The King said: "Go! Make them all work!" [158]

When they all were again made to do work in the King's house, they once again said to the Venerable Pilindaka: "Noble One, we again in the same way were made to work in the King's house. Has the Noble One not spoken to him?"

"Good men, I have spoken to him (103a), but I must do so again."

The Venerable Pilindaka, when King Śreṇya Bimbisāra approached him again in the same way, said: "What is this, Great King? Have you again come to have regrets?"

"Noble One, what have I done wrong?"

"The servants have again been made to work in the same way."

"Noble One, I am not able to order anyone. When I order someone, they say 'We belong to the Noble Ones.' Ah! If I had built at some place quarters for the proper bondmen (*lha 'bangs*, *kalpikāra*) of the Noble Ones, then we would know—'These belong to the King. These belong to the Noble Ones' (*'di dag ni rgyal po'i 'o / 'di dag ni 'phags pa dag gi 'o /*)."

The Venerable Pilindaka said: "I will ask the Blessed One."

The Venerable Pilindaka reported the matter in detail to the Blessed One.

The Blessed One said: "Henceforth having quarters for the proper bondmen constructed is approved [ordered]."

The monks did not know where to have the quarters for the proper bondmen constructed. The Blessed One said: "Quarters for the proper bondmen should be built outside of the King's house and outside of the Bamboo Grove Monastery, but in between where, when they have heard the sound of a summons, they can accomplish the needs of the Community."

The monks informed the subministers: "The Blessed One has said that 'the quarters for the proper bondmen should be built in this place.' You should make that known!"

The subministers had the bell sounded in Rājagṛha and proclaimed: "It is determined that those who are proper bondmen of the Noble Ones are to live outside of Rājagṛha and outside of the Bamboo Grove, but in between. Quarters must now be built there!" They went there and built quarters.

When they had built their bondmen's quarters, they went to the *vihāra* and (103b) worked. The monks explained to them the work: "Since this task is proper, you should do it. Since this task is not proper, you should not do it." Because they performed the proper tasks, the designation "proper bondman," "proper bondman," came into being. Because they took care of the *ārāma* of the Community, the designation "proper slave," "proper slave" (*rtse rgod*, *kapyāri*) came into being. When all the bondmen were in the *vihāra*, the monks were not able to achieve mental concentration because of the noise.

The Blessed One said: "Only those who have finished their work should enter the *vihāra*, not all of them."

When the monks had food and clothing distributed to all the bondmen, the Blessed One said: "To those who work, food and clothing are to be distributed, but not to all."

When the monks ignored those who were sick, the Blessed One said: "To those who are sick, food and clothing are to be distributed and they should be attended to."

There can be, it seems, little doubt that the Mahāvihārin and Mūlasarvāstivādin accounts of Pilinda represent two different redactions [159] of the same tradition. That would mean that both the *Vinaya* that is purported to be the earliest (the Mahāvihārin), and the *Vinaya* that is purported to be the latest (the Mūlasarvāstivādin), have this tradition in common. Putting aside the possibility of other redactions in other *vinayas*—the Sarvāstivādin *Vinaya* preserved in Chinese may well contain yet another version of the account[32]—conventional wisdom would dictate that the Mūlasarvāstivādin version must be the latest version and must somehow be based on or borrow from the Mahāvihārin *Vinaya*, through however many intermediaries: it must come after it. But a comparison of the two versions, rather than confirming this, produces a series of anomalies.

To start with, the Mahāvihārin account, which should represent the earliest version, has itself been labeled a probable "late interpolation." Moreover, both the beginning and the end of the Mahāvihārin account may well reflect not early Indian but Sri Lankan practice, and even formally the Mahāvihārin version looks—if anything—like an abbreviated or an abridged version of a longer account. There is, for example, the abrupt and awkward introduction into the Mahāvihārin account of the technical term *ārāmika* before the term itself has been defined. Equally awkward and equally abrupt is the insertion, at the end, of the reference to the *ārāmikagāma*, or "Village of Monastery Attendants"—the clumsiness of the original is nicely reflected in Horner's translation: "and a distinct village established itself" (*pāṭiyekko gāmo nivisi*). Unlike in the Mūlasarvāstivādin version, there is no reason given for this, no explanation as to why it should have occurred. This same final passage also underlines the secondary character of the Mahāvihārin account: here the account is framed in such a way that it becomes not a story of primary origins—as in the Mūlasarvāstivādin account—but of secondary origins. It is presented not as the story of the origins of *ārāmikas* but as the story of the origins of "villages of *ārāmikas*," a [160] term or concept that the Mūlasarvāstivādin version knows nothing about.

Then there are the matters of content. The Mūlasarvāstivādin version addresses and negotiates a whole series of "legal" and practical issues that the acceptance of such property by monastic groups would almost certainly have entailed—the question of where ownership inheres; the retention of rights or interest in the property by the donor; the obligations of the community, etc.—none of which, as we have seen, are addressed by the Mahāvihārin account. The first of these issues is particularly interesting, and the way in which it is handled in the two accounts would seem to point to a striking anomaly: the latest version (the Mūlasarvāstivādin) takes a far more conservative and restricted position in regard to the ownership of "proper bondmen" (*kalpikāra*) or "monastery attendants" than does what should be the earliest version (the Mahāvihārin). The former takes some pains to have Pilindaka point out that as an individual he is a *pravrajita* and as such "does his own work" (*rgyal po chen po rab tu byung ba ni rang nyid kyis byed pa yin te /*) and that he has renounced personal servants (*rgyal po chen po kho bo rang gi g-yog nyid spangs te /*). Moreover, the Mūlasarvāstivādin text explicitly says the servants were given, allowed by the Buddha, and accepted "for the benefit of the Community" (*dge 'dun gyi don du*), not as personal property. That ownership inheres not in Pilindaka but in the monastic group is then repeatedly reaffirmed by the consistent use of the plural: the servants say they were given not to Pilindaka but to "the Noble Ones" (*'phags pa dag gi, āryānāṃ*); they say they "belong" not to Pilindaka but "to the Noble Ones"; the king establishes separate quarters to institutionalize the distinction between those servants who "belong to the king" and those who "belong to the Noble Ones" (*'di dag ni rgyal po'i 'o / 'di dag ni 'phags pa dag gi 'o /*).[33] The Mahāvihārin account, on the other hand, articulates a [161] different conception of ownership. It has nothing to correspond to the Mūlasarvāstivādin repeated clause "for the benefit of the Community," and it just as consistently uses the singular: the king promises to give an attendant not to "the Noble Ones," but to "the Noble One" (*ayyassa*), i.e., to Pilindavaccha; likewise when the king finally gives five hundred, they are given specifically to "the Noble One," or Pilindaka himself. The Mahāvihārin text seems to want to emphasize that the *ārāmikas* were the personal property of Pilinda. It specifically notes that the village was called the "Village of Pilinda" or "Pilinda's Village," and this name—not *Ārāmikagāma*—is repeatedly used in the continuation of the story. The conception of ownership that is articulated in the Mahāvihārin account of Pilinda may be only one instance of a far broader Mahāvihārin attitude toward the "private" possession by monks of "monastic" property, an attitude for which, again, there is little Indian evidence. S. Kemper, for example, has said that "the precedent for the individual holding and willing of property by monks [in Sri Lanka] dates to a tenth-century dedication of property to the use of a particular monk and his pupils."[34] But there is good evidence that this happened much, much earlier. There is at least one early Sri Lankan Brāhmī inscription that dates to the end of the first or beginning of the second century C.E. and records that a *vihāra* was built not for the Community but "for the Elder Godhagatta Tissa," and Paranavitana has noted that "the chronicle has recorded the founding by Vaṭṭagāmaṇī Abhaya of the Abhayagiri-*vihāra*, and some other *viharās* by his generals, to be given to certain *theras* in recognition of the aid rendered to the king and his followers in their days of adversity."[35] Evidence for anything like this is both hard to find in Indian Buddhist inscriptions [162] and, then, only very late.[36] Moreover, in specific regard to the personal possession of *ārāmikas*, at least some Indian *vinayas* explicitly forbid this. In the 8th *Prakīrṇaka* of the *Mahāsāṃghika-Lokottaravādin Bhikṣuṇī-vinaya*, for example, the Buddha is made to say:

> Désormais, il ne convient pas d'entretenir une jardinière personnelle (*tena hi na kṣamati paudagalikām* [read: *paudgalikām*] *ārāmikinīm upasthāpayitum*).
>
> Il ne convient pas [d'entretenir] une jardinière, ni une servante, ni une laïque au service de la communauté (*na kṣamati ārāmikinī / na kṣamati ceṭī / na kṣamati kalpiyakārī*).
>
> Si une nonne entretient une jardinière personnelle, elle commet une infraction à la discipline. C'est ce qu'on appelle la règle concernant les jardinières.[37]

This passage from the Mahāsāṃghika-Lokottaravādin tradition also directs our attention to a final anomaly, or at least distinct difference, between the Mahāvihārin and Mūlasarvāstivādin accounts of Pilinda: it both distinguishes between and conflates the two terms *ārāmika*, "monastery attendant," and *kalpiyakāra*, a form of the term I have translated "proper bondman." The Mahāvihārin account of Pilinda deals with the first, but the Mūlasarvāstivādin is concerned with the second, and the question naturally arises about the relationship between the two terms or categories they designate. The Mahāsāṃghika-Lokottaravādin passage, [163] if in no other way than by using them separately, distinguishes between the two terms or categories but then lumps them together with *ceṭa* ("servant" or "slave") by saying that the rule that applies to all three is called "the rule concerning *ārāmikas*."

This confusion or conflation appears to occur in one form or another almost everywhere. In referring to the *Cūlavaṃsa*, Geiger, for example, says that "the terms *kappiyakāraka* 'who does what is appropriate' . . . *paricāraka* 'attendant' . . . and *parivārajana* 'people for service' . . . seem to be synonymous with *ārāmika*."[38] In the "old" commentary embedded in the Mūlasarvāstivādin *Vinayavibhaṅga*, for another example, in the section dealing with the rule against "touching" gold and silver, the text says: "'*ārāmika*' means 'one who does what is proper'" (*kun dga' ra ba pa zhes bya ba ni rung ba byed pa'o*).[39] Sorting this out—if even possible—will certainly not be easy and would require a separate study. Here we need only stick to our particular context.

The context in both the Mahāvihārin and the Mūlasarvāstivādin accounts of

Pilinda makes it clear that the individuals called *ārāmikas* or *kalpikāras* are individuals who engage in or do the physical labor connected with monastic living quarters. In regard to *ārāmikas* this is not problematic—in the *Vinayas* of both Orders, *ārāmikas* continue to be associated with physical or manual labor. But, again in both *Vinayas*, individuals of the serving class also come to be given more specific or specialized functions; in both they are sometimes assigned the role of *kappiyakārakas* or *kalpikāra*. The specialized nature of this role is clear in both *Vinayas* in regard to the vexed question of monks accepting money. The Mahāvihārin *Vinaya*, for example, says:

> There are, monks, people who have faith and are believing. They deposit gold (coins) in the hands of those who make things allowable [*kappiyakāraka*], saying: "By means of this, give the master that which is allowable [*kappiya*]." I allow you, monks, thereupon to consent to that which is allowable.[40]

And in the *Bhaiṣajyavastu* of the *Mūlasarvāstivāda-vinaya*, in a discussion of the acceptance by monks of "travel money," we find [164]

> Though it was said by the Blessed One "money (*kārṣāpaṇa*) is to be accepted," the monks did not know by whom and how it was to be accepted.
>
> The Blessed One said: "It is to be accepted by one who makes things allowable (*kalpikāra*)."[41]

In these and numerous other passages in both *Vinayas*, the *kappiyakāraka* or *kalpikāra* is an individual who acts as a middleman by accepting things that monks cannot (e.g., money) and converting them into things that they can. This specialized function is well established in both *Vinayas*, but the Mūlasarvāstivādin account of Pilinda seems to know nothing of this particular development and appears to be using the term *kalpikāra* in an old, if not original, sense of one who does the manual labor that was deemed proper to him. There is no hint of the developed middleman role. The Tibetan translators too appear to have recognized this. When *kalpikāra* is used in the sense of a middleman "who makes things proper"—as it is in the passage from the *Bhaiṣajyavastu* just cited—it is rendered into Tibetan by *rung ba byed pa*, which means just that. But in the account of Pilinda it is rendered into Tibetan by *lha 'bangs*, a term that seems to carry some of the same connotations as Sanskrit *devadāsa*, "temple slave," which it sometimes translates.[42] Moreover, that the Mūlasarvāstivādin account of Pilinda is old—though it is supposed to be the latest of such accounts—may be further confirmed by the fact that it also uses the even more obscure *kapyāri* precisely where the term *ārāmika*, if then well established, would have both naturally and "etymologically" been expected. After "because they took care of the *ārāma* of the Community," we do not find "the designation [165] '*ārāmika, ārāmika*' came into being," but rather "the designation '*kapyāri, kapyāri*' came into being."[43] In other words, the Mūlasarvāstivādin story of Pilinda appears to have been used to account for the origin of both an old, if not obsolete, sense of *kalpikāra* and the equally—if not more—obsolete term *kapyāri*. Such obsolescence is hard to account for in what should be a late text, whereas the use of *ārāmika* in the Mahāvihārin account creates, in this sense, no difficulties: in that account an old story may well have been used to explain a relatively late term.

Most of the anomalies that arise from a comparison of the story of Pilinda in the purportedly early Mahāvihārin *Vinaya* and the purportedly late *Mūlasarvāstivādin-vinaya* can perhaps be explained in two conventional ways. It is possible, for example, to take the account of Pilinda in the Mahāvihārin *Vinaya* as another instance of the "strong northern influence" on the Buddhist literature of Sri Lanka. E. Frauwallner—in referring to several remarks of S. Lévi—said almost forty years ago:

> Now it has been remarked long ago that the Buddhist literature of Ceylon, and above all the commentaries, show a strong northern influence. It is met with at every step when one scans the pages of the *Dhammapadaṭṭhakathā*. And some legends show unmistakably the form which they have received in the school of the Mūlasarvāstivādin. . . . There was rather a borrowing of themes, above all in the field of narrative literature, which took place on a large scale.[44] [166]

The account of Pilinda might well fall into line with what is suggested here; it is a "legend," presumably, and certainly falls within "the field of narrative literature." Its late borrowing and adaptation by the Mahāvihārin tradition would seem to account for both its basic narrative similarity with the Mūlasarvāstivādin tradition and the Sri Lankan elements it appears to contain. Such an explanation, moreover, would fit with Jaworski's suggestion that the account was a "late interpolation" in the Mahāvihārin *Vinaya*. But notice that if this explanation is correct, then the account of Pilinda presents us with a case of "northern influence" not on the commentaries but directly on the canon. And it would, indeed, have been strong: if the account is interpolated, then it was interpolated twice into the canonical Mahāvihārin *Vinaya*, once into the *Suttavibhaṅga* and once into the *Bhesajja-khandhaka*.

But it is also possible, perhaps, to explain the anomalies in another way. The account of Pilinda may present us with yet another instance where on close study the Mūlasarvāstivādin tradition, though it is supposed to be late, turns out not to be so. Again almost forty years ago A. Bareau—referring to Przyluski's *Légende d'açoka* and Hofinger's *Concile de vaiśālī*—said:

> However, after deep but very incomplete comparative studies the *Vinayapiṭaka* of the Mūlasarvāstivādins appears clearly to be more archaic than that of the Sarvāstivādins, and even than the majority of other *Vinayapiṭakas*.[45]

A case, then, can be made for thinking—contrary to what might have been expected—that the Mahāvihārin account of Pilinda represents a Sri Lankan borrowing and adaptation of the Mūlasarvāstivādin account; and a case can be made for thinking that the Mūlasarvāstivādin account, rather than being the latest, is the earliest. But this may not exhaust what we might learn from the comparison of the two versions, nor do these explanations address the distinct possibility that the Mūlasarvāstivādin version itself is not very early. Notice, for example, that it need not have been early for it to have been borrowed by the Sri Lankan Mahāvihārins along with other "themes" and "narrative literature." As is suggested by Frauwallner himself, the most likely period for the Sri Lankan borrowing of Mūlasarvāstivādin material was during the period [167] from the second to the fifth or sixth century C.E.[46] There are in fact reasons for thinking that the Mūlasarvāstivādin account is not much earlier than the second century and that what separates the two versions is not so much time as cultural and physical geography.

There has been a marked tendency to ignore the remarkable degree of institutional development and sophistication reflected in virtually all of the *vinayas* as we have them, to avoid, in effect, asking how a given ruling attributed to the Buddha could have possibly been put into effect or implemented, or what conditions or organizational elements were presupposed by a given rule. It may be, however, just such questions that will begin to reveal the various layers of institutional forms that were known or presupposed by the redactors of the various *vinayas* that have come down to us. The Mūlasarvāstivādin account of Pilinda may serve as a good example.

The Mūlasarvāstivādin account of Pilinda would at first seem to presuppose permanent monastic establishments whose repair and maintenance required a large nonmonastic workforce—notice that both it and the Mahāvihārin account concern the gift not of single servants or bondmen but of large numbers, though we need not take the number five hundred too seriously. Such establishments, to judge by the archaeological record, were not early. It seems that they begin to appear only around the beginning of the Common Era and, even then, were probably not the norm.[47] Moreover, a variety of *vinaya* literatures suggest that monks in other instances did, and in many places may have continued to do, their own maintenance and repair work. In the *Suttavibhaṅga* of the Mahāvihārin *Vinaya* there is a long series of cases, for example, dealing with the deaths of monks that resulted from construction accidents—monks building *vihāras* or walls had stones or bricks dropped on their heads, they fell off scaffolds while making repairs, had adzes and beams dropped on them, fell off the roof when thatching the *vihāra*, and so on.[48] [168] Elsewhere, in the Mahāsāṃghika *Abhisamācārikā*, for example, there is an explicit ruling made that *all* monks are to do repair and maintenance work on the *vihāra*—claiming exemption by virtue of being a "Reciter of Dharma" (*dharmakathika*) or a "Preserver of the *Vinaya*" (*vinayadhara*), or the like is an offense and will not work.[49] In light of texts like these, we may begin to see that the redactors of the Mūlasarvāstivādin account of Pilinda may not simply have presupposed a community that could use large nonmonastic labor forces but may also have had in mind a community that found itself in a cultural milieu in which at least prominent monks were not expected to do manual labor and had achieved the status and means whereby they could avoid it.[50]

A related presupposition must of necessity lie behind the seemingly simple ruling that "to those who work, food and clothing are to be distributed." This ruling presupposes that the monastic community had the means to do so, that it had—or was expected to have—sufficient surplus to meet its obligations to feed and clothe a large workforce. But in addition to presuppositions in regard to the monastic communities' access to a considerable economic surplus, the redactors of the Mūlasarvāstivādin account also presuppose that the conception of the *saṅgha* as a juristic personality that could, and did, own property was well [169] established and, more importantly, publicly recognized by the state. At least that was what they were asserting.

None of these considerations argue well for an early date for the Mūlasarvāstivādin account of Pilinda, and this in turn leaves us with two redactions of the same text—the Mahāvihārin and the Mūlasarvāstivādin—neither of which could be early. It is, therefore, unlikely that their relative chronology can in any way explain their significant differences: something else must be involved. What that something is, I would suggest, is that already suggested in regard to the beginning and the end of the Mahāvihārin account: locality. These two versions may differ from each other not so much because they were redacted at different times but because they were redacted in different places and there were different social and, more especially, legal forces at work in these different areas.

A number of recent studies on specific topics in the *Mūlasarvāstivāda-vinaya*, for example, have demonstrated, I think, a remarkable degree of contact between that *Vinaya* and Indian *dharmaśāstra*, or "orthodox" brahmanical values. These studies have suggested, for instance, that Mūlasarvāstivādin "monastic regulations governing the distribution of a dead monk's property were framed to conform to, or be in harmony with, classical Hindu laws or *dharmaśāstric* conventions governing inheritance."[51] They have shown as well that this *Vinaya* and the *Yājñavalkya-smṛti* have remarkably similar rules governing lending on interest and written contracts of debt.[52] The redactors of this *Vinaya* frequently appear to be trying to come to terms or negotiate with an established legal system and set of values that surrounded them.[53] Here, in the cultural milieu in which the redactors of this *Vinaya* found themselves, a gift—for example—was not a simple spontaneous act without complications but a legal procedure involving rights of ownership that had to be defined and [170] defended.[54] It is, I think, fairly obvious that the Mūlasarvāstivādin account of Pilinda differs from the Mahāvihārin account almost entirely in terms of legal detail. The former takes pains to distinguish between private and corporate ownership of the property involved; it carefully distinguishes between the rights of the king in regard to the labor of those individuals who belong to the king and those who belong to the Community; it insists that the two groups be physically separated, that those that belong to the Community be in effect removed from the general population (they must live outside of the royal house and the city), and that this distinction be formally recognized and publicly proclaimed (the ministers sound the city bell and formally announce it); it also clearly defined the Community's obligations to feed, clothe, and give medical aid to their bondmen, and the bondmen's obligation to work.[55] All of this—even an awareness of the problems—is, as has already been noted, completely absent from the Mahāvihārin account, and this can hardly be unrelated to the fact that the Mahāvihārin *Vinaya* as a whole shows little awareness of the early and elaborate Indian legal system articulated in the *Dharmasūtras* and *Dharmaśāstras*. Indeed, there is little trace of either in any of the extant sources for early Sri Lankan cultural history, nor is there any strong evidence in these same sources for any clearly established indigenous, formal system or systems of law. That so little is known of the history of Sri Lanka law prior to the Kandy period would seem to suggest that in early Sri Lanka—in marked contrast to brahmanized areas of early India—formal law and legal literature were little developed.[56] A monastic community in such an [171] environment would have had considerable latitude in the way in which they would or could frame their own ecclesiastical law, and there would almost certainly have been far less need for precise legal definition, far less need to distinguish one set of rights from another. The absence of a strong legal tradition in Sri Lanka, and the presence of an established, competing system of nonecclesiastical law in the brahmanical milieu in which the *Mūlasarvāstivāda-vinaya* seems to have been redacted, are sufficient, it seems, to account for the significant differences between the Mahāvihārin and Mūlasarvāstivādin accounts of Pilinda. They can, in any case, not be simply a function of time.

A few loose ends remain, and there is still room for another conclusion.

First of all, it would appear that the accounts of Pilinda in both the Mahāvihārin and Mūlasarvāstivādin *Vinayas* contain or deliver the initial rule allowing for the acceptance by monks or monastic communities of *ārāmikas* or *kalpikāras*.

They were the charters for such practices. But because it also seems that neither account in either *vinaya* can be early, then it would also appear that references to *ārāmikas* and *kalpikāras* elsewhere in their respective *vinayas* also cannot be early. It would seem unlikely that incidental references to *ārāmikas* or *kalpikāras* would precede the rule allowing their acceptance. But because such references are scattered throughout both *vinayas* as we have them, the implications of this are both far-reaching and obvious.

Then there is the problem of what to call *ārāmikas* or *kalpikāras*: are they servants, forced laborers, bondmen, slaves? This is a problem reflected in the clumsiness of my own translation, but also one that goes way beyond Indian studies. The definition of "slavery," for example, is beset in every field by academic debate and ideological wrangling.[57] [172] About all that can be done here is to report what our specific texts can contribute to the discussion. We might note first that the language of the Mahāvihārin account is not particularly helpful. It does, however, indicate that *ārāmikas* were human beings who could be, and were, given (*dātu-*, *dammi*, *dinna*, *detha*, *pādāsi*) by one person (the king) to another (the Venerable Pilinda) and appear to have been, in this sense, chattels. The language of the Mūlasarvāstivādin account is richer but also has to be filtered through the Tibetan translation. The preponderant verb for the action of the king is the same as in the Mahāvihārin text: it is in Tibetan some form of *'bul ba*, a well-attested equivalent of forms from √*dā*. What the king offers and gives is expressed, up until a certain point in the text, by two apparently interchangeable Tibetan terms: *zhabs 'bring ba*, which frequently translates *parivāra*, "suite, retinue, dependents," etc., and *g-yog*, which also translates *parivāra* but translates *dāsa*, "slave, servant," as well, and *bhṛtya*, "dependent, servant." These terms are used throughout the text until, significantly, the king determines that a distinction between "those who belong to the king" and "those who belong to the Community" must be institutionalized, and the latter must be physically removed from the city. From this point and this point only, the text begins to use the term that I have translated "proper bondmen": *lha 'bangs*. The term *lha 'bangs* is a well-attested equivalent for *kalpikāra*, but it is by no means an etymological translation of it. In Tibetan its etymological meaning is "subjects of the god(s)," and Jäschke defines it as "slaves belonging to a temple." In fact, the only Sanskrit equivalent other than *kalpikāra* that Chandra gives is *devadāsa*.[58] For what it is worth, then, the Tibetan translators seem to have understood *kalpikāras* to be a special category of slaves.[59] In the Mūlasarvāstivādin account too they are human beings who are owned and can be given, although there they also have conditional rights: if they work, they have rights to food, clothing, and medical attention from their monastic owners. [173]

Finally, and by way of conclusion, we should probably note what should be obvious from the above discussion: the accounts of Pilinda can almost certainly not tell us anything about what early Buddhist groups were. They, and the *vinayas* as we have them, can, however, tell us a great deal about what those groups had become. There are good reasons for thinking that neither account could have been redacted much before the first or second century C.E. Such a suggested date is, of course, usually enough to have a text or passage dismissed as "late" and of little historical value. But to do so, I think, is to miss completely the importance of such documents: they are important precisely because they are "late." Such "late" documents would provide us, for example, with written sources close to, if not contemporaneous with, the remarkable florescence of monastic Buddhisms visible in the archaeological record between the beginning of the Common Era and the fifth or sixth century and would help us make sense of it. Such "late" documents would provide us with important indications of the activities and interests of the "mainstream" monastic Orders during the period when the majority of Mahāyāna *sūtras* were being composed, and, again, help us make sense of them. The apparent fact, for example, that the redactors of two very different *vinayas*, the canon lawyers of two very different Orders, were occupied with and interested in framing rules governing the monastic acceptance and ownership of servants, bondmen, or slaves in the early centuries of the Common Era can hardly be unrelated to the attacks on and criticisms of certain aspects of institutionalized monasticism found in Mahāyāna *sūtra* literature. Indeed, it may well turn out that the institutional concerns that dominate the various *vinayas* as we have them played an important—and largely overlooked—role in the origins of what we call the Mahāyāna. But that, too, is another story.

Notes

1. J. Burton, *Monastic and Religious Orders in Britain, 1000–1300* (Cambridge, U.K.: 1994) x. As a small sampling of the richness of historical studies on Western monasticisms, see esp. B. D. Hill, *English Cistercian Monasteries and Their Patrons in the Twelfth Century* (Urbana, Ill.: 1968); R. B. Dobson, *Durham Priory 1400–1450* (Cambridge, U.K.: 1973); D. J. Osheim, *A Tuscan Monastery and Its Social World. San Michele of Guamo (1156–1348)* (Rome: 1989); B. H. Rosenwein, *To Be the Neighbor of Saint Peter. The Social Meaning of Cluny's Property, 909–1049* (Ithaca, N.Y., and London: 1989).

2. The distinctive differences between Christian monasticism in early Ireland and most of the rest of Europe are commonly said to have been conditioned, if not determined, by the absence of towns in early Ireland, by the fact that Ireland had never been part of the Roman Empire, and by the fact that Irish society was essentially tribal; see J. F. Webb and D. H. Farmer, *The Age of Bede* (London: 1988) 13, and, much more fully, L. M. Bitel, *Isle of*

the Saints. Monastic Settlement and Christian Community in Early Ireland (Ithaca, N.Y., and London: 1990) esp. 1, 87.

3. The most elaborate study based on this assumption is still E. Frauwallner, *The Earliest Vinaya and the Beginnings of Buddhist Literature* (Rome: 1956). For a succinct discussion of some of the larger problems involved in this approach, and for references to other conceptualizations of the relationship among the various *vinayas*, see G. Schopen, "The Ritual Obligations and Donor Roles of Monks in the Pāli *Vinaya*," *JPTS* 16 (1992) 87–107, esp. 104–106 and notes [= *BSBM* 72–85].

4. S. Lévi, "Les saintes écritures du bouddhisme. Comment s'est constitué le canon sacré," *Mémorial Sylvain Lévi* (Paris: 1937) 83: "Réduits par élagage à leurs éléments communs, les Vinaya de toutes les écoles se ramènent sans effort à une sorte d'archétype unique, qui n'est pas le Vinaya primitif, mais la moyenne des Vinaya."

5. I. B. Horner, *The Book of the Discipline*, Vol. I (Oxford: 1938) xvi–xvii; cf. xxviii–xxix.

6. J. Jaworski, "Le section de la nourriture dans le vinaya des mahīśāsaka," *Rocznik Orientalistyczny* 7 (1929–1930) 94. Something like this sense—though not so clearly expressed—may be lurking in the corresponding passage in the Mahāvihārin *Vinaya*: see Pāli *Vinaya* i 250–251.

7. Horner, *The Book of the Discipline*, iv 263.

8. R. W. Lariviere, *The Nāradasmṛti* (Philadelphia: 1989), Pt.1, 18 (1.34); Pt. 2, 11 (I.34); see also V. N. Mandlik, *Mānava-Dharma-Śāstra* (Bombay: 1886; repr. 1992) VIII.46.

9. For a recent reaffirmation of this view, see O. von Hinüber, "The Arising of an Offence: Āpattisamuṭṭhāna. A Note on the Structure and History of the Theravāda-Vinaya," *JPTS* 16 (1992) 68 n. 13.

10. For some references to the sometimes contradictory assessments of the chronological position of the *Mūlasarvāstivādin-vinaya*, see G. Schopen, "On Avoiding Ghosts and Social Censure: Monastic Funerals in the *Mūlasarvāstivāda-vinaya*," *JIP* 20 (1992) 36–37 n. 69 [= *BSBM* 235–236]. Regardless of the date of its compilation, the Tibetan translation is clearly later than the Sanskrit manuscripts from Gilgit and the Chinese translation and should represent the latest form of this *Vinaya*.

11. Pāli *Vinaya* i 206.34–208.1; trans. in T. W. Rhys Davids and H. Oldenberg, *Vinaya Texts*, Pt. II (Sacred Books of the East, Vol. XVII) (Oxford: 1882) 61–63; Horner, *The Book of the Discipline* iv 281–282. I have intentionally used the title "Mahāvihārin *Vinaya*" to refer to what is usually called "*The* Pāli Vinaya" or "*The* Theravāda Vinaya" or—still worse—simply "The Vinaya." My usage is intended to problematize the status of this *Vinaya*, which is too often assumed to be self-evident. Though we know little or nothing of the details, we do know that there were, or appear to have been, competing versions or understandings of "The Theravāda Vinaya" in both Sri Lanka (see H. Bechert, "On the Identification of Buddhist Schools in Early Sri Lanka," in *Indology and Law. Studies in Honour of Professor J. Duncan M. Derrett*, ed. G.-D. Sontheimer and P. K. Aithal [Wiesbaden: 1982] 60–76; V. Stache-Rosen, *Upālipariprcchāsūtra. Ein Text zur buddhistischen Ordensdisziplin*, ed. H. Bechert [Göttingen: 1984] esp. 28–31), and in South India (see P. V. Bapat, "Vimati-Vinodani, A Vinaya Commentary and Kundalkesi-Vatthu, A Tamil Poem," *JIH* 45.3 [1967] 689–694; P. Kieffer-Pülz, "Zitate aus der Andhaka-Aṭṭhakathā in der Samantapāsādikā" in *Studien*

zur Indologie und Buddhismuskunde. Festgabe des Seminars für Indologie und Buddhismuskunde für Professor Dr. Heinz Bechert zum 60. Geburtstag am 26. Juni 1992, ed. R. Grünendahl et al. [Bonn: 1993] 171–212), and this must at least raise the question of the representativeness of the redaction of this *Vinaya* that we have.

12. For the sake of convenience—and nothing more—I have adopted Horner's translation of *ārāmika* here. Rhys Davids and Oldenberg fall back on an etymological rendering, "park-keeper," but that fits clumsily into the account because there is no *ārāma* here; cf. below.

13. There is some uncertainty about where this part of the story ends. Oldenberg has paragraphed the same text in two different ways. I follow that found at Pāli *Vinaya* iii 249; cf. n. 28 below.

14. R. A. L. H. Gunawardana, *Robe and Plough. Monasticism and Economic Interest in Early Medieval Sri Lanka* (Tucson: 1979) 97.

15. J. Jaworski, "Le section des remèdes dans le vinaya des mahīśāsaka et dans le vinaya pali," *Rocznik Orientalistyczny* 5 (1927) 100: "Le début du chapitre XV, qui est très développé en pali, n'a pas d'equivalent en chinois. Il s'agit de la fondation d'un village appelé Pilinda-gāma. Cette légende locale, où le vénérable Pilinda vaccha tient un grand rôle, n'a que peu de rapports avec le médecine."

16. Jaworski, *Rocznik Orientalistyczny* 7 (1929–1930) 55 n. 7.

17. Edgerton, *BHSD* 390. He gets this sense from Tibetan *bya skyibs*, "lit. bird-shelter," but the equivalence is well attested by the *Mahāvyutpatti*, where, as Edgerton notes, *prāgbhāra* follows *parvata* and precedes *darī*.

18. S. Paranavitana, *Inscriptions of Ceylon*, Vol. I (Ceylon: 1970) ii; see also—especially for the dates assigned to these inscriptions, which in many cases may turn out to have been too early—P. E. E. Fernando, "Palaeographical Development of the Brahmi Script in Ceylon from the 3rd Century B.C. to the 7th Century A.D.," *UCR* 7 (1949) 282–301; W. S. Karunaratne, "The Date of the Brāhmī Inscriptions of Ceylon," in *Paranavitana Felicitation Volume*, ed. N. A. Jayawickrama (Colombo: 1965) 243–251; S. K. Sitrampalam, "The Brahmi Inscriptions of Sri Lanka. The Need for a Fresh Analysis," in *James Thevathasan Rutnam Felicitation Volume*, ed. K. Indrapala (Jaffna: 1975) 89–95; and, in particular, A. H. Dani, *Indian Palaeography* (Oxford: 1963) 214ff.

19. W. Rahula, *History of Buddhism in Ceylon. The Anurādhapura Period 3rd Century B.C.—10th Century A.C.* (Colombo: 1956) 113.

20. Rahula, *History of Buddhism in Ceylon*, 114; see also W. M. A. Warnasuriya, "Inscriptional Evidence Bearing on the Nature of Religious Endowment in Ancient Ceylon," *UCR* 1.1 (1943) 71–72: "The majority of these caves gifted to the Saṅgha were natural rock caves—for excavated caves are rare in Ceylon—whose insides were doubtless whitewashed and even plastered, and a mud or brick wall (the latter occurring about the 9th Century, A.D., says Hocart) built so as to form protected or enclosed rooms under the shelter of the rocks." See also "*VbhA* 366," cited in the Pāli Text Society dictionary under *leṇa*.

21. M. Carrithers, *The Forest Monks of Sri Lanka. An Anthropological and Historical Study* (Delhi: 1983), esp. the second and sixth plates between pp. 128–129.

22. See the recently discovered and still not fully published early monastic site at Pan-

guraria in Madhya Pradesh: B. K. Thapar, ed., *Indian Archaeology 1975–76—A Review* (New Delhi: 1979) 28–30, pls. xxxix–xli; H. Sarkar, "A Post-Asokan Inscription from Pangoraria in the Vindhyan Range," in B. N. Mukherjee et al. *Sri Dinesacandrika. Studies in Indology. Shri D. C. Sircar Festschrift* (Delhi: 1983) 403–405, pls. 73–75.

23. W. Geiger, *Culture of Ceylon in Mediaeval Times*, 2d ed., ed. H. Bechert (Stuttgart: 1986) 194 (§ 187); the numbers refer to chapter and verse of the *Cūlavaṃsa.*

24. Gunawardana, *Robe and Plough*, 98–99; note in particular here the term *ārāmikagāma*.

25. Pāli *Vinaya* ii 175–177; Horner, *The Book of the Discipline* v 246–249; cf. M. Njammasch, "Hierarchische Strukturen in den buddhistischen Klöstern Indiens in der ersten Hälfte des ersten Jahrtausends unserer Zeitrechnung," *Ethnographisch-Archäologische Zeitschrift* 11 (1970) 513–539, esp. 522–524, 529ff.

26. *Śayanāsanavastu* (Gnoli) 53–56. It does refer to a *preṣaka*, but this term—which is unrecorded in Edgerton—has no connection here with *ārāmika* and appears to designate a general comptroller.

27. Pāli *Vinaya* v 204–205; Horner, *The Book of the Discipline* vi 328; *Aṅguttara-Nikāya* iii 275.

28. Pāli *Vinaya* iii 248–249; Horner, *The Book of the Discipline* ii 126–228.

29. The translation given here is based on *Vinayavibhaṅga*, Derge, 'dul ba Ca 101a.7–103b.4. This was the only edition available to me.

30. *de'i tshe na tshe dang ldan pa pi lin da'i bu gtsug lag khang de na ral ba dang 'drums par rang nyid kyis phyir 'chos par byed do*, 101b.4.

31. *rgyal po de brjed ngas pas rgyal po de'i kun tu spyod pa ni gang yang rung ba la chung zad khas blangs pa ci yang rung ste / de thams cad phyi na 'dug pa'i mis yi ger 'dri bar byed pas* . . . , 102a.4.

32. See J. Gernet, *Les aspects économiques du bouddhisme dans la société chinoise du vᵉ au xᵉ siècle* (Paris: 1956) 124 (citing Taishō 1435). But to judge by Gernet's brief remarks, this text could hardly be the source for the Mūlasarvāstivādin account. Moreover, if it is a version of the Pilinda story, then it—like the Mahāvihārin account—may also contain distinct local elements that in this case could be either Chinese or Central Asian; e.g., the reference to Bimbisāra's giving not "servants" but "500 brigands qui méritaient la peine capitale"—such a practice, says Gernet, was "courante à l'époque des Wei," but there is not, as far as I know, any evidence for this sort of thing in India.

33. The only exception to this in the Mūlasarvāstivādin account occurs in the continuation of the story. There, when a band of thieves is about to set upon the *kalpikāras*, the gods who are devoted to Pilinda (*lha gang dag tshe dang ldan pa pi lin da'i bu la mngon par dad pa*) warn him. In speaking to him, they use the expression "Your servants" (*khyed kyi zhabs 'bring ba*; 104a.2); but this is an isolated and strictly narrative usage. Note that in both accounts the continuation of the story deals with Pilinda's coming to the aid of the *ārāmikas / kalpikāras*, but the story line and details are completely different in each. Note, too, that the continuation of the Mūlasarvāstivādin account also contains at 106a.3–113a.6 another, largely unnoticed, Mūlasarvāstivādin version of the text now found in the *Dīghanikāya* under the title of the *Aggañña-suttanta*. The Tibetan text there differs in many small

ways from the Tibetan translation that occurs in the *Saṅghabhedavastu* at Ga 257b.1ff (cf. *Saṅghabhedavastu* [Gnoli] i 7–16).

34. S. Kemper, "The Buddhist Monkhood, the Law, and the State in Colonial Sri Lanka," *Comparative Studies in Society and History* 26.3 (1984) 401–427, esp. 417; cf. H.-D. Evers, *Monks, Priests and Peasants. A Study of Buddhism and Social Structure in Central Ceylon* (Brill, Netherlands: 1972) 16; H.-D. Evers, "Kinship and Property Rights in a Buddhist Monastery in Central Ceylon," *American Anthropologist*, n.s., 69 (1967) 703–710.

35. S. Paranavitana, *Inscriptions of Ceylon*, Vol. II, Pt. I (Moratuwa: 1983) 21–22.

36. The Guṇaighar Copper-plate Inscription of Vainyagupta (507 C.E.) might present an Indian case, but it is difficult to interpret on this point (see D. C. Bhattacharyya, "A Newly Discovered Copperplate from Tippera," *IHQ* 6 [1930] 45–60, esp. "Obverse," lines 3–5; D. C. Sircar, *Select Inscriptions Bearing on Indian History and Civilization*, 2d ed., Vol. I [Calcutta: 1965] 341–345). And in several of the Valabhī grants we find wording like *ācāryya-bhadanta-sthiramati-kārita-śrī-bappapādīyavihāre* (G. Bühler, "Further Valabhī Grants," *IA* 6 [1877] 12, l.3–.4), which might be—but has not been—taken to mean "in the monastery called that of Śrī Bappapāda, which had been built *for* the Ācārya Bhadanta Sthiramati." Bühler takes it to mean "built *by* the Ācārya . . ." (p. 9); so too does Lévi: "l'un [monastery] avait été élevé à Valabhī *par* le savant docteur (*ācārya bhadanta*) Sthiramati" (S. Lévi, "Les donations religieuses des rois de valabhī," in *Mémorial Sylvain Lévi* [Paris: 1937] 231). [For the private or personal ownership of monasteries by individual monks in the *Mūlasarvāstivāda-vinaya*, see Ch. VIII below, 224–225 and 244].

37. É. Nolot, *Règles de discipline des nonnes bouddhistes* (Paris: 1991) 344–345 (§ 262), translating G. Roth, *Bhikṣuṇī-vinaya. Including Bhikṣuṇī-Prakīrṇaka and a Summary of the Bhikṣu-Prakīrṇaka of the Ārya-Mahāsāṃghika-Lokottaravādin* (Patna: 1970). There is, however, good narrative evidence—which I hope to deal with elsewhere—that the Mūlasarvāstivādin tradition allowed individual monks to own what would have to be called "child oblates," and that these child oblates frequently functioned as menials or acolytes.

38. Geiger, *Culture of Ceylon in Mediaeval Times*, 195.

39. Derge, 'dul ba Cha 149a.4.

40. Pāli *Vinaya* i 245.2–.5; Horner, *The Book of the Discipline* iv 336.

41. GMs iii 1, 248.7–.10. This is the only passage cited by Edgerton, *BHSD* 173, for the form *kalpakāra*, but if there are no others, *kalpakāra* would represent yet another ghost word in *BHSD* based on a misreading in Dutt's edition of the *Mūlasarvāstivāda-vinaya*. In both occurrences of the term in this passage, the manuscript has clearly *kalpikāra*- (GBMs vi 772.2). Note too that here *kalpikāra* is translated into Tibetan by *rung ba byed pa*; 'dul ba Ga 31b.7.

42. Cf. below. Note that Edgerton too at least hints at a differentiation of meanings for his *kalpikāra* and notes that the connection with Pāli *kappiyakāraka* is only possible. His whole entry reads: "*kalpikāra*, m. (cf. *kapyāri*; possibly connected with Pali *kappiya-kāraka*, Vin i.206.12, but the traditional interpretation is different; . . .), Mvy 3840; ? acc. to confused definitions in Tib., Chin., and Jap., would seem to mean some kind of *servant* of monks in a temple or monastery"; *BHSD* 173.

43. *dge 'dun gyi kun dga' ra ba skyong bar bred pas rtse rgod rtse rgod ces bya ba'i ming du*

gyur to, Ca 103b.1. As noted, this would have been a perfect place to find *kun dga' ra ba pa*, the standard equivalent of *ārāmika*. What we do find, *rtse rgod*, is given as an equivalent by the *Mahāvyutpatti* for *kapyāri* and *kalpikāra*, suggesting that the two are closely related. Edgerton says that *kapyāri* "appears to be Sktization of MIndic form representing *kalpikāra* or *'rin* (something like *kappiyāri)"; *BHSD* 168. He also cites the Chinese as meaning "male or female slave." The Tibetan would seem, however, to be somehow related to the etymological meaning of *ārāma* or *ārāmika*: Jäschke, gives for *rtse rgod* only the meaning "sport and laughter"; *Bod rgya tshig mdzod chen mo* gives, as the second meaning of *rtse rgod*: *(rnyin) lha 'bangs dang g-yog po*, Vol. II, 2225.

44. Frauwallner, *The Earliest Vinaya and the Beginnings of Buddhist Literature*, 188–189; see also H. Bechert, "Zur Geschichte der buddhistischen Sekten in Indien und Ceylon," *La nouvelle clio* 7–9 (1955–1957) 311–360, esp. 355–356.

45. A. Bareau, *Les sectes bouddhique du petit véhicule* (Paris: 1955) 154; cf. K. R. Norman, "The Value of the Pali Tradition," *Jagajjyoti. Buddha Jayanti Annual* (Calcutta: May 1984) 7; etc.

46. Frauwallner, *The Earliest Vinaya and the Beginnings of Buddhist Literature*, 187ff.

47. On the late appearance of the large, well-organized, walled, quadrangular *vihāra* presupposed by the *vinayas*, see J. Marshall et al., *The Monuments of Sāñchi*, Vol. I (Delhi: 1940) 61–64; J. Marshall, *Taxila. An Illustrated Account of the Archaeological Excavations Carried out at Taxila under the Orders of the Government of India between the Years of 1913 and 1934*, Vol. I (Cambridge, England: 1951) 233, 320. Both, however, need to be read critically—see the work cited below in n. 52.

48. Pāli *Vinaya* iii 80–82; Horner, *The Book of the Discipline* i 140–142.

49. B. Jinananda, *Abhisamācārikā* [*Bhikṣuprakīrṇaka*] (Patna: 1969) 65.5–.9.

50. There is, of course, a distinct possibility that different Buddhist Orders in India, like different monastic Orders in the West, took different positions in regard to monks engaging in manual labor and that, again as in the West, those positions could and did change over time, especially when an Order's financial condition improved. This is a topic hardly touched in the study of Buddhist monasticisms. For the West, see, at least, H. Dörries, "Mönchtum und Arbeit," *Forschungen zur Kirchengeschichte und zur christlichen Kunst* (Festschrift Johannes Ficker) (Leipzig: 1931) 17–39; E. Delaruelle, "Le travail dans les règles monastiques occidentales du quatrième au neuvième siècle," *Journal de psychologie normale et pathologique* 41 (1948) 51–62. But note too: "It has been a romantic notion only with difficulty dispelled by historical research, that the typical (or perhaps ideal) monk laboured in the fields so as to be almost self-supporting. The truth of the matter was far different. Even in the general recommendations of the rule of St. Benedict manual labour was only part and not a necessary part, of a programme of moral culture" (J. A. Raftis, "Western Monasticism and Economic Organization," *Comparative Studies in Society and History* 3 [1961] 457). For passages in the *Mūlasarvāstivāda-vinaya* that place a positive value on monks doing manual labor, see *Śayanāsanavastu* (Gnoli) 37.27–38.3; GMs iii 1, 285.8ff. For a text that seems to implicitly allow monks to continue practicing certain secular trades, see GMs iii 1, 280.8–281.18.

51. Schopen, "On Avoiding Ghosts and Social Censure," 12. Note that in medieval

and modern Sri Lanka, practices in regard to the inheritance of a deceased monk's property had developed in a completely different way—see the sources cited above in n. 34.

52. G. Schopen, "Doing Business for the Lord: Lending on Interest and Written Loan Contracts in the *Mūlasarvāstivāda-vinaya*," *JAOS* 114.4 (1994) [= Ch. III above].

53. G. Schopen, "Ritual Rights and Bones of Contention: More on Monastic Funerals and Relics in the *Mūlasarvāstivāda-vinaya*," *JIP* 22 (1994) 31–80, esp. 62–63 [= Ch. X below].

54. A systematic study of gifts and giving in *Dharmaśāstra* has yet to be done, but see P. V. Kane, *History of Dharmaśāstra*, Vol. II, Pt. II (Poona: 1941) 837–888; V. Nath, *Dāna: Gift System in Ancient India (c. 600 B.C.–c. A.D. 300). A Socio-economic Perspective* (Delhi: 1987).

55. Note that even the reference to the king's having his promises recorded in a written document (see the text cited in n. 31) seems to place the Mūlasarvāstivādin account in a *dharmaśāstric* environment; see the texts on a king's use of written documents conveniently collected in L. S. Joshi, *Dharmakośa. Vyavahārakāṇḍa*, Vol. I, Pt. I (Wai, India: 1937) 348ff. Note too that—as in, for example, the Carolingian West—the use of writing in early India may be closely connected with the development of formal legal systems; cf. R. McKitterick, *The Carolingians and the Written Word* (Cambridge, U.K.: 1989), esp. Ch. 2.

56. See, for example, A. Huxley, "How Buddhist Is Theravāda Buddhist Law," in *The Buddhist Forum*, Vol. I, ed. T. Skorupski (London: 1990) 41– 85: "Sri Lanka has produced no lasting tradition of written secular law texts . . ." (p. 42); "Sri Lankan Buddhists, despite 1800 years of literate culture, did not produce a lasting textual tradition of secular laws" (p. 82). Huxley suggests this may be because of, or related to, the absence of "brahmins" to carry such a tradition in Sri Lanka, and the peculiar role of the king there.

57. See M. I. Finley, *Ancient Slavery and Modern Ideology* (New York: 1980); Y. Garlan, *Slavery in Ancient Greece*, rev. and expanded ed., trans. J. Lloyd (Ithaca, N.Y., and London: 1988). Garlan refers to E. Herrmann, *Bibliographie zur antiken Sklaverei*, published in 1983, which alone contains 5,162 works. For India, see now J. A. Silk, "A Bibliography on Ancient Indian Slavery," *StII* 16/17 (1992) 277–285. For an early inscriptional reference to the giving of male and female "slaves" (*dāsidāsa-*) to a Buddhist monastic community, see S. Sankaranarayanan, "A Brahmi Inscription from Alluru," *Sri Venkateswara University Journal* 20 (1977) 75–89; it has generally been assigned to the second century C.E.—cf. D. C. Sircar, *Successors of the Satavahanas in Lower Deccan* (Calcutta: 1939) 328–330.

58. *TSD* 2530.

59. The only inscriptional reference to *kalpikāras* that I know occurs in an early seventh-century Valabhī grant made to a Buddhist monastery. There the grant is made in part *kalpikāra-pāda-mūla-prajīvanāya* (D. B. Diskalkar, "Some Unpublished Copper-plates of the Rulers of Valabhī," *JBomBRAS* 1 [1925] 27, 1.5), with *pāda-mūla* and *prajīvana* being two additional—and largely undefinable—categories of "servants," the former frequently attached to temples in Indian inscriptions.

CHAPTER VIII

The Lay Ownership of Monasteries and the Role of the Monk in Mūlasarvāstivādin Monasticism

THE EARLIEST BUDDHIST inscriptions that have survived do not refer to monasteries (*vihāra*). In fact, the numerous monks and nuns who made donations at Sāñcī, for example, identify themselves not by reference to a monastery or Order, but—exactly as lay men and women donors do—by reference to their place of birth or residence. We find, for example:

> The gift of the Nun Yakhī from Vedisa.
> The gift of the Nun Saghadanā from Vāghumata.
> The gift of the Monk Kāboja from Nadinagara.
> The gift of the Elder (*thera*), the Noble One (*aya-*) Nāga, a monk from Ujenī.[1]

The wording here—exactly parallel to the wording in the records of lay donors—would appear to suggest that these nuns and monks lived in villages.[2] [82]

But when references to monasteries begin to occur after the beginning of the Common Era, they sometimes seem already to carry hints of what might be an unexpected form of ownership. Both monastic seals and inscriptions, for example, suggest that some early Buddhist monasteries were named after private or particular individual laypersons. A late-second- or early-third-century sealing from Inṭwā, near Jūgaḍh, is a case in point. The legend on this sealing reads:

> *mahārāja-rudrasena-vihāre bhikṣu-saṃghasya.*[3]

Without yet being able to say what the genitive or possessive implies, this should probably be rendered:

Originally published in *The Journal of the International Association of Buddhist Studies* 19.1 (1996) 81–126. Reprinted with stylistic changes with permission of the editor.

of the Community of Monks in the Monastery of the Great King Rudrasena

or

. . . in the Great King Rudrasena's Monastery

Likewise in the well-known Wardak Vase Inscription the gift recorded was made "in Vagramarega's Monastery" or "the Monastery of Vagramarega" (*vagramareg(r)a-viharam(r)i*), and Vagramarega is certainly the name of a layperson, although we still do not get any explicit indication of the relationship of the individual to the *vihāra* [83] that is named after him or said to be his. We are not explicitly told in what sense it might have "belonged" to him.[4] But another well-known Kharoṣṭhī inscription would seem to make this a little more clear.

The inscription on the Tōr Ḍherai Potsherds begins in the following way:

shahi-yola-mirasya viharasvamisya deyadharmo yaṃ prapa svakiya-yola-mira-shahi-vihare saṃghe caturdiśe acaryanaṃ sarvastivadinaṃ pratigrahe[5]

This hall for providing water is the religious gift of the Shāhi Yola-Mīra, the Owner of the Monastery, to the Community from the Four Directions, for the acceptance of the Teachers of the Sarvāstivādin Order, in his own—Yola-Mīra, the Shāhi's—monastery.

The gift is made here to the monastic community in "Yola-Mīra, the Shāhi's monastery," so that once again we have a monastery that is named after or said—in some sense—to belong to a particular layman.[6] But in addition we are told not only that the gift was made by the Shāhi Yola-Mīra himself but that "the monastery of Yola-Mīra, the Shahī" was his own (*svakiya*) and that he was the *vihārasvāmin.* This last term or title may be particularly significant because—although the discussion of it has given rise to some red herrings[7]—its basic meaning is on one level seemingly straightforward. B. G. Gokhale, for example, says: "That a [84] person described as *vihārasvāmin* had control of the *vihāra*, or monastery, is beyond doubt as the second part, *svāmin*, indicates."[8] And Sircar has defined the term as "'the master of a monastery'; the builder or owner of a monastery."[9] But since in virtually all unambiguous cases the individual who has the title *vihārasvāmin* or *vihārasvāminī* is not a monk or a nun but a layperson of some sort, and since the term *svāmin* cannot itself mean either "donor" or "builder" and must rather mean "owner," "proprietor," or "master," it is difficult to avoid the conclusion—however jarring—that some Buddhist monasteries in India were thought to be in some sense the property of laymen or laywomen. The fact that we are not used to thinking in these terms probably explains why most translators of the title *vihārasvāmin* have preferred the more ambiguous "master," rather than "owner," in their renderings. "Owner," however, may well turn out to be, as we will see, the better translation.

Understood in this way the Tōr Ḍherai Inscription would appear, of course, to be particularly striking evidence for the private ownership of Buddhist monasteries in India, but it is by no means unique. We have already seen other evidence, and there are other references to *vihārasvāmins*. There is in fact a wide range of expressions in inscriptions that seems to point in the same direction.

Like the Tōr Ḍherai Inscription, a number of inscriptions from Mathurā record religious gifts made by a donor in his or her "own monastery." We find it said, for example, that "a Bodhisattva (image) was set up by Amohāāsi, the mother of Budharakhita, together with her mother and father, in her own monastery (*sake vihāre*); or that what Lüders takes to be a group of "merchants" made a gift "in their own *vihāra*" (*s[va]ke vihāre*); or that Puśyada(tā), the daughter of Gunda, an owner of a *vihāra* (*vihārasvāmin*), also set up an image in "her own monastery" (*svake vih[ā]re*).[10] At Mathurā, however, the adjective [85] *svaka*, "own," is applied not just to *vihāras* but to what must have been smaller units within a monastery as well. We find that a monk named Nāgadatta, for example, set up yet another Bodhisattva image "in the Kaṣṭikīya Monastery in his own shrine" (*kaṣṭi[k]īy[e v]ihāre svakā[yaṃ ce]ti[ya]kuṭiyaṃ*); likewise, that a lay-sister (*upāsika*) named Nāgapiyā also set up a Bodhisattva "in her own shrine for the acceptance of the Teachers of the Dharmaguptaka Order (*svakāyā cet[i]yākaṭ[i]y[ā] acāryana dharmagutakāna pratigrahe*).[11]

In Kharoṣṭhī materials the expression can be even more varied, although the basic idea seems to remain much the same. We find reference to a donor establishing relics "in his own bodhisattva chapel" (*tanuvae bosi(dhi)satva-gahami*) in the monastic compound at the Dharmarājikā in Taxila; a seal from Taxila with the legend "of Mudrasata, in his own *Vihāra*" (*atavihare mudrasatasa*); a donor who describes himself as the *horamurta*—which Lüders says is "a Scythian word with the same meaning as Skr. *dānapati*"—in "his own *vihāra*" (*apanage vihare*);[12] and so forth.

There is really nothing new in all of this. Nearly all these references have been noted before by others. But their fuller or more precise significance may not yet have been recognized. G. Fussman, for example, has said recently in regard to the expression *svakāyaṃ cetiyākuṭeyaṃ* that—when the individual using it is a layperson—"l'expression peut seulement signifier 'dans le sanctuaire qu'elle a fait construire, ou donné.'"[13] M. Njammasch, speaking more broadly, has observed: "Die Inschriften bestätigen uns die Vermutung, dass der Stifter, der ein Kloster oder einen Tempel erbauen liess, diesem als eine Art Mäzen vorstand."[14] Both remarks are undoubtedly true in one way or another, but neither probably goes far enough. To suggest that the term *svaka* indicates *only* that the individual concerned built or donated the shrine or [86] monastery is, again, to ignore what the term etymologically means and to avoid the question of who actually owned the shrine or *vihāra* once it was built, or who had control of it once it was donated—it ducks the distinct possibility that "the conveyance of a piece of property into the possession of another did not irrevocably suppress the claims and rights of former owners";[15] it ignores the question of the continuing relationship—if any—of the "donor" to that which he or she donated. To say that the donor or founder continued, once a *vihāra* or shrine had been built, to superintend or preside over it as a "patron" is better, but it too avoids the question of actual ownership.

Part of the problem here must lie in the sources so far used. The inscriptions we have are undoubtedly records of actual gifts and transactions, but the kinds of things that we would like to know are often precisely those things they take for granted: they assume an understanding of phrases like *svake vihāre* and never explain them. Literary sources, on the other hand, have not—insofar as I know—been considered germane to the kind of issues raised by our inscriptions. This may be an oversight.

There are, for example, several passages in the Pāli or Mahāvihārin *Vinaya* that either suggest or assert the private ownership of Buddhist monasteries. Sometimes these are little more than incidental elements in a narrative dealing with some other matter—and are important for that reason. In the *Suttavibhaṅga* there is an interesting case in point. Here a monk indirectly claims to be an Arhat by saying to a lay-brother (*upāsaka*): "That monk who lives in your *vihāra* (*tuyhaṃ vihāre*) is an Arhat." The narrator then immediately adds: "But he (the monk himself) was living in his (the lay-brother's) *vihāra*" (*so ca tassa vihāre vasati*).[16] Both statements are delivered in such a way as to suggest that it was perfectly natural and in no way unusual to refer to a *vihāra* as belonging to a lay-brother or to call it "his."

Another text that occurs twice in the Mahāvihārin *Vinaya* as we have it—once in the *Suttavibhaṅga* and once in the *Cullavagga*[17]—both confirms that the redactors of this *Vinaya* saw nothing unusual in describing a monastery or monastic property as being a layman's and reveals a little more about what this might have meant: [87]

> On one occasion, moreover, monks used in another place the bedding and seats that were articles for use in the monastery of a certain lay-brother (*tena kho pana samayena bhikkhū aññatarassa upāsakassa vihāraparibhogaṃ senāsanaṃ aññatra paribhuñjanti*).
>
> That lay-brother, then, was contemptuous, critical, and complained: "How is it, indeed, that the Reverend Ones will use articles for use in one place somewhere else?"
>
> They related this matter to the Blessed One. He said: "Monks, an article for

use in one place must not be used somewhere else. Who would use it thus—that is an offense of wrongdoing.

The text is admittedly ambiguous, though this does not affect the main point. The text is saying, it seems, either that the monastery belonged to a certain lay-brother or that the property "for use" in the monastery did. In either case his apparent possession or ownership was sufficiently strong to allow him to criticize the monks for asserting control over it—they took elsewhere what belonged to him or to his *vihāra*. At the very least, then, the rights of the monks to "monastic" property would appear here to have been limited: they could not do whatever they wanted to with it. But the ability to do *quidquid facere voluerint* ("whatever they want to do with it") was in Roman and medieval Western law, as in Indian law, the defining characteristic of absolute possession or ownership.[18] Our Pāli text is confirming that [88] ownership of this sort did not inhere in the monks in regard either to the monastery of a lay-brother or to the property "for use" in such a monastery. And this ruling is given the sanction of the Buddha himself.[19]

Passages of this sort are perhaps sufficient to indicate that a study of the conceptions of property in the Pāli or Mahāvihārin *Vinaya* might well be fruitful. Such a study, however, is not undertaken here. Here I would rather show that there is as well another body of material—and perhaps a better one—that can provide important data on the conceptions and role of property exchanges in Indian monastic Buddhism; here I would rather give some idea of the range of materials bearing on the notions of property and ownership to be found in the *Mūlasarvāstivāda-vinaya* preserved in Sanskrit and Tibetan. It is, though, important to note that what follows is in no sense intended as an exhaustive or even a systematic study of these notions in this literature. What follows is meant only as a hint of what might be discovered there; it is intended only to give some idea of the complexity of the conceptions of ownership found in this *Vinaya* and to point to the intricate web of ongoing relationships and mutual obligations between monks and laymen that transfers of property created and sustained.

We might begin with two cases involving the mischievous Monk Upananda. In one case the ownership of a *vihāra* appears to inhere in Upananda himself; in the other the *vihāra* is said to belong to the Community; but in both cases there are further complications. Because the texts dealing with these two cases—and most of the others dealt with below—[89] are not yet easily available in a Western language, I will generally translate them in full.[20]

A certain householder had a *vihāra* made for Upananda (*upanandasyānyatamena gṛhapatinā vihāraḥ kāritaḥ*).[21] Upananda did not live there. He gave space (*vastu*) to whatever visiting monk came, but he took himself any acquisition (*lābha*).

Once an ascetic monk who limited himself to only the three robes (*traicīvarika*) came. He saw that that *vihāra* was empty, and he asked: "Whose *vihāra* is this?" (*kasyāyaṃ vihāraḥ iti*).

The monks told him: "The Monk Upananda's" (*upanandasya bhikṣoḥ*).

The ascetic monk went and asked Upananda.[22]

Upananda said: "This *vihāra*? You may live there. But any acquisition is mine" (*prativasa, yo 'tra lābhaḥ sa mama iti*). [90]

The ascetic monk stayed there, but he never cleaned that *vihāra*, nor applied fresh cow dung.[23] Once when he went away from the *vihāra*, another monk came. He too, having asked Upananda, stayed in that *vihāra*. He saw that the *vihāra* was full of rubbish. He cleaned it, and when he had thrown the rubbish out and was standing near the rubbish dump still holding the broom, another monk saw him. That monk said: "Why, Venerable One, are you standing here still holding the broom? Should you not leave the broom?"

He responded: "Who, indeed, has stayed here so fastidious about his hands that he never set foot toward a broom?"[24]

The other monk said: "So-and-so, an ascetic monk who limits himself to the three robes, stayed here."

When he saw that ascetic monk while going about for alms and reproached him, the ascetic monk said: "Upananda takes the acquisition. Why should I clean out his *vihāra*?" (*upanando lābhaṃ gṛhṇāti ahaṃ tasya vihāraṃ śodhayāmi*[25]).

The monks reported this matter to the Blessed One, and the Blessed One said in regard to this situation: "Whoever takes the acquisition, he must clean the *vihāra*" (*yo lābhaṃ gṛhṇāti tena vihāraḥ saṃmārṣṭavyaḥ iti*).

In this passage—which comes from the *Śayanāsanavastu*—the simple genitive is three times used to indicate possession or ownership: first interrogatively in the initial question of the ascetic monk: *kasyāyaṃ vihāraḥ iti*, "whose *vihāra* is this?"; then in the response to that question by the monks: *upanandasya bhikṣoḥ*, "the Monk Upananda's," and in the [91] ascetic monk's justification of his inaction: *ahaṃ tasya vihāraṃ śodhayāmi*, "why should I clean out his *vihāra*?" Notice that nowhere in the account does the apparent private ownership of a *vihāra* by a monk receive comment or criticism. It seems to be taken for granted. The problem for our text appears to be not the private ownership of a *vihāra* by a monk but rather certain abuses that such ownership might give rise to. This would probably have been clear already to the reader by the choice of Upananda as the main character: he is in this *Vinaya* the stock figure of the scheming monk who is always trying to find an angle to benefit, and usually enrich, himself.

The problem for our text seems to be that some monks—condensed into the figure of Upananda—did not live in *vihāras* that they owned but, while living elsewhere, used or were using them as sources of income. They allowed other monks to live in their *vihāras*, but they claimed for themselves any income or property that came to the *vihāra*. This income or property was called *lābha*. To translate this by "acquisition" is admittedly not elegant, but it has the advantage of signaling that this is commonly a technical term in this *Vinaya* for property that came to an individual or the *vihāra* over time, that was, quite literally, acquired.[26]

Our text, then—without directly raising the issue of private ownership—seems to have been intended to encourage monks who owned *vihāras* to live in them. It says that those who claimed ownership of any acquisition that came to a *vihāra* must themselves clean that *vihāra*. But to keep the *vihāra* clean would inevitably require the regular and active presence there of the monk claiming the acquisitions. Read in this way what might otherwise seem to be a simple, if not silly, story turns out to be an attempt to deal with matters of some moment. It appears to be an attempt to force monks to live in—or themselves properly maintain—any *vihāra* that they received benefits from. It is perhaps also worth noting here that a similar tendency toward encouraging or [92] reinforcing "stability" can be detected in the terms of many of the gifts recorded in the inscriptions from the Western Caves[27] and that the preoccupation of monks with "acquisitions" (*lābha*) is a common object of criticism in many early Mahāyāna *sūtras*.[28]

The second case concerning Upananda comes immediately after the first in the *Śayanāsanavastu*. Here Upananda does not own the *vihāra* in question; it has only been "assigned" (*uddiṣṭa*) to him. Its actual ownership is ambiguous. Its donor twice refers to it as his; and he retains an active interest in its condition. The monks refer to it as *sāṃghika*, "of or belonging to the Community."[29]

> The Blessed One had said: "The reward must be assigned in the name of dead donors!" (*abhyatītakālagatānāṃ dānapatīnām namnā dakṣiṇā ādeṣṭavyā iti*). The Elder of the Community (*saṃghasthavira*) was reciting the verse for the sake of dead donors, and a certain householder came to the *vihāra*. He heard him assigning the reward. He approached the Elder and said: "Noble One, if I have a *vihāra* built, will you assign a reward in my name also?"
>
> The Elder said: "Do so! I will duly make the assignment."
>
> When that householder had had a *vihāra* built, he had not given anything to it. It remained entirely empty. When the householder saw that, he went [93] to the first *vihāra* and said to the Elder: "Noble One, my *vihāra* (*madīyo vihāraḥ*) remains empty. Not a single monk lives there."
>
> The Elder of the Community said: "Sir, it should be made productive (*utsvedya*)."
>
> The householder said: "But, Noble One, it has been built on sterile saline soil (*ūṣare jaṃgale kāritaḥ*). How is it to be made productive?"
>
> "Householder, I did not mean it in that sense (*nāham etat saṃdhāya kathayāmi*), but rather that there is no acquisition (*lābha*) there."

The householder said: "Noble One, whoever now lives in my *vihāra* (*idānīṃ yo madīye vihāre prativasati*), to him I present cloth."

Thinking "an acquisition is obtained," Upananda [got the *vihāra* assigned to him],[30] but he still lived elsewhere. The *vihāra* stood empty. When a mendicant pilgrim monk (*anyatamaḥ piṇḍapātiko caityābhivandakaḥ*)[31] [94] came to Śrāvastī and saw that the *vihāra* was empty, he asked the monks: "Whose *vihāra* is this?" (*kasyāyaṃ vihāraḥ iti*).

They explained the situation, saying: "This *vihāra* belongs to the Community but has been assigned to the Monk Upananda" (*sāṃghiko 'yaṃ vihāraḥ kiṃ tūpanandasya bhikṣor uddiṣṭa iti*).

The mendicant monk approached Upananda: "This *vihāra* has been assigned to you (*tavoddiṣṭo 'yaṃ vihāro*). May I stay here?"

Upananda said: "You may do so."

The mendicant monk stayed there. He was industrious and not lazy. Everyday he smeared that *vihāra* with cow dung and cleaned it.—There are five blessings in sweeping: one's own mind becomes clear; the mind of others becomes clear; the gods are delighted; one accumulates roots of merit that are conducive to that which is attractive; and when one's body is destroyed, having departed easily, one is reborn in the heavenly world among the gods.

Those who saw that *vihāra* smeared and swept went to that householder and told him about it. When he heard that, he was delighted. Then later he himself went to that *vihāra* and saw that it was indeed well smeared and swept. He was very grateful (*abhiprasanna*) and presented that mendicant with cloth.

Upananda heard about it. He scurried to the *vihāra* and said: "Mendicant, this *vihāra* was assigned to me (*mamāyaṃ vihāra uddiṣṭaḥ*). You must give me the cloth!"

The mendicant thought to himself: "This monk is by nature acquisitive (*lābhātmaka*). If I do not give it to him, he will most certainly take it by force and drive me out of the *vihāra*." He handed it over to him.

The monks reported this matter to the Blessed One, and the Blessed One said in regard to this situation: "When someone is grateful to a person and gives him a token of his gratitude, that belongs to that person alone (*yasya prasannaḥ prasannādhikāraṃ karoti tasyaiva sa*). But an acquisition connected with the rainy season retreat belongs to Upananda" (*upanandasya tu vārṣiko lābhaḥ iti*).

Certain elements of the first part of this text have already been dealt with elsewhere.[32] Here we might note the motive that our text attributes to the donor or builder of a *vihāra*. The donor here is moved to act as a result of hearing the Elder of the Community reciting a verse and assigning the reward or merit to dead donors. This is apparently what the present donor wants as well. He acts—if you will—not so much out of concern for this life as for the next, and the Elder assures him that should he [95] have a *vihāra* built, this will be done for him too. The recitation of verses for the benefit of donors was apparently a regular part of a Mūlasarvāstivādin monastic community's activity. It was apparently not only a public event—the householder heard it being done when he went to the *vihāra*—but one text indicates that it was done daily as a part of the regular round of monastic chores. The text in question now forms a part of the *Kṣudrakavastu* and describes "the rules of customary behavior for monks who have been given a penance" (*bslab pa byin pa'i dge slong gi kun tu spyad pa'i chos*). The activities of such a monk are severely restricted—he cannot accept any form of greeting or salutation from monks in good standing, cannot sit with them, and so forth—but he must also perform the daily round of chores and rituals:

> Having risen early in the morning, he must open the door. The lamp-pots are to be cleaned. The *vihāra* must be watered down, swept, and smeared with fresh cow dung. The latrine is to be swept, and earth and leaves and cold or hot water—depending on the season—are to be provided. The openings of the drains must be cleaned. . . .[33]

And:

> When it is time to assemble, he must arrange the bedding and seats and set out the incense and censer. He must recite the Qualities of the Teacher (*ston pa'i yon tan bsgrags par bya*[34]). He must announce the date, saying: [96] "Reverend Ones, may the Community hear! Today is the first day of the winter month. The verse for the benefit of the Owner of the *Vihāra* (*vihārasvāmin*), and for the gods of the *vihāra*, must be recited." But if he is not able to do it, he must entrust it to a monk! (*dge 'dun btsun pa rnams gsan du gsol / deng dge 'dun gyi tshes gcig lags te / gtsug lag khang gi bdag po dang / gtsug lag khang gi lha rnams kyi don du tshigs su bcad pa gsungs shig ces nyi ma brjod par bya / ci ste mi nus na dge slong la bcol bar bya'o /*).

Although here the announcement of the day and the call to recite the verse for the Owner of the *Vihāra* are made by a monk undergoing a penance, it appears from the closely parallel passage in the *Pārivāsikavastu* preserved in Sanskrit that this was otherwise done by the *Upadhivārika*, the Provost, or monk-in-charge-of-physical-properties, in a monastery:

> The day must be announced: "Reverend Ones, may the Community hear! Today is the tenth of the half-month"—and so on in the same way as the monks-in-charge-of-physical-properties announce it" (*divasa ārocayitavyaḥ /* [97] *śṛṇotu bhadantaḥ saṃghaḥ / adya pakṣasya daśamīty evamādi yathā upadhivārikā ārocayanti/*).[35]

The *Śayanāsanavastu*, the *Kṣudrakavastu*, and the *Vinayasūtra* all refer to a formally announced ritual recitation of verses. The fact that the first says that it is done for deceased *dānapatis*, or donors, whereas the second two say it is for the *vihārasvāmin*, or Owner of the *Vihāra*, would seem to suggest, if all are referring to the same activity, that the two titles—*dānapati* and *vihārasvāmin*—could be used interchangeably or that the two titles could be carried by the same person. *Vihārasvāmin*, of course, is the title we have already met in inscriptions and will meet again in our *Vinaya*.

It is also incidentally worth noting that our text suggests that a *vihāra*, to be inhabitable, must carry benefits or "be made productive" and that the terms of the donor's grant of cloth appear once again to have been designed to encourage "stability" or continued residence in a *vihāra*: the first grant of cloth is not to the monastery but to the monk who lives in it. The [98] second gift of cloth is equally interesting. It is made out of personal gratitude—not out of obligation nor as a part of the regular benefits attached to the monastery—and it is made to a specific individual, not to anyone who resides in the monastery. The text, moreover, explicitly says that this sort of gift "belongs to that person alone." It is the private property of the monk involved and forms thus—along with inheritance of family property—a part of the private wealth that the *Mūlasarvāstivāda-vinaya* allows monks to have.[36] Such a gift, made as a token of personal gratitude, also tells us something important about a donor's relationship to his *vihāra*.

Our text uses the expression *prasannaḥ prasannādhikāraṃ karoti*, which I have understood here, in light of two instances of its use in a text from the Mūlasarvāstivādin *Vinayavibhaṅga* now preserved in Sanskrit in the *Divyāvadāna*, to mean something like: "being grateful, he gives a token of his gratitude." The *Vibhaṅga* text[37] concerns a boy who, as a result of seeing the Wheel of Rebirth with its five possible destinations painted on the porch of the Veṇuvana Monastery (*sa vayasyakena sārdhaṃ veṇuvanaṃ gato vihāraṃ praviṣṭaḥ paśyati dvārakoṣṭhake pañcagaṇḍakaṃ cakram abhilikhitam*), is determined to be reborn in heaven. Told by a monk that he can achieve this by feeding the Buddha and his monks, but lacking the means to do so, he hires himself out to a householder who is building a house. Because of his ability to keep the other laborers at their work—he tells great stories—twice the work usually done in a day is finished. As a consequence the householder starts to give the boy twice his promised wage, and the boy asks why he is giving him two days' wages. The householder says: *putra na dvidaivasikāṃ dadāmy api tu prasanno 'haṃ prasannādhikāraṃ karomīti*. Edgerton suggests that *prasannādhikāra* means here "service tendered by one who [99] is kindly disposed, i.e. service of friendship,"[38] but this seems to be a little off. The householder is not tendering a "service" but making a gift, and not from friendship but from gratitude for a service done for him. He is, then, perhaps more precisely saying: "Son, I am not giving two days' wages, but I, being grateful, am giving a token of my gratitude." Later in the same story, the boy gives food left over from the meal intended for the Buddha and his monks to a group of merchants. They are described as *abhiprasanna*, which here certainly cannot mean "believing in" and must mean something more than Edgerton's "favorably disposed." They are more accurately "pleased" or "moved" or "grateful" for a service done for them. The boy had given them food when they were unable to buy any in Rājagṛha because it was a holiday (*rājagṛhe ca parva pratyupasthitam iti na kiṃcit krayeṇāpi labhyate*—some things never change!). The merchants gave the boy a heap of jewels, but the boy initially refuses it, saying that he does not give for a price (*na mayā mūlyena dattam iti*). The merchants respond by saying that they are not paying him for the food—*kiṃtu vayam tavābhiprasannāḥ prasannādhikāraṃ kurmaḥ*, which again would seem to mean "but we, being very grateful to you, are giving a token of our gratitude."[39]

In these two passages the meaning of *prasannādhikāra* seems to be unusually clear. Both take some pains to point out that a *prasannādhikāra* is neither a wage nor a payment. And both indicate that it is something given in response to action that personally benefits or affects the giver. It is hard to imagine that its sense is any different in our passage from the *Śayanāsana-vastu*. This would then mean, however, that something done for a *vihāra* was thought to personally benefit its *dānapati*, or donor, that *vihāra* and donor remained intimately linked, and that the interests—however defined—of the latter in the former continued over time.

Defining precisely the interests of the donor in the *vihāra* described in the *Śayanāsanavastu* is, at this stage, still difficult. In the monks' response to the direct question "Whose *vihāra* is this?" the text has them say: "This *vihāra* belongs to the Community (*sāṃghika*)." But when the donor speaks, he twice refers to it as "my *vihāra*" (*madīyo vihāro*). The use of the form *madīya*, rather than the usual genitive of the first-person pronoun, would seem to want to emphasize his ownership. [100] Moreover, our text also implies that even if the Community in some sense owns the *vihāra*, it does not hold it outright or without obligation. If actually given, the gift of the *vihāra* was made on the understanding that at least a recitation of verses and an assigning of merit would be performed for the donor, and it appears that this was both a daily obligation and an obligation that continued even after the death of the donor. This arrangement looks less and less like a gift than an exchange of mutual benefits.

The same language of possession occurs elsewhere in the *Mūlasarvāstivāda-vinaya* in a variety of other contexts as well. Three further examples must suffice. In yet another passage from the *Śayanāsanavastu*,[40] for example, it is said that a householder had built two *vihāras* and that it was his "usual practice" (*ācarita*) to distribute cloth to each of the monks who had entered the rainy season retreat in them. When he went to one of the *vihāras* to do so, Upananda had arranged for

Nanda, another monk, to get a share for him there, while he ran off to the second *vihāra* to get a second share at that *vihāra* as well. The following exchange occurred:

> Nanda held out his hand. The householder gave him cloth.
> He held it out again.
> The householder said: "Noble One, you have been given cloth. Why do you hold out your hand again?"
> Nanda said: "Householder, Upananda has entered into the rainy season retreat in your *vihāra* (*tava vihāre*). I seek something that he can have."

The householder, of course, does not give it to him, ironically citing the Buddha's authority to a monk: "Noble One, the Blessed One has praised giving with one's own hand. So with my own hand I will give."[41] Here the person who built the *vihāra* is the same person who also regularly distributes cloth there during the rainy season. And the Monk Nanda, at least, refers to the *vihāra* as that person's. [101]

There is—as a second example—yet another interesting passage from the *Vinayavibhaṅga*.[42] Here, when *vihāras* in Vaiśālī fall into disrepair, the donors (*sbyin bdag dag*, *dānapati*) are said to have made the following observation and determination:

> If even the *vihāras* of those who are still living, abiding, continuing, and alive fall into ruin like this, how will it be for the *vihāras* of those who are dead? We should give a perpetuity to the Community for building purposes (*bdag cag gson zhing 'dug ste / 'tsho zhing sdod pa rnams kyi gtsug lag khang dag kyang 'di ltar 'jig na shi ba rnams kyi ji ltar 'gyur / bdag cag gis mkhar len gyi rgyur dge 'dun la mi zad pa dbul bar bya'o. . .*).

Here again, lay donors are presented as thinking of the *vihāras* in question as their own. There are *vihāras* of donors who are still living and *vihāras* of those who are dead, but none of the *vihāras* are said to belong to the Community. The sense of ownership here seems in addition to have created specific obligations. The donors themselves determine that they should provide the financial resources for the future maintenance of their *vihāras*. Both their interest and their obligation are long-term, and to service both, they provide permanent endowments.

The last example of the language of possession to be cited here is also, perhaps, the strongest and comes from the *Vinayavibhaṅga*:[43]

> Once when one householder had two *vihāras*, a forest *vihāra* and a village *vihāra* (*khyim bdag gcig la gtsug lag khang dgon pa dang / grong mtha' pa gnyis yod nas*), there was an abundance of bedding and seats in his (*de'i*) village *vihāra*, but in the forest *vihāra* there were few. On one occasion when there was a festival

(*dus ston*) in the *vihāra* in the forest, the forest monks were going to borrow (*g-yar ba*) bedding and seats from the village *vihāra*, but the village monks would not let them.

The Blessed One said: "They must be lent! (*brnyan par bya'o*). If there is rain or the threat of rain, they must not be lent!"

While on the way, they were spoiled by wind and rain.

The Blessed One said: "They should be piled under a large tree or near a wall and covered with something!"

The monks covered them with something good.

The Blessed One said: "They should be covered with things of little value!" [102]

When the festival had ended, the monks thought: "This *vihāra* too belongs to that householder" (*gtsug lag khang 'di yang khyim bdag de'i yin no snyam nas*) and did not give them back.

The Blessed One said: "They must be brought back with force!" (*mthus dgug par bya'o*).[44]

The monks did not know which was which.

The Blessed One said: "Write on them 'This bedding and seat belong to the forest *vihāra* of the householder so-and-so,' 'this belongs to the village monastery' (*gnas mal 'di ni khyim bdag cha ga ma zhig gi dgon pa'i gtsug lag khang gi yin no / 'di ni grong mtha'i gtsug lag khang gi yin no zhes yi ge bri zhing*[45]), and as the bedding and seats are clearly identified, so they are to be used!"

The references here to the lay possession of *vihāras* can hardly be called casual. The entire purpose of the text is to deal with a situation in which a layman has not one, but two *vihāras*, and the relationship of the layman to the *vihāras* is expressed in a variety of ways. [103] Strictly speaking, Tibetan has no verb corresponding to the English "have," but it commonly expresses the notion of "to have"—as it does in the opening clause of our text—by the construction: "subject" + *la* particle + thing or things + the existential verb "to be," *yod*. The force of the construction is clear from some examples in our grammars. Hahn, for example, gives *rgyal po de la sras gsum mnga'o* (respect form for *yod pa*): "Für jenen König sind drei Söhne da; jener König hat drei Söhne"; Bacot, *bdag la dam pa'i chos yod do*, "J'ai le bonne Loi," or *mi 'di la pha ma yod*, "Cet homme a ses parents."[46] It therefore expresses possession in the broadest possible sense. In addition to this, the village *vihāra* is said to be "his," by use of the genitive of the pronoun (*de'i*), and, by use of yet another common construction, the forest *vihāra* is said "to belong" to him (*khyim bdag de'i yin no*).

But perhaps the most interesting statement of ownership in the text is the last one. The Buddha rules that the property of a *vihāra* should be labeled, but not—be it noted—by writing on it "this is the property of the Community" or something like that. It is, rather, to be identified as belonging to the *vihāra of the householder so-and-so*. If nothing else, the generic nature of this formula—it is essentially a form in which the blank "so-and-so" is to be filled in with an actual name—points to how common it might have been that a *vihāra* belonged to householders. There is one other text that might suggest that all *vihāras* did.

The account in the *Kṣudrakavastu* of the *Mūlasarvāstivāda-vinaya* that describes the conditions under which the Buddha ruled that monks should use the kind of seals that have been recovered from a number of monastic sites in India, and which we have already referred to, starts—like the last part of our *Vibhaṅga* text—with a confusion over property:[47]

> In the *vihāra*, thieves stole from the Community's strong room and from the individuals' cells. Moreover, when what belonged to other monks was mislaid, having mislaid their belongings, they did not know what they had received. The monks reported this matter to the Blessed One.
>
> The Blessed One said: "Since it is henceforth authorized, a seal should be carried!" [104]
>
> *gtsug lag khang du ma byin par len pa rnams kyis / dge 'dun gyi mdzod dang / gang zag gis* [read: *gi*] *gnas khang dag nas brkus so / dge slong gzhan dag cig gi yang stor na / bdag cag gi stor nas ji tsam lon pa ma tshor ro / skabs de dge slong rnams kyis / bcom ldan 'das la gsol ba dang / bcom ldan 'das kyis bka' stsal pa / de lta bas na gnang gis / rgya bcang bar bya'o /*

But once allowed to have seals, "the group of six" had lewd scenes engraved on them—"a man and woman having sex." In response to lay criticism of such seals, the Buddha is then made to say:

> There are two sorts of seals, those of the Community (*dge 'dun gyi*) and those of the individual (*gang zag gi*). For the seal of a Community, when a wheel has been engraved in the middle, on each side of it a deer should be engraved, and below this the name of the Owner of the *Vihāra* (*'og tu gtsug lag khang gi bdag po'i ming bri bar bya'o*).[48]

This passage would seem to suggest that the name found on a seal, like that from Inṭwā discussed above, is the name of the *vihārasvāmin*, even if that title is not actually used. More importantly, it is obvious that the instructions given in our text were intended to be general, that they were meant to apply to all Mūlasarvāstivādin monasteries. But since this would mean that the seals of all monasteries should have below the wheel and deer the name of the *vihārasvāmin*, this would in turn strongly suggest that the redactors of this text assumed that *every* monastery had a *vihārasvāmin*. And it is worth repeating that in both inscriptions and texts the *vihārasvāmin* is—in all unambiguous cases—a layperson.

It would seem, then, that the evidence cited so far for the lay ownership of Buddhist monasteries in India is strong, if not yet specific: we have yet to see in what sense or senses we are to understand that "ownership," or what specific legal rights that ownership entailed. Of course, the fact that specifics are hard to come by might itself be significant. It, and the pervasive use of the language of possession as if it were perfectly straightforward and unproblematic, may suggest that such ownership and its attendant rights were assumed to be so well known and [105] understood that they did not require explanation.[49] There are, however, some texts in which the nature of that ownership and some of its attendant rights are more explicitly stated. Although there are undoubtedly others, I limit myself here to two examples. The first comes from the *Śayanāsanavastu*:[50]

When the householder Anāthapiṇḍada had covered the grove with ten million (*koṭī*) and had bought it from Prince Jeta and presented it (*niryātita*) to the Community of Monks headed by the Buddha, then pious pilgrims from various places (*nānādeśanivāsinaḥ śrāddhāś caityābhivandakā*) came to Śrāvastī.[51] Some of them were greatly affected (*abhiprasanna*) and said: "Noble One, we too would have a site built here in the Jetavana for the Noble Community" (*ārya vayam apy āryasaṃghāya jetavane kiṃcid vastu kārayema iti*).

The monks said: "When you have bought the land for a price (*mūlyena bhūmiṃ kritvā*), you may do so."

"Noble Ones, for what price is it given?" (*kiyatā mūlyena dīyate*).

"For so much gold" (*iyatā hiraṇyena*).

"Noble One, where are we going to get that much? But if we get a place on this spot we are going to have it built on" (*ārya kuto 'smākam etāvad bhavati*; *tathāpi tu yady etasmin pradeśe labhāmahe karayāma iti*).

The monks reported this matter to the Blessed One. [106]

The Blessed One said: "The householder must be asked for permission! (*gṛhapatir avalokayitavyaḥ*). If he authorizes it (*anujānīte*), it should be built."[52]

The monks asked the householder Anāthapiṇḍada permission (*bhikṣubhir anāthapiṇḍado gṛhapatir avalokitaḥ*).

He said: "I authorize pious brahmins and householders to do a meritorious work that depends on me for the sake of the Community. I do not authorize doing it for the sake of an individual" (*sa kathayati. māṃ āgamya śrāddhā brāhmaṇagṛhapatayaḥ saṃghasyārthāya puṇyakriyāvastu kurvanti anujānāmi*; *pudgalasya kurvanti nānujānāmi iti*).

The monks reported this matter to the Blessed One, and the Blessed One said: "Therefore, I authorize (*anujānāmi*) that it is to be built for the sake of the Community. When it is for the sake of an individual, the donor must be asked

> for permission (*danāpatir avalokayitavyaḥ*). If he authorizes (*anujānīte*) it, it is to be built. If he does not authorize it, it is not to be built."[53]

Although they do not affect the main point of the passage, some elements of the language here are difficult to render smoothly and certainly into English. The pious pilgrims, for example, say *vastu kārayema*. *Vastu* here is almost certainly used for what in Classical Sanskrit is more commonly spelt *vāstu*. Edgerton defines *vastu* as "site" or "place," giving as examples the site on which a hut stands or a city is to be built. But *vastu* itself also can mean "building"—as in *Vāstuśāstra*, "the science of architecture"—or "a building." In his translation of the *Arthaśāstra*, Kangle translates *vāstu* as "a building site" and as "immovable property," and the text itself includes "a house, a field, a park, an embankment, a tank or a reservoir" under the term.[54] It is, of course, difficult to get all of this into a translation, but it is clear that the pious pilgrims want both [107] to build and a site on which to build within the Jetavana. Likewise difficult to translate is the compound *puṇyakriyāvastu*, which here may in part be punning off *vāstu*. Edgerton, again, defines the expression as an "object or item of meritorious action"; de la Vallée Poussin, whom I follow, translates it in the plural as "oeuvres méritoires."[55]

In spite of these difficulties, however, the basic situation of our text is not in doubt. Anāthapiṇḍada had presented (*niryātita*) the Jetavana to the Community. Then other laypersons also wanted to build there. The monks tell them they must, in effect, first buy the land on which they would build. The monks, in other words, are purposing to "sell" what should belong to them. But when—in spite of a stiff price—the laymen agree, the text makes it clear that the monks do not themselves have the exclusive rights to do so. They cannot act without the donor's permission. If he does not authorize it, it cannot be done. The donor then retains control and certain rights of ownership even after he has "presented" the property in question to the Community.

The text goes on, however, to modify these rights, and we may be seeing in our text two stages in what might have been a historical process. Anāthapiṇḍada is made to concede some of his rights of ownership for certain purposes. He allows others to perform "oeuvres méritoires" at *his vihāra if* it is for the sake or benefit of the Community but not if it is for the sake of an individual. But this too is not quite the end. Anāthapiṇḍada's judgment would have categorically disallowed actions "for the sake of an individual" if it had become the general rule. The general rule articulated by the Buddha at the end of the text, however, is more flexible. The Buddha is made to allow building activity by others at a *vihāra* that appears to still belong to and be under the control of the original donor if it is for the benefit of the Community; but it is also allowed if it is for the benefit of an individual *and* the original donor also allows it. The solution here is—as it frequently is in the *vinaya*—a complicated one. But even after several modifications it is clear that the original donor or owner of a *vihāra* continued to have some control over who could or could not participate in and add to his pious foundation.

The donor in our text retained this control over his monastery in regard to, above all else, meritorious works done "for the sake of an individual," [108] *pudgalasyārthāya*, but what precisely this expression might intend is not immediately determinable. Generally in both the Mūlasarvāstivādin and the Pāli *Vinayas* the contrastive categories *sāṃghika* and *paudgalika* are used to distinguish that which belongs to or refers to the Community as a whole from that which belongs to or refers to an individual monk. This is the case, for example, in the passage concerning seals cited above. If this same contrast or distinction is intended in our present text, then the donor's control does not extend to meritorious works done at his *vihāra* that are for the sake of the entire Community but is restricted to works done for the benefit of individual monks. This, however, is only one possibility.[56] In light of what we sometimes find in inscriptions, there is also one other. In a Kuṣān inscription from Mathurā, for example, it is said that an image was set up by a monk donor "in his own shrine in the *vihāra* belonging to the timber merchants" (*kaṣṭi*[*k*]*īy*[*e v*]*ihāre svakā*[*yaṃ ce*]*ti*[*ya*]*kuṭiyaṃ*).[57] The language here suggests—as has already been indicated—that individuals could and did own smaller units within a monastery. There is a distinct possibility that it is this sort of "individual" (*pudgala*) ownership of a shrine or chapel in a monastery that our text is putting directly under the control of the original donor or owner of the *vihāra*. It is not inconceivable that the monk Nāgadatta—the donor of the image in the Mathurā inscription—was required, and had sought the authorization of the timber merchants, to establish his own shrine, or *cetiyakuṭi*, in their *vihāra*, and that it was precisely this sort of situation that our text envisioned.

If the language in regard to the phrase "for the sake of an individual" is ambiguous, the language used to express the force of the donor's authority is not. The verb used to express the donor's authority is *anujānīte*, "to authorize [order], allow, or permit." This verb occurs hundreds, if not thousands, of times in canonical *vinaya* texts, and it is its frequency that makes its use here a little startling. It is the verb used whenever the Buddha himself sanctions a practice, as he does at the end of our text or in the text concerning monastic seals already cited. But here in our text it is not only the Buddha who "authorizes"; the *dānapati* does so as well. In this one case—and I can cite no others—a layman actually performs the same action in regard to the monks as the Buddha himself does. The *dānapati* here is allowed to determine what the monks [109] can and should do. Like the Buddha and only the Buddha, he too—in regard to his *vihāra*—determines what is allowed. This would appear to be a remarkable admission of the strength of his rights.

The second text that we might look at that explicitly deals with some of the continuing ownership rights of a donor—again called the *vihārasvāmin*—is yet another text from the *Kṣudrakavastu*. Our text describes the proper procedure to be followed in abandoning a *vihāra*.[58]

The Buddha, the Blessed One, was staying in Śrāvastī, in the Jetavana, in the Park of Anāthapiṇḍada.

A householder living in a mountain hamlet (*ri 'or*)[59] had a *vihāra* built. He supplied it with all the requisites (*yo byad*) and gave it (*phul ba*) to the Community of Monks from the Four Directions. Later that householder was seized in the court of the king. The monks heard about this, and when they heard, they abandoned the *vihāra* and ran away. Thieves stole the riches of the Three Jewels (*dkon mchog gsum gyi dkor*).

In time the householder was released. When the monks heard how the Owner of the *Vihāra* (*gtsug lag khang gi bdag po*) had been released, they went to that householder. Since he had already heard how the monks had abandoned the *vihāra* and run away, and how thieves had stolen the riches of the Three Jewels, he was ashamed (*bskyengs pa*) of them. "Noble Ones," he said, "why did you run away?"

They said: "We heard how you had been seized in the court of the king, and when we heard that, we were afraid and ran away."

"But, Noble Ones, even if I had been seized in the court of the king, why did all of you run away? Since my relatives were not seized, would they not have provided your requisites?"

The monks had no response and remained silent.

The monks reported this matter to the Blessed One, and the Blessed One said: "You should not run away like that. Rather, you should ask the relatives of the Owner of the *Vihāra*: 'Since the Owner of the *Vihāra* has been seized in the king's court, are you able to provide the requisites of alms for us?' (*ci khyed kyis bdag cag gi bsod snyoms kyi yo byad sbyar nus sam*). If they provide them, that is good. But if they do not provide them, you should for five years beg alms and remain there (*ji ste mi sbyor na lo lnga'i bar du bsod snyoms bya zhing 'dug par bya'o*). If after five years the [110] Owner of the *Vihāra* is released, that is good. But if he is not released then, after performing a formal act of twofold motion, those who are the guardians of *vihāras*[60] in the neighborhood of that *vihāra*, and their common acquisitions, and their fortnightly meetings, should remain distinct for five more years (*gtsug lag khang de'i nye 'khor gyi gtsug lag khang dag yongs su skyong bar byed pa rnams dang / rnyed pa thun mong dang / gso sbyod tha dad pa dag gis lo gzhan lnga'i bar du 'dug par bya'o /*).

[The standard procedure for making a formal motion is then described, and the text continues:]

"If under these conditions the Owner of the *Vihāra* comes to the residents (*gnas pa rnams*) during the ten years, that is good. But if he does not come then, when the seats and bedding, the vessels, and the requisites have been stored (*bzhag*

> *nas*) in neighboring *vihāras*, and the inner door locked, one should go away. When the Owner of the *Vihāra* is released then, when he claims (*phyir blangs te*) the goods as they were stored from the neighboring *vihāras*, they must indeed be given to him! If the monks residing in the neighboring *vihāra* give them up, that is good. If they do not give them up, they come to be guilty of an offense (*'gal tshabs can du 'gyur ro*)."[61] [111]

As in the text from the *Śayanāsanavastu* dealing with the Jetavana where the entire discussion of the donor's rights takes place in reference to property that had already been "presented" (*niryātita*) to the Community of Monks headed by the Buddha, so here too in our text the entire discussion is taken up with questions that concern a *vihāra* that had already been given (*'bul ba = dadāti*) to the Community of Monks from the Four Directions. These texts in particular, but in effect all the passages that have been cited, raise therefore, and fundamentally, the question of what verbs like *dadāti*, "to give," and *niryātayati*, "to present," were understood to mean in both a practical and a legal sense. All of the passages we have seen—but particularly our last two texts—make it almost impossible to believe that they expressed an outright gift or the complete alienation of the property involved. However understood, the transaction did not involve the extinction of either the donor's interest or, apparently, his legal rights. The text from the *Kṣudrakavastu* indicates that such interests and rights continued to be felt for a long time—even after ten years in the case of absence—and, moreover, as in the case of the donor who had two monasteries, were attached not only to the *vihāra* but to its contents as well: "the seats and bedding, the vessels, and the requisites." Notice that neither the *vihāra* nor its contents can be merged with the common property of neighboring *vihāras* for at least ten years after their donor or owner comes to be absent, and that this is proclaimed by a formal motion. Notice too that even after ten years, and even after the *vihāra* itself has been closed down, the contents of the *vihāra* still cannot be merged with the property of other *vihāras* but can only be stored in those other *vihāras*: when the *vihārasvāmin* returns and claims them, they must be returned to him. And the text explicitly says they must be returned *to him* (*de nyid du sbyin par bya'o*), not, be it noted, to the original *vihāra*. They could, it seems, only have remained his property. The same conclusion is reached when we look at the text from yet another angle. [112]

Our *Kṣudrakavastu* text calls the householder the *vihārasvāmin*, or "Owner of the *Vihāra*." The relationship of the monks to the *vihāra* is, however, expressed differently. They are described only as its residents (*gnas pa rnams*). Even the monks associated with the neighboring *vihāras* are said not to own them but only to reside in them (*nye 'khor gyi gtsug lag khang na gnas pa'i dge slong rnams*), and although it is less certain, they also seem to be called "the guardians of *vihāras*," *gtsug lag khang dag yongs su skyong bar byed pa rnams*, which—whatever its precise meaning—strongly implies something other than ownership.

The role of the *vihārasvāmin* in our text, on the other hand, seems clear: he builds the *vihāra* and supplies it with the requisites; in his absence there is an expectation, confirmed by the Buddha's initial instructions, that his relatives will or might provide the latter; but in any case it appears that he continues to own—even though he has "presented" or "given" them to the Community—both the *vihāra* and its contents. The role of the monks is obviously different, but still not entirely what might have been expected.

The monks' role—indeed their obligation—is first of all to remain there, to reside in the *vihāra*. They must not abandon the *vihāra* even if the *vihārasvāmin* is seized by the king; even when the *vihārasvāmin* is absent and his relatives are unable to meet his obligations the monks are obliged to remain there for at least five years and to meet their needs by begging—which apparently they normally do not do—so that they might do so. The monks, in other words, are under heavy obligation to the donor or owner to remain in his *vihāra* or to use it. The monks, then, have not ownership rights to the *vihāra* but rather obligations in regard to it and its owner, and even if it means they must revert to begging, those obligations must be met.

The obligation of monks to live in or use the *vihāras* that are "given" or "presented" to them is even more explicitly addressed in a text from the *Śayanāsanavastu* that I have already treated elsewhere from a somewhat different angle, but it is worth citing here again in a fuller form. It not only explicitly articulates the obligation we are concerned with but also allows us to see that the monks' obligation to use what is "given" to them is, in fact, their obligation to make merit for their donors—they are one and the same.[62] [113]

> The devout had had many *vihāras* built, but few monks entered into the rainy season retreat in Śrāvastī, and they stood empty. For the donors there was no merit resulting from use (*dānapatīnāṃ paribhogānvayaṃ puṇyaṃ na bhavati*). And they were inhabited by ne'er-do-wells (*vātaputra*).
>
> The Blessed One said: "All *vihāras* must be assigned (*uddeṣṭavya*). To each one individually two or three or four, depending on how many there are. All must be used (*sarve paribhoktavyāḥ*). One should stay in one place in the morning, in another at midday, at another in the afternoon, and one should pass the night in yet another!"
>
> The monks did not then perform the work. The *vihāras* fell into disrepair.[63]
>
> The Blessed One said: "The donor should be encouraged (to make repairs) (*dānapatir utsāhayitavyaḥ*). If just that succeeds, that is good. If it does not succeed, then they are to be repaired with that belonging to the Community

> (*sāṃghikena*).[64] If that is not possible, insofar as it is possible, to that extent restoration is to be done. The rest should be tolerated (*vyupekṣitavya*)!"[65] [114]

There is much here in common with the *Kṣudrakavastu* passage just treated. The obligation for monks to use all *vihāras* is here, and in fact far more explicitly, stated. Here, as in the *Kṣudraka*, provisions are made for when the donor cannot supply what is required—here not from absence but from inability—though they are not the same: rather than begging, the monks in our present text are allowed to use—insofar as it is available—what belongs to the Community. But in both texts the monks must continue to use the *vihāras* even if doing so creates some inconvenience by causing them to have to beg or put up with a certain amount of disrepair. There are, however, two things that are particularly striking in our present text: the explicit connection of use with merit, and the length to which our text suggests that it is necessary to go to make sure that what donors "give" is used. In regard to the first, our text makes explicit what seems to be implied in almost all the passages we have seen so far. Almost all the passages that have been cited promulgate rules that seem—in one way or another—designed to ensure that *vihāras* or other property "donated" would be continuously used. Our text goes one step further and explains the reason for this by indicating quite explicitly the consequence of their not being used: if *vihāras* stand empty and are not used, the donors are deprived of "the merit resulting from use" (*paribhogānvayaṃ puṇyam*, *longs spyod las byung ba'i bsod nams*). It is, therefore, the monks' obligation to make sure that this does not happen, or, to phrase it positively, the monks' obligation is to continuously make merit for their "donors" by using what those individuals have made available. The expression "merit resulting from use" is, moreover, not unique to this passage from the *Śayanāsanavastu*, nor is the idea it expresses applied only to *vihāras*. In the *Kṣudrakavastu*, for example, it is applied to plates or dishes:[66]

> When devout brahmins and householders gave dishes (*sder spyad* = *bhājana*) to the monks, the monks would not accept them. The brahmins and householders said: "Noble Ones, when the Buddha, the Blessed One, had not yet appeared in the world, then those belonging to other religious groups (*mu stegs can*, *tīrthika*) were the ones worthy of receiving reverential gifts (*yon gnas*, *dakṣiṇīya*). Now, however, since the Buddha, the Blessed One, has appeared in the world, you are the ones worthy of receiving reverential gifts. If you will not accept them, how can we, being deprived of provisions of merit for the journey (*dge ba'i lam brgyags ma mchis par*), go from this world to the other world? You must accept these!" [115]
>
> The monks reported this matter to the Blessed One, and the Blessed One said: "For the sake of the Community (*dge 'dun gyi phyir*), dishes should be accepted!"

> When the Blessed One had said that dishes should be accepted for the sake of the Community, the monks, after they had accepted them, put them in the storeroom and left them there and continued to eat in the same way from their bowls. The devout brahmins and householders saw that and said: "Noble Ones, are there no dishes that we gave?" (*phul ba*).
>
> The monks said: "Gentleman, they remain in the storeroom."
>
> They said: "Noble Ones, could we not have stored them in our own houses? Did we not give them to you (*bdag cag gis khyed la phul lam*)? When they are used then for us, there is the merit that comes from use (*yongs su longs spyad na / bdag cag la yongs su longs spyad pa'i rgyu las byung ba'i bsod nams su 'gyur ba zhig na*), but still you put them in the storeroom!"[67]
>
> The monks reported this matter to the Blessed One, and the Blessed One said: "Dishes that are given by donors must be used!" (*sbyin bdag gis byin pa'i sder spyad dag yongs su longs spyad par bya'o*).

The argument put here in the mouth of the donors—"If you will not accept them, how can we . . . go from this world to the other world?"—is worthy of note. It is something of a trope in this literature,[68] but it nicely encapsulates an important *monastic* view of the role of the monk in-the-world: his role is to accept gifts so that their donors might be able to gain the merit necessary to achieve "the other world." This conception of the monk makes no mention of the monks' own wishes or religious goals and seems to leave little room for them. A monk here is one who accepts gifts so others can make merit, and he is obligated to do so by the authority of the Buddha. But added to this trope is the further obligation already met in regard to *vihāras* in the *Śayanāsanavastu*. Acceptance of movable property—like the acceptance of *vihāras*—was not, or came to be thought not, sufficient to generate the full complement of the donor's merit. Like *vihāras*, all such property had not only to be accepted but also to be used, and the monks were under obligation to do so; they were under obligation to ensure that the donor was not denied the "merit resulting from use." Both texts use the same expression. In the Sanskrit [116] text of the *Śayanāsanavastu* this is *paribhogānvayaṃ puṇyam*, which the Tibetan translators there rendered as *longs spyod las byung ba'i bsod nams*. In the *Kṣudrakavastu* we find what can only be another attempt to render the same expression, a rendering that is, if anything, slightly more precise: *yongs su longs spyad pa'i rgyu las byung ba'i bsod nams*.[69] How strongly the obligation to use was felt might be suggested by the complexity, if not convolutions, of the rules put in place by the *Śayanāsanavastu* to ensure that it occurred.

The *Śayanāsanavastu*, to ensure that all *vihāras* were used, has recourse to what would have been—if put into practice—a clumsy and inconvenient system. Depending on the number of *vihāras* and the number of monks, one monk could be held responsible for, and obligated to use, two or three or four or more *vihāras* in the same day. In order to do so, he is explicitly told to divide his time in such a way that each *vihāra* was used for at least a part of each day. Such an arrangement would have almost certainly been disruptive, requiring each monk to move from place to place, and hardly conducive to anything like a contemplative life. That the religious advantages that might accrue to the individual monk from undisturbed time could be sacrificed in order to meet obligations to their donors would seem to indicate how strongly such obligations—especially the obligation to use—were felt. But the monk's obli[117]gation to use what donors had provided could take other, though no less extreme, forms as well. We might look at one last text from the *Kṣudrakavastu* as an example.

Like the text cited above dealing with the proper way to abandon a *vihāra*, the last text we will look at also deals with disposing of property that was given by and in some sense still belonged to a lay donor.[70] In this case, although the property involved is cloth, the concern is still with ensuring that the full complement of merit accrue to the donor or owner.

> The monk-in-charge-of-physical-properties (*dge skos*, *upadhivārika*) put coverlets (*mal stan*) on mats that were full of dust, and when they were ruined, the Blessed One said: "Coverlets are to be spread on mats that have been beaten."
>
> The monk-in-charge-of-physical-properties did not know what to beat them with.
>
> The Blessed One said: "They should be beaten with one of the cloths."
>
> When the monk beat them with a good cloth, the Blessed One said: "They should be beaten with one of little value."
>
> The monk-in-charge-of-physical-properties beat them with one of little value and when it was old and ruined and incapable of being mended, and he threw it away, the Blessed One said: "You should cut it into small pieces and strips and tie it to a piece of wood; then the mats are to be beaten with that."
>
> When that became completely useless and he threw it away, the Blessed One said: "Even when it is completely useless, the cloth should not be thrown away. You should mix it with dung or mud and use it as a filler for cracks in the pillars or holes in the wall. The merit of the donor will then be multiplied over a long period of time (*sbyin bdag gi bsod nams yun ring du 'phel bar 'gyur ro*).[71] [118]

This set of rules arose out of a situation in which a donor observed that an expensive cloth that he had given (*phul ba*) to the Community had been ruined and he had complained, using the kind of language now familiar, saying to the monks: "Now you have gotten *my* cloth (*bdag gi gos*) all dirty." It is also followed by another set of rules that are very similar and end in exactly the same way: *sbyin bdag gi bsod nams yun ring du 'phel bar 'gyur ro*. Such passages point—as has already been noted—to the apparent seriousness with which the obligation to use was viewed and the extremes to which the redactors of this *Vinaya* were willing to go in formulating rules designed to ensure that the obligation was met. But beyond that, these mundane rules governing seemingly insignificant domestic matters bear heavily on the monks' ability to dispose of any property as they might want, and therefore these rules carry severe restrictions that would seriously compromise any claims to ownership the monks might make on the property made available to them. We have already seen in the passage from the Pāli or Mahāvihārin *Vinaya* concerning articles for use in one monastery being transferred elsewhere, or in the similar text in the Mūlasarvāstivādin *Vinayavibhaṅga* dealing with monks from one *vihāra* borrowing property from another, that monks could not do whatever they might want with movable properties and that in this sense at least—and that is an important sense—they did not own them. The *Kṣudrakavastu* ruling on dishes only establishes the same point in a different way. But the passage from the *Śayanāsanavastu* dealing with building sites in the Jetavana extends to real or immovable property the limitations on the monks' ability to act freely, limiting, if [119] not denying, their ability to alienate land within a pious foundation established by a specific layman. To this then are added the important restrictions in the *Kṣudrakavastu* text in regard to abandoning a *vihāra*, where it is clear that monks could not dispose of *either* real *or* movable property as they might wish. And the inability of monks to dispose of property of any kind as they might want is then, finally, applied in our last text to objects even of little or no appreciable value like a worn-out piece of cloth. The cumulative weight of these rulings is, indeed, substantial. Monks can neither *move*, nor *alienate*, nor *dispose* of what should have been their property. They cannot, in other words, exercise any of the most basic rights that classically define ownership. Put into practice, these rulings would, of course, have severely restricted, if not entirely impeded, the ability of Mūlasarvāstivādin monastic communities to hold clear or outright "title" to the property they used, and this, in fact, may have been the original intention of the *Vinaya* masters who developed these ideas. Seen in this light, the passages we have discussed might be taken as yet another indication of the conservative character of the *Mūlasarvāstivāda-vinaya*. One final point in the last passages, however, deserves to be noted separately.

It may well be—although this for now remains to be demonstrated—that the concept of "merit resulting from use" requires that the monks *not* own the property they use. Although I have yet to see it explicitly stated, several passages seem to imply that the merit resulting from use accrues only to the owner of the property used. If this is so, and if the monks themselves were to actually own the property they used, then—paradoxically—they, not the donor, would get the merit that should result from its use. Such a result seems to be clearly contrary to the spirit of the idea that would have produced it. This point, however, like almost all of what has been discussed here, will require a great deal more study.

In a study of this sort the impulse to form conclusions should surely be suppressed. What has been presented here is only a small sample drawn from an enormous and largely unstudied body of monastic literature, nor is it, as noted already at the outset, a systematic sample.[72] In short, it [120] does not allow, nor was it intended to produce, definitive conclusions. It would seem, however, to at least make possible some observations.

The first and most general observation that might be made is that, to judge by the *Mūlasarvāstivāda-vinaya*, transactions involving property between Buddhist monks and laymen may have been far more complicated than has heretofore been realized. So too may have been the conceptions and facts of ownership of what has usually been thought of as monastic property. Indeed, the texts that have been presented here seem to raise fundamental questions concerning the meaning—both linguistic and legal—of religious "giving" in early classical India.

Our texts fairly consistently use forms of the verbs *dadāti*, "to give," or *niryātayati*, "to present," to describe what laymen do with property in regard to monastic communities. But these same texts just as consistently continue to refer to the property that was "given" to the monastic community as still belonging to the "donor": it is "his" or "mine," depending on whether the donor is speaking or being spoken about. That this is not simply a necessary linguistic or narrative convention seems fairly certain from the kinds of obligations, interests, and control that the donor continues to have in regard to the property even after it has been given. A donor, for example, not only provides "his" *vihāra* with its initial requisites or benefits, but he—or even his relatives in his absence—continues to do so. He also continues to be concerned about its physical maintenance: he personally rewards a monk who keeps it up, or he provides endowments for that purpose. Moreover, the monastic seal of the *vihāra* bears his name, and its movable property is to be labeled as belonging to "his" *vihāra*. More specifically still, building sites on property donated by him cannot be sold, except for the specific purpose of benefiting the Community as a whole, without his permission; nor can a *vihāra* or any movable property donated by him be abandoned or disposed of at will by the monks. Even after being absent for more than ten years, he may claim as his own, even [121] property that has been removed from his *vihāra* and stored in another. In light of all this, it is hard to know what to call that which the donor did with his property: if he gave it, that act of giving did not annul or even necessarily diminish the donor's obligations, interests, or rights in regard to the property given. This is obviously not what we generally understand as a gift.

But the ownership especially of *vihāras* is complicated in another way as well. *Vihāras*, even in our small sample, have three different kinds of owners: a *vihāra* is once said to belong to an individual monk and once said to belong to the Community, but *vihāras* are most frequently referred to in our sample as the property of laymen who are sometimes called *vihārasvāmins*, sometimes *dānapatis*, and sometimes simply *gṛhapatis*, or "householders." How representative our sample is in this regard I cannot at this stage say. In part, that is because most references to *vihāras* in the *Mūlasarvāstivāda-vinaya* do not contain any indication of ownership. My impression—and that is all it is at the moment—is, however, that if we limit ourselves to references that do contain some kind of explicit indication of ownership, then our sample is at least not hopelessly distorted. References to the ownership of a *vihāra* by an individual monk will, I think, turn out to be rare, even extremely rare.[73] References to corporate ownership by the Community will also probably not occur nearly as often as one might have expected, and—conversely—references to, or indications of, lay ownership of *vihāras* will be far more frequent than anyone would have guessed. Although there are passages, like that giving rules concerning monastic seals, that might suggest that the redactors of this *Vinaya* assumed that all *vihāras* had a *vihārasvāmin* or lay owner, in the end, and on balance, the evidence will probably show that they assumed, or were familiar with, several different patterns of ownership. But one point seems certain: the redactors of the *Mūlasarvāstivāda-vinaya* took it for granted that Buddhist monasteries could be, and were, owned by laymen and that they [122] continued to be so owned even after they were "given" or "presented" to the monastic community.

Whether they were making rules in regard to *vihāras* owned by laymen, or even in regard to those said to belong to individual monks or the Community, the redactors of our *Vinaya* seem, however, to have had the same basic concerns. The rules that they were framing all seem designed to effect, to encourage, even to force, in one way or another, both the proper maintenance and upkeep of physical properties, and the residential stability of the monks. Over and over again the rules promulgated in these texts are formulated in such a way that their implementation would require or at least foster the continual residence of a monk at a given *vihāra*—the monk who claims the acquisitions that come to a *vihāra* must himself clean and maintain it; for a monk to receive the benefits of the distributions of cloth at a *vihāra*, he must be physically present; all *vihāras* that are presented must be lived in, even if for only a part of each day, and at least minimally maintained, even if that means using what belongs to the Community as a whole to do so. Rules of this sort may suggest two things about the situation that the redactors of the *Mūlasarvāstivāda-vinaya* might have been responding to. Such rules may suggest that—as in the West at the time of St. Benedict—wandering and itinerancy were, or had become, a problem, at least in the eyes of those who were engaged in formulating rules for Mūlasarvāstivādin monastic communities.[74] It is at least fairly certain that, contrary to some standard theories on the institutionalization and development of monastic Buddhism, itinerancy always remained a significant element in Buddhist monasticism in India even when a part of the Community might have permanently settled down. But these same rules may reflect a period when, or situations in which, property was starting to accrue to Buddhist monastic groups who did not yet have any effective mechanisms to assure responsibility for it. Clearly, and like so many monasticisms elsewhere, once Buddhist monastic groups got involved with property—and if they were to survive, this was a necessary involvement[75]—they were no longer able to do whatever they might want. And this brings us to the last observation we might make. [123]

The study of Buddhist monasticism can gain much from the work of medieval historians on Western religious Orders—they have already worked much more fertile fields. It is, for example, probably now commonly accepted in the study of Western monasticism that "in the first place it is important to understand that the monasteries did not exist solely or even mainly for the sake of the monks who sought within their walls a personal salvation."[76] Moreover—and as a kind of corollary to this—it has been more recently suggested that there is a "need to distinguish much more clearly than is at present customary between what monks liked to do and what the tyranny of founders and benefactors often obliged them to do."[77] It is not difficult to see how both these observations might apply to the conception of monasticism that is embedded in the texts we have seen here. It is clear—if no less surprising—that both monasteries and their movable property are presented in our texts not in terms of what they can or should do for the monks who inhabit or use them but rather in terms of what those monks must do to ensure that their use properly and fully benefits their donors or owners. Monasteries—to put it crudely—are presented here primarily not as residences for monks to live in but rather as potential and permanent sources of merit for their donors.

It is perhaps equally clear that the monks in our texts are, by virtue of their own monastic rule, monks under heavy obligations and that those obligations were not determined by the religious life or needs of monks but by the religious needs of donors. Whether or not it might be conducive to his spiritual life and development, a Mūlasarvāstivādin monk was required by his rule to both accept dishes or plates and to use them; regardless of how disruptive it might be to anything like a contemplative life, a Mūlasarvāstivādin monk was required by his own rule, and under certain conditions, to spend some time each day in several different *vihāras*—not, be it noted, because he might like to but because he had an obligation to their donors or owners to do so. According to his own [124] monastic rule, such a monk was not even free to decide when to throw an old rag away—that too was determined by obligations to its donor, regardless of what the monk himself might choose. The monk redactors of this *Vinaya*, therefore, seem to have had a conception of the role and function of a Buddhist monk that differs markedly from that found commonly in our scholarly sources. For these monks—at least in the texts we have seen—the primary role of their fellow Buddhist monks was not to "work out their own salvation with diligence" but to diligently generate merit for lay donors by using what they provided or what belonged to them. This is a conception of the Buddhist monk that we need to know much more about if we are ever to understand the social history of monastic Buddhism in India, and if we are ever to understand how Indian Buddhist monks saw themselves. It is possible, of course, that they would not recognize themselves in our textbooks.[78]

Notes

1. J. Marshall et al., *The Monuments of Sāñchī* (Delhi: 1940) Vol. 1, nos. 137, 138, 169, and 303.

2. For something like this pattern in the early history of Western monasticism, see G. E. Gould, "The *Life of Antony* and the Origins of Christian Monasticism in Fourth-Century Egypt," *Medieval History* 1.2 (1991) 3–11; but see also B. Harvey, *Living and Dying in England 1100–1540. The Monastic Experience* (Oxford: 1993) 75–77, who refers to "the old-established practice of naming a novice after his local village or town" in Benedictine monasticism (e.g., John Cambridge, Nicholas Salisbury, etc.). On Sri Lankan usage in regard to monastic names, see R. F. Gombrich, *Theravāda Buddhism. A Social History from Ancient Benares to Modern Colombo* (London and New York: 1988) 5. In Indian donative inscriptions, whether referring to monks or laypersons, it is really impossible to tell whether the toponyms refer to place of residence or place of birth, though it is usually assumed to be the former. On the onomasticon of early Buddhist inscriptions in general and its value for the historian, see G. Schopen, "What's in a Name: The Religious Function of the Early Donative Inscriptions," *Unseen Presence: The Buddha and Sanchi*, ed. V. Dehejia (Bombay: 1996) 58–73 [= Ch. XIII below], and contrast this with Lamotte, *Histoire du bouddhisme indien*, 454–455. On the development of the standard *vihāra*, see G. Schopen, "Doing Business for the Lord: Lending on Interest and Written Loan Contracts in the *Mūlasarvāstivāda-vinaya*," *JAOS* 114 (1994) 527–554, esp. 547–552 [= Ch. III above, 73–80]. It is also worth noting that—as the texts cited in this paper amply demonstrate—it is becoming increasingly obvious that the single term *vihāra* is used in both texts and inscriptions to refer to what must have been a wide range of types of buildings that differed enormously in both size and construction. Though I will frequently not translate the term *vihāra*, I also frequently use the term "monastery." Because we rarely know *precisely* what sort of building a given text is referring to, this should be taken as nothing more than a convenient gloss. Note that the *Vinayavibhaṅga*, Derge 'dul ba Ca 249b.3 defines *vihāra* in the widest possible way: "'*vihāra*' means: where there is room for the four bodily postures—walking, standing, sitting and lying down" (*gtsug lag khang zhes bya ba ni gang du spyod lam bzhi po 'chag pa dang / 'greng ba dang / 'dug ba dang / nyal ba dag shong ba'o*). Pāli *Vinaya* iv 47.27, for example, offers another definition, which, though different, is no less broad.

3. B. Ch. Chhabra, "Intwa Clay Sealing," *EI* 28 (1949–1950) 174–175.

4. Konow, *Kharoshṭhī Inscriptions*, 165–170, no. LXXXVI.

5. Ibid., 173–176, no. XCII; see also S. Konow, "Note on the Tōr Ḍherai Inscriptions," in A. Stein, *An Archaeological Tour in Wazīristān and Northern Balūchistān* (*MASI* 37) (Calcutta: 1929) 93–97. For the sake of orthographic simplicity, I have cited the text from the latter.

6. Konow, *Kharoshṭhī Inscriptions*, 175, says of Yola-Mīra: "His title *shāhi* shows that he was not a private person but a local governor or chief, probably under Kushāṇa suzerainty." The *Kṣudrakavastu*, Tog, 'dul ba Ta 164a.3–167a.2 = Derge, 'dul ba Tha 108a.6–110a.4, has an interesting account of drinking facilities for passersby, and the origin, location, and rules governing "water-houses" (*chu'i khang pa*) in Mūlasarvāstivādin monasteries. In part, the text says, these facilities grew out of brahmanical concerns for purity.

7. See, for example, J. F. Fleet, *Inscriptions of the Early Gupta Kings and Their Successors* (Corpus Inscriptionum Indicarum 3) (Calcutta: 1888) 263 n. 7, 272 n. 3, 279 n. 5; V. V. Vertogradova, "Notes on the Indian Inscriptions from Kara-Tepe," *Summaries of Papers Presented by Soviet Scholars to the VIth World Sanskrit Conference* (Moscow: 1984) 160–171, esp. 166; and n. 8, below.

8. B. G. Gokhale, "Buddhism in the Gupta Age," *Essays on Gupta Culture*, ed. B. L. Smith (Delhi: 1983) 114, though he himself then goes on to suggest that the *vihārasvāmin* was a kind of government official in charge of monasteries, which is unsupportable and almost certainly incorrect.

9. D. C. Sircar, *Indian Epigraphical Glossary* (Delhi: 1966) 371.

10. Lüders, *Mathurā Inscriptions*, nos. 1, 65, 136 (Though the readings differ widely, Lüders no. 136 is almost certainly the same inscription edited in B. Ch. Chhabra, "Curzon Museum Inscription of Kanishka's Reign; Year 23," *EI* 28 [1949–1950] 42–44. The two editions have sometimes been wrongly cited as if they contained two different inscriptions, e.g., M. Njammasch, "Hierarchische Strukturen in den buddhistischen Klöstern Indiens in der ersten Hälfte des ersten Jahrtausends unserer Zeitrechnung," *EAZ. Ethnographisch-Archäologische Zeitschrift* 11 [1970] 534, 535.)

11. Lüders, *Mathurā Inscriptions*, nos. 157, 150.

12. Konow, *Kharoshṭhī Inscriptions*, 77, no. XXVII; 101, no. XXXVII.10; 148–150, no. LXXVI.

13. G. Fussman, "Documents épigraphiques kouchans (V). Buddha et bodhisattva dans l'art de mathura: deux bodhisattvas inscrits de l'an 4 et l'an 8," *BEFEO* 77 (1988) 12.

14. Njammasch, "Hierarchische Strukturen in den buddhistischen Klöstern Indiens," 535.

15. B. H. Rosenwein, *To Be the Neighbor of Saint Peter. The Social Meaning of Cluny's Property, 909–1049* (Ithaca, N.Y., and London: 1989) 114.

16. Pāli *Vinaya* iii 102.5.

17. Pāli *Vinaya* ii 174.4, iii 65.38.

18. Rosenwein, *To Be the Neighbor of Saint Peter*, 111. For India, see J. D. M. Derrett, "The Development of the Concept of Property in India c. A.D. 800–1800," *Zeitschrift für vergleichende Rechtswissenschaft* 64 (1962) 15–130, but esp. his discussion of the expression *yatheṣṭa-viniyoga-bhāva*, "the presence of an application at pleasure," at 113ff. The compil-

ers of the *Mūlasarvāstivāda-vinaya* too apparently already knew a similar conception of property according to which individual ownership was characterized by the individual's ability to do what he pleased with the property involved. In the *Cīvaravastu*, GMs iii 2, 124.3, a dying monk promises his property to another monk, saying *madīyaṃ pātracīvaraṃ mṛte mayi tava yathāsukham*, "When I am dead, my bowl and robe are yours to treat as you please"; in the *Kṣudrakavastu*, Tog, 'dul ba Ta 379a.3 the Buddha is made to say that a monk should accept property "willed" to him by his father and that, when it has been accepted, "it should be used as property in whatever way one wishes," *ji ltar 'dod pa bzhin du longs spyod du yongs su spyad par bya'o*. (Both these texts—the latter in fact quotes the former—are discussed in some detail in G. Schopen, "Monastic Law Meets the Real World: A Monk's Continuing Right to Inherit Family Property in Classical India," *HR* 35 [1995] 101–123 [= Ch. VI above]). Still within the Indian cultural sphere but farther afield, see T. Burrow, *A Translation of the Kharoṣṭhi Documents from Chinese Turkestan* (London: 1940) 90, 127, 136, 137, 143.

19. For a particularly interesting passage concerning the ambiguity of ownership in the Pāli *Vinaya*, see the "court case" at iv 223. Here a "shed" or "stable" (*?uddosita*) given to the Community of Nuns by a lay-brother is claimed by his heirs after his death, and the nuns take the case to "the chief ministers of justice" (. . . *vohārike mahāmatte pucchiṃsu*) for adjudication. (The Mūlasarvāstivādin "parallel" to this—found at *Bhikṣuṇī-vinayavibhaṅga*, Derge, 'dul ba Ta 123a.5–124a.2—is particularly interesting. It too involves a "court case," but not in regard to a building. It concerns a nun's attempt to collect on what appears to be a written, negotiable promissory note, *chags rgya*. Moreover, *chags rgya* is here defined in the following way: *chags rgya zhes bya ba ni bu lon bda' ba'i dpang rgya'o*: "'promissory note' means: a witnessed marker that calls in a debt." Since this is exactly the same definition that is given at *Bod rgya tshig mdzod chen mo*, 779, the former must here be the latter's source—the definition is cited there simply as "old," *rnyin pa*.)

20. *Śayanāsanavastu* (Gnoli) 36.14–37.5 = Tog, 'dul ba Ga 285b.4–286a.6 = Derge, 'dul ba Ga 211a.3–b.1; cf. *Vinayasūtra* (Sankrityayana) 111.2, where the entire text is condensed into a restatement of its concluding rule: *lābhagrāhiṇo vihārasya sammārjanam*, "For he who takes the acquisition there is the cleaning of the *vihāra*." Here and throughout when an extended passage from the canonical *Vinaya* is cited, I cite in the notes the passage corresponding to it in Guṇaprabha's *Vinayasūtra*. This procedure, it is hoped, will allow the reader to see something of how the author of this fundamental, but little studied, Mūlasarvāstivādin handbook used his canonical sources. Moreover these citations from the *Vinayasūtra* will provide some of the Sanskrit vocabulary for those canonical passages that I can cite only from their Tibetan version. In most cases I have *attempted* translations of these citations from the *Vinayasūtra*, but they are almost all extremely tentative and rough. The only complete published edition of the Sanskrit text of the *Sūtra* is—as will be seen—full of corruptions and conjectural readings, and the Tibetan version, in addition to not yet being critically edited, frequently and significantly differs from the available Sanskrit text. The succinctness of expression and their numerous lexical problems, moreover, make both versions difficult to understand even when the text seems certain.

21. The Tibetan seems to imply a different text here: *nye dgas khyim bdag cig gtsug lag*

khang brtsig tu bcug nas: "When Upananda had caused (compelled) a householder to build a *vihāra*"; cf. n. 73 below.

22. The Sanskrit here reads simply *sa tena gatvā yācitaḥ*, and an inordinate reliance on pronouns whose referents are not always immediately clear is characteristic of the style of the *Mūlasarvāstivāda-vinaya* in both Sanskrit and Tibetan. I have frequently supplied the referents for such pronouns in my translations.

23. Applying *gomaya* as a cleaning agent is frequently referred to in the *Mūlasarvāstivāda-vinaya* but not, I think, in the Pāli *Vinaya*. A careful study of "bull-shit" in the two *vinayas* may, therefore, tell us something important about the geographical and cultural place of origin of these *vinayas*.

24. The translation here is doubtful. Gnoli prints *sa kathayati*: *ko 'py atra hastarakṣāsthitaḥ tena na kadācit saṃmārjanī padam api dattam iti*, but emends the text at least twice in so doing. The Tibetan has *des smras pa / 'di na lag srung ba 'ga' zhig gnas gnas pa lta ste / des phyags ma'i rjes kyang med do /*. The tone here is almost certainly sarcastic or ironic and probably involves a wordplay on "hands" and "foot."

25. This is clearly marked in the Tibetan as a question: *rnyed pa ni nye dgas khyer la de'i gtsug lag khang kho bos phyag bdar bya 'am zhes* . . . and such sharp retorts are also characteristic of the earthy, sometimes humorous style of this *Vinaya*. See, for another example, *Cīvaravastu*, GMs iii 2, 123.1, where the distributor-of-robes tells the attendant of a monk who has died to wash the latter's robes and the attendant says: *tvaṃ pariṣkāraṃ bhājayiṣyasi. ahaṃ socayiṣyāmi. tvam eva śocaya*, "You will just distribute these belongings. Why should I clean them? Clean them yourself!" [See also Ch. V above, 130.]

26. See *Cīvaravastu*, GMs iii 2, 108.16–113.10, for a long and detailed discussion of the eight kinds of "acquisitions" (*lābha*), and *Vinayavibhaṅga*, Derge, 'dul ba Cha 208b.5–211b.4, for an even more detailed enumeration of rules governing the transfer of "acquisitions" intended for one thing or purpose to another. For some idea of the range of things that can fall under the heading *lābha*, see, for example, Pāli *Vinaya* iii 266.2: *lābho nāma cīvara-piṇḍapāta-senāsana-gilānapaccayabhesajja-parikkhārā antamaso cuṇṇapiṇḍo pi dantakaṭṭhaṃ pi dasikasuttaṃ pi*, "'an acquisition' means: the belongings—robes, bowls, bedding and seats, medicine for the sick—even a lump of chunam, a tooth-stick, a bit of thread."

27. See, for example, E. Senart, "The Inscriptions in the Caves at Karle," *EI* 7 (1902–1903) 57 (no. 13), 64 (no. 19); E. Senart, "The Inscriptions in the Caves at Nasik," *EI* 8 (1905–1906) 65 (no. 3), 71 (no. 4), 73 (no. 5), 78 (no. 10), 82 (no. 12), 88 (no. 15), 90 (no. 17)—all of which indicate in one way or another that the gifts they record are intended *only* for monks who are in residence at a particular *vihāra*, or monastery.

28. See, for example, A. von Staël-Holstein, *The Kāśyapaparivarta. A Mahāyānasūtra of the Ratnakuṭa Class* (Shanghai: 1926) §§ 2.8, 5.4, 15.2, 15.6, 22.3, 112.2, 112.6, 125.2, 126.18, 131.3; and L. Finot, *Rāṣṭrapālaparipṛcchā. Sūtra du mahāyāna* (St. Petersburg: 1901) 15.1, 17.4, 17.5, 17.10, 19.10, 19.14, 31.16, 33.2, 34.4, 34.11, 35.2, 35.11, 35.13, 35.17, 36.4, etc. Notice too that in a remarkable passage at the beginning of the Pāli *Suttavibhaṅga* (iii 9.20ff), a passage that presents both a developmental view of the *vinaya* and an explicit enumeration of the "conditions" that worked to create it, the text itself has the Buddha

say, in effect, that certain problems will not arise in the Order until it has accumulated considerable acquisitions (*lābhaggamahatta*).

29. *Śayanāsanavastu* (Gnoli) 37.6–38.13 = Tog, 'dul ba Ga 286a.6–287b.2 = Derge, 'dul ba Ga 211b.1–212a.5. Here again the whole of this text seems to be represented in the *Vinayasūtra* by a restatement of the first part of its concluding rule: *na prasādalābhasya vaihāratvam*, 111.2: "In regard to an acquisition (given) from gratitude, it does not belong to the *vihāra*."

30. The text here is uncertain. Gnoli prints *upanandena anupūrveṇa svabhāga iva udgṛhītaḥ*, but this is "ex conject." He says the manuscript reads *upanandena svagātryā uddiśita*. The Tibetan has *gral rims kyis bab pa na rang gi skal bar blangs nas*, which both here and below seems to presuppose a somewhat different text: where the Sanskrit text has *tūpanandasya bhikṣor uddiṣṭa*, the Tibetan has *dge slong nye dga'i skal bar dbang ngo*; where the Sanskrit has *tavoddiṣṭo 'yaṃ vihāro 'tra tiṣṭhāmi*, the Tibetan has *khyod kyi skal ba'i gtsug lag khang 'dir 'dug go*; and where the former reads *mamāyaṃ vihāra uddiṣṭaḥ*, the latter has *gtsug lag khang 'di kho bo'i skal ba yin gyis*. The Sanskrit text, then, uses throughout a form of *ud √diś* to express the relationship of Upananda with the *vihāra*, and this is in conformity with monastic procedure elsewhere in this *Vinaya*; cf. *Śayanāsana* (Gnoli) 35.4, 39.15, 43.4, 53.24ff, etc., where *vihāras* and "cells" (*layana*) are consistently referred to as "assigned" to monks.

31. *caityavandaka* (*mchod rten la phyag tshal ba*), which I have translated "pilgrim," is the designation of a specific category of itinerant monk frequently referred to in the *Mūlasarvāstivāda-vinaya*; see *Śayanāsanavastu* (Gnoli) 33.26 (where such monks are also described as *āgantukas*, "visitors," "guests"), 49.13 (where such a monk is said to "have come from the country," *janapadād bhikṣuś . . . āgataḥ*); *Carmavastu*, GMs iii 4, 196.9 (where a monk so designated is explicitly said to "have arrived at Śrāvastī from the South," *dakṣiṇāpathāt śrāvastīm anuprāpto*); *Bhaiṣajyavastu*, Tog, 'dul ba Ka 439b.6 (= *Divyāvadāna* [Cowell and Neil] 47.26); *Saṅghabhedavastu* (Gnoli) i 60.2, 60.27, 91.6, 93.14 (in the last five references the title occurs in what is an interesting editorial comment inserted into the text; in each case a certain place or *stūpa* is referred to and then the redactors add: *adyāpi caityavandakā bhikṣavo vandante*, "Even today pilgrim monks venerate it"—such editorial comments [there are several other kinds as well] will richly reward careful study). The title also occurs at *Mahāparinirvāṇasūtra* (Waldschmidt) 41.7, 41.12, and in two inscriptions from Amarāvati; see Lamotte, *Histoire du bouddhisme indien* 580, 582–583, where both are wrongly taken to refer to the *Caitika* "sect." For an instance in which laymen are referred to as *caityābhivandakas*, see *Śayanāsanavastu* (Gnoli) 33.11, cited below, p. 233.

32. Schopen, "Doing Business for the Lord," 545 ff [= Ch. III above, 70].

33. *Kṣudrakavastu*, Tog, 'dul ba Ta 156b.1–157b.4 = Derge, 'dul ba Tha 103b.1–104a.5; cf. *Vinayasūtra*, cited in n. 35, below.

34. The Sanskrit that *ston pa'i yon tan bsgrags par bya* is translating is virtually certain because of a close parallel for this passage in the *Pārivāsikavastu*, GMs iii 3, 97.17: *sacet pratibalo bhavati śāstur guṇasaṃkīrtanaṃ kartum svayam eva kartavyam. no ced bhāṣaṇakaḥ praṣṭavyaḥ*, "If he is able to perform the Proclamation of the Qualities of the Teacher, he himself should do it. If he is not able, a reciter is to be asked." In the Tibetan translation

of the *Pārivāsikavastu* (Tog, 'dul ba Ga 241.lff), *śāstur guṇasaṃkīrtanaṃ* is translated by *ston pa'i yon tan bsgrag par*, which corresponds exactly to what we find in our *Kṣudrakavastu* passage. When *śāstur guṇasaṃkīrtanaṃ* occurs a little later in the same passage, the Tibetan renders it *ston pa'i yon tan yang dag par bsgrags pa*. Unfortunately, I do not know whether the "Proclamation of the Qualities of the Teacher" involved a specific text and, if so, what that text might be. That it involved a ritualized recitation is, however, almost certain. Sylvain Lévi, in what remains a remarkable piece of scholarship, cited—among a wealth of other texts—a passage from the Chinese translation of the *Mūlasarvāstivāda-vinaya* in which the Buddha is made to say that only two things are to be recited with "the intonations of a chant": "Il y a exactement deux choses qu'on fait avec des intonations de cantilène: l célébrer les vertus du Grand Maître; 2 réciter le livre sacré des Trois Ouvertures" (S. Lévi, "La récitation primitive des textes bouddhiques," *JA* [1915] 432). The Tibetan version of this text is found at *Kṣudrakavastu*, Tog, 'dul ba 67b.3–69a.3 = Derge Tha 45b.6–46b.5, and the passage in question reads: *'di ltar ston pa'i yon tan yang dag par bsgrag pa dang / rgyud chags gsum pa gdon pa dag ni skad kyi gtang rag gis gdon par bya'o*. Given the correspondences already established, it is virtually certain that Lévi's "célébrer les vertus du Grand Maître" is the same as the *śāstur guṇasaṃkīrtanaṃ kartum* of the *Pārivāsikavastu* (his "le livre sacré des Trois Ouvertures" corresponds to what in Sanskrit is called the *Tridaṇḍaka*, on which see G. Schopen, "On Avoiding Ghosts and Social Censure: Monastic Funerals in the *Mūlasarvāstivāda-vinaya*," *JIP* 20 (1992) 32–34 n. 62 [= *BSBM* 231–233], and, independently, *Poṣadhavastu* [Hu-von Hinüber] 209–210). For the corresponding passage to *Pārivāsikavastu*, GMs iii 3, 97.17, see *Vinayasūtra* (Sankrityayana), 104.28ff, which also refers to *śāstur guṇasaṃkīrtana*; and for what appears to be the corresponding passage to *Kṣudrakavastu*, Tog, 'dul ba 67b.3–69a.3, see *Vinayasūtra* (Sankrityayana) 55.10: *kuryāt śāstṛguṇasaṃkīrttane tridaṇḍakadāne ca svaraguptim*, and Derge, bstan 'gyur, 'dul ba Wu 43b.7, where *svaragupti* is translated by *dbyangs kyi nga ro*.

35. *Pārivāsikavastu*, GMs iii 3, 98.7, and n. 34, above. *Upadhivārika*, "the Provost, or monk-in-charge-of-physical-properties," is one of the numerous monastic administrative titles that have yet to be closely studied. The *upadhivārika* sometimes appears as a monk of some status and sometimes as almost a janitor; see *Bhaiṣajyavastu*, GMs iii 1, 249.8; *Cīvaravastu*, GMs iii 2, 146.15; *Kṣudrakavastu*, Tog, 'dul ba Ta 242a.1–243a.2 = Derge, 'dul ba Tha 159b.3–160a.6 (cited below, n. 70); *Vinayavibhaṅga*, Derge, 'dul ba Ca 103b.4ff, 152b.1ff, etc.; and also *Vinayasūtra* (Sankrityayana) 115.3ff, 119.1–.10. It will have been noticed that, in explicit regard to the reciting of the verse and assigning the reward to dead donors, the *Śayanāsanavastu* says this was done not by the *upadhivārika* but by the *saṃghasthavira*, or "Elder of the Community," and the assigning of the reward is also elsewhere said to be the responsibility of the *saṃghasthavira* (see *Poṣadhavastu*, GMs iii 4, 80.8–.12). But a passage in the *Vinayasūtra*—which, if not drawn from the *Kṣudrakavastu*, is based on a text remarkably close to it—again attributes these activities to the *upadhivārika*: *upadhivārikena tata āgamyārocanaṃ saṃghe / viśeṣitasya / pakṣabhedena / vihārasvāmidevatārthañ ca gāthābhāṣaṇe bhikṣūṇāṃ niyogasya vacanaṃ / anantaram / adya śuklapakṣasya pratipad vihārasvāmino vihāradevatānāṃ cārthāya gāthāṃ bhāṣadhvam iti* (76.14–.20): "By the monk-in-charge-of-physical-properties then, when it is determined, there is the announcing to the

Community of the particulars, of the time of the month, (and) the declaration of the duty of the monks in regard to the recitation of verses for the benefit of the Owner and the gods of the *vihāra*. To wit: 'Today is the first day of the bright half of the fortnight. You must recite the verses for the benefit of the Owner of the *vihāra* and for the gods of the *vihāra*!'" [All of this will be discussed further in Ch. IX, below.]

36. See *Kṣudrakavastu*, Tog, 'dul ba Ta 377a.2–379a.4 = Derge, 'dul ba Tha 252b.3–254a.1; cf. Schopen, "Monastic Law Meets the Real World," 110ff [= Ch. VI above, 176ff].

37. For the Sanskrit text, see *Divyāvadāna* (Cowell and Neil) 298.24–311.10; for the Tibetan, see *Vinayavibhaṅga*, Derge, 'dul ba Ja 113b.3–122a.7; the first part of this text has been translated from the Chinese version of the *Mūlasarvāstivāda-vinaya* in J. Przyluski, "La roue de la vie à ajaṇṭā," *JA* (1920) 314–319; on the identification of *Divyāvadāna* (Cowell and Neil) 298.14ff with the *Vibhaṅga* text, see S. Lévi, "Les éléments de formation du divyāvadāna," *TP* 8 (1907) 105–122, esp. 107; on the relationship of the *Divyāvadāna* and the *Mūlasarvāstivāda-vinaya*, see, more recently, S. Hiraoka, "The Relation between the *Divyāvadāna* and the *Mūlasarvāstivāda-vinaya*. The Case of *Divyāvadāna* Chapter 31," *IBK* 49.2 (1991) 1038–1036.

38. Edgerton, *BHSD*, s.v. *adhikāra*.

39. *abhiprasanna* is sometimes better rendered by "very pleased," "gratified," or—and perhaps even here—when it involves a reaction to fine, beautiful, or expensive things, "greatly affected"; cf. the text cited below, p. 233.

40. *Śayanāsanavastu* (Gnoli) 40.13–41.6 = Tog, 'dul ba Ga 289a.4–290a.1 = Derge, 'dul ba Ga 213a.7–b.7.

41. *svahastena bhagavata* [read: *-tā*] *dānaṃ praśastam svahastenaiva dāsyāmi iti*. The same statement also occurs elsewhere, e.g., *Kṣudrakavastu*, Tog, 'dul ba Ta 64a.6 = Derge, 'dul ba Tha 43b.3: *bcom ldan 'das kyis rang lag nas dbul ba bsngags pas / rang gi lag nyid nas dbul gyis. . . .*

42. *Vinayavibhaṅga*, Derge, 'dul ba Cha 154b.3ff. This text is discussed in some detail in Schopen, "Doing Business for the Lord," 527ff, and the corresponding passage from the *Vinayasūtra* is also treated there, 541ff. [= Ch. III above, 47ff and 66ff].

43. *Vinayavibhaṅga*, Derge, 'dul ba Ja 15a.3–b.1.

44. Though this seems fairly strong talk, it is hard to interpret otherwise, because *mthus* here almost certainly is translating something like *balāt*, as it does at *Śayanāsanavastu* (Gnoli) 38.9, cited above, p. 226. What I have there translated as "will take it by force" is in Sanskrit *balāt grahīṣyati*, and this is rendered into Tibetan as *mthus khyer nas*. Moreover, what appears to be the corresponding passage in the *Vinayasūtra* has *balād adāne grahaṇam* (*mi ster na mthus gzhung bar bya'o*): "In regard to what was not given, it is to be taken (back) by force."

45. I have taken *cha ga ma* to be the same as, or intended for, *che ge mo* (= *amuka*). For the *Vinayavibhaṅga*, I unfortunately have access only to the Taipei reprint of the Derge, but the *Vinayasūtra*, cited below, also seems to suggest an intended *che ge mo*. If I am correct, the rules generated by this *Vinayavibhaṅga* text are treated in two widely separated places in the *Vinayasūtra*. First at *Vinayasūtra* (Sankrityayana) 36.3–.5 (= Derge Tanjur, 'dul ba Wu 28 b.6–.7), where we find: *dāsyatvam eṣām apratilambhane / dānatve 'pi gṛhapater niyater abhaṅgaḥ*

| balād adāne grahaṇam | dadyur yācitakatvena | (*mi ster na de dag gis sbyin par bya ba nyid yin no | khyim bdag de nyid yin yang nges pa la gzhig pa med do | mi ster na mthus gzhung bar bya'o | g-yar po nyid du sbyin par bya'o |*). Then at *Vinayasūtra* (Sankrityayana) 119.1–.2 (= Derge Tanjur, 'dul ba Wu 98b.3): *adoṣaṃ nimittakaraṇam | sāṃghike nāmnaḥ śayanāsane lekhanam | deyadharmo 'yam amukasyedaṃ nāmni vihāra iti* (*mtshan ma byas pa nyid la nyes ba med do | dge 'dun gyi gnas mal la ming yi ger bri'o | 'di ni che ge mo'i gtsug lag khang ming 'di zhes bya ba'i sbyin par bya ba'i chos so zhes so |*). Enough is clear in these two passages to make it fairly sure that both are related to, or based on, our *Vibhaṅga* text, but enough is not so clear that I, at least, do not have the confidence to attempt a translation of either.

46. M. Hahn, *Lehrbuch der klassischen tibetischen Schriftsprache* (Bonn: 1985) 84 (114.b); J. Bacot, *Grammaire du tibétain littéraire* (Paris: 1948) t. II, 102, s.v. *yod pa*.

47. *Kṣudrakavastu*, Tog, 'dul ba Ta 11a.2–b.6 = Derge, 'dul ba Tha 7b.6–8a.7.

48. Cf. *Vinayasūtra* (Sankrityayana) 54.25: *dhārayet mudrān . . . cihnaṃ sāṃghikāyāṃ madhye cakraṃ pārśvayor mṛgāv adhstād vihārasvāmino nāma*: "They should keep (or wear) seals. . . . The insignia on a Community's (seal should be) a wheel in the middle with a deer on each side (of it); beneath it the name of the owner of the monastery."

49. Cf. the remarks in N. Hunt, *Cluny under Saint Hugh. 1049–1109* (London: 1967) 166, in regard to monastic donors in eleventh- and twelfth-century France: "Some donors liked to retain the *advocatio* or *defensio*, whereby they remained the lawful protectors of their monasteries, especially in temporals and against other lay interference. Their rights, regarded by contemporaries as natural to the owner or founder of a monastery, were nowhere clearly defined." Notice how the terms "donor," "founder," and "owner" are used in this quotation. Such usage points to the same sort of fluidity and overlapping of titles and statuses that occur in our texts where the "founder" or "donor" also appears to be the "owner." In a situation of this sort the term "donor" is—like the term "monastery"; see n. 2 above—only a convenient gloss for a much more complicated status and is used as such throughout this chapter.

50. *Śayanāsanavastu* (Gnoli) 33.9–.25 = Tog, 'dul ba Ga 283a.4–b.4 = Derge Ga 209a.7–b.5; for the *Vinayasūtra*, see n. 53 below.

51. Here the title *caityābhivandaka* appears to be applied to laymen; see n. 31 above.

52. Except when translating the phrase *puṇyakriyāvastu kurvanti* immediately below, the Tibetan consistently translates forms of *kṛ-* in our text by forms of *rtsig pa*, which means much more specifically "to build."

53. See *Vinayasūtra* (Sankrityayana) 110.23 (= Derge, Tanjur Wu 92b.1), where this text from the *Śayanāsana* is represented by *anujānīyur anyeṣāṃ sāṃghike vastuni saṃghāya pudgalāya va bhikṣave vāsavastukaraṇaṃ | saṃśce(?)d* [read: *sacet*] *dānapatir anujñātena* (*gal te sbyin bdag yod na des rjes su gnang na'o*): "They should authorize the making of a dwelling place by others for the Community or an individual monk on a site belonging to the Community. If there is a donor (it should be done) through being authorized (by him)."

54. Edgerton, *BHSD* 475, s.v. *vastu*; R. P. Kangle, *The Kauṭilīya Arthaśāstra*, 2d ed. (Bombay: 1969) Pt. 1, III, 8, 1ff; 332.

55. L. de La Vallée Poussin, *L'abhidharmakośa de vasubandhu*, t. III (repr. Brussels: 1971) 15, 94 ("bonnes oeuvres"), 231ff. For passages where monks exhort laymen by praising the

puṇyakriyāvastus, see *Vinayavibhaṅga*, Derge, 'dul ba Ca 246b.6ff; *Kṣudrakavastu*, Derge, 'dul ba 192a.3ff; etc.

56. But note, however, that the corresponding passage in the *Vinayasūtra* (cited above in n. 53) has clearly also adopted this possibility.

57. Lüders, *Mathurā Inscriptions*, 191–192, no. 157.

58. *Kṣudrakavastu*, Tog, 'dul ba Ta 343a.2–344b.1 = Derge, 'dul ba Tha 230a.2–231a.2; for the corresponding passage in the *Vinayasūtra*, see n. 61.

59. *ri 'or* is the conventional translation of Sanskrit *karvaṭaka*, which itself seems rather to mean "a (mean, poor) village," or "a (small, mean) village"; so Edgerton, *BHSD*, s.v. *karpaṭaka* and *karvaṭaka*. Though the term occurs frequently in the canonical *Vinaya*, the precise nature of the settlement that it refers to is not known.

60. I am unable to say whether *gtsug lag khang dag yongs su skyong bar byed pa rnams*, which I have translated "guardians of *vihāras*," is an administrative title that refers to a certain category of monks or simply refers to the monks who lived in, used, or looked after the neighboring *vihāras*. [See also Ch. V n. 80 above, and Ch. IX below, 272–273.]

61. This text appears to have been summarized at *Vinayasūtra* (Sankrityayana) 35.29ff: *na sahasaiva nirāvāsatākaraṇaṃ vihārasya / sānunayasya tatrāvalokaṃ(?)dāne / anupanatau daśavarṣāṇy atinamanaḥ / pañcapiṇḍapātena / anudbhūtav atra kāle dānapater aparāṇi sāmantakavihāreṇa sārdham / hidukyo(?) ṣadhaikalābhatāyāḥ karaṇaṃ karmakaraṇāt / sāmantakavihāreṣu pramīlane vastūnāṃ nikṣepaḥ /* (= Derge, bstan 'gyur, 'dul ba Wu 28b.4: *gya tshom du gtsug lag khang dor bar mi bya'o / rjes su chags pa dang bcas pa der srung mar gzhug go / ma lhags na lo bcur 'da' bar bya'o / lnga ni bsod snyoms kyis so / der dus so sbyin bdag ma byung na lo gzhan lnga ni nye 'khor gyi gtsug lag khang dang lhan cig tu'o / gos sbyong tha dad pa dang rnyed pa thun mong ba'i las bya'o / 'gro ba na dngos po rnams nye 'khor gyi gtsug lag khang dag tu gdams par bya'o*): "The abandonment of a *vihāra* should not be done precipitously. When one who is solicitous has been provided to look after that, (and even) when nothing is received, he should remain ten years (maintaining himself) by begging for five (years). If the donor does not appear in that time, after a further (five then the *vihāra*) is brought together with a neighboring *vihāra* by performing a formal act in regard to their distinct fortnightly assembly and common property. When closing (the abandoned *vihāra*) the property is deposited in neighboring *vihāras*." Note that I have followed the Tibetan where the Sanskrit is marked as questionable, and that I have taken *pramīlana* to mean "close"; it normally means "to close the eyes" (Tibetan has, unaccountably, *'gro ba na*). Note too that Guṇaprabha does not here deal with the claims of the *Vihārasvāmin* but rather shifts to what appears to be a paraphrase of *Vibhaṅga* Ja 15a.3–b.1 cited above, p. 230–231; see n. 45. Finally, notice that Guṇaprabha uses the title *dānapati* where the canonical text has *vihārasvāmin*, suggesting that he too took the titles to be interchangeable. This suggestion is strengthened further if Guṇaprabha is the author of the *Ekottarakarmaśataka*—the latter also digests our text, and there the title is *gtsug lag khang gi bdag po* (Derge, bstan 'gyur, 'dul ba Wu 156a.6).

62. *Śayanāsanavastu* (Gnoli) 35.1–.10 = Tog, 'dul ba Ga 284b.4–285a.2 = Derge, 'dul ba Ga 210a.7–b.3; for *Vinayasūtra*, see n. 65 below.

63. Gnoli reads *pralubhyante*, but the Tibetan has *'drums par gyur nas*, and one meaning of *'drums* is, according to *Bod rgya tshig mdzod chen mo* 1427, *'tshe ba*, "hurt" or "dam-

age." This might suggest the intended reading was *pralupyante*, which would appear to be supported both by what follows in the text and by the paraphrase in the *Vinayasūtra*. I have so read.

64. Again, Gnoli reads *pratisaṃstartavyaḥ* and refers to Pāli *paṭisamthāra*, but the Tibetan—which he cites—reads *phyir bcos par bya*, and this would rather favor *pratisaṃskartavyaḥ*. Because in addition both the context and the *Vinayasūtra*'s *pratisaṃskurvīta* also favor such a reading, I have adopted it.

65. *Vinayasūtra* (Sankrityayana) 78.30–.33 condenses our text into *sarve paribhuñjīta / pūrvāhṇe kvacit pāṭhasvādhyāyāvasthānacaṃkramāṇāṃ kvacid madhyāhne paratrānyatra* [Tib. suggests reading *paratra pātra-*] *cīvarasthāpanam āvāso 'paratra rātrāv ity asya yogaḥ / khaṇḍaphullam upagato vāsavastunaḥ pratisaṃskurvīta* / (= Derge Tanjur, 'dul ba Wu 62 a.4: *thams cad yongs su spyad par bya'o / la lar klog pa dang kha ton dang 'dug pa dang bcag pa dag las gang yang rung ba bya / la lar lhung bzed dang chos gos gzhag par bya / la lar mtshan mo nyal bar bya / la lar snga dro dang gung tshigs dang phyi dro 'dug pas de la sbyar bar bya'o / gnas par khas blangs pas gnas kyi gzhi ral ba dang 'grums pa bcos par bya'o /*): "In regard to all (*vihāras*, one) must make use of them. The procedure for this is thus: in the morning someplace (is used) for reading, reciting, staying, and walking; at midday he stores his bowl and robe at some other place; he spends the night at still another. He who has entered (into residence) must repair the cracks and holes in the property of the residence."

66. *Kṣudrakavastu*, Tog, 'dul ba Ta 78a.5–79a.2 = Derge Tha 52b.6–53a.6.

67. The narrative beginning from "When the Blessed One had said that dishes should be accepted . . ." up until this point is very similar to the narrative used to describe the acceptance by the monastic community of perpetuities that gave rise to the rules governing lending on interest in the *Mūlasarvāstivāda-vinaya*; see Schopen, "Doing Business for the Lord," 529 [= Ch. III above, 48].

68. See, for example, Tog, 'dul ba Ta 7a.5, 15b.1, 293a.1, 294a.1.

69. It is important to note that the idea of the "merit resulting from use" is by no means limited to Mūlasarvāstivādin *vinaya* sources. It is discussed on more than one occasion in the *Abhidharmakośa*, for example (de La Vallée Poussin, *L'abhidharmakośa*, t. III, 20, 244: "Le mérite du don est de deux sortes: 1. mérite produit par l'abandon (*tyāgānvaya*), le mérite qui résulte du seul fait d'abandonner; 2. mérite produit par la jouissance (*paribhogānvaya*), le mérite qui résulte de la jouissance, par la personne qui reçoit, de l'objet donné. . . . Le mérite du don au Caitya est mérite produit par l'abandon.") The same idea—under the heading *paribhogamayaṃ puññaṃ vaḍḍhatīti*—is also a matter of dispute in the *Kathāvatthu* (A. C. Taylor, *Kathāvatthu* [London: 1894–1897] VII.5). The Theravādins reject the idea, but the text from *Aṅguttara* ii 54–55 cited in the discussion there might well support it and deserves closer study. The phrase *tyāga-paribhogānvayam aupadhikañ ca puṇyakriyāvastv* occurs once even in a remarkable fifth- or sixth-century copperplate grant from Andhra (see S. Sankaranarayanan, "Two Vishṇukuṇḍi Charters from Tummalagudem," *Epigraphia Andhrica* 2 [1974] 4–20, esp. 11.20; S. Sankaranarayanan, *The Vishṇukuṇḍis and Their Times* [Delhi: 1977] 154.20; V. V. Mirashi, "Fresh Light on Two New Grants of the Vishṇukuṇḍins," *JIH* 50 [1972] 1–8; V. V. Mirashi, *Indological Research Papers*, Vol. 1 [Nagpur: 1982] 121–141, esp. 140.20).

70. *Kṣudrakavastu*, Tog, 'dul ba Ta 242a.1–243a.2 = Derge, 'dul ba Tha 159b.3–160a.6.

71. Even this text—and in surprising detail—is represented in the *Vinayasūtra* (Sankrityayana) 115.11–.16: *śayanāsanaṃ malinaṃ prasphoṭayet / atīva ced dhāvet / ūrdhaṃ* (?-*rdhvaṃ* [confirmed by Tib.]) *sekāt saṃsṛṣṭiḥ* [Tib. suggests *saṃmṛṣṭiḥ*] / *tataś ca prajñapanam / na prasphoṭite sarajaskatāyām ādhāre / prajñapanīyebhyo vastrasyaikasya prasphoṭane viniyogaḥ / lūhasya / pratisaṃskaraṇam asya / aśakyatāyāṃ cīrīkṛtya yaṣṭyām upanibadhya prasphoṭanam / tathāpy ayogyatve gomayamṛdā stambhasuśi*(?*ṣi* [confirmed by Tib.])-*re kuṇya*(?)*sya* [Tib. suggests *kuḍyasya*] *vā lepanam / puṇyābhivṛddhiciratāyai dātraḥ*(*tuḥ*? [confirmed by Tib.]) / (= Derge, bstan 'gyur, 'dul ba Wu 96a.2: *mal cha dri mas gos pa sprug par bya'o / gal te ha cang na bkru'o / chag chag btab pa'i 'og tu phyag bya'o / de'i 'og tu stan bsham mo / gzhi rdul dang bcas pa ma sprugs pa la mi bya'o / bsham par bya ba dag la gos gcig sprug par spyad do / ngan pa'o / de bcos so / mi nus pa nyid na ras mar byas te shin bu'i rtse mo la btags nas sprug go / de ltar na yang mi rung ba nyid yin na sbyin pa po'i bsod nams mdon par spel pa dang / yun ring ba nyid du bya ba'i phyir lci ba dang sa bsregs te ka' dang rtsig pa'i ser kar glan par bya'o /*): "He must beat dirty bedding and seats. If (they are) very (dirty) he must wash them. After watering down (the ground) he should sweep. And then (the bedding and seats) are to be arranged. [The preceding two sentences summarize a part of the canonical text I have not cited.] But not on a support that has not been beaten (or) on what itself is dusty. For those (seats) that are to be arranged a single cloth is to be used for beating them. It should be of little value. It should be mended. When that is no longer possible, after cutting it into strips and tying it to a stick, the beating is to be done (with that). When it is useless even for that, then (mixed) with cow dung and clay, it should be smeared in cracks in pillars or in the walls, so that the merit of the giver will (continue to) increase for a long time."

72. One set of passages that has been consciously excluded here, but will certainly have to have a significant place in future discussions, is made up of the Sanskrit text of the 6th and 7th *saṃghāvaśeṣa* infractions in the Mūlasarvāstivādin *Prātimokṣa* (A. C. Banerjee, *Two Buddhist Vinaya Texts in Sanskrit* [Calcutta: 1977] 17.3–.14) and their treatment in the *Vinayavibhaṅga* (Derge, 'dul ba Ca 240a.1–252a.3), in the *Vinayasūtra* (Sankrityayana) 25.17ff, and in the *Ekottarakarmaśataka* (Derge, bstan 'gyur, 'dul ba Wu 141a.4 ff), where a *kuṭi*, or "hut" (?), is characterized as *asvāmika*, "without an owner," and at least a certain kind of *vihāra* is called *svāmika*, "with or having an owner." But the textual problems here are many: Banerjee's edition of the *Prātimokṣa* is almost unbelievably careless, the Gilgit Manuscript is fragmentary, and the Tibetan translation appears to reflect a text that differed in at least one significant way. All of this, together with the numerous parallels in other versions, will have to be sorted out before this material can be used with any confidence.

73. Notice that there may be some doubt even about the one case of ownership of a *vihāra* by an individual monk that we have discussed above, 223. The Sanskrit text begins by saying "a certain householder had a *vihāra* made for Upananda," but the Tibetan translation—as already noted in n. 21—presupposes a different reading that suggests that Upananda prevailed upon the householder to do so. Such solicitation by a monk would itself be disapproved of, and since the individual ownership of a *vihāra* is here associated with Upananda, that may also point to disapproval of it.

74. Cf. B. Upadhyay, "The Monastic Economy and Eradication of Beggary in Ancient India," *Journal of the Bihar Research Society* 54.1–4 (1968) 45–50.

75. Cf. Dom U. Berlière, *Le recrutement dans les monastères bénédictins aux xiii*ᵉ *et xiv*ᵉ *siècles* (Académie royale de belgique: Classe des lettres et des sciences morales et politiques, Mémoires) (Brussels: 1924) 3: "Assurément la [monastic] richesse peut engendrer des abus, mais elle est un facteur nécessaire à la prospérité des institutions, et l'on pourrait affirmer avec autant de raison que l'appauvrissement des maisons religieuses eut pour conséquence nécessaire un arrêt dans leur développement et une décadence dans leur discipline."

76. R. W. Southern, *Western Society and the Church in the Middle Ages* (Harmondsworth, England: 1970) 224.

77. Harvey, *Living and Dying in England*, 33. One might, of course, doubt the suitability of the word "tyranny." English monks—like Indian monks—undoubtedly chose freely to put themselves under their respective obligations for their own reasons and with their own advantages in mind.

78. A final note on the composition of the *Vinayasūtra* and Guṇaprabha's sources and methods: The citation of a significant sampling of extended passages from the canonical text of the *Mūlasarvāstivāda-vinaya* in the body of the present chapter, together with the citation, in the notes, of the corresponding passages in Guṇaprabha's *Vinayasūtra* (nn. 20, 29, 34, 35, 42, 44, 45, 48, 53, 61, 65, and 70), seemed to present an opportunity to—using an un-Buddhist turn of phrase—kill two birds with one stone. Such citations could economically serve a dual purpose. The Sanskrit text of the *Vinayasūtra*—though itself by no means free of problems—could often supply the basic Sanskrit vocabulary for canonical texts preserved in Tibetan. *Kṣudrakavastu*, Tog, 'dul ba Ta 242a.1 = *Vinayasūtra* (Sankrityayana) 115.11 (241 and n. 71), dealing with the obligation of monks to fully utilize and not throw away cloth that was given to them, is a particularly good example. Still others are *Kṣudrakavastu*, Tog, 'dul ba Ta 11a.2 = *Vinayasūtra* (Sankrityayana) 54.25 (232 n. 48) and *Vinayavibhaṅga*, Derge, 'dul ba Ja 15a.3 = *Vinayasūtra* 36.3 and 119.1 (231 n. 45), the first dealing with monastic seals, the second with monasteries lending their property to other monasteries and the proper labeling of monastic property; or *Kṣudrakavastu*, Tog, 'dul ba Ta 156b.1 = *Vinayasūtra* 76.17 (227 and n. 35), which deals with the recitation of verses for the "owner" and gods of the *vihāra*. There is a very large number of similar cases not quoted here; see, for example, *Vinayasūtra*, 33.12, which gives us the Sanskrit vocabulary behind the passage on lending on interest found at *Vinayavibhaṅga*, Derge, 'dul ba Cha 154b.3, discussed in Schopen, "Doing Business for the Lord" [= Ch. III above]; or *Vinayasūtra* 114.16, which does the same for the text at *Kṣudrakavastu*, Tog, 'dul ba Ta 335b.6, which deals with paintings and their placement in the *vihāra* (cf. M. Lalou, "Notes sur la décoration des monastères bouddhiques," *RAA* 5.3 [1930] 183–185); or *Vinayasūtra* 54.31 = *Kṣudrakavastu*, Tog, 'dul ba Ta 7a.4, 292b.6–294b.2, on the acceptance and use by monks of perfumes and garlands; or *Vinayasūtra* 88.16 = *Kṣudrakavastu*, Tog, 'dul ba Ta 332a.4, on the restrictions imposed on monks who wear robes made from burial cloth.

But equally important, the juxtaposition of the canonical texts with the *sūtras* of the *Vinayasūtra* could allow us to actually catch a glimpse of Guṇaprabha at work, to see, in effect, how this important Mūlasarvāstivādin monastic handbook was composed (for the life of Guṇaprabha and the date and influence of the *Vinayasūtra*, see G. Schopen, "Ritual Rights and Bones of Contention: More on Monastic Funerals and Relics in the *Mūlasarvāstivāda-vinaya*," *JIP* 22 (1994) 63–64 [= Ch. X below, 312–313] and nn. 63–65 and the sources cited there). Such a juxtaposition reveals, indeed, both the precise sources that Guṇaprabha used and the remarkable degree to which he depended on those sources. The mere fact that his sources can so often be precisely identified, and that such a juxtaposition can be made, already indicates some important things about the composition of the *Vinayasūtra*.

Even a quick and cursory reading of the *Vinayasūtra* will show that the correspondences cited in the notes here are only a small fraction of such correspondences. My impression—though it is only that—is that there is probably very little in the *sūtras* that does not occur in the canonical *vinaya*. But only when both have been thoroughly studied will we actually be able to determine this for certain, or to know, in other words, if, and to what degree, Guṇaprabha added new material.

There are cases where Guṇaprabha *seems* to add details not found in the canonical text. A good example is *Śayanāsanavastu* (Gnoli) 35.1–10, cited above p. 238. Here the canonical text says: "All [*vihāras*] must be used. One should stay in one place in the morning, in another at midday, at another in the afternoon, and one should pass the night in yet another!" But *Vinayasūtra* 78.30 (cited in n. 65) says: "In regard to all (*vihāras*, one) must make use of them. The procedure for this is thus: in the morning someplace (is used) for reading, reciting, staying, and walking; at midday he stores his bowl and robe at some other place; he spends the night at still another." Here Guṇaprabha omits reference to the afternoon but adds explicit references to specific activities to be performed in the morning and at midday that the canonical text knows nothing about. Another good example—this one not cited above—concerns the problem of monks dying on bedding that belonged to the Community. *Cīvaravastu*, GMs iii 2, 123.16 says: "Having recognized the (dying monk's) physical condition, having moved him on a pretext onto his personal bedding, he is to be laid out" (*śarīrāvasthāṃ jñātvā paudgalike śayanāsane vyājenāvatārya śāyitavya iti*). But Guṇaprabha (11.5) has: "That one [the attendant], when death is certain, having raised him [the dying monk] from bedding belonging to the Community, should settle him on his personal [bedding]. It is to be done on the pretext of its being preparatory to rubbing [him] with unguents and bathing [him]" (*sāṃghikād enam asau maraṇāśaṃkāyāṃ śayanāsanād utthāpya paudgalike niveśayet / abhyaṅganasnāpanapūrvakatāvyājena*). Here too we have in the *Vinayasūtra* what appears to be added material—the canonical text says nothing about rubbing with unguents and bathing. In this case, however, and this case probably also explains the previous one too, Guṇaprabha's additions only explain the otherwise curious "pretext" (*vyāja*) of the canonical text. They explain what kind of a "pretext" might be used and in this sense are commentary or gloss, not addition. Seen in the light of this case, the previous case appears to be of exactly the same sort: the specification of activities at certain periods of the day appears to be simply commentarial. In both cases if you remove the "commentarial" matter, what you have left is a close restatement of the canonical rule; and in both cases something like the "commentarial" matter itself will also undoubtedly be found somewhere else in the canonical *vinaya* (e.g., for rubbing and bathing the sick, see GMs iii

2, 129.15). I would foresee the vast majority of "new" or "additional" material in Guṇaprabha falling into precisely this category. This, of course, is not meant to deny all innovation, nor, especially, to deny Guṇaprabha's remarkable intellectual achievement, but rather to emphasize his close and careful adherence to the canonical texts that he was dealing with. This itself is no mean achievement.

CHAPTER IX

Marking Time in Buddhist Monasteries

On Calendars, Clocks, and Some Liturgical Practices

ANYONE WHO IS even vaguely interested in how a typical day was spent in the Buddhist monasteries of India must be thankful that either some Mūlasarvāstivādin monks got into serious trouble or the redactors of their *Vinaya* thought they would. This is so because the closest thing we have in the *Mūlasarvāstivāda-vinaya* to something like a daily work schedule occurs in two sets of rules redacted to govern the behavior not of monks "in good standing" (*prakṛtisthaka*) but of monks who were either on probation (*pārivāsika*) or undergoing penance (*śikṣādattaka*). Both sets of rules start with a long list of things that such monks cannot do—for example, they cannot accept any form of respectful greeting or salutation from monks in good standing; they cannot sit or walk with them; they cannot approach brahmin families or perform or take part in formal monastic acts or procedures. But both sets of rules also contain lists of what such monks must do, and these are the lists of most immediate interest because, as has been noted elsewhere, these lists contain references to both menial chores and liturgical practices that must, it seems, be performed on a daily basis at certain times of day.[1] They constitute, in effect, a kind of daily monastic schedule.

The first of these lists is preserved in Sanskrit in the Gilgit text of the *Pārivāsikavastu* and describes the duties of a Mūlasarvāstivādin monk on probation. The text—at least as Dutt prints it—reads:[2]

> *kālyam evotthāya dvāraṃ moktavyam / dīpasthālaka udvartavyaḥ / vihāraḥ sektavyaḥ-saṃmārṣṭratyaḥ sukumārī gomayakārṣī anupradātavyā / prasrāvoccārakuṭī dhāvayitavyā / mṛttikā upasthāpayitavyā pātrāṇi pāṇīyaṃ śītalaṃ vā kālānurūpataḥ / praṇāḍikāmukhāni dhāvayitavyāni /*

Originally published in *Sūryacandrāya. Essays in Honour of Akira Yuyama on the Occasion of His 65th Birthday* (Indica et Tibetica 35), ed. P. Harrison and G. Schopen (Swisttal-Odendorf: 1998) 157–179.

kālaṃ jñātvāsanaprajñaptiḥ kṛtvā dhūpakaṭacchuke dhūpaś copasthāpayitavyaḥ / sa cet pratibalo bhavati śāstur guṇasaṃkīrtanaṃ kartuṃ svayam eva kartavyam noced bhāṣaṇakaḥ praṣṭavyaḥ /

upānvāhāraṃ pratyavekṣyopānvāhṛtaṃ cec charaṇapṛṣṭham abhiruhya gaṇḍir [158] *dātavyā /*

nidāghakāle bhikṣūṇāṃ vyajanaṃ grahītavyam tataḥ sarvopasampannānāṃ copariṣṭāc chānteneryāpathavartinā bhikṣusaṃgham upasthāpya bhoktavyam /

kṛtabhaktakṛtyena śayanāsanaṃ channe gopayitavyam / pātrādhiṣṭhānaṃ chorayitavyam /

kālaṃ jñātvā tathāgatakeśanakhastūpāḥ saṃmārṣṭravyāḥ sukumārī gomayakārṣī anupradātavyā /

sāmagrīvelāyāṃ punaḥ śayanāsanaprajñaptiḥ kartavyā / dhūpakaṭacchuke [*dhūpa*] *upasthāpayitavyaḥ / śāstur guṇasaṃkīrtanaṃ pūrvavat kartavyam / divasa ārocayitavyaḥ / śṛṇotu bhadantaḥ saṃghaḥ / adya pakṣasya daśamīty evamādi yathā upadhivārikā ārocayanti /*

tataḥ pārivāsa ārocayitavyaḥ / śṛṇotu bhadantaḥ saṃghaḥ / aham evaṃ nāmā bhikṣur . . .

Once the major misreadings in Dutt's edition are corrected on the basis of the published facsimile of the Gilgit manuscript, the Tibetan translation of the *Pārivāsika*, and the Sanskrit text of the *Vinayasūtra*—as they are in the following notes[3]—this might be translated, keeping always in mind that the logical subject is the monk on probation, as follows:

Having risen at the very break of day, the door must be opened. The lamp-pot must be removed.[4] The *vihāra* must be watered down, swept, and a coat of fresh cow dung applied. The privy must be cleaned. Earth and leaves[5] must be set out, or cool water, depending on the season.

The mouths of the drains[6] must be cleaned. [159]

When he knows that it is time and has arranged the seats, the censer[7] and incense must be set out. If he is able to perform the Proclamation of the Qualities of the Teacher,[8] he himself must perform it. If not, a reciter must be asked.[9]

The food-preparation must be checked.[10] If it is prepared, having gone up on the roof, the *gaṇḍī* must be struck.[11] [160]

In the hot season the monks must be fanned. Then, after all those who are ordained but before those who are unordained, he, with a pliant demeanor and keeping firmly in mind the awareness that he is not a monk, must eat.[12]

When what has to be done in regard to eating has been done, the bedding and seats must be concealed in a safe place. The bowl-rest must be thrown out.[13]

When he knows that it is time, the *stūpas* of the hair and nail clippings of the Tathāgata must be swept and a coat of fresh cow dung must be applied.[14] [161]

> At the evening meeting time[15] the bedding and seats must again be arranged and the censer[16] set out. The Proclamation of the Qualities of the Teacher must be performed as before. The day must be announced as the Monks-in-Charge-of-Physical-Properties announce it, beginning with such as "Today is the tenth of the fortnight. . . ."[17]
>
> Then his period of probation must be announced, saying, "Reverends, may the community hear! I, the monk named so-and-so . . ." [and he then enumerates the specifics of his own case].

The second set of rules in the *Mūlasarvāstivāda-vinaya* that contains a fairly detailed daily work schedule occurs in the *Kṣudrakavastu* and is of particular interest because these rules were apparently designed to allow "defrocked" monks to remain in their monasteries. These rules, in fact, are meant to govern the behavior of a monk who has had sexual intercourse and therefore has committed [162] the first of the four *pārājika* offenses. Such an offense should result in immediate expulsion from the order, but even though the question was still being discussed as late as the *Abhidharmakośa*,[18] according to Sasaki "all vinayas except the Pāli Vinaya" already had provisions that both allowed a monk who was guilty of this particular offense to remain a member of the community and, at the same time, stripped him "forever" of most of the rights of a monk.[19] The *Mūlasarvāstivāda-vinaya* certainly had such provisions. In this *Vinaya* such a "monk" was allowed a continuing place in the monastery on two conditions: first, that he had no intention of concealing the offense; and second, that he himself asked to be given the lifelong penance (*ji srid 'tsho'i bar du bslab pa'i sdom pa*), which, in turn, entailed giving up almost all the rights and privileges of a monk—in this *Vinaya* he retained the right to a cell and a share of the donations—and becoming responsible for the daily round of chores in the monastery. It is, of course, as a part of the requirements of this "penance" that we find the parallel to our passage in the *Pārivāsikavastu*, and it is a very close one. Like the monk on probation, the monk undergoing the lifelong penance cannot interact normally with the other monks, go to the house of a brahmin, take part in formal monastic acts and procedures, and so on. And like the monk on probation, the monk undergoing the lifelong penance has a long list of daily duties:[20]

> *nang par sngar langs te sgo dbye bar bya / mar me'i snod bsal bar bya / gtsug lag khang chag chag gdab par bya / phyag bdar bya / ba lang gi lci ba sar pa bzang pos byug par bya / bshang gci khang phyag bdar bya / sa dang / lo ma dag dang / chu grang mo 'am / dron mo dus dang mthun par gzhag par bya /*
>
> *de nas wa'i kha phyag par bya /*[21]
>
> *dus shes par bya ste / stan bsham par bya / bdug pa'i snod dang bdug pa nye bar*

gzhag par bya / gal te ston pa'i yon tan sgrog par nus na / bdag nyid kyis bya / ci ste mi nus na smra ba po la gsol par bya'o /

zas kyi skos sa la brtag par bya zhing / zas bskos zin nas khang steng du song ste / gaṇḍī brdung bar bya /

tsha ba'i dus su dge slong rnams la bsil yab kyis g-yab par bya / de nas bsnyen par rdzogs pa thams cad kyi ni 'og / bsnyen par ma rdzogs pa rnams kyi ni [163] *gong du spyod lam zhi bas dge slong gi 'du shes nye bar bzhag ste*[22] *zas bza' bar bya /*

zas kyi bya ba byas nas gnas mal phug tu brtul bar bya / lhung bzed kyi gzhi dor bar bya /

dus shes par byas nas / de bzhin gshegs pa'i dbu skra dang sen mo'i mchod rten dag phyag bdar bya zhing / ba lang gi lci ba sar pa bzang pos byug par bya /

'du ba'i dus su gnas mal bsham par bya zhing / bdug pa dang bdug pa'i snod gzhag par bya / ston pa'i yon tan bsgrags par bya / dge 'dun btsun pa rnams gsan du gsol / deng dge 'dun gyi tshes gcig lags te / gtsug lag khang gi bdag po dang / gtsug lag khang gi lha rnams kyi don du tshigs su bcad pa gsungs shig ces nyi ma brjod par bya / ci ste mi nus na dge slong la bcol bar bya'o /

Apart from the final paragraph and some minor differences already cited in some previous notes, this list of duties in the *Kṣudrakavastu* is virtually identical to the list that occurs in the *Pārivāsikavastu*. In fact, when the text of the *Kṣudrakavastu* is compared with the Tibetan version of the parallel in the *Pārivāsika-vastu*, the two look like only variant Tibetan translations of essentially the same Sanskrit text—they exhibit the same sort of differences that can be seen at a glance in, for example, Hartmann's presentation of the two Tibetan translations of the *Ambāṣṭasūtra*, which are still embedded in the *Mūlasarvāstivāda-vinaya*, the one in the *Bhaiṣajyavastu*, the other in the *Kṣudraka*.[23] Where, for example, the *Kṣudraka* translates *dīpasthālaka* by *mar me'i snod*, the *Pārivāsika* renders it *mar me'i sdong bu*; where the *Kṣudraka* has *ba lang gi lci ba sar pa bzang pos* for *sukumārī gomayakārṣī*, the *Pārivāsika* has *ba'i lci ba 'jam pos*; where *bhāṣaṇaka* is translated by *smra ba po* in the *Kṣudraka*, the *Pārivāsika* has *'chad pa po*; where the *Kṣudraka* translates the sentence *nidāghakāle bhikṣūṇāṃ vyajanaṃ grahītavyam* by *tsha ba'i dus su dge slong rnams la bsil yab kyis g-yab par bya*, the *Pārivāsika* has *sos ka tsha ba'i dus su bsil yab blangs te dge slong rnams la g-yab par bya'o*; and so forth. This sort of inconsistency in the Tibetan translations is—it is becoming increasingly clear—commonly seen even in "canonical" renderings when we have two or more Tibetan translations of the same text; and although such differences might occasionally reflect slight differences in the Sanskrit originals that were used, in most cases they probably do not.

Whether or not the Sanskrit text underlying the *Kṣudrakavastu* was exactly the same as the Sanskrit text now preserved in the Gilgit *Pārivāsika*, the fact remains that—apart again from the final paragraph—the Tibetan translation of [164] the *Kṣudrakavastu* says virtually the same thing and therefore need not be translated. But the concluding paragraph merits some attention because, if for no other reason, it may supply what was omitted by abbreviation in the penultimate section of the *Pārivāsikavastu*.

In spite of the textual problem there, it is virtually certain that the penultimate section of the *Pārivāsika* passage says something like "the day must be announced as the Monks-in-Charge-of-Physical-Properties announce it, beginning with such as . . . ." The redactor of the *Pārivāsikavastu*, in other words, assumes that his audience will know how the *upadhivārikas*, "the Monks-in-Charge-of-Physical-Properties," announce the date and therefore gives only the beginning of such an announcement: "Today is. . . ." In the *Kṣudrakavastu* no such assumption is made, nor any apparent abbreviation used. It says, "The day must be announced, saying, 'Today is the first day of winter. The verses for the benefit of the Owner of the *Vihāra* and the gods of the *vihāra* must be said!'" And not only do we have good reasons to think—as we shall see—that this was the way in which the day was normally announced, but we also have, thanks to a passage in the *Vinayasūtra*, a good idea of what this statement looked like in Sanskrit: *adya śuklapakṣasya pratipad vihārasvāmino vihāradevatānāṃ cārthāya gāthāṃ bhāṣadhvam iti*.[24] Only the specific date differs, and because this was a prescribed formula, any date, when appropriate, could be used. Moreover, given that Guṇaprabha explicitly says that this formula is spoken by the *upadhivārika*, it is relatively certain that it does indeed represent what the redactors of the *Pārivāsika* were referring to when they said "the day must be announced as the Monks-in-Charge-of-Physical-Properties announce it . . . ," and that the two texts—the *Pārivāsika* and the *Kṣudraka*—are even more closely parallel than might appear at first sight.

The lists, or list, of duties found in both the *Kṣudrakavastu* and the *Pārivāsikavastu* are, or is, of interest, then, from several points of view. But here we can note only a few particular points, one of the most important of which is that these are daily duties that are listed, and their sequential ordering appears to reflect, therefore, the structure of a typical day in a Mūlasarvāstivādin monastery. The day started early for the monk or monks on probation or undergoing penance or for the *upadhivārika* who, as we know from other passages, was otherwise responsible for many of the same chores.[25] They had to get up at dawn, turn off the night-lights, and open shop, as it were, getting the *vihāra*—especially the bathroom—ready for the day. When this was done, and sometime before the main meal, they had to make the preparations for what appears to have been a communal gathering during which the other monks sat, incense was used, and the praises of the Buddha were recited. When this recitation was over and when the other monks were still seated—at least the seats had not yet been removed—the monk on probation or his counterpart had to keep an eye on the food preparations, and [165] when the meal was ready, he had to strike the *gaṇḍī* to signal such and gather all the remaining monks who had not yet assembled. Then the community ate in groups, according to their status. This must have been just before noon. After lunch the seats had to be put away and eating places cleaned—incidentally, any formal act (*karman*) of the community would, it seems, have been atypical and would have occurred in the afternoon after the seats had been removed, given that the descriptions of such events invariably begin with instructions to "arrange the bedding and seats": they would already have been arranged in the morning and at the time of the evening meeting. Also sometime in the afternoon the *stūpas* would have been cleaned and "purified." Then in the evening the bedding, seats, and censer had again to be set out, and a second liturgical recitation of the praises of the Buddha took place, the day was "announced," and verses for the benefit of the Owner of the *Vihāra* and the gods of the *vihāra* were recited. Finally, to judge by what happened in the morning, the seats had to be removed again, the door closed, and the lamp-pot set out.

At least two things stick out in this schedule. There is a clear emphasis on liturgical recitations: the monastic day begins and ends with recitations of the praises of the Buddha, recitations that apparently required some expertise to perform, because all monks could not apparently do it, and recitations that we know from another passage in the *Kṣudrakavastu* involved "chant" or a particular kind of intonation. In that passage the Buddha himself says that "the Proclamation of the Qualities of the Teacher . . . must be recited with measured intonation," *'di ltar ston pa'i yon tan yang dag par bsgrag pa . . . skad kyi gtang rag gis gdon par bya'o*, which Guṇaprabha paraphrases as *kuryāt śāstṛguṇasaṃkīrttane . . . svaraguptim.*[26] And only this "proclamation" and one other recitative sequence called the *Tridaṇḍaka* may be "recited with measured intonation."

There is also the recitation of verses for the Owner and gods of the *vihāra* in the daily schedule. We will see further reference to both and here might only note that there are frequent references in the *Mūlasarvāstivāda-vinaya* to the liturgical or ritualized recitation of unspecified verses, although such verses are frequently characterized as *ārṣā gāthās*, "verses of the Sage."[27] Of such recitations the closest to those referred to in the daily schedule are probably the ones referred to in the *Śayanāsanavastu*, where it is said that the Elder-of-the-Community recites a verse for the benefit of dead donors (*saṃghasthaviro 'bhyatītakālagatānāṃ dānapatīnām arthāya gāthāṃ bhāṣate*),[28] or the one referred to in the *Kṣudrakavastu* in a set of rules meant to govern the behavior of a Mūlasarvāstivādin monk who is on the road. In the latter, it is said: "At a resting place a verse of the Sage must be [166] recited. When taking water, a verse must be recited for him to whom it belongs and for its deva" (*ngal bso ba'i gnas kyi phyogs su gtsug lag gi tshigs su bcad pa gdon par bya'o / chu chu ba na chu de gang gi yin pa dang / de'i lha la tshigs su bcad pa gdon par bya'o*).[29] The latter looks much like an extension of the final recitative obligations found in the daily schedule to the road: whether in the *vihāra* or traveling, the monk must recite verses for those who provide for his needs. Apart from these instances, in the *Bhaiṣajyavastu* the Buddha himself says: "After having eaten, you must recite a verse of the Sage" (*yuṣmābhir bhuktvā ārṣā gāthā vaktavyā*);[30] in the *Kṣudrakavastu* a monk is instructed to recite a verse of the Sage (*gtsug lag gi tshigs su bcad pa*) over the water used to wash the bowls of the monks before it is given as a curative agent to laypersons;[31] again in the *Kṣudraka* the monks are instructed to recite such a verse before stepping on the shadow cast by an image or by the pole of a *stūpa*;[32] and finally both in the *Kṣudraka*[33] and repeatedly in the *Vibhaṅga* there are references to individuals—usually laymen—coming to a *vihāra* and, before engaging the monks, first worshipping the monastery's *stūpa* "with the singing of verses" (*tshigs su bcad pa'i dbyangs kyis mchod rten la phyag 'tshal te*).[34] Clearly, much here remains to be learned. [167]

But if references to liturgical or recitative practices are prominent in the daily monastic schedule embedded in our *Pārivāsika* and *Kṣudraka* passages, so too—and not surprisingly—are references to time, the time of day and the time of the week or fortnight. The schedule—again not surprisingly—is punctuated with such references: "at the very break of day," "when he knows that it is time" (twice), "at the evening meeting time." Of course, at the risk of being even more than usually obvious, it might be noted that the existence of rules dictating a daily monastic schedule, or rules requiring the formal announcement of the date, would seem to presuppose that the monastic communities these rules were meant to govern had the means to determine, or keep track of, both the time of day and the date of the month, that they had, in other words, something like clocks and calendars; and there are other passages in our *Vinaya* that suggest, indeed, that they did.[35]

It has been known for a long time that I-ching's seventh-century *Record of the Buddhist Religion*—in many ways a kind of Mūlasarvāstivādin handbook—describes two different devices used in India to keep track of time. One—and the one that has received the most attention—is the water clock, or clepsydra; the other was a kind of sundial, and I-ching describes how it was made: "[One] has to form a small earthen elevation at a suitable place. This mound is to be made round, of one foot diameter, and five inches high, at the centre part of which a slender stick is to be fixed. Or, on a stone stand, a nail is to be fixed, as slender as a bamboo chop-stick, and its height should be four fingers' width long."[36] I-ching also describes his water clock—a copper vessel filled with water on which a copper bowl floats that has a small pinhole in its bottom—and says that "clepsydrae are much used in great monasteries in India." The "dials," on the other hand, he says "are made everywhere" and are called, he says, *velācakras*.[37]

Though interesting, I-ching's remarks are late and chiefly important only because they specifically refer to practices in Buddhist monasteries. Outside of such monasteries both types of device are already referred to, for example, in Kauṭilya's *Arthaśāstra*, where the water clock is called a *nālikā* and the "dial," apparently, a *chāyā*.[38] But they may also be important because they are able to [168] suggest that the device for measuring time that is referred to in the *Vibhaṅga* of the *Mūlasarvāstivāda-vinaya* was not—in spite of its name—like either one of these.

The reference in the *Vibhaṅga* to a device that measures time occurs in a story that might well suggest that Islamic invaders like Muhammad Bakhtiyar may not have been the first persons bent on plunder to mistake a Buddhist monastery for a fort.[39] The story[40] concerns a beautiful *vihāra*, which is described in terms that are frequently repeated in this *Vinaya*: "[This *vihāra*] was ornamented with lofty gateways, windows, latticed windows, and railings. It captivated both the heart and the eye and was like a stairway to the heavens."[41] It was also said that it "possessed every sort of flower and every sort of fruit and was altogether delightful"; it had "every requisite," cloth racks "hung and heaped with cloth," and cells "full of copper vessels." It also, not surprisingly, had been burgled. In fact, although the topic has been little studied, the redactors of this *Vinaya* appear to have been preoccupied with the problems of theft and burglary—usually at the hands of organized gangs. The monasteries they knew or envisioned appear to have been frequent and attractive targets for such activities, and the presence of burglars was explicitly cited as the justification for the Buddha's authorization of the use of both individual and monastic seals to mark property,[42] for example, or his insistence that at least forest monasteries keep dogs and that a monk be specially assigned as their keeper (*kukkuraposaka*).[43] In our *Vibhaṅga* story, as a result of previous burglaries, the Buddha instructs the monks to post a monk as a guard and indicates that at the first sign of thieves that monk must sound a specific warning.

Thieves, of course, return, and the monk on guard shouts out exactly what the Buddha himself told him to shout: "Bring the *gaṇḍī* and the *gaṇḍī*-striker! Bring the time wheel, the waist cloths, the sevens, the fives, the bags and sashes, belts, girdles, and small belts!" (*gal te chom rkun pa 'ongs na gaṇḍī 'on cig / gaṇḍī'i the'u 'on cig / dus kyi 'khor lo 'on cig / snam sbyar dang / bdun pa dang / lnga pa dang / gtur bu dang / rgya cang dang / shur bu dang / lcag pod dang / shur bu phre'u 'on cig ces tsham dam bya'o /*). This—as well it might—confuses the [169] thieves but also terrifies them, and they run away. They ran, it turns out, because they thought—like Muhammad Bakhtiyar—that they were dealing with military men, not monks.

> One of their number who knew about monks said: "Why, you guys, are you running away?"
>
> They said: "Because you yourself said: 'All sixty of the renunciants who are

living there are masters of archery (*'phong gi slob dpon*)'—why shouldn't we run away like this? Moreover, we have never before even heard the names of such weapons as a *gaṇḍī* and so forth."

The other thief then points out their error:

"But these," he said, "are not weapons."
"Then what are they?"

And here we get a kind of commentary:

"That which is called a *'gaṇḍī'* is what they strike to make a sound. A *'gaṇḍī-*striker' is what they strike it with. A 'time wheel' is what accurately measures time (*dus kyi 'khor lo zhes bya ba ni dus yongs su gcod par byed pa'o*). 'A waist cloth, a seven, a five' are names for kinds of robes, etc."

Given that our text implies that the same warning is to be shouted at all monasteries—all *vinaya* rules, unless otherwise stated, had universal application—thanks to the ignorance or stupidity of your average thief, we can conclude, then, that the redactors of the *Mūlasarvāstivāda-vinaya* assumed that all monasteries had a "time wheel" and grouped or associated it with the *gaṇḍī*, the instrument used to signal timed events. They also seem to have assumed that like the *gaṇḍī*, which was small enough to be thrown at someone, the time wheel was easily portable and of sufficient value to be worth saving from thieves. Unfortunately, apart from this we know little about it. Even the ancillary sources that are so often helpful are not here. Guṇaprabha's *Vinayasūtra*, for example, does not seem to treat our passage, restating only the final rule that it produces: *rkun po spa bkong ba'i phyir tsham dam bya'o / gaṇḍī la sogs pa mi 'phog par 'phang ngo*[44]—the Sanskrit appears to be corrupt. Bu-ston's *'Dul ba pha'i gleng 'bum chen mo*, which frequently supplies helpful glosses or paraphrases, here only repeats the canonical vocabulary: *dus kyi 'khor lo* and *dus yongs su gcod pa*. Even Vinītadeva's *Vinayavibhaṅgapadavyākhyāna* is of little help, at least to me. It does gloss the term, but I do not understand the gloss: *dus kyi 'khor lo zhes bya ba ni gnyis bzhur gyi 'khor lo'o*, "the 'wheel of time' means: a wheel of two *bzhurs*"[45]—but *bzhur* in any contextually meaningful sense does not seem to occur in the standard dictionaries. Perhaps the most that can be taken from this is the apparent fact that already in Vinītadeva's time the term may have needed explanation, and the possibility that the "wheel of time" or "time wheel" was actually some kind [170] of wheel consisting of two parts. We can, though, perhaps take a little more from our story.

In spite of the similarity or even identity of their names, the particulars of our story would, for example, seem to make it unlikely that the device that it says "accurately measures (*yongs su gcod par byed pa = paricchidyate*) time" and that it calls a *dus kyi 'khor lo* (= *kālacakra* or *velācakra*) was identical to either form of I-ching's "dial." First of all, both forms of I-ching's dial were apparently common—they were "made everywhere"—and therefore hardly worth saving. The materials used in their construction would point in the same direction—a little earthen mound and a stick, a "stone stand" and a nail. Moreover, neither form, and most certainly not the first, was portable, and neither form would have been inside the *vihāra* in any case. It is perhaps equally unlikely that *dus kyi 'khor lo* was a clepsydra, or water clock. The sort of thing I-ching describes in this category would also not have been easily transportable, at least in working condition, that is to say, full of water. And again, although he describes the components of his water clock as made of copper, Fleet long ago pointed out that for the earlier Indian form of this device "the ordinary earthen water-jar (*kumbha, ghāṭa*) served the purpose."[46] Then there is the name—regardless of what it was made of, the water clock almost certainly did not involve a wheel (*'khor lo, cakra*). Whatever it was, however it was made, the *kālacakra* referred to by the *Vibhaṅga* must have been some other sort of device.[47] But, before turning from the time of day to the day of the month, it might well be worth noting with J. D. North that "a time piece is much more than a mechanism."

North, speaking of course of medieval Europe, has noted: "Through the close regulation of the monastic day a measure of regularity was imposed on society at large. With or without automatic control, the canonical hours of the monastic life were struck eight times daily on a tower bell which, in summoning the monks to prayer by day and by night, was heard far beyond the confines of [171] the cloister."[48] And something like this might well apply to the monasteries that were known or envisioned by the compilers of the *Mūlasarvāstivāda-vinaya*. The *gaṇḍī* they would have struck at certain times of day was to be struck on the roof of the *vihāra*, and there are ample indications that they took for granted that it could be heard for a considerable distance: a text in the *Vibhaṅga*, for example, assumes that when the *gaṇḍī* was struck in the environs of the Jetavana, it could be heard in Śrāvastī; in the *Poṣadhavastu*, when the *gaṇḍī* is sounded inordinately, the townsmen of the region (*spyod yul gyi grong mi rnams*) hear it and come running, thinking the *vihāra* is being robbed; in the *Śayanāsana* it is assumed that the sound of the *gaṇḍī* could be heard across a river that was large enough to have a strong current.[49] The *gaṇḍī* too, then, could have punctuated more than just the monastic day, and our text at least would have us believe that monks and members of other religious groups also provided the local people with other types of temporal information that would have ordered their lives.

Unlike the device that "accurately measured" the time of day, the nature of what might be called the monastic "calendar" is not in doubt: we have in the

Mūlasarvāstivāda-vinaya a clear description of both how it was made and how it was used. The descriptions occur in the final and probably least-studied section of this monstrous *Vinaya*, the *Uttaragrantha*. There appear to be two texts in this concluding section that have the same Sanskrit title, or two versions of the same text, one incomplete, at least in the Tibetan Kanjur. This remains to be sorted out.[50] Still to be sorted out too is the relationship between the work or works called the *Uttaragrantha* in the Tibetan tradition and the work preserved in Chinese translation under the reconstructed title "[*Mūlasarvāstivāda*]*nidānamātṛkā*?" (Taishō 1452). The works so titled at least seem to share in common a good deal of material.[51] There is also some evidence to suggest that the text(s) [172] known to the Tibetans under the title *Uttaragrantha(s)* was (were) known to the Indian tradition under the title *Mātṛkā*. Guṇaprabha, for example, cites in his *Svavyākhyānābhidhānavinayasūtravṛtti* a text dealing with lending on interest from what he calls the *Mātṛkā*, but exactly the same passage occurs in the *Uttaragrantha*.[52] In fact a considerable amount of material in Guṇaprabha's *Vinayasūtra* and, consequently, Bu-ston's *'Dul ba pha'i gleng 'bum chen mo* has been taken from what the Tibetans call the *Uttaragrantha*, and it is therefore clear that Banerjee's remark that "this work tells us nothing new; it is only an abridgement of the *Vinaya* texts"[53] is very far off the mark.[54] But it is not just from the evidence of Guṇaprabha's use of it that the *Uttaragrantha* appears to be an integral and important part of his *Vinaya*. The relationships of dependence or interdependence between the various parts of the *Mūlasarvāstivāda-vinaya* would also seem to indicate the same. The passage that most concerns us here is as good an example as any of this "intertextuality."

Both the *Pārivāsikavastu* and the *Kṣudrakavastu* take for granted—as we have seen—that an established part of the daily monastic routine was the formal announcement of the date. The former indicates that this function normally fell to the *upadhivārika*, and the latter associates the announcement with the equally formal and daily recitation of verses for the benefit of the Owner of the *Vihāra* and its gods, but neither actually contains the warrant for these practices nor an account of their authorization by the Buddha. That warrant, the "origin tale" of both practices, is—insofar as I know—found only in the *Uttara*[173]*grantha*, making it awkward to try to argue that the *Uttara* was a late "appendix."

The text of that origin tale falls quite naturally into several parts, and its translation does not present any serious difficulties:[55]

> At a time when the Buddha, the Blessed One, was staying in Śrāvastī, in the Jetavana, in the Park of Anāthapiṇḍada, when brahmins and householders came to the monks and asked them, "What, Noble Ones, is today's date?" (*'phags pa de ring tshes grangs du zhes dris pa*), the monks said: "Sorry, we don't know."
>
> But the brahmins and householders said: "When members of other reli-

gious groups know not only the date but the position of the sun and the stars and the moment as well, how can you, when you have entered the religious life, not even know the date?" (*mu stegs can gyis kyang tshes grangs dang / nyi ma dang / skar ma dang / yud tsam yang shes na / khyed cag rab tu byung na tshes grangs tsam yang mi shes sam /*).

The monks, having no response, sat there saying nothing.

The monks then reported what had occurred to the Blessed One, and the Blessed One said: "I order[56] that henceforth the date is to be counted (*bgrang ba*)!" But then all the monks started to count.

The monks then reported to the Blessed One what had occurred, and the Blessed One said: "All must not count! Both the Elder-of-the-Community (*dge 'dun gyi gnas brtan* = *saṃghasthavira*) and the Guardian-of-the-*Vihāra* (*gtsug lag khang skyong*) must count!" But when both the Elder-of-the-Community and the Guardian-of-the-*Vihāra* also forgot to do it, their calculations were off (*nyes pa'i dmigs su gyur pa*).

The monks reported to the Blessed One what had occurred, and the Blessed One said: "Fifteen small balls of clay must be made, and they must be strung and arranged on a cord; then each day one must be slid over (*'jim pa'i ril bu bco lnga byos la srad bu la brgyus te zhog la nyin re re zhing drang bar gyis shig*)!" But the cord sagged (*'phyongs par gyur pa*), and the Blessed One said: "Fifteen strips of bamboo must be made, and they must be strung and arranged on a cord, then each day one must be slid over (*'od ma'i byang bu bco lnga byos la srad bu la brgyus te zhog la de la nyin gcig re re bzhin drongs shig*)!" But all the monks did the [174] sliding. And their memories being bad, the Blessed One said: "The Elder-of-the-Community must slide the strips!"

To this point in our text, several things are of interest. First, according to the *Mūlasarvāstivāda-vinaya*, Buddhist monasteries started to keep track of the date as the result of lay criticism and as a way to compete with other religious groups (*tīrthikas*). Virtually the same justification is also given by the redactors of this *Vinaya* to account for the adoption by the Buddhist community of a number of other practices as well. In the *Poṣadhavastu*, for example, lay criticism and the unfavorable comparison of the Buddhist community with other religious groups (*tīrthikaparivrājakas*) are presented as the reason why the Buddha ruled that Buddhist monks should practice meditation (*niṣadyā—niṣadyā ucyate yogaḥ*) and hold the fortnightly assembly (*poṣadha*).[57] In the *Kṣudrakavastu*, unfavorable comparison of Buddhist practice with that of other religious groups (*mu stegs can*) leads the Buddha to authorize the recitation of Buddhists texts "with measured intonation."[58]

Then there is the narrative fact that Buddhist monks were not good at math, nor endowed with very good memories. The *Kṣudrakavastu*, for example, has a set of rules on how to make up the narrative details of canonical texts, because the monks could not always remember them,[59] and—even more germane—it justifies recourse to another crude counting device, the *śalākā*, or "stick used in counting," by pointing out that the monks had no head for numbers. A brahmin who wished to invite the monks to a meal asked how many monks there were in the Jetavana, and the monks—as in our text—say they do not know. When the brahmin—again much like in our text—castigates them, the Buddha orders that the monks must be counted. The monks first count them out loud, but then forget the total. Next they count them on their fingers but still forget, and the Buddha finally says: "Tally sticks (*śalākā*) must be distributed! When they have been distributed, they must be counted! When they have been counted, it must be announced to the community: 'There are so many monks.'" This last text from the *Kṣudraka* obviously has a good deal in common with our text from the *Uttaragrantha*.[60] [175]

There is also the description of the calendar, and we are particularly fortunate to have a Sanskrit text of the *Vinayasūtra*, for Guṇaprabha, while ignoring the first and unsuccessful form of the device that used clay balls that proved to be too heavy, describes the second in the following *sūtra*: *divasasya gaṇanaṃ saṃghasthavireṇa sūtraprotavaṃśaśalākāsaṃcāreṇa*, "the counting of the day (is to be done) by the Elder-of-the-Community by moving a strip of bamboo strung on a cord."[61] Both the nature and the operation of the device are therefore not in doubt: it was a bit like an abacus with only one row of counters—primitive technologically, but easily used. Here too it should be noted that—as with the time wheel—the mere existence of this rule in the *Mūlasarvāstivāda-vinaya* suggests that its redactors assumed that all monasteries that they were writing for had such a device: the rule applies not to some or to a specific monastery but to all.

Up to this point in the text, then, the only thing that is problematic is the title that I have translated as "the Guardian-of-the-*Vihāra*"—*gtsug lag khang skyong*. Context and its pairing with the title *saṃghasthavira* point toward its being a monastic office held by a monk. It is, moreover, almost certainly quite distinct from the title *vihārasvāmin*, *gtsug lag khang gi bdag po*, "the Owner-of-the-*Vihāra*," which occurs a little later in our text, where it refers to a layperson, as it normally does elsewhere in both texts and inscriptions.[62] What might be a variant translation of the same title—*gtsug lag khang dag yongs su skyong bar byed pa rnams*—also occurs, for example, in the *Kṣudrakavastu* in a text dealing with the proper procedure for abandoning a *vihāra* whose Owner (*gtsug lag khang gi bdag po*) is not able to provide for it, but this title too is marked by the same sort of uncertainties.[63] It does not, of course, necessarily help that the *Uttaragrantha* passage itself shifts in the same line from *gtsug lag khang skyong* to simply *khang skyong*, or that both the *Vinayasūtra* and *'Dul ba pha'i gleng 'bum chen mo* seem to substitute the more familiar title *upadhivārika* (*dge skos*) for *gtsug lag khang skyong* in their handling of the text. It is even not impossible that *gtsug lag khang skyong* is a nonstandard rendering of *upadhivārika*—much of the language of the *Uttara* is nonstandard—but this, like so much having to do with monastic titles and administrative offices, remains to be sorted out.

The *Uttaragrantha* passage up to this point provides, then, at least a clear warrant for monks keeping track of the date and a description of the device used [176] to do so. The section that follows in the text—much of which can be summarized—adds a further warrant and a familiar theme.

When brahmins and householders now came to the *vihāra* and asked for the date, the monks referred them to the Elder-of-the-Community and the Guardian-of-the-*Vihāra*, who had been charged with keeping track of it. The laymen, however, are once again critical, insisting that the monks themselves should know the date, and the Buddha responds to this criticism by ordering that "the date must be announced in the midst of the community!" (*de lta bas na dge 'dun gyi nang du tshes grangs brjod par gyis shig*), providing thus the initial warrant for a part of the practice we have met with in the schedule of activities enumerated in the *Pārivāsikavastu* and the *Kṣudrakavastu*. But this initial procedure only exposed an important weakness in both the method and the device used to keep track of the date: "The monks, although the date was announced in the midst of the community, did not have the fortnight determined" (*dge slong rnams kyis dge 'dun gyi nang du tshes grangs brjod kyis zla ba phyed po 'dzin par mi byed do*), and again laymen point out the problem involved—if the day is announced without determining the fortnight, how can anyone know whether it refers to the waxing or the waning fortnight? Without explaining how it is to be done, the Buddha orders that the fortnight has to be determined, then gives a revised version of the procedure for announcing the date and, not incidentally, the warrant for the recitation of verses for the Owner and devas of the *vihāra*. He says: "The announcement must be announced in this way: when the entire community is seated and assembled, a single monk seated first at the Seniors' end of the assembly[64] must say this with reverence and his hands in the gesture of supplication: 'Today is the first day of the waning fortnight. Separate verses for the benefit of the Owner and gods of the *vihāra* must be recited!'" (*brjod pa ni 'di bzhin du brjod par bya ste / dge 'dun thams cad 'dus shing 'khod pa dang / dge slong gcig gis rgan rims kyi dang por 'dug la rim gro dang bcas pas thal mo sbyar la tshig 'di skad du smros shig / de ring ni zla ba mar gyi tshes gcig ste / gtsug lag khang gi bdag po dang lha rnams kyi phyir tshigs su bcad pa re re rjod cig /*).

Here it would seem we finally have—in close conjunction with a calendrical device that would have made it possible—an explicit warrant for the monastic practice of announcing the day, as well as for the recitation of verses for the Owner and gods of the *vihāra*, two of the practices that were taken for granted in the daily schedules that we started with in the *Pārivāsikavastu* and the *Kṣudrakavastu*. By linking these two practices, however, our passage and those who redacted it gave the donor of a Mūlasarvāstivādin monastery a prominent place in the daily life of the monks who lived in it. Every day those monks—to use a Christian idiom—"prayed" for him in a communal, liturgical setting.[65] As if to confirm all [177] this, and to make it absolutely clear that these recitations were for specific individuals, not for nameless categories like "patrons" or "donors," the final part of the *Uttaragrantha* passage that concerns us[66] says:

> Although the monks announced the date, they did not call the Owner-of-the-*Vihāra* by name, and the Blessed One said: "The name of the Owner-of-the-*Vihāra* must also be announced! Just so, since the donor named so-and-so has invited the communities of monks for a meal tomorrow, you, Reverends, with generous minds, must show consideration toward him! As you do toward the Owner-of-the-*Vihāra*, so too you also, with generous minds, must show consideration toward donors and benefactors! As you show consideration with generous minds, their good qualities will increase; they will not decrease! Thus too the names must be announced individually for all those who are involved in that cause. The monks too, after all the words are finished, must individually read a verse for each!"

dge slong rnams kyis tshes grangs ni brjod kyis / gtsug lag khang gi bdag po'i ming nas ma smos pa dang / bcom ldan 'das kyis bka' stsal pa / gtsug lag khang gi bdag po'i ming nas kyang brjod par bya'o / di skad du sbyin bdag ming 'di zhes bya bas sang dge slong gi dge 'dun rnams bshos la spyan drangs kyis / de la btsun pa rnams kyis dge ba'i yid kyis brtse bar mdzod cig [Vinayasūtra: evaṃ nāma dānapati[ḥ] śvo bhikṣusaṃghaṃ bhaktenopanimantrayate taṃ bhadant[āḥ] kalyāṇaiḥ manobhiḥ pratyanukampantām iti] / gtsug lag khang gi bdag po la ji lta ba gzhan yang sbyin par byed pa dang / sbyin pa'i bdag po la yang dge ba'i yid kyis brtse bar mdzod cig / ji ltar dge ba'i yid kyis brtse bar mdzad pas na / de'i dge ba'i chos rnams 'phel bar 'gyur gyis 'grib par mi 'gyur ro / de bzhin du gzhan yang de na rkyen du gnas pa'i sems can thams cad la yang so so'i ming nas brjod par bya'o / dge slong dag gis kyang tshig thams cad rdzogs pa'i rjes la so so nas tshigs su bcad pa re re lhogs shig /

The point here, perhaps, could not be clearer, but note that if the ritual or recitative protocol described in this final passage were actually put into practice, it would produce something like an oral version of a Buddhist donative inscription: both inscription and recitation announce the date, name the gift or invitation, and recite the donor's name and the names of anyone associated with the act. It may well be that what Buddhist monks recorded in inscriptions they also may have celebrated in their daily liturgical practices. Note too that at least in this concluding passage the obligation to recite verses for donors and benefactors was both communal and individual. Both the community as a whole was required to do so, then [178] each individual monk. If the obligation extended to all donors and benefactors—and there is no reason to think that it did not—it could have taken up a great deal of the monks' time, and once again it is beginning to look as if Buddhist monks, at least Mūlasarvāstivādin monks, may have been much more like their Western medieval counterparts than anyone has yet imagined. Certainly, the presence of daily schedules, the preoccupation with marking and recording time, the development of devices to do so, and recitative activities for the religious benefit of donors—all the things we have seen here—point in that direction. But, more broadly still, they point as well to how important it is for both communities and individuals to mark their days and meet their obligations, so I can only hope that today, the eleventh day of August, 1998, Yuyama Sensei will accept this little essay as a token payment of the very large debt that I owe to him.[67]

Notes

1. See G. Schopen, "The Lay Ownership of Monasteries and the Role of the Monk in Mūlasarvāstivādin Monasticism," *JIABS* 19.1 (1996) 81–126, esp. 95–97 [= Ch. VIII above, esp. 226–227], for some preliminary remarks on both lists.

2. GMs iii 3, 97.12–98.10.

3. The following materials have been used: GBMs vi, fol. 933.1–.5; *Spo ba'i gzhi*, Tog, dul ba Ga 240b.6–241a.7 = Derge, 'dul ba Ga 179a.7–b.6; *Vinayasūtra* (Sankrityayana) 105.11ff = *'Dul ba'i mdo*, Derge, bstan 'gyur, 'dul ba Wu 87b.2ff.

4. Dutt reads *udvartavyaḥ*; Edgerton (*BHSD*, s.v. *sthālaka*) follows him and translates "is to be set up." But the facsimile, which is—as it frequently is for this passage—hard to read, seems rather to have *uddhartavyaḥ*; *Vinayasūtra* has *-oddharaṇa-* and would seem to confirm this. Tibetan for both the *Pārivāsika* and the *Vinayasūtra* has a form of *bsal pa*, adding further support. At *Vibhaṅga*, Derge Ca 152b.5, the lamp-pots (plural) are in a similar context said to be "collected" (*mar me'i kong bu dag bsdus*), that is to say, removed—read: *uddhartavyaḥ*.

5. Dutt reads *pātrāṇi*, "bowls," but the facsimile clearly has *patrāṇi*, for *pattrāṇi*. *Vinayasūtra* is corrupt; Tibetan for *Pārivāsikavastu* has *lo ma*, confirming *patrāṇi*—so read. For the uninitiated it should be noted that we are dealing here with culturally specific Indian toilet practices. The list in the *Kṣudraka* rules for monks undergoing penance is slightly different: *sa dang / lo ma dag dang / chu grang mo 'am / dron mo dus dang mthun par gzhag par bya /*: "Earth and leaves and either cool or hot water, depending on the season, must be set out"; and still another enumeration occurs in the *Poṣadhavastu* (Hu-von Hinüber) § 18: *patravaibhaṅgukā sthāpayitavyā[ḥ] mṛttikāpānīyaṃ sthāpayitavyam*, "Zerkleinerte Blätter sollen hingelegt werden. Tonerde und Wasser sollen hingestellt werden." See, finally, the

rather outlandish frame-story for the *Kośāmbakavastu* (GMs iii 2, 173.5ff), in part at least a spoof of learned monks who end up arguing about how much water (= toilet paper) must be left in the privy to avoid an offense!

6. Dutt reads *praṇāḍikā-*, but the facsimile has *pranāḍikā-*. Both the spelling and the referent of the term remain unsettled. I have treated this injunction separately because I am not certain where in the monastery we are, whether, indeed, the reference to "drains" refers to drains in the privy or, for example, to drains in the courtyard or throughout the monastery as a whole; cf. n. 21 below.

7. Dutt reads *dhūpakaṭacchuke*, as if a locative, but this does not take account of the *ca* following *dhūpaś* and does not reflect the manuscript reading. The facsimile clearly has *-chukā*, and that two things are set out, not one *in* another, is also clear from the Tibetan: *bdug pa dang pog por gzhag par bya'o*. *Vinayasūtra* has *dhūpatatkaṭacchukayor upasthāpanam*, *bdug spos dang de'i pog phor dag nye bar gzhag go*—read: *dhūpakaṭacchukā*. Though explicitly stated neither here nor in the *Kṣudraka* rules for the monk undergoing penance, it would seem from other passages in this *Vinaya* that the censer and incense were set out in the *stūpa* court. At *Vibhaṅga*, Derge Ca 152b.5, which describes the morning activities of a young monk acting as the *upadhivārika*, the text says: *dus shes par byas nas stan bshams shing mchod rten gyi 'khor sar bdug spos brims te* /. . . , "When he knew it was time, he arranged the seats and distributed the incense in the *stūpa* court . . ." A little more than a leaf later in the same text it is said of a layman who had built the monastery in question: *rang nyid kyis pog phor thogs te dge slong gi dge 'dun dang lhan cig mchod rten la phyag 'tshal nas gtsug lag khang du zhugs te* (Ca 154a.4), "When he, himself carrying the censer, had venerated the *stūpa* with the community of monks, they entered the *vihāra*." That the censer was a necessary element *carried* in a variety of liturgical practices is also confirmed by yet another passage in the *Vibhaṅga* that describes the monk Udāyin taking a group of pious ladies around the Jetavana to venerate the Perfume Chamber and the *vihāras* of the great arhats. The text here (Derge Ca 207a.1) says: *des me tog dang / bdug spos la sogs pa mchod pa rnam pa sna tshogs thogs te pog phor lag tu blangs nas go rims ji lta ba bzhin du bstan par brtsams te* /, "Taking the various accoutrements of worship—incense, perfumes, etc.—he (Udāyin) took the censer in his hand and began to show them around (the *vihāras*) according to the monastic rank (of their inhabitants)." Note finally that the Tibetan used to translate *dhūpakaṭacchukā* is sometimes spelled *pog par* and sometimes *pog phor*.

8. For "the Proclamation of the Qualities of the Teacher," see Schopen, *JIABS* 19.1 (1996) 95 n. 34 [= Ch. VIII above, 227 n. 34].

9. Dutt reads *praṣṭavyaḥ*, but to judge by the facsimile—which here again is difficult to read—this cannot be right. The first syllable, at least, cannot be *pra-* and is almost certainly *-ādhye-*. The *Vinayasūtra* has *bhāṣaṇakādhyeṣaṇam*, which not only confirms the unusual *bhāṣaṇaka* but also suggests that the manuscript should be read as *adhyeṣṭavyaḥ*—so read.

10. Dutt reads *upānvāhāraṃ pratyavekṣyopānvāhṛtaṃ*. . . . I, however, cannot see a long *ā* marker in the facsimile on the first syllables of either *upānvāhāraṃ* or *-opānvāhṛtam*, and Sankrityayana prints the reading in *Vinayasūtra* as *up*[*ā*]*nvāhṛte*. Apart from this, the facsimile clearly has *pratyavekṣyam*, a gerundive, not *pratyavekṣyo-*, a gerund, which would seem

to indicate that *upānvāhāraṃ* here is neuter and not masculine, as Edgerton (*BHSD* 148), citing Dutt, suggests. Both here and in the rules governing monks undergoing penance, the references to "food preparation" are interesting in that they suggest the absence of daily begging in the monasteries envisioned and instead the preparation of food in the monastery itself. The *Mūlasarvāstivāda-vinaya* in fact, on more than one occasion, distinguishes between monks who obtain their food from the Community (*saṃghalābhin*) and monks who beg for their food (*piṇḍapātika*)—see, for example, *Poṣadhavastu* (Hu-von Hinüber) § 20. In some instances our *Vinaya* suggests that the two categories of monks lived in separate *vihāras*: so *Śayanāsanavastu* (Gnoli) 41.11: . . . *nadyā ubhayakūle dvau vihārau, ekaḥ saṃghalābhikānām dvitīyo piṇḍapātikānām*.

11. On the *gaṇḍī*, often translated as "gong" although it was almost certainly made of wood, see H. Hu-von Hinüber, "Das Anschlagen der Gaṇḍī in buddhistischen Klöstern," in Li, Zheng a.o. *Ji Xianlin Jiaoshou Bashi Huayan Jinian Lunwenji* (Papers in honour of Prof. Dr. Ji Xianlin on the Occasion of His 80th Birthday), ed. Zheng Li et al., (Nanchang: 1991) Vol. 2, 737–768; G. Schopen, "On Avoiding Ghosts and Social Censure: Monastic Funerals in the *Mūlasarvāstivāda-vinaya*," *JIP* 20 (1992) 5–7 and n. 27 [= *BSBM* 207–209 and n. 27] and references cited there, though the textual references could easily be multiplied; and the interesting modern work, Thubten Legshay Gyatsho, *Gateway to the Temple*, trans. D. P. Jackson (Kathmandu: 1979) 77–78. The expression *śaraṇapṛṣṭham* here is a little vague, and elsewhere the reference is explicitly to the roof of the *vihāra*. In the *Vibhaṅga* text describing the young monk acting as the *upadhivārika*, for example, we find *gtsug lag khang gi steng du 'greng nas gaṇḍī brdungs par brtsams so* (Derge Ca 152b.6). The fact that the *gaṇḍī* was, it seems, normally kept on the roof could even have strategic advantages. In a *Vibhaṅga* text that we will return to, when a thief is trying to climb up onto the roof on a ladder, a monk is able to knock him off by throwing the *gaṇḍī* at him (Derge Ca 158 b.2).

12. Dutt reads: *tataḥ sarvopasaṃpannānāṃ copariṣṭāc chānteneryapathavartinā bhikṣusaṃgham upasthāpya* . . . , but there are several problems here. Dutt apparently did not notice that the *ca* after *sarvopasaṃpannānāṃ* would seem to suggest that something might have dropped out of the manuscript, and a glance at the Tibetan would have confirmed this. It has *de'i 'og tu bsnyen par rdzogs pa thams cad kyi ni tha ma bsnyen par ma rdzogs pa rnams kyi gong du* . . . , "Then, after all those who are ordained but before those who are not ordained . . . ," and the parallel in the rules governing monks undergoing penance has virtually the same thing. Something like *anupasaṃpannānāṃ ca purastāt* has indeed apparently dropped out of the manuscript. But the problems do not end here. What Dutt read as *-saṃghaṃ* is (and it is uncharacteristically clear in the facsimile) *-saṃjñām*. Moreover, the Tibetan translation of the *Pārivāsika* indicates that Dutt has missed the *sandhi* operating between *-vartinā* and what follows. It should be resolved as *-vartinā + abhikṣusaṃjñāṃ*: the Tibetan here is *dge slong ma yin pa'i 'du shes bzhag la* . . . . The Tibetan translators of the parallel in the rules governing monks undergoing penance seem, on the other hand, to have made the same mistake that Dutt did. See n. 22 below.

13. The reading here is not in doubt. Dutt's *pātrādhiṣṭhānaṃ chorayitavyaṃ* is confirmed, for example, by *Vinayasūtra*'s *pātrādhiṣṭhānachoraṇam*, *lhung bzed kyi gzhi dor ro*. What is not so clear is what a *pātrādhiṣṭhāna* was. Edgerton (s.v. *chorayati*) translates our sentence: "He

must put away the (food-)bowl stand," but the problem here is that *chorayati* in the *Mūlasarvāstivāda-vinaya* almost always means "to throw out or away," not "put away." At *Śayanāsanavastu* (Gnoli) 36.24, for example, it is used to describe what is done with rubbish (*saṃkāraṃ chorayitvā*); at 39.3 the same verb is used in regard to dogshit (*uccāraprasrāvaś chorayitavyaḥ*); at *Cīvaravastu* (GMs iii 2, 127.5) it is a dead body that is the object of this action (*śmaśāne chorayitvā*); etc. Even Edgerton's own examples overwhelmingly favor this sense. Whatever, then, a *pātrādhiṣṭhāna* was, it was almost certainly not "put away" or "saved" but discarded after a meal.

14. On "the *stūpas* of the hair and nail clippings of the Tathāgata," see Schopen, "An Old Inscription from Amarāvatī and the Cult of the Local Monastic Dead in Indian Buddhist Monasteries," *JIABS* 14.2 (1991) 320 n. 34 [= *BSBM* 196 n. 34], but once again the textual references for our *Vinaya* could be greatly multiplied. In fact, all references to otherwise unspecified *stūpas* in the *Mūlasarvāstivāda-vinaya* were probably understood to refer to such *stūpas*. Notice, for example, that while our canonical text says *tathāgatakeśanakhastūpāḥ saṃmārṣṭavyāḥ*, etc., Guṇaprabha's *Vinayasūtra* says simply *stūpānāṃ saṃmārjanam*; and the rules that Guṇaprabha presents as applying to *stūpas* in general (120.7) are taken almost exclusively from two passages in the *Uttaragrantha* that actually refer only to *stūpas* for the hair and nails of the Buddha (see Derge Pa 114a.3ff, 119b.6ff; cf. Bu-ston, *'Dul ba pha'i gleng 'bum chen mo*, 'A 416a.2ff; some of this material has recently been treated—with some room for improvement—in P. Dorjee, *Stūpa and Its Technology: A Tibeto-Buddhist Perspective* [New Delhi: 1996] 3–7. That this material in what the Tibetan tradition knows as the *Uttaragrantha* corresponds very closely to the material on *stūpas* cited by Bareau from the Chinese version of a Mūlasarvāstivādin *vinaya* text called the *Nidānamātṛkā* [Taishō 1452] may be a first clue that the *Uttaragrantha* and the *Nidānamātṛkā* may be different versions of the same text [see A. Bareau, "La construction et le culte des stūpa d'après les vinayapiṭaka," *BEFEO* 50 (1960) passim]—see n. 51 below).

15. For Sanskrit *sāmagrīvelāyāṃ*, the Tibetan translation of the *Pārivāsikavastu* has *dgongs ka'i dus su*; the *Kṣudrakavastu* parallel and the Tibetan translation of the *Vinayasūtra* both have *'du ba'i dus so*. The latter must mean something like "at meeting time," but the former can mean only "in the evening," suggesting that the translators of the *Pārivāsika* understood that the *sāmagrī*, or "meeting," referred to here was to take place in the evening. Such a placement appears to conform to the time sequence implied in this set of duties, and so I have tried to combine both Tibetan renderings in my own translation. *BHSD* (s.v. *sāmagrī*) translates our sentence: "but at the time of a meeting he must arrange the seats"—in its actual context *punaḥ*, which Edgerton appears to translate as "but," must obviously mean "again." Śīlapālita's commentary on the *Kṣudraka* passage (*Āgamakṣudrakavyākhyāna*, Derge, bstan 'gyur, 'dul ba Dzu 44 a.2) appears to place the activity undertaken in regard to the *stūpa* also at the time of the evening meeting: *dus shes par byas la zhes bya ba ni nyi ma nub pa'i dus la tshogs pa'i dus so*.

16. Dutt's suggested emendation *dhūpakaṭacchuke* [*dhūpa*] has no support in the manuscript, which has only *dhūpakaṭacchuka* (not *-ke*; cf. n. 7 above), nor in the Tibetan translation of the *Pārivāsikavastu*, which has *pog por nye bar gzhag par bya'o* only. The *Kṣudrakavastu* parallel alone has *bdug pa dang bdug pa'i snod gzhag par bya*.

17. The Tibetan corresponding to what Dutt reads as *adya pakṣasya daśamīty* is *deng du zla ba byed kyi tshes bcu yang 'das lags so zhes bya ba*, "saying, 'Today the tenth day of the fortnight has also passed.'" This would again suggest that something has dropped out of the Sanskrit text. It has no word for "day" and no indication—adjective? suffix?—that it is a lapsed day. Moreover, although I cannot say for sure what the facsimile does say, it certainly does not say *daśamīty*. The last syllable looks more like *-īve* or *ndhe*. I have translated Dutt's text until this can be cleared up, perhaps by recourse to the manuscript itself or at least to a better reproduction.

18. For convenience's sake, see L. de La Vallée Poussin, *L'abhidharmakośa de vasubandhu* (Paris and Louvain: 1923–1931) T. III, 95ff.

19. S. Sasaki, "Buddhist Sects in the Aśoka Period (4)—The Structure of the Mahāsāṃghika Vinaya," *Buddhist Studies (Bukkyō Kenkyū)* 23 (1994) 55–100, esp. 63, 83, and n. 17.

20. *Kṣudrakavastu*, Derge, 'dul ba Tha 103b.6–104a.4 = Tog, 'dul ba Ta 157a.1–b.2. The Tog text is cited. There are the usual sorts of minor variants between the Derge and the Tog versions that will not be noted here.

21. In light of the uncertainty noted above (n. 6) in regard to where these drains are, it is worth noticing that here instructions referring to them are separated from instructions dealing with the privy by a *de nas*.

22. As already suggested at the end of n. 12 above, there is a good chance in light of the Tibetan translation of the *Pārivāsika* parallel—*dge slong ma yin pa'i 'du shes*—that the Tibetan translators, like Dutt, here did not recognize nor correctly resolve the *sandhi* operating in *-vartinābhikṣusaṃjñāṃ*, though this, of course, assumes that the original of the *Kṣudraka* had the same reading.

23. J.-U. Hartmann, "Fragmente aus dem Dīrghāgama der Sarvāstivādins," in *Sanskrit-Texte aus dem buddhistischen Kanon: Neuentdeckungen und Neueditionen* (Sanskrit-Wörterbuch der buddhistischen Texte aus den Turfan-Funden. Beiheft 2), Bearbeitet von F. Enomoto et al. (Göttingen: 1989) 37– 67, esp. 65–67.

24. *Vinayasūtra* (Sankrityayana) 76.19—on the *vihārasvāmin* and *vihāradevatā*, see below.

25. See, for example, *Vibhaṅga*, Derge, 'dul ba Ca 152b.3 = *'Dul ba pha'i gleng 'bum chen mo*, 'A 210b.3.

26. *Kṣudraka*, Derge, 'dul ba Tha 46b.7 = *'Dul ba pha'i gleng 'bum chen mo*, 'A 207b.5 = Śīlapālita, Derge, bstan 'gyur, 'dul ba Dzu 25a.7 = *Vinayasūtra* (Sankrityayana) 55.10.

27. For some interesting observations on the Buddhist uses of the term *ārṣa*, see D. S. Ruegg, "Allusiveness and Obliqueness in Buddhist Texts: Saṃdhā, Saṃdhi, Saṃdhyā and Abhisaṃdhi," in *Dialectes dans les littératures indo-aryennes*, ed. C. Caillat (Paris: 1989) 295–328, esp. 295–296, 320–321.

28. *Śayanāsanavastu* (Gnoli) 37.6 = *'Dul ba pha'i gleng 'bum chen mo*, 'A 389b.3.

29. *Kṣudraka*, Derge, 'dul ba Tha 198b.1 = *Vinayasūtra* (Sankrityayana) 87.29: *viśrāmasthāne gāthāṃ bhāṣetāṣā(?)m / pānīyagrahaṇasya ca / yasya tad pāyanīyaṃ tam uddiśya / aparāṃ ca devatām /*. The corruption *bhāṣetāṣā(?)m* can probably be corrected in light of the canonical text's *gtsug lag* to *bhāṣetārṣam*.

30. *Bhaiṣajyavastu*, GMs iii 1, 20.1. The Tibetan translation here—at least in Derge Kha 131b.2 and Tog Kha 170a.1—is corrupt. It has *gtsug lag khang gi tshigs su bcad pa* for what should be *gtsug lag gi* . . . . This must be a scribal error that crept into the translation in the course of its subsequent transmission, because it is hard to account for it as a mistranslation. *'Dul ba pha'i gleng 'bum chen mo*, 'A 351b.4, reproduces the corruption.

31. *Kṣudraka*, Derge, 'dul ba Tha 227a.2 = *Vinayasūtra* (Sankrityayana) 63.9 = *'Dul ba pha'i gleng 'bum chen mo*, 'A 44 b.4 and 248b.1.

32. *Kṣudraka*, Derge Tha 176a.1 = *Vinayasūtra* (Sankrityayana) 115.9 (*cāryāḥ gāthāḥ* here should probably be corrected to *ārṣāḥ gāthāḥ* in light of the canonical text [*gtsug lag gi tshigs su bcad pa*] and the Tibetan translation of the *Vinayasūtra* itself, although the Derge version of the latter also requires correction, for it has the same corruption noted in n. 30: *gtsug lag khang gi tshigs su bcad pa*, Derge, bstan 'gyur, 'dul ba Wu 96a.1; the Peking version has the expected *gtsug lag gi* . . . , Zu 104b.2) = *'Dul ba pha'i gleng 'bum chen mo*, 'A 397b.1.

33. *Kṣudraka*, Derge, 'dul ba Da 172b.5 = *'Dul ba pha'i gleng 'bum chen mo*, 'A 405b.1; for a detailed discussion of the canonical text, see G. Schopen, "The Suppression of Nuns and the Ritual Murder of Their Special Dead in Two Buddhist Monastic Texts," *JIP* 24 (1996) 563–592, esp. 575ff [= Ch. XI below, esp. 341ff].

34. *Vibhaṅga*, Derge Ca 155b.2; Cha 184a.6, 187b.3; Nya 146b.3; etc. Vinītadeva in his commentary on the first of these passages, for example, says: *tshigs su bcad pa'i dbyangs kyis zhes bya ba ni / rta brgya dang ni gser brgya dang / dre 'u dang shing rta brgya dag dang / zhes bya ba la sogs pa'i tshigs su bcad pa 'don bas so /* (Derge, bstan 'gyur, 'dul ba Tshu 64b.7). He in other words cites, as the appropriate verses for such a setting, a variant translation of the first line of a set of verses extolling the value of *padāvihāra* that occur at *Śayanāsana* (Gnoli) 16.1ff = Derge, 'dul ba Ga 196b.3ff. Though the term *padāvihāra* remains difficult—*BHSD* 505 says: "walking, marching on foot (refers to passing around a holy place to the right)"—the suitability of such verses seems clear enough.

35. This of course is not to say that other means might not have been used to determine time of day and date—observation of the sun or the regular course of the stars, for example. For comparative purposes see, for example, J. D. North, "Monasticism and the First Mechanical Clocks," in *The Study of Time II*, ed. J. T. Fraser and N. Lawrence (New York, Heidelberg, and Berlin: 1975) 381–398; J. Biarne, "Le temps du moine. d'après les premières règles monastiques d'occident (IV–VIe siècles)," in *Le temps chrétien de la fin de l'antiquité au moyen âge IIIe-XIIIe siècles* (Paris: 1984) 99–128; S. C. McCluskey, "Gregory of Tours, Monastic Timekeeping, and Early Christian Attitudes to Astronomy," *Isis* 81 (1990) 9–22.

36. J. Takakusu, *A Record of the Buddhist Religion as Practiced in India and the Malay Archipelago* (A.D. 671–695), by I-tsing (London: 1896) 143.

37. Takakusu, *A Record of the Buddhist Religion*, 143–146; see also O. von Hinüber, "Probleme der Technikgeschichte im alten Indien," *Saeculum* 29.3 (1978) 215–230, esp. 224–226.

38. R. P. Kangle, *The Kauṭilīya Arthaśāstra*, 2d ed. (Bombay: 1969) Part I, 1.7.8, 1.19.6, 2.20.34–35, 2.20.39.

39. For the sake of convenience, see the passages brought together in A. K. Warder, *Indian Buddhism* (Delhi: 1970) 502ff.

40. *Vibhaṅga*, Derge, 'dul ba Ca 153b.1–158b.7 = *'Dul ba pha'i gleng 'bum chen mo*, 'A 86b.5–88a.3.

41. *Vibhaṅga*, Derge, 'dul ba Cha 184a.1; Nya 141a.6, 146b.4, 147b.3. *Pravrajyāvastu*, (Näther/Vogel/Wille) ii 254.28, 273, 274–275, and n. 16.

42. *Kṣudraka*, Derge, 'dul ba Tha 7b.6–8 a.7 = *Vinayasūtra* (Sankrityayana) 54.25 = *'Dul ba pha'i gleng 'bum chen mo*, 'A 204a.6.

43. *Śayanāsana* (Gnoli) 38.15–39.5 = *Vinayasūtra* (Sankrityayana) 111.7 = *'Dul ba pha'i gleng 'bum chen mo*, 'A 390a.1.

44. *'Dul ba'i mdo*, Derge, bstan 'gyur, 'dul ba Wu 17b.3.

45. *'Dul ba rnam par 'byed pa'i tshig rnam par bshad pa*, Derge, bstan 'gyur, 'dul ba Tshu 65b.2.

46. J. F. Fleet, "The Ancient Indian Water-Clock," *JRAS* (1915) 224. Fleet also treats here the passages on the measurement of time in the *Śārdūlakarṇāvadāna*, ch. 33 of the *Divyāvadāna*.

47. Part of the obstacle to a clearer understanding may of course be related to Tibetan lexicography. All of the sources directly related to our passage—the *Vibhaṅga* itself, Vinītadeva, and Bu-ston—all use the same term, *dus kyi 'khor lo*, the standard equivalent of which is *kālacakra*, as in the famous *tantra* of that name. But I have found it nowhere else used to refer to a device to measure time. I-ching's *velācakra*, on the other hand, occurs in the *Mahāvyutpatti*, but its Tibetan equivalent is there given as "<*nyi/nying* N> *tshod kyi 'khor lo*" (*A New Critical Edition of the Mahāvyutpatti* [Tokyo: 1989] Vol. 1, no. 9092 = S.9157), and, as *BHSD* 509 points out, *velācakra* itself is problematic, having several Chinese and Japanese renderings. *nyi tshod*—but not *nyi tshod 'khor lo*—is listed in *Bod rgya tshig mdzod chen mo* (950) and defined first as *nyi ma'i dus tshod*, but then it is clearly distinguished from *chu tshod* (which Jäschke defines as "the clepsydra or water-clock of ancient India . . . clock in general, *chu tshod 'khar lo*, a wheel clock"): *chu tshod med skabs nyi tshod la bltas na dus tshod snga phyi shes thub*. It is at least worth noting that the *Mahāvyutpatti*, like our *Vibhaṅga* passage, lists a device for marking time together with the *gaṇḍī* and *gaṇḍīkoṭanaka*, and that both list them in the same order. But much still needs to be sorted out here.

48. North, "Monasticism and the First Mechanical Clocks," 382.

49. *Vibhaṅga*, Derge, 'dul ba Ca 159b.3 = *'Dul ba pha'i gleng 'bum chen mo*, 'A 88 a.6 (although there is no reason to assume that the redactors of this text knew it, the actual Jetavana was located "about 500 meters" from the mud and [later] brick rampart walls of Śrāvastī; K. K. Sinha, *Excavations at Śravasti—1959* [Varanasi: 1967]); *Poṣadhavastu* (Hu-von Hinüber) § 19.2 = *'Dul ba pha'i gleng 'bum chen mo*, 'A 251a.7; *Śayanāsana* (Gnoli) 41.11 = *'Dul ba pha'i gleng 'bum chen mo*, 'A 127b.3.

50. See, for the moment, G. Schopen, "If You Can't Remember, How to Make It Up: Some Monastic Rules for Redacting Canonical Texts," in *Bauddhavidyāsudhākaraḥ*, 581 n. 30 [= Ch. XIV below, 402 n. 30].

51. For the moment, again, note that the passages cited, for example, in A. Bareau, "La construction et le culte des stūpa d'après les vinayapiṭaka," *BEFEO* 50 (1960) 229–274, from the [*Mūlasarvāstivāda*]*nidānamātṛkā*, Taishō 1452, almost always have clear parallels in the *Uttaragrantha(s)*; so too do the passages on art, architecture, and images cited from the same source in E. Zürcher, "Buddhist Art in Medieval China: The Ecclesiastical View," *Function and Meaning in Buddhist Art. Proceedings of a Seminar Held at Leiden University*, October 21–24, 1991, ed. K. R. van Kooij and H. van der Veere (Groningen: 1995) 1–20. Note incidentally that most of the material in the final sections of Guṇaprabha's *Vinayasūtra* on *stūpas* and images is also based on the *Uttaragrantha(s)*.

52. G. Schopen, "Doing Business for the Lord: Lending on Interest and Written Loan Contracts in the *Mūlasarvāstivāda-vinaya*," *JAOS* 114 (1994) 543 [= Ch. III above, 66], where I was unable to locate the text that Guṇaprabha cited at Derge, bstan 'gyur, 'dul ba Zhu 165b.1 as coming from the *Ma mo*. It now appears that a version of that passage—or a variant Tibetan translation of the passage—occurs at *Uttaragrantha*, Derge, 'dul ba Pa 265a.6. There are some interesting differences in the two texts or translations, but their essential similarity can hardly be in doubt.

53. A. C. Banerjee, *Sarvāstivāda Literature* (Calcutta: 1957) 99–100.

54. Even when the *Uttaragrantha* appears to "repeat" a text or topic that occurs elsewhere in the *Mūlasarvāstivāda-vinaya*—and there is a significant number of such cases—it is by no means obvious that the version found elsewhere is necessarily earlier, and in some cases there is actual evidence that it is not. In G. Schopen, "Monastic Law Meets the Real World: A Monk's Continuing Right to Inherit Family Property in Classical India," *HR* 35 (1995) 101–123 [= Ch. VI above], for example, I treated in some detail a text from the *Kṣudrakavastu* dealing with the rights of Buddhist monks to family property even after their ordination. Now it turns out that the *Uttaragrantha* has what appears to be a similar text (Derge, 'dul ba Pa 130a.4–131a.3 = *'Dul ba pha'i gleng 'bum chen mo*, 'A 294b.6ff). The text in the *Kṣudraka* says that when the monk's father died, he thought that he should return home to recite Dharma for, and give consolation to, his "foster mother (*ma yar mo*) and elder brothers," and I noted the difficulty that the use of the term "foster mother" created because there was no prior reference to a "foster mother" in the text or any indication that the monk's actual mother was no longer available. Curiously, the *Uttaragrantha* "version" of the text uses exactly the same expression—*ma yar mo*—but here, and here alone, is it appropriate, for the *Uttaragrantha* had already indicated that the monk's own mother had died and that his father had remarried. This little detail, in other words, suggests that the text in the *Kṣudraka* was in fact a careless adaptation of the text in the *Uttaragrantha* and therefore later.

55. *Uttaragrantha*, Derge, 'dul ba Pa 71b.4–74a.2 = *'Dul ba pha'i gleng 'bum chen mo*, 'A 257b.7–258b.4 = *Vinayasūtra* (Sankrityayana) 76.16–.23.

56. *Rjes su gnang ba* = *anujñā-*. Although unfortunately still not always heeded, H. Bechert has pointed out more than once that forms of this verb in this kind of *vinaya* context have been "generally mistranslated": "This word [*anujānāmi*] has been generally mistranslated here as 'I allow.' Its meaning in this context is clearly 'I order' or 'I command.' The imperative form of the command is emphasized by the part. fut. pass." H. Bechert, "Some

Remarks on the Kaṭhina Rite," *Journal of the Bihar Research Society* 54 (1968) 320–321; Bechert, "The Laws of the Buddhist Sangha: An Early Juridical System in Indian Tradition," *Hokke-bunka kenkyū* 19 (1993) 7. But note too that the problem goes beyond *vinaya* law—see J. D. M. Derrett, "'Must' and 'Ought': Problems of Translation in Sanskritic Hindu Law," in *Language and Thought. Anthropological Issues*, ed. W. C. McCormack and S. A. Wurm (The Hague and Paris: 1977) 251–259.

57. *Poṣadhavastu* (Hu-von Hinüber) §§ 3.2ff = *'Dul ba pha'i gleng 'bum chen mo*, 'A 250b.7ff.

58. See the references in n. 26 above.

59. Schopen, "If You Can't Remember"; in that essay, I noted the "distinct possibility that parallel sets of rules may still come to light in other *vinayas*" (n. 25), and one such set already had! I had overlooked the paraphrase of a passage from the *Mahāsāṅghika-vinaya* given in Sasaki, "Buddhist Sects in the Aśoka Period (4)" (n. 19 above): "(Regulation concerning reciting the *nava-aṅga-vacana*: if a *bhikṣu* forgets the place where the Buddha preached while reciting a *sūtra*, he may select and use the name of one of eight famous places)" (p. 71). See also *'Dul ba pha'i gleng 'bum chen mo*, 'A 408a.6; *Vinayasūtra* (Sankrityayana) 118.30; *Svavyākhyānābhidhānavinayasūtravṛtti*, Derge, bstan 'gyur, 'dul ba Zu 267b.6.

60. *Kṣudraka*, Derge, 'dul ba Tha 256a.6–258a.3; cf. H. Durt, "Chū," *Hōbōgirin* 5 (Paris and Tokyo: 1979) 431–456.

61. *Vinayasūtra* (Sankrityayana) 76.16. Note the term *śalākā* here. What is almost certainly the same, or a similar, device also appears to be described in a similar context in the Chinese translation of the *Mahāsāṅghika-vinaya*: ". . . si on craint d'oublier [the day], il faut prendre des fiches et une corde, enfiler, et suspendre devant la salle d'explication ou devant le réfectoire. Le directeur des occupations (. . . *karmadāna*) 'préposé au mois' . . . chaque jour enlève une fiche" (S. Levi et Éd. Chavannes, "Quelques titres énigmatiques dans la hiérarchie ecclésiastique du bouddhisme indien," *JA* (1915) 204.

62. Schopen, "The Lay Ownership of Monasteries," 82ff.

63. *Kṣudraka*, Derge, 'dul ba Tha 230b.2 = *'Dul ba pha'i gleng 'bum chen mo*, 'A 135a.4; cf. Schopen, "The Lay Ownership of Monasteries," 109–112 and n. 60.

64. The expression *dge slong gcig gis rgan rims kyi dang por 'dug la* . . . here is a little odd or circuitous. Normally it seems the person so seated would have been the *saṃghasthavira*.

65. The role of "the gods of the *vihāra*" in Mūlasarvāstivādin monasteries remains to be studied and potentially of great interest. For some references to "gods" associated with monasteries, see *Kṣudraka*, Derge, 'dul ba Tha 223a.3 (*rgyal byed kyi tshal na sangs rgyas la mngon par dad pa'i lha dang / klu dang / gnod sbyin dag 'dug pas* . . .) = *'Dul ba pha'i gleng 'bum chen mo*, 'A 76a.6; *Bhaiṣajyavastu*, Derge, 'dul ba Kha 1a.2 (*rgyal bu rgyal byed kyi tshal na gnas pa'i lha* . . .) = *Divyāvadāna* (Cowell and Neil) 46.21 (*jetavananivāsinī devatā*).

66. The text has a concluding section of a rather technical nature dealing with the problems of adjusting the lunar calendar that should be read in conjunction with, and added to, the important discussion in C. Vogel, "On the Date of the Poṣadha Ceremony as Taught by the Mūlasarvāstivādins," in *Bauddhavidyāsudhākaraḥ*, 673–686. This section is also briefly treated in the *Vinayasūtra* (76.23), where the term *ūnarātra-* is used.

67. It might, perhaps, have been noticed that in many of the previous notes when reference was made to passages in the canonical *Vinaya*, they were followed by parallel references to the *'Dul ba pha'i gleng 'bum chen mo*, and it might be that this work is not well known to some. As noted along the way, this work was written—perhaps compiled is more accurate—by the famous Tibetan polymath Bu-ston Rin po che of the thirteenth and fourteenth centuries. But in spite of its title it is far more than a collection of "stories" from the *Vinaya*. It is, rather, a condensed version of the *entire Mūlasarvāstivāda-vinaya*, reducing some 4,000 folios of Tibetan to about 420. It follows the rearrangement of the canonical material effected by Guṇaprabha in his *Vinayasūtra*, bringing together in one place passages dealing with the same or closely related topics that are scattered throughout the canonical collection. It therefore retains the great advantage gained by Guṇaprabha's work, but it also goes a long way toward avoiding its major disadvantage. Guṇaprabha's condensation was achieved by a degree of concision and economy of expression that not infrequently renders the *Vinayasūtra* all but incomprehensible on its own—hence the *Vinayasūtra* itself quickly generated four commentaries of almost two thousand folios. Bu-ston's work, on the other hand, by not restating the canonical text in tight *sūtras*, can by and large be read on its own. It is a remarkable work and deserves to be better known. Some sense of its completeness can be seen in the previous notes, and it—unlike the canonical *Vinaya* in its entirety—might actually be translatable by one person in something less than a lifetime. It should also be noted that—as is clear from its title—the *'Dul ba pha'i gleng 'bum chen mo* does not deal with the *Bhikṣuṇī-vinaya*. That is dealt with in a separate, much smaller work of Bu-ston's entitled *'Dul ba dge slong ma'i gleng 'bum*, at the end of which Bu-ston once again suggests that the *Bhikṣuṇīvibhaṅga* translated into Tibetan does not belong to the Mūlasarvāstivādin tradition; see C. Vogel, "Bu-ston on the Schism of the Buddhist Church and on the Doctrinal Tendencies of Buddhist Scriptures," in *Zur Schulzugehörigkeit von Werken der Hīnāyāna-Literatur*, T. I, ed. H. Bechert (Göttingen: 1985) 110. The *'Dul ba dge slong ma'i gleng 'bum* is in the same volume of Bu-ston's collected works as the *'Dul ba pha'i gleng 'bum chen mo*.

CHAPTER X

Ritual Rights and Bones of Contention

More on Monastic Funerals and Relics in the *Mūlasarvāstivāda-vinaya*

IT IS BEGINNING to appear that the treatment of dead monks in Buddhist monastic communities may turn out to be a lively issue. There has in the last few years been a trickle of papers and parts of books addressing the issue and—in Buddhist studies—such trickles are usually as close as we get to a flood. Much of this work has dealt with China and Japan. That work is detailed, historically textured, and theoretically interesting.[1] The work on India, however, has been—as it usually is by comparison—thin and uneven. Especially in regard to the treatment of textual sources dealing with monastic funerals, the presentation of the Indian material is inadequate. The one paper I know of lacks anything like historical boundaries; is limited largely to one monastic Order, and even then to only a part of that order's monastic code; and is flawed by a tendency toward premature generalization.[2]

I cannot, of course, presume to solve all these problems but here only hope to widen the evidential base for the discussion of monastic funerals in the one Indian Order that has received some attention, the Mūlasarvāstivāda Order. In so doing, statements already made can be corrected, qualified, or assigned to the bin.

Certainly one of the things about the *Mūlasarvāstivāda-vinaya* that makes, and will continue to make, any generalization in regard to it precarious, if not entirely foolhardy, is its size. It has been referred to in the scholarly literature as "this enormous *vinaya*," as "monumental" and "huge," as an "enormous compilation" or a "vast compilation," as an "immense pot-pourri of Buddhist discipline," and—perhaps most accurately—as "this monstrous Vinaya . . . in itself a canon already complete."[3] In its complete form presented in Tibetan translation it consists, depending on the "edition," of from twelve to sixteen bulky volumes. Probably few, if any, modern scholars apart from Csoma, who was stuck in an unheated monastic

---

Originally published in *Journal of Indian Philosophy* 22 (1994) 31–80. Reprinted with stylistic changes with permission of Kluwer Academic Publishers.

cell for a long Himalayan [32] winter, have been able to read all of it even quickly, let alone carefully study it. I have not, and each time I dip into it I find more and more of interest.[4]

What has been reported so far, though presented under the subtitle "Monastic Funerals in the *Mūlasarvāstivāda-vinaya*," reflects—and that imperfectly—only what is found in two sections of this "monstrous Vinaya," the *Vinayavastu* and the *Vinayakṣudrakavastu*, which correspond roughly to what in the Pāli *Vinaya* is called the *Khandaka*. These two sections contain at least two separate, though similar, sets of formal rules governing the performance of monastic funerals, and a significant number of narrative references to such funerals or to elements thereof. This might suggest that the topic was of some concern to the monk or monks who compiled these two sections of the *Mūlasarvāstivāda-vinaya*, but it tells us nothing about the extent of that concern, or whether it is addressed as well in other sections of this *Vinaya*, notably in the Mūlasarvāstivādin *Vinayavibhaṅga*, the counterpart to the Pāli *Suttavibhaṅga*. It also does not tell us about the presence or absence of this concern in what may have been, from a historical point of view, an even more important part of an Order's *vinaya* literature.

Charles Hallisey has suggested recently:

> Theravādins found the [canonical] *Vinaya* both too little and too much. They found it too little in so far as the canonical text required elucidation and clarification, and as a result, massive commentaries and glossaries were written on it. . . . They found it too much in so far as the size of the canonical *Vinaya* made it unwieldy and they consequently wrote diverse summaries and compendiums. . . . Such works were written to present the *Vinaya*'s practical message in a more manageable fashion. . . . This associated literature makes relating the canonical *Vinaya* to actual practice in diverse contexts more complex than has generally been admitted by students of Buddhism.[5]

The suggestion here may allow in turn at least the possibility that the Pāli *Vinaya* reached the typical monk—if it reached him at all—not in its canonical form but in the form of "summaries," "compendiums," or "handbooks" and that it was sources of this sort that had some impact on actual monastic behavior.

Obviously, if the Theravādins had problems with an "unwieldy" *vinaya*, the Mūlasarvāstivādins might well have been overwhelmed, and they would have had even more pressing need for "the *Vinaya*'s [33] practical message in more manageable form." Although we know much less about them, the Mūlasarvāstivādins too did indeed produce "summaries" and "compendiums" of their *vinaya*, the most authoritative of which seems to have been Guṇaprabha's *Vinayasūtra*, with its auto-commentary, the *Svavyākhyānābhidhānavinayasūtravṛtti*. If, in fact, the

Mūlasarvāstivāda-vinaya too reached the majority of its monks in the form of "summaries," then clearly it will be important to determine what such a summary has to say about monastic funerals if we are to get a sense of the significance that such ritual forms might have had over time.[6]

What is presented here, then, is intended to address these specific lacunae, to correct, as I said above, some of what has gone before, and to provide a more comprehensive *sketch*, though by no means a complete study, of the place of monastic funerals in *Mūlasarvāstivāda-vinaya* sources. Nothing more.

We can start with the observation that rules regarding monastic funerals in the *Mūlasarvāstivāda-vinaya* are not, indeed, found only in its *Vinayavastu* or *Kṣudrakavastu*. There is as well at least one set of such rules in its *Vinayavibhaṅga*. They occur as a part of the long account devoted to the 80th *Pāyantikā* rule, which makes it an offense for a monk to enter a village at an "irregular," or "wrong," time except when there is a reason (*anyatra tadrūpāt pratyayāt*), and they are promulgated in connection with the death of the Monk Kālodāyin. Kālodāyin was designated by the Buddha as "the Best of Those (Monks) Who Make Families Pious" (*kulaprasādakānāṃ . . . agro*),[7] and several stories are given—one quite funny[8]—illustrating his power to convert. But a married woman who has been sleeping with the leader of a group of thieves is afraid that the Monk Kālodāyin has found her out and conspires with her lover to kill the monk. The monk is enticed into a house—and below we pick up the account from that point, translating from the Ṭibetan text of the Derge edition found in the Taipei reprint.[9]

The Funeral of the Monk Kālodāyin

Vinayavibhaṅga

(Derge Nya 65a.2–66a.4)

The ringleader of thieves, having pulled his sword from its sheath, waited at the door. [34]

Then the Venerable Udāyin came out, and the ringleader, with a mind devoid of compassion and without concern for the other world, severed his head, and it fell to the ground.

An old woman saw him killing the Noble One and standing there—"Who is this," she said, "who has done such a rash thing?"

The ringleader said: "You must tell no one or I will make sure that you too end up in the same condition!"

She was terrified and was then unable to speak. Thinking that perhaps someone following the tracks of the Eminent One would come by later,[10] she—given the circumstances—remained silent.

The two of them, with minds devoid of compassion and without concern for the other world, hiding the body of the Venerable Udāyin in a heap of rubbish, left it there.

That day the Monk-in-Charge-of-the-Fortnightly-Gathering, sitting at the seniors' end of the assembly, said: "Has someone determined the inclination of the Reverend Udāyin? The Reverend Udāyin is not here."

Then the Blessed One said to the monks: "Monks, that one who is the Best of Those Who Make Families Pious has been killed. His monastic robes must be brought back, and the honors for his body should be performed!"

The Blessed One set forth until having been stopped by the gate of Śrāvastī. The Blessed One then caused a brightness like that of gold to shoot forth. He filled all of Śrāvastī with a luminosity like that of pure gold.

Prasenajit, the King who had arisen in Kośala, thought to himself: "Why (65b) has all of Śrāvastī been filled with a luminosity like that of pure gold?" He thought further: "Without a doubt, the Blessed One wishes to come!"

Together with his retinue of wives, and taking the key to the city, he unlocked the gate, and the Blessed One entered Śrāvastī.

Prasenajit, the King who had arisen in Kośala, thought: "But why has the Blessed One come into Śrāvastī at an irregular time?" But since Buddhas, Blessed Ones, are not easy to approach and are difficult to resist, he was incapable of putting a question to the Buddha, the Blessed One.

The Blessed One, together with the community of disciples, having gone ahead, Prasenajit, the King who had arisen in Kośala, together with his retinue of wives, went following everywhere behind the Blessed One, until they came to the place where that heap of rubbish was.

The Blessed One then addressed the monks: "Monks, he who was the Best of Those Who Make Families Pious is hidden here. Remove him!"

He was removed, and those who had depended on the Venerable Udāyin, seeing there what had truly happened in regard to the Noble One, said: "Since he was our Good Spiritual Friend, does the Blessed One allow us to perform the honors for his body?"

The Blessed One did not allow it.

Prasenajit, the King who had arisen in Kośala, said: "Since he was a friend of mine from our youth, does the Blessed One allow me to perform the honors for his body?"

The Blessed One did not allow it.

The Queen Mālikā said: "Since he was my teacher, does the Blessed One allow me to perform the honors for his body?"

The Blessed One allowed it. [35]

The Queen Mālikā, then, having had the dirt removed from the body of the Venerable Udāyin with chalk, had it bathed with perfumed water. Having adorned a bier with various-colored cotton cloths, she put the body onto it and arranged it.

Then the Blessed One, together with the community of disciples, having gone ahead, the King, together with his retinue of wives, went following behind them.

Having put the bier down at an open, extensive spot, Queen Mālikā, heaping up a pile all of aromatic woods, cremated the body. She extinguished the pyre with milk, and having put the bones into a golden pot, she had a mortuary *stūpa* erected at a crossing of four great roads. Raising an umbrella, a banner, and a flag, doing honor with perfumes, strings of garlands, incense, aromatic powders, and musical instruments, she venerated both its feet.[11] After that, the Blessed One, having assigned the reward, departed.

In addition to a number of details concerning the language of the text, there are as well several interrelated points of interest in this account, most of which cluster around the exhortation attributed to the Buddha that signals the beginning of monastic participation in the affair. The Buddha is made to say: "Monks, that one who is the Best of Those Who Make Families Pious has been killed. His monastic robes must be brought back, and the honors for his body should be performed": *dge slong dag khyim dad par byed pa rnams kyi mchog de bsad kyis / chos gos dag long shig dang de'i lus la mchod pa bya'o.* There are, as it were, two injunctions here, two matters of monastic concern: attending to the deceased monk's property, and attending to the deceased monk's body. Both concerns are addressed elsewhere in the *Mūlasarvāstivāda-vinaya*. In the set of rules governing monastic funerals in the *Cīvaravastu* of the *Vinayavastu*, the distribution of the deceased monk's property is, in fact, the central issue, and proper attendance to the body is made a precondition to its successful and proper completion.[12] Elsewhere in the *Cīvaravastu* several long paragraphs are given over to ruling on what should occur when a monk dies at a monastery other than his "own," and the central concern is, again, with the property of the dead monk. Typical of the form and content of these paragraphs is the following case: *upagatakānām āvāse anupagatako bhikṣur āgatya kālaṃ kuryāt. upagatakair anupagatakānāṃ dūto 'nupreṣayitavyaḥ. sabrahmacārī vaḥ kālagataḥ. haratāsya pātracīvaram iti.* ("A monk who has not entered into the retreat there, having come, might die in a parish of those who have entered the retreat there. Those who have entered the retreat there must send a [36] messenger to those who have not, saying 'A fellow monk of yours has died. You must come and get his bowl and robe!'")[13] The wording here, though clumsy in translation, makes it clear that the status of "fellow monks" (*sabrahmacārin*) is determined by where a monk has entered into retreat and that fellow monks have a right to, and responsibility to go and get, the estate of a deceased fellow monk regardless of where he might die. These rulings also occasionally are given narrative expression. Perhaps the most famous account—and one we will return to—concerns the death of Śāriputra. After Śāriputra's death, according to the Tibetan *Kṣudrakavastu*, the following occurred:

His attending novice (*dge sbyong gi ched*) Cunda performed the honors for the body on the remains of the Venerable Śāriputra (*tshe dang ldan pa śā ri'i bu'i ring bsrel*

> *la lus kyis mchod pa byas te*), and taking the remains (*ring bsrel*), his bowl and monastic robes, set off for Rājagṛha. Going in due order, he arrived at Rājagṛha. . . . Being seated to one side, the attending novice Cunda said this to the Venerable Ānanda: "Reverend Ānanda, you should know that my preceptor (*mkhan po*), the Reverend Śāriputra, has entered into final nirvāṇa—these are his remains and his bowl and monastic robes."[14]

All of these considerations seem to be telescoped into the first part of the injunction attributed to the Buddha in our account of the death of Kālodāyin: "His monastic robes must be brought back." But the second part of this injunction is also of interest.

The Buddha is made to say in regard to the Monk Kālodāyin: *dge slong dag . . . de'i lus la mchod pa bya'o*, "Monks . . . the honors for his body should be performed!" This same injunction occurs elsewhere, and there is virtually no doubt about what it translates. Significantly, as we will see, the first statement Guṇaprabha makes in his *Vinayasūtra*, in regard to monastic funerals is *tshangs pa mtshungs par spyod pa shi ba'i lus la mchod pa bya'o*, "Honor is to be done to the body of a deceased fellow monk." But such an injunction had already occurred in the *Cīvaravastu*, and for that we have the Sanskrit: *bhagavān āha*: *bhikṣubhis tasya pūrvaṃ śarīrapūjā kartavyeti*, "The Blessed One said: 'By the monks the honor for the body of him (i.e., the deceased monk) is first to be performed" (*dge slong rnams kyis sngar de'i ro* [= *lus*] *la mchod pa byas la* . . .).[15] What the Buddha is made to say in the account of the death of Kālodāyin is, then, that the monks have an obligation to perform what in these texts is commonly, though not [37] exclusively, called *śarīra-pūjā*. In the context of the 80th *Pāyantikā* rule in which this account occurs, the monastic obligation to perform *śarīra-pūjā* is apparently important enough to abrogate the otherwise strict rule against entering a village at an "irregular," or "wrong," time (*dus ma yin par*).

It has recently been suggested that the term *śarīra-pūjā* in Sanskrit and its equivalent in Pāli have given rise to some major textual and historical misinterpretations. Though the term has been habitually taken to refer to the "worship of relics," a close examination of the texts themselves does not seem to support such an interpretation, and the evidence appears to be overwhelming that the term originally—and for a long time—referred to the ritual handling or preparation of the body prior to cremation, though sometimes it seems also to include the latter.[16] Although it is true that the term *śarīra-pūjā* is not always used in accounts of monastic funerals, the terms that are used in its place only strengthen the suggestion that it refers to the ritual preparation of a dead body. We find, for example, phrases like *bhikṣavas tam ādāya dahanaṃ gatāḥ . . . bhikṣavas tam ādahane saṃskārya vihāram āgatāḥ*, "The monks, having taken that (i.e., the dead monk's body) up, had gone to the cremation . . . after having performed the funeral ceremonies for him at the cremation ground, the monks returned to the *vihāra*"; or *bhikṣavas tam ādahanaṃ nītvā saṃskārya vihāram āgatāḥ*, which is almost identical.[17] Likewise in the rules governing monastic funerals in the *Kṣudrakavastu* the Buddha is made to say *dge slong dag de lta bas na gnang gis dge slong shi ba'i rim gro bya'o*, "Now then, monks, with my authorization, funeral ceremonies for a deceased monk are to be performed."[18] Where elsewhere the term *śarīra-pūjā* is used, here in exactly the same sort of contexts we find *saṃskārya* and *rim gro bya*. All these terms are clearly interchangeable, but *saṃskārya* and *rim gro bya* can in such cases only denote "funeral ceremonies" directed toward the body. The fact that they are used interchangeably with *śarīra-pūjā* would seem to confirm that this is what that term too denoted.[19]

Although, then, it is virtually certain that all these texts are mandating or referring to funeral ceremonies, to the ritual handling of a dead monk's body, it is still not certain what was included in such ceremonies or what *śarīra-pūjā* entailed. It is here that our *Vinaya*[38]*vibhaṅga* passage is able to add one detail. It contains one of the very few references I have met so far to what one would expect to have been a common element of such procedures. Having gained permission to perform the *śarīra-pūjā* for the Monk Kālodāyin, Queen Mālikā first had "the dirt removed from the body of the Venerable Udāyin with chalk" (*tshe dang ldan pa 'char ka'i lus de sa dkar gyis dril phyi byed du bcug nas*). This is the only reference I know to the use of "chalk" in such a context. In fact, I am not sure what *sa dkar* refers to here. The only Sanskrit equivalent in Chandra's *Tibetan-Sanskrit Dictionary* for *sa dkar* is *makkola*, which seems to mean "chalk," but also "white-wash," "plaster." The standard Tibetan dictionaries, moreover, give *sa dkar* as the same as *dkar rtsi*, "whitewash, consisting of lime or some other earthy colour." In any case, there is a good chance that this operation may have been exceptional, being necessitated by the fact that the body had first been dumped in a heap of garbage.[20] The second operation that Queen Mālikā had performed, however, was probably much more standard.

Our text says that "having had the dirt removed from the body," Queen Mālikā "had it bathed with perfumed water" (*spos chus 'khur bcug ste*). Given that the body had already been cleaned, this obviously was not the function of this procedure, and in fact some form of purely ritual washing of the corpse is an extremely common element in funeral practices almost everywhere. But although such ritual washing may have formed a common element of *śarīra-pūjā*, I have so far only met with one other reference to something even like it. In a curious story in the *Vinayavibhaṅga* concerning a monk appropriately named Mahākāla, people began to suspect—because Mahākāla "was one who obtained everything from a cemetery" (*thams cad dur khrod pa dang ldan pa yin te*)—that he was eating corpses. Some brahmin boys decided to try to find out. They said, "One of us should pretend to be a dead person; the rest of us will perform the honors in the cemetery" (*bdag cag las gcig shi ba'i cha lugs su byas pa de bdag cag gis dur khrod du bkur bar bya'o*). As a part of this "performance," the text says the "dead body" was "anointed with bdellium and oil" (*yang ba dang l'bru mar gyis bskus te*).[21]

Again, although explicit reference to a bier adorned with colored cloths is a common element of secular funerals described in these [39] *vinaya* texts,[22] there are few such references in the accounts of monastic funerals. Apart from our account of the funeral of Kālodāyin, such biers are, however, also mentioned in the account of the funeral of Mahāprajāpatī found in the *Kṣudrakavastu*.[23]

But in addition to the washing or anointing of the corpse and the use of biers, our text also presents us with two other elements not noted before: explicit reference to the erection of a *stūpa* as, seemingly, a part of the funeral ritual itself; and the performance of the *śarīra-pūjā* for a monk by a layperson. In regard to the first, it has been maintained—somewhat disconcertingly—both that "it appears . . . that at least Mūlasarvāstivāda texts do not seem to link funeral activity per se with the erection of *stūpas* for the local monastic dead" and that "the construction of a *stūpa*—if it is included at all—signaled the end of *śarīra-pūjā*, not its beginnings."[24] Obviously we cannot have it both ways, and our text—the first Mūlasarvāstivādin text so far reported explicitly to "link" funeral activity with the making of a *stūpa*—makes the first assertion no longer viable, but it also points to another problem: the term *stūpa*—like the term *vihāra*—is used as if it had a single known referent, as if, in other words, we all know what we and our texts are talking about. But the *stūpa* referred to in the account of Kālodāyin's funeral cannot possibly be the sort of thing we find in books on Buddhist architecture, if for no other reason than it was, as it were, built in a day. For the narrator of our text, the washing of the body, the procession, the cremation, the collecting of the bones, and the erection of the *stūpa* were clearly conceived of only as different moments in a single process: they all took place on the same day. If nothing else, the conclusion of our account would indicate this. The rules governing monastic funerals in the *Cīvaravastu*, the *Kṣudrakavastu*, and, as we will see, Guṇaprabha's *Vinayasūtra* all agree that the final moment in the actual funeral, the final act before the participants in the funeral disperse, is the assigning of the reward or merit of a recitation of Dharma to the deceased (*tam uddiśya dharmaśravaṇaṃ dattvā dakṣiṇāṃ uddiśya*; *yon bsngo zhing rgyun chags gsum gyi chos mnyan pa byin nas 'dong bar bya'o*; *chos mnyan pa dang yon bshad pa dag bya'o*). But this final act of a monastic funeral does not take place in our text until after Mālikā has had the *stūpa* erected, and the Buddha himself is continuously present narratively throughout all of the pro[40]cedures. It is only after Mālikā has had the *stūpa* raised, has honored it, and has "venerated its feet," that the Buddha, "having assigned the reward," is said to have departed (. . . *gdugs dang / rgyal mtshan dang / ba dan bsgreng zhing / dri dang / phreng brgyu dang / bdug spos dang / phye ma dang / sil snyan dag gis mchod pa byas / rkang pa gnyis la phyag 'tshal nas / bcom ldan 'das kyis yon bshad pa mdzad de gshegs so /*).

Considerations of this kind would seem effectively to rule out the possibility that the *stūpa* envisioned was a major architectural form, and an old observation of A. H. Longhurst is undoubtedly here—and in many other cases—pertinent:

> The famous *stūpas* of Bharhut, Sāñchī and Amarāvati have been so often described and illustrated by different writers on Indian art, that one is apt to regard these once magnificent Buddhist shrines as typical examples of *stūpas*; but as a matter of fact, *stūpas* of this class were the exception. . . . The *stūpas* erected over the remains of ordinary members of the Buddhist community were very humble little structures. The ashes of the dead were placed in an earthenware pot and covered with a lid, and the humble little *stūpas* erected over it. Plenty of Buddhist *stūpas* of this class may still be seen in the Madras Presidency and also in Ceylon.[25]

It is quite likely, then, that it was a "very humble little structure" of this kind that our account of the funeral of Kālodāyin is referring to and that, indeed, the construction of a *stūpa* "of this class" may well "have signaled the end of *śarīra-pūjā*, not its beginnings."[26] The "humble" nature of these little structures may explain why we have so little certain knowledge of them in the archaeological record, but the recognition of this class of humble funeral *stūpa* does not in itself completely solve the problem of the relationship of Buddhist funeral activity to what might more legitimately be called a cult of relics. Some further clarification, however, might be had by looking at the second of the additional elements noted above that have so far been found only in the *Vinayavibhaṅga*'s account of Kālodāyin's funeral.

We have already had occasion to cite the injunctions attributed to the Buddha in regard to the imperative to perform *śarīra-pūjā* for a deceased fellow monk. They all either, like that in the *Cīvaravastu*, explicitly declare that it is to be performed by monks (*bhikṣubhis tasya pūrvaṃ śarīra-pūjā kartavyeti*) or, like that in the *Vinayasūtra*, occur in contexts where this is clearly implicit. In narrative references to the funerals of monks it is, as well, virtually always monks [41] who perform those funerals, and even in accounts where there is some reference to a lay presence—as in the account of the funeral of Mahāprajāpatī—it is the monks who feel the obligation, and the monks who have the active role. When the Nun Mahāprajāpatī dies and monks in various distant places become aware of it, the text says those monks thought, "If the person of the Buddha passed away into final *nirvāṇa*, we would go to take care of the performance of the superior honors for his body" (*sangs rgyas kyi sku yongs su mya ngan las 'das na / de'i lus la mchod pa lhag par bya ba la brtson par byas 'dong ngo snyam nas*), and then set off for her residence to do so. Monks too are explicitly said to have even carried her bier, and the biers of the nuns who died with her, and to have performed "the great honor": "The Venerables Nanda, Aniruddha, Ānanda, and Rāhula then lifted up the bier of Mahāprajāpatī Gautamī. The Blessed One also held on to it with his right hand. The remaining monks too lifted up the biers of the remaining nuns. Then performing the great honor, having carried them away, they laid the biers down at an appropriate, isolated spot" (*de nas tshe dang ldan pa dga' bo dang / ma 'gags pa dang / kun dga' bo dang / sgra gcan zin gyis skye dgu'i bdag mo chen mo go'u ta mi'i khyogs bteg go / bcom ldan 'das kyis kyang phyag g-yas pas bzung ngo / dge slong lhag ma rnams kyis kyang / dge slong ma lhag ma rnams kyi khyogs bteg go / de nas mchod pa chen po byas te khyer nas / sa phyogs bar skabs dben par khyogs rnams bzhag go /*).[27] The laypersons present—and there is a large group of them, including King Prasenajit, Anāthapiṇḍada, and others—are said to have provided only the requisite materials like biers, perfume, incense, and so forth and to have cremated the bodies: nothing more.

On the basis of these kinds of considerations, and the passages in the *Mūlasarvāstivāda-vinaya* then known, it has been said—with typical overstatement—"that the laity was allowed no place in these [funeral] procedures, that the funeral of a local monk was an exclusively monastic affair, participation being limited to monks and monks alone."[28] That these remarks will need some qualification is obvious in light of the account of the funeral of Kālodāyin in the *Vinayavibhaṅga*. However, it is worth noting that this account itself seems to start from something like the same position, seems to assume that it is, at least, the general rule. [42]

We have seen already that the injunction to perform *śarīra-pūjā* for Kālodāyin is addressed to monks (*dge slong dag . . . de'i lus la mchod pa bya'o*) even in the *Vinayavibhaṅga* and that it is this monastic obligation that allows the monks to enter a village at what would otherwise be an "irregular," or "wrong," time. It seems, then, to be both assumed and accepted by the redactor of the account that monks, and monks alone, are responsible for the performance of *śarīra-pūjā* for a fellow monk. But as the account develops, a series of competing claims are put forth for what now appears as the "privilege" of such a performance. First "those who had depended on the Venerable Udāyin" (*gang dag tshe dang ldan pa 'char ka la brten nas*)—and these by context appear to be monks—seek permission to perform the *śarīra-pūjā* on the grounds that Kālodāyin was their "Good Spiritual Friend," or *kalyāṇamitra* (*'di bdag cag gi dge ba'i bshes gnyen lags na / bcom ldan 'das kyis bdag cag 'di'i lus la mchod pa bgyid par ci gnang*). But they are denied. Then King Prasenajit seeks permission on the grounds that Kālodāyin was a friend of his from their youth (*'di bdag gi chung po grogs lags na*), but he too is denied. The successful claim is that of Queen Mālikā: "Since he was my teacher, does the Blessed One allow me to perform the honors for his body?" (*'di bdag gi slob dpon lags na / bcom ldan 'das kyis bdag 'di'i lus la mchod pa bgyid par ci gnang*).

These competing claims appear to be based on the degree of relationship between the person or persons making them and the deceased monk, and the successful claim seems to be that which is based on the closest formally acknowledged ecclesiastical bond. If we start from what appears to be taken as given—that the general rule was indeed that monks had the responsibility and privilege of performing *śarīra-pūjā*—then the king's claim appears to be the weakest: although it might have had some weight in secular contexts, long-standing friendship would have had little or no ecclesiastical force. The claim of "those who had depended on the Venerable Udāyin"—a claim made apparently by one group of monks within the larger Community—would have been stronger, but their grounds lack ecclesiastical or formal specificity. The term *dge ba'i bshes gnyen* or *kalyāṇamitra* denotes not a formal ecclesiastical relationship but rather an informal spiritual bond.[29] Mālikā, finally, appears to [43] have been not simply a layperson but a "lay-sister," an *upāsikā*, a woman who had a formally acknowledged connection with the monastic community.[30] She in any case claimed that the Monk Kālodāyin was her *slob dpon* or *ācārya*, and this would make her his *antevāsin*. This is a formal relationship with a specific set of mutual obligations, and it is this relationship that our text allows, it seems, to determine who receives the privilege of performing the "honor for the body" in this case.[31]

It is important to note two further things. First, although our text might establish a precedent that might allow for the occasion when a wealthy lay-sister might seek and gain permission to perform the funeral of a monk who was her *ācārya*, it does not establish or allow this as a general rule. In fact, our text seems to carefully avoid making any rule here and, in so doing, appears to reinforce what is elsewhere explicitly delivered as just such a general rule: that it is the responsibility and privilege of monks and only monks to perform the funeral rites for a fellow monk.

The second point concerns the very idea of privilege. There has been very little analysis of what might be called relationships of power among different sections of Buddhist communities, and what little has been said in this regard has not been distinguished by its subtlety. Such a lack may be particularly unfortunate for an understanding of at least a part of the *vinaya*, in terms of both its style and its content. One of the things that any successful religious institution must do, it seems, is to continuously negotiate and renegotiate questions of privilege and access to religiously important people, objects, and activities. This, it seems, may well be an important function of at least a part of the *vinaya*. What emerges from our text, for example, is a clear indication that the performance of the funeral ritual for a monk was not thought of simply as an obligation but was presented as a privilege sought after by competing constituencies or groups. Though by general rule assigned to fellow monks, access to and participation in this ritual form apparently had to be negotiated in certain circumstances, and this—above all else—may be the purpose behind our text. Such negotiations can sometimes be complex.

In the Mūlasarvāstivādin *Bhikṣuṇī-vinayavibhaṅga* there is, for example, a general rule that "if a nun accepts an image of the [44] Buddha containing relics, it is a *pātayantikā* offense" (*dge slong mas sangs rgyas kyi sku gzugs brnyan ring bsrel dang bcas pa len na ltung byed do*). Such a rule, if consistently enacted, would, of course, have made it all but impossible for nuns to establish their own and independent shrines or places of worship, and this may well have been the original intent. But the formulation of the rule as we now have it is followed by a series of amendments, the first of which is that "if there are no relics," such acceptance is only a minor offense (*ring bsrel med pa yin na nyes byas so*), allowing at least some flexibility. And the rule is then finally and seriously softened: "If (such an image) is accepted with the idea of doing worship to the Teacher, and if it is placed in the hands of a female novice or of one who makes things allowable (*kalpikāra*, *kappiya-kāraka*), there is no offense" (*gal te ston pa la mchod pa'i du shes kyis len par byed cing / dge tshul ma 'am rung bar byed pa'i lag tu bzhang pa la ni ltung ba med do*).[32] It is not at all improbable that we have condensed in this rule of but a line and a half a whole series of negotiations and an outline of the significant stages in a "struggle" by Mūlasarvāstivādin nuns to achieve ritual independence. It is even not improbable that a considerable number of *vinaya* rules as we now have them reflect the "histories" of similar sorts of negotiations.

Questions of privilege and access, however, almost certainly did not arise only between monks and nuns. Such questions almost certainly formed a continuous and delicate part of the relationships between monastic communities and "lay" communities. I would see the account of the funeral of the Monk Kālodāyin in the *Vinayavibhaṅga* as an attempt to negotiate one such question, the question of who gets to perform and participate in monastic funerals. But there certainly were others, at least one of which may be of particular interest to us for a variety of good reasons. The question at issue presumably would have been an important one—it comes down to who had control of and greatest access to what might legitimately be considered the most sacred of Buddhist "objects": what we call relics. The account that to my knowledge treats this question most fully is the account of the deposition of the relics of the Monk Śāriputra found in the *Kṣudrakavastu* of the *Mūlasarvāstivāda-vinaya*. Strictly speaking—at least according to the internal [45] chronology adopted by the texts—it is this account, and not the *Mahāparinirvāṇasūtra*, that records the beginnings of the relic cult. It is, of course, important because of that, but it is particularly interesting for us because (1) it seems further to clarify the relationship between monastic funerals and what can be considered an ongoing relic cult; (2) it involves a particularly clear case of protracted negotiations of privilege and access between the monastic and the lay communities; and (3) it forms a background to some of what we will see in Guṇaprabha's *Vinayasūtra*.

The whole story is a long one.[33] It begins in the *Kṣudrakavastu* immediately after the rules governing monastic funerals have been given, but the accompanying *uddāna*, or summary of contents, makes it clear that the redactors considered the two as separate sections, giving key words for each (*ro ni bsreg par bya ba dang / śā ri'i bu yi mchod rten dang*).[34] It starts with a curious story—the first part of which is also found in the *Saṅghabhedavastu*—about Śāriputra and Maudgalyāyana making a visit to the hells. There they encounter the non-Buddhist Teacher Purāṇa undergoing some fairly unpleasant torments, and he asks the two monks to take a message back to his disciples. Śāriputra and Maudgalyāyana are to say to Purāṇa's disciples that he says, "Since whenever you honor my *stūpa*, my suffering just then becomes intolerably great, hereafter it should not be done!" (*khyed kyis ji lta ji ltar nga'i mchod rten la brjed pa byas pa de lta de ltar nga la sdug bsngal ches mi bzad par gyur gyis / phyin chad ma byed par thong zhig ces* [Ta 355a.1], *yathā yathā ca śrāvakā stūpakārān kurvanti tathā tathā tīvravedanāṃ vedayāmi. tad arhasi madīyām avasthāṃ teṣāṃ nivedya nivārayitum. mā tasya stūpakāraṃ kariṣyatheti*[35]). This is a rare and clear expression of what was probably a widely held belief: the belief that what was done to a deceased individual's *stūpa* affected the "individual" himself.

When Śāriputra and Maudgalyāyana return and deliver the message, the disciples of Purāṇa are not pleased and plot the demise of the two monks. They succeed in waylaying Maudgalyāyana and beat him—literally—to a pulp ("They smashed his limbs and appendages like sugarcane," *de dag gis de'i yan lag dang nying lag 'dam bu bzhin bcom nas* . . . ; Ta 356 a.3). Śāriputra returns and finds Maudgalyāyana's "limbs and appendages having been smashed like sugarcane scattered on the [46] ground" and—because somehow Maudgalyāyana is still alive—the text says: "The Venerable Śāriputra, having tucked the Venerable Maudgalyāyana into his upper robe like a little baby, carried him away to a *vihāra* (*de nas tshe dang ldan pa śā ri'i bus / tshe dang ldan pa mo'u 'gal gyi bu byis pa chung ngu bzhin du bla gos kyi nang du bcug nas gtsug lag khang du khyer ba dang*; Ta 356a.7). Maudgalyāyana manages to—if you will—pull himself together for one last begging round in Rājagṛha but forms the intention to "pass away into final *nirvāṇa*." Śāriputra, becoming aware of this, says, "Since the Venerable Maudgalyāyana will pass away into final *nirvāṇa*, why should I remain?" (*tshe dang ldan pa mo'u 'gal gyi bu chen po yongs su mya ngan las 'da' na / bdag ci ste 'dug*; Ta 358b.2), and he too makes the decision to die, which he then does.

According to the text, Śāriputra dies at the village of Nalada, some distance away from Rājagṛha, where the narrator has situated the text itself. This may account for the fact that there is no description of a funeral. We are, however, told—as we have seen—that the funereal *śarīra-pūjā* for Śāriputra was performed by his attending novice Cunda (*tshe dang ldan pa śā ri'i bu'i ring bsrel la lus kyis mchod pa byas te*), and only after that were his remains (*ring bsrel*), bowl, and robe taken back to Rājagṛha. Though small, this is an important detail, for it establishes a boundary between the funereal *śarīra-pūjā* and everything in the account that follows it: here, too, then—as we have seen elsewhere everywhere except in the account of the funeral of Kālodāyin—the funereal *śarīra-pūjā* was an exclusively monastic affair.

When Cunda hands the remains of Śāriputra over to Ānanda—and here we can begin to use our word "relic"—Ānanda expresses his dismay and disconsolation at the news of Śāriputra's death: when he heard that Śāriputra was dead, Ānanda says: "My body was afflicted, my bearings confused, the various teachings I had heard too were left aside" (*bdag gi lus gdung bar gyur cing / phyogs kyang bslad / chos thos pa'i rnams kyang bskyung bar gyur ro*; Ta 359b.1). The Buddha then delivers to Ānanda a long homily on death, a good part of which has echoes in, or itself echoes, passages in the *Mahāparinirvāṇasūtra*. But its beginning is distinct and worthy of note. The Buddha's initial response to Ānanda's grief is to say: [47]

> "But, Ānanda, did the Monk Śāriputra, taking the accumulation of morality with him, enter into final *nirvāṇa*?" (*kun dga' bo ci dge slong śā ri'i bus tshul khrims kyi phung po khyer te yons su mya ngan las 'das sam*; Ta 395b.2).
>
> "No, Reverend."

The Buddha then asks in the same way about concentration, wisdom, release, and the knowledge and vision of release, and Ānanda again says no. This too is followed with the same question in regard to a standard list of the "limbs of enlightenment," with the same answer.

We have, then, to this point in the account two statements—both indirect—about what is left behind or remains after Śāriputra's death: the narrative says, in effect, that first of all what remains are "relics" (*ring bsrel*); but the homily says that the "accumulation, heap, substratum, or material form" (*phung po = rāśi, skandha, upadhi*) of morality, concentration, wisdom, release, and knowledge and vision of release is what remains. The relationship between the two—between relics and the accumulation or substratum of morality, concentration, wisdom, and so on—is here neither stated nor resolved and could, of course, have been interpreted in a number of ways. It is, however, hard to imagine that what we see in some early inscriptions from the Northwest, in the learned Aśvaghoṣa, and in a late book of the *Milindapañha* is not somehow related to our account, or to one like it, and does not represent at least one fairly widespread interpretation or resolution of the relationship between these two seemingly disparate categories of things. These various sources seem to dissolve the distinction between the two and to suggest that one—the "relic"—is permeated, saturated, infused, and enlivened by the other. It seemingly cannot be an accident that we find in inscriptions, for example, that relics—one of the things our account says Śāriputra left behind—are said to be permeated or saturated by the other things that our account says remain. The inscriptions use what is almost exactly the same vocabulary and refer—as has been noted elsewhere—to relics as "infused with morality, infused with concentration, wisdom, release, and knowledge and vision" (*ima dhadu śila*[*pari*]*bhavita samasipraṅavimutiñaṇadra*[*śa*]*paribhavita*) or simply as "infused with morality, infused with concentration, infused with wisdom" (*śilaparibhavida sama*[*s*]*iparibhavemtu praṅaparibhavida*).[36] [48] The fourth book of the *Milindapañha* says almost exactly the same as the first of these, and Aśvaghoṣa says that relics are "full of virtue" (*dge legs gang ba*).[37] In the present state of our ignorance there is, of course, no way to connect directly any of these sources with our text or to know if what they assert was even a part of the intention of the original author of that text. But it is hard to rule out the distinct possibility that our account of the death of Śāriputra, its Pāli parallel in the *Saṃyutta*, or a similar account, forms at least a part of the background to these other sources, hard to rule out that the conception of a relic as saturated with morality, concentration, wisdom, and so on resulted in part from the kind of purely narrative conjunction found in our account of Śāriputra.

Apart from considerations of this kind, we need to note two things. None of the narrative dealing with relics—their return to Rājagṛha, their presentation to Ānanda, the homily they seem to give rise to—has anything to do with Śāriputra's funeral: they all take place after Cunda has performed what the Tibetan text somewhat unhappily calls *tshe dang ldan pa śā ri'i bu'i ring bsrel la lus kyis mchod pa*, "the honors for the body on the remains of the Venerable Śāriputra." There is no part in any of this assigned to laypersons. Not only does the redactor of our text take it very much as a given that the performance of a monk's funeral is a monastic concern but also—and this is the second point of note—he takes it as a given that any "relics" that result are to remain in the keeping of other monks: the novice Cunda initially collects and returns them to Rājagṛha, he presents them to the monk Ānanda, and Ānanda continues to keep them in his possession. In fact, the long homily delivered by the Buddha has no bearing on the disposition of Śāriputra's relics. After the homily a narrative break occurs, with the text simply saying: "Then the Venerable Ānanda, having praised and rejoiced in that which was spoken by the Blessed One, and honoring with his head the feet of the Blessed One, departed from his presence." But this, of course, is not the end of the story, because if monks retain unmodified the privilege of possession of such relics, the laity will have no access—we might expect, then, the kinds of negotiations we have seen in the account of Kālodāyin's funeral.

Without indicating how much time elapses, the account [49] immediately continues with what I translate below in full interspersed with some remarks.[38]

Negotiating the Control of Relics

Then the Blessed One, having stayed as long as he pleased at Rājagṛha, set off and went toward Śrāvastī. Having set off and gone, he in due course arrived at Śrāvastī. In Śrāvastī he stayed at the Park of Anāthapiṇḍada in the Jetavana.

The Householder Anāthapiṇḍada heard it said that the Noble Śāriputra had passed away into final *nirvāṇa* and that his relics (*ring bsrel*) were in the hands of the Noble Ānanda. Having heard that, he went to the Venerable Ānanda. Having arrived there, and honoring with his head the feet of the Venerable Ānanda, he sat down to one side. Having sat down to one side, the Householder Anāthapiṇḍada said this to the Venerable Ānanda: "May the Noble Ānanda hear! Since for a long time the Noble Śāriputra was to me dear, beloved, a guru, and an object of affection, and since he passed away into final *nirvāṇa* and his relics are in your possession, would you please hand them over to me! The honor due to relics should be done to his relics! (*'phags pa śā ri'i bu ni bdag gi yun ring po nas sdug pa dang / yid du 'ong ba dang / bla ma dang / dran par bgyi ba lags na / de yongs su mya ngan las 'das te / de'i ring bsrel khyod kyi phyag na mnga' ba de dag bdag la stsol cig dang / de'i ring bsrel la ring bsrel gyi mchod pa bgyi*; Ta 364b.6).

Ānanda said: "Householder, because Śāriputra for a long time was to me dear, beloved, a guru, and an object of affection, I myself will perform the honor due to relics for his relics" (*bdag nyid de'i ring bsrel la ring bsrel gyi mchod pa byed do*).

To this point, our text presents us with a lay claim and a monastic counterclaim, both expressed in the same terms, terms that parallel in part those found in the various claims made on the Buddha's relics in the *Mahāparinirvāṇasūtra*. The result is a stalemate, with the relics remaining in monastic hands.

Notice too that the competing claims concern both who will have possession of the relics and who is to perform "the honor due to relics for his relics." The Tibetan here—*ring bsrel la ring bsrel gyi mchod pa*—is undoubtedly a translation of a Sanskrit *śarīre śarīra-pūjā*. This Sanskrit phrase—as has already been pointed out elsewhere—has been translated in at least a half a dozen different ways by Tibetan translators. *Śarīra* in this phrase has often been translated, for example, by *rus bu* ("bone") or *sku gdung* (respect form of *rus bu*) in places where the context makes it clear that it can mean only "body" (*lus*) or "corpse" (*ro lo*). Part of the problem is, of course, that *śarīra* in the singular means "body" but in the plural or in compound [50] can mean what we call "relics" or bone. But in spite of this muddle the Tibetan of our account makes a verbal distinction between what Cunda did as a part of Śāriputra's funeral, *ring bsrel la lus kyis mchod pa*, and what Ānanda and Anāthapiṇḍada want to do to his relics, *ring bsrel la ring bsrel gyi mchod pa*. It is a small, somewhat clumsy attempt to mark a distinction, but it is an important additional piece of evidence indicating that the tradition did not consider funeral activity and activity in regard to relics as the same thing.[39]

> Then the Householder Anāthapiṇḍada went to the Blessed One. Arriving there, and honoring with his head the feet of the Blessed One, he sat down to one side. Having sat down to one side, the Householder Anāthapiṇḍada said this to the Blessed One: "May the Reverend One hear! For a long time the Noble Śāriputra was to me dear, beloved, a guru, and an object of affection. His relics are in the hands of the Noble Ānanda. May the Blessed One please grant that they be given to me! I ask for the honor due to relics for his relics" (*bdag de'i ring bsrel la ring bsrel gyi mchod pa 'tshal lo*; Ta 365a.5).
>
> The Blessed One then, having summoned Ānanda through a messenger, said this to him: "Ānanda, give the relics of the Monk Śāriputra to the Householder Anāthapiṇḍada! Allow him to perform the honors! (*de mchod pa byed du chung cig*). On account of this advantage brahmins and householders are possessed of faith. Moreover, Ānanda, through only this, there is by you neither benefit nor recompense for my teaching. Therefore you should cause to go forth, you should ordain, you should give the requisites, you should attend to the business of a monk, to them you should cause to be proclaimed as it was proclaimed, cause it to be taken up, teach it, and through only this, there is by you profit and recompense for my teaching" (*kun dga' bo gzhan yang 'di tsam gyis ni khyod kyis nga'i bstan pa la phan byas pa 'am lan lon pa ma yin no / de lta bas na khyod kyis rab tu phyung zhig / bsnyen par rdzogs par gyis shig / gnas byin cig / dge slong gi ched nye bar zhog ci / de dag la yang ji ltar thon pa bzhin 'don du chug cig / 'dzin du chug cig / slobs shig dang / 'di tsam gyis na khyod kyis nga'i bstan pa la phan btags pa dang lan lon pa yin no*; Ta 365a.6).
>
> Then the Venerable Ānanda, by the order of the Teacher, gave the relics of Śāriputra to the Householder Anāthapiṇḍada—this was so because the Blessed One, when formerly a *bodhisattva*, never violated the words of his father and mother or of his preceptor or teacher or other such person of respect (*'di ltar bcom ldan 'das sngon byang chub sems dpar gyur par na / lan 'ga' yang yab yum dang / mkhan po dang / slob dpon dang gzhan bla ma'i gnas lta bu dag gi tshig ma bcag pas so /*; Ta 365b.1).
>
> The Householder Anāthapiṇḍada, having taken up the relics of the Venerable Śāriputra, went to his own house. Having arrived there, having placed them at a height in the best of his house (*de dag khyim gyi mchog gi nang du mthon po zhig tu bzhag nas*),[40] he, together with members of his household, together with his friends, relations, and older and younger brothers, undertook to honor them with lamps, incense, flowers, perfumes, garlands, and unguents.

Here is something more like what our handbooks would lead us to [51] expect: a monk is told to hand over the relics to the laity and to stick to "the business of a monk"—ordaining, teaching, and training other monks. But it is important to note that narratively this was not the original monastic impulse. That impulse was to retain possession of any relics. The authority of the Buddha had to be invoked to change it. And the Buddha's explicit directive was apparently not felt by the redactor to be sufficient—he apparently felt the need to reinforce the directive by adding a kind of editorial admonition that explains Ānanda's obedience: the Buddha himself, "when formerly a *bodhisattva*," always obeyed figures of authority. One may sense that this—for the redactor—was not a simple issue and that there may have been a good deal of monastic resistance to what was being proposed. The continuation of the text would seem only to confirm this, because if it were a simple issue, we would expect the tale to end here by saying that "everyone lived happily thereafter." But they did not. The text so far has in fact only substituted one private cult for another. The problem of access remains, and our redactor certainly had something more to say.

> The multitude of men who lived in Śrāvastī heard thus that the Noble Śāriputra had passed away into final *nirvāṇa* in the village of Nalada in the country of Magadha, that the Noble Ānanda, after having obtained his relics, presented them to the Householder Anāthapiṇḍada, and that the latter, together with members of his household, together with his friends, relatives and acquaintances, and elder and younger brothers, honored them with lamps, incense, flowers, perfumes, garlands, and unguents. Likewise Prasenajit, the King of Kośala, having heard this, went to the house of the Householder Anāthapiṇḍada together with his wife Mālikā, the Kṣatriyā Varṣākārā, both Ṛṣidatta and Purāṇa, and Viśākhā, the mother of Mṛgāra, as well as many of the devout, all of them carrying the requisites for doing honor. From undertaking to honor them with the requisites of honor, several of them there obtained accumulations of good qualities. But when, on another occasion, some business arose in a mountain village, the Householder Anāthapiṇḍada, having locked the door of his house, had gone away. But a great crowd of people came then to his house, and when they saw the door locked, they were derisive, abusive, and critical, saying, "Seeing that the Householder Anāthapiṇḍada has locked the door and gone off, he has created an obstacle to our merit" (*des bdag cag gi bsod nams kyi bar chad byas so*).
>
> Later the Householder Anāthapiṇḍada returned from that mountain village, and members of his household said: "Householder, a great multitude of people carrying the requisites of honor came, but seeing the door locked, they were derisive, abusive, and critical, saying, 'Anāthapiṇḍada has created an obstacle to our merit.'"
>
> Anāthapiṇḍada, having thought to himself, "This indeed is what I must do," went to the Blessed One. Arriving there, and honoring with his head the feet of the Blessed [52] One, he sat down to one side. Seated to one side, he said this to the Blessed One: "Reverend, when a great multitude of men who were deeply devoted to the Venerable Śāriputra came to my house carrying the requisites of honor,

> I, on account of some business, had closed the doors and gone elsewhere. They became derisive, abusive, and critical, saying, 'Seeing that the Householder Anāthapiṇḍada has locked the door and gone away, he has created an obstacle to our merit.' On that account, if the Blessed One would permit it, I would build a *stūpa* for the Noble Śāriputra in a suitably available place (*phyogs snang yal can zhig tu*). There the great multitudes of men would be allowed to do honor as they wish."
>
> The Blessed One said: "Therefore, Householder, with my permission, you should do it!"

Unless I am much mistaken, the monk redactor of our text here has either himself made a particularly dexterous narrative move or written into his account an equally dexterous move made by the monastic community at some point in the process of negotiations concerning access to sought-after relics. Notice that the account has doubled back on itself, but with a difference. The Buddha had been presented as wanting to allow the laity to possess the relics of saintly monks. He even ordered it. The monks themselves, in the figure of Ānanda, were presented as—if not entirely enthusiastic—obedient to the wishes of the Buddha in this regard. Buddha and monk have both done their part to make access to the relics available. But alas, the narrator implies, look what happens when laypersons are allowed to keep and control access to relics. Even such a devout layperson as Anāthapiṇḍada turns the opportunity into something like a private domestic cult—"he, together with members of his household, together with his friends, relations, and older and younger brothers, undertook to honor them"—and, even if inadvertently, effectively restricts access to the relics in yet another way, creating an obstacle to others' merit. People complain, and it is these complaints, *not* the will of the Buddha or the monks, that justify and account for yet another arrangement's being devised, an arrangement that, although it will benefit the monks, was motivated—or so it appears—purely by the laity's actions and the gracious desire to remove obstacles to their merit.

> Although the Blessed One said, "with my permission, you should do it," Anāthapiṇḍada did not know how it should be done.
>
> The Blessed One said: "Successively make four terraces; then make the base for [53] the dome; then the dome and the *harmikā* and the crowning pole and, having made one or two or three or four umbrellas, make up to thirteen, and the rain receptacles are to be put in place."
>
> Although the Blessed One said "a *stūpa* of this sort is to be made," because Anāthapiṇḍada did not know if a *stūpa* of such a form was to be made only for the Noble Śāriputra or also for all Nōble Ones (*'phags pa*), the monks asked the Blessed One concerning this matter, and the Blessed One said: "Householder, in regard to the *stūpa* of a Tathāgata, a person should complete all parts. In regard to the

> *stūpa* of a Solitary Buddha, the rain receptacle should not be put in place; for an Arhat, there are four umbrellas; for One Who Does Not Return, three; for One Who Returns, two; for One Who Has Entered the Stream, one. For ordinary good men (*so so'i skye bo dge ba rnams*; Ta 367a.4), the *stūpa* is to be made plain."
>
> The Blessed One said, "In regard to a *stūpa* for the Noble Ones it has this form, for ordinary men (*so so'i skye bo*) this," but Anāthapiṇḍada did not know by whom and in which place they were to be made. The Blessed One said: "As Śāriputra and Maudgalyāyana sat when the Tathāgata was seated, just so the *stūpa* of one who has passed away into final *nirvāṇa* is also to be placed. Moreover, in regard to the *stūpas* of each individual Elder, they are to be arranged according to seniority. Those for ordinary good men are to be placed outside the monastic complex" (*ji ltar de bzhin gshegs pa bzhugs pa na / śā ri'i bu dang mo'u 'gal gyi bu dag 'dug pa de bzhin du yongs su mya ngan las 'das pa'i mchod rten yang bya'o / gzhan yang gnas brtan gnas brtan rnams kyi mchod rten ni rgan rims bzhin sbrang bar bya'o / so so'i skye bo dge ba rnams kyi ni dge 'dun gyi kun dga' ra ba'i phyi rol tu bya'o /*; Ta 367a.6).

Apart from the description of the various categories of *stūpas*, which has been treated more than once in detail,[41] perhaps the most important element of the text here is the last sentence: "Those for ordinary good men are to be placed outside the monastic complex." What this means, of course, is that all others, *all the stūpas of extraordinary monks must be placed within the monastic complex*, or—to phrase it otherwise—under monastic control. We obviously have come full circle: laypersons might be permitted to build *stūpas*, but they must build them within a monastic complex.

Fortunately, we have some idea of who fell into the different categories. The Sanskrit text of the *Poṣadhasthāpanavastu*, for example, says: *saṃvṛttisaṃghaḥ katamaḥ. sarve pṛthagjana-kalyāṇakāḥ. paramārthasaṃghaḥ katamaḥ. śaikṣāśaikṣā aṣṭau mahāpuruṣapudgalāḥ*; *kun rdzob kyi dge 'dun gang zhe na / so so'i skye bo dge ba dang ldan pa thams cad do / don dam pa'i dge 'dun gang zhe na / slob pa dang mi slob pa'i skyes bu gang zag brgyad do /*: "What is the conventional Saṅgha? All the ordinary good men. What is the true Saṅgha? Those undergoing training and those no longer needing training, the [54] eight kinds of great persons."[42] In the *Divyāvadāna*, moreover, Aśoka is said to have fed three thousand monks, "one thousand of Arhats, and two of those undergoing training and ordinary good men" (*yatraiko 'rhatāṃ dvau śaikṣāṇāṃ pṛthagjanakalyāṇakānāṃ ca*).[43] And de la Vallée Poussin has said, "According to the *Mahāsāṃghikavinaya* . . . ordinary monks (*pṛthagjana*) also have a right to a *stūpa*, that is to say, the Vinayadharadharmācārya, the Vaiyāpṛtya-bhikṣu, the Virtuous-bhikṣu. As they are not Āryas, there is no lou-pan [rain-receptacle] and [their *stūpa*] is in a private place."[44] There is not a perfect agreement among these sources, but the basic point is clear—only the *stūpa* of ordinary monks, monks of little formally acknowledged religious attainment, could be erected outside the monastic complex.[45] The monks, it seems, were to keep the best very much under their jurisdiction.

The general agreement of the Mūlasarvāstivādin and Mahāsāṃghika *Vinayas* that "ordinary" monks are worthy of a *stūpa*, and that such *stūpas* are to be placed outside the complex or "dans un lieu caché," also presents us with another instance where the Sri Lankan tradition appears to be aberrant or unrepresentative. In a passage found in the commentaries to both the *Aṅguttara* and the *Dīgha Nikāyas*, it is asserted that the Buddha *did not* allow *stūpas* for "ordinary" monks (*na sīlavato puthujjana-bhikkhussa*). But, to judge by the reason given to justify it, this assertion appears to be late and of Sri Lankan origin. The reason the Buddha did not allow *stūpas* for ordinary monks was as follows: "for were a *stūpa* to be allowed for puthujjana monks there would be no room for any villages or cities in Tambapaṇṇadīpa (Ceylon), likewise in other places" (*puthujjana-bhikkhūnaṃ hi thūpe anuññāyamane tambapaṇṇadīpe gāmapaṭṭanānaṃ okāso ca na bhaveyya tathā aññesu ṭhānesu*).[46] This assertion, however, which is justified in purely Sri Lankan terms, appears to be not only in conflict with Indian *vinayas* but at variance with what some very early Indian archaeological and epigraphical evidence indicates actually occurred.

Epigraphical evidence indicates that *stūpas* were raised for monks beginning as early as the second century B.C.E., first at Sāñcī, Sonāri, and Andher, then at Amarāvatī, Mathurā, Bedsā, Kanheri, and Bhājā, and probably at Pitalkhora, Nāgārjunikoṇḍa, and a number of other widely separated sites in India. These monks are called *āryas* ("Noble Ones"), [55] *peṇḍavatikas* ("Mendicants"), *bhikṣus*, *āraṇakas* ("Forest-dwellers"), or *theras* ("Elders"), but never until the sixth and seventh centuries—and only then at Kanheri—are they given titles like *arhat*, "non-returner," or any of the other titles assigned to "the eight kinds of great persons." These monks appear to have been *pṛthagjana* monks.[47]

Not all these *stūpas* were placed outside the complex, but the larger number were either so placed or placed in isolated areas at the extremities of their sites. Several that were not had—unlike the majority of such *stūpas*—named and private individual sponsors. Fortunately, the earliest case of what appears to be the textually sanctioned placement is the clearest and most certain.

The main *stūpa* at Sāñcī sits on the top of the hill. Near it is the *stūpa* of Śāriputra and Maudgalyāyana. This is as it "should be." But *stūpa* number 2, which held the remains of ten local monks "stands on a small terrace projecting out from the hill-side some 350 yards down its western slope," according to Marshall, who also notes: "The location of the *stūpa* on this terrace is significant, since at the time when it was built there must still have been a considerable area unoccupied on the hill-top above, and it is not at first sight clear why so much trouble was taken to build up this small terrace *apart from, and below*, the other *stūpas*." He goes on to say that "whatever the achievements and fame of the dead [in *stūpa* number 2] may have been, there must manifestly have been an objection to burying their remains side by side with those of the Buddha and his personal disciples."[48] Obviously, the arrangements at Sāñcī correspond almost exactly with the directions given in our text, and our text—now found in the *Kṣudrakavastu* of the *Mūlasarvāstivāda-vinaya*—may well explain the "objection" Marshall refers to. Given that Bénisti has suggested that the rail around *stūpa* number 2 "goes back, in virtually its entirety, to the first half of the 2nd century before our era," this would date some version of our text—or, perhaps more importantly, the practices it refers to—to the second or third centuries B.C.E. And Sāñcī is not the only early site that testifies to this arrangement: the monastic cemetery at Bhājā is situated on what originally must have been the northern perimeter of the site; at Pitalkhora, what appears to be the monastic cemetery is completely removed from the main site on the other side of a deep ravine. This is enough, perhaps, to establish that the practices described in our text [56] are very old and widespread. But if this is what occurred in regard to ordinary monks, we still need to understand the monastic communities' interest in those monks who were extraordinary. The final section of our text will give us one good reason.

> The Householder Anāthapiṇḍada said: "If the Blessed One were to give permission, I will celebrate festivals (*dus ston dag*) of the *stūpa* of the Noble Śāriputra."
>
> The Blessed One said: "Householder, with permission, you should do it!"
>
> Prasenajit, the King of Kośala, had heard how, when the Householder Anāthapiṇḍada asked of the Blessed One to institute a festival of the *stūpa* of the Noble Śāriputra, the Blessed One had permitted the institution. Prasenajit, having thought, "It is excellent! I too should help in that," and having the bell sounded, declared: "Sirs, city dwellers who live in Śrāvastī, and the multitudes of men who have come together from other places, hear this: 'At the time when the festival of the *stūpa* of the Venerable Śāriputra occurs, for those who have come bringing merchandise there is no tax, no toll, nor transportation fee. Therefore, they must be allowed to pass freely here!'"
>
> At that time five hundred overseas traders who had made a great deal of money from their ships arrived at Śrāvastī. They heard then how the king, sounding the bell in Śrāvastī, had ordered, "Whoever, at the time when the festival of the *stūpa* of the Noble Śāriputra occurs, comes bringing merchandise, for them there is no tax, no toll, nor transportation fee. Therefore, they must be allowed to pass freely here!" Some thought to themselves: "This king abides in the fruit of his own merit but is still not satisfied with his merit. Since gifts given produce merit, why should we not give gifts, not make merit?" They, becoming de-

> vout in mind, on the occasion of that festival gave tortoise shell and precious stones and pearls, and so on.
>
> The monks, however, did not know how to proceed.
>
> The Blessed One said: "Those gifts that are the 'first fruit' offerings (*bud dung*) are to be given to the 'Image That Sits in the Shade of the Jambu Tree.' Moreover, a small part is to be put aside for the repair of the *stūpa* of Śāriputra. The remainder is to be divided by the assembly of monks—this is not for a *stūpa* of the Tathāgata, this is for a *stūpa* of Śāriputra: therefore one does not commit a fault in this case."

Perhaps because of the protestantization—or at least romanticization—of early Buddhism, we are not in the habit of thinking about the economic aspects of Buddhist monastic practice. It is, however, becoming increasingly clear that the compilers of the various *vinayas* were, and our text may represent a particularly good example of how such concerns were addressed. Our text is certainly about merit, about access to important religious objects and who controls them. But it is also about money and who gets it.

There is probably nothing unique in what we see being negotiated in our text—first, as has been noted, monastic control of the relics of extraordinary monks; but then monastic rights to the offerings that the [57] presence of such relics generates. Notice, too, the linkage with trade and commerce. All of these things—variously linked—can be found in the histories of any number of saints' shrines in the medieval West. We might only note here what may be some particularly pertinent Indian parallels. In discussing the early Sufi tomb-shrines, or *dargahs*, in India, Siddiqui noted, for example: "Evidence from fourteenth-century hagiographic as well as historical literature suggests that the dargah of Shaikh Bakhtiyar Kaki did not take long to emerge as a popular centre of pilgrimage . . . the more popular it became, the greater seems to have been the flow of wealth to it." He notes too that "as the annual *'urs* [death anniversary] celebrated at the dargahs of the Sufi saints were the most important event of the dargah, this gave impetus to trade and commerce."[49] Still on *dargahs*, Mann has noted both that "the dargah is the medium through which the individual may perform deeds to ensure religious merit" and that "the dargah itself is a religious institution not only associated with spiritual values but also with material assets." He continues: "The spiritual and material resources of the shrine create an arena where powerful local interests converge, which constantly conflict with each other. Benefits associated with the shrine thus generate intense competition over their control."[50]

We know, of course, much much less about the *stūpas* of early Buddhist monastic saints than about Sufi *dargahs*,[51] but it is not difficult to see that our text is negotiating much the same issues. And although we know little about what was involved in the "festival" (*dus ston* = *maha*) of the *stūpa* of a dead Buddhist monastic saint, Fa-hsien's travel account would seem to suggest that—especially in regard to Śāriputra—such festivals were widespread and annual in the late fourth and early fifth centuries.

> "Wherever monks live," he [Fa-hsien] says, "they build stūpas in honor of the saints Sariputra, Maudgalaputra and Ananda. . . . A month after the summer retirement, all devout families collect offerings for the monks . . . while the monks hold a great assembly to expound the Law. The assembly at an end, they offer all manner of incense and flowers at the stūpa of Sariputra, and keep the lamps there burning throughout the night. Actors are hired to perform a play in which Sariputra, who was originally a Brahman, goes to Buddha to ask for ordination. The lives of Maudgalaputra and Kasyapa are also performed in this way."[52]

The monastic interest in the *stūpas* of saints, as opposed to *stūpas* of the Buddha, may very well be explained—at least in part—by the [58] fact that they in particular were for the monks "material assets" and "material resources." Establishing this point may in fact be the raison d'être of our entire account.

Our account ends with a statement that acknowledges and plays off of one of the most widely attested and deeply anchored principles of the economy of Buddhist monastic organizations: what is given to a *stūpa* belongs *inalienably* to that *stūpa*. We need only cite two expressions of this principle from two widely different sorts of sources. Twice in the Pāli *Suttavibhaṅga* we find the following statement:

> If he appropriates what was apportioned to the Order [*saṃghassa*] for another (part of the) Order or for a shrine [*cetiyassa*], there is an offense of wrong-doing. If he appropriates what was apportioned to a shrine [*cetiyassa*] for another shrine or for an Order or for an individual [*puggalassa*], there is an offense of wrong-doing, etc.[53]

There can be little doubt that *cetiya*, "shrine," refers here to *stūpas* of the Buddha, whatever else it might include, and no doubt that the statement asserts the inalienable character of property "apportioned" to such a *stūpa*. But perhaps even stronger still is the expression of the same principle found in the *Ratnarāśisūtra*, an early Mahāyāna text. The passage in question first allows under certain conditions—if the *stūpa* falls into disrepair, and the *Saṅgha* has abundant resources—that the property belonging to the *Saṅgha* can be used for the *stūpa*, but the passage then goes on immediately to insist that the reverse cannot occur under any circumstances:

> Kāśyapa, even if the property of the *stūpa* were to be however large, it is not to be transferred to the local *Saṅgha* or the *Saṅgha* of the four directions by the supervising monk. What is the reason for that? That which is given to the *stūpa* by those with devotion and great faith—even so much as a single fringe of cotton cloth—that is itself a shrine for the world together with the gods. How much more so is that the case in regard to precious stones and things of value!" (*dad cing dang ba mang po dag gis mchod rten la phul ba ni tha na ras kyi kha tshar gcig tsam gang yin pa de yang lha dang bcas pa'i 'jig rten gyi mchod rten yin na rin po che 'am / rin po cher smos pa dag lta smos kyang ci dgos*).[54]

Property belonging to the *stūpa* is, then, in monastic rule, both inviolable and inalienable, and itself "sacred." This does not leave much room to move, but the *vinaya*-master who recorded or put together the account of Śāriputra's relics seems concerned to negotiate this particular strait. [59]

The final episode in the account starts with the gift of valuable property (*dung dang / nor bu dang / mu tig la sogs pa*) made by rich merchants during the festival of the *stūpa* of Śāriputra, and the monks not knowing what should be done with them (*dge slong dag gis ji ltar bsgrub pa mi shes nas*).[55] Notice that the rule this situation gives rise to both begins with and ends with the established rule that what is given to the *stūpa* belongs to the *stūpa*—but here, of course, a distinction is introduced. The Buddha is first made to say "those gifts that are the 'first fruit' offerings are to be given to the 'Image that Sits in the Shade of the Jambu Tree,'" *bud dung gang dag yin pa de dag ni shing 'dzam bu'i grim ma na bzhugs pa'i sku gzugs la dbul bar bya'o.* One of two important terms here, *bud dung*, has given me a lot of trouble, and I owe the suggestion that I think successfully solves the problem to my former student and colleague Yael Bentor. She noticed what is certainly the same term in Bu-ston's *mchod rten la mchod pa byas pa'i phan yon*, but there it is spelled not *bud dung* but *phud dud*,[56] and indeed Jäschke's entries show that the orthography of what seems to be the basic form is unsettled: *phud*, *phu dug*, *phu dud*. The term *bud dung* appears to be yet another variant. Jäschke defines *phud* as "a thing set apart, used particularly of the first fruits of the field"; he cites *rdo phud* and *sa phud* as "an offering of stones or earth, when a house is first built," and gives the most general meaning as "initiatory present, e.g. the first produce of a work, that has been committed to one."[57] The "first fruits" of the merchants' labor, then, are to be given to the Buddha—that is, the Image That Sits in the Shade of the Jambu Tree. This image—one inscribed Kuṣān exemplar of which was discovered at Sāñcī—was apparently a specific type that represented the Buddha as a *bodhisattva* during his first youthful spontaneous meditation. It is also referred to as the recipient of specific property elsewhere in the *Mūlasarvāstivāda-vinaya*.[58]

Apart from this "first fruits" offering and a "small part . . . put aside for the repair of the *stūpa* of Śāriputra," the remainder—which having been given to the *stūpa* should have continued to belong to it—"is to be divided by the assembly of monks." This is a significant departure from established rule or monastic law but is justified by introducing a distinction that plays off that same rule: "This [all of what has been given] is not for a *stūpa* of the Tathāgata, this is for [60] a *stūpa* of Śāriputra: therefore one does not commit a fault in this case" (*de de bzhin gshegs pa'i mchod rten gyi ma yin gyi / śā ri'i bu'i mchod rten gyi yin te / de lta bas na 'di la 'gyod par mi bya'o*). Guṇaprabha appears to have seen—as we will see—that the rule framed here in terms of Śāriputra's *stūpa* has categorical application. He says: "That which is given to the *stūpa* of a disciple (*nyan thos kyi mchod rten*) belongs indeed to his fellow monks" (*tshangs pa mtshungs par spyod pa = sabrahmacārin*), the same category of people for whom monks are obligated to perform funerals (*tshangs pa mtshungs par spyod pa shi ba'i lus la mchod pa bya'o*).

It is not hard to see that the legal distinction affirmed in our account could have had considerable economic implications for monks who had no access to, or claim on, property given to "a *stūpa* of the Tathāgata" and could easily account for at least a part of the impulse that produced what Fa-hsien appears to have seen: "Wherever monks live, they build stūpas in honor of the saints Sariputra, Maudgalaputra and Ananda." Such *stūpas*, and their associated "festivals," may have been an important part of the monk's bread and butter.[59] But as important, perhaps, as making these economic connections is what our discussions may tell us about the "style" of Buddhist monastic codes and the legal minds that produced them.

If the readings of these *Mūlasarvāstivāda-vinaya* accounts that are suggested above are even remotely correct, then the world we have been reconnoitering—the world of monastic law—appears to be not a simple one of fables and fiction or half-remembered "historical" accounts but a complex one of carefully constructed "cases" in which concerns of power, access, and economics were being or had been negotiated. We have seen two such cases, one concerned with whether or not laypersons could participate in monastic funerals, the other dealing with the question of whether or not laypersons could possess or have control over the relics of extraordinary monastic saints. Because, it seems, these cases may be neither mindless fables nor historical records but rather the juridical decisions—delivered in canonical form—of an Order's *vinaya* redactors, they appear to be, more than anything, like certain systems of formal Buddhist philosophy: they work from certain presuppositions; they establish general principles, introduce category distinctions, and negotiate exceptions. They do not [61]—or only very rarely—establish definitive positions. And this, indeed, may be a characteristic of all successful law.

Notice that in our cases there is not—as there was not on so many points of formal Buddhist doctrine—a single, definitive position, even within one Order.

In our first case, for example, the answer to the question "can lay persons participate in monastic funerals?" is first, and most generally, no (that is an obligation and prerogative of fellow monks); then the answer is maybe, under certain circumstances (it occurred once when a lay-sister was able to assert an ecclesiastically recognized relationship between herself and the dead monk). But no general definitive statement was made in this instance that would establish it as a rule. In our second question, "can laypersons possess, or control access to, or participate in the cult of, the relics of extraordinary monks?" the answer is again fluid—first no; then definitively yes; then sort of, under certain conditions of monastic control.

Considerations of this kind would seem to have at least two effects: they would seem to doom the endless series of papers on "*the* Buddhist position on this or that" to a not undeserved oblivion; and they would make in yet another way "relating the canonical *Vinaya* to actual practice in diverse contexts more complex than has generally been admitted by students of Buddhism." If *vinaya* cases are neither fables nor historical accounts but rather the forms that *vinaya*-masters chose narratively to frame the issues that concerned them, then they do provide us a record of such concerns and the various legal attempts to resolve them. They do not, however, provide any direct evidence for what actually occurred.

These *vinaya* cases also can be—like all legal cases—arcane. They are embedded in, and presuppose, an accumulated body of related cases. The significance of one case often assumes a knowledge of other cases. The conclusion of the account of the relics of Śāriputra, for example, does not by itself make a great deal of sense: "The remainder is to be divided by the assembly of monks—this is not for a *stūpa* of the Tathāgata, this is for a *stūpa* of Śāriputra: therefore one does not commit a fault in this case." Its significance requires a knowledge of the general principles stated elsewhere that what is given to a *stūpa* belongs to the *stūpa*. Again, unless one knows the sets of rules governing monastic funerals given elsewhere, the account [62] of the funeral of the Monk Kālodāyin seems like just a curious story, and what is being negotiated is not at all evident. In some instances one case will even explicitly refer to another.

One of the clearest instances of such an explicit cross-reference in the *Mūlasarvāstivāda-vinaya* that I know occurs in an important case—important both for Buddhist monastic law and "Hindu" law—involving inheritance. The case to which the reference is made concerns a monk named Upananda.[60] Upon his death, he left a large estate. Government officials got wind of the estate, and while the monks were away performing the funeral ceremonies (*tam ādahane saṃskārya*), they sealed Upananda's room with the king's seal (*layanaṃ rājamudrāmudritam*). The Buddha then sent Ānanda to the king with a series of questions designed to determine if the king had had any specific relationship with the dead monk. The king said no and was made to assent to the principle that the text puts into the mouth of the Buddha: "Great King, the affairs of the house of householders are one thing; those of renouncers quite another. . . . These possessions fall to the fellow monks of Upananda" (*pṛthaṅ mahārāja gṛhiṇāṃ gṛhakāryāṇi pṛthak pravrajitānām . . . sabrahmacāriṇām eṣa lābhaḥ prāpadyate*).

This case occurs in the *Cīvaravastu*, and so does the case that refers to it, but they are separated by more than twenty pages treating unrelated matters. The case that refers to the first case also treats the question of inheritance. Here the estate at issue was left by a wealthy layman who had started to enter the order, had had his head shaved, and had begun to undertake the rules of training but had fallen sick. Though attended to by the monks, he died. He, however, had made a "will" before he died and sent it to the Jetavana (*tatas tena maraṇakālasamaye sarvaṃ santakasvāpateyaṃ patrābhilekhyaṃ kṛtvā jetavane preṣitam*). It is, of course, the reference to the written "will" that makes this case so interesting from the point of view of Hindu law, where such written instruments are very rarely attested.[61] In any case, government officials again hear of the estate and report it to the king, noting that the deceased was *aputra*, without son or heir. But the king does not contest the rights to inherit and simply says, referring to the first case: [63]

> Even in the absence of a written document, I did not obtain the possessions of the Noble Upananda; how much less will I obtain such goods when there is a written document (*āryopanandasantakam eva mayā apatrābhilikhitaṃ na pratilabdhaṃ prāg eva patrābhilikhitaṃ pratilapsye*).[62]

Here, then, not only does one case explicitly refer to another case as a partial precedent but we see as well—from the Buddhist side—Buddhist monastic law playing off and negotiating with "secular" law. There are a number of allusions to, and—I suspect—paraphrases of, secular law in this *Vinaya*.

It is, in short, beginning to appear that Buddhist *vinayas* may represent a far more sophisticated and a far more artificial system of thought than has heretofore been recognized. Ironically, this may have made canonical *vinayas* even less accessible to ordinary monks, and—as if their sheer size were not enough—even less useful for the governance of actual behavior: we arrive again at the "summaries" and "handbooks," and a quick look at Guṇaprabha's *Vinayasūtra* will not only introduce us to one such Mūlasarvāstivādin summary but also, in fact, allow us to summarize much of what has been discussed.

We have for the life of Guṇaprabha the usual pastiche of biographical bits from late sources and colophons. Dates between the fifth and seventh centuries have been suggested for him, and at least two Tibetan colophons connect him with the reign of Harṣavardhana (606–647 C.E.), one of which also says he was Harṣa's "preceptor"—a tradition Tāranātha also repeats. Guṇaprabha may have been from Mathurā and is mentioned by both I-ching and Tāranātha in the same breath with some pretty heavy-duty company: Dignāga, Sthiramati, Bhavya, Dharmakīrti, and others.[63]

Bu-ston refers to Guṇaprabha as "a great authority in the Vinaya of the Ārya-mūlasarvāstivādins" and twice cites his *Vinayasūtra* as a model of the kind of treatise that is "condensing excessively large (portions of) scripture" or of those that "render the contents of many different parts of scripture, taken together." The *Vinayasūtra* is, in fact, the only work on *vinaya* that Bu-ston treats in any detail.[64]

A Sanskrit text of the *Vinayasūtra* has come down to us in a Tibetan transliteration, a single manuscript of which was discovered and photographed by R. Sāṅkṛityāyana at the Ṣhalu monastery. [64] Sāṅkṛityāyana also photographed a manuscript of the auto-commentary on the text, but whereas the text of the *sūtra* appears to be complete, the manuscript of the commentary is described as "mostly fragmentary," although it is in an "ancient Indian script." So far only the first chapter of the Sanskrit text of both *sūtra* and commentary have been published, but both are available in their entirety in Tibetan translation.[65]

Looking even quickly at Guṇaprabha's *Vinayasūtra* will tell us at least two things: it will tell us whether an eminent early medieval *vinaya*-master thought that any of what we have been discussing was worthy of being included in what appears to have been intended as a comprehensive handbook or summary of the *Mūlasarvāstivāda-vinaya*; and it will tell us something about the form in which what we have been discussing may have reached a significant number of medieval monks. In regard to the first of these questions, the answer is, on one level, simple and straightforward: Guṇaprabha treats *both* monastic funerals *and* the questions concerning monastic relics. In fact, he ends his *sūtra* with the treatment of three spheres of monastic ritual, in the following order: monastic funerals, activity in regard to *stūpas*, and activity in regard to images. This grouping might well suggest that for Guṇaprabha monastic funeral ritual had the same importance as ritual connected with both *stūpas* and images.[66] But what Guṇaprabha chose to exclude is as interesting as what he included, and it is connected, of course, with the form in which he presented what we have seen in the canonical text of this *Vinaya*. Nothing conveys a better sense of this than a translation of the relevant sections, which I give here after the Tibetan text from the Taipei reprint of the Derge edition. The translation, again, is tentative: Guṇaprabha's style is—in keeping with his genre—extremely terse, and the commentary is not always helpful. I have had, moreover, access only to the Derge text.[67]

Rules Governing Monastic Funerals and Relics in Guṇaprabha's Vinayasūtra

(Derge, bstan 'gyur, 'dul ba Wu 99a.1–.6)

tshangs pa mtshungs par spyod pa shi ba'i lus la mchod pa bya'o.

de bsreg par bya'o—gal te srog chags dang bcas pa'i rma med pa nyid yin no—so sor brtags pas nges par bya'o.

brko ba 'am chu klung la bskur ro—mi rung na tshang tshing gi dbus su gzhag go—glo g-yas pas bsnyal te mgo byang phyogs su bstan no—sngas su rtsva'i chun po gzhug go—rtsva dag gam lo ma dag gis g-yogs so. {65}

chos mnyan pa dang yon bshad pa dag bya'o.

reg pa dag gis gos dang bcas te khrus bya'o—gzhan dag gis ni rkang lag bkru'o.

mchod rten la phyag byas te 'jug par bya'o.

mchod rten ni rnam pa gnyis te: gtsang khang can nyid dang ka ba lta bu nyid do.

da rab tu byung ba rnams la 'os pa nyid de—gal te dge ba yin na'o.

sangs rgyas rnams kyi rnam pa thams cad do—rnam pa ni bang rim bzhi dang 'dab ma dang bum pa dang pu shu dang srog shing dang gdugs bcu gsum dang char gab dag go.

rang sangs rgyas rnams kyi ni char gab med ba'o.

nyan thos rnams kyi ni 'bras bu'i tshad dag gis de'i gdugs gcig lhag pa'o.

de bzhin gshegs pa'i phyogs kyi yul nyid du gang ru de dag gnas par gyur pa'i phyogs der de'i 'khor du bya'o—'di la rgan rims su mi bya bar mi bya'o.

so so'i skye bo rnams kyi ni byi bo'o—de dag ni dge 'dun gyi kun dga' ra ba'i phyi rol tu bya'o.

'phags pa la ni mchod rten gyi dus ston rigs so.

nyan thos kyi mchod rten la phul ba ni tshangs pa mtshungs par spyod pa rnams dbang ba nyid yin no.

mu tig dag ni bstan pa bzhin bya'o.

bud dung dag ni sangs rgyas la dbul lo—de las zhig ral bcos ba'i phyir gzhag par bya'o—mchod par rung ba nyid kyang ngo.

Honor is to be done to the body of a deceased fellow monk.

It is to be cremated—if there is an absence of wounds containing living things—it should be made certain by examining each one.

It should be consigned to a grave[68] or a river—if that is not suitable it will be deposited in the middle of a thicket—laying it on its right side, its head will face north—on a bolster bunches of grass will be placed—it should be covered with grass or leaves.

Both a recitation of Dharma and an assigning of the reward (to the deceased) is to be made.[69]

Those who had contact with the corpse should bathe themselves together with their robes—others will wash feet and hands.

Having venerated the *stūpa,* they should go in.

There are two types of *stūpa*: that within a chamber[70] and that which is like a pillar (i.e., freestanding).

Now, in regard to renunciants, that one is worthy (of a *stūpa*)—if he is meritorious.

For Buddhas a *stūpa* has all its parts—the parts are four terraces, the petal, the dome, the enclosure, the crowning pole, thirteen umbrellas, and the rain receptacle.[71]

For Solitary Buddhas there is no rain receptacle.

For disciples there are one or more umbrellas depending on the measure of their achievement.

When the spots where they are lodged are within an area that is a Tathāgata's spot, they should encircle that[72]—in this case the order of seniority must be observed.

For ordinary men a *stūpa* is plain (i.e., without any crowning members)—they are to be placed outside the monastic complex.

In regard to Noble Ones a festival for the stūpa is necessary. [66]

That which is given to the *stūpa* of a disciple belongs indeed to his fellow monks.

Pearls are to be used thus for the Teaching.

The initiatory respect offerings will be for the Buddha—from that will be put aside what is required for repairs—that is also suitable for costs of worship.

What is first and most immediately obvious here is that we have shifted worlds. We are no longer in the leisurely world of the monastic jurist where narrative cases can be slowly built up, concerns negotiated, flexibility allowed—even deliberate ambiguity. We have moved to the world of the disciplinarian who tacks up lists on walls. There is no room here for contingency. What has above all else been lost in the move is any consideration of the laity.

Guṇaprabha had, presumably, at least three canonical passages to draw on for rules regarding monastic funerals: those found in the *Cīvaravastu*, those found in the *Kṣudrakavastu*, and the account of the funeral of the Monk Kālodāyin. A glance at the *Kṣudrakavastu* will immediately show that Guṇaprabha has faithfully reproduced the rules found there, entirely shorn of their narrative frame.[73] Although he alludes to them in a much earlier section,[74] here in the more relevant section he ignores the rules found in the *Cīvaravastu*. Most significantly, however, he completely ignores the account of the funeral of Kālodāyin, the one text that allows for some lay participation in such ritual events. Obviously Guṇaprabha had to make some choices, *but they did not have to take this form*.

Notice too that his selections of material concerning *stūpas* have the same result. He is once again depending closely on the account of Śāriputra's relics now found in the *Kṣudrakavastu*. But his presentation entirely excludes any reference to the frame-story or case that had been built up and, thereby, entirely excludes any place for the laity. Regardless, then, of the care and flexiblity with which the canonical jurist might have considered an issue, it is more than likely that the majority of monks received and knew that issue in a much more rigid form. It is also not impossible that Guṇaprabha's selections—and the consequent exclusion of the laity—are related to other changes that led to a precipitous decline in the number of lay donors clearly visible in Buddhist inscriptions dating from the fifth and sixth centuries.[75] [67]

In terms of more specific details, it is worth noting that—like his source text—Guṇaprabha appears to maintain, and therefore confirm, a clear distinction between funereal activity and activity in regard to *stūpas*, although his wording is somewhat cryptic. In the *Kṣudrakavastu* the discussion of a monastic funeral ends with the Buddha specifying what should presumably form its last moment: "The *stūpa* is to be worshiped" (*mchod rten la phyag 'tshal bar bya'o*). The *stūpa* in question here is almost certainly that of the Buddha—however anachronistic this might be—for the discussion itself has made no reference to building one for the deceased. Guṇaprabha adds a clause and thereby appears to emphasize the closure: "Having venerated the *stūpa*, they (the monks) should go in"—presumably, into the *vihāra*. The distinction also seems to be marked in another way. Guṇaprabha opens by saying, "Honor is to be done to the body of a deceased fellow monk," without any qualification: all monks are to get a funeral. But, significantly, all are not to get a *stūpa*. When he talks about *stūpas*, he adds a qualification: "Now, in regard to renunciants (*pravrājin*), that one is worthy (of a *stūpa*)—if he is meritorious." The commentary here on *da rab tu byung ba rnams la 'os pa nyid de—gal te dge ba yin na'o* fleshes it out thus: "When it is said 'Now, in regard to renunciants, that one is worthy,' this refers to a *stūpa*. But it might be asked if this is so for all. For that reason it is said: 'if he is meritorious'" (*de rab tu byung ba rnams la 'os pa nyid do zhes bya ba ni mchod rten de'o / ci thams cad la 'am zhe na de'i phyir / gal te dge ba yin na'o zhes bya ba smos te*).[76] Therefore, though all monks got a funeral, only the "meritorious" got a *stūpa*, and funeral and *stūpa* were determined by two quite different sets of considerations.

Guṇaprabha also confirms other distinctions. He confirms that *stūpas* for "ordinary men . . . are to be placed outside the monastic complex." The text of the *sūtra* has here only *so so'i skye bo*, or simply *pṛthagjana*, but both it and the text of its canonical source use *so so'i skye bo* and *so so'i skye bo dge ba* = *pṛthagjanakalyāṇa* interchangeably and are always referring to a category of monks. This is of note because it suggests that the masses of mostly anonymous mortuary *stūpas* and deposits that so often and so early transformed [68] "monastic sites into fields of funerary urns" were those of laypersons. This is confirmed in the rare cases in which such deposits are inscribed.[77]

Guṇaprabha confirms as well, by clearly stating it, that "festivals" were required for the *stūpas* of all *āryas*—not just Śāriputra. In fact, he states as a rule what is only implied in his source text, which refers to Śāriputra alone. The same applies to the question of ownership: what is, again, only implied in the *Kṣudrakavastu* Guṇaprabha states as an explicit rule: "That which is given to the *stūpa* of a disciple belongs indeed to his fellow monks." Here too the auto-commentary fills this out: *de la ras dang snam bu dang rdzas gang yang rnam pa gzhan gang dag phul ba de dag ni dge slong rnams kyis bgo bar bya'o*, "Here whatever cotton cloth and woolen cloth and object of possession (*dravya*), and any other type of thing that is given, that is to be divided by the monks" (Zu 271a.3).

Finally, Guṇaprabha both confirms that "first fruit" offerings go to the Buddha, but adds as well a stipulation not found in his immediate source text that may well have been intended to "correct" it. The account of Śāriputra's relics seems to imply that pearls (*mu tig*) were to be divided among the monks. But, as Guṇaprabha certainly knew,[78] this runs counter to other rulings in his *Vinaya* that specifically exclude pearls from such distribution or indicate that if pearls are divided, one share is "for the Buddha" (*ekaṃ buddhāya*). That share, moreover, is to be used to plaster the Perfume Chamber (*yo buddhasya bhāgas tena gandhakuṭyām pralepaṃ dadata*).[79] In his *Sūtra* Guṇaprabha says that pearls are to go to the Teaching (*śāsana*), but in his commentary he specifically says: "'A coat of plaster is to be given to the Perfume Chamber,' this is the meaning of the words 'to be used thus for the Teaching'" (*dri gtsang khang gi zhal zhal du bya'o zhes bstan pa bzhin du bya'o zhes bya ba'i don to*; Zu 271a.4). It is, of course, possible that a part of Guṇaprabha's insistence here is related to the fact that—to judge by Buddhist inscriptions—the Perfume Chamber was becoming an increasingly prominent part of Buddhist monastic institutions.[80] But regardless of his motivations, he is obviously trying to bring some order or system out of his source material. This last point leads us to the first of our final and more general observations. [69]

As we have seen, in regard to canonical passages on monastic funerals, Guṇaprabha had to make some choices; in regard to the disposition of pearls, he had to impose some order or consistency: Guṇaprabha had to do both because the compilers of the *Mūlasarvāstivāda-vinaya* appear to have done neither. This *Vinaya* is not only large but also messy. We have—to stick to our first example—at least three different formulations of rules governing monastic funerals in three different sections of the same *Vinaya*. Though basically similar, they are not the same and there is significant variation or development from one to another. It is difficult, given the presuppositions about how the Buddhist monastic codes were constructed, to account for this. But it seems at least possible that (1) each section of the *Mūlasarvāstivāda-vinaya* was organized, transmitted, and used by a different group within the same Order; or (2) this *Vinaya* never underwent the same processes of revision and systemization that some—if not all—other *vinayas* did. Certainly in comparison to the Pāli *Vinaya* the *Mūlasarvāstivāda-vinaya* is terribly untidy. Sylvain Lévi noticed this long ago and made his usual insightful observation: The

Mūlasarvāstivāda-vinaya's "tumultuous and chaotic liveliness," he said, "contrasts with the dry and cold regularity of the Pāli Vinaya. But," he added, "the systematic and rigorous ordering of material—not the confusion of genres—marks an advanced stage of an art or technique."[81] Moreover, the presence—repeatedly noted—of some seemingly very old material in this *Vinaya* may also suggest that it was never revised.[82]

There are, however, other inconsistencies in this *Vinaya* that seem to reflect something that goes beyond form or redactional history and points to a fissure that seems to appear throughout the history of Indian Buddhism—one side of the line has been clearly acknowledged and much studied, the other not. Much in Indian Buddhism seems to project a decidedly mixed message in regard to the body—certainly the *Mūlasarvāstivāda-vinaya* does. Everybody knows, for example, what the last words of the Buddha were supposed to have been: "All compounded things are by nature liable to change." But much less attention has been paid to what was—according to an equally good or equally bad authority—his last act. The Mūlasarvāstivādin *Mahāparinirvāṇasūtra*, which still forms a [70] part of its *Vinaya*, gives the following report of what took place immediately before the Buddha's death:

> There was this, however, that remained to be done by the Tathāgata, namely, taking pity on this final gathering.
>
> Then the Blessed One, having removed to one side the upper robe from his body, addressed the monks: "Behold, monks, the body of the Tathāgata! Look closely, monks, at the body of the Tathāgata."
>
> *api tu karaṇīyam etat tathāgatena yathāpi tat paścimāṃ janatāṃ anukampamānaḥ. atha bhagavān svakāyād uttarāsaṅgam ekānte vivṛtya bhikṣūn āmantrayate: avalokayata bhikṣavas tathāgatasya kāyam vyavalokayata bhikṣavas tathāgatasya kāyaṃ.*[83]

An equally startling display of bodies occurs in the account of the funeral of Mahāprajāpatī. After the bodies of Mahāprajāpatī and the five hundred nuns who died with her are set down at the place for cremation, the text says:

> The Blessed One then, having laid aside the upper robes from the bodies of Mahāprajāpatī Gautamī and those five hundred nuns, spoke to the monks: "Look, monks! Although Mahāprajāpatī Gautamī and these five hundred nuns have lived for a hundred and twenty years, there are no wrinkles or white hair on their bodies—they look like girls of sixteen."
>
> *de nas bcom ldan 'das kyis skye dgu'i bdag mo chen mo go'u ta mi dang / dge slong ma lnga brgya po dag gi lus las bla gos phud nas / dge slong rnams la bka' stsal pa / dge slong dag skye dgu'i bdag mo chen mo go'u ta mi dang / dge slong ma lnga brgya po 'di dag lo brgya nyi shu long yang / lus la gnyer ma dang skra dkar med cing / bu mo lo bcu drug lon pa lta bu la ltos /* (Ta 172a.3)

Notice that both exhibitions are intended for and explicitly directed toward monks. They are apparently meant for their edification, not for that of a group of admiring lay devotees. They both, moreover, reflect a strong positive value placed on holy bodies.

That there be some ambivalence in regard to the bodies of the founders of the monastic communities may not be too surprising. But it is precisely for that reason that it is important to note that the ambivalence appears to be much wider and appears to arise in regard to ordinary Buddhist bodies as well.

One pole of the monastic attitude to the body—the pole that is widely acknowledged in the scholarly literature—can be documented within this *Vinaya* itself. In one of the infrequent passages in the *Mūlasarvāstivāda-vinaya* that refers to "mental cultivation" we find the following:

> The Blessed One said: "The practice of sitting is called yoga (*niṣadyā ucyate yogaḥ*). Monks, you should observe that this body (*kāya*), from the soles of the feet upward, [71] from the hair of the head downward, is bounded by skin, and as it stands, as it obtains, is full of various sorts of impurity. There are in this body hairs of the head, body hairs, nails, teeth, dirt, filth, skin, flesh, bone, sinew, veins, kidneys, spleen, lung, intestines, mesentery, stomach, abdomen, bladder, liver, shit, tears, sweat, phlegm, grease, lymph, marrow, fat, bile, mucus, pus, blood, and piss. The body thus is to be observed."[84]

Passages of this sort are, of course, widely passed off as "good Buddhism," and they certainly give expression to one important part of what appears to have been a complex attitude. What has been much less frequently noted, though, are other expressions of other aspects of this attitude. In the *Mūlasarvāstivāda-vinaya*, for example, it may be these other aspects that are more frequently found. Certainly alongside passages that describe the body as full of dirt, filth, shit, and piss we find as well elaborate rules specifying that it is to be washed, anointed, carefully handled, and reverently honored. Its "parts" too are to be carefully preserved. Both types of passages must be considered.

Finally, we need at least to ask again how these "parts" were thought of. We have seen above that both texts and inscriptions suggest that they were thought to contain or to be enlivened by the spiritual qualities of the person they belonged to—that they were alive. There is further confirmation of this in yet another text from the *Mūlasarvāstivāda-vinaya*, and citing it will allow us to end as we began—with a story. The story is a curious pendant to the equally curious case given in the Pāli *Bhikkhunīvibhaṅga* under *Pācittiya* LII. Both involve the destruction by an angry monk of *stūpas* that groups of nuns had erected for the remains of the bodies of deceased persons honored by their communities. The text of the Mūlasarvāstivādin case says that when the nuns heard that the *stūpa* had been destroyed, they said, "Our brother beginning from today is, indeed, dead" (*bdag cag gi ming po deng gdod shi ba lta zhes*), and wept.[85] The redactors do not comment on this expression. Perhaps we would do well to follow their lead.

Notes

1. See B. Faure, *The Rhetoric of Immediacy. A Cultural Critique of Chan/Zen Buddhism* (Princeton, N.J.: 1991), esp. 149–208; R. H. Sharf, "The Idolization of Enlightenment: On the Mummification of Ch'an Masters in Medieval China," *HR* 32 (1992) 1–31; W. M. Bodiford, "Zen in the Art of Funerals: Ritual Salvation in Japanese Buddhism," *HR* 32 (1992) 146–164; cf. K. Shinohara, "Two Sources of Chinese Buddhist Biographies: Stupa Inscriptions and Miracle Stories," in *Monks and Magicians. Religious Biographies in Asia*, ed. P. Granoff and K. Shinohara (Oakville: 1988) 119–228; J. Hubbard, "Chinese Reliquary Inscriptions and the San-chieh-chiao," *JIABS* 14.2 (1991) 253–280; etc.

2. I am particularly aware of the weakness of the work on Indian materials, given that I wrote it—see G. Schopen, "On Avoiding Ghosts and Social Censure: Monastic Funerals in the *Mūlasarvāstivāda-vinaya*," *JIP* 20 (1992) 1–39 [= *BSBM* 204–237] [I here thank my friend Richard Hayes for having drawn so much undeserved attention to this piece that it justified another]; Schopen, "An Old Inscription from Amarāvatī and the Cult of the Local Monastic Dead in Indian Buddhist Monasteries," *JIABS* 14.2 (1991) 281–329 [= *BSBM* 165–204]; cf. Schopen, "Monks and the Relic Cult in the Mahāparinibbānasutta: An Old Misunderstanding in Regard to Monastic Buddhism," in *From Benares to Beijing. Essays on Buddhism and Chinese Religion in Honour of Prof. Jan Yün-Hua*, ed. K. Shinohara and G. Schopen (Oakville: 1991) 187–201 [= *BSBM* 99–113]; Schopen, "Burial Ad Sanctos and the Physical Presence of the Buddha in Early Indian Buddhism," *Religion* 17 (1987) 193–225 [= *BSBM* 114–147]; Schopen, "*Stūpa* and *Tīrtha*: Tibetan Mortuary Practices and an Unrecognized Form of Burial Ad Sanctos at Buddhist Sites in India," *Buddhist Forum II. Papers in Honour of D. S. Ruegg*, ed. T. Skorupski (London: 1993) 273–293 [= *FFMB* Ch. XIV].

3. So—in order of citation—M. Lalou, "Notes sur la décoration des monastères bouddhiques," *RAA* 5.3 (1930) 183; J. Przyluski, "Fables in the Vinaya-Piṭaka of the Sarvāstivādin School," *IHQ* 5 (1929) 5; E. Huber, "Le roi kaniṣka dans le vinaya des mūlasarvāstivādins," *BEFEO* 14 (1914) 18; S. Lévi, "Les saintes écritures du bouddhisme. Comment s'est constitué le canon sacré," in *Mémorial Sylvain Lévi* (Paris: 1937) 78, 84.

4. The most detailed and useful "table of contents" that I know for this *Vinaya* is to be found in T. Skorupski, *A Catalogue of the Stog Palace Kanjur* (Tokyo: 1985) 1–28, which follows the division of the text according to the types and numbers of offense. It is, however, not cross-referenced to other editions.

5. C. Hallisey, "Apropos the Pāli Vinaya as a Historical Document: A Reply to Gregory Schopen," *JPTS* 15 (1991) 206–207.

6. To my knowledge, little work has been done on Mūlasarvāstivādin summaries or handbooks of the *Vinaya*. The *Ārya-mūlasarvāstivādi-śrāmaṇera-kārika*, sometimes attributed to Nāgārjuna, has been translated into English: L. Dagpa et al., *The Discipline of the Novice Monk* (Mussoorie, India: 1975), and works of this sort designed for novices may be a good place to start. (R. E. Buswell in speaking of Korean monasticism says, for example, that a text entitled *Admonitions to Beginners* was "the first text read by every incoming postulant" and that this text meant for novices is "the basic handbook of Korean monastic regulations and lifestyle"—*The Zen Monastic Experience. Buddhist Practice in Contemporary Korea* [Princeton, N.J.: 1992] 191, 80.) A start has also been made on what appears to be a promising genre of texts for Tibetan monasticism, the so-called *bca' yig*, "the name for a document outlining the basic principles, institutions, roles, and rules governing the organization and operation of a Tibetan monastic community"—see T. Ellingson, "Tibetan Monastic Constitutions: The Bca' Yig," in *Reflections on Tibetan Culture. Essays in Memory of Turrell V. Wylie*, ed. L. Epstein and R. F. Sherburne (Lewiston, N.Y.: 1990) 205–229, which contains a short discussion of the relationship of such *bca' yig* to the canonical *vinaya*.

7. Cited from Edgerton, *BHSD* 181, who is correcting *Mahāvastu* iii 104.7; see also G. P. Malalasekera, *Dictionary of Pāli Proper Names* (London: 1937) i 589–590, s.v. Kāḷudāyī Thera.

8. It concerns a brahmin who gains control of a non-human-being (*mi ma yin pa*) by means of *mantras*, hooks him to a cart, and drives around Śrāvastī. Kālodāyin sees the brahmin get off his cart to have a piss and—to allow the *mi ma yin pa* to escape—causes the brahmin to continue to piss interminably through his supernatural powers (*byin gyis brlabs nus*). Such stories—sometimes crude but always funny—are a significant part of *vinaya* literature that has been sadly overlooked.

9. In the present essay, I have sometimes used this Derge edition—*The Tibetan Tripitaka. Taipei Edition*, ed. A. W. Barber (Taipei: 1991)—which is the only complete edition now available to me; and sometimes *The Tog Palace Manuscript of the Tibetan Kanjur* (Leh: 1979), only part of which I now have access to. This in itself should warn the reader that the translations presented here are not based on a critically established text and are therefore tentative in this regard (the immense labor that will be required to establish such a text can be seen in H. Eimer, *Rab tu 'byuṅ ba'i gži. Die tibetische Übersetzung des Pravrajyāvastu im Vinaya der Mūlasarvāstivādins*, T. I und II (Asiatische Forschungen Band 82) (Wiesbaden: 1983). The translations are, however, tentative in other ways as well. The *Mūlasarvāstivāda-vinaya* in both Sanskrit and Tibetan is not only huge but largely unstudied. It is written in an elliptical, often almost colloquial style, bristles with uncommon constructions and obscure or virtually unknown lexical items, and is haunted by textual uncertainties. In dealing with these texts, I have frequently felt that I was not—to use a favorite phrase of J. W. de Jong's—"equal to the task." To at least partially offset the quality of the translations, I have felt it necessary to cite the original more often than I would have liked, and certainly more often than will be convenient for many readers. I have, however, tried to keep textual and lexical notes to a minimum—they will have to wait until another time.

10. *bdag nyid chen po 'di'i rjes gcod pa 'ga' zhig phyis 'ong grang snyams nas* is ambiguous;

it might also mean "thinking that perhaps someone coming by later would obliterate the tracks of the Eminent One."

11. *rkang pa gnyis la phyag 'tshal nas*; this is an interesting anthropomorphic turn of phrase not uncommonly applied—as here—to *stūpas* in this *Vinaya*; for some instances in Sanskrit, see *Adhikaraṇavastu* (Gnoli) 70.12: *tasmin stūpe samāropitam tīvreṇa ca prasādena pādayor nipatya*; *Saṅghabhedavastu* (Gnoli) i 161: *yāvat paśyati stūpam . . . pūjāṃ kṛtvā pādayor nipatya*; see also *Śayanāsanavastu* (Gnoli) 32.18, where the same expression is applied not to a *stūpa* but to a pot (*kumbha*) containing the bones of a Pratyekabuddha.

12. Schopen, "On Avoiding Ghosts and Social Censure," 3–14 [= *BSBM* 206–215].

13. *Cīvaravastu*, GMs iii 2, 115.8.

14. *Kṣudrakavastu*, Tog, 'dul ba Ta 358b.7–359a.4.

15. *Cīvaravastu*, GMs iii 2, 127.10; Tog, 'dul ba Ga 138b.4; Schopen, *JIP* 20 (1992) 9.

16. Schopen, "Monks and the Relic Cult," 187–201 [= *BSBM* Ch. VI].

17. *Cīvaravastu*, GMs iii 2, 118.15, 125.14.

18. *Kṣudrakavastu*, Tog, 'dul ba Ta 353a.7.

19. The use of the term *śarīra-pūjā* to refer to funeral ceremonies is also not limited to accounts dealing with monks; see *Saṅghabhedavastu* (Gnoli) ii 40–41, where a *kinnarī* (Yaśodharā in a former life) asks the king, who slayed her husband (Śākyamuni), to wait before taking her away so she could perform *śarīra-pūjā* for her dead mate: *deva tiṣṭhatu tāvat anujānīhi māṃ yāvad asya kinnarasya śarīrapūjāṃ kariṣyāmi*. The king agrees, thinking to himself: *kva gamiṣyati, paśyāmi, tāvat katham asya śarīrapūjāṃ karoti iti*.

20. Cf. *TSD* 2394; for *dril phyi*, see *Bod rgya tshig mdzod chen mo* 1332, where *dril phyis* is defined as *lus kyi dreg pa phyis pa*. [For both it and *sa dkar*, see now G. Schopen, "Hierarchy and Housing in a Buddhist Monastic Code," *Buddhist Literature* 2 (2000) 160 (V. 16)].

21. *Vinayavibhaṅga*, Derge, 'dul ba Ja 155b.4.

22. See *Saṅghabhedavastu* (Gnoli) i 70.15, 163.5, etc.

23. See below, pp. 294 and 318.

24. Schopen, "On Avoiding Ghosts and Social Censure," 35; Schopen, *From Benares to Beijing*, 195 [= *BSBM* 234, 108].

25. A. H. Longhurst, *The Story of the Stūpa* (Colombo: 1936) 13–14.

26. As the above allusion to *vihāras* hopefully suggests, the same perceptions or assumptions that distort our reading of textual references to *stūpas* almost certainly distort our reading of such references to *vihāras*. When the term *vihāra* is translated by "monastery," this undoubtedly conceals more than it reveals. Some of the problems involved have already been acknowledged elsewhere. S. Foot, for example, has said, "No writer from the early Anglo-Saxon period defined precisely what a *monasterium* (in Old English a *mynster*) was. . . . *Monasterium*, *coenobium*, and the Old English *mynster* were in fact used synonymously, and very imprecisely, to denote a wide variety of types of establishment" (S. Foot, "What Was an Early Anglo-Saxon Monastery?" in *Monastic Studies. The Continuity of Tradition*, ed. J. Loades [Bangor, Maine: 1990] 48). E. James, in regard to yet another context, has pointed to another part of the problem and to an obvious, if often overlooked, source for arriving at some clarification. He starts by citing J. Hourlier to the effect that "scholars study the history of monasticism, analyse its institutions and even explore its economic

and social problems with little or no reference to a factor which is necessarily central to all monastic life, the monastery itself." But then he adds: "In the future we are likely to learn just as much about early medieval monastic life from the archaeologist as from the ecclesiastical or social historian" (James, "Archaeology and the Merovingian Monastery," in *Columbanus and Merovingian Monasticism*, ed. H. B. Clarke and M. Brennan [Oxford: 1981] 33). That all these considerations apply as well to the study of Buddhist monasticism in India probably does not need to be belabored.

27. The Tibetan text here and just above is cited from *Kṣudrakavastu*, Tog, 'dul ba Ta 171b.1 and 172a.1. When Mahāprajāpatī died, five hundred of her fellow nuns died with her, but this is only one example of what is something of a commonplace in the accounts of the death of the great disciples—when Śāriputra died, eighty thousand monks also died with him; when Maudgalyāyana died, seventy-seven thousand monks also passed away, Tog, 'dul ba Ta 358b.5. Ānanda too was joined in death by a Ṛṣi and five hundred of his attendants who had just previously become monks, Tog, 'dul ba Tha 469b.6ff.

28. Schopen, "On Avoiding Ghosts and Social Censure," 21 [= *BSBM* 221].

29. Cf. S. Collins, "*Kalyāṇamitta* and *Kalyāṇamittatā*," *JPTS* 11 (1986), for a treatment of the term in Pāli sources.

30. There is much, I suspect, that we do not understand, or have glossed over, in regard to the technical sense of the terms *upāsikā* and *upāsaka*. Though habitually translated by "laywoman" or "layman," it is beginning to appear that individuals so designated may have constituted a small group that fell somewhere between monks and nuns and the general population; they appear to have had a particularly close and formally acknowledged relationship with their monastic communities; and monks and nuns appear to have had a specific set of ritual obligations in regard to such individuals. See G. Schopen, "The Ritual Obligations and Donor Roles of Monks in the Pāli *Vinaya*," *JPTS* 16 (1992) 87–107 [= *BSBM* 72–85], esp. 103–104, but a great deal more work needs to be done here.

31. As one of a number of possible sources on the mutual obligations between an *ācārya* and an *antevāsin*, see J. Filliozat and H. Kuno, "Fragments du vinaya des sarvāstivādin," *JA* (1938) 51–52 and esp. 51 n. 4.

32. *Bhikṣuṇīvinayavibhaṅga*, Derge, 'dul ba Ta 245b.5. Two additional points are worth noting here. First, this is not the only indication we have of friction between nuns and monks concerning objects of worship—both the Pāli *Bhikkhunīvibhaṅga* and the Mūlasarvāstivādin *Kṣudrakavastu* contain accounts of monks destroying *stūpas* that nuns had erected (see below, Ch. XI). Second, this passage in the *Bhikṣuṇīvibhaṅga* presents us with a rare canonical reference to an image containing a relic.

33. *Kṣudrakavastu*, Tog, 'dul ba Ta 354a.5–368a.5.

34. For these *uddānas*, see J. L. Panglung, "Preliminary Remarks on the Uddānas in the Vinaya of the Mūlasarvāstivādin," in *Tibetan Studies in Honour of Hugh Richardson*, ed. M. Aris and A. S. S. Kyi (Warminster: 1980) 226–232.

35. *Saṅghabhedavastu*, GMs iii 4, 239.17; (Gnoli) ii 264.18.

36. For the first of these inscriptions—"securely dated to . . . about the first half of the 1st century A.D."—see R. Salomon, "The Inscription of Senavarma, King of Oḍi," *IIJ* 29 (1986) 265 (lines 7a–d), and G. Fussman, "Documents épigraphiques kouchans (III).

L'inscription kharoṣṭhī de senavarma, roi d'oḍi: une nouvelle lecture," *BEFEO* 71 (1982) 4 (7a–d). Note, too, that in line 12b of this inscription the relic is described as *amuda* = *amṛta* or "immortal." For the second inscription—dating to 25–26 C.E.—see G. Fussman, "Nouvelles inscriptions śaka (II)," *BEFEO* 73 (1984) 39 (lines b11–13).

37. For references and further discussion, see Schopen, "Burial Ad Sanctos," 205–206. For some remarks on the Pāli parallel to the *Kṣudraka's* account of the death of Śāriputra, see Schopen, "An Old Inscription from Amarāvāti," n. 111 [= *BSBM* 127–128, 203].

38. The text translated here has been briefly summarized in W. W. Rockhill, *The Life of the Buddha and the Early History of His Order* (London: 1884) 111–112; L. de La Vallée Poussin, "Staupikam," *HJAS* 2 (1935) 276–279; G. Roth, "Symbolism of the Buddhist Stūpa According to the Tibetan Version of the Caitya-vibhāga-vinayodbhāva-sūtra, the Sanskrit Treatise Stūpa-lakṣaṇakārikā-vivecana, and a Corresponding Passage in Kuladatta's Kriyāsaṃgraha," in *The Stūpa. Its Religious, Historical and Architectural Significance*, ed. A. L. Dallapiccola and S. Z. Lallemant (Wiesbaden: 1980) 183–185. None of these summaries, it seems, does justice to the complexities of the account, and G. Roth in particular leaves—I think—a distorted impression of its point when he says: "The narration of this important passage illustrates that it is the laymen who are concerned with the construction and worship of a *stūpa* and the relics."

39. On the Tibetan treatment of the expression, see Schopen, "On Avoiding Ghosts and Social Censure," 28–29 n. 38 [= *BSBM* 227 n. 38].

40. What is meant here by *khyim gyi mchog gi nang du mthon po zhig tu* is particularly unclear to me. Rockhill has "put them in a high place," Roth "on a prominent place of his house."

41. For full discussions of the terms used here to designate the different parts of a *stūpa*, see the papers by de La Vallée Poussin and Roth cited in n. 38 above.

42. *Poṣadhasthāpanavastu*, GMs iii 3, 117.1; Tog, 'dul ba Ga 250b.6.

43. *Divyāvadāna* (Cowell and Neil) 419.16, 429.17.

44. De La Vallée Poussin, *HJAS* 2 (1939) 288.

45. It is worth noting that, as with the term *vihāra* (see n. 26 above), the exact significance of *ārāma*, *kun dga' ra ba*, or what precisely it designates, is not yet clear. It will be noticed both here and below that the narrative of the funeral of the Monk Kālodāyin, and a number of other texts, including the *Mahāparinirvāṇasūtra*, conflict with the ruling in the *Kṣudrakavastu*'s account of the remains of Śāriputra and Guṇaprabha's *Vinayasutra* in regard to the placement of the *stūpas*. The former say that the *stūpa* is, or should be, erected "at a crossing of four great roads." This is a question that cannot be treated here, but it is worth noting two things. First, none of the hundreds of *stūpas* discovered in India are—to my knowledge—situated literally "at a crossing of four great roads," but rather they are situated in, or in close association with, a Buddhist monastery. Second, "crossroads" have in Indian culture a decidedly ambivalent value (see D. D. Kosambi, "At the Crossroads: A Study of Mother-Goddess Cult Sites," in Kosambi, *Myth and Reality. Studies in the Formation of Indian Culture* [Bombay: 1962] 82–109: "The crossroads, according to Varāhamihira, bring evil repute upon any house situated near the junction [*Bṛhatsaṃhitā* 53.89]. In *Br.* 51.4, the location is listed among inauspicious places, below the cemetery

and the deserted temple"). The *Mūlasarvāstivāda-vinaya* itself repeatedly refers to a category of gods associated with crossroads (*catvaradevatā*) who are supplicated by people in the hope of obtaining offspring (*Cīvaravastu*, GMs iii 2, 139.11; *Adhikaraṇavastu* [Gnoli] 69.25; etc.), and they are as well a kind of no-man's-land that cannot be included in a "parish boundary" (*sīmāhṛta*) (*Cīvaravastu*, GMs iii 2, 111.10ff). The whole question needs further work.

46. Both the Pāli and its English translation are cited from P. Masefield, *Divine Revelation in Pali Buddhism* (London: 1986) 23.

47. For references and a discussion of this material, see Schopen, "An Old Inscription from Amarāvāti," 281–329 [= *BSBM* Ch. IX].

48. J. Marshall et al., *The Monuments of Sāñchī* (Delhi: 1940) Vol. I, 79.

49. I. H. Siddiqui, "The Early Chisthi Dargahs," in *Muslim Shrines in India. Their Character, History and Significance*, ed. C. W. Troll (Delhi: 1989) 11, 21–22.

50. E. A. Mann, "Religion, Money and Status: The Competition for Resources at the Shrine of Shah Jamal, Aligarh," in *Muslim Shrines in India*, ed. Troll, 166, 145.

51. One of the things we know even less about is the exact historical relationship between Sufi *dargahs* and Buddhist *stūpas*, though there are some indications, and some reasons to suspect, that their similarities might well be more than simply typological. In *JA* 280 (1992) there is a brief description of a paper delivered by C. Servan-Schreiber entitled "'Dargah sur stoupa.' Une modèle d'implantation du culte des saints musulmans au Bihar (Inde)," in which she speaks of "un réseau de tombes de saints musulmans établies sur des stoupas bouddhistes" (p. 401). Jackson too has pointed out that the Sufi Saint Sharafuddin Maneri lived the last forty years of his life, and was entombed, on the outskirts of the township of Bihar, the latter being, according to him, the site of the then recently occupied Vihāra of Odantapuri (P. Jackson, *The Way of a Sufi. Sharafuddin Maneri* [Delhi: 1987] 17ff). The same scholar, in speaking about "the most imposing dargah in Patna proper, that of Shah Arzan," says "very likely the elevated area where the dargah is situated marks the site of some Buddhist ruins" (P. Jackson, "Perceptions of the Dargahs of Patna," in Troll, *Muslim Shrines in India*, 106). For the same sort of thing in a much wider area, see A. Stein, "Note on Buddhist Local Worship in Muhammadan Central Asia," *JRAS* (1910) 839ff; A. Stein, *An Archaeological Tour in Wazīristān and Northern Balūchistān* (Calcutta: 1929) 20, 24, 27, 65, etc. In addition to this topographical overlay, an overlay of a different sort has also been asserted. Haq has said, for example, "The Buddhist practice of *Chaitya-pūjā*, i.e. worship of gravemounds of the departed saintly men (*sthavīra* or *thera*—an old man) is undoubtedly at the basis of Pīr-[saint] adoring practices . . . the descendants of *Chaitya* worshippers, when converted to Islam, became the tomb-worshippers (*Gūr-purast*) or saint-worshippers (*Pīr-purast*)" (M. E. Haq, *A History of Sufi-ism in Bengal* [Dacca: 1975] 324–325). It does not matter much that Haq has confused Hindu *samadhis* with Buddhist *stūpas*. His assertion—rephrased as a hypothesis—is well worth pursuing. This, of course, will involve much more work on the neglected "late" periods of Indian Buddhism.

52. Li Yung-hsi, trans., *A Record of the Buddhist Countries by Fa-hsien* (Peking: 1957) 36. The older translations of this passage differ considerably for the last two sentences—

J. Legge, *A Record of Buddhistic Kingdoms* (Oxford: 1886) 44–45; H. A. Giles, *The Travels of Fa-Hsien* (Cambridge, England: 1923) 22–23.

53. Pāli *Vinaya* iii 266, also iv 156. The translation cited is from I. B. Horner, *The Book of the Discipline* (Oxford: 1940) ii 162. When I cited Horner's translation in G. Schopen, "The Stūpa Cult and the Extant Pāli Vinaya," *JPTS* 13 (1989) 89 [= *BSBM* 86–98], I inadvertently omitted the phrase "for another shrine or."

54. *'phags pa rin po che'i phung po lung bstan pa*, Derge, dkon brtsegs, Cha 164a.7ff. There is a Sanskrit text for this passage from the *Ratnarāśi* in *Śikṣāsamuccaya* (Bendall) 56.5ff, but to judge by the Tibetan, the passage there has suffered somewhat in transmission or—as frequently happens—has been telescoped in quotation.

55. Some sense of the value these gifts might have had can be gotten by noticing that all three things listed—but especially "tortoise shell"—were all much sought-after items of the international maritime trade at the beginning of the Common Era in which India played a major role. See the richly annotated L. Casson, *The Periplus Maris Erythraei* (Princeton, N.J.: 1989), esp. 42.

56. See G. Schopen, "The Buddha as an Owner of Property and Permanent Resident in Medieval Indian Monasteries," *JIP* 18 (1990) 199 [= *BSBM* 258–289], where I express my ignorance of the meaning of *bud dud* and which now, I think, can be corrected. For Buston's *mchod rten la mchod pa byas pa'i phan yon*, see L. Chandra, ed., *The Collected Works of Bu Ston* (New Delhi: 1969) Part 14, Pha 560–573, esp. 561.3.

57. Jäschke, 343, 342.

58. See for this type of image and references to it Schopen, "The Buddha as an Owner of Property," 199–200 and n. 77 [= *BSBM* 286 n. 77].

59. It is worth noting, although I do not understand either reference fully, that the *Sphuṭārthā Śrīghanācāra-saṃgraha-ṭīkā* certainly, and the *Cīvaravastu* possibly, refer to *mahas*, or "festivals," connected with some or all of the four main events of the Buddha's biography—birth, enlightenment, turning the wheel of Dharma, and *parinirvāṇa*—as specific sources of revenue for the monks; see *Sphuṭārthā Śrīghanācāra-saṃgraha-ṭīkā* (Sanghasena) 41.12; J. D. M. Derrett, *A Textbook for Novices. Jayarakṣita's "Perspicuous Commentary on the Compendium of Conduct by Śrīghana"* (Torino: 1983) 49–50; *Cīvaravastu*, GMs iii 2, 113.8. Note that the latter does not actually use the term *maha* but speaks, in part, of goods (*lābha*) received at the shrines connected with these events (*caturmahācaityeṣu*). A close study of these passages promises to give us a glimpse, at least, of the economic functions of both such festivals and these important sites. Guṇaprabha also refers to festivals and goods received at these sites; see *Vinayasūtra*, bstan 'gyur, 'dul ba Wu 28b.7, 99b.5.

60. *Cīvaravastu*, GMs iii 2, 117.8ff.

61. See R. Lingat, *The Classical Law of India*, trans. J. D. M. Derrett (Berkeley: 1973) xiii; P. V. Kane, *History of Dharmaśāstra* (Poona: 1941) Vol. II, Part I, 118 ("nor was there in Ancient India any practice of making wills whereby large estates came to the Church as in England"); cf. Vol. II, Part II, 887–888. It is Yājñavalkya who "gives preference to documentary evidence . . . and gives very detailed rules about the drawing up of legal documents"—so Lingat (p. 99), who cites Kane as placing Yājñavalkya "in the first two centuries of the Christian Era . . . even . . . as early as the first century B.C."

62. *Cīvaravastu*, GMs iii 2, 139.6ff, esp. 140.15–141.1.

63. Tāranātha, *History of Buddhism in India*, trans. L. Chimpa and A. Chattopadhyaya (Simla: 1970) 176–177 and n. 1; Bu-ston, *History of Buddhism (Chos-ḥbung)*, trans. E. Obermiller (Heidelberg: 1931–1932) ii 160–161; I-ching, *A Record of the Buddhist Religion as Practiced in India and the Malay Archipelago* (London: 1896) lviii, 181, and n. 3; J. Naudou, *Les bouddhistes kaśmīriens au moyen age* (Paris: 1968) 57, 88; M. Tatz, *Asanga's Chapter on Ethics* (Lewiston, N.Y.: 1986) 28–29 and n. 36; see also the works cited in n. 65 below.

64. Bu-ston, *History of Buddhism* ii 160; i 43, 58.

65. See R. Sāṅkṛityāyana, "Second Search of Sanskrit Palm-leaf Mss. in Tibet," *JBORS* 23 (1937) 34–35. The first chapter of the Sanskrit text of both *sūtra* and commentary is edited in P. V. Bapat and V. V. Gokhale, *Vinaya-sūtra and Auto-Commentary on the Same* (Patna: 1982); see also P. V. Bapat, "Discovery of a Sanskrit Text: *Vinaya-sūtra*," in *Proceedings of the Twenty-sixth International Congress of Orientalists*, Vol. III, Part I (Poona: 1969) 343–344; Bapat, "Kṛt in a Buddhist Sanskrit Vinaya Text," *Journal of the Department of Sanskrit* (University of Delhi) December 1971, 58–62; Bapat, "Guṇaprabha's *Vinaya-sūtra* and His Own Commentary on the Same," *JIABS* 1.2 (1979) 47–51. [This note was written before I knew about Sāṅkṛityāyana's edition—see Ch. III above, n. 55.]

66. I am now preparing a paper dealing with the section on images, to be called "Bringing the Buddha into Town: Rules Governing Monastic Image Processions from an Early Medieval Text." [This paper never materialized—see, however, *FFMB*, Ch. IV.]

67. I have corrected obvious spelling mistakes in the text without notice, the "correct" form being found in the canonical text that Guṇaprabha is drawing on or in the auto-commentary. But in addition to a complete edition of the Sanskrit text, there is a pressing need for a critical edition of the Tibetan translation. There are a number of places where, for example, a reading in the Tibetan translation of the commentary, which cites in full the text of the *sūtra* it is commenting on, differs from the reading in the *sūtra* itself. Several centuries separate the translation of the *sūtra* (c. ninth century) from the translation of the commentary (twelfth century), according to Bapat and Gokhale (xviii, nn. 2 and 3), and this may account for some of these differences. Cf. n. 76 below.

68. For *brko ba*, which I have translated "grave," the commentary says: *sa brkos par gzhug pa*—*Svavyākhyānābhidhānavinayasūtravṛtti*, Derge, bstan 'gyur, 'dul ba Zu 270a.4.

69. Notice that here Guṇaprabha appears to have reworked the canonical text he appears to have been relying on. It has *yon bsngo zhing rgyun chags gsum gyi chos mnyan pa byin nas*. He therefore establishes a more "natural" order and omits reference to the *Tridaṇḍaka* (see Schopen, "On Avoiding Ghosts and Social Censure," 15, 20, n. 62). He does, however, refer to the *Tridaṇḍaka* elsewhere (Derge, Wu 30a.4, 56b.6, 71a.2). The Tibetan here—as elsewhere, Wu 68a.7—also prefers *yon bshad pa* to the canonical *yon bsngo ba* for translating *dakṣiṇām ādiś-*. But the canonical text itself occasionally also uses *yon bshad pa*: *Poṣadhavastu*, GMs iii 4, 80.8, *dakṣiṇāṁ nādiśanti* = Tog Ka 202b.2, *yon bshad par mi byed nas*.

70. The translation "within a chamber" is not certain; cf. *dri gtsang khang* = *gandhakuṭī* where *gtsang khang* translates *kuṭī*.

71. There is some variation here from the canonical vocabulary used to describe the various parts of a *stūpa*—see n. 41 above.

72. I do not understand this sentence; cf. the canonical text on which it is presumably based cited above, p. 304.

73. The *Kṣudrakavastu* passage is cited and translated in full in Schopen, "On Avoiding Ghosts and Social Censure," 15–17 [= *BSBM* 215–218].

74. *dbyung ba dang rim gro dang chos mnyan pa dang yon bshad ma byas par byin gyis brlab par mi bya'o*—Derge, Wu 68a.7, requiring thus all the elements individually stipulated in the *Cīvaravastu*. See Schopen, "On Avoiding Ghosts and Social Censure," 7–11 [= *BSBM* 210–213].

75. Cf. G. Schopen, "The Inscription on the Kuṣān Image of Amitābha and the Character of the Early Mahāyāna in India," *JIABS* 10.2 (1987) 120 [= *FFMB* Ch. VIII]; Schopen, "On Monks, Nuns, and 'Vulgar' Practices: The Introduction of the Image Cult into Indian Buddhism," *ArA* 49 1/2 (1988/89) 164–165 [= *BSBM* 238–257].

76. Derge, Zu 270a.7. This citation is a good example of the sort of thing referred to above n. 67: the text of the *sūtra* reads *da rab tu byung ba rnams* . . . , but the commentary quotes the *sūtra* as *de rab tu byung ba rnams*. . . .

77. The phrase is from G. Fussman and M. Le Berre, *Monuments bouddhiques de la région de caboul*, I. *Le monastère de gul dara* (Paris: 1976) 46. The examples I know where such deposits are inscribed come from outside India: C. Duroiselle, "Excavations at Hmawza, Prome," *ARASI for 1911–12* (Calcutta: 1915) 147ff; S. Paranavitana, "Recent Discoveries at the Ruvanväli Dāgaba (Mahāthūpa) of Anurādhapura," *Annual Bibliography of Indian Archaeology*, Vol. XV for the years 1940–1947 (Leiden: 1950) xlii–xlv.

78. See *Vinayasūtra*, Derge Wu 68b.6, which is ambiguous.

79. *Cīvaravastu*, GMs iii 2, 143.1–.5; *Adhikaraṇavastu* (Gnoli) 68.9ff; cf. *Sphuṭārthā Śrīghanācārasaṃgraha-ṭīkā* (Sanghasena) 42.7, but the reading here is *muktāphala-*.

80. See Schopen "The Buddha as an Owner of Property," 193ff [= *BSBM* 268ff].

81. Lévi, *Mémorial Sylvain Lévi*, 84.

82. Cf. Schopen, "On Avoiding Ghosts and Social Censure," n. 69 [= *BSBM* 235].

83. *Mahāparinirvāṇasūtra* (Waldschmidt) §§ 42.8–.10. Edgerton, *BHSD*, s.v. *paścima*, gives *paścimā janatā* as "vulgar folk," but that sense can hardly be in play here; Tibetan is *dus phyi ma'i sems can rnams la*.

84. *Poṣadhavastu*, GMs iii 4, 72.16ff.

85. *Kṣudraka*, Derge, 'dul ba Da 172b.2–174b.5.

CHAPTER XI

The Suppression of Nuns and the Ritual Murder of Their Special Dead in Two Buddhist Monastic Codes

THE COMPILERS OF THE various Buddhist monastic codes that we have appear to have been very anxious men. They were anxious about—even obsessed with—maintaining their public reputation and that of their Order, and avoiding any hint of social scandal or lay criticism.[1] They were anxious about their body and what went into it, and they were anxious about women.[2] They appear, moreover, to have been particularly anxious about nuns, about containing, restraining, and controlling them. At every opportunity they seem to have promulgated rules toward these ends. Some scholars, seeing the resulting maze of legislation, have taken it to suggest that the monks were very much in charge, and these scholars have suggested that the Order of nuns was never more than a marginalized minority that had little, if any, influence in the Buddhist community as a whole.[3] Obviously that is only one reading. That same body of legislation could be read to suggest something like the opposite. The mere existence of such rules might rather suggest that, at the time our monastic codes were compiled, the Order of nuns was a force of considerable consequence, if not an actual powerful and potentially competitive rival in the world that the compilers of the *vinayas* were trying to construct.

Certainly, when we move outside of texts and look—insofar as we can—at actual monastic communities in India, nuns and groups of nuns do not appear to have been a marginalized minority without influence. During the period at or before the beginning of the Common Era up until the fourth or fifth century—the period during which I would place the final redaction, if not the composition, of all the monastic codes as we have them[4]—donative inscriptions from a significant number of Buddhist sites show clearly that approximately the same number of nuns as monks, and sometimes more, acted as donors.[5] This donative activity would seem to sug-

---

Originally published in *Journal of Indian Philosophy* 24 (1996) 536–592. Reprinted with stylistic changes with permission of Kluwer Academic Publishers.

gest, if nothing else, that nuns during this period had equal and sometimes superior access to private wealth.[6] This parity, moreover, is taken for granted by the monastic codes themselves: the Pāli, the Mūlasarvāstivādin, and the Mahāsāṅghika-lokottaravādin *Vinayas* all, for example, have rules to govern situations in which nuns—exactly like monks and lay-brothers [564] and lay-sisters—donate monasteries, land for monasteries, permanent alms, meals, *stūpas*, etc., to the monastic community, and they all assume that nuns had the financial means to do so.[7]

The fact that sizable numbers of individual nuns—and some groups—could and did act independently as donors, and had the means to do so, added to the fact that some of these nuns had their own disciples and significant ecclesiastical titles, might well have raised the possibility in the minds of anxious men that these nuns might also act independently in other ways as well, that, for example, their private wealth and energies might well be channeled toward more independent religious projects and away from sites or *stūpas* that appear to have been under the control of monks and that were in part an important source of revenue for them.[8]

Alas, some of this must remain, for now at least, another example of the sort of "exciting tale" I have been said to author elsewhere.[9] I sketch these possibilities only as a prelude to an attempt to make some sense of two otherwise even stranger tales, in two different *vinayas*, of violence and aggression directed first by monks toward nuns and their special dead, then by nuns toward monks and each other—all of it passing without sanction or censure. It may be that these two tales are in part about the ritual murder by monks of the special dead claimed by groups of nuns. We shall see.

The first of our tales—and the hardest still to interpret—has been available in translation for a long time. It forms the frame-story for the 52nd *Pācittiya* rule in the Pāli *Bhikkunīvibhaṅga* and was translated in 1942 by I. B. Horner.[10] I give here another translation not so much because I can improve on hers—her translation of the Pāli *Vinaya* as a whole remains, in spite of enormous problems, a remarkable achievement—but simply to highlight and nuance certain elements of vocabulary that are used.

On that occasion the Buddha, the Blessed One, was living in Vesāli, in the Great Grove, in the Hall of the Peaked Dwelling.

At that time as well the Venerable Kappitaka, the preceptor (*upajjhāya*) of Upāli, was living in the cemetery. And at that time too a comparatively great nun among the nuns of the group of six had died.[11] When the nuns of the group of six had taken that nun out, had cremated her near the Venerable Kappitaka's *vihāra*, and had made a *stūpa*, they went there and lamented at that *stūpa*.

The Venerable Kappitaka, then, was annoyed by the noise. Having demolished that *stūpa*, he scattered it around (*taṃ thūpaṃ bhinditvā pakiresi*).

The group of six nuns talked among themselves, saying "The *stūpa* of our Noble One was demolished by this Kappitaka (*iminā kappitakena amhākaṃ ayyāya thūpo bhinno*). Come, we are going to kill him!" [565]

Another nun reported this matter to the Venerable Upāli. The Venerable Upāli reported this matter to the Venerable Kappitaka. The Venerable Kappitaka, then, having left the *vihāra*, remained in hiding.

The group of six nuns went, then, to the Venerable Kappitaka's *vihāra*. When they got there and had covered the Venerable Kappitaka's *vihāra* with rocks and clods of earth, they departed saying, "Kappitaka is dead."

Then, however, when that night had passed, and when the Venerable Kappitaka had dressed in the morning and taken his bowl and robe, he entered Vesāli for alms. The nuns of the group of six saw the Venerable Kappitaka going around for alms and, having seen him, spoke thus: "This Kappitaka is alive. Who now has told of our plan?"

The group of six nuns then heard that it was certainly the Noble One Upāli who had told of their plan. They verbally abused and reviled the Venerable Upāli, saying "How is it, indeed, that this barber, this low-born dirt wiper, will tell of our plans?"

Those nuns who were decorous (*appiccha*) were critical, saying "How is it, indeed, that nuns of the group of six will verbally abuse the Noble One Upāli?". . .

The Blessed One said: "Is it true in fact, Monks, that nuns of the group of six verbally abuse Upāli?"

"It is true, Blessed One."

The Buddha, the Blessed One, upbraided them, saying "How is it, indeed, Monks, that the group of six will be verbally abusive? This will not, Monks, inspire devotion in those who have none. . . . therefore, Monks, nuns should proclaim this rule of training: whichever nuns were to verbally abuse or revile a monk—this is an offense involving expiation."

The vocabulary here seems largely and at first sight to be straightforward, but it almost immediately reveals our awkward ignorance about the realia of Buddhist monasticism. The text tells us that Kappitaka lived in a or the *susāna*—in Sanskrit *śmaśāna*. This is usually—really as a matter of convention—translated as "cemetery" but sometimes as "burning ground," although we know next to nothing about the precise nature of such a place or the range of activities or kinds of depositions that took place there. Our text and others suggest that corpses were cremated there, whereas other monastic texts seem to indicate that whole, uncremated bodies were left there—as well as food for and the possessions of the deceased—but were not buried.[12] Then there is the question of the definite or indefinite article: is our text referring to *a* or *the cemetery*? The archaeological record makes it certain that Buddhist monastic communities had what would seem to qualify as cemeteries—Bhojpur would be an early example, and Kānheri a large and late one.[13] There is too the term *vihāra*: Kappitaka's *vihāra* is in the cemetery. The term *vihāra* is—again conventionally—translated as "monastery," but even a quick reading of Buddhist monastic literature will show that the word is used to designate a large and wide range of types of dwelling places. The compiler of our tale could almost certainly not have had in mind the sort of thing still visible at places like Nālandā, given that he suggests that a group of nuns could seal it over with rocks [566] and dirt all in a day's work. Moreover, although it is virtually certain that a significant number of Buddhist monastic complexes were intentionally sited near, in, or on top of old, protohistorical graveyards,[14] there is little evidence to suggest that they were established in still functioning *susānas* or *śmaśānas*; and although literary sources rarely suggest that a *vihāra* was at least close enough to a cemetery to be off-putting,[15] they far, far more commonly indicate that cremations took place well away from the monastic residence: like our text, descriptions of monastic funerals in both Pāli and Sanskrit commonly use a verb like *nīharitvā*, *abhinirhṛtya*, or *nītvā*—all of which mean "to take away" or "to remove"—in their accounts of the initial parts of the procedure.[16] Finally, in terms of realia, it should be noted that, as with Kappitaka's *vihāra*, the exact nature of the *stūpa* erected for the deceased nun is not clear. In her translation of the text, Horner renders the term *thūpa* simply as "tomb," and although elsewhere she uses the term *stūpa* in her brief discussion of the text, about all that can be said with certainty is that our author or compiler understood it to be something that could be destroyed by a single person in a short period of time.

If there is considerable uncertainty about "things" in our text, the same can be said about persons. If, for example, the Monk Kappitaka were any more obscure, he would be virtually unknown. Outside of our text, a monk named Kappitaka appears to be referred to in only one other place in the entire Pāli Canon. The *Petavatthu* refers to an elder by that name, but the latter has little in common with our Kappitaka except for the name, and there is no reason—in spite of the commentarial tradition—to assume that the two are necessarily the same.[17] As for the deceased nun, she is so obscure as to not have a name, unless *mahatarā*—a strange reading—might be a corrupt version thereof. *Mahatarā*, which I have translated as "comparatively great," Horner renders by "an older nun" and adds in a note, "perhaps a leading nun." But in his spare critical apparatus, Oldenberg clearly doubts even the reading and suggests "read, *aññatarā*?" which of course would produce the even less specific "a certain nun" or "some nun."

The imprecision of our Pāli text in regard to place and person occurs as well in regard to the action of Kappitaka: we do not know precisely what he did, why he did it, and—most important—what it meant. At first sight the phrase *taṃ thūpaṃ bhinditvā pakiresi* appears, again, to be straightforward, and I have conservatively translated it "Having demolished that *stūpa*, he scattered it around." But although the verb *bhindati* in Pāli can mean "destroy" or "demolish," its basic sense seems to be "to break, break apart, split," and the same verb [567] in Sanskrit ranges from "to split, cleave" to "transgress, violate, open, disturb." Moreover, there is no stated object for the verb *pakiresi*, "scattered." I have supplied "it," and Horner translates: "The Venerable Kappitaka . . . having destroyed that tomb, scattered (the materials)." In light of these considerations, it is possible to arrive at what from our point of view would be an altogether more sinister translation: "Having broken open (or violated) that *stūpa*, he scattered (its contents) around."

The question of why he did it also remains. If the text had said that the nuns' activities disturbed or negatively affected Kappitaka's profound meditations, then we might see here an epic struggle between two competing styles of religiosity, the contemplative and the devotional. But of course it says no such thing. The text in fact passes no judgment on what the nuns had done in building a *stūpa* for their deceased fellow nun—they had, after all, done only what the Buddha twice elsewhere in the Pāli Canon instructed monks to do.[18] Nor does the text indicate any disapproval on the part of even Kappitaka in regard to the activities the nuns engaged in at the *stūpa*: it is not mourning per se that he reacts to but its volume. Kappitaka's reaction, moreover, is not one of moral outrage or indignation. He was said to be simply "annoyed" or "bothered"—*ubbāḷha*. The same verb is used elsewhere in the Pāli *Vinaya*: monks are said to be "bothered" or "annoyed" by animals and "creeping things" and "demons" (*pisāca*) or by "mosquitoes"; the Buddha himself is said to be "annoyed" by the unruly monks of Kosambī, but he does not then go out and smash them, nor do any of the monks act similarly.[19] Both Kappitaka's reaction and his actions may seem out of context, if not altogether out of control. The compilers of our text, however, give us no indication that they thought so.

In the same way that our text passes no judgment on the initial activities of the nuns in regard to the *stūpa*, it also passes no judgment on Kappitaka's destruction of it, leaving us to surmise that it too was sanctioned. In fact, in the entire tale the compilers of this document find fault only in the nuns' verbal abuse of Upāli after he has betrayed their plans—verbal abuse of a monk appears, therefore, to have been considered far more serious than attempted murder and what might look to us like the desecration of a grave. The only outrage at the latter in particular that I know of is in I. B. Horner. She clearly did not approve. She—in spite of the text's silence—says: "Kappitaka's indecent and selfish behavior is symptomatic of the extremely low state to which monkdom could fall at that time"—without, unfortunately, ever making it clear when that was. She also refers to "the horror felt by these [568] [nuns of the group of six] at the dishonor done to their dead."[20] But since the text itself again says nothing of the sort, this must simply be the projection onto another time and another place of modern Western sensibilities. The text itself says nothing about how the nuns felt. It gives no indication that they were horrified or angry or outraged. They appear to be simply resolute: "That monk did this and we must kill him." If anything, this looks like an old-fashioned (?) blood feud or—being biblical, which at least would put us closer to the desired time frame—an eye for an eye. Putting such a construction on the text, however, would seem to require that the first murder was of a dead person.

Clearly, the more carefully one looks at this text, the more curious it becomes, and when we look elsewhere in the Pāli Canon for aid in understanding it, or in determining what the intentional destruction of a *stūpa* might have meant, we get only equally obscure hints. There are—as far as I know—only two other texts in the Canon that seem to talk about the destruction of a *stūpa*, though one of them occurs several times. The latter occurs twice in the *Dīgha-nikāya* and once in the *Majjhima*, and in all three places the statement that is of interest is repeated two or three times.[21] This statement is the concluding part of the description of the sorry state of the Community of "the Nigaṇṭhas, the followers of Nātaputta"—a religious group that competed with the Buddhists—after Nātaputta's death. This community, the text says, was divided and at each other's throats:

> Even the lay disciples of the white robe, who followed Nātaputta, showed themselves shocked, repelled and indignant at the Nigaṇṭhas, so badly was their doctrine and discipline set forth and imparted, so ineffectual was it for guidance, so little conducive to peace, imparted as it had been by one who was not supremely enlightened, and now wrecked as it was of his support and without a protector.

The phrase "wrecked as it was of his support and without a protector" is Rhys Davids' translation of *bhinna-thūpe appaṭisaraṇe*, to which he adds the note: "lit. having its *stūpa* broken—a metaphor, says the Com[mentar]y, for foundation (platform, *patiṭṭhā*)."[22] Various other renderings have been given of the phrase that vacillate between the metaphoric and the literal meaning of the terms: "with its support gone, without an arbiter" (Walshe); "deren Kuppel geborsten, die keine Zuflucht gewährt" (Neumann); "the foundations wrecked, without an arbiter" (Horner); "its shrine broken, left without a refuge" (Ñāṇamoli and Bodhi); and so forth.[23] Here then, however nuanced, the expression *bhinna-thūpa*, "a broken or demolished *stūpa*," seems to have no reference to the desecration of a grave, or anything like that. It seems rather to refer to the destruction of the central focus and—significantly—the support, [569] refuge, or shelter of a religious community or group. Ñāṇamoli and Bodhi, in a note added to their translation already cited, give a statement that they attribute to the Commentary: "The 'shrine' and 'refuge' are the Nigaṇṭha Nātaputta, who is now dead." But this ignores the *bhinna*, "broken or wrecked." When the qualifier is allowed in, it seems almost unavoidable to suggest that if the *stūpa* is Nigaṇṭha Nātaputta, then the broken or wrecked *stūpa*—not the *stūpa* itself—signifies that he is truly dead. The necessary corollary of this is, of course, that as long as the *stūpa* is not demolished, Nātaputta remains alive and—importantly—his community has a continuing shelter and refuge.[24]

Seen in this light—which is admittedly dim—Kappitaka's actions too take on a different significance: he did not desecrate a tomb; he killed a "person" who was a religious focus of the group of nuns; he destroyed their refuge and support. This is an act that it seems would have been understood to involve or precipitate the kind of chaos and disarray that befell the Nigaṇṭhas when Nātaputta's *stūpa* was destroyed. Kappitaka cut at the root of their Community. Note that a form of the same verb that produced the qualifier applied to Nātaputta's *stūpa* (*bhinna-*) is used to express Kappitaka's action (*bhinditvā*)—he did to the nun's *stūpa* exactly what was said to have happened to Nātaputta's.

The second text that seems to refer to the destruction of a *stūpa* is in its Pāli version both obscure in sense and uncertain in reading. The text in question makes up the 35th *Sekhiya* Rule in the Pāli *Pātimokkha* and, on the surface, seems to deal with monks playing with their food. The text in the Pāli Text Society edition reads:

> *na thūpato omadditvā piṇḍapātaṃ bhuñjissāmīti sikkhā karaṇīyā.*[25]

Straining to make some kind of natural sense of this, and depending almost entirely on the interpretation of the commentary, Rhys Davids and Oldenberg translate this as follows:

> "Without pressing down from the top will I eat the alms placed in my bowl." This is a discipline which ought to be observed.

And Horner:

> "Not having chosen from the top will I eat almsfood," is a training to be observed.[26]

It is probably fair to say that neither the commentator nor our modern translators were very sure about what this meant. Nor is it altogether clear that the compilers of the *Vibhaṅga* did—they essentially just restate the rule. There is, moreover, in regard to *thūpato*, taken to mean "from the top," a whole series of variants: *dhūpakato*, *thupato*, *thutho*, *thūpikato*, *thūpakato*—and this list is certainly not complete.[27] There [570] is a distinct possibility that both the correct reading and the meaning of the rule were lost by the time the Pāli manuscripts we have were written.

Interpreted as it generally has been, this rule would seem to have little to offer to our discussion. But at least one other interpretation has been suggested, one that several variants in the Pāli manuscript tradition and one set of thoroughly unambiguous parallels also would seem to support. André Bareau, for example, has seen in this rule an interdiction against making a *stūpa* with one's food, then demolishing and eating it ("les Theravādin . . . interdisent de faire un *stūpa* avec la nourriture puis de le démolir et de le manger").[28] He has also said that the Theravādins shared this rule with the Mūlasarvāstivādins. But in Mūlasarvāstivādin sources there are much less serious doubts about the readings for this rule and virtually none about how it was generally understood. The one verifiable Gilgit manuscript reading for this rule in the Mūlasarvāstivādin *Prātimokṣasūtra* is

> *na stūpākṛtim avamṛdya piṇḍapātaṃ paribhokṣyāma iti śikṣā karaṇīyā.*[29]
>
> We will not eat alms food after having crushed that which has the form of a *stūpa*—this is a rule of training that must be followed.

The Tibetan renderings of this differ somewhat—as they frequently do—depending on where they are found. In the Derge edition of both the *Prātimokṣasūtra* and the *Bhikṣuṇīprātimokṣasūtra*, we find:

> *mchod rten 'dra bar bcos te zas mi bza' bar . . .*[30]
>
> We must not eat food forming it like a *stūpa* . . .

But in the *Vinayavibhaṅga* the same rule appears as

> *mchod rten 'dra ba bcom ste zas mi bza' bar . . .*[31]
>
> We must not eat food destroying that which has the form (or is like) a *stūpa* . . .

And in the *Bhikṣuṇīvinayavibhaṅga*:

> *mchod rten 'dra bar sbrus te zas za bar mi bya bar . . .*[32]
>
> We must not eat food kneading it like (or into the form of) a *stūpa* . . .

It can be seen here that if *bcos te* ("forming") is not simply a graphic error for *bcom ste* ("destroying")—and there is a good chance that it is—then the Tibetan translators wavered in regard to how best to translate *avamṛdya*. Given that the latter can mean not only "crush" or "destroy" but also "rub," the same verb can by extension even account for *sbrus te*, "knead." When Guṇaprabha restated our rule in *sūtra* form in his *Vinayasūtra*, he did so as *na stūpākṛtyavamardam*, "not (eating after) crushing (food) having the form of a *stūpa*"; this in turn was translated [571] into Tibetan as *mchod rten 'dra bar byas te mi gzhom mo*, "not (eating after) destroying (food) that was made into the form of a *stūpa*," and glossed by Dharmamitra in his commentary *zan la mchod rten gyi dbyibs 'dra bar byas te gzhom zhing bza' bar mi bya'o*, "making food into the likeness of the form of a *stūpa* he must not destroy and eat it."[33]

A number of niggling details will have to be worked out here, but the important point for us is that Mūlasarvāstivādin texts in both Sanskrit and Tibetan make it all but absolutely certain that this tradition—over a long period of time, Guṇaprabha may have written as late as the seventh century, and Dharmamitra still later—understood our rule to interdict forming food into the shape of a *stūpa*, then crushing or demolishing and eating it. This virtual certainty may well support Bareau's interpretation of the Pāli text—we will have to return to this—but by itself it does not necessarily allow us to establish a link between it, Kappitaka's action, and the wrecked *stūpa* of Nātaputta. The Mūlasarvāstivādin *Vinayavibhaṅgas*, however, I think, will.

The possibility has already been suggested that the compilers of the Pāli *Suttavibhaṅga* that we have did not understand our rule, and it has been noted that the explanatory or frame-story found there does little more than restate the rule itself. Bareau, however, has noted that this is not the case in the Mūlasarvāstivādin *Vibhaṅga*, but I cannot agree with him when he characterizes the elements of the Mūlasarvāstivādin frame-story as "in fact very poor and of little interest."[34] There are actually two Mūlasarvāstivādin frame-stories—one in the *Vinayavibhaṅga* and one in the *Bhikṣuṇīvinayavibhaṅga*—and although in many ways similar they are both of interest. They establish a clear and coherent, if somewhat unexpected, understanding of the rule, and they both associate the destruction of a *stūpa*, however ritualistic or symbolic, with aggression by one religious group against another.

Vinayavibhaṅga

(Derge, 'dul ba Nya 257b.7–258a.4)[35]

A certain householder living in Śrāvastī was very devoted to the naked ascetics (*gcer bu pa* = *nirgrantha*). When at a later time he had become devoted to the Blessed One and had invited the community of monks to a meal in his other house (*khyim gzhan du*), he distributed flour (*phye dag*) there, and the group of six kneaded it (*sbrus te* = *avamṛdya*)[36] and arranged it (*rnam par bzhag go* = *vyavasthāpita*) like a *stūpa*. He distributed split pieces of radish, and they were also stuck into that flour arranged like the central pole of a *stūpa*. He distributed cakes, and they too were arranged like umbrellas on top of that radish. Then the monks of the group of six said: "Nanda, Upananda![37] This is the *stūpa* of Pūraṇa, Pūraṇa gone to hell." Then destroying (*bcom ste*) and eating it, they said: "Nanda, Upananda! The *stūpa* of Pūraṇa, Pūraṇa gone to hell, is broken (*rdib pa = bhinna*)!"

When the householder heard that, he said: "Noble Ones, although I am rid of that form of evil view, you persist in not being rid of hostility (*zhe sdang = dveṣa*)." [572]

The monks of the group of six sat there saying nothing.

The monks reported this matter to the Blessed One, and the Blessed One said: "Henceforth, my disciples should recite thus this rule of training in the Discipline: 'We must not eat food destroying that which has the form of (or is like) a *stūpa*. So we should train!'"

Note here first of all that unlike what we see in the Pāli *Vinaya*, this frame-story makes perfect—if, again, somewhat unexpected—sense of our rule: for the Mūlasarvāstivādin *vinaya* tradition it is not simply a rule about food but a rule about ritual aggression through the use of food. This frame-story gives some interesting and precise details in regard to what making the form or likeness of a *stūpa* from one's food entailed;[38] it indicates that crushing and eating such a *stūpa* was perceived as an act motivated by hostility, hatred, or aggression and that its avowed purpose and end was to do to a named person's *stūpa* what was said to have happened to the *stūpa* of Nātaputta and what Kappitaka is said to have done to the *stūpa* of the dead nun. As Nātaputta's *stūpa* is said to have been "broken" (*bhinna*), and Kappitaka is said to have "demolished" (*bhinditvā*) that of the dead nun, so when the group of six have destroyed and eaten the *stūpa* formed from food, they declare, "The *stūpa* of Pūraṇa . . . is broken" (*rdib pa = bhinna*)—all three use forms of the same verb.

Secondarily, it might be noted that the *Vibhaṅga* text employs in one passage the whole range of verbs or meanings that occurs in the various Tibetan translations of the actual rule: "knead," "form," "destroy." In so doing, it seems to make explicit what is implied in the rule: that forming food into the shape of a *stūpa*, destroying it, and eating it are *all* forbidden. It is, moreover, difficult to avoid the conclusion that the procedure described was anything other than what we might call an act of ritual or sympathetic magic or causation. Notice that in the text once the *stūpa* is formed, and before it is demolished, the monks are made to verbally declare, "This is the *stūpa* of Pūraṇa." This formal verbal declaration was presumably—given the power of verbal declarations of several sorts in India—thought to make it so. It is the *stūpa* of Pūraṇa, not a *stūpa* made of food, that is likewise declared to have been broken at the end of the procedure. Finally, the fact that the procedure is aimed at the *stūpa* of Pūraṇa is also of interest because this same *stūpa* is referred to as well elsewhere in the *Mūlasarvāstivāda-vinaya*. In a text that is found in two slightly different versions in both the *Saṅghabhedavastu* and the *Kṣudrakavastu*, for example, we read that on one of their periodic visits to hell Śāriputra and Maudgalyāyana see Pūraṇa there undergoing some fairly uncomfortable tortures. Pūraṇa says to them: [573]

> O Noble Śāriputra and Maudgalyāyana, when you return to the world, you must tell my fellow practitioners (Tib. *tshangs pa mtshungs par spyod pa rnams*, but Skt. *śrāvakā*) that I said this: ". . . whenever you pay reverence to my *stūpa*, then my suffering becomes intolerably severe—hereafter you must not do it! (*khyed kyis ji lta ji ltar nga'i mchod rten la brjed pa byas pa de lta de ltar nga la sdug bsngal ches mi bzad par gyur gyis / phyin chad ma byed par thong zhig . . . ; yathā yathā ca śrāvakā stūpakārān kurvanti tathā tathā tīvravedanāṃ vedayāmi . . . mā tasya stūpakāraṃ kariṣyatheti*).[39]

Found in a Buddhist text, this passage would seem to be an instance of preaching to the converted. The fact that it is repeated, and that the *Vibhaṅga* and—as we will shortly see—the *Bhikṣuṇīvinayavibhaṅga* both take aim at this same *stūpa*, would seem to suggest that, for reasons I cannot explain, the compilers of the *Mūlasarvāstivāda-vinaya* saw or cast Pūraṇa and the *stūpa* of Pūraṇa in the roles of major competitor, rival, or threat.[40] In addition, this passage would seem to establish in an even more explicit way the "principle" that what is done to the *stūpa* of someone who is dead directly affects the dead person himself or herself. This in turn implies in yet another way that to destroy someone's *stūpa* is to definitively destroy his or her person. The *Bhikṣuṇīvinayavibhaṅga* takes this out of the realm of implication.

Bhikṣuṇīvinayavibhaṅga

(Derge, 'dul ba Ta 321b.7–322a.4)

The nuns of the group of twelve were then making their way through the countryside and came to the house of a farmer. When they had shaken out their robes there and washed their feet and hands, they got ready to eat. Naked ascetics (*gcer bu po*) had also assembled then in the other house (*khyim cig shos su*), and they too then got ready to eat.

The group of twelve then, with derisive intentions, having made in their food a *stūpa* that they named Pūraṇa (*kha zas la rdzogs byed ces bya ba'i mchod rten byas nas*), and sticking a radish into it as the central pole, said to the naked ascetics: "This is the *stūpa* of your teacher" (*'di ni khyed kyi ston pa'i mchod rten yin no zhes smras nas*). Then, breaking chunks from that *stūpa* and eating them, they said in unison: "The *stūpa* of Pūraṇa is demolished" (*zhig go* = [?] *bhinna*).

The naked ascetics were then aggrieved, and having become dejected, they said, weeping: "Today our teacher is truly dead" (*de ring bdag cag gi ston pa dus las 'das pa lta zhes zer ro*).

> The Blessed One said: "One must train such that . . . we must not eat food kneading it like (or into the form of) a *stūpa*!"

The frame-story here from the *Bhikṣuṇīvinayavibhaṅga* has obvious similarities with that cited above from the *Vibhaṅga*, although they are by no means identical. There is a small piece of evidence that in this case the latter may have been derived from the former. In the text of the *Vibhaṅga* it is said that the monks were invited to a meal in the householder's "other house," but in this text there is only one. It is only in the *Bhikṣuṇīvinayavibhaṅga* that there is reference to two [574] houses, and only there that the reference to the "other" makes any sense. It looks as though the compilers of the *Vibhaṅga*, in adapting the *Bhikṣuṇīvinayavibhaṅga* story, may have mechanically taken over the reference to the "other" of two houses without noticing that it did not fit in its new context.[41]

The text in the *Bhikṣuṇīvinayavibhaṅga*, however, seems to make it even more clear than in the *Vibhaṅga* that what is being described is a ritual procedure: the *stūpa* is formed, then named, then declared to be what it had been named. When it has been torn apart and eaten, the nuns then publicly and "in unison" declare that what had been created is now demolished—that is to say, that the same thing happened to it as was said to have happened to the *stūpa* of Nātaputta, and that Kappitaka is described as having done to the deceased nun's *stūpa*. The verb in this case too was probably the same. But the *Bhikṣuṇīvinayavibhaṅga* text—as we have already intimated—also goes beyond this. It makes perfectly explicit what the destruction of a *stūpa* entailed, what it was understood to *mean*. When the *stūpa* of Pūraṇa is declared demolished, the naked ascetics are made to say: "Today our teacher is truly dead." To destroy one is to kill the other, and that—it would seem—is the point of the whole procedure. To judge by the words put into the mouths of the naked ascetics, moreover, it would appear that the compilers of this *vinaya* thought that their "readers" would think that such a procedure actually worked. Naked ascetics are also not the only ones to express such sentiments in the *Mūlasarvāstivāda-vinaya*.

Having come this far, we are almost back to the frame-story for the 52nd *Pācittiya* rule in the Pāli *Bhikkhunīvibhaṅga* that we started with. A parallel for it might simply summarize what we have seen along the way. When, however, we look for a parallel for this rule in the Mūlasarvāstivādin *Bhikṣuṇīvinayavibhaṅga*, it is not there. The 52nd *Pācittiya* in the Pāli tradition dealt—as we have seen—with the verbal abuse of monks by nuns. It seems at some stage to have come to form a pair with its 51st *Pācittiya*, which requires nuns to ask permission of the monks before entering a monk's residence, an *ārāma* or a *vihāra*. According to Waldschmidt's tables, the same two rules in the same relative order as in the Pāli also occur in the *Bhikṣuṇī-prātimokṣas* of the Dharmaguptas and Sarvāstivādins, but neither occur in that of the Mūlasarvāstivādins.[42] There is, however, in the Mūlasarvāstivādin *Kṣudrakavastu*—a rich and little-studied collection of odds and ends that sometimes have a prominent place in other *vinayas*—an account that is similar to, though not the same as, the frame-story about Kappitaka attached to the 52nd *Pācittya* in the Pāli *Bhikkhunīvibhaṅga* [575] and, curiously, it delivers a ruling that is parallel to that found in the Pāli's 51st *Pācittiya*. It does, indeed, in many respects summarize or recapitulate most of what we have seen.

Kṣudrakavastu

(Derge, 'dul ba Da 172b.2–174b.5)

The Buddha, the Blessed One, was staying in Śrāvastī, in the park of the Jetavana.

When the Venerable Phalguna had died, then the nuns of the group of twelve, after collecting his bones (*rus*), built a *stūpa* with great veneration at a spacious spot. They also attached umbrellas and banners and flags to it, and adorned it with perfume and flowers, and assigned to it two nuns who spoke sweetly. Every day they provided earth and water and incense and flowers there. Then they gave to those monks who came there from other countries the washing of hands and had them pay reverence to the *stūpa* with flowers and incense and the singing of verses.

Once the Venerable Udakapāna was moving through the countryside with a retinue of five hundred and arrived at Śrāvastī. Now, since *arhats* do not enter into knowledge and vision without focusing their mind (*dgong pa*), when he saw that *stūpa* from a distance he thought to himself: "Since this is a new *stūpa* of the hair and nails of the Blessed One, I should go and pay reverence!"[43]

They went there, and the two attendant nuns gave them earth and water for washing their hands and feet. Then the monks paid reverence to the *stūpa* by presenting flowers and incense and the singing of verses. Having paid reverence there with the retinue of five hundred, Udakapāna left.

Not very far from that *stūpa* a nun, the Venerable Utpalavarṇā, was sitting at the root of a tree for the purpose of spending the day. Having watched them, she said: "Venerable Udakapāna, you should focus your mind when you pay reverence to someone's *stūpa*!" (*khyed kyis su'i mchod rten la phyag bgyis pa dgongs shig*).

The Venerable Udakapāna thought to himself: "Why would the Venerable Utpalavarṇā say, 'Venerable Udakapāna, you should focus your mind when you pay reverence to someone's *stūpa*!'?" Having thought that, he said: "There is something here I should concentrate on." When that thing entered into his mind, and he saw that the *stūpa* was a *stūpa* of the bones of the Monk Phalguna, he was infected with a passion that was totally engulfed by hostility and went back and said to the Venerable Utpalavarṇā: "When an abscess has appeared in the teaching, you have sat there and ignored it!" (*bstan pa la chu bur byung na khyod 'di na 'dug bzhin du yal bar bor ro zhes byas pa*).

> She sat there, saying nothing.
>
> The Venerable Udakapāna said then this to his pupils and disciples: "Venerables, those who are fond of the Teacher and would spare him (*ston pa la sdug pa dang phangs par byed pa gang yin pa de dag gis . . .*) must on that account tear out and pull down every single brick from this heap of bones and bone chunks!" (*rus pa dang rus gong gi phung po*).
>
> Since that was a large group, they, tearing out every single brick from that heap of bones and bone chunks and throwing them away, demolished that *stūpa* in the snap of a finger. The two attendant nuns were crying and ran hurriedly to the retreat house and told the nuns. When the nuns of the group of twelve, and others who were not free of commitment to and feelings of affection for Phalguna, heard that, they sat there crying and said: "Our brother is as of today truly dead!" (*bdag cag gi ming po deng gdod shi ba lta zhes . . .*). And the Nun Sthūlanandā said: "Sisters, who has revealed this?"
>
> The other nuns said: "It occurs to us immediately, although we do not actually know, that the Noble Utpalavarṇā was sitting there and that she actually told them." [576] Sthūlanandā said: "Seeing that she has entered the Order from among barbers and is therefore naturally inferior, it is clear to me from what little has been said that this is her doing. Seeing too that the Blessed One has well said 'one who defames the assembly is not to be allowed in the midst of the assembly,' how could there therefore be any considerations in regard to her?[44] Come—we must go!"
>
> Being totally engulfed by anger and taking up weapons and needles and daggers of hard wood, they went to kill her. . . .

The rest of the text—although of considerable interest in other regards—adds little that is germane to our specific interests here and is in any case too long to cite in its entirety. Utpalavarṇā sees the group of twelve coming, and realizing their intentions, she wraps herself in a protective mantle and enters into the meditative state of cessation (*nirodhasamāpatti*). They attack her and leave her for dead. When she rouses herself from her meditative state, she sees that she is badly punctured and goes to the monks' *vihāra*. They ask what has happened to her, and when told, they themselves become angry and make an ordinance (*khrims*) forbidding all nuns to enter the Jetavana. Mahāprajāpatī comes and is turned away. The Buddha, although he already knows why, asks Ānanda why Mahāprajāpatī no longer comes to see him, and Ānanda tells him about the ordinance. The Buddha, although he does not forbid the making of such ordinances,[45] then promulgates a rule that nuns must ask permission to enter a *vihāra*, as a part of which he requires that the monks, when asked for permission, must in turn inquire of the nuns if they are carrying concealed weapons!—"Sisters, having some grudge, are you not carrying weapons and needles?" (*sring mo dag 'khon can mtshon cha dang khab dag 'chang ba ma yin nam zhes dris shig*).

This Mūlasarvāstivādin tale about, in part, the Monk Udakapāna is both clearly like and clearly different from the Pāli tale about, in part, the Monk Kappitaka. Their similarities and differences may both be informative. What is perhaps most generally striking about both is that in neither case is the behavior of their respective monks anything like the main focus of the text. In both it is simply a narrative element in a larger story, an introductory device that allows the compilers to tell the main story that gave rise to the rule they presumably want to deliver. In neither is any judgment passed on the monk's behavior, and in both the unedifying and definitionally, if not doctrinally, perplexing picture of an infuriated *arhat* or an irascible senior monk—the preceptor of the monk both traditions centrally associate with the *Vinaya*—is allowed to stand. We will have to return to this.

In terms of details, the first point that might be noticed is that although the compilers of both texts use the term *stūpa* or *thūpa*, they clearly [577] did not have in mind the same thing: in the Pāli text the *thūpa* appears to have been a small, relatively insubstantial construction—it could be destroyed by one man in a short time—in or near a cemetery; in the Mūlasarvāstivādin text the *stūpa* was more substantial, being made of brick—it took five hundred men to destroy it, although they made quick work of it—and sited "at a spacious spot." The *stūpa* in each was also the object of different kinds of activity and had different clientele: the Pāli text presents its *thūpa* as a focal point for mourning—at least no other forms of activity are mentioned—and it draws, apparently, only local nuns; the *stūpa* in the Mūlasarvāstivādin text, on the other hand, is clearly the focal point of cult activity—although this too may have included mourning—had two attendant nuns assigned to it, and drew, apparently, monks from far away ("monks who came there from other countries" are explicitly mentioned). Differences of this sort are, of course, almost chronically "explained" by chronology, but here—as in many other cases—they might be explained as well by cultural geography. We admittedly know little about any cult of the local monastic dead in Sri Lanka, though the Pāli commentaries—as I have pointed out elsewhere—seem to suggest some resistance to it.[46] Moreover, what little we know about *stūpas* for local monks in Sri Lanka suggests that they were insubstantial affairs. Long ago Longhurst reported in regard to what he had seen in Sri Lanka that "the *stūpas* erected over the remains of ordinary members of the Buddhist community were very humble little structures"; Richard Gombrich, more recently, that "small *stūpas* (closer to molehills than mountains) cover the ashes of monks in Sri Lanka to this day."[47] In communities accustomed to this sort of thing, the architectural detail suggested by the story of Kappitaka would have made narrative and cultural sense—"readers" of the text in Sri Lanka could have easily envisioned what was said to have occurred. But the same account probably would not, perhaps could not, have been written on the subcontinent. There things seem to have been very different very early.

Although the situation is somewhat better than it is in regard to Sri Lanka, still we are far from fully informed about the cult of the local monastic dead in India proper. What is clear, however, is that from our earliest datable evidence *stūpas* for the local monastic dead could and did take impressive and substantial monumental form. *Stūpa* number 2 at Sāñcī, for example, which contained the inscribed reliquaries of several local monks, was forty-seven feet in diameter and twenty-nine feet high. It was provided with a crowning umbrella, which raised its height to thirty-seven feet, was made of carefully cut and finished stone, and eventually surrounded by a sculpted [578] railing.[48] This substantial construction—which could have easily taken five hundred men to dismantle—is, moreover, not late: it stands at the very beginning of the series of known *stūpas* of this sort. Bénisti has argued that the carvings on the rail of *Stūpa* number 2 predate Bharhut and that they go back to the first half of the second century B.C.E.[49] There is general agreement that they are early, but given that the *stūpa* itself must already have been in existence before the railing was erected, that would make it even earlier—although by how much is not clear. To judge by the inscriptions on the rail, this *stūpa*—like that of Phalguna—attracted people and gifts from other regions or "countries." Likewise, some of the inscribed *stūpas* of the local monastic dead at Bhaja are both substantial and early. Carved from the living rock, they are—or were when complete—at least fifteen to twenty feet high, and some of them have been assigned to the late third century B.C.E.[50] These and other examples would seem to suggest that the Pāli tale told on the continent might well not make good cultural sense, whereas the monks of Central or Western India would have no difficulty in understanding the details of the story of Udakapāna. There need not necessarily be, therefore, any chronological gap between the two tales, and it may well only be that each is simply telling its story in a language of detail adapted to its local environment.[51] The important point for us, however, is that in both a monk was allowed to destroy without censure or blame an important focus—however that was understood—of the activities of a group of nuns.

The individual monks who did the deed in the two tales also have some things in common, though here too the specific details differ. Both were not just monks but monks with disciples and therefore senior monks. One is specifically said to have been an *arhat*, the other a cemetery dweller. But above all else, they have in common that they are virtually unknown elsewhere. Kappitaka may be referred to nowhere else in the Pāli Canon; Udakapāna is so obscure that I probably do not even have his name right. In Tibetan the name occurs as *chu 'thung*, but I have not been able to find an attested Sanskrit equivalent for this, and Udakapāna is simply a wild guess. Given that in Tibetan the name seems to mean something like "a drink of water," it is not impossible that it might be connected with the Pāli name Udakadāyaka, "provider of water," carried by two monks and a nun—all equally obscure—in the *Apadāna*. But this too is a wild guess.[52] This obscurity of the main actors may point in two directions. Given the enormous degree of standardization of both personal names and place-names that the "editing" process seems to have imposed on both the Pāli and the Mūlasarvāstivādin [579] *Vinayas*—the latter contains a set of rules telling monks exactly how to do this—the strikingly nonstandard nature of our characters' names may point to the relative authenticity of the account. But it is equally possible that there might have been some unease in ascribing the actions described to a Śāriputra or a Maudgalyāyana, so the choice of characters we find may be connected to an attempt to avoid indelicate questions. Ironically, this would also have lessened the authority of the model.

Obscurity of character, however, does not mark just the main actors—the deceased are equally unknown. In the Pāli text the *stūpa* was built for the remains of an apparently nameless nun. In the Mūlasarvāstivādin text the *stūpa* contains the bones of a monk who appears to have been named Phalguna, that is, if I am right in thinking that the Tibetan *gre las skyes* is an alternative translation of the second element of the name Mūlaphalguna, which occurs in the *Cīvaravastu*. The monk so named there—and only there as far as I know—*may* be the same as Moliya-Phagguna in Pāli sources. The latter is described as excessively close to the nuns and their staunch defender; and Mūlaphalguna as "fondly looked after by the nuns." Although much remains uncertain here, if the *Kṣudrakavastu* account is referring to this same monk, then he was, indeed, an important figure for groups of nuns, though he, typically, receives little attention in monastic sources.[53]

Curiously, the only role occupied by individuals of any standing elsewhere in monastic literature is that of *révélateur*, and in both texts these are precisely the individuals who are the objects of the censored attacks, both verbal and actual. Upāli is, of course, in both traditions one of the most prominent of the Buddha's immediate disciples—it was he who is said to have preserved the whole of the *vinaya*. In the Pāli tradition Utpalavarṇā is almost equally eminent and is said to have been "one of the two chief women disciples of the Buddha."[54] In the *Mūlasarvāstivāda-vinaya* she has a more checkered career—she is rebuked by the Buddha for showing off her magical powers, for example—but is still well known.[55] As a kind of final inversion, note that whereas the obscure characters in both the Pāli and the Mūlasarvāstivādin tales have clear roles, the roles of the well-known characters are ambivalent—in both cases they start what the compilers seem to have seen as the real trouble. Both, incidentally, are also slurred for their low birth or inferior social status. This is, however, the only indication that I know that would suggest that Utpalavarṇā was of low caste origin.

When we turn to the explicit motives behind Udakapāna's action, it is clear that they are not. Although Udakapāna expresses himself [580] much more verbally than Kappitaka, this is not difficult, given that the latter does not say anything. But what Udakapāna says is itself difficult to interpret. He is described as extremely angry, but the narrative leaves the impression that this might be because he was hoodwinked by a bunch of nuns. Apparently referring to the *stūpa*, he says "an abscess has appeared in the teaching" and, clearly referring to the *stūpa*, calls it a "heap of bones and bone chunks." But if this strong talk is based on a disapproval of the Monk Phalguna, the text, as we have noted, gives no indication of this, and he presumably could not—if he knew his *vinaya*—be objecting to the erection of a *stūpa* for a deceased monk: this is elsewhere explicitly allowed with rules provided to govern it, and narratively described.[56] Perhaps the most significant thing Udakapāna says is in his exhortation to his disciples to tear the *stūpa* down. They should do it, he says, because they "are fond of the Teacher and would spare him." But spare him from what? It can only be, it seems, from a loss of veneration as a result of what was meant for him being "misdirected" toward something else: "a heap of bones and bone chunks." Notice that those concerned with the *stūpa* of Phalguna are described as having "feelings of affection" (*mdza' ba 'dod chags*) for him, and Udakapāna's monks are exhorted to act because they are "fond of the Teacher" (*ston pa la sdug pa . . . byed pa*). The conflict, it seems, is about competing loyalties, if not affections. And the real point that is narratively made is that from the monks' point of view it is a dangerous conflict, because even an *arhat* can, if he is not careful, be led astray. The whole text turns in a sense on the fact that Udakapāna thought he was worshiping a *stūpa* of the Buddha.[57]

The *stūpa* of Phalguna—erected, maintained, and promoted by the nuns—appears, therefore, as a potentially dangerous competitor to the *stūpa* of the Buddha and the monks' response is a brutal one, one that we view differently from the way in which the nuns are reported to have viewed it. Where we would see the destruction of a monument, they—confirming much of what has been said above—are presented as seeing the death of a person. When the nuns are informed of the destruction of Phalguna's *stūpa*, they say almost exactly what the followers of Pūraṇa said when the nuns ritually demolished his *stūpa*: "Our brother is as of today truly dead!" He too appears to have been ritually murdered.

It is not just our analysis, then, that links the rule about food and the text concerning the *stūpa* of Phalguna: they are linked by a shared key statement. The end result of the ritual manipulation of food triggers exactly the same exclamation as the end result of the actual destruction of the *stūpa*. But if one is ritual, so too must be the other, at least in [581] meaning. They both moreover effect a definitive change in one thing by manipulating another: in the one case a person is destroyed by the destruction of kneaded food; in the other case this is effected by the destruction of an arrangement of bricks; in both cases the person destroyed is—from our point of view—already dead. Here I think it is important to note that both kneaded food and arranged bricks are also employed in brahmanical rites for manipulating the "dead." The most obvious, perhaps, is the use of balls of rice to "be" the dead in the *sapiṇḍa* ritual; or the use of brick in the fire altar to reconstitute the dismembered Puruṣa. The pattern runs deep.[58]

But our texts also intersect or link up with another Indian pattern as well, this one more specifically Buddhist. It has been argued elsewhere on the basis of both archaeological and epigraphical sources that the *stūpa* of the Buddha was—to use again the formulation of the late Professor Bareau—"more than the symbol of the Buddha, it is the Buddha himself"; it is the living Buddha.[59] It has also been suggested that this must apply as well to the *stūpas* of local monks like those of Gobhūti at Bedsa or the Elder Aṃpikiṇaka at Bhaja.[60] But if this is correct, if the *stūpa* is the living person, then it would seem that as a necessary corollary such a "person" must also be subject to death. If, in other words, a *stūpa* could live, it also—by necessity—should be able to die or even, indeed, be murdered. Our texts, it seems, explicitly establish this. They confirm, if you will, from yet another angle that *stūpas* were thought to be living, by showing that it was also thought that they could be killed. And they show as well that this conception was a monastic one found in decidedly monastic sources.[61]

Then there are the compulsory caveats and "final" conclusions. It may not be too difficult to assent to the suggestion that the Pāli account of the destruction of the nameless nun's *stūpa* be read in light of the more explicit Mūlasarvāstivādin text, and to see in it that the destruction of her *stūpa* meant both the destruction of her and the suppression by a monk of a focal point for the activities of the group of nuns that sought it and her out, the destruction—if you will—of either an actual or potential organizational center. We have, after all, the repeated reference elsewhere in the Pāli Canon to fragmented religious groups who are characterized as having their "*stūpa* broken or demolished," *bhinna-thūpa*. There may, however, be more resistance to reading the Pāli rule about food in light of the Mūlasarvāstivādin "parallel."

The Mūlasarvāstivādin understanding of the rule in question may indeed be "late." One person has in fact asserted that this Mūlasarvāstivādin reading "is clearly a later derivation which was [582] produced by mistaking the first member of the compound [*stūpākṛti*] *stūpa* aṣ 'a tope.'" But this observation is based on a rather confused presentation and analysis of purely philological data and the questionable assumption that there was an *ur* or "original" text of such rules rather than a number of competing versions.[62] Moreover, the data could as easily be argued the other way around. Sylvain Lévi, for example, has shown that in other cases where other *vinaya* traditions are confused or garbled, or where the sense of a term appears to have been forgotten, that sense has been accurately preserved in the Mūlasarvāstivādin tradition.[63] We could well be dealing with a similar case, especially if the Mūlasarvāstivādin interpretation can indeed be linked to old Indian patterns. The confusion in the manuscript tradition for the Pāli rule has already been noted, as has the fact that the compilers of the Pāli *Vibhaṅga* seem no longer to have known what it meant—at least they give no explanation.[64] Over against this stands the Mūlasarvāstivādin tradition in considerable contrast. It has everywhere understood the rule in the same way—in its two *Prātimokṣas*, in both the *Bhikṣu-* and the *Bhikṣuṇī-vinayavibhaṅgas*, and even in Guṇaprabha's *Vinayasūtra* and its four commentaries. It has, moreover, consistently given an interpretation of the rule that is clear and in conformity with both its readings and with texts like the tale of Phalguna's *stūpa* found elsewhere in its *Vinaya*. Ironically, even if the Mūlasarvāstivādin interpretation would turn out to be relatively "late," it would still give us a consistent Buddhist interpretation of a difficult text that would otherwise remain all but meaningless, an interpretation, moreover, that would be much closer in time and culture to the compilers of the Pāli Canon than anything that could be produced in modern Europe or America—the latter leaves us with little more than a seemingly silly rule about monks playing in their food. Moreover, in assessing the Mūlasarvāstivādin interpretation of the rule, it must always be kept in mind that we have an extant manuscript containing this rule that predates anything we have for the Pāli by six centuries or more. The Gilgit manuscript of the Mūlasarvāstivādin *Prātimokṣa* contains—as far as I know—the earliest attested form of this rule in an Indian language, and there are at least two comparatively early manuscripts from Central Asia ascribed to the Sarvāstivādins that have very similar readings.[65]

Finally, we might conclude by trying to place the Pāli tale of the nameless nun's *stūpa* and the Mūlasarvāstivādin account of the *stūpa* of Phalguna in the context of what else has been said—or not said—about *stūpas* elsewhere in the literatures they come from. Both the Pāli Canon and the Mūlasarvāstivādin *Vinaya*, for example, explicitly mandate the [583] erection of *stūpas* by monks for deceased fellow monks, but in neither is there—as far as I know—a similar statement in regard to nuns. This omission is also narratively or hagiographically highlighted in the *Mūlasarvāstivāda-vinaya*: when the Monk Śāriputra dies, he gets a *stūpa*; when the Monk Kāśyapa dies, he too gets a *stūpa*; when the Monk Ānanda dies, he gets two—he also refers to the *stūpas* of the others when, on the point of dying, he describes himself by saying, "I am alone, isolated, like the remaining tree in a forest of *stūpas*." When, however, Mahāprajāpatī—the seniormost nun and in a sense the foundress of the Order of nuns—dies, she gets none, and the funeral proceedings, which are elaborately described, are entirely in the hands of the monks.[66]

The Pāli tale of the nameless nun's *stūpa* and the Mūlasarvāstivādin account of the *stūpa* of Phalguna are the only references I know in either *Vinaya* to *stūpas* built for or by nuns, and in both cases these *stūpas* are destroyed by monks who receive no censure for their acts. Generally speaking, the attitude toward such destruction in Buddhist literature is firm and unequivocal: "to destroy a *stūpa* is a grave offence which could be committed only by men who have no faith in the law."[67] If the interpretation of the *prātimokṣa* rule proposed above is correct, even the purely symbolic or ritual destruction of the *stūpa* of a "heretic" is strictly forbidden to both monks and nuns. Moreover, apart from the two *stūpas* built by nuns that we have studied here, the only other *stūpas* whose destruction is contemplated or referred to are those of "heretics" or members of rival religious groups. If by nothing else, then, nuns are by association classified with such groups.

It is clear from the references to the *stūpa* of Nātaputta in the Pāli Canon that the destruction of a group's *stūpa* was associated with that group's disarray and loss of an organizational center. It is clear as well from the *Mūlasarvāstivāda-vinaya* that the *stūpa* of a monk was a source of revenue and support for his fellow monks: what was given to it belonged to them.[68] The actions of the Monks Kappitaka and Udakapāna would, then, have left the two groups of nuns involved with neither an important means of support nor an organizational focus. Such actions would have been not just ritual murder but something more akin to the political assassination of a group's special dead. That such actions did occur in Buddhist India may account, far better than does historical accident, for the fact that nowhere in either the archaeological or the epigraphical records do we find an instance of a *stūpa*'s having been built for a nun. It is perhaps unlikely that once having built such structures, and having had them pulled down, groups of nuns [584] would have continued doing so, knowing that this would be again for them—as it must now be for us—the end.[69]

Notes

1. See G. Schopen, "On Avoiding Ghosts and Social Censure: Monastic Funerals in the *Mūlasarvāstivāda-vinaya*," *JIP* 20 (1992) 1–39 [= *BSBM* 204–237], esp. 17ff.

2. There is as yet no good study of food in the various *vinayas*, but the potential of such can be glimpsed in what has been done in studies of food in other Indian contexts: see, for example, R. S. Khare, ed., *The Eternal Food: Gastronomic Ideas and Experiences of Hindus and Buddhists* (Albany, N.Y.: 1992); P. Olivelle, "Food in India," *JIP* 23 (1995) 367–380, and the sources cited in this review of Khare. In spite of a growing list of monk-bashing papers, there is still not a good study of the complex monastic attitudes toward women either.

3. This position—still influential—was early in place; see H. Oldenberg, *Buddha: His Life. His Doctrine. His Order*, trans. W. Hoey (London: 1882) 381. Recently it has been said: "The findings of Paul [D. Y. Paul, *Women in Buddhism: Images of the Feminine in the Mahāyāna*

Tradition, 2d ed. (Berkeley: 1985)] and Lang [K. C. Lang, "Lord Death's Snare: Gender-Related Imagery in the Theragāthā and the Therīgāthā," *Journal of Feminist Studies in Religion* 2.2 (1986)] would suggest that, in the period prior to the composition of *Apadāna*, Buddhist women were decidedly marginalized"—J. S. Walters, "A Voice from the Silence: The Buddha's Mother's Story," *HR* 33.4 (1994) 370. Here, as I think Walters suggests, this position is in part maintained so as to cast "the Mahāyāna" in a supposedly more favorable light.

4. See G. Schopen, "Deaths, Funerals, and the Division of Property in a Monastic Code," in *Buddhism in Practice*, ed. D. S. Lopez (Princeton, N.J.: 1995) 473–502, [= Ch. IV above, esp. 93–95]. esp. 475–477.

5. G. Schopen, "On Monks, Nuns, and 'Vulgar' Practices: The Introduction of the Image Cult into Indian Buddhism," *ArA* 49.1/2 (1988/89) 153–168 [= *BSBM* 238–257], esp. 163–165; the findings here seem now to be confirmed by P. Skilling, "A Note on the History of the Bhikkunī-saṅgha (II): The Order of Nuns after the Parinirvāṇa," in *Pāli and Sanskrit Studies. Mahāmakut Centenary Commemorative Volume and Felicitation Volume Presented to H. H. the Supreme Patriarch on the Occasion of His 80th Birthday*, ed. P. Bodhiprasiddhinand (Bangkok: 1993) 208–251, esp. 211–216, 229, and n. 167. I cannot account for the assertion in A. Hirakawa, *A History of Indian Buddhism. From Śākyamuni to Early Mahāyāna*, trans. P. Groner (Honolulu: 1990) 226, that at Sāñcī "the names of many more nuns than monks are recorded." He cites no source, and my own count indicates that the numbers were about equal: 129 monks and 125 nuns.

6. On the private means of Buddhist monastics, see most recently G. Schopen, "Monastic Law Meets the Real World: A Monk's Continuing Right to Inherit Family Property in Classical India," *HR* 35.2 (1995) 101–123 [= Ch. VI above].

7. See G. Schopen, "The Ritual Obligations and Donor Roles of Monks in the Pāli *Vinaya*," *JPTS* 16 (1992) 87–107 [= *BSBM* 72–85].

8. Two of the three main *stūpas* at Sāñcī contained the remains of deceased monks. Stūpa number 2 was built for the deposit of the remains of several local monks, number 3 for those of Śāriputra and Maudgalyāyana, and at least the Mūlasarvāstivādin tradition explicitly declares, "That which is given to the *stūpa* of a disciple belongs indeed to his fellow monks." See G. Schopen, "Ritual Rights and Bones of Contention: More on Monastic Funerals and Relics in the *Mūlasarvāstivāda-Vinaya*," *JIP* 22 (1994) 31–80, esp. 56ff [= Ch. X. above, esp. 306ff]. See also the second version of the *Vinaya-uttaragrantha*, Derge, 'dul ba Na 260 b.5: *nan thos kyi mchod rten la bsngos par gyur pa ni shi ba'i yo byad pas na bgo bar bya'o*: "Since what is dedicated to the *stūpa* of a disciple (*śrāvaka*) is (a part of) the estate of the deceased (*mṛtapariṣkāra*), it should be distributed (among the monks)." It has been said that "the *Vinaya-uttara-grantha*, just like the Pāli *Parivāra*, is an appendix to the Vinaya" and that "this work tells us nothing new" (A. C. Banerjee, *Sarvāstivāda Literature* [Calcutta: 1957] 99); neither assertion, however, has yet been demonstrated, and the latter is far from true. Here the *Uttaragrantha* has assimilated what is given to the *stūpa* of a deceased *śrāvaka* to his estate. This, of course, means in turn that the rules that apply to the latter (which are detailed, for example, at *Cīvaravastu*, GMs iii 2, 120.3ff, and digested in the *Ekottarakarmaśataka*, Derge, bstan 'gyur, 'dul ba Wu 221b.3–.7) now apply to the

former as well. This same *Vinaya* also lists as one of the eight categories of "acquisitions" (*lābha*), or revenue, that which is offered at "the Four Great Shrines," i.e., those shrines at the sites of the Buddha's birth, awakening, first teaching, and *parinirvāṇa*—see *Cīvaravastu*, GMs iii 2, 113.8, and note that these four are not relic or mortuary *stūpas* and therefore, technically, not subject to the rules that govern *stūpas* of the Buddha.

9. R. Gombrich, "Making Mountains without Molehills: The Case of the Missing *Stūpa*," *JPTS* 15 (1991) 141–143. Notice, however, that, in a characteristically fine paper that revisits the question of the role of nuns in early and medieval Sri Lanka, Gunawardana uses some of the same sort of language for some of the same reasons: he notes the economic independence of women in Sri Lankan inscriptions and refers to "the independent spirit displayed by nuns," "the concern shared by some monks about this situation," and the "challenge" this presented (R. A. L. H. Gunawardana, "Subtile Silk of Ferreous Firmness: Buddhist Nuns in Ancient and Early Medieval Sri Lanka and Their Role in the Propagation of Buddhism," *The Sri Lanka Journal of the Humanities* 14 [1988, but 1990] 1–59). It is ironic that whereas in most areas of Buddhist studies interpretation, analysis and conjecture frequently go far beyond their available evidential base, the study of the history of the order of nuns in India has yet to fully use even the rich textual data that have accumulated over the years. In 1884, Rockhill published a translation of the Mūlasarvāstivādin *Bhikṣuṇī-prātimokṣa* (W. W. Rockhill, "Le traité d'émancipation ou Pratimoksha Sutra traduit du tibétan," *RHR* 9 [1884] 3–26, 167–201); in 1910, Wieger translated both the Dharmaguptaka *Bhikṣuṇī-prātimokṣa* and extracts of its *Vibhaṅga* (L. Wieger, *Bouddhisme Chinois 1: Vinaya: Monachisme et discipline; Hinayana. Véhicule inférieur* [Paris: 1910], reprinted in 1951); in 1920 appeared C. M. Ridding and L. de la Vallée Poussin, "A Fragment of the Sanskrit Vinaya. Bhikṣunikarmavacana," *BSOAS* 1 (1920) 123–143; the important study of E. Waldschmidt, *Bruchstücke des Bhikṣuṇī-prātimokṣa der Sarvāstivādins. mit einer Darstellung der Überlieferung des Bhikṣuṇī-prātimokṣa in den verschiedenen Schulen*, was published in Leipzig in 1926; then followed significant work on Mahāsāṅghika texts dealing with nuns: G. Roth, *Bhikṣuṇī-vinaya, Including Bhikṣuṇī-prakīrṇaka and a Summary of the Bhikṣu-prakīrṇaka of the Ārya-Mahāsāṃghika-Lokottaravādin* (Patna: 1970); A. Hirakawa, *Monastic Discipline for the Buddhist Nuns. An English Translation of the Chinese Text of the Mahāsāṃghika-Bhikṣuṇī-Vinaya* (Patna: 1982); É. Nolot, *Règles de discipline des nonnes bouddhistes* (Paris: 1991); etc. Little of this or similar work has made its way into more general works, and we still get studies like that of R. Pitzer-Reyl's, which, in spite of its title *Die Frau im frühen Buddhismus* (Berlin: 1984), is based almost exclusively on Pāli or Theravādin sources.

10. Pāli *Vinaya* iv 308–309; Horner, *BD* iii 343–44.

11. "The nuns of the group of six," *chabbaggiyā*, are of course the female counterparts to "the group of six monks," the latter being described in T. W. Rhys Davids and W. Stede, *The Pali Text Society's Pali-English Dictionary* (London: 1921–1925) 273, as "a set of (sinful) Bhikkhus taken as exemplification of trespassing the rules of the *Vinaya*" (the dictionary makes no reference to the nuns' group!). The *Mūlasarvāstivāda-vinaya* has an exact counterpart to the Pāli's group of monks who are called *ṣaḍvārgika*. Edgerton, *BHSD* 538, says: "In Pali they seem to be represented as followers of the Buddha, though very imperfect ones, often transgressing rules of propriety. In *BHS*, at least in Divy., they seem to be heretics

from the Buddhist standpoint"—the last sentence here must be corrected. In the *Mūlasarvāstivāda-vinaya* and in the *Divyāvadāna* (much of which appears to have been borrowed from the former), there can be no doubt that the *ṣaḍvārgika* monks were Buddhists. Interestingly, the Mūlasarvāstivādin counterpart to the Pāli's group of six nuns is called, as we will see, "the group of twelve," *dvādaśavargīya*, making them, presumably, twice as bad (here too Edgerton, 273, needs to be corrected and supplemented, though he does recognize that they cannot be "heretics"). The members of both groups, male and female, appear as stereotypical rogues, scoundrels, tricksters, deviants, and sometimes downright nasty customers, but they are always represented as regular members of the Order, and some of their stories provide some of the finest humor in both *Vinayas*. At the same time, though, the compilers of the various *vinayas* seem to have used these groups or individuals belonging to them to articulate and work out some of the most disturbing and highly charged issues that confronted them. (For a representative sampling of passages from the Pāli *Vinaya* in which the group of six occurs, see the references given in *DPPN* i 926; J. Dhirasekera, *Buddhist Monastic Discipline. A Study of Its Origin and Development in Relation to the Sutra and Vinaya Pitakas* [Colombo: 1982], is one of the few works that gives serious consideration to the group; see 46, 135, 150–151 [nuns], 164–170. For references to the groups or individuals belonging to them in the *Mūlasarvāstivāda-vinaya*, see *Cīvaravastu*, GMs iii 2, 98.9, 117.8; *Śayanāsanavastu* [Gnoli] 36.14, 37.19, 39.7, 40.13, 41.13, 43.4, 53.24; *Vinayavibhaṅga*, Derge, 'dul ba Nya 257b.7; *Bhikṣuṇīvinayavibhaṅga*, Derge, 'dul ba Ta 123a.5, 321b.7; *Kṣudrakavastu*, Tog, 'dul ba Ta 6a.6, 8b.4, 11a.2, 91b.7, 151a.4, 304a.3, 332a.4, 337b.2, 346b.1—all references here are to the beginning of the texts in which the group or its members appear.)

12. Pāli *Vinaya* iii 58.11 = Horner, *BD* i 97 = *Kṣudrakavastu*, Tog, 'dul ba Ta 332a.4ff; Pāli *Vinaya* iv 89.17 = *BD* ii 344 = *Vinayavibhaṅga*, Derge, 'dul ba Ja 154b.2ff; etc. (Note that when a *Mūlasarvāstivāda-vinaya* text is joined to a Pāli text by an equal sign this implies not that it is an exact equivalent but only that it is more or less parallel or broadly similar.)

13. See G. Schopen, "An Old Inscription from Amarāvatī and the Cult of the Local Monastic Dead in Indian Buddhist Monasteries," *JIABS* 14.2 (1991) 281–329 [= *BSBM* 165–203].

14. See G. Schopen, "Immigrant Monks and the Proto-Historical Dead: The Buddhist Occupation of Early Burial Sites in India," in *Festschrift Dieter Schlingloff zur Vollendung des 65. Lebensjahres dargebracht von Schülern, Freunden und Kollegen*, ed. F. Wilhelm (Reinbek: 1996) 215–238 [= Ch. XII below].

15. See, for example, *Bhaiṣajyavastu*, GMs iii 1, 223.7–224.12.

16. See *JIP* 20 (1992) 27 nn. 31–33.

17. See *DPPN* i 524, s.v. Kappitaka Thera.

18. References at *JIABS* 14.2 (1991) 281 n. 1.

19. Pāli *Vinaya* i 148–149 = Horner, *BD* iv 196; Pāli *Vinaya* ii 119 = Horner, *BD* v 163 (here translated by "pestered"); Pāli *Vinaya* i 353 = Horner, *BD* iv 505.

20. I. B. Horner, *Women under Primitive Buddhism. Laywomen and Almswomen* (London: 1930) 158.

21. *Dīgha-nikāya* iii 117–118, 209–210; *Majjhima-nikāya* ii 244.

22. T. W. and C. A. F. Rhys Davids, *Dialogues of the Buddha* (Oxford: 1921) Part III, 111–112 n. 1, also 203–204.

23. M. Walshe, *Thus Have I Heard. The Long Discourses of the Buddha* (London: 1987) 427, 480; K. E. Neumann, *Die Reden Gotamo Buddhos. Aus der Mittleren Sammlung Majjhima-nikāyo des Pāli-Kanons* (München: 1922) III, 52–53; I. B. Horner, *The Middle Length Sayings* (London: 1959) Vol. III, 30–31; Bhikkhu Ñāṇamoli and Bhikkhu Bodhi, *The Middle Length Discourses of the Buddha* (Boston: 1995) 853, 854.

24. There are a number of problems with the Pāli passages about the *stūpa* of "the *Nigaṇṭha Nātaputta*," not the least of which is whether this refers to the Jains. A. L. Basham, *History and Doctrines of the Ājīvikas* (London: 1951) 75, suggests that it does not, but refers rather to the death and community of Gosala, a founding figure of the Ājīvakas, another group competing with the Buddhists (cf. K. R. Norman, "Observations on the Dates of the Jina and the Buddha," *The Dating of the Historical Buddha/Die Datierung des historischen Buddha* [Göttingen: 1991] 300–312, esp. 301). If it does refer to the Jains, then there is the problem of the *stūpa* in Jainism (see P. Dundas, *The Jains* [London and New York: 1992] 188, 97–98; K. W. Folkert, "Jain Religious Life at Ancient Mathurā: The Heritage of Late Victorian Interpretation," in *Mathurā. The Cultural Heritage*, ed. D. M. Srinivasan [New Delhi: 1988] 102–112), and this will involve the further questions of the relative age and exact nature of Jain *nisidhis* (see A. N. Upadhye, "A Note on *Nisidhi* [Nisīdiya of Khāravela Inscription]," *Annals of the Bhandarkar Oriental Research Institute* 14 [1932–1933] 264–266). None of this will, however, affect the basic interpretation of the passages: regardless of which religious group is being referred to, the fact remains that the compilers of the Pāli texts used the expression *bhinna-thūpa* to characterize the destruction of the central focus of a competing religious group and that group's fragmentation. There is in fact a great deal of confusion about other religious groups in "early" Buddhist literature (see, for example, C. Vogel, *The Teachings of the Six Heretics* [Abhandlungen für die Kunde des Morgenlandes, XXXIX.4] [Wiesbaden: 1970]; D. Schlingloff, "Jainas and Other 'Heretics' in Buddhist Art," in *Jainism and Prakrit in Ancient and Medieval India. Essays for Prof. Jagdish Chandra Jain*, ed. N. N. Bhattacharyya [New Delhi: 1994] 71–82). Note, finally, that the one Sanskrit parallel to the Pāli passages that I have noticed has—as it has been reconstructed—a different reading; see V. Stache-Rosen, *Dogmatische Begriffsreihen im älteren Buddhismus II. Das Saṅgītisūtra und sein Kommentar Saṅgītiparyāya* (Berlin: 1968) T. 1, 45.

25. Pāli *Vinaya* iv 192.15. See also Sekhiya 30, . . . *chabbaggiyā bhikkhū thūpikataṃ piṇḍapātaṃ paṭigaṇhanti*, which is also problematic but ignored here in spite of its similarity.

26. T. W. Rhys Davids and H. Oldenberg, *Vinaya Texts* (The Sacred Books of the East, XIII) (Oxford: 1885) Part I, 63 and n. 2; Horner, *BD* iii 130.

27. The first three variants are cited from Pāli *Vinaya* iv 374 (the only edition that is available to me); the last two, from H. Matsumura, "A Lexical Note on the Vinaya Literature: *Stūpa* in the Śaikṣa Rules," *WZKS* 33 (1989) 57. (I cite this paper here and below with some hesitation, because it seems that one cannot be sure whose work appears under this author's name—see Professor Bechert's postscript to K. Wille, *Die handschriftliche Über-*

lieferung des Vinayavastu der Mūlasarvāstivādin [Verzeichnis der orientalischen Handschriften in Deutschland. Supplementband 30] [Stuttgart: 1990] 173–174. This "author" has made the same sort of unacknowledged "use" of material from my Canberra dissertation: "his" paper entitled "The *Stūpa* Worship in Ancient Gilgit," *Journal of Central Asia* 8.2 (1985) 133–147, for example, is almost entirely based on texts I refer to or cite and translate in that dissertation; cf. G. Schopen, "The Bhaiṣajyaguru-sūtra and the Buddhism of Gilgit," Ph.D. Dissertation, Australian National University [1978] 148–150, 298ff, 315. The inane comments, however, are entirely his own.)

28. A. Bareau, "La construction et le culte des stūpa d'après les vinayapiṭaka," *BEFEO* 50 (1960) 271.

29. A. C. Banerjee, *Two Buddhist Vinaya Texts in Sanskrit. Prātimokṣa Sūtra and Bhikṣukarmavākya* (Calcutta: 1977) 51.10, but in light of Matsumura, "A Lexical Note on the Vinaya Literature," 49.

30. *So sor thar pa'i mdo*, Derge, 'dul ba Ca 18b.7; *Dge slong ma'i so sor thar pa'i mdo*, Derge, 'dul ba Ta 23a.5.

31. *'Dul ba rnam par 'byed pa*, Derge, 'dul ba Nya 258a.4.

32. *Dge slong ma'i 'dul ba rnam par 'byed pa*, Derge, 'dul ba Ta 322a.4.

33. *Vinayasūtra* (Sankrityayana) 63.4; *'Dul ba'i mdo*, Derge, bstan 'gyur, 'dul ba Wu 49b.2; *'Dul ba'i mdo'i rgya cher 'grel pa*, Derge, bstan 'gyur, 'dul ba Yu 16b.7.

34. Bareau, "La construction et le culte des stūpa," 272.

35. There is—to use an expression he himself applies to the translation of another—a "queer translation" of this passage in Matsumura, "A Lexical Note on the Vinaya Literature," 49–50, where he has completely misunderstood the structure of the first part of the text.

36. So *TSD* 1755, citing *Mahāvyutpatti*.

37. Nanda and Upananda are the names of the first two monks of the group of six in the *Mūlasarvāstivāda-vinaya*. But they are often—as here—compounded and used as a vocative at the head of an exclamation by the group of six. E. B. Cowell and R. A. Neil, *The Divyāvadāna. A Collection of Early Buddhist Legends* (Cambridge, England: 1886), index, 682, recognize something of this ejaculatory function when they say "Nandopananda, in exclamation (Gemini!)."

38. Compare the instructions for making "miniature" *stūpas* of the Buddha out of a lump of clay in Y. Bentor, "The Redactions of the *Adbhutadharmaparyāya* from Gilgit," *JIABS* 11.2 (1988) 21–52, esp. 40 and 41. Although going in two different directions, and having quite different ends, the two practices appear to be based on the same sort of thinking: by making a model or miniature of the thing—whether in clay or food—one makes the thing itself.

39. *Kṣudrakavastu*, Tog, 'dul ba Ta 354b.6; *Saṅghabhedavastu* GMs iii 4, 239.14 = (Gnoli) ii 264.14.

40. The traditions about Pūraṇa are as confused as are the traditions about other "heretical" teachers—see *BHSD* 351 for references, and the sources cited at the end of n. 24 above.

41. Although this is obviously only one case, it is perhaps sufficient to suggest that the relationship between the *Bhikṣu-* and *Bhikṣuṇī-vinayavibhaṅgas* in the Mūlasarvāstivādin

tradition differs, at least in part, from that posited, but not yet proven, for the Pāli *Bhikkhu-* and *Bhikkhunī-vibhaṅgas*; cf. O. von Hinüber, "Sprachliche Beobachtungen zum Aufbau des Pāli-Kanons," *StII* 2 (1976) 27–40, esp. 34 [= O. von Hinüber, *Selected Papers on Pāli Studies* (Oxford: 1994) 69]. But note also that there is a Tibetan tradition, starting, it seems, with Bu-ston, that the Tibetan translation of the *Bhikṣuṇīvinayavibhaṅga* is not a Mūlasarvāstivādin text "(but has been taken over) from the Āgama of another sect by mistake"; C. Vogel, "Bu-ston on the Schism of the Buddhist Church and on the Doctrinal Tendencies of Buddhist Scriptures," *Zur Schulzugehörigkeit von Werken der Hīnayāna-Literatur*, ed. H. Bechert (Göttingen: 1985) T. I, 104–110. At this stage of our knowledge it is possible neither to confirm nor to deny this, however.

42. Waldschmidt, *Bruchstücke des Bhikṣuṇī-Prātimokṣa der Sarvāstivādins*, 61 (3.I.A); the references in both C. Kabilsingh, *A Comparative Study of Bhikkhunī Pāṭimokkha* (Varanasi: 1984) 124, and Hirakawa, *Monastic Discipline for the Buddhist Nuns*, 285 n. 104, seem to have gone awry.

43. *Arhats* getting themselves into awkward situations by not focusing their mind (*asamanvāhṛtya*) before they act is something of a narrative motif in the *Mūlasarvāstivāda-vinaya* (see *Bhaiṣajyavastu*, GMs iii 1, 79.3ff) and literature associated with it (cf. *BHSD*, s.v. *asamanvāhṛtya*); for a discussion of the problem in scholastic literature, see P. S. Jaini, "On the Ignorance of the Arhat," in *Paths to Liberation. The Mārga and Its Transformation in Buddhist Thought*, ed. R. E. Buswell Jr. and R. M. Gimello (Honolulu: 1992) 135–145. References to *stūpas* of the hair and nails of the Buddha (*keśanakhastūpa*) are also frequent in the *Mūlasarvāstivāda-vinaya*: *Cīvaravastu*, GMs iii 2, 143.12; *Pārivāsikavastu*, GMs iii 3, 98.4; *Kṣudrakavastu*, Derge, 'dul ba Ta 7b.2, 137a.5, 138a.4, 157a.7, 185b.1, 293a.4, 293a.6, etc.

44. One of the characteristics of the group of six monks and the group of twelve nuns in the *Mūlasarvāstivāda-vinaya* is that they—far more than other "good" monks and nuns—quote "scripture" (i.e., passages from the *vinaya*) to justify their actions or make a point (for some examples, see *Kṣudrakavastu*, Tog, 'dul ba Ta 154a.2, 346b.7; *Cīvaravastu*, GMs iii 2, 101.7; *Śayanāsanavastu* [Gnoli] 43.27). The obvious incongruity of this could hardly be unintentional and was almost certainly a source of some amusement for both the compilers and their readers.

45. For other texts in the *Mūlasarvāstivāda-vinaya* that deal with local monasteries making their own "ordinances" and some of the problems this could create, see *Kṣudrakavastu*, Tog, 'dul ba Ta 107a.4–108a.6, 318a.1–319a.6 (that the Sanskrit being translated by *khrims su bya ba* or *khrims su bca' ba*, "to make an ordinance," was *kriyākāraṃ kṛ-* is made relatively certain by Guṇaprabha's restatement of Ta 107a.4–108a.6 at *Vinayasūtra* (Sankrityayana) 9.22, but with a better reading at *Vinayasūtra* [Bapat and Gokhale] 42.13). Evidence for the compilation of local monastic ordinances comes from several places. The earliest such compilation that I know was found among the Kharoṣṭhī documents from the third century A.D. that Stein recovered from Niya, Sāca, and Lou-lan (see A. M. Boyer, E. J. Rapson, and E. Senart, *Kharoṣṭhi Inscriptions. Discovered by Sir Aurel Stein in Chinese Turkestan* [Oxford: 1927] Part II, 176 [no. 489]; T. Burrow, *A Translation of the Kharoṣṭhi Documents from Chinese Turkestan* [London: 1940] 95 [no.489])—the document is headed

bhichusaṃgasa kriyakara, "Regulations for the community of monks," and because only the beginning has been preserved, it is impossible to know how long it was. It is likely, though now hard to tell, that a sadly fragmentary inscription from Amarāvatī that has been assigned to the fifth or sixth century, also contained local monastic ordinances (see R. Sewell, *Report on the Amaravati Tope and Excavations on Its Site in 1877* [London: 1880] 63–66). For Sri Lanka, see the references to inscriptions given by N. Ratnapala, *The Katikāvatas. Laws of the Buddhist Order of Ceylon from the 12th Century to the 18th Century* (München: 1971) 7 nn. 13–18 (following earlier Sri Lankan usage, Ratnapala calls these "Vihāra katikāvatas" as opposed to "Sāsana katikāvatas"); for Tibet, see T. Ellingson, "Tibetan Monastic Constitutions: The Bca'-yig," in *Reflections on Tibetan Culture. Essays in Memory of Turrell V. Wylie*, ed. L. Epstein and R. F. Sherburne (Lewiston, N.Y.: 1990) 205–229; etc.

46. See G. Schopen, "The Stūpa Cult and the Extant Pāli Vinaya," *JPTS* 13 (1989) 91 [= *BSBM* 86–98] end of n. 9.

47. A. H. Longhurst, *The Story of the Stūpa* (Colombo: 1936) 14; Gombrich, "Making Mountains without Molehills," 142.

48. J. Marshall, A. Foucher, and N. G. Majumdar, *The Monuments of Sāñchī* (Delhi: 1940) Vol. I, 79; Vol. III, pls. LXXIff.

49. M. Bénisti, "Observations concernant le stūpa n°2 de sāñcī," *BEI* 4 (1986) 165–170, esp. 165.

50. There is a fine old photograph of some of these *stūpas* in H. Bechert and R. Gombrich, *The World of Buddhism. Buddhist Monks and Nuns in Society and Culture* (London: 1984) 64 (6); for the inscriptions and dates, see Schopen, "An Old Inscription from Amarāvatī," 293–294 [= *BSBM* 175–177].

51. For what might be another case of the adaptation of a canonical *vinaya* text to local architectural traditions, see G. Schopen, "The Monastic Ownership of Servants or Slaves: Local and Legal Factors in the Redactional History of Two *Vinayas*," *JIABS* 17.2 (1994) 145–173 [= Ch. VII above].

52. *DPPN* i 368.

53. For Moliya-Phagguna, see *DPPN* ii 674 and in particular *Majjhima* i122ff; for Mūlaphalguna, *BHSD* 437 (Edgerton says of him: "evidently same as Pali Moliya-Phagguna; like him a friend of the nuns"); in the *Cīvaravastu* (GMs iii 2, 143.15), where the "group of twelve" is explicitly mentioned in association with him, the name is translated by *khrums stod*.

54. *DPPN* i 418–421.

55. *BHSD* 125; also the passages cited and summarized in Panglung, *Die Erzählstoffe des Mūlasarvāstivāda-Vinaya* 123, 140, 159–160, 193; Ét. Lamotte, *Le traité de la grand vertu de sagesse* (Louvain: 1949) T. II, 634–636, 844–846; in the Mūlasarvāstivādin *Bhikṣuṇīvinayavibhaṅga*, she is declared to be the foremost of those possessed of miraculous power (Derge, 'dul ba Ta 295a.5); she is, finally, the only nun clearly identifiable, or even visible, in early Buddhist art (see the good photograph of a "panel" from Swat illustrating "The Buddha's Descent at Sankissa" in V. Dehejia, "Aniconism and the Multivalence of Emblems," *ArO* 21 (1991) 563, fig. 9.

56. Schopen, "Ritual Rites and Bones of Contention" [= Ch. X below].

57. Though it is not formally parallel, the text at *Cīvaravastu*, GMs iii 2, 49.1–51.6, in which the Buddha prescribes a distinct and identifiable form of robe to distinguish Buddhist monks from members of other religious groups, seems to be addressing a part of the same issue that our text may be. That text says that it was the usual practice of Bimbisāra to dismount from his elephant whenever he saw a monk or nun and to venerate their feet. Once he did this in view of others to an Ājīvaka whom he mistook for a Buddhist monk, much to the consternation (*sandigdhamanas*) of devout Buddhists. When this was reported to the Buddha, he pointed out that the problem was that the Ājīvaka "appropriated as his own the veneration intended for one who had seen the truths" (*dṛṣṭasatyasyāntikād vandanā svīkṛteti*). However, in neither case do the texts indicate that there was a conscious deception: the Ājīvaka did not claim to be a Buddhist, nor did the nuns of the group of twelve present their *stūpa* as a *stūpa* of the Buddha. But in both cases similarity provided an opportunity for confusion and the "misdirection" of veneration.

58. For the *sapiṇḍa*, especially see D. M. Knipe, "Sapiṇḍīkaraṇa: The Hindu Rite of Entry into Heaven," in *Religious Encounters with Death. Insights from the History and Anthropology of Religions*, ed. F. E. Reynolds and E. H. Waugh (University Park and London: 1977) 111–124. It is worth noting that the compilers of the *Mūlasarvāstivāda-vinaya* were well aware of brahmanical funeral practices; see *Kṣudrakavastu*, Tog, 'dul ba Ta 377a.2ff, which refers to two sons performing *śrāddha* (*shing btang ba*) for their deceased father, and *Saṅghabhedavastu* (Gnoli) ii 34.14ff, which refers to the giving of five *piṇḍas* at the site of the cremation of a dead relative (*pañca piṇḍān datvā*—this text is also of interest because it contains what may be, comparatively, an early reference to depositing the postcremational bones in the Ganges: *asthīnāṃ bhasmanāṃ ca karparakaṃ pūrayitvā gaṅgāyāṃ prakṣipya* . . .).

59. Bareau, "La construction et le culte des stūpa," 269. For the archaeological and epigraphical evidence, see G. Schopen, "Burial 'ad sanctos' and the Physical Presence of the Buddha in Early Indian Buddhism. A Study in the Archeology of Religions," *Religion* 17 (1987) 193–225 [= *BSBM* 114–147].

60. See Schopen, "An Old Inscription from Amarāvatī," esp. 299–301 [= *BSBM* 179–180].

61. There is also evidence that Indian Buddhist images, like *stūpas*, could both live and, significantly, die; see G. Schopen, "The Buddha as an Owner of Property and Permanent Resident in Medieval Indian Monasteries," *JIP* 18 (1990) 181–217 [= *BSBM* 258–289], esp. 203. And "dead" *sūtras* and other texts were also handled like "dead" Buddhas; see, for example, A. F. R. Hoernle, *Manuscript Remains of Buddhist Literature Found in Eastern Turkestan* (Oxford: 1916) 1ff.

62. Matsumura, "A Lexical Note on the Vinaya Literature," 59. The idea or assumption of an *ur* text has probably nowhere been more influential than in studies of the *prātimokṣa*, where virtually all the energies have been directed toward finding a hypothetical "original" of the various rules. This has frequently been done by forcing disparate versions together and rejecting those that cannot be so forced as "late" or "corrupt." The whole procedure is in need of reappraisal and may be particularly unsuitable for the *Sekhiya/Śaikṣa*

rules. The latter are frequently described as the most "disparate" or "divergent," but this is only a negative and misleading way of saying that it is in these rules that the individual orders express and define themselves most individually. This, I should think, would make them not less but more valuable. Matsumura's argument—insofar as he has one—is very much of the *ur* variety. He tries to force a good deal of material together that probably should not be and, in doing so, ignores or questions what would otherwise appear to be clear.

63. See, for example, S. Lévi, "Observations sur une langue précanonique du bouddhisme," *JA* (1912) 495–514, esp. 510.

64. Cf. some of the cases in D. Schlingloff, "Zur Interpretation des Prātimokṣasūtra," *ZDMG* 113.3 (1964) 536–551.

65. Matsumura, "A Lexical Note on the Vinaya Literature," 72–73 cites both. The more sure of the two reads: *na stūpākāraṃ piṇḍapātaṃ paribhokṣyāma iti*. He says "the meaning of the whole sentence is not very intelligible," but it seems to me to be perfectly straightforward: "we will not eat alms food having the shape of a *stūpa*." He also says that the Chinese translation of the Kāśyapīya *Prātimokṣa* gives the rule as "not to eat making a shape of [a] tope." The Mūlasarvāstivādin understanding of the rule is, therefore, not an isolated one. (Incidentally, the Chinese translations "like a well" that he cites might be accounted for by a confusion somewhere in the transmission that transformed *stūpākāra* into *kūpākāra*.)

66. For the death of Śāriputra, see *Kṣudrakavastu*, Tog, 'dul ba Ta 354a.5–368a.5 (Schopen, "Ritual Rites and Bones of Contention," 45–56; Schopen, in "Death, Funerals, and the Division of Property in a Monastic Code," 491–494); for Kāśyapa, *Kṣudrakavastu*, Tog, 'dul ba Tha 463b.4–465b.7 (J. Przyluski, "Le nord-ouest de l'inde dans le vinaya des mūlasarvāstivādin et les texts apparentés," *JA* (1914) 522–528, from the Chinese); for Ānanda, *Kṣudrakavastu*, Tog, 'dul ba Tha 467b.2–470b.7 (Przyluski, "Le nord-ouest de l'inde dans le vinaya," 529–535); for Mahāprajāpatī, *Kṣudrakavastu*, Tog, 'dul ba Ta 167a.6–172b.3. Walters, "A Voice from the Silence," 358ff, makes an interesting argument to the effect that in the *Apadāna* Mahāprajāpatī is being presented as "the female counterpart of Buddha" or "the Buddha's counterpart." If that is the case, then it is particularly interesting that the equation is not complete in one significant way: neither in the *Apadāna* nor elsewhere in canonical literature, insofar as I know, is there any reference to a *stūpa* for Mahāprajāpatī. (The text Walters is referring to is now available in translation: J. S. Walters, "Gotamī's Story," in *Buddhism in Practice*, 113–138; it gives evidence of some possible contact with the Mūlasarvāstivādin text, especially in regard to the "sneezing" incident that in both texts occasions Mahāprajāpatī's decision to enter *parinirvāṇa*. Walters fudges his translation here by rendering *vandiya* and *vandasi* as "bless" and misses the fact that this is a rebuke of Mahāprajāpatī similar to the one addressed to the trees that drop their flowers on the Buddha in the Pāli version of the *Mahāparinirvāṇa-sūtra* [V. 3]. The absence of any reference to *stūpas* for female "saints" is also noticeable in, and creates some problems for, the interesting study of R. A. Ray, *Buddhist Saints in India. A Study in Buddhist Values and Orientations* (New York/Oxford: 1994), 101–123.

67. Bareau, "Le construction et le culte des stūpa," 253. Also, among many other possibilities, see L. de la Vallée Poussin, "À propos du cittaviśuddhiprakaraṇa d'āryadeva,"

BSOAS 6.2 (1931) 412, where he says in regard to the destruction of a *stūpa*: "On sait que ce sacrilège est un des cinq *upānantaryas*, un des cinq péchés quasi mortels: c'est détruire le corps même du Bouddha."

68. Schopen, "Ritual Rites and Bones of Contention," 68 [= 316–317 above].

69. I hasten to add, though, that much remains to be seen. The accounts treated here are drawn from only two *vinayas*, the Pāli (often said to be the earliest) and the Mūlasarvāstivādin (equally often said to be the latest). But the chances of there being similar or related accounts in other *vinayas* are very good. In fact, J. Silk in a not yet published paper entitled "The Yogācāra Bhikṣu" refers to what seems to be just such an account in the *Dharmaguptaka Vinaya* (T. 1428 [XXII] 766c 3–10) [see now J. A. Silk, "Further Remarks on the *yogācāra bhikṣu*," in *Dharmadūta. Mélanges offerts au Vénérable Thích Huyên-Vi*, ed. Bh. T. Dhammaratana and Bh. Pāsādika (Paris: 1997) 233–250, esp. 244]. More may well show up.

CHAPTER XII

Immigrant Monks and the Protohistorical Dead

The Buddhist Occupation of Early Burial Sites in India

THAT CHAMELEON-LIKE collection of startling "metaphysics," complex cults, and sometimes cantankerous monks that we call Buddhism—and flatter ourselves that we thereby have understood it—seems to have been restless from the start and always moving. It moved—and surprisingly quickly—across Central Asia not only to China, Korea, and Japan but also, perhaps, to the borders of Syria and certainly to the Eastern marches of Iran and beyond, where it left its mark both on the land and on Arabic and Persian literature.[1] It immigrated not just to Nepal or Tibet but also to Sri Lanka and Southeast Asia and to the distant Maldives, where recent excavations have shown it to have been a not insignificant presence,[2] as well as to Java and Malaysia.

These migrations or movements to foreign lands have, of course, been studied—though unevenly—and the recurring problem of Buddhism's finding roots in foreign countries has been discussed more than once, in some cases very extensively. What has been much less considered is that Buddhism had almost certainly faced [216] the same problem already in what we call India. The fact that for the immigrant Buddhist—whether "missionary," monk, or merchant—Andhra, for example, was linguistically, culturally, and religiously as much a foreign country as China has rarely been discussed. But it is virtually certain that as soon as Buddhism moved out of the Gangetic plain—and, again, it seems to have done so quickly—it found itself, in effect, in foreign countries, often in areas where the kind and level of culture differed markedly from that which had produced it. Finding itself in foreign places, it had, of course, to find some roots or wither. It had above all else to forge some links with the local land, to find a place in the local

Originally published in *Festschrift Dieter Schlingloff zur Vollendung des 65. Lebensjahres dargebracht von Schülern, Freunden und Kollegen*, ed. F. Wilhelm (Reinbeck: 1996) 215–238. Reprinted with stylistic changes with permission of the editor.

landscape. Our surviving textual sources for India—with rare exceptions—tell us little about this. In part, perhaps, because of their anachronizing program these sources avoid the purely local. Archaeological material, on the other hand, is at least suggestive of some elements of what must have been a complex process. Unfortunately, because archaeological data have often been poorly reported, they are not always conclusive; they do, however, suggest what appears to be at least one distinct pattern in the process by which Buddhist monastic communities settled into local "foreign" landscapes. It suggests that immigrating Buddhist monks in India may have intentionally sought out places that were—oddly enough—already occupied, but the current occupants were not in a good position to object.

A cursory survey of the archaeological literature seems to indicate that many Buddhist monastic sites in India were already occupied by the protohistorical dead before they were taken over by the immigrant monks. Unfortunately, again, the presence of these dead is often poorly reported, and frequently all we know is that they were there. Goli, for example, is a Buddhist site in Andhra with a small *stūpa* that has been assigned to the third or fourth century C.E. But this *stūpa* was not, apparently, the first structure at the site. Although they give no details or references, both Venkataramanayya and Rao signal the presence at the site of what they simply call "dolmens."[3] Likewise, it is only from a remark regarding future work that should be undertaken that we learn that there are "megalithic" burials at the site of [217] the "monastic establishment" at Chandavaram, again in Andhra.[4] At Panigiri—yet another site in Andhra—we are told: "Between the hill on which the [modern] Irrigation Bungalow is situated and the hill where there are vestiges of Buddhist structures upon it, there is a vast field of pre-historic tombs which can be identified by the presence of huge slabs of rock which cover the tops of the cists below."[5] Somewhat more detailed but still unsatisfactory are Sewell's remarks on a discovery of his "near the town of Jaggayyapeta." There he found a "large circle of stone," which, he said, "contained little more than the bones of a horse buried with its head at the center." He added: "At the cardinal points there were four small vessels of earth." The exact relationship of this—in some ways—typical megalithic horse burial to the Buddhist structures at the site is not, however, ever stated.[6] Again badly reported, but of great potential significance, is yet another case—this time from the north.

The one major Buddhist sacred site with the most obvious funereal association is, of course, Kusinārā, a place the texts themselves describe as in the middle of nowhere and as a "miserable little town of wattle-and-daub." It is here that the Buddha himself is said to have decided he was to die and to be cremated—although the [218] redactors of the texts appear to have felt that his choice needed some explanation.[7] The texts, of course, do not say so, but it is not impossible that these events were placed here precisely because Kusinārā was a site already associated with such events. In any case it would appear that if the Buddha was actually cremated here, he very possibly was not the first person who had been. Cunningham's map of 1861–1862, for example, shows close to and to the northeast of the main *stūpa* at the site an area covered with more than twenty "*tumuli*." The local people, according to Cunningham, said that "gypsys were formerly very numerous about Kasia, and that these mounds are the *tumuli* of their dead." Curiously, since—as Rao has shown—such explanations are in India frequently given by local peoples to account for megalithic burials, it is not improbable that this story inadvertently points toward the true nature of these mounds. Cunningham, however, first wrote that he opened three of these mounds "but without making any discovery." He continued: "They were all formed of plain earth, without any trace of bones, ashes, or broken bricks." In a later note, though, he added a typical archaeological lament in regard to his initial observations: "I believe now that I did not dig deeply enough. That they are tombs I feel quite certain. . . ."[8] Carlleyle, more than a dozen years later, was able to augment and confirm to some degree Cunningham's belated belief.

> I counted nearly fifty of these small mounds, or *barrows*, altogether. They are probably sepulchral. I only excavated two of these small *barrows*, and I could not find anything in them, except a small quantity of pale whitish-coloured powdery substance resembling bone-ash, and a few minute black or dark-coloured particles resembling charcoal. But I did not find even this little until I dug down into the centre of the base of the mounds below the level of the surrounding plain.[9]

Because later workers at the site like Vogel and Sastri completely ignored these "*tumuli*" or "mounds" or "barrows," this is all we know about them: they were [219] numerous; they were almost certainly funereal; and they were—to judge by the depth at which Carlleyle found what he found—old. Given what a close examination of these *tumuli* might have told us about the pre-Buddhist history of the site, it is a great pity that no such examination was ever pursued. If, however, some brief remarks of Hsüan-tsang refer to this area, it is not impossible that the contents of these *tumuli* might already have been "found" long ago. Referring to "the place where they burnt the body of the Tathāgata," Hsüan-tsang says: "The earth is now of a blackish yellow, from a mixture of earth and charcoal. Whoever with true faith seeks here, and prays, is sure to find some relics of Tathāgata." Moreover, much the same is said in later Tibetan guidebooks.[10] There is as well just a hint of the presence of the protohistorical dead at another northern site, a site also connected with the biography of the Buddha, which has been much more recently published. In a confused summary of archaeological work done in 1970–1971 at Lumbinī, Rijal says that "a circular burial containing some portions of the human skull, one iron sickle, and a few bones of birds and animals were found kept in a larger number of pots which were mainly full of encised designs."[11]

But if what we know about the presence of the "protohistorical" dead at places like Goli, Chandavaram, Panigiri, Jaggayyapeta, Kusinārā, and Lumbinī is more frustrating than fulfilling, the situation in regard to other sites is somewhat more satisfying. For Amarāvatī, for example, we have both anecdotal evidence and hard description. From the first, we know that "an extensive area around Amarāvatī appears to have been occupied by megalith builders."[12] Burgess' incidental description of the larger setting of the Amarāvatī *stūpa* is typical of the kind of observations that could be quoted: to the east of Dharaṇikoṭa, he says, "and between this old city and the foot of the neighbouring hills, where so many dolmens or [220] rude-stone burying places are still to be seen, stood the great Mahāchaitya."[13] Fergusson before him had also noted "the sepulchral circles of which such numbers exist in the neighbourhood." According to Fergusson, "In Colonel Mackenzie's maps they are represented as extremely numerous, both to the eastward and westward of the city." But Fergusson provides us as well with a precious woodcut showing both the plan and the elevation of one of these "sepulchral stone circles," and its megalithic character is unmistakable.[14] It would appear from just this much, then, that the Amarāvatī *stūpa* and monastic complex were built very near or even in the midst of a megalithic cemetery. The broad similarity of what we see at Amarāvatī with the much more poorly documented setting of Kusinārā, for example, may provide an additional argument for suggesting that the latter, too, was situated in a preexisting cemetery. For Amarāvatī, at least, there is even more evidence for such an argument.

In 1908–1909, Alexander Rea brought to light a small *stūpa* near the northwestern quadrant of the main *stūpa* at Amarāvatī. This *stūpa*—which is twenty-one feet in diameter—is significant not so much for what it contained as for what in part it covered. "Adjacent to, and partly under" this *stūpa*, Rea discovered a group of what he called "seventeen neolithic pyriform tombs." Referring to these "huge urn burials," Rao notes that although Rea assigned them to the Neolithic, we, "taking into account the recent evidence, . . . can safely assign them to the megalithic period."[15] This find, of course, makes it absolutely certain that the Buddhist complex at Amarāvatī was built not just near a megalithic cemetery but on top of one. And Amarāvatī is not the only Buddhist site in Andhra where this occurred.

Yeleśwaram lies directly across the Krishna River from the much better known Nāgārjunakoṇḍa. Here, too, we find Buddhist structures built directly over megalithic burials. Although both of Khan's accounts are badly written and at times confused, this much is clear: a "domenoid cist" burial containing three skulls, "fractional bones," and pottery underlay the northeastern quadrant of a Buddhist *stūpa*;

under "the south-eastern quadrant of a *stūpa* at the temple complex" a "cairn circle" came [221] to light containing pottery, "a bone probably of a horse," and two complete human skeletons, one on top of the other in an extended position; under the northwest quadrant of—apparently—the same *stūpa* an "urn burial" was found. The diversity of burial types that were discovered at Yeleśwaram is, of course, striking, but for us it is sufficient to note that, regardless of type, these megalithic burials had—as they had at Amarāvatī—been overlaid by a Buddhist *stūpa*.[16] Something similar occurs as well at neighbouring Nāgārjunakoṇḍa.

According to Subrahmanyam et al., the megalithic burials at Nāgārjunakoṇḍa are confined to two localities. The first and most thoroughly documented group occurs "in a cluster in close proximity to the south-east corner of the Ikshvaku citadel." A good number of these burials have been properly excavated, and they are important for the types of deposits they contain—a topic we will return to. For the moment, though, it is the second group that must most directly concern us.

Subrahmanyam et al. call this group "the minor cluster" but then almost immediately admit that we do not actually know its original extent. The reason we are unable to determine the original size of this cluster is, however, of considerable interest in itself: "It was not possible to arrive at the total number of tombs here, because, the later [Buddhist] monastic complex crowning the hill Kshuladhammagiri, on the southern slopes of which the site was situated, very likely utilized the boulders of these burials for forming a pedestal for its *stūpa*."[17] The two burials of this group that have been examined are also of interest. The one studied during the 1954–1960 excavations was marked by a "cairn circle" of unhewn granite boulders, only a part of which remained. Below the cairn were multiple capstones covering "an oblong [222] rectangular cist." The cist contained, in turn, "four human skulls along with several long bones, and among the "primary offerings" were typical megalithic pottery, some iron objects, and animal bones.[18] The other burial belonging to this group that has been examined was opened by Longhurst. Although he uses a different vocabulary from that now in vogue, it is obvious that it too was marked by a "cairn-circle" and had multiple capstones, but it—obviously a construction requiring some effort—was empty.[19] In this regard it is important to note, however, that it is by no means unique. Carefully constructed megalithic tombs that are empty or devoid of human mortuary remains have been frequently encountered at Khapa, for example, or Khairwara in Maharashtra, and at Chinnamarur and Uppalapadu in Andhra.[20] Empty megalithic tombs of this type almost unavoidably call to mind the other mortuary monuments at Buddhist sites that are sometimes found empty: the secondary *stūpas* that have been called "votive." A connection—as we shall see—is not entirely out of the question. But for the moment we need only note that at least one of the monastic establishments at Nāgārjunakoṇḍa was not just built near or on a megalithic cemetery: it appears to have actually been built, in part, of materials that originally belonged to such a cemetery. Similar cases are, moreover, found elsewhere.

The sites we have so far looked at are mostly in the south, and although all are by no means well reported, even the available evidence establishes the presence of the protohistorical dead at a significant number of Buddhist monastic sites there. But there is, in addition, even in the uneven reporting a potentially significant pattern: *the more we know in general about a site, the stronger is the evidence for the presence of the protohistorical dead.* Goli and Jaggayyapeta, for example, where the evidence is thin, have never actually been excavated. Amarāvatī, Nāgārjunakoṇḍa, and Yeleśwaram, on the other hand, where our evidence is strongest, have all been excavated in modern times and each in its own way carefully studied. This must suggest, as a good possibility, that as our knowledge of other sites increases—if it does—so too will the evidence for the presence of the protohistorical dead at such sites. In any case, the same pattern seems to hold for the north as well. [223]

Although an important site, Kusinārā is not the only northern monastic site that has revealed a close connection between Buddhist monastic establishments and the presence of the protohistorical dead. But—again as in the south—that connection is most fully and firmly established at sites that have been most thoroughly studied and excavated.

The work of the Italian Archaeological Mission in Swat not only was carefully done but also has, happily, been well published. The detailed excavations that were carried out at several sites fully confirmed what had already been suggested by preliminary survey work: they fully confirmed that "many of the *stūpas* still existing in Swat have been built on or near the [protohistorical] graveyards."[21] At Butkara II, for example, forty-eight tombs have been found, forming a part of an extensive protohistorical cemetery. According to D. Faccenna: "An analysis of the stratigraphy has shown [that] the cemetery area was later occupied by a Buddhist sanctuary. Three badly-preserved *stūpas* . . . are visible today. West of the spur down by the foot of the ravine there are traces of large and complex buildings . . . probably contemporary with the layout of the Sacred Precinct."[22] Likewise at Katelai another "necropolis" came to light. Here forty-five tombs were noted, and—again according to Faccenna—"the tangled mass of burials testifies to the cemetery's long life."[23] Here too "rise the ruins of a [Buddhist] *stūpa* which has not yet been excavated nor studied," Antonini notes. "As in the case of Butkara we are in the presence of a locality which has carried its sacred character through time."[24] An observation similar to Antonini's has also been made in regard to the one other well-documented northern site we might look at.

J. E. van Lohuizen–de Leeuw has noted in regard to the Buddhist monastic complex at Mohenjo-daro that "although its report is far better than that of any other early historical site in Sind examined previously, it never received the attention it deserved because it was written after the publication of Cousens' monumental work on 'The Antiquities of Sind' and was hidden away as a short chapter of 18 pages among the 716 pages of Sir John Marshall's three epoch making volumes on [224] 'Mohenjo-daro and the Indus Civilization.' . . ."[25] It is, however, this monastic complex in regard to which Mackay has said: "When further excavations take place on this site, the axiom that once a site becomes sacred it remains so, even to the followers of other religions who may occupy it later, will probably once more prove true."[26]

The point, of course, and Mackay's prediction turn on the character of the structures that underlie the Buddhist complex, which stands "at a height of some sixty feet above the level of the surrounding plain." This complex—according to Mackay—is "known to cover a building which may well have been a temple." Because it has not been possible to fully excavate the underlying structure, however, its exact character remains uncertain. But its original discoverer discovered as well that it had had funereal associations at some stage or stages in its career.

Funeral practices at Mohenjo-daro have been the subject of considerable disagreement and debate, and the whole question is made even more complicated by the fact that early Indus pottery vessels appear to have been reused in some cases for much later Buddhist mortuary deposits. The recent publication of R. D. Banerji's original report, rather than resolving these disagreements and uncertainties, has served only to reinvigorate them. But, for the moment, we might merely note the following. Referring to what he calls "the post-cremation period," Banerji says: "The ashes of the dead were collected and placed in some urns. Such urns were brought to the temples and grouped round some favorite sanctuary." One of the "favorite places for the deposit of such post-cremation burial urns" was—according to Banerji—at "the bottom of the grand staircase along the eastern facade of the front retaining wall of the main platform" on which the Buddhist complex came to the built.[27]

The stratigraphical context of these deposits is not entirely clear, nor, as a consequence, is the period to which they belong. But there are at least two further funereal deposits about which we can be more certain. Banerji reports "several" jar burials under the layer of ashes below the platform on which the Buddhist *stūpa* at Mohenjo-daro was built. He also found a similar burial jar below the foundations of the [225] eastern wall of one of the residental cells of the monastery.[28] Even Marshall concedes in regard to this jar that "the position of this . . . vessel under the foundations of the monastery and the presence of the flint scrapers [found in it] indicate that it appertained to the prehistoric stratum immediately below the Buddhist sanctuaries."[29]

In spite, then, of all the uncertainties, it seems sure that at Mohenjo-daro—as at Butkara and Katelai—the Buddhist monastic complex was built on and over an area that formerly had been used for, and still contained, deposits of the protohistorical dead. The Mohenjo-daro monastic complex had also been constructed largely from materials taken from such an area—as had that at Nāgārjunakoṇḍa but even more so—although this reutilization of materials at both sites is certainly not the most significant aspect of the repeated pattern that has emerged from our necessarily short survey.

The significance of what we have seen here is simply put: the association of Buddhist monastic sites with the presence of the protohistorical dead occurs too often to be coincidental and suggests that Buddhist monastic communities in "India"—like the early Christian monastic communities in, for example, Ireland, Britain and France—intentionally chose to build their residences and sacred structures on sites that already housed the dead of former occupants. Although this pattern is common in the history of religions, it has almost never been noted in specific regard to Buddhist monastic sites. Mackay, it is true, suggested something like this—as we have seen—in regard to Mohenjo-daro; and Professor Tucci too came close when he said that "the fact that many of the *stūpas* still existing in Swat have been built on or near the graveyards" was "a mark, so to say, of the occupation by the new religion of previous religious centres."[30] But more typical, perhaps, are Rao's more recent remarks in regard to Amarāvatī and Yeleśwaram. [226]

Referring to the chronology of the megaliths in Maharashtra and Andhra, Rao starts by saying that "by far the most reliable dates on stratigraphical grounds come from Amarāvatī and Yeleśwaram." This "reliability" is, of course, based on the fact that at both sites the megalithic material was overlaid by Buddhist *stūpas*. From here, though, Rao takes two further steps—one unproblematic, the other not. If we date the *stūpa* at Amarāvatī, for example, as prior to 200 B.C.—which he does—then the underlying megalithic remains must be earlier than that. This, if nothing else, has the advantage of being obvious. But then he adds: "Now this date can be further pushed back if we consider the fact that nobody would construct a religious monument over a burial ground knowingly," and from this he further concludes: "So, it appears that the local people at that time had no knowledge of the existence of these urn burials."[31] There are problems with this argument even apart from its circularity.

In specific regard to Amarāvatī, for example, Rao assumes that there was no surface marker or "lithic appendage" over these urns, but the presence of the *stūpa* itself establishes that the surface layer had been "disturbed." Moreover, even if we were to grant Rao's assumption that there was no "lithic appendage" over *this* particular group of urns, the fact remains—as Mackenzie's and Fergusson's observations prove—that there were such "lithic appendages" scattered over the entire area on which the main *stūpa* stood. If these were still clearly visible in the nineteenth century, it is hard to imagine how they could not have been even more so in the first. The builders of both the main *stūpa* and the smaller *stūpa* covering in part the urns could not, it seems, have been unaware of the general nature of the site. But if this is true, then Amarāvatī itself disproves Rao's more obvious assumption—the one he calls a "fact"—that "nobody would construct a religious monument over a burial ground knowingly," and it is not the only case that can be cited.

Although one could, one need not cite here the numerous cases outside India where someone knowingly built a religious monument over a burial ground, nor need one note that something of this sort occurred as late as the eighteenth century at Sept-Saints on the Côte-du-Nord in Brittany, for example.[32] Indian material, particularly South Indian material, may make this unnecessary. Although not yet fully studied and a topic perhaps too often avoided, an association of Hindu temples, especially Shivite [227] temples, with cemeteries and burial grounds is not difficult to detect. Venkataramanayya, for example, says: "There is ample epigraphical evidence to show that, in certain cases, Temples of Śiva were actually built upon graves," and he goes on to cite three epigraphical records from the south that record that someone "caused to be built a temple to Iśvara (Śiva) on the spot where his father had been buried" or "built a shrine over or near the burial ground," etc. In fact, he says:

> The numerous temples that are dedicated to the god Śmaśāneśvara in many places in South India might have had a similar origin. They generally stand in or near the graveyards. The custom of building Śiva's temples over graves is by no means dead. Many communities in South India, such as the Lingāyats, Kammālans, Jāṇḍras, Vellālars, etc., still observe it.[33]

It is not impossible, moreover, that the entire temple complex at Aihoḷe may have had a similar origin and that "the temple-like structures found at Aihoḷe and Paṭṭadakal or Tigowa" are funerary monuments.[34] But, again, it is not necessary to prove this to render Rao's assumption unsupportable. That is already effected—as we have seen—by Amarāvatī. It is made even more untenable by other Buddhist sites as well. The builders of the monastery on the "Kshuladhammagiri" at Nāgārjunakoṇḍa could hardly have been unaware of what had earlier been on the site; nor could the builders of the Mohenjo-daro monastery: in both cases they reused material from the structures that they chose to build over. The more general argument too remains, I think, persuasive: if Buddhist builders were unaware of the presence of the protohistorical dead, how do we account for the fact that they repeatedly built at places where those dead were found? It occurs too often to be coincidence. There are as well other considerations that suggest a clear awareness.

The chronology of the megalithic period in the south, for example, is rough and approximate, but whatever view we take of it is suggestive. The Allchins, for example, say: [228]

> The South Indian graves appear as a developing complex, first arising around the end of the second millennium, and lasting for many centuries, probably not less than a thousand years. Modern burial customs in many parts of South India reveal direct continuation of the tradition into modern times . . .
>
> That, once established, the burial customs continued for many centuries is attested by stray finds of Roman or other coins in graves. It is to be expected that there are many more graves belonging to the later centuries than to the earlier.[35]

Rao—in speaking about Andhra—says:

> Thus, broadly speaking we can place the megalithic culture . . . in Andhra Pradesh between 6th century B.C. to the 2nd–3rd centuries A.D.[36]

More recently still, McIntosh has assigned the megalithic culture to a period starting around 1100 B.C.E. and ending around 100 B.C.E.[37]

Regardless, then, of which formulation we accept, and regardless of when precisely we date the initial appearance of Buddhism in the south at such sites as Bhaṭṭiprolu and Amarāvatī, there will be a more or less lengthy period of overlap between Buddhist presence and megalithic practice, a more or less lengthy period when the two coexisted. This continuity and overlap has been noted in far more general terms as well. Maloney, for example, has said that "in Deccan sites such as Māski and Brāhmagiri the [megalithic] Iron Age comes up to the Sātavāhana historic level" and that "the megalithic Iron Age culture persisted to the beginning of the Andhra period."[38] Begley too has noted that "there is no stratigraphic break between the Iron Age and Early Historical period—on the contrary, an overlap is demonstrated at most of the excavated sites."[39] Megalithic monuments were, then, almost certainly still being constructed in Andhra after—perhaps long after—Buddhist monastic [229] communities had already been established in the area. To argue that these communities would have been unaware of the funereal function of such monuments would, as a consequence, be difficult. Moreover, if Tucci is correct in assigning the graveyards in Swat to the Assakenoi, there could be little, if any, gap between them and the Buddhist complexes built over them. Here too there was probably overlap.[40] Here too the Buddhists must have been fully aware of the nature of the sites and must have consciously and intentionally chosen to establish themselves among, or above, the local protohistorical dead. But there is also one more and final argument for asserting a Buddhist awareness of megalithic practice.

The general resemblance and possible connection between an equally generalized Indian megalith and the Buddhist *stūpa* have been noted more than once. F. R. Allchin, for example, has said in regard to the "relic chamber" in a Buddhist *stūpa* that "these chambers were no more than stone cists and were often identical to the cists of the southern graves." He has as well noted that "there is close proximity in time of the earliest surviving *stūpas* and the cist graves" and asserted an "essential correspondence of their parts"; but he has declined to discuss the origins of either.[41] Piggot too has argued for a "correspondence" between the wooden pillars surrounding the old *stūpa* at Bairat and presumed "wooden fences . . . surrounding cairns and barrows" in pre-Mauryan India.[42] To these we could possibly add the rough "correspondence" between the "svastika-patterned cists" found at several southern megalithic sites and the much more precisely labeled "svastika-insets" in the cores of at least three *stūpas* at Nāgārjunakoṇḍa and, perhaps, in "the Nirvāṇa *Stūpa*" at Kusinārā.[43] There is also the striking *stūpa* recently discovered at Vaddamanu—a site situated 8.5 kilometers southeast of Amarāvatī. Here the constructional components of [230] the foundation seem to reflect an intentional combination of the elements of a megalithic cairn circle with those of an Andhran *stūpa*. It is, in fact, not impossible that the Vaddamanu structure actually presents us with a case where an earlier cairn circle was converted architecturally into a Buddhist *stūpa*. We will, however, have to have a better report to go further.[44]

Up to now what little work has been done on the question of the relationship of the *stūpa* and the megalith has been largely limited to noting generalized structural "correspondences" and similarities, and little attention has been paid to the possible parallel correspondences between the kinds of deposits they contain. In part, of course, this is because surprisingly little attention has been paid to the nature of the contents of Buddhist *stūpas*, and in part, perhaps, because there are few sites where we have a large enough number of both types of structure to make a comparison meaningful. I know of only one such site, but even a cursory examination of the deposits found there in both *stūpas* and megaliths produces interesting results.

The excavations at Nāgārjunakoṇḍa have revealed more than twenty megaliths in two groups, and more than thirty individual *stūpas*. A complete comparison of all these is neither possible nor necessary here. We need only concentrate on certain types of deposits found in both kinds of structures to arrive at some suggestive conclusions.

The *stūpa* at Ramachandran's site 5 is an elaborate construction almost 40 feet in diameter, but it—like a number of Buddhist *stūpas* here and elsewhere—was, in spite of the obvious labor involved in its construction, found to be empty.[45] Curiously, there are a number of megaliths where much the same thing occurs. The megalith excavated by Longhurst on the Kshuladhammagiri, for example, was marked by a cairn circle some 20 feet in diameter and had two huge capstones. Although Longhurst felt "sure the tomb had not been tampered with by treasure-seekers," it was empty.[46] Likewise, Megalith IV, "the largest pit-circle" found at Nāgārjunakoṇḍa, [231] although "built of huge untrimmed boulders" and having an internal diameter of 9.15 meters, was also virtually empty. This is particularly striking, for the "pit"—3.05 × 1.22 meters—had been "dug into the hard granitic rock to a depth of 2.37m." In spite of "the enormous labour and material that went into the making of this grave," the only things it contained were "a couple of unidentified small splinters of bones, perhaps belonging to an animal and an iron object of indeterminate shape," and even these may not have been intentional deposits. "It was," moreover, "devoid of pottery or any other furnishing goods."[47] *Stūpas* like that at Nāgārjunakoṇḍa site 5 are, of course, commonly called *uddesika* and are not considered mortuary, but the empty megaliths at Nāgārjunakoṇḍa, for example, may suggest that the "commemorative" (*uddesika*) explanation is a later literary rationalization of megalithic mortuary practices that we still do not understand.[48]

The contents of Longhurst's *stūpa* number 9 and those found in the *stūpa* described by Fábri are also interesting. Both of these structures are undoubtedly Buddhist *stūpas*, but neither contained "relics." Instead, the first contained, in addition to two earthenware waterpots and two bowls, "the calcined bones of the ox, deer and hare," and Longhurst's description and photograph make it clear that these were large bones, not fragments.[49] Fábri's *stūpa* too contained the same kinds of pottery and "a few bones of an ox and a deer."[50] With these deposits must also be grouped what Longhurst found in one of the chambers of the Great *Stūpa*: "the burnt bones of a peafowl lying in a heap of charcoal as though the body of the bird had been cremated on the spot before the chamber was filled in with earth."[51] [232]

Longhurst seems to offer two tentative explanations for the contents of his *stūpa* number 9. He asserts that some of "these animals were regarded as sacred as we are told that the Buddha had assumed their forms in previous births" and suggests what Fábri calls "the surmise that *stūpas* have been erected to commemorate the Buddha's former existence in the shape of an animal." But seemingly as an alternative Longhurst suggests too that these deposits—and other animal remains found in association with the monasteries—might be explained by assuming that the resident monks had made "pets" of these animals and that when these "pets" died, the monks placed their remains in *stūpas*, etc.[52]

Although there is some evidence much later of "memorial stones" being erected for "pets," these were by and large animals of war and the chase and would scarcely support Longhurst's second suggestion.[53] Moreover, the remains themselves do not favor it: a "pet" ox is hard to imagine as a monastic mascot, and the condition of the "peafowl" hardly suggests a mark of affection. Longhurst's suggestion that these remains—at least those in *stūpa* number 9—were somehow connected with the former animal incarnations of the Buddha is ingenious but otherwise unsupported. A much more likely explanation than either of these two may, however, be suggested by evidence from Nāgārjunakoṇḍa that was not yet available when Longhurst wrote.

Rao has noted, for example, that "very interesting evidence revealing the importance accorded to animals comes from Nāgārjunakoṇḍa, where a separate [megalithic] burial was constructed for a bovine animal."[54] He is referring here to Subrahmanyam et al.'s Megalith III. It had a stone circle with an internal diameter of 4.27meters, and in the "pit" covered by this circle were discovered "a few bones probably of [233] a bovine animal."[55] Megalith III, however, was not the only grave of this kind. Number IX is described as having a multiple capstone composed of seven oblong slabs covered by a low cairn within a stone circle. It yielded, in addition to numerous pots and iron objects, a portion of an animal jaw with teeth and a few small bones.[56] In neither megalith number III nor number IX were human remains found. But if these megaliths containing animal remains present us only with clear parallels to Longhurst's *stūpa* number 9 and the *stūpa* noted by Fábri, there is still more. Nearly half of the twelve megaliths from Nāgārjunakoṇḍa described by Ghosh, for example, whatever else they contained, contained animal bones, often as "secondary" offerings. In Megalith XIV, for example, "a few animal bones" were found "lying over an ashy deposit covering a skeleton."[57] This presents an interesting parallel to the "bones of a peafowl lying on a heap of charcoal" discovered by Longhurst in one of the chambers of the main *stūpa* at the site. These bones too have the appearance of being secondary offerings, and the *stūpa* in which they were found appears to have been not only the main such structure at the site but the earliest as well.

The similarities in the deposits found in both types of structures are seemingly too strong to be merely coincidental. Given the proximity in place and, probably, time, given the strong evidence for a period of overlap and therefore contemporarity of the two types of structures, the likelihood of an adventitious similarity is even less. The Buddhist deposits, then, would probably best be explained as a reflection of the incorporation or continuation of elements of local megalithic practice in Buddhist mortuary rites. But if this is true, it would mean that the Buddhist community not only was aware of the nature of the megalithic monuments they encountered and built upon, but had actually continued some of the practices associated with these monuments—at least at Nāgārjunakoṇḍa. How far beyond Nāgārjunakoṇḍa we can generalize is, of course, unclear. It is, however, worth noting that animal remains have also been found in Buddhist structures outside of the south.

One of the most interesting instances of animal remains in a Buddhist *stūpa* outside Andhra may involve the oldest *stūpa* that we have any certain [234] knowledge of. It is well known that Aśoka says in the Nigālī Sagar inscription that he "enlarged to double its size," or "increased for the second time," the *stūpa* of the Buddha Konākamuni (*budhasa konākamanasa thube dutiyaṃ vaḍhite*).[58] The two pieces of the pillar on which this inscription was incised were found near a tank belonging to the Nepalese village of Nigliva. The early reports of its discovery declared that the pillar was in situ, but these statements were based on Führer's monograph on the site, which was "withdrawn from circulation by the Government of India" when it was discovered that the "facts" it contained were a product of "Dr. Führer's fertile imagination": the pillar was not in situ, and the *stūpa* that Führer had described in some detail did not, in fact, exist.[59]

Much more recently Mitra has made a good case for saying that "it is very likely" that the two fragments of the inscribed Aśokan pillar "at present lying at Nigali-Sagar" originally formed the upper parts of what is now the broken stump of an "Aśokan" pillar still in situ at Gotihawa, a site some seven miles southwest of Nigali Sagar. Because the lower part of the pillar that is still in situ at Gotihawa stands very near "a large brick *stūpa*" there, Mitra—not unreasonably—says that if her presumption is correct, "the *stūpa* (which by the size of the bricks looks Aśokan) in front of the pillar at Gotihawa is the one of Kanakamuni which Aśoka claims to have enlarged."[60]

If Mitra is correct—and, again, her case is good—then it is of considerable interest to note that this *stūpa*, the one Buddhist *stūpa* we know for certain predated Aśoka, did not contain human remains but, like Longhurst's *stūpa* number 9 and the *stūpa* Fábri excavated at Nāgārjunakoṇḍa, the remains of one or more animals. According to Mukherji, when Waddell "opened" this *stūpa*, "he found a large number of bones, which did not appear to have belonged to man." He continued, "The teeth were many and [235] certainly belonged to animals. A few pieces of charcoal were also discovered. There was nothing interesting in them[!]"[61]

Again in the north, but this time in the northwest, in Afghanistan, Masson found "the beak of a bird, supposed to have been a maina," in *stūpa* number 1 at Kotpur. This, too, appears to have been a "secondary offering" and was not unique. Masson specifically says: "This was not an accidental deposit; a similar one having occurred in a tope at Chahár-Bágh, and again in a tumulus at Darunta." The "tumulus" referred to here was particularly impressive. Masson says that "on this tumulus a greater expense was necessary than on any of the topes we had examined." It had a circumference of 220 feet. But its elaborate cupola—8 feet deep, "coated with cement, and decorated with coarsely coloured flowers"—contained nothing but "the beak of a bird."[62] This tiny deposit can only remind us of "the largest pit-circle" at Nāgārjunakoṇḍa. Although its construction too required "enormous labour and material," it contained little more than "small splinters of bones, perhaps belonging to an animal." It is also worth noting that the association especially of birds and bird remains with burials and *stūpa* deposits at such widely seperated sites as Nāgārjunakoṇḍa and Kotpur may also be reflected in Gandharan narrative art. Recently De Marco has published and discussed an interesting series of Gandharan reliefs—many unfortunately fragmentary—in which *stūpas* or *stūpa*-like structures are clearly represented as tombs or funerary monuments. In at least a half a dozen of these reliefs a bird is shown perched on these structures, and in most cases the bird is identifiable as a parrot.[63]

It would appear from all of this that what occurred at Nāgārjunakoṇḍa was not unique. Buddhist communities in the north too may well have been familiar with—and in part continued—megalithic or protohistorical mortuary practices. [236]

It would seem, then, that in even a quick survey of the often imperfect archaeological literature at least one distinct pattern is discernible. It would appear that immigrant Buddhist monastic communities, when they settled in many "foreign" areas of what we call India, intentionally and knowingly chose to establish their monasteries and *stūpas* in, near, or on sites already occupied by protohistorical cemeteries or burials. It is worth noting that we may eventually come to see that a similar thing occurred in Sri Lanka. Certainly, until recently there has been little interest in protohistorical archaeology in Sri Lanka, but there are already some indications that may point toward the same sort of pattern that can be seen from Andhra to Swat. Begley, for example, refers to a cist burial site near Kokebe that "covers an area of over two acres." She notes too that "the burial site is to the southwest of an early Buddhist settlement using partly natural rock outcrops and partly supplemental brick structural remains" and that it is possible that "the two can not be far removed in time and the burials could either antedate or be contemporaneous with the earliest phase of the Buddhist settlement." There may as well be some connection between the huge urn-burial "cemetery" at Pomparippu and the Galge Vihara.[64]

But Sri Lanka aside, there is no doubt that what Buddhist monks did in Andhra, Swat, and elsewhere is in no way unique in the history and spread of monastic communities. To cite only one of a large number of possible examples, L. M. Bitel—in speaking of monastic settlements in Ireland—has said:

> Monks also built in the shadow of the ancestors' tombs. Over three thousand years at Fidnacha (Fenagh), in Leitrim, the [same] site hosted a portal tomb, a court tomb, two or three passage tombs, standing stones, mounds, a ring-fort, an early Christian and medieval monastery, and associated secular settlements. Some thirty miles to the Northwest, on the coast of Donegal, Saint Columcille raised his little [monastic] community of Druim Cliab . . . a few miles from the monastery

> were vast neolithic necropolises . . . the monks used [237] the tombs to find a holy place: a place where the dead of four thousand years watched over the living, where the living could reach the realm of the dead, and the monks could build a church to the Christian Savior.[65]

But if the Irish and Andhran patterns are similar, so too may have been some of the advantages, and some of the consequences.

The advantages gained by Buddhist monks doing what they did in Andhra, Swat, and elsewhere are not difficult to tease out. Their choice of such sites would have placed the Buddhist complex at an already established focal point in the local landscape and in the local community. It would have established the Buddhist monastic community as the keepers, the guardians of the native dead, and claimed thereby an important function for the newly arrived monks. It also would have assimilated the newcomers' own central focus—the *stūpa*—to local, preexisting structures. Modern scholars, as we have seen, have frequently remarked on the structural similarities between megalith and *stūpa*. But if they have noticed this, it is unlikely that early Buddhist monks did not. It would appear likely that these early immigrant monks not only noticed these similarities but also intentionally exploited them to effect the transfer of the religious and cultural values attached to the megalith in the local communitiy to the Buddhist *stūpa*, to—in effect—assimilate by association and similarity their *stūpa* to the already sacred. But although there are similarities, there are also important differences. The Buddhist *stūpa* is architecturally more rigorously structured, more monumentally and technologically finished and impressive. It is not only similar to but—importantly—also *superior to* the surrounding megaliths. The message must have been clear.

But the choice of this kind of site must also have had some consequences. It would almost certainly have forged a link in the local perception between Buddhist complexes and the dead and the deposition of the dead. It almost certainly would have committed the Buddhist monastic communities to the continuance of the local tradition and reinforced and further strengthened what appears to have been an early monastic inclination toward sheltering their own dead—the Buddha himself, Śāriputra, and a host of local monks.[66] It very likely played a role in and extended the [238] process that turned so many Buddhist monastic complexes and *stūpa* sites in India into bone yards or "champs d'urnes funéraires."[67] In short, what was from one point of view an advantage may have had unforeseen and significant repercussions. It may well have conditioned—if not determined—how the local populations thought of the new monastic groups, regardless of how the monks thought of themselves or otherwise might have preferred to have been thought of. But the selection by the immigrant monks of early burial sites for their settlements undoubtedly would also have reinforced and given prominence to some elements and aspects of their "new" religion at the expense and exclusion of others. It would have channeled the development of "local Buddhism" in a certain direction, and the monks would have had to live with the consequences of their choices in every sense of the term. Where you lived undoubtedly determined to a large degree who and what you were. Some things never change.

Notes

1. See, for example, A. Stein, *An Archaeological Tour in Wazīristān and Northern Balūchistān* (MASI, no. 37) (Calcutta: 1929), esp. 64–70; A. S. Melikian-Chirvani, "L'evocation littéraire de bouddhisme dans l'iran musulman," *Le monde iranien et l'islam II* (Paris and Geneva: 1974) 1–77; Melikian-Chirvani, "Recherches sur l'architecture de l'iran bouddhique," *Le monde iranien et l'islam III* (Paris and Geneva:1975); Melikian-Chirvani, "The Buddhist Ritual in the Literature of Early Islamic Iran," in *SAA* 1981, ed. B. Allchin (Cambridge: 1984) 272–279; G. Schopen, "Hīnayāna Texts in a 14th Century Persian Chronicle. Notes on Some of Rashīd al-Dīn's Sources," *CAJ* 26 (1982) 225–235; D. M. Lang, *The Wisdom of Balahvar. A Christian Legend of the Buddha* (London: 1957), esp. 30–39; S. M. Stern and S. Walzer, *Three Unknown Buddhist Stories in an Arabic Version* (Columbia, S. C.: 1971) [The last of these three stories should be compared with the curious Manichean text in Uigur discussed in H.-J. Klimkeit, "Stūpa and Parinirvāṇa as Manichean Motifs," in *The Stūpa. Its Religious, Historical and Architectural Significance*, ed. A. L. Dallapiccola and S. Z. Lallemant (Wiesbaden: 1980) 234–235].

2. See C. H. B. Reynolds, "Buddhism in the Maldives: Excavations in 1958," in *Buddhist Studies in Honour of Hammalava Saddhatissa*, ed. G. Dhammapala et al. (Colombo: 1984) 228–235; and the popular T. Heyerdahl, *The Maldive Mystery* (Bethseda, Md.: 1986) for some interesting photographs.

3. For the Buddhist remains at Goli, see T. N. Ramachandran, *Buddhist Sculptures from a Stūpa near Goli Village, Guntur District* (Bulletin of the Madras Government Museum, n.s.—General Section I, Pt. I) (Madras:1929); D. Barrett, "The Later School of Amarāvatī and Its Influence," *Arts and Letters* 28.2 (1954) 41–53, esp. 41; O. C. Gangoly, *Andhra Sculptures* (Government of Andhra Pradesh Archaeological Series 36) (Hyderabad:1973) 33, 78–81, 89–90. For the "dolmens," see N. Venkataramanayya, "Pre-Historic Remains in Andhra Pradesh," *Journal of the Andhra Historical Research Society* 32 (1971–1972) 40; K. P. Rao, *Deccan Megaliths* (Delhi: 1988) 23.

4. For the relatively recently discovered Buddhist monastic complex at Chandavaram, see M. N. Deshpande, ed., *IAR* 1972–1973 (New Delhi: 1978) 3; V. V. Krishna Sastry, ed., *Annual Report of the Department of Archaeology and Museums, Government of Andhra Pradesh, 1976–77* (Hyderabad: 1978) 17–24 and pl. 7; B. K. Thapar, ed., *IAR* 1973–1974 (New Delhi: 1979) 7, 35, and pl. XIII a and b; Thapar, ed., *IAR* 1974–1975 (New Delhi: 1979)

6–7; Thapar, ed., *IAR* 1975–1976 (New Delhi: 1979) 3–4; Thapar, ed., *IAR* 1976–1977 (New Delhi: 1980) 9–10, 58; V. V. Krishna Sastry, ed., *Annual Report of the Department of Archaeology and Museums, Government of Andhra Pradesh, 1975–76* (Hyderabad:1986) 12–16 and nine good photographs [the remark about megalithic burials occurs on p. 15]; R. S. Sharma, *Urban Decay in India (c. 300–c. 1000)* (New Delhi: 1987) 97.

5. The only published reference to Panigiri that I know is P. Sreenivasachar, *The Archaeological Bulletin*, no. II (Andhra Pradesh Government Archaeological Series) (Hyderabad: 1963) 5 and fig. 35. The description of the site there—a part of which I have quoted—is extremely brief, but there is what appears to be a reasonably detailed site plan.

6. R. Sewell, *Quelques points d'archéologie de l'inde méridionale* (Paris: 1897), esp. 5–6. On the Buddhist site at Jaggayyapetta, which had been all but destroyed by the time it was discovered, see G. Bühler, "Inscriptions from the *Stūpa* of Jaggayyapaṭṭā," *IA* 11 (1882) 256–259; J. Burgess, *The Buddhist Stūpas of Amarāvatī and Jaggayyapeta in the Krishna District, Madras Presidency, Surveyed in 1882* (Archaeological Survey of South India, n.s. 1) (London: 1887), esp. 107–113; D. Mitra, "Observations on the Buddhist Remains at Jaggayyapeta," *IHQ* 35 (1959) 274–275; D. Barrett, "Early Phase at Amarāvatī," *British Museum Quarterly* 32.1–2 (1967) 35–48, esp. 41–42, 45; V. Dehejia, "Early Activity at Amarāvatī," *Archives of Asian Art* 23 (1969–1970) 41–54, esp. 48, 53.

7. *Mahāparinirvāṇāsūtra* (Waldschmidt) 304ff; *Dīgha Nikāya* i 146ff—an entire text, the *Mahāsudarśanasūtra*, was inserted here to supply the "explanation."

8. A. Cunningham, *Four Reports Made During the Years 1862–63–64–65* (Archaeological Survey of India, Vol. I) (Simla: 1871) 79, 76 n; pl. xxvi. Cunningham himself noted, in regard to the "mounds," that though he counted twenty-one, "it is probable that their actual number is much greater." For local traditions about megalithic remains, see Rao, *Deccan Megaliths*, 3–8.

9. A. C. L. Carlleyle, *Report of a Tour in the Gorakhpur District in 1875–76 and 1876–77* (Archaeological Survey of India, Vol. XVIII) (Calcutta: 1883) 94.

10. S. Beal, *Buddhist Records of the Western World* (London: 1884) ii 39; L. A. Waddell, "A Tibetan Guide-book to the Lost Sites of the Buddha's Birth and Death," *Journal of the Asiatic Society of Bengal* 65 (1896) 275–279, esp. 278 [Waddell says that the author of this guidebook says it is compiled in part "from the records of Hiuen-Tsiang," and this may well be referring to the Tibetan translation of Hsüan-tsang done by Mgon po skyab—see Kyōgo Sasaki, "A Note on the Study of the Ta-T'ang Hsi-Yu-Chi," *EB* 8 (1958) 8–9].

11. B. K. Rijal, "Archaeological Activities in Lumbini 1976–77," *Ancient Nepal. Journal of the Department of Archaeology* 30–39 (1975–1977) 28–37, esp. 30. On animal bones in burials and *stūpa* deposits, see below.

12. N. S. Ramaswami, *Amarāvatī. The Art and History of the Stūpa and Temple* (The Government of Andhra Pradesh Archaeological Series, no. 41) (Hyderabad: 1975) 2.

13. J. Burgess, "Is Bezawāḍa on the Site of Dhanakaṭaka?" *IA* 11 (1882) 95–98, esp. 97–98.

14. J. Fergusson, "Description of the Amarāvatī Tope in Guntur," *JRAS* (1868)

132–166, esp. 143 and fig. 6—compare the drawing with pl. 1 in Rao, *Deccan Megaliths*, which is a photo of a "stone circle" at Bhagimahari.

15. A. Rea, "Excavations at Amarāvatī," *ARASI 1908–1909* (Calcutta: 1912) 88–91, esp. figs. 1 and 2; Rao, *Deccan Megaliths*, 46.

16. M. A. W. Khan, "Yeleśwaram Excavations," *Journal of the Andhra Historical Research Society* 19 (1963) 1–8; Khan, *A Monograph on Yelleshwaram Excavations* (Hyderabad: 1963). Khan himself notes that "some scholars" have called into question the Buddhist affiliation of the structures overlaying the burials, and so, too, has Sarkar much more recently (H. Sarkar, "Yelleswaram, Yeleswaram, Elleswaram, Yellaisharam," in *An Encyclopedia of Indian Archaeology*, ed. A. Ghosh [New Delhi: 1989] Vol. II, 468–469).

17. R. Subrahmanyam et al., *Nagarjunakonda* (1954–1960) (MASI, no. 75) (New Delhi: 1975) 165–166, 212. Subrahmanyam points to another factor that may have been in play in the Buddhist selection of such sites. "These two megalithic localities," he says, "were unsuitable to serve as fields of cultivation. . . . In general an effort to confine their sepulchral monuments to an uncultivable area is discernable in the megalithic distribution in the valley, as it was usually observed in megalithic burial patterns" (p. 166). This may suggest not only that immigrant Buddhist monastic communities settled on burial sites but that—in some cases at least—they were initially so economically impoverished that they had few options and were forced to take up worthless lands.

18. Subrahmanyam et al., *Nagarjunakonda* (1954–1960), Vol. I, 166–167.

19. A. H. Longhurst, *The Buddhist Antiquities of Nāgārjunakoṇḍa, Madras Presidency* (MASI, no. 54) (Delhi: 1938) 7.

20. Rao, *Deccan Megaliths*, 38, 41, 49, 51.

21. G. Tucci, "The Tombs of the Asvakayana-Assakenoi," *EW* 14 (1963) 27.

22. D. Faccenna, *A Guide to the Excavations in Swat (Pakistan) 1956–1962* (Rome: 1964) 62; see 73–74, 76, for a fuller bibliography on the Italian work on Swat.

23. Ibid., 65.

24. C. S. Antonini, "Preliminary Notes on the Excavations of the Necropolises Found in Western Pakistan," *EW* 14 (1963) 16.

25. J. E. van Lohuizen-de Leeuw, "The Pre-Muslim Antiquities of Sind," in *SAA 1975*, ed. J. E. van Lohuizen–de Leeuw (Leiden: 1975) 155.

26. E. Mackay, *The Indus Civilization* (London: 1935) 19.

27. R. D. Banerji, *Mohenjodaro. A Forgotten Report* (Varanasi: 1984) 117. This volume is a facsimile of Banerji's original typescript, or a copy of it, with an interesting—if somewhat inflammatory—"Publisher's Note."

28. Ibid., 166.

29. J. Marshall, *Mohenjo-daro and the Indus Civilization. Being an Official Account of Archaeological Excavations at Mohenjo-daro Carried Out by the Government of India between the Years 1922 and 1927* (London: 1931) Vol. I, 113–130, esp. 121–122. There are some interesting inscribed potsherds from the Buddhist complex at Mohenjo-daro. Marshall refers to several (p. 317 and pl. lxxviii), but several more are found in E. J. H. Mackay, *Further Excavations at Mohenjo-Daro. Being an Official Account of Archaeological Excavations at Mohenjo-Daro Carried Out by the Government of India between the Years 1927 and 1931* (New Delhi:

1938) Vol. I, 187. One of these—and probably a second—contained the *vinaya* term *karaka*, "drinking vessel": . . . *tasa saghar[a]kshitasa ida karaka i . . . ; bhadata-(sangha) rakshasa aya kara(ka)*.

30. Tucci, "The Tombs of the Asvakayana-Assakenoi," 27.

31. Rao, *Deccan Megaliths*, 130–131.

32. A. Burl, *Megalithic Brittany* (London: 1985) 45. Burl refers to other examples from Guernsey, Spain, and Portugal.

33. N. Venkataramanayya, *An Essay on the Origin of the South Indian Temple* (New Delhi: 1985) [first published 1930] 1–2.

34. M. S. Mate and S. Gokhale, "Aihole: An Interpretation," in *Studies in Indian History and Culture*, ed. S. Ritti and B. R. Gopal (Dharwar: 1971) 501–504. See also H. Bakker, "Memorials, Temples, Gods and Kings. An Attempt to Unravel the Symbolic Texture of Vākāṭaka Kingship," in *Ritual, State and History in South Asia. Essays in Honour of J. C. Heesterman*, ed. A. W. van den Hoek et al. (Leiden: 1992) 7–19.

35. B. and R. Allchin, *The Rise of Civilization in India and Pakistan* (Cambridge, U.K.: 1982) 341, 345.

36. Rao, *Deccan Megaliths*, 134.

37. J. R. McIntosh, "Dating the South Indian Megaliths," in *SAA 1983*, ed. J. Schotsmans and M. Taddei (Naples: 1985) Vol. 2, 467–493, esp. 469.

38. C. Maloney, "Archaeology in South India: Accomplishments and Prospects," in *Essays on South India*, ed. B. Stein (Honolulu: 1975) 1–40, esp. 6, 25.

39. V. Begley, "From Iron Age to Early Historical in South Indian Archaeology," in *Studies in the Archaeology of India and Pakistan*, ed. J. Jacobson (New Delhi: 1986) 297–319, esp. 298–299.

40. Tucci, "The Tombs of the Asvakayana-Assakenoi," 27–28; C. S. Antonini and G. Stacul, *The Proto-Historic Graveyards of Swat (Pakistan)* (Rome: 1972); G. Stacul, "The Sequence of the Proto-Historical Periods at Aligrāma (Swat, Pakistan)," in *SAA 1975*, ed. J. E. van Lohuizen-de Leeuw (Leiden: 1979) 88–90; cf. E. Benveniste, "Coutumes funéraires de l'arachosie ancienne," in *A Locust's Leg. Studies in Honour of S. H. Taqizadea* (London: 1962) 39–43.

41. F. R. Allchin, "Sanskrit *eḍūka*—Pali *eluka*," *BSOAS* 20 (1957) 1–4 [on the elusive etymology, cf. P. Shah, "Aiḍūka," *Journal of the Oriental Institute* 1 (1952) 278–285; U. P. Shah, "A Note on Aiḍūka," in *Neue Indienkunde/New Indology. Festschrift Walter Ruben zum 70. Geburtstag* (Berlin: 1970) 353–356].

42. S. Piggot, "The Earliest Buddhist Shrines," *Antiquity*, Vol. 17, no. 65 (1943) 1–10.

43. For examples of the so-called svastika-patterned cists, see Rao, *Deccan Megaliths*, 11, 48, 50, 52, and fig. 3.3; on *stūpas* "with svastika-insets" in Andhra, see H. Sarkar, *Studies in Early Buddhist Architecture of India* (Delhi: 1966) 85, 90 n. 2, pl. xii.a.

44. T. V. G. Sastri, *Excavations of Vaddamanu and Exploration in the Krishna Valley Basin* (Hyderabad: 1983) 1–21, esp. plate between pp. 4 and 5; cf. I. K. Sarma, *Studies in Early Buddhist Monuments and Brāhmī Inscriptions of Āndhra Desa* (Nagpur: 1988) 9–11, 37, 49, 106–107.

45. T. N. Ramachandran, *Nāgārjunakoṇḍa 1938* (MASI, no. 71) (Calcutta: 1953) 21.

46. Longhurst, *The Buddhist Antiquities of Nāgārjunakoṇḍa*, 7.

47. Subrahmanyam et al., *Nagarjunakonda* (1954–1960) Vol. I, 169.

48. The notion itself of an *uddesika stūpa* or *caitya* may be both late and of Sri Lankan origin. E. W. Adikaram, *Early History of Buddhism in Ceylon* (Colombo: 1946) 135, for example, says: "As far as I am aware, the word [i.e., *uddissa-cetiya*] occurs only in this commentary [i.e., the *Dhammapadaṭṭhakathā*] and even there it appears to be an interpolation." Although the term *uddesika* applied to a type of *cetiya* occurs in a difficult passage in the *Kāliṅga-bodhi-jātaka* (*Jātaka* iv 228) as well, it does not appear to be any earlier. Cf. the probably earlier, and certainly continental, discussion of kinds of *pūjā* in U. Wogihara, ed., *Bodhisattvabhūmi* (Tokyo: 1930–1936) 231–237, and L. de la Vallée Poussin, "Staupikam," *HJAS* 2 (1937) 276–289, esp. 281–283.

49. Longhurst, *The Buddhist Antiquities of Nāgārjunakoṇḍa*, 23 and pl. xviii c; see also A. H. Longhurst, "Excavations at Nagarjunakonda," *ARASI 1929–30* (Delhi: 1935) 148–149.

50. C. L. Fábri, "Excavations at Nāgārjunakoṇḍa," *ARASI 1930–34* (Delhi: 1936) 108.

51. Longhurst, *The Buddhist Antiquities of Nāgārjunakoṇḍa*, 23.

52. Ibid., 23–24; Fábri, "Excavations at Nāgārjunakoṇḍa," 108.

53. See, for example, C. V. Rangaswami, "Memorials for Pets, Animals and Heroes," in *Memorial Stones. A Study of Their Origin, Significance and Variety*, ed. S. Settar and G. D. Sontheimer (Dharwad: 1982) 235–241; A. V. Narasimha Murthy, "Memorials to Household Animals in Ancient Karnataka," *The Journal of the Bihar Research Society* 67–68 (1981–1982) 140–145; cf. D. Eliasberg, "Pratiques funéraires animales en chine ancienne et médiévale," *JA* (1992) 115–144.

54. Rao, *Deccan Megaliths*, 69.

55. Subrahmanyam et al., *Nagarjunakonda* (1954–1960), Vol. I, 168–169. There are some grounds for thinking that number III is a very late construction: see Subrahmanyam et al., 183.

56. Ibid., Vol. I, 174–175.

57. A. Ghosh, ed., *IAR* 1959–1960 (New Delhi: 1960) 9; see also nos. I, III, IV, VI, VII, IX, XII, and XIV in Subrahmanyam et al., *Nagarjunakonda* (1954–1960).

58. E. Hultzsch, *Inscriptions of Asoka* (CII, Vol. I) (Oxford: 1925) 165; J. Bloch, *Les inscriptions d'Asoka* (Paris: 1950) 158.

59. On Führer's frauds, see P. C. Mukherji, *A Report on a Tour of Exploration of the Antiquities in the Tarai, Nepal, The Region of Kapilavastu; during February and March, 1899*, with a Prefatory Note by Vincent A. Smith (Calcutta: 1901) 3ff; H. Lüders, "On Some Brāhmī Inscriptions in the Lucknow Provincial Museum," *JRAS* (1912) 161ff; D. K. Chakrabarti, *A History of Indian Archaeology. From the Beginning to 1947* (New Delhi: 1988) 110–112.

60. D. Mitra, *Buddhist Monuments* (Calcutta: 1971) 252. For a drawing of the two pieces from Nigliva and the stump in situ at Gotihawa together, see Mukherji, *A Report on a Tour of Exploration*, pl. xvii, figs. 1 and 2.

61. Mukherji, *A Report on a Tour of Exploration*, 32, 55; for the teeth, see pl. xvii [the second one so marked], fig. 3.

62. H. H. Wilson, *Ariana Antiqua. A Descriptive Account of the Antiquities and Coins of Afghanistan: With a Memoir on the Buildings Called Topes, by C. Masson, Esq.* (London: 1841) 65, 95.

63. G. De Marco, "The *Stūpa* as a Funerary Monument. New Iconographical Evidence," *EW* 37 (1987) 191–246, esp. his reliefs A2, B2, B6, B8, B13, B15; also n. 82.

64. V. Begley, "Archaeological Exploration in Northern Ceylon," *Expedition. The Bulletin of the University Museum of the University of Pennsylvania* 9.4 (1967) 21–29, esp. 28–29; see also V. Begley, "Proto-Historic Material from Sri Lanka (Ceylon) and Indian Contacts," in *Ecological Backgrounds of South Asian Prehistory*, ed. K. A. R. Kennedy and G. L. Possehl (Ithaca, N.Y.: n.d.) 191–196. For a sample of more detailed work on Pomparippu, see V. Begley, J. R. Lukacs, and K. A. R. Kennedy, "Excavations of Iron Age Burials at Pomparippu, 1970," *Ancient Ceylon. Journal of the Archaeological Survey of Sri Lanka* 4 (1981) 49–141. For some very interesting remarks on the spread of "urn burials" *from* Sri Lanka *to* South India, see McIntosh, "Dating the South Indian Megaliths," 488–489.

65. L. M. Bitel, *Isle of the Saints. Monastic Settlement and Christian Community in Early Ireland* (Ithaca, N.Y., and London: 1990), esp. 43–56.

66. G. Schopen, "An Old Inscription from Amarāvatī and the Cult of the Local Monastic Dead in Indian Buddhist Monasteries," *JIABS* 14.2 (1991) 281–329 [= *BSBM* 165–203]; Schopen, "Ritual Rights and Bones of Contention: More on Monastic Funerals and Relics in the *Mūlasarvāstivāda-vinaya*," *JIP* 22 (1994) 31–80 [= Ch. X above].

67. G. Schopen, "Burial 'ad sanctos' and the Physical Presence of the Buddha in Early Indian Buddhism. A Study in the Archaeology of Religions," *Religion* 17 (1987) 193–225 [= *BSBM* 114–147]; Schopen, "*Stūpa* and *Tīrtha*: Tibetan Mortuary Practices and an Unrecognized Form of Burial Ad Sanctos at Buddhist Sites in India," *Buddhist Forum III: Ruegg Felicitation Volume*, ed. T. Skorupski and U. Pagel (London: 1994) 273–293 [= *FFMB* Ch. XIV].

CHAPTER XIII

What's in a Name

The Religious Function of the Early Donative Inscriptions

THERE ARE HUNDREDS of early donative inscriptions at Sāñcī, and they have been invaluable to modern scholars studying the site. Though no early records are themselves dated, they have, for example, still enabled scholars to approximately date the site and various parts of the *stūpas*. This has been accomplished largely by comparing the forms of letters in these undated records with the forms found in other inscriptions that either contain a date or can be more or less securely assigned one.[1]

These inscriptions have also allowed modern scholars to establish, at least in part, how the construction of the early site was funded, to determine, in effect, some of the patterns of patronage at the site, and something about the donors. They make it clear, for example, that work at early Sāñcī was funded not by royal or political patronage but by a large number of separate gifts made by individuals, mostly ordinary monks, nuns, and laypeople. Because these people frequently indicated where they were from or where they were born, such early records have also inadvertently allowed modern scholars to determine what might be called the "catchment area," or the geographical area served by the monastic complex at Sāñcī, and to establish links between Sāñcī and other sites. Most of the place-names that occur in these early records seem, not surprisingly, to be the names of villages or towns in Malwa, the area in which Sāñcī itself is situated, and some of the individuals who made gifts at Sāñcī appear to have come from villages and towns that had their own Buddhist establishments. Seven inscriptions refer to donors from Tubavana, for example, one of whom was a nun. If K. D. Bajpai is correct in identifying Tubavana with present-day Tumain, then these donors came from a place that itself appears to have had several early Buddhist *stūpas*.[2] Sometimes too linkages with Sāñcī can be established—or suggested—from inscriptions found else-

---

Originally published in *Unseen Presence. The Buddha and Sanchi*, ed. V. Dehejia (Bombay 1996) 58–73. Reprinted with stylistic changes with permission of the editor.

where. S. S. Iyer, for example, has suggested that an inscription on an umbrella shaft from a *stūpa* at Panguraria records the activity of a nun named Koramika and that this is the same nun who made at least one gift at Sāñcī.[3]

However, not only have these early donative records provided modern scholars with information on where the numerous donors came from, but they have also made it possible to determine a number of other things about them. Sāñcī, for instance, was one of the earliest Buddhist sites known that provided clear—if sometimes reluctantly accepted—evidence that Buddhist monks and nuns themselves acted as donors and financed the construction and decoration of *stūpas*. Almost 40 percent of the donors at Sāñcī were monks or nuns. The percentage is even higher for specific projects: at *stūpa* 2, monks and nuns made up nearly 60 percent of the donors. To fully appreciate these numbers, one has to keep in mind that it is very unlikely that monks and nuns made up more than a small fraction of the total population of the Sāñcī catchment area. If, for the sake of illustration, one were to say that monks and nuns made up 10 percent of the total population of Malwa (and this figure is almost certainly way too high), this would mean that 10 percent or less of the total population made nearly 60 percent of the donations to *stūpa* 2 at Sāñcī, or, in other words, monks and nuns made proportionately far, far more donations to this *stūpa* than did laypeople.[4]

Although they probably should not have, these figures created a certain sense of unease among scholars studying Indian Buddhism. Many early scholars believed, and some still do, that Buddhist monks and nuns renounced all private property or wealth, that they had no private means, and that they could not therefore have acted as donors. To sustain this belief required that the evidence from Sāñcī, and from a significant number of other early Buddhist sites, for the active participation of monks and nuns in donative activities be either [61] ignored or explained away.[5] A closer reading and fuller awareness of Buddhist monastic literature, or *vinaya*, has made it clear, for example, that Buddhist monastic codes themselves take it as a given that monks and nuns do and will act as donors, and the codes contain detailed rulings on the obligations of other monks when they do.[6] The Pāli *Vinaya* has as well a long series of rulings allowing monks to possess things that are normally forbidden, such as new alms bowls, if they acquired them by means of their "private wealth."[7] Another *vinaya*, the *Mūlasarvāstivāda-vinaya*, explicitly recognizes a monk's continuing right to inherit family property upon the death of his father.[8]

Many aspects of the patronage at early Sāñcī have been recently and well summarized by Vidya Dehejia and need not, therefore, be discussed here.[9] But the early donative inscriptions at Sāñcī also contain—again inadvertently—other kinds of information, and much of this has been less well studied, if at all. The onomasticon, or inventory of personal names, at Sāñcī has, for example, received little attention, and yet it may be able to tell us some interesting things. Two in particular might be noted.

The appearance of Arabic names in what had been a Persian onomasticon in medieval Iran has been used to good effect to track the spread and penetration of Islam there; likewise "onomastic change"—the appearance of Christian names—in early Byzantine Egypt has been used to determine the degree and depth of "conversion" to Christianity that was occurring at that time.[10] Though they remain to be systematically pursued, many of the same methods may hold considerable promise for determining something about the local history and the degree of penetration of Buddhism in various parts of early India. At *stūpa* 2 at Sāñcī (and this is only meant as an example of how such a study might work), only a limited number of men had distinctly Buddhist names like Budhaguta ("Protected by the Buddha[s]"), Budhapālita ("Guarded by the Buddha[s]"), or Saghamita ("Friend of the Saṅgha"), and even a smaller number of women had such names. Of prominent citizens there, one of the "bankers" is named Budhapālita, but the other two have names connected with the *nāgas*, or divine snakes: Nāgapiya ("Beloved of the Snakes") and Nagasena ("Dependent on the Snakes"). One of the women is also called Nāgapālitā, and one has what appears to be a distinctly Hindu name, Viṇhukā. The number of distinctly Buddhist names—only about one fifth of the total—at Sāñcī *stūpa* 2 is comparatively small and may indicate that the Buddhist presence in Central India at the time of these records was neither old nor extensively rooted, although it must have already been a presence for at least a generation. Such a study may also show that a significant number of individuals may have made donations to Buddhist establishments without, however, ever being "Buddhist" to the degree that they had been given or took Buddhist names: "Buddhism," in other words, may never have been a significant component of these individuals' self-identity.

This same stock of personal names that was current in Malwa when *stūpa* 2, or at least its railing, was being built is, however, also able to provide the only information available concerning the conception of the Buddha that was current in Malwa at that time. It can, in other words, provide us with some indication of a *local* Central Indian conception of the Buddha, as opposed to the textual conceptions provided and presented by canonical literature. Here we need go no further than several of the names already cited. If, to oversimplify, we might say that the Buddha is frequently presented as a teacher in textual sources, we can then note that there is no evidence for this in the Sāñcī onomasticon. The names found at Sāñcī rather suggest, and that consistently, that the Buddha was thought of [62] as a protector or defender. Moreover, whereas canonical sources sometimes emphasize human elements in regard to the conception of the Buddha and assimilate him to, again, the type of human teacher, early Central Indian names—by implication—assimilate him to the category *nāga*, or "divine" and powerful serpent. The parallel names Nāgapālitā and Budhapālitā suggest that both Buddha and Nāga were thought to function in the same role and in the same way. It was this Buddha, presumably, that the monks, nuns, and ordinary people of Central India were attracted to at the beginning of the Common Era.

The early donative inscriptions from Sāñcī, then, can and do provide a variety of kinds of information. Yet, it is important to keep in mind that they do so unintentionally or even accidentally. It is virtually certain that neither the donors who paid for the inscriptions, nor the scribes or stone masons who engraved them, had any intention of providing future historians with the kind of data that they do. Their intentions, in fact, remain to be determined, and we have yet to understand what value they saw in their own inscriptions.

Any attempt to determine how the donors themselves might have understood the value of their own records immediately encounters some curious facts. There are, indeed, a number of odd things about early Buddhist donative inscriptions, not the least of which is that they exist. There is little or no textual warrant for the practice of inscribing a donor's name on the object he or she has given, and what warrant there is does not seem to apply to the kind of inscriptions that have survived from most early sites. Both the *Vinayavibhaṅga* of the Mūlasarvāstivādin *Vinaya* and Guṇaprabha's commentary on his own *Vinayasūtra* contain passages that refer to the admissibility of writing the names of a donor or a monastery on certain kinds of property belonging to the *saṅgha*—specifically bedding, seats, and pots—but this is for the purpose of determining ownership and applies, apparently, only to property belonging to the Community, whereas the surviving inscriptions from Sāñcī are on objects that technically belong to the Buddha or *stūpa*, and they do not refer to a Community or monastery. In the *Vinayavibhaṅga* it says that once, when there was a festival, monks residing in a forest monastery borrowed bedding and seats from a village monastery but they did not return them at the conclusion of the festival, because they did not know for sure whom they belonged to. In response to this situation, the Buddha is made to say that "this . . . belongs to the forest monastery of such-and-such a householder donor," "this belongs to the village monastery," should be written on the bedding and seats.[11] In his *Vinayasūtra*, Guṇaprabha says, "There is no fault in marking property. In regard to what belongs to the *Saṅgha*, the name is written on bedding and seats: 'This is the religious gift of so-and-so, this the name of the monastery'"; and in justification of this he quotes in his auto-commentary a canonical passage that reads: "The Blessed One said: 'On the bedding it is to be written: "This is the religious gift of King Bimbisāra."'"[12]

Passages like these are interesting and have not, I think, been noted before, but they do not explain what we find in connection with the Sāñcī *stūpas*. There, for example, the need to mark ownership and thereby avoid confusion does not arise. In fact, the textual sources seem to be exclusively concerned with certain types of movable property—largely domestic furnishings and utensils—not with things like parts of *stūpas*.

If, then, the practice of engraving a donor's name in stone on parts of a *stūpa* has little or no textual support, it of course is not alone: much of early Buddhist practice may not appear in, or be sanctioned by, its canonical literature. However, in this particular case, there is in addition a clear doctrinal position that would seem to render such inscriptions pointless, if not completely useless. [63]

Buddhist literature of almost all types and periods abounds with explicit statements such as the following:

> Whatever action a man does, good or evil, he is the heir of whatever action he does.
>
> For no man's action disappears . . . truly it comes back. Its owner assuredly obtains it(s result).
>
> The Householder Sahasodgata performed and accumulated these acts—how could someone else experience (their results)?
>
> Actions never perish even after a hundred aeons, but having arrived at the optimum time, they bear fruit for the man.[13]

In the light of passages like these—and they are legion—the inscriptional records at early Sāñcī look distinctly odd. These records say no more and no less than, for example:

> The gift of Agila, an inhabitant of Adhapura.
>
> The gift of the Monk Arahaka, the Reciter.
>
> The gift of the Monk Nāgarakhita, an inhabitant of Pokhara.

Such inscriptions look as if they were intended as records of specific gifts, but it is far from clear what possible function such records could have in a world that was governed by the certain inexorability of karma: if every act inexorably had its consequence, if Agila, for example, was "the heir of whatever action he does," then any act was already in the most important sense indelibly, automatically, and unavoidably entered into the "record," and there could be no doubt about who did it. To record it in stone would seem at best redundant, if not, again, completely pointless. It is, of course, possible that the mere existence of such seemingly senseless records itself may indicate that the formal doctrine of karma expressed in texts had little or no hold outside of them, that actual people were far less sure of an inevitable consequence for their religious acts, that a lack of certainty, a sense of doubt in regard to formal doctrine, impelled them to "get it in writing." But this, in turn, raises the equally awkward question of who it was who was supposed to read these records.

Several factors must be taken into account in trying to determine the intended readership of these records, the first of which is their placement. To judge by their placement, however, it would appear that a large number of early Buddhist donative inscriptions were never intended even to be seen, let alone read. The Bajaur Inscription of Menandros, and a sizable number of other early Kharoṣṭhī inscriptions, the famous inscription on the Piprawa vase, the Bhaṭṭiprolu casket inscriptions—all of these and dozens more were written on, or placed within, containers that in turn were buried deep within the solid fabric of monumental *stūpas*. Once deposited, probably no one expected that they would be seen again, let alone carefully studied in twentieth-century India or Europe or America.

It is not just inscriptions connected with relic deposits that were not intended to be read. A. Barth noted long ago that the inscription on the Mathurā Lion Capital was never intended to be read and that, in fact, when the capital was put in place a significant part of [64] the inscription would have been completely invisible.[14] Likewise, A. V. Naik noted that a significant number of inscriptions in the Western Caves "are noticeable only after a deliberate search with a torch or lamp and accessible only with assistance of such appliances as the ladder." At Junnar, Kuda, and Nāsik, he says of some important records: "Besides being too high for the ordinary human eye, these inscriptions always remain in the dark."[15] At Bhājā, two donative records were carved on the wooden ribs in the ceiling, more than twenty feet from the floor level. Similar considerations hold for a surprisingly large number of inscriptions at Sāñcī as well. To cite just two examples from *stūpa* 1:

> The gift of Ānaṃda, son of Vāsiṭhī, the foreman of the artisans of the Rājan Sirī Sātakaṇi.

> The gift of Balamitra, a pupil of the Reciter of Dhamma, Aya Cuḍa.

The first of these is on the top architrave of the south gateway, facing the *stūpa*; the second, on the middle architrave of the same gate, facing outward. Both are six meters or more in the air and would have been scarcely visible from the ground, let alone readable. [65]

Naik says in regard to the placement of such inscriptions that "they seem to defeat their own purpose which is primarily public intimation." However, given the number of early Buddhist donative inscriptions so placed, one must begin to suspect that this was not their function at all. Moreover, there are so many cases where the placement of inscriptions indicates that they were never meant to be seen or read, that it is reasonable to assume that, even in those cases in which they can be seen, this visibility was either fortuitous or secondary and that the primary function of even these records was not to make their content public. We seem, on the whole, to be confronted not only with unnecessary written records but also with unnecessary written records that were never meant to be seen. And there are still other questions.

There is, in regard even to those inscriptions that were plainly visible, the question of how many people who saw them could actually read them. Any definite answer to such a question would require, of course, knowledge of a number of things. Nothing definite is known about the level of literacy in India at the time of any of these records, although it is commonly assumed to have been low. Sten Konow, in referring to the inscriptions at Jauliāñ said with no hesitation: "Only very few who saw the images were able to read the inscriptions."[16] Unless the level of literacy in early Central India was far higher than commonly suspected, the same would almost certainly apply to the inscriptions at Sāñcī.

We also do not know anything certain about the spoken language or languages of Central India at the beginning of the Common Era, or whether someone there, even if he or she could read the Brāhmī script, could understand the Prakrit of these records. But the situation elsewhere is clearer and may be instructive. There is a good chance that there were as many donative inscriptions at early Amarāvatī as there were at Sāñcī—those that have survived must be only a small proportion of the number that must once have existed, and they are in form much the same as those from Sāñcī.[17] But at Amarāvatī—indeed at Jaggayyapeta, Bhaṭṭiprolu, Guṇṭupalli, Nāgārjunakoṇḍa, and everywhere else in Andhra—although the Buddhist donative inscriptions are written in a "North" Indian Prakrit, it is virtually certain that the people themselves spoke then, as they do today, some form of Telugu.[18] These records, then, were written not only in a "foreign" script but also in a distinctly "foreign" language, and they could not therefore have been intended to communicate any information to the local populations who visited and supported the sites even if, as was often the case, they were placed in readily visible locations. One is back to the question of why such inscriptions were written at all.

Many of the curious characteristics of early Buddhist donative inscriptions that have been noted here had already been observed by earlier scholars who had worked with them. One of the best of these earlier scholars, Auguste Barth, had said, in writing about the Piprawa vase inscription, that the recording of the names of the donor, and the names he wanted associated with his gift, in early Buddhist inscriptions "was certainly not a case of mere ostentation, on objects destined to be buried deep underground and never again to see the light of day." He continued:

> When we see how on the reliquary of Bhaṭṭiprolu, for instance . . . there is a long enumeration of names not only of the promoters of the foundation but of all those who took even the least part in it . . . we are bound to reflect that there was in this something more than a gratification of vanity, and that a mystic efficacy was attributed to the recording of such names.[19]

Konow, another fine earlier scholar, both quoted Barth and noted as well that "such [66] records are not therefore historical documents or proclamations in the ordinary sense," adding:

> The inscriptions are sometimes dug down in *stūpas* or placed in such a way that it is evident that they were never meant to be seen by mortal eyes. And we understand the care which was taken in order to have the names of the donors written and to include many of their friends and relatives, and also why the *navakarmika* [the monk who supervised the work] seems to have added his name subsequently in the Patika and Manikiala records. This was, as says M. Barth, something more than a gratification of vanity, and a mystic efficacy was attributed to the recording of such names.[20]

It is a pity that no one—as far as this writer knows—has pursued these old observations, because, regardless of what one might think of the concept of "mystic efficacy," both Barth and Konow were undoubtedly pointing, as they almost always did, in the right direction. Their remarks emphasize the important place that personal names had in these inscriptions, and in so doing, they provide us with something we can pursue: the power and properties of personal names in early India,

Most of the early Buddhist inscriptions are, as they are at Sāñcī, little more than names. The two engraved on the wooden beams at Bhājā already referred to read:

> The gift of Dhamabhāga.
>
> By Śrī Dharasa.[21]

At early Amarāvatī, one has the following:

> Of Tikana, son of Satula.
>
> The pillar of Hupahena.
>
> Of Dhamarakhita.

On pavement slabs surrounding the interesting little *stūpa* at Kesanapalli, Andhra, one finds these inscriptions:

> The slab of Turukalā.
>
> The slab of Nāgī.
>
> The gift of the Elder Ayapu[sa] and the pupil Deva and Aya Badhaka.[22]

From the railings surrounding *stūpa* 1 at Sāñcī, one gets, finally, these:

> The gift of the Monk Budharakhita, the inhabitant of Ujjayinī.
>
> The gift of the Nun Devabhāgā, an inhabitant of Madhuvana.
>
> The gift of the Reciter (*bhāṇaka*) Selaka.

All of these, and the vast majority of other early Buddhist donative inscriptions, consist of little more than names with, sometimes, a place of origin or residence. They are carved in stone and permanently placed in proximity to a sacred object. They are, to be sure, records—they indicate who paid for the architectural piece on which they are written, but it looks as though, perhaps, a donor did not just get a permanent record. He got what may have been more important: he got, for a price, the privilege of having his name permanently in the presence of the *stūpa* of the Buddha, and Professor Bareau reminds us that even "before the beginning of our era . . . the *stūpa* is more than the symbol of the Buddha, it is the Buddha himself."[23] A good part of the significance of these "records," then, may turn on conceptions connected with a person's [71] name, and of those at least something is known.

Renou, for example, in speaking of the corpus of Vedic literature has said that *naman*, name or personal name, "is the essential characteristic of identity"; and Gonda too has observed that in early India, "representing its owner, the name makes him, whether he be a god or a human being, present"; or that "over and over again [early Indian] authors give evidence of their conviction that the connection between a name and its bearer . . . is so intimate that there is for all practical purposes question of identity, interchangeability, or inherent participation." The latter notes as well that "there is indeed an intimate connection between name and origin: in magic practices the exact name and origin (cf. e.g. Av. 5, 21, 3) of the object dealt with must be given wherever possible; if 'father and mother' can be named so much the better." It is probably not an accident that this is almost exactly the kind of information found in Buddhist donative records: personal name, place of origin, parents' names, and so on.[24]

Gonda also describes what he calls "a curious rite" found in the *Taittirīya-saṃhitā* that involves an individual's name. The individual, who is about to go on a long journey and will therefore be separated from his all-important sacrificial fires, exchanges names with the god Agni—in effect leaving his name at home. Gonda interprets the whole by saying that the individual "so to say, bears his fires with him and his name, i.e. his representative, which is left behind, guards his fires or protects them from 'estrangement.'"[25] This particular ritual does not, of course, involve the name in written form, but even when exchanged and left only in oral form, the name functions as the active "representative" of the person.

There are, however, other brahmanical rituals that do make use of one's personal name in written form. Gonda refers to "one of the witchcraft performances" that involves making an "image" of the victim from flour, "scratching" his name on it, and then doing some unpleasant things to it and, therefore, to the person.[26] This sort of thing had a long life in early India. The *Bhaiṣajyagurusūtra*, a Mahāyāna text probably composed sometime around the third or fourth century, addresses the problem as if it were still current. It refers to people who "after having made the name or an image of the body of their enemy" try to create "an impediment to his life or the destruction of his body." However, the text promises that no such impediment can arise—that is, the procedure is ineffective—for those who have heard the name of the Buddha Bhaiṣajyaguruvaiḍūryaprabha.[27] It is, of course, hard to avoid the impression that one has here of competing forms of "magic," but notice, if nothing else, that in both cases the name "represents" the living person. In the first case, what is done to the name is done to the person. They are identical.

The same kind of equation between written name and actual person occurs as well in other Buddhist contexts, noticeably in Buddhist rituals for the dead. In the *Sarvakarmāvaraṇaviśodhanīdhāraṇī*, one of the almost interminable list of undatable Indian texts, the following recommended procedure is found:

> If, writing the name of the deceased and reciting this Dhāraṇī, one would make a hundred thousand miniature *stūpas*, and after having worshiped them fully . . . one were to throw them into a great ocean or river, by that means the deceased would be freed from the hells, etc.[28]

Likewise, several times in the *Sarvadurgatipariśodhana-tantra*, where rituals for the benefit of the dead who have landed in unfortunate places are described, both deceased and [72] living individuals are represented by, and acted on through, their written names. For example:

> The *mantrin* who takes delight in acting for the benefit of other people draws with saffron their effigy or their name. Out of compassion he should consecrate it in order to liberate those beings from the great fear of the three evil destinies.[29]

If ideas like these, which are embedded in a wide range of Indian literary sources over long periods of time, ever circulated outside of texts—and given their nature, chances are that they did—then it is not difficult to see how they must change the way one understands early donative inscriptions. Konow has noted "the care which was taken in order to have the names of the donors written," but if "representing its owner, the name makes him . . . present," if both deceased and living individuals are represented by, and acted on through, their written names, then this "care" is with something more than a mere record. If it is true that when a person's name is present, the person is present; if it is true that, in physical absence by journey or death, if a person's name is left behind, so too is his person, then we must begin to suspect that having one's name carved in stone and permanently placed near a powerful religious "object" must have placed the person there as well, regardless of whether that person was otherwise occupied, absent, or what we call dead. And this, I suggest, is precisely the purpose behind the early donative inscriptions at Sāñcī when seen from the point of view of the donor. They did not intend to leave a record, so it did not much matter whether it could be seen or read or understood. Like their cousins elsewhere or later who had small figures of themselves carved on the bases of images, they wanted only, it seems, to leave their presence in proximity to another, more powerful presence, and in this, it seems, they succeeded: the Monk Budharakhita, the inhabitant of Ujjayinī; the Nun Devabhāgā from Madhuvana; Balamitra, the pupil of Aya Cuḍa—they have all been dead for almost two thousand years and yet are still encountered at modern Sāñcī, surrounding that other presence that we can only vaguely sense.[30] [73]

Notes

1. The best discussions of the dates of the early donative inscriptions at Sāñcī are still A. H. Dani, *Indian Palaeography* (Oxford: 1963) 64ff; and V. Dehejia, *Early Buddhist Rock Temples. A Chronology* (London: 1972) 35–48, 186–188. N. G. Majumdar published what is still the standard collection of the early inscriptions in J. Marshall et al., *The Monuments of Sanchi* (Delhi: 1940) Vol. 1, 263–383.

2. K. D. Bajpai, "Some Place-names of the Sanchi Inscriptions," *Studies in Indian Place Names*, Vol. II, ed. M. N. Katti and C. R. Srinivasan (Mysore: 1981) 15; K. D. Bajpai and S. K. Pandey, *Excavation at Tumain* (Bhopal: 1985) 2.

3. S. S. Iyer, "Panguraria Brahmi Inscription," *EI* 40 (1973, but 1986) 119–120.

4. *Stūpa* 2 was, of course, not a *stūpa* of the Buddha but contained the "relics" of at least three generations of, it seems, local monks; cf. G. Schopen, "An Old Inscription from Amarāvatī and the Cult of the Local Monastic Dead in Indian Buddhist Monasteries," *JIABS* 14.2 (1991) 281–329, esp. 297–298 [= *BSBM* 165–203]. I will cite material from *stūpa* 2 several times here as an example only because it has received less explicit attention. It is interesting to note, however, that in spite of its contents, the inscriptions from *stūpa* 2 do not significantly differ from those associated with *stūpa* 1, the *stūpa* of the Buddha himself. Both *stūpas* received virtually the same sorts of attention and donations. Moreover, though the percentage of monastic donors is somewhat higher at *stūpa* 2, it is still in line with what is found elsewhere in donative inscriptions connected with *stūpas* and with other sorts of donations as well. It is now clear, for example, that the majority of early Buddhist images were also donated by monks and nuns; see G. Schopen, "On Monks, Nuns, and 'Vulgar' Practices: The Introduction of the Image Cult into Indian Buddhism," *ArA* 49 (1988–1989) 153–168 [= *BSBM* 238–257].

5. For examples and some discussion, see G. Schopen, "Archaeology and Protestant Presuppositions in the Study of Indian Buddhism," *HR* 31 (1991) 1–23, esp. 6–8 [= *BSBM* 1–22].

6. G. Schopen, "The Ritual Obligations and Donor Roles of Monks in the Pāli *Vinaya*," *JPTS* 16 (1992) 87–107 [= *BSBM* 72–85].

7. I. B. Horner, *The Book of the Discipline* (Oxford: 1940) Vol. II, 27, 49, 52, 57, 91, 125, 144, 150, 260, 325, 343, etc. = Pāli *Vinaya* iii, 204, 213, 215, 217, 234, 248, 257, 260; iv, 48, 81, 89, etc.

8. *Kṣudrakavastu*, Derge, 'dul ba Tha 252b.3–254a.1.

9. V. Dehejia, "The Collective and Popular Basis of Early Buddhist Patronage: Sacred Monuments, 100 B.C.–A.D. 250," in B. S. Miller, ed., *The Powers of Art. Patronage in Indian Culture* (Delhi: 1992) 35–45, esp. 36–39. Note, however, that one point made here needs to be corrected. Professor Dehejia says that "inscriptions on the railing pieces occasionally speak of the gift of entire villages . . . to the Sāñcī monks" and goes on to say that "the services and produce from such, collected by the brotherhood, may well have paid for the bulk of the work of the sculptors." It is virtually certain, though, that the inscriptions alluded to do not record the gift *of* entire villages but gifts *by* entire villages as corporate or collective donors.

10. R. W. Bulliet, *Conversion to Islam in the Medieval Period. An Essay in Quantitative History* (Cambridge: 1979); R. S. Bagnall, "Religious Conversion and Onomastic Change in Early Byzantine Egypt," *The Bulletin of the American Society of Papyrologists* 19.3 and 4 (1982) 105–124.

11. *Vinayavibhaṅga*, Derge, 'dul ba Ja 15a.7.

12. *Vinayasūtra* (Sankrityayana) 119.2; and Derge, bstan 'gyur, 'dul ba Zu 268a.6.

13. *Theragāthā* v. 144; *Suttanipāta* v. 666; *Divyāvadāna* (Cowell and Neil) 311.17; *Saṅghabhedavastu* (Gnoli) i 145.31.

14. A. Barth, "Inscription P. on the Mathura Lion-Capital," *IA* 37 (1908) 246.

15. A. V. Naik, "Inscriptions of the Deccan: An Epigraphical Survey (circa 300 B.C.–1300 A.D.)," *Bulletin of the Deccan College Research Institute* 11 (1948) 3–4.

16. Konow, *Kharoshṭhī Inscriptions*, 93.

17. See, for example, the inscriptions published in A. Ghosh, "The Early Phase of the *Stūpa* at Amaravati, South-East India," *Ancient Ceylon* 3 (1979) 97–103.

18. K. M. Sastri, *Historical Grammar of Telugu* (Anantapur: 1969) Ch. III.

19. A. Barth, "The Inscription on the Piprahwa Vase," *IA* 36 (1907) 121.

20. Konow, *Kharoshṭhī Inscriptions*, cxviii.

21. M. N. Deshpande, "Important Epigraphical Records from the Chaitya Cave, Bhaja," *Lalit Kala* 6 (1959) 30–32.

22. A. W. Khan, *A Monograph on an Early Buddhist Stupa at Kesanapalli* (Hyderabad: 1969) 2–4.

23. A. Bareau, "La construction et le culte des *stūpa* d'après les vinayapiṭaka," *BEFEO* 50 (1960) 269.

24. All of these quotations, including that from Renou, come from J. Gonda, *Notes on Names and the Name of God in Ancient India* (Amsterdam and London: 1970) 4, 23, 7, 21.

25. Ibid., 12–13.

26. Ibid., 27.

27. N. Dutt, *Gilgit Manuscripts* Vol. I (Srinagar: 1939) 13.9ff.

28. Derge, bka' 'gyur, rgyud 'bum, Tsha 236b.3.

29. T. Skorupski, ed., *Sarvadurgatipariśodhana Tantra* (Delhi: 1983) 81; cf. 33, 68–70.

30. Though there seems an obvious connection between donative inscriptions and donor figures—note, too, that in most of the texts cited here the name *or* the "effigy" of a person can be used interchangeably to represent him or her—a discussion of it would lead too far afield. However, in inscribed donor images something of their function is sometimes explicitly stated. In a twelfth-century inscribed donor image from Rajasthan, for example, the donor says, "He, through his image, performs worship constantly"; K. V. Soundara Rajan, "An Interesting Stone Inscription from Menal (Rajasthan)," *JIH* 40 (1962) 9–14.

CHAPTER XIV

If You Can't Remember, How to Make It Up

Some Monastic Rules for Redacting Canonical Texts

SCHOLARLY OPINION HAS naturally varied in regard to the importance and value of the "historical" elements—the names of places and persons—in the narrative frames found in early Buddhist canonical literatures. L. S. Cousins, for example, in discussing the "kind of variation which is actually found in the different versions of the four nikayas preserved by various sects and extant today in Pali, Sanskrit, Chinese and Tibetan," says that "these divergences are typically greatest in matters of little importance—such items as the locations of suttas, the names of individual speakers or the precise order of occurrence of events."[1] A. K. Warder, however, sees something quite different in these "matters of little importance." He says: "The individual '*Suttantas*,' however, mostly have their place of origin noted, and sometimes the time, and they generally give a detailed and circumstantial account of the events leading up to the main discourse or dialogue. . . . These records of the activity of the Buddha were regarded by the Schools which rehearsed them as authentic historical records of the events connected with the foundation of their order (*Saṅgha*) and the promulgation of their doctrine. The records are circumstantial and realistic and purport to be eye-witness accounts of the events. It seems we must accept the conclusion that some such eye-witness reports, at least, formed the model for this apparently unique style of literature."[2]

Still other scholars have seen still other things in these elements and in their patterns of occurrence. In a series of observations, C. A. F. Rhys Davids noted the overwhelming preponderance of Śrāvastī as the setting for the "talks" of the Buddha—Woodward even counted the cases: 871 of the *suttas* of the four *nikāyas*

Originally published in *Bauddhavidyāsudhākaraḥ. Studies in Honour of Heinz Bechert on the Occasion of His 65th Birthday* (Indica et Tibetica 30), ed. P. Kieffer-Pülz and J.-U. Hartmann (Swisttal-Odendorf: 1997) 571–582. Reprinted with stylistic changes with permission of the editors.

are set there. Mrs. Rhys Davids came to the following conclusion: "Either the founder *mainly* resided there, or else Sāvatthi was the earliest emporium (? library) for the collection and preservation [572] (however it was done) of the talks."[3] Woodward preferred the latter explanation ("I think it likely, as Mrs. Rhys Davids has conjectured . . . that the whole collection was stored and systematized at Sāvatthī"[4]), G. P. Malalasekera the former ("The first alternative is the more likely, as the Commentaries state that the Buddha spent twenty-five rainy seasons in Sāvatthi"[5]). Thich Minh Chau, who pursued a comparative analysis of the Chinese *Madhyama-āgama* and the Pāli *Majjhima-nikāya*, arrived at still stronger conclusions. Noting that there was "nearly 80% agreement" between the two collections in regard to the setting of the individual *sūtras*, he said: "This proves that both versions drew their contents from almost the same source, perhaps the old lost canon, and that at the time of compilation of these *sūtras*, Sanskrit and Pāli, the oral traditions handed down were still fresh in the memory of the compilers."[6]

For "matters of little importance" these narrative elements have, then, entered into a surprisingly large number of discussions bearing on such things as the biography of the Buddha and the transmission of Buddhist literature. But they may have played an even greater role in the increasingly frequent discussions of the relationship between early Buddhism and the reemergence of urbanism in early historic India. Here one example might suffice. B. G. Gokhale begins his paper entitled "Early Buddhism and the Urban Revolution" by saying: "It is now generally accepted that early Buddhism rode to popular acceptance on the crest of a significant urban revolution." He then goes on to say, "Statistically, the number of *suttas* delivered in urban centers, even in our limited sample, is overwhelmingly large (83.43%) while the rest (16.57%) are distributed over 76 different places, among which are included some towns, *nigamas*, villages and the 'countryside' (*janapada*). The share of rural areas in the total sample is thus very small." His numbers are impressive: "The total number of place names thus collected is 1009. Of these, 842 (83.43%) refer to five cities, while the rest, 167 (16.57%) cover 76 separate places." His methods and assumptions are also unusually clear: "Every place name associated with the delivery of the rule or *sutta* was carefully noted . . . The authenticity of place-association has been assumed, as it is based on a long tradition of faithful text-transmission with little possibility of interpolation or extrapolation."[7] [573]

Remarks like these of Gokhale's have gained wide currency[8] and are delivered as virtual facts even outside Indian studies. E. Zürcher, for example, has said in a paper on Han Buddhism: "The urban setting of Buddhism is amply confirmed by the scriptural tradition: the Buddha's sermons are generally situated at or near big cities like Vaiśālī, Śrāvastī, Rājagṛha and Benares, and the first famous donations made by lay supporters are not only reported to have been made by the local rulers, but also by prominent citizens: the rich bankers Anāthapiṇḍada at Śrāvastī. . . ."[9] Once again these narrative elements appear to be carrying some fairly weighty matters, matters that one might want to be sure of, and here we strike a problem.

We know next to nothing for certain about what Gokhale has assumed—the "authenticity" of the association of texts and their settings—because we know next to nothing for certain about how early Buddhist texts were redacted and transmitted. Apart from the traditional accounts of the first council, our literary sources seem to say very little about such issues. This more general silence makes a short text tucked away in the second volume of the *Kṣudrakavastu* of the *Mūlasarvāstivāda-vinaya* that much more remarkable, although—as I think will become evident—it is remarkable in other ways as well.

The *Kṣudrakavastu* passage deals with a specific problem of textual transmission: what is to be done when elements of texts are no longer remembered or are lost or unknown; it also deals with a problem of preservation: how the loss of texts can be avoided. Given that the various *vinayas* give little evidence for a clearly organized system that could carry over time even a moderately sized textual corpus—let alone the enormous collections that have been taken to constitute "early" Buddhist literature—both problems could well have been frequent. At least the *Mūlasarvāstivāda-vinaya*, moreover, seems to have taken for granted a low level of textual knowledge on the part of monks: its *Vinayavibhaṅga* contains rules governing a situation [574] where monks were unable to explain to visitors the wheel of rebirth painted on the porch of the monastery;[10] its *Kṣudrakavastu* has rules that are to be applied when monks—even the most senior monks—are incapable of reciting the *Prātimokṣa-sūtra*,[11] and both its *Pārivāsikavastu* and *Kṣudrakavastu* have specific provisions for dealing with the situation in which a monk was incapable of reciting even the daily recitation of "the Qualities of the Teacher."[12] The presence of such rules is not reassuring. The text we are most concerned with, however, addresses a specific form of this incompetence.

Kṣudrakavastu

(Tog Tha 56b.5–57a.5; Derge Da 39b.3–40a.1)

gleng gzhi ni mnyan yod na'o /

sangs rgyas bcom ldan 'das la / tshe dang ldan pa nye bar 'khor gyis zhus pa / btsun pa ma 'ongs pa'i dus na dge slong dran pa nyams pa / dran pa zhan pa dag 'byung ste / de dag gis gnas dang / grong dang / grong rdal gang dang gang du mdo sde gang bshad pa dang / bslab pa'i gzhi gang bcas pa ma 'tshal bar gyur pa na / de dag gis ji ltar bsgrub par bgyi / gzhan yang mdo sde dang / 'dul ba dang / chos mngon pa bskyud par 'gyur na / de dag gis ji ltar bsgrub par bgyi / gzhan yang rgyal po dang / khyim bdag dang / dge bsnyen rnams kyi sngon gyi bka' mchid dag (57a) *la gnas dang / rgyal po dang / grong khyer dang / grong rdal dang / khyim bdag dang / dge bsnyen rnams kyi ming bskyud par gyur na / de dag gis ji ltar bsgrub par bgyi /*

bcom ldan 'das kyis bka' stsal pa / nye bar 'khor gang gis gnas la sogs pa'i ming brjed par gyur pa de dag gis grong khyer chen po drug las gang yang rung ba 'am / yang na de bzhin gshegs pa gang du lan mang du bzhugs pa brjod par bya'o / ji ste rgyal po'i ming brjed na ni gsal rgyal lo / khyim bdag gi ming ni mgon med zas sbyin no / dge bsnyen ma ni ri dags sgra'i ma sa ga'o / sngon gyi gtam gyi gnas ni wā rā ṇā si'o / rgyal po ni tshangs sbyin no / khyim bdag [575] *ni khyim bdag sdums byed do / dge bsnyen ma ni khyim bdag gso sbyong skyes kyi chung ma brjod par bya'o / mdo sde dang / 'dul ba dang / chos mngon pa rnams brjed par 'gyur na / glegs bu la bris nas bcang bar bya ste / 'di la 'gyod par mi bya'o /*[13]

The setting (*nidāna*) is in Śrāvastī.

The Venerable Upāli asked the Buddha, the Blessed One: "Reverend One, in the future monks will appear who have imperfect memories, feeble memories. If they do not know in which place, village (*grāma*), or town (*nigama*) which *sūtra* was taught and which rule of training was promulgated, how are they to supply (*samudānayitavya*, *vidhātavya*) them? If, moreover, they were to forget the *sūtra* or *vinaya* or *abhidharma*, how are they to supply them? Or again, if they were to forget the name of the place or the king or the city (*nagara*) or the town or the householder or the lay-brother in a story of the past about a king or householder or lay-brother, how are they to supply them?"

The Blessed One said: "Upāli, those who forget the name of the place, et cetera, must declare that it was one or another of the six great cities, or somewhere where the Tathāgata stayed many times. If he forgets the name of the king, he must declare it was Prasenajit; if the name of the householder, that it was Anāthapiṇḍada; of the lay-sister, that it was Mṛgāramātā; of the place of a story of the past, that it was Vārāṇasī; of the king, that it was Brahmadatta; of the householder, that it was the householder Saṃdhāna; of the lay-sister, that it was the wife of the householder Poṣadhajāta.[14] If he would forget the *sūtra* or *vinaya* or *abhidharma*, when he has written it down on a folio it should be preserved. In this there is no cause for remorse.

The basic rules delivered by our text are straightforward. They indicate that when the name of the place or village or town where a *sūtra* or rule was delivered is lost or unknown, the reciter or redactor should supply the name of one of "the six great cities" (*ṣaṇ-mahānagara*), or the name of a place "where the Tathāgata stayed many times." Anyone at all familiar with early Buddhist canonical literature as we have it will know that the two categories "places where the Buddha stayed many times" and "the six great cities" are [576] almost, if not entirely, coterminous: the Buddha—according to that literature—stayed "many times" *only* in one or another, but mostly one, of the great cities. But notice, too, that even according only to our text when the name of a "village" or "town" was lost, it was to be replaced by the name of "a great city"—this alone would shift the setting of Buddhist teaching more and more to major urban sites.

Our rules are, moreover, not as flexible as they might at first sight seem. At first sight it would seem that the unknown or forgotten name could be replaced by that of any of the six great cities—Śrāvastī, Sāketā, Vaiśālī, Vārāṇasī, Rājagṛha, and Campā, according to the Mūlasarvāstivādin tradition (the Pāli tradition substitutes Kosambī for Vaiśālī but is otherwise the same).[15] But this range of options is then severely restricted by the additional provisions of our rule. If the names of a king or householder or lay-sister are lost, they *must* be replaced with the names Prasenajit, Anāthapiṇḍada, and Mṛgāramātā—there are no options. All three of these worthies are, however, from Śrāvastī and inextricably bound up with it. To replace the lost name of a king, for example, with that of Prasenajit would therefore, it seems, almost by necessity require that the setting—if preserved—also be changed to Śrāvastī. Although Buddhist redactors seem sometimes cavalier about consistency, it almost certainly would not do to have a text associated with Prasenajit or Anāthapiṇḍada set in Campā or Vārāṇasī. Our rules clearly favor Śrāvastī.

In regard to "stories of the past" there can be no doubt and there are, again, no options. If the setting or the name of the king associated with such a story is not known, it must be declared to have been set in Vārāṇasī, and the king must be said to have been Brahmadatta.

The absence or narrow limitation of options allowed in our short text would suggest that, however unsophisticated, it was intended to provide a systematic solution to what could have been a frequent problem, to in effect systematically limit a redactor's choices in regard to where he set a text whose provenance was unknown. But before we attempt to find evidence for the application of such a system, we might make some attempt, however unsophisticated, to date it.

Our text appears to present only one crude marker that might be of use in dating it. It refers to three categories of Buddhist texts: *sūtra*, *vinaya*, and *abhidharma*. This list does not correspond with what appears to be the standard list found elsewhere in the *Mūlasarvāstivāda-vinaya*. There we find [577] *sūtra*, *vinaya*, and *mātṛkā*.[16] If *mātṛkā* represents the forerunner or earlier form of *abhidharma*, there can, of course, be no doubt about which list is earlier, and this would suggest that our text could be relatively late, later at least than the bulk of the literature of which it now forms a part.[17] If we add to this that this literature, the *Mūlasarvāstivāda-vinaya*, is itself considered by many to be late—Lamotte, for example, thinks it is the latest of the *vinayas* and says "we cannot attribute to this work a date earlier than the fourth–fifth centuries of the Christian era"[18]—then our text may represent a late piece of a late compilation and could, if Lamotte is right, be as late as the fourth–fifth centuries C.E.

Obviously, even the moderately frequent operation of our apparently late, perhaps fourth or fifth century, rules would have generated a *sūtra* and *vinaya* literature dominated by Śrāvastī, and a *Jātaka* literature dominated by Vārāṇasī. It is therefore worth noting that the collections that have come down to us and that we conventionally take to be "early," appear to represent just such literatures.

The Pāli collection of *Jātakas* as we have it, for example, might be taken to instance in a particularly striking way the results that a set of rules like those found in our Mūlasarvāstivādin text would—almost by necessity—generate. All of its texts are "stories of the past," so that if their settings were unknown, they would, by the rule, have to be set in Vārāṇasī, or Benares, and any reference to a king would have to be to Brahmadatta. Now, Franklin Edgerton noted almost incidentally in his great dictionary that Brahmadatta was the name "of various kings of Benares city and the land of Kāśī" and that reference to a Brahmadatta was "in many Pali *Jātakas* formulaic at the beginning of the story . . . playing no part in the story itself."[19] What Edgerton might have meant by "many" can be made a bit more precise by thumbing quickly through the text of the *Jātakas* published by the Pāli Text Society. Slightly more than 400 of the 547 [578] *jātakas* found in that collection are set, by their opening phrase, in Benares during the reign of King Brahmadatta. Thirty-six additional *jātakas* that do not explicitly refer to Brahmadatta are also set in Benares. And there are as well some curious anomalies like that found in the *Gaṅgamāla Jātaka* where a king of Benares named Udaya is, in spite of his name, addressed as Brahmadatta. The numbers involved here—something approaching consistency—make it unlikely that the setting of these texts was accidental or, even, whimsical. The choice appears to have been made according to some sort of system, and that system must have looked very much like the rules in our late Mūlasarvāstivādin text.[20] Evidence, perhaps, for the operation of that same system might also be found in the Pāli *sūtra* collection.

Rules like those found in our Mūlasarvāstivādin text would have required that any *sūtra* whose setting was unknown be set in one of the six great cities or—and as we have seen this comes down to the same—in a place where the Buddha had stayed many times. This would allow placing it in Śrāvastī, Sāketā, Vaiśālī/Kosambī, Vārāṇasī, Rājagṛha, or Campā. But if the name of a king or householder were also unknown, other rules determining their choice would—as we have also seen—restrict the first choice to Śrāvastī. Again, assuming even a moderate operation of such rules, we should find a *sūtra* literature dominated by Śrāvastī, and that is exactly what we find in the Pāli collection. For brevity's sake we might simply cite Gokhale's figures. His sample contained 1,009 texts, 842 (83.43%) of which were set in five cities, with the following breakdown: 593 are set in Sāvatthī, 140 in Rājagaha, 56 in Kapilavatthu, 38 in Vesāli, and 15 in Kosambī.[21] The same basic pattern occurs—to judge by Thich Minh Chau's analysis—in the

Chinese version of the *Madhyama-āgama*: out of 94 *sūtras*, 44 are set in Śrāvastī, 13 in Rājagṛha, and so on.[22] We do not have a certain unified *sūtra* collection for the Mūlasarvāstivādins,[23] but a quick look at its *Vinaya* would seem to indicate that the pattern holds there as well: a rough count of the settings in the first 100 folios of the first volume of the *Kṣudrakavastu*, for example, produces 67 settings. Of these 67 settings, 55 are Śrāvastī, 4 each are Rājagṛha and Vaiśālī, and so on.[24] A more random sample produces much the same thing: I have been working lazily for the last couple of years on a representative anthology of translations of texts [579] from the *Mūlasarvāstivāda-vinaya*; of those completed, 78, drawn from all parts of this *Vinaya*, contain a setting; of these 78, 58 are set in Śrāvastī, 6 in Rājagṛha, 4 in Kapilavastu, and so on.

It would appear, then, that in regard to their "historical" settings the collections of "early" Buddhist literature that we have look remarkably like what would necessarily have been expected if our rules, or a similar set of rules, had been applied to collections of texts whose settings—in a significant number of cases—were unknown: in stories of the past, Benares and Brahmadatta would overwhelmingly predominate; in *sūtra* and *vinaya* it would be Śrāvastī, Prasenajit, and Anāthapiṇḍada. And so it is. The similarity between the patterns that would necessarily be created by the application of rules like those in the *Kṣudrakavastu*, and the patterns that actually occur in our collections, is almost certainly too great to be explained by coincidence and would appear to require that we conclude, for the moment, that our collections of "early" Buddhist literatures reflect—in regard to their "historical" settings—the application of redactional rules that themselves cannot, as of now, be shown to have been "early," and may be as late as the fourth or fifth century of the Common Era. The shape of all our collections would, moreover, seem to suggest that redactional rules very similar to those in the *Kṣudrakavastu* operated in all traditions or monastic groups, even if the Mūlasarvāstivādin version is the only one so far discovered.[25]

Our little text also has something to offer to the discussion of the problem of preservation. Much has been said about the "writing down" of the Buddhist canon—as if there were only one. But virtually all of it has concerned events in Sri Lanka, not in India. Although Professor Bechert has wisely argued otherwise, the general tendency has been to present the writing down of the canon in Sri Lanka as a significant, even definitive, event and to ignore India. Indian sources, in turn, appear by and large to ignore any such "event," but our text may suggest one reason why: our text suggests that for the Mūlasarvāstivādin tradition the writing down of canonical texts was not an event but rather—as Professor Bechert has suggested it really was in Sri Lanka—a process,[26] and a process to which no great significance [580] was attached. The *Mūlasarvāstivāda-vinaya* is, for example, familiar with a range of written legal instruments—written loan contracts, a written will, and written negotiable contracts of debt.[27] In this regard it is—apart, it seems, from the will—in conformity with contemporary (?) Indian legal texts. That such instruments are not known to the Pāli Canon may have resulted from a lack of contact with the Indian legal environment and the apparent absence of a parallel system of law in early Sri Lanka. The *Mūlasarvāstivāda-vinaya* also contains specific rules requiring monks to mark movable property by writing on it "This belongs to the *vihāra* of so-and-so."[28] The *Mūlasarvāstivāda-vinaya* is familiar with books as well, both Buddhist and non-Buddhist, and suggests that, as in early medieval Europe, they were of such value that they were included in wills; it also suggests that their sale could generate significant income,[29] and it contains specific sanctions for the theft of books by monks.[30] This same *Vinaya* also gives evidence of a system—never [581] detailed—for funding the copying of texts,[31] and on more than one occasion it specifies that individuals who had been scribes (*kāyastha*) before entering the Order should keep their equipment, apparently so that they could continue to practice their trade.[32] None of this, however, is presented as out of the ordinary. This too may be a result of the fact that the history of writing in India may by no means have been the same as the history of writing—both sacred and secular—in Sri Lanka.[33] In any case, our *Kṣudrakavastu* text [582] contains—insofar as I know—the earliest and main Mūlasarvāstivādin rule regarding committing canonical material to writing, and this ruling is delivered in such a way as to suggest that those who delivered it saw in it nothing of particular note. They do not even refer to writing texts down in books (*glegs bam = pustaka*) but rather on folios (*glegs bu = pattra*), perhaps even scraps—they seem to have had in mind something like notes, and clearly did not envision a major systematic enterprise. Again, our text suggests that for the Indian Mūlasarvāstivādin tradition the writing down of Buddhist texts was simply not—unlike Professor Bechert's sixty-fifth birthday—a major event. We send our congratulations!

Notes

1. L. S. Cousins, "Pali Oral Literature," *Buddhist Studies. Ancient and Modern*, ed. P. Denwood and A. Piatigorsky (London and Dublin: 1983) 5; cf. R. Gombrich, "How the Mahāyāna Began," *The Buddhist Forum*, ed. T. Skorupski (London: 1990) Vol. I, 21–22.

2. A. K. Warder, "The Pali Canon and Its Commentaries as an Historical Record," *Historians of India, Pakistan and Ceylon*, ed. C. H. Philips (London: 1961) 47.

3. C. A. F. Rhys Davids, *The Majjhima-nikāya* (London: 1925) Vol. IV, vi; F. L. Woodward, *The Book of the Kindred Sayings* (London: 1925) Vol. III, x–xii; F. L. Woodward, *The Book of the Kindred Sayings* (London: 1927) Vol. IV, xiv–v.

4. F. L. Woodward, *The Book of the Kindred Sayings* (London: 1930) Vol. V, xvii–xviii.

5. *DPPN* ii 1127.

6. Thich Minh Chau, *The Chinese Madhyama Āgama and the Pāli Majjhima Nikāya. A Comparative Study* (Saigon: 1964) 52–56, esp. 55.

7. B. G. Gokhale, "Early Buddhism and the Urban Revolution," *JIABS* 5.2 (1982) 7, 20, 10, 10.

8. For a sampling of citations concerning the urban settings of early Buddhism and the six great cities, see N. Wagle, *Society at the Time of the Buddha* (Bombay: 1966) 12, 27; A. Ghosh, *The City in Early Historical India* (Simla: 1973) 15–16, 64–65; R. Thapar, *From Lineage to State. Social Formations in the Mid-First Millennium* B.C. *in the Ganga Valley* (Bombay: 1984) 109; R. F. Gombrich, *Theravāda Buddhism. A Social History from Ancient Benares to Modern Colombo* (London and New York: 1988) 54; H. Härtel, "Archaeological Research on Ancient Buddhist Sites," in *The Dating of the Historical Buddha/Die Datierung des historischen Buddha*, ed. H. Bechert, Part I (Göttingen: 1991) 63ff; G. Erdosy, "The Archaeology of Early Buddhism," *Studies on Buddhism. In Honour of Professor A. K. Warder*, ed. N. K. Wagle and F. Watanabe (Toronto: 1993) 52–53; F. R. Allchin, *The Archaeology of Early Historic South Asia. The Emergence of Cities and States* (Cambridge: 1995) 110, 115; D. K. Chakrabarti, *The Archaeology of Ancient Indian Cities* (Delhi: 1995) 215.

9. E. Zürcher, "Han Buddhism and the Western Region," in *Thought and Law in Qin and Han China. Studies Dedicated to Anthony Hulsewé on the Occasion of His Eightieth Birthday*, ed. W. L. Idema and E. Zürcher (Leiden: 1990) 170.

10. *Vinayavibhaṅga*, Derge, 'dul ba Ja 113b.3ff = *Divyāvadāna* (Cowell and Neil) 298.24ff; J. Przyluski, "La roue de la vie à ajaṇṭā," *JA* (1920) 316ff.

11. *Kṣudrakavastu*, Derge, 'dul ba Tha 201b.2–202b.5 = Tog, 'dul ba Ta 302a.5–303b.7.

12. *Pārivāsikavastu*, GMs iii 3, 97.17 = Tog, 'dul ba Ga 241a.1; and *Kṣudrakavastu*, Tog, 'dul ba Ta 157a.4 = Derge, 'dul ba Tha 103 b.7. The Recitation or Proclamation of the Qualities of the Teacher, *śāstur guṇasaṃkīrtana*, is referred to several times in the *Mūlasarvāstivāda-vinaya* and Guṇaprabha's *Vinayasūtra*. Whether it refers to a specific text is not clear, although it appears that, like the *Tridaṇḍaka*, with which it is often paired, it was a recitative formulary; see G. Schopen, "The Lay Ownership of Monasteries and the Role of the Monk in Mūlasarvāstivādin Monasticism," *JIABS* 19.1 (1996) 95 n. 34 [= Ch. VIII above, 227 n. 34].

13. The text as it occurs in Tog is cited here. Although there are no significant variations here between Tog and Derge—the only two editions available to me—this is certainly not the case for the *Kṣudrakavastu* as a whole. There are in fact significant differences between these two editions in regard to numerous texts now found in the *Kṣudraka*—compare, for example, Tog, 'dul ba Tha 127a.2–b.7 and Derge, 'dul ba Da 87a.6–b.6, or Tog, 'dul ba Tha 213b.2–216a.5 and Derge, 'dul ba Da 143b.1–145a.4. These differences may prove of use to students of Kanjur history.

14. This reconstruction is doubtful; I have not been able to find an attested equivalent for *gso sbyong skyes*. In fact, personal names are a particular problem in the *Kṣudrakavastu*. At Tog, 'dul ba Tha 213b.2ff, for example, the name of the nun involved is consistently given as *gub ta*, and it is only in the *Ekottarakarmaśataka*, Derge, bstan 'gyur, 'dul ba Wu

191b.3ff, that we get the name written *sbed ma*. Panglung, *Die Erzählstoffe des Mūlasarvāstivāda-Vinaya*, 306, gives Guptika as the equivalent of *sbed pa*, so our nun's name was probably Guptikā. This sort of nonstandard rendering is even used sometimes in regard to well-known names in the *Kṣudrakavastu*. The standard translation for Jetavana is, of course, *rgyal byed kyi tshal*, but it is not uncommon to find it rendered as *'dze ta'i tshal* in the *Kṣudraka* (see Tog, 'dul ba Tha 204b.3, 206a.7, 212a.l, etc.); see also J.-U. Hartmann, "Fragmente aus dem Dīrghāgama der Sarvāstivādins," *Sanskrit-Texte aus dem buddhistischen Kanon: Neuentdeckungen und Neueditionen*, ed. von F. Enomoto, J.-U. Hartmann, and H. Matsumura (Göttingen: 1989) 62–63. Apart from Poṣadhajāta, all the other names in our text have attested equivalents, which I have used. I have also occasionally inserted Sanskrit equivalents for other terms when they are well attested.

15. For the Mūlasarvāstivādin tradition see, for example, *Cīvaravastu*, GMs iii 2, 119.19–120.3 (= G. Schopen, "Deaths, Funerals, and the Division of Property in a Monastic Code," in *Buddhism in Practice*, ed. D. S. Lopez Jr. [Princeton, N.J.: 1995] 497) [= Ch. IV above, 116]; for the Pāli, *Dīghanikāya* ii 146.13.

16. See, for example, *Śayanāsanavastu* (Gnoli) 3.18, 44.15; *Adhikaraṇavastu* (Gnoli) 71.6; *Kośāmbakavastu*, GMs iii 2, 173.7; *Poṣadhasthāpanavastu*, GMs iii 3, 116.21; *Poṣadhavastu*, GMs iii 4, 97.12; etc. (cf. *Poṣadhavastu* (Hu-von Hinüber) 227–231). But see also *Saṅghabhedavastu* (Gnoli) ii, 205.8 where *sūtravinayadharābhidhārmikāraṇyakas* are referred to, and *Kośāmbakavastu*, GMs iii 2, 173.16.

17. On the relationship of *mātṛkā* and *abhidharma*, see the recent discussion and sources cited in R. Gethin, "The Mātikās: Memorization, Mindfulness, and the List," in *In the Mirror of Memory. Reflections on Mindfulness and Remembrance in Indian and Tibetan Buddhism*, ed. J. Gyatso (Albany, N.Y.: 1992) 149–172, esp. 156ff.

18. Ét. Lamotte, *History of Indian Buddhism. From the Origins to the Śaka Era*, trans. S. Webb-Boin (Louvain-La-Neuve: 1988) 657. My own view is that such a date is too late by more than one century, and Lamotte himself seems to have changed his mind after 1958. But the question cannot be appropriately discussed here [see Ch. II above, 20 and the sources cited in its n. 3].

19. *BHSD*, 403, s.v. Brahmadatta.

20. Though very many years ago, my friend and colleague Patrick Olivelle remembered from his boyhood in Sri Lanka that all stories told of past times started: *ĕkamat ĕka raṭaka baranäs nuvara brahmadatta nam rajakĕnĕk rajakaraṇakalhi*, "In a certain kingdom, in the city of Benares, during the reign of a king named Brahmadatta. . . ."

21. Gokhale, "Early Buddhism and the Urban Revolution," 10.

22. Chau, *The Chinese Madhyama Āgama and the Pāli Majjhima Nikāya*, 52–56.

23. See, however, F. Enomoto, *A Comprehensive Study of the Chinese Saṃyuktāgama* (Kyoto: 1994) Part I, xiii, and the sources cited in n. 1.

24. Notice that our text that contains the rules favoring Śrāvastī is itself also set there and looks as if it had been subjected to its own rules, its original setting being "unknown."

25. There is, of course, a distinct possibility that parallel sets of rules may still come to light in other *vinayas*, and this may allow some adjustments in dating such rules [see now Ch. IX above, n. 59]. It is, moreover, worth noting that, in dating our rules, we are

strictly speaking dating only their explicit and formal expression or redaction. One could, of course, argue that such "rules" circulated and were applied long before they themselves were formally or "officially" redacted, but it is unlikely that this could ever be anything other than an argument, and it does not answer the question of why, if such rules were circulating earlier, they were not formally expressed. We have, after all, formally expressed and apparently "early" rules governing other aspects of the transmission and authenticity of texts; see Ét. Lamotte, "La critique d'authenticité dans le bouddhisme," in *India Antiqua* (Leyden: 1947) 213–222.

26. H. Bechert, "The Writing Down of the Tripiṭaka in Pāli," *WZKS* 36 (1992) 45–53. See, however, Bu-ston's discussion, and the sources he cites, which is translated in C. Vogel, "Bu-ston on the Schism of the Buddhist Church and on the Doctrinal Tendencies of Buddhist Scriptures," *Zur Schulzugehörigkeit von Werken der Hīnayāna-Literatur*, ed. H. Bechert, Vol. I (Göttingen: 1985) 104–110, esp. 108–109.

27. For loan contracts, see the text from the Mūlasarvāstivādin *Vinayavibhaṅga* cited and discussed in G. Schopen, "Doing Business for the Lord: Lending on Interest and Written Loan Contracts in the *Mūlasarvāstivāda-vinaya*," *JAOS* 114 (1994) 527–54 [= Ch. III above]; for the will, *Cīvaravastu*, GMs iii 2, 140.15ff (trans. in Schopen, "Deaths, Funerals, and the Division of Property in a Monastic Code," 498–500). [= Ch. IV above, 117–119]. Note that although it has not been recognized as such, there may also be a reference to a will in the *Divyāvadāna*'s account of the death of Aśoka. There Aśoka, on the point of death, declares that he is giving everything—except the treasury—to the Community of monks. Then, after reciting some verses describing the gift and his intentions, the text says: *yāvat patrābhilikhitaṃ kṛtvā dattaṃ mudrayā mudritam / tato rājā mahāpṛthivīṃ saṃghe dattvā kālagataḥ* (*Divyāvadāna* [Cowell and Neil] 433.1). This, of course, looks strikingly like *Cīvaravastu*, GMs iii 2, 140.15 ff: *tatas tena maraṇakālasamaye sarvaṃ santa{ka}svāpateyaṃ patrābhilekhyaṃ kṛtvā jetavane preṣitam / sa ca kālagataḥ*. In this second passage, the context makes it all but certain that *patrābhilekhya* refers to some sort of written will. A few lines later on, *patrābhilekhya* is three times replaced by *patrābhilikhita*, exactly the same term as in the *Divyāvadāna*. For negotiable contracts of debt, see *Bhikṣuṇīvinayavibhaṅga*, Derge, 'dul ba Ta 123a.5–124a.2.

28. *Vinayavibhaṅga*, Derge, 'dul ba Ja 15a.3–15b.1. This text is cited and translated in G. Schopen, "The Lay Ownership of Monasteries and the Role of the Monk in Mūlasarvāstivādin Monasticism," *JIABS* 19.1 (1996) 101–103 [= Ch. VIII above, 230–231].

29. *Cīvaravastu*, GMs iii 2, 143.5; Schopen, "Deaths, Funerals, and the Division of Property in a Monastic Code," 500 [= Ch. IV above, 119].

30. *Uttaragrantha*, Derge, 'dul ba Na 6b.2: *btsun pa re zhig dge slong gis glegs bam brkus na cir 'gyur lags / glegs bam gyi rin thang brtsi bar bya'o /* "Reverend One if then a monk steals a book, what will be done?" "The price of the book must be paid" (see also Na 96b.3). Kalyāṇamitra in his *Vinayāgamottaraviśeṣāgamapraśnavṛtti*, a commentary on the text, seems to take "book" here as meaning *śāstra* (*glegs bam ni bstan bcos kyi snod do*; Derge, bstan 'gyur, 'dul ba, Dzu 238a.1), but this is probably because he has already treated "canonical" books (*mdo sde dang 'dul ba dang / chos mngon pa la sogs pa'i chos bzung ba'i ngo bo*) under a previous heading. There (Dzu 236b.lff) he makes an interesting distinction between making a copy

of a *sūtra*, etc.—which could, after all, be considered a form of theft—and stealing a book that had already been written. In regard to the former, he says *'di la ni rku sems med pa'i phyir nyes pa med pa nyid do / 'di ltar mdo sde la sogs pa'i chos bri bar bya ba'i glegs bam mthong nas 'dri ba dang / 'dzin pa gang yin pa des ni pha rol po las cung zad kyang god par mi 'gyur te / 'di ltar bri bar bya ba'i gzugs brnyan son 'dug pa'i phyir ro / rku ba ni god pa yin te de lta bas na 'dir de ma gtogs so / 'o na glegs bam brim pa brkus pa la tshul ji lta bu zhe na / de brkus na rin thang dang mthun par nyes pa sbom po la sogs pa'i ltung bar 'gyur par shes par bya'o /*. For the theft of *sūtras* in the Chinese translation of the *Sarvāstivāda-vinaya* (T .1435), see M. Hofinger, "Le vol dans la morale bouddhique," in *Indianisme et bouddhisme. Mélanges offerts à Mgr. Étienne Lamotte* (Louvain-La-Neuve: 1980) 177–189, esp. 185 n. 38: "voler des rouleaux de *sūtra* pour une valeur de cinq sapèques constitue un péché d'Exclusion"; this has an almost exact counterpart in Kalyāṇamitra's commentary: *ma śa ka lngar tshad na des 'dis pham par 'gyur la*. There are also close parallels to the passages cited by Hofinger on the theft of relics and goods from *stūpas* in this commentary and both Tibetan versions of the *Uttaragrantha*. However, there is some confusion about the latter. Although the Derge Kanjur—at least in the recent reprint published in Taipei—has two texts that are given the same Sanskrit title, *bi na ya ud ta ra gran tha*, they do not have the same Tibetan title. The first ('dul ba Na 1.1–92a.7) is entitled *'dul ba gzhung bla ma*; the second (Na 92b.1–Pa 313a.5), *'dul ba gzhung dam pa*. At least in this edition both have their own long colophons, that to *'dul ba bla ma* explaining in part how there came to be two versions (it also contains a reference to Puṣyamitra's "persecution" that corresponds closely to the beginning of that cited by Lamotte [*History of Indian Buddhism*, 387] from the Chinese translation of the *Vibhāṣā*, and a reference to monks collecting all the books of the Tripiṭaka from various countries and places and attempting to make a complete collection in Mathurā). In spite of this, the Tōhoku Catalog (p. 2, no. 7), for example, gives no indication that two works are involved, whereas the Otani Catalog both recognizes two works (nos. 1036 and 1037) and translates the colophon of the first into Japanese. There is confusion in the secondary literature as well. A. C. Banerjee (*Sarvāstivāda Literature* [Calcutta: 1957] 99–100) does not recognize that two works are involved; nor, it seems, does C. Vogel ("Bu-ston on the Schism of the Buddhist Church and on the Doctrinal Tendencies of Buddhist Scriptures," 110 n. 60). P. Harrison ("In Search of the Source of the Tibetan Bka' 'Gyur: A Reconnaissance Report," *Tibetan Studies. Proceedings of the 6th Seminar of the International Association for Tibetan Studies*, ed. P. Kvaerne [Oslo: 1994] Vol. 1, 306) recognizes the importance of some of the colophon material and makes a start on sorting it out, but even here it is not entirely clear that there are two *Uttaragranthas* (cf. his n. 61).

31. *Adhikaraṇavastu* (Gnoli) 68.23; *Cīvaravastu*, GMs iii 2, 143.13, 146.4, etc.

32. *Bhaiṣajyavastu*, GMs iii 1, 281.18; *Kṣudrakavastu*, Derge, 'dul ba Da 87b.5; etc.

33. On the early history of writing in Sri Lanka, and especially on recent archaeological evidence that would seem to indicate "that the use of writing began [in Sri Lanka] some two centuries earlier than the first datable inscriptions currently known from any other part of South Asia," see Allchin, *The Archaeology of Early Historic South Asia*, 176–179, 215–216; but also the cautionary note in K. R. Norman, "The Development of Writing in India and Its Effect upon the Pāli Canon," *WZKS* 36 (Supplementband; 1992),

239–249, esp. 247, and the sources cited in both. For India we now fortunately have O. von Hinüber, *Der Beginn der Schrift und frühe Schriftlichkeit in Indien* (Akademie der Wissenschaften und der Literatur. Mainz. Abhandlungen der Geistes- und Sozialwissenschaftlichen Klasse, Jahrgang 1989. Nr. 11) (Stuttgart: 1989), and H. Falk, *Schrift im alten Indien. Ein Forschungsbericht mit Anmerkungen* (Tübingen: 1993), although in neither has discussion of the Mūlasarvāstivādin material found a place (von Hinüber has been thoughtfully reviewed by P. Kieffer-Pülz in *Göttingische Gelehrte Anzeigen* 246.3/4 [1994] 207–224; and both von Hinüber and Falk in R. Salomon, "On the Origin of the Early Indian Scripts," *JAOS* 115.2 [1995] 271–279).

INDEX OF ARCHAEOLOGICAL SITES

INDEX OF TEXTS

(Those numbers printed in **bold** mark passages that are cited, translated, or discussed in some detail.)

INDEX OF SUBJECTS